McDOUGAL · LITTELL

LITERATURE & LANGUAGE

ANNOTATED TEACHER'S EDITION

GRADE 7

Art and Photo Credits for the Annotated Teacher's Edition

Table of Contents

OVERVIEW OF LITERATURE AND LANGUAGE

TEACHING WITH LITERATURE AND LANGUAGE

THE PHILOSOPHY OF LITERATURE AND LANGUAGE

STRATEGIES FOR SUCCESSFUL TEACHING

ANNOTATED STUDENT TEXT

SKILLS TRACE (LOCATED AT THE BACK OF THE TEXT)

Program Overview

Literature and Language, an entirely new kind of textbook, was developed with two major goals in mind. First, to motivate students —helping them to see what most English teachers already know: that reading literature can be fun, that discussing literature can be stimulating, and that writing about what is read can be meaningful and satisfying. Second, using literature as a base, to integrate the language arts in a way that makes sense to both students and teachers.

1 GOAL 1: *Motivating Students*

Literature and Language was developed to give students a positive attitude toward literature, writing, and language study. Every aspect of the series was planned to engage the student and encourage him or her to become part of a community of writers and lifelong readers.

1. SELECTIONS

The tables of contents in the series represent a carefully chosen combination of old favorites and classics as well as fresh new fiction and nonfiction selections that have not previously appeared in classroom anthologies. Such combinations bring new meaning and relevance to the classics and add depth and importance to the contemporary works. In addition, a broad range of authors reflects the cultural diversity of today's world.

2. THEMATIC ORGANIZATION

An organization based on theme allows students to begin their study of literature with what they find most interesting—the meaning of the selection and how it relates to them. In addition, thematic groupings build broader contexts in which to consider what is read. Selections may be discussed in relation to larger issues as well as to other selections.

To gain insight from readers themselves, a student board of diverse ethnicity, geographic location, and ability was asked to read and comment on many of the selections in each book. Their responses were both thoughtful and revealing.

3. SELECTION AND WORKSHOP LESSON STRUCTURE

The lesson design for literature selections is based on the reader-response approach developed by Senior Consultants Judith Langer and Arthur Applebee (see pages T18-T21). The design consists of three parts: *Explore* (prereading) and *Explain* and *Extend* (postreading). All of the activities and questions on these pages are designed to help students connect with the text in meaningful ways. Questions have no "right" answers and allow all students to build and share their personal responses to the text. For a detailed description of the lesson design, see pages T6 and T7 of this Teacher's Edition.

Workshops in writing, language, and related skills are thematically connected to the selections. Instruction is brief, clear, practical, and leads quickly to actual work. Students write instead of reading about writing, and they learn language skills that are necessary and useful as they write.

4. VISUAL ELEMENTS

The typography and layout of the series were designed with a fresh, contemporary look and color palette meant to invite readers into the text. Design elements such as callout quotes, graphic organizers, expanded capital letters, and so on, help to break the monotony of long passages of dense text. The fine art illustrating the series was chosen for its direct relationship to the selections and for its appeal to students.

Reading, writing, grammar, and vocabulary are all parts of the whole we call language. In the past, however, each part has been taught as a discrete subject with separate texts and time periods —a semester of literature, six weeks of grammar, and so on. This fragmented curriculum has resulted in students who have also treated these subjects as discrete, generally failing to transfer information from one area of study to the next.

During the past few years, educational researchers have encouraged the integration of the language arts, and most teachers have been quick to recognize the logic of an integrated program. Indeed, many teachers have already tried to integrate their language arts curriculum. They have

spent long hours attempting to coordinate lessons from separate texts. They have developed lesson plans, created and duplicated assignments and activities, and asked students to juggle a confusion of mismatched texts and materials. In the end, despite long hours and good intentions, the results have often been frustrating and unsuccessful.

In an effort to combat "integration through teacher exhaustion," textbooks were published that promised an integrated approach. However, since these programs seldom did more than insert new activities into existing texts, the outcome was disappointing.

In contrast, *Literature and Language* is an entirely new series with an innovative organization,

intriguing tables of contents, and a dynamic lesson design based on the work of education's most respected researchers.

Teachers will discover that *Literature and Language* offers an entirely new framework for the study of language arts. It is a complete program in one book with all of the language arts strands woven together in a meaningful, relevant way. Students receive instruction (not merely activities) in writing, reading, grammar, vocabulary, and other related areas. Lessons occur when they are needed and when they fit logically into the instructional program, thus allowing students to understand why they are learning and how each part of language relates to the next.

INTEGRATION IN *LITERATURE AND LANGUAGE*

Each book in the *Literature and Language* series is arranged in thematic units of mixed-genre selections.

Since the unit themes are broad in scope, units have been divided into more focused subunits which deal with specific aspects of the unit theme. At the end of each subunit, a series of three instructional workshops is presented: a Writer's Workshop, a Language Workshop, and a Related Skills Workshop. The workshops are integrated with each other and with the literature in the subunit. The graphic below provides a visual picture of this organization.

THEMATIC UNIT ⟶

Unit Three

REACHING FOR THE STARS

SUBUNITS ⟶

1 DRIVEN BY DREAMS

Anne McCaffrey	**The Smallest Dragonboy**
Georgia Douglas Johnson	**Wishes**
Langston Hughes	**Dream Deferred**
Ana Maria Iza	**Formula**
William Jay Jacobs	**Eleanor Roosevelt**
Eleanor Roosevelt	*from* **The Autobiography of Eleanor Roosevelt** / INSIGHT

Literature–based Workshops

WORKSHOPS ⟶

WRITER'S WORKSHOP
Informative Writing
Guided Assignment:
Magazine Article

LANGUAGE WORKSHOP
Avoiding Fragments and
Run–ons

READER'S WORKSHOP
Skimming and
Scanning

2 FIGHT TO THE FINISH

Russell Gordon Carter	**Old Sly Eye**
Nadja Salerno–Sonnenberg	*from* **Nadja on My Way**
Lillian Morrison	**The Women's 400 Meters**
Frank Horne	**To James**
Rudyard Kipling	**Rikki-tikki-tavi**

WRITER'S WORKSHOP
Informative and
Persuasive Writing

Guided Assignment:
Problem-Solution

Literature–based Workshops

LANGUAGE WORKSHOP
Words Often Confused
or Misspelled

READER'S WORKSHOP
The Language of
Persuasion

READING ON YOUR OWN
Suggested Novels for Unit Three

The Design of the Literature Lesson

A Three-Part Structure with a Variety of Options

Selection lessons in *Literature and Language* are divided into a three-part design that surrounds the literature. Each part of the lesson offers a wide variety of activities. However, it is not expected that every activity will be used for every selection. Rather, it is assumed that each teacher will select those options most useful for his or her class.

EXPLORE

PREPARING STUDENTS TO READ

The cream-tinted *Explore* page provides three prereading activities designed to prepare students for the selection they are about to read. Research shows that such preparation improves reading comprehension and enhances reader response.

Examine What You Know
Helps students activate what they already know about the events and ideas in the selection they are about to read

Expand Your Knowledge
Provides important background information relevant to the selection

Enrich Your Reading
Presents direct instruction in a reading skill designed to improve comprehension of the selection

OR

Write Before You Read
Serves as an alternate to Enrich Your Reading. Allows students to explore selection-related ideas in writing before they read

---

EXPLORE

Fiction

Flowers for Algernon
DANIEL KEYES

Examine What You Know

What if you woke up tomorrow and realized you had become a genius overnight? In your journal or on a sheet of paper, answer the following questions:
- What personal goals could you achieve if you were a genius?
- What drawbacks, if any, might there be to becoming a genius?
- How might your friends and family react to your intelligence?

Expand Your Knowledge

What if we could increase our intelligence? Researchers are currently exploring drugs that might help us do just that. These drugs—"smart drugs" or "brain drugs"—are combinations of vitamins, nutrients, amino acids, and prescription drugs. Some people say that smart drugs improve people's memory as well as boost their intelligence. Smart drugs, however, have not yet been thoroughly tested by the Food and Drug Administration for safety and effectiveness.

Enrich Your Reading

Character Change In this story Charlie Gordon goes through some dramatic changes. His personality and intelligence change—and so does the way others treat him. To better understand and keep track of what happens to Charlie, fill in a chart like the one below as you read.

	March 5– March 10	March 15– June 4	June 5– July 28
What is Charlie's personality like?			
What is his intelligence like?			
How do others see and treat him?			
What does he think about other people?			

■ *Author biography on Extend page*

FLOWERS FOR ALGERNON

EXPLAIN

Responding to Reading

First Impressions

1. What events in this story affected you the most? Write about them in your journal or on a sheet of paper.

Second Thoughts

2. Look back at the chart you made for Enrich Your Reading. Which of the changes that Charlie goes through do you think are most difficult for him? Why?

3. Why do you think Charlie's co-workers and acquaintances treat him the way they do before and after his operation?

4. If Charlie were asked to participate in another experiment to increase his intelligence, do you think he would accept? Why or why not?

   Think about
   - whether Charlie is happier before or after becoming a genius
   - Charlie's reaction to Fanny Girden's reference to the tree of knowledge
   - the relationship, if any, between intelligence and happiness

5. Have your ideas about being a genius changed after reading this story? Why or why not?

Broader Connections

6. Giving "informed consent" means agreeing to undergo a medical procedure only when one thoroughly understands the possible risks and benefits of the procedure. Do you think Charlie was capable of giving informed consent to his surgery? Do you feel that it was right for the doctors to have operated on him? Why or why not?

Literary Concept: Foreshadowing

Giving hints to suggest events that will happen later in a story is called **foreshadowing**. In "Flowers for Algernon," for example, Algernon is operated on before Charlie, what happens afterward to Algernon foreshadows what will happen to Charlie. Find and explain one other example of foreshadowing in this story.

FLOWERS F

EXTEND

Options for Learning

1 • **Dare to Compare** With your classmates, watch the film version of "Flowers for Algernon," called *Charly*. Then get together in small groups and write a comparison of the film and the short story. When you have finished, share your group's comparison with the other groups.

2 • **Look into It** Choose a topic related to this story and research and write about it. You may want to study some aspect of psychological testing, such as *Rorschach* or IQ tests, or you may prefer to find out more about "smart drugs." To share your report, put it in a large binder with the reports of other classmates who chose this activity.

3 • **Clean Up His Act** Rewrite Charlie's progress report for "March 6," using correct spelling, punctuation, and grammar. When you have finished, compare your entry with the entries of others who chose this activity.

4 • **To Be or Not to Be** Hold a debate about whether or not the operation should have been performed on Charlie. To begin preparing for the debate, you may want to think back to what you and your classmates said in response to the Broader Connections question on page 293.

◆ **FACT FINDER** SCIENCE
What part of the brain is responsible for intelligence?

Daniel Keyes
1927–

Daniel Keyes grew up in Brooklyn, New York. Keyes has taught high school in New York and is presently the director of the creative writing center at Ohio University.

Keyes is interested in abnormal psychology. Since he is, as he says, "fascinated by the complexities of the human mind," Keyes has written several books on psychological

because several of his "selves" had read "Flowers for Algernon" and agreed that Keyes was the perfect author to tell their story.

The short story "Flowers for Algernon" won Keyes a Hugo Award at the World Science Fiction Convention in 1959. Later, when he developed the story into a novel, the Science Fiction Writers of America awarded the new, longer version the coveted Nebula

2 EXPLAIN

POSTREADING QUESTIONS AND ACTIVITIES

3 EXTEND

POSTREADING ACTIVITIES

Each selection is followed by an *Explain* section which challenges students to investigate literature through their own personal responses in an atmosphere of shared exploration. These discussion questions, which are based on the conviction that all students have something of value to contribute, motivate students to develop personally meaningful interpretations and to build connections between the literature and the world around them. Finally, students are challenged to expand their reading experience to literary analysis, informal writing, and vocabulary enrichment.

Responding to Reading Provides a framework for meaningful class discussion
First Impressions Initiates discussion by encouraging each reader's personal response
Second Thoughts Encourages critical thinking as students develop more complex and sophisticated interpretations
Broader Connections Establishes relevance by making connections between the selection and the students' world

Literary Concept Introduces a literary element found in the selection and often reviews previously taught elements

Writing Options Presents a variety of informal, imaginative, "write-to-learn" assignments for further exploration of the selection

Vocabulary Practice Reinforces the vocabulary words presented in the selection

The activities on the *Extend* page allow students to respond to the selection in a variety of modes and cross-curricular content areas.

Options for Learning Presents opportunities for students to express understanding of the selection in their preferred mode of expression and in various content areas

Fact Finder Challenges students to research and answer questions in other subject areas

About the Author Provides information about the author

A SPECIAL NOTE ON VOCABULARY

The vocabulary program is based on two research conclusions: first, that new words are best learned and remembered when taught in context; second, that readers need not know the meaning of every unfamiliar word in order to understand what they read.

Vocabulary words in **Literature and Language** were chosen based on the following criteria:
1. words that would be useful additions to a reader's vocabulary
2. words that add important meaning to the selection
3. words that are not easily inferred from context

These words are underlined in the text and defined in boxes at the bottom of the pages where they appear. An alphabetized list of these words can be found in the glossary at the back of each text. Other unfamiliar words and terms are footnoted.

17

$\mathcal{T}$he Design of the Workshops

Integrated Lessons in Writing, Language, and Related Skills

The series of three workshops that follows each subunit in *Literature and Language* is the foundation of the integrated program. Although the workshops are integrated with each other and with the literature, each workshop may also be taught independently.

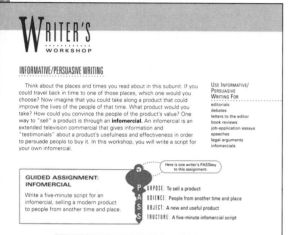

Eleven Writer's Workshops at each grade level guide students through the writing process from prewriting to presentation. The workshops introduce a broad range of writing modes and formats while providing a flexible framework that allows students to make their own decisions about what and how to write.

The Writer's Workshops include the following:

- literature-based writing assignments
- clear, practical instruction in the writing process
- complete student models
- extensive use of graphic organizers and other writing strategies
- peer and self-evaluation
- text-supported portfolio use

The Language Workshops support the Writer's Workshops by providing skill instruction that students can put to immediate use as they write.

Language Workshop highlights include the following:

- a focus on the most common usage problems of student writers
- **Looking at Style** exercises that send students back to the literature to see how professional writers use language
- **Revising Your Writing** activities that allow students to apply the skills to their own writing

The Related Skills Workshops cover three important content areas: **Reading, Vocabulary,** and **Speaking and Listening.** The lessons can be used as part of the integrated workshop program or at anytime during the year.

The Design of the Teacher's Edition

Unit Planning Guides and Cooperative Projects

Special planning pages at the beginning of each unit provide a clear, comprehensive overview of the skills, objectives, and integrated language activities found in each unit. Also included are suggestions for community and parental involvment plus audiovisual resources. This unit preview will allow you to tailor your plans to the needs of your students and to prepare in advance for the kinds of enrichment that make lessons stimulating and exciting.

The materials that precede each unit also include detailed directions for completing a cooperative project related to the unit theme. These projects may be done simultaneously with the unit or as a culminating activity after the unit is completed.

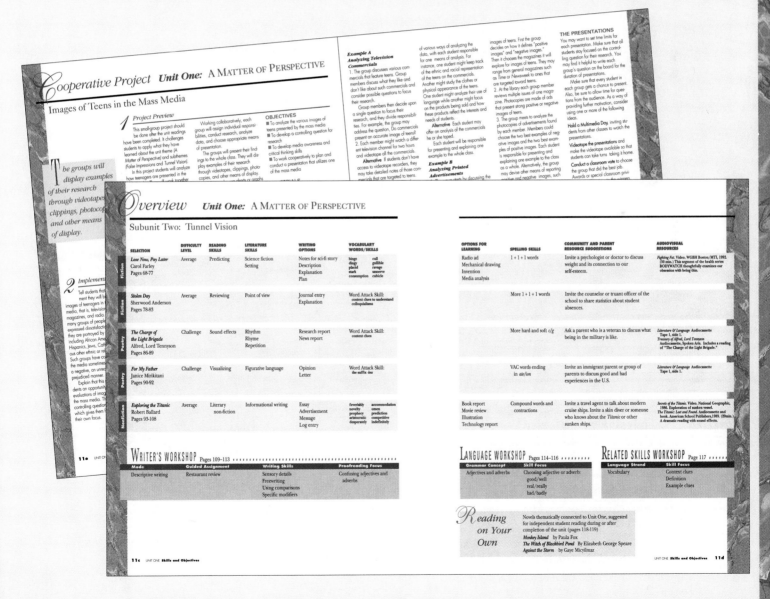

The Design of the Teacher's Edition

Teaching the Literature Selections and the Workshops

The Annotated Teacher's Edition of *Literature and Language* is a professional sourcebook designed to promote effective and efficient teaching. Every page contains intelligent, thoughtful material that addresses teachers as professionals and reflects current trends in educational research.

Strategies for Individualizing Instruction

include the following:

- Guided reading for less-proficient students
- Challenge questions and activities
- Suggestions for LEP students
- Tips for teaching to alternative learning styles

Guided Reading for Less-Proficient Students

Multicultural Connections

Looking at Style

Speaking . . . Listening . . . Viewing

Comprehension Check

The Spelling Connection

Cross-Curricular Projects

Reinforcement, Extension, and Enrichment

suggestions are signaled by yellow bands at the bottom of the page.

Objective

■ To learn how to make inferences while reading

Teaching Strategies

Remind students that to make an inference, they must use given facts and their own knowledge to make a logical guess. Caution them against making wild assumptions—their inferences should be firmly grounded in the evidence. Read students the following sentences, asking them to make inferences and support their guesses with facts.

The seventh-grade girls' basketball team has won all its games. Elizabeth is the best player both offensively and defensively.

(logical inferences: Elizabeth makes a lot of baskets; she defends the basket well; she is probably fast.) Point out that an assumption such as "Elizabeth is tall" may be correct but is not supported by the facts given.

TEACHING TIP: LEP

Since the ability to make inferences depends on good reading skills, be sure to make provisions for LEP and at-risk students. Pairing such students with excellent readers or experienced classroom aides should make a great difference.

Have students make conscious efforts to draw inferences as they read. Remind them that whenever they use context clues or try to figure out why a character acts in a certain way, they are making inferences. Suggest that students jot down their inferences as they read and check the correctness of the inferences when they finish reading.

Answers to Exercise

1. He was a child, since there were Ghost-Slayer toys, posters, and comic books in "our bedroom."

2. The puppy made the noises; the clues are "yowling" and "clawing."

3. He thought a ghost made the noises, since the sounds were "eerie," the yowling and clawing could have been ghost or monster noises, and he knew nothing about the puppy.

Objectives

■ To use subject, object, and possessive forms of personal pronouns correctly

■ To use personal pronouns correctly in compound constructions

Teaching Strategies

Personal Pronouns

Have students study the pronouns in the chart on page 63. Then write the following sentences on the board and use them for the oral activity described below:

For subject pronouns: _____ enjoyed the first day of school.

For object pronouns: Shannon gave _____ a tour of the library.

For possessive pronouns: That is _____ classroom. That classroom is _____.

Ask students to use all the pronoun forms in the chart to complete these sentences—first the subject pronouns, then the object pronouns, and then the possessives.

One of the biggest problems students have with personal pronouns is a tendency to use object forms as predicate pronouns because the subject forms "just don't sound right." Try this strategy. First, have students read Using the Subject Form on page 64. Point out item 2 in the Reminder in the margin, noting that a pronoun that is in the predicate of a sentence and that renames or refers to the subject must be in the subject form. Next, provide some practice with sentences like these:

The chosen student was she.

Our award recipients are they.

It is I.

The owner of the book is he.

The hosts will be Davin and she.

USING PERSONAL PRONOUNS CORRECTLY

Personal pronouns have three forms: subject, object, and possessive.

Personal Pronouns

When you do personal writing, as in an autobiographical incident, you use many personal pronouns. Choosing the correct forms of these pronouns can help to keep your writing clear. You probably remember that a **pronoun** is a word used to take the place of a noun or another pronoun. The pronouns underlined in the excerpt below are personal pronouns.

Then he saw her. She was sitting with a girlfriend under a plum tree. . . . When the bell sounded, Teresa looked up, and their eyes met. She smiled sweetly and gathered her books.

◄ LITERARY MODEL from "Seventh Grade" by Gary Soto

Each of the personal pronouns has a subject form, an object form, and a possessive form. The form that a personal pronoun takes depends on how the pronoun is used. Study the following chart.

Forms of Personal Pronouns			
	Subject	**Object**	**Possessive**
Singular	I	me	my, mine
	you	you	your, yours
	she, he, it	her, him, it	her, hers, his, its
Plural	we	us	our, ours
	you	you	your, yours
	they	them	their, theirs

◄ SPELLING TIP Notice that possessive pronouns are spelled without apostrophes: hers, its, ours, yours, theirs.

ADDITIONAL RESOURCES

Unit One Resource Book
Language Workshop Practice, p. 44

Technology and Enrichment
Grammar and Usage Copymasters, pp. 34, 35
Grammar Test Generator

Links to Writer's Craft

For more about personal pronouns, see The Writer's Craft, Grade 7, "Using Pronouns," pages 432–442.

Student-Centered Teaching

is reflected in the innovative, research-based strategies that include:

■ Discussion prompts

■ Think-Aloud models for reading

■ Modeled writing

■ Graphic organizers

■ Writing conference support

■ Alternative assessment options

■ Teaching to all modalities

Cross-Series Correlations

to McDougal, Littell's The Writer's Craft are provided with every lesson.

USE PERSONAL WRITING FOR
journals
logs
notes
letters
diaries
autobiographies

PERSONAL WRITING

Each of us remembers misunderstandings like those experienced by the characters in this subunit. We have all believed a false impression or have purposely or mistakenly created a false impression. In this workshop you will write about such an experience. Like Jean in Little by Little, you could write about a false impression you gave of yourself. Or, you can focus on a false impression you had of someone else. A personal experience of this kind is called an **autobiographical incident**. Writing about these experiences can help you understand them. You are sharing a moment in your life with readers—and with yourself.

GUIDED ASSIGNMENT: AUTOBIOGRAPHICAL INCIDENT

Write about a time when you either received or gave a false impression. Explain what happened as a result.

Here is one writer's PASSkey to this assignment.

PURPOSE: To tell about a personal experience
AUDIENCE: Classmates, friends, family
SUBJECT: A false impression
STRUCTURE: Autobiographical incident

STUDENT MODEL
Before you write, read how one student responded to the assignment.

The pronoun I shows that this piece is personal or autobiographical writing.

The Turnaround
by Zachary Hurston

I had to grin when Mike introduced us. "Your name is Eel-ya?" I asked. "Eel-ya?" The new kid's name sounded like a joke. Is he named after an eel, or what, I wondered. It was the first day of sixth grade, and he was sitting right behind me.

"Ilya," he corrected in a fed-up voice. "It's a Russian name."

"Oh—are you from Russia?" I was trying to be friendly.

"No!" he snapped. "I'm American." He sure didn't sound Russian—but he did sound as if he

ADDITIONAL RESOURCES

Unit One Resource Book
Writer's Workshop Worksheet, p. 39
Writer's Workshop: Peer and Self-Evaluation, p. 40
Writer's Workshop: Assessment Guidelines, p. 41

Technology and Enrichment
Guidelines for Writing Assessment and Portfolio Use
Elaboration, Revision, and Proofreading Transparencies 1–4
Writer's Databank Software: File 2, Starting Points
Fine Art Transparency Pack

Links to Writer's Craft

For more about personal writing, see The Writer's Craft, Grade 7, "Personal and Expressive Writing," pages 27–47. See also pages 218–220, "Finding Writing Ideas."

Objectives

■ To understand the elements of an autobiographical incident

■ To write about a personal experience from the first-person point of view

■ To organize writing in chronological order or cause-and-effect order

■ To draft, revise, edit, and share personal writing

Draft and Discover

If students aren't sure how to begin their incidents, suggest the following strategies:

■ Describe a person involved in the incident other than yourself.

■ Begin with some lively dialogue, as Zachary did in the model incident. Have the characters themselves show what they are like and tell what is going on.

■ Begin with the result of the incident and work backward.

Remind students that they can always go back and replace missing details or rearrange the ones they've written. If they get a better idea while they're writing, they can scrap what they've done and begin again.

Modeling: On an overhead, write a paragraph about an incident in your own memory for students. Explain that this draft is imperfect and that you will change it as you develop your incident more fully.

Teaching Strategies

DISCUSSING THE ASSIGNMENT

Have students read the first paragraph on page 58, and be sure they know that an autobiographical incident is a person's true story of something that happened to him or her, and that a false impression is a wrong idea that someone forms about someone else. Emphasize that this assignment calls for not only how a false impression was given but also what happened as a result.

Then point out the PASSkey for the Guided Assignment. Help students understand the relationship between the directions in the box and the "shorthand" in the graphic. Point out that the PASSkey provides them with a way of planning their writing. Deciding their purpose, audience, subject, and structure before they begin will keep them on target in prewriting and in drafting and revising their work. Explain that they may change parts of their PASSkey during their writing process.

If you wish, you may give students the option of writing about something else that is important to them. Alternative Writing and Research Topics at the bottom of the following page offers additional suggestions. Remind students too that the Writer's Handbook, pages 694–696, provides an overview of each step of the writing process and explains the PASSkey in detail.

ANALYZING THE MODEL

Ask a volunteer to read aloud the student model on pages 58–59. Have students evaluate Zachary's work to see if it conforms to the assignment. (Possible response: Yes, the first part tells how Zachary formed a false impression of

TEACHING TIP: CHALLENGE

Students who are strong writers might be encouraged to model all or part of their autobiographical incident on the style of an author whose work appears in the subunit, such as Toni Cade Bambara. Not only will such an activity be an exercise in analysis, but it will also illustrate how important word choice and phrasing can be to the finished project.

TEACHING TIP: COMPUTER

Suggest that students who draft on a computer use the Insert edit mode. Then, if they should suddenly have an idea or recall an important detail while drafting, they can hit the Page Down key and input the idea or fact. Afterward, they can hit the Page Up key and continue where they left off. After finishing a page or draft, students will have a collection of useful notes at the end of their document.

Paragraphs at Work

If students are having trouble deciding where each paragraph should begin, offer these guidelines:

1. Start a new paragraph whenever you begin a different part of your story. For example, if you have been describing your hard work on a plan, the first sentence of the next paragraph might begin, "On Monday morning I put my plan into action."

2. Start a new paragraph when you begin describing new settings. For example, if you've just told what's going on in the kitchen and now you want to tell

what happened in the garage, your new paragraph might begin, "Meanwhile, out in the garage, Dad was painting the racer."

3. Start a new paragraph when the story moves toward or backward in time. For example, if you've been narrating an event and want to describe what happened later, your new paragraph might begin, "Back then I had no idea how hard it is to live on a budget, but I found out when I turned thirteen."

Alternative Writing and Research Topics

Paragraphs at Work

Assessment Guidelines

Collaborative Writing

Managing the Paper Load

Grammar Games

Additional Practice

The Design of the Teacher's Resource File

Innovative Resource Materials Organized for Convenience

The Teacher's Resource File holds all the resource material for *Literature and Language*. The first part of the file contains lesson-specific materials organized by order of use. The second part includes supplementary materials. Every item in the file is thoughtfully designed to reflect the teaching philosophy of the text and the commitment to integrated language arts.

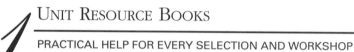

1 UNIT RESOURCE BOOKS

PRACTICAL HELP FOR EVERY SELECTION AND WORKSHOP

Each unit in *Literature and Language* has its own resource book. All support materials for the selections and workshops are grouped together by order of use so that you will not have to hunt for what you need. Each *Unit Resource Book* contains the following items:

- **Reader's Guidesheets**
- **Reading Skills**
- **Literature Skills**
- **Vocabulary Connections**
- **Spelling Connections**
- **Comprehension and Vocabulary Check Tests**
- **Selection Tests**
- **Writer's Workshop: Worksheets**

- **Writer's Workshop: Peer and Self-Evaluation**
- **Writer's Workshop: Assessment Guidelines**
- **Language Workshop: Practice**
- **Related Skills Workshop: Practice**
- **Unit Tests**
- **Answer Keys**

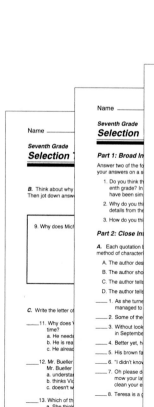

ℰ NRICHMENT MATERIALS

CREATIVE IDEAS AND ENGAGING ACTIVITIES

In addition to the *Unit Resource Books*, the Teacher's Resource File includes a remarkable range of supplementary materials including the following:

- **Active Reading Transparencies and Worksheets**
- **Thinking Skills Transparencies and Worksheets**
- **Fine Art Transparencies and Worksheets**
- **Elaboration, Revision, and Proofreading Transparencies and Worksheets**
- **Guidelines for Reading and Literature Assessment**
- **Guidelines for Writing Assessment and Portfolio Use**
- **Sentence Composing Copy Masters**
- **Grammar & Usage Copy Masters**
- **Family and Community Involvement Sourcebook**

ℒ LSO AVAILABLE

Writer's DataBank Software

A collection of useful tools and techniques that helps students write more effectively. Includes journal starters, ideas for writing, creativity prompts, elaboration techniques, usage and spelling help, and much more. Available for Apple II, Macintosh, and IBM PC.

Grammar Test Generator

A database of 1600 multiple choice questions allows teachers to easily create customized exams, quizzes, and worksheets. Available in IBM, Apple, or Macintosh versions.

Audiocassette Tapes

Professional actors read many of the more challenging selections in each text. The two 60-minute tapes per grade level provide an enjoyable option for students—especially auditory learners or those who need additional reading support.

JAMES MARSHALL, SENIOR CONSULTANT

Why should we try to integrate the language arts in our English classrooms? Perhaps the best answer comes from the students themselves. Listen, for instance, to Jake, a seasoned veteran of schools:

> In English class, they always give you that line about how they're preparing you for college. Whenever you ask teachers why you're doing what you're doing, that's the definitive answer. The teacher picks out the books that are on the list of classics, but I don't know what makes them a great work of art. I guess it has to be abstruse and have a lot of hidden meanings. You're not allowed to read it for pleasure. You have to think about the symbols.
> What does the fish mean? What does the merry-go-round mean? It doesn't mean anything to me. What teachers want is an opinion, and they have an opinion also, and they grade you against that opinion. And it really gets hard to write to please the teacher instead of writing what you're thinking. Sometimes I know what they want and I give it to them. Sometimes I know what they want and I refuse to give it to them because it's so absurd. And sometimes I have no idea what they want.

How would we answer Jake? What exactly *do* we want? In Jake's experience, the purpose driving the teacher of literature is to prepare students for something else—college perhaps, or maybe a job. The activity is not pleasurable, or even meaningful, in itself. It is a means to some other end. And the purpose is accomplished by taking apart the texts that Jake and his friends might read ("What does the fish mean?" "What does the merry-go-round mean?"), eliciting opinions about those texts, and then grading the students' opinions against the teacher's. The

end result of such an approach, of course, is a profound alienation from the process of reading and understanding literature—an alienation that Jake articulates with a clear and discouraging force.

Jake's observations obviously do not apply to all English classrooms, but recent research on the teaching of literature suggests that they do apply to many. Arthur Applebee's study of schools with strong reputations in the teaching of English, for instance, found that literature instruction today looks largely the same as it did twenty-five years ago, even though many teachers have made significant changes in the way they teach writing.

In other words, while students have been encouraged to value process, ownership, and small group work in learning to write, they have continued to search, in Jake's words, for those "abstruse" and "hidden" meanings when learning about literature. My own studies of classroom discussions of literature suggest how that search is usually carried out. In most discussions, regardless of grade or ability level, teachers talk three to five times more than their students; when students speak, they usually contribute one sentence or less. And that sentence is usually an abbreviated answer to the teacher's question.

Perhaps even more disturbing, both Applebee's research and my own suggest that it is the programs for non-academic students that are in the most trouble. It was those students, Applebee found, "the very students in most need of help," who received the least attention in curriculum planning and revision. And it was those students who expressed the most frustration about the patterns of classroom discussion that I have described. Given such findings, it is little wonder that both teachers and students have come to express increasing frustration with the models we have been using to guide our teaching in literature. Clearly it is time for a fresh approach.

What Integration Means

What alternatives do we have? One of the most promising is a model of teaching English that begins with the assumption that the basic components of language use—reading, writing, speaking and listening—cannot be learned well in isolation from one another. Rather, they are learned best when they are learned together within meaningful activities that call all of them into play. Young children, after all, first learn about language not by studying it, but by using it. For them it is not an end in itself, but a

*P*erhaps the best answer comes from the students themselves.

Young children first learn about language not by studying it, but by using it. For them it is a tool to get things done.

tool to get things done. And because it is a useful tool—because controlling language empowers children to become increasingly competent in their world—they will practice the craft of language with an energy and a curiosity that seems long since lost by the time they enter secondary school.

What happens, of course, is that in school, reading and writing and speaking and listening are often treated as if they were isolated skills, and mastering those skills becomes an end in itself. Thus students are given reading assignments so that they will learn to read better and writing assignments so that they will learn to write better. We certainly want our students to grow in their ability to read and write, but the best way to accomplish that goal is to engage them in activities that call for extended practice in reading and writing—activities in which reading and writing become tools to get things done.

It is just such an approach that we have taken in *Literature and Language*. Here the skills of writing, language use, and vocabulary development have not been isolated from one another or from the study of literature. Instead, we have structured lessons and units so that the literature provides a context for practice in writing, language, and vocabulary. At the same time, the writing, language, and vocabulary exercises will provide students with a variety of tools for more deeply exploring the literature they read. We feel that when the language arts are integrated in this way, students will more clearly see the purposes driving the activities and thus will be more fully empowered to participate in the larger community of literate persons.

New Developments in the Study of Literature

Even teachers who are taking an integrated approach to the study of English, however, must still face questions about the kinds of literature they will ask their students to read and about the kinds of literary understanding that they will attempt to foster. On the one hand, it seems clear that at least part of our job is to introduce students to the great traditions of Western literature. But on the other hand, recent scholarship and massive changes in our school population have awakened us to the necessity of teaching other traditions as well. There is the rich legacy of African-American, Native American, Asian-American, and Hispanic literature that has for far too long gone unexplored in school. There is new and old literature written by women. There is an increasingly diverse range of contemporary fiction and nonfiction—some of the best of it directed specifically to adolescents. There is, in short, a whole new world of literature that our teaching cannot ignore.

At the same time, there is a whole new world of thought about what it means to understand a piece of literature—and this too we cannot ignore. The process of reading, it appears, is not a matter of extracting meanings from texts but a matter of making meaning in interaction with texts. Readers bring a wide range of prior knowledge and personal history to bear on their reading, and what they bring helps to shape what they take away. What this means in practice, of course, is that students should be given wider opportunities to connect their reading in class to their lives outside of

class, to use what they know to make sense of what they read. In addition to asking them what they think about a text, then, we can also ask them what the text makes them remember, what it makes them feel, what it helps them understand. Instead of reading to find answers about what texts mean, this new approach asks teachers and students to move together through a process of making meaning, drawing on both knowledge of the text and knowledge of themselves. The questions we ask will be different, the answers we seek will be different, and the end result may well be a richer and more deeply reasoned understanding of literature.

Related Reading

■ Applebee, A. N. (1989). "The Teaching of Literature in Programs with Reputations for Excellence in English." Technical Report. Center for the Learning and Teaching of Literature. State University at Albany, Albany, NY.
■ Beach, R., & Marshall, J. (1991). *Teaching Literature in the Secondary School.* San Diego, CA: Harcourt, Brace, Jovanovich.
■ Marshall, J. (1989). "Patterns of Discourse in Classroom Discussions of Literature." Technical Report. Center for the Learning and Teaching of Literature, State University at Albany, Albany, NY.
■ Marshall, J. (1988). "Classroom Discourse and Literary Response." In Nelms, B. (Ed.). *Literature in the Classroom: Readers, Texts, Contexts.* Urbana, IL: National Council of Teachers of English.
■ Rosenblatt, L. (1977). *The Reader, the Text, the Poem.* Carbondale, IL: Southern Illinois University Press.
■ Scholes, R. (1985). *Textual Power.* New Haven, CT: Yale University Press.

In Literature and Language . . .

In *Literature and Language*, we directly address these new developments in the study of literature and, again, the key word for our approach is integration. Classic works are represented here, but they are connected within thematic units to contemporary works and works from other traditions as well. Questions about the texts are here, but they are preceded and followed by questions about students' responses to those texts. We have attempted, in other words, to interrelate texts with one another and students with texts, to provide a structured occasion for students and teachers to explore the full range of opportunities that the study of literature affords.

Literature and Language can help teachers provide their students with a fresh point of departure in their study of literature, and in so doing, provide them with new reasons to continue reading and thinking about what they read. And that, after all, is probably what we want most for Jake and students like him.

SUSAN HYNDS, SENIOR CONSULTANT

Middle school students are, indeed, in the middle of childhood and young adulthood. But rather than living in some nether world between the two, they seem to be straddling them. Sometimes they tip more to the side of childhood, at other times to the side of young adulthood. That very quality is what makes them a delight to teach on one day and an exercise in hair-pulling exasperation the next.

Physically, socially, intellectually, and emotionally, young adolescents seem more different from each other and seem to change more dramatically in four short years than children of almost any other age. For example . . .

> *Middle school students have three main characteristics: energy, energy, and energy!*

Physically...

Middle school students have three main characteristics: energy, energy, and energy! Just stand in a middle school hallway during the change of classes and feel the vibrating chaos as hundreds of spirited young bodies stream from classrooms, banging their lockers, flying up stairways, screaming at their peers, and streaming past their teachers. But this seemingly endless reservoir of energy is fluctuating and unpredictable. The same students who were just screaming and hitting each other in the hallways can be seen a few minutes later, lounging in their desks in a near-catatonic state the minute classes begin again.

Because they always seem poised on the brink of hyperactivity or boredom, middle school students need to be invited to read about, write about, and explore topics that are personally meaningful and easily related to their own worlds in some way. They also need language activities that allow them to get up from their desks, to switch intellectual gears, and to interact with other students.

Socially...

There is no question that middle school students are very social creatures. Often, it's only through the support of their peers that they discover and develop their own personal identities. Their social identities, like their moods, are in a perpetual and dramatic state of flux.

The move from the safe, self-contained classroom of the elementary school to the middle school with its changes of classes and teachers makes young adolescents needy of little touches that say they are cared about and part of a classroom family. If you are a middle school teacher, you know how often you seem to be dispensing paper clips, pencils, hall passes, hugs, and bandaids.

Young adolescents need to belong in another way as well. The friends of elementary school are often quickly forgotten, but middle school students are beginning to forge the bonds of friendships that can last a lifetime. At the same time, they are beginning to think of themselves as members of a society. They are curious about how issues of race, gender, poverty, and crime touch their own lives or neighborhoods.

They are also becoming aware of social and cultural differences. For this reason, they need reading materials that allow them to explore a variety of human relationships and cultural perspectives. Teachers need to invite them to write and talk about these perspectives with others, and to capitalize on their irrepressibly social natures.

Intellectually...

For many years, it was assumed that students between the ages of ten and fourteen were beginning to move from what Piaget called "concrete operations" into what he called "formal operations"—basically, that they could think abstractly about themselves and the world. For that reason, many instructional materials for junior high school students were geared to lead students up through the ranks from concrete to more abstract levels of thinking.

Today, we know that most middle school students, indeed, many high school students, and even adults, have not yet moved fully into formal operational thinking in the purest sense of that term. This doesn't mean that middle school learners can't think abstractly. It means that they need teachers who can help them make concrete connections between abstract ideas and their own personal worlds.

A middle school student reading one of the Greek myths might remark: "He's just a male chauvinist!"

> *As productive members of society, middle school students are, quite literally, useless.*

or "She's just stupid!" They don't typically gravitate to more abstract comments like "Greed is a common human characteristic" or "People should follow the spirit and not the letter of the law." Because young adolescents often believe that all eyes are on them, it's hard for them to look past their own viewpoints.

This doesn't mean that middle school learners can't think abstractly about people and events; it means that they need to be invited to think beyond themselves. They need to be challenged with prompts like "Tell me all the reasons why you think this character did that" or "Does this historical event remind you of anything in today's world?" or "Tell me how you'd solve the problem that this character has just encountered." They need to be led back and forth from the world of concrete, personal experience, into the realm of imagining, speculating, and hypothesizing.

Emotionally...

Middle school students are intense! Perhaps because life seems so intense for them, middle school students have a powerful need to be recognized and listened to. They need to have opportunities to perform, to be at center stage, and to explore the dramatic potential in what they read. Oral interpretation, creative dramatics, readers' theater, and choral reading are excellent ways for young adolescents to discover the endless creative possibilities in literature.

At the same time, because they are so intense, they have a very strong need for routine. This does not mean a need for boring drill and practice exercises, but for comfortable rituals which invite them to take risks and be creative. They need little routines that say, "We are a classroom family, and we do things this way in *our* room." Providing predictable structures for such things as portfolio conferences and writers' and readers' workshops will give students this sense of safety and comfort.

The Nineties: Harsh Realities

Unfortunately, there are many issues that may not have faced us in the days when we went to junior high school. We are beginning to see some of the effects of parental substance abuse, sexual abuse, and domestic violence on the intellectual and emotional capacities of young adolescents. Perhaps these problems and issues were always with us and are simply made more visible today by stricter child abuse reporting laws. Whatever the case, parental abuse and neglect know no racial, ethnic, or socioeconomic lines. They are as present in suburbs as they are in cities.

There is also a great deal of media explicitness that encourages early sexuality, promotes materialism, and makes a life of crime seem like a glamorous occupation. On top of this, young adolescents are reaching puberty earlier than their cohorts did at the turn of the century, and, perhaps regrettably, many of them are experimenting with issues and experiences that once were considered beyond the realm of children their age.

Finally, as productive members of society, middle school students are, quite literally, useless. Years ago, young people worked on farms or in the village when they weren't in school. They were an integral part of the larger social community. Today, although they might be loved, they aren't *needed* for much of anything. And so, they often become consumers of junk food, video games, or other kinds of mindless diversion.

Teachers need to realize that through the teaching of literature and writing they can open the doorway to topics that help young adolescents to feel integral and involved in their community and the larger world.

Related Reading

■ George, P. S., Stevenson, C., Thomason, J., & Beane, J. (1992). *The Middle School and Beyond.* Alexandria, VA: Association for Supervision and Curriculum Development.

■ Hester, J. P., & Hester, P. J. (1983) Brain Research and the Middle School Curriculum. *Middle School Journal* 15 (1), pp. 4–7.

■ Hynds, S. (1994). *Making Connections: Language and Learning in the Classroom.* Norwood, MA: Christopher-Gordon.

■ Johnson, J. H., & Markle, G. C. (1986). *What Research Says to the Middle Level Practitioner.* Columbus, OH: National Middle School Association.

■ Lawrence, V. (1988). The Teacher in the Middle School. *Early Adolescence Magazine* 2 (3), pp. 19–21.

■ Silvern, S. B. (1990). Connecting Classroom Practice and Research. *Journal of Research in Childhood Education* 5 (1), pp. 85–86.

■ Wiles, J., & Bondi, J. (1986). *Making Middle Schools Work.* Alexandria, VA: Association for Supervision and Curriculum Development

In Literature and Language . . .

Literature and Language invites young adolescents to explore a whole array of personally meaningful topics and issues from a variety of cultural perspectives. A host of language activities invites students to work collaboratively or individually, moving beyond their own perspectives and considering the viewpoints of others. Best of all, *Literature and Language* invites you to create a sense of classroom community and to give your middle school students the self-confidence to become more involved in the world beyond the walls of school.

JUDITH A. LANGER, ARTHUR N. APPLEBEE, SENIOR CONSULTANTS

Recent studies of the English Language Arts curriculum have highlighted a number of problems in most programs:

■ Teachers' goals for the teaching of literature stress student response and understanding, but the questioning strategies in most programs treat literature as a source of "right answers."

■ In part as a result, the teaching of literature has remained a teacher-centered and text-centered activity, in contrast to an increasingly student-centered approach in composition.

■ The literature program is often completely separate from the writing program; writing is not treated as a context for enriching and extending student response to literature.

■ The selections chosen for study remain unnecessarily narrow; generally, they do not represent the many rich and diverse traditions that are part of the students' literary heritage. Even when a broader range of materials has been included in literature anthologies, teachers have avoided these materials because they are unfamiliar and often because the accompanying teaching support has been less than satisfactory.

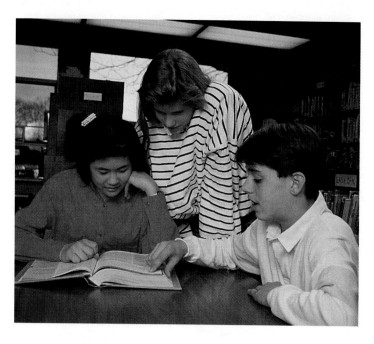

> *The teaching of literature has remained a teacher-centered and text-centered activity, in contrast to an increasingly student-centered approach in composition.*

Text-Based and Reader-Based Approaches

During the twentieth century, the major debates about the teaching of literature have centered on the relative contributions of the text and the reader's own understanding to "good" reading. New critical approaches, which dominated decades of instruction, involve close and careful textual analyses. They focus on the text as a source of knowledge, and by and large, emerge from a more generalized view that the text has a "message" that needs to be extracted by a reader following certain procedures. Recent studies indicate that the analytical procedure itself too often becomes the focus of instruction rather than a support for the reading process.

In contrast, approaches that focus on the reader—reader response theory, for example—consider meaning to reside in the reader or in the transaction between the reader and the text, with the reader's interpretations as evidence of good reading. Reader-based approaches are the views most consonant with current research on reading comprehension as an interactive and constructive process and with process-oriented research on reading, writing, and reasoning. Reader-based approaches also underlie the theoretical framework of the *Literature and Language* series, which builds upon current theories of writing, literature, and the teaching of literature. The series is designed to remedy the problems that have been identified in recent studies of the English curriculum.

Literature and Language: *Conceptual Framework*

For the past few years, Judith Langer has been developing a theory for the teaching of literature, which describes the process of coming to understand literature and the contribution that the teaching of literature can make to the intellectual and cultural development of the growing student. Langer's theory is based on research that has shown the following:

■ The meaning-making processes used in reading literature are not necessarily the same as those used in other coursework.

■ The special contribution of literary understanding to the developing intellect needs to be acknowledged.

■ The teaching of critical thinking in literature—the kinds of questions asked and the kinds of responses sought—needs to differ from the teaching of critical thinking in other subjects, focusing instead on helping students engage more successfully in the processes involved in literary understanding.

■ Instructional focus in the process of understanding can help poorer as well as more successful readers engage in higher literacy and literature learning.

The Process of Reading Literature.

A process view of reading suggests that making sense of a work of literature involves building envisionments, with understanding changing and growing over time. The term *envisionment* refers to a world of understanding a reader has about a text. When you read *Driving Miss Daisy*, for instance, what you read in the first few scenes provides you with only the scantest hints of what will unfold later in the play. The conversation is important at that time because it provides you with the necessary information to begin building an understanding of what will happen later. Thus the conversation is only of momentary importance, soon disappearing from your awareness, replaced with a deepening and ever-changing understanding of the main characters and their relationships with each other.

Meaning-Making Through Envisionment-Building.

An envisionment includes what a reader understands about a text, the questions the reader has, and the reader's hunches about how the piece will unfold. A reader has a different envisionment at each point in a reading; the envisionment changes as the reading progresses. As more is read, some details are dropped from the envisionment as no longer important, and new details are added. The effect is a continuing elaboration upon the reader's knowledge. Meaning gained from one portion of the reading is shaped by earlier interpretations and continues to change in light of interpretations developed later in the reading. This changing understanding is at the heart of the reader's response to literature, and needs to be at the heart of meaningful reader-based instruction.

Envisionment as Response.

Envisionment is the way in which a reader experiences a text—the reader's total understanding or response at any point in time. During the reading of a novel, story, play, or poem, a reader's envisionment changes as new information from the text and new inferences from the reader influence the reader's response. This evolving envisionment might be thought of as a series of envisionments, which leads to an envisionment at the end of a reading. This end point is not the sum total of all the other envisionments but rather a result of all the changes and modifications in understanding that have occurred along the way.

The envisionment at the end of a reading—the text world of ideas, questions, and quandaries that every reader comes away with after reading a work of literature—is a reader's starting point for contemplation and discussion. This envisionment can become fodder for further modification, as other readers offer alternative ways of making sense of a text.

The concept of envisionment as response is a critical one for instruction. The belief that when students read they continually modify their understandings demands questions that are not structured according to traditional hierarchies. These hierarchies, based on distinctions such as literal questions and inferential questions or on Bloom's taxonomy, are text-based and do not reflect the reader's process of sense-making. Words "on the page," for instance, are quite different from the ways in which those words are combined in a reader's mind at any given point in time. Talking about particular words from the text outside of the reader's text world disregards the response-building process the reader has engaged in. Rather than helping readers, discussions that begin by focusing on the "literal"

meaning of the text rather than on what sense students have made of the text can actually get in the way of students' understanding. Similarly, retracing the plot line to check understanding ignores the envisionment-building process that led to the readers' response to the text as a whole. Rather than building on what students already understand, such activities force them to retreat from their understandings to focus on details out of context. Focusing on details may be helpful at a later point, however, as readers begin to sort out why their interpretations of the same text differ.

Readers naturally want to discuss their envisionments (or initial responses). Recall, for example, the experience of finishing a good book, a mystery perhaps. You probably ended up with ideas and questions you wanted to talk about with others who had read the same book. What you experienced was a desire to share your envisionment.

The best reader-based questions teachers can ask immediately after students have read a selection are questions that tap students' envisionments. These questions might be similar to the following: *What were you thinking as you finished the story? Is there anything you'd like to talk about? What did the poem mean to you?*

What Is Unique About Literary Understanding?

While readers use envisionment-building in both literary and informative contexts, the essential concerns are different for each type of reading. When engaged in informative reading (for example, to get information from social studies and science materials), readers early on establish a sense of the topic and of the author's slant, and they use this judgment as a point of reference to monitor new and growing understandings. Once a sense of direction is established, it takes a great deal of countervailing information to change a reader's notion of the whole.

The reading of literature involves a great deal of thinking that is different from the kinds of thinking required by informative texts.

In contrast, literary reading abounds with the exploration of possibilities. Readers continually open new possibilities for meaning, for alternative interpretations and changing points of view. The possibilities change over time, growing out of the readers' developing envisionments.

The reading of literature involves a great deal of critical thinking that is different from the kinds of thinking required by informative texts. For example, in social studies or science materials, students must focus on understanding an argument or on learning specific content. As with literary texts, the reader works with a sense of the whole. However, in informational reading the sense of the whole serves as a steady point of reference, while in literary reading it is a constantly changing horizon of possibilities.

Instruction that helps students become competent readers of literature needs to reflect an awareness of these distinctions. Teachers must encourage students to recognize ambiguities, to explore possibilities, and to seek ways of "filling out" meanings, using their knowledge of the text and of human experience to develop deeper insights. The goal is to support students in becoming mature, sophisticated readers, capable of dealing with complex texts in increasingly thoughtful ways.

Putting Theory into Practice

The ideal literature classroom is a literary community where students are active meaning-makers: where they have room to respond, interpret, think critically, and contrast their ideas with those of other readers. To move toward this ideal, the questions asked need to change dramatically, so that they support the process of understanding from the student's point of view. Rather than seeking right answers and predetermined interpretations, questions need to serve as "thought tappers." Students should respond to these open-ended questions individually, in small groups, or as a class, sharing their initial questions and understandings and then moving beyond into more fully developed interpretations.

The following are guidelines for supporting students through the rethinking process, after they have read a literary selection. The boldface heads correspond to those on the **Explain** pages of *Literature and Language*.

1. First Impressions. Begin with a question that encourages students to share their initial responses to the piece. For example: *What were your thoughts as you finished reading this story? What were your reactions to Victor?*

2. Second Thoughts. Ask open-ended questions that operate as scaffolds, helping students to move beyond their initial understandings toward fuller and more carefully reasoned responses. Students might explore motivations, causes and effects, and implications, and might relate the parts to one another and to their understanding of the whole. Students might also consider how their ideas and feelings have changed as a result of their reading experience. The questions asked might be similar to the following: *What are the effects of Ernie's crush? How do you think Dolores would react if she found out who was sending her flowers? Think about your previous discussion about retarded people. Have your feelings changed after reading the story?*

3. Broader Connections. After the students have worked through their understandings, ask them to make connections between the selection and the world around them. For example, after reading and discussing an excerpt from Jackie Robinson's autobiography, students might be asked: *Many saw Jackie Robinson as a role model for young people. Should we expect profes-*

sional athletes to be role models, or should they be judged only on their athletic performance?

In addition to conducting discussions, it is important to involve students in collaborative activities and in writing both before and after reading. The following are guidelines for further analysis and for making writing an integral part of the meaning-making process.

Literary Concepts. After students have had a chance to develop their own interpretations, they can then turn their attention to the literary elements that underlie the work. Students' appreciation of language and structure and of the effects these engender is enhanced when you assign groups of students to work collaboratively on literary analysis: for example, when pairs of students identify parts of the text that were particularly vivid for them and then analyze what created this effect, or when groups of students debate and defend their interpretation of the ending of a selection.

T he ideal literature classroom is a literary community where students are active meaning-makers.

Writing Options. Writing offers a powerful context for thinking about literature, for clarifying understandings, and for sharing them with others. Writing before reading helps students connect the reading they will do with what they already know, thus providing a way into a new text or orienting the reader toward that text. Writing after reading provides students with opportunities to connect the reading they have done to other ideas and experiences.

This variety of questions and activities provides students with an array of vantage points from which to reflect upon a text. The guidelines for questions are not meant to imply that only one sequence of question types is effective or that each type of question and activity needs to be addressed during every lesson. However, one guideline is almost always applicable: Begin a discussion with an open-ended question that taps students' initial responses (not the teacher's understandings), thus inviting students to take an active role in building their own understandings of literature.

Effective Instruction: Underlying Principles

A teacher's techniques, and the activities within which they are embedded, are likely to be different in every classroom. The teacher alone has the professional knowledge to tailor instruction to the needs of a particular class. Across classrooms, however, the following principles underlie programs that effectively involve students in learning to develop rich, thoughtful interpretations of literature.

1. Students are active makers of meaning. Students are treated as thinkers, as if they can and will have interesting and cogent thoughts about a work of literature, which they will want to discuss.

2. Literature reading generates questions. Effective programs assume that after reading a work, students come away with initial responses and with questions that are part of their envisionments. Good instruction acknowledges that the process of understanding literature involves the raising of questions.

3. Content questions tap student knowledge. When teachers ask questions about content, they are tapping into student knowledge and understandings. Such questions have no predetermined right answers and are meant to prompt extended thought and sharing of ideas.

4. Class meetings are a time to develop understandings. Meaningful class discussions support the process of coming to understand. With the help of the teacher, students develop their envisionments. Thus, the cognitive behaviors students engage in during discussion are the same envisionment-building behaviors they engage in during reading.

5. Instruction scaffolds the process of understanding. All questions, activities, and assignments are designed to help students develop their own understandings, not memorize (or guess) the "right" interpretation of a text.

6. Control is transferred from teacher to students. Students work through their ideas alone, in small groups, and in class discussion. While students work, they are encouraged to interact collaboratively, to respond to and communicate with each other.

Related Reading

■ Andrasick, K. D. (1990). *Opening Texts; Using Writing to Teach Literature.* Portsmouth, NH: Heinemann.

■ Applebee, A. N. (1992). *Literature in the Secondary School: Studies of Curriculum and Instruction in the United States.* Urbana, IL: National Council of Teachers of English.

■ Applebee, A. N., Langer, J. A., & Mullis, I. (1989). *Crossroads in American Education.* Princeton, NJ: National Assessment of American Progress, Educational Testing Service.

■ Diaz, P., & Hayhoe, M. (1988). *Developing Response to Poetry.* Philadelphia: Open University Press.

■ Langer, J. A. (1990). "Understanding Literature." *Language Arts,* December.

■ Langer, J. A. (ed.) (1992). *Literature Instruction: A Focus on Student Response.* Urbana, IL: National Council of Teachers of English.

■ Langer, J. A. (ed.). (1990) "The Process of Understanding: Reading for Literary and Informative Purposes." *Research in the Teaching of English* 23, pp. 229-260.

■ Langer, J. A., & Applebee, A. N. (1987). *How Writing Shapes Thinking: Studies of Teaching and Learning.* Urbana, IL: National Council of Teachers of English.

■ Langer, J. A., Bartolome, L., Vasquez, O., & Lucas, T. (1990). "Meaning Construction in School Literacy Tasks: A Study of Bilingual Students." *American Educational Research Journal.*

■ Newell, G. E., & Durst, R. K. (eds.) (1992). *Exploring Texts: The Role of Discussion and Writing in the Teaching and Learning of Literature.* Norwood, MA: Christopher-Gordon.

■ Probst, R. E. (1988). *Response and Analysis: Teaching Literature in the Junior and Senior High School.* Portsmouth, NH: Boynton/Cook.

*I*N LITERATURE AND LANGUAGE . . .

Literature and Language is a program designed to help the teacher put into practice these principles for effective instruction. The activities and questions in the program support envisionment-building, build confidence in dealing with literary texts, and encourage active participation in the classroom literary community.

VALUES OF MULTICULTURAL LITERATURE

DONNA E. NORTON, SENIOR CONSULTANT

The literary heritage associated with folklore, whether folk tales, fables, myths, or legends, is especially important for developing multicultural understandings.

Appreciating Our Literary Heritage

Developing understandings of our literary heritage whether it is European, African, Native-American, Hispanic, or Asian is one of the most important tasks for educators. Experts in multicultural education frequently emphasize the value of using literature to increase cultural awareness.

Through carefully selected and shared literature, students begin to understand and to appreciate a literary heritage that comes from many diverse backgrounds. Through this literature, students learn to identify with people who created the stories, whether from the past or the present. From the past, they discover folk tales, fables, myths, and legends that clarify the values and beliefs of the people — the great stories on which whole cultures have been founded. From the present, they discover the threads that weave the past with the present and the themes and values that continue to be important.

Folklore as Catalyst for Multicultural Understanding

The literary heritage associated with folklore, whether folk tales, fables, myths, or legends, is especially important for developing multicultural understandings. Joseph Campbell (1988) stresses that myths from all cultures are powerful literature and should be read and understood by everyone. He maintains that myths are as important today as they were in earlier times because the myths (a) allow people to experience the awe of the universe, (b) show the shape and mystery of the universe, (c) support and validate the social order within the culture, and (d) teach people how to live within that culture. By reading Native-American myths, for example, students discover that Native-American cultures had strong foundations and powerful beliefs long before the arrival of the Spaniards in 1492. Chinese folklore

leads students toward an understanding of an ancient culture that influenced peoples from around the world. Through African folklore students learn about the proverbs and legends that have helped to shape the thoughts and deeds of current African leaders. African folklore is also the foundation of African-American slave tales in which students discover the bravery of the human spirit and the will to survive in even the most terrible circumstances. Folk tales from the ancient Aztec and Mayan civilizations demonstrate to their descendents and to the population at large, the rich traditions of many of the Hispanic peoples. By comparing this folklore with the folklore from European origins, students begin to learn about both the similarities and the differences among people.

All Students Benefit

Multicultural literature is of value to both students who are members of a racial or ethnic minority and to students who are not. Through multicultural literature, minority students realize that they have a cultural heritage of which they can be proud and recognize that their culture has made important contributions to the United States and to the world. Pride in their heritage helps minority students improve their self-concepts and develop cultural identity.

Learning about other cultures allows students to see that people who belong to other racial or ethnic groups are real people, with feelings, emotions, and needs similar to their own — individual human beings, not stereotypes.

Folklore Is Culture-Rich

Studying the folklore from diverse cultures is especially meaningful because, according to Diane Wolkstein (1992), "Every story is rooted in a culture, and the world of culture is limitless—music, dance, religion, art.... Storytelling is a challenge, an art, a possibility, a doorway into other cultures, a momentary opening into the universe" (p. 704). This momentary glimpse into the universe may be one of the most powerful reasons for sharing folklore from different cultures with students. Folklore helps students improve their understanding of the world in the following ways:

■ by showing the inter-relatedness of various types of stories that are found in cultures from around the world
■ by introducing the idea of cultural diffusion as students observe how different versions of a tale are dispersed
■ by developing an appreciation for the culture and art of different countries

- by introducing information about geography, family patterns, and celebrations from different countries
- by familiarizing students with the many languages and dialects of cultures around the world through names and other language patterns that are found in authentic tales
- by providing a stimulus for creative drama, writing, and other forms of artistic expression that helps students interact with their own imaginations and gain respect for the people who created such tales
- by encouraging students to realize that people from all over the world have inherent goodness, mercy, courage, and industry
- and, as stated previously, by helping them understand the values and beliefs of diverse cultures

Classic and Contemporary Nonfiction

Equaling the values of reading folklore are the personal gains acquired by students when they study classic and contemporary works from their own cultural backgrounds and those of other cultures. As they read **autobiography, biography,** and other nonfiction works, they develop social sensitivity to the needs of others and realize that people have similarities as well as differences. Heightened sensitivity and awareness hopefully increase the concern for the rights of all people as students raise their own levels of moral consciousness. Biography and autobiography about people from many cultures are excellent for encouraging high aspirations and respect for the social contributions of outstanding people. By reading about people who achieve, students discover that achievement in such areas as science, art, literature, music, and politics is possible for people from all backgrounds. In addition, the students may discover that the subjects of these biographies have many personal characteristics in common. Developing these characteristics could encourage students to search for and try to attain their own areas of excellence.

Fiction and Poetry

As students read poetry and other fictional works, look at art from various cultures, and listen to music developed by the culture, students gain aesthetic appreciation as they learn to understand and respect the artistic contributions of people from many cultural backgrounds. They may also expand their knowledge of geography and natural history, and increase their understanding of historical and sociological change. For example, reading **authentic historical fiction** about people from the past, allows students to be in touch with their own historical past as well as to make their cultural world seem alive and vivid. Students who are not members of the cultural group gain historical understandings and develop respect for those people who made contributions or battled unjust causes in their will to survive. It is only through historical fiction, that students can vicariously live through the past and gain new understandings of the people and the issues of the time. Historical fiction allows students to accompany characters during times of both triumph and tragedy and to respond to injustice as they vicariously accompany the Cherokee Indians as they walk "The Trail of Tears," live in Aztec Mexico at the time of the Spanish conquest, or be on a slave ship as it nears the coast of an unknown land.

Poetry is another genre of literature that helps students develop respect for and understanding of other cultures. By reading the work of poets from numerous cultures, students develop an appreciation for the vividness of the language and the ability of the poet to create images that allow readers to visualize the world in new ways. Whether it is the poetry of African-American poet Langston Hughes, the poetic texts of Native-American author Byrd Baylor, the haiku of the Japanese poet Issa, or the poetic experiences developed by British poet Robert Louis Stevenson, students can respond to beautiful images and vivid language.

Contemporary realistic fiction provides another window on the diverse multicultural world. Through reading realistic fiction, students

identify with characters of their own age who have similar interests and problems. Realistic fiction can help students discover that their problems and desires are not unique, and that they are not alone in experiencing certain feelings and situations. Realistic fiction also extends students' horizons by broadening their interests, allowing them to experience new adventures, and showing them different ways to view and deal with conflicts in their own lives. Many of the themes in realistic fiction, such as "dreams for the future," "the importance of ethnic heritage," and "love of family" are found in contemporary realistic fiction books that have settings in different cultures.

Through sharing multicultural literature, students discover that while not all people may share their personal beliefs and values, individuals can and must learn to live in harmony. Through multicultural literature, students learn to respect the values and contributions of all people. The wide range of multicultural themes helps students develop an understanding of social change and realize that all groups have made notable achievements.

Related Reading

- Campbell, J. (1988). *The Power of Myth.* New York: Doubleday. (Campbell discusses mythology from around the world and presents reasons for studying mythology.)
- Hayden, D., ed. (1992). *Venture into Cultures: A Resource Book of Multicultural Materials and Programs.* Chicago: American Library Association. (The text includes an annotated list of books and program ideas for using multicultural literature. The cultures include African-American, Arabic, Asian, Hispanic, Jewish, Native-American, and Persian.)
- Norton, D. E. (September 1990). "Teaching Multicultural Literature in the Reading Curriculum." *The Reading Teacher.* Vol. 44: 28-40. (The article includes a sequence for multicultural literature study and recommendations for Native-American, African-American, and Hispanic literature.)
- Norton, D. E. (1991). *Through the Eyes of a Child: An Introduction to Children's Literature,* Third Edition, Columbus: Merrill/Macmillan. (Chapter 11, Multicultural Literature, includes numerous literature sources and suggestions for activities to accompany multicultural literature.)
- Williams, H. (1991). *Books by African-American Authors and Illustrators for Children and Young Adults.* Chicago: American Library Association. (This text identifies books written and illustrated by black writers and artists.)
- Wolkstein, D. (Nov.–Dec. 1992). "Twenty-Five Years of Storytelling: The Spirit of the Art." *The Horn Book.* Vol. LXVIII: 702–708. (The author is a storyteller and a teacher who discusses the requirements of multicultural storytelling.)

*I*N LITERATURE AND LANGUAGE . . .

Multicultural literature is an essential part of each unit.
- Selections from a broad range of ethnic traditions provide an added dimension to the exploration of the unit themes.
- Unit Six in grades 6, 7, and 8 presents a rich mosaic of folklore arranged in groupings that make thematic connections with the other units in each book. In grades 6 and 7 the focus is on world folklore. Grade 8 is dedicated to the folklore of the Americas.
- Art and artifacts pictured throughout the texts are carefully chosen to represent a rich array of cultures and traditions.
- **Explore** pages in the pupil books provide a wealth of cultural, historical, and geographical information to support the literature selections.

LEP STUDENTS IN THE LITERATURE CLASSROOM

ANDREA B. BERMÚDEZ, SENIOR CONSULTANT

The contemporary classroom reflects the diversity of language and cultures in the United States at the present time. The 1990 U.S. Census, for example, suggests that there are over sixteen million homes where people communicate in a non-English language. The culturally and linguistically diverse students from these homes bring with them a wealth of potential and experiences that should be utilized by teachers to enrich the learning environment of all students. Transition to a mainstream classroom may not be dependent exclusively on the efforts of the students but on the degree of sensitivity of a teacher who can successfully mediate between the learner and instruction. Developing multicultural sensitivity is a fourfold process which involves: (a) acceptance of the students' circumstances, (b) a genuine search for information regarding the background and prior knowledge of the students, (c) an updated bank of teaching strategies, and (d) a desire to find the best options for the students.

> *To avoid misunderstanding, it is critical that teachers disregard the assumption that all students have the same, or similar, frames of reference or perceptions about the world.*

A Profile of the LEP Learner

While many culturally and linguistically diverse students experience limited English proficiency (LEP), LEP students are not necessarily from homes whose first language is other than English. Many monolingual English-speaking students, regardless of ethnic background, experience difficulty when dealing with text and written expression. These difficulties include problems in the following areas: (a) comprehending text, (b) expressing ideas clearly, and (c) negotiating meaning regarding the context and symbolism expressed by words and/or phrases.

There are certain cultural and linguistic characteristics of learners that may set the LEP learner apart from the "standards" operating within a mainstream classroom. Teachers expect certain behaviors in response to the learning environment offered

to students and often become frustrated when these behaviors do not occur. To avoid misunderstanding, it is critical that teachers disregard the assumption that all students have the same, or similar, frames of reference or perceptions about the world. The following is a partial list of behaviors that teachers commonly experience with LEP students.

■ LEP students generally **focus attention on style,** not content. This is often a result of teachers who are very insistent on error-free products to the detriment of original ideas and creative expression.

■ These students are often **unaware of learning strategies** that could facilitate comprehension, such as brainstorming, mapping, and cooperative learning. These strategies must be taught directly to ensure their effectiveness.

■ LEP students **may become disorderly** and disobedient as a result of frustration created by their inability to relate to the learning environment.

■ LEP students often **do not make eye contact** when addressing others. Unlike mainstream U.S.A., many cultures consider eye contact a sign of disrespect to teachers or others of high status.

■ LEP students may seem to **have difficulty meeting deadlines.** The concept of time varies across cultures. A teacher should not assume that students are familiar with the very precise chronology by which the mainstream classroom operates. Students need to be taught how to function within a deadline-driven curriculum.

■ LEPs **may not seem to understand classroom "rules."** Discipline is not a universally defined concept. Schools and homes need to establish common parameters of discipline to obtain positive results.

■ LEPs generally **show a different speaking-listening style.** Not all cultures communicate in tandem. In some cultures, it is considered acceptable to interrupt others while talking, finish their stories, or talk and listen simultaneously.

■ LEPs may **organize thoughts in a pattern that does not correspond to the expected linear-sequential pattern** characteristic of English communication. For example, they may be redundant when trying to express ideas, or they may explain a situation in a "roundabout" manner.

■ LEPs may exhibit an **external locus of control.** Students sometimes seem dependent on teachers or peers for validation of their responses or for vital information related to the learning task. Self-dependence can be learned and should be taught, not expected.

Common Problem Areas

The following areas pose special challenges to LEP students in trying to comprehend literary selections.

Vocabulary difficulty. If students do not have prior experience with the words appearing in the selection, the normal links between the concept and its label will not occur. Problems often arise when a selection contains low frequency words, idiomatic or dialectal expressions, and/or jargon.

Unfamiliar content. The message in the literature may be misunderstood if students are not placed in the proper context of the selection. This often happens as a result of: (a) lack of prior experience with the context, (b) abstract nature of the ideas expressed (e.g., poetry), or (c) culture-specificity of ideas expressed.

Grammatical features of the selection. Comprehension problems arise when students encounter: (a) dialectal forms, (b) outdated grammatical forms, (c) unusual word order, and/or (d) above average length of the selection.

Effective Teaching/ Learning Strategies

The following instructional strategies have been shown to be successful with LEP learners.

Cognitive Mapping. Every individual has a unique history of experiences which play a vital part in acquiring new knowledge. Many students, however, have poor strategies for organizing and categorizing this information. Instruction in cognitive mapping can enable students to integrate previous experience with new knowledge.

An Integrated Approach. The integrated approach to learning is particularly successful with LEP learners. Students learn about reading and writing while listening; they learn about writing from reading and gain insights into reading from writing. Any strategy or approach based on dissecting language into mutually exclusive components jeopardizes second language acquisition by not drawing on the prior knowledge and strengths of the learner.

> *Differing language backgrounds and prior cultural experiences will determine the degree of difficulty with the language and "culture" of the classroom.*

Cooperative Learning. Cooperative learning is a generic term that refers to a variety of approaches to integrating students into group activities where each participant is responsible for contributing to group outcomes and products. Cooperative learning strategies significantly improve students' achievement and productivity for a wide range of subjects and grade levels. This approach also improves self-esteem and respect for others.

Lesson Format

Using scientific inquiry to present literature selections to LEP students maximizes learning. This format includes the following steps:

1. Exploration Phase
Probe prior knowledge.

■ Use brainstorming, mapping, and discussion probes to assess how familiar the student is with the context of the selection, and to introduce new ideas.

2. Instructional Phase
Provide familiarity with context.

■ Preteach any concepts for which students may not have a cultural reference. These may include historical references, mythological references, obscure terms, and dialect.
■ Define abstract concepts such as *opinion* or *evaluation* in concrete terms, giving specific examples.

Teach new vocabulary in clusters.

■ When possible, present key vocabulary in clusters related by meaning or word family.

Present in a variety of modes.

■ Present concepts in a variety of media, for example: pictures, signs, films, graphic organizers, videos, sketches, and so on.
■ Read some selections aloud as LEP students follow, or use commercially or student-produced audio tapes.

3. Application Phase
Provide opportunities to relate groups of concepts/words.

■ Use webbing or mapping to help students establish relationships among concepts.
■ Have students write summaries of what they have read.
■ Develop (and encourage students to develop) cross-cultural analogies for concepts, characters, plots, and themes.

Encourage alternate modes of expression.

■ Allow students to express themselves in various media.

Differing language backgrounds and prior cultural experiences will determine the degree of difficulty with the language and "culture" of the classroom. The teacher's ability to assess the strengths that students bring to the learning experience as well as a commitment made to continually search for better instructional alternatives will, to a great extent, determine the academic success of LEP students.

In Literature and Language . . .

LEP students are provided with the support they need to succeed.

■ A rich variety of multicultural literature fosters self-esteem and cultural worth.
■ The integrated design of the series allows students to draw on prior knowledge while learning new material.
■ The reader-based approach to literature allows all students to develop meaningful interpretations.
■ Successful LEP learning strategies such as brainstorming, mapping, and cooperative learning are found throughout the series.
■ Special LEP support is provided in the **Annotated Teacher's Edition** and **Unit Resource Books.**
■ Options for Learning on **Extend** pages provide opportunities for alternative modes of expression.

Cooperative learning is not the traditional small group situation common in classrooms, in which students work in proximity toward individual goals. Nor is cooperative learning just a group of students working together in which one or two students do all of the work.

In cooperative learning:

■ Students work interdependently to ensure that all of the group's members master the assigned material.
■ Individuals are accountable, and each student's mastery is assessed.
■ The membership of the group is heterogeneous in ability.
■ All members participate actively in a group.
■ The teacher monitors behavior and learning and gives feedback to groups on their effectiveness.
■ Members of the group evaluate their own effectiveness.

Advocates of cooperative learning assert that it motivates students to learn, improves social skills, promotes self-esteem in students of all abilities, and lessens dependence on the teacher. Recent classroom research appears to validate claims about the effectiveness of the cooperative learning experience.

The Cooperative Learning Group

No more than three students in a group are recommended for the class that does not have much experience with cooperative learning. Six is probably the most members a group can have and still be effective.

Advocates of cooperative learning assert that it motivates students to learn, improves social skills, promotes self-esteem in students of all abilities, and lessens dependence on the teacher.

The makeup of a cooperative learning group depends on its purpose. Grouping by interests and by a cross-section of ability are just two possibilities. Grouping might also be random: for example, students might count off to create groups in which no one has the same number. Then, when an assignment is made, the task may be divided into parts. All the students with the same number then become experts on one part and are held responsible for reporting on it. This technique is sometimes called *jigsawing*. All the pieces of the puzzle are put together so that everyone in a group sees the whole picture. Not only do members of the group pool their knowledge, but they also teach the others what they need to know.

While the groups are working, the teacher circulates and observes for appropriate behavior and also listens for any misunderstandings. Sometimes a teacher may intervene by asking a question that directs the students' thinking toward a solution. Even then, the emphasis should be on having the group, rather than the teacher, work through the problem. At other times, especially if more than one group is having difficulty, teachers may interrupt to discuss the point of confusion with the entire class.

Accountability and Assessment

When a group has completed an assignment, there remains the issue of accountability for both the group and the individuals in it. Some ways of assuring accountability are as follows:

1. Have the group produce a single report, paper, or other end result. Every member signs off on the final product to indicate agreement with its conclusions or answers. The teacher then chooses individual students at random to respond to additional questions: for example, to explain the rationale behind an answer.
2. If members produce individual products, randomly choose one product to evaluate as representative of the group, or have the group make the choice. You might also have one member demonstrate understanding of a concept.
3. Keep a progress chart on which the performance of each group and its individuals is charted, or have each group keep the chart. Hold students responsible for improving the performance of the group and its members.
4. Divide the tasks so that each member completes a different one. However, don't accept any work until all the group's members have completed their individual tasks and have compiled the results.

Grades, the most obvious rewards in most classrooms, can be used to encourage cooperative learning. A teacher might average individual scores; give a group score for a product, which all members receive; randomly score one member's paper or exam; give individual scores plus bonus points for successful group performance; or give all members the lowest score.

IN LITERATURE AND LANGUAGE . . .

Opportunities for cooperative work appear throughout the text.

■ Prereading and postreading activities and questions on the **Explore** and **Explain** pages are particularly well-suited to small group discussion.
■ Multimodal activities on the **Extend** pages include cooperative learning projects.
■ **Writer's Workshop** assignments call for group work at all stages of the writing process.
■ Cooperative projects based on unit themes are outlined in the **Teacher's Edition** at the beginning of each unit.

Schools tend to favor students who are strong in linguistic and logical-mathematical intelligences and discriminate against those who are weak in those areas. . . .

We are all unique. We have different sets of characteristics, abilities, and needs. It should not be surprising, therefore, to learn that we have different learning styles as well. Yet it is only recently (the early 1980s) that this theory of learning gained acceptance, based largely on the initial research of Harvard psychologist Howard Gardner. Gardner recognizes seven types of intelligence: linguistic, logical-mathematical, spatial, musical, bodily-kinesthetic, interpersonal, and intrapersonal. Everyone has all seven intelligences, but in different proportions.

Research indicates that the different kinds of intelligences are located in different parts of the brain. There seems to be a correlation between behavior and hemisphericity (the dominance of either the right or the left side of the brain). The various parts of the brain do cooperate with each other, which suggests that the seven types of intelligence interact as well.

Different environments favor and encourage the development of specific intelligences. From Chart A, which shows the characteristic strengths of each intelligence, you can infer how certain environments are likely to be more favorable to some intelligences than to others. As Gardner points out, when we address the notion of high intelligence in our society, we are usually talking about only two or three types: linguistic, logical-mathematical, and sometimes intrapersonal. Other researchers have suggested that because of their emphasis on formal testing, schools tend to favor students who are strong in linguistic and logical-mathematical intelligences and discriminate against those who are weak in those areas though strong in others.

The theory of multiple intelligences is the basis for recognizing that not only do all learners have different abilities but, because they do, they also have different styles of learning. Biological and developmental characteristics can determine how we learn, what we learn most easily, and what we have difficulty with. The same teaching method is not equally effective with all students. Student performance does improve markedly when learning styles are accommodated.

There are five elements to consider when accommodating various learning styles: environmental, emotional, sociological, physical, and psychological. Studies show that the individual needs of students are best met when classrooms are organized and teaching approaches are developed with learning styles in mind. As Chart B shows, these needs include the physical conditions of the classroom as well as interpersonal and pedagogical considerations.

Within every group a significant number of students has needs that are different enough from the standard to inhibit learning. Classroom design, for example, can affect students' achievement. Students tend to need more light as they grow older. The need for sound also tends to increase during adolescence. Yet often a class includes a minority of students who require less light and some who need complete silence—to the point of needing ear plugs—when they work. Temperature variations may also affect some students more than others. And while a majority of adolescents show a preference for sitting casually in soft chairs, some require the more formal support of a desk.

Chart A

Linguistic	Is verbal; thinks in words; has highly developed auditory skills; likes to read and write
Logical-Mathematical	Thinks conceptually; capable of highly abstract thinking, logic, reasoning
Spatial	Thinks in visual images and pictures; enjoys drawing, designing, building, daydreaming, inventing
Musical	Is sensitive to music, nonverbal sounds, rhythm; enjoys listening to, singing, moving to, playing music
Bodily-Kinesthetic	Processes knowledge through bodily sensations; has fine-motor coordination; communicates through body language
Interpersonal	Understands other people; organizes, communicates, socializes
Intrapersonal	Prefers working alone; intuitive, independent, private, self-motivated

Chart B

Stimuli	Elements
Environmental	Sound, Light, Temperature, Design
Emotional	Motivation, Persistence, Responsibility, Structure
Sociological	Peers, Self, Pair, Team, Adult, Varied
Physical	Perceptual, Intake, Time, Mobility
Psychological	Analytic/Global, Hemispheric Preference, Impulsive/Reflective

[Rita Dunn and Kenneth Dunn. "Can Students Identify Their Own Learning Styles?" *Educational Leadership,* February 1983, p. 61.]

To accommodate these varying physical needs, a classroom might include an informal area with cushions, couches, and carpeting; quiet areas for some; and an area where students can work while listening to music with a headset on. Loosening a bulb in one corner of the classroom creates an area for those who prefer low light.

The older students get, the less teacher-motivated they become, preferring peer learning. By the ninth grade, there also is a greater need to learn and study alone. At all levels, though, some students have needs that are contrary to the general tendencies of the age group. Allowing for variation can accommodate the different styles. Thus, students might set mutual objectives within a small group under teacher guidance, go off to study by themselves, and then return to share their findings with the group and the class.

Not all students learn verbally. If a student's modality is kinesthetic, for example, he or she will learn more if at least the initial instruction is presented through manipulatives. The students who require more mobility than others need to be able to move around the classroom. Instruction can be so organized that different learning takes place in different parts of the room, requiring

students to move from one part to the other. Students with kinesthetic learning styles benefit from activities such as performing skits and observing the natural world. Students with a spatial orientation will enjoy building models and sketching illustrations. Students who have musical style will respond to activities such as composing ballads and choosing music to reflect the mood of a literary selection.

The majority of teachers teach analytically, reaching students with linguistic and logical-mathematical strengths. Teachers need to become aware of their own learning and teaching styles so that they can better meet student needs, and this will improve classroom performance. One goal should be for teachers to integrate the multimodal activities into their lessons. Another goal should be to help all students move from their single, favored modes to a mix of instructional modes from which they might benefit. (The essay "Alternative Assessment in the Literature Classroom," on page T29 provides strategies for evaluating students with various learning styles.)

> *Teachers need to become aware of their own learning and teaching styles so that they can better meet student needs.*

Related Reading

■ Dunn, K., & Dunn, R. (1987). "Dispelling Outmoded Beliefs About Student Learning." *Educational Leadership.* March.

■ Dunn, R. (1983). "Can Students Identify Their Own Learning Styles?" *Educational Leadership.* February.

■ Dunn, R. (1987). In *Their Own Way: Discovering and Encouraging Your Child's Personal Learning Styles.* Los Angeles: Tarcher.

■ Dunn, R., Beaudry, J. S., & Klavas, A. (1989). "Survey of Research on Learning Styles." *Educational Leadership.* March.

■ Gardner, H. *(1983). Frames of Mind, The Theory of Multiple Intelligences.* New York: Basic Books, Inc.

■ Keefe, J., M. Languis, C., & Dunn, R. (1986). *Learning Style Profile.* Reston, VA: National Association of Secondary School Principals.

■ Wheeler, R. (1980). "An Alternative to Failure: Teaching Reading According to Students' Perceptual Strengths." *Kappa Delta Pi Record 17,* (2), pp. 59–63.

*I*N LITERATURE AND LANGUAGE . . .

Addressing the variety of student learning styles is a primary focus of this text.

■ Reader response questions on the **Explain** page allow all students to participate—not just those who can memorize "correct" answers.

■ "Options for Learning" activities on the **Extend** page provide students with opportunities to express their knowledge using a wide variety of intelligences and learning modes.

■ Innovative assessment options allow students to be evaluated on their particular strengths, not their weaknesses.

■ **Writer's, Language,** and **Related Skills Workshops** are focused toward cooperative learning.

Historically, the term *assessment* has been almost synonymous with testing and with pencil-and-paper testing in particular. Often, however, this form of evaluation does not ascertain how well students have learned the comprehension, thinking, and problem-solving skills they must be able to carry over to other learning situations.

In recent years, many attempts have been made to extend the concept of assessment to other strategies that may be more reliable in measuring both student growth and mastery of subject matter. They include self-assessment, interactive assessment, and multimodal assessment, as well as other strategies that go beyond the traditional pencil-and-paper methods. (Strategies for the assessment of writing are discussed in a separate essay, "Assessment and Response to Student Writing," on pages T30–T32 of this Teacher's Edition.)

Self-Assessment

One of the most popular, new self-assessment tools is the **portfolio.** Much like the portfolios of artists and writers, assessment portfolios are usually collections of the students' best work. While portfolios are most often used for student writing, the portfolio may also include drawings and illustrations, tape recordings or videotapes of group work, or readings and dramatic presentations. The significant factor is that students have a voice in what goes into the folder. For more about portfolios and developing a portfolio assessment plan, see "Assessment and Response to Student Writing," pages T30–T32.

Observation Assessment

Unlike a written test, observation assessment goes beyond asking a question and getting a response; this method allows the questioners/evaluators to follow the students' thinking process. After hearing responses,

they can ask students to clarify or justify what they have said, give reasons for their conclusions, or explain why they think as they do.

Through classroom observation, the evaluator can also follow the development of other skills, such as the ability to work effectively in peer groups, the willingness to participate in class discussion, the level of preparedness, and the depth of involvement in the subject matter. For example, during classroom discussion, teachers can observe how well students interact with their peers. Are they open-minded about accepting alternative answers? Do they raise important issues suggested by the questions? Do they stick to the main point of the discussion, indicating that they recognize what is relevant to it? Using observation forms such as those included in the Guidelines for Reading and Literature Assessment booklet in the Teacher's Resource File, allows the teacher to observe a number of students in one discussion period.

Journals and Logs

Journals and logs can be used in a directed manner as a place where students are asked to comment or report on particular issues. An example would be reader responses on assigned or elective reading. Student comments may be general or may be responses to specific questions.

The teacher would evaluate the responses on the basis of general qualities, such as critical thinking or open-mindedness, and of specific understandings of skills.

Another source of information is the teacher's own journal or log, in which entries may report examples that can be used to assess student growth.

Multimodal Assessment

Recognizing students' learning styles and allowing them the option of demonstrating knowledge through their preferred mode of learning and presentation offers other assessment options. Such students might choose to focus on drama, art, oral reports, dance, music, construction, or a variety of other forms to show their understanding of a work of literature. For further information see "Multimodal Learning" on pages T27–T28.

There is no doubt that teachers will continue to use more traditional testing devices to make their evaluations of students' skills. However, if teachers use these tools in conjunction with other, more innovative, evaluation techniques, they can form a more complete picture of students' skills and progress.

> *I n recent years, many attempts have been made to extend the concept of assessment to other strategies that may be more reliable in measuring both student growth and mastery of the subject.*

IN LITERATURE AND LANGUAGE . . .

Possibilities for alternative assessment can be found in all parts of the text.

■ **Writer's Workshops** include "Reflect on Your Writing" questions for self-assessment.

■ Portfolio use and journal writing, which are encouraged and supported by the text, offer assessment alternatives.

■ Specific guidelines for observation assessment are listed in the Teacher's Edition on the first page of each subunit.

■ "Options for Learning" activities on **Extend** pages provide opportunities for multimodal assessment.

ARTHUR N. APPLEBEE, JUDITH A. LANGER, SENIOR CONSULTANTS

Traditionally, much of the work in the teaching of writing has occurred in the process of responding to and assessing what students write. Teachers have given students topics to write about and then have spent a great deal of time marking the papers that result—giving grades, making suggestions for ways the writing could have been improved, and correcting errors.

Such an approach is exhausting for teachers—the paperload quickly becomes overwhelming—and discouraging for students, whose papers "bleed" with the teachers' red pencilling. Such an approach also works against what we know about the writing process. When students write about topics that have substance and depth, we can expect their work to be characterized by growth and change over time. They will try out and abandon ideas. They will reorganize sections. Beginnings and endings will drift out of alignment with the rest of the text and need to be redrafted. During the process of writing, grammar and usage often falter in the rush of new ideas—because the writer's immediate concerns are momentarily (and appropriately) focused more on the generation of ideas and on the growing clarity of the message than on the surface presentation of the paper. This is the "normal" state of affairs among the best of writers and characterizes the *process* of crafting a text. Rather than "errors" to be corrected and deplored, tentativeness and exploration of ideas and the accompanying imprecision of spelling and mechanics need to be accepted and encouraged, as a natural and productive part of the process of exploring new forms and new ideas.

> **W**riters need frequent responses from interested readers, but that does not mean that the teacher needs to read everything that is written.

Response vs. Evaluation

For students to engage in this kind of thoughtful exploration, evaluation—judgments about how well the work has been done—needs to be separated from response—reactions to the paper and ideas for further development that come from an interested reader. *Response* is the critical feature in writing instruction; it helps students know what works, what doesn't, and how to go about improving what they have written. The ideal writing environment invites students to engage in exploratory writing and offers response to work-in-process. However, for this to succeed, evaluation and grades must be postponed until later.

Although well-intentioned, evaluation that comes too early and that becomes too much a part of ongoing instruction is inhibiting to students—it shifts their focus from the development of ideas to the way things look. While writing instruction should encourage students to ponder ideas and try out new ways to present them, when they face early judgments, students learn instead not

to take risks, not to try new forms, not to draft and redraft, but to concentrate on letter-perfect work that says little and goes nowhere.

Evaluation is, of course, necessary. Report cards demand grades and students want to know how they are doing. But there are a number of ways in which response and evaluation can be managed so they support rather than subvert teaching and learning.

1. Limit the amount of writing to which you, the teacher, respond. Writers need frequent responses from interested readers, but that does not mean that the teacher needs to read everything that is written. The workshops in the present series are structured to give students responses at many different points, when those responses can be helpful rather than evaluative. Thus students may be asked to share initial brainstorming about a topic, to reflect upon one another's notes and journals, to respond to early drafts, and to help polish a work for final publication. Such activities often work best in pairs or small groups, where everyone can receive some constructive response to his or her work quickly and directly. At other times the whole class may benefit from sharing ideas or discussing questions that have arisen as they work on their writing.

These early writings, like students' journals or logs, have served their purpose once they have been discussed with an interested reader or mined for the nuggets that will become parts of later drafts. There is no reason for the teacher to read them, too; indeed, the teacher can become a bottleneck.

2. Respond to work in progress as a collaborator rather than an evaluator.

Teachers can, of course, be very helpful while students are working on their drafts. They can show new ways to solve writing problems, suggest other issues to consider, and offer their own responses as readers about what parts are clear, what parts are interesting, and what parts fail to convince. These kinds of responses are instructional in the best sense: the teacher's suggestions about work in progress can become part of the developing writer's repertoire of strategies and models, available for use in other contexts.

It is important to avoid evaluations of work in progress, however. Students should not get the sense that their writing is "wrong" because it still needs work. They need, instead, to learn that it is normal to revise and rework what one has done, particularly when the topics being written about have substance and weight.

3. Be clear and consistent about criteria for evaluation.

Even when evaluation is separated from the process of writing, it is important to keep in mind what "counts." In this textbook, the workshops stress writing as a process for exploring ideas and sharing them with others. The conventions of writing are treated as part of this process rather than as the focus of instruction. It is easy, however, for evaluation to provide a different picture of what counts as important. If grading means primarily correcting errors and adding a summative comment about the need for more careful spelling and grammar, the student will quickly learn what "counts" in this classroom, and become more concerned with mechanics than with message.

Setting Criteria for Evaluation

In recent years, teachers have developed a number of different ways to formalize their evaluations of student writing. Most of these have been used in the context of large-group assessment, where the concern is with how well students are doing *relative to* one another or to some external criterion. Using such procedures (for example, general impression or holistic scoring, analytic scoring, or primary trait scoring) is generally inappropriate within a classroom when used in a formal sense, but can be extremely helpful when used informally to guide teachers' and students' mutual understandings of the goals of the writing task. While many teachers have begun to use such scoring systems to judge student papers, they are certain to look at many papers over an extended period of time before making overall judgments about students' writing abilities.

We know that evaluations of student performance will vary depending upon how important the evaluator considers each of the following to be: originality, correctness, amount of support provided, handwriting, spelling, word choice, and awareness of genre conventions. Because students are quick to concentrate on what "counts" in a particular classroom, it is important to have clear, consistent standards about what "writing well" will mean in your class. If "writing well" is to mean exploring ideas and experimenting with ways to share them effectively, then students who try to do this should be rewarded with higher grades—even if their experiments lead them to make mistakes. A new and difficult task, completed with some uncertainty, may reflect much more growth in writing achievement than a simple task completed with little thought and no "error."

Writing Portfolios

Writers vary in how well they write from topic to topic and day to day. Again this is normal and natural, but we often forget about it when judging how well a writer writes. To offer a well-grounded evaluation of a student's writing skills, we need to examine a broad sample of that student's work.

Portfolios of student work offer one of the best vehicles for classroom-based assessment, for two reasons:
1) They typically contain a variety of different samples of student work, and 2) they make it easy to separate evaluation from the process of instruction. Evaluation can be based on the diverse samples of work in the portfolio rather than on the day-to-day progress of an individual piece of classroom work.

Portfolios take almost as many forms as there are teachers and can be tailored to virtually any classroom situation. The major options involve the form that portfolios take, what is included in them, and how they are evaluated.

Form. Portfolios are just a cumulative collection of the work students have done. The most popular forms

Portfolios will give students, parents, administrators, and other teachers a much richer sense of what a child can do than can be conveyed by any list of grades from a gradebook.

include: 1) a traditional "writing folder" in which students keep their work, 2) a bound notebook with separate sections kept for work in progress and final drafts, 3) a loose-leaf notebook in which students keep their drafts and revisions, 4) a large artist's portfolio, or 5) a published collection of carefully selected and hand-bound work.

Content. Portfolios provide an ideal way to illustrate how a student's work has developed over time, and will give students, parents, administrators, and other teachers a much richer sense of what a child can do than can be conveyed by any list of grades from a gradebook. Portfolios may contain 1) everything a student writes for a particular class; 2) a selection of "best work" representing the diverse kinds of writing that a student has done; 3) a cumulative collection of work that is passed on from grade to grade; 4) a diverse collection of a student's performance including drawings and illustrations, tape recordings or videotapes of group work, and readings or dramatic presentations of the student's writing; 5) drafts and revisions; or 6) a selection of finished work, chosen by the student, the teacher, or the student and teacher working together.

Evaluation. With portfolios, evaluation and grading can be planned to reflect the range of a student's writing skills, across topics and modes of writing. Just as teachers vary in the form and content of the portfolios they ask their students to build, they also vary in how they use portfolios to determine students' grades. Evaluation can be based on: 1) everything a student has written, 2) selections chosen by the student or teacher to represent the best work during a grading period, 3) selections chosen to represent each of the types of writing the student has done during a grading period, 4) the student's and teacher's judgments about progress represented in accumulated drafts and revisions, or 5) "best and final" examples of the student's writing.

An approach that many teachers have found to be particularly effective is to base grading on a selection of work from the portfolio—chosen to reflect the range of types of writing that students have done during the grading period. Students can be asked to select the pieces to be graded, making the choice themselves or in conjunction with the teacher.

The ability to choose works to be graded—rather than being graded on everything—can be a powerful motivational device as well. Many teachers give their students the opportunity to work further on the selections they want to have graded. Returning to these writings at a later point, students often recognize for themselves ways to make their writing more effective.

Students can also be encouraged to reflect further upon their own progress as writers by providing an essay summarizing their work as they see it in the portfolio. Like the reflective activities included at the end of most workshops in this textbook, such reflection can help students become aware of and take control over their own growth as writers. Note that the final workshop in this text provides guidelines for a summarizing essay.

Changing to a Workshop Approach

Many teachers who are new to a workshop approach, postponing evaluation rather than interjecting it into the writing process, worry that students want quicker grades. One transitional device that works well in many classrooms is to give points when students have completed each separate part of the work. Everyone who completes a first draft, for example, might get a point, with another for doing a revision. And these points can be totaled across the marking period to become part of the final grade.

If evaluation is separated from instruction, if criteria for evaluation are kept consistent with those stressed during instruction, and if response becomes a responsibility shared with students, assessment can become an effective complement to the process of learning to write.

---

*I*N LITERATURE AND LANGUAGE . . .

Writing response and assessment is supported in the following ways:

■ **Writer's Workshops** encourage peer response during all stages of the writing process.
■ Reflection questions at the end of **Writer's Workshops** help students become aware of their process and then progress as writers.
■ The final **Writer's Workshop** in each text asks students to assess their year as writers and to set future writing goals.
■ Portfolio use is encouraged and supported in the student text.
■ The **Unit Resource Book** provides student Peer and Self-Evaluation Guidelines and teacher Writing Assessment Guidelines for each workshop.

McDOUGAL, LITTELL

LITERATURE

AND LANGUAGE

• RED LEVEL •

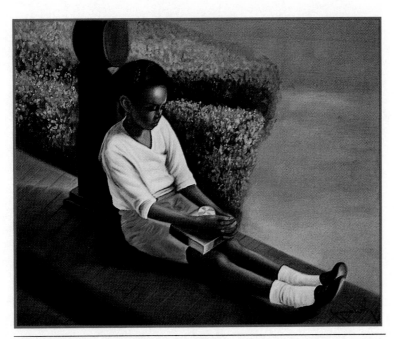

DAYDREAMING   Raymond Lark   Collection of Mary Moran, New Jersey.
Photo courtesy, Edward Smith, Los Angeles.

McDOUGAL, LITTELL
LITERATURE AND LANGUAGE

Red Level

Senior Consultants

Arthur N. Applebee
State University of New York at Albany

Andrea B. Bermúdez
University of Houston–Clear Lake

Susan Hynds
Syracuse University, Syracuse, New York

Judith A. Langer
State University of New York at Albany

James Marshall
University of Iowa, Iowa City

Donna E. Norton
Texas A&M University, College Station

McDOUGAL, LITTELL & COMPANY

Evanston, Illinois
New York · Dallas · Columbia, SC

Acknowledgments

Ricardo E. Alegría: "Lazy Peter and His Three-Cornered Hat," from *The Three Wishes* by Ricardo E. Alegría. By permission of the author.

Terry D. Allen: "Looking North to Taos" by Rudy Bantista, from *Writer's Reader* (Fall 1970).

Américas/Organization of American States: "Formula" by Ana Maria Iza, from *Américas,* a bimonthly magazine published by the General Secretariat of the Organization of American States in English and Spanish.

Arte Publico Press: "Graduation Morning" by Pat Mora, from *Chants* (Houston: Arte Publico Press–University of Houston, 1984). "Primary Lessons" by Judith Ortiz Cofer, excerpted from *Silent Dancing: A Partial Remembrance of a Puerto Rican Childhood* by Judith Ortiz Cofer (Houston: Arte Publico Press, 1990).

Toni Cade Bambara: "The War of the Wall" by Toni Cade Bambara; copyright © 1981 by Toni Cade Bambara. By permission of the author.

Susan Bergholz Literary Services: "Bums in the Attic," from *The House on Mango Street* by Sandra Cisneros; copyright © 1989 by Sandra Cisneros. Published in the United States by Vintage Books, a division of Random House, Inc., New York, and distributed in Canada by Random House of Canada Limited, Toronto. Originally published in somewhat different form by Arte Publico Press in 1984 and revised in 1989. Reprinted by permission of Susan Bergholz Literary Services, New York.

BOA Editions, Ltd.: "in the inner city," from *good woman: poems and a memoir, 1969–1980* by Lucille Clifton; copyright © 1987 by Lucille Clifton. With the permission of BOA Editions, Ltd., 92 Park Avenue, Brockport, NY 14420.

Don Congdon Associates, Inc.: "All Summer in a Day" by Ray Bradbury, published in *Magazine of Fantasy and Science Fiction,* March 1954; copyright © 1954, renewed 1982 by Ray Bradbury. Reprinted by permission of Don Congdon Associates, Inc.

Copp Clark Pitman Ltd.: "Phaëthon" and "Echo and Narcissus," from *Myth* by Moira Kerr and John Bennett; copyright © 1966, Copp Clark Pitman Ltd. Used by permission of the publisher.

The Crisis/NAACP: "Wishes" by Georgia Douglas Johnson, from *The Crisis,* April 1927 issue. By permission of *The Crisis* magazine.

Continued on page 806

Cover Art
DAYDREAMING (detail) Raymond Lark Collection of Mary Moran, New Jersey. Photo courtesy, Edward Smith, Los Angeles. Background photograph by Andrew Lawson.

ISBN: 0-8123-8042-8

Copyright © 1994 by McDougal, Littell & Company
Box 1667, Evanston, Illinois 60204

93 94 95 96 - DWO - 10 9 8 7 6 5 4 3 2

Senior Consultants

The senior consultants guided conceptual development for the *Literature and Language* series. They participated actively in shaping prototype materials for major components, and they reviewed completed prototypes and/or completed units to ensure consistency with current research and the philosophy of the series.

Arthur N. Applebee
Professor of Education, State University of New York at Albany; Director, Center for the Learning and Teaching of Literature; Senior Fellow, Center for Writing and Literacy

Andrea B. Bermúdez
Professor of Multicultural Education; Director, Research Center for Language and Culture, University of Houston–Clear Lake

Susan Hynds
Associate Professor and Director of English Education, Syracuse University, Syracuse, New York

Judith A. Langer
Professor of Education, State University of New York at Albany; Co-director, Center for the Learning and Teaching of Literature; Senior Fellow, Center for Writing and Literacy

James Marshall
Associate Professor of English and Education, University of Iowa, Iowa City; Executive Secretary, High School Task Force, National Standards Project for English Language Arts K-12.

Donna E. Norton
Professor of Children's Literature, Texas A & M University, College Station

Senior Writers

The senior writers participated in the conceptual development of the series and wrote all the lessons for the literature selections in this text.

Jane N. Beatty
Reading Specialist; formerly, Haverford High School, Haverford, Pennsylvania

William L. McBride, Ph.D.
Educational Materials Specialist; formerly Curriculum and Reading Specialist, Department of Defense Dependents School, Bonn, Germany

Writers

Susanna Nied (Workshops)
Educational Materials Consultant; formerly Instructor, Comparative Literature, San Diego State University, San Diego, California

Wordworks (Language Handbook)
Educational Publishing Services, Gloucester, Massachusetts

Multicultural Advisory Board

The multicultural advisors reviewed literature selections for appropriate content and made suggestions for teaching lessons in a multicultural classroom.

Andrea B. Bermúdez, Professor of Multicultural Education; Director, Research Center for Language and Culture, University of Houston–Clear Lake
Alice A. Kawazoe, Director of Curriculum and Staff Development, Oakland Unified School District, Oakland, California
Sandra Mehojah, Project Coordinator, Office of Indian Education, Omaha Public Schools, Omaha, Nebraska
Alexs D. Pate, Writer and columnist on multiculturalism, literature, and teaching; Adjunct faculty member, University of Minnesota and Macalester College

Contents

Unit One

A MATTER OF PERSPECTIVE   12

Unit Two

SCALES OF JUSTICE 120

Literature–based
Workshops

Unit Three

REACHING FOR THE STARS

Unit Six

THEMES IN WORLD FOLKLORE   **580**

Handbook Section

CONTENTS OVERVIEW

Introducing *Literature and Language*

Since the philosophy and structure of the program are simple and user-friendly, you may wish to use the introduction as a motivational tool on the first day of class.

Objectives

■ To become familiar with the content and structure of the text

■ To recognize that the text draws upon each student's personal knowledge and experience, inviting a wide range of individual interpretations

Teaching Strategies

Have students read the opening two paragraphs. Point out that this text represents an alternative to the use of separate books for literature, writing, and grammar. Ask students to identify possible advantages of using one book instead of multiple books in their language arts or reading class. Ask them if they would like to have been on the student board that helped select the literature in this textbook. Finally, ask them to think of other times in school that they have been asked to form their own opinions, rather than search for right answers.

Unit Organization

Have students read this section and look at the Table of Contents, on pages vii–xviii. Point out that in this book different genres of literature—short stories, poems, nonfiction, and drama—are mixed together according to common themes. The writing and language lessons are also based on those themes.

INTRODUCING *LITERATURE* AND LANGUAGE

Literature and Language is different from other books you have used in two important ways. First, it is organized to help you tie together your study of the language arts—literature, writing, and language. The literature, chosen for its appeal to your life, serves as the starting point for all your learning. Students like you helped to select the stories, plays, articles, and poems that appear in this book (see their names on page vi). You'll find stories that have been favorites for many generations, as well as works by current writers.

Second, as you use this book, you will find that it does not present a "right" way to understand a story or to write a paper. Instead, it requires you to think for yourself. It asks you to form your own opinions and make your own decisions.

Unit Organization

All the parts of this book fit closely together. If you look at the Table of Contents, on pages vii–xviii, you will see that the book is divided into six units. Each unit is organized around a theme, such

2

Technology and Enrichment
Guidelines for Reading and Literature Assessment,
    Reader's Self-Evaluation Forms

Family and Community Involvement Source Book, pp.
    1–5

 Fine Art Transparency Pack

as "Scales of Justice" or "Reaching for the Stars," that connects to your life and the world around you. To narrow the focus of these broad themes, each unit is further divided into two subunits. For example, "Scales of Justice" is divided into "Victims or Victors?" and "Turning the Tables."

After the literature selections in each subunit, you will find a Writer's Workshop, a Language Workshop, and a third workshop that varies in content. These workshops are based upon the literature selections, so that all the parts of the subunit work together.

Organization of the Literature Lessons

Each literature lesson follows a carefully designed pattern, described below.

EXPLORE: *Before You Read*   An **Explore** page, marked by a green band at the top, appears before each selection. Its three parts prepare you for reading.

• **Examine What You Know** provides an activity or discussion question based on your own experiences to help you get into the selection.

• **Expand Your Knowledge** gives you useful background information about the selection.

• **Enrich Your Reading** or **Write Before You Read** provides a specific reading or writing activity to help you better understand the literature you are about to read.

3

EXPLORE: *Before You Read*

After students read this section, have them skim the Explore page for "The War of the Wall" (page 26), and ask the following questions:

■ What does the Examine What You Know paragraph focus on? *(students' own neighborhood)*

■ What do you learn more about in the Expand Your Knowledge section? *(walls and wall artists)*

■ What does the information in Enrich Your Reading help you understand? *(dialect)*

Reading the Selection After students read this section, let them locate the blue box at the bottom of page 31. Have them find the words *drawled* and *scheme* underlined in the story. Point out that footnotes, such as the one on page 27, will help them understand the selections but do not need to be learned.

EXPLAIN: *After You Read*

After students read this section, have them skim the material on the Explain pages for "The War of the Wall" (pages 34–35). Call attention to phrases such as "your impressions" and "do you think" as indications that there are no "right" and "wrong" answers to these questions. Point out that students are, however, expected to back up their opinions with details from the selection. Then call to their attention the Literary Concepts feature and explain that after they are introduced to a new literary concept or technique, they will review it later in the book.

Point out to students that each of them can choose one of the four Writing Options at the top of page 35. In addition, vocabulary exercises will help them learn the words presented in the Words to Know and Use boxes.

EXTEND: *Beyond the Reading*

Invite students to read this section and then look at the Extend page for "The War of the Wall" (page 36). Ask which of the Options for Learning they might have the most fun doing. Also direct their attention to the biography of the author.

Reading the Selection Useful words that you should add to your vocabulary are underlined in the selection. These words are defined in a blue box at the bottom of the page where they first appear. Other difficult words and phrases are defined in footnotes, which appear beneath a black line at the bottom of the page.

EXPLAIN: *After You Read*

You'll find one or two **Explain** pages at the end of the selection, marked by a red band at the top. This section starts with discussion questions about the literature. The questions, which have no "right" or "wrong" answers, help you develop your own ideas and interpretations.

After the discussion questions, a literary concept is presented to help you become aware of literary techniques and their importance. In addition, writing activities give you another way of thinking about the literature. Finally, a vocabulary practice is provided if the selection includes vocabulary words.

EXTEND: *Beyond the Reading* This page,

marked by a purple band at the top, gives you creative ways to display your understanding. These **Options for Learning** allow you to show what you have learned in many different ways such as group projects, dramatics, art, storytelling, and debates. An author biography also appears here.

4

A MINI-COURSE IN ART APPRECIATION
To help students better understand and appreciate the fine art that illustrates the selections in this text, a series of art-appreciation transparencies has been included in the Teacher's Resource File. These transparencies are part of the Fine Art Transparency Pack. Before proceeding to Unit One, you may wish to use the transparencies to teach a one- or two-class mini-course on the fundamental elements of art.

FINE-ART PROMPTS FOR WRITING
The Fine Art Transparencies are designed for enrichment in the different modes of writing. Use them as appropriate.

Literature-based Workshops

Three workshops appear at the end of each subunit.

Writer's Workshop Each Writer's Workshop guides you through an entire writing assignment closely related to the literature and theme of the subunit. Clear instructions, helpful hints, optional suggestions, examples from literature, and models of student writing will help you write your own compositions.

Language Workshop Each Language Workshop focuses on skills that are related to your work in the Writer's Workshop as well as other writing that you do.

Related Skills Workshop The third workshop gives you additional tips in reading, vocabulary, or speaking and listening.

Reading on Your Own

Two pages at the end of each unit suggest novels that tie in with the unit theme. The plot summaries of these novels will help you choose books to read on your own.

Handbook Section

At the back of the book, you'll find three reference handbooks to round out your language-arts studies—a **Reader's Handbook,** a **Writer's Handbook,** and a **Language Handbook.**

5

Literature-based Workshops

Writer's Workshop Direct students to the Writer's Workshop on pages 58–62. Call attention to the organization of this feature: first an explanation of the assignment, then a student model, then step-by-step instructions for completing the assignment independently.

Language Workshop Direct students to the Language Workshop on pages 63–65. Point out that each Language Workshop gives a quick lesson in grammar that will help them in completing the assignment in the preceding Writer's Workshop.

Related Skills Workshop Have students read this section and then look at the Reader's Workshop on page 66. Point out that the concluding workshop is one page long and focuses on a skill that will improve their reading or communicating.

Reading on Your Own

Have students read this section and then turn to the Reading on Your Own feature on pages 118–119. Remind them about this feature at the end of each unit throughout the year, encouraging them to read the featured novels or the books listed under "Other Recommended Books."

Handbook Section

Ask students to read this sentence and then to turn to the back of their text. Point out the Glossary (pages 674–679), and have them leaf together through the rest of the handbooks, stopping at pages that might help them with their reading, writing, and grammar. Explain that they can use these handbooks as a reference tool at any time.

WRITING TO THE PUBLISHER
During the year, encourage students to write to the publisher about their opinions of the text. They may wish to share comments about the selections, the unit and subunit themes, the workshops, the art, or other features. When students write, remind them to include their name, school, and grade level, along with the date, the book title, and page references. Correspondence may be sent to
    Editors, Language Arts
    McDougal, Littell & Company
    Box 1667
    Evanston, IL 60204

Strategies for
READING

Objective

■ To teach students how to read actively through questioning, connecting, predicting, reviewing, and evaluating

Motivation

Ask volunteers to recall exciting stories they have read. Ask how a friend might recognize their active involvement in a story just by looking at them. *(Possible responses: by the emotions shown in their faces, by their eager turning of pages, by their obliviousness to outside events)* Explain that the strategies on page 6 are the "secrets" of good readers—things they do to help them get more from what they read. Point out that all students can learn to use these strategies regularly so that their reading experiences will be easier and more enjoyable.

Teaching Strategies

Invite students to read aloud and discuss the descriptions of the strategies for active reading on page 6. Explain that the model they are about to read shows what one reader thought as she was reading the story "Charles." Suggest that as they read the story, they cover the remarks in the margin and think their own thoughts first; then they can compare their thoughts with the printed ones. Stress that the comments in the margin are not "right" responses but simply one reader's thoughts—their own thoughts are just as valid.

Have you ever been so involved in reading that you ignored the world around you? A herd of elephants stampeding through your room, a flying saucer landing outside your window, or even your mom reminding you for the fifth time to take out the trash—none of these could tear you away from your book! When you are that excited about what you are reading, you are an active reader. Active readers not only step into the actions, times, and places of stories and poems but also become more involved in the issues and events they read about in magazines, newspapers, and textbooks. Try the strategies below. They describe the kinds of thinking good readers engage in as they read.

- **Questioning** Ask questions about what is happening. Exploring possible reasons for what is going on in the selection and how characters feel can help you "get into" the selection. Also, make mental notes about words or statements that confuse you, but don't get sidetracked. Things may get clearer as you read further in the selection.

- **Connecting** Think of similarities between what is described in the selection you are reading and what you have experienced, heard about, or read about.

- **Predicting** Try to figure out what will happen next and how the selection might end.

- **Reviewing** Stop occasionally for a quick review of what you understand so far. Then draw conclusions about what is "between the lines," that is, what is suggested but not stated directly.

- **Evaluating** Form opinions about what you read, both during and after reading. Develop your own images of and ideas about characters and events.

The reading model on the next page shows how one reader used these strategies as she read the story "Charles." Naturally, your thoughts would be different from hers, since you think in your own way. You might have different questions, and you would make different connections based on your own experiences.

ADDITIONAL RESOURCES

Technology and Enrichment
Guidelines for Reading and Literature
 Assessment

- ■ Student Strategies for Taking Literature and Language Tests
- ■ Selection Practice Test (on "Charles")
- ■ Model Test Answers

 Active Reading Transparencies 1–5

Reading Support in Literature and Language

Pupil Edition The Explore page for each selection taps into students' prior knowledge, provides them with additional background information, and frequently introduces a reading skill that students can practice as they read. Some selections have interlinear questions (see pages 79–81) that focus on the five reading strategies introduced on this page.

Teacher's Edition Active Reading annotations identify passages that can be used to teach specific reading skills and strategies. Guided Reading for Less-Proficient Students provides questions that can be used to direct and structure the reading of students who need more help.

Teacher's Resource File The Unit Resource Books contain, for every selection, a Reading Skills page for all students and a Reader's Guidesheet for students who need extra help. The Active Reading Transparency Pack provides transparencies and worksheets for more practice in the reading strategies listed on this page.

Charles

SHIRLEY JACKSON

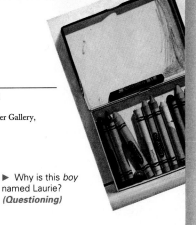

CRAYON BOX II
David Brega
Courtesy, Alexander Gallery,
New York.

The day Laurie started kindergarten, he renounced corduroy overalls with bibs and began wearing blue jeans with a belt. I watched him go off the first morning with the older girl next door, seeing clearly that an era of my life was ended, my sweet-voiced nursery-school tot replaced by a long-trousered, swaggering character who forgot to stop at the corner and wave goodbye to me.

▶ Why is this *boy* named Laurie? *(Questioning)*

He came home the same way, the front door slamming open, his cap on the floor, and the voice suddenly become raucous shouting, "Isn't anybody *here?*"

1 At lunch he spoke insolently to his father, spilled Jannie's milk, and remarked that his teacher said that we were not to take the name of the Lord in vain.

▶ Laurie's a bad boy! *(Evaluating)*

"How *was* school today?" I asked, elaborately casual.

"All right," he said.

"Did you learn anything?" his father asked.

Laurie regarded his father coldly. "I didn't learn nothing," he said.

▶ All parents correct their kids' language. *(Connecting)*

"Anything," I said. "Didn't learn anything."

"The teacher spanked a boy, though," Laurie said, addressing his bread and butter. "For being fresh," he added with his mouth full.

▶ What does "being fresh" mean? *(Questioning)*

"What did he do?" I asked. "Who was it?"

2 Laurie thought. "It was Charles," he said. "He was fresh. The teacher spanked him and made him stand in a corner. He was awfully fresh."

"What did he do?" I asked again, but Laurie slid off his chair, took a cookie, and left, while his father was still saying, "See here, young man."

▶ Laurie's rude. *(Evaluating)*

3 The next day Laurie remarked at lunch, as soon as he sat down, "Well, Charles was bad again today." He grinned enormously and said, "Today Charles hit the teacher."

▶ That's excessive—unless there's something wrong with Charles. *(Evaluating, Questioning)*

TEXT ANNOTATIONS

Some of these annotations complement the marginal notes in the Pupil Edition; others suggest alternative ways of applying the reading strategies to "Charles."

1. ACTIVE READING: Review
Tell students that *reviewing* literally means "taking another look" and that active readers stop from time to time to review what they have read and make inferences about it. Choose volunteers to review this paragraph and make an inference about Laurie. *(Possible responses: Laurie tends to misbehave at home; Laurie is feeling upset.)*

2. ACTIVE READING: Predict
Explain that predicting what might happen in a story is a fun way to get involved. Give as a sample prediction, "I predict that Charles is a boy whom Laurie will become friends with." Stress the need for students to check and update their predictions as they read.

3. ACTIVE READING: Evaluate
Point out that the opinions we form when evaluating are based on our personal judgments. Ask volunteers to evaluate Laurie and Charles. *(Possible responses: Both boys tend to be rude; Charles seems much worse than Laurie.)*

Reading Assessment in Literature and Language

Pupil Edition The Explain pages allow the teacher to assess students' understanding of their reading through discussion (Responding to Reading) and writing (Writing Options). The Options for Learning on the Extend pages allow students to show understanding through multimodal, cross-curricular activities.

Teacher's Edition A Comprehension Check for each selection tests students' literal understanding of the piece.

Teacher's Resource File The Unit Resource Books include a Comprehension Check Test and a Selection Test for every selection, as well as a Unit Test. The *Guidelines for Reading and Literature Assessment* booklet provides Observation Assessment Forms.

4. ACTIVE READING: Evaluate
Have students evaluate the techniques Laurie's teacher uses to discipline Charles—spanking him and telling the other kids not to play with him. Are these effective techniques? *(Any response is valid.)*

5. ACTIVE READING: Evaluate
Ask students which of Laurie's parents they agree with more. Is it better to avoid or get used to a classmate who might be a "bad influence"? *(Any response is valid.)*

6. ACTIVE READING: Review
Ask students how likely they think it is that all the children would stay late to watch Charles being kept after school. Then ask if there is anything in the story so far to suggest that Laurie might not be giving accurate information about Charles. *(Any response is valid.)*

"Good heavens," I said, mindful of the Lord's name, "I suppose he got spanked again?"

"He sure did," Laurie said. "Look up," he said to his father.

"What?" his father said, looking up.

"Look down," Laurie said. "Look at my thumb. Gee, you're dumb." He began to laugh insanely.

▶ That's typical of a kindergartner—stupid baby joke. *(Connecting)*

"Why did Charles hit the teacher?" I asked quickly.

4 "Because she tried to make him color with red crayons," Laurie said. "Charles wanted to color with green crayons, so he hit the teacher, and she spanked him and said nobody play with Charles; but everybody did."

The third day—it was Wednesday of the first week—Charles bounced a seesaw onto the head of a little girl and made her bleed, and the teacher made him stay inside all during recess. Thursday Charles had to stand in a corner during story time because he kept pounding his feet on the floor. Friday Charles was deprived of blackboard privileges because he threw chalk.

▶ Something's wrong with Charles. *(Evaluating)*

On Saturday I remarked to my husband, "Do you think kindergarten is too unsettling for Laurie? All this tough-**5** ness and bad grammar, and this Charles boy sounds like such a bad influence."

"It'll be all right," my husband said reassuringly. "Bound to be people like Charles in the world. Might as well meet them now as later."

▶ That's true. (Dad's statement) *(Evaluating)*

On Monday Laurie came home late, full of news. "Charles," he shouted as he came up the hill; I was waiting anxiously on the front steps. "Charles," Laurie yelled all the way up the hill, "Charles was bad again."

"Come right in," I said, as soon as he came close enough. "Lunch is waiting."

"You know what Charles did?" he demanded, following me through the door. "Charles yelled so in school they **6** sent a boy in from first grade to tell the teacher she had to make Charles keep quiet, and so Charles had to stay after school. And so all the children stayed to watch him."

"What did he do?" I asked.

"He just sat there," Laurie said, climbing into his chair at the table. "Hi, Pop, y'old dust mop."

▶ Sounds like Laurie is maturing too fast. *(Evaluating)*

"Charles had to stay after school today," I told my husband. "Everyone stayed with him."

"What does this Charles look like?" my husband asked Laurie. "What's his other name?"

"He's bigger than me," Laurie said, "and he doesn't ever wear a jacket."

Monday night was the first Parent-Teachers meeting, and only the fact that Jannie had a cold kept me from going; I wanted passionately to meet Charles's mother. On Tuesday Laurie remarked suddenly, "Our teacher had a friend come to see her in school today."

"Charles's mother?" my husband and I asked simultaneously.

"Naaah," Laurie said scornfully. "It was a man who came and made us do exercises. Look." He climbed down from his chair and squatted down and touched his toes. "Like this," he said. He got solemnly back into his chair and said, picking up his fork, "Charles didn't even *do* exercises."

"That's fine," I said heartily. "Didn't Charles want to do exercises?"

"Naaah," Laurie said. "Charles was so fresh to the teacher's friend he wasn't *let* do exercises."

"Fresh again?" I said.

"He kicked the teacher's friend," Laurie said. "The teacher's friend told Charles to touch his toes like I just did, and Charles kicked him."

"What are they going to do about Charles, do you suppose?" Laurie's father asked him.

Laurie shrugged elaborately. "Throw him out of school, I guess," he said.

Wednesday and Thursday were routine; Charles yelled during story hour and hit a boy in the stomach and made him cry. On Friday Charles stayed after school again and so did all the other children.

With the third week of kindergarten, Charles was an institution in our family. Jannie was being a Charles when she cried all afternoon. Laurie did a Charles when he filled his wagon full of mud and pulled it through the kitchen. Even my husband, when he caught his elbow in the telephone cord and pulled telephone, ash tray, and a bowl of flowers off the table, said, after the first minute,

▶ What does he mean by "his other name"?
(Questioning)

YOUTH WITH TOY   James Lloyd
Courtesy, Portal Gallery, London.

▶ Charles should just have been kicked out of school right away.
(Evaluating)

7. ACTIVE READING: Predict
Remind students that you earlier predicted that Laurie would befriend Charles in kindergarten. Explain that this does not seem likely now, so you are going to revise your prediction. Say that since the story is more than half over and we still have not met Charles or learned anything about his family, you now predict that Laurie is making up some of the stories about Charles.

Art Note
James Lloyd (1905–1974) was a self-taught artist from the town of Cheshire in England. He created nearly all of his paintings by using an extra-fine brush to apply tiny dots. His works are noted for their simple and powerful honesty. *Describe the boy's expression in this painting. Do you think it reflects the attitude of Laurie in "Charles"? Explain.*

8. ACTIVE READING: Evaluate
Ask students what they think the school should do with Charles. Is there any way to change his behavior so that he can stay in the class? *(Any response is valid.)*

9. ACTIVE READING: Review
Ask students to explain how Charles has become "an institution" in the narrator's family. *(Possible responses: The name Charles has become a metaphor for any unpleasant, naughty, or clumsy act; Charles has been referred to so often that he has become a fixture in the family's life.)*

10. ACTIVE READING: Question
Ask students why Laurie would report the news of the change in Charles "grimly." (Possible responses: Maybe kindergarten was more fun when Charles was naughty; Laurie would like to be as naughty as Charles was.)

11. ACTIVE READING: Predict
Have students predict what will happen in the kindergarten now that things are "back to normal." (Possible responses: Charles will resume his naughty ways; Charles will be punished.)

12. ACTIVE READING: Review
Ask students what they can infer about Laurie from the fact that he whispers the bad word "joyfully" to his father. (Possible responses: Laurie gets great pleasure from Charles's behavior; Laurie may be making these stories up; Laurie likes to say the bad word.)

"Looks like Charles."

10 During the third and fourth weeks there seemed to be a reformation in Charles. Laurie reported grimly at lunch on Thursday of the third week, "Charles was so good today the teacher gave him an apple."

"What?" I said, and my husband added warily, "You mean Charles?"

"Charles," Laurie said. "He gave the crayons around and he picked up the books afterward, and the teacher said he was her helper."

"What happened?" I asked incredulously.

"He was her helper; that's all," Laurie said, and shrugged.

"Can this be true, about Charles?" I asked my husband that night. "Can something like this happen?"

"Wait and see," my husband said cynically. "When you've got a Charles to deal with, this may mean he's only plotting."

He seemed to be wrong. For over a week, Charles was the teacher's helper. Each day he handed things out, and he picked things up; no one had to stay after school.

"The PTA meeting's next week again," I told my husband one evening. "I'm going to find Charles's mother there."

"Ask her what happened to Charles," my husband said. "I'd like to know."

"I'd like to know myself," I said.

11 On Friday of that week things were back to normal. "You know what Charles did today?" Laurie demanded at the lunch table, in a voice slightly awed. "He told a little girl to say a word, and she said it; and the teacher washed her mouth out with soap, and Charles laughed."

"What word?" his father asked unwisely, and Laurie said, "I'll have to whisper it to you; it's so bad." He got down off his chair and went around to his father. His **12** father bent his head down, and Laurie whispered joyfully. His father's eyes widened.

"Did Charles tell the little girl to say *that*?" he asked respectfully.

"She said it *twice*," Laurie said. "Charles told her to say it *twice*."

"What happened to Charles?" my husband asked.

► All of a sudden, Charles seems to change.
(Reviewing)

► Why doesn't she ask, "What did you do to make Charles's behavior change?"
(Questioning, Evaluating)

► Teacher should have washed *both* their mouths out with soap.
(Evaluating)

"Nothing," Laurie said. "He was passing out the crayons."

Monday morning Charles abandoned the little girl and said the evil word himself three or four times, getting his mouth washed out with soap each time. He also threw chalk.

My husband came to the door with me that evening as I set out for the PTA meeting. "Invite her over for a cup of tea after the meeting," he said. "I want to get a look at her."

"If only she's there," I said prayerfully.

"She'll be there," my husband said. "I don't see how they could hold a PTA meeting without Charles's mother."

At the meeting I sat restlessly, scanning each comfortable, matronly face, trying to determine which one hid the secret of Charles. None of them looked to me haggard enough. No one stood up in the meeting and apologized for the way her son had been acting. No one mentioned Charles.

After the meeting, I identified and sought out Laurie's kindergarten teacher. She had a plate with a cup of tea and a piece of chocolate cake; I had a plate with a cup of tea and a piece of marshmallow cake. We maneuvered up to one another cautiously and smiled.

"I've been so anxious to meet you," I said. "I'm Laurie's mother."

"We're all so interested in Laurie," she said.

"Well, he certainly likes kindergarten," I said. "He talks about it all the time."

"We had a little trouble adjusting, the first week or so," she said primly, "but now he's a fine little helper. With lapses, of course."

"Laurie usually adjusts very quickly," I said. "I suppose this time it's Charles's influence."

"Charles?"

"Yes," I said, laughing, "you must have your hands full in that kindergarten, with Charles."

"Charles?" she said. "We don't have any Charles in the kindergarten."

13

14

15

▶ Charles gets other people to do things for him while he still acts good.
(Reviewing)

▶ She's finally going to find out about Charles.
(Predicting)

▶ I like the ending. I was really involved with Charles when I found out it's really Laurie. Laurie's a good story-maker for his age.
(Evaluating)

13. ACTIVE READING: Question
Whom does the narrator's husband want his wife to invite over so that he can "get a look at her"? *(Charles's mother)* Why does he want to see her? *(Possible responses: He's fascinated by Charles and curious about the boy's mother; he wants to find out why Charles is so bad.)*

14. ACTIVE READING: Predict
Ask students whether there are any hints in this paragraph that can help them predict the ending of the story. *(Any response is valid.)*

15. ACTIVE READING: Evaluate
Ask students to share their reactions to the story. What effect did the story have on them? *(Any response is valid.)*

How to Model Think-Alouds

Teacher think-alouds are a simple way of modeling active reading. By sharing your own responses to a passage, you help students become more aware of strategies they can use to monitor their own comprehension. These examples of short think-alouds might be used with the final paragraphs of "Charles":

■ Make predictions. "At last we're going to learn the truth about Charles and Laurie. I still think Laurie's stories about Charles aren't true."

■ Describe visual images. "In my mind, I see Laurie's mother's face when she learns there is no Charles. Her mouth drops open in surprise."

■ Share an analogy or use prior knowledge. "What a shock for Laurie's mother! It reminds me of the time I learned that . . ."

■ Demonstrate rethinking strategies. "Is it possible that Laurie has been 'Charles' all along? I think I'll go back and look for clues that led up to this surprise ending."

Overview
Unit One: A MATTER OF PERSPECTIVE

Subunit One: False Impressions

	SELECTION	DIFFICULTY LEVEL	READING SKILLS	LITERATURE SKILLS	WRITING OPTIONS	VOCABULARY WORDS/SKILLS
Fiction	*Seventh Grade* Gary Soto Pages 17–25	Average	Evaluating actions and motives	Characterization	Note Scene Advice column Journal	conviction elective ferocity linger scowl
Fiction	*The War of the Wall* Toni Cade Bambara Pages 26–36	Average	Dialect	Plot Setting	Letter Comparison Explanation Personal narrative	beckon drawl inscription liberation scheme
Fiction	*Hearts and Hands* O. Henry Pages 37–41	Challenge	Inferences	Surprise ending Characterization	Dialogue Description	Word Attack Skill: familiar roots in new words
Nonfiction	*Homeless* Anna Quindlen Pages 44–47	Challenge	Author's purpose	Author's opinion	Editorial Essay	Word Attack Skill: the prefix *en-*
Nonfiction	*Little by Little* Jean Little Pages 48–57	Easy	Infer character's feelings	Autobiography	Diary entry School rules Script Description	abrasion ominously anguished quiver detention spellbound glower stupendous jeering transfixed

WRITER'S WORKSHOP Pages 58-62 ·····························

Mode	Guided Assignment	Writing Skills	Proofreading Focus
Personal writing	Autobiographical incident	First-person writing Colorful details Organizational patterns Strong beginning	Personal pronouns

OPTIONS FOR LEARNING	SPELLING SKILLS	COMMUNITY AND PARENT RESOURCE SUGGESTIONS	AUDIOVISUAL RESOURCES
Research report Song lyrics Acting Survey	Words ending in *ly/ally*	Invite a school counselor to talk about peer pressure.	*The No-Guitar Blues*, 16mm film or video. Phoenix/BFA, 1991. (27 min). Based on the book *Baseball in April*, by Gary Soto. The quest of Fauso Sanchez to earn money to buy a guitar.
Research murals Speech Mural Dictionary	Words ending in *ate/ion*	Invite parents to cook and share soul-food recipes. Get permission for the class to paint a mural on a community wall.	*Toni Cade Bambara.* Two audiocassettes. American Audio Prose Library. (110 min) An interview with the author and reading of her short story, "The Organizer's Wife."
	More words ending in *ate/ion*	Invite a law-enforcement person to discuss transporting prisoners.	*O. Henry's Jimmy Valentine.* 16mm film or video. Coronet/MTI, 1985. (46min) Award-winner examines O. Henry's life and relates his tale "A Retrieved Reformation."
	More words ending in *ly/ally*	Invite a volunteer from a homeless shelter to discuss experiences.	*Literature & Language* Grade 7 Audiocassette Tape 1, Side 1 *A Place Called Home.* Video. PBS video. 1991. (28 min) An intimate portrait of homeless children and their families.
Read book Debate Research technology Storytelling	Hard and soft *c/g*	Invite an opthomologist or other eye-care expert to discuss testing, eye care, and blindness.	*Meet the Author: Jean Little.* Video. School Services/Clearvue/EAV, 1987. An intimate portrait of the popular award-winning author

LANGUAGE WORKSHOP Pages 63–65 ··········

Grammar Concept	Skill Focus
Personal pronouns	Subject forms Object forms Using compound pronouns correctly

RELATED SKILLS WORKSHOP Page 66 ······

Language Strand	Skill Focus
Reading	Inferences

Subunit Two: Tunnel Vision

	SELECTION	DIFFICULTY LEVEL	READING SKILLS	LITERATURE SKILLS	WRITING OPTIONS	VOCABULARY WORDS/SKILLS
Fiction	*Lose Now, Pay Later* Carol Farley Pages 68-77	Average	Predicting	Science fiction Setting	Notes for sci-fi story Description Explanation Plan	binge cull dingy gullible placid ravage stark unnerve consumption cubicle
Fiction	*Stolen Day* Sherwood Anderson Pages 78-83	Average	Reviewing	Point of view	Journal entry Explanation	Word Attack Skill: context clues to understand colloquialisms
Poetry	*The Charge of the Light Brigade* Alfred, Lord Tennyson Pages 86-89	Challenge	Sound effects	Rhythm Rhyme Repetition	Research report News report	Word Attack Skill: context clues
Poetry	*For My Father* Janice Mirikitani Pages 90-92	Challenge	Visualizing	Figurative language	Opinion Letter	Word Attack Skill: the suffix *-less*
Nonfiction	*Exploring the Titanic* Robert Ballard Pages 93-108	Average	Literary non-fiction	Informational writing	Essay Advertisement Message Log entry	feverishly accommodation novelty omen prophecy prediction aristocratic competitive desperately indefinitely

WRITER'S WORKSHOP Pages 109–113 ································

Mode	Guided Assignment	Writing Skills	Proofreading Focus
Descriptive writing	Restaurant review	Sensory details Freewriting Using comparisons Specific modifiers	Confusing adjectives and adverbs

OPTIONS FOR LEARNING	SPELLING SKILLS	COMMUNITY AND PARENT RESOURCE SUGGESTIONS	AUDIOVISUAL RESOURCES
Radio ad Mechanical drawing Invention Media analysis	1 + 1 + 1 words	Invite a psychologist or doctor to discuss weight and its connection to our self-esteem.	*Fighting Fat.* Video. WGBH Boston/MTI, 1992. (30 min.) This segment of the health series BODYWATCH thoughtfully examines our obsession with being thin.
	More 1 + 1 + 1 words	Invite the counselor or truant officer of the school to share statistics about student absences.	
	More hard and soft *c/g*	Ask a parent who is a veteran to discuss what being in the military is like.	*Literature & Language* Audiocassette Tape 1, side 1. *Treasury of Alfred, Lord Tennyson* Audiocassette, Spoken Arts. Includes a reading of "The Charge of the Light Brigade."
	VAC words ending in *ate/ion*	Invite an immigrant parent or group of parents to discuss good and bad experiences in the U.S.	*Literature & Language* Audiocassette Tape 1, side 1.
Book report Movie review Illustration Technology report	Compound words and contractions	Invite a travel agent to talk about modern cruise ships. Invite a skin diver or someone who knows about the *Titanic* or other sunken ships.	*Secrets of the Titanic.* Video. National Geographic, 1986. Exploration of sunken vessel. *The Titanic: Lost and Found.* Audiocassette and book. American School Publishers,1989. (20min.) A dramatic reading with sound effects.

LANGUAGE WORKSHOP Pages 114–116 · · · · · · · · ·

Grammar Concept	Skill Focus
Adjectives and adverbs	Choosing adjective or adverb: good/well real/really bad/badly

RELATED SKILLS WORKSHOP Page 117 · · · · · ·

Language Strand	Skill Focus
Vocabulary	Context clues Definition Example clues

Reading on Your Own

Novels thematically connected to Unit One, suggested for independent student reading during or after completion of the unit (pages 118-119)

Monkey Island   by Paula Fox
The Witch of Blackbird Pond   By Elizabeth George Speare
Against the Storm   by Gaye Micyilmaz

Cooperative Project **Unit One:** A MATTER OF PERSPECTIVE

Images of Teens in the Mass Media

1 Project Preview

*T*he groups will display examples of their research through videotapes, clippings, photocopies, and other means of display.

This small-group project should be done after the unit readings have been completed. It challenges students to apply what they have learned about the unit theme (*A Matter of Perspective*) and subthemes (*False Impressions* and *Tunnel Vision*).

In this project students will analyze how teenagers are presented in the mass media. They will work together in groups of four, with each group focusing on a separate topic, such as commercials, magazine ads, or television shows.

Each group will develop a controlling question to focus their research, such as "Are teens presented accurately by the media?" Groups will develop their own criteria to help them analyze materials in response to the question.

Working collaboratively, each group will assign individual responsibilities, conduct research, analyze data, and choose appropriate means of presentation.

The groups will present their findings to the whole class. They will display examples of their research through videotapes, clippings, photocopies, and other means of display. Groups may also use charts or graphs to present their findings.

The scope and time allotted to the project can be easily narrowed or expanded according to the needs and interests of your class. What follows is a general description, examples of implementation, and a possible time frame.

OBJECTIVES
■ To analyze the various images of teens presented by the mass media
■ To develop a controlling question for research
■ To develop media awareness and critical thinking skills
■ To work cooperatively to plan and conduct a presentation that utilizes one of the mass media

MATERIALS
■ a range of magazines that focus on teens or display them prominently
■ television shows with teens as main characters
■ television or radio commercials
■ a bulletin board or other means of display
■ a videocassette recorder (if available) and blank tapes
■ an audiocassette player

2 Implementing the Project

Tell students that in this assignment they will be studying the images of teenagers in the mass media, that is, television, newspapers, magazines, and radio. Point out that many groups of people have expressed dissatisfaction with how they are portrayed by the media, including African Americans, women, Hispanics, Jews, Catholics, and various other ethnic or religious groups. Such groups have complained that the media sometimes presents them in a negative, an unrealistic, or a prejudiced manner.

Explain that this project gives students an opportunity to form their own evaluations of images of teenagers in the mass media. They will create a controlling question for their research, which gives them freedom to choose their own focus.

WARM-UP ACTIVITY
Display a magazine that is targeted at teens and acceptable for classroom discussion. Read aloud the titles of the articles, various lead paragraphs, captions, any highlighted type, and some of the advertisements. Show photographs of teens that are depicted on the pages. Then lead a class discussion focused on the following questions:
1. In your opinion does the magazine create a positive or negative impression of teens? Explain.
2. Do the teens featured in the magazine look or act like people you know?
3. If beings from another planet read this magazine, what impression might they form of teenagers?
4. Do you think this magazine presents a fair and accurate view of teenagers today?

At the end of this discussion, tell students that these are the types of questions they will use for research.

GROUP PLANNING SESSIONS

Assigning Groups
At the beginning of class, divide students into groups of four. Assign or allow students to choose the focus of their group's research. Possible assignments:
■ Group 1: printed advertisements in magazines and newspapers aimed at teenagers
■ Group 2: popular television shows with teenage main characters
■ Group 3: the editorial content (i.e., types of articles) of magazines directed toward teenagers
■ Group 4: television commercials directed toward teenagers
■ Group 5: radio commercials directed toward teenagers

Planning Research
Advise students of the resources that are available in the school library or media center or at the community library.

Tell students that groups will need to divide responsibilities among their members. Each group will need to create a controlling question to guide its research. Examples of such questions follow:
■ Does the media present an accurate image of teens?
■ Does the media do justice to the cultural diversity of teenagers?
■ Does the media pay too much attention to the appearance of teens?
■ Does the media promote prejudices or stereotypes of teens?
Once students understand the assignment, allow them to meet in their groups for preliminary planning.

GATHERING AND ANALYZING INFORMATION
Allow adequate time for each group to complete its research. If desired, discuss the following examples of how the project might be completed.

Example A
Analyzing Television Commercials

1. The group discusses various commercials that feature teens. Group members discuss what they like and don't like about such commercials and consider possible questions to focus their research.

Group members then decide upon a single question to focus their research, and they divide responsibilities. For example, the group may address the question, Do commercials present an accurate image of teens?

2. Each member might watch a different television channel for two hours and videotape all the commercials.

Alternative If students don't have access to videotape recorders, they may take detailed notes of those commercials that are targeted to teens.

3. The group meets to review the videotapes that focus on teens and to discuss the accuracy of how they present to teens. Group members think

of various ways of analyzing the data, with each student responsible for one means of analysis. For instance, one student might keep track of the ethnic and racial representation of the teens on the commercials. Another might study the clothes or physical appearance of the teens. One student might analyze their use of language while another might focus on the products being sold and how these products reflect the interests and needs of students.

Alternative Each student may offer an analysis of the commercials he or she taped.

Each student will be responsible for presenting and explaining one example to the whole class.

Example B
Analyzing Printed Advertisements

1. The group starts by discussing the ways in which printed advertisements can create positive or negative

images of teens. First the group decides on how it defines "positive images" and "negative images." Then it chooses the magazines it will explore for images of teens. They may range from general magazines such as *Time* or *Newsweek* to ones that are targeted toward teens.

2. At the library each group member reviews multiple issues of one magazine. Photocopies are made of ads that present strong positive or negative images of teens.

3. The group meets to analyze the photocopies of advertisements found by each member. Members could choose the two best examples of negative images and the two best examples of positive images. Each student is responsible for presenting and explaining one example to the class as a whole. Alternatively, the group may devise other means of reporting positive and negative images, such as graphs or charts.

THE PRESENTATIONS

You may want to set time limits for each presentation. Make sure that all students stay focused on the controlling question for their research. You may find it helpful to write each group's question on the board for the duration of presentations.

Make sure that every student in each group gets a chance to present. Also, be sure to allow time for questions from the audience. As a way of providing further motivation, consider using one or more of the following ideas.

Hold a Multimedia Day, inviting students from other classes to watch the presentations.

Videotape the presentations and make the videotape available so that students can take turns taking it home.

Conduct a classroom vote to choose the group that did the best job. Awards or special classroom privileges may be given to the winners.

3 Project Assessment

You may wish to give two grades to each student, one for the group as a whole and one for each student's presentation. The following questions may help you evaluate the project.

Group Assessment

1. Did the group delegate responsibility effectively?
2. Did all group members stay focused on the controlling question?
3. Did the group present an interesting and thought-provoking range of evidence?
4. Did the group present a reasonable analysis of their findings?

Individual Assessment

1. Did the student present his or her ideas clearly?

2. Was the presentation well supported by examples or other data?
3. Did the information clearly address the controlling question?
4. Did the presentation show signs of thoughtful and thorough preparation?
5. Did the presentation demonstrate proficiency in public speaking and listening?

For the Portfolio

Videotapes of the group presentations can be a useful addition to student portfolios. You may be able to make duplicate tapes so that a separate copy can be made for each student's portfolio.

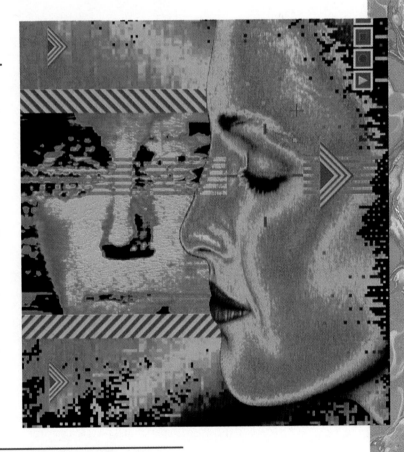

4 Team Teaching Options

Social Studies

Explore images of teens in other eras, such as the 1920s or 1950s, making use of popular magazines from the era.

Math

Help students do a statistical analysis of their findings. For example, students might figure ethnic representation by percentages, and create a bar graph to present the information.

Foreign Language

Study images of teens in other cultures, as presented by popular foreign language magazines.

Unit Preview

In Unit One, "A Matter of Perspective," students will explore how people's interpretations of events depends largely on their points of view. The unit contains two subunits:

- Subunit 1, "False Impressions"
- Subunit 2, "Tunnel Vision"

Connections to Unit Six

Unit Six, "Themes in World Folklore," contains literature from the oral tradition that connects with the themes in Unit One. You may wish to begin or end Unit One with selections from Unit Six that relate to the theme "A Matter of Perspective":

- "The Arrow and the Lamp," p. 587
- "Lazy Peter and His Three-Cornered Hat," p. 593
- "The Force of Luck," p. 597

ADDITIONAL RESOURCES

Unit One Resource Book
Unit Test, pp. 86–89

Technology and Enrichment
Family and Community Involvement Source Book, pp. 6–8

Fine Art Transparency Pack: Art Appreciation Transparencies

About the Art

Stop Light is by C. J. Yao (1941–), a painter from Taiwan. This painting combines two different styles of art: photorealism and abstraction. A photorealist painting is intended to resemble a photograph; abstract art is not realistic. In Yao's painting, the traffic signals and sign are realistic, but the reflections in the building windows are nearly abstract. *What idea of a city do you get from this painting? Why do you think the artist has not shown any people?*

A MATTER OF PERSPECTIVE

It is difficult to see

the picture when you

are inside the frame.

R. S. Trapp

STOP LIGHT 1986 © C. J. Yao.
Courtesy, Styria Studio, New York.

13

To help students probe connections between the art, the quotation, and the unit theme, have them consider the following questions:

1. What is meant by the word *perspective*? *(Possible responses: a point of view, an angle from which you look at something)*

2. How does the quotation relate to the title "A Matter of Perspective"? *(Possible responses: It expresses the idea that a person cannot view something objectively when he or she is very involved with the subject matter; it implies that people have a hard time judging fairly things to which they are emotionally linked.)*

3. Do you agree with the quotation? Why or why not? *(Possible responses: Yes, because people's emotions cloud their perspectives; yes, because people are unable to see themselves clearly without a mirror or another external aid.)*

4. How does the art relate to matters of perspective? *(Possible responses: The viewer's perspective determines whether he or she sees the buildings or their distorted reflections; the painting shows two perspectives—the traffic lights and sign are realistic, and the reflections of the buildings are abstract; it shows how ordinary things can be perceived in different ways.)*

5. On the basis of the quotation and the art, what kinds of selections do you imagine this unit will contain? *(Possible responses: selections about people who view the same situation in very different ways, selections about people who change their ideas when they see a subject from another viewpoint)*

Subunit Preview

Have students read the introduction to Subunit 1, "False Impressions." Ask them to explain how getting the wrong impression of someone relates to perspective. How does the angle from which you are looking affect the way you see something or someone? How do your own views affect how you see someone else? Has someone ever formed a false impression of you?

INTEGRATING THE LANGUAGE ARTS

The literary selections in this subunit focus on the theme of false impressions. Reading skills, literature skills, writing options, language study, vocabulary, and spelling skills are all based on these literary selections.

Writer's Workshop After reading several selections that deal with false impressions, students will use personal writing to describe their own experiences with false impressions.

Language Workshop The Language Workshop in this subunit focuses on using personal pronouns correctly. Students will see how the proper use of personal pronouns is important in writing about their experiences.

Reader's Workshop The Reader's Workshop in this subunit discusses inferences—logical guesses based on facts. Students will see how their understanding of what they read depends on their ability to draw correct inferences from the given facts.

FOR ADDITIONAL CHALLENGE

The following selections offer extra challenge in the exploration of the subunit theme:

"A Day's Wait," short story by Ernest Hemingway

"Let's Steal the Moon," folktale retold by Blanche Serwer-Bernstein

ADDITIONAL RESOURCES

Technology and Enrichment
Family and Community Involvement Source Book, p. 6

Guidelines for Reading and Literature Assessment: Observation Assessment Forms

A thirty-story building looks huge when seen from the ground. The same building looks tiny when seen from an airplane. The size of the building is a matter of perspective. It depends on your point of view. The same is true of people and situations. Your understanding of events and your opinions about people are also a matter of perspective—and the focus of Unit One.

Seeing things clearly is not always easy.

Have you ever been surprised to find out that your first impression of someone was totally false? You may have drawn the wrong conclusion because the person wanted to mislead you, or you may have simply made an error in judgment.

Sometimes we receive false impressions of others, and sometimes we give false impressions of ourselves. You will see both situations in the following selections.

Observation Assessment

Observing how students respond to the text, to the classroom instruction, and to peers is an important part of an assessment program. The following suggestions and the form in each *Guidelines for Reading and Literature Assessment* booklet can be used to implement observation assessment.

■ **Reading Behavior** As students work through the subunit, assess how they comprehend both when reading aloud and when reading silently. Evaluate how well and how long they are able to concentrate. Note whether lack of concentration is shown by one student only or by a larger group. Try to pinpoint specific passages that may be especially challenging because of unfamiliar vocabulary. Throughout the subunit, look for growth in students' abilities to maintain concentration and to demonstrate comprehension of difficult passages.

Elements of
FICTION

When you read a story, you are reading a work of fiction. **Fiction** is writing that comes from an author's imagination. Although the author makes the story up, he or she might base it on real events.

Fiction writers write either short stories or novels. A **short story** usually revolves around a single idea and is short enough to be read at one sitting. A **novel** is much longer and more complex. In this textbook, the fiction selections that you will read are short stories. However, at the end of each unit you will find recommendations for novels that you can read on your own.

Understanding Fiction

Character **Characters** are the people, animals, or imaginary creatures that take part in the action of the story. Usually, a short story centers on events in the life of one person or animal. He or she is the **main character.** Generally, there are also one or more **minor characters** in the story. Minor characters sometimes provide part of the background for the story. More often, however, minor characters interact with the main character and with one another. Their words and actions help to move the plot along.

Setting The **setting** is the time and place in which the story happens. The time may be the past, present, or future; day or night; and any season. The place where the action of the story occurs may be imaginary or real.

Plot The sequence of events in a story is called the **plot.** The plot is the writer's blueprint for what happens, when it happens, and to whom it happens. One event causes another, which causes another, and so on until the end of the story.

Generally, plots are built around a **conflict**—a problem or struggle between two or more opposing forces. Conflicts can range from a life-or-death struggle to a disagreement between friends.

While the development of each plot is different, traditional works of fiction generally follow a pattern that includes the following stages:

- **Exposition** Exposition sets the stage for the story. Characters are introduced, the setting is described, and the conflict begins to unfold.
- **Complications** As the story continues, the plot gets more complex. While the characters struggle to find solutions to the conflict, suspense and a feeling of excitement and energy build.
- **Climax** The climax is the highest point of interest or suspense in the story. It is the turning point when the action reaches a peak and the outcome of the conflict is decided. The climax may occur because of a decision the characters reach or because of a discovery or an event that changes the situation. The climax usually results in a change in the characters or a solution to the problem.
- **Resolution** The resolution occurs at the conclusion of the story. Loose ends are tied up and the story ends.

ADDITIONAL RESOURCES
Technology and Enrichment
Active Reading Transparencies 2–5

Plot Point out that a fiction writer must plan a way of shaping events into an interesting story with a beginning, a middle, and an end. This plan determines the plot.

After students have read about the four stages of a plot, ask them to identify these stages in the plot of a simple, familiar story such as "Cinderella."

Elements of Fiction

This feature provides students with an opportunity to develop a common vocabulary to use in discussing fiction. The terms on these pages are discussed in depth in the fiction selections that follow.

Objectives

- To understand and appreciate fiction
- To understand the elements of fiction—character, setting, plot, and theme
- To learn strategies for reading fiction

Motivation

Invite volunteers to describe clay objects that they have crafted. Point out that over the ages craftspeople have used their imagination to mold new and unusual objects from clay—pottery, for example, and figures of gods and beasts. Then explain that the word *fiction* is related to Latin verb meaning "to mold" and ask students how the writing of stories is like molding clay. Elicit that like a sculptor molding clay, a fiction writer shapes words and ideas into something imaginative and new.

Teaching Strategies

Understanding Fiction

Character Invite students to name some favorite fictional characters from books, television shows, and movies. Point out that the characters they remember are probably main characters, although minor characters are sometimes memorable as well. Ask if any minor characters come to mind.

Setting Ask students to name some times and places that they would like to visit in a time machine. Point out that there are stories that can "transport" them to these settings, as well as stories that explore times and places much like their own. Then invite volunteers to describe the settings of their favorite novels.

Theme Have students name a few familiar proverbs, such as "All that glitters is not gold" and "Where there's a will, there's a way." Point out that the theme of a story can often be expressed as a simple statement like a proverb. Then invite students to use the three bulleted suggestions to unlock the theme of a familiar story or tale.

Strategies for Reading Fiction

Make sure students understand that a strategy is a plan or method used to reach a goal. Then invite students to paraphrase the explanation of each of the strategies in this section, focusing on how they have used or might use the strategy to achieve the goal of understanding a short story or novel.

Refer students back to the short story "Charles" (pp. 7–11), noting that the student reactions shown in the margins illustrate some of the reading strategies, such as questioning and evaluating. Invite volunteers to demonstrate how they might use the strategies listed here to understand and appreciate "Charles" better.

Closure

To close the lesson, invite students to work together to outline the elements of an original short story. Write the terms *Characters* and *Setting* on the board and have students suggest possibilities for these elements. Next, list the names of the stages of a plot—*Exposition, Complications, Climax,* and *Resolution*—and ask students to brainstorm events that might happen at each stage. Finally, write *Theme* and have students note a message that the story might convey. Encourage interested students to use the outline to write a story draft.

Theme The **theme** of a story is the main message the writer wishes to share with the reader. This message might be a lesson about life or a belief about people and their actions. Most themes are not stated directly. They are like hidden messages that the reader must decode. You will find, however, as you discuss literature, that different readers discover different themes in the same selection. The following suggestions will help you unlock the theme.

- Review what happened to the main character. Did he or she change during the story? What did he or she learn about life?

- Skim the selection for key phrases and sentences—statements that move beyond the action of the story to say something important about life or people.

- Think about the title of the selection. Does it have a special meaning that could lead you to the main idea of the piece?

Strategies for Reading Fiction

1. **Preview** a story before you read it by looking at the title and the pictures, or even skimming through the pages, reading some words here and there.

2. Try to **visualize** the setting and the characters. Can you picture a similar place in your mind? Can you "see" the action and the characters?

3. As you read, **make connections.** Do any of the characters have the same thoughts or experiences that you have had? Does the story remind you of an event or person you've heard of or read about?

4. While you read, **question** events, characters, and ideas. "Why is the door unlocked?" "Why is she so rude?" Asking good questions is at the heart of good reading.

5. During your reading, stop occasionally and **predict** what might happen next and how the story will end.

6. As you read, **build** on what you're learning about the characters and events in the story. Let your thoughts change and grow as you learn more about the situation.

7. Continually **evaluate** the story as you read. Think about your feelings toward the characters and their actions. Also consider how well the author is telling his or her story.

When you have finished reading, discuss your understandings and questions about the story with someone else.

Remember, a story never tells you everything. It leaves room for you to build your own ideas. When you read, you are left with first impressions, but you need to be able to elaborate and explain them based on the story, your own experiences, and other stories you have read.

Fiction

Seventh Grade
GARY SOTO

Examine What You Know (Prior Knowledge)

How do seventh graders try to impress each other? Think about what you and your friends do to make others admire you. Create a chart that lists ways seventh graders show off. An example of such a chart is shown below. Share your ideas with your classmates.

Words or Actions	Appearance
bragging	designer jeans

Expand Your Knowledge (Building Background)

For some students, wearing the right clothes is a way to gain admiration and acceptance. They often work summer jobs in order to purchase a back-to-school wardrobe. The main character in the next story earns his clothing money by picking grapes near his home in Fresno. Fresno is an important farming center in central California. One of the largest crops grown in the Fresno area is grapes, a seasonal crop that requires thousands of workers to harvest. During summers, both migrant workers, those who follow harvests from one town to another, and residents pick grapes for money.

Write Before You Read (Journal Writing)

In your journal or notebook, write about a time you used clothing, money, or actions to impress someone. What did you do? What were the results?

■ *Author biography on Extend page*

Objectives

■ To understand and analyze a short story

■ To understand methods of characterization

■ To enrich reading by evaluating characters' actions and motives

■ To express understanding of the story through a choice of writing forms, including a note, a scene, an advice column, and a journal

Prereading/Motivation

Examine What You Know

Discussion Prompts What kinds of things do people do to impress their friends? to impress someone they admire? How do people try to show that they are smart or interesting or cool or important?

Expand Your Knowledge

Additional Background Fresno, California, is an important marketing center for United States agriculture. Nearly all of the country's raisins come from the Fresno area. Since the 1950s, economic growth has caused a population boom in Fresno, including an increase in the number of Mexican-American laborers. In 1962, Cesar Chavez, a labor leader, helped to organize California grape pickers and to win for them significant union rights, which helped improve both their standard of living and education for their children.

Thematic Link— False Impressions

Victor and his friends try to impress girls through their actions. Victor gives Teresa the false impression that he knows French, and his teacher doesn't give him away.

MORE JOURNAL WRITING IDEAS

■ Describe a time when you pretended to know something.

■ How do you react when you feel someone is working hard to make a good impression on you?

■ How do adults try to impress one another?

COLLABORATIVE LEARNING OPTIONS

Opportunities for collaborative learning include Options for Learning 1, 3, and 4 (p. 25) and Cross-Curricular Projects (p. 25).

ADDITIONAL RESOURCES

Unit One Resource Book
Reader's Guidesheet, p. 1
Reading Skills, p. 2
Literature Skills, p. 3
Vocabulary Connections, p. 4
Spelling Connections, p. 5
Comprehension and Vocabulary Check Tests, p. 6
Selection Test, pp. 7–8

VOCABULARY PREVIEW

These vocabulary words are defined at the bottom of the selection pages on which they appear.

conviction a strong belief

elective a school subject chosen by the student

ferocity extreme fierceness

linger to continue to stay

scowl to look angry by frowning

LIMITED ENGLISH PROFICIENCY

■ Use the Reader's Guidesheet, *Unit One Resource Book,* page 1.

■ Some of the characters in this story use foreign words as well as slang and dialect. You may wish to read certain passages aloud to help clarify pronunciation and meaning.

★ Text annotations marked with a red star (2, 4, 9) may be particularly helpful for students with limited English proficiency.

TEXT ANNOTATIONS

1. ACTIVE READING: Review
Ask students if they can infer the characters' ethnic identities based on the first two paragraphs. *(The reference to "brown people," the names Rodriguez and Torres, and some Spanish dialogue all hint that the characters are Hispanic Americans.)*

2. VOCABULARY: Cultural References
Some students may not be familiar with GQ magazine or a bookmobile. Have volunteers explain the terms if possible. *(GQ, which stands for Gentleman's Quarterly, is a men's fashion magazine. A bookmobile is a library van that brings reading materials for people to borrow, often in small towns where no regular library exists.)* ★

3. LITERARY CONCEPT: Characterization
Point out that throughout the story, the author reveals Victor's private thoughts. Ask students what they learn about Victor from his thoughts here and elsewhere in the story. *(Possible responses: He has a down-to-earth attitude; he is less sophisticated than Michael.)*

Seventh Grade

GARY SOTO

On the first day of school, Victor stood in line half an hour before he came to a wobbly card table. He was handed a packet of papers and a computer card on which he listed his one <u>elective</u>, French. He already spoke Spanish and English, but he thought someday he might travel to France, where it was cool; not like Fresno, where summer days reached 110 degrees in the shade. There were rivers in France, and huge churches, and fair-skinned people everywhere, the way there were brown people all around Victor.

Besides, Teresa, a girl he had liked since they were in catechism classes[1] at Saint Theresa's, was taking French, too. With any luck they would be in the same class. Teresa is going to be my girl this year, he promised himself as he left the gym full of students in their new fall clothes. She was cute. And good at math, too, Victor thought as he walked down the hall to his homeroom. He ran into his friend, Michael Torres, by the water fountain that never turned off.

They shook hands, *raza*-style[2], and jerked their heads at one another in a *saludo de vato*[3]. "How come you're making a face?" asked Victor.

"I ain't making a face, *ese*[4]. This *is* my face." Michael said his face had changed during the summer. He had read a *GQ* magazine that his older brother borrowed from the Book Mobile and noticed that the male models all had the same look on their faces. They would stand, one arm around a beautiful woman, and <u>scowl</u>. They would sit at a pool, their rippled stomachs dark with shadow, and *scowl*. They would sit at dinner tables, cool drinks in their hands, and *scowl*.

"I think it works," Michael said. He scowled and let his upper lip quiver. His teeth showed along with the <u>ferocity</u> of his soul. "Belinda Reyes walked by a while ago and looked at me," he said.

Victor didn't say anything, though he thought his friend looked pretty strange. They talked about recent movies, baseball, their parents, and the horrors of picking grapes in order to buy their fall clothes. Picking grapes was like living in Siberia,

---

1. **catechism classes:** formal classes in religious instruction.
2. *raza*-**style** (rä′ zä-) *Spanish:* in the familiar manner that local Hispanics greet each other.
3. *saludo de vato* (sä lōō dō dä vä′ tō) *Spanish:* greeting between Hispanic buddies.
4. *ese* (e′ sā) *Spanish:* a slang term used when addressing someone, as in "Hey, man."

Words to Know and Use	**elective** (ē lek′ tiv) *n.* a school subject or course chosen by the student rather than assigned
	scowl (skoul) *v.* to look angry by drawing the eyebrows together and frowning
18	**ferocity** (fə räs′ ə tē) *n.* extreme fierceness; savagery

---

Guided Reading for Less-Proficient Students

These questions can help guide students through the reading. Ask each question at the point of the selection where the capital letter and arrow appear in the margin. In addition, you may wish to use appropriate Active Reading annotations.

A. Why does Victor decide to take French? *(Teresa is taking it; he may go to France someday; he already knows Spanish.)* Recalling

B. Why does Victor practice scowling? *(His friend Michael has told him that girls find it attractive.)* Recalling

C. How does Victor show that he likes Teresa? *(He waits for her after homeroom, he mentions her name in English, and he looks for her during lunch.)* Summarizing

Continued on page 19

BOY SEATED IN THE STUDIO 1980 Claudio Bravo Private collection.
Courtesy, Marlborough Gallery, New York.

Guided Reading for Less-Proficient Students

Continued from page 18

D. In Mr. Bueller's class, why does Victor pretend to know French? *(He wants to impress Teresa.)* Recalling

E. How does Teresa react to Victor's performance in French class? *(She compliments him and asks if he will help her with French.)* Recalling

F. How does Teresa's response after French class affect Victor's attitude toward seventh grade? *(He goes from feeling worried and unsure about school to feeling self-confident and motivated.)* Evaluating

4. VOCABULARY: Idioms

Ask students if they can figure out the meaning of "She would be a good bet" and "He watched her on the sly" by using context clues. (*Possible responses: "She would be a good person to ask"; "He watched her secretly."*) ★

5. ACTIVE READING: Review

Ask the students to **infer** the reason Victor does not speak to Teresa in a more friendly way. (*Possible responses: He is nervous; he wants to seem manly, or macho; he wants to seem in control, not in love.*)

except hot and more boring.

"What classes are you taking?" Michael said, scowling.

"French. How 'bout you?"

"Spanish. I ain't so good at it, even if I'm Mexican."

"I'm not either, but I'm better at it than math, that's for sure."

A tinny, three-beat bell propelled students to their homerooms. The two friends socked each other in the arm and went their ways, Victor thinking, man, that's weird. Michael thinks making a face makes him handsome.

On the way to his homeroom, Victor tried a scowl. He felt foolish, until out of the corner of his eye he saw a girl looking at him. Umm, he thought, maybe it does work. He scowled with greater <u>conviction</u>.

In homeroom, roll was taken, emergency cards were passed out, and they were given a bulletin to take home to their parents. The principal, Mr. Belton, spoke over the crackling loudspeaker, welcoming the students to a new year, new experiences, and new friendships. The students squirmed in their chairs and ignored him. They were anxious to go to first period. Victor sat calmly, thinking of Teresa, who sat two rows away, reading a paperback novel. This would be his lucky year. She was in his homeroom, and would probably be in his English and math classes. And, of course, French.

The bell rang for first period, and the students herded noisily through the door. Only Teresa <u>lingered</u>, talking with the homeroom teacher.

"So you think I should talk to Mrs. Gaines?" she asked the teacher. "She would know about ballet?"

"She would be a good bet," the teacher said. Then added, "Or the gym teacher, Mrs. Garza."

Victor lingered, keeping his head down and staring at his desk. He wanted to leave when she did so he could bump into her and say something clever.

He watched her on the sly. As she turned to leave, he stood up and hurried to the door, where he managed to catch her eye. She smiled and said, "Hi, Victor."

He smiled back and said, "Yeah, that's me." His brown face blushed. Why hadn't he said, "Hi, Teresa," or "How was your summer?" or something nice?

As Teresa walked down the hall, Victor walked the other way, looking back, admiring how gracefully she walked, one foot in front of the other. So much for being in the same class, he thought. As he trudged to English, he practiced scowling.

In English they reviewed the parts of speech. Mr. Lucas, a portly man, waddled down the aisle, asking, "What is a noun?"

"A person, place, or thing," said the class in unison.

"Yes, now somebody give me an example of a person—you, Victor Rodriguez."

"Teresa," Victor said automatically. Some of the girls giggled. They knew he had a crush on Teresa. He felt himself blushing again.

"Correct," Mr. Lucas said. "Now provide

Words to Know and Use	**conviction** (kən vik' shən) *n.* a strong belief **linger** (lin' gər) *v.* to continue to stay; delay leaving

20

Multicultural Connections

In the 1990 census, 9 percent of Americans identified themselves as Hispanics. Hispanic Americans are the second largest minority group in the United States, after African Americans. Many speak English most of the time, while others make Spanish their primary language.

Ask students why they think some Hispanic Americans might prefer Spanish to English. If students were Hispanic Americans living in Fresno, which language might they prefer? Why?

me with a place."

Mr. Lucas called on a freckled kid who answered, "Teresa's house with a kitchen full of big brothers."

After English, Victor had math, his weakest subject. He sat in the back by the window, hoping that he would not be called on. Victor understood most of the problems, but some of the stuff looked like the teacher made it up as she went along. It was confusing, like the inside of a watch.

After math he had a fifteen-minute break, then social studies, and, finally, lunch. He bought a tuna casserole with buttered rolls, some fruit cocktail, and milk. He sat with Michael, who practiced scowling between bites.

Girls walked by and looked at him.

6

"See what I mean, Vic?" Michael scowled. "They love it."

"Yeah, I guess so."

They ate slowly, Victor scanning the horizon for a glimpse of Teresa. He didn't see her. She must have brought lunch, he thought, and is eating outside. Victor scraped his plate and left Michael, who was busy scowling at a girl two tables away.

The small triangle-shaped campus bustled with students talking about their new classes. Everyone was in a sunny mood. Victor hurried to the bag lunch area, where he sat down and opened his math book. He moved his lips as if he were reading, but his mind was somewhere else. He raised his eyes slowly and looked around. No Teresa.

He lowered his eyes, pretending to study, then looked slowly to the left. No Teresa. He turned a page in the book and stared at some math problems that scared him

because he knew he would have to do them eventually. He looked to the right. Still no sign of her. He stretched out lazily in an attempt to disguise his snooping.

7

Then he saw her. She was sitting with a girlfriend under a plum tree. Victor moved to a table near her and daydreamed about taking her to a movie. When the bell sounded, Teresa looked up, and their eyes met. She smiled sweetly and gathered her books. Her next class was French, same as Victor's. ◄ C

They were among the last students to arrive in class, so all the good desks in the back had already been taken. Victor was forced to sit near the front, a few desks away from Teresa, while Mr. Bueller wrote French words on the chalkboard. The bell rang, and Mr. Bueller wiped his hands, turned to the class, and said, *"Bonjour."*[5]

"Bonjour," braved a few students.

"Bonjour," Victor whispered. He wondered if Teresa heard him.

Mr. Bueller said that if the students studied hard, at the end of the year they could go to France and be understood by the populace.

One kid raised his hand and asked, "What's 'populace'?"

"The people, the people of France."

Mr. Bueller asked if anyone knew French. Victor raised his hand, wanting to impress Teresa. The teacher beamed and said, *"Très bien. Parlez-vous français?"*[6]

8

Victor didn't know what to say. The teacher wet his lips and asked something else in French. The room grew silent. Victor felt all eyes staring at him. He tried to bluff

---

5. ***Bonjour*** (bōn zhōōr′) *French:* Good day.
6. ***Très bien. Parlez-vous français?*** (tre byän pär′ le vü frän′ se) *French:* Very good. Do you speak French?

---

6. ACTIVE READING: Evaluate
Ask students whether they agree that the girls look at Michael's scowl because "they love it." If not, what else might the girls be thinking as they look at his face? *(Possible responses: They simply think Michael is strange; his behavior seems weird to them; they are curious.)*

7. LITERARY CONCEPT:
Characterization
Ask how Victor's character is further revealed through his actions here. Why does he pretend to be studying while secretly looking at Teresa? *(He doesn't want her to know he is interested in her.)* Ask students how his actions are another example of a false impression he creates for other people. *(He wants people to think he is too cool to have a crush; he doesn't want to be embarrassed if Teresa doesn't like him.)*

8. ACTIVE READING: Predict
What do students predict Victor will do or say after Mr. Bueller speaks to him in French? *(Any response is valid.)* Encourage students to explain their predictions.

Looking at Style

These ideas may be helpful in discussing Soto's writing style in "Seventh Grade."

Have students read these sentences from page 22:

■ <u>Great rosebushes of red bloomed</u> on Victor's cheeks.

■ <u>A river of nervous sweat</u> ran down his palms.

■ Better yet, <u>he wished he could start his life over.</u>

Have students note the underlined portion of each sentence. Then ask the following questions:

1. Why do you think Soto uses such exaggerated images and statements? How does each exaggeration help express a character's thoughts or feelings?

2. Try creating an exaggerated statement of your own to express a character's thoughts or feelings. You may want to begin your sentence with "She was so nervous, she felt . . ."

his way out by making noises that sounded French.

"La me vava me con le grandma," he said uncertainly.

Mr. Bueller, wrinkling his face in curiosity, asked him to speak up.

Great rosebushes of red bloomed on Victor's cheeks. A river of nervous sweat ran down his palms. He felt awful. Teresa sat a few desks away, no doubt thinking he was a fool. Without looking at Mr. Bueller, Victor mumbled, "Frenchie oh wewe gee in September."

Mr. Bueller asked Victor to repeat what he had said.

"Frenchie oh wewe gee in September," Victor repeated.

Mr. Bueller understood that the boy didn't know French and turned away. He walked to the blackboard and pointed to the words on the board with his steel-edged ruler.

"Le bateau," he sang.

"Le bateau," the students repeated.

"Le bateau est sur l'eau,"[7] he sang.

"Le bateau est sur l'eau."

Victor was too weak from failure to join the class. He stared at the board and wished he had taken Spanish, not French. Better yet, he wished he could start his life over. He had never been so embarrassed. He bit his thumb until he tore off a sliver of skin.

The bell sounded for fifth period, and Victor shot out of the room, avoiding the stares of the other kids, but had to return for his math book. He looked sheepishly at the teacher, who was erasing the board, then widened his eyes in terror at Teresa who stood in front of him. "I didn't know you knew French," she said. "That was good."

Mr. Bueller looked at Victor, and Victor looked back. Oh please, don't say anything, Victor pleaded with his eyes. I'll wash your car, mow your lawn, walk your dog—anything! I'll be your best student, and I'll clean your erasers after school.

Mr. Bueller shuffled through the papers on his desk. He smiled and hummed as he sat down to work. He remembered his college years when he dated a girlfriend in borrowed cars. She thought he was rich because each time he picked her up, he had a different car. It was fun until he had spent all his money on her and had to write home to his parents because he was broke.

Victor couldn't stand to look at Teresa. He was sweaty with shame. "Yeah, well, I picked up a few things from movies and books and stuff like that." They left the class together. Teresa asked him if he would help her with her French.

"Sure, anytime," Victor said.

"I won't be bothering you, will I?"

"Oh no, I like being bothered."

"Bonjour," Teresa said, leaving him outside her next class. She smiled and pushed wisps of hair from her face.

"Yeah, right, *bonjour,*" Victor said. He turned and headed to his class. The rosebushes of shame on his face became bouquets of love. Teresa is a great girl, he thought. And Mr. Bueller is a good guy.

He raced to metal shop. After metal shop there was biology, and after biology a long sprint to the public library, where he checked out three French textbooks.

He was going to like seventh grade. 🐾 ◄ F

---

7. *Le bateau est sur l'eau* (lə bà tō′ e sür lō) *French:* The boat is on the water.

Comprehension Check

✓ 1. Why does Victor take French rather than Spanish? *(He knows Spanish; Teresa is taking French; he wants to visit France some day.)*

2. For what purpose do Michael and Victor scowl? *(to attract girls)*

3. What does Victor do to embarrass himself? *(He speaks fake French in class.)*

4. Why is Teresa impressed with Victor? *(She thinks he really knows French.)*

5. Why is Victor grateful to Mr. Bueller? *(Mr. Bueller doesn't expose the fake French.)*

6. What did Teresa ask Victor after French class? *(to help her with French)*

7. What did Victor think of seventh grade after his first day? *(He thinks he will like it.)*

Responding to Reading

First Impressions

1. What were your reactions to Victor? Jot down your ideas in your journal or on a sheet of paper.

Second Thoughts

2. Do you think Victor should feel proud or ashamed of his actions? Explain your answer.

> **Think about**
> - why he claimed to know French
> - what happens, or might happen, as a result of his claim

3. The French teacher, Mr. Bueller, realizes that Victor is faking his knowledge of French. Why do you think he keeps the truth to himself?

4. It seems that Victor succeeds in impressing Teresa. What is your opinion of Teresa? Support your answer with evidence from the story.

Broader Connections

5. Why do people feel the need to create false impressions of themselves? Are they always wrong to do so? Use the experiences you wrote about before reading to help you think through your response.

Literary Concept: Characterization

Characterization refers to the methods that writers use to make their characters seem real. Writers can use any of the following methods to make their characters come alive for readers.

1) Show the character in action or conversation.
2) Express the character's thoughts.
3) Describe his or her physical appearance.
4) Tell how other characters respond to him or her.

Look back through the story to find an example of each of the methods that Soto uses. Share your examples with your classmates.

Student Response

Responding to Reading

1. Any response is valid.

2. **Possible responses:** He should feel proud because he has won Teresa's admiration and will try hard to help her in French this year; proud because he has survived a difficult situation; he should feel ashamed because he lied both to Teresa and to his teacher; ashamed because he acted foolishly by speaking fake French; ashamed because he has impressed Teresa through a falsehood.

3. **Possible responses:** Mr. Bueller does not wish to embarrass Victor in front of Teresa and the rest of the class. He recalls a time that he too used a falsehood to impress a girl, and he therefore understands Victor's behavior.

4. **Possible responses:** She is a friendly girl who shows her fondness for Victor through her sweet smiles and complimentary words for him. She is naive to be taken in by Victor's fake French.

5. **Possible responses:** People create false impressions because they feel that they are inadequate or not well liked. They are not always wrong to do so, especially if the false impression makes everyone feel more comfortable; giving a false impression is always wrong because it puts relationships on a false basis.

Challenge Question

Based on details from the story, what do you think Teresa's attitude toward school and learning is? *(Possible responses: Some students might say she genuinely wants to learn, while others may believe she's just trying to impress others. Details include her reading between classes, asking advice of teachers, and asking for Victor's help.)*

Literary Concept: Characterization

Victor's character is shown by his actions when he secretly watches Teresa and when he bluffs knowledge of French. His character is shown by his thoughts when he wonders about Michael's scowl and prays desperately that Mr. Bueller will not embarrass him in front of Teresa. His character is shown by his appearance in the description of his blushing face when he meets Teresa and of the river of sweat when he is embarrassed by his lie. His character is shown through other characters in his friendship with Michael and in Victor's reaction when Teresa compliments him after French class.

Writing Options

The Writing Options are designed to meet varied student interests and abilities. Have each student choose one writing activity to complete.

Journal Update Suggest that students write about a time when they embarrassed themselves and felt the way Victor did.

Links to
Writer's Craft

Writing Option 4 is an exercise in personal writing. For more practice, see *The Writer's Craft, Grade 7,* "Personal and Expressive Writing," pages 26–46.

Vocabulary Practice

Answers to Exercise

1. linger

2. conviction

3. elective

4. scowl

5. ferocity

For Alternative Learning Styles

Encourage students to use facial expressions and/or body gestures to demonstrate the meanings of *scowl, linger,* and *ferocity.* Then ask them to pantomime how they would speak or act *with conviction.*

Closure

Tell students that when they read the excerpt from *Little by Little,* they will encounter another character who, like Victor and Michael, is concerned with making an impression in a school setting. Ask students to explain why young people may be especially concerned with the impression they are making in school. Discuss how the pressures felt in school might lead students to try to create a false impression.

Writing Options

1. Write the **note** Teresa might hand to her best friend describing what happened in French class and her reaction to Victor.

2. Extend the story by describing what might happen next. You might wish to create a **scene** between Victor and Teresa, or one between him and his friends.

3. Write an **advice column** to Victor and his friends, giving them suggestions on how to get a girl's attention.

4. Record your first impressions of seventh grade in your **journal.** Include what you expect to like about seventh grade as well as what you may not like about it or what worries you.

Vocabulary Practice

Exercise On your paper, write the word from the list that best completes the sentence.

1. Victor wanted to ___?___ in the hallway to see Teresa, even though he might be late for class.

2. Victor's friend changed his appearance because of his ___?___ that girls cared mainly for looks.

3. When a course is offered as an ___?___, students do not have to take it.

4. Most people probably would not consider a ___?___ to be more attractive than a smile.

5. Michael believed that a look of ___?___, not gentleness, would win the hearts of girls.

Words to Know and Use

conviction
elective
ferocity
linger
scowl

The Spelling Connection

Spelling Pattern: ly/ally To spell the adverb form of adjectives that end in **al**, just add **ly**. To spell the adverb form of words that end with the letter **c**, add **ally**.
Examples: intentional + ly = intentionally
basic + ally = basically

ly/ally Words from the Selection
eventual + ly = eventually
final + ly = finally
automatic + ally = automatically

Other ly/ally Words
traditionally   systematically
accidentally   dramatically

Exercise Fill in the blanks with **ly/ally** words.
1. The Parker family _____ went bowling every Friday night.
2. Tom _____ dropped the heavy bowling ball.
3. Susan's ball went into the gutter _____.
4. After trying hard, she _____ got two strikes.

*O*ptions for Learning (Multimodal/Cross-Curricular Activities)

1 • A Bunch of Trouble   Grape pickers drew national attention in the 1960s and 1970s. Research the problems that grape pickers faced and their efforts to improve conditions. Report your findings to the class. Be sure to report both sides of the problems.

2 • A Tuneful Telling   Write lyrics for a song that Victor might use to impress Teresa. The lyrics should boast about his imaginary achievements. You might want to include some fake French to impress her.

3 • On Stage   With other students, act out one scene from "Seventh Grade" for your class. Study the story carefully for details about the characters.

4 • In Another Language   Ask at least twenty students which foreign language they are most interested in learning. It may be one that they have already begun studying. Chart the results and share your findings with your class.

 FACT FINDER SOCIAL STUDIES
What other crops are grown in the Fresno area?

*G*ary Soto
1952 –

Gary Soto grew up in a Mexican-American community in Fresno, California. His father worked for a raisin company, and his mother peeled potatoes at a food-processing company. At various times during his childhood, Soto wanted to be a priest, a hobo, and a paleontologist (a scientist who studies fossils).

In college he planned to study geography, until he discovered poetry. "I don't think I had any literary aspirations when I was a kid," says Soto. "In fact, we didn't have books, and no one encouraged us to read. So my wanting to write poetry was a sort of fluke."

He has been writing poetry, novels, and short stories for young readers and adults ever since college. A collection of autobiographical pieces, *Living Up the Street*, won an American Book Award. His recently published young adult novels include *Taking Sides, Pacific Crossing*, and *The Skirt*.

Soto lives with his wife and daughter in Berkeley, California, where he occasionally teaches at the University of California.

Options for Learning

These activities suit a variety of learning styles and modes of expression.

Collaborative Learning Activities
See Options 3 and 4.

1. A Bunch of Trouble Students can find information in encyclopedias and books. They can also use the *Readers' Guide to Periodical Literature* and *The New York Times Index* to find articles in magazines and newspapers from the 1960s and 1970s.

2. A Tuneful Telling If students have difficulty choosing a form for their song, they might take an already popular song and rewrite the lyrics to fit their subject.

3. On Stage Encourage students to write out their scenes before performing them. Students may need to write dialogue that does not appear in the story.

4. In Another Language Have students display their survey results in a box or bar graph.

 FACT FINDER SOCIAL STUDIES
Students can use an encyclopedia to find that Fresno's other crops include cotton and figs.

Gary Soto

■ **More About the Author** A teacher as well as a writer, Soto takes literature seriously. He says: "I stress mechanics—how a piece is put together, characterization, dialogue, pace, symbolism—so that students can . . . deepen their understanding of writing. I want them to understand how a writer puts things together, to see that it's not simply a mishmash of feelings."

■ **Other Works** Short stories: *Baseball in April and Other Stories*; poetry: *The Tale of Sunlight, Father Is a Pillow Tied to a Broom, Black Hair*

 ■ **Awards** Academy of American Poets Prize, 1975; creative writing fellowship from National Education Association, 1982; Levinson Award from *Poetry* magazine, 1984.

Cross-Curricular Projects

Art Have students color or paint a picture of a "typical" seventh grader, using careful detail to show the subject's clothing, posture, and facial expression.
Social Studies Have groups of students research Fresno, California, to learn about its demographics, topography, economy, and history to create a "Welcome to Fresno" guide.
Science Invite students to find out how raisins are processed from grapes and to try it themselves by drying green grapes in the sun for ten to fifteen days. Have them take daily notes about the changes that occur.
Geography/Math Have students make a map of the United States showing concentrations of Hispanic Americans. Students may wish to make these maps for times in the past as well, showing the growth of the Hispanic-American population.

Objectives

- To understand and analyze a short story

- To examine the significance of plot and setting

- To enrich reading by understanding the meaning and use of dialect

- To express understanding of the story through a choice of writing forms, including a letter, a comparison, an explanation, and a personal narrative

Prereading/Motivation

Examine What You Know

Discussion Prompts What makes your place a good or special place to be? With whom do you share it? Has anyone ever intruded on it? How did you feel and what did you do?

Expand Your Knowledge

Additional Background When a group of artists painted *The Wall of Respect* in Chicago in the 1960s, they inspired the movement of painting murals on walls to reflect community culture. Chicago artist William Walker describes such art as a form of "artist-to-people communication." Bambara says this movement was later adopted by Hispanic-American and Asian-American communities and is now part of Arab-American communities.

Enrich Your Reading

For Alternative Learning Styles To reinforce oral language skills, invite volunteers to take the parts of story characters and read aloud some of the passages containing dialect.

Thematic Link— False Impressions

The narrator and Lou have a false first impression of the "painter lady" in this story. First they see her as an intruder who has no regard for what their wall means to them. Later, however, they realize she is painting the wall to show her respect for their culture and heroes.

Fiction

The War of the Wall

TONI CADE BAMBARA

Examine What You Know (Prior Knowledge)

Is there a place in your neighborhood that seems to belong to young people? Perhaps it is a park or a schoolyard or a mall. Describe that place in your journal and tell how people feel about it.

Expand Your Knowledge (Building Background)

In the 1960s, some African-American artists began the "wall of respect" movement. The artists began creating special places by painting walls within the community that became symbols of their respect for their own neighborhoods.

Walls have also been regarded as symbols for even larger ideas. The Berlin Wall was a negative symbol for the split between the Communist and free worlds. On the other hand, the Vietnam Veterans Memorial has a wall engraved with the name of every American killed or missing in action in the Vietnam conflict. It is a wall of honor.

Enrich Your Reading (Reading Skill)

Dialect   Dialect is the particular type of language spoken in a particular place by a certain group of people. Dialect includes the way words are pronounced, as well as the colorful expressions used in informal conversation. The chart below explains some of the dialect used in the story.

■ *Author biography on Extend page*

Dialect	Meaning
pot likker:	liquid left after meat and/or vegetables have cooked
full of sky:	as if in another world
fix her wagon:	tell her off
hunching each other:	bumping someone with a shoulder or elbow
laying down a heavy rap:	saying something important
sounded very tall:	sounded proud

26   UNIT ONE   FALSE IMPRESSIONS

JOURNAL WRITING IDEAS

■ Use the title to predict what this story might be about.

■ If you were to design a "wall of respect" for your neighborhood, what would it look like and why?

■ How have walls figured in wars or conflicts of the past? Consider such examples as ancient walled towns, the Great Wall of China, or the Berlin Wall.

COLLABORATIVE LEARNING OPTIONS

Opportunities for collaborative learning include Options for Learning activities 1, 3, and 4 (p. 36) and Cross-Curricular Options (pp. 32 and 36).

ADDITIONAL RESOURCES

Unit One Resource Book
Reader's Guidesheet, p. 9
Reading Skills, p. 10
Literature Skills, p. 11
Vocabulary Connections, p. 12
Spelling Connections, p. 13
Comprehension and Vocabulary Check Tests, p. 14
Selection Test, pp. 15-16

The War of the Wall

TONI CADE BAMBARA

Me and Lou had no time for courtesies. We were late for school. So we just flat out told the painter lady to quit messing with the wall. It was our wall, and she had no right coming into our neighborhood painting on it. Stirring in the paint bucket and not even looking at us, she mumbled something about Mr. Eubanks, the barber, giving her permission. That had nothing to do with it as far as we were concerned. We've been pitching pennies against that wall since we were little kids. Old folks have been dragging their chairs out to sit in the shade of the wall for years. Big kids have been playing handball against the wall since so-called integration[1] when the crazies 'cross town poured cement in our pool so we couldn't use it. I'd sprained my neck one time boosting my cousin Lou up to chisel Jimmy Lyons's name into the wall when we found out he was never coming home from the war in Vietnam to take us fishing.

2   "If you lean close," Lou said, leaning hip-shot against her beat-up car, "you'll get a whiff of bubble gum and kids' sweat. And that'll tell you something—that this wall belongs to the kids of Taliaferro Street." I thought Lou sounded very convincing. But the painter lady paid us no mind. She just snapped the brim of her straw hat down and A ▶ hauled her bucket up the ladder.

"You're not even from around here," I hollered up after her. The license plates on her old piece of car said "New York." Lou dragged me away because I was about to grab hold of that ladder and shake it. And then we'd really be late for school.

Why is the narrator angry? *question*   3

When we came from school, the wall was slick with white. The painter lady was running string across the wall and taping it here and there. Me and Lou leaned against the gum ball machine outside the pool hall and watched. She had strings up and down and back and forth. Then she began chalking them with a hunk of blue chalk.

The Morris twins crossed the street, hanging back at the curb next to the beat-up car. The twin with the red ribbons was hugging a jug of cloudy lemonade. The one with yellow ribbons was holding a plate of dinner away from her dress. The painter lady began snapping the strings. The blue chalk dust measured off halves and quarters up and down and sideways too. Lou was about to say how hip it all was, but I dropped my book satchel on his toes to remind him we were at war. ◀ B

---

1. **since so-called integration**: from the time in the 1960s when segregation, the separation of the races in public places, was outlawed. The narrator is being sarcastic, suggesting that integration never took effect.

THE WAR OF THE WALL   27

SUNNY SIDE OF THE STREET   1950   Philip Evergood   Collection of The Corcoran Gallery of Art, Washington, D.C. Museum purchase, Anna E. Clark Fund.

28   UNIT ONE   FALSE IMPRESSIONS

Guided Reading for Less-Proficient Students

Continued from page 27

C. Why does the painter ignore the people of the neighborhood? *(She is totally focused on preparing to paint the wall.)* Recalling

D. What does the late news say kids in New York are doing to the subway trains? *(They are using spray cans to paint graffiti on the trains.)* Recalling

E. What kinds of people has the woman painted on the wall? *(heroes of African-American history and people from the neighborhood)* Drawing conclusions

F. Why is the wall dedicated to Jimmy Lyons? *(He was the painter's cousin, a respected member of the community, who died in Vietnam.)* Recalling

Some good aromas were drifting our way from the plate leaking pot likker onto the Morris girl's white socks. I could tell from where I stood that under the tinfoil was baked ham, collard greens, and candied yams. And knowing Mrs. Morris, who sometimes bakes for my mama's restaurant, a slab of buttered cornbread was probably up under there too, sopping up some of the pot likker. Me and Lou rolled our eyes, wishing somebody would send us some dinner. But the painter lady didn't even turn around. She was pulling the strings down and prying bits of tape loose.

Side Pocket came strolling out of the pool hall to see what Lou and me were studying so hard. He gave the painter lady the once-over, checking out her paint-spattered jeans, her chalky T-shirt, her floppy-brimmed straw hat. He hitched up his pants and glided over toward the painter lady, who kept right on with what she was doing.

"Whatcha got there, sweetheart?" he asked the twin with the plate.

"Suppah," she said, all soft and country-like.

"For her," the one with the jug added, jerking her chin toward the painter lady's back.

Still she didn't turn around. She was rearing back on her heels, her hands jammed into her back pockets, her face squinched up like the masterpiece she had in mind was taking shape on the wall by magic. We could have been gophers crawled up into a rotten hollow for all she cared. She didn't even say hello to anybody. Lou was muttering something about how great her concentration was. I butt him with my hip, and his elbow slid off the gum machine.

◄ C

"Good evening," Side Pocket said in his best ain't-I-fine voice. But the painter lady was moving from the milk crate to the step stool to the ladder, moving up and down fast, scribbling all over the wall like a crazy person. We looked at Side Pocket. He looked at the twins. The twins looked at us. The painter lady was giving a show. It was like those old-timey music movies where the dancer taps on the table top and then starts jumping all over the furniture, kicking chairs over, and not skipping a beat. She didn't even look where she was stepping. And for a minute there, hanging on the ladder to reach a far spot, she looked like she was going to tip right over.

"Ahh," Side Pocket cleared his throat and moved fast to catch the ladder. "These young ladies here have brought you some supper."

"Ma'am?" The twins stepped forward. Finally the painter turned around, her eyes "full of sky," as my grandmama would say. Then she stepped down like she was in a trance. She wiped her hands on her jeans as the Morris twins offered up the plate and the jug. She rolled back the tinfoil, then wagged her head as though something terrible was on the plate.

"Thank your mother very much," she said, sounding like her mouth was full of sky too. "I've brought my own dinner along." And then, without even excusing herself, she went back up the ladder, drawing on the wall in a wild way. Side Pocket whistled one of those oh-brother breathy whistles and went back into the pool hall. The Morris twins shifted their weight from one foot to the other, then crossed the street and went home. Lou had to drag me away, I

5

THE WAR OF THE WALL 29

4. LITERARY CONCEPT: Characterization
Based on what students have read so far, ask what kind of person they think the painter is, and why. Encourage them to **skim** the text for clues to help them **make inferences** about the painter's character. (Possible responses: She intrudes where she doesn't belong and isn't wanted; she is rude to people who have gone out of their way to help her. She is also single-minded, focusing on her painting.)

5. VOCABULARY: Idiom
Ask students what they think the narrator meant by saying that the painter lady was giving a show. If necessary, help students **reread** to note what the painter was doing and to **infer** that giving a show means "showing off" or "trying to attract attention." ★

6. LITERARY CONCEPT: Setting
Ask students for details that show that Taliaferro Street is located in an urban area. If necessary, help them **skim** the story to find clues. (*Possible clues: The characters in the story hang out in the streets of a neighborhood; the neighborhood contains a pool hall, a firehouse, and a restaurant; the narrator's family takes a trip to the country.*)

7. CULTURAL SIDELIGHT
When Mama tells the painter, "I don't care who your spiritual leader is. If you eat in the community, sistuh, you gonna eat pig by-and-by, one way or t'other," her comment is in reference to the fact that some people's religious beliefs prohibit them from eating pork. Examples are Muslims and Jews.

8. ACTIVE READING: Review
Why is Mama becoming annoyed? (*Possible responses: The painter is being fussy about the food. Also, Mama thinks that even though the painter is a visitor, she should observe the community's way of life.*)

9. ACTIVE READING: Review
Ask students why they think the painter doesn't want the Morris twins' food or Mama's food. If necessary, help students by reading the following example of a think-aloud, or model one of your own.

Think-Aloud Script Why is the painter getting dinner in the restaurant? She told the Morris twins she brought her own food. I remember that the painter "wagged her head as though something terrible was on the plate" when the Morris twins brought her baked ham, collard greens, and yams. Now she is asking Mama all kinds of questions about the food. Since she didn't eat the ham that the twins brought her, and since she wants to know if there are any vegetables cooked without meat, I am going to **infer** that the painter is a vegetarian or is on a special diet. ★

was so mad. We couldn't wait to get to the firehouse to tell my daddy all about this rude woman who'd stolen our wall.

All the way back to the block to help my mama out at the restaurant, me and Lou kept asking my daddy for ways to run the painter lady out of town. But my daddy was busy talking about the trip to the country and telling Lou he could come too because Grandmama can always use an extra pair of hands on the farm.

Later that night, while me and Lou were in the back doing our chores, we found out that the painter lady was a liar. She came into the restaurant and leaned against the glass of the steam table, talking about how starved she was. I was scrubbing pots and Lou was chopping onions, but we could hear her through the service window. She was asking Mama was that a ham hock in the greens, and was that a neck bone in the pole beans, and were there any vegetables cooked without meat, especially pork.

"I don't care who your spiritual leader is," Mama said in that way of hers. "If you eat in the community, sistuh, you gonna eat pig by-and-by, one way or t'other."

review **Why is Mama becoming annoyed?**

Me and Lou were cracking up in the kitchen, and several customers at the counter were clearing their throats, waiting for Mama to really fix her wagon for not speaking to the elders when she came in. The painter lady took a stool at the counter and went right on with her questions. Was there cheese in the baked macaroni, she wanted to know? Were there eggs in the

salad? Was it honey or sugar in the iced tea? Mama was fixing Pop Johnson's plate. And every time the painter lady asked a fool question, Mama would dump another spoonful of rice on the pile. She was tapping her foot and heating up in a dangerous way. But Pop Johnson was happy as he could be. Me and Lou peeked through the service window, wondering what planet the painter lady came from. Who ever heard of baked macaroni without cheese, or potato salad without eggs?

"Do you have any bread made with unbleached flour?" the painter lady asked Mama. There was a long pause, as though everybody in the restaurant was holding their breath, wondering if Mama would dump the next spoonful on the painter lady's head. She didn't. But when she set Pop Johnson's plate down, it came down with a bang.

When Mama finally took her order, the starving lady all of a sudden couldn't make up her mind whether she wanted a vegetable plate or fish and a salad. She finally settled on the broiled trout and a tossed salad. But just when Mama reached for a plate to serve her, the painter lady leaned over the counter with her finger all up in the air.

"Excuse me," she said. "One more thing." Mama was holding the plate like a Frisbee, tapping that foot, one hand on her hip. "Can I get raw beets in that tossed salad?"

"You will get," Mama said, leaning her face close to the painter lady's, "whatever Lou back there tossed. Now sit down." And the painter lady sat back down on her stool and shut right up.

All the way to the country, me and Lou tried to get Mama to open fire on the

---

Speaking . . . Listening . . . Viewing

The following activities may be especially useful for introducing students to some of the famous African Americans referred to on page 32 of this selection.

Speaking/Listening Invite volunteers to read aloud favorite passages from the following books:

■ *Stride Toward Freedom* by Martin Luther King, Jr.
■ *Malcolm X Talks to Young People* by Malcolm X
Listening Students may enjoy listening to some of the following recordings, as a class or in groups:

■ *Louis Armstrong Plays W. C. Handy* by Louis Armstrong, Columbia Records
■ *God Bless the Child* by Billie Holiday, Columbia Records
■ *Ellington at Newport* by Duke Ellington, Columbia Records

Viewing Students can watch Dr. Martin Luther King, Jr., deliver his famous "I Have a Dream" speech in *A Day to Remember: August 28, 1963*, PBS Video.

Urban artist Meg Fish portrays people from the neighborhood in her murals painted on Philadelphia buildings.
Mural in Philadelphia   1992   Meg Fish   Courtesy of the artist.

10

painter lady. But Mama said that seeing as how she was from the North, you couldn't expect her to have any manners. Then Mama said she was sorry she'd been so impatient with the woman because she seemed like a decent person and was simply trying to stick to a very strict diet. Me and Lou didn't want to hear that. Who did that lady think she was, coming into our neighborhood and taking over our wall?

"Welllll," Mama drawled, pulling into the filling station so Daddy could take the wheel, "it's hard on an artist, ya know. They can't always get people to look at their work. So she's just doing her work in the open, that's all."

Me and Lou definitely did not want to hear that. Why couldn't she set up an easel downtown or draw on the sidewalk in her own neighborhood? Mama told us to quit fussing so much; she was tired and wanted

to rest. She climbed into the back seat and dropped down into the warm hollow Daddy had made in the pillow.

All weekend long, me and Lou tried to scheme up ways to recapture our wall. Daddy and Mama said they were sick of hearing about it. Grandmama turned up the TV to drown us out. On the late news was a story about the New York subways. When a train came roaring into the station all covered from top to bottom, windows too, with writings and drawings done with spray paint, me and Lou slapped five. Mama said it was too bad kids in New York had nothing better to do than spray paint all over the trains. Daddy said that in the cities, even grown-ups wrote all over the trains and buildings too. Daddy called it "graffiti." Grandmama called it a shame.

We couldn't wait to get out of school on Monday. We couldn't find any black spray

11

◀ D

Words to Know and Use	**drawl** (drôl) *v.* to speak in a slow manner, stretching the vowel sounds **scheme** (skēm) *v.* to plot or plan in a secretive way

31

10. ACTIVE READING: Evaluate
Ask students to evaluate Mama's arguments in defense of the painter. *(Any response is valid.)*

11. LITERARY CONCEPT: Plot
Ask students how the painter's actions and attitude toward the people of the neighborhood have helped build the conflict in the plot. *(Possible response: Her turning down food, annoying the narrator's mother, and ignoring people have all contributed to their poor opinions of her. She has upset the narrator and Lou so much that they have planned to ruin her painting and recapture the wall.)*

Looking at Style

In order to begin discussing Bambara's writing style, point out these sentences to students:

■ "If you lean close," Lou said, leaning hipshot against her *beat-up* car, "you'll get a whiff of bubble gum and sweat." (p. 27)

■ "Good evening," Side Pocket said in his best *ain't-I-fine* voice. (p. 29)

■ Side Pocket whistled one of those *oh-brother*

breathy whistles and went back into the pool hall. (p. 29)

Draw students' attention to the hyphenated adjectives and ask the following questions:

1. Why do you think Bambara chose to use these particular adjectives?
2. How do these adjectives help you better understand or envision what Bambara is describing?
3. How would you describe Bambara's writing style?

12. ACTIVE READING: Predict
What are the kids planning to do?
(They are planning to spray white epoxy paint all over the lady's painting and reclaim the wall.) Ask students what clues tell them this. *(Possible clues: the discussion of graffiti, during which the kids "slapped five"; their search for spray paint.)*

paint anywhere. But in a junky hardware store downtown we found a can of white epoxy[2] paint, the kind you touch up old refrigerators with when they get splotchy and peely. We spent our whole allowance on it. And because it was too late to use our bus passes, we had to walk all the way home lugging our book satchels and gym shoes, and the bag with the epoxy.

12

predict   What are the kids planning to do?

When we reached the corner of Taliaferro and Fifth, it looked like a block party or something. Half the neighborhood was gathered on the sidewalk in front of the wall. I looked at Lou, he looked at me. We both looked at the bag with the epoxy and wondered how we were going to work our scheme. The painter lady's car was nowhere in sight. But there were too many people standing around to do anything. Side Pocket and his buddies were leaning on their cue sticks, hunching each other. Daddy was there with a lineman[3] he catches a ride with on Mondays. Mrs. Morris had her arms flung around the shoulders of the twins on either side of her. Mama was talking with some of her customers, many of them with napkins still at the throat. Mr. Eubanks came out of the barbershop, followed by a man in a striped poncho, half his face shaved, the other half full of foam.

"She really did it, didn't she?" Mr. Eubanks huffed out his chest. Lots of folks answered right quick that she surely did when they saw the straight razor in his hand.

Mama beckoned us over. And then we saw it. The wall. Reds, greens, figures outlined in black. Swirls of purple and orange. Storms of blues and yellows. It was something. I recognized some of the faces right off. There was Martin Luther King, Jr. And there was a man with glasses on and his mouth open like he was laying down a heavy rap. Daddy came up alongside and reminded us that that was Minister Malcolm X. The serious woman with a rifle I knew was Harriet Tubman because my grandmama has pictures of her all over the house. And I knew Mrs. Fannie Lou Hamer 'cause a signed photograph of her hangs in the restaurant next to the calendar.

Then I let my eyes follow what looked like a vine. It trailed past a man with a horn, a woman with a big white flower in her hair, a handsome dude in a tuxedo seated at a piano, and a man with a goatee holding a book. When I looked more closely, I realized that what had looked like flowers were really faces. One face with yellow petals looked just like Frieda Morris. One with red petals looked just like Hattie Morris. I could hardly believe my eyes.

"Notice," Side Pocket said, stepping close to the wall with his cue stick like a classroom pointer. "These are the flags of liberation," he said in a voice I'd never heard him use before. We all stepped closer while he pointed and spoke. "Red, black, and green," he said, his pointer falling on the leaflike

13

◀ E

---

2. **epoxy** (i päk′ sē): a substance used to make glue or a tough lacquer.
3. **lineman:** a person who sets up and maintains telephone or electric power lines.

Words to Know and Use | **beckon** (bek′ ′n) *v.* to summon or call someone, usually by a gesture or nod
liberation (lib ər ā′ shən) *n.* the state of freedom reached after a struggle

---

Multicultural Connections

Heroes The narrator recognizes four African-American heroes on the wall: Malcolm X, Dr. Martin Luther King, Jr., Harriet Tubman, and Fannie Lou Hamer. Hamer, a poor, uneducated farmer, gained prominence in the early 1960s as a civil-rights activist in Mississippi. She helped lead the voting rights movement.

Ask students how they might feel about these heroes if they were residents of the narrator's community.

What have such heroes contributed to our country?

Symbols The red, black, and green flag that Side Pocket calls "our liberation flag" is the African-American flag. This flag, introduced by Marcus Garvey in the 1920s, represents the blood (red), race (black), and hopes (green) of African Americans.

Ask students why some African Americans feel a need to have their own flag. What other groups or peoples may feel a similar need?

flags of the vine. "Our liberation flag. And here Ghana, there Tanzania. Guinea-Bissau, Angola, Mozambique." Side Pocket sounded very tall, as though he'd been waiting all his life to give this lesson.

Mama tapped us on the shoulder and pointed to a high section of the wall. There was a fierce-looking man with his arms crossed against his chest guarding a bunch of children. His muscles bulged, and he looked a lot like my daddy. One kid was looking at a row of books. Lou hunched me 'cause the kid looked like me. The one that looked like Lou was spinning a globe on the tip of his finger like a basketball. There were other kids there with microscopes and compasses. And the more I looked, the more it looked like the fierce man was not so much guarding the kids as defending their right to do what they were doing.

Then Lou gasped and dropped the paint bag and ran forward, running his hands over a rainbow. He had to tiptoe and stretch to do it, it was so high. I couldn't breathe either. The painter lady had found the chisel marks and had painted Jimmy Lyons's name in a rainbow.

"Read the inscription, honey," Mrs. Morris said, urging little Frieda forward. She didn't have to urge much. Frieda marched right up, bent down, and in a loud voice that made everybody quit oohing and ahhing and listen, she read,

> To the People of Taliaferro Street
> I Dedicate This Wall of Respect
> Painted in Memory of My Cousin
> Jimmy Lyons

I N S I G H T

in the inner city
LUCILLE CLIFTON

in the inner city
or
like we call it
home
we think a lot about uptown
and the silent nights
and the houses straight as
dead men
and the pastel lights
and we hang on to our no place
happy to be alive
and in the inner city
or
like we call it
home

Words to Know and Use | **inscription** (in skrip′ shən) *n.* a brief message permanently marked or engraved on a surface

33

14. LITERARY CONCEPT: Character
Ask students what changes they see in Side Pocket at this point in the story. *(Possible responses: His voice changes, he becomes proud, and he shows his knowledge of Africa.)*

15. ACTIVE READING: Connect
If you were the narrator, how would you feel at this point in the story? Why? *(Any response is valid.)*

16. ACTIVE READING: Review
Why is Jimmy Lyons important to the story? *(He is a community hero who died serving his country in Vietnam and whose name the narrator and Lou had chiseled on the wall. As the painter's cousin, he connects the painter to the neighborhood and is the reason she paints the wall.)*

I N S I G H T

This poem is a reflection on the ideas in the main selection and is suggested for students' independent reading. Optional discussion questions follow.

1. How are the setting of "The War of the Wall" and this poem similar? *(Both take place in an urban area.)*

2. What is similar about the way the story's characters and the poem's speaker view the places they live? *(They all see the city as home and are happy to be there.)*

3. How does the poem's speaker describe uptown? *(It is silent, with houses "straight as dead men" and with "pastel lights.")*

4. How is the inner city different from uptown? *(Possible response: It is noisy, alive, confused, and bright by comparison.)*

ENCOURAGING INDEPENDENT READING

Gorilla My Love, novel by Toni Cade Bambara

Light, short stories by Nancy White Carlstrom

Comprehension Check

1. What was the painter lady preparing to do at the beginning of the story? *(paint the wall)*

2. Why did this upset the narrator and Lou? *(They considered the wall theirs; they thought the lady had no business intruding.)*

3. In what ways did the painter seem rude to the Morris twins and to Mama? *(She turned down the food that the twins offered her; she annoyed Mama with questions about how the restaurant food had been prepared.)*

4. How did the narrator and Lou plan to recapture the wall? *(They planned to cover the mural with spray paint.)*

5. What changed their minds? *(They saw that the painting respectfully portrayed their community.)*

Student Response

Responding to Reading

1. Any response is valid.

2. Possible responses: Yes, because the painter didn't explain why she was there, so the narrator felt that the painter was a "rude woman who'd stolen their wall"; no, because the painter said she had been given permission to paint the wall and so had a right to be there.

3. Possible responses: Some of them probably know of her intentions and her relationship to Jimmy Lyons; many of them probably don't share the narrator's possessive feelings toward the wall.

4. Possible responses: The artist has paid her respects to her cousin Jimmy Lyons, his neighbors, and his friends. By incorporating portraits of famous African Americans with those of neighborhood people, she has made them all heroes of a sort and has shown the connections among them. The painter's mural has inspired pride among the neighborhood characters, especially Mr. Eubanks and Side Pocket.

5. Any response is valid. Encourage students to explain why they consider each person to be a neighborhood hero.

Challenge Question

The artist could have avoided a lot of trouble by talking to the people of the neighborhood. Why do you think she didn't tell the kids who she was? (Possible responses: She didn't consider the kids important; she wanted to surprise people in the neighborhood; she was shy; painting the wall took all of her attention; she told the grown-ups and assumed they would tell the kids.)

Responding to Reading

First Impressions

1. Did your impressions of the painter change during the course of the story? In your journal or notebook, briefly describe your reactions.

Second Thoughts

2. Do you think the narrator was right to be upset with the painter when she first appeared? Why or why not?

3. An army of only two tries to wage war against the painter lady. Why do you think other family members or neighbors don't join the battle?

4. What do you think the artist accomplished by painting the mural?

   Think about
   - the people and faces on the wall
   - what the "wall of respect" means to the neighborhood
   - the impact that the wall has on various characters

Broader Connections

5. If an artist painted a mural in your neighborhood, which heroes do you think your neighbors would want represented? Why?

Literary Concepts: Plot and Setting

Plot is what happens in a story. You can think of the plot as a sequence of related actions. The actions center on a conflict—a problem or situation faced by the main character. The conflict builds up during the story. At the end, the conflict is usually settled. What is the main conflict of this story? How is the conflict settled?

Setting consists of the time and place of a story. Could this story occur in a rural rather than urban setting? Explain your opinion.

Literary Concept: Plot and Setting

Plot The main conflict of this story is the narrator and Lou's struggle to prevent the painter lady from "stealing" the wall. The conflict is settled when they see that the mural reflects and respects the neighborhood's people, values, and heroes.

Setting Students may say that kids in the countryside would be unlikely to become attached to a wall, unlike kids in a city, where streets are the location of much social activity.

Writing Options

1. Put yourself in the shoes of the narrator and Lou. Write a **letter** they might send to the artist after seeing her work.

2. Think about the ways that the narrator and the narrator's mother respond to the painter. Make a list that shows the differences between their responses. Then make another list that shows similarities. Use your lists to write a **comparison** of their reactions.

3. Write an **explanation** that tells why you think the narrator of "The War of the Wall" would agree with the feelings expressed in the poem "in the inner city."

4. Think about the place in your neighborhood that seems to belong to the young people who live there—the one you wrote about earlier. Now write a **personal narrative** that illustrates the things that make this place special.

Vocabulary Practice

Exercise Some words seem to fit certain subjects or situations. For instance, you would expect to find the word *exercise* in a book about healthy living. Read each book title below. Choose a word from the list that you would expect to find in that book. Write the number and the word on your paper.

1. *The Speech Patterns of Slow Talkers*
2. *The True Story of a Million-Dollar Bank Robbery*
3. *Ways of Welcoming: A Study of Gestures and Their Meanings*
4. *Memoirs of a Former Slave*
5. *History Recorded on Tombstones*

> **Words to Know and Use**
>
> beckon
> drawl
> inscription
> liberation
> scheme

The Spelling Connection

Spelling Pattern: *-ate/-ion* endings. Most words ending in *-ate* are verbs; most words ending in *-ion* are nouns. Many verbs ending in *-ate* can be changed to nouns by taking off the e and adding *-ion*.

Example: separate + **ion** = separation

-ate/-ion Words from the Selection

integr**ate** + **ion** = integr**ation**
liber**ate** + **ion** = liber**ation**
segreg**ate** + **ion** = segreg**ation**

Other *-ate/-ion* Words

consolida**tion**	complica**tion**	evalua**tion**
opera**tion**	educa**tion**	narra**tion**

Exercise

1. The Civil Rights Act helped the cause of _____.
2. Before then, many schools practiced _____.
3. At first integration caused many _____s.
4. It was hard for students to concentrate on their _____s.

Writing Options

The Writing Options are designed to meet varied student interests and abilities. Have each student choose one writing activity to complete.

Journal Update Invite students to jot down new ideas they might have about whom they would feature on their own "wall of respect." Some might want to describe a place in their community where such a wall might be appropriate.

Links to Writer's Craft

Writing Option 4 is an exercise in personal writing. For more practice, see *The Writer's Craft,* Grade 7, "Personal and Expressive Writing," pages 26–46.

Vocabulary Practice

Answers to Exercise
1. drawl
2. scheme
3. beckon
4. liberation
5. inscription

For Alternative Learning Styles
Have students play Charades with the words *beckon, inscription, liberation,* and *scheme.* While one student acts out the meaning of a word, have the others *drawl* the answer.

Closure

Ask students to compare this story with "Seventh Grade." Ask which characters are alike in giving and in receiving false impressions. Point out that receiving a false impression of someone else can be just as embarrassing as someone else receiving a false impression of you.

Extending the Lesson

Options for Learning

These activities suit a variety of learning styles and modes of expression.

Collaborative Learning Activities
See Options 1, 3, and 4.

1. **Art Detective** Art books are another possible source of information. More recent murals may be mentioned in newspaper indices, such as *Newsbank*, or the *New York Times Index*.

2. **A Toast to Heroes** Students can find information in encyclopedias or books on American history, especially those dealing with the civil rights movement.

3. **Mural Maker** Be sure that planning and sketching stages precede the actual painting. Groups may wish to divide the paper into sections.

4. **Dialect Dictionary** Cartoon art may be appropriate for this activity.

 FACT FINDER SOCIAL STUDIES
Students can use an encyclopedia to find out that the memorial was dedicated on November 13, 1982.

Toni Cade Bambara

■ **More About the Author** Bambara credits much of her success to her mother, to whom she dedicated her book *The Salt Eaters* with these words:

"To my first friend, teacher, mapmaker, landscape aide:
    Mama
Helen Brent Henderson Cade Brehon who in 1948, having come upon me daydreaming in the middle of the kitchen floor, mopped around me."

■ **Other Works** Novel: *If Blessing Comes*; screenplays: *Tar Baby, Zora, The Bombing of Osage, The Long Night, Raymond's Run, Epitaph for Willie*

■ **Awards** The Black Community Award, The George Washington Carver Distinguished African-American Lecturer Award, *Ebony's* Achievement in the Arts Award, Best Documentary of 1986 for *The Bombing of Osage*.

Options for Learning (Multimodal/Cross-Curricular Activities)

1 • Art Detective Research public murals and mural artists from the past and present. Look under "murals" in an encyclopedia or "mural decoration" in the *Readers' Guide to Periodical Literature*. Share your findings with your class.

2 • A Toast to Heroes Read about one of the heroes of the wall: Martin Luther King, Jr., Malcolm X, Harriet Tubman, or Fannie Lou Hamer. Prepare and deliver a speech about that person's life.

3 • Mural Maker On a large sheet of paper or cardboard, paint or draw your own version of a mural. Like the mural in the story, your creation should reflect the people and heroes of your own neighborhood.

4 • Dialect Dictionary Create a dictionary of the words and expressions that are popular among students in your school. Illustrate some of the terms.

 FACT FINDER SOCIAL STUDIES
When was the Vietnam Veterans Memorial in Washington, D.C., dedicated?

Toni Cade Bambara
1939 –

Toni Cade Bambara has written numerous short stories, collected in *Gorilla, My Love* and *The Sea Birds Are Still Alive*. She is also a screenwriter and a novelist, having won an American Book Award for *The Salt Eaters*. She believes that writers "are everyday people who write stories that come out of their neighborhoods." "The War of the Wall" is inspired by her own memories. As a child, she and her companions created a park in a vacant city lot. One day they found a large advertisement there. "We were incensed," she recalls. "We went to city hall and got the billboard removed."

She has also worked in a welfare department, planned recreation for mentally ill patients, held community action workshops, and taught at a college. In recent years she has produced documentaries and videos for organizations that help needy people. One of her works, "The Bombing of Osage Avenue," won several awards. Bambara was born in New York City, has lived in Atlanta, and currently resides in Philadelphia.

Cross-Curricular Projects

Biology/Math Have some students research the nutritional content of the foods mentioned in the story. How much fat, iron, carbohydrates, and salt do they contain, and how many vitamins and calories? Does soul food provide a balanced diet? Have students present their findings to the class.

Art Obtain permission for students to make a chalk drawing on your school grounds. Volunteers may poll the class for ideas and then plan and draw a wall of respect.

Music Invite volunteers to write and perform a rap song about the arrival of the painter lady on Taliaferro Street. You may want to suggest that they include verses that describe figures in the mural, such as Harriet Tubman and Malcolm X.

Home Arts Interested students might find a soul food cookbook and prepare a meal for the class that includes the foods mentioned in the story—baked ham, collard greens, cornbread, and candied yams.

Fiction

Hearts and Hands
O. HENRY

Examine What You Know
(Prior Knowledge)

How much do you judge people by their appearance? How closely does a person's appearance reflect his or her personality? Share your ideas with your classmates.

Expand Your Knowledge (Building Background)

In the late 1800s, the train was an important means of travel. Due to its speed and power, it won the affection of many Americans. It provided fast and comfortable transportation, and it often proved to be an interesting place to meet people from all walks of life. The odd mix of passengers often resulted in wealthy ladies in their finery sitting next to rough-looking characters who might even spit in the aisles.

Enrich Your Reading (Reading Skill)

Inferences An inference is a logical guess based on the information that is known. For example, if you saw a man who was shabbily dressed, you might infer that he was poor. When reading this story, draw inferences about the three main characters. Base your judgment on how they appear and act. While you read, fill out a chart like the one started below. After finishing the selection, change each inference that you no longer agree with.

- *Author biography in Reader's Handbook*

Character	Appearance	Inference
young woman	"dressed in elegance"	she's wealthy
Mr. Easton	a "bold" manner	he's confident
other man	"glum-faced"	he's unhappy

JOURNAL WRITING IDEAS

- Predict what a story entitled "Hearts and Hands" will be about.

- Have you ever run into a friend somewhere you didn't expect to? Describe the experience.

- What do you need to be a good judge of character?

COLLABORATIVE LEARNING OPTIONS

Opportunities for collaborative learning include a Literary Concept activity (p. 41).

ADDITIONAL RESOURCES
Unit One Resource Book
Reader's Guidesheet, p. 17
Reading Skills, p. 18
Literature Skills, p. 19
Vocabulary Connections, p. 20
Spelling Connections, p. 21
Comprehension Check Test, p. 22
Selection Test, p. 23

Objectives

- To understand and analyze a short story

- To examine the use of a surprise ending and to review the concept of characterization

- To enrich reading by drawing inferences

- To express understanding of the story through a choice of writing forms, including dialogue and description

Prereading/Motivation

Examine What You Know

Discussion Prompts What kind of judgments do you make about people based on the clothes they wear? How does someone's appearance influence your impressions of him or her? Can you think of someone you know whose appearance gives a false impression of his or her personality?

Expand Your Knowledge

Additional Background Train travel was introduced in the United States in the 1820s, and in succeeding decades thousands of miles of track were laid from coast to coast. Improvements in passenger service—the advent of the dining car (1868), steam heat (1881), and electric lighting (1887)—helped people ride in comfort.

Enrich Your Reading

For Alternative Learning Styles To stimulate aural language skills, have students fill out their charts as they listen to a reading of selected passages from the story.

Thematic Link— False Impressions

Miss Fairchild forms a false impression of two men she sees on the train. She mistakenly assumes that the scruffy stranger is a prisoner and that her friend Mr. Easton is a marshal. Her false impression is based on the real marshal's fib and her own assumption that the well-dressed Easton is in charge.

The focus of vocabulary study for this selection is familiar roots in unfamiliar words. See *Unit One Resource Book,* Vocabulary Connections, page 20.

LIMITED ENGLISH PROFICIENCY

■ Use the Reader's Guidesheet, *Unit One Resource Book,* page 17.

■ Students may have difficulty with the opening of the story because of its old-fashioned tone and unfamiliar words. **Read aloud** the first paragraph and have volunteers **paraphrase** it.

★ Text annotations marked with a red star (1, 2, 6) may be particularly helpful for students with limited English proficiency.

TEXT ANNOTATIONS

1. LITERARY SIDELIGHT
Reversing the usual order of subject and verb was a popular literary device in the 1800s. Point out that its use here creates both an old-fashioned feeling and the sense that a story is beginning in the style of a folk tale or legend. ★

2. VOCABULARY: Technical Terms
Terms describing the train (*coach, express,* a *reversed* seat, a *smoker*) may be unfamiliar. As necessary, explain that a coach is a passenger car, express trains make few or no stops, a reversed seat has been set to face backward, and a smoker is a car in which smoking is allowed. ★

3. ACTIVE READING: Connect
If you were Miss Fairchild, how would you feel when you saw the handcuffs? Why? *(Any response is valid.)*

4. LITERARY CONCEPT:
Characterization
Ask students what kind of person they think Miss Fairchild is. *(Possible responses: She is a strong, self-confident woman; she looks down on people who don't come from her social class, but she seems willing to start a new life in the West; she is a refined lady who is not used to hardships or crime.)*

Hearts and Hands

O. HENRY

1

At Denver there was an influx of passengers into the coaches on the eastbound B. & M. express. In one coach there sat a very pretty young woman dressed in elegant taste and surrounded by all the luxurious comforts of an experienced traveler. Among the newcomers were two young men, one of handsome presence with a bold, frank countenance and manner; the other a ruffled, glum-faced person, heavily built and roughly dressed. The two were handcuffed together.

2

As they passed down the aisle of the coach the only vacant seat offered was a reversed one facing the attractive young woman. Here the linked couple seated themselves. The young woman's glance fell upon them with a distant, swift disinterest; then with a lovely smile brightening her countenance and a tender pink tingeing her rounded cheeks, she held out a little gray-gloved hand. When she spoke her voice, full, sweet, and deliberate, proclaimed that its owner was accustomed to speak and be heard.

"Well, Mr. Easton, if you *will* make me speak first, I suppose I must. Don't you ever recognize old friends when you meet them in the West?"

The younger man roused himself sharply at the sound of her voice, seemed to struggle with a slight embarrassment which he threw off instantly, and then clasped her fingers with his left hand.

"It's Miss Fairchild," he said, with a smile. "I'll ask you to excuse the other hand; it's otherwise engaged just at present."

He slightly raised his right hand, bound at the wrist by the shining "bracelet" to the left one of his companion. The glad look in the girl's eyes slowly changed to a bewildered horror. The glow faded from her cheeks. Her lips parted in a vague, relaxing distress. Easton, with a little laugh, as if amused, was about to speak again when the other forestalled him. The glum-faced man had been watching the girl's countenance with veiled glances from his keen, shrewd eyes.

"You'll excuse me for speaking, miss, but I see you're acquainted with the marshal here. If you'll ask him to speak a word for me when we get to the pen he'll do it, and it'll make things easier for me there. He's taking me to Leavenworth prison. It's seven years for counterfeiting."

"Oh!" said the girl, with a deep breath and returning color. "So that is what you are doing out here? A marshal!"

Guided Reading for Less-Proficient Students

These questions can help guide students through the reading. Ask each question at the point in the selection where the capital letter and arrow appear in the margin. In addition, you may wish to use appropriate Active Reading annotations.

A. Which characters sit across from Miss Fairchild? *(two men who are handcuffed together)* Recalling

B. Whom does Miss Fairchild recognize? *(the younger man, an old friend of hers named Mr. Easton)* Clarifying

C. What has Miss Fairchild learned about the identities of the two men opposite her? *(One is a marshal and the other is a prisoner being delivered to the Leavenworth prison.)* Summarizing

(Continued on page 39)

TRAIN INTERIOR   E. Boyd Smith   Collection of Oliver Jensen.

Art Note

Boyd Smith's illustration from the railroads' heyday gives an idea of the thrill of riding a passenger train. The artist uses perspective to make the car seem long and roomy. He emphasizes the passengers' pleasure at watching the world pass by. *How does the artist show that a train ride was a special occasion?*

Guided Reading for Less-Proficient Students

(Continued from page 38)

D. Why won't Mr. Easton be in Washington again soon? *(His "butterfly days"—or carefree days—are over.)* Clarifying

E. What do we learn about Mr. Easton from the conversation between the two nearby passengers? *(Mr. Easton is the prisoner, not the marshal.)* Clarifying

5. ACTIVE READING: Question
Ask students to read this exchange of dialogue carefully. What inferences can they make about Mr. Easton's and Miss Fairchild's past? *(Mr. Easton's mention of the ambassador and Miss Fairchild's response suggest that Mr. Easton may have competed with the ambassador as the lady's suitor.)*

6. VOCABULARY: Idiom
Ask students what they think Mr. Easton means by saying that his "butterfly days are over." If necessary, help them use **context clues** and **associations** of the word *butterfly* to infer that a carefree time in Mr. Easton's life is over. ★

7. LITERARY CONCEPT: Surprise Ending
After students have read the story's ending, ask them to **reread** this passage and infer why the glum-faced man interrupted and what Miss Fairchild seemed about to say. *(Since Miss Fairchild seemed about to reveal her feelings for Mr. Easton, the marshal probably interrupted to save Mr. Easton the embarrassment of having either to put her off or reveal his true status as prisoner.)*

ENCOURAGING INDEPENDENT READING

Tracks Across America: The Story of the American Railroad, 1825–1900, nonfiction by Leonard Everett Fisher

"A Retrieved Reformation," a short story by O. Henry

"My dear Miss Fairchild," said Easton, calmly, "I had to do something. Money has a way of taking wings unto itself, and you know it takes money to keep step with our crowd in Washington. I saw this opening in the West, and—well, a marshalship isn't quite as high a position as that of ambassador, but—"

"The ambassador," said the girl, warmly, "doesn't call anymore. He needn't ever have done so. You ought to know that. And so now you are one of these dashing Western heroes, and you ride and shoot and go into all kinds of dangers. That's different from the Washington life. You have been missed from the old crowd."

The girl's eyes, fascinated, went back, widening a little, to rest upon the glittering handcuffs.

"Don't you worry about them, miss," said the other man. "All marshals handcuff themselves to their prisoners to keep them from getting away. Mr. Easton knows his business."

"Will we see you again soon in Washington?" asked the girl.

"Not soon, I think," said Easton. "My butterfly days are over, I fear."

"I love the West," said the girl irrelevantly. Her eyes were shining softly. She looked away out the car window. She began to speak truly and simply, without the gloss of style and manner: "Mamma and I spent the summer in Denver. She went home a week ago because father was slightly ill. I could live and be happy in the West. I think the air here agrees with me. Money isn't everything. But people always misunderstand things and remain stupid—"

"Say, Mr. Marshal," growled the glum-faced man. "This isn't quite fair. I'm needin' a drink, and haven't had a smoke all day. Haven't you talked long enough? Take me in the smoker now, won't you? I'm half dead for a pipe."

The bound travelers rose to their feet, Easton with the same slow smile on his face.

"I can't deny a petition for tobacco," he said lightly. "It's the one friend of the unfortunate. Goodbye, Miss Fairchild. Duty calls, you know." He held out his hand for a farewell.

"It's too bad you are not going East," she said, reclothing herself with manner and style. "But you must go on to Leavenworth, I suppose?"

"Yes," said Easton, "I must go on to Leavenworth."

The two men sidled down the aisle into the smoker.

The two passengers in a seat nearby had heard most of the conversation. Said one of them: "That marshal's a good sort of chap. Some of these Western fellows are all right."

"Pretty young to hold an office like that, isn't he?" asked the other.

"Young!" exclaimed the first speaker, "why—Oh! didn't you catch on? Say—did you ever know an officer to handcuff a prisoner to his *right* hand?" ☙

Comprehension Check

1. Who are the story's three main characters? *(Miss Fairchild, Mr. Easton, and the marshal)*

2. In what setting does the story take place? *(on a passenger train in the West)*

3. Why does Mr. Easton use his left hand to greet Miss Fairchild? *(His right hand is handcuffed to another man's left hand.)*

4. Where is the marshal taking his prisoner? *(Leavenworth prison)*

5. Why does Mr. Easton say he went out West? *(He had a business opportunity.)*

6. What did you learn about the two men at the end? *(Mr. Easton is really the prisoner; the other man is the marshal.)*

Responding to Reading

First Impressions

1. What was your reaction to the ending of this story? Jot down a word or phrase to describe your response.

Second Thoughts

2. Review the inferences that you made about the characters. How did these inferences set the scene for the surprise ending?

   Think about
   - the appearance of Miss Fairchild and the men
   - what all three characters do and say

3. Based on what happens in the story, what can you infer about the personalities of Miss Fairchild and the two men?

4. A white lie is a lie about an unimportant matter, often told to spare someone's feelings. How does that term apply to the actions of the marshal and Mr. Easton? Why?

Literary Concept: Surprise Ending

A **surprise ending** is an unexpected twist in the plot at the end of a story. Most readers are surprised by the ending of "Hearts and Hands" because they have wrongly inferred that Mr. Easton is the marshal. However, there are clues earlier in the story that suggest the truth. Working with a partner, make a list of clues about the real identity of Mr. Easton.

Concept Review: Characterization Which method of characterization listed on page 23 does O. Henry use most in this story?

Writing Options

1. Give the marshal's account of what happened on the train. Write a **dialogue** to show how he tells his wife or his superior his version of the events.

2. Write two **descriptions** of Mr. Easton. One should be from Miss Fairchild's viewpoint. The other should be from the viewpoint of the passenger who speaks at the story's end.

HEARTS AND HANDS   41

Closure

In both "Seventh Grade" and in "Hearts and Hands," a male character misleads a female character with a false impression of himself. Invite students to discuss what the male characters risk by being deceptive. Then have students brainstorm about how each might have made a good impression by presenting a true image of himself.

Student Response

Responding to Reading

1. Any response is valid.

2. Possible responses: The reader is likely to infer from the two men's appearances that the prisoner is the poorly dressed man; Miss Fairchild seems to think highly of Mr. Easton; since neither man contradicts the other, it seems that their words are true.

3. Possible responses: Neither Mr. Easton nor Miss Fairchild is as shrewd as the marshal, who introduces the deception; the marshal feels sympathy for others; Miss Fairchild might be sheltered or spoiled but is sincere about her feelings; and Mr. Easton is a slick talker keeping up appearances.

4. Possible responses: The marshal's lie could be seen as a white lie because he told it to spare Miss Fairchild's, and possibly Mr. Easton's, feelings; Mr. Easton's going along with the deception might also be a white lie, since it is possible he too did not wish to hurt or shock Miss Fairchild. Some students may feel the lie was not about an unimportant matter, so it cannot be called a white lie.

Literary Concept: Surprise Ending

Clues about the real identity of Mr. Easton include the following: his "slight embarrassment" and "little laugh" on meeting Miss Fairchild; the marshal's closely watching Miss Fairchild's face just before he tells his lie; the marshal's familiarity with criminal procedure; Mr. Easton's admissions that he came west to make money and that his "butterfly days are over."

Concept Review: Characterization
Primarily, O. Henry uses conversation and action to provide characterization.

Writing Options

The Writing Options are designed to meet varied student interests and abilities. Have each student choose one writing activity to complete.

Journal Update: Invite students to review their journal entries for "Hearts and Hands." What does the title of the story mean to them now? In their opinion, why did O. Henry use this title?

Elements of Nonfiction

This feature provides students with an opportunity to develop a vocabulary to use in discussing different types of nonfiction. The terms on these pages are discussed in depth in the nonfiction selections that follow.

Objectives

■ To understand and appreciate nonfiction

■ To recognize types of nonfiction

■ To learn strategies for reading nonfiction

Motivation

Invite volunteers to recall the titles of fiction selections that they have read in Unit One. (*"Seventh Grade," "The War of the Wall," "Hearts and Hands"*) Elicit that these stories are fiction because they tell about imaginary people, places, and events. Then write the term *nonfiction* on the board, pointing out that the prefix *non-* means "not." Ask students what writing that is "not fiction" might tell about. (*real people, places, and events*)

Copy the following comparison chart on the board and ask students to copy it and fill in the column for fiction. As students read page 42, have them fill in the nonfiction column. Ask them to list examples of nonfiction that they have read.

	Fiction	Nonfiction
What It Tells About	imaginary people, places, and events	real people, places, and events
Purpose	to entertain	to inform, to entertain, to persuade
Types	short story, novel	article, essay, biography
Examples	"Hearts and Hands"	

Elements of
NONFICTION

While some readers enjoy getting lost in the imaginary world of fiction, others prefer the authenticity of stories from real life. **Nonfiction** is writing about real people, places, and events.

There are two broad categories of nonfiction. One category, called **informative nonfiction,** is mainly written to provide factual information. Nonfiction of this type includes science and history texts, informational books, encyclopedias, pamphlets, and most of the articles in magazines and newspapers.

The other category of nonfiction is called **literary nonfiction** because it is written to be read and experienced in much the same way you experience fiction. However, literary nonfiction differs from fiction in that real people take the place of fictional characters, and the settings and plots are not imagined but are actual places and true events.

The following are the types of literary nonfiction you will read in this book.

Understanding Nonfiction

Autobiography An **autobiography** is the true story of a person's life, told by that person. It is almost always written using the first-person point of view. In this book you will read excerpts from several autobiographies. In each, the author focuses on a significant event in his or her life.

An autobiography is usually book length because it covers a long period of the writer's life. However, there are shorter types of autobiographical writing such as **journals, diaries,** and **memoirs.**

Biography A **biography** is the true story of a person's life told by someone else. The writer, or **biographer,** interviews the subject if possible and also researches the person's life by reading letters, books, diaries, and any other information he or she can find. A short biography of Eleanor Roosevelt is included in this book.

As you will see, biographies and autobiographies often seem like fiction because they contain many of the same elements such as character, setting, and plot.

Essay An **essay** is a short piece of nonfiction writing that deals with one subject. Essays are often found in newspapers and magazines. The writer might share an opinion, try to entertain or persuade the reader, or simply describe an incident that has special significance. These essays that explain how the author feels about a subject are called **informal,** or **personal,** essays. In this book, the selection "Homeless" is an example of an informal essay. **Formal essays** are serious and scholarly and are rarely found in literature textbooks.

Discuss the two categories of nonfiction described in the opening paragraphs, and have students list types of nonfiction that belong in each category, as shown below.

Informative Nonfiction
textbooks
informational books
pamphlets
articles

Literary Nonfiction
autobiographies
biographies
essays

ADDITIONAL RESOURCES
Technology and Enrichment
Active Reading Transparencies 6–9

Strategies for Reading Nonfiction

Nonfiction can be read as a piece of literature or as a source of information. The nonfiction you will read in this book has been included because of the interesting story it has to tell—because of its literary quality.

Use the following strategies when you read nonfiction.

1. **Preview** a selection before you read. Look at the title, pictures, diagrams, subtitles, and any terms in boldfaced print or italics. All of these will give you an idea of what the selection is about.

2. **Figure out the organization.** If the work is a biography or autobiography, the organization is probably chronological, that is, in the order that events happened. Other articles may be arranged around ideas the author wants to discuss. Understanding the organization can help you predict what to expect next.

3. **Separate facts and opinions.** Facts are statements that can be proved, such as "There are several autobiographies in this book." **Opinions** are statements that cannot be proved. They simply express the writer's beliefs, such as "*Boy* is the best autobiography in this book." Writers of nonfiction sometimes present opinions as if they were facts. Be sure you recognize the difference.

4. **Question** as you read. Why did things happen the way they did? How did people feel? What is the writer's opinion? Do you share the writer's opinion, or do you have different ideas on the subject?

5. During your reading, stop now and then and try to **predict** what will come next. Sometimes you will be surprised by what happens or by what the author has to say about an issue.

6. As you read, **build** on your understanding. Add new information to what you have already learned and see if your ideas and opinions change.

7. Continually **evaluate** what you read. Evaluation should be an ongoing process, not just something that is done when you have finished reading. Remember that evaluation means more than saying a selection is good or bad. Form opinions about people, events, and ideas that are presented. Decide whether or not you like the way the piece was written.

Finally, it is important to recognize that your understanding of a selection does not end when you stop reading. As you think more about what you have read and discuss it with others, you will find that your understanding continues to grow.

Closure

To close the lesson, encourage students to list some titles of works of literary nonfiction. Ask them to recommend nonfiction that they have read, classifying the titles by types—autobiographies, biographies, and essays.

Teaching Strategies

Understanding Nonfiction

Autobiography Have students identify some autobiographical writing of their own, such as diaries. Encourage them to speculate on what events they might include if they were writing complete autobiographies.

Biography Ask students to recall true stories they have read or have seen on film. Encourage them to describe ways in which biographers make real people's stories vivid.

Essay Show students essays from the editorial page or the op-ed page of a local newspaper. If any students have taken part in essay contests, have them relate their experiences.

Strategies for Reading Nonfiction

Invite volunteers to read aloud the explanations of the strategies. Then use the following examples, or model ones of your own, to show ways in which students might use some of the strategies when reading the next selection, "Homeless," on pages 45–46.

Preview "By reading the title and skimming the paragraphs I see that the essay focuses on what it means to be homeless."

Figure Out the Organization "The essay begins with a vivid, specific incident—meeting Ann in the terminal. From there Ms. Quindlen seems to move on to general ideas about home and homelessness."

Separate Facts and Opinions "As I read, I note mainly opinions—'You are where you live,' 'Home is where the heart is.' The author is using her feelings and opinions to persuade me to view the homeless more sympathetically."

Question "As I read, many questions spring to mind: What would I miss most about losing my home? How do I feel deep down about homeless people?"

Predict "From the opening paragraph, I predict that I will come away from the essay with a more personal, perhaps painful, awareness of the meaning of homelessness."

Objectives

- To understand and analyze an informal essay

- To examine an author's expression of feelings and opinions

- To enrich reading by understanding an author's purpose

- To express understanding of the essay through a choice of writing forms, including an editorial and an essay

Prereading/Motivation

Examine What You Know

Discussion Prompts How have you learned about the homeless? What images of the homeless stand out in your mind? Have you ever had any personal contact with a homeless person?

Expand Your Knowledge

Additional Background Various factors have contributed to the growth of the homeless population, including a shortage of low-cost housing, a decline in government rent assistance, and a decline in the employment and wages of unskilled workers. Since this essay was written, homeless people have been evicted from the Port Authority Bus Terminal in New York City.

Enrich Your Reading

Name examples of different types of writing, such as television commercials, editorials, owner's manuals, and movie scripts. Ask students the purpose of each type of writing. Point out that a writer can have more than one purpose for writing.

Thematic Link— False Impressions

Quindlen realizes that her readers share many false impressions of "the homeless" as a group. By focusing on one individual, Quindlen seeks to persuade her readers to form new impressions of homeless people.

Nonfiction

Homeless

ANNA QUINDLEN

Examine What You Know (Prior Knowledge)

What are your impressions of the homeless people you have seen on the street or on television? Draw a word web on a sheet of paper, as shown below. On the spokes around the word *homeless*, write the words that describe your impressions. Then share your responses with your classmates.

(homeless)

Expand Your Knowledge (Building Background)

Every night in cities across the country, thousands of homeless people sleep on sidewalks, in bus stations, in cardboard boxes, or in other temporary shelters. In the last ten years, the number of homeless people has increased dramatically. Estimates of our nation's homeless population range from a quarter of a million to three million.

People are homeless for a number of reasons. Many simply cannot find low-cost housing. Others have lost their jobs, are mentally ill, or are victims of abuse. The woman featured in this article lived in the Port Authority Bus Terminal in New York City, a "home" for hundreds.

Enrich Your Reading (Reading Skill)

■ *Author biography in Reader's Handbook*

Author's Purpose Authors write for many reasons: to entertain, to explain or inform, to express an opinion, or to persuade the reader to do or believe something. As you read this selection, think about Quindlen's purpose for writing. What might she want to accomplish by writing this essay? Do you think she has more than one goal?

JOURNAL WRITING IDEAS

■ If you could keep and carry only one photo, of whom or what would it be? Explain.

■ Have you ever been locked out of your house or apartment? How did you feel?

■ Describe your image of a homeless person.

COLLABORATIVE LEARNING OPTIONS

Opportunities for collaborative learning include Broader Connections, the Literary Concept, and Writing Option 1 (p. 47).

ADDITIONAL RESOURCES

Unit One Resource Book
Reader's Guidesheet, p. 24
Reading Skills, p. 25
Literature Skills, p. 26
Vocabulary Connections, p. 27
Spelling Connections, p. 28
Comprehension Check Test, p. 29
Selection Test, p. 30

Technology and Enrichment
Audiocassette Tape 1, Side 1

Homeless

ANNA QUINDLEN

Her name was Ann, and we met in the Port Authority Bus Terminal several Januarys ago. I was doing a story on homeless people. She said I was wasting my time talking to her; she was just passing through, although she'd been passing through for more than two weeks. To prove to me that this was true, she rummaged through a tote bag and a manila envelope and finally unfolded a sheet of typing paper and brought out her photographs.

They were not pictures of family, or friends, or even a dog or cat, its eyes brown-red in the flashbulb's light. They were pictures of a house. It was like a thousand houses in a hundred towns, not suburb, not city, but somewhere in between, with aluminum siding and a chain-link fence, a narrow driveway running up to a one-car garage, and a patch of backyard. The house was yellow. I looked on the back for a date or a name, but neither was there. There was no need for discussion. I knew what she was trying to tell me, for it was something I had often felt. She was not adrift, alone, anonymous, although her bags and her raincoat with the grime shadowing its creases had made me believe she was. She had a house, or at least once upon a time had had one. Inside were curtains, a couch, a stove, potholders. You are where you live. She was somebody.

1

A ▶

I've never been very good at looking at the big picture, taking the global view, and I've always been a person with an overactive sense of place, the legacy of an Irish grandfather. So it is natural that the thing that seems most wrong with the world to me right now is that there are so many people with no homes. I'm not simply talking about shelter from the elements, or three square meals a day, or a mailing address to which the welfare people can send the check—although I know that all these are important for survival. I'm talking about a home, about precisely those kinds of feelings that have wound up in cross-stitch and French knots on samplers[1] over the years.

2

Home is where the heart is. There's no place like it. I love my home with a ferocity totally out of proportion to its appearance or location. I love dumb things about it: the hot-water heater, the plastic rack you drain dishes in, the roof over my head, which occasionally leaks. And yet it is precisely those dumb things that make it what it is—a place of certainty, stability, predictability, privacy, for me and for my family. It is where I live. What more can you say about a place than that? That is everything.

Yet it is something that we have been ◀ **B**

3

---

1. **cross-stitch and French knots on samplers:** two kinds of fancy stitches on hand-embroidered cloths.

Teaching Strategies

VOCABULARY PREVIEW

The focus of vocabulary study for this selection is on words with the prefix *en-*. See *Unit One Resource Book*, Vocabulary Connections, p. 27.

LIMITED ENGLISH PROFICIENCY

Use the Reader's Guidesheet, *Unit One Resource Book*, page 24.

★ Text annotations marked with a red star (2, 3, 5, 7) may be particularly helpful for students with limited English proficiency.

TEXT ANNOTATIONS

1. ACTIVE READING: Review
Ask students to **infer** why Ann carries the picture of her former house with her. (*Possible responses: It makes her feel important; it shows that she wasn't always homeless.*)

2. LITERARY CONCEPT: Essay
Ask students to find wording that indicates that the author is expressing her personal opinion. (*"seems most wrong in the world to me right now"*) ★

3. ACTIVE READING: Connect
Ask students to give the root words of *certainty, stability, predictability,* and *privacy.* (*certain, stable, predict, private*) Then ask them why a home is associated with those qualities. (*Possible responses: When you have a home, you don't have to worry about where to sleep; you have time to yourself; you know that it won't change from day to day.*) ★

Guided Reading for Less-Proficient Students

These questions can help guide students through the reading. Ask each question at the point of the selection where the capital letter and arrow appear in the margin. In addition, you may wish to use appropriate Active Reading annotations.

A. What do you know about Ann so far? (*She lives in a bus terminal; she used to have a house; she's poor and alone.*) Reviewing

B. How does the author feel about her own home? (*She loves her home; it makes her feel secure.*) Recalling

C. What do homeless people want that is not available in shelters? (*a place of their own, their own private space*) Inferring

D. How does Quindlen want us to think about homeless people? (*as individual people who happen to be without homes*) Recalling

SHADOW © Maureen Fennelli.

edging away from gradually during my lifetime and the lifetimes of my parents and grandparents. There was a time when where you lived often was where you worked and where you grew the food you ate and even where you were buried. When that era passed, where you lived at least was where your parents had lived and where you would live with your children when you became enfeebled. Then, suddenly, where you lived was where you lived for three years, until you could move on to something else and something else again.

And so we have come to something else again, to children who do not understand what it means to go to their rooms because they have never had a room, to men and women whose fantasy is a wall they can paint a color of their own choosing, to old people reduced to sitting on molded plastic chairs, their skin blue-white in the lights of a bus station, who pull pictures of houses out of their bags. Homes have stopped being homes. Now they are real estate.

People find it curious that those without homes would rather sleep sitting up on benches or huddled in doorways than go to shelters. Certainly some prefer to do so because they are emotionally ill, because they have been locked in before and they are determined not to be locked in again. Others are afraid of the violence and trouble they may find there. But some seem to want something that is not available in shelters, and they will not compromise, not for a cot, or oatmeal, or a shower with special soap that kills the bugs. "One room," a woman with a baby who was sleeping on her sister's floor once told me, "painted blue." That was the crux[2] of it; not size or location, but pride of ownership. Painted blue.

This is a difficult problem, and some wise and compassionate people are working hard at it. But in the main I think we work around it, just as we walk around it when it is lying on the sidewalk or sitting in the bus terminal—the problem, that is. It has been customary to take people's pain and lessen our own participation in it by turning it into an issue, not a collection of human beings. We turn an adjective into a noun: the poor, not poor people; the homeless, not Ann or the man who lives in the box or the woman who sleeps on the subway grate.

Sometimes I think we would be better off if we forgot about the broad strokes and concentrated on the details. Here is a woman without a bureau. There is a man with no mirror, no wall to hang it on. They are not the homeless. They are people who have no homes. No drawer that holds the spoons. No window to look out upon the world. My God. That is everything. ❧

---

2. **crux:** the most important point.

Comprehension Check

1. Why doesn't Ann consider herself among the homeless even though she is living in a bus station? (*Sometime in the past she had a home.*)

2. What does the author think is "most wrong with the world"? (*that there are so many people without homes*)

3. How does the author feel about her own home? (*She loves it; it gives her privacy and security.*)

4. What reasons does the author give to explain why homeless people do not go to shelters? (*emotional illness, fear of being locked in, fear of violence, wanting a place of one's own*)

5. Why does the author suggest that we concentrate on the details of homelessness? (*The details make the problem seem real; they focus attention on individuals.*)

Responding to Reading

First Impressions

1. What is the strongest feeling you had about Ann when you finished this selection? Share your ideas with your class.

Second Thoughts

2. Look back at your word web about homeless people. Does this essay change your impression of the homeless? Why or why not?

3. One of the ways the dictionary defines home is "a dwelling place." Compare Quindlen's thoughts and feelings about home with your own.

4. In your opinion, did Quindlen accomplish her purpose in writing this essay?

Think about
- why she focused on only one homeless person
- why she described her own home and her feelings about it
- what might have been her purpose for writing

Broader Connections

5. What is being done now to help homeless people like Ann? What other actions do you think should be taken?

Literary Concept: Essay

As you recall, an **essay** is a short nonfiction piece in which a writer gives her or his opinion on one subject. **Informal** or **personal** essays reflect a writer's feelings about a topic. Find places in Quindlen's essay where she expresses her own feelings and opinions about the homeless.

Writing Options

1. Work with a partner to brainstorm about ways students like you can help homeless people. Then write a student newspaper **editorial** that expresses these ideas.

2. Write an **essay** about the space or object in your home that you would miss most if you were homeless. Describe it so others will understand why it is so important to you.

HOMELESS 47

Writing Options

The Writing Options are designed to meet varied student interests and abilities. Have each student choose one writing activity to complete.

Journal Update Encourage students to think about what everyday problems they or others they know would have if they became homeless.

Closure

Ask students what false impressions Quindlen addresses in her essay. Point out that false impressions can keep us from understanding the needs and desires of a homeless person. False impressions can also lead us to make hasty judgments based only on appearances.

Student Response

Responding to Reading

1. Any response is valid.

2. Possible responses: Yes, because the author made me realize that homeless people are individuals who want what everyone wants; no, my impressions that homeless people are just like other people were reinforced.

3. Possible responses: Students who regard their home as a treasured place will have thoughts and feelings similar to Quindlen's; other students may not be able to relate to the depth of Quindlen's feelings; some may view home mainly as a place to eat and sleep.

4. Possible responses: Yes, because in describing Ann, Quindlen fulfilled her purpose of persuading the reader that each homeless person is an individual with unique problems; yes, because in describing her own feelings, she persuaded the reader how important it is to have a home; no, because I think her purpose was to persuade people to do something about the homeless and she offered no solutions for the problem; no, because she did not give enough information about the problems of the homeless.

5. Possible responses: Shelters provide a temporary place for them to live; community and church groups provide food, shelter, and support; social agencies provide money and food stamps; some programs provide job training and counseling. The homeless could be given their own places free of charge until they are able to pay for housing.

Literary Concept: Essay

Examples: "The thing that seems most wrong with the world to me right now is that there are so many people with no homes"; "I think we work around it [the problem of homelessness], just as we walk around it when it is lying on the sidewalk or sitting in the bus terminal"; "I think we would be better off if we forgot about the broad strokes and concentrated on the details."

Objectives

- To understand and analyze an excerpt from an autobiography

- To identify the literary elements of an autobiography

- To infer a character's feelings through dialogue and behavior

- To express understanding of the work through a choice of writing forms, including a diary entry, a set of school rules, a script, and a description

Prereading/Motivation

Examine What You Know

Discussion Prompts Did your embarrassing moment come after something you did or said? Were you concerned about how you appeared to others? What did you learn from that experience?

Expand Your Knowledge

Additional Background Students may have had their vision tested using an eye chart like the one pictured. From a distance of twenty feet, the person reads aloud the letters that he or she can see, first with one eye covered and then the other. A person with normal vision is said to have 20/20 vision. The first 20 refers to the 20-foot distance from the eye to the letters on the chart. The second 20 indicates the distance at which a normal eye is able to read the letters in the second row from the bottom. A person is legally blind if his or her vision is 20/200 or worse while wearing corrective lenses; at 20 feet, he or she sees what normal-sighted people see at 200 feet.

Thematic Link— False Impressions

Jean's classmates have a falsely narrow impression of her, seeing her as nothing more than a person to make fun of. Then Jean invents a story that gives them a false impression of her heroism but a true impression of her wit and imagination.

Nonfiction

from Little by Little
A Writer's Education
JEAN LITTLE

Examine What You Know (Prior Knowledge)

Everyone has embarrassing moments. They are often hard to forget. Think of an embarrassing moment you've had. Remember what caused your embarrassment and how you felt? In small groups, talk about embarrassing moments and what causes them.

Expand Your Knowledge (Building Background)

As a child, Jean Little frequently faced embarrassment because of her poor eyesight. Not only was she born almost blind, she was also cross-eyed.

Cross-eye is a condition that most commonly occurs in children under the age of four who have poor vision. They sometimes force their pupils close together in an effort to see more clearly. Cross-eye can also be inherited or result from weak eye muscles. Usually the condition can be treated successfully. However, in Jean's case, it was not corrected, and in the fifth grade her eyesight was so poor that she could only make out the *E* at the top of the eye chart. In school she could not even read the words on the board.

Write Before You Read (Journal Writing)

Think about a time when you went out of your way to avoid being embarrassed. What did you do? In your journal, write about that time. As you read, compare your experience to the author's.

■ *Author biography on Extend page*

MORE JOURNAL WRITING IDEAS

■ Recall a time when someone made you feel bad about yourself. How did you handle the situation?

■ How do you react when you see a person whose eyes are unusual?

COLLABORATIVE LEARNING OPTIONS

Opportunities for collaborative learning include Examine What You Know (above), Writing Option 2 (p. 56), Options for Learning 2 and 3 (p. 57), and Cross-Curricular Projects (p. 57).

ADDITIONAL RESOURCES

Unit One Resource Book
Reader's Guidesheet, p. 31
Reading Skills, p. 32
Literature Skills, p. 33
Vocabulary Connections, p. 34
Spelling Connections, p. 35
Comprehension and Vocabulary Check Tests, p. 36
Selection Test, pp. 37-38

from *Little by Little*

A Writer's Education

JEAN LITTLE

I was eating my porridge when Hugh, hurrying too fast, fell down the back stairs. Before Mother could get up, he limped in, sniffling slightly, and displayed a bumped elbow for her inspection. Mother examined it gravely.

"A slight hematoma," she said in a serious voice. "And an <u>abrasion</u> almost invisible to the naked eye. You'll live."

Hugh, who always recovered with the speed of light and who won Mother's admiration with his bravery, chuckled at the impressive words.

"What does that mean?" he asked.

"A little bruise and a scrape I can hardly see."

I <u>glowered</u> at my oatmeal. Why did she have to smile at him like that? He was not so special. I searched my mind for something terrible he had done that I could tell her about.

"Jean, hurry up or you'll be late," Grandma said.

I did not want to go to school. We were going to have another mental arithmetic test, and I still did not know my times tables. If only I could fall down and break my leg . . .

Four-year-old Pat grinned at me.

"Huwwy up, Jean," she parroted. "You'll be late."

I wanted to slap the wide smile off her silly little face. Instead I scooped up a few drops of milk on the tip of my spoon and let fly. The tiny bit of milk splashed her on the nose. I laughed. Before anyone could stop her, Pat grabbed up her mug filled to the brim with milk and sent its entire contents sloshing over me, soaking me to the skin.

The next thing I knew, I was back upstairs changing out of my wet serge dress, cotton petticoat, long brown stockings, and underwear into clean, dry clothes. Not only was this going to make me really late, but Mother handed me the knitted suit Aunt Gretta had made for my tenth birthday. The ribbed blue skirt was sewn onto a sleeveless cotton vest. Over it went a horizontally striped blue and pink sweater with short sleeves. Nobody else in Miss Marr's class had a homemade knitted suit anything like it.

"I can't wear it," I said in <u>anguished</u> tones. ◄ A

"It's lovely," my mother said calmly. "Gretta worked hard to make it for you.

Words to Know and Use

abrasion (ə brā′ zhən) *n.* a scrape on the skin
glower (glou′ ər) *v.* to stare in an angry way; scowl
anguished (an′ gwisht) *adj.* filled with pain, mental or physical; extremely upset
 anguish *v.*

49

VOCABULARY PREVIEW

These vocabulary words are defined at the bottom of the selection pages on which they appear.

abrasion a scrape on the skin

anguished extremely upset

detention punishment of being kept unwillingly

glower to stare angrily

jeering taunting

ominously in a threatening way

quiver to tremble

spellbound as if in a trance

stupendous huge; tremendous

transfixed unable to move

LIMITED ENGLISH PROFICIENCY

■ Use the Reader's Guidesheet, *Unit One Resource Book*, page 31.

■ This selection is set several decades ago in Canada. You might define such unfamiliar words as *porridge* (hot cereal), *serge* (a type of woolen fabric), and *petticoat* (an underskirt or slip). Also, you may wish to help students recognize some melodramatic elements that appear in Jean's tall tale.

★ Text annotations marked with a red star (2, 5) may be particularly helpful for students with limited English proficiency.

TEXT ANNOTATIONS

1. LITERARY CONCEPT: Autobiography
Ask students what two meanings the title "Little by Little" has. (*"Little by little" denotes gradual progress; the autobiography is about and by a woman named Little.*)

2. ACTIVE READING: Connect
Ask volunteers to explain "times tables" and to give an example. (*the tables of multiplication: 1 x 5 = 5, 2 x 5 = 10, etc.*) Ask students if they would have dreaded a mental arithmetic test as Jean did. (*Answers will vary depending on how well students think they know their tables and whether they need to write out math problems.*) ★

Guided Reading for Less-Proficient Students

These questions can help guide students through the reading. Ask each question at the point of the selection where the capital letter and arrow appear in the margin. In addition, you may wish to use appropriate Active Reading annotations.

A. Why is Jean upset during her morning at home? (*She is jealous of Hugh, angry at her little sister for spilling milk on her, and embarrassed at having to wear an ugly dress.*) Summarizing

B. Why is Jean so determined to save herself from writing her name on the board? (*She is afraid of being ridiculed because she cannot see exactly how her name should be written.*) Recalling

C. What is Jean planning to do? How well do you suppose her plan will work? (*She is planning to make up a story about an emergency. Predictions will vary.*) Inferring/Predicting

Continued on page 50

3. LITERARY CONCEPT:
Autobiography

Why does Jean blame her sister for "all the trouble"? Do you think she still thinks this way as an adult? *(Possible responses: Even though Jean began the milk incident herself, her sister over-reacted; little sisters are annoying and easy to blame; Jean does not want to feel guilty; she probably does not feel this way as an adult.)*

4. ACTIVE READING:
Question/Connect

Ask students why Jean thinks she'll be ridiculed. *(She is not sure how other students write their names on the board and expects to be made fun of if she does it differently.)* Ask students if they can understand her dread at being ridiculed and if they have ever had a similar fear. *(Any response is valid.)*

LE PETIT DEJEUNER 1986
Jennifer Hornyak
Courtesy, Gallery Claude Lafitte,
Montreal, Canada.

Don't be ridiculous. Of course you will wear it."

3 In ten minutes I was gobbling toast and honey, gulping down milk, and hating my cheerful little sister who was the cause of all the trouble and who got to stay home and be spoiled by everybody.

When I reached the street, it was <u>ominously</u> quiet. I really was going to be late, and it was all Pat's fault. I ran the first three blocks, but slowed down when I got a stitch[1] in my side. There was still not a single child in sight.

As I passed St. John's School, I could hear the grade four class singing "God Save the King." I sent the small building a look of longing. Mr. Johnston had not had these horrid mental arithmetic tests.

Then I stood stock still. When I got to school, Miss Marr would tell me to put my name on the board to stay after four. I didn't mind staying late–lots of the others got <u>detentions</u>–I wasn't sure what to write, though I had a strong suspicion that you did not write out your whole name. Did you **4** just write your initials? Or one initial and your surname? Or your first name and your last initial?

I had to get it right. The others still called me names when no teacher was near enough to hear. The only game I had ever been invited to play was Crack the Whip, and they always made me go on the end. Then, when the big girl at the front swung

---

1. **stitch:** a sharp, sudden pain.

Words to Know and Use

ominously (äm′ ə nəs lē) *adv.* in a threatening or evil way
detention (di ten′ shən) *n.* punishment of being held against one's will, as in having to stay after school

50

Guided Reading for Less-Proficient Students

Continued from page 49

D. In the tale Jean makes up, what is the most important thing that she does? *(She saves a girl's life.)* Summarizing

E. In what way was Jean's story a success? *(She avoided both taking the arithmetic test and writing her name on the board; she fascinated her listeners.)* Recalling

F. Why doesn't Jean want to go out for recess? *(She doesn't want people to see that her knee is not bandaged.)* Clarifying

G. Why do you think the boy's snowballs missed Jean? *(Possible responses: Jean stood up to him; he meant to miss her; his aim was off because of his surprise.)* Inferring

everybody around in a long *Crack!*, I ended
up flying through the air and landing with a
jarring crash on my hands and knees. As I
picked myself up, I'd try to look as though I
thought crash landings were fun. Nobody
was fooled.

If I wrote my name up there differently
than the others did, they would have a new
thing to tease me about. I could hear the
jeering voices already.

"You're not just cross-eyed, you're so
dumb you don't even know how to write
your name on the board!"

I stood there, thinking hard. How could I
save myself? Once in a while, when a child
brought a note from home, he got out of
putting his name on the board. Well, my
mother would not write me a note.

I had to invent the most convincing lie of my life.

Perhaps, if your parents were not at
home, and some emergency cropped up and
you had to deal with it, Miss Marr just
might let you sit down without asking for a
note. It would have to be a desperate emergency . . .

I began to walk again, taking my time. I
had to invent the most convincing lie of my
life. Bit by bit, I worked it out. As I imagined how it must have happened, it grew so
real that I began to believe it myself. I had
every detail ready as I turned the last corner. Then I began to run.

I knew it was essential that I be out of

breath when I arrived.

I dashed up the stairs, puffing hard. I
opened the door, said a private prayer for
help, and entered the grade five classroom.
Miss Marr was at her desk. Out of the corner of my eye, I could see monitors collecting the test papers. So far so good.

"Jean," said my teacher, "you're late."

"Yes," I panted, facing her and opening
my eyes wide so that I would look innocent
and pitiful. "I know. I couldn't help it."

"Why are you late?" she asked.

I took a deep breath.

"Well, I was all ready in plenty of time.
But just as I was going out the door, the telephone rang. I knew I should not go back to
answer it, but you know my mother and
father are both doctors, and I was afraid it
might be an emergency."

Miss Marr opened her mouth to ask a
question, but I rushed on, not giving her
time to get a word in edgewise.

"The trouble was, you see, that nobody
was home but me. So I took the receiver off
the hook and I said, 'Dr. Littles' residence.'"

Everybody was listening now, even the
boys who never paid attention. I kept going.

"MY DAUGHTER IS DYING! MY DAUGHTER
IS DYING!"

I saw my teacher jump as I shrieked
the words at the top of my lungs.
Her eyes were wide with shock.
The class gasped. I did not stop
for effect. I could not give the teacher time
to interrupt.

"It was a man's voice. He sounded frantic
with worry. 'I'm sorry,' I told him, 'my par-

5. ACTIVE READING: Connect
Invite volunteers to describe, draw, or
demonstrate in slow motion the game of
Crack the Whip, in which players form
a line, join hands, and swing around
like a whip. Ask how students feel
about being at the end of the line: Does
it seem fun, dangerous, or frightening? ★

6. ACTIVE READING: Review
Have students **summarize** Jean's problems at school and their causes.
*(Possible responses: Jean is behind in
arithmetic because she didn't study; she
is late for school because of the spilled
milk; she cannot read the board
because of her sight; her classmates
make fun of her because she is cross-
eyed.)*

7. LITERARY CONCEPT:
Characterization
Have students explain the steps Jean
has taken to carry out her plan and
what that shows about her personality.
*(She is ready with every detail of her
story; she is clever, thorough, plans
ahead, and is a little devious.)*

8. ACTIVE READING: Question
Ask students whether they think the
teacher believes Jean's story at first.
*(Possible response: Yes, because the
teacher is shocked and because the
story is not too unbelievable up to this
point.)*

Words to Know and Use	**jeering** (jir' iŋ) *adj.* mocking; rude, taunting **jeer** *v.*

9. ACTIVE READING: Evaluate
Ask students to evaluate the details of Jean's story at this point for believability. (Possible response: Details such as the father asking a child to save his daughter's life, a log cabin in the middle of the city, and the weeping crowd at the church door seem hard to believe.)

10. LITERARY CONCEPT: Characterization
Have students explain why Miss Marr's face quivered and her mouth twitched. (Possible response: Miss Marr is amused by Jean's story and is trying not to laugh at it.)

11. ACTIVE READING: Connect
Ask students to make a generalization about the rewards the people offer Jean. (Possible response: They are story-book or fairy-tale rewards.)

ents are out. If you call back, they should be home in one hour.' 'No! Please, don't hang up,' he begged. 'You must come and save her life. If I wait for your parents, she will surely die.' 'Well, I guess if she is dying, I'd better come. Where do you live?' I asked him. '111 King Street,' he told me."

Miss Marr did not even try to ask a question as I paused to catch my breath. The entire class was sitting spellbound. The silence was absolute. Not a desk seat squeaked. Not a giggle broke the hush.

"I hurried in and got the right medicine from the office, and then I ran out the door. I didn't go the long way around by the Norwich Street bridge. I was afraid it would take too long. I went down London Road and across some stepping stones down there. When I got to King Street, there was the house. It was a log cabin with wind whistling through the cracks. And as I came up to it, I saw the door was standing open and there were a bunch of people in the doorway and they were all crying. 'What's wrong?' I asked them. 'You are too late,' they sobbed. 'She's dead already.' "

This time, as I snatched a breath, Miss Marr choked back a small sound. She made no attempt to stem the flood of my story. I pressed on.

" 'Oh, I am so sorry,' I told them. 'Take me to see her.' So they took me into the cabin, and there lay the girl on a trundle bed.[2] Her face was blue, and her eyes had rolled up till you could just see white, and her teeth were clenched. And her fingers

and toes all curled over backwards."

I watched Miss Marr carefully at this point, because I was not absolutely sure what a dead person looked like. The last bit worried me especially. I had heard someone say that when people died, they turned their toes up. That could only mean that their toes curled over backwards, but I was not sure about the fingers.

Miss Marr's face quivered a little and her mouth twitched, but she did not speak. I hurried, eager to finish. It would be a relief to sit down. Even so, in spite of myself, I kept putting in extra bits as they occurred to me.

*S*he's just on the point of death. I think I can save her.

" 'She's not quite dead,' I cried. 'She's just on the point of death. I think I can save her.' I hit her chin and her mouth opened. I poured in the medicine. She fluttered her lashes and turned a normal color and said weakly, 'Where am I?' I turned and hurried toward the door. But before I could escape, all the weeping people went down on their knees and grabbed hold of my skirt and they said, 'You saved her life! We want to give you a reward. Gold, silver, a bag of emeralds, a horse that will come when you whistle . . . tell us the one thing you want

2. **trundle bed:** a low bed on wheels that is stored under a larger bed when not needed.

Words to Know and Use	**spellbound** (spel' bound') *adj.* as if in a trance; fascinated **quiver** (kwiv' ər) *v.* to tremble or shake

52

Speaking . . . Listening . . . Viewing

Speaking/Listening Introduce the concept of melo-drama—a kind of play in which emotions and actions are greatly exaggerated and overacted. Then ask students who tend to be hams to retell Jean's imaginary story in a melodramatic way, overacting and exaggerating emotions and using gestures where appropriate. Allow them to practice and then to deliver their performance for the class.

more than anything else in the world and you can have it.' "

I paused for effect this time. I knew no one would break the hush. I wanted my teacher to take in the next bit.

" 'The one thing I want more than anything else in the world,' I told them, 'is to be on time for school.' So they let me go, and I ran down the hill and across the stepping stones. When I got to the third last stone, though, I slipped and fell in the river and cut my knee. I had to get to shore, go home and bandage my knee and put on dry clothes. Then I hurried here as fast as I could. And that is why I am late."

There was a stunned silence in the classroom. Miss Marr and I stared at each other for a long, long minute. I waited for her to tell me to write my name on the board. Instead she pointed her finger at my desk. Speaking extremely slowly and wearily, she said, "Take . . . your . . . seat. Just . . . take . . . your . . . seat."

I tried to keep a solemn expression on my face. But it was hard not to grin. I sat down and did not turn my head as a buzz of whispers broke out behind me. I had missed the mental arithmetic test. I had not had to write my name on the board. And I had kept every single person transfixed with my exciting story.

At least three blissful minutes went by before I realized I had no cut on my knee and no bandage, either. Not only that, but I could not remember whether I had told her which knee I was supposed to have cut.

She had believed me. I was sure of that. Yet any second she was going to discover

Jean Little as a child.   Courtesy Jean Little.

that I had told her a stupendous lie.

I hooked one knee over the other and clasped my hands around the knee on top. I spent the entire morning that way. When I was required to write, I used only one hand. Miss Marr did not ask me a direct question. When recess time came and she said, "Class, stand," I stayed where I was.

"Jean, aren't you going out for recess?" she asked when the others had marched out and there I still sat.

"Oh, Miss Marr," I said in my smallest, most pathetic voice, "I am so tired from saving that girl's life that I have to stay in and have a rest."

Still clutching my knee with both hands, I

D ▶

12

13
E ▶

14

Words to Know and Use	**transfixed** (trans fikst') *adj.* unable to move because of awe or fear **transfix** *v.*
	stupendous (stoo pen' dəs) *adj.* huge; tremendous

53

12. ACTIVE READING: Evaluate
Ask students why they think the teacher doesn't challenge the truth of Jean's story. *(Possible responses: She wants to save Jean's pride in front of the class; she is impressed with Jean's storytelling skill.)*

13. LITERARY CONCEPT: Fiction
Point out to students that although Little's autobiography is nonfiction, Jean's tall tale is a short work of fiction. Have them describe the elements of fiction within her story. *(Possible responses: Her story has a life-and-death conflict, a heroic main character, a suspenseful plot with a climax and a satisfying resolution.)*

14. LITERARY CONCEPT: Autobiography
As a child, Jean was certain that the teacher believed her story. Ask students whether Jean as an adult still believes that. *(Possible response: No. As an adult, she realizes that her teacher could not have believed such an exaggerated tale.)*

Multicultural Connections

Near the end of the story, on page 54, Jean obtains self-respect and dignity when she educates the seventh-grade bully on how to refer to her disability appropriately. Have students write in their journals about the "power of words" when naming social groups. What social or ethnic groups do they identify with, and what names do they prefer for those groups? Have they ever been hurt by a slur used against them? What does the use of such slurs indicate about the person who uses them?

laid my head down on my desk and shut my eyes.

F ▶ She did not say a word.

At noon, when she had her back turned, I ran out of the classroom, dashed home, sneaked bandaids from my parents' office and plastered them over both knees, to be on the safe side. When I returned to school, Miss Marr smiled and did not ask why both my knees were bandaged.

I sat through the afternoon thinking over what had happened. Did she really guess? The other kids did not seem to have figured out that I had lied. One girl had even smiled at me, as though she might be my friend. Nobody in my class had called me cross-eyed. A boy in grade seven had, though. If only I could shut him up the way I had hushed everybody that morning.

Then I remembered Hugh's knee. That night I asked Mother, "What are the long words for what's wrong with my eyes?"

I was standing beside her chair. She looked up at me.

"Why?" she asked.

"I want to know, that's all. They call me cross-eyed. I want to know the long words, the ones doctors use."

She rhymed off a whole list.

"Say it again. Slowly."

"Strabismus, nystagmus, corneal opacities, and eccentric pupils."[3]

I practiced.

The next day I was late coming out of school. The same grade-seven boy was waiting for me. He had his first snowball ready.

"Cross-eyed, cross-eyed," he chanted and waited for me to start running so that he could chase me, pelting me with hard-packed snowballs.

I turned on him instead.

"I am not cross-eyed," I said in a strong, clear voice. "I have corneal opacities and eccentric pupils."

I glared at him as I spoke, and my eyes were as crossed as ever. But he was so surprised that he stood there, his mouth gaping open like a fish's.

Then I turned my back and walked away. Perhaps his aim was off because he was so used to firing his missiles at a running target. But the first snowball flew past me harmlessly. The second exploded with a smack against a nearby tree.

◀ G

I kept walking, chin in the air.

In the last two days, I had learned a lot about the power of words. Snowballs would hit me again, and I would run away and cry. I would be late, and, eventually, I would even have to write my name on the board.

But I had found out what mere words could do. I would not forget. ❧

---

3. **Strabismus** (strə biz′ məs), **nystagmus** (nis tag′ məs), **corneal opacities** (kôr′ nē əl ō pas′ ə tēs), **and eccentric pupils** (ək sen′ trik pyo͞o′ pəlz).

Comprehension Check

✓ 1. Who did Jean blame for her being late for school? (*her little sister Pat*)

2. Why didn't Jean want to be late for school? (*She was afraid she would have to write her name on the board, and she didn't know how.*)

3. Why did her classmates make fun of Jean? (*She was cross-eyed.*)

4. What desperate emergency did Jean invent? (*She had to save a dying girl.*)

5. How did the class respond to Jean's story? (*They were fascinated.*)

6. How did Jean act toward the seventh-grade boy? (*She stood up to him and told him the proper name for her condition.*)

7. What power has Jean learned about? (*the power of words*)

Responding to Reading

First Impressions

1. How did you feel about Jean Little? Jot down your thoughts in your journal or on a piece of paper.

Second Thoughts

2. Little hoped to invent "the most convincing lie" of her life to avoid standing at the board. Do you think she really convinced her classmates and teacher? Explain why or why not.

3. Imagine that you are Little's teacher or her parent. How would you respond to her invented story?

   Think about
   - how the rest of the class might react if she gets away with her lie
   - the pride that she takes in her story

4. Little says that she "found out what mere words could do." Do you agree that words are important? Support your opinion with examples from the story and your own experience.

5. Compare Jean Little's embarrassing situation with the one you wrote about on page 48.

Broader Connections

6. What could have been done at Jean's school to help her deal with her disability? What is being done by your school and your community to help people with physical disabilities? Does more need to be done?

Literary Concept: Autobiography

An **autobiography** is the story of a person's life, written by that person. Even though it is based on real events, an autobiography shares many of the elements of fiction. In what ways is this chapter of Little's autobiography like a short story? How does it differ from a short story?

Student Response

Responding to Reading

1. Any response is valid.

2. **Possible responses:** Jean did not convince her teacher, as is shown by Miss Marr's quivering face, her wearily telling Jean to sit down after the story was finished, her smiling when Jean returned with bandaged knees, and the story's being so far-fetched that no adult would believe it. Jean may have convinced her classmates, since they were spellbound by her story.

3. **Possible responses:** Jean's teacher or parent might let Jean know she is not fooling anyone with her invented story so that she and the class realize that lying is wrong, or they might let Jean shine in front of classmates who have taunted her.

4. **Possible responses:** Words helped Jean impress classmates who had ridiculed her. They also helped her defend herself against a bully. Students may give examples of times when words helped them provide explanations or apologies, entertain others, bring humor to a situation, obtain help, teach a skill, or share feelings.

5. Any response is valid.

6. **Possible responses:** Jean's school could have seated her closer to the chalkboard, provided large-print textbooks or large-print lessons for what was written on the board; her teacher could have been more aware of her problems and how the class was treating her and provided counseling both for Jean and the class. Communities can help people with disabilities by providing accessible parking spots, ramps for wheelchairs, sign-language interpreters for hearing-impaired people, and specially equipped washrooms and other facilities.

Literary Concept: Autobiography

This chapter is like a short story in that it contains dialogue, depicts characters through the use of thoughts and actions, has a particular setting, and contains a conflict, climax, and resolution. It differs from a short story in that it is based on real events.

Challenge Question

Ask how this episode fits with Little's subtitle, *A Writer's Education.* (Possible responses: It describes how she discovered that she had a talent for creating fiction; it explains how her discovery of the power of words led her to be a writer.)

Writing Options

The Writing Options are designed to meet varied student interests and abilities. Have each student choose one writing activity to complete.

Journal Update Have students review and add to their journal entries. What did they learn from Jean's handling of her predicament that might help them in their own lives? What advice might Jean give to them?

Links to Writer's Craft

Writing Option 4 is an exercise in personal writing. For more practice, see *The Writer's Craft,* Grade 7, "Personal and Expressive Writing," pages 26–46.

Vocabulary Practice

Answers to Exercise

1. c	6. d
2. b	7. d
3. b	8. a
4. a	9. b
5. d	10. d

For Alternative Learning Styles

Have students pair off. Supply each pair with drawing paper and pens of different colors. Give each student five of the ten Words to Know and Use from this selection. Then tell students to illustrate each of their words for their partners and to let partners guess the words.

Closure

Invite students to compare the theme of creating "false impressions" in this selection to the theme of "Seventh Grade," noting similarities in the actions of Jean and Victor, the responses of the teachers and students, and the final outcomes. Then discuss similarities between this selection and "The War of the Wall" in how false impressions are created.

Writing Options

1. Suppose Jean Little moved to the "War of the Wall" neighborhood. How do you think she would be treated? Write a **diary entry** in which she tells about a typical day.

2. Work with a partner or a small group to write a **set of school rules** for treating disabled people respectfully and fairly.

3. What if the principal had listened to Little's invention and Miss Marr's response? Write a **script** of the conversation that the principal and the teacher might have had.

4. Describe an **incident** in your own life in which you experienced the power of words. You may describe a time when words gave you a sense of your own power or a time when words were used against you.

Vocabulary Practice

Exercise Write the letter of the word that is least like the other words in the set.

1. (a) jeering   (b) mocking   (c) cheering   (d) hissing
2. (a) fascinated   (b) bored   (c) spellbound   (d) interested
3. (a) worried   (b) calm   (c) upset   (d) anguished
4. (a) smile   (b) glower   (c) scowl   (d) stare
5. (a) great   (b) huge   (c) stupendous   (d) minor
6. (a) quiver   (b) shake   (c) tremble   (d) steady
7. (a) frozen   (b) transfixed   (c) motionless   (d) nervous
8. (a) reward   (b) punishment   (c) penalty   (d) detention
9. (a) threateningly   (b) encouragingly   (c) ominously   (d) evilly
10. (a) cut   (b) abrasion   (c) scrape   (d) paint

> **Words to Know and Use**
>
> abrasion
> anguished
> detention
> glower
> jeering
> ominously
> quiver
> spellbound
> stupendous
> transfixed

The Spelling Connection

Spelling Pattern: Hard and soft c/g When the letters c and g have a hard sound, they will be followed by a, o, or u. When they have a soft sound, they will be followed by i, e, or y. Suffixes that follow the soft c or g will always begin with i or e.

Examples: ca**p**a**c**ity   ga**ra**ge   intelli**g**ence

c/g Words from the Selection

ridi**c**ulous   silen**ce**   residen**ce**   convin**c**ing

anguished   game   serge   emergency

Other hard and soft c/g Words

circular   garage   tragedy

conceal   gorgeous   gymnastics

Exercise Add the correct vowels. Use the clues.

1. ang_ished (hard g)
2. c_rc_lar (soft c/hard c)
3. trag_dy (soft g)
4. ridic_lous (hard c)
5. c_nvinc_ng (hard c/soft c)

Options for Learning (Multimodal/Cross-Curricular Activities)

1 • Read the Book This selection is one chapter from Jean Little's autobiography. Read the rest of her book and share more anecdotes from her life with your class.

2 • Debate the Question Is it ever acceptable to tell a lie? Plan a debate with three students on each team. One team will argue the affirmative (yes), the other team the negative (no). Each group should list reasons to support its position and plan a concluding statement. Stage the debate and let the class vote for the winner.

3 • Sight Technology Find out what equipment is now available to help blind or nearly blind people lead lives closer to the lives of sighted people. Use your library or contact institutions that deal with the blind. Share your information with the class.

4 • A Tall Tale Create another story that Jean might tell to excuse her lateness. Tell your tale to your classmates.

 FACT FINDER SCIENCE
Use a dictionary to explain what a corneal opacity might be.

Jean Little
1932 –

Jean Little was born in Taiwan, where her parents, both doctors, were missionaries. She considers herself "very fortunate" that her parents never treated her as "the handicapped child," despite her eye problems. Her family settled in Guelph, Ontario, when she was in third grade. Continual teasing about her eyes forced her to the public library. "I read, I daydreamed and I lied prodigiously—so I prepared myself for becoming a writer."

Her first book, *Mine for Keeps,* won the Canadian Children's Book Award. Her other popular books include *Spring Begins in March* and *From Anna.* These books portray characters with physical disabilities.

Little's eye problems now prevent her from reading, though she continues to write by using a talking computer. She lives in Guelph with her guide dog. To young writers, she advises, "Read and write a lot. You have a storehouse in your head. If you don't put anything in it, there's nothing to draw on."

Options for Learning

These activities suit a variety of learning styles and modes of expression.

Collaborative Learning Activities
See Options 2 and 3.

1. Read the Book Little's book is highly readable and entertaining for a middle school audience. A sequel entitled *Stars Come Out Within* was published in 1990.

2. Debate the Question Remind students that the most convincing arguments are supported with facts rather than with opinions.

3. Sight Technology Students may write to the American Foundation for the Blind (15 West 16th Street, New York, New York 10011) to obtain a copy of its catalog. It contains many examples of technology to aid the blind.

4. A Tall Tale Recall other characters from Little's own life that students may want to draw upon to build a story—for example, her younger sister Pat.

 FACT FINDER SCIENCE
In the dictionary students can learn that the cornea is the clear covering of the eyeball. Opaque means "not letting light through." A corneal opacity is a cornea that is partly or entirely clouded.

Jean Little

■ **More About the Author** Translations of Little's books appear in Braille and in French, German, Dutch, Danish, Norwegian, Japanese, and Greek.

■ **Other Works** Novels: *Mine for Keeps, Look Through My Window, Kate, From Anna, Mama's Going to Buy You a Mockingbird, Different Dragons;* poetry: *Hey, World, Here I Am!*

 ■ **Awards** Canadian Children's Book Award, Vicky Metcalf Award, Boston Globe-Horn Book Honor Award, several Junior Literary Guild awards, and numerous other awards.

Cross-Curricular Projects

Social Studies Ask volunteers to research other people in history or contemporary society who overcome disabilities. You may suggest such contemporary figures as Stevie Wonder and Ray Charles (blind musicians) as well as such historical figures as Ludwig van Beethoven (deaf composer), John Milton (blind poet), and Thomas Edison (hearing-impaired scientist and inventor).

Science Have volunteers find out how eyeglasses correct vision. Ask them to draw a diagram to demonstrate their findings to the class. Interested students can research medical advances in eye care, starting with the invention of eyeglasses and working up to recent developments in radial keratotomy and laser surgery.

- To understand the elements of an autobiographical incident

- To write about a personal experience from the first-person point of view

- To organize writing in chronological order or cause-and-effect order

- To draft, revise, edit, and share personal writing

Teaching Strategies

DISCUSSING THE ASSIGNMENT

Have students read the first paragraph on page 58, and be sure they know that an autobiographical incident is a person's true story of something that happened to him or her, and that a false impression is a wrong idea that someone forms about someone else. Emphasize that this assignment calls for not only how a false impression was given but also what happened as a result.

Then point out the PASSkey for the Guided Assignment. Help students understand the relationship between the directions in the box and the "shorthand" in the graphic. Point out that the PASSkey provides them with a way of planning their writing. Deciding their purpose, audience, subject, and structure before they begin will keep them on target in prewriting and in drafting and revising their work. Explain that they may change parts of their PASSkey during their writing process.

If you wish, you may give students the option of writing about something else that is important to them. Alternative Writing and Research Topics at the bottom of the following page offers additional suggestions. Remind students too that the Writer's Handbook, pages 694–696, provides an overview of each step of the writing process and explains the PASSkey in detail.

ANALYZING THE MODEL

Ask a volunteer to read aloud the student model on pages 58-59. Have students evaluate Zachary's work to see if it conforms to the assignment. *(Possible response: Yes, the first part tells how Zachary formed a false impression of*

WRITER'S
WORKSHOP

**USE PERSONAL
WRITING FOR**

journals
logs
notes
letters
diaries
autobiographies

PERSONAL WRITING

Each of us remembers misunderstandings like those experienced by the characters in this subunit. We have all believed a false impression or have purposely or mistakenly created a false impression. In this workshop you will write about such an experience. Like Jean in *Little by Little*, you could write about a false impression you gave of yourself. Or, you can focus on a false impression you had of someone else. A personal experience of this kind is called an **autobiographical incident**. Writing about these experiences can help you understand them. You are sharing a moment in your life with readers—and with yourself.

> Here is one writer's PASSkey to this assignment.

**GUIDED ASSIGNMENT:
AUTOBIOGRAPHICAL INCIDENT**

Write about a time when you either received or gave a false impression. Explain what happened as a result.

PURPOSE: To tell about a personal experience
AUDIENCE: Classmates, friends, family
SUBJECT: A false impression
STRUCTURE: Autobiographical incident

STUDENT MODEL
Before you write, read how one student responded to the assignment.

▶

The pronoun *I* shows that this is personal or **autobiographical** writing.

▶

The Turnaround
by Zachary Hurston

I had to grin when Mike introduced us. "Your name is Eel-ya?" I asked. "Eel-ya?" The new kid's name sounded like a joke. Is he named after an eel, or what, I wondered. It was the first day of sixth grade, and he was sitting right behind me.

"Ilya," he corrected in a fed-up voice. "It's a Russian name."

"Oh—are you from Russia?" I was trying to be friendly.

"No!" he snapped. "I'm American." He sure didn't sound Russian—but he did sound as if he

ADDITIONAL RESOURCES
Unit One Resource Book
Writer's Workshop Worksheet, p. 39
Writer's Workshop: Peer and Self-Evaluation, p. 40
Writer's Workshop: Assessment Guidelines, p. 41

Technology and Enrichment
Guidelines for Writing Assessment and Portfolio Use
Elaboration, Revision, and Proofreading
   Transparencies 1–4
Writer's Databank Software: File 2,
   Starting Points
Fine Art Transparency Pack

Links to
Writer's Craft

For more about personal writing, see *The Writer's Craft*, Grade 7, "Personal and Expressive Writing," pages 27–47. See also pages 218–220, "Finding Writing Ideas."

were talking to a pesky four-year-old. I knew right then that I wasn't going to like this guy. He looked like he didn't think much of me either.

Sure enough, when Ilya, Mike, and I were put in the same science-project group that week, Ilya turned out to be a pain. When Mike and I joked around, Ilya wouldn't even smile. It was like he was all brains and no fun. I wished I didn't have to sit in front of him for the whole year.

Now, finally, I'm in seventh grade. On the first day, I walked to school with my best friend—Ilya Penoff.

What caused the turnaround? For one thing, sometime during sixth grade, Ilya finally broke down and started laughing at my jokes. He admitted later that it had just about killed him to keep a straight face, but he thought I was a brainless clown and didn't want to get me going. For another thing, I started really listening to him. Ilya has a mind like some kind of wild video game, always coming up with new twists. Also I think he found out that I'm not exactly brainless myself. In fact, Mr. Sykes gave Ilya and me A's in science. We were the only two who earned them. My friend Ilya and I did learn a lot about science last year. We also learned a lot about judging people too quickly.

◀ Details about words, voices, and facial expressions help readers to imagine the incident.

◀ The writer uses time order to tell the story.

◀ Details show how the writer's original impressions were proved false.

◀ The writer explains reasons and results.

Now that you've read Zachary's paper, it's time to begin your own.

Prewrite and Explore

1 **Wake up your memory**   To find ideas for personal writing, look in personal places. Rummaging is one way to waken memories. Look through family photo albums or watch family videos; check your old diaries, scrapbooks, notebooks, or calendars; swap memories with family members. Focus on times when you got—or gave—the wrong impression.

Ilya, and the second part explains how the boys learned that their first impressions were wrong.)

You may wish to ask questions such as those listed below to help the class further analyze the model.

■ Who is the "I" referred to in the model? How do you know?

■ What does dialogue contribute to Zachary's work?

■ How can you tell what kind of order Zachary uses?

■ How does he help you picture the incidents in your own mind?

Prewrite and Explore

Encourage students to think of times when they were the receivers of false impressions and times when they were the givers. Suggest that they choose to write about an incident that stands out in their mind and has a clear results.

As they remember their incident, students may want to think about it in terms of cause and effect. To help them crystallize their thoughts, you might copy this cause-and-effect chart on the board.

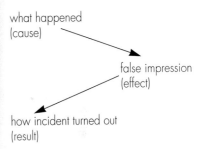

what happened
(cause)

false impression
(effect)

how incident turned out
(result)

TEACHING TIP: LEP

Since students with limited English proficiency are often better speakers than writers, try pairing them with advanced writers who will work through the assignment with them. Encourage advanced writers to

■ listen to their partner's ideas and help them convert the ideas into written drafts

■ offer help with wording, spelling, and sentence structure

■ assist in revising and proofreading

■ take notes while LEP students relate incidents orally

Alternative Writing and Research Topics

Personal Writing Write about a time when you did something silly or foolish, like the boys in "Seventh Grade," because you thought it would "improve" you. Include the results.

Short Story In "Hearts and Hands" giving a false impression becomes an act of kindness. Write another short story that illustrates this theme.

Research—Visual Handicaps Jean Little had a visual handicap. Research and write a report about another

type of visual handicap. Choose one specific condition, such as glaucoma or cataracts.

Historical Essay Sometimes false impressions cause people to make errors in judgment. Write an essay describing a time in history when a person or group acted on a false impression. For example, Columbus had the false impression that he had reached the East Indies.

Draft and Discover

If students aren't sure how to begin their incidents, suggest the following strategies:

■ Describe a person involved in the incident other than yourself.

■ Begin with some lively dialogue, as Zachary did in the model incident. Have the characters themselves show what they are like and tell what is going on.

■ Begin with the result of the incident and work backward.

Remind students that they can always go back and replace missing details or rearrange the ones they've written. If they get a better idea while they're writing, they can scrap what they've done and begin again.

Modeling: On an overhead, write a paragraph about an incident in your own memory for students. Explain that this draft is imperfect and that you will change it as you develop your incident more fully.

TEACHING TIP: CHALLENGE

Students who are strong writers might be encouraged to model all or part of their autobiographical incident on the style of an author whose work appears in the subunit, such as Toni Cade Bambara. Not only will such an activity be an exercise in analysis, but it will also illustrate how important word choice and phrasing can be to the finished project.

TEACHING TIP: COMPUTER

Suggest that students who draft on a computer use the Insert edit mode. Then, if they should suddenly have an idea or recall an important detail while drafting, they can hit the Page Down key and input the idea or fact. Afterward, they can hit the Page Up key and continue where they left off. After finishing a page or draft, students will have a collection of useful notes at the end of their document.

2 **Choose your topic and gather information**   By yourself or with a friend, sift through your memories. Which incident would be most fun to write about? Which one means the most to you today? Either would make a good topic. After you've chosen a topic, you can start gathering the details that will help you write.

STUDENT MODEL ▶

GATHERING INFORMATION

Try closing your eyes and reliving the incident you've chosen. Take your time. Think about why the incident happened and about the results it had. After you open your eyes, you can fill in an idea chain like the one below, which Zachary used. Jot down as many details as you can remember.

```
False Impression
Ilya seemed all brains, no fun.
Like no one was home in there.
Seemed like he felt so superior.
```

```
Reasons
When we first met,
  Ilya treated me like
  a little kid.
I tried to be friendly,
  and he got offended.
He never laughed at my
  jokes.
```

```
Results
I hated him at first.
  Now we're tight.
We both learned about
  snap judgments.
We both got A's!
```

Draft and Discover

1 **Begin drafting**   You don't have to start at the beginning of your incident. You can start with the part you're most interested in right now. When you run out of steam, your idea chain will remind you of what else to put in.

2 **Use paragraphs to organize**   You might write a paragraph for each main "link" in your idea chain, or you might write a paragraph for each main time segment in your story.

Paragraphs at Work

If students are having trouble deciding where each paragraph should begin, offer these guidelines:
1. Start a new paragraph whenever you begin a different part of your story. For example, if you have been describing your hard work on a plan, the first sentence of the next paragraph might begin, "On Monday morning I put my plan into action."
2. Start a new paragraph when you begin describing new settings. For example, if you've just told what's going on in the kitchen and now you want to tell what happened in the garage, your new paragraph might begin, "Meanwhile, out in the garage, Dad was painting the racer."
3. Start a new paragraph when the story moves forward or backward in time. For example, if you've been narrating an event and want to describe what happened later, your new paragraph might begin, "Back then I had no idea how hard it is to live on a budget, but I found out when I turned thirteen."

3 **Color your writing with details** Adding details can turn a pale, washed-out piece of writing into a lively, interesting story. Details can include descriptive phrases, colorful verbs and nouns, and interesting comparisons. Look at this example.

> She was rearing back on her heels, her hands jammed into her back pockets, her face squinched up like the masterpiece she had in mind was taking shape on the wall by magic. We could have been gophers crawled up into a rotten hollow for all she cared.

◀ **LITERARY MODEL**
from "The War of the Wall" by Toni Cade Bambara

Revise Your Writing

1 **Build on your pattern** When you have finished drafting, notice the pattern your paragraphs make. They may follow **time order,** or they may follow the **cause-and-effect** order of your idea chain. (For cause-and-effect order, you first write about the reasons or causes of something, then you write about the results or effects.) If the order of your draft does not seem clear, you may have to move paragraphs or add information.

2 **Write a strong beginning** Now that you have a draft, you can write a "grabber" beginning for it. One way is to start with action rather than with explanation. For instance, reread the first part of Gary Soto's "Seventh Grade" on page 18. Notice that the author doesn't explain who Victor is. He just shows Victor moving through the registration line.

◀ **COMPUTER TIP**
On a word processor you can easily move blocks of text. So you can write two or three action beginnings, try each at the front of your draft, and decide which you like best.

3 **Try a peer reader** You might ask a friend to respond to your draft. The following questions can help.

◀ **WRITER'S CHOICE**
If you don't feel ready to share your writing yet, you can use the For You questions as a guide for rethinking your work.

Revision Questions

For You

1. What's my favorite part of this writing?
2. Could I add details that would make other parts more like my favorite part?
3. Have I shown what this incident meant to me?

For a Peer Reader

1. Which part seemed most interesting to you?
2. Is there anything that confuses you?
3. How would you sum up the incident I wrote about?

CONFERENCING TIP

As you conference with individual writers for this workshop, you may wish to focus on

■ being flexible about changing ideas

■ adding details

■ appropriate paragraphing

Revise Your Writing

At this stage students should be encouraged to check their PASSkeys to see whether their purpose and audience are the same or have changed along the way. Remind those who are writing an autobiographical incident that their subject and structure should be the same as those in the PASSkey in their text. As students revise the part of their work in which they explain the results of their false impression, have them identify the causes and effects in their explanation. Point out that in the model graphic organizer on page 60, the reasons are actually causes and the first result is an effect. If students need more help with this concept, you may want to stop and teach a short lesson on it, such as the workshop on page 182.

As they revise, students might want to have several classmates read their drafts. Suggest that students keep notes on peer reactions to their incidents and then review their revisions against these comments.

As students evaluate the peer responses, encourage them to distinguish between criticisms they feel are helpful and those that are not. Help students understand that their classmates' comments may lead to new ideas and better ways of constructing their incidents. On the other hand, the writers have the option of ignoring ideas that they disagree with.

Proofread

Note that the Editor's Eye feature in this workshop previews the content of the Language Workshop that follows. If students do not need extra help in using personal pronouns, the brief review in The Editor's Eye may be enough for them. If the class or individual students might benefit from additional work, you may choose to teach the Language Workshop, pages 63–65, before students proofread their work.

Use the following models as needed for extra reinforcement of the Editor's Eye topic:

1. Ilya and (I, me) love science.

2. Simon asked Erika and (we, us) for help.

3. Grace and (he, him) didn't understand the experiment.

4. Erica and (we, us) worked with them.

5. Finally, both (she, her) and (he, him) understood.

Have students proofread for details of mechanics and usage that apply to dialogue. Remind them, for example, to enclose the exact words of speakers in quotation marks and to set them off with commas or other punctuation. Make sure students remember to start a new paragraph whenever a different speaker talks. Refer students to pages 778 and 784–785 of the Language Handbook for help with these proofreading tasks.

Publish and Present

If students present their incidents as pantomimes, remind them to convey the actions and emotions in the incidents clearly. Because the actors will not be speaking, they should exaggerate their movements and facial expressions to emphasize the emotions on their faces.

Reflect on Your Writing

You may choose to have students answer the following questions in addition to or instead of those in their text:

■ Was sharing a personal experience embarrassing or fun? Why?

■ Was writing about your own life easier or harder than writing about something you know less well?

Closure

Now that students have written an autobiographical incident, have them find autobiographical articles in newspapers or magazines. Discuss with the class the kind of organization the writers use most often and the kinds of incidents that they relate.

Proofread

Check your work for errors in grammar, spelling, punctuation, and capitalization. If possible, ask a friend to check your writing. Pay special attention to personal pronouns.

NEED MORE HELP?
See the Language Workshop on pages 63–65 and pages 735–736 of the Language Handbook.

THE EDITOR'S EYE: PERSONAL PRONOUNS

Use personal pronouns correctly in compound objects.

When you use pronouns as objects, you choose their object forms: *me, you, him, her, it, us,* and *them.* Sometimes you use two pronouns together, or a noun and a pronoun, as compound objects. Then it can be harder to choose the correct form. The object form is still the correct choice.

Problem	Mr. Sykes gave *Ilya and I* A's in science.
Revised	Mr. Sykes gave *Ilya and me* A's in science.
Also Correct	Mr. Sykes gave *him and me* A's in science.

Publish and Present

Here is a suggestion for sharing your work with others.

Mime Show With two or three friends, recast your autobiographical incidents as pantomimes. Plan how to convey your impressions using only gestures, props, and music. Then perform your pantomimes for the class.

Reflect on Your Writing

Briefly answer the following questions. Put your answers with your paper and add both to your portfolio.

FOR YOUR PORTFOLIO ▶

1. What surprised you as you worked on this assignment?
2. If you had more time to work on this assignment, which part would you change? Why?

62 UNIT ONE FALSE IMPRESSIONS

Assessment Guidelines

These guidelines may help you assess student writing:

Content

1. The writing relates an incident in which someone gave or received a false impression.

2. The sequence of events is easy to follow.

3. The narrative tells the result of the false impression.

Style

4. The point of view is clear and consistent.

5. Description, details, or dialogue add to the narration.

6. The writing is organized in chronological or cause-and-effect order.

Usage and Mechanics

7. The correct forms of personal pronouns are used.

8. Capitalization is handled correctly.

See also *Unit One Resource Book*, page 41.

LANGUAGE WORKSHOP

USING PERSONAL PRONOUNS CORRECTLY

Personal pronouns have three forms: subject, object, and possessive.

Personal Pronouns

When you do personal writing, as in an autobiographical incident, you use many personal pronouns. Choosing the correct forms of these pronouns can help to keep your writing clear. You probably remember that a **pronoun** is a word used to take the place of a noun or another pronoun. The pronouns underlined in the excerpt below are personal pronouns.

> Then <u>he</u> saw <u>her</u>. <u>She</u> was sitting with a girlfriend under a plum tree. . . . When the bell sounded, Teresa looked up, and <u>their</u> eyes met. <u>She</u> smiled sweetly and gathered <u>her</u> books.

◀ LITERARY MODEL
from "Seventh Grade" by Gary Soto

Each of the personal pronouns has a subject form, an object form, and a possessive form. The form that a personal pronoun takes depends on how the pronoun is used. Study the following chart.

Forms of Personal Pronouns

	Subject	Object	Possessive
Singular	I	me	my, mine
	you	you	your, yours
	she, he, it	her, him, it	her, hers, his, its
Plural	we	us	our, ours
	you	you	your, yours
	they	them	their, theirs

◀ SPELLING TIP
Notice that possessive pronouns are spelled without apostrophes: *hers, its, ours, yours, theirs.*

LANGUAGE WORKSHOP   63

ADDITIONAL RESOURCES
Unit One Resource Book
Language Workshop Practice, p. 44

Technology and Enrichment
Grammar and Usage Copymasters, pp. 34, 35
 Grammar Test Generator

Links to Writer's Craft

For more about personal pronouns, see *The Writer's Craft*, Grade 7, "Using Pronouns," pages 432–442.

Objectives

■ To use subject, object, and possessive forms of personal pronouns correctly

■ To use personal pronouns correctly in compound constructions

Teaching Strategies

Personal Pronouns

Have students study the pronouns in the chart on page 63. Then write the following sentences on the board and use them for the oral activity described below:

For subject pronouns: _____ enjoyed the first day of school.

For object pronouns: Shannon gave _____ a tour of the library.

For possessive pronouns: That is _____ classroom. That classroom is _____.

Ask students to use all the pronoun forms in the chart to complete these sentences—first the subject pronouns, then the object pronouns, and then the possessives.

One of the biggest problems students have with personal pronouns is a tendency to use object forms as predicate pronouns because the subject forms "just don't sound right." Try this strategy. First, have students read Using the Subject Form on page 64. Point out item 2 in the Reminder in the margin, noting that a pronoun that is in the predicate of a sentence and that renames or refers to the subject must be in the subject form. Next, provide some practice with sentences like these:

The chosen student was *she.*

Our award recipients are *they.*

It is *I.*

The owner of the book is *he.*

The hosts will be Davin and *she.*

However, once students have practiced, explain that they don't have to use such constructions in their own writing. Instead, all they have to do is recast their sentences, as in the example below.

- The winners of the race were Agnes and he.

- Agnes and he (or He and Agnes) were the winners of the race.

For Alternative Learning Styles Read this tip aloud: When a pronoun is part of a compound subject or object and you can't figure out which form to use, read aloud each part of the compound with the rest of the sentence. Then provide examples like these:

- Janice and (he, him) will be there on time. (Test: "He will be there" sounds right; "him will be there" sounds wrong.)

- Will your sister ride with you and (I, me)? (Test: "With you" sounds right; "with I" sounds wrong; "with me" sounds right.)

Answers to Exercise 1

1. his, P

2. you, S; your, P

3. him, O; he, S

4. her, O; She, S; me, O; he, S; It, S

5. they, S; them, O

6. their, P; her, P

7. He, S; she, S; his, P

8. her, O; he, S

9. I, S; you, S; me, O

10. It, S; us, O

REMINDER
1. Predicate pronouns follow linking verbs such as *am, is, was,* and *were.*
2. Predicate pronouns rename or refer to the subject of the sentence.
3. A sentence with a predicate pronoun will make sense if the subject and the predicate pronoun are reversed.
The winner was *he.*
He was the winner.

Exercise 1 Concept Check Copy the personal pronouns that you find in each sentence. Above each, write *S, O,* or *P,* for subject form, object form, or possessive form.

1. Victor notices that his friend looks different.
2. "What did you do to your face?" asks Victor.
3. Victor's friend thinks that girls will like him if he scowls.
4. "See her? She looked at me!" he says. "It really works!"
5. As the boys talk, they watch girls watching them.
6. In their homeroom, Victor sees Teresa reading her novel.
7. He hopes that she will be his girlfriend.
8. To impress her, he pretends to speak French.
9. "If I have trouble with French, will you help me?" Teresa asks.
10. It might just be a great year for us, thinks Victor.

Using the Subject Form

You use the subject form for a personal pronoun that is the subject of a sentence. You also use the subject form for a **predicate pronoun**—a pronoun that follows a linking verb and renames, or refers to, the subject. Study the following examples.

Subject	**Predicate Pronoun**
She won the race.	The winner was she.
Tory and I visited the school.	The visitors were Tory and I.
Either he or she called.	The caller was either he or she.

Subject and predicate pronouns can be **compound**. One type of compound pronoun consists of two pronouns joined by *and, or,* or *nor.* Another type consists of a noun and a pronoun. In these cases, choosing the correct pronoun form can be confusing. However, as in the second and third examples above, the subject form is correct.

Using the Object Form

The examples below show the three uses of object pronouns.

Direct Object	Lou saw her.
Indirect Object	The twins gave her some supper.
Object of Preposition	The children walked toward her.

Grammar Games: Personal-Pronoun Bee

Prepare about fifty sentences beforehand, each containing at least one noun that can be replaced with a personal pronoun. Be sure there is a good mix of sentences with predicate nouns and compound constructions. Group students into four teams and line them up spelling-bee style. Provide for each team a set of poster-board cards on which are written all the personal pronouns.

Read the first sentence, and name the noun to be replaced. The first player on each team holds up an answer card, and the first player with the correct answer wins a point for his or her team. Then the next player on each team takes a turn. Play continues as long as your sentences hold out. The team with the most points wins.

You use the object form when the pronoun is a **direct object** or an **indirect object**—when the pronoun receives the action of a verb. You also use the object form when the pronoun is the **object of a preposition**—when it is part of a prepositional phrase.

Problems with object pronouns are most likely to occur when the object pronoun is part of a compound. Just remember—if the pronoun is used as an object, you must use the object form.

Direct Object	The painter ignored Lou and <u>me</u>.
Indirect Object	Mama gave <u>him</u> and <u>me</u> the dishes.
Object of Preposition	Daddy heard about <u>her</u> and <u>us</u>.

Exercise 2   Concept Check   For each sentence, choose the correct subject or object pronoun.

1. Lou stumbled when I nudged (he, him) in the ribs.
2. The first one to notice the painter lady was (I, me).
3. (She and I, Her and me) were enemies from the start.
4. (We, Us) and the twins stood around watching her work.
5. It was (they, them) who offered her some dinner.
6. I hoped my friends and (I, me) would get some cornbread.
7. Mama and (I, me) agreed that the lady was too fussy about her food.
8. Mama told (Lou and I, Lou and me) to stop criticizing her.
9. It was (we, us) who planned to spray paint the wall.
10. The finished mural amazed (he and I, him and me).

Exercise 3   Looking at Style   Professional writers sometimes use nonstandard pronoun forms. For example, in "The War of the Wall," "me and Lou" is the subject of several sentences.

1. Explain why "me and Lou" used as a subject is incorrect.
2. Do you think that the tone or mood of the story would change if it were rewritten with only correct pronoun forms? Why?
3. Why did the writer deliberately misuse pronouns?

◀ **BREAKING THE RULES**

Exercise 4   Revising Your Writing   Reread the autobiographical incident you wrote for the Writer's Workshop on pages 58–62, and lightly underline each personal pronoun you used. Correct any errors in the pronoun forms that you find.

HELP!

Here's an easy way to choose the right pronoun for a compound. Take out one part of the compound and see how the sentence sounds with only one pronoun.
The teacher smiled at Teresa and (me, I).
The teacher smiled at I. (This sounds wrong, and it is!)
The teacher smiled at me. (This sounds better; it's correct!)

LANGUAGE HANDBOOK
For review and practice: Section 5, Using Pronouns, pages 732–736.

Answers to Exercise 2
1. him
2. I
3. She and I
4. We
5. they
6. I
7. I
8. Lou and me
9. we
10. him and me

Answers to Exercise 3

1. "Me and Lou" is incorrectly used as a subject because *me* is the object form of the pronoun. The correct form is *I*.

2. If correct pronouns were used, the story would lose some of its appealing colorful details and natural dialogue.

3. The writer obviously wanted her characters to seem as realistic as possible. She wanted readers to feel that they were actually hearing the language of city kids.

Answers to Exercise 4

Answers will vary. Check students' writing to assess their grasp of the workshop lesson.

Closure

Remind students that the points made in the Language Workshop should prove especially useful as they revise their autobiographical incidents for correct pronoun usage.

Additional Practice

Choose the correct personal pronouns to complete these sentences. (Correct pronouns are underlined.)
1. Sue and (<u>I</u>, me) paddled down the river with George and Luis.
2. (<u>We</u>, Us) were in one canoe, and (<u>they</u>, them) were in another.
3. Then George and Luis hit some rapids. Luis called out to (I, <u>me</u>), "Help (we, <u>us</u>)!"
4. So (<u>we</u>, us) paddled around the rapids and saved (they, <u>them</u>).
5. It was (<u>I</u>, me) whom Luis had called, but he thanked both Sue and (I, <u>me</u>).
6. The next day the principal called Sue and (I, <u>me</u>) into her office.
7. (<u>She</u>, Her) had heard about the canoe accident.
8. The principal congratulated (she and I, <u>her and me</u>) for saving the boys.
9. "It is (<u>I</u>, me) who am truly grateful," said Luis.
10. "If you ever need help," added George, "just call Luis and (I, <u>me</u>)."

Objective

■ To learn how to make inferences while reading

Teaching Strategies

Remind students that to make an inference, they must use given facts and their own knowledge to make a logical guess. Caution them against making wild assumptions—their inferences should be firmly grounded in the evidence. Read students the following sentences, asking them to make inferences and support their guesses with facts.

The seventh-grade girls' basketball team has won all its games. Elizabeth is the best player both offensively and defensively.

(Logical inferences: Elizabeth makes a lot of baskets; she defends the basket well; she is probably fast.) Point out that an assumption such as "Elizabeth is tall" may be correct but is not supported by the facts given.

TEACHING TIP: LEP

Since the ability to make inferences depends on good reading skills, be sure to make provisions for LEP and at-risk students. Pairing such students with excellent readers or experienced classroom aides should make a great difference.

Have students make conscious efforts to draw inferences as they read. Remind them that whenever they use context clues or try to figure out why a character acts in a certain way, they are making inferences. Suggest that students jot down their inferences as they read and check the correctness of the inferences when they finish reading.

Answers to Exercise

1. He was a child, since there were Ghost-Slayer toys, posters, and comic books in "our bedroom."

2. The puppy made the noises; the clues are "yowling" and "clawing."

3. He thought a ghost made the noises, since the sounds were "eerie," the yowling and clawing could have been ghost or monster noises, and he knew nothing about the puppy.

READER'S WORKSHOP

INFERENCES

Making **inferences**—logical guesses based on facts—is an important reading skill. You already know how to do this mental detective work. As you were reading each selection, you picked up clues that let you understand what was going on. You made inferences about the setting, how the characters felt, and why they acted as they did.

For example, look at the paragraph below.

LITERARY MODEL
from "Homeless," by Anna Quindlen

▶ Her name was Ann, and we met in the Port Authority Bus Terminal several Januarys ago. I was doing a story on homeless people. She said I was wasting my time talking to her; she was just passing through, although she'd been passing through for more than two weeks. To prove to me that this was true, she rummaged through a tote bag and a manila envelope and finally unfolded a sheet of typing paper and brought out her photographs.

From the fact that the narrator was "doing a story on homeless people," you can infer that she is a newspaper or magazine writer. What can you infer about Ann from this paragraph?

IN OTHER CLASSES
In science class, skill at making inferences can help you form reasonable hypotheses based on your experiments or reading.

▶ **Exercise   Drawing Inferences**   Read the paragraph below. Then use inferences to answer the questions that follow it.

The night my brother heard the ghost, he and I had gone to bed early. Our bedroom, crammed with Ghost-Slayer toys and posters, was just above the garage. I had read a comic book and dropped off to sleep, but my brother lay awake, excited because the next day was his birthday. Neither of us knew that our parents had bought him a puppy and hidden it in the garage. So, in the middle of the night, when the eerie yowling and the sound of clawing began, my brother immediately assumed the worst.

1. Was the narrator an adult or a child at the time of this incident? On which facts can you base your inference?
2. What can you infer about the cause of the noises? Which clues tell you this?
3. What can you infer about what the brother thought? What evidence supports your inference?

ADDITIONAL RESOURCES
Unit One Resource Book
Reader's Workshop Practice, p. 43

Additional Practice

Draw at least one inference from each statement.

1. Rhonda is a scuba diver. She has a large collection of coral, shells, and sponges. *(Possible responses: She loves to swim and is good at it; she may have gathered the items in her collection herself.)*

2. Simon belongs to the school orchestra. He plays the cello, the violin, and the bass. *(Possible responses: He loves music, especially that played on stringed instruments; he is probably a good musician.)*

TUNNEL VISION

In medical terms, *tunnel vision* is a condition that limits what a person can see. People with this condition can only see what is directly in front of them—as if they were looking through a tube or a straw.

Sometimes, however, people act as if they have tunnel vision when their eyesight is perfectly normal. They seem to see the world from a very narrow point of view.

This kind of tunnel vision can be positive or negative—it can keep people focused on their goals, but it might also keep them from seeing something important that is right under their nose! In this subunit, you will discover many characters who have tunnel vision and you will decide whether it works for them or against them.

Observation Assessment

Observing how students respond to the text, to the classroom instruction, and to peers is an important part of an assessment program. The following suggestions and the forms in the *Guidelines for Reading and Literature Assessment* booklet can be used to implement observation assessment.

■ **Group Interaction** As students work through the subunit, assess how they interact in small-group and whole-class situations. Note whether students show courtesy and concern while others in the group express themselves. Also note how closely students listen to comments made by others. See if their own comments reflect an understanding of remarks made prior to their own. Throughout the subunit, watch for growth in students' abilities to listen carefully to others and to share their own thoughts with others.

Subunit Preview

Have students read the introduction to Subunit 2, "Tunnel Vision." Ask them to explain how tunnel vision is related to perspective. How is tunnel vision an example of limited perspective? What are advantages and disadvantages of this kind of perspective?

INTEGRATING THE LANGUAGE ARTS

The literary selections in this subunit focus on the theme of tunnel vision. Reading skills, literature skills, writing options, language study, vocabulary, and spelling skills are all based on these literary selections.

Writer's Workshop After reading several selections that deal with tunnel vision, students will use descriptive writing to review a restaurant or other eating place they know well.

Language Workshop The Language Workshop in this subunit deals with correct use of adjectives and adverbs. Students will discover how vivid adjectives and adverbs can lend a specific point of view to their descriptions.

Vocabulary Workshop The Vocabulary Workshop in this subunit deals with using context clues to figure out the meanings of unfamiliar words. Paying attention to context clues is a way for students to widen their perspectives when reading.

FOR ADDITIONAL CHALLENGE

The following selections offer challenge in exploring the subunit theme:

"The Speckled Band," short story by Sir Arthur Conan Doyle

"Pandora's Box," myth retold by Jay Macpherson

ADDITIONAL RESOURCES

Technology and Enrichment
Family and Community Involvement Source Book, page 7

Guidelines for Reading and Literature Assessment, Observation Assessment Forms

Objectives

- To understand and analyze a short story

- To examine characteristics of science fiction and to review the concept of setting

- To predict characters' actions and the outcome of a story

- To express understanding of the story through a choice of writing forms, including notes for a science fiction story, an explanation, a plan, and a description

Prereading/Motivation

Examine What You Know

Discussion Prompts Are your favorite foods sweet, juicy, spicy, hot, or sour? Do you crave the "bad stuff"—cookies and candy bars—or do you just adore roast beef and a baked potato?

Expand Your Knowledge

Additional Background Trying to be thin at all costs is costing women more than they think; most of the money spent on dieting in the United States is spent by women. Half of all U.S. women diet each year, but only a fourth of all men.

Enrich Your Reading

For Alternative Learning Styles Invite students to make a chart with headings like these:

What I Think   *What Happens*
Will Happen   *in the Story*

Ask them to jot down, as they read, predictions in the first column and what actually happens in the second column.

Thematic Link— Tunnel Vision

Lost in a sweet lover's paradise, Deb and Trinja are blinded by their passion for swoodies. Their tunnel vision prevents them from accepting the warning of Deb's brother, who believes that they and the rest of the population are being manipulated by aliens and are losing control over their lives.

Fiction

Lose Now, Pay Later

CAROL FARLEY

Examine What You Know   (Prior Knowledge)

Is there any one food that you simply cannot resist? For example, if a steaming hot pizza were put in front of you right now, could you turn away from it—even if you were on a diet? Think of your favorite foods and list them in your journal. Circle those that might cause you to lose your self-control.

Expand Your Knowledge
(Building Background)

Dieting is one of our society's greatest passions. At any given time, more than 20 million people in the United States are on a diet. In 1992, the amount of money spent on diet products and weight loss programs in the United States was about 36 billion dollars. Although Americans lose millions of pounds every year, only two to five percent of dieters do not regain the weight they lost. Most dieters try to lose weight rapidly, usually resulting in only a temporary victory.

Enrich Your Reading   (Reading Skill)

Predicting   Reading a story is more fun when you try to figure out what will happen next. For example, what do you think a story called "Lose Now, Pay Later" might be about? Use the title, pictures, and large blue quotes to make an educated guess. Then as you read the story, predict what the characters will do next. To make a prediction, think about what you've learned about the characters. Look for clues along the way. After you make your predictions, read on to see what actually happens.

■ *Author biography on Extend page*

JOURNAL WRITING IDEAS

■ What does the expression "You get what you pay for" mean? Did you ever get something free that turned out not to be a bargain after all?

■ Describe a time when you tried to resist a temptation, such as a favorite food. Why did you try to resist it? Did you succeed?

COLLABORATIVE LEARNING OPTIONS

Opportunities for collaborative learning include Options for Learning 1, 3, and 4 (p. 77) and Cross-Curricular Projects (p. 77).

ADDITIONAL RESOURCES

Unit One Resource Book
Reader's Guidesheet, p. 44
Reading Skills, p. 45
Literature Skills, p. 46
Vocabulary Connections, p. 47
Spelling Connections, p. 48
Comprehension and Vocabulary Check Tests, p. 49
Selection Test, pp. 50–51

Lose Now, Pay Later

CAROL FARLEY

I think my little brother is crazy. At least I hope he is. Because if his looney idea is right, then all of us are being used like a flock of sheep, and that's a pretty gruesome thought. Humans just can't be that stupid. My brother has a dumb idea, that's all. It's just a dumb idea.

This whole situation started about eight months ago. That's when I first knew anything about it, I mean. My best friend, Trinja, and I were shopping when we noticed a new store where an old insurance office used to be. It was a cubbyhole, really, at the far end of the mall where hardly anybody ever goes. We were there because we'd used that entrance as we came home from school.

"Swoodies!" Trinja said, pointing at the letters written across the display window. "What do you think they are, Deb?"

I stared through the glass. The place had always looked dim and dingy before, full of desks, half-dead plants, and bored-looking people; but now it was as bright and glaring as a Health Brigade Corp office. There weren't any people inside at all, but there were five or six gold-colored machines lining the walls. Signs were hung everywhere.

SWEETS PLUS GOODIES = SWOODIES, one said. Flavors were posted by each machine; peanut-butter-fudge-crunch . . . butter-rum-pecan . . . chocolate-nut-mint . . . Things like that. The biggest sign of all simply said FREE.

The place gave me the creeps . . .

I have to admit that the place gave me the creeps that first time I saw it. I don't know why. It just looked so bare and bright, so empty and clean, without any people or movement. The glare almost hurt my eyes. And I guess I was suspicious about anything that was completely free. Still, though, there was a terrific aroma drifting out of there—sort of a combination of all those flavors that were listed on the signs.

"Let's go in," Trinja said, grabbing my arm. I could see that the smell was getting to her too. She's always on a diet, so she thinks about food a lot.

"But it's so empty in there," I said, drawing away.

"They've just opened, that's all," she told me, yanking my arm again. "Besides, machines and robots run lots of the stores. Let's go inside and see what's in there."

◀ A

Words to Know and Use	**dingy** (din′ jē) *adj.* somewhat dark and unclean; shabby

69

LOSE NOW, PAY LATER **Teacher's Edition**   **69**

Teaching Strategies

VOCABULARY PREVIEW

These vocabulary words are defined at the bottom of the selection pages on which they appear.

binge a period of uncontrolled eating

consumption the act of eating or drinking

cubicle a small compartment

cull to remove an inferior item from a group

dingy unclean; shabby

gullible easily fooled

placid at peace

ravage to violently attack

stark completely

unnerve to make nervous

LIMITED ENGLISH PROFICIENCY

■ Use the Reader's Guidesheet, *Unit One Resource Book*, page 44.

■ This story is set in the future. Terms—such as *kitcho machine, heliobiles, calshow,* and *bodivision*—that refer to fictional futuristic objects may confuse some students. Students may also need help with slang and informal language.

★ Text annotations marked with a red star (2, 5, 10) may be particularly helpful for students with limited English proficiency.

TEXT ANNOTATIONS

1. LITERARY CONCEPT: Plot
Ask students why Farley might have opened her story with Deb's reference to her conflict with her brother but without giving any details. *(Possible responses: to arouse curiosity about a "gruesome" idea; to hint that something is wrong)*

2. LANGUAGE: Word Blends
Invite volunteers to write on the board "equations" that show how some words in use today are **blends** of other words.

Examples: breakfast + lunch = brunch; smoke + fog = smog; motor + hotel = motel. ★

Guided Reading for Less-Proficient Students

These questions can help guide students through the selection. Ask each question at the point in the selection where the capital letter and arrow appear in the margin. In addition, you may wish to use appropriate Active Reading annotations.

A. Why does the swoodie shop give Deb "the creeps" at first? *(It is too bright and clean; there are no people inside; she is suspicious because the swoodies are free.)* Recalling

B. What is it like to eat a swoodie? *(The texture is like a blend of ice cream and cooked pudding; eating a swoodie brings to mind happy memories associated with each flavor.)* Summarizing

C. What big questions about the swoodie shops are ignored? *(who put them there and why)* Recalling

Continued on page 70

SOFT FUR GOOD HUMOR 1963
Claes Oldenburg   Courtesy,
BlumHelman Gallery, New York.

Do you know that wonderful spurt of air that rushes out when you first open an expensive box of candy? The inside of that store smelled just like the inside of one of those boxes. For a few seconds we just stood there sniffing and grinning. My salivary glands started swimming.

Trinja turned toward the nearest machine. "Coconut-almond-marshmallow." She was almost drooling. "I've got to try one, Deb." She pressed the button, and a chocolate cone dropped down, like a coffee cup from a kitcho machine. Then a mixture, similar to the look of soft ice cream, filled it. "Want to try it with me?" she asked, reaching for the cone. We both took a taste.

It was absolutely the neatest sensation I've had in my whole life. Swoodies aren't cold like ice cream or warm like cooked pudding, but they're a blending of both in temperature and texture. The flavor melts instantly, and your whole mouth and brain are flooded with tastes and impressions. Like that first swoodie I tried, coconut-almond-marshmallow; suddenly, as my mouth separated the individual tastes, my brain burst into memories associated with each flavor. I felt as if I were lying on a warm beach, all covered with coconut suntan oil—then I heard myself giggling and singing as a group of us roasted marshmallows around a campfire—then I relived the long-ago moments of biting into the special Christmas cookies my grandmother made with almonds when I was little.

"Wow!" Trinja looked at me, and I could see that she had just experienced the same kind of reactions. We scarfed up the rest of that swoodie in just a few more bites, and we moved on to another flavor. With each

70   UNIT ONE   TUNNEL VISION

one it was the same. I felt a combination of marvelous tastes and joyous thoughts. We tried every flavor before we finally staggered out into the mall again.

"I'll have to diet for a whole year now," Trinja said, patting her stomach.

"I feel like a blimp myself," I told her, but neither one of us cared. We both felt terrific. "Go ahead in there," I called to some grade-school kids who were looking at the store. "You'll love those swoodies."

"It's a publicity stunt, we think," Trinja told them. "Everything is free in there."

In no time at all the news about the swoodie shop had spread all over town. But days passed, and still everything was absolutely free. Nobody knew who the new owners were or why they were giving away their product. Nobody cared. The mall directors said a check arrived to pay for the rent, and that was all they were concerned about. The Health Brigade Corp said swoodies were absolutely safe for human consumption.

Swoodies were still being offered free a month later, but the shop owners had still not appeared. By then nobody cared. There were always long lines of people in front of the place, but the swoodies tasted so good nobody minded waiting for them. And the supply was endless. Soon more shops like the first one began opening in other places around the city, with machines running in the same quiet, efficient way. And everything was still absolutely free.

Soon all of us were gaining weight like crazy.

"It's those darn swoodies," Trinja told me as we left the mall after our daily binge. "I can't leave them alone. Each one must have a thousand calories, but I still pig out on them."

I sighed as I walked out into the sunshine. "Me too. If only there was some easy way to eat all the swoodies we want and still not gain any weight!"

The words were hardly out of my mouth when I noticed a new feature in the mall parking lot. Among all the usual heliobiles there was a tall white plastic box, sort of like those big telephone booths you see in old pictures. A flashing sign near the booth said THE SLIMMER. A short, thin woman was standing beside it. She was deeply tanned, and her head was covered with a green turban almost the same color as the jumpsuit she was wearing.

Trinja looked at the sign, then glanced at the woman. "What's that mean?"

"It means that this machine can make you slimmer," the woman answered. She had a deep, strange-sounding voice. "Just step inside, and you'll lose unwanted fat."

She seemed so serious and confident that I was startled. In the old days people thought they could lose weight in a hurry, but those of us who live in 2041 aren't that gullible. No pills or packs or wraps or special twenty-four-hour diets can work. There isn't any easy way to get rid of fat, and that's all there is to it. I knew this booth was a scam or a joke of some kind, but the woman acted as if it were a perfectly respectable thing. Her seriousness sort of unnerved me. I looked into the booth half

Words to Know and Use	**consumption** (kən sump' shən) *n.* the act of eating or drinking **binge** (binj) *n.* a period of uncontrolled eating or drinking **gullible** (gul' ə bəl) *adj.* easily fooled or tricked **unnerve** (un nurv') *v.* to take away courage; to make nervous

71

6. LITERARY CONCEPT: Character
Ask students in what ways Deb and Trinja seem like kids they know. *(Possible responses: They like to shop or hang out at a mall; they worry about their weight; they are best friends who are always together; they use slang.)*

7. ACTIVE READING: Connect
Ask students what in our world the Health Brigade Corp is similar to. *(Possible responses: the U.S. Food and Drug Administration, consumer agencies that check the safety of new food products)*

8. ACTIVE READING: Review
Ask students to **summarize** how swoodies have changed people's lives. *(People stand in long lines at the swoodies shop, but don't complain at all; no one cares where swoodies come from; everyone is gaining weight; Deb and Trinja binge on swoodies daily.)* Have students **draw conclusions** about what is happening to people. *(Possible responses: They are abandoning common sense in pursuit of swoodies; they seem unable to control themselves.)*

Looking at Style

Ask students to identify and define the slang expressions in the following sentences:

- We scarfed up the rest of that swoodie. . . . (p. 70)
- "Each one must have a thousand calories, but I still pig out on them." (p. 71)
- "I think that woman was wacko . . . ." (p. 72)

Then ask the following questions:

1. How does Carol Farley's use of slang help sharpen the picture of Deb and Trinja?

2. Do you think people in 2041 will use the same slang as people today?

Invite students to invent futuristic slang expressions to replace this twentieth-century slang.

9. ACTIVE READING: Question

Why are prices in yen—Japanese money? *(Possible responses: Japan now controls the world's economy; the world has converted to a single currency, the yen.)*

10. LANGUAGE: Nonstandard Usage

Point out that authors sometimes use nonstandard English to make dialogue sound realistic. Ask students to suggest some standard alternatives. *(Do you have any money? Have you got any money?)* ★

11. ACTIVE READING: Evaluate

Ask students to **review** what they know about the woman in green and to decide whether she seems trustworthy. If necessary, help students by reading the following example of a think-aloud, or model one of your own.

Think-Aloud Script The woman is really skinny herself. She sure seems confident—even when the girls laugh at her, she doesn't drop her act. Maybe she's just a good salesperson. On the other hand, she never smiles, and there's something weird about the tone of her voice. The way she pushes Deb is scary, since at first she acted as if she didn't care if they tried the slimmer or not. I am suspicious of her. She seems bossy and cold and kind of mean.

expecting someone to jump out laughing. But it was empty, <u>stark</u> white, and, except for some overhead grill work, it was completely smooth and bare.

"How can a thing like this make you slimmer?" I asked.

The woman shrugged. "A new process. Do you care to try? Twenty-five yen to lose one pound of body fat."

Trinja and I both burst into laughter. "And how long is it before the pound disappears?" she asked.

The woman never even cracked a smile. "Instantly. Body fat is gone instantly." She gestured to a small lever on the side nearest to her. "I regulate the power flow according to your payment."

My mouth dropped open. "But that's impossible! No exercise? No chemicals? No starving on a retreat week?"

"No." The woman folded her arms and leaned against the smooth white sides of her <u>cubicle</u>, as if she didn't much care whether we tried her new process or not. Trinja and I stared at each other. I was wondering if the woman had tried her machine herself—she didn't have an ounce of fat.

"You got any money?" I asked Trinja. As she was shaking her head, I was rummaging through my pack. "I've got a hundred and thirty yen."

"Five pounds then," the woman said, taking my money with one hand and setting her lever with the other. She literally pushed me into the booth, and the door slammed behind me.

At first I wanted to scream because I was so scared.

At first I wanted to scream because I was so scared. The whole thing had happened too fast. I wanted to prove that this woman and her slimmer were a big joke, but suddenly I was trapped in a coffinlike structure as bare and as bright as an old microwave oven. My heart was hammering, and the hair on the back of my neck stood up straight. I opened my mouth, but before I could scream, there was a loud humming sound, and instantly the door flew open again. I saw Trinja's frightened face peering in at me.

"Are you all right, Deb? Are you okay? I guess she decided not to do anything after all. You ought to get your money back."

"Five pounds are gone," the woman said in her strange voice.

Trinja pulled me away. "I'll just bet!" she shouted back at the woman. "Somebody ought to report you and that phony machine! We might even call the Health Brigade Corp!" She leaned closer to me. "Are you really okay, Deb?"

I took a deep breath. "My jeans feel loose."

Frowning, Trinja shook her head. "It's just your imagination, that's all. What a fake! I think that woman was wacko, Debbie, really weird. The only thing slimmer after a treatment like that is your bank account. Nobody but nobody can lose weight that easily. We'll go to my house,

Words to Know and Use
stark (stärk) *adv.* entirely; completely
cubicle (kyōō′ bi kəl) *n.* a small compartment used for work or sleep

72

and you can weigh yourself. You haven't lost an ounce."

But Trinja was wrong. I really *was* five pounds lighter. I know it sounds impossible, but Trinja's calshow is never wrong. The two of us hopped and howled with joy. Then we ravaged her bedroom trying to find some more money. We ran all the way back to the mall, worrying all the way that the woman and her miracle machine might have disappeared. But the slimmer was still there. Within minutes Trinja had used up her three hundred yen, and she looked terrific.

"I can't believe it! I just can't believe it!" she kept saying as she notched her belt tighter. "Twelve pounds gone in seconds!"

"For safety's sake I'll have to prick your wrist, my dear," the woman said. "For every ten pounds you lose we give a tiny little mark. Nobody will ever notice it."

"It didn't even hurt," Trinja said as we walked home. And neither of us could see the tiny blue pinprick unless we looked closely. We were both so happy about the weight loss that we almost floated. All our worries and problems about calories and fat and diets were over forever.

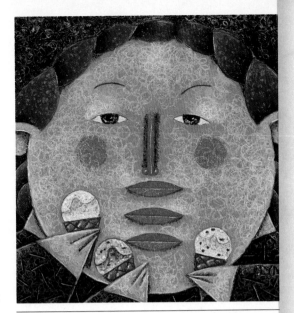

Illustration by Lynn Rowe Reed.

*N*ow there's hardly a fat person left . . .

In no time at all the slimmers were all over the city, near all the swoodie stores. They've been a real blessing. Everybody says so. Now there's hardly a fat person left

on the streets. A few people have so many blue marks on their wrists that you can see them, but most have just four or five pinpricks.

◄ E

Nobody really understands how these slimmers work. The attendants, all just as strange sounding as the woman in our mall, get so technical in their explanations that none of us can follow the principles they're talking about, so we don't much worry about it. The process has something to do with invisible waves that can change fat cells into energy, which then radiates away from the body.

"I don't care how the slimmers work," Trinja says happily. "Now I can eat swoodies all day long if I want, and I never gain an ounce. That's all I care about."

Everybody feels that way, I guess. We're

13

73

Speaking...Listening...Viewing

14

14. ACTIVE READING: Question
Ask students if they can think of other explanations of why there is nothing about the swoodies or the slimmers in the media. *(Possible responses: Journalists are as thrilled with the swoodies and slimmers as everyone else; governments have censored mention of them; the owners of the shops and machines control the media.)*

15. LITERARY CONCEPT: Character
Ask students what purpose the character of Trevor serves in the story. *(Possible response: to provide an objective view of the swoodies and slimmers; to offer contrast to characters who are obsessed with the machines)*

16. ACTIVE READING: Predict
Ask students to speculate about what it might take to arouse more suspicions about the swoodies and the slimmers. *(Possible responses: for people's wrists to become solid blue with marks; for people to start disappearing because they are being "culled")*

ENCOURAGING INDEPENDENT READING

The Garden Is Doing Fine, a novel by Carol Farley

This Star Shall Abide, a novel by Sylvia Louise Engdahl

The White Mountains, a novel by John Christopher

Z for Zachariah, a novel by Robert C. O'Brien

---

14 too happy to want to upset anything by asking questions. Maybe that's why you don't hear about the swoodies or slimmers on the fax or the bodivision or read about them anywhere. Nobody understands them well enough to sound very intelligent about them. But people all over Earth are beginning to use them. My cousin in Tokyo faxed to say that they have them in her area now and people there are just as happy as we are.

Except for my brother, Trevor. He's not the least bit happy, he says. Of course, few ten-year-olds worry about weight, so he doesn't know the joy of being able to eat everything in sight and still stay thin.

"Suppose the swoodies and the slimmers are run by aliens from outer space," he says. "From lots farther than we've been able to go. Maybe they have big starships posted around Earth, and they're gathering up the energy from human fat that's sent up from the slimmers. Maybe the swoodies are here so people will get fat quicker so that there'll be more to harvest through the slimmer machines. Then they'll take the fat back to

F ▶ their planet and use it as fuel."

"That's the dumbest thing I ever heard of!" Trinja has told him. "Why don't we hear about the spaceships, then? Why doesn't the Health Brigade Corp tell us to stop doing this if it isn't good for us?"

Trevor thinks he has the answers. He says the spaceships are invisible to human detection, and he says the aliens have hypnotized **15** our leaders into being as calm and placid as we all are. The blue marks on our wrists play a big role. He says maybe after each of us has had so many blue marks, we'll be culled from the flock because our fat content won't be as good anymore.

He's crazy, isn't he? He must think we all have the brains of sheep. Ten-year-old brothers can be a real pain. He simply doesn't know people yet, that's all. Humans would never sacrifice their freedom and dignity just so they could eat and still be thin. Even aliens ought to know that.

I could quit eating swoodies and using those slimmers any time I want to.

But all those little blue marks Trinja and I have are beginning to look like delicate tattooed bracelets, and we both think they look really neat on our wrists. **16** ✤

Words to Know and Use

74

placid (plas' id) *adj.* calm; at peace
cull (kul) *v.* to remove from a group something or someone that is not as good as the rest

---

Comprehension Check

1. When does the story take place? *(the year 2041)*

2. How much do swoodies cost, and how many are there? *(Swoodies are free, and the supply is endless.)*

3. What do slimmers do? *(remove body fat instantly)*

4. Why do Deb and Trinja like the slimmers? *(They can eat swoodies all day and not gain weight.)*

5. What signs show that people have used the slimmers? *(blue marks on their wrists)*

6. What does Trevor think the purpose of swoodies and slimmers is? *(Space aliens are using them to gather human fat to use as fuel.)*

Responding to Reading

First Impressions

1. What were your thoughts as you finished reading this story? Write your reactions in your journal.

Second Thoughts

2. Are Deb and Trinja right to reject Trevor's theory?

> **Think about**
> - how most of the people react to swoodies and slimmers
> - what Deb says about her little brother
> - the title of the story

3. At the end of the story, Deb says, "Humans would never sacrifice their freedom and dignity just so they could eat and still be thin." Do you agree? Explain your opinion using evidence from the story and your own experience.

4. Which **characters** in this story have tunnel vision? Explain the effects their tunnel vision has on them.

Broader Connections

5. Nowadays, there are advertisements in newspapers and on television for products that may be unhealthy or unsafe. While some people believe that these ads should be banned, others feel that consumers should make their own decisions. Explain your opinion on this issue, using examples from the story and your own experiences.

Literary Concept: Science Fiction

"Lose Now, Pay Later" is a work of **science fiction**. Science fiction stories are frequently based on possible scientific developments and are usually set in the future. Often, realistic characters with attitudes and values of present-day society are projected into an imaginary future world. This lets the reader examine current values in a different setting. What values of our society are reflected in this story? How do you know?

Concept Review: Setting Science fiction writers sometimes use imaginary terms and inventions to set their stories in the future. Find several examples of this in "Lose Now, Pay Later."

LOSE NOW, PAY LATER   75

Student Response

Responding to Reading

1. Any response is valid.

2. Possible responses: Yes, everyone, including the Health Brigade Corp, seems to think that swoodies and slimmers are great; yes, there is no reason to believe a ten-year-old boy with a ridiculous "alien" theory; no, Trevor is the only character who can see the truth, since he isn't hooked on swoodies or worried about his weight; no, the title suggests there will be a price to pay.

3. Possible responses: No, because the characters in the story have already given up some freedom and dignity for swoodies and slimmers; in real life many people are hooked on things that offer instant gratification but are not good for them (drugs, alcohol, cigarettes, certain foods); real people often give up dignity because of an inability to control their appetites.

4. Possible responses: Deb, Trinja, and other swoodie lovers have tunnel vision; they spend their days waiting to eat swoodies and going to slimmers and lose their ability to think critically. Trevor has tunnel vision that causes him to make up a crazy explanation for the swoodies and slimmers.

5. Possible responses: Consumers should make up their own minds, but ads and labels should give complete information about products; consumers don't have the time and equipment to test all products, so ads for unsafe products should be banned; people should have the freedom to make their own choices without government interference.

Challenge Question

Do you think Deb's behavior is typical of someone who has a serious addiction? Explain, using evidence from the story. (*Possible responses: Yes, she is unable to stop eating swoodies but believes she can stop if she wants to; her unwillingness to believe Trevor could be seen as denial. No, she just likes sweets, as everyone else seems to; if she is an addict, everyone else is one too.*)

Literary Concept: Science Fiction

Possible responses: We love to indulge ourselves, like eating swoodies; we want quick solutions to problems, as in slimmers; we value thinness (slimmers); we want things free (swoodies); we don't question things that please us.

Concept Review: Setting Coffee is dispensed from a *kitcho machine* (p. 70), the mall parking lot is full of *heliobiles* (p. 71), Deb checks her weight with Trinja's *calshow* (p. 73), and people watch the news on the *bodivision* (p. 74).

Writing Options

The Writing Options are designed to meet varied student interests and abilities. Have students choose one writing activity to complete.

Journal Update Invite students to return to their journal entries for "Lose Now, Pay Later" and write responses to the following: How do you feel and what do you think when someone offers you a "freebie"?

Links to Writer's Craft

Writing Option 4 is an exercise in personal writing. For more practice, see *The Writer's Craft,* Grade 7, "Observation and Description," pages 48–68.

Vocabulary Practice

Answers to Exercise

1. Antonyms	6. Synonyms
2. Antonyms	7. Synonyms
3. Synonyms	8. Synonyms
4. Antonyms	9. Antonyms
5. Antonyms	10. Synonyms

For Alternative Learning Styles

Have students think of other words in the word families of *consumption* and *unnerve (consumer, consume, nerve, nervous).* Ask someone to display facial expressions reflecting the meanings of the words *placid, gullible,* and *unnerved.*

Closure

Tell students that in the remainder of this subunit they will meet other characters who see only what they want to see.

Demonstrate tunnel vision by having students hold a rolled sheet of paper up to one eye while closing the other. Have students look through this "tunnel," and ask whether they would like to walk home that way. Point out that a narrow focus can keep people from seeing what matters.

Writing Options

1. If you were to write your own science fiction story, what would be the setting? Write **notes** that you could develop into a science fiction story of your own.

2. Assume that Trevor's theory is wrong. Write your own **explanation** of the swoodie and slimmer machines.

3. Assume that Trevor's theory is right. Write the **plan** that the aliens are using to obtain all the fat they need from humans. Add steps to the plan that Trevor was unable to guess.

4. Reread the description of how swoodies taste. Then write a detailed **description** of your own favorite snack for someone who has never tried the snack.

Vocabulary Practice

Exercise Decide if the following pairs of words are synonyms (words that have the same meaning) or antonyms (words that have opposite meanings). On a separate sheet of paper, identify each pair as *Synonyms* or *Antonyms.*

1. gullible—suspicious
2. consumption—production
3. ravage—wreck
4. placid—disturbed
5. unnerve—comfort
6. stark—completely
7. cull—select
8. binge—spree
9. dingy—clean
10. cubicle—compartment

Words to Know and Use

**binge
consumption
cubicle
cull
dingy
gullible
placid
ravage
stark
unnerve**

The Spelling Connection

Spelling Pattern: 1 + 1 + 1 Words A word that has 1 syllable, 1 vowel, and 1 final consonant is called a 1 + 1 + 1 word. In such words, the last consonant is doubled before a suffix beginning with a vowel but not before a suffix beginning with a consonant.

Examples: plan/planning   fit/fitter/fitness

1 + 1 + 1 Words from the Selection
fat/fatter/fatness   slim/slimmer/slimness
run/runner/running   slam/slammed/slamming

Other 1 + 1 + 1 Words
ship/shipped/shipment   sad/saddest/sadness
grab/grabbed/grabbing   slip/slipped/slippery
jog/jogged/jogging

Exercise Add needed letters to complete words.
The dieters group met to discuss their __ ness. Their goal was to become __ er by ten pounds each. Twice a week they went __ ing together. Anyone who __ ed off his or her diet was chided by everyone else.

Options for Learning (Multimodal/Cross-Curricular Activities)

1 • Be Fat — Be Fit Plan and perform a radio ad for either swoodies or the slimmer. Use descriptive words that appeal to the senses.

2 • Mechanical Drawings Make a drawing or painting of one of the machines described in this story.

3 • Inventions of Tomorrow Think up your own marvelous invention for the future. Design and sketch your invention and present it to the class. Explain what it will do and how it will help people.

4 • Any Connection? Check through a current newspaper and count the total number of advertisements. As you go through the ads, jot down how many are related to weight-loss programs or products, and how many are for the food industry (restaurants, bakeries, supermarkets, and so on). Using a calculator, divide the number of each kind of ad by the total number of ads and multiply both results by 100. Report your final figures, which will be the percentages of the newspaper's ads that are devoted to food and weight loss in that paper.

 FACT FINDER SCIENCE
How many calories do you have to burn to lose one pound?

Carol Farley
1936-

For Carol Farley, writing is an extension of what she always loved about school. She says that her "happiest memories of school years are centered on classes I had in literature when we read fiction and talked about what we had read."

Farley has done many things besides write, however. She has taught school, picked fruit, and sold women's clothing. As an army wife, she once moved thirteen times in fifteen years. Her varied experiences have taught her that "we all look at life from our own viewpoint, often unaware or unconcerned about the views of others." Such concerns prompt her to write stories like "Lose Now, Pay Later" to show "that sometimes small children—like the boy in the story about the emperor's new clothes (or lack of them)—are the first to notice and report on something that is perfectly obvious."

LOSE NOW, PAY LATER   77

Extending the Lesson

Options for Learning
These activities suit a variety of learning styles and modes of expression.

Collaborative Learning Activities
See Options 1, 3, and 4.

1. Be Fat—Be Fit Suggest that students recall and discuss familiar radio ads to get ideas. Point out that a script will be necessary for smooth performance.

2. Mechanical Drawings Have students refer to the brief descriptions of swoodie and kitcho machines on pages 69 and 70 and of the slimmer on pages 71 and 72. No descriptions of heliobiles and the calshows are given, so students must envision them.

3. Inventions of Tomorrow Suggest that students find ideas by considering the problems of society and then imagining machines that might solve them.

4. Any Connection Suggest that students work in small groups, dividing their newspapers into sections to share the task of counting ads.

 FACT FINDER SCIENCE
Students can refer to an encyclopedia or a book about nutrition or dieting to find that a person must burn about 3,500 calories to lose one pound.

Carol Farley

■ More About the Author Carol Farley notes, "Writing helps me bring order to what seems to be chaotic existence. I marvel that so many people seem content to float across the surface of life without ever delving deeply. . . ." The mother of four children, Ms. Farley likes writing for young people "because they're eager to try to understand the unknowable too."

■ Other Works Novels: *Mystery of the Fog Man, The Garden Is Doing Fine, Loosen Your Ears, Settle Your Fidgets*

 ■ Awards Franklin Watts Mystery Medal; Golden Kite Award, Society of Children's Book Writers; Wel-Met Children's Book Award, Child Association of America; IRA/CBC Children's Choice Book.

Cross-Curricular Projects

Health Invite volunteers to make a food chart showing the vitamins and calories supplied by various types of food. Other students can make an exercise chart that shows how many minutes of different exercises are needed to burn off 100 calories.

Science/Social Studies Have students imagine that teenagers from 1930 have traveled through time to visit our world. Ask students to list technological advances that will surprise these time travelers. Have them discuss whether the travelers will think that our gadgets have changed people's attitudes and values.

Art Ask students to imagine that they have been hired to design sets and costumes for a play based on "Lose Now, Pay Later." Encourage them to draw futuristic designs for the mall and the costumes.

Objectives

- To understand and analyze a short story

- To examine a writer's use of point of view

- To use reviewing while reading to improve understanding

- To express understanding of the story through a choice of writing forms, including a journal entry and an explanation

Prereading/Motivation

Examine What You Know

Discussion prompts What caused you to miss school? Did you enjoy having a day away from school, or was the whole day miserable? What did you do that day?

Expand Your Knowledge

Additional Background One form of rheumatism is called rheumatoid arthritis, a disease that affects about 200,000 Americans under the age of 16. Extreme cases of this disease can lead to crippling or deformity of the joints. Another type of rheumatism is rheumatic fever, which is brought on by bacteria and can lead to heart failure or death.

Thematic Link— Tunnel Vision

The narrator yearns for a day off from school after he sees a sick neighbor boy fishing. Through tunnel vision and a lively imagination, he persuades himself that he has the same disease and has to come home from school. Members of his family also have tunnel vision—they see only the boy's antics and not his needs.

Fiction

Stolen Day

SHERWOOD ANDERSON

Examine What You Know (Prior Knowledge)

A missed day at school can be many things. You might be happy to miss school, or nervous about missing assignments, or you might just be too sick to care! Think about times when you have missed school. How did you feel? Compare your reactions with your classmates'.

Expand Your Knowledge (Building Background)

In this selection, a neighbor of the narrator suffers from an illness called inflammatory rheumatism. Rheumatism is a general name for several painful conditions that make a person's joints and muscles hurt, swell up, and get stiff, so that it is hard to move. Although most people think only the elderly have rheumatism, children can get it too. When that happens, the children may have to miss weeks or months of school, as well as undergo special medical treatments.

■ *Author biography in Reader's Handbook*

Write Before You Read (Journal Writing)

In your journal or on a separate piece of paper, tell about the last time you missed school. Include all the details—Why couldn't you go to school? What happened when you returned to class?

MORE JOURNAL WRITING IDEAS

■ Use the title and clues you already have about the story to predict what it might be about.

■ What is a "stolen day"? From whom or what would you steal it?

COLLABORATIVE LEARNING OPTIONS

Opportunities for collaborative learning include Examine What You Know (above) and Literary Concept (p. 83).

ADDITIONAL RESOURCES

Unit One Resource Book
Reader's Guidesheet, p. 52
Reading Skills, p. 53
Literature Skills, p. 54
Vocabulary Connections, p. 55
Spelling Connections, p. 56
Comprehension Test, p. 57
Selection Test, p. 58

Stolen Day

SHERWOOD ANDERSON

It must be that all children are actors. The whole thing started with a boy on our street named Walter, who had inflammatory rheumatism. That's what they called it. He didn't have to go to school.

Still, he could walk about. He could go fishing in the creek or the waterworks pond. There was a place up at the pond where in the spring the water came tumbling over the dam and formed a deep pool. It was a good place. Sometimes you could get some big ones there.

I went down that way on my way to school one spring morning. It was out of my way but I wanted to see if Walter was there.

He was, inflammatory rheumatism and all. There he was, sitting with a fish pole in his hand. He had been able to walk down there all right.

1

A ▶

It was then that my own legs began to hurt. My back, too. I went on to school but, at the recess time, I began to cry. I did it when the teacher, Sarah Suggett, had come out into the schoolhouse yard.

She came right over to me.

"I ache all over," I said. I did, too.

I kept on crying and it worked all right.

"You'd better go on home," she said.

So I went. I limped painfully away. I kept on limping until I got out of the schoolhouse street.

Then I felt better. I still had inflammatory rheumatism pretty bad but I could get along better.

I must have done some thinking on the way home.

"I'd better not say I have inflammatory rheumatism," I decided. "Maybe if you've got that, you swell up."

Why doesn't the boy want to say he has the disease?

review **2**

I thought I'd better go around to where Walter was and ask him about that, so I did—but he wasn't there.

"They must not be biting today," I thought.

I had a feeling that, if I said I had inflammatory rheumatism, Mother or my brothers and my sister Stella might laugh. They did laugh at me pretty often, and I didn't like it at all.

3

"Just the same," I said to myself, "I have got it." I began to hurt and ache again.

I went home and sat on the front steps of our house. I sat there a long time. There wasn't anyone at home but Mother and the two little ones. Ray would have been four or five then and Earl might have been three.

It was Earl who saw me there. I had got tired of sitting and was lying on the porch. Earl was always a quiet, solemn little fellow.

He must have said something to Mother, for presently she came.

STOLEN DAY   79

Teaching Strategies

VOCABULARY PREVIEW

The focus of vocabulary study for this selection is on the use of context clues to understand colloquialisms. See Vocabulary Connections, *Unit One Resource Book*, p. 55.

LIMITED ENGLISH PROFICIENCY

■ Use the Reader's Guidesheet, *Unit One Resource Book*, page 52.

■ The narrator of this story uses colloquialisms that reflect the speech patterns of the rural Midwest in the early part of this century. You may wish to read certain passages aloud to students to help clarify meanings.

★ Text annotations marked with a red star (6, 9) may be particularly helpful for students with limited English proficiency.

TEXT ANNOTATIONS

1. LITERARY CONCEPT: Point of View
Ask who is telling this story and what pronouns are used to identify the narrator. *(A schoolboy is the narrator; I and my are used to identify him.)*

2. ACTIVE READING: Review
Why doesn't the boy want to say he has the disease? *(Possible response: He is unsure of its symptoms and is afraid people won't believe him.)*

3. ACTIVE READING: Connect
Ask students how the narrator feels about his family's treatment of him and whether they would feel the same way. *(Possible responses: His family laughs at him, which he doesn't like; no one enjoys being embarrassed.)*

Guided Reading for Less-Proficient Students

These questions can help students through the reading. Ask each question at the point of the selection where the capital letter and arrow appear in the margin. In addition, you may wish to use appropriate Active Reading annotations.

A. Why does the boy suddenly have pains in his legs and back? *(He imagines he is sick like Walter.)* Inferring

B. What does the narrator hear about inflammatory rheumatism that frightens him? *(The disease affects the heart.)* Recalling

C. How does the boy's mother react to his coming home? Why? *(She does not show deep concern. She may suspect that the boy is not really ill.)* Drawing conclusions

Continued on page 80

4. ACTIVE READING: Question
Does the boy actually believe he has inflammatory rheumatism? (Possible responses: Yes, he thinks his racing heartbeat was caused by rheumatism; no, he's just grasping for reasons to believe it.)

5. LITERARY CONCEPT:
Characterization
Ask students why the mother appeared so unconcerned about her son. (Possible responses: She did not believe he was really sick; she was too busy to pay much attention to him.) What did the boy want his mother to do? (to worry about him; to reassure him; to pay attention to him)

6. VOCABULARY: Colloquialisms
Some students may have difficulty understanding the expressions on this page ("sore at Mother," "I'd pitch forward," "I'd drown sure"). Point out that these expressions are Midwestern small-town dialect used in the early part of the century. As necessary, help students use **prior knowledge** or **context clues** to figure out what the terms mean. (angry with Mother; I would fall forward; I would surely drown) ★

"What's the matter with you? Why aren't you in school?" she asked.

I came pretty near telling her right out that I had inflammatory rheumatism, but I thought I'd better not. Mother and Father had been speaking of Walter's case at the table just the day before. "It affects the heart," Father had said. That frightened me when I thought of it. "I might die," I thought. "I might just suddenly die right here; my heart might stop beating."

B ▶

On the day before, I had been running a race with my brother Irve. We were up at the fairgrounds after school, and there was a half-mile track.

"I'll bet you can't run a half mile," he said. "I bet you I could beat you running clear around the track."

And so we did it and I beat him, but afterward my heart did seem to beat pretty hard. I remembered that, lying there on the porch. "It's a wonder, with my inflammatory rheumatism and all, I didn't just drop down dead," I thought. The thought frightened me a lot. I ached worse than ever.

"I ache, Ma," I said. "I just ache."

She made me go in the house and upstairs and get into bed.

It wasn't so good. It was spring. I was up there for perhaps an hour, maybe two, and then I felt better.

I got up and went downstairs. "I feel better, Ma," I said.

Mother said she was glad. She was pretty busy that day and hadn't paid much attention to me. She had made me get into bed upstairs and then hadn't even come up to see how I was.

I didn't think much of that when I was up

there; but when I got downstairs where she was, and when, after I had said I felt better and she only said she was glad and went right on with her work, I began to ache again.

I thought, "I'll bet I die of it. I bet I do."

I went out to the front porch and sat down. I was pretty sore at Mother.

"If she really knew the truth, that I have inflammatory rheumatism and I may just drop down dead any time, I'll bet she wouldn't care about that either," I thought.

I was getting more and more angry the more thinking I did.

"I know what I'm going to do," I thought; "I'm going to go fishing."

I thought that, feeling the way I did, I might be sitting on the high bank just above the deep pool where the water went over the dam, and suddenly my heart would stop beating.

And then, of course, I'd pitch forward, over the bank into the pool; and, if I wasn't dead when I hit the water, I'd drown sure.

They would all come home to supper and they'd miss me.

"But where is he?"

Then Mother would remember that I'd come home from school aching.

She'd go upstairs, and I wouldn't be there. One day during the year before, there was a child got drowned in a spring. It was one of the Wyatt children.

Right down at the end of the street there was a spring under a birch tree, and there had been a barrel sunk in the ground.

Everyone had always been saying the spring ought to be kept covered, but it wasn't.

◀ C
5

6

Guided Reading for Less-Proficient Students

Continued from page 79

D. What does the boy catch? (a huge carp)
Recalling

E. What makes the boy feel sick at the end of the story? (His family laughs at his supposed illness.)
Drawing Conclusions

Illustration by David Barnett.

7. ACTIVE READING: Review
Ask students what caused the boy to remember this incident from the past. *(He is upset that his mother ignored him and remembers a time when she was very concerned; he's going fishing alone and worries that something bad may happen.)*

8. ACTIVE READING: Review
What has the boy imagined? *(his own death as a drowning victim, resulting from inflammatory rheumatism)*

9. VOCABULARY: Colloquialisms
Point out the colloquialisms on this page ("making for," "turn out," "lit out") and ask students to paraphrase them. *(heading for, appear, left quickly)* ★

So the Wyatt child went down there, played around alone, and fell in and got drowned.

Mother was the one who had found the drowned child. She had gone to get a pail of water, and there the child was, drowned and dead.

This had been in the evening when we were all at home, and Mother had come running up the street with the dead, dripping child in her arms. She was making for the Wyatt house as hard as she could run, and she was pale.

She had a terrible look on her face, I remembered then.

"So," I thought, "they'll miss me, and there'll be a search made. Very likely there'll be someone who has seen me sitting by the pond fishing, and there'll be a big alarm and all the town will turn out and they'll drag the pond."[1]

What has the boy imagined?

review

I was having a grand time, having died. Maybe, after they found me and had got me out of the deep pool, Mother would grab me up in her arms and run home with me as she had run with the Wyatt child.

I got up from the porch and went around the house. I got my fishing pole and lit out

---

1. drag the pond: pull a net over the bottom to find the body of a drowning victim.

Looking at Style

These ideas may be helpful for discussing Anderson's writing style in "Stolen Day."

Read aloud the first five paragraphs of the story. Then have students answer these questions.

1. Why doesn't Anderson tell us who the narrator is right away?

2. How old do you think the narrator is, based on the language that he uses?

3. How does the writer make it seem as if the narrator is speaking directly to you, as though you were one of his friends or classmates?

4. If you wanted to make this story sound more modern, how would you change the opening paragraphs? Explain.

11. ACTIVE READING: Predict
Ask students what they think will spoil the boy's day. *(Any response is valid.)* Encourage students to explain their predictions.

12. ACTIVE READING: Evaluate
Do you feel sorry for the boy at the end? Why or why not? *(Yes, he's been ridiculed by his family; no, he's acted silly and deserves to be laughed at.)*

ENCOURAGING INDEPENDENT READING

"A Day's Wait," short story by Ernest Hemingway

A Hero Ain't Nothin' but a Sandwich, a novel by Alice Childress

Winesburg, Ohio, collection of short stories by Sherwood Anderson

for the pool below the dam. Mother was busy—she always was—and didn't see me go. When I got there, I thought I'd better not sit too near the edge of the high bank.

By this time I didn't ache hardly at all, but I thought,

"With inflammatory rheumatism you can't tell," I thought.

"It probably comes and goes," I thought.

"Walter has it and he goes fishing," I thought.

I had got my line into the pool and suddenly I got a bite. It was a regular whopper; I knew that. I'd never had a bite like that.

I knew what it was. It was one of Mr. Fenn's big carp.

Mr. Fenn was a man who had a big pond of his own. He sold ice in the summer, and the pond was to make the ice. He had bought some big carp and put them into his pond; and then, earlier in the spring when there was a freshet, his dam had gone out.

So the carp had got into our creek, and one or two big ones had been caught—but none of them by a boy like me.

The carp was pulling and I was pulling and I was afraid he'd break my line, so I just tumbled down the high bank, holding onto the line and got right into the pool. We had it out, there in the pool. We struggled. We wrestled. Then I got a hand under his gills and got him out.

He was a big one all right. He was nearly half as big as I was myself. I had him on the bank and I kept one hand under his gills and I ran.

I never ran so hard in my life. He was slippery, and now and then he wriggled out of my arms; once I stumbled and fell on him, but I got him home.

So there it was. I was a big hero that day. Mother got a washtub and filled it with water. She put the fish in it, and all the neighbors came to look. I got into dry clothes and went down to supper—and then I made a break that spoiled my day.

There we were, all of us, at the table, and suddenly Father asked what had been the matter with me at school. He had met the teacher, Sarah Suggett, on the street, and she told him how I had become ill.

"What was the matter with you?" Father asked; and before I thought what I was saying, I let it out.

"I had the inflammatory rheumatism," I said—and a shout went up. It made me sick to hear them, the way they all laughed.

It brought back all the aching again, and like a fool I began to cry.

"Well, I *have* got it—I *have,*" I cried, and I got up from the table and ran upstairs.

I stayed there until Mother came up. I knew it would be a long time before I heard the last of the inflammatory rheumatism. I was sick all right, but the aching I now had wasn't in my legs or in my back. 🐟

Comprehension Check

1. What is wrong with Walter? *(He has inflammatory rheumatism.)*

2. What does the narrator do to get sent home from school? *(He cries and tells the teacher that he aches.)*

3. How does the narrator's mother react when he comes home from school? *(She puts him to bed and pays little attention to him.)*

4. What bad thing does the narrator imagine might happen to him while he is fishing? *(He might drown.)*

5. Why does the boy consider himself a hero? *(He catches a huge carp.)*

6. What makes the boy feel terrible at the end of the story? *(His family laughs at him.)*

Responding to Reading

First Impressions

1. What do you think of the boy in this story? Share your reactions with your classmates.

Second Thoughts

2. What do you think was really wrong with the boy? Explain, using information from the story.

3. What is your opinion of the way the boy is treated by his family? Find evidence to explain your answer.

4. What advice would you give to either the boy or his family?

Literary Concept: Point of View

When planning a story, the writer must decide who will narrate or tell the story. This is called the story's **point of view.** In first-person point of view, a narrator who is also a character in the story speaks directly to the reader using pronouns such as *I, me,* and *we.* In third-person point of view, the story is told by someone outside the story using pronouns like *he, she,* and *they.* From which point of view is "Stolen Day" written? What other stories have you read that were told from this point of view?

Writing Options

1. Using first-person point of view, write the narrator's **journal entry** at the end of the day, expressing his feelings about what happened. Before you write, skim the story and try to make your writing sound like the narrator's.

2. Which character or characters in this story have tunnel vision? Write an **explanation** to identify your choice and explain the effect of tunnel vision on the character.

Student Response

Responding to Reading

1. Any response is valid.

2. **Possible responses:** The boy was jealous of Walter, whose illness gave him plenty of free time; the boy wanted attention from his mother and other family members; thinking about rheumatism actually made him feel sick.

3. **Possible responses:** They treated him badly by not giving him the attention he needed and by laughing at him; they acted normally, and he is too sensitive about being teased; most people would laugh at a boy who imagines he has a deadly disease.

4. **Possible responses:** The mother should set aside time to spend with her son each day; the boy should be given more responsibility at home so that he feels a part of the family; family members should not laugh at the boy if it makes him feel bad.

Literary Concept: Point of View

"Stolen Day" is written from the first-person point of view; "The War of the Wall" is also written in the first person.

Writing Options

The Writing Options are designed to meet varied student interests and abilities. Have each student choose one writing activity to complete. You may wish to guide some students to an option that requires less writing.

Journal Update Invite students to review their journal entries for "Stolen Day." What advice would they give the boy from their own experience? What advice might the boy give them?

Closure

Like the girls in "Lose Now, Pay Later," the boy in "Stolen Day" sets his sights on something he wants. Invite students to compare the tunnel vision of the boy, or of other members of his family, with that of the two girls. Ask them to think of other examples of tunnel vision, perhaps from their own experience.

Elements of Poetry

This feature offers students an opportunity to develop a vocabulary of terms that they can use to discuss poems. All the terms introduced here are taught in depth in the poetry selections that follow.

Objectives

- To understand and appreciate poetry
- To recognize the elements of poetry
- To examine strategies for reading poetry

Motivation

Read the opening paragraph on page 84 aloud, and then divide the class into two groups—those who like poetry and those who don't. Call on members of each group to give reasons for their feelings. Use these opinions and the discussion prompts that follow to talk about poetry.

- In what ways are songs like poems? In what ways are songs and poems different?
- Have you ever tried to write a limerick or another kind of humorous poem? Did you have fun?
- Do you have a favorite poem? What do you like about it?
- Is it important for poems to rhyme? In what other situations do people use rhythm and rhyme?

Teaching Strategies

Some students may find these explanations of poetic terms difficult to understand. You may want to read the information about each term aloud to the class, stopping to discuss it before going on to the next term. Here are some suggestions for discussion.

Form To emphasize the wide range of poetic forms, have students contrast the form of "in the inner city" (page 33) with the form of "The Charge of the Light Brigade" (page 87).

Elements of
POETRY

Poetry is the most compact form of literature. A poem packs all kinds of ideas, feelings, and sounds into a few carefully chosen words. The look, sound, and language of poetry all work together to create a total effect.

Understanding Poetry

Form   The way a poem looks—or its arrangement on the page—is **form.** Poetry is written in **lines,** which may or may not be sentences. Sometimes the lines are separated into groups called **stanzas.** Remember that poets choose the arrangements of words and lines deliberately. The form of a poem can add to its meaning.

Sound   Poems are meant to be read aloud. Therefore, poets choose and arrange words to create the sounds they want the listener to hear. There are many techniques that poets can use to achieve different sounds. Three of these are described below.

- **Rhyme**   When words end with the same sounds, the words rhyme. In Western cultures, traditional poems such as "The Charge of the Light Brigade" on page 86, often contain rhyming words at the ends of the lines:

    Theirs not to reason *why,*
    Theirs but to do and *die.*

- **Rhythm**   The rhythm is sometimes called the "beat" of the poem. It is the pattern of stressed (′) and unstressed (⌣) sylla-

bles, or those word parts that are read with more and less emphasis, in a line of poetry. In these lines from "The Charge of the Light Brigade," listen for a beat that sounds like the pounding of horses' hooves.

    Cánnŏn tŏ ríght ŏf thĕm,

    Cánnŏn tŏ léft ŏf thĕm,

Poems that do not have a regular rhythm and sound more like conversation are called **free verse.** "For My Father" on page 90 is written in free verse.

- **Repetition**   Poets often choose to repeat sounds, words, phrases, or whole lines in a poem. Repetition helps the poet emphasize an idea or create a certain feeling.

Imagery   Imagery involves words and phrases that appeal to the five senses. Poets use imagery to create a picture in the reader's mind, or to remind the reader of a familiar sensation. Notice how these lines from "in the inner city" on page 33 give you a visual picture as well as a sound picture. They help bring the poem "inside" of you.

    we think a lot about uptown
    and the silent nights
    and the houses straight as
    dead men

Figurative Language   Poets use figurative language when they choose words and phrases that help the reader to picture ordinary things in new ways. These special

Sound Ask students to give examples of how "the three R's"—rhyme, rhythm, and repetition—are used in their favorite rock or rap songs to create a memorable sound.

Imagery Invite students to suggest some images that they might include in a poem called "Sounds." What images might belong in poems called "Smells" and "Tastes" and "Touching"?

ADDITIONAL RESOURCES
Technology and Enrichment
Active Reading Transparency 10

descriptions are called **figures of speech.** Three figures of speech are explained below.

• **Simile** A comparison that uses the words *like* or *as* is called a simile. This simile from "Dream Deferred" on page 268 compares a raisin to a dream that has not come true:

> What happens to a dream deferred:
> Does it dry up
> like a raisin in the sun?

• **Metaphor** A comparison that does *not* use the words *like* or *as* is called a metaphor. To what is the road compared in this line from "The Highwayman" on page 408?

> The road was a ribbon of moonlight over the purple moor

• **Personification** When a poet describes an animal or object as if it were human or had human qualities, he or she is using personification. In these lines from "Formula" on page 268, the poet gives human characteristics to the night and the fish.

> Perhaps the night dreams
> that it is no longer night;
> the fish, that they are boats;

Theme All the poetic elements you have read about help the poet establish the theme. Just as in fiction, the message about life that the poem conveys is the poem's theme.

---

*S*trategies *for Reading Poetry*

1. **Preview the poem.** Notice the poem's form on the page: its shape, its length, the length of the lines, and whether or not it has stanzas.

2. **Read the poem aloud.** Pause at the ends of complete thoughts, not necessarily at the ends of lines. Look for end punctuation to help you find the end of a complete thought. As you read, see if there is rhyme and listen for rhythm as well as the overall sound of the words in the poem.

3. **Visualize the images.** In your mind's eye, picture the images and comparisons the poem makes. Do the images remind you of feelings or experiences you have had?

4. **Think about the words and phrases.** Allow yourself to wonder about any

phrases or words that seem to stand out. Think about what that choice of words adds to the poem.

5. **Try to figure out the theme.** Ask yourself, What's the point of the poem? What message is the poet trying to send or help you create?

6. **Let your understanding grow.** When you finish reading, you are left with first impressions of the poem. Over time, you will add to your understanding based on the poem, your discussions in class, and other poetry you read.

7. **Allow yourself to enjoy poetry.** Remember that poetry is about feelings. You may connect with a particular poem because it expresses feelings that you yourself have felt.

Closure

To close the lesson, encourage students to write brief descriptions of poems that they find meaningful, using some of the terms they have learned.

Figurative Language Volunteers might create their own examples of similes, metaphors, and personification to describe aspects of the classroom or school. Give them some examples to start them off.
Simile: Students swarmed like bees around the teacher's desk.
Metaphor: School is the key that unlocks a world of ideas.
Personification: Books take their readers by the hand.

Theme Have students look back at "in the inner city" and briefly state what they think the poem's theme, or main message, is. (*Possible response: The inner city is not some abstract sociological concept but home to the people who live there.*)

Strategies for Reading Poetry

Invite volunteers to read the explanation of each strategy. You might model some of these strategies while reading the next selection, "The Charge of the Light Brigade," on pages 87 and 88. Use the following suggestions, or develop your own.

Modeling
Preview the Poem "On first glance, I notice that all the lines of this poem are about the same length. The lines are divided into six stanzas that vary in length."

Read the Poem Aloud "As I read the first few stanzas, I hear end-of-line rhymes, such as *reply*, *why*, and *die*. The poet repeats important phrases, such as 'Rode the six hundred.' I also hear a strong, regular rhythm—like the galloping of cavalry or the pounding of cannon shells."

Visualize the Images "In my mind's eye, I see the soldiers riding into a death-trap. Cannons all around are aimed right at them. The flashing sabers and smoke are signs of a terrible battle."

Think About the Words and Phrases "The phrases 'valley of death,' 'jaws of death,' and 'mouth of hell' stand out for me. These phrases emphasize the horrible devastation of war."

Try to Figure Out the Theme "The poem says that it was a blunder to ride into a deathtrap and take heavy losses, yet it honors the soldiers who faced death so bravely and loyally."

Objectives

- To understand and analyze a poem

- To understand the concept of rhythm in poetry

- To understand how rhyme, rhythm, and repetition add to a poem's meaning and effect

- To express understanding of the poem through a choice of writing forms, including a research report and a news report

Prereading/Motivation

Examine What You Know

Discussion Prompts What would happen if a soldier refused to follow an order? if many soldiers did so? Why does the military insist that soldiers obey orders? Does a soldier ever have the right to refuse to obey an order?

Expand Your Knowledge

Additional Background Tennyson wrote "The Charge of the Light Brigade" immediately after reading a newspaper report about the battle. Historians believe that the tragedy was caused by rivalry between two stubborn British commanding officers.

Enrich Your Reading

Ask students to name popular songs that have strong rhythms. Ask them what instruments produce the strong beats. Suggest that often a poem has a strong or regular beat, like that of some music, when read aloud. Remind them to listen for the beat in this poem as they would listen for the beat in a song.

Thematic Link— Tunnel Vision

The soldiers of the Light Brigade charge into battle knowing that the order is a mistake and that they will probably die. They have been taught to obey without question, showing a kind of tunnel vision that leads to death for many of them.

Poetry

The Charge of the Light Brigade
ALFRED, LORD TENNYSON

Examine What You Know (Prior Knowledge)

The following poem is based on a tragedy that took place because of orders given during wartime. What do you know about the military and the giving and taking of orders? Must all orders be obeyed? As a class, discuss what you know about military orders.

Expand Your Knowledge (Building Background)

The real Charge of the Light Brigade came during the Crimean War, 1853–1856, a war between Russia and a group of nations that included Great Britain. Russia eventually lost the war. On October 25, 1854, a British brigade was mistakenly ordered to attack a Russian artillery post. The Light Brigade, so called because it was lightly armed with swords, made a suicidal charge and actually overran the Russian guns and gunners. That victory came at a tragic cost, however. Of the 673 soldiers who made the charge, 247 were wounded or killed.

Enrich Your Reading (Reading Skill)

Sound Effects Poetry is meant to be read aloud. Often the sounds of the words add to the poem's meaning and overall effect. In the poem you are about to read, the poet has created short lines of carefully chosen words that suggest the sounds of battle. Read the poem once silently to yourself. Then read it again aloud. Notice the **repetition** of short words and phrases that suggest the **rhythm,** or regular beat, of soldiers riding into battle. Listen for the rhyme and for other sound effects that suggest a wild and desperate struggle.

■ *Author biography in Reader's Handbook*

JOURNAL WRITING IDEAS

■ Use the title to predict what this poem might be about.

■ Write about what you think it would be like to be a soldier in battle.

■ Tell about a time when you or someone you know obeyed a person's orders and then regretted it afterwards. What happened?

COLLABORATIVE LEARNING OPTIONS

Opportunities for collaborative learning include the Literary Concept and Writing Option 1 (p. 89).

ADDITIONAL RESOURCES

Unit One Resource Book
Reader's Guidesheet, p. 59
Reading Skills, p. 60
Literature Skills, p. 61
Vocabulary Connections, p. 62
Spelling Connections, p. 63
Comprehension Check Test, p. 64
Selection Test, pp. 65

Technology and Enrichment
Audiocassette Tape 1, Side 1

The Charge of the Light Brigade

ALFRED, LORD TENNYSON

Half a league,[1] half a league,
Half a league onward,
All in the valley of death
    Rode the six hundred.
5 "Forward, the Light Brigade!
Charge for the guns!" he said:
Into the valley of death
    Rode the six hundred.

    "Forward, the Light Brigade!"
10 Was there a man dismayed?
Not though the soldier knew
    Someone had blundered;
Theirs not to make reply,
Theirs not to reason why,
15 Theirs but to do and die;
Into the valley of death
    Rode the six hundred.

Cannon to right of them,
Cannon to left of them,
20 Cannon in front of them
    Volleyed and thundered;
Stormed at with shot and shell,
Boldly they rode and well,
Into the jaws of death,
25 Into the mouth of hell
    Rode the six hundred.

---

1. **league:** distance of about three miles

Teaching Strategies

VOCABULARY PREVIEW

The focus of vocabulary study for this selection is the use of context clues to determine meaning. See *Unit One Resource Book*, Vocabulary Connections, p. 62.

LIMITED ENGLISH PROFICIENCY

■ Use the Reader's Guidesheet, *Unit One Resource Book*, p. 62.

■ Some students may have difficulty understanding poetry because of its lines and stanzas. You may wish to read the poem aloud and then have students reread it in small groups.

■ You might help students visualize the battle by sketching the setting on the chalkboard, showing the charge of the soldiers into the valley, with enemy artillery positions in front of them and on the heights on either side.

★ Text annotations marked with a red star (3, 5) may be particularly helpful for students with limited English proficiency.

TEXT ANNOTATIONS

1. ACTIVE READING: Review
Point out that the poet often repeats words and phrases to create a feeling or an effect. Have students read the poem's first stanza aloud. Ask them what effect is created by the repetition of "half a league," "the valley of death," and "rode the six hundred." *(Possible responses: movement, marching, galloping)*

2. LITERARY CONCEPTS: Repetition Rhyme
Have students identify the repetition of the phrase "theirs not to." Then ask what other element of poetry can be found in these three lines. *(rhyme: reply, why, die).*

3. ACTIVE READING: Question
Ask students how the phrases "jaws of death" and "mouth of hell" help them **visualize** events. *(Possible responses: The jaws seem to open up and close on the soldiers; the mouth is like a narrow opening from which there is no escape; the mouth seems ready to swallow the soldiers.)*

Guided Reading for Less-Proficient Students

These questions can help guide students through the reading. Ask each question at the point of the selection where the capital letter and arrow appear in the margin. In addition, you may wish to use appropriate Active Reading annotations.

A. What orders are given to the Light Brigade? *(to move forward and charge the guns)* Recalling

B. Why do the soldiers charge, knowing that the command is a mistake? *(Their job is simply to follow orders.)* Summarizing

C. What weapons do the Light Brigade and the enemy have? *(The Light Brigade has sabers; the enemy has cannons.)* Inferring

D. What is the result of the battle? *(The Light Brigade fights well, but many die.)* Summarizing

E. How does the poet want the Light Brigade to be remembered? *(as heroes)* Reviewing

THE CHARGE OF THE LIGHT BRIGADE (detail) early 20th century Christopher Clark
Historical Pictures/Stock Montage.

Flashed all their sabers bare,
Flashed as they turned in air
Sab'ring the gunners there,
30 Charging an army, while
   All the world wondered.
Plunged in the battery smoke,
Right through the line they broke;
4 | Cossack and Russian
35 | Reeled from the saber-stroke,
   Shattered and sundered.[2]
Then they rode back, but not,
C ▶   Not the six hundred.

Cannon to right of them,
40 Cannon to left of them,
Cannon behind them
   Volleyed and thundered;   **5**
Stormed at with shot and shell,
While horse and hero fell,
45 They that had fought so well
Came through the jaws of death,
Back from the mouth of hell,
All that was left of them,
   Left of six hundred. ◀ **D**

50 When can their glory fade?
Oh, the wild charge they made!
   All the world wondered.
Honor the charge they made,
Honor the Light Brigade,
55   Noble six hundred! ᚚ   ◀ **E**

---

2. **sundered:** split; broken apart

Comprehension Check

1. How many men are in the Light Brigade? *(six hundred)*

2. What weapons does the brigade face? *(cannons)*

3. What weapons does the Light Brigade fight with? *(sabers)*

4. In what way does the Light Brigade suffer? *(Many men die.)*

5. How does the poet want the Light Brigade to be remembered? *(with honor)*

Responding to Reading

First Impressions

1. What images went through your mind as you read this poem? Discuss them with your classmates.

Second Thoughts

2. Do you consider the soldiers of the Light Brigade to be heroes? Why or why not?

   Think about
   - lines 11–12 of the poem
   - the outcome of the soldiers' decision

3. How do you think the speaker of the poem feels about the Light Brigade? Why do you think so?

4. Do you think an incident like this suicidal charge could happen today? Why or why not?

Literary Concept: Rhythm

Rhythm is the pattern of stressed and unstressed syllables in a line of poetry. You can understand the rhythm of a poem more clearly if you mark the stressed and unstressed syllables. The words or word parts you read with more emphasis (stress) are marked with ´. The weaker-sounding syllables (unstressed) are marked with ˘.

Example   "Fórwărd, thĕ Líght Brĭgáde!
                Chárge fŏr thĕ gúns!" hĕ sáid:

Working in pairs, copy the first stanza on a separate piece of paper. Then chart the rhythmic pattern as shown in the example.

Writing Options

1. Research and write a short **research report** on the causes and outcome of the Crimean War. Share your information with the class.

2. Imagine that you are a reporter on the field of battle. Write a **news report** describing what you see.

THE CHARGE OF THE LIGHT BRIGADE   89

Student Response

Responding to Reading

1. Any response is valid.

2. **Possible responses:** They are heroes because they nobly followed orders and endangered their lives in battle; they are not heroes because they foolishly followed orders that they knew were a mistake.

3. **Possible responses:** He feels that they deserve to be honored for their bravery, as evidenced by lines 53 and 54; even though the world questions the charge, they should be admired.

4. **Possible responses:** Yes, because human error continues to occur on the battlefield and soldiers are still expected to obey orders; yes, because some commanders are willing to sacrifice human lives in order to win; no, because today's soldiers would disobey a foolish order.

Literary Concept: Rhythm

Hálf ă léague, hálf ă léague,
Hálf ă léague ónward,
Áll ĭn thĕ válley ŏf déath
   Róde thĕ síx húndred.
"Fórward, thĕ Líght Brĭgáde!
Chárge fŏr thĕ gúns!" hĕ sáid:
Íntŏ thĕ válley ŏf déath
   Róde thĕ síx húndred.

Alternative:
Líght Brĭgáde! / gúns!" hĕ sáid:

Point out that the basic rhythm of the poem is ´ ˘ ˘ . Also point out that even experts sometimes disagree on which syllables should be stressed in lines of poetry, depending on how they read the lines aloud.

Writing Options

The Writing Options are designed to meet varied student interests and abilities. Have each student choose one writing activity to complete.

Journal Update Invite students to write any new thoughts they have about war and about obeying orders. Some might want to imagine that they are survivors of the charge and write the journal entry they think such a survivor would write.

Closure

Both the men in charge of the *Titanic* and those commanding the Light Brigade exhibited tunnel vision, as did the people who took their orders. Have students discuss how tunnel vision might be necessary or helpful to people who take or give orders and how it might be harmful or even dangerous.

Objectives

- To understand and analyze a poem
- To examine the way figurative language creates meaning
- To enrich reading by visualizing images in a poem
- To express understanding of the poem through a choice of writing forms, including an opinion and a letter

Prereading/Motivation

Examine What You Know

Discussion Prompts Does talking help when you are hurt or angry? Have you ever solved problems like this by "talking them out"? Are there other ways to communicate besides talking?

Expand Your Knowledge

Additional Background In the early 1900s, some U.S. labor unions joined other political forces to fight for immigration restrictions, fearing that cheap immigrant labor would make it harder for them to win better wages for their members. However, prejudice against Asians led to more severe restrictions on them than on other ethnic groups. In the "gentleman's agreement" of 1907, Japan agreed to stop allowing its laborers to emigrate to the United States.

Enrich Your Reading

Suggest to students that visualizing is like daydreaming or like imagining or remembering scenes or pictures from one's own life. They can think of their mind as a camera that zooms in for a close up of a detail or scene.

Thematic Link—
Tunnel Vision

Both the father and the speaker of the poem might be said to have tunnel vision. The father expresses his narrow view with harsh discipline and silence. The speaker remembers viewing the father through a child's eyes, without understanding the father's burdens.

Poetry

For My Father

JANICE MIRIKITANI (mi' ri ki tän' ē)

Examine What You Know (Prior Knowledge)

Very often the conflicts we have with others are caused by communication gaps. Sometimes people are unable to express their feelings. Think about times when you have had a problem with someone else. In your journal, draw and fill in a chart like the one below.

Conflict between	Problem about	Who couldn't communicate?
Jill & me	borrowing clothes	both of us

Expand Your Knowledge (Building Background)

The father in the poem you are about to read is a Japanese immigrant. Although the Japanese people who moved to the United States were good citizens and hard workers, they faced a great deal of prejudice. Resentment against them grew so strong that in 1924 a law was passed that excluded any more Japanese and other nonwhite people from entering the country. In 1941, during World War II, Pearl Harbor was bombed by Japan, and Japanese Americans faced even worse discrimination. Although 20,000 Japanese Americans served in the U.S. military during World War II, Japanese Americans on the West Coast were forced to give up their homes and belongings and go to special camps that were like prisons. One of these camps, Tule Lake, is mentioned in the poem.

Enrich Your Reading (Reading Skill)

- *Author biography in Reader's Handbook*

Visualizing Poets often select words that put a mental picture in the mind of the reader. As you read this poem, try to visualize, or picture in your mind, the images described by the writer. Take time to try to picture each thing that is described. Not only will visualizing help you remember details, it will also help you enjoy the poem more.

JOURNAL WRITING IDEAS

- Write about a particular problem you had in communicating with a family member or friend.
- Write a brief description of a family member or friend you knew when you were a very young child, recalling how that person seemed to you then.

COLLABORATIVE LEARNING OPTIONS

Opportunities for collaborative learning include the discussion questions in Second Thoughts and the Literary Concept (p. 92).

ADDITIONAL RESOURCES

Unit One Resource Book
Reader's Guidesheet, p. 66
Reading Skills, p. 67
Literature Skills, p. 68
Vocabulary Connections, p. 69
Spelling Connections, p. 70
Comprehension Check Test, p. 71
Selection Test, p. 72

Technology and Enrichment
Audiocassette Tape 1, Side 1

For My Father

JANICE MIRIKITANI

He came over the ocean
carrying Mt. Fuji[1] on
1 │ his back / Tule Lake on his chest
hacked through the brush
5 of deserts
and made them grow
A ▶ strawberries

we stole berries
from the stem
10 we could not afford them
for breakfast

his eyes held
nothing
as he whipped us
15 for stealing.

2 │ the desert had dried
his soul.

wordless
he sold
20 the rich,
full berries
to hakujin[2]
whose children
pointed at our eyes

25   they ate fresh   3
    strawberries
    on corn flakes.   ◀ B

Father,
i wanted to scream
30 at your silence.   ◀ C
Your strength
was a stranger   4
i could never touch.

iron
35 in your eyes
to shield
the pain   ◀ D
to shield desert-like wind
from patches
40 of strawberries
grown
from
tears.

---

1. **Mt. Fuji** (fōō′ jē): the highest mountain in Japan.
2. **hakujin** (hä kōō jən): a Japanese term for Caucasians.

Teaching Strategies

VOCABULARY PREVIEW

The focus of vocabulary study for this selection is adjectives formed with the suffix -less. See *Unit One Resource Book*, Vocabulary Connections, p. 69.

LIMITED ENGLISH PROFICIENCY

■ Use the Reader's Guidesheet, *Unit One Resource Book*, p. 66.

■ This poem's form may cause difficulty for some readers. Read it aloud, demonstrating where pauses occur, to make the meaning clearer.

★ Text annotations marked with a red star (3, 4) may be particularly helpful for students with limited English proficiency.

TEXT ANNOTATIONS

1. LITERARY CONCEPT: Figurative Language
Ask students what idea is suggested by the father's carrying Tule Lake on his chest. *(Possible responses: the suffering of Japanese Americans in the camp; the heavy weight of an unhappy past)*

2. ACTIVE READING: Connect
Ask students to **visualize** a man whose soul has been dried by the desert. Invite volunteers to describe the man's facial expression and posture. Ask them what words they would use to describe this person? *(Possible responses: old, harsh, stooped, brittle, raspy)*

3. ACTIVE READING: Review
Ask students to **contrast** the children of the *hakujin* with the speaker's family. *(The* hakujin *children can afford strawberries for breakfast, whereas the speaker's family cannot; the* hakujin *children's eyes are different from those of the speaker's family.)* ★

4. LITERARY CONCEPT: Metaphor
Ask what things are being compared in lines 31-33. *(The father's strength is compared to an untouchable stranger.)* Discuss what idea is meant by this metaphor. *(Possible response: The father's harshness made it impossible for the speaker to be close to him.)* ★

Guided Reading for Less-Proficient Students

These questions can help guide students through the reading. Ask each question at the point of the selection where the capital letter and arrow appear in the margin. In addition, you may wish to use appropriate Active Reading annotations.

A. What difficult thing does the man in the poem do to make a living? *(He grows strawberries in the desert.)* Clarifying

B. What do the children of the *hakujin* have that the man's children do not have? *(strawberries for breakfast)* Reviewing

C. Why does the speaker resent the father's silence? *(The speaker can't get close to him and feel his love.)* Inferring

D. Why does the father have "iron" in his eyes? *(His toughness shields him from pain and disappointment.)* Reviewing

Student Response

Responding to Reading

1. Any response is valid.

2. **Possible responses:** No, because he showed no love or closeness; no, because he was too hard on them and himself; yes, because he was working hard for his family's survival and they should have understood his problems.

3. **Possible responses:** He might say that he needed to expend all his energy supporting his family, that the bitterness of his past closed up his feelings, or that he was preparing his children for the harshness of life.

4. **Possible responses:** The speaker is angry at him for giving neither love nor communication, as shown by the statements that blame him; the speaker finally feels sympathy for his pain and respect for all he did to ensure the family's survival, as shown by the word *For* in the title, his pain, and the tears.

Literary Concept: Figurative Language

Possible responses: Being a Japanese immigrant and facing prejudice in the United States has been a difficult burden; the father is weighed down by old ideas and customs. Other examples: "Tule Lake on his chest," "desert had dried / his soul," "strength / was a stranger," "iron / in your eyes," "strawberries / grown / from / tears."

Writing Options

The Writing Options are designed to meet varied student interests and abilities. Have each student choose one writing activity to complete.

Journal Update Invite students to list questions they would like to ask an immigrant about the difficulties in adjusting to a new life.

Closure

Ask students how both the father and the child exhibit tunnel vision in their behavior and perceptions. Have students discuss in small groups how the speaker of this poem might advise the family in "Stolen Day."

Responding to Reading

First Impressions

1. Choose one word to describe your feelings about this poem. Then explain your choice to the class.

Second Thoughts

2. Do you feel that the father's treatment of his child was fair? Why or why not?

3. How do you think the father would explain his side of the issue?
   Think about
   • the reference to Tule Lake
   • the tears mentioned in the last stanza

4. How do you think the speaker feels about the father? Why do you think so?

Literary Concept: Figurative Language

The creative use of words to extend ideas beyond their literal or dictionary meanings is called **figurative language.** The words in a figurative expression are not literally true but instead paint vivid images in the minds of readers. For example, the speaker begins this poem by saying the father carried Mount Fuji on his back. What do you think this might mean? What other examples of figurative language can you find in this poem?

Writing Options

1. Think back to "The Charge of the Light Brigade." Write your **opinion** about whether both Tennyson's poem and "For My Father" were good choices for a subunit called "Tunnel Vision."

2. Imagine you are either the father or the child in this poem. Write a **letter** to the other person fully describing how you feel about him or her and about the events in the poem. Try to include some figurative language.

Comprehension Check

1. From what country does the father come? *(Japan)*

2. What kind of work does the father do? *(He grows strawberries.)*

3. For what does the father punish his children? *(for stealing berries)*

4. What makes the child want to scream at the father? *(his silence)*

5. What does the speaker say that the strawberries are grown from? *(tears)*

Objectives

- To understand and analyze a work of nonfiction

- To examine methods of organizing informational writing

- To contrast literary nonfiction with informational nonfiction

- To express understanding of the selection through a choice of writing forms, including an essay, an advertisement, a message in a bottle, and a log entry

Nonfiction   *from* **Exploring the Titanic**

ROBERT BALLARD

Examine What You Know   (Prior Knowledge)

You probably know something about the sinking of the great ship *Titanic*, but what else would you like to learn about it? Copy the following chart on the board. As a class, fill in the first two columns now, and the last column when you finish reading the piece.

What We Know	What We Want to Learn	What We Learned

Expand Your Knowledge
(Building Background)

As with most specialized fields, the shipping industry has its own special vocabulary, or **jargon.** To understand this selection more clearly, review the definitions of the terms below and refer to them as you read.

bow: front of a ship
stern: rear of a ship
hull: outside frame of a ship
deck: any floor on a ship
funnel: smokestack
mooring rope: rope that ties ship to dock

mast: tall pole that holds a sail or radio equipment
crow's nest: small platform on the mast for the lookout
hold: cargo compartment below deck
keel: beam along the bottom of a ship

Enrich Your Reading   (Reading Skill)

Literary Nonfiction   If you read about the *Titanic* in an encyclopedia, you could learn the facts about the sinking in a few minutes. Giving facts is the purpose of informational nonfiction.
    Literary nonfiction such as the selection you will read next also provides factual information. However, this type of nonfiction is often written in narrative form. Like a story, it might introduce characters—real people—and allow you to live through an event with them. As you read the following account, compare it to the informational nonfiction you read in encyclopedias. Think about when you might use each type.

■ *Author biography on Extend page*

EXPLORING THE TITANIC   93

Prereading/Motivation

Examine What You Know

Set aside room on the chalkboard for the KWL chart. Help students discover what they know by asking questions such as, What have you learned about the *Titanic* from books, magazines, television, or other people? Then ask them what they would like to find out about the ship and its passengers. Encourage students to suggest entries for the third column when they finish reading.

Expand Your Knowledge

Additional Background Have students use the cutaway diagram of the *Titanic* on pages 96 and 97 to identify the features named by these terms.

Enrich Your Reading

To clarify the difference between literary and informational nonfiction, read aloud examples of each. For instance, you might contrast factual excerpts from textbooks and newspapers with the narrative from *Little by Little* (pp. 49–54).

Thematic Link— Tunnel Vision

Everyone—owners, crew, and passengers—believed that the *Titanic* was unsinkable. This narrow perspective led the crew to minimize serious warnings about icebergs. The tunnel vision of various people resulted in tragedy.

JOURNAL WRITING IDEAS

■ Imagine taking a long trip on a luxurious ocean liner. Tell whether you would enjoy such a trip and why or why not.

■ List some well-known disasters. Tell why you think people are so fascinated by them.

COLLABORATIVE LEARNING OPTIONS

Opportunities for collaborative learning include Writing Option 2 (p. 107), Options for Learning 1, 2, and 4 (p. 108), and Cross-Curricular Projects (p. 108).

ADDITIONAL RESOURCES
Unit One Resource Book
Reader's Guidesheet, p. 73
Reading Skills, p. 74
Literature Skills, p. 75
Vocabulary Connections, p. 76
Spelling Connections, p. 77
Comprehension and Vocabulary Check Tests, p. 78
Selection Test, pp. 79–80

Technology and Enrichment
Active Reading Transparencies 11–12; Worksheets

VOCABULARY PREVIEW

These vocabulary words are defined at the bottom of the selection page on which they appear.

accommodation a room and food

aristocratic wealthy, privileged people

competitive relating to rivalry

desperately showing extreme need

feverishly in a highly emotional way

indefinitely for an unlimited time

novelty something new

omen a sign of a future happening

prophecy a prediction

tribute an act or gift to honor someone

LIMITED ENGLISH PROFICIENCY

■ Use the Reader's Guidesheet, *Unit One Resource Book,* page 73.

■ Students may have difficulty with the proper nouns in the first few pages of the selection. Some expressions, such as "trellised walls" and "sultan's palace," may also prove difficult.

★ Text annotations marked with a red star (1, 3, 4, 7, 8, 10, 13, 16, 20) may be particularly helpful for students with limited English proficiency.

TEXT ANNOTATIONS

1. VOCABULARY: Word History
Ask students if they know who the Titans were in Greek mythology and what the words *titan* and *titanic* now mean. *(The Titans were a family of giants who ruled the world before the Olympian gods; titan means "anyone or anything that is very large or strong," and titanic means "having great size or strength.")* ★

2. HISTORICAL SIDELIGHT
The Olympic made over five hundred safe Atlantic crossings before being retired in 1934. She was nicknamed Old Reliable. The other huge ocean liner built by the White Star Line, the *Britannic,* was sunk during World War I by German mines.

from # Exploring the Titanic

ROBERT D. BALLARD

1 The story of the *Titanic* began before anyone had even thought about building the great ship. In 1898, fourteen years before the *Titanic* sank, an American writer named Morgan Robertson wrote a book called *The Wreck of the Titan.* In his story, the *Titan,* a passenger ship almost identical to the *Titanic,* and labeled "unsinkable," sails from England headed for New York. With many rich and famous passengers on board, the *Titan* hits an iceberg in the North Atlantic and sinks. Because there are not enough lifeboats, many lives are lost.

The story of the *Titan* predicted exactly what would happen to the *Titanic* fourteen years later. It was an eerie prophecy of terrible things to come.

A ▶

In 1907, nearly ten years after *The Wreck of the Titan* was written, two men began making plans to build a real titanic ship. At a London dinner party, as they relaxed over coffee and cigars, J. Bruce Ismay, president of the White Star Line of passenger ships, and Lord Pirrie, chairman of Harland & Wolff shipbuilders, discussed a plan to build three enormous ocean liners. Their goal was to give the White Star Line a competitive edge in the Atlantic passenger trade with several gigantic ships whose accommodations would be the last word in comfort and elegance.

The two men certainly dreamed on a grand scale. When these floating palaces were finally built, they were so much bigger than other ships that new docks had to be built on each side of the Atlantic to service them. Four years after that London dinner party, the first of these huge liners, the *Olympic,* safely completed her maiden voyage.

2

On May 31, 1911, the hull of the *Titanic* was launched at the Harland & Wolff shipyards in Belfast, Ireland, before a cheering crowd of 100,000. Bands played, and people came from miles around to see this great wonder of the sea. Twenty-two tons of soap, grease, and train oil were used to slide her

Words to Know and Use	**prophecy** (präf′ ə sē) *n.* a prediction; foretelling of future events **competitive** (kəm pet′ ə tiv) *adj.* relating to rivalry among businesses, groups, or individuals **accommodation** (ə käm′ ə dā′ shən) *n.* a room and food in hotels, ships, trains, and so on

94

Guided Reading for Less-Proficient Students

These questions can help guide students through the reading. Ask each question at the point of the selection where the capital letter appears in the margin. In addition, you may wish to use appropriate Active Reading annotations.

A. Why was the book "an eerie prophecy of terrible things to come"? *(The Titan was very similar to the Titanic. In the book, the Titan hits an iceberg and sinks, just as the Titanic would.)* Reviewing

B. Why might many wealthy passengers choose to travel on the *Titanic?* *(The Titanic is the largest and most luxurious ship ever built, so that its first voyage attracts the rich and powerful.)* Inferring

C. Why do all the passengers aboard the *Titanic* feel so safe? *(They have been assured that the ship is unsinkable.)* Summarizing

Continued on page 95

The Grand Staircase was five stories high and covered by a glass dome.

3 into the water. In the words of one eyewitness, she had "a rudder as big as an elm tree . . . propellers as big as a windmill. Everything was on a nightmare scale."

For the next ten months the *Titanic* was outfitted and carefully prepared down to the last detail. The final size and richness of this new ship was astounding. She was 882 feet long, almost the length of four city blocks. With nine decks, she was as high as an eleven-story building.

4 Among her gigantic features, she had four huge funnels, each one big enough to drive two trains through. During construction an astonishing three million rivets[1] had been hammered into her hull. Her three enormous anchors weighed a total of thirty-one tons—the weight of twenty cars. And for her maiden voyage, she carried enough food to feed a small town for several months.

As her name boasted, the *Titanic* was indeed the biggest ship in the world. Nicknamed "the Millionaires' Special," she was also called "the Wonder Ship," "the Unsinkable Ship," and "the Last Word in Luxury" by newspapers around the world.

The command of this great ocean liner was given to the senior captain of the White Star Line, Captain Edward J. Smith. This proud, white-bearded man was a natural leader and was popular with both crew members and passengers. Most important, after thirty-eight years' service with the White Star Line, he had an excellent safety record. At the age of fifty-nine, Captain Smith was going to retire after this last trip, a perfect final <u>tribute</u> to a long and successful career.

On Wednesday, April 10, 1912, the *Titanic*'s passengers began to arrive in Southampton for the trip to New York. Ruth Becker was dazzled as she boarded the ship with her mother, her younger sister, and two-year-old brother, Richard. Ruth's father was a missionary in India. The rest of the family was sailing to New York to find medical help for young Richard, who had developed a serious illness in India. They had booked second-class tickets on the *Titanic*.

5 Twelve-year-old Ruth was delighted with the ship. As she pushed her little brother about the decks in a stroller, she was impressed with what she saw. "Everything was new. New!" she recalled. "Our cabin was just like a hotel room, it was so big. The dining room was beautiful—the linens, all the bright, polished silver you can imagine."

---

1. **rivets:** metal bolts used to fasten beams.

Words to Know and Use | **tribute** (trib′ yo͞ot) *n.* an action or gift that honors a deserving individual

95

Continued from page 94

D. How does the *Titanic* reflect the society of its day? *(The levels of the ship reflect the different levels of society, with the wealthy on top.)* Summarizing

E. Why don't the captain and crew pay more attention to the warnings about ice? *(No one thinks that ice presents a danger to the ship; the crew is distracted by other duties.)* Inferring

F. Once the iceberg has been sighted, why doesn't the crew steer the *Titanic* out of the way? *(They try, but there isn't enough time to avoid a collision.)* Clarifying

Continued on page 96

First Class
Second Class
Third Class

Crew Living and Eating Areas
Crew Working Areas
Cargo and Stores

The forecastle area held giant anchor chains and bollards for tying the ship when in port.

Purser and Captain stand outside the officers' quarters.

1. The swimming pool was 33 feet long.
2. A wrought-iron and glass dome covered the first-class staircase.

The ship's gymnasium held rowing machines.

6. LITERARY CONCEPT: Setting
Point out details in this paragraph and the previous one that show that the *Titanic* was indeed "the Last Word in Luxury," with thick carpets, carved paneling, marble sinks, the opulent Verandah and Palm Court, and the squash court, pool, Turkish bath, and exercise equipment on the lower decks.

7. VOCABULARY: Jargon
Invite students to identify in the cutaway view of the ship the various places mentioned in the narrative, such as the holds, the first-class rooms, and the lower decks. ★

Meanwhile, seventeen-year-old Jack Thayer from Philadelphia was trying out the soft mattress on the large bed in his cabin. The first-class rooms his family had reserved for themselves and their maid had thick carpets, carved wooden panels on the walls, and marble sinks. As his parents were getting settled in their adjoining stateroom, Jack decided to explore this fantastic ship.

On A Deck, he stepped into the Verandah and Palm Court and admired the white wicker furniture and the ivy growing up the trellised walls. On the lower decks, Jack discovered the squash court,[2] the swimming pool, and the Turkish bath decorated like a room in a sultan's palace. In the gymnasium, the instructor was showing passengers the latest in exercise equipment, which included a mechanical camel you could ride on, stationary bicycles, and rowing machines.

Daylight shone through the huge glass dome over the Grand Staircase as Jack went down to join his parents in the first-class reception room.

There, with the ship's band playing in the background, his father pointed out some of the other first-class passengers. "He's supposed to be the world's richest man," said his father of Colonel John Jacob Astor, who was escorting the young Mrs. Astor. He also identified Mr. and Mrs. Straus, founders of Macy's of New York, the world's largest department store. Millionaire Benjamin Guggenheim was aboard, as were Jack's parents' friends from Philadelphia, Mr. and Mrs. George Widener and their son, Harry. Mr. Widener had made a fortune building streetcars. Mr. and Mrs. William Carter were also friends of the Thayers. Stowed in one of the holds below was a new Renault car that they were bringing back from England.

There was absolutely nothing to worry about.

J. Bruce Ismay, president of the White Star Line, moved about the room saying hello to people. He wanted to make sure

---

2. **squash court:** a walled court for playing squash, a racquet game in which a rubber ball is hit off walls.

Continued from page 95

G. What do the crew do to attract rescue ships? *(fire rockets and send radio calls for help)* Recalling

H. Why can't all of the passengers aboard the *Titanic* be saved? *(There are not enough lifeboats.)* Drawing conclusions

I. How do Ruth Becker, Jack Thayer, and Harold Bride manage to survive? *(Ruth is placed in a lifeboat; Jack and Harold jump into the water and cling to an overturned lifeboat; all three are rescued by the Carpathia.)* Reviewing

The boilers were over 15 feet high.

Stokers had to shovel coal to power the boilers.

Middle-income people stayed in second-class state rooms.

The first-class promenade deck allowed passengers to walk outside.

Three huge propellers, two of which were 23 feet across, powered the ship.

that his wealthy passengers were comfortable, that they would feel relaxed and safe aboard his floating palace.

Indeed, when Ruth Becker's mother had asked one of the second-class staff about the safety of the ship, she had been told that there was absolutely nothing to worry about. The ship had watertight compartments that would allow her to float indefinitely. There was much talk among the passengers about the *Titanic*

C ▶ being unsinkable.

8 | In 1912, people were divided into social classes according to background, wealth, and education. Because of these class lines, the *Titanic* was rather like a big floating layer cake. The bottom layer consisted of the lowly manual workers sweating away in the heat and grime of the boiler rooms and engine rooms. The next layer was the third-class passengers, people of many nationalities hoping to make a new start in America. After that came the second class—teachers, merchants, and professionals of moderate means like Ruth's family. Then, finally,

there was the icing on the cake in first class: the rich and the aristocratic. The differences between these groups were enormous. While the wealthy brought their maids and valets and mountains of luggage, most members of the crew earned such tiny salaries that it would have taken them years to save the money for a single first-class ticket. ◀ D

9

A t noon on Wednesday, April 10, the *Titanic* cast off. The whistles on her huge funnels were the biggest ever made. As she began her journey to the sea, they were heard for miles around.

10

Moving majestically down the River Test, and watched by a crowd that had turned out for the occasion, the *Titanic* slowly passed two ships tied up to a dock. All of a sudden, the mooring ropes holding the passenger liner *New York* snapped with a series of sharp cracks like fireworks going off. The enormous pull created by the *Titanic* moving past her had broken the *New York*'s ropes and was now drawing her stern toward the *Titanic*.

Words to Know and Use	**indefinitely** (in def′ ə nit lē) *adv.* for an unlimited length of time **aristocratic** (ə ris′ tə krat′ ik) *n.* wealthy, privileged people

97

8. CULTURAL SIDELIGHT
Point out that the *Titanic* was a British ship and reflected the sharp distinctions between social classes that existed in Great Britain at the time and still exist to a lesser extent today. Third-class passengers were prevented, by gates and other physical barriers, from entering the areas reserved for the other classes. ★

9. ACTIVE READING: Review
Ask students how the author uses a comparison to describe the *Titanic*. (*Possible response: The Titanic is compared to a layer cake, with each class of accommodations compared to a layer.*) Invite students to explain why the first-class passengers are like the icing on the cake. (*Possible responses: The first-class cabins are at the top of the ship; the rich are often regarded as the "top" of society.*)

10. VOCABULARY: Jargon
Have students determine the meaning of "cast off." (*to be unfastened from a dock and leave*) ★

How do you know that some time has passed since the event described in the last two paragraphs? *(Possible responses: The Titanic is now in the vicinity of icebergs, so it must have traveled some distance since the start of the journey; the space between paragraphs indicates the passage of time.)*

12. HISTORICAL SIDELIGHT
Wireless (radio) communications were pioneered by Guglielmo Marconi in the 1890s. The ability of the *Titanic* to radio rescue ships after it collided with the iceberg emphasized the importance of the wireless at sea. Soon all large ships were required by law to have wireless equipment.

13. VOCABULARY: Definitions
On a map of the world, point out Greenland and explain that a five-thousand foot-thick sheet of ice covers nearly all of this island's surface. Explain that icebergs are formed when sections of this ice sheet, extending into the sea, are broken off by the motion of the waves. Pack ice is formed when the frozen surface of the sea breaks into chunks, which then freeze together. ★

Jack Thayer watched in horror as the two ships came closer and closer. "It looked as though there surely would be a collision," he later wrote. "Her stern could not have been more than a yard or two from our side. It almost hit us." At the last moment, some quick action by Captain Smith and a tugboat captain nearby allowed the *Titanic* to slide past with only inches to spare.

It was not a good sign. Did it mean that the *Titanic* might be too big a ship to handle safely? Those who knew about the sea thought that such a close call at the beginning of a maiden voyage was a very bad omen.

Jack Phillips, the first wireless operator[3] on the *Titanic* quickly jotted down the message coming in over his headphones. "It's another iceberg warning," he said wearily to his young assistant, Harold Bride. "You'd better take it up to the bridge." Both men had been at work for hours in the *Titanic*'s radio room, trying to get caught up in sending out a large number of personal messages. In 1912, passengers on ocean liners thought it was a real novelty to send postcard-style messages to friends at home from the middle of the Atlantic.

Bride picked up the iceberg message and stepped out onto the Boat Deck. It was a sunny but cold Sunday morning, the fourth day of the *Titanic*'s maiden voyage. The ship was steaming at full speed across a calm sea. Harold Bride was quite pleased with himself at having landed a job on such a magnificent new ship. After all, he was only twenty-two

years old and had just nine months' experience at operating a "wireless set," as a ship's radio was then called. As he entered the bridge area, he could see one of the crewmen standing behind the ship's wheel steering her course toward New York.

What danger could a few pieces of ice present?

Captain Smith was on duty in the bridge, so Bride handed the message to him. "It's from the *Caronia*, sir. She's reporting icebergs and pack ice ahead." The captain thanked him, read the message, and then posted it on the bulletin board for other officers on watch to read. On his way back to the radio room, Bride thought the captain had seemed quite unconcerned by the message. But then again, he had been told that it was not unusual to have ice floating in the sea lanes during an April crossing. Besides, what danger could a few pieces of ice present to an unsinkable ship?

Elsewhere on board, passengers relaxed on deck chairs, reading or taking naps. Some played cards, some wrote letters, while others chatted with friends. As it was Sunday, church services had been held in the morning, the first-class service led by Captain Smith. Jack Thayer spent most of the day walking about the decks getting

---

3. **wireless operator:** a person who works a telegraph transmitter.

Words to Know and Use

omen (ō′ mən) *n.* an event or sign believed to point toward a future happening
novelty (näv′ əl tē) *n.* something new, original, or unusual

some fresh air with his parents.

14 Two more ice warnings were received from nearby ships around lunch time. In the chaos of the radio room, Harold Bride only had time to take one of them to the bridge. The rest of the day passed quietly. Then, in the late afternoon, the temperature began to drop rapidly. Darkness approached as the bugle call announced dinner.

Jack Thayer's parents had been invited to a special dinner for Captain Smith, so Jack ate alone in the first-class dining room. After dinner, as he was having a cup of coffee, he was joined by Milton Long, another passenger going home to the States. Long was older than Jack, but in the easy-going atmosphere of shipboard travel, they struck up a conversation and talked together for an hour or so.

At 7:30 P.M., the radio room received three more warnings of ice about fifty miles ahead. One of them was from the steamer *Californian* reporting three large icebergs. Harold Bride took this message up to the bridge, and it was again politely received. Captain Smith was attending the dinner party being held for him when the warning was delivered. **15** He never got to see it. Then, around 9:00 P.M., the captain excused himself and went up to the bridge. He and his officers talked about how difficult it was to spot icebergs on a calm, clear, moonless night like this with no wind to kick up white surf around them. Before going to bed, the captain ordered the lookouts to keep a sharp watch for ice.

After trading travel stories with Milton Long, Jack Thayer put on his coat and walked around the deck. "It had become

Jack Thayer at age sixteen.

very much colder," he said later. "It was a brilliant, starry night. There was no moon, and I have never seen the stars shine brighter . . . sparkling like diamonds. . . . It was the kind of night that made one feel glad to be alive." At eleven o'clock, he went below to his cabin, put on his pajamas, and got ready for bed.

In the radio room, Harold Bride was exhausted. The two operators were expected to keep the radio working twenty-four hours a day, and Bride lay down to take a much-needed nap. Phillips was so busy with the passenger messages that he actually brushed off the final ice warning of the night. It was from the *Californian*. Trapped in a field of ice, she had stopped for the night about nineteen miles north of the *Titanic*. She was so close that the message literally blasted in Phillips's ears. Annoyed by the loud interruption, he cut off the *Californian's* radio operator with the words, "Shut up, shut up. I'm busy."

The radio room had received a total of seven ice warning messages in one day. It was quite clear that floating icebergs lay ahead of the *Titanic*. ◄ E

14. ACTIVE READING: Evaluate
Point out that the author mentions every warning about ice that the *Titanic* receives. Ask students to keep track of them and to decide whether the captain and crew acted on these warnings responsibly.

15. LITERARY CONCEPT:
Chronology
Have students identify clues in this paragraph that indicate the author is beginning to pay close attention to the time and sequence of events, such as the references to what happens at 7:30 and 9:00 P.M. As students continue to read, help them notice the frequent references to time and encourage them to think about why these references are important in this part of the selection.

16. VOCABULARY: Definitions
Help students use prior knowledge and context clues to determine that "glancing blow" refers to one object hitting another on its side before scraping by or bouncing off. ★

17. LITERARY CONCEPT: Literary Nonfiction
Through whose experiences does the author present the moment when the ship's engines stop? *(Ruth Becker, her mother, and Jack Thayer)* How do these different perspectives make this moment come alive? *(Possible responses: They indicate that the moment was memorable; they foreshadow terrible things to come; they allow the reader to be in more than one place at that moment.)*

18. ACTIVE READING: Predict
Refer students to the phrase "something was very wrong" and ask them to predict what the next section will be about. *(Possible response: the disastrous effects of the ship's collision with the iceberg)*

The *Titanic* collides with the iceberg, most of which lay hidden under water.

High up in the crow's nest on the forward mast, Fred Fleet had passed a quiet watch. It was now 11:40 P.M., and he and his fellow lookout were waiting to be relieved so they could head below, perhaps for a hot drink before hopping into their warm bunks. The sea was dead calm. The air was bitterly cold.

Suddenly, Fleet saw something. A huge, dark shape loomed out of the night directly ahead of the *Titanic*. An iceberg! He quickly sounded the alarm bell three times and picked up the telephone.

"What did you see?" asked the duty officer.

"Iceberg right ahead," replied Fleet.

Immediately, the officer on the bridge ordered the wheel turned as far as it would go. The engine room was told to reverse the engines, while a button was pushed to close the doors to the watertight compartments in the bottom of the ship.

The lookouts in the crow's nest braced themselves for a collision. Slowly the ship

started to turn. It looked as though they would miss it. But it was too late. They had avoided a head-on crash, but the iceberg had struck a glancing blow along the *Titanic*'s starboard bow. Several tons of ice fell on the ship's decks as the iceberg brushed along the side of the ship and passed into the night. A few minutes later, the *Titanic* came to a stop.

Many of the passengers didn't know the ship had hit anything. Because it was so cold, almost everyone was inside, and most people had already gone to bed. Ruth Becker and her mother were awakened by the dead silence. They could no longer hear the soothing hum of the vibrating engines from below. Jack Thayer was about to step into bed when he felt himself sway ever so slightly. The engines stopped. He was startled by the sudden quiet.

Something was very wrong.

Sensing trouble, Ruth's mother looked out of the door of their second-class cabin and asked a steward[4] what had happened. He told her that nothing was the matter, so Mrs. Becker went back to bed. But as she lay there, she couldn't help feeling that something was very wrong.

Jack heard running feet and voices in the hallway outside his first-class cabin. "I hurried into my heavy overcoat and drew on my slippers. All excited, but not thinking anything serious had occurred, I called in to

---

4. **steward:** a worker on a ship who attends to the needs of passengers.

100   UNIT ONE   TUNNEL VISION

Speaking . . . Listening . . . Viewing

Viewing Allow students to watch the video documentary *Search for the* Titanic, produced by the National Geographic Society and dealing with the discovery of the sunken *Titanic*. As they watch, have them try to identify some of the main structures of the ship, such as the funnels, the hull, and the bridge.

After they view the video, ask what they learned about the ship's size and importance, about the damage caused by the collision, and about the

waters in which the *Titanic* was traveling when it sank. Then encourage them to compare what they saw in the video with the photographs and drawings that illustrate the excerpt from *Exploring the* Titanic. Ask what different ideas about the ship they gained from these different media.

my father and mother that I was going up on deck to see the fun."

On deck, Jack watched some third-class passengers playing with the ice that had landed on the forward deck as the iceberg had brushed by. Some people were throwing chunks at each other, while a few skidded about playing football with pieces of ice.

Down in the very bottom of the ship, things were very different. When the iceberg had struck, there had been a noise like a big gun going off in one of the boiler rooms. A couple of stokers[5] had been immediately hit by a jet of icy water. The noise and the shock of cold water had sent them running for safety.

Twenty minutes after the crash, things looked very bad indeed to Captain Smith. He and the ship's builder, Thomas Andrews, had made a rapid tour below decks to inspect the damage. The mail room was filling up with water, and sacks of mail were floating about. Water was also pouring into some of the forward holds and two of the boiler rooms.

Captain Smith knew that the *Titanic*'s hull was divided into a number of watertight compartments. She had been designed so that she could still float if only the first four compartments were flooded, but not any more than that. But water was pouring into the first five compartments. And when the water filled them, it would spill over into the next compartment. One by one all the remaining compartments would flood, and the ship would eventually sink. Andrews told the captain that the ship could last an hour, an hour and a half at the most.

Harold Bride had just awakened in the radio room when Captain Smith stuck his head in the door. "Send the call for assistance," he ordered.

"What call should I send?" Phillips asked.

"The regulation international call for help. Just that." Then the captain was gone. Phillips began to send the Morse code "CQD" distress call, flashing away and joking as he did it. After all, they knew the ship was unsinkable.

Five minutes later, the captain was back. "What are you sending?" he asked.

"CQD," Phillips answered. Then Bride cut in and suggested that they try the new SOS signal that was just coming into use. They began to send out the new international call for help—it was one of the first SOS calls ever sent out from a ship in distress.

Ruth and her family had stayed in their bunks for a good fifteen minutes or so after the room steward had told them nothing was wrong. But Ruth's mother couldn't stop worrying as she heard the sound of running feet and shouting voices in the hallway. Poking her head out of the cabin, she found a steward and asked what the matter was.

"Put on your things and come at once," said the steward.

"Do we have time to dress?" she asked.

"No, madam. You have time for nothing. Put on your life jackets and come up to the top deck."

Ruth helped her mother dress the children quickly. But they only had time to throw their coats over their nightgowns and put on their shoes and stockings. In their

---

5. **stokers:** people who tended the boilers that powered steamships.

21. ACTIVE READING: Evaluate

Ask students why Andrews tells the Thayers the news in a "low voice." *(He doesn't want everyone to know that the ship is sinking.)* Ask them whether they think the captain should have announced to all passengers that the ship was going to sink in an hour. *(Possible responses: Yes, all the passengers have a right to know that their lives are in danger; no, the announcement would cause great panic.)*

22. ACTIVE READING: Review

Ask students how the behavior of Harold Bride and Jack Phillips has changed as they have become more aware of the danger. *(Earlier, they were not worried about the danger. Now they are frantically trying to get help.)*

23. HISTORICAL SIDELIGHT

About 75 percent of the people aboard the *Titanic* were men. The evacuation tore families apart, since many husbands and older sons went down with the ship. Only about 20 percent of the men were saved.

rush, they forgot to put on their life jackets.

Just after midnight, Captain Smith ordered the lifeboats uncovered. The ship's squash court, which was thirty-two feet above the keel, was now completely flooded. Jack Thayer and his father came into the first-class lounge to try to find out exactly what the matter was. When Thomas Andrews, the ship's builder, passed by, Mr. Thayer asked him what was going on. He replied in a low voice that the ship had not much more than an hour to live. Jack and his father couldn't believe their ears.

From the bridge of the *Titanic*, a ship's lights were observed not far away, possibly the *Californian's*. Captain Smith then ordered white distress rockets fired to get the attention of the nearby ship. They burst high in the air with a loud boom and a shower of stars. But the rockets made no difference. The mystery ship in the distance never answered.

In the radio room, Bride and Phillips now knew how serious the accident was and were feverishly sending out calls for help. A number of ships heard and responded to their calls, but most were too far away to come to the rescue in time. The closest ship they had been able to reach was the *Carpathia* about fifty-eight miles away. Immediately, the *Carpathia* reported that she was racing full steam to the rescue. But could she get there **G** ▶ in time?

Not far away, the radio operator of the *Californian* had gone to bed for the night and turned off his radio. Several officers and

crewmen on the deck of the *Californian* saw rockets in the distance and reported them to their captain. The captain told them to try to contact the ship with a Morse lamp. But they received no answer to their flashed calls. No one thought to wake up the radio operator.

On board the *Titanic*, almost an hour after the crash, most of the passengers still did not realize the seriousness of the situation. But Captain Smith was a very worried man. He knew that the *Titanic* only carried lifeboats for barely half the estimated twenty-two hundred people on board. He would have to make sure his officers kept order to avoid any panic among the passengers. At 12:30 A.M. Captain Smith gave the orders to start loading the lifeboats—women and children first. Even though the *Titanic* was by now quite noticeably down at the bow and listing slightly to one side, many passengers still didn't want to leave the huge, brightly lit ship. The ship's band added to a kind of party feeling as the musicians played lively tunes.

About 12:45 A.M. the first lifeboat was lowered. It could carry sixty-five people, but left with only twenty-eight aboard. Indeed, many of the first boats to leave were half empty. Ruth Becker noticed that there was no panic among the crowds of passengers milling about on the decks. "Everything was calm, everybody was orderly." But the night air was now biting cold. Ruth's mother told her to go back to their cabin to get some blankets. Ruth hurried down to the cabin

Words to Know and Use

feverishly (fē′ vər ish lē) *adv.* in a highly emotional or nervous way

102

Looking at Style

These ideas may be helpful for discussing Ballard's writing style in *Exploring the* Titanic.

Point out the following sentences to students, noting the use of questions:

■ It was not a good sign. Did it mean that the *Titanic* might be too big a ship to handle safely? (p. 98)

■ Immediately, the *Carpathia* reported that she was racing full steam to the rescue. But could she get there in time? (p. 102)

Then discuss these points:

1. Did Ballard need to include these questions in order to explain what happened to the *Titanic*?

2. Reword the questions, making them statements. How does this change affect your response to the passages?

3. Do you think the use of these questions is effective in creating suspense? Why or why not?

24. ACTIVE READING: Connect
For Alternative Learning Styles
Ask students to visualize the scene in
which another lifeboat almost comes
down on top of Ruth's. Then invite them
to illustrate the scene or describe it in
their own words.

The last lifeboats pull away from the sinking *Titanic*, leaving 1,500 people on board.

and came back with several blankets in her arms. The Beckers walked toward one of the lifeboats, and a sailor picked up Ruth's brother and sister and placed them in the boat.

"That's all for this boat," he called out. "Lower away!"

"Please, those are my children!" cried Ruth's mother. "Let me go with them!"

The sailor allowed Mrs. Becker to step into the lifeboat with her two children. She then called back to Ruth to get into another lifeboat. Ruth went to the next boat and asked the officer if she could get in. He said,

"Sure," picked her up, and dumped her in.

Boat No. 13 was so crowded that Ruth had to stand up. Foot by foot it was lowered down the steep side of the massive ship. The new pulleys shrieked as the ropes passed through them, creaking under the weight of the boat and its load of sixty-four people. After landing in the water, Ruth's lifeboat began to drift. Suddenly Ruth saw another lifeboat coming down right on top of them! Fearing for their lives, the men in charge of her boat shouted, "Stop!" to the sailors up on the deck. But the noise was so great that nobody noticed. The second

24

25. HISTORICAL SIDELIGHT
Most of the passengers who were lost with the *Titanic* were third-class passengers. Only 1 child was lost in first class and none in second class, whereas 52 of the 79 children in third class were lost.

26. LITERARY CONCEPT: Theme
Point out that the "unsinkable" *Titanic* is now "sinking fast," and ask the students what theme, or main message, this outcome suggests. *(Possible responses: Thinking we are unbeatable can blind us to weaknesses; the forces of nature are stronger than human technology.)*

27. ACTIVE READING: Connect
Have students imagine that they are Jack Phillips or Harold Bride and that the captain has just told them, "Now it's every man for himself." Ask them if they would keep trying to work the radio or would leave immediately. *(Possible responses: keep trying the radio, because everyone's chances of survival, including mine, are better if I can get help; leave immediately to save my life)*

lifeboat kept coming down, so close that they could actually touch the bottom of it. All of a sudden, one of the men in Ruth's boat jumped up, pulled out a knife, and cut them free of their lowering ropes. Ruth's boat pushed away from the *Titanic* just as boat No. 15 hit the water inches away from them.

Below, in the third-class decks of the ship, there was much more confusion and alarm. Most of these passengers had not yet been able to get above decks. Some of those who did finally make it out had to break down the barriers between third and first class.

By 1:30 A.M. the bow was well down, and people were beginning to notice the slant of the decks. In the radio room, Bride and Phillips were still <u>desperately</u> sending out calls for help: "We are sinking fast . . . women and children in boats. We cannot last much longer." The radio signal gradually got weaker and weaker as the ship's power faded out. Out on the decks, most passengers now began to move toward the stern area, which was slowly lifting out of the water.

By 2:05 A.M. there were still over fifteen hundred people left on the sinking ship. All the lifeboats were now away, and a strange stillness took hold. People stood quietly on the upper decks, bunching together for warmth, trying to keep away from the side of the tilting ship.

Captain Smith now made his way to the radio room and told Harold Bride and Jack Phillips to save themselves. "Men, you have done your full duty," he told them. "You can do no more. Abandon your cabin. Now it's every man for himself." Phillips kept working the radio, hanging on until the very last moment. Suddenly Bride heard water gurgling up the deck outside the radio room. Phillips heard it, too, and cried, "Come on, let's clear out."

Some of the passengers and crew began to jump overboard . . .

Near the stern, Father Thomas Byles had heard confession and given absolution[6] to over one hundred passengers. Playing to the very end, the members of the ship's brave band finally had to put down their instruments and try to save themselves. In desperation, some of the passengers and crew began to jump overboard as the water crept up the slant of the deck.

Jack Thayer stood with his friend Milton Long at the railing to keep away from the crowds. He had become separated from his father in the confusion on deck. Now Jack and his friend heard muffled thuds and explosions deep within the ship. Suddenly the *Titanic* began to slide into the water. The water rushed up at them. Thayer and Long quickly said goodbye and good luck to each other. Then they both jumped.

---

6. **heard confession and given absolution:** in some religions, the action of the priest who listens to people tell their sins and then declares their forgiveness.

Words to Know and Use	**desperately** (des′ pər it lē) *adv.* acting in a manner that shows extreme need or hopelessness

As he hit the water, Jack Thayer was sucked down. "The cold was terrific. The shock of the water took the breath out of my lungs. Down and down I went, spinning in all directions." When he finally surfaced, gasping for air and numbed by the water, the ship was about forty feet away from him. His friend Milton Long was nowhere to be seen. Jack would never see him again.

Jack Thayer was lucky. As he struggled in the water, his hand came to rest on an overturned lifeboat. He grabbed hold and hung on, barely managing to pull himself up out of the water. Harold Bride had been washed overboard and now also clung to this same boat.

Both Jack and Harold witnessed the mighty ship's last desperate moments. "We could see groups of . . . people aboard, clinging in clusters or bunches, like swarming bees; only to fall in masses, pairs, or singly, as the great part of the ship . . . rose into the sky. . . ." said Thayer. "I looked upwards—we were right under the three enormous propellers. For an instant, I thought they were sure to come right down on top of us.

Then . . . she slid quietly away from us into the sea."

Out in the safety of her lifeboat, Ruth Becker also witnessed the end of the *Titanic*. "I could look back and see this ship, and the decks were just lined with people looking over. Finally, as the *Titanic* sank faster, the lights died out. You could just see the stern remaining in an upright position for a couple of minutes. Then . . . it disappeared."

Then, as Ruth recalled, "there fell upon the ear the most terrible noise that human beings ever listened to—the cries of hundreds of people struggling in the icy cold water, crying for help with a cry we knew could not be answered." In Thayer's words, they became "a long continuous wailing chant." Before long this ghastly wailing stopped, as the freezing water took its toll.

Jack Thayer and Harold Bride and a number of other survivors clung to their overturned lifeboat, inches away from an icy death in the North Atlantic. Numb from the cold and not daring to move in case the boat sank under their weight, they prayed and waited for help. Then, as the first light of dawn crept on the horizon, a rocket was seen in the distance. The *Carpathia* had come to their rescue. ❧

28

28. LITERARY CONCEPT: Literary Nonfiction
How has the author brought the last terrible moments of the Titanic to life for readers? *(Possible responses: He quotes the words of eyewitnesses; he describes the disaster in words that appeal to the senses of sight, hearing, and touch.)* In what ways is this passage like fiction? *(Possible responses It has a climax, "characters" who are real people, and vivid details that convey the setting and events.)*

ENCOURAGING INDEPENDENT READING

The Discovery of the Titanic, nonfiction by Robert D. Ballard

A Night to Remember, nonfiction by Walter Lord

Titanic: *An Illustrated History,* nonfiction illustrated by Ken Marschall

Twentieth-Century Shipwrecks: A Pictorial History, nonfiction by Associated Press Editors and Dan Perkes

Comprehension Check

1. How did the *Titanic* rank in size among ships? *(It was the world's biggest.)*

2. Why did people consider the *Titanic* safe? *(It was said to be unsinkable.)*

3. What did other ships warn the *Titanic* about by radio? *(ice and icebergs ahead)*

4. What caused the damage to the *Titanic?* *(hitting an iceberg)*

5. What indication of trouble did the captain discover below decks after the collision? *(flooding)*

6. How did the *Titanic* alert other ships of its trouble? *(by radioing an S O S signal)*

7. Why were some people unable to leave the sinking ship? *(There were not enough lifeboats.)*

8. How were the survivors rescued? *(by another ship, the Carpathia)*

Student Response

Responding to Reading

1. Any response is valid.

2. **Possible responses:** Yes, because traveling on the maiden voyage of the world's largest ship would be a memorable experience; yes, the *Titanic* was said to be unsinkable and was commanded by a captain with an excellent safety record; no, the "unsinkable" label would make me suspicious.

3. **Possible responses:** The advance publicity, which claimed the ship was unsinkable, might have caused the crew to be careless about spotting icebergs, as evidenced by the fact that no one took the ice warnings seriously; Captain Smith probably was not to blame because his safety record was excellent; Captain Smith was to blame because he should have shut the *Titanic* down; the radio operators were to blame for not giving the captain the final warning from the *Californian*.

4. **Possible responses:** The passengers remained remarkably calm and were either very brave or unaware of the danger; the crew bravely carried out their duties; the crew should have filled all the lifeboats to capacity and informed everyone of the crisis; the radio operators should have tried harder to get the messages to the captain; they acted bravely in manning their station to the very end.

5. **Possible responses:** An informational nonfiction article would not be written in narrative form; it would present the facts plainly, without trying to stir readers' emotions; there would be no effort to introduce characters through whom we relive the event.

6. Any response is valid.

Challenge Question

If a member of your family had died on the *Titanic*, would you have filed a lawsuit? If so, whom would you have sued and why? *(Possible responses: No, because the tragedy was caused by chance; no, because there was no one left who could have paid; yes, I'd have sued the White Star Line for neglecting safety and claiming that the ship was unsinkable)*

Responding to Reading

First Impressions

1. What were you thinking about as you finished this selection? Jot down some notes and be prepared to share them with your classmates.

Second Thoughts

2. Based on the description of the *Titanic* early in the selection, would you have wanted to travel on it? Would you have felt safe? Explain why, citing evidence from the passage in your explanation.

3. Was anyone to blame for the sinking of the ship? Cite details from the story to support your judgment.

   Think about
   • the advance publicity about the *Titanic*
   • the safety record of the captain

4. Evaluate the behavior of passengers and crew as the *Titanic* was sinking.

5. How might this account differ from an article on the same topic written as informational nonfiction?

Broader Connections

6. Are people more or less cautious about new technology than they used to be? Give some examples to support your opinion.

Literary Concept: Informational Writing

Writers of nonfiction material use whatever organization works best for their topic and purpose. In this selection, Ballard describes the *Titanic* using paragraphs organized by topic sentence. When the ship is sinking, he uses chronological order. Find an example of each kind of organization in the article. Why do you think he changed the type of organization he used?

Literary Concept: Informational Writing

At first, the author wants to give us a detailed portrait of the *Titanic*. The topic sentence method of organization is a good way to do this, because the characters, settings, events, and details in each paragraph fill out the main idea. Good examples include the second paragraph on page 95 and the fourth paragraph on page 96. Once the *Titanic* begins to receive ice warnings (p. 98), time is all-important and is the natural way to organize the story of the ship's last hours. Focusing on time also heightens the suspense. Examples include the first and third paragraphs on page 99.

Writing Options

1. The *Titanic* was evacuated traditionally, "women and children first." Write an **essay** on whether you agree or disagree with this principle.

2. Write an **advertisement** for the *Titanic*. Before you begin, skim the description of the *Titanic* to find details and features that you could use to entice customers.

3. Write a **message in a bottle** you might have thrown overboard if you had been one of the passengers in a crowded lifeboat.

4. Imagine that you are the captain of the *Carpathia*. Write the ship's **log entry** describing what you see when you arrive, too late, at the scene.

Vocabulary Practice

Exercise   On a separate sheet of paper, write the word from the list that best completes the sentence.

1. The passenger ship business in 1907 was just as __?__ as the airline industry is now.

2. Even today, people pay __?__ to the courage of the *Titanic's* captain and crew.

3. Given a choice, most people would choose first class rooms over a third class __?__.

4. The rich and __?__, like the Astors, were physically separated from the lower classes.

5. The swimming pool on board was a real __?__; it was the first to be built on a steamship.

6. A near collision at the *Titanic's* launching seemed to be an __?__ of bad things to come.

7. Even though it was called "unsinkable," the *Titanic* did not stay afloat __?__.

8. In fearful haste, grim sailors __?__ lowered lifeboats into the cold water.

9. With no lifeboats left, some passengers leaped __?__ into the icy waters.

10. No one would have believed a __?__ that predicted the *Titanic's* sinking.

> **Words to Know and Use**
>
> accommodation
> aristocratic
> competitive
> desperately
> feverishly
> indefinitely
> novelty
> omen
> prophecy
> tribute

Writing Options

The Writing Options are designed to meet varied student interests and abilities. Have each student choose one writing activity to complete.

Journal Update Invite students to write about whether their feelings about traveling on a luxury ocean liner have changed.

Links to Writer's Craft

Writing Option 4 is an exercise in personal writing. For more practice, see *The Writer's Craft*, Grade 7, "Observation and Description," pages 48–68.

Vocabulary Practice

Answers to Exercise

1. competitive   6. omen
2. tribute   7. indefinitely
3. accommodations   8. feverishly
4. aristocratic   9. desperately
5. novelty   10. prophecy

For Alternative Learning Styles

Assign students to small groups. Have each group write sentences that contain the vocabulary words as well as clues to their meanings. Then have the groups copy their sentences, leaving a blank where each vocabulary word goes. Tell the groups to exchange their sentences and to fill in each other's blanks.

Closure

Ask students how the tunnel vision portrayed in the excerpt from *Exploring the Titanic* compares with that portrayed in "Lose Now, Pay Later" and "The Charge of the Light Brigade." Note that each selection shows what can happen when people don't heed warnings or see "the whole picture."

The Spelling Connection

Compound Words and Contractions When two words are connected with no change in either word or are joined by a hyphen, the word formed is called a **compound word**. When an apostrophe is used to show that one or more letters have been omitted, the word is called a **contraction**.

Compound Words/Contractions from the Selection
eyewitness   nightmare   nearby   overboard
background   first-class   twenty-two   that's   it's

Other Compound Words and Contractions
nighttime   meanwhile   everywhere   someone
blue-eyed   one-half   would've   ninety-four

Exercise Make up an imaginary news report, using compound words and contractions, that answers these questions.

1. What happened during the night? Where? Why?

2. What exactly did an eyewitness tell you?

3. Who was involved? What is known about them?

Extending the Lesson

Options for Learning

These activities suit a variety of learning styles and modes of expression.

Collaborative Learning Activities
See Options 1, 2, and 4.

1. Facts to Fathom Ballard has also written *The Discovery of the Titanic,* a longer work that contains many before-and-after photographs of the ship.

2. See the Movie! Invite students to read and report on *A Night to Remember* by Walter Lord (1955), the historical novel on which the movie is based.

3. Dramatic Drawing Ballard's books, as well as the November 1987 issue of *National Geographic* magazine, contain detailed chronologies and artist's renderings of the ship's sinking.

4. On the Rocks You might also assign some students to research the International Ice Patrol and the International Safety of Life at Sea conventions.

 FACT FINDER SCIENCE

Students can use an encyclopedia or a dictionary to find out that about 90 percent of an iceberg's mass is below the surface of the water.

Robert D. Ballard

■ **More About the Author** Robert Ballard is one of the world's leading marine geologists. He helped discover volcanic vents nine thousand feet beneath the Pacific Ocean near the Galápagos Islands. He played a major role in the development of the Argo/Jason underwater exploration system that was used to find the *Titanic.*

■ **Other Works** Nonfiction: *The Discovery of the Bismarck, The Discovery of the Titanic, Exploring Our living Planet, The Wreck of the Isis.*

 ■ **Awards** Compass Distinguished Achievement Award, Marine Technology Society; Newcomb Cleveland Prize, American Association for the Advancement of Science; Cutty Sark Science Award, *Science Digest.*

Options for Learning (Multimodal/Cross-Curricular Activities)

1 • Facts to Fathom Read the rest of *Exploring the Titanic,* or use other resources, to find out how the sunken ship was finally discovered. Report on your findings to the class.

2 • See the Movie! Rent either *The Titanic* (1953) or *A Night to Remember* (1958). Screen it for your class and lead a discussion on the differences between the movie version and Ballard's written account.

3 • Dramatic Drawing Based on what you've learned, illustrate a dramatic scene from the sinking of the *Titanic.*

4 • On the Rocks Using articles from magazines such as *National Geographic,* report to the class on modern technologies that now help prevent disasters like the sinking of the *Titanic.*

 FACT FINDER SCIENCE

What percentage of an iceberg lies under water?

Robert D. Ballard
1942-

Robert Ballard has been fascinated by the sea since childhood, when he explored beaches and read about famous sailors such as Captain Cook and Admiral Byrd. As an adult, Ballard helped pay for his education in oceanography by training dolphins at a marine park. Eventually, Ballard joined the staff at Woods Hole Oceanographic Institute in Massachusetts. There he began his search for and eventual discovery of the *Titanic,* using remote-control underwater robots. Among the first things the robot cameras saw were the empty lifeboat racks— "the last thing many of the people saw as they were looking for a lifeboat," Ballard says.

The explorer has now set his sights on inspiring children to learn. "We need to declare war on ignorance, and the only way is through education. I want to recruit people to study science, just as a coach recruits basketball players."

Cross-Curricular Projects

Science Have a group of students research icebergs in the North Atlantic. Have students detail their origin, size, and appearance and the way in which they enter shipping lanes.

Social Studies Although class differences in our society are not as obvious as the differences aboard the *Titanic,* they do exist. Have students discuss and list ways in which class differences are manifested in our society.

Art/Math Students can do research to find diagrams and measurements of the *Titanic* in order to make a class model of the ship. Students should build their model to scale and include an explanation of the scale.

Music Musical students may enjoy collaborating on a ballad or a round that pays tribute to the crew or passengers of the *Titanic.* Some students may already know songs about the *Titanic.*

WRITER'S WORKSHOP

DESCRIPTIVE WRITING

What's one food that you know you'll never forget? In the subunit you've just read, a poem describes the taste of stolen strawberries, freshly picked. A short story describes a mysterious dessert called swoodies. What are your own best or worst—or strangest— experiences with food? This workshop will let you share some of them as you write a restaurant review. You may review an eating place you love, one you hate, or one you have mixed feelings about. You'll use **observation** and **description** as you put your impressions into words.

USE DESCRIPTIVE WRITING FOR

character sketches
letters
stories
poems
reports
reviews
advertisements
travel guides

GUIDED ASSIGNMENT: RESTAURANT REVIEW

Write a review describing a restaurant or another eating place you know well. In your review make your opinion clear.

> Here is one writer's PASSkey to this assignment.

PURPOSE: To observe and describe

AUDIENCE: People in your community

SUBJECT: A local restaurant or eating place

STRUCTURE: Review

◄ **STUDENT MODEL**

The Real Thing
by Lee Granville

Buck, buck, ba-gawk! I can almost hear clucking as we step through the door. Inside, the walls are covered with pictures of chickens and a cartoon mural of two puzzled chickens looking at an ax and a chopping block. This is the Chicken Pie Shop, my favorite restaurant.

My mother and I find an empty booth. The clatter of dishes and silverware being dumped into bus trays rings in my ears. Under the fluorescent lights, the yellow plastic seats look greenish, and the Formica tables look old. A waitress in a yellow uniform zooms up,

◄ A surprising first line catches readers' interest.

◄ The writer sets a positive focus.

◄ Sensory details describe sights and sounds.

WRITER'S WORKSHOP   109

ADDITIONAL RESOURCES

Unit One Resource Book
Writer's Workshop Worksheet, p. 81
Writer's Workshop: Peer and Self-Evaluation, p. 82
Writer's Workshop: Assessment Guidelines, p. 83

Technology and Enrichment
Thinking Skills Transparency 2

Elaboration, Revision, and Proofreading
   Transparencies 5–8
Fine Arts Transparency Pack

Links to
Writer's Craft

For more about descriptive writing, see *The Writer's Craft*, Grade 7, "Observation and Description," pages 49–61. See also pages 221–223, "Writing Techniques."

Objectives

■ To understand the purpose and elements of a restaurant review

■ To describe and evaluate a restaurant

■ To draft, revise, edit, and share descriptive writing

Teaching Strategies

DISCUSSING THE ASSIGNMENT

Invite a few volunteers to describe what they remember most about their favorite (or least favorite) restaurants. Have them talk about times when the food was wonderful and times when it was not. Encourage them to recall other impressions about their experiences. Then point out the PASSkey for the Guided Assignment, reminding students that their work should include an opinion. Note that students' PASSkeys may be different from this one, but that listing their own purpose, audience, subject, and structure will help keep them aware of the elements of the assignment.

If you wish, you may give students the option of writing about something else that is important to them. Alternative Writing and Research Topics at the bottom of the following page offers additional suggestions.

Remind students that pages 694–696 of the Writer's Handbook provide an overview of each step of the writing process and explain the PASSkey in detail.

ANALYZING THE MODEL

Call on a volunteer to read aloud the student model on pages 109–110. Note that Lee describes the whole restaurant experience, not just the food. Then ask students how Lee feels about the place. *(He likes it; the food is delicious and the tacky setting and surly service are part of the whole fun package.)* You may want to suggest that students adopt a particular tone for their reviews, such as humorous or horrified, to pull the description together.

Have students work in pairs to analyze the model further. You may wish to write these questions on the board to guide discussion.

■ How does Lee begin his review of the Chicken Pie Shop?

■ Which words help you to see, feel, hear, smell, and taste things in the restaurant? Which words reveal Lee's opinion about the dinner?

■ Why is Lee's choice of time order appropriate for the review?

■ How does his description of the waitress and the restaurant itself add to the review?

Afterward, have volunteers share with the class any other observations they made about the review.

Prewrite and Explore

You might have the class brainstorm words that describe hearing, smell, taste, and touch. If you list the words on the board, students can use them in their writing.

Modeling Explain that freewriting is a way of brainstorming on paper and is best done individually. On an overhead, show an example of your own freewriting. Explain that from your freewriting, you might choose an idea and freewrite again about that idea.

An unusual comparison describes the waitress. ▶

takes our order without smiling, and zooms off again like a taxi. However, the tacky atmosphere and grouchy service don't bother us. We're about to eat the world's tastiest chicken pies.

Here they are, steaming on the plates that the waitress has just slapped down in front of us. The only problem with eating here is the danger of burning your mouth. This happens when you can't wait to dig in to the moist chunks of chicken and the creamy gravy you see through the hole in the crust. The crust is not thin or greasy like the crusts of frozen chicken pies. It's smooth and sort of floury and smells like warm pie crust fresh from the oven.

Specific adjectives and adverbs describe the food. ▶

As you carefully begin eating, you discover that this pie is the real thing. It has huge pieces of chicken, thick gravy, and no peas or carrots to get in your way. Next to the pie is an ice-cream scoop of real, not fake, mashed potatoes, covered in spicy gravy.

My mother and I don't talk—we're too busy shoveling in the food. As soon as we finish, the waitress is back. All in one swoop she clears the table, gives us the bill, and asks if we want dessert. She can't wait to be rid of us. Another load of dishes crashes into a bus tray as we pass the chicken mural on our way out. This place is definitely not elegant—but it does serve really good chicken pie.

The writer clearly states an opinion. ▶

Now that you've read Lee's review, start your own.

Prewrite and Explore

1 **Let your taste buds talk** Imagine your taste buds brainstorming about eating places they especially like and hate. Try jotting down the places they'd probably put in each category. Think of places you visit often, like fast-food shops or the school cafeteria, as well as places you've visited only once or twice.

Alternative Writing and Research Topics

Descriptive Writing Find a favorite spot outdoors like the narrator's fishing pond in "Stolen Day." Go there to observe and take notes on what you see and hear. Then write a description of the place, using sensory details.

Narrative Writing Imagine what happens to the characters in "Lose Now, Pay Later" after some time has passed. Write the next episode of the story.

Poetry Think about the contrasting feelings the speaker in "For My Father" has toward her father. Write a short poem dealing with your own mixed feelings about someone you know.

Research: Disasters Research and write an article about a real disaster like the sinking of the *Titanic*. Try to make your nonfiction article literary, like Ballard's article, rather than purely factual.

When you've listed several places, you can take a quick mental tour of them. Any place you remember well or have strong feelings about will make a good subject.

2 **Set your focus** In a restaurant review you explain your opinion of the restaurant. Your opinion may be positive or negative. It may be based on the way the food tastes, looks, and is prepared or on the service or the atmosphere. It may be based on several of these factors. Freewrite briefly to focus on your opinion. In **freewriting** you write whatever comes to your mind about the subject for three to five minutes. Don't worry about using complete sentences or proper spelling or punctuation. When you finish, see if you know yet which factors your opinion is based on.

GATHERING INFORMATION

Now you have time to recall details about the place you've chosen. Your freewriting can guide your memory. Using a chart like the one below can help you think of details. Fill in the sections you can. Notice what Lee filled in about the Chicken Pie Shop.

◀ **TIP**
Use "tunnel vision" to zero in on one sense at a time.

Hear	Smell	Touch
dishes clanking not much talk	oven-fresh	hot!

◀ **STUDENT MODEL**

See	Taste
chicken pictures old Formica tables faded yellow seats steaming pies	smooth, floury crust moist chicken rich gravy real mashed potatoes

---

Draft and Discover

1 **Begin drafting** As you draft, go into as much detail as possible. Your prewriting chart will help. You might start by describing the first thing you notice when you walk into the restaurant, then move on to other things you notice. If you prefer, you may start by stating your opinion, then describe the factors that support it.

As an alternative to the graphic organizer shown in the text, students may prefer making time lines or inventing their own graphic organizers. Note that ideas for other graphic organizers can be found in the Thinking Skills Transparency Pack.

Draft and Discover

One effective way to begin drafting is to choose a sensory word and use it to describe something in the restaurant. For example, a student who chooses the word *crusty* might write, "With my first bite of the warm, crusty roll dripping with honey, I closed my eyes and enjoyed every crumb." Using this as an opening sentence, the student can then continue the description. Later, that sentence and the ones that follow can be used wherever they fit best.

TEACHING TIP: COMPUTER

Most word processing programs give students the option of formatting their pages in one column or in multiple columns. Suggest that those who draft on a computer use a two-column format. Students can then write their drafts in the column at the left of the screen, leaving the column at the right free for questions, comments, notes, possible revisions, and points they may want to discuss with you or a peer reader. Finally, just before the last rewrite, students can delete whatever is in the column at the right and then reformat to print their work in one column.

Paragraphs at Work

As students write, encourage them to think in paragraphs—that is, in groups of related sentences. For example, a student writing in time order might decide that the first paragraph should describe entering the restaurant. In that case, all the sentences in the paragraph should have something to do with that idea. A sentence about dessert should be moved to a later paragraph. It might be a good idea to list the following reminders on the board.

■ Make sure that each paragraph has a single focus.

■ Make sure that every sentence in a paragraph is related to the focus.

■ Delete sentences or details that don't belong, or move them to other paragraphs.

Tell students that more help on writing strong and effective paragraphs appears in Tips for Better Paragraphs, pages 697–701.

Revise Your Writing

As students begin revising, move around the room and encourage them to replace boring, vague modifiers with crisp, precise ones. Students unfamiliar with a thesaurus might benefit from a quick lesson.

Some students might want to read their work quietly to their peer reviewers so that they can identify paragraphs that need to be reworked. At the same time, students might be able to help one another with transitions to aid coherence.

Before students complete the revising process, remind them that a review should include an opinion. Suggest that they place their opinion toward the end of the review, but that they provide a clue or two about it earlier so that the audience is not surprised when they finally read the verdict.

CONFERENCING TIP

As you conference with individual writers for this workshop, you may wish to focus on

- progress in expressing an opinion
- using strong beginnings
- proper use of adjectives and adverbs

LITERARY MODEL
from "Lose Now, Pay Later," by Carol Farley

COMPUTER TIP
A search feature can find all the places you've used a certain word. Try searching for vague adjectives like *nice* and *gross,* then replace them with a more specific modifier.

2 Use comparisons   One way to help a reader imagine what you are describing is by comparing it to something else. Look at the following example. Which two things are compared?

▶ Do you know that wonderful spurt of air that rushes out when you first open an expensive box of candy? The inside of that store smelled just like the inside of one of those boxes.

3 Be specific   Go for specific adjectives and adverbs. Describing a hamburger as *bad, gross, fine,* or *delicious* is vague. Specific modifiers—like *greasy, dry,* or *tender*—convey stronger sensory details. General terms like *good* and *bad* weaken description, but you may need them to sum up your opinion. Ask a friend whether you're using them effectively.

Revise Your Writing

1 Showcase your reasons and opinion   As you read your draft, look again for the reasons that support your opinion. They will be clearer now, and you can revise to spotlight them. For example, you may decide that the food is only average but you love the atmosphere. Then you might write a paragraph about each, or you might add more details about food and atmosphere to each body paragraph.

2 Get a strong start   After you have a draft you like, try adding a catchy first sentence: a vivid description, an unusual comparison, or a surprising statement. When you are satisfied with your introduction, use the questions below to help you polish your work.

Revision Questions

For You	For a Peer Reader
1. How do I use sensory details to support my opinion?	1. What would you expect to find if you ate at this place?
2. Where might I use a comparison or a more specific modifier?	2. How would you sum up my opinion? On which factors do you think I based it?
3. Does my first sentence catch the readers' interest?	3. Which part of my review was most vivid or surprising?

Managing the Paper Load

Some teachers manage their paper load by looking only at the results of the writing process, ignoring the intermediate stages. Although this practice takes less time, it doesn't help students learn at what point in the process they could have improved their work.

The best idea is to compromise. You don't need to see the results of brainstorming or of small-group sessions unless students themselves request it. However, you should work with students on an individual basis when it comes to drafts and revisions. Even the proofreading stage of students' work may show you where grammar, usage, and mechanics errors proliferate and may suggest refresher lessons for you to teach.

Proofread

Correct errors in grammar and mechanics. Look carefully at your use of adjectives and adverbs. If you wish, ask a peer to help.

THE EDITOR'S EYE: CONFUSING ADJECTIVES AND ADVERBS

Choose adjectives to modify nouns and pronouns. Choose adverbs to modify verbs, adjectives, and other adverbs.

Sometimes you may not be sure whether to choose an adjective or an adverb. Ask yourself which kind of word the modifier describes.

Problem   But it does serve *real* good chicken pie.

The modifier *real* describes *good,* an adjective. Only adverbs describe adjectives, so the adverb form is needed.

Revised   But it does serve *really* good chicken pie.

NEED MORE HELP?

See the Language Workshop on pages 114–116 and pages 752–753 of the Language Handbook.

Publish and Present

Here is a suggestion for sharing your work with others.

A Restaurant Guide   Gather the class's reviews, grouping together reviews of similar places. Create a table of contents, design a cover, and distribute copies to class members and friends.

Reflect on Your Writing

Write answers to the following questions. Then attach them to your review and add it to your portfolio.

1. Which part of this review was most fun to write? Why?
2. As I worked, what did I discover about my writing process?

◄ FOR YOUR PORTFOLIO ......

Assessment Guidelines

These guidelines may help you assess student writing:

Content
1. The review describes a restaurant experience in detail.
2. An opinion of the restaurant is clearly stated.
3. The opinion is consistent with the description that precedes it.

Style
4. The opening sentence captures interest.

5. Specific modifiers provide colorful details.

Usage and Mechanics
6. The review follows rules of standard grammar and usage.
7. Adjectives and adverbs are used correctly.
8. Names of places and foods are spelled correctly.

See also *Unit One Resource Book,* page 83.

Proofread

Note that The Editor's Eye feature previews the content in the Language Workshop that follows. If the class or individual students might benefit from additional work, you may choose to teach the Language Workshop, pages 114–116, before the students proofread.

Use the following models for reinforcement. (Correct answers are underlined.)

1. This is my (<u>honest</u>, honestly) opinion.

2. Diners here are (usual, <u>usually</u>) happy with the food.

3. We were (prompt, <u>promptly</u>) seated at our table.

4. This restaurant prepares vegetables (amazing, <u>amazingly</u>) well.

5. This is a (<u>terrific</u>, terrifically) dinner.

Publish and Present

Restaurant reviews might be arranged alphabetically or be clustered according to the type of food served. Students might attach a copy of the restaurant's menu to their review. They might also decorate the cover with copies of the logos of several of the restaurants.

Writing for the Community You might encourage individual students to send their reviews to the restaurants they described. A school or local newspaper might publish some of the reviews. Finally, the public library might be given a copy of the finished booklet to be used as a resource for teenagers.

Reflect on Your Writing

You may choose to have students answer the following questions in addition to or instead of those in their text:

1. Did freewriting work for me?

2. Did I observe well enough to write a good description?

Closure

Point out to students that description is a fundamental part of almost every kind of writing. Explain that description gives life, color, and clarity to the writing.

Objectives

■ To understand that adjectives modify nouns

■ To understand that adverbs modify verbs, adjectives, and other adverbs

■ To use adjectives and adverbs correctly

Teaching Strategies

WHICH MODIFIER IS CORRECT?

Begin the workshop by reviewing with students that adjectives modify nouns and that adverbs modify verbs, adjectives, and other adverbs. On the chalkboard write the following:

■ Adjectives answer the questions *what kind? which one? how much? how many?*

■ Adverbs answer the questions *how? when? where? to what extent?*

Then read the following sentences to students as a review. Ask students to determine whether the italicized word is an adjective or adverb by figuring out what question it answers. If necessary, try all eight of the adjective/adverb questions with each sentence. Although it takes time, students will soon see that only one question out of eight really fits.

1. The Purple Pheasant is a *really* good restaurant. (To what extent is it good?—adverb)

2. I had a *delicious* meal. (What kind of meal was it?—adjective)

3. We had *four* people in our party. (How many people were there?—adjective)

4. The waiter brought our menus *immediately.* (When did he bring them?—adverb)

5. He *carefully* described the day's specials. (How did he describe them?—adverb)

6. I chose *this* dinner on the menu. (Which one did I choose?—adjective)

7. We certainly had *enough* food! (How much did we have?—adjective)

8. Of course we'll go *there* again. (Where will we go?—adverb)

USING ADJECTIVES AND ADVERBS

Use **adjectives** to describe nouns and pronouns. Use **adverbs** to describe verbs, adjectives, and other adverbs.

The more specific and vivid your adjectives and adverbs are, the stronger your descriptions will be.

Adjectives

Adjectives modify, or describe, nouns and pronouns. In the sentences below, the words in italics are adjectives.

> The ship was about *forty* feet away. . . .

> "I could look back and see *this* ship, and the decks were just lined with people looking over. . . .

> Before long this *ghastly* wailing stopped, as the *freezing* water took its toll.

Adjectives tell *which one* (this ship), *how much* or *how many* (forty feet), or *what kind* (freezing water). Specific adjectives are as exact as possible. For example, *forty* is more specific than *several*, and *ghastly* is a vivid way to describe *wailing*.

LITERARY MODEL
from *Exploring the Titanic,* by Robert D. Ballard ►

Adverbs

Adverbs modify verbs, adjectives, and other adverbs. In the sentences below, the words in italics are adverbs.

> I limped *painfully away.* . . .

> They did laugh at me *pretty often.* . . .

Adverbs answer the question *how* (I limped painfully), *where* (I limped away), *when* (they laughed often), or *to what extent* (pretty often). Many adverbs are formed by adding *-ly* to adjectives (painful/painfully). Specific, vivid adverbs bring your writing to life.

SPELLING TIP
When you form an adverb by adding *-ly* to an adjective that ends in *l*, keep both *l*'s: *painful + -ly = painfully* ►

114   UNIT ONE   TUNNEL VISION

ADDITIONAL RESOURCES
Unit One Resource Book
Language Workshop Practice, p. 84

Technology and Enrichment
Grammar and Usage Copy Masters, pp. 4, 5, 60

Grammar Test Generator

Links to
Writer's Craft

For more about adjectives and adverbs, see *The Writer's Craft,* Grade 7, "Using Adjectives," pages 495–513, and "Using Adverbs," pages 515–531.

Common Errors in Using Adjectives and Adverbs

This, These, That, and Those   *This, these, that,* and *those* can be **demonstrative adjectives,** or adjectives that point out *which one* or *which ones. This* and *that* are singular and modify singular nouns and pronouns. *These* and *those* are plural and modify plural nouns and pronouns. In addition, the nouns *kind* and *sort* are singular; *kinds* and *sorts* are plural. Use the correct demonstrative adjectives with them.

Singular	Plural
this shoe	these shoes
that shoe	those shoes
this kind	these kinds
that sort	those sorts

Never use the words *here* or *there* with demonstrative adjectives.

Incorrect	Correct
Look at that there cabin.	Look at that cabin.

Never use the pronoun *them* in place of a demonstrative adjective.

Incorrect	Correct
Who sent them messages?	Who sent those messages?

Exercise 1   Concept Check   Write the correct adjective.

1. I wonder if (this, these) life jacket is the right size.
2. You may not enter (that, those) lifeboats without permission.
3. Have you ever seen (this, these) type of flare before?
4. Quickly, grab (that, that there) rope and pull!
5. (Them, Those) radio operators stayed on the job all night.

Good/Well, Real/Really, Bad/Badly

Because the adjectives *good, real,* and *bad* and their adverb partners *well, really,* and *badly* are used in similar situations, writers sometimes confuse them. To make the correct choice, first decide which part of speech the modifier is describing.

Sherwood Anderson writes (good, well).

The modifier tells how Anderson *writes;* it describes a verb. So you would choose the adverb, *well.*

His story is (real, really) funny.

Begin the review with easy sentences without "problems" like extra clauses, gerunds, and infinitive phrases. However, as students become more secure in choosing the correct modifiers, challenge them with sentences such as these:

1. Sentences with predicate nouns, pronouns, or adjectives:

My favorite dish is *this* one. (Which one?—adjective)

It is *absolutely* wonderful! (To what extent is it wonderful?—adverb)

2. Sentences with more than one clause (although you don't have to discuss clauses here):

Someday Tanya will become a chef, because she *really* wants that career. (When will she become a chef?—adverb; to what extent does she want it?—adverb)

For Alternative Learning Styles   Visual learners may profit from keeping a list of adjective suffixes handy. Point out that they can often recognize adjectives by identifying typical suffixes such as *-ful* in *plentiful* and *powerful* and *-ous* as in *courageous.* Have them draw up a list of other suffixes commonly used to form adjectives, such as *-able/-ible, -ant/-ent, -ive, -less, -like,* and *-some.* Challenge students to write an adjective that ends in each suffix.

Answers to Exercise 1

1. this
2. those
3. this
4. that
5. Those

Grammar Games: Adjective-Adverb Dash

Prepare beforehand approximately fifty sentence strips in which either an adjective or an adverb is missing. Have students form two or three teams.

Reveal the first sentence to the first players on each team. These players dash to the chalkboard and write an adjective or an adverb that would make sense in the sentence. The first person to write a correct word wins one point for his or her team. Then these players go to the end of their teams' lines, and the next player on each team takes a turn. The team with the most points wins the game.

Answers to Exercise 2

1. brightly
2. Suddenly
3. cool
4. badly
5. heavy
6. proudly
7. good
8. really
9. happily
10. Tired

Answers to Exercise 3

Responses may vary slightly. Possible response:

Have you tried <u>these</u> new desserts called swoodies? Those shops offering them are everywhere now. The scent of <u>these</u> swoodies is irresistible. My favorite flavor is <u>that</u> chocolate almond. I enjoy this kind of treat as often as I want. Since I've gained a few pounds, my clothes fit <u>tightly</u>, but if I use the slimmer, they'll look <u>good</u> again. The slimmer seems <u>really</u> eerie at first. It's a tall plain booth without windows. Still, it works really <u>well</u>.

Answers to Exercise 4

Answers will vary. Check students' writing to assess their grasp of the Workshop lesson.

Closure

Remind students that no matter what kinds of writing they do, they are likely to use adjectives and adverbs. Have a volunteer choose a paragraph in any fiction or nonfiction selection in the book and read it aloud, omitting every adjective and adverb. Ask the class what is left out when the modifiers are omitted. *(information, preciseness, color, size, sensory details)*

The modifier tells how *funny* the story is; it describes an adjective. So you would choose the adverb, *really*.

At school, the boy's legs hurt (bad, badly).

The modifier tells how the boy's legs *hurt*; it describes a verb. So you would choose the adverb, *badly*.

Watch for modifiers that follow linking verbs (*is, seems, looks, smells, tastes, sounds, feels*, and so forth). These modifiers are not adverbs but predicate adjectives.

He feels (bad, badly) when his family laughs at him.

The modifier describes a pronoun, *he*. So you would choose the adjective, *bad*.

Exercise 2　Concept Check　Write the correct modifier.

1. The pond sparkles (bright, brightly) in the sun.
2. (Sudden, Suddenly) the boy decides to go fishing.
3. To his bare toes the water feels (cool, coolly).
4. He wants (bad, badly) to catch the giant carp.
5. The carp is (heavy, heavily) in his arms, but he gets it home.
6. He (proud, proudly) shows the carp to his family.
7. The boy feels (good, well) about his accomplishment.
8. His family is (real, really) surprised at the size of the fish.
9. His brothers and sisters shout (happy, happily).
10. (Tired, Tiredly) after a long day, the boy finally goes to bed.

Exercise 3　Revision Skill　Copy the paragraph correctly.

Have you tried this new desserts called swoodies? Those shops offering them are everywhere now. The scent of them swoodies is irresistible. My favorite flavor is that there chocolate almond. I enjoy this kind of treat as often as I want. Since I've gained a few pounds, my clothes fit tight, but if I use the slimmer, they'll look well again. The slimmer seems real eerie at first. It's a tall plain booth without windows. Still, it works real good.

LANGUAGE HANDBOOK
For review and practice:
Section 7, Using Adjectives and Adverbs, pages 749–752, 756–758.

Exercise 4　Revising Your Writing

1. Reread the descriptive writing you did for the Writer's Workshop.
2. Correct any errors in your use of adjectives and adverbs.
3. Add five specific, vivid modifiers to your writing.

Additional Practice

Choose the correct modifier from each pair in parentheses. Write the new sentences. (Correct modifiers are underlined.)

1. (<u>This,</u> These) restaurant looks (real, <u>really</u>) tacky, but (<u>that</u>, those) kind of tackiness is part of its charm.

2. In fact, people flock in (constant, <u>constantly</u>) to see the (<u>wonderful,</u> wonderfully) decorations.

3. (Them, <u>Those</u>) decorations are not of (<u>great,</u> greatly) importance, however.

4. The (<u>delicious,</u> deliciously) food, which is prepared (creative, <u>creatively</u>) by a (<u>famous,</u> famously) chef, is the restaurant's most (<u>popular,</u> popularly) attraction.

5. (<u>That,</u> That there) pasta is (true, <u>truly</u>) my favorite kind, and (this, <u>these</u>) omelets are the ones that Dee (real, <u>really</u>) enjoys.

VOCABULARY
WORKSHOP

CONTEXT CLUES

Part of reading is discovering new words. Often, you can figure out the meanings of unfamiliar words by using context clues. A word's **context** is the sentences and paragraphs surrounding it. If you didn't know the meaning of *saber,* which clues in the sentence below could help you figure it out?

> The men of the Light Brigade charged, their sharp sabers flashing in the air, slashing at the enemy.

When you read that a saber is sharp, can flash in the air, and is used to slash at an enemy, you can guess that it is a kind of sword.

A **definition,** one kind of context clue, directly states the meaning of a word. Definition clues may be set off with commas, dashes, or parentheses. They may follow the key terms *or, is, that is, who is, which is,* or *in other words.*

> The enemy forces were shattered, *or* completely broken.

An **example,** another kind of context clue, may follow the key terms *like, such as, for example, for instance,* or *other.*

> Did no soldiers feel misgivings, *such as* the uneasy sense that the order was a mistake or the fear that they were outnumbered?

◄ **NOTE**
Use inference to help you guess what an example clue reveals about a word's meaning.

Exercise   Using Context Clues   With the help of context clues, explain the meaning of each italicized word as it is used below.

1. The men rode a *league,* or three miles, into the valley and back.
2. Of the entire *brigade*—a group of hundreds of soldiers—only a few survived.
3. None of the soldiers showed signs of *dismay,* such as trembling or running away.
4. Like other famous mistakes, the order to charge was a *blunder.*
5. The unexpected charge of the Light Brigade *sundered,* or divided, the enemy forces.
6. Tennyson's poem praises the soldiers' *fortitude;* for example, the soldiers attacked bravely, though they knew they couldn't win.

ADDITIONAL RESOURCES
Unit One Resource Book
Vocabulary Workshop Practice, p. 85

Objectives

■ To learn to use context clues in reading

■ To use context clues to find the meanings of new words

Teaching Strategies

Have a volunteer read aloud the paragraphs on page 117 in which the words *definition* and *example* are bold-faced. Have the class repeat the words or name the kinds of punctuation signaling context clues. Then provide oral practice by having students define the italicized term in each sentence below and name the clue that helped them know its meaning.

1. Some restaurants use French words to name dishes; *brulée,* for example, tells that a dish has been browned. (Brulée *means browned; the clue is "for example."*)

2. Fans of spicy food might enjoy chicken *moutard,* that is, chicken in mustard sauce. (Moutard *indicates a mustard sauce; the clue is "that is."*)

3. Lasagna Florentine, or noodles layered with spinach, is tasty. (Florentine *means "with spinach"; "or" is the clue.*)

TEACHING TIP: LEP

Help students whose first language is not English understand how context clues work by having them write context-clue sentences in English in which the new words come from their own first languages.

Answers to Exercise

1. A *league* is a distance of three miles.

2. A *brigade* is a group of hundreds of soldiers.

3. *Dismay* has something to do with fear, because signs of dismay are trembling and running away.

4. A *blunder* is a mistake.

5. *Sundered* means "divided."

6. *Fortitude* involves bravery.

Additional Practice

Use context clues to explain the meaning of the bold-faced words. (Context clues are in italics.)

1. Benjamin Franklin is known for his **aphorisms**—*short statements expressing wise observations.*

2. Cara claimed the painting of Washington was **bona fide,** but nothing about it seemed *genuine.*

3. Ancient Sumer is an example of a **hagiocracy** because it was a *land ruled by its religious leaders.*

Objectives

- To extend the study of the unit theme, "A Matter of Perspective," to novels and other longer works

- To read independently for personal enrichment and enjoyment

MONKEY ISLAND

Study Focus

- False impressions people have about the homeless

- The setting and its effect on the main character

- A character's conflicts with society

About Paula Fox

Fox's books for young people are noted for their intelligence and originality. She incorporates many autobiographical details in her writing, and her story-telling reflects a strong social concern.

- **Other Works** Novels: *Maurice's Room, The Village by the Sea, Lily and the Lost Boy, A Place Apart, Hungry Fred*

 - **Awards** Newbery Medal, 1974, for *The Slave Dancer;* American Book Award, 1983, for *A Place Apart;* Newbery Honor Book, 1985, for *One-Eyed Cat*

Reading on Your Own

Suggested Novels for Unit One

The novels introduced on these pages allow you to explore the unit theme, "A Matter of Perspective," in more depth and in different ways.

118

MONKEY ISLAND
PAULA FOX ©1991

After his father and his mother both leave him, eleven-year-old Clay becomes a homeless person living on the streets of New York City. Clay's new life is a sad and frightening change from his former life. His father has lost his job and is gone; his mother is unable to bear life in a welfare hotel and disappears. Clay's new circumstances completely change his perspective. While he searches for his mother, Clay makes friends with two homeless men, who become his family. Clay now must survive cold, hunger, and vicious street gangs that prey on homeless people. Throughout this exciting urban survival story, Clay discovers that although homelessness can happen to anyone, only the strong survive. Read to find out . . .

- whether Clay can survive on his own in this nightmarish environment

- whether Clay will find his mother

- whether Clay and his mother will be able to make a decent life together

THE WITCH OF BLACKBIRD POND
ELIZABETH GEORGE SPEARE ©1958

How would you feel if you were accused of witchcraft and put on trial because of your actions and beliefs? In this exciting historical novel set in New England in the late 1600s, a girl named Kit faces persecution by the entire community when she moves to a Puritan village. Read to find out how she tries to overcome the tunnel vision of people who are suspicious of everyone. As you read, consider the following questions:

• What if everything you normally do were suddenly seen as unnatural?

• How would you have responded to the fear and persecution common during this time of witch hunts?

• How would it feel to suddenly become the target of a whole community's suspicions?

AGAINST THE STORM
GAYE HICYILMAZ ©1992

From the perspective of twelve-year-old Mahmet, life in his Turkish village is wonderful—he has friends, flowers, and plenty of space. When his family decides to improve their lives by moving to the large, unfamiliar city of Ankara, Mahmet finds himself living in a shantytown, surrounded by poverty. Based on a real-life incident, this modern survival story shows how a false impression—the idea that city life will be better—can almost ruin a family. Read to discover . . .

• what has become of Mahmet's best friend, who has moved to the city

• what Mahmet can do when he sees his family changing

• whether Mahmet can survive and help his family

Other Recommended Books

Commodore Perry in the Land of the Shogun by Rhoda Blumberg (©1985). In this nonfictional book, the author describes how Commodore Perry helped to open Japan to world trade in the 1850s.

Reflections on a Gift of Watermelon Pickle . . . and other Modern Verse edited by Stephen Dunning, Edward Lueders, and Hugh Smith (©1967). This classic collection of poetry contains engaging poems by many well-known poets.

The Wright Brothers: How They Invented the Airplane by Russell Freedman (©1991). The fascinating activities of the Wright brothers as they develop the airplane are related and illustrated with numerous original photographs by Wilbur and Orville Wright.

A Solitary Blue by Cynthia Voigt (©1983). In a contemporary realistic novel, a boy discovers that he may have false impressions of family members and friends. As he develops new insights, he also makes valuable discoveries about himself.

119

THE WITCH OF BLACKBIRD POND

Study Focus
■ Historical setting as it relates to societal beliefs in witches

■ External conflicts

■ Tunnel vision exemplified by the villagers' persecution

About Elizabeth George Speare

Speare enjoys writing works with historical settings. She says, "New Englanders have not changed much in three hundred years." About her writing methods she says, "Every book begins with questions. How must it have seemed to the people who lived through this experience? What choices would I have made in their place? I must find the answers by going back in the past, by living side by side with them."

■ Other Works Novels: *Calico Captive, The Bronze Bow;* nonfiction: *Life in Colonial America*

 ■ Awards Newbery Medal, 1959, for *The Witch of Blackbird Pond;* Newbery Medal, 1962, for *The Bronze Bow*

AGAINST THE STORM

Study Focus
■ Contrasts between wealthy and poor segments of society

■ A family's false impressions about wealth in the city

■ A character's false impressions about his best friend

About Gaye Hiçyilmaz

Hiçyilmaz was born in England but lived in Turkey for many years, working as a British Council teacher in Ankara. She used her experiences in Ankara as a background for her novel *Against the Storm,* noting how poverty can destroy the very root of a society.

■ Other Works Hiçyilmaz is currently writing an adult novel about Turkey in the 1970s; she has published several novels for older children.

 ■ Awards Short-listed for the Whitbread Award and runner-up for the Guardian Award, both for *Against the Storm*

Subunit One: Victims or Victors?

	SELECTION	DIFFICULTY LEVEL	READING SKILLS	LITERATURE SKILLS	WRITING OPTIONS	VOCABULARY WORDS/SKILLS	
Fiction	*All Summer in a Day* Ray Bradbury Pages 123-130	Average	Finding contrasts	Simile Metaphor	Opinion Story Poem	concussion resilient slacken tumultuously	immense savor surge
Fiction	*Upon the Waters* Joanne Greenberg Pages 131-142	Challenge	Appreciating humor	Satire Characterization	Report Letter Essay Anecdote	ascertain divert humility senile surplus	disabled genially pending sluggish tyrant
Nonfiction	*The Noble Experiment* Jackie Robinson Pages 143-154	Average	Problem-solving	Motivation Autobiography	Comparison Profile Definition Rap	cynical incredulous insinuation shrewdly taunt	eloquence indignant retaliate speculating ultimate
Drama	*The Monsters Are Due on Maple Street* Rod Serling Pages 157-173	Average	Reading a teleplay	Dialogue Theme	Summary Stage directions Teleplay Letter to editor	antagonistic defiant idiosyncrasy intense optimistic	contorted flustered incriminate legitimate persistent

WRITER'S WORKSHOP Pages 174–178 ▪▪

Mode	Guided Assignment	Writing Skills	Proofreading Focus
Narrative writing	Personal narrative	Using dialogue Using signal words Using flashback	Punctuating dialogue

OPTIONS FOR LEARNING	SPELLING SKILLS	COMMUNITY AND PARENT RESOURCE SUGGESTIONS	AUDIOVISUAL RESOURCES
	Proofreading for Spelling	Invite a high school or college science teacher or an astronomer to discuss Venus or other planets. Take a field trip to a planetarium.	*All Summer in a Day.* 16mm film or video. Learning Corporation of America, 1983. (25 min) A dramatic adaptation. *The Electric Grandmother.* 16mm film or video. Learning Corporation of America, 1982. (32 min.) Based on Bradbury's story "The Body
News report Distribution plan Oral history Panel cartoon	Compound words and contractions	Invite local welfare workers to discuss the problems they face in working with clients and bureaucracy.	*Literature & Language* Audiocassette Tape 1, side 1.
Research teams Research players Acting a scene Reading autobiography	Suffixes *ance/ant* and *ence/ent*	Invite a high school or college coach to discuss how athletes, especially baseball players, go on to the next level, and to explain the farm team system.	*Jackie Robinson.* Video. Library Video Co., 1992. (30 min.) This video probes deeply into Robinson's life. *The Jackie Robinson Story,* film, 1950 (76 min.) Starring Jackie Robinson.
Diagram Trial Videotape play Research UFO's	Final silent *e* words and suffixes	Invite any parent who works in a television station to discuss how TV productions are made.	

LANGUAGE WORKSHOP Pages 179–181 ....

Grammar Concept	Skill Focus
Punctuating dialogue	Direct quotations Divided quotations Quotation marks/end punctuation Paragraphing dialogue

RELATED SKILLS WORKSHOP Page 182 ....

Language Strand	Skill Focus
Reading	Cause and effect

Overview

Subunit Two: Turning the Tables

	SELECTION	DIFFICULTY LEVEL	READING SKILLS	LITERATURE SKILLS	WRITING OPTIONS	VOCABULARY WORDS/SKILLS
Fiction	*The Revolt of the Evil Fairies* Ted Poston Pages 184-191	Challenge	Cause and effect	External and internal conflict Climax	Rewrite climax Conversation Opinion Account	distinctive expire inconsolable pigmentation sneering / elite impromptu intervening rationalize vanquish
Fiction	*Aunt Millicent* Mary Steele Pages 192-210	Average	Predicting Evaluating Reviewing	Humor Exaggeration Sarcasm	Letter Article Compare/contrast Pen-portrait	baseless enterprising exotic intrepid tedious / capsize exasperation hoax prolific wielding
Fiction	*Gentleman of Río en Medio* Juan A. A. Sedillo Pages 211-216	Average	Inferring character traits	Narrator	Opinion Letter	Word Attack Skill: context clues
Poetry	*old age sticks* E.E. Cummings *The Rebel* Mari Evans Pages 217-221	Challenge	Reading modern poetry	Free verse	Free-verse poem Letter	Word Attack Skill: using familiar words to understand unfamiliar words
Nonfiction	from *Boy: Tales of Childhood* Roald Dahl Pages 222-236	Easy	Predicting	Dialect	Ballad Persuasive essay Memo Story	cauldron glimmer malignant venom / flourish loathsome sullen

WRITER'S WORKSHOP Pages 237–241

Mode	Guided Assignment	Writing Skills	Proofreading Focus
Narrative writing	Story to drama	Dramatic form Dialogue Stage directions Writing scenes	Subject/verb agreement

OPTIONS FOR LEARNING	SPELLING SKILLS	COMMUNITY AND PARENT RESOURCE SUGGESTIONS	AUDIOVISUAL RESOURCES
Speech Stage play Research teams	Prefixes and base words	Invite a director of a local theater group to discuss the problems and challenges of casting a play.	*With All Deliberate Speed.* 1976. Phoenix/BFA Films and Video. Order 71725. Focuses on civil rights and desegregation during the 1970s.
Group story Research women Topographical map Play episode	The letters *qu*	Take a field trip to a local curio shop and have the owner discuss interesting items.	
	More prefixes and base words	Invite a real estate agent or real estate lawyer to tell anecdotes about sales that had unusual conditions.	*The Southwest.* Video. Encyclopedia Britannica, 1988. Order 4316
Oral interpretation Share poetry	Proofreading for Spelling	Arrange to have students visit a senior citizens' center and plan an activity that both groups can do together.	*Literature & Language* Audiocassette Tape 1, side 1. *A Gathering of Great Poetry for Children.* Audiocassette, Caedmon. Performed by Julie Harris and others. Includes E.E. Cummings.
Research candy Health codes British schools Read *Boy*	Silent letters	Invite a local shopowner near the school to discuss the problems of having students as customers. Take a trip to a candy factory or have a confectioner explain candy-making.	*Author's Eye: Roald Dahl.* Video. American School Publishers, 1988. (25 min.) The author discusses inspiration for his writing in an informal setting in his apple orchard in England.

LANGUAGE WORKSHOP Pages 242–244 . . . .

Grammar Concept	Skill Focus
Subject/verb agreement	Singular/plural compound subjects Verbs in unusual positions: questions, here/there

RELATED SKILLS WORKSHOP Page 245 . . . .

Language Strand	Skill Focus
Speaking and listening	Dramatic reading skills

Reading on Your Own

Novels thematically connected to Unit Two, suggested for independent student reading during or after completion of the unit

Roll of Thunder, Hear My Cry by Mildred D. Taylor
Brother Eagle, Sister Sky: A Message from Chief Seattle by Susan Jeffers
Maniac Magee by Jerry Spinelli

Cooperative Project

A Mock Town-Council Session

Students will investigate community problems, recommend solutions, and present their points of view before a mock town-council.

1 Project Preview

This project challenges students to apply what they have learned about the unit theme, "Scales of Justice."

Students will work together in task groups of four or five to draft resolutions that will be discussed and debated in a mock town-council session. They will investigate community problems, recommend solutions, and present their points of view in one-to-three-minute speeches before the town council. Each group will also respond to the resolutions proposed by other groups. If possible, the class will choose the best resolution to present to the actual legislative body of the community.

Depending upon your resources and time, you may want to modify the following teaching suggestions according to your students' needs, abilities, and interests.

OBJECTIVES
■ To identify community problems that are of interest to students
■ To research different perspectives on and possible solutions to these problems
■ To work cooperatively to devise resolutions that address the problems
■ To prepare and deliver speeches that support the resolutions
■ To respond critically to resolutions proposed by other groups

MATERIALS
■ Community or neighborhood newspapers that call attention to local problems
■ If available, a videotape of a debate in your town or city council

2 Implementing the Project

INTRODUCTION
Before students begin work on the project, you might wish to show a tape of a local government body discussing an issue. Point out that the purpose of such discussion is to allow for the expression of various points of view.

Tell students that this project gives them a chance to identify a local problem and to offer their own solution. Begin by naming some concrete examples of problems, such as unsafe parks, unsightly public places, a lack of recreational facilities for teenagers, and a need for supervised afterschool activities. Lead students in a discussion of these or other problems in your community and possible ways of addressing them. For example, students might propose an annual or semiannual community cleanup day as a way of dealing with litter problems in public places.

ASSIGNING GROUPS
Break students into task forces of four or five members. The purpose of each task force is to choose one problem in need of community action and to draft a resolution that recommends a specific course of action.

Alternative The entire class might agree upon a single problem. In that case, each group can propose its own solution to the problem, and the class as a whole can choose the best proposed solution.

Point out that each group will need to offer a specific plan of action. A resolution that all community residents should be treated with respect, for instance, offers no concrete solution. A resolution that calls for the local government to help poor people improve their lives is too general and vague for action.

Give students an example of a resolution, such as the one in the next column, to serve as a model for content and format.

Whereas the railroad viaducts in our town are unsightly;

and whereas the railroad is not willing to paint or renovate them;

and whereas the entire community will appreciate the improvement of the viaducts;

be it resolved, that our class be given permission by town officials to paint murals on the viaduct walls.

PLANNING RESEARCH
Each task force will first need to choose a problem. The group should consider the interests and viewpoints of all members. Students might find it helpful to enlist parents or other adults to suggest problems in the community. The following questions may help students focus their attention:

1. Is the problem one that you or community residents care about?
2. Is information about the problem readily available?
3. Do you know enough, or can you learn enough, about the issue to

recommend a practical solution?
4. Is the problem narrow enough for a specific plan of action to be recommended?

After choosing a topic, the group should divide research responsibilities. Caution students that they will need to be flexible and that plans may need to be changed.

GATHERING AND ANALYZING INFORMATION
Encourage students to explore a variety of sources. For example, a group that is investigating a lack of recreational facilities for teenagers might interview people in public service agencies, officials with the YMCA or other private service organizations, and teenagers themselves. Students can work individually, bringing what they find to daily group meetings, or they can gather information in teams.

Keeping a Project Log
A project log is an individual record of

each student's research. It can be in the form of loose-leaf paper in a manila folder or a spiral notebook. Tell students to keep a detailed record of the information they gather, including notes from interviews, a complete list of the resources they consult, and an account of other research activities. This project log can eventually serve as the basis for a "preparation" grade that you can give each student.

Considering Solutions

After students have gathered various kinds of information about their problem, the group should brainstorm possible solutions and list them on chart paper. They can then discuss each idea, offering both positive and negative comments. Tell students that they need to agree on a single solution.

Students may want to consider the following questions at this stage.
1. Is the solution practical—that is, can it actually be put into effect?
2. Will the solution be supported by the community?

3. What are the biggest obstacles to the solution?
4. Does the solution create any additional problems for the community?

Writing a Resolution

When students have decided upon a reasonable solution, they should write up a resolution. Students may write collectively, or they may give one student the responsibility for drafting the resolution, with the group as a whole editing it.

PREPARING SUPPORTING SPEECHES

Each member of the group should prepare a one-to-three-minute speech in support of the resolution. The group may decide to assign subtopics for each speaker. For example, one student might present the group's analysis of the problem, one might summarize what is currently being done about it, one might explain the group's solution, and one might explain why this solution is better than other possible ones.

PRESENTATION: THE MOCK TOWN COUNCIL

If possible, move desks around to create an appropriate physical environment for a town council. The town council will consist of the entire class, which will vote on the groups' resolutions after hearing the presentations and discussing them.

Designate a timekeeper each day. Stress that speeches cannot go over the time limit and that students will be asked to sit down immediately when time is called.

Each member of a group should speak for one to three minutes. After the group has presented its case, allow consultation time so that the other groups in the classroom can meet to consider the strengths and weaknesses of the resolution. After the consultation, open the floor to speakers from the rest of the class. Students can ask for further clarification, speak against the proposal, or offer alternative ways of looking at the problem.

Allow members of the group proposing the resolution to give short responses.

In some cases, you may wish to give groups a chance to rework their proposals in order to respond to criticism. Point out that making such revisions is common in most forms of government.

After allowing a reasonable time for discussion and, if desired, revision, call the roll of the entire class, with each student voting yes or no for each resolution. A simple majority is needed for a resolution to pass.

After all resolutions have been addressed, lead students in a discussion of which proposal is best suited for submission to the actual legislative body of your own community. Conduct a vote to choose the most appropriate one. If possible, arrange for students to submit their idea, either in writing or in person, to the local government.

3 Project Assessment

Group Assessment

Each group can be given a single grade, based on the quality of its preparation and delivery. The highest grade may be given to the group whose proposal was submitted to the real local government.

Individual Assessment

The following factors may be considered in assigning a separate grade for each student.
1. An individual's presentation can be graded on the basis of quality of evidence and argument, poise and delivery, and persuasiveness.

2. The student's project log can be graded on the basis of extent of research, quality of notes, and evidence of effort.
3. The student's comments about the resolutions of other groups can also be a factor. Points may be assigned for each comment made about the other resolutions, or each comment may be graded on a simple one-to-three-point scale.

For the Portfolio

If possible, videotape each group's presentation. The tapes may be kept in a master file, or a copy might be added to each student's portfolio.

4 Team-Teaching Options

Social Studies

Have students analyze how a local, state, or federal legislative body passes a law.

Math

Help students to calculate the following ratios, which require current census data:

1. In your community, what is the ratio of elected officials to citizens?
2. What is the proportion of elected state officials to the number of citizens in your state?
3. What is the ratio of U.S. representatives to citizens in your state?

Art

Suggest that students create a photographic display illustrating one of more of the community problems addressed in the mock town-council.

Science

Have students choose one kind of mammal, such as wolves or gorillas, and research how these animals work in groups to deal with problems.

Unit Preview

In Unit Two, "Scales of Justice," students will examine situations in which justice either prevails or is denied. The unit contains two subunits:

- Subunit 1: "Victims or Victors?"
- Subunit 2: "Turning the Tables"

Connections to Unit Six

Unit Six, "Themes in World Folklore," contains literature from the oral tradition that connects with the themes in Unit Two. You may wish to begin or end Unit Two with selections from Unit Six that relate to the theme "Scales of Justice":

- Aesop's fables "The Wolf in Sheep's Clothing" and "The Travelers and the Purse," page 608
- "Anansi and His Visitor, Turtle," page 610
- "A Blind Man Catches a Bird," page 612
- "The Old Grandfather and His Little Grandson," page 615

ADDITIONAL RESOURCES

Unit Two Resource Book
Unit Test, pp. 83–86

Technology and Enrichment
Family and Community Involvement
   Source Book, pages 9–11

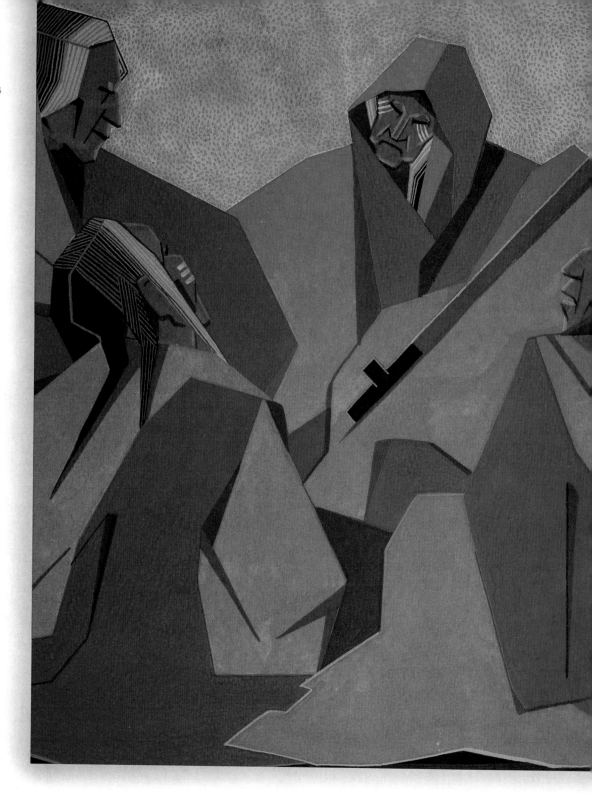

About the Art

Oscar Howe (1915–) was born on the Crow Creek Reservation in South Dakota. He graduated from the University of Oklahoma and now teaches at the University of South Dakota. In his posterlike *Dakota Pipe Clan Magic,* he treats the ritual of pipe smoking as a kind of pattern, with the shapes of the robes dominating the work. *In what way might these shapes add to the religious air of the ritual?*

SCALES OF JUSTICE

It does not require many words to speak the truth.

Chief Joseph

DAKOTA PIPE CLAN MAGIC
Oscar Howe
Courtesy, Mr. and Mrs. Peter A. Hassrick.

121

Discussion Questions

To help students probe connections between the fine art, the quotation, and the unit theme, have them consider the following questions:

1. What does the phrase "scales of justice" suggest to you? *(Possible responses: justice must be weighed carefully; justice can easily be thrown off balance if the judge does not give equal weight to each side.)*

2. How do you think Chief Joseph's words relate to the theme of justice? *(Possible responses: justice demands honesty and integrity; sometimes people use long speeches to cloud the truth and create injustice.)*

3. Do you agree with the quote? Why or why not? *(Possible responses: Yes, because truthful actions can replace the need for words; yes, because lies often need long explanations to seem believable, but truths do not.)*

4. How does the art relate to the idea of justice? *(Possible responses: The figures appear to be deliberating; it depicts a ritual that implies justice and peace.)*

5. Based on the quotation and the art, what kinds of selections do you imagine this unit will contain? *(Possible responses: Selections about individuals who seek justice or who mete out justice; selections in which people are treated unjustly or justly.)*

About the Quoted Author

Chief Joseph was born in about 1840. When his father became ill, Joseph replaced him as chief of the Nez Percé people in Oregon. In 1877, the U.S. government ordered Joseph's people onto a reservation in Idaho to make their land available for white settlers. The Nez Percés refused to go, and fighting broke out between them and the U.S. Army. Chief Joseph then bravely led his people on a one-thousand-mile retreat to Canada, fighting off troops along the way. Eventually they were defeated and forced to move to Oklahoma.

Have students read the introduction to Subunit 1, "Victims or Victors?" Ask them to explain how victims and victors might relate to the concept of justice. How do you judge whether someone is a victor or victim? Where do victors and victims sit on the scales of justice? Do victims and victors sometimes change places?

INTEGRATING THE LANGUAGE ARTS

The literary selections in the subunit focus on the theme of victims and victors. Reading skills, literature skills, writing options, language study, vocabulary, and spelling skills are all based on these literary selections.

Writer's Workshop After reading several selections that deal with victims and victors, students will use narrative writing to tell about an experience in which they or another individual was a victim.

Language Workshop The Language Workshop in this subunit focuses on punctuating dialogue correctly. Students will find the rules for dialogue punctuation valuable because narrative writing often incorporates dialogue.

Reader's Workshop The Reader's Workshop in this subunit deals with identifying cause and effect. Students will see how important cause and effect is when they read the selections concerning victims and victors.

FOR ADDITIONAL CHALLENGE

The following selections offer extra challenge in the exploration of the subunit theme.

Barrio Boy, novel by Ernesto Galarza

Rifles for Watie, novel by Harold Keith

ADDITIONAL RESOURCES

Technology and Enrichment
Family and Community Involvement Source Book, p. 9

Guidelines for Reading and Literature Assessment: Observation Assessment Forms

VICTIMS OR VICTORS?

Have you ever seen justice portrayed as a blindfolded woman holding a pair of scales in her hand? The scales show the importance of fairness when making a decision. Before a just decision can be made, both sides of a conflict must be studied. In this unit you will be reading about issues of justice. Like the blindfolded woman, you must weigh the evidence and come to your own decisions.

In "Victims or Victors?" you will meet some characters who are defeated by injustice and others who rise in triumph. You will need to decide who really is the victor and who is the victim.

Observation Assessment

Observing how students respond to the text, to the classroom instruction, and to peers is an important part of an assessment program. The following suggestions and the form in each *Guidelines for Reading and Literature Assessment* booklet can be used to implement observation assessment.

■ **Writing Behavior** As students work through the subunit, assess how well they incorporate the steps of the writing process in their work. Determine how well they brainstorm for ideas to write about. Also evaluate how well they organize their ideas in a rough draft. See how carefully they revise their work and how conscientiously they proofread it. Also judge the creative ways that students find to share their writing. As they work through the subunit, look for growth in the ability to use the writing process as an effective tool of expression.

Fiction

All Summer in a Day

RAY BRADBURY

Examine What You Know (Prior Knowledge)

Think of times when a group has excluded or picked on a person who was somehow different from the members of the group. Why do you think groups feel the need to exclude people unlike themselves? Discuss your ideas with the class.

Expand Your Knowledge (Building Background)

One source of differences among people is their reaction to the environment. The **setting** of the following science fiction story is a classroom on the planet Venus—an imaginary Venus unlike the real planet—in the future. The author has created a world without sunshine. Although most of us feel slightly depressed when deprived of sunlight for a long time, some people develop serious cases of depression. One treatment for such depression involves the use of special lights that give off ultraviolet rays similar to those found in sunlight. Patients are exposed to the lights for limited periods, and their depression is usually relieved.

Enrich Your Reading (Reading Skill)

Finding Contrasts When two things are examined together, the differences between them are called **contrasts.** Writers use contrasts to help readers get a clear picture of a character, an event, a place, or an idea. As you read, think about the differences between Margot (the main character) and her classmates. As soon as you finish reading, jot down some of those differences in a chart like the one below. Share your ideas when you finish.

Margot	Her Classmates
would not sing or play games	played and sang happily

■ *Author biography in Reader's Handbook*

ALL SUMMER IN A DAY   123

Objectives

■ To understand and analyze a short story

■ To examine the use of simile and metaphor

■ To enrich reading by finding contrasts

■ To express understanding of the story through a choice of writing forms, including an opinion and a story or poem

Prereading/Motivation

Examine What You Know

Discussion Prompts: Is the behavior of people in groups different from the behavior of people who are by themselves? Why?

Expand Your Knowledge

Additional Background The rain that falls constantly on Bradbury's fictional Venus would boil away on the real Venus. Though the planet Venus is always covered by clouds, its surface is actually hot and dry, with a temperature of about 850 degrees Fahrenheit. However, lack of enough sunlight is a real problem for some humans on Earth. The serious depression caused by lack of sunlight is called Seasonal Affective Disorder (SAD) and is treated by exposing patients to high-intensity light before dawn and after dusk in order to lengthen their day.

Enrich Your Reading

For Alternative Learning Styles To stimulate visual learners, have students mime a scene from the story that shows the contrasting behavior of Margot and her classmates. Then have students fill out their charts.

JOURNAL WRITING IDEAS

■ Using the paintings on pages 125 and 128 and the title, predict what this story might be about.

■ How are you different from your classmates?

■ How does weather affect you? What feelings do you associate with storms, wind, rain, sun, snow?

COLLABORATIVE LEARNING OPTIONS

Opportunities for collaborative learning include the Literary Concept and Closure (p. 130).

ADDITIONAL RESOURCES

Unit Two Resource Book
Reader's Guidesheet, p. 1
Reading Skills, p. 2
Literature Skills, p. 3
Vocabulary Connections, p. 4
Spelling Connections, p. 5
Comprehension and Vocabulary Check Tests, p. 6
Selection Test, pp. 7–8

Technology and Enrichment
Thinking Skills Transparency, 10

Thematic Link— Victims or Victors?

Sensitive Margot is a victim of her peers' jealousy and cruelty. Her classmates seem to be victors, since they enjoy the hour of sunshine and prevent Margot from doing the same. Yet they too are victims of an almost unbearable environment.

All Summer in a Day

RAY BRADBURY

R eady?"
"Ready."
"Now?"
"Soon."
"Do the scientists really know? Will it happen today, will it?"
"Look, look; see for yourself!"

1 The children pressed to each other like so many roses, so many weeds, intermixed, peering out for a look at the hidden sun.

It rained.

2 It had been raining for seven years; thousands upon thousands of days compounded and filled from one end to the other with rain, with the drum and gush of water, with the sweet crystal fall of showers and the concussion of storms so heavy they were tidal waves come over the islands. A thousand forests had been crushed under the rain and grown up a thousand times to be crushed again. And this was the way life was forever on the planet Venus, and this was the schoolroom of the children of the rocket men and women who had come to a raining world to set up civilization and live out

A ▶ their lives.

"It's stopping, it's stopping!"

"Yes, yes!"

Margot stood apart from them, from these children who could never remember a time when there wasn't rain and rain and rain. They were all nine years old, and if there had been a day, seven years ago, when the sun came out for an hour and showed its face to the stunned world, they could not recall. Sometimes, at night, she heard them stir, in remembrance, and she knew they were dreaming and remembering gold or a yellow crayon or a coin large enough to buy the world with. She knew that they thought they remembered a warmness, like a blushing in the face, in the body, in the arms and legs and trembling hands. But then they always awoke to the tatting drum, the endless shaking down of clear bead necklaces upon the roof, the walk, the gardens, the forest, and their dreams were gone.

3

All day yesterday they had read in class about the sun. About how like a lemon it was, and how hot. And they had written small stories or essays or poems about it:

I think the sun is a flower
That blooms for just one hour.

| *Words to Know and Use* | **concussion** (kən kush′ ən) *n.* a strong shaking |

Guided Reading for Less-Proficient Students

These questions can help guide students through the reading. Ask each question at the point of the selection where the capital letter and arrow appear in the margin. In addition, you may wish to use appropriate Active Reading annotations.

A. Describe the setting of this story, including the weather. *(Venus in the future, where it rains all the time)* Recalling

B. In what ways is Margot different from the other children? *(Unlike them, she lived on Earth for four years; she remembers the sun, and they do not; she is pale and quiet, but they are noisy and playful; she is alone, and they are a group.)* Summarizing

C. How do the children feel about Margot's being different? *(They hate her for being different.)* Recalling

Continued on page 125

PORTRAIT OF A SICK GIRL
1901   Paula Modersohn-Becker
Courtesy, Westfälisches Landesmuseum
für Kunst und Kulturgeschichte,
Münster, Germany.

That was Margot's poem, read in a quiet voice in the still classroom while the rain was falling outside.

"Aw, you didn't write that!" protested one of the boys.

"I did," said Margot. "I *did*."

"William!" said the teacher.

But that was yesterday. Now, the rain was slackening, and the children were crushed to the great thick windows.

"Where's teacher?"

"She'll be back."

"She'd better hurry; we'll miss it!"

They turned on themselves, like a feverish wheel, all tumbling spokes.

Margot stood alone. She was a very frail girl who looked as if she had been lost in the rain for years and the rain had washed out the blue from her eyes and the red from her mouth and the yellow from her hair. She was an old photograph dusted from an album, whitened away, and if she spoke at all, her voice would be a ghost. Now she stood, separate, staring at the rain and the loud, wet world beyond the huge glass.

"What're *you* looking at?" said William.

Margot said nothing.

"Speak when you're spoken to." He gave her a shove. But she did not move; rather, she let herself be moved only by him and nothing else.

They edged away from her; they would not look at her. She felt them go away. And this was because she would play no games

Words to Know and Use | **slacken** (slak′ ən) *v.* to lessen; let up

125

6. ACTIVE READING: Question
Ask students why would the other children call Margot a liar when she describes the sun. *(Possible responses: They are jealous; they do not want to admit that she knows more than they do.)*

7. ACTIVE READING: Review
Ask students to name the big and the small reasons for the other children's hatred of Margot. *(She refuses to play games and to sing about "happiness and life and games" with them; they resent that she has lived on Earth and that she may return to live there again; they dislike her appearance.)*

with them in the echoing tunnels of the underground city. If they tagged her and ran, she stood blinking after them and did not follow. When the class sang songs about happiness and life and games, her lips barely moved. Only when they sang about the sun and the summer did her lips move, as she watched the drenched windows.

She was different, and they knew her difference and kept away.

And then, of course, the biggest crime of all was that she had come here only five years ago from Earth, and she remembered the sun and the way the sun was and the sky was when she was four, in Ohio. And they, they had been on Venus all their lives, and they had been only two years old when last the sun came out and had long since forgotten the color and heat of it and the way that it really was. But Margot remembered.

"It's like a penny," she said, once, eyes closed.

"No, it's not!" the children cried.

"It's like a fire," she said, "in the stove."

"You're lying; you don't remember!" cried the children.

But she remembered and stood quietly apart from all of them and watched the patterning windows. And once, a month ago, she had refused to shower in the school shower rooms, had clutched her hands to her ears and over her head, screaming that

the water mustn't touch her head. So after that, dimly, dimly, she sensed it; she was different, and they knew her difference and kept away.

There was talk that her father and mother were taking her back to Earth next year; it seemed vital to her that they do so, though it would mean the loss of thousands of dollars to her family. And so the children hated her for all these reasons, of big and little consequence. They hated her pale, snow face, her waiting silence, her thinness, and her possible future.

"Get away!" The boy gave her another push. "What're you waiting for?"

Then, for the first time, she turned and looked at him. And what she was waiting for was in her eyes.

"Well, don't wait around here!" cried the boy, savagely. "You won't see nothing!"

Her lips moved.

"Nothing!" he cried. "It was all a joke, wasn't it?" He turned to the other children. "Nothing's happening today. *Is* it?"

They all blinked at him and then, understanding, laughed and shook their heads. "Nothing, nothing!"

"Oh, but," Margot whispered, her eyes helpless. "But, this is the day, the scientists predict, they say, they *know,* the sun . . ."

"All a joke!" said the boy, and seized her roughly. "Hey, everyone, let's put her in a closet before teacher comes!"

"No," said Margot, falling back.

They surged about her, caught her up and bore her, protesting and then pleading and then crying, back into a tunnel, a room, a closet, where they slammed and locked

| *Words to Know and Use* | **surge** (sɜrj) *v.* to suddenly push forward in a violent way |

the door. They stood looking at the door and saw it tremble from her beating and throwing herself against it. They heard her muffled cries. Then, smiling, they turned and went out and back down the tunnel, just as the teacher arrived.

"Ready, children?" She glanced at her watch.

"Yes!" said everyone.

"Are we all here?"

"Yes!"

The rain slackened still more.

They crowded to the huge door.

The rain stopped.

It was as if, in the midst of a film concerning an avalanche, a tornado, a hurricane, a volcanic eruption, something had, first, gone wrong with the sound apparatus, thus muffling and finally cutting off all noise, all of the blasts and repercussions and thunders, and then, secondly, ripped the film from the projector and inserted in its place a peaceful tropical slide which did not move or tremor. The world ground to a standstill. The silence was so <u>immense</u> and unbelievable that you felt that your ears had been stuffed or you had lost your hearing altogether. The children put their hands to their ears. They stood apart. The door slid back, and the smell of the silent, waiting world came in to them.

The sun came out.

It was the color of flaming bronze, and it was very large. And the sky around it was a blazing blue tile color. And the jungle burned with sunlight as the children, released from their spell, rushed out, yelling, into the summertime.

"Now, don't go too far," called the teacher after them. "You've got only one hour, you know. You wouldn't want to get caught out!"

But they were running and turning their faces up to the sky and feeling the sun on their cheeks like a warm iron; they were taking off their jackets and letting the sun burn their arms.

"Oh, it's better than the sunlamps, isn't it?"

"Much, much better!"

They stopped running and stood in the great jungle that covered Venus, that grew and never stopped growing, <u>tumultuously</u>, even as you watched it. It was a nest of octopuses, clustering up great arms of flesh-like weed, wavering, flowering in this brief spring. It was the color of rubber and ash, this jungle, from the many years without sun. It was the color of stones and white cheeses and ink.

The children lay out, laughing, on the jungle mattress and heard it sigh and squeak under them, <u>resilient</u> and alive. They ran among the trees, they slipped and fell, they pushed each other, they played hide-and-seek and tag; but most of all they squinted at the sun until tears ran down their faces, they put their hands up at that yellowness and that amazing blueness, and they breathed of the fresh air and listened and listened to the silence which suspended them in a blessed sea of no sound and no motion. They looked at everything and <u>savored</u> everything. Then, wildly, like animals

8

E ▶

9

10

Words to Know and Use	**immense** (im mens') *adj.* very large; enormous **tumultuously** (too mul' choo əs lē) *adv.* in a wild and disorderly way **resilient** (ri zil' yənt) *adj.* flexible and springy **savor** (sā' vər) *v.* to take great pleasure in

127

8. ACTIVE READING: Predict
Ask students to predict whether Margot will be released in time to see the sun. *(Any response is valid.)*

9. LITERARY CONCEPT: Setting
Ask students to identify the sensory details that Bradbury uses to describe the way the sun transforms the setting. *(Details include "silence was so immense"; "smell of the silent, waiting world"; "blazing blue tile color"; and "jungle burned with sunlight.")* Then ask how this change might affect the children's mood. *(Possible responses: They will be excited; they will be awe-struck and quiet.)*

10. VOCABULARY: Definitions
Some students may have difficulty identifying two popular games mentioned in this sentence, hide-and-seek and tag. Allow volunteers to explain the games. ★

Looking at Style

Point out to students the following sentence on page 127, and have them follow along as you read it aloud:

They ran among the trees, they slipped and fell, they pushed each other, they played hide-and-seek and tag; but most of all they squinted at the sun until tears ran down their faces, they put their hands up at that yellowness and that amazing blueness, and they breathed of the fresh air and listened and listened to the silence which suspended them in a blessed sea of no sound and no motion.

Point out the italicized phrases. Then ask,

1. Why do you think Bradbury chose to write such a long sentence containing so much repetition?

2. Is this sentence effective in helping you visualize the children's movement? Why or why not?

3. How does the rhythm of the sentence help you imagine the children's excitement?

11. ACTIVE READING: Review
Ask students to read this passage carefully to discover the contrasts between the children's behavior before and after the raindrops fall. *(Possible response: Before the rain the children behave with joy and enthusiasm, but when the rain begins they react with grief and sorrow.)*

JAPANESE RAIN ON CANVAS   1972   David Hockney   Acrylic on canvas, 48" x 48".
© David Hockney 1972.

escaped from their caves, they ran and ran in shouting circles. They ran for an hour and did not stop running.

And then–

In the midst of their running, one of the girls wailed.

Everyone stopped.

The girl, standing in the open, held out her hand.

"Oh, look, look," she said, trembling.

They came slowly to look at her opened palm.

In the center of it, cupped and huge, was a single raindrop.

She began to cry, looking at it.

They glanced quickly at the sky.

"Oh. Oh."

A few cold drops fell on their noses and their cheeks and their mouths. The sun faded behind a stir of mist. A wind blew cool around them. They turned and started to walk back toward the underground house, their hands at their sides, their smiles vanishing away.

A boom of thunder startled them, and like leaves before a new hurricane, they tumbled upon each other and ran. Lightning struck ten miles away, five miles away, a mile, a half mile. The sky darkened into midnight in a flash.

F ▶

They stood in the doorway of the underground for a moment until it was raining hard. Then they closed the door and heard the gigantic sound of the rain falling in tons and avalanches everywhere and forever.

"Will it be seven more years?"

"Yes. Seven."

Then one of them gave a little cry.

12

"Margot!"

"What?"

"She's still in the closet where we locked her."

"Margot."

13

They stood as if someone had driven them, like so many stakes, into the floor. They looked at each other and then looked away. They glanced out at the world that was raining now and raining and raining steadily. They could not meet each other's glances. Their faces were solemn and pale. They looked at their hands and feet, their faces down.

"Margot."

One of the girls said, "Well . . . ?"

No one moved.

"Go on," whispered the girl.

They walked slowly down the hall in the sound of cold rain. They turned through the doorway to the room, in the sound of the storm and thunder, lightning on their faces, blue and terrible. They walked over to the closet door slowly and stood by it.

Behind the closet door was only silence. **| 14**

They unlocked the door, even more slowly, and let Margot out. ❧

I N S I G H T

What Do We Do with a Variation?

JAMES BERRY

What do we do with a difference?
Do we stand and discuss its oddity
or do we ignore it?

Do we shut our eyes to it
or poke it with a stick?
Do we clobber it to death?

Do we move around it in rage
and enlist the rage of others?
Do we will it to go away?

Do we look at it in awe
or purely in wonderment?
Do we work for it to disappear?

Do we pass it stealthily
or change route away from it?
Do we will it to become like ourselves?

What do we do with a difference?
Do we communicate to it,
let application acknowledge it
for barriers to fall down?

Comprehension Check

Student Response

Responding to Reading

1. Any response is valid.

2. **Possible responses:** They are ashamed of themselves—they cannot look each other in the eye; they are sorry for the terrible thing they've done—they stand stock-still for a moment and then walk slowly to release Margot.

3. **Possible responses:** They are jealous of her past—and possible future—on Earth; they resent her seriousness and sensitivity; her standing apart makes them feel she has rejected them.

4. **Possible responses:** Margot's classmates are victors because they punished Margot and got an hour in the sun; the children are victims because no matter how they treat Margot, they cannot leave Venus; the children are victims because they will always feel guilty about their terrible deed.

Literary Concepts: Simile and Metaphor

Simile Similes in the story include "children pressed to each other like so many roses"; "warmness, like a blushing"; "they turned on themselves, like a feverish wheel"; "like a penny"; "like a fire . . . in the stove"; "the sun on their cheeks like a warm iron"; "like animals escaped from their caves"; and "like leaves before a new hurricane"; and "like so many stakes."

Metaphor Accept any metaphors that make sense.

Writing Options

The Writing Options are designed to meet varied student interests and abilities. Have each student choose one writing activity to complete.

Journal Update Suggest that students review their journal entries for "All Summer in a Day," and write their new thoughts and insights. They may also want to imagine what happened after the children let Margot out of the closet. They may write more about Venus's weather, using similes and metaphors.

Responding to Reading

First Impressions

1. What feeling do you have at the end of the story? Why?

Second Thoughts

2. How do you think Margot's classmates feel about what they've done? Support your answer with evidence from the story.

3. Why do you think the class picks on Margot?
   Think about
   • your discussion about why groups exclude those who are different
   • the ways in which the writer contrasts Margot with the group

4. Margot is a victim in this story. In your opinion, are her classmates victims or victors? Explain your answer.

Literary Concepts: Simile and Metaphor

Similes and metaphors help create images and make a story more vivid. A **simile** compares two things using words such as *like, as, than,* or *resembles:* The sun is *like a lemon.* Find two similes in the story.

A **metaphor** is also a comparison of two things, but a metaphor does not contain the words *like* or *as.* Metaphors are sometimes harder to find than similes. "She was an old photograph dusted from an album, whitened away" is a metaphor describing Margot. In pairs or small groups, use your ideas about the story to make up metaphors that begin with the phrases *The rain was _____, Margot's classmates were _____; The classroom was _____.* Share your best metaphors with the rest of the class.

Writing Options

1. Do you think Margot's classmates are entirely at fault, or did some of her actions encourage their behavior? Write your **opinion** about the responsibility of both Margot and the class in the incident.

2. Write your own **story** or **poem** about how you or your friends might deal with someone who is different. Include three *Words to Know and Use.*

130 UNIT TWO VICTIMS OR VICTORS?

Closure

Tell students that like "All Summer in a Day," all the selections in this subunit include individuals who stand alone, apart from the crowd, and who face things that are new and unknown. Assign students to small groups and have them outline their own story ideas on the theme "Victims or Victors?" Each outline should include descriptions of setting, characters, plot, and theme.

Fiction

Upon the Waters

JOANNE GREENBERG

Examine What You Know (Prior Knowledge)

Have you ever felt frustrated filling out a complicated form? Have you ever tried to sign up for an activity at a park or school, only to find yourself in an endless line? If so, you have encountered a **bureaucracy**—an organization having numerous rules and complicated procedures. Make a concept map of *bureaucracy*. Copy the model below on a sheet of paper. Use the dictionary to define *bureaucracy*, and then fill in the other boxes with examples and descriptions.

Dictionary Definition — BUREAUCRACY — Example
Descriptive Words — BUREAUCRACY — Example

Expand Your Knowledge (Building Background)

Today, the welfare system in the United States is a giant bureaucracy. It started out, however, as a response to the Great Depression. Between 1929 and 1932, the U.S. economy nearly collapsed, and almost a third of the nation's workers lost their jobs. Franklin Roosevelt, elected president in 1932, created the New Deal to get the country back on track. The New Deal programs provided food and clothing, jobs, and other forms of relief.

Enrich Your Reading (Reading Skill)

Appreciating Humor This story pokes fun at the bureaucracy of the welfare system. As you read, think about the humor that arises from the different perceptions of the main character and the office workers.

■ *Author biography on Extend page*

Objectives

■ To understand and analyze a short story

■ To understand satire and to review the concept of character

■ To enrich reading by appreciating humor

■ To express understanding of the story through a choice of writing forms, including a report, a letter, an essay, and an anecdote

Prereading/Motivation

Examine What You Know

Discussion Prompts Have you ever applied for a cash card or a part-time job? How would you describe the experience?

Expand Your Knowledge

Additional Background Roosevelt's New Deal established emergency organizations to hire jobless people to work on dams, on public roads and buildings, and in national forests. Because many banks had failed and many people had lost all their money, agencies were created to regulate businesses and banks in order to protect workers and restore confidence in banks.

Enrich Your Reading

To help students understand the humor in this selection, suggest that students make a chart like this to record what characters are thinking, which may be very different from what they are saying.

What Cephas Thinks	What the Office Worker Thinks
She wants to know about me.	Why is he wasting my time?

JOURNAL WRITING IDEAS

■ Use the pictures on pages 133 and 138 and clues on page 131 to predict what this story might be about.

■ What do you think of the welfare system and people who receive welfare?

COLLABORATIVE LEARNING OPTIONS

Opportunities for collaborative learning include the Concept Review (p. 140), Options for Learning activities 1 and 2 (p. 142), and Cross-Curricular Projects (p. 142).

ADDITIONAL RESOURCES

Unit Two Resource Book
Reader's Guidesheet, p. 9
Reading Skills, p. 10
Literature Skills, p. 11
Vocabulary Connections, p. 12
Spelling Connections, p. 13
Comprehension and Vocabulary Check Tests, p. 14
Selection Test, pp. 15–16

Technology and Enrichment
🎧 Audiocassette Tape 1, Side 1

📺 Thinking Skills Transparency 1

Thematic Link—
Victims or Victors?

Workers at the Welfare Office think Cephas is just another poor victim applying for aid, but in fact, he is a victor, a successful man who has come to return the help he received during the Depression. The Welfare Office workers become victims of Cephas's goodwill.

VOCABULARY PREVIEW

These vocabulary words are defined at the bottom of the selection pages on which they appear.

ascertain to find out

disabled physically handicapped

divert to shift; turn aside

genially in a friendly way

humility lack of pride; humbleness

pending while waiting for; until

senile showing mental confusion due to old age

sluggish moving slowly

surplus extra

tyrant a ruler with unlimited power

LIMITED ENGLISH PROFICIENCY

■ Use the Reader's Guidesheet, *Unit Two Resource Book,* page 9.

■ The main character speaks a dialect. To help clarify, you may want to read some dialogue aloud.

★ Text annotations marked with a red star (8, 9) may be particularly helpful for students with limited English proficiency.

TEXT ANNOTATIONS

1. LITERARY CONCEPT: Character
Have students **review** what they know about Cephas so far, and tell what these details reveal about him. (*Possible responses: He has thin gray hair; he is an older man; he wants to make a good impression; he is patient.*)

2. ACTIVE READING: Review
Have students describe how the office workers are behaving toward Cephas and **draw conclusions** about how the workers see him. (*Possible responses: They are ignoring him; they don't see him as a person; they see him as just another faceless client.*)

3. LITERARY CONCEPT: Figurative Language
Make sure students understand that *issue* means "offspring" here and that Greenberg is talking about the minutes as though they were alive. They go through a "life cycle"—are born, mature, grow old, and die with no "children"—they produce nothing.

Upon the Waters

JOANNE GREENBERG

It was a bright green day. Big trees on the side streets were raining seeds, and the wind stirred in its second sleep. A long flatbed truck came rattling down one of the streets and stopped by the new steel, chrome, and glass building. The building's lines were so "functional" it made Cephas wonder if anyone actually worked in it. Then he saw some women going in. Good.

He checked his appearance by hitching up to the rearview mirror. He was wearing a clean white shirt and a bow tie, and his thin gray hair had been slicked down with water. When he was sure he was presentable, he got down out of the cab of the truck, dusted himself off, and began to walk slowly toward the building.

It had been many years . . . perhaps they had moved. No, there was the sign: BOONE COUNTY DEPARTMENT OF PUBLIC WELFARE. The last time he had been here the building had been a temporary shed, and people had been lined up outside waiting for the relief trucks to come. That had been in 1934, in the winter. His father had been proud of holding out until '34.

Cephas stopped and looked at the building again. Some secretaries came out, laughing and talking. They didn't look at him, being used to seeing people who came hesitantly to their offices to acknowledge failure in life.

Cephas checked himself again in the big glass door and then went in. There was a large booth with a woman behind it and eight or nine rows of benches facing it. People were sitting quietly, staring at nothing, waiting. To the right there were a series of chutes with numbers over them. Cephas went up to the booth.

"Take a number," the woman said without looking at him.

"Ma'am?"

"You take a number and wait your turn. We'll call you."

He took one of the plastic number cards. It said 15. He sat down and waited.

"Five," the woman called. A heavy woman got up slowly and went to the booth and then to one of the chutes.

Cephas waited. Minutes were born, ripened, aged, and died without issue.

"Number six." Around him the springtime asthmatics[1] whistled and gasped in their season. He looked at the cracks in his fingers.

"Number seven." An hour went by; another. He was afraid to go out and check his truck lest the line speed up and he lose his place.

"Number thirteen," the woman called. . . . ◀ A
They came to his number at last, and he

---

1. **springtime asthmatics:** people who wheeze and have difficulty breathing in the spring season.

Guided Reading for Less-Proficient Students

These questions can help guide students through the reading. Ask each question at the point of the selection where the capital letter and arrow appear in the margin. In addition, you may wish to use appropriate Active Reading annotations.

A. When Cephas is in the Welfare Office, what does he have to do? *(wait for a long time)* Recalling

B. What do the Welfare Office workers assume that Cephas wants? *(aid)* Recalling

C. What do the office workers think about Cephas's mental condition? *(They think he is senile, maybe even crazy.)* Recalling

D. What gift has Cephas brought? *(four hundred chickens, many barrels of fruit and vegetables, milk, and butter)* Summarizing

E. Why is Cephas giving this gift? *(to pay back aid he received during the Depression)* Inferring

Continued on page 133

STATION   1980-1982   Billy Morrow Jackson   Courtesy, Jane Haslem Gallery, Washington, D.C.

Art Note

Although *Station,* by Billy Morrow Jackson, shows a scene in a crowded bus or train station, the mood of the piece is typical of waiting rooms in many other settings. In this realistic painting we see the jammed room and the boredom of the people who are waiting. *Choose a person in the painting. Describe what you think the person's life might be like, why he or she is in the waiting room, and how he or she feels.*

4. ACTIVE READING: Review
Ask students to use the questions of the woman at the desk to decide what she is trying to do and how she probably feels. *(Possible responses: She is trying to find out what kind of aid Cephas needs; she feels bored, impatient, and frustrated.)*

went up to the desk, gave back the plastic card, and was directed to his chute. Another woman was there at another desk. She took his name, Cephas Ribble, and his age, sixty-eight.

Had he been given aid before?

Yes.

Had he been on General Assistance, Aid to the Needy, <u>Disabled</u> or Tuberculosis Aid?

"It was what they called Relief."

"But under what category was it?"

"It was for people that was off their farms or else didn't have nothin' to eat. They called it 'goin' on the county.' It was back in nineteen and thirty-four. We held out till thirty-four."

"I see. . . . Now you are applying for the old-age pension?"

He said he wasn't.

"Are you married, Mr. Ribble?" She sighed.

"Never had the pleasure," he said.

"Are you without funds, in emergency status?"

He said he wasn't.

"Then take this card and go to Room Eleven, to your left." She pressed a little light or something, and he felt the people shifting their weight behind him, Number Sixteen, he supposed. He made his way to Room Eleven.

The lady there was nice; he could see it right off. She told him about the different requirements for what they called Aid, and then she had him sign some forms: permission to inquire into his bank account, accep-

Words to Know and Use	**disabled** (dis ā′ bəld) *n.* people with an illness or physical handicap that limits their activities

133

Guided Reading for Less-Proficient Students

Continued from page 132

F. How does Cephas think the Welfare Office workers feel about his gift? *(He thinks they are pleased by his generosity.)* Recalling

G. Why don't the Welfare Office workers know what to do about Cephas's donation? *(They have no way to distribute food; their office mostly just gives out checks and processes paperwork.)* Inferring

H. Sum up in a few words the result of Cephas's generosity. *(Political groups protest and picket, a riot follows, and the mayor calls for an investigation.)* Summarizing

I. What makes Cephas's idea at the end of the story humorous? *(He thinks he is doing a great thing, but the reader knows that the same terrible mess will occur next year.)* Clarifying tance of surplus or donated food, release of medical information, and several others. Then she said sympathetically, "In what way are you disabled?"

He thought about all the ways a man might be disabled and checked each one off. It was a proud moment, a man sixty-eight without one thing in the world to complain of in his health.

5 "I ain't disabled no way. I am pleased you asked me, though. A man don't take time to be grateful for things like his health. If the shoe don't pinch, you don't take notice, do you?" He sat back, contented. Then he realized that the sun was getting hotter, and what with everything in the truck, he'd better get on.

The woman had put down her ballpoint pen. "Mr. Ribble, if you aren't disabled or without funds, what kind of aid do you want?" A shadow of irritation crossed her

B ▶ face.

"No aid at all," he said. "It's about somethin' different." He tried to hold down his excitement. This was his special day, a day for which he had waited for over a decade, but it was no use bragging and playing the boy, so he said no more.

6

 question

Why is Cephas at the Welfare Office if he doesn't need aid?

The woman was very annoyed. "Then why didn't you tell the worker at the desk?"

"She didn't give me no chance, ma'am, an' neither did that other lady. I bet you don't have many repairmen comin' in here

to fix things—not above once, anyway, except them gets paid by the hour." **7**

"Well, Mr. Ribble, what is it you want?" She heard the noise of co-workers leaving or returning on their coffee breaks. She sighed and began to drum her fingers, but Cephas wasn't aware of her impatience. He was beginning back in 1934. Good God, she thought, he's senile. She knew that she would have to listen to all of it. In his time, in his way.

"'Thirty-four cleaned us out—cleaned us bare. You wonder how *farmers* could go hungry. I don't know, but we did. After the **8** drought hit, there was nothin' to do but come in town an' sign up on the County. Twice a month my pa would come in an' bring back food. Sometimes I came with him. I seen them lines of hungry men just standin' out there like they was poleaxed[2] an' hadn't fallen yet. I tell you, them days was pitiful, *pitiful*." He glanced at her and then smiled. "I'm glad to see *you* done good since—a new buildin' an' all. Yes, you come right up." He looked around with approval at the progress they had made.

"Mr. Ribble . . . ?"

He returned. "See, we taken the Relief, but we never got to tell nobody the good it done for us. After that year, things got a little better, and soon we was on toward bein' a payin' farm again. In 'forty-six we built us **9** a new house—every convenience—an' in 'fifty-two we got some of them automated units for cattle care. Two years ago we dug out of debt, an' last year, I knew it was time

---

2. **poleaxed:** attacked with a long-handled spiked tool.

134

to think about my plan for real. It was time to thank the Welfare."

"Mr. Ribble, thanks are not necessary—"

"Don't you mind, ma'am; you just get your men an' come with me."

"I beg your pardon. . . ."

"I don't just talk, ma'am; I act. You just bring your men."

Mr. Morrissey had come back from his coffee break and was standing in the hall.

The woman signaled him with her eyes as she followed Cephas Ribble, now walking proud and sure out the door to his truck. Mr. Morrissey sighed and followed, wondering why he was always around when somebody needed to make a madness plain. Why

C ▶ did it never happen to McFarland?

Cephas reached into his pocket, and both of the Welfare people thought, *Gun.* He took out a piece of paper and turned to them as

10 they stood transfixed and pale, thinking of death. "I got it all here, all of what's in the truck. Get your men, ma'am, no use wastin' time. It's all in the truck, and if it don't get unloaded soon, it's gonna spoil."

"What is this *about*, Mr. Ribble?"

"My gift, ma'am; my donation. I'm giving the Relief four hundred chickens, thirty barrels of tomatoes, thirty barrels of apricots—I figured, for variety. Don't you think the apricots was a good idea—ten barrels Eyetalian beans, six firkins of butter. . . . Ma'am, you better get the chickens out—it don't do to keep 'em in the sun. I thought about milk, so I give two cans—that's a hundred gallons of milk in case there's hungry

D ▶ babies."

They were dumbfounded. Cephas could see that. He wanted to tell them that it

wasn't a case of trying to be big. He'd fig-
◀ E ured that everybody gave when they could. He'd even signed a form right there in the office about promising to accept donated food and clothing. Their amazement at his gift embarrassed him. Then he realized that it was probably the only way they could thank him—by making a fuss. People on the State payroll must have to walk a pretty nar-

11 row line. They'd have to be on the lookout for people taking advantage. That was it. It was deep work, that Welfare—mighty deep

12 work.

What is Cephas trying to do?   *review*

"What are we supposed to do with all that food?" Mr. Morrissey asked.

Cephas knew that the man was just making sure that it wasn't a bribe. "Why, give it to the poor. Call 'em in an' let 'em get it. You can have your men unload it right now, an' I'd do it quick if I was you. Like I said, it won't be long till it starts to turn in all this heat."

Mr. Morrissey tried to explain that modern welfare methods were different than those in 1934. Even then, the food had been U. S. surplus, not privately donated. It had come from government warehouses.

Cephas spoke of the stupidity and waste

13 of Government in Farming and rained invective on the Soil Bank.[3]

Mr. Morrissey tried again to make his point. "We don't *give* out any food. There hasn't been any food *donated* since nineteen sixteen!"

---
3. **rained . . . Soil Bank:** Cephas complained about a government program in the late 1950s that paid farmers not to grow crops.

10. LITERARY CONCEPT: Humor
Ask students how this incident shows the great contrast between Cephas and the office workers. (*Possible response: The office worker's fear that Cephas is reaching for a gun contrasts with his innocent action of reaching for a piece of paper. It shows they totally misunderstand him.*)

11. ACTIVE READING: Question
Ask what Cephas means when he says that Welfare is "mighty deep work." If necessary, help students by reading the following example of a think-aloud script or model one of your own.

Think-Aloud Script: "Mighty deep work" suggests that something is complicated and involves deep thinking. But what makes Cephas think that? I see he thinks the workers "have to walk a pretty narrow line." That must mean they aren't free to react naturally; something holds them back. Cephas's next thought explains. He says they have to watch out for "people taking advantage." I guess he means people trying to break rules or get something they are not entitled to. All the rules and regulations make Welfare look like "mighty deep work" to Cephas, who is a plain farmer and a straightforward guy.

12. ACTIVE READING: Review
What is Cephas trying to do? (*He's trying to donate food from his farm to the needy; he wants to pay back what he received, now that he can.*)

13. LITERARY CONCEPT: Characterization
Ask students what Cephas's criticism of the government's farm program adds to their knowledge of his personality. (*Possible responses: He freely expresses his opinion of the government's actions, even to people who work for a government agency; he doesn't play games and is open and honest.*)

Speaking . . . Listening . . . Viewing

Viewing Students can see the conditions that caused Cephas's family to turn to relief agencies in the Depression-era photographs of Dorothea Lange, Walker Evans, Russell Lee, Jack Delano, Arthur Rothstein, and others. Explain that the works of sever-al photographers of the era helped generate popular support for government efforts to help farmers and other workers. Have students study the pictures in order to see how the photographers tried to get their message across.

14. ACTIVE READING: Review
Ask students to contrast Cephas's belief about the old law "that never got taken off the books" with the Welfare people's feelings about it. Why is this passage humorous? *(Because the Welfare people had him sign a form that mentioned donations and surplus food, Cephas thinks that they are proudly following an honored tradition by obeying an old law; the Welfare people know that the law doesn't apply anymore but that it remains in place because nobody bothered to repeal it. The strong contrast in their attitudes and the failure of each to understand what the other is thinking produces the humor.)*

15. ACTIVE READING: Question
What is the misunderstanding between Cephas and Mr. Morrissey? *(Cephas thinks that Mr. Morrissey is thunderstruck by his generosity and that the Welfare office has no storage place because food is distributed so quickly; Mr. Morrissey is trying to explain that they have no system for accepting donations of food.)*

No doubt of it, these Welfare people had to be awful careful. Cephas nodded. "The others do what they can—don't blame 'em if it don't seem like much," he said sympathetically. "I signed that slip in there about the donated food, so there must *be* a lot of donated food."

"It's an old law," Morrissey argued tiredly. "It's one of the old Poor Laws[4] that never got taken off the books."

14

"An' here you folks are followin' it, right today," Cephas mused. "It must make you mighty proud."

"Mr. Ribble, *we have no place to store all this!*"

Cephas found his throat tightening with happiness. He had come in <u>humility</u>, waited all morning just so he could show his small gratitude and be gone, and everyone was thunderstruck at the plenty. "Mister," he said, "I pay my taxes without complainin', but I never knowed how hard you people was workin' for your money. You got to guard against every kind of bribes an' invitations to break the law; you got to find ways to get this food to the poor people so fast you can't even store it! By God, Mister, you make me proud to be an American!"

F ▶

15

review

What is the misunderstanding between Cephas and Mr. Morrissey?

A policeman had stopped by the truck and was tranquilly writing a ticket. Cephas excused himself modestly and strode off to defend his situation. The two Welfare work-ers stood staring after him as he engaged the officer.

It was, after all, State law that food could be donated. Were there no loading ramps, no men attending them? Had the department no parking place for donors? The policeman began to look at the two stunned bearers of the State's trust. He had stopped writing.

"Could that truck fit in the workers' parking lot?" Morrissey murmured.

"What are we going to *do* with it all?" Mrs. Traphagen whimpered.

"All those chickens—four hundred chickens!"

Mrs. Traphagen sighed. "The poor will never stand for it."

"First things first," Mr. Morrissey decided, and he went to confront the policeman.

Cephas's truck in the workers' parking lot blocked all their cars. As a consequence, the aid applications of eight families were held <u>pending</u> investigation. Six discharged[5] inmates of the State hospital remained incarcerated[6] for a week longer pending home checkups. Thirty-seven women washed floors and children's faces in the expectation of home visits which did not come about. A meeting at the Midtown Hotel was one speaker short, and high school students who had been scheduled to hear a lecture entitled "Social Work, Career of Tomorrow"

---

4. **Poor Laws:** rules that allow a government to give money or food to the needy.
5. **discharged:** legally released.
6. **incarcerated:** confined or imprisoned.

Words to Know and Use	**humility** (hyōō mil' ə tē) *n.* lack of pride **pending** (pen' diŋ) *prep.* while waiting for; until

remained unedified[7]. Applicants who came to apply for aid that afternoon were turned away. There was no trade in little plastic cards, and the hive of offices were empty. But the people of the Boone County Department of Public Welfare were not idle. It was only that the action had moved from the desks and files and chutes to the workers' parking lot and into the hands of its glad tyrant, Cephas Ribble.

All afternoon Cephas lifted huge baskets of apricots and tomatoes into the arms of the Welfare workers. All afternoon they went from his truck to their cars, carrying baskets, or with chickens festooned limply over their arms. When they complained to Mr. Unger, the head of the department, he waved them off. Were they to go to every home and deliver the food? He said he didn't care—they were to get rid of it. Were big families to get the same amount as small families? He said that the stuff was political dynamite and that all he wanted was to be rid of it before anybody noticed.

Cephas, from the back of his flatbed, was a titan[8]. He lifted, smiling, and loaded with a strong hand. He never stopped to rest or take a drink. The truck steamed in the hot spring light, but he was living at height, unbothered by the heat, or the closeness, or the increasing rankness of his chickens. Of course he saw that the Welfare people weren't dressed for loading food. They were dressed for church, looked like. It was deep work, very deep, working for the State. You had to set a good example. You had to dress up and talk very educated so as to give the poor a moral uplift. You had to be honest. A poor man could lie; Cephas had been poor himself, so he knew; but it must be a torment to deal with people free to lie and not be able to do it yourself.

By three-thirty the truck had been unloaded, and Cephas was free to go home and take up his daily life again. He shook hands with the director and the casework supervisor, the head bookkeeper and the statistician. To them he presented his itemized list, with weights carefully noted and items given the market value as of yesterday, in case they needed it for their records. Then he carefully turned the truck out of the parking lot, waved goodbye to the sweating group, nosed into the sluggish mass of afternoon traffic, and began to head home.

A cacophony[9] of high-pitched voices erupted in the lot behind him:

"I've got three mothers of dropouts to visit!"

"What am I going to *do* with all this stuff?"

"Who do we give this to? . . . My people won't take the Lady Bountiful[10] bit!"

"Does it count on their food allowance? Do we go down Vandalia and hand out apricots to every kid we see?"

"I don't have the time!"

"Which families get it?"

---

7. **unedified:** uneducated; not taught.
8. **titan:** person of great power.
9. **cacophony:** harsh sound.
10. **Lady Bountiful:** a person who gives away money or other things in a showy way; originally from George Farquhar's 1707 comedy, *The Beaux' Strategem*.

Words to Know and Use

tyrant (tī′ rənt) *n.* a ruler with unlimited power
sluggish (slug′ ish) *adj.* moving at a slow pace

137

19. LITERARY CONCEPT: Satire
Remind students of their concept maps for the word *bureaucracy*. Ask what the dialogue here says or implies about people who work in a bureaucracy. *(Possible response: They have to follow so many rules and regulations that they have trouble getting anything done.)*

20. LITERARY CONCEPT: Humor
Ask students how the author's description of the chickens increases the humor of this passage. *(Possible responses: The chickens are personified as indignant people who agree with Mrs. Traphagen; the use of words like decorum and righteously implies that the chickens are also obsessed with rules and regulations, which makes the rules and the Welfare people seem even more silly.)*

Art Note

The New York City artist Emily Steadman has painted an elderly man as he sits waiting—for what? He looks directly at the viewer with a steady gaze. In this realistic work one can see the subject as someone courageously facing life. *Choose three adjectives that describe the man. Could the same adjectives be used to describe Cephas in "Upon the Waters"?*

21. CULTURAL SIDELIGHT
As groups develop their cultural identities, they frequently change the names they use to identify themselves. African-American people have been known at different times in the past century as colored, Negro, and Black.

22. EDITORIAL NOTE
Two sentences in Greenberg's original story that might be offensive have been omitted here. The paragraph ended: "A rumor began that the food had been impregnated with contraceptive medicine to test on the poor and that three people had died from it. The Health Department denied this, but its word was not believed."

"Do we take the value off next month's check?"

"It's hopeless to try to distribute this fairly," the supervisor said.

"It will cost us close to a thousand dollars to distribute it at all," the statistician said.

"It would cost us close to two thousand dollars to alter next month's checks," the bookkeeper said, "and the law specifies that we have to take extra income-in-kind off the monthly allowance."

"If I were you," the director said, "I would take all this home and eat it and not let anyone know about it."

"Mr. Morrissey!" Mrs. Traphagen's face paled away the red of her exertion. "That is fraud! You know as well as I do what would happen if it got out that we had <u>diverted</u> Welfare commodities to our own use! Can you imagine what the Mayor would say? The Governor? The State Department of Health? The HEW, The National Association of Social Workers?!" She had begun to tremble, and the two chickens that were hanging limply over her arm nodded to each other with slow decorum, their eyes closed righteously against the thought.

Cars began to clot the exit of the parking lot. The air was redolent[11].

But many of the workers didn't take the food home. The wolf of hunger was patient in shadowing the poor, even in summer, even on Welfare. As the afternoon wore on, apricots began to appear in the hands of children from Sixteenth and Vandalia Street all the way to the Boulevard. Tomatoes flamed

ANONYMOUS MAN   Emily Steadman   Courtesy of the artist.

briefly on the windowsills of the Negro ghetto between Fourteenth and Kirk, and on one block there was a chicken in every pot.

The complaints began early the next day. Sixteen Negroes called the Mayor's Committee on Racial Harmony, claiming that chickens, fruit, and vegetables had been given to the White Disadvantaged, while they had received tomatoes, half of them rotten. . . .

There were eighteen calls at the Department of Welfare protesting a tomato fight which had taken place on Fourteenth and

---

11. **redolent:** sweet-smelling.

Words to Know and Use	**divert** (də vurt′) *v.* to shift; to turn aside

138

Looking at Style

To discuss Greenberg's writing style in "Upon the Waters," read these descriptions:

■ "Cars began to clot the exit of the parking lot."

■ "Tomatoes flamed briefly on the windowsills. . . ."

Discuss these questions and activities with students:

1. What unusual verb choices help us visualize the cars and the tomatoes?

2. To what are cars and tomatoes being compared?

3. Try writing a description of your own in which you use an unusual verb.

4. For Alternative Learning Styles Scan the story for other passages that help readers visualize scenes. Illustrate one of the passages on a poster with the words copied beneath.

Vandalia, in which passersby had been pelted with tomatoes. The callers demanded that the families of those involved be stricken from the Welfare rolls as Relief cheaters, encouraging waste and damaging the moral fiber of working people.

23 *review* How is the community responding to Cephas's gift?

Eighteen mothers on the Aid to Dependent Children program picketed the Governor's mansion, carrying placards that read HOPE, NOT HANDOUTS and JOBS NOT CHARITY.

Sixty-eight welfare clients called to say that they had received no food at all and demanded equal service. When they heard that the Vandalia Street mothers were picketing, a group of them went down as counter-pickets. Words were exchanged between the two groups, and a riot ensued in which sixteen people were hospitalized for injuries, including six members of the city's riot squad. Seven of the leaders were arrested and jailed pending investigation. The FBI was called in to the case in the evening to ascertain if the riot was Communist-inspired.

At ten o'clock the Mayor appeared on TV with a plea for reason and patience. He stated that the riot was a reflection of the general decline in American morals and a lack of respect for the law. He ordered a six-man commission to be set up to hear testimony and make recommendations. A political opponent demanded a thorough investigation of the county Welfare system, the War on Poverty, and the local university's radicals.

The following day, Mrs. Traphagen was unable to go to work at the Welfare Office, having been badly scalded on the hand while canning a bushel of apricots.

Cephas Ribble remembered everyone at the Welfare Office in his prayers. After work, he would think about the day he had spent in the city, and of his various triumphs: the surprise and wonder on the faces of the workers, the open awe of the lady who had said, "You don't need to thank us." How everyone had dropped the work they were doing and run to unload the truck. It had been a wonderful day. He had given his plenty unto the poor, the plenty and nourishment of his own farm. He rose refreshed to do his work, marveling at the meaning and grandeur with which his chores were suddenly invested.

"By God," he said, as he checked the chickens and noted their need for more calcium in the feed, "a man has his good to do. I'm gonna do it every year. I'm gonna have a day for the poor. Yessir, every year." And he smiled genially on the chickens, the outbuildings, and the ripening fields of a generous land. ❧

◄ H

25

26

◄ I

Words to Know and Use

ascertain (as' ər tān) *v.* to find out
genially (jēn' yəl lē) *adv.* in a friendly way

139

---

23. ACTIVE READING: Review
How is the community responding to Cephas's gift? *(They complain; they respond in comical and exaggerated ways that show greed or arrogance; they voice current political ideas that don't fit the situation.)*

24. ACTIVE READING: Connect
Invite students to imagine that they are members of the community and explain how they feel about the free food. *(Any response is valid.)*

25. ACTIVE READING: Question
Ask students why this detail about Mrs. Traphagen is particularly funny. *(Mrs. Traphagen was outraged at Mr. Morrissey's suggestion that Welfare workers take food home, yet she took apricots home for herself.)*

26. CULTURAL SIDELIGHT
The title of the story comes from the Bible, Ecclesiastes 11:1, "Cast thy bread upon the waters: for thou shalt find it after many days." The verse is usually interpreted as meaning that trust and generosity are their own reward. In this story, Cephas has cast his bread upon the waters and been spiritually rewarded.

ENCOURAGING INDEPENDENT READING

Brother Can You Spare a Dime?, nonfiction by Milton Meltzer

Hard Times: An Oral History of the Great Depression by Studs Terkel

Let Us Now Praise Famous Men, nonfiction by James Agee, photographs by Walker Evans

---

Comprehension Check

1. How does Cephas earn a living? *(He is a farmer.)*

2. When the story opens, what brings him to the welfare office? *(He has brought food for the poor as thanks for the help he received during the Depression.)*

3. Why does Cephas have to stand in line and answer questions? *(The Welfare workers think he is applying for aid.)*

4. Why do the Welfare workers feel upset and confused by Cephas's gift? *(They have no rules to follow and no way to store and distribute food.)*

5. What does Cephas decide at the end of the story? *(to donate to the Welfare Office every year)*

Student Response

Responding to Reading

1. Any response is valid.

2. Possible responses: The welfare system's rules get in the way of its ability to help people with a donation of food; the welfare bureaucracy is set up to give money or food stamps, not actual food; the bureaucracy deals with papers and forms, not real people.

3. Possible responses: Each group competes for benefits; people are surprised at something new and unfamiliar; the Welfare Office's usual rules and regulations have been broken. The community's reaction is unreasonable—its members behave in selfish, competitive, and paranoid ways. The community's reaction is exaggerated but reasonable—different groups do compete and argue this way in real life, and people may feel that the food should have been fairly divided among needy groups.

4. Possible responses: Yes, because he is following his own code of right and wrong by repaying those who helped him; no, because he creates havoc and his gift does more harm than good—he could have given the food to a soup kitchen or another more appropriate recipient.

5. Possible responses: Originally, welfare was supposed to help people just for a little while; people got food instead of money. Now the welfare system provides money, housing, food, medical care, and other benefits to the poor, the aged, and the disabled—often for extended periods of time, even generations of the same families.

Responding to Reading

First Impressions

1. What are your impressions of Cephas? Jot down your thoughts on a sheet of paper.

Second Thoughts

2. Why is the bureaucratic welfare system unable to deal with Cephas's simple act of gratitude?

    Think about
    - the differences between Cephas's view of welfare and that of the office workers
    - the problems Cephas's gift might cause
    - the concept map you made for *bureaucracy*

3. Why do you think Cephas's donation causes so much trouble in the community? Is the community's reaction reasonable?

4. Do you think Cephas does the right thing by thanking the government in the manner that he does? Explain why or why not.

Broader Connections

5. In 1934, Cephas's family sought temporary relief to help them through hard times. Compare the welfare system then with the welfare system now.

Literary Concept: Satire

To criticize someone or something in a humorous way is to use **satire.** Satire exposes foolishness, stupidity, or wrongdoing in people or institutions. In your opinion, what are the targets of Greenberg's satire? Whom or what is she criticizing?

Concept Review: Characterization Work with a partner to identify details in the story that show the kind of person Cephas is. Share your findings with the class.

Literary Concept: Satire

Possible responses: Her main targets seem to be the Welfare workers, who are so interested in rules and regulations that they can't cope with a real gift. Other students may say Greenberg's targets are the suspicious and hostile factions and leaders in the community; Cephas, who is rendered foolish by his innocence and good-heartedness; and our entire society for its failure to appreciate simple generosity.

Concept Review: Characterization Cephas cares about his appearance, waits patiently, speaks in a friendly way, takes pride in his health, shows himself to be a generous and practical man of action by his donation of food, shows humility about the fuss the Welfare people make, and is naive about a modern Welfare Office. In unloading the food, he shows himself to be hard-working and a successful farmer. He enjoys life and is optimistic, as shown by his thoughts and plans at the end.

Writing Options

1. Write Mr. Morrissey's official **report** about Cephas's gift and its results. Remember that officials, or bureaucrats, can usually find an excuse when things go wrong.

2. Write a **letter** to Cephas, telling him what you think of his actions at the Welfare Office.

3. This story is in a subunit called "Victims or Victors?" Identify the victims and the victors in "Upon the Waters" and write an **essay** explaining your opinion.

4. Write an **anecdote,** or very short true story, about a time when you tried to help someone and got unexpected results.

Vocabulary Practice

Exercise   Refer to the word list to answer the questions below. Use each word once.

1. What word could be used for Cephas when he acted like a tough boss?

2. Instead of being boastful, Cephas showed what quality?

3. If Cephas had many more apricots than he needed, what did he have?

4. If Cephas had been forgetful and weak in the mind because of old age, what word would describe him?

5. What word should *not* be applied to Cephas as he energetically unloaded his truck?

6. What word describes the friendly manner in which Cephas gave away his chickens?

7. What verb describes how the welfare workers make sure a statement is true?

8. If Cephas were handicapped in some way, what word would describe him?

9. What word is associated with waiting?

10. What word would the police use to ask for traffic to be directed to a different street?

> *Words to Know and Use*
>
> ascertain
> disabled
> divert
> genially
> humility
> pending
> senile
> sluggish
> surplus
> tyrant

Writing Options

The Writing Options are designed to meet varied student interests and abilities. Have each student choose one writing activity to complete.

Journal Update Ask students to evaluate "Upon the Waters" in their journals. How would they rate the humor in this story? Which aspects of the story did they find the funniest and why? Ask them to evaluate whether this story effectively criticizes the welfare system.

Links to Writer's Craft

Writing Option 4 is an exercise in narrative writing. For more practice, see *The Writer's Craft,* Grade 7, "Narrative and Literary Writing," pages 70–93.

Vocabulary Practice

Answers to Exercise

1. tyrant
2. humility
3. surplus
4. senile
5. sluggish
6. genially
7. ascertain
8. disabled
9. pending
10. divert

For Alternative Learning Styles
Have students pair up to act out and guess the meanings of the following vocabulary words: *tyrant, humility, senile, sluggish, disabled,* and *divert.*

Closure

Anyone can be both victim and victor. Like Cephas, for example, millions of people in the United States have been victims of a poor economy and have required government assistance. Later, also like Cephas, they have become victors, in work and in life. Have students think of other real-life examples in which victims have become victors.

UPON THE WATERS **Teacher's Edition**   **141**

The Spelling Connection

Spelling Pattern: The Letters *j, ge,* **and** *dge.* The letter *j* is used at the beginning and in the middle of words. The letters **ge** spell the soft sound of *j* at the end of words. The letters **dge** are usually used in one-syllable words with short vowels.

Examples: *j*ustice langua**ge** do**dge**

Words from the Selection with *j, ge,* **and** *dge*

*j*ust   in*j*uries   advanta**ge**

exchan**ge**   dischar**ge**   enga**ge**

Other Words with *j, ge,* **and** *dge*

*j*acket   *j*eopardy   *j*ournal   challen**ge**
dama**ge**   le**dge**   bri**dge**   ba**dge**

Exercise Fill in the blanks with words above.

The ship was in danger when the movable __ didn't open. The captain and crew were faced with a __. The ship was in great __. __ at the last moment, the bridge rose. The ship suffered only slight __. There were no __ to the crew.

Extending the Lesson

Options for Learning

These activities suit a variety of learning styles and modes of expression.

Collaborative Learning Activities
See Options 1 and 2.

1. Live at Five Suggest to actors that a borrowed trench coat can give a reporter the proper air of authenticity, and that the bureaucrats can be in suits and ties. Cephas should wear a clean white shirt and a bow tie.

2. Feed the Poor In many places, there are organizations that handle the distribution of surplus food donated by farms and supermarkets. Students can research the problems of distributing fresh food by consulting one of these organizations.

3. Oral History Have students do some background research before formulating their questions. They might consult *An Album of the Great Depression* by William Loren Katz.

4. Cephas Comics Provide large sheets or rolls of paper for art. Allow students to display their work somewhere in the classroom.

📕 FACT FINDER History
An encyclopedia will tell students that the new agencies became known by their initials, such as NRA (National Recovery Administration) and AAA (Agricultural Adjustment Administration).

Joanne Greenberg

■ **More About the Author** Greenberg teaches anthropology at the Colorado School of Mines. Greenberg's best-known work is the novel *I Never Promised You a Rose Garden.* The story of a young woman struggling with a bout of mental illness, it has been widely acclaimed.

■ **Other Works** Novels: *Of Such Small Differences, Simple Gifts, A Season of Delight;* short story collections: *Summering, Rites of Passage.*

 ■ **Awards:** Fiction awards from the National Jewish Welfare Board; Marcus L. Kenner Award, New York Association of the Deaf; Christopher Book Award for *In this Sign.*

Options for Learning (Multimodal/Cross-Curricular Activities)

1 • Live at Five Present a "live" news report that shows Cephas unloading his truck in the middle of the confusion at the Welfare Office. Some students can play the roles of Cephas and various bureaucrats, while another student can be an "on the scene" reporter who interviews them.

2 • Feed the Poor Work in small groups to devise fair plans for dealing with Cephas's donation. Take into account each item he brought. Report the plans to the whole class. Then, as a class, vote on which plan is the best.

3 • Oral History Interview someone who lived during the Great Depression. Before the interview, draw up a list of questions that will prompt your source to give vivid descriptions of the times. Tape record the interview, and play the most interesting part for your class.

4 • Cephas Comics Reduce the plot of this story to five important scenes. Then draw these scenes as a panel cartoon showing the events of the day. Add dialogue balloons with humorous comments by the characters.

📕 FACT FINDER History
Why were Roosevelt's new government agencies called alphabet soup?

Joanne Greenberg
1932-

Joanne Greenberg, who lives in the Colorado mountains, drew the inspiration for "Upon the Waters" from an incident related by her husband, who worked in a welfare office. She says that she "started laughing" from the time she invented Cephas Ribble and has "not stopped since."

Greenberg, a native of Brooklyn, New York, has written nine novels and four collections of short stories. Her most famous novel is *I Never Promised You a Rose Garden,* published in 1964 under the pseudonym, or pen name, Hannah Green. This novel, which was made into a movie in 1977, deals with schizophrenia, a type of mental disorder. Greenberg herself suffered from this disease and courageously overcame it. More recently, Greenberg wrote *In This Sign,* about communication between deaf people, which was later dramatized for television.

Cross-Curricular Projects

Math Ask interested students to create a chart showing the approximate weight of all the food Cephas gave to the Welfare Office. Have them list the resources they used to obtain the information.

Art/Architecture Have students consider the description of the Boone County Department of Public Welfare and then design a more humane and comfortable building. Have them draw a rough blueprint of the layout of the building.

Social Studies Have students present a panel discussion of the welfare services in your area. If possible, have students visit a local agency and interview its workers about the problems they face, how they feel about the rules and regulations under which they work, and how they assess the agency's goals and achievements.

Nonfiction

The Noble Experiment
from I Never Had It Made
JACKIE ROBINSON *as told to* **ALFRED DUCKETT**

Examine What You Know (Prior Knowledge)

Prejudice is the result of *prejudging*, or judging before all the facts are known. It often consists of judging a whole group of people by their appearance or by the actions of a few members of the group. Usually it results in negative and unfair treatment of individuals. Share with your classmates some examples of prejudice you have experienced or seen, and the effects on the people involved.

Expand Your Knowledge
(Building Background)

In the 1940s, African Americans faced many barriers created by prejudice. In the South, "Jim Crow" laws kept African Americans from mixing with whites in schools, restaurants, hospitals, and parks. African Americans were forced to use separate restrooms and water fountains.

Athletic competition did not escape this segregation. Even in baseball, blacks played in separate "Negro leagues"; they were barred from the major leagues. In 1947, Jackie Robinson became the first African American to break the major-league "color barrier." A superb athlete, he helped the Brooklyn Dodgers win six league championships and was named the league's most valuable player in 1949. He was voted into the Baseball Hall of Fame in 1962.

JACKIE ROBINSON 3b of BROOKLYN DODGERS

Enrich Your Reading (Reading Skill)

Problem Solving   In this selection, Branch Rickey, the owner of the Brooklyn Dodgers, faces a difficult problem. Create a chart like that below to track the steps in Rickey's problem-solving strategy.

Problem	Problem-Solving Strategy
No blacks are allowed in baseball.	1. Identify best black player. 2.

■ *Author biography on Extend page*

THE NOBLE EXPERIMENT   143

JOURNAL WRITING IDEAS
■ What does the expression "had it made" (from the title of the book) mean to you? Who do you know who "has it made"?

■ Would you enjoy being the first ever to do something difficult? Why or why not? What qualities does such a person need most?

COLLABORATIVE LEARNING OPTIONS
Opportunities for collaborative learning include Writing Option 4 (p. 153), Options for Learning activities 1, 2, and 3, and Cross-Curricular Projects (p. 154).

ADDITIONAL RESOURCES
Unit Two Resource Book
Reader's Guidesheet, p. 17
Reading Skills, p. 18
Literature Skills, p. 19
Vocabulary Connections, p. 20
Spelling Connections, p. 21
Comprehension and Vocabulary Check Tests, p. 22
Selection Test, pp. 23–24

Objectives

■ To understand and analyze an autobiographical excerpt

■ To examine motivation in a person's life and to review the concept of autobiography

■ To enrich reading by identifying steps in problem solving

■ To express understanding of the story through a choice of writing forms, including a comparison, a profile, a definition, and a rap song

Prereading/Motivation

Examine What You Know

Discussion Prompts Is it possible to be completely free from prejudice? Can prejudice ever have a positive effect?

Expand Your Knowledge

Additional Background Jack Roosevelt Robinson was born in Cairo, Georgia, in 1919. He attended college at UCLA, where he excelled in football, track, basketball, and baseball. He was named Rookie of the Year in 1947 and led the National League in batting average in 1949 and stolen bases in 1947 and 1949. A commemorative stamp was issued in his honor in 1982.

Enrich Your Reading

Problems: No blacks allowed in baseball; players, umpires, press, and public will resist; black player will want to fight back.
Problem-Solving Strategy: Identify best black player; find player with courage to take abuse; keep plan a secret until ready; prepare player for possible abuse; convince player of importance of "turning the other cheek."

Thematic Link— Victims or Victors?

Jackie Robinson was a victim of racial prejudice in both baseball and American society in general. His entrance into the major leagues was a victory for him, Branch Rickey, baseball, African Americans, and American society.

VOCABULARY PREVIEW

These vocabulary words are defined at the bottom of the selection pages on which they appear.

cynical mistrustful of others' sincerity

eloquence forceful speech

incredulous unable to believe something

indignant angry due to a wrongful action

insinuation an insulting suggestion

retaliate to get revenge

shrewdly wisely

speculating guessing

taunt to make fun of

ultimate most important

LIMITED ENGLISH PROFICIENCY

■ Use the Reader's Guidesheet, *Unit Two Resource Book,* page 17.

■ Robinson sometimes uses technical language to describe the business of baseball. You may wish to have students who are sports enthusiasts explain some of these terms to the class.

★ Text annotations marked with a red star (5, 7, 13) may be particularly helpful for students with limited English proficiency.

TEXT ANNOTATIONS

1. ACTIVE READING: Review
As necessary, help students see that the speaker changes from Charley Thomas to Branch Rickey. Thomas's dialogue appears within single quotations marks, Rickey's appears within regular quotation marks, and Robinson's appears without quotation marks.

2. LITERARY CONCEPT:
Characterization
Ask students how the incident with Charley Thomas influenced Rickey's career in baseball. *(Possible responses: Rickey never forgot the incident in the hotel; he tried to integrate the seating in the St. Louis ballpark.)* Ask students what they learned about Rickey's character here. *(Possible responses: He believed in equality; he tried to change things that were wrong.)*

The Noble Experiment
from I Never Had It Made

JACKIE ROBINSON
as told to Alfred Duckett

In 1910 Branch Rickey was a coach for Ohio Wesleyan. The team went to South Bend, Indiana, for a game. The hotel management registered the coach and team but refused to assign a room to a black player named Charley Thomas. In those days college ball had a few black players. Mr. Rickey took the manager aside and said he would move the entire team to another hotel unless the black athlete was accepted. The threat was a bluff because he knew the other hotels also would have refused accommodations to a black man. While the hotel manager was thinking about the threat, Mr. Rickey came up with a compromise. He suggested a cot be put in his own room, which he would share with the unwanted guest. The hotel manager wasn't happy about the idea, but he gave in.

Years later Branch Rickey told the story of the misery of that black player to whom he had given a place to sleep. He remembered that Thomas couldn't sleep.

"He sat on that cot," Mr. Rickey said, "and was silent for a long time. Then he began to cry, tears he couldn't hold back. His whole body shook with emotion. I sat and watched him, not knowing what to do until he began tearing at one hand with the other—just as if he were trying to scratch the skin off his hands with his fingernails. I was alarmed. I asked him what he was trying to do to himself.

"'It's my hands,' he sobbed. 'They're black. If only they were white, I'd be as good as anybody then, wouldn't I, Mr. Rickey? If only they were white.'"

"Charley," Mr. Rickey said, "the day will come when they won't have to be white."

Thirty-five years later, while I was lying awake nights, frustrated, unable to see a future, Mr. Rickey, by now the president of the Dodgers, was also lying awake at night, trying to make up his mind about a new experiment.

He had never forgotten the agony of that black athlete. When he became a front-office executive in St. Louis, he had fought, behind the scenes, against the custom that consigned black spectators to the Jim Crow section of the Sportsman's Park, later to become Busch Memorial Stadium. His pleas to change the rules were in vain. Those in power argued that if blacks were allowed a free choice of seating, white business would suffer.

Branch Rickey lost that fight, but when he became the boss of the Brooklyn Dodgers in 1943, he felt the time for equality in baseball had come. He knew that achieving it would

◀ A

1

2

Guided Reading for Less-Proficient Students

These questions can help guide students through the reading. Ask each question at the point of the selection where the capital letter and arrow appear in the margin. In addition, you may wish to use appropriate Active Reading annotations.

A. What incident makes Charley Thomas cry and scratch at the skin on his hands? *(He was denied a hotel room because of his color.)* Recalling

B. What was Branch Rickey's "noble experiment"? *(a plan to end segregation in major-league baseball by bringing in a black player)* Summarizing

C. Why was Robinson reluctant to try out for the Dodgers? *(Possible responses: He was afraid of being fired by the Monarchs; he didn't think anything would come of it)* Summarizing

Continued on page 145

be terribly difficult. There would be deep resentment, determined opposition, and perhaps even racial violence. He was convinced he was morally right, and he shrewdly sensed that making the game a truly national one would have healthy financial results. He took his case before the startled directors of the club, and using persuasive eloquence, he won the first battle in what would be a long and bitter campaign. He was voted permission to make the Brooklyn club the pioneer in bringing blacks into baseball.

Winning his directors' approval was almost insignificant in contrast to the task which now lay ahead of the Dodger president. He made certain that word of his plans did not leak out, particularly to the press. Next, he had to find the ideal player for his project, which came to be called "Rickey's noble experiment." This player had to be one who could take abuse, name-calling, rejection by fans and sportswriters and by fellow players not only on opposing teams but on his own. He had to be able to stand up in the face of merciless persecution and not retaliate. On the other hand, he had to be a contradiction in human terms; he still had to have spirit. He could not be an Uncle Tom.[1] His ability to turn the other cheek had to be predicated[2] on his determination to gain acceptance. Once having proven his ability as player, teammate, and man, he had to be able to cast off humbleness and stand up as a full-fledged participant whose triumph did not carry the poison of bitterness.

Unknown to most people and certainly to me, after launching a major scouting program, Branch Rickey had picked me as that player. The Rickey talent hunt went beyond national borders. Cuba, Mexico, Puerto Rico, Venezuela, and other countries where dark-skinned people lived had been checked out. Mr. Rickey had learned that there were a number of black players, war veterans mainly, who had gone to these countries, despairing of finding an opportunity in their own country. The manhunt had to be camouflaged. If it became known he was looking for a black recruit for the Dodgers, there would have been all kinds of trouble. The gimmick he used as a coverup was to make the world believe that he was about to establish a new Negro league. In the spring of 1945 he called a press conference and announced that the Dodgers were organizing the United States League, composed of all black teams. This, of course, made blacks and prointegration whites indignant. He was accused of trying to uphold the existing segregation and, at the same time, capitalize on black players. Cleverly, Mr. Rickey replied that his league would be better organized than the current ones. He said its main purpose, eventually, was to be absorbed into the majors. It is ironic that by coming very close to telling the truth, he was able to conceal that truth from the enemies of integrated baseball. Most people assumed that when he

---

1. **Uncle Tom:** a black person who tries overly hard to please white people; originally from the novel *Uncle Tom's Cabin* written by Harriet Beecher Stowe in 1852.
2. **predicated:** based

Words to Know and Use	**shrewdly** (shrōōd′ lē) *adv.* wisely; in a clever way **eloquence** (el′ ə kwens) *n.* forceful, convincing speech **retaliate** (ri tal′ ē āt′) *v.* to get revenge; get even **indignant** (in dig′ nənt) *adj.* angry because of an action that seems wrong

145

3. ACTIVE READING: Review
Ask students to identify the first battle that Rickey had to win in order to integrate the major leagues. (*He had to win over the directors of the Brooklyn Dodgers.*)

4. ACTIVE READING: Connect
Make sure students understand the meanings of *merciless persecution* and *turn the other cheek.* (*constant cruel treatment, take more abuse without fighting back*) Ask how they would feel if they had to take abuse and not fight back. (*Any response is valid.*) Then ask why Rickey feels the player should not fight back. (*Possible responses: The player needs to be completely above reproach; the persecutors, not the player, need to look bad; retaliation may distract him from playing well.*)

5. VOCABULARY: Compound Words
Students with limited English proficiency may have difficulty understanding such compound words as *manhunt* and *coverup.* Explain that breaking compounds into two simple words will enable students to figure out the words' meanings. (*man + hunt = "search for a person"; cover + up = "an effort to hide or conceal"*) Explain also that *gimmick* in this sense means "a trick." ★

Guided Reading for Less-Proficient Students

Continued from page 144

D. What is the real reason Robinson was invited to Brooklyn? (*Rickey is interested in hiring Robinson for Brooklyn's major-league team.*) Recalling

E. As Branch Rickey speaks, what does Jackie Robinson realize about Rickey's attitude toward his "noble experiment"? (*He realizes that Rickey is sincere and passionate about justice and about bringing blacks into major-league baseball.*) Summarizing

F. What does Rickey say may happen if Jackie Robinson enters the major leagues? (*He could be hit with beanballs, called terrible names, and physically attacked.*) Summarizing

G. For what people does Robinson accept the challenges of entering major league baseball? (*for black youth, for his mother, for his girlfriend, for himself, and for Branch Rickey.*) Recalling

7. ACTIVE READING: Question
Ask students what *cynical* means here. (*a person who is suspicious of others or who doesn't trust them*) Ask why blacks had "to learn to protect themselves by being cynical." (*Blacks needed to guard themselves against whites who deceived them.*) Ask what Robinson meant by the statement, "We go through life walking a tightrope to prevent too much disillusionment." (*Possible responses: If blacks become too distrustful, they might end up missing out on actual opportunities. If they become too trustful, they might get taken advantage of.*) ★

spoke of some distant goal of integration, Mr. Rickey was being a hypocrite on this issue as so many of baseball's leaders had been.

Black players were familiar with this kind of hypocrisy. When I was with the Monarchs, shortly before I met Mr. Rickey, Wendell Smith, then sports editor of the black, weekly Pittsburgh *Courier*, had arranged for me and two other players from the Negro league to go to a tryout with the Boston Red Sox. The tryout had been brought about because a Boston city councilman had frightened the Red Sox management. Councilman Isadore Muchneck threatened to push a bill through banning Sunday baseball unless the Red Sox hired black players. Sam Jethroe of the Cleveland Buckeyes, Marvin Williams of the Philadelphia Stars, and I had been grateful to Wendell for getting us a chance in the Red Sox tryout, and we put our best efforts into it. However, not for one minute did we believe the tryout was sincere. The Boston club officials praised our performance, let us fill out application cards, and said "So long." We were fairly certain they wouldn't call us, and we had no intention of calling them.

Incidents like this made Wendell Smith as cynical as we were. He didn't accept Branch Rickey's new league as a genuine project, and he frankly told him so. During this conversation, the Dodger boss asked Wendell whether any of the three of us who had gone to Boston was really good major league material. Wendell said I was. I will be forever indebted to Wendell because, without his even knowing it, his recommendation was in the end partly responsible for my career. At the time, it started a thorough investigation of my background.

In August 1945, at Comiskey Park in Chicago, I was approached by Clyde Sukeforth, the Dodger scout. Blacks have had to learn to protect themselves by being cynical but not cynical enough to slam the door on potential opportunities. We go through life walking a tightrope to prevent too much disillusionment. I was out on the field when Sukeforth called my name and beckoned. He told me the Brown Dodgers were looking for top ballplayers, that Branch Rickey had heard about me and sent him to watch me throw from the hole.[3] He had come at an unfortunate time. I had hurt my shoulder a couple of days before that, and I wouldn't be doing any throwing for at least a week.

Sukeforth said he'd like to talk with me anyhow. He asked me to come to see him after the game at the Stevens Hotel.

Here we go again, I thought. Another time-wasting experience. But Sukeforth looked like a sincere person, and I thought I might as well listen. I agreed to meet him that night. When we met, Sukeforth got right to the point. Mr. Rickey wanted to talk to me about the possibility of becoming a Brown Dodger. If I could get a few days off and go to Brooklyn, my fare and expenses would be paid. At first I said that I couldn't leave my team and go to Brooklyn just like that.

---

3. **throw from the hole:** ability to throw from deep in the infield to first base.

| Words to Know and Use | **cynical** (sin' i kəl) *adj.* mistrustful of others' sincerity |

146

Multicultural Connections

In the years before Robinson broke "the color line," African-American athletes played baseball in the American "Negro leagues." The Negro National League (1920–1948) and Negro American League (1937–1950) produced such sports legends as Robinson, Willie Mays, Henry Aaron, and Roy Campanella—each of whom earned a place in the Baseball Hall of Fame after a major-league career. In 1971 four other men—Satchel Paige, Josh Gibson, Monte Irvin, and James (Cool Papa) Bell—were inducted in the Hall of Fame for their Negro league accomplishments. Since then, other players from the Negro leagues have been voted into the Hall of Fame by a special committee.

Ask students why Negro league players deserve to be honored by major-league baseball. Would such players be happy or bitter to receive recognition from the baseball establishment?

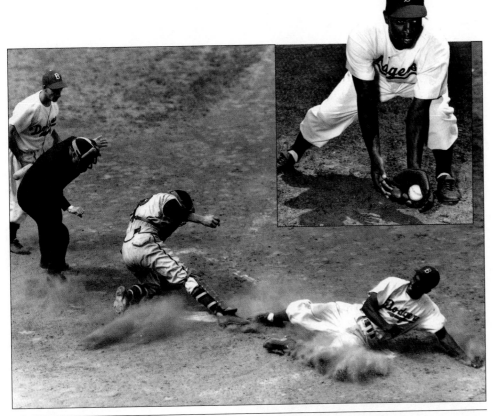

Jackie Robinson stealing home during a Braves–Dodgers game at Ebbets Field in Brooklyn, 1948.
UPI/Bettmann, New York.

8. LITERARY CONCEPT: Motivation
Why was Robinson reluctant to go to Brooklyn for a tryout? (*Possible responses: He was afraid he'd lose his position with the Kansas City Monarchs; he had already been deceived by the Red Sox.*)

9. LITERARY CONCEPT: Character
Ask how the qualities in Branch Rickey's personality would help him to succeed in a difficult project. (*Possible responses: His air of command would help him be seen as a leader; his directness would enable him to get things done; his friendliness would help win people's trust.*)

Sukeforth wouldn't take no for an answer. He pointed out that I couldn't play for a few days anyhow because of my bum arm. Why should my team object?

I continued to hold out and demanded to know what would happen if the Monarchs fired me. The Dodger scout replied quietly that he didn't believe that would happen.

I shrugged and said I'd make the trip. I figured I had nothing to lose.

Branch Rickey was an impressive-looking man. He had a classic face, an air of command, a deep, booming voice, and a way of cutting through red tape and getting down to basics. He shook my hand vigorously and, after a brief conversation, sprang the first question.

"You got a girl?" he demanded.

It was a heck of a question. I had two reactions: why should he be concerned about my relationship with a girl; and, second, while I thought, hoped, and prayed I had a girl, the way things had been going, I was afraid she might have begun to consider me a hopeless case. I explained this to Mr. Rickey and Clyde.

10. ACTIVE READING: Connect
Ask students how they would feel if they were in Jackie Robinson's shoes at this moment. *(Possible responses: I'd feel as if I were dreaming; I'd be afraid that I might not do well in the major leagues; I'd be angry that lies had been told to get me there.)*

11. HISTORICAL SIDELIGHT
A "farm club" is a baseball team in the minor leagues that is affiliated with a major-league team. Farm clubs train and develop players for their parent teams in the major leagues. The farm system was established by Branch Rickey in 1919, when he was working for the St. Louis Cardinals.

12. ACTIVE READING: Evaluate
Ask students to identify the reason for Branch Rickey's "exhaustive" background search of Jackie Robinson. *(He was trying to be sure that Robinson was the right candidate for this experiment.)* Was such an investigation necessary? *(Any response is valid.)*

Mr. Rickey wanted to know all about Rachel. I told him of our hopes and plans.

"You know, you *have* a girl," he said heartily. "When we get through today, you may want to call her up because there are times when a man needs a woman by his side."

My heart began racing a little faster again as I sat there speculating. First he asked me if I really understood why he had sent for me. I told him what Clyde Sukeforth had told me.

"That's what he was supposed to tell you," Mr. Rickey said. "The truth is you are not a candidate for the Brooklyn Brown Dodgers. I've sent for you because I'm interested in you as a candidate for the Brooklyn National League Club. I think you can play in the major leagues. How do you feel about it?"

My reactions seemed like some kind of weird mixture churning in a blender. I was thrilled, scared, and excited. I was incredulous. Most of all, I was speechless.

Robinson after signing his contract with the Brooklyn Dodgers. AP/Wide World Photos, New York.

"You think you can play for Montreal?" he demanded.

I got my tongue back. "Yes," I answered.

Montreal was the Brooklyn Dodgers' top farm club. The players who went there and made it had an excellent chance at the big time.

I was busy reorganizing my thoughts while Mr. Rickey and Clyde Sukeforth discussed me briefly, almost as if I weren't there. Mr. Rickey was questioning Clyde. Could I make the grade?

Abruptly, Mr. Rickey swung his swivel chair in my direction. He was a man who conducted himself with great drama. He pointed a finger at me.

"I know you're a good ballplayer," he barked. "What I don't know is whether you have the guts."

I knew it was all too good to be true. Here was a guy questioning my courage. That virtually amounted to him asking me if I was a coward. Mr. Rickey or no Mr. Rickey, that was an insinuation hard to take. I felt the heat coming up into my cheeks.

Before I could react to what he had said, he leaned forward in his chair and explained.

I wasn't just another athlete being hired by a ball club. We were playing for big stakes. This was the reason Branch Rickey's search had been so exhaustive. The search had spanned the globe and narrowed down to a few candidates, then finally to me. When it looked as though I might be the number-one choice, the investigation of my life, my habits, my reputation, and my character had become an intensified study.

"I've investigated you thoroughly,

Words to Know and Use	**speculating** (spek′ yōō lāt′ iŋ) *adj.* thinking about different possibilities; guessing what might happen **speculate** *v.* **incredulous** (in krej′ ōō ləs) *adj.* unable or unwilling to believe something **insinuation** (in sin′ yōō ā′ shən) *n.* a suggestion or hint intended to insult

Speaking . . . Listening . . . Viewing

Viewing The following activities may be useful for helping students to compare film and literature. Invite students to watch a video (black and white, 76 minutes) of the 1950 film, *The Jackie Robinson Story*, in which Robinson plays himself. Then encourage students to compare the film with what they have read in "The Noble Experiment." Ask such questions as these:

1. What advantages does the filmed version have?

2. What advantages does the written version have?

3. Which version seems more emotionally powerful to you? Which version gives you more information? What other differences do you notice?

Robinson," Mr. Rickey said.

One of the results of this thorough screening were reports from California athletic circles that I had been a "racial agitator"[4] at UCLA. Mr. Rickey had not accepted these criticisms on face value. He had demanded and received more information and came to the conclusion that if I had been white, people would have said, "Here's a guy who's a contender, a competitor."

After that he had some grim words of warning. "We can't fight our way through this, Robinson. We've got no army. There's virtually nobody on our side. No owners, no umpires, very few newspapermen. And I'm afraid that many fans will be hostile. We'll be in a tough position. We can win only if we can convince the world that I'm doing this because you're a great ballplayer and a fine gentleman."

He had me transfixed as he spoke. I could feel his sincerity, and I began to get a sense of how much this major step meant to him. Because of his nature and his passion for justice, he had to do what he was doing. He continued. The rumbling voice, the theatrical gestures, were gone. He was speaking from a deep, quiet strength.

"So there's more than just playing," he said. "I wish it meant only hits, runs, and errors—only the things they put in the box score. Because you know—yes, you would know, Robinson, that a baseball box score is a democratic thing. It doesn't tell how big you are, what church you attend, what color you are, or how your father voted in the last election. It just tells what kind of baseball player you were on that particular day."

I interrupted. "But it's the box score that really counts—that and that alone, isn't it?"

"It's all that *ought* to count," he replied.

(From left) Gil Hodges, Gene Hermanski, Branch Rickey, and Jackie Robinson in Yankee Stadium, 1949.
The Bettmann Archive, New York.

"But it isn't. Maybe one of these days it *will* be all that counts. That is one of the reasons I've got you here, Robinson. If you're a good enough man, we can make this a start in the right direction. But let me tell you, it's going to take an awful lot of courage."

He was back to the crossroads question that made me start to get angry minutes earlier. He asked it slowly and with great care.

"Have you got the guts to play the game no matter what happens?"

"I think I can play the game, Mr. Rickey," I said.

The next few minutes were tough. Branch Rickey had to make absolutely sure that I knew what I would face. Beanballs[5] would be

---

4. racial agitator (rā shəl aj′ i tāt′ ər): a negative term used for someone who tried to stir up trouble between the races.

5. beanballs: pitches thrown purposefully at a batter's head.

13. VOCABULARY: Technical Terms
Some students may have difficulty with the baseball terminology on this page. Ask baseball "experts" in the class to explain the terms or have volunteers look up the terms in a reference book. The definition of a box score is "a printed statistical summary of players' performances in a game." Among other things, a box score tallies the hits (*"plays in which one hits the ball and safely reaches base"*), runs (*"points scored by players' crossing home plate"*) and errors (*"fielders' mistakes that allow an opposing player to reach base or advance between bases."*) ★

14. Literary Concept: Motivation
Ask students why Rickey keeps testing Robinson's courage. (*He knows how difficult Robinson's task will be; he wants to make absolutely certain that Robinson knows what he's getting into.*)

The Brooklyn Dodgers in 1949. Robinson is second from the right in the third row.   UPI/Bettmann, New York.

F ▶ thrown at me. I would be called the kind of names which would hurt and infuriate any man. I would be physically attacked. Could I take all of this and control my temper, remain steadfastly loyal to our <u>ultimate</u> aim?

15 He knew I would have terrible problems and wanted me to know the extent of them before I agreed to the plan. I was twenty-six years old, and all my life–back to the age of eight when a little neighbor girl called me a nigger[6]–I had believed in payback, retalia-tion. The most luxurious possession, the richest treasure anybody has, is his personal dignity. I looked at Mr. Rickey guardedly, and in that second I was looking at him not as a partner in a great experiment, but as the enemy–a white man. I had a question, and it was the age-old one about whether or not you sell your birthright.

"Mr. Rickey," I asked, "are you looking for a Negro who is afraid to fight back?"

I never will forget the way he exploded.

"Robinson," he said, "I'm looking for a ballplayer with guts enough not to fight back."

After that, Mr. Rickey continued his lec-ture on the kind of thing I'd be facing.

He not only told me about it, but he acted out the part of a white player charging into me, blaming me for the "accident" and call-ing me all kinds of foul racial names. He talked about my race, my parents, in lan-guage that was almost unendurable.

"They'll <u>taunt</u> and goad you," Mr. Rickey said. "They'll do anything to make you react.

---

6. **nigger:** *slang,* a derogatory name for an African American. The word is offensive and insulting.

Words to Know and Use	**ultimate** (ul' tə mit) *adj.* final; most important **taunt** (tônt) *v.* to make fun of; jeer

They'll try to provoke a race riot in the ballpark. This is the way to prove to the public that a Negro should not be allowed in the major league. This is the way to frighten the fans and make them afraid to attend the games."

If hundreds of black people wanted to come to the ballpark to watch me play and Mr. Rickey tried to discourage them, would I understand that he was doing it because the emotional enthusiasm of my people could harm the experiment? That kind of enthusiasm would be as bad as the emotional opposition of prejudiced white fans.

Suppose I was at shortstop. Another player comes down from first, stealing, flying in with spikes high, and cuts me on the leg. As I feel the blood running down my leg, the white player laughs in my face.

"How do you like that, nigger boy?" he sneers.

Could I turn the other cheek? I didn't know how I would do it. Yet I knew that I must. I had to do it for so many reasons. For black youth, for my mother, for Rae, for myself. I had already begun to feel I had to do it for Branch Rickey.

I was offered, and agreed to sign later, a contract with a $3,500 bonus and $600-a-month salary. I was officially a Montreal Royal. I must not tell anyone except Rae and my mother. ❧

◀ G

INSIGHT

I'll Walk the Tightrope

MARGARET DANNER

I'll walk the tightrope that's been stretched for me,
and though a wrinkled forehead, perplexed why,
will accompany me, I'll delicately
step along. For if I stop to sigh
at the earth-propped stride
of others, I will fall. I must balance high
without a parasol to tide
a faltering step, without a net below,
without a balance stick to guide.

THE CIRCUS (detail) 1961 Romare Bearden Courtesy, The Estate of Romare Bearden and ACA Galleries, New York.

THE NOBLE EXPERIMENT 151

Comprehension Check

1. What does Branch Rickey show about his beliefs when he shares a room with a black athlete? (*He rejects racism; he believes in equality for all.*)

2. What is Rickey looking for in his search of baseball teams? (*the best candidate for ending segregation in the Major Leagues*)

3. What are Rickey's plans for Robinson? (*to make him the first black to break the color barrier in the major leagues.*)

4. What does Rickey warn Robinson about? (*that Robinson must be prepared for beanballs, insults, and abuse*)

5. How does the interview between Rickey and Robinson end? (*Robinson accepts Rickey's offer and signs a contract.*)

Student Response

Responding to Reading

1. Any response is valid.

2. **Possible responses:** It was most ingenious of Rickey to keep his master plan secret so that it couldn't be sabotaged by others, to insist on hiring a particular type of person as the first black major-league ballplayer, to test Robinson before hiring him.

3. **Possible responses:** Both men showed courage by defying the wishes and expectation of others; Robinson had the courage to take a job where he would be facing anger, abuse, and possible physical danger; Rickey possessed the courage to stand up against long-standing traditions of segregation.

4. **Possible responses:** I would have played because of my responsibility to other black players and because of my right to play at the highest level my abilities would allow; I would not have played because being publicly challenged and resented would have been too difficult.

5. **Possible responses:** The first and sixth lines apply to Robinson's life, for Branch Rickey had "stretched" the challenge before him and Robinson achieved a much higher position than any black player had previously; the last four lines apply to Robinson because he risked being hurt, and he had no model to guide him.

6. **Possible responses:** They should be expected to be role models, because they are the most widely known heroes for young people in society; they should not be expected to be role models, because they are hired strictly for their athletic ability, and like other people, they are just trying to do a job.

Challenge Question

This is Robinson's autobiography. Why does he bother to explain Rickey's point of view so thoroughly? *(Possible responses: to show his admiration for Rickey, to show the difficulties of integrating major league baseball.)*

---

*R*esponding to Reading

First Impressions

1. What was your reaction to Branch Rickey as you finished reading? Jot down words and phrases to describe your thoughts about him.

Second Thoughts

2. In your opinion, what were the most ingenious parts of Rickey's plan to integrate major-league baseball?

   Think about
   • his search for "a great ballplayer and a fine gentleman"
   • how and why he kept his plan secret
   • his meeting with Jackie Robinson

3. Consider the difficulties both men faced in fighting prejudice. How do you think both Rickey and Robinson showed courage? Explain.

4. If you had been in Robinson's shoes, would you have agreed to play for the Dodgers? Give your reasons.

   Think about
   • your discussion of prejudice and its effects
   • Rickey's predictions of what Robinson would face

5. Reread the poem "I'll Walk the Tightrope" on page 151. What lines of this poem apply to Robinson's life? Explain why you think so.

Broader Connections

6. Many saw Jackie Robinson as a role model for young people. Should we expect professional athletes to be role models, or should they be judged only on their athletic performance?

*L*iterary Concept: Motivation

The reasons for a person's action are known as **motivation.** What motivated Branch Rickey and Jackie Robinson? Were their motivations the same or different? Explain.

Concept Review: Autobiography An **autobiography** usually focuses on events that shape or change a person's life. How did the meeting with Branch Rickey change Jackie Robinson's life?

152   UNIT TWO   VICTIMS OR VICTORS?

Literary Concept: Motivation

Possible response: Both Rickey and Robinson were motivated by their sense of justice, their competitiveness, and their desire to have African Americans play in the major leagues; both may also have been motivated by personal pride.

Concept Review: Autobiography The meeting changed Robinson's career by giving him the opportunity to play at the highest professional level; it changed his life by helping him to become a world-famous leader and role model.

Writing Options

1. Jackie Robinson had to become a victim in order to become a victor. Can you think of any other real or fictional characters who have had to do the same thing? Write a **comparison** of Robinson with someone else in a similar situation.

2. Baseball programs include profiles of each player, noting the player's strengths and special qualities. Write a **profile** of Jackie Robinson for a Brooklyn Dodgers program.

3. Branch Rickey said that he was "looking for a ballplayer with guts enough not to fight back." Write a **definition** of *courage* with which Rickey would agree.

4. A **rap** is a spoken song with a strong rhythm. Some raps tell a story. Write a rap that tells the story of "The Noble Experiment." Practice speaking it, and then share it with your classmates.

Vocabulary Practice

Exercise On a separate sheet of paper, write the word from the list that is the best substitute for each word or phrase in dark type.

1. Rickey **cleverly** devised a cover story for the press.

2. Some **unbelieving** fans gasped when Robinson walked onto the field for his first major-league game.

3. The majority of fans were wrong about Rickey's plans as they sat home, **guessing.**

4. Many African Americans felt very **mistrustful** about promises made by whites.

5. Some ballplayers on other teams would **mock** Robinson and try to anger him.

6. Robinson was not allowed to **fight back.**

7. The **final** goal of the experiment was to integrate the major leagues.

8. Sportswriters filled their columns with many a **sly negative comment** about Robinson's character.

9. Several ministers spoke with **great speaking skill** about the evils of prejudice.

10. Many people were **upset** about the treatment of the rookie Robinson.

> **Words to Know and Use**
>
> cynical
> eloquence
> incredulous
> indignant
> insinuation
> retaliate
> shrewdly
> speculating
> taunt
> ultimate

THE NOBLE EXPERIMENT   153

Writing Options

The Writing Options are designed to meet varied student interests and abilities. Have each student choose one writing activity to complete.

Journal Update Invite students to review their journal entries for "The Noble Experiment." They may wish to write about a time when they, like Robinson, had to face a difficult situation or had to show spirit.

Links to Writer's Craft

Writing Option 4 is an exercise in narrative writing. For more practice, see *The Writer's Craft,* Grade 7, "Narrative and Literary Writing," pages 70–92.

Vocabulary Practice

Answers to Exercise

1. shrewdly

2. incredulous

3. speculating

4. cynical

5. taunt

6. retaliate

7. ultimate

8. insinuation

9. eloquence

10. indignant

For Alternative Learning Styles

Have students work in small groups to act out the meanings of *cynical, incredulous, indignant, taunt,* and *retaliate,* using words, facial expressions, and body gestures. Assign one word to each group; then have each group demonstrate their word and have the rest of the class guess the word. ★

The Spelling Connection

The Suffixes *ance/ant* and *ence/ent* The suffixes **ance** and **ant** are commonly added to complete words. The suffixes **ence** and **ent** are commonly used with roots and after the letters **ci, qu,** and **sc.**

Examples: attend + **ance** = attend**ance**
inhabit + **ant** = inhabit**ant**

ance/ant and *ence/ent* Words from the Selection
accept**ance** perform**ance** viol**ence** experi**ence**
eloqu**ence**

Other Words with *ance/ant* and *ence/ent*
defend**ant**   inhabit**ant**   frequ**ent**
contest**ant** appli**ance**   suffici**ent**

Exercise Complete each analogy.
1. seldom is to **infrequent** as often is to __.
2. awkward is to **graceful** as inadequate is to __.
3. **assistant** is to **assist** as __ is to **contest.**
4. **rejection** is to **reject** as __ is to **accept.**
5. **gentleness** is to __ as honesty is to **cheating.**

Extending the Lesson

Options for Learning

These activities suit a variety of learning styles and modes of expression.

Collaborative Learning Activities
See Options 1, 2, and 3.

1. A League of Their Own Suggest that students consult general encyclopedias, *The Baseball Encyclopedia*, and books such as *Only the Ball Was White*, a history of the Negro leagues by Robert Peterson.

2. Now and Then Encyclopedias of African-American biography, sports books, annual publications of baseball statistics, and *The Baseball Encyclopedia* will be helpful.

3. A Telling Moment Students will find a literary model of dialogue on page 177 and information on punctuating dialogue on page 178.

4. Robinson Report Encourage students to include their own personal responses to the events of Robinson's life.

 FACT FINDER SPORTS

Students can use The Baseball Encyclopedia, general encyclopedias, or a good biography of Robinson to find out that Robinson's lifetime batting average was .311.

Alfred A. Duckett

■ **Other Works** Nonfiction: *Changing of the Guard: The New Breed of Black Politicians, Soul in Type: The Romance and History of the Black American Press.* Poetry: *Raps.*

Closure

"The Noble Experiment" concerns Jackie Robinson's struggle against forces that sought to hold him and all African Americans down. His true story shows how the triumph of a single individual can influence society. Ask students to be alert for true stories in the media that indirectly demonstrate the influence of Jackie Robinson on the world of professional sports.

Options for Learning (Multimodal/Cross-Curricular Activities)

1 • A League of Their Own Research the various Negro leagues that existed earlier in this century. Then make a display featuring interesting facts, such as team nicknames, locations of teams, names of star players, and uniform designs.

2 • Now and Then Research the progress that African Americans have made in baseball since Robinson's time. Gather information about blacks in major-league baseball. Find out about stars, the percentage of black players today, and the numbers of black managers, umpires, and owners. Share your statistics by making a chart to display in class.

3 • A Telling Moment Write the dialogue that might have taken place between Jackie and his girlfriend, Rachel, when he told her that he planned to join the Brooklyn Dodgers. Have him explain his decision, and have Rachel voice her concerns. Then act out the scene for your classmates.

4 • Robinson Report Read the rest of Robinson's autobiography, *I Never Had It Made*. Give a report on his experiences in baseball and his other achievements.

 FACT FINDER SPORTS

What was Jackie Robinson's lifetime batting average?

Alfred A. Duckett
1917–1984

It seems natural that Alfred Duckett would want to tell Jackie Robinson's story, since he was born in Brooklyn and was a baseball fan as well as a journalist. Robinson and Duckett worked together to produce *I Never Had It Made: The Autobiography of Jackie Robinson*.

Besides writing books, Duckett also wrote poetry, magazine articles, and speeches.

Perhaps his most famous speech was written with Martin Luther King, Jr. Dr. King delivered this "I Have a Dream" speech in Washington, D.C., in 1963.

Duckett also cofounded *Equal Opportunities* magazine and was the director of Associated Negro Press International, Inc. He appeared on national television programs and lectured in many schools, churches, and universities. Duckett ran a public relations firm in Chicago until his death in 1984.

Cross-Curricular Projects

Math Have some students prepare a report on Robinson's statistical record during his career. Have them calculate yearly averages for Robinson's achievements in batting average, home runs, triples, doubles, bases on balls, games played, errors, and stolen bases. Have them provide a clear explanation of how to determine a player's batting average.

Art Have interested students prepare a collage in honor of Jackie Robinson and his achievements, made up of images both drawn and collected by students.

History Have students research and present a report about the career of Branch Rickey. Encourage students to locate information on Rickey in histories of baseball's early years, encyclopedias, and sports anthologies.

Elements of
DRAMA

A **drama,** or **play,** is a form of literature that is performed for an audience, either on stage or before a camera.

The elements of drama are similar to the elements of fiction. Like fiction, drama usually tells a story with characters, plot, and setting. Unlike fiction, drama is written to be performed for an audience. For this reason, drama is written in a special form called a **script,** in which lines are written out for the characters to speak. The script has various parts, which are described below.

Understanding Drama

Cast of Characters   A script usually begins with a list of the characters in the play. Often a short description appears next to a character's name.

Dialogue   A play consists almost entirely of dialogue—conversation between the characters. Both the plot of the play and the characters' personalities are revealed through dialogue. The dialogue appears in lines next to the characters' names, as in this example from *The Monsters Are Due on Maple Street*, page 157:

> **Steve.** What was that? A meteor?
>
> **Don.** That's what it looked like. I didn't hear any crash though, did you?

Stage Directions   A play includes instructions for the director, the performers, and the stage crew. These are called stage directions and are printed in italics in this book; often they are also enclosed in parentheses. Many stage directions tell actors how to speak or move. Stage directions also describe the **scenery**—all the decorations on stage that help create the setting. Some stage directions describe **props**—the objects that actors need during the play. Many scripts also include suggestions for lighting and sound. Notice how these stage directions from *Funny Boy*, in Unit 5, tell the actor what to do and what props to use.

> **Kaufman.** Thank you. *(He sits down, eyes the trayful of food, sighs, picks up his glass of juice, and starts to take a sip of it.)*

The stage directions in dramas that are meant to be filmed must also include camera directions. Through the medium of the camera, the audience might see a close-up of a character, a look between characters while someone else is speaking, or a quick shot of the outside of a high school. These types of camera shots are carefully planned by the playwright and are an important element in the play.

Acts and Scenes   The action of a play is divided into scenes. A scene changes whenever the setting—time, place, or both time and place—changes. Sometimes scenes are grouped into acts. In *The Monsters Are Due on Maple Street*, four scenes are grouped into two acts.

In a movie or television script, the scenes

Elements of Drama

This feature gives students an opportunity to develop a vocabulary to use in discussing drama. The terms introduced on these pages are discussed in depth in the drama selections of this book.

Objectives

- To understand and appreciate drama
- To recognize the elements of drama
- To learn strategies for reading drama

Motivation

Write the word *dramatic* on the chalkboard, explain that it can mean "striking" or "vivid," and invite a volunteer to make a dramatic entrance into the classroom. Explain that *dramatic* also means "characteristic of drama."

Encourage students to compare and contrast dramas—stage, TV, or movie—with novels. Place this comparison-and-contrast chart on the board and have students complete it together as they read.

	Fiction	Drama
Elements	*characters, plot, setting*	*characters, plot, setting*
Written Form	*prose form, sentences and paragraphs*	*script form with stage directions*
Division of Work	*chapters*	*scenes, acts*
Intended Audience	*individual readers*	*live audience*

Understanding Drama

Cast of Characters Ask students to look at the cast of characters for *The Monsters Are Due on Maple Street*, on page 158. Then have them imagine rewriting "All Summer in a Day" as a play. Have them name its cast of characters.

Dialogue Ask students to recall some memorable lines of dialogue from a favorite movie or play. Have them discuss what it means for an author to "have a good ear" for dialogue.

Stage Directions Encourage students to find, in *The Monsters Are Due on Maple Street*, examples of various types of stage directions. Explain to students that if they were watching the drama, they would see the settings and actions described in these directions. The script gives the plan for these settings and actions. The stage directions are not meant to be read aloud.

Acts and Scenes Explain that just as novels are divided into chapters, plays are divided into scenes and acts to indicate changes in time or place. Point out that in a TV drama a commercial break often comes between scenes or acts. Have students note how ends of scenes and acts are shown to the audience in stage plays. *(Possible responses: by dimming the lights, by closing the curtain)*

Strategies for Reading Drama

Invite volunteers to read the explanations of the strategies to the class. Then use the following suggestions to help students use the strategies when reading *The Monsters Are Due on Maple Street.*

Read the play silently. Before students begin to read the play, ask them to set a purpose for reading. Their purpose might be to answer the question, Who are the monsters on Maple Street?

Figure out what is happening. After students read the first four pages of the play, call on volunteers to discuss what the play seems to be about. *(Possible response: The strange loss of power has all the neighbors on Maple Street looking for someone or something to blame.")*

Read the stage directions carefully. Remind students that important actions are described in stage directions. Point out the block of stage directions in the first column on page 159 and ask students to find an important action in those directions. *(Something roars and flashes in the sky.)*

Get to know the characters. Suggest that students copy the cast of characters, leaving several blank lines after each name and make notes about each character as they read.

Keep track of the plot. Remind students of the plot stages that they have already studied—exposition, complications, climax, and resolution. Suggest that they identify these stages in the play.

Read the play aloud with others. Even before students complete the entire play, have them read short segments aloud. For each segment, assign different students to read the parts.

---

might not be labeled by number. In *Driving Miss Daisy,* in Unit 4, scene changes are simply marked with extra space, followed by the location of the next scene in capital letters. Here is an example:

Daisy. No, thank you.
FRONT HALL. *Daisy puts on her hat and gathers her gloves and purse.*

Strategies for Reading Drama

1. **Read the play silently.** Before you try to read the play aloud with others, read it to yourself. You need to know the entire plot and understand the characters before you perform the play.

2. **Figure out what is happening.** When you watch a movie, it takes you a while to understand exactly what the movie is about. The same is true when you read a play. Be patient and read several pages to understand what is happening.

3. **Read the stage directions carefully.** If you were watching a drama on stage or on television, you would see the action and the scenery. When you read a drama, you have to imagine both. The stage directions tell exactly where and when each scene is happening and help you visualize the action. If you skip over the stage directions, you will miss important information.

4. **Get to know the characters.** In drama, you get to know the characters through dialogue. Just as if you were reading fiction, analyze the characters' words carefully and try to discover the feelings behind the words.

5. **Keep track of the plot.** As in fiction, the plot of a drama centers on a main conflict that the characters try to resolve. Look for the conflict and let yourself become involved in the story. Watch for the action to build to a climax, and evaluate how the conflict is resolved.

6. **Read the play aloud with others.** When drama is performed, it takes on a whole new aspect; it becomes almost like real life. When you read the part of a character, you become an actor. You will play the part differently from anyone else because you bring your own interpretation to the role. Let yourself become that character for a while. React to what other characters say and do to you. Be ready with your character's lines and read only the words your character says. Do not read the stage directions aloud. You may find that you really enjoy playing the part of someone totally different from yourself.

Closure

To close the lesson, direct students to the play *Driving Miss Daisy* (page 421) and have them identify the cast of characters and examples of stage directions and dialogue.

Drama

The Monsters Are Due on Maple Street

ROD SERLING

Examine What You Know (Prior Knowledge)

How do you react to fear of the unknown? What happens to you when danger lurks around the corner? How does your body react? What goes through your mind? As a class, brainstorm the ways people react to fear using a chart like the one below.

Individuals		Groups
dry mouth		cling together
	FEAR	

Expand Your Knowledge (Building Background)

The Twilight Zone was a television series created by Rod Serling that ran from 1959 through 1965. It was an eerie and very suspenseful series that became one of the most popular shows in television history. The action often took place in suburbs typical of the late 1950s, and the characters were ordinary people. The events, however, were far from ordinary because they involved an imaginary world beyond ours—the twilight zone. The characters faced the unknown—and reacted in both typical and unexpected ways.

■ *Author biography on Extend page*

Enrich Your Reading (Reading Skill)

Reading a Teleplay The script for a television show is called a teleplay. Like all drama scripts, a teleplay includes stage directions. These directions provide suggestions for the actors and the director, explain the setting, and describe the lighting, sound effects, and props. A teleplay also includes camera instructions. Pay careful attention to these directions, printed in italic type.

THE MONSTERS ARE DUE ON MAPLE STREET   157

JOURNAL WRITING IDEAS

■ Predict from the title *The Monsters Are Due on Maple Street* what this drama will be about.

■ Describe the scariest movie you ever saw. What made it so scary?

COLLABORATIVE LEARNING OPTIONS

Opportunities for collaborative learning include Writing Options 2 and 3 (p. 172), Options for Learning 2, 3, and 4 (p. 173), and Cross-Curricular Projects (p. 173).

ADDITIONAL RESOURCES

Unit Two Resource Book
Reader's Guidesheet, p. 25
Reading Skills, p. 26
Literature Skills, p. 27
Vocabulary Connections, p. 28
Spelling Connections, p. 29
Comprehension and Vocabulary Check Tests, p. 30
Selection Test, pp. 31–32

Objectives

■ To understand and analyze a drama

■ To examine the use of dialogue and theme

■ To understand the use of stage directions in a teleplay

■ To express understanding of the selection through a choice of writing forms, including a summary, stage directions, a teleplay, and a letter to the editor

Prereading/Motivation

Examine What You Know

Discussion Prompts What sorts of new situations or unfamiliar places make you afraid? When you are afraid, what is your breathing like? How does your heart feel? Would you prefer to face a fearful situation alone or with others? Why?

Expand Your Knowledge

Additional Background Rod Serling introduced each episode of *The Twilight Zone* himself, with such provocative words as these: "You're traveling through another dimension, a dimension not only of sight and sound but of mind; a journey into a wondrous land whose boundaries are that of imagination. That's the signpost up ahead! Your next stop . . . the Twilight Zone!"

Enrich Your Reading

Stress the importance of paying attention to the stage directions. Remind students that much of the action is described only in the stage directions. Suggest that students imagine the drama as they would see it on television.

Thematic Link— Victims or Victors?

The people of Maple Street are victimized by a sudden, unexplained loss of power. This mysterious event fuels people's fears and prejudices, turning them into a murderous mob in search of victims. At the end, it is revealed that aliens caused the events. They are confident of victory over the suspicious and fearful humans.

VOCABULARY PREVIEW

These vocabulary words are defined at the bottom of the selection pages on which they appear.

antagonism hostility; unfriendliness

contorted twisted out of shape

defiant refusing to obey

flustered nervous or confused

idiosyncrasy an odd mannerism

incriminate to give evidence of someone's guilt

intense firm; serious

legitimate according to the rules

optimistic hopeful about the future

persistent refusing to stop

LIMITED ENGLISH PROFICIENCY

■ Use the Reader's Guidesheet, *Unit Two Resource Book,* page 25.

■ The dialogue in this teleplay makes frequent use of nonstandard English, idioms, and sentence fragments. Explain any expressions that students don't understand.

★ Text annotations marked with a red star (3, 6, 14, 15, 18, 23, 25, 26, 27) may be particularly helpful for students with limited English proficiency.

TEXT ANNOTATIONS

1. ACTIVE READING: Question
How does this opening make Maple Street seem to you? *(Possible responses: There must be something special about Maple Street, even though it looks ordinary; something in space is looking down on Maple Street.)*

2. LITERARY CONCEPT: Setting
Remind students that this play is set in the late 1950s. Then have them think about the description of Maple Street in the stage directions on this page, and ask what they think the narrator means by "Maple Street, U.S.A." *(Possible response: Maple Street is a typical small-town street that could be anywhere in the United States in the 1950s.)*

The Monsters Are Due on Maple Street

ROD SERLING

CHARACTERS

Narrator	**Voice Four**	**Man Two**
Tommy	**Voice Five**	**Figure One**
Steve Brand	**Pete Van Horn**	**Figure Two**
Don Martin	**Charlie**	**Ice-cream vendor**
Myra Brand, *Steve's wife*	**Sally,** *Tommy's mother*	**Second Boy buying ice cream**
Woman	**Man One**	**Charlie's wife**
Voice One	**Les Goodman**	**Other Residents of Maple Street**
Voice Two	**Ethel Goodman,** *Les's wife*	
Voice Three		

ACT ONE

(*Fade in on a shot of the night sky. The various heavenly bodies stand out in sharp, sparkling relief. The camera moves slowly across the heavens until it passes the horizon and stops on a sign that reads "Maple Street." It is daytime. Then we see the street below. It is a quiet, tree-lined, small-town American street. The houses have front porches on which people sit and swing on gliders, talking across from house to house. Steve Brand is polishing his car, which is parked in front of his house. His neighbor,* Don Martin, *leans against the fender watching him. An ice-cream vendor riding a bicycle is just in the process of stopping to sell some ice cream to a couple of kids. Two women gossip on the front lawn. Another man is watering his lawn with a garden hose.*

As we see these various activities, we hear the Narrator's *voice.*)

Narrator. Maple Street, U.S.A., late summer. A tree-lined little world of front-porch gliders, hopscotch, the laughter of

---

Guided Reading for Less-Proficient Students

These questions can help guide students through the reading. Ask each question at the point of the selection where the capital letter and arrow appear in the margin. In addition, you may wish to use appropriate Active Reading annotations.

A. What startling event happens on Maple Street at 6:43 P.M.? *(With a giant roar and flash, something streaks over Maple Street.)* Recalling

B. Judging from the actions described in these stage directions, what would you say has just happened? *(some kind of power failure)* Drawing conclusions

C. Why are the people staring at Steve just because his car won't start? *(They realize that something more mysterious than a power failure has occurred.)* Inferring

D. What does Tommy think the "meteor" really was? *(an alien spaceship)* Drawing conclusions children, and the bell of an ice-cream vendor.

(There is a pause, and the camera moves over to a shot of the ice-cream vendor and two small boys who are standing alongside just buying ice cream.)

Narrator. At the sound of the roar and the flash of the light, it will be precisely six-forty-three P.M. on Maple Street.

(At this moment Tommy, *one of the two boys buying ice cream from the vendor, looks up to listen to a tremendous screeching roar from overhead. A flash of light plays on the faces of both boys and then*

A ▶ *moves down the street and disappears.*

Various people leave their porches or stop what they are doing to stare up at the sky.

Steve Brand, the man who has been polishing his car, stands there transfixed, staring upwards. He looks at Don Martin, *his neighbor from across the street.)*

Steve. What was that? A meteor?

Don. That's what it looked like. I didn't hear any crash though, did you?

Steve. Nope. I didn't hear anything except a roar.

3 **Myra** *(from her porch).* What was that?

Steve *(raising his voice and looking toward the porch).* Guess it was a meteor, honey. Came awful close, didn't it?

Myra. Too close for my money! Much too close.

(The camera moves slowly across the various porches to people who stand there watching and talking in low conversing tones.)

Narrator. Maple Street. Six-forty-four P.M. on a late September evening. *(He pauses.)* Maple Street in the last calm and reflective moment *(pause)* before the monsters came!

4

(The camera takes us across the porches again. A man is replacing a light bulb on a front porch. He gets off his stool to flick the switch and finds that nothing happens.

Another man is working on an electric power mower. He plugs in the plug, flicks the switch of the mower off and on, but nothing happens.

Through a window we see a woman pushing her finger up and down on the dial hook of a telephone. Her voice sounds far away.) **◀ B**

Woman. Operator, operator, something's wrong on the phone, operator! *(Myra Brand comes out on the porch and calls to Steve.)*

Myra *(calling).* Steve, the power's off. I had the soup on the stove, and the stove just stopped working.

Woman. Same thing over here. I can't get anybody on the phone either. The phone seems to be dead.

(We look down again on the street. Small, mildly disturbed voices are heard coming from below.) **5**

Voice One. Electricity's off.

Voice Two. Phone won't work.

Voice Three. Can't get a thing on the radio.

Voice Four. My power mower won't move, won't work at all.

Voice Five. Radio's gone dead!

4. ACTIVE READING: Predict

Read the narrator's words aloud to the class. Then invite students to make some predictions about the play, based on his comment that this is Maple Street's "last calm and reflective moment." *(Possible responses: The street will be reduced to chaos; we will see what the "monsters" in the title are.)*

5. LITERARY CONCEPT: Stage Directions

Ask volunteers to speculate on how this aerial view might influence our attitudes toward events on Maple Street. *(Possible responses: The people on the street would seem small and helpless; the view would give us the feeling that the street is being watched.)*

Guided Reading for Less-Proficient Students

E. What has Tommy said that makes the people look at one another? *(He has said that aliens make themselves look like human beings.)* Recalling

F. Predict what will happen when the group of neighbors reaches Les Goodman's house. *(Any response is valid.)* Predicting

G. Why are Les Goodman's neighbors paying so much attention to his house as Act Two opens?

(Possible responses: They are keeping watch on him and his family; because Les's car started, they suspect him of being an alien.) Summarizing

H. What does Steve really mean when he suggests a firing squad "so we can get rid of all the suspects"? *(Steve is showing how dangerous the situation is becoming; he's criticizing the way people are looking for individuals to blame.)* Drawing conclusions

Continued on page 160

6. VOCABULARY: Clipped Words
Tell students that *pan* is a clipped, or shortened, form of *panorama* ("a continuous view of all parts of a scene"). Explain that scriptwriters use *pan* to instruct a camera operator to move the camera slowly to keep an object in view or to give a panoramic effect. ★

7. ACTIVE READING: Review
Invite volunteers to explain why the news about the portable radio upsets the neighbors. *(Possible response: Since a portable radio is battery operated, the people realize that this is no ordinary electric power failure.)*

Illustration by Tim O'Brien.

(Pete Van Horn, a tall, thin man, is seen standing in front of his house.)

Pete. I'll cut through the back yard to see if the power's still on, on Floral Street. I'll be right back!

(He walks past the side of his house and disappears into the back yard.
The camera pans down slowly until we are looking at ten or eleven people standing around the street and overflowing to the curb and sidewalk. In the background is Steve Brand's car.).

Steve. Doesn't make sense. Why should the power go off all of a sudden and the phone line?

Don. Maybe some kind of an electrical storm or something.

Charlie. That don't seem likely. Sky's just as blue as anything. Not a cloud. No lightning. No thunder. No nothing. How could it be a storm?

Woman. I can't get a thing on the radio. Not even the portable.

(The people again begin to murmur softly in wonderment.)

Charlie. Well, why don't you go downtown and check with the police, though they'll probably think we're crazy or something. A little power failure and right away we get all <u>flustered</u> and everything—

Steve. It isn't just the power failure, Charlie. If it was, we'd still be able to get a broadcast on the portable.

(There is a murmur of reaction to this. Steve looks from face to face and then at his car.)

Steve. I'll run downtown. We'll get this all straightened out.

(He gets in the car and turns the key.
Looking through the open car door, we see the crowd watching Steve from the other

Words to Know and Use	**flustered** (flus′ tərd) *adj.* nervous or confused **fluster** *v.*

Guided Reading for Less-Proficient Students

Continued from page 159

I. Why does Charlie shoot Pete? *(In the darkness Charlie can't see Pete and thinks he is a monster.)* Summarizing

J. Why does the mob suddenly turn on Charlie? *(Possible responses: The lights mysteriously come on in his house; the mob suspects Charlie of shooting Pete to cover up his own involvement with aliens.)* Recalling

K. Why do the aliens think that the situation on Maple Street is typical of the way humans act? *(They've conducted this experiment before, getting the same destructive results each time.)* **Summarizing** side. *He starts the engine. It turns over sluggishly and then stops dead. He tries it again, and this time he can't get it to turn over. Then very slowly he turns the key back to "off" and gets out of the car.*

The people stare at Steve. He stands for a moment by the car and then walks toward them.)

8

C ▶

Steve. I don't understand it. It was working fine before–

Don. Out of gas?

Steve *(shakes his head)*. I just had it filled.

Woman. What's it mean?

Charlie. It's just as if *(pause)* as if everything had stopped. *(Then he turns toward Steve.)* We'd better walk downtown.

(Another murmur of assent to this.)

Steve. The two of us can go, Charlie. *(He turns to look back at the car.)* It couldn't be the meteor. A meteor couldn't do this.

9

(He and Charlie exchange a look. Then they start to walk away from the group.

Tommy comes into view. He is a serious-faced young boy in spectacles. He stands halfway between the group and the two men, who start to walk down the sidewalk.)

Tommy. Mr. Brand–you'd better not!

Steve. Why not?

Tommy. They don't want you to.

(Steve and Charlie exchange a grin, and Steve looks back toward the boy.)

Steve. *Who* doesn't want us to?

Tommy *(jerks his head in the general direction of the distant horizon)*. Them!

Steve. Them?

Charlie. Who are them?

Tommy *(intently)*. Whoever was in that thing that came by overhead.

(Steve knits his brows for a moment, cocking his head questioningly. His voice is intense.*)*

Steve. What?

Tommy. Whoever was in that thing that came over. I don't think they want us to leave here.

(Steve leaves Charlie, walks over to the boy, and puts his hand on the boy's shoulder. He forces his voice to remain gentle.)

10

Steve. What do you mean? What are you talking about?

Tommy. They don't want us to leave. That's why they shut everything off.

Steve. What makes you say that? Whatever gave you that idea?

Woman *(from the crowd)*. Now isn't that the craziest thing you ever heard?

Tommy *(persistent but a little frightened)*. It's always that way, in every story I ever read about a ship landing from outer space.

◀ D

Woman *(to the boy's mother, Sally, who stands on the fringe of the crowd)*. From outer space yet! Sally, you better get that boy of yours up to bed. He's been read-

---

| *Words to Know and Use* | **intense** (in tens') *adj.* firm; very serious
persistent (per sist' ent) *adj.* refusing to stop; continuing stubbornly |

161

---

8. LITERARY CONCEPT: Plot
Ask students how Steve's failure to start his car is connected to other events. *(Possible responses: If this were a simple power failure, the car would not be affected; the failures of both the car engine and the portable radio show that something strange and perhaps dangerous is going on.)*

9. ACTIVE READING: Connect
For Alternative Learning Styles Call on volunteers to enact the look that Steve and Charlie exchange. Invite them to express its meaning in words. *(Possible responses: "If it's not a meteor, it might be something worse." "Let's be ready for anything.")*

10. LITERARY CONCEPT: Characterization
Tell students that stage directions often reveal the traits of characters in a play. Ask students what they can **infer** about Steve from his actions toward Tommy. *(Possible responses: Steve treats children gently; he is kind and considerate to others.)*

162

11. LITERARY CONCEPT:
Characterization
Invite volunteers to tell what these stage directions reveal about Steve's feelings. (Possible response: Although he tries to put up a brave front, he actually feels nervous and frightened about the situation.)

12. SCIENCE SIDELIGHT
Sunspots are dark, cooler areas on the sun's surface caused by changes in the sun's magnetic field. It is not unusual for a large sunspot to have a diameter many times greater than the diameter of the earth. Depending on its size, a sunspot can last for only a few hours or for as long as several months. The solar storms associated with sunspots interfere with our radio and television reception and sunspots are thought to influence the earth's weather.

13. ACTIVE READING: Evaluate
Ask students whether they agree with Man One that it is crazy for the neighbors to listen to Tommy's "comic book plot." (Any response is valid.) Ask why people are still listening to Tommy. (Possible responses: They are hungry for an explanation of the mysterious power failure; they don't know what else to do with themselves.)

---

ing too many comic books or seeing too many movies or something!

Sally. Tommy, come over here and stop that kind of talk.

Steve. Go ahead, Tommy. We'll be right back. And you'll see. That wasn't any ship or anything like it. That was just a . . . a meteor or something. Likely as not—(*He turns to the group, now trying very hard to sound more optimistic than he feels.*) No doubt it did have something to do with all this power failure and the rest of it. Meteors can do some crazy things. Like sunspots.

Don (*picking up the cue*). Sure. That's the kind of thing—like sunspots. They raise Cain[1] with radio reception all over the world. And this thing being so close— why, there's no telling the sort of stuff it can do. (*He wets his lips and smiles nervously.*) Go ahead, Charlie. You and Steve go into town and see if that isn't what's causing it all.

(*Steve and Charlie walk away from the group down the sidewalk as the people watch silently.*
Tommy *stares at them, biting his lips, and finally calls out again.*)

Tommy. Mr. Brand!

(*The two men stop.* Tommy *takes a step toward them.*)

Tommy. Mr. Brand . . . please don't leave here.

(*Steve and* Charlie *stop once again and turn toward the boy. In the crowd there is a murmur of irritation and concern, as if the boy's words—even though they didn't make sense—were bringing up fears that shouldn't be brought up.*
Tommy *is both frightened and <u>defiant</u>.*)

Tommy. You might not even be able to get to town. It was that way in the story. Nobody could leave. Nobody except—

Steve. Except who?

Tommy. Except the people they sent down ahead of them. They looked just like humans. And it wasn't until the ship landed that—(*The boy suddenly stops, conscious of the people staring at him and his mother and of the sudden hush of the crowd.*)

Sally (*in a whisper, sensing the <u>antagonism</u> of the crowd*). Tommy, please son . . . honey, don't talk that way—

Man One. That kid shouldn't talk that way . . . and we shouldn't stand here listening to him. Why this is the craziest thing I ever heard of. The kid tells us a comic book plot, and here we stand listening—

(*Steve walks toward the camera and stops beside the boy.*)

Steve. Go ahead, Tommy. What kind of story was this? What about the people they sent out ahead?

---

1. **raise Cain:** cause problems. As told in the Bible, Adam and Eve's son Cain killed his brother Abel.

Words to Know and Use	**optimistic** (äp′ tə mis′ tik) *adj.* hopeful about the future; confident **defiant** (dē fī′ ənt) *adj.* refusing to obey or act in a way acceptable to others **antagonism** (an tag′ ə niz′ əm) *n.* hostility; unfriendliness

162

Speaking . . . Listening . . . Viewing

Viewing Fear of alien takeovers and the transformation of people by aliens was one of the richest themes of science fiction in the 1950s. You might show students one of the movies listed below.

Invaders from Mars (1953), Fox Hills Video
Invasion of the Body Snatchers (1956), Republic Pictures
It Came from Outer Space (1953) MCA/Universal

I Married a Monster from Outer Space (1958) Paramount Home Video

Then ask students these questions:

1. What did you see in the movie that could have influenced Tommy?
2. What do the aliens want most from the earth or from humankind?
3. How do people respond to the presence of invaders?

Tommy. That was the way they prepared things for the landing. They sent four people. A mother and a father and two kids who looked just like humans . . . but they weren't.

(*There is another silence as Steve looks toward the crowd and then toward Tommy. He wears a tight grin.*)

14 **Steve.** Well, I guess what we'd better do then is to run a check on the neighborhood and see which ones of us are really human.

AMERICAN STREET 1983 Roger Brown
Courtesy, Phyllis Kind Gallery, Chicago and New York.

(*There is laughter at this, but it's a laughter that comes from a desperate attempt to lighten the atmosphere. The people look at one another in the middle of their laughter.*) ◄ E

Charlie (*rubs his jaw nervously*). I wonder if Floral Street's got the same deal we got. (*He looks past the houses.*) Where is Pete Van Horn anyway? Isn't he back yet?

(*Suddenly there is the sound of a car's engine starting to turn over.*
We look across the street toward the driveway of Les Goodman's *house. He is at the wheel trying to start the car.*)

Sally. Can you get started, Les?

(*Les Goodman gets out of the car, shaking his head.*)

Les. No dice. **15**

(*He walks toward the group. He stops suddenly as, behind him, the car engine starts up all by itself. Les whirls around to stare at the car.*
The car idles roughly, smoke coming from the exhaust, the frame shaking gently.
Les's eyes go wide, and he runs over to his car.
The people stare at the car.)

Man One. He got the car started somehow. He got *his* car started! **16**

(*The people continue to stare, caught up by this revelation and wildly frightened.*)

Woman. How come his car just up and started like that?

Sally. All by itself. He wasn't anywheres near it. It started all by itself.

---

14. ACTIVE READING: Connect
Invite a volunteer to demonstrate Steve's "tight grin" and to read Steve's speech. Then ask the class what that kind of grin suggests about Steve's feelings. (*Possible responses: He feels uncomfortable; he fears that the situation may be getting out of control.*) ★

Art Note
Roger Brown (1941–) first gained critical recognition as a member of the Chicago Imagists, a group of Chicago artists who mocked familiar features of American life. His *American Street* shows a suburban-like "home town" street with shade trees and tidy box-shaped houses. However, the eerie mood of the painting contrasts with the cheery, peaceful atmosphere usually connected with suburban life. *What is the mood of this painting? How does the artist create this mood?*

15. VOCABULARY: Slang
Help students use **context clues** and **prior knowledge** to explain what Les means when he says "No dice." (*Possible responses: No luck. No success.*) ★

16. LITERARY SIDELIGHT
Point out that Rod Serling's literary hero was the playwright Arthur Miller, whose 1953 play *The Crucible*, an exploration of the Salem witch trials, shows a community destroying itself in a vain effort to find the evil ones in its midst.

17. ACTIVE READING: Review
Ask students to **infer** what Don is suggesting about Les. (*Possible response: Les knew that the flying object was coming.*) Ask what Charlie is suggesting about Les and his family. (*They might not be human; they might be working for the aliens.*)

18. VOCABULARY: Connotation
Ask students what words or images they associate with the word *mob*. (*Possible responses: violence, danger, riots, chaos, destruction*) Ask why they think Steve uses that word here. (*Possible responses: He wants to warn his neighbors about what they're becoming; he's trying to keep them from hurting Les.*) ★

19. ACTIVE READING: Evaluate
Invite students to **reread** Steve's words here. Then ask them to **draw conclusions** about whether Steve really believes that there are aliens on Maple Street. (*Any response is valid.*)

(Don Martin *approaches the group and stops a few feet away to look toward* Les's *car.*)

Don. And he never did come out to look at that thing that flew overhead. He wasn't even interested. (*He turns to the group, his face taut and serious.*) Why? Why didn't he come out with the rest of us to look?

Charlie. He always was an oddball. Him and his whole family. Real oddball.

Don. What do you say we ask him?

(*The group starts toward the house. In this brief fraction of a moment, it takes the first step toward changing from a group into a mob. The group members begin to head purposefully across the street toward the house.* Steve *stands in front of them. For a moment their fear almost turns their walk into a wild stampede, but* Steve's *voice, loud, incisive, and commanding, makes them stop.*)

Steve. Wait a minute . . . wait a minute! Let's not be a mob!

(*The people stop, pause for a moment, and then, much more quietly and slowly, start to walk across the street.*
Les *stands alone facing the people.*)

Les. I just don't understand it. I tried to start it, and it wouldn't start. You saw me. All of you saw me.

(*And now, just as suddenly as the engine started, it stops, and there is a long silence that is gradually intruded upon by the frightened murmuring of the people.*)

Les. I don't understand. I swear . . . I don't understand. What's happening?

Don. Maybe you better tell us. Nothing's working on this street. Nothing. No lights, no power, no radio, (*then meaningfully*) nothing except one car—yours!

(*The people's murmuring becomes a loud chant filling the air with accusations and demands for action. Two of the men pass* Don *and head toward* Les, *who backs away from them against his car. He is cornered.*)

Les. Wait a minute now. You keep your distance—all of you. So I've got a car that starts by itself—well, that's a freak thing—I admit it. But does that make me a criminal or something? I don't know why the car works—it just does!

(*This stops the crowd momentarily, and* Les, *still backing away, goes toward his front porch. He goes up the steps and then stops, facing the mob.*)

Les. What's it all about, Steve?

Steve (*quietly*). We're all on a monster kick, Les. Seems that the general impression holds that maybe one family isn't what we think they are. Monsters from outer space or something. Different from us. Aliens from the vast beyond. (*He chuckles.*) You know anybody that might fit that description around here on Maple Street?

Les. What is this, a gag? (*He looks around the group again.*) This a practical joke or something?

(*Suddenly the car engine starts all by itself, runs for a moment, and stops. One woman begins to cry. The eyes of the crowd are cold and accusing.)*

Les. Now that's supposed to <u>incriminate</u> me, huh? The car engine goes on and off, and that really does it, doesn't it? *(He looks around at the faces of the people.)* I just don't understand it . . . any more than any of you do! *(He wets his lips, looking from face to face.)* Look, you all know me. We've lived here five years. Right in this house. We're no different from any of the rest of you! We're no different at all. . . . Really . . . this whole thing is just . . . just weird–

Woman. Well, if that's the case, Les Goodman, explain why–*(She stops suddenly, clamping her mouth shut.)*

Les *(softly).* Explain what?

Steve *(interjecting).* Look, let's forget this–

Charlie *(overlapping him).* Go ahead, let her talk. What about it? Explain what?

Woman *(a little reluctantly).* Well . . . sometimes I go to bed late at night. A couple of times . . . a couple of times I'd come out here on the porch, and I'd see Mr. Goodman here in the wee hours of the morning standing out in front of his house . . . looking up at the sky. *(She looks around the circle of faces.)* That's right, looking up at the sky as if . . . as if he were waiting for something, *(pauses)* as if he were looking for something.

(There's a murmur of reaction from the crowd again as Les backs away.)

Les. She's crazy. Look, I can explain that. Please . . . I can really explain that . . . . She's making it up anyway. *(Then he shouts.)* I tell you she's making it up!

(He takes a step toward the crowd, and they back away from him. He walks down the steps after them, and they continue to back away. Suddenly he is left completely alone, and he looks like a man caught in the middle of a menacing circle as the scene slowly fades to black.)

ACT TWO

Scene 1.

(Fade in on Maple Street at night. On the sidewalk, little knots of people stand around talking in low voices. At the end of each conversation they look toward Les Goodman's *house. From the various houses, we can see candlelight but no electricity. The quiet that blankets the whole area is disturbed only by the almost whispered voices of the people standing around. In one group* Charlie *stands staring across at the* Goodmans' *house. Two men stand across the street from it in almost sentrylike poses.)*

Sally *(in a small, hesitant voice).* It just doesn't seem right, though, keeping watch on them. Why . . . he was right when he said he was one of our neighbors. Why, I've known Ethel Goodman ever since they moved in. We've been good friends–

20. ACTIVE READING: Question
Point out that the name Les Goodman sounds like "less good man." Ask volunteers to speculate on why Rod Serling might have given this name to the character. *(Possible response: The author suggests that people sometimes blame their problems on someone who they think is "less good" than they are.)*

21. ACTIVE READING: Evaluate
Invite students to tell what they think the main conflict of the play is so far—the people of Maple Street versus Les Goodman? the people versus monsters from outer space? the people versus their own fears? Urge students to support their opinions with quotations from the text. *(Any response is valid.)*

22. LITERARY CONCEPT: Contrast
When Act Two opens, Maple Street is very different from what it was at the beginning of Act One. Have students contrast the descriptions in the stage directions that open the two acts. *(Possible responses: Act One opens during the day; the characters are relaxed and friendly; cheerful sounds can be heard. Act Two opens at night; the sounds are the low voices of people tightly grouped together; men stand guard outside Les's house; the peaceful, relaxed community is now like a community at war.)*

Words to Know and Use	**incriminate** (in krim′ i nāt′) *v.* to cause someone to appear guilty

165

Multicultural Connections

Rod Serling used the science fiction format of *The Twilight Zone* to explore controversial issues, such as prejudice and intolerance. Remind students that prejudice and intolerance can be based on differences in ethnic background, race, religion, age, or behavior.

Ask students to share stories of individuals or groups in their community who have been blamed or victimized simply because they were different.

Have students describe how they would feel if they found themselves being wrongly blamed for something just because they were different from their neighbors.

23. LANGUAGE: Nonstandard Usage
Point out the nonstandard usage in Charlie's dialogue here—for example, "That don't prove a thing" and "that ain't legitimate." Ask what Charlie's language reveals about his personality and background. *(Possible response: It makes him seem poorly educated and therefore, perhaps, open to irrational ideas.)* ★

24. LITERARY CONCEPT: Plot
Point out the new conflict developing between former friends, Charlie and Steve. Ask volunteers for the cause of this conflict. *(Possible response: Steve's open-minded, rational search for answers conflicts with Charlie's narrow-minded, quick-to-judge attitude.)*

25. VOCABULARY: Idiom
Help students use **prior knowledge** and **context clues** to see that "One of 'em'll tip their hand" means "One of them will give away his secret." Ask students what they think Charlie means by this. *(Possible response: Either Les or Steve will accidentally reveal his identity as a monster from space.)* ★

26. VOCABULARY: Idiom
To control a horse's movements, a rider uses the reins to put pressure on the bit, a steel bar that rests in the soft part of a horse's mouth. If a horse "takes the bit in its teeth," it no longer feels the pressure and takes control away from the rider. Ask students what Don trying to do here. *(Take control of the situation)* ★

23

Charlie. That don't prove a thing. Any guy who'd spend his time lookin' up at the sky early in the morning—well, there's something wrong with that kind of person. There's something that ain't <u>legitimate</u>. Maybe under normal circumstances we could let it go by, but these aren't normal circumstances. Why, look at this street! Nothin' but candles. Why, it's like goin' back into the Dark Ages or somethin'!

(Steve walks down the steps of his porch, down the street to the Goodmans' house, and then stops at the foot of the steps. Les is standing there; Ethel Goodman behind him is very frightened.)

Les. Just stay right where you are, Steve. We don't want any trouble, but this time if anybody sets foot on my porch—that's what they're going to get—trouble!

Steve. Look, Les—

Les. I've already explained to you people. I don't sleep very well at night sometimes. I get up and I take a walk and I look up at the sky. I look at the stars!

Ethel. That's exactly what he does. Why, this whole thing, it's . . . it's some kind of madness or something.

Steve *(nods grimly).* That's exactly what it is—some kind of madness.

24

Charlie's Voice *(shrill, from across the street).* You best watch who you're seen with, Steve! Until we get this all straightened out, you ain't exactly above suspicion yourself.

Steve *(whirling around toward him).* Or you, Charlie. Or any of us, it seems. From age eight on up!

Woman. What I'd like to know is—what are we gonna do? Just stand around here all night?

Charlie. There's nothin' else we *can* do! *(He turns back, looking toward Steve and Les again.)* One of 'em'll tip their hand. They got to.

25

Steve *(raising his voice).* There's something you can do, Charlie. You can go home and keep your mouth shut. You can quit strutting around like a self-appointed judge and climb into bed and forget it.

Charlie. You sound real anxious to have that happen, Steve. I think we better keep our eye on you, too!

Don *(as if he were taking the bit in his teeth, takes a hesitant step to the front).* I think everything might as well come out now. *(He turns toward Steve.)* Your wife's done plenty of talking, Steve, about how odd you are!

26

Charlie *(picking this up, his eyes widening).* Go ahead, tell us what she's said.

(Steve walks toward them from across the street.)

Steve. Go ahead, what's my wife said? Let's get it all out. Let's pick out every <u>idiosyncrasy</u> of every single man, woman, and child on the street. And then we might as well set up some kind of citizens' court. How about a firing squad at dawn,

Words to Know and Use

legitimate (lə jit′ ə mət) *adj.* normal; according to the rules
idiosyncrasy (id′ ē ō′ siŋ′ krə sē) *n.* a personal way of acting; odd mannerism

Charlie, so we can get rid of all the suspects. Narrow them down. Make it easier for you.

Don. There's no need gettin' so upset, Steve. It's just that . . . well . . . Myra's talked about how there's been plenty of nights you spent hours down in your basement workin' on some kind of radio or something. Well, none of us have ever seen that radio—

(By this time Steve *has reached the group. He stands there defiantly.)*

Charlie. Go ahead, Steve. What kind of "radio set" you workin' on? I never seen it. Neither has anyone else. Who do you talk to on that radio set? And who talks to you?

Steve. I'm surprised at you, Charlie. How come you're so dense all of a sudden? *(He pauses.)* Who do I talk to? I talk to monsters from outer space. I talk to three-headed green men who fly over here in what look like meteors.

(Myra Brand steps down from the porch, bites her lip, calls out.)

Myra. Steve! Steve, please. *(Then looking around, frightened, she walks toward the group.)* It's just a ham radio set, that's all. I bought him a book on it myself. It's just a ham radio set. A lot of people have them. I can show it to you. It's right down in the basement.

Steve *(whirls around toward her).* Show them nothing! If they want to look inside our house—let them go and get a search warrant.

Charlie. Look, buddy, you can't afford to—

Steve *(interrupting him).* Charlie, don't start telling me who's dangerous and who isn't and who's safe and who's a menace. *(He turns to the group and shouts.)* And you're with him, too—all of you! You're standing here all set to crucify—all set to find a scapegoat—all desperate to point some kind of a finger at a neighbor! Well now, look, friends, the only thing that's gonna happen is that we'll eat each other up alive—

(He stops abruptly as Charlie *suddenly grabs his arm.)*

Charlie *(in a hushed voice).* That's not the only thing that can happen to us.

(Down the street, a figure has suddenly materialized in the gloom. In the silence we hear the clickety-clack of slow, measured footsteps on concrete as the figure walks slowly toward them. One of the women lets out a stifled cry. Sally grabs her boy, as do a couple of other mothers.)

Tommy *(shouting, frightened).* It's the monster! It's the monster!

(Another woman lets out a wail, and the people fall back in a group staring toward the darkness and the approaching figure.

The people stand in the shadows watching. Don Martin *joins them, carrying a shotgun. He holds it up.)*

Don. We may need this.

Steve. A shotgun? *(He pulls it out of* Don's *hand.)* No! Will anybody think a thought around here! Will you people wise up. What good would a shotgun do against—

27. LITERARY CONCEPT: Theme
Explain that a *scapegoat* is someone who is blamed for everyone's problems or who is the object of people's irrational anger. Ask students who the crowd's first scapegoat was. *(Les Goodman)* Ask who the scapegoat seems to be now. *(Steve)* Then ask students to discuss the meaning of Steve's remark that the neighbors are about to "eat each other up alive." *(Possible responses: The people will keep turning on their neighbors, looking for someone to blame; sooner or later, everyone might become a scapegoat.)* ★

28. ACTIVE READING: Predict
Invite students to predict who or what the "monster" coming down the street might be. *(Any response is valid.)*

(The dark figure continues to walk toward them as the people stand there, fearful, mothers clutching children, men standing in front of their wives.)

Charlie *(pulling the gun from* Steve's *hands)*. No more talk, Steve. You're going to talk us into a grave! You'd let whatever's out there walk right over us, wouldn't yuh? Well, some of us won't!

(Charlie swings around, raises the gun, and suddenly pulls the trigger. The sound of the shot explodes in the stillness.

The figure suddenly lets out a small cry, stumbles forward onto his knees, and then falls forward on his face. Don, Charlie, and Steve race forward to him. Steve is there first and turns the man over. The crowd gathers around them.)

Steve *(slowly looks up)*. It's Pete Van Horn.

Don *(in a hushed voice)*. Pete Van Horn! He was just gonna go over to the next block to see if the power was on—

Woman. You killed him, Charlie. You shot him dead!

Charlie *(looks around at the circle of faces, his eyes frightened, his face <u>contorted</u>)*. But . . . but I didn't know who he was. I certainly didn't know who he was. He comes walkin' out of the darkness—how am I supposed to know who he was? *(He grabs* Steve.*)* Steve—you know why I shot! How was I supposed to know he wasn't a monster or something? *(He grabs* Don.*)* We're all scared of the same thing. I was just tryin' to . . . tryin' to protect my

RUSH HOUR   1983   George Segal
Courtesy, Sidney Janis Gallery, New York.

home, that's all! Look, all of you, that's all I was tryin' to do. *(He looks down wildly at the body.)* I didn't know it was somebody we knew! I didn't know—

(There's a sudden hush and then an intake of breath in the group. Across the street all the lights go on in one of the houses.)

Woman *(in a hushed voice)*. Charlie . . . Charlie . . . the lights just went on in your house. Why did the lights just go on?

Don. What about it, Charlie? How come you're the only one with lights now?

Les. That's what I'd like to know.

(Pausing, they all stare toward Charlie.*)*

Les. You were so quick to kill, Charlie, and you were so quick to tell us who we had to be careful of. Well, maybe you had to

Words to Know and Use	**contorted** (kən tôrt´ əd) *adj.* twisted or pulled out of shape **contort** *v.*

kill. Maybe Pete there was trying to tell us something. Maybe he'd found out something and came back to tell us who there was amongst us we should watch out for—

(Charlie backs away from the group, his eyes wide with fright.)

Charlie. No . . . no . . . it's nothing of the sort! I don't know why the lights are on. I swear I don't. Somebody's pulling a gag or something.

(He bumps against Steve, who grabs him and whirls him around.)

Steve. A gag? A gag? Charlie, there's a dead man on the sidewalk, and you killed him! Does this thing look like a gag to you?

(Charlie breaks away and screams as he runs toward his house.)

Charlie. No! No! Please!

(A man breaks away from the crowd to chase Charlie.

As the man tackles him and lands on top of him, the other people start to run toward them. Charlie gets up, breaks away from the other man's grasp, and lands a couple of desperate punches that push the man aside. Then he forces his way, fighting, through the crowd and jumps up on his front porch.

Charlie is on his porch as a rock thrown from the group smashes a window beside him, the broken glass flying past him. A couple of pieces cut him. He stands there perspiring, rumpled, blood running down from a cut on the cheek. His wife breaks away from the group to throw herself into his arms. He buries his face against her. We can see the crowd converging on the porch.)

Voice One. It must have been him.

Voice Two. He's the one.

Voice Three. We got to get Charlie.

(Another rock lands on the porch. Charlie pushes his wife behind him, facing the group.)

Charlie. Look, look I swear to you...it isn't me . . . but I do know who it is . . . I swear to you, I do know who it is. I know who the monster is here. I know who it is that doesn't belong. I swear to you I know.

Don *(pushing his way to the front of the crowd).* All right, Charlie, let's hear it!

(Charlie's eyes dart around wildly.)

Charlie. It's . . . it's . . .

Man Two *(screaming).* Go ahead, Charlie.

Charlie. It's . . . it's the kid. It's Tommy. He's the one!

(There's a gasp from the crowd as we see Sally holding the boy. Tommy at first doesn't understand and then, realizing the eyes are all on him, buries his face against his mother.)

Sally *(backs away).* That's crazy! He's only a boy.

Woman. But he knew! He was the only one! He told us all about it. Well, how did he know? How could he have known?

(Various people take this up and repeat the question.)

Voice One. How could he know?

Voice Two. Who told him?

Voice Three. Make the kid answer.

---

31. ACTIVE READING: Evaluate
Ask students if Steve is becoming a member of the mob now. *(Possible responses: Yes, he's showing signs of violence; and he's letting his emotions get out of control; no, he's understandably upset about the death of Pete Van Horn and is still trying to be reasonable.)*

32. ACTIVE READING: Review
Ask the class if the shooting of Pete Van Horn has made the people of Maple Street see the dangers of their behavior. *(Possible response: No, they are already attacking a new target—Charlie; they have become more hysterical.)*

33. LITERARY CONCEPT: Characterization
Ask students what these comments reveal about Charlie. *(Possible responses: He's a desperate man, willing to do or say anything to save himself; he's vicious, blaming a boy to save his own skin.)*

CULTURAL SIDELIGHT
The MGM studios in Hollywood, where *The Twilight Zone* was filmed, had acres of useful sets left over from older productions, not to mention all kinds of costumes. The set used for Maple Street had been used for the *Andy Hardy* movies, which were wholesome comedies of American life. The costumes of the aliens, who appear in the last scene of this teleplay, had been worn in the 1956 science fiction hit *Forbidden Planet*.

34. ACTIVE READING: Connect
Ask students to imagine they live on Maple Street. Would they be chasing after Tommy like everyone else, or would they be voices of reason? *(Any response is valid.)*

35. LITERARY CONCEPT: Plot
Point out that the play reaches its climax in a frenzy of wild accusations, flashing lights, and screaming. Ask students why they think Rod Serling ends the scene on Maple Street in such chaos. *(Possible responses: to show how far the neighborhood has deteriorated since the opening scene, to show how everyone has lost control)*

36. LITERARY CONCEPT: Surprise Ending
Invite students to share what they found surprising and thought-provoking in the plot twist at the end of the play. *(Possible responses: the fact that aliens were responsible for the strange events, the idea that aliens could throw a neighborhood into chaos by tampering with the simplest household appliances)*

37. HISTORICAL SIDELIGHT
The fear of nuclear warfare was especially strong in the 1950s and early 1960s, when tensions between the United States and the Soviet Union were high. The fallout produced by a nuclear explosion can lead to death, serious illness, or birth defects. Ask students why the narrator says that the "search for a scapegoat" produces fallout that can harm future generations. *(Possible responses: People pass on their own fears and prejudices to their children; our prejudices are like a disease that keeps spreading.)*

ENCOURAGING INDEPENDENT READING

"The Lottery," short story by Shirley Jackson

Series TV: How a Show Is Made, nonfiction by Malka Drucker and Elizabeth James

Stories from the Twilight Zone, short stories by Rod Serling

34

(The crowd starts to converge around the mother, who grabs Tommy and starts to run with him. The crowd starts to follow, at first walking fast, and then running after him.
   Suddenly Charlie's lights go off and the lights in other houses go on, then off.)

Man One *(shouting).* It isn't the kid . . . it's Bob Weaver's house.

Woman. It isn't Bob Weaver's house, it's Don Martin's place.

Charlie. I tell you it's the kid.

Don. It's Charlie. He's the one.

35

(People shout, accuse, and scream as the lights go on and off. Then, slowly, in the middle of this nightmarish confusion of sight and sound, the camera starts to pull away until, once again, we have reached the opening shot looking at the Maple Street sign from high above.)

Scene 2.

(The camera continues to move away while gradually bringing into focus a field. We see the metal side of a spacecraft that sits shrouded in darkness. An open door throws out a beam of light from the illuminated interior. Two figures appear, silhouetted against the bright lights. We get only a vague feeling of form.)

Figure One. Understand the procedure now? Just stop a few of their machines and radios and telephones and lawn mowers . . . . Throw them into darkness for a few hours, and then just sit back and watch the pattern.

36

Figure Two. And this pattern is always the same?

Figure One. With few variations. They pick the most dangerous enemy they can find . . . and it's themselves. And all we need do is sit back . . . and watch.

Figure Two. Then I take it this place . . . this Maple Street . . . is not unique.

Figure One *(shaking his head).* By no means. Their world is full of Maple Streets. And we'll go from one to the other and let them destroy themselves. One to the other . . . one to the other . . . one to the other—

◀ K

Scene 3.

(The camera slowly moves up for a shot of the starry sky, and over this we hear the Narrator's voice.)

37

Narrator. The tools of conquest do not necessarily come with bombs and explosions and fallout.[2] There are weapons that are simply thoughts, attitudes, prejudices—to be found only in the minds of men. For the record, prejudices can kill and suspicion can destroy. A thoughtless, frightened search for a scapegoat has a fallout all its own for the children . . . and the children yet unborn, *(a pause)* and the pity of it is . . . that these things cannot be confined to . . . The Twilight Zone!

(Fade to black.) ✒

---

2. **fallout:** radioactive particles that fall to earth after a nuclear explosion.

170   UNIT TWO   VICTIMS OR VICTORS?

Comprehension Check

1. What happens on Maple Street at 6:43 P.M.? *(There is a bright flash and a roar overhead as something streaks by.)*

2. What causes the neighborhood to become concerned? *(Electricity goes off and appliances stop working.)*

3. What does Tommy say to make the neighbors mistrust each other? *(that one family in the neighborhood are aliens sent ahead to prepare for an invasion)*

4. Why do the neighbors suddenly become suspicious of Les Goodman? *(His car starts all by itself.)*

5. Why does Charlie shoot Pete Van Horn? *(He can't see Pete and thinks he might be a monster from space.)*

6. Who do the aliens say is humans' worst enemy? *(humans themselves)*

Responding to Reading

First Impressions

1. In your notebook or journal, jot down words and phrases to describe your reaction to the end of the play.

Second Thoughts

2. Do you think the aliens were correct in their judgment of human behavior? Why?

3. In your opinion, who are the monsters on Maple Street? Why?

    Think about
    - who shares responsibility for the death of Pete Van Horn
    - what the aliens and the narrator say at the end

4. Consider your earlier discussion of how people react to fear. Is the crowd's reaction of searching for someone to blame a common reaction? Explain your opinion.

5. Why do you think the author chose Maple Street as the **setting?**

Broader Connections

6. This play shows what can happen when a crowd becomes a mob. How does being in a crowd change the way people act? What other examples of "mob mentality" can you name?

Literary Concepts: Dialogue and Theme

In drama, the story is told mostly through the conversations, or **dialogue,** between the characters. The dialogue also reveals the beliefs and values of the characters. According to the dialogue in this play, which characters are most eager to find a scapegoat for the unusual events?

The **theme** of a literature selection is the main message about life or human nature that an author presents. Often, the theme is not stated directly. A selection might have more than one theme, and different readers might find different themes. For example, one theme from "The War of the Wall" might be, "Don't jump to conclusions." What do you think is the theme of *The Monsters Are Due on Maple Street*?

THE MONSTERS ARE DUE ON MAPLE STREET   171

Student Response

Responding to Reading

1. Any response is valid.

2. **Possible responses:** Yes; because humans faced with threatening circumstances do tend to find and destroy scapegoats; no; because humans have shown the ability to act reasonably even when faced with great danger.

3. **Possible responses:** Except for Steve, the residents of Maple Street are the monsters, because they accuse and threaten friends and neighbors and kill one of their own; the aliens who set in motion the events on Maple Street are the monsters; the real monsters are the prejudice and ignorance of people.

4. **Possible responses:** Yes, when fearful, people often blame someone instead of facing uncertainty or taking responsibility; yes, a crowd of people may protest or riot, for example, because they blame someone else for their misfortune; no, most human beings deal with their fears in a less destructive fashion.

5. **Possible responses:** By choosing Maple Street, a comfortable suburban neighborhood, the author suggests that prejudice and fear can get out of control anywhere. The ordinary setting suggests that everyone must be on guard against succumbing to monsters within.

6. **Possible responses:** When people are in a crowd, or especially a mob, their sense of individual responsibility fades. They become caught up in the emotions that motivate the mob. A mob also provides anonymity, or cover, that makes it easier to commit illegal or antisocial acts. Examples of mob actions include looting, rioting, and crushing people at sports and rock-music events.

Challenge Question

What does the role of the narrator contribute to the play? Think about what he says at the beginning and at the end. *(Possible response: The narrator explains the setting, prepares the audience for action, gives a warning about events to come, and summarizes the theme at the end.)*

Literary Concepts: Dialogue and Theme

Dialogue Charlie seems most eager to find a scapegoat among his neighbors; he calls Les "oddball" and accuses Steve and Tommy as well. Don is quick to follow Charlie's lead.

Theme Possible responses: Our worst enemy is ourselves; we can destroy society with prejudice just as easily as we can with bombs or guns; fear can turn people into monsters; the human mind can be a dangerous weapon.

Writing Options

The Writing Options are designed to meet varied student interests and abilities. Have each student choose one writing activity to complete.

Journal Update Invite students to add to their journal entries for this selection by describing what they learned about the behavior of people in a mob.

Links to Writer's Craft

Writing Option 4 is an exercise in persuasive writing. For more practice, see *The Writer's Craft*, Grade 7, "Persuasion," pages 139–163.

Vocabulary Practice

Answers to Exercise

1. a	6. a
2. c	7. b
3. d	8. b
4. b	9. a
5. d	10. c

For Alternative Learning Styles
Allow student partners to work together to compose five sentences. Explain that each sentence must contain two or more of the vocabulary words. For example, they might use *antagonism* and *defiant* in one sentence and *intense* and *contorted* in another.

Closure

Point out that many types of "monsters" are depicted in this subunit—monsters such as prejudice, injustice, and intolerance. In "All Summer in a Day," Margot is a victim of intolerance; Cephas faces the indifference of a bureaucracy in "Upon the Waters"; and Jackie Robinson and Branch Rickey battle racial bigotry in "The Noble Experiment." Ask students to recall other situations in which the monsters of Serling's teleplay have appeared.

Writing Options

1. Write a short **summary** of the play as it might appear in the coming-attractions section of a video catalog. Remember to tempt the readers to watch the show.

2. Write **stage directions** to describe what a visitor would find on Maple Street if he or she arrived the next day.

3. Imagine that the aliens have targeted your school next. With classmates, write a **teleplay** that presents your version of the events.

4. Choose one victim from the selections in this subunit. Write an angry **letter to the editor** of a local newspaper, blasting those who mistreated the victim.

Vocabulary Practice

Exercise Use your understanding of the meanings of the boldfaced words to complete the following sentences. Write the letter of each correct answer on your paper.

1. A student who is **flustered** is probably (a) confused (b) happy (c) asleep (d) mean.

2. **Intense** fans might (a) clap softly (b) show boredom (c) scream (d) leave early.

3. **Optimistic** students expect (a) punishment (b) failure (c) homework (d) success.

4. A **legitimate** answer to a question is (a) silly (b) correct (c) false (d) dishonest.

5. If one's face is **contorted,** it is (a) clean (b) red (c) pale (d) twisted.

6. A child who is **defiant** answers (a) boldly (b) promptly (c) cautiously (d) timidly.

7. A **persistent** talker would be (a) shy (b) seldom quiet (c) dishonest (d) bragging.

8. If the police found evidence to **incriminate** you, you would be (a) relieved (b) in trouble (c) thankful (d) released.

9. A nurse may feel **antagonism** toward a patient who (a) is insulting (b) is considerate (c) arrives on time (d) feels feverish.

10. An **idiosyncrasy** is (a) a persistent drip (b) a repeated sound (c) an annoying habit (d) a stupid person.

Words to Know and Use

antagonism
contorted
defiant
flustered
idiosyncrasy
incriminate
intense
legitimate
optimistic
persistent

172   UNIT TWO VICTIMS OR VICTORS?

The Spelling Connection

Final Silent e and Suffixes When a suffix that begins with a vowel is added to a word that ends with a silent **e**, the final **e** is usually dropped.
Example: literate + ure = literature

Final-Silent-*e* Words and Suffixes from the Selection
cause/caus**ing**   realize/realiz**ati**on
converge/converg**ing**   incriminate/incrimin**ati**on
confuse/confus**ion**   irritate/irrit**ati**on
continue/continu**ous**   intense/intens**ity**

Other Final Silent -e Words and Suffixes
create/creat**ive**   survive/surviv**al**
believe/believ**able**   ridicule/ridicul**ous**
refuse/refus**al**

Exercise Use words with suffixes as answers.
1. In art class, students try to be __.
2. They don't want their work to look __.
3. __ loud noise and laughter create __.
4. We reached the __ that artists need silence.

Options for Learning (Multimodal/Cross-Curricular Activities)

1 • Map Maple Using details from the play, draw a diagram of what you think Maple Street looks like. Include houses, cars, and other objects mentioned in the teleplay.

2 • Day in Court Put Charlie on trial for the unlawful killing of Pete Van Horn. Have class members play the parts of judge, jury, trial lawyers, and witnesses from the neighborhood. The jury should decide whether Charlie killed Pete in self-defense or he is guilty of manslaughter.

3 • Shoot the Monsters Using the stage directions as a guide, videotape one act or both acts of the play. Assign class members to play the characters and to work on the production crew, for which you will need a director, a camera operator, and a sound crew.

4 • What Saucer? Research the controversy about the existence of UFO's (unidentified flying objects). Find out what the U. S. Air Force and others have to say about whether or not aliens have visited the earth. Present your findings to the class.

 FACT FINDER VOCABULARY

What is the origin of the word scapegoat?

Rod Serling
1924–1975

Though the public knew Rod Serling as the creator of exciting television shows, those in the entertainment business knew him as "the angry young man of television." Serling began his career by writing for radio and television in Cincinnati. In 1955, he scored his first big hit with his television drama *Patterns,* which won an Emmy Award. He hoped to write meaningful plays about important social issues. However, television sponsors and executives often found his topics too controversial. Thus began his long battle with those who controlled the networks.

Serling turned to writing science fiction and fantasy with series such as *The Twilight Zone* and *Night Gallery.* Because these shows were not realistic, he had more freedom to deal with issues such as prejudice and intolerance. Serling eventually won six Emmy Awards and many other honors for the extraordinary quality of his work.

Cross-Curricular Projects

Social Studies Have students prepare nominations for a Scapegoat of the Year Award. Suggest that they use their knowledge of current events, along with newspaper and magazine research, to choose some person or group that they think has been unfairly blamed for problems.

Art Interested students can write and draw a comic book based on this teleplay. Encourage them to create a new ending that describes the demise or survival of the residents of Maple Street.

Music Invite volunteers to compose or choose appropriate background music for different scenes in the teleplay. They can play the music for the class and explain why each selection is appropriate for a particular scene.

Options for Learning

These activities suit a variety of learning styles and modes of expression.

Collaborative Learning Activities
See Options 2, 3, and 4.

1. Map Maple If possible, supply students with graph paper to help them draw their diagrams to scale. Looking at local street maps may give them ideas.

2. Day in Court Allow students to prepare for their roles ahead of time. You might want to videotape the trial so that it can be shown to another class or to parents at an open house.

3. Shoot the Monsters Students will find tips in a book entitled *Lights! Camera! Scream!: How to Make Your Own Monster Movies* by Stephen Mooser.

4. What Saucer? Useful books about the UFO controversy include *The World of UFO's* by Daniel Cohen and *The Encyclopedia of UFO's* by Ronald D. Story.

FACT FINDER VOCABULARY
Students can use a dictionary to discover that a scapegoat was an actual goat used by the people of Israel in the Yom Kippur ceremony described in the Bible. The people symbolically placed sins on the goat and then sent it into the wilderness.

Rod Serling

■ **More About the Author** Rod Serling grew up in Binghamton, New York, and served as a paratrooper in World War II before going to college. *Patterns,* his first big success, was about power struggles in big business. *Requiem for a Heavyweight* (1956) and *The Comedian* (1957) were studies of troubled characters.

■ **Other Works** Teleplays: *Requiem for a Heavyweight* and *The Comedian* for the series *Playhouse 90;* screenplays: *Saddle the Wind, Requiem for a Heavyweight, The Yellow Canary, Seven Days in May, Planet of the Apes*

 ■ **Awards:** Rod Serling won five Emmy Awards for his television screenwriting achievements. In 1975, he was awarded a special posthumous Emmy.

Objectives

■ To understand the purpose and elements of a personal narrative

■ To use narrative techniques of time order, flashbacks, or dialogue

■ To write about a time when someone became a victim

■ To draft, revise, edit, and share narrative writing

Teaching Strategies

DISCUSSING THE ASSIGNMENT

Write the word *victimize* on the board, and share with students that it means to treat someone badly or to make him or her the target of unfair treatment. To check students' understanding, ask volunteers to use the word *victimize* in a sentence about one of the selections in the unit. Then ask whether anyone they know has ever been victimized and how it happened.

Have students read the first paragraph on page 174; review with them that a personal narrative is a true story in which they tell about something they themselves experienced.

Call students' attention to the PASSkey for the Guided Assignment and the boxed explanation. Point out that their PASSkeys may be a little different from the model, but that listing a purpose, audience, subject, and structure may help them keep their writing on track.

If you wish, you may give students the option of writing about something else that is important to them, such as the topics listed under Alternative Writing and Research Topics on the bottom of page 175.

ANALYZING THE MODEL

Have someone read aloud the model on pages 174–175. Ask the class to identify the victim in the model *(a new math teacher)* and the person who made her a victim *(the writer, Chris Nelson)*. Ask students how Chris feels about her prank *(guilty and ashamed)*. Point out that as they write their own narratives, students should be sure to include these three important ideas.

WRITER'S WORKSHOP

NARRATIVE WRITING

USE NARRATIVE
WRITING FOR
- - - - - - - - - - -
stories
narrative poems
oral histories
plays
skits
biographies

Like the characters in this subunit, each of us has experienced unfair treatment at one time or another. We have been victims, seen victims, and maybe even victimized someone else. In this workshop you will write the true story of such an experience. The victim might be you or someone you know. When you write a story, true or imagined, you are using **narrative** writing. In a **personal narrative**, you base your story on the experiences of someone you know better than anyone else—you.

> Here is one writer's PASSkey
> to this assignment.

GUIDED ASSIGNMENT:
PERSONAL NARRATIVE

Write about a time when you were a victim, saw someone being victimized, or helped make someone else a victim.

P URPOSE: To tell a true story

A UDIENCE: Classmates, friends

S UBJECT: A victim

S TRUCTURE: Personal narrative

- - - - - - - - - - - - -
STUDENT MODEL
Before you write, read how one student responded to the assignment.

▶

The Perfect Victim
by Chris Nelson

Mrs. King, the new math teacher, smiled her odd smile and moved clumsily back and forth as she erased the board. It was between classes, and as kids passed Mrs. King, they grinned and giggled. She probably thought they were finally beginning to like her. Peering through her thick glasses at those friendly faces, she didn't realize that they were laughing at her.

Class started. "Today," she began, "I have a brain teaser for you." The kids giggled again, and Mrs. King smiled again. When she turned back to the board, however, the reason for the giggles was clear. On the back of her skirt was a sign saying "I need a face lift."

Signal words such as *when* make the order of events clear.

▶

174   UNIT TWO   VICTIMS OR VICTORS?

ADDITIONAL RESOURCES

Unit Two Resource Book
Writer's Workshop Worksheet, p. 33
Writer's Workshop: Peer and Self-Evaluation, p. 34
Writer's Workshop: Assessment Guidelines, p. 35

Technology and Enrichment
Elaboration, Revision, and Proofreading
   Transparencies 1–4
Writer's Databank Software: File 3,
   Ideas for Writing
Fine Arts Transparency Pack

Links to
Writer's Craft

For more about narrative writing, see *The Writer's Craft,* Grade 7, "Personal and Expressive Writing," pages 27–39.

You might think the author of this nasty trick was the class clown or some other troublemaker. You'd be wrong. The person who did it was always polite, got good grades, and was probably Mrs. King's favorite student. I know a lot about this person because I did it.

Before class I had my friend Lon go up to Mrs. King. He had trouble with math, and she knew it. "I didn't understand the third homework problem," he complained, as I had told him to.

"Just remember our four steps, Lon," she began patiently. While she talked, I went behind her and hung the sign from her belt loop. I felt like I was going to throw up. I was nervous, excited, and scared, all at once.

When I think back, it's hard to figure out why I did such a mean thing. I know I wanted to be popular—part of the "in" group. I thought doing something really crazy might make me an instant member. Mrs. King was my way in. She was the perfect victim.

Mrs. King didn't return this year. I hope my stupid trick didn't have anything to do with it. At the time I was thinking only about myself. I never thought about Mrs. King at all. Now I think about her a lot.

◀ Notice that the writer began her story in the middle. Now a **flashback,** a jump back in time, tells how it all started.

◀ **Dialogue**— conversation between characters—gives readers insights into characters and adds life to your writing.

◀ The writer tells what the incident meant to her.

Prewrite and Explore

1 **Search your memory**   If you can't think of anything to write about, try listing times when you, or someone you know, felt like a victim. Think of recent experiences as well as experiences from the past. Remember times when you have felt guilty or felt sorry for yourself or someone else.

2 **Choose your topic and gather information**   Be sure to choose an experience you will feel comfortable sharing with others. Once you've made a choice, you can begin to gather information.

◀ **WRITER'S CHOICE**
Another way to find ideas is to brainstorm aloud while a partner takes notes. Then take notes for your partner.

Remind students that they can use some familiar strategies to read and respond to the model narrative: question, connect, predict, review, and evaluate. The questions that follow may also be useful. Students can write the answers in their journals and use them later to prewrite and draft their own narratives.

■ Why is time order a good method of organization for a narrative?

■ What does a flashback do in a narrative? Why use it?

■ What qualities does Chris Nelson describe in Mrs. King?

■ What qualities does the writer reveal in herself? What words does she use?

■ How does the writer end her narrative? Considering her topic, why is this kind of ending appropriate?

Prewrite and Explore

Because students may not want others to know about the role they played in a victimizing situation, they may be reluctant to brainstorm with a partner or group. For this reason you might let them prewrite on their own, perhaps by freewriting in their journals.

To help students come up with a topic, suggest that they review the selections in the subunit to see whether one or another jogs a memory. For instance, do they know anyone like Margot in "All Summer in a Day," or have they ever taken part in a similar prank?

Point out that the graphic on page 176 is a good one to use for a narrative because it spells out the elements that this kind of writing should include. However, students might also explore a cause-effect diagram or a spider diagram with the situation in the center and the other elements jotted around it.

Alternative Writing and Research Topics

Narrative Writing Retell "All Summer in a Day" from the point of view of the student who suggested the prank. Include how William feels later about what he did.

Persuasive Letter The story of Cephas in "Upon the Waters" pits one simple man against the entire welfare system. How do you think the people in the welfare office should have handled Cephas's generous gift? Write a letter persuading the city council to accept gifts for the poor and to find a good way to distribute them.

Drama Think about why the residents of Maple Street became "monsters." Work in a group to come up with a plot that does not involve the neighbors turning against one another. Together, write a different, happier ending for the play.

Draft and Discover

Share with students that one good place to begin a narrative is in the middle of the action. Note that this strategy engages the reader's attention immediately and often points the writer in likely directions for continuing the story. However, remind students who begin this way to go back later and explain how and why the action happened in the first place.

As an alternative, suggest that students begin with a sentence about the dominant emotion they want to communicate, and freewrite from there. Example: "I never knew how the shame of one small deed could haunt me until I took part in a harmless little prank not long ago."

TEACHING TIP: CHALLENGE

Sometimes even the best students can't figure out where to start a narrative. Try this technique with strong writers: have them write several lines of dialogue that could come from any part of their story. Then instruct them to continue the dialogue until the scene is complete.

Now suggest that they use the dialogue to begin the story, even if that means they'll need to write a flashback later.

Remind students that in drafting their narratives they should let the characters' personalities emerge—either in the words they speak themselves or in the words of others.

Modeling On an overhead, write a few lines of ordinary, mediocre dialogue that might reflect a conversation between yourself and a student. With students' input, change the dialogue to reflect strong emotion such as anger or excitement. Point out how the use of strong verbs, exclamations, and modifiers makes the dialogue more interesting and more revealing.

·····••• STUDENT MODEL ◀

GATHERING INFORMATION

Begin by visualizing the experience you've chosen. Use your mind as a camera, zooming in for close-ups. Next, make a **story map**—a set of notes that breaks the story into its literary elements—to focus your thoughts. Jot notes as you search through your memories. To see how this works, look at the story map and notes Chris made.

Plot—what happened?	Characters—who was involved and what were they like?
I played a practical joke on a teacher. I got Lon to distract her. I hung a sign on her back. Everyone cracked up. This year she's gone.	Me: a goody-goody—felt excited, scared, guilty Mrs. King: new math teacher—strange and sad Lon: my friend—no good at math Other kids: the "in" kids—laughing
Setting—where and when?	Motivation—why did it happen?
November, sixth grade Between classes	I wanted to be liked.

Draft and Discover

1 **Begin drafting** You may want to start with the part of the story you remember most clearly. Your story map will remind you what else to put in. Remember to write more than just the facts—include your feelings and impressions too.

Paragraphs at Work

Point out that when students are writing dialogue, they should begin a new paragraph every time the speaker changes. However, a paragraph change is not necessary when a character speaks more than one sentence of dialogue consecutively, even if the words are interrupted by action or by explanatory words such as "challenged Joey." An example:

Two different speakers Begin a new paragraph when the second speaker starts:

"C'mon, Estrellita, are you in on this plan or not?" challenged Joey.

"Yeah," Tina parroted, her chin barely two inches from Estrellita's nose, "is that a spine in your back or a yo-yo cord?"

Only one speaker Do not begin a new paragraph.

"Sure," said Estrellita, secretly planning a way to get out of the prank. "I'll help you soap Mr. Leslie's car windows. What kind of soap do you want?"

2 **Bring it to life** To make your narrative vivid, you can include **dialogue**—words that the characters say. As you learned on page 155, writers use dialogue to reveal characters' personalities. Look at this example and decide what it shows about Margot and the boy. Then try putting a few lines of dialogue in your own writing.

> "Oh, but," Margot whispered, her eyes helpless. "But, this is the day, the scientists predict, they say, they *know,* the sun. . . ."
> "All a joke!" said the boy, and seized her roughly. "Hey, everyone, let's put her in a closet before teacher comes!"

◀ **LITERARY MODEL** .... from "All Summer in a Day" by Ray Bradbury

Revise Your Writing

1 **Find your angle** As you read your draft, decide what the event you're narrating meant to you. Try to sum up its meaning in one sentence. Then you can add details that will make the meaning clearer to readers.

ASK FOR HELP .... Need more details? Try telling your story to a classmate. See if any new ideas come out as ◀ you talk.

2 **Shape your draft** Narratives are usually organized in chronological order. You might devote one paragraph to each major part of the story. You could also begin your story in the middle, as Chris did. In such a case, you can use a flashback to help readers understand how the beginning of the story came about. A **flashback** explains the events that happened before the story begins. Since Chris's story begins with the kids laughing at the sign on the teacher, a flashback is needed to explain how the sign got there.

Use the following questions to review your work.

COMPUTER TIP .... Will it work best to narrate events from the beginning, to start in the middle, or even to start at the end? Try moving sections of your story around on the computer.

Revision Questions

For You	For a Peer Reader
1. Should I add details or dialogue to make the important parts stand out?	1. Which parts of my story could you imagine most clearly?
2. Should I add signal words to make the order of events clearer?	2. Were there any parts that you had to reread to understand?
3. Would a flashback help explain events more clearly?	3. How do you think I felt about the events in the story?

SIGNAL WORDS .... Signal words such as *first, then, before, when, after,* and *while* help keep the events clear for readers.

Revise Your Writing

Students who have chosen to begin with a sentence about an emotion might appreciate help in weaving that feeling into their narratives. Suggest these methods:

■ Describe the setting in words that echo the emotion.

■ In dialogue, work the feeling into explanatory words and into descriptions of actions.

Be sure students use the revision questions on this page before proceeding to Proofread. If students read each other's drafts (remembering that some may not want to share this assignment), have them use the comments to decide what changes to make. Remind students that they don't have to make every change—or any change—but only those they think will strengthen their narratives.

TEACHING TIP: LEP

To achieve natural-sounding dialogue, have LEP students write in their first languages. Then during the revision stage, ask a bilingual student or classroom aide to translate the dialogue into English. This strategy might also be used with descriptive passages. When translations are complete, suggest that LEP students enter into their journals their best dialogue and descriptions in both languages. These passages may serve as inspiration for subsequent writings.

CONFERENCING TIP

As you conference with individual writers for this workshop, you may wish to focus on

■ organization of the narrative

■ expression of feelings in the writing

■ punctuating dialogue

Proofread

Note that The Editor's Eye feature pre-views the content in the Language Workshop that follows. If students do not need extra help in punctuating dialogue, the brief review in the feature may be enough for them. If the class or individual students might benefit from additional work, you may choose to teach the Language Workshop, pages 179–181, before students proofread.

Use the following dialogue models as needed for extra reinforcement. Have students name the rule that governs each passage.

1. Mrs. King said, "Today I have a brain teaser for you."

"Well, we'll see whose brain is teased," I thought.

2. "If you help me, Lon," I said, "no one will ever know the part you played."

3. "Yes," I admitted, "I've always felt that my prank drove Mrs. King away. I'll never lose that guilt."

As students proofread, make them aware of the need for commas to separate dialogue passages from explanatory words. Remind them that more practice is available on pages 778–779 of the Language Handbook.

Publish and Present

An additional way to publish the narratives is to make a class audio recording, with partners reading each others' dialogue.

Reflect on Your Writing

You may choose to have students answer the following questions in addition to or instead of those in their text:

■ What new strategy did I try? Did I like using it?

■ How can I improve my writing of dialogue?

Closure

Suggest that when students read other personal narratives they look for the techniques the writers used, such as flashback, dialogue, and chronological order.

Proofread

Review your work for errors in grammar, spelling, capitalization, and punctuation. If possible, ask a peer editor to review your work. Check dialogue carefully for correct punctuation.

THE EDITOR'S EYE: PUNCTUATING DIALOGUE

Enclose dialogue in quotation marks. Start a new paragraph each time the speaker changes.

When you write a character's exact words, put quotation marks around them. Each time a different character begins speaking, indent the sentence to start a new paragraph.

Problem   I didn't understand the third homework problem, he complained, as I had told him to. Just remember our four steps, Lon, she began patiently.

Revised   "I didn't understand the third homework problem," he complained, as I had told him to.

"Just remember our four steps, Lon," she began patiently.

NEED MORE HELP? See the Language Workshop on pages 179–181 and pages 784–785 of the Language Handbook.

Publish and Present

Here is a suggestion for sharing your work with others.

A Memory Album   Put all the stories into an album that can be borrowed by class members. Add photographs or drawings if you wish.

Reflect on Your Writing

Write answers to the following questions. Attach your answers to your paper, and add it to your writing portfolio.

FOR YOUR PORTFOLIO ▶

1. Which part of your story do you like best now? Why?

2. Which part of the writing process was most difficult for you this time? Why?

Assessment Guidelines

These guidelines may help you assess student writing:

Content

■ The narration tells how someone was treated unfairly.

■ The writing includes a narrative technique, such as flashback or dialogue.

■ The narrative indicates the student's feelings about the event.

Style

■ The organization is appropriate and consistent.

■ Flashbacks, if used, are handled correctly.

Usage and Mechanics

■ The narrative uses standard grammar and usage.

■ Dialogue is punctuated correctly.

■ Words are capitalized correctly.

See also *Unit Resource Book Two*, page 35.

LANGUAGE WORKSHOP

PUNCTUATING DIALOGUE

A **dialogue** is a conversation between two or more people.

Using Dialogue in Writing

When you write a story, you can use indirect quotations, in which you report secondhand what characters say, as in this sentence:

Cephas explained that the chickens wouldn't keep long in the sun.

However, if you use direct quotations instead, your characters speak for themselves. Then your stories come alive.

"Ma'am, you better get the chickens out—it don't do to keep 'em in the sun."

Direct quotations need careful punctuation. Careless punctuation can leave your readers wondering who said what and when. The following rules can help you keep the speakers and their words clear.

1. Use quotation marks to enclose direct quotations.

A direct quotation gives a speaker's exact words. Use quotation marks to show where this speech begins and ends.

"Take a number," the woman said without looking at him.

2. Use quotation marks to enclose both parts of a divided quotation.

"The food might spoil," said Mr. Ribble, "if you don't hurry."
"In 1934 we came here for help," he remembered. "Today I'm here for a different reason."

Notice that when the words in quotation marks are a complete sentence, the quotation begins with a capital letter.

◀ **GRAMMAR TIP**
The word *that* often signals an indirect quotation.

LITERARY MODELS
from "Upon the Waters" by Joanne Greenberg

Objectives

■ To capitalize and punctuate dialogue correctly

■ To begin a new paragraph whenever the speaker changes

Teaching Strategies

Using Dialogue in Writing

With students, work through the five rules for dialogue on pages 179–180, noting that the rules are mostly based on common sense. Point out that students are well attuned to the sound of dialogue even though they may have difficulty writing it. Prove this by noting that when they read a story aloud, their own voices automatically rise and fall as each speaker's part begins and ends.

For Alternative Learning Styles: You may want to have kinesthetic learners work with cut-apart sentences and punctuation flash cards to practice assembling passages of dialogue. Suggest that these students copy their best passages into their journals.

PUNCTUATION IN QUOTATIONS

For students who need extra help in punctuating quotations, provide these practice sentences on the board or overhead projector. Work with them to punctuate the sentences.

"Ouch" said Susie. "I scraped my head on the ceiling of this cave"

"I told you to wear the hard hat I offered you when we came in" said Michael "By the way, where is Bob"

He was right behind me answered Susie. "Oh, no You don't suppose he's lost, do you"

"Aaaargh" wailed Bob, back in the last cavern. "I crawled halfway into this passage" Bob continued "and now I'm stuck"

ADDITIONAL RESOURCES
Unit Two Resource Book
Language Workshop Practice, p. 36
Grammar Test Generator

Links to
Writer's Craft

For more about punctuating dialogue, see **The Writer's Craft**, Grade 7, "Punctuation," pages 648–651.

Answers to Punctuation Exercise

"Ouch!" said Susie. "I scraped my head on the ceiling of this cave!"

"I told you to wear the hard hat I offered you when we came in," said Michael. "By the way, where is Bob?"

"He was right behind me," answered Susie. "Oh, no! You don't suppose he's lost, do you?"

"Aaaargh!" wailed Bob, back in the last cavern. "I crawled halfway into this passage and now I'm stuck!"

Answers to Exercise 1

1. "Exactly why are you here?" the woman asked impatiently.

2. Cephas announced, "I have a whole truckload of food outside."

3. "It's for the poor. There are even apricots," he added with pride.

4. "But," the woman sputtered, "we have no way to handle this!" or But the woman sputtered, "We have no way to handle this!"

5. Why didn't the director say "Just take it back home"?

6. Mrs. Traphagen exclaimed, "The poor won't stand for it!"

7. "I put in some milk," confided Cephas, "in case there are hungry babies."

8. As Cephas spoke to the police officer, Mr. Morrissey asked, "Can the truck fit into the parking lot?"

9. Mrs. Traphagen told a friend, "I'll never know how we got rid of it all."

10. "Imagine how happy they'll be when they see me coming back with more next year!" Cephas said to himself.

.... MEMORY TIP
Here's an easy way to remember rule 3: Commas and periods always go inside quotation marks— they're too little to stay outside.

▶ **3. Put commas and periods inside quotation marks.**

Cephas Ribble said, "I didn't come for aid**.**"
"I'm grateful**,**" he added, "and I want to show it."

4. If an exclamation point or a question mark is part of a quotation, put it inside the quotation marks. Otherwise, put it outside.

The woman asked**,** "Are you married, Mr. Ribble**?**"
Did she look up as she said**,** "Go to Room Eleven"**?**

Notice that commas set off **explanatory words**—the words that come before, after, or in the middle of a quotation and tell who is speaking. In the examples above, *The woman asked* and *she said* are explanatory words.

5. Begin a new paragraph every time the speaker changes.

The woman was very annoyed. "Then why didn't you tell the worker at the desk?"
"She didn't give me no chance, ma'am. . . ."

Exercise 1 Concept Check   Rewrite the following sentences. Add quotation marks and commas in the correct places.

1. Exactly why are you here? the woman asked impatiently.
2. Cephas announced I have a whole truckload of food outside.
3. It's for the poor. There are even apricots he added with pride.
4. But the woman sputtered We have no way to handle this!
5. Why didn't the director say Just take it back home?
6. Mrs. Traphagen exclaimed The poor won't stand for it!
7. I put in some milk confided Cephas in case there are hungry babies.
8. As Cephas spoke to the police officer, Mr. Morrissey asked Can the truck fit into the parking lot?
9. Mrs. Traphagen told a friend I'll never know how we got rid of it all.
10. Imagine how happy they'll be when they see me coming back with more next year! Cephas said to himself.

Exercise 2 Proofreading Skill   Work in small groups to punctuate the following dialogue. Decide together how each sentence should be punctuated, and have one person write the dialogue according to your decisions. Remember to start a new paragraph each time the speaker changes.

Grammar Games: Comic Strip Caper

Group students into teams and explain that each team is to draw a comic strip with a great deal of action (stick figures are fine). Students may base their work on an existing comic strip or create a new one.

Instruct the teams in the proper way to handle dialogue in comic strips: word balloons for regular speech, thought balloons for thoughts, and no balloons for sound effects such as ZAP! and BLAM! Remind the teams that every speaker must have his or her own speech/thought balloon.

When the comic strips are complete, teams must reformat their comic strips as ordinary stories with narration, dialogue, and correct capitalization and punctuation. Finally, the reformatted stories are displayed next to the appropriate comic strips, and the team with the fewest errors in reformatting wins.

There's nothing as good as fresh-picked apricots Gram began brightly. Why do you mention that? my cousin inquired as we edged toward the door. We had a pretty good idea what was coming. Well, that tree out in back is getting loaded down Gram said sweetly, and I'd hate to see the birds get all the fruit. Besides, I've been wanting to make some jam. But Gram I protested we were just going to go Rollerblading with our friends. Can't the apricots wait? You can go Rollerblading another time Gram stated firmly. Right now there's work to be done, and you're just the two I need to do it!

Exercise 3   Looking at Style   Work with a partner to find a passage containing dialogue in one of the selections in Unit 1. Together, rewrite the passage to make it a narrative without dialogue, using indirect quotations if necessary. When you finish, decide which passage you prefer—the original, written in dialogue, or the one you rewrote without dialogue. Share your rewritten passage with others.

Exercise 4   Revising Your Writing   Reread your personal narrative. Where you have used dialogue, check your punctuation and paragraphing. Correct any errors you find.

LANGUAGE HANDBOOK
For review and practice:
Section 10, Punctuation, pages 784–785.

Answers to Exercise 2
"There's nothing as good as fresh-picked apricots," Gram began brightly.

"Why do you mention that?" my cousin inquired as we edged toward the door. We had a pretty good idea what was coming.

"Well, that tree out in back is getting loaded down," Gram said sweetly, "and I'd hate to see the birds get all the fruit. Besides, I've been wanting to make some jam."

"But Gram," I protested, "we were just going to go Rollerblading with our friends. Can't the apricots wait?"

"You can go Rollerblading another time," Gram stated firmly. "Right now there's work to be done, and you're just the two I need to do it!"

Answers to Exercise 3
Students will probably prefer the version with dialogue because it is more immediate and more personal than the indirect quotations.

Answers to Exercise 4
Students' work will vary.

Closure

Remind students that the practice they had in this Language Workshop should help as they proofread the dialogue they write in narratives. Point out that if writers don't punctuate correctly, few readers will be willing to wade through their words and search for meaning.

Additional Practice

Punctuate correctly the following passage.

Mr. Mac, I hope Al knows his lines said Ann. I'm sure he does, replied the drama teacher Just then Al arrived. All is cool he said. I know my lines.
Good! answered Ann. And I hope you know your stage directions too. Directions? asked Al uncertainly. Uh, sure.
OK, actors, take your places, called Ann. Al, here's your mop. Let's go!

Answers to Additional Practice *(Answers may vary.)*
"Mr. Mac, I hope Al knows his lines," said Ann.
"I'm sure he does," replied the drama teacher.
Just then Al arrived. "All is cool," he said. "I know my lines!"
"Good!" answered Ann. "And I hope you know your stage directions too!"
"Directions?" asked Al uncertainly. "Uh, sure."
"OK, actors, take your places," called Ann. "Al, here's your mop. Let's go!"

Objectives

■ To understand how causes and effects are related

■ To identify causes and effects in narratives

Teaching Strategies

Review with students the definitions of cause and effect as presented in the text. Then provide the following oral practice, having students identify the causes and effects.

1. The trellis collapsed because of the weight of the snow. *(The weight of the snow is the cause; the collapse of the trellis is the effect.)*

2. When the alarm clanged right above Elizabeth, she jumped and knocked the book off her desk. *(The clanging alarm is the cause; Elizabeth's knocking the book off her desk is the effect.)*

Answers to Exercise 1
Possible responses:

Causes
2. Aliens turn off the phones and the electricity.

3. Les Goodman's car begins to run.

4. Steve makes a ham radio set.

Effects
2. The neighbors begin to panic.

3. People think that Les is involved.

4. People think Steve must talk to the aliens.

Answers to Exercise 2
Responses will vary.

READER'S WORKSHOP

CAUSE AND EFFECT

Events in stories are often linked as **cause and effect.** In other words, one event is the reason why another event happens. The event that happens first in time is called the **cause.** What follows is the **effect.** Try to identify the cause and the effect in the following excerpt:

▸ LITERARY MODEL
from "All Summer in a Day" by Ray Bradbury ▸

> A boom of thunder startled them, and like leaves before a new hurricane, they tumbled upon each other and ran.

The thunder booms first; this is the cause. The effect is that the children tumble upon each other and run.

Effects do not always come after causes in a story. A story or incident might begin with an effect. Then the events in the plot explain the causes. For example, in the student model in the Writer's Workshop, the writer states first that the students were laughing at Mrs. King. The reader learns the cause of this laughter later in the piece—that the laughter was the effect of the prank the writer played on her teacher.

As you read, look for the ways events are connected. Picture the order of events in your mind. Look for signal words such as *because, therefore, since, in order that, so that,* and *if . . . then,* which point out causes and their effects.

Exercise 1 Look back at the play *The Monsters Are Due on Maple Street.* On a chart like the one below, note examples of cause and effect in the play. One example has been filled in for you.

Cause	Effect
1. The power goes off on Maple Street.	Steve decides to drive downtown.
2.	

Exercise 2 In the personal narrative you wrote for the Writer's Workshop on pages 174–178, identify at least one example of cause and effect.

182   UNIT TWO   VICTIMS OR VICTORS?

ADDITIONAL RESOURCES
Unit Two Resource Book
Reader's Workshop Practice, p. 37

Additional Practice

Identify the causes and effects in these statements.

1. Sachiko could not ride the old bike because it was so badly rusted. *(Cause: the bike was badly rusted; Effect: Sachiko could not ride it)*

2. Gustav poured too much water in the flowerpot, and a puddle began to form on the floor. *(Cause: too much water in the flowerpot; Effect: puddle on the floor)*

TURNING THE TABLES

The phrase "turning the tables" comes from backgammon, a game that was originally called Tables and often involves dramatic reversals of fortune.

Today, we turn the tables on someone when we put that person in a situation we have been in ourselves. When a doctor becomes a patient, when a thief's wallet is stolen, or when a losing sports team wins a game, the tables are turned.

Putting another person in your position can sometimes lead to a well-earned reward. However, when turning the tables is motivated by revenge, people may go beyond what is right or legal. In the following selections you will discover rewards, revenge, and satisfaction as the tables are turned.

Subunit Preview

Have students read the introduction to Subunit 2, "Turning the Tables." Ask them to explain how turning the tables relates to the idea of justice. What happens when people's roles and situations are suddenly reversed? How can turning the tables balance the scales of justice?

INTEGRATING THE LANGUAGE ARTS

The literary selections in the subunit focus on the theme of turning the tables. Reading skills, literature skills, writing options, language study, vocabulary, and spelling skills are all based on these literary selections.

Writer's Workshop After reading several selections that deal with turning the tables, students will use narrative writing to rewrite a selection as a stage drama.

Language Workshop The Language Workshop in this subunit deals with subject-verb agreement. Students will see how errors in subject-verb agreement can make their writing sound jarring.

Speaking and Listening Workshop The Speaking and Listening Workshop in this subunit deals with techniques to develop students' skills in dramatic reading. These techniques will come in handy when students read their dramas aloud.

FOR ADDITIONAL CHALLENGE

The following selections offer extra challenge in the exploration of the subunit theme.

"Beauty and the Beast," folk tale retold by Virginia Hamilton

"The Birdman," short story by Mari Sandoz

"The Ransom of Red Chief," short story by O. Henry

ADDITIONAL RESOURCES

Technology and Enrichment
Family and Community Involvement Source Book, p. 10

Guidelines for Reading and Literature Assessment: Observation Assessment Forms.

Observation Assessment

Observing how students respond to the text, to the classroom instruction, and to peers is an important part of an assessment program. The following suggestions and the form in each *Guidelines for Reading and Literature Assessment* booklet can be used to implement observation assessment.

■ **Group Interaction** As students work through the subunit, assess how individuals work best with class-mates. Evaluate whether students are most productive and effective with a single partner, a small group, or the entire class. See what type of grouping makes students most willing to share their ideas aloud. Also see what type of grouping makes students listen the best. Throughout the subunit, try to place individuals in interactive situations that prove effective.

Objectives

■ To understand and analyze a short story

■ To identify internal and external conflict and to review the concept of climax

■ To recognize cause and effect

■ To express understanding of the story through a choice of writing forms, including a story climax, a conversation, an opinion, and a personal account

Prereading/Motivation

Examine What You Know

Discussion Prompts Did you ever know someone who got tired of being pushed around and decided not to take it anymore? What made him or her decide to do something about it?

Expand Your Knowledge

Additional Background Discrimination based on shades of skin color can be traced to the days of slavery. Lighter-skinned slaves, often the offspring of white fathers, were preferred as house servants and skilled artisans. Dark-skinned slaves were generally forced to do field work. As a result, light-skinned slaves learned the manners and customs of their owners. They were then viewed by blacks and whites as having a higher social status. This attitude continued long after the Civil War.

Enrich Your Reading

The rest of the chart may be filled out as follows: Narrator must be Head Evil Fairy again, *so that* narrator resents Leonardius, who "accidentally" hits the narrator, *so that* the narrator hits Leonardius later and starts a brawl, *so that* the play is stopped, *so that* the narrator will not be in the play next year.

Thematic Link— Turning the Tables

Tired of having to play the "bad guy" role in a school play because of his skin color, the narrator turns the tables by leading a revolt against light-skinned classmates and prejudiced teachers.

184 UNIT TWO **Turning the Tables**

Fiction

The *Revolt of the Evil Fairies*

TED POSTON

Examine What You Know (Prior Knowledge)

What do you know about rebels and revolts? You have probably read about group rebellions in your history class, but what individual rebels have you known? Perhaps you know someone who has rebelled against unfair treatment. What caused the rebellion? What were the results? Discuss your ideas with your classmates.

Expand Your Knowledge (Building Background)

The **setting** of this story is a small town in the South during the early 1900s, long before the "rebellion" of the civil rights movement. At that time, segregated schools, or schools for one race only, were legal. Although all African Americans experienced discrimination to some degree, those with lighter complexions fared better than those with darker skin. Even within the black community, certain prejudices existed. Lighter-skinned blacks were considered superior to those who were darker, and those with lighter skins were often the wealthiest and most favored members of African-American society.

Enrich Your Reading (Reading Skill)

Cause and Effect Events in a story are often related as causes and effects. One event causes another event, the effect, to occur. For example, mistreatment (the cause) might lead to rebellion (the effect). Sometimes clue words or phrases, such as *because*, *since*, and *so that* signal cause-and-effect relationships. When you finish reading, create a cause-and-effect chart like the one started below. As you write, notice how some effects become the causes of other effects.

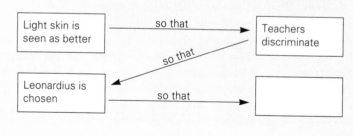

■ *Author biography on Extend page*

184   UNIT TWO TURNING THE TABLES

JOURNAL WRITING IDEAS

■ Recall a time when you very much wanted something that you couldn't have.

■ Were you ever rejected for a part in a play? Describe the situation and your feelings.

■ What do you know about racial segregation?

COLLABORATIVE LEARNING OPTIONS

Opportunities for collaborative learning include Options for Learning activities 2 and 3 and Cross-Curricular Projects (p. 191).

ADDITIONAL RESOURCES

Unit Two Resource Book
Reader's Guidesheet, p. 38
Reading Skills, p. 39
Literature Skills, p. 40
Vocabulary Connections, p. 41
Spelling Connections, p. 42
Comprehension and Vocabulary Check Tests, p. 43
Selection Test, pp. 44–45

The Revolt of the Evil Fairies

TED POSTON

The grand dramatic offering of the Booker T. Washington Colored Grammar School was the biggest event of the year in our social life in Hopkinsville, Kentucky. It was the one occasion on which they let us use the old Cooper Opera House, and even some of the white folks came out yearly to applaud our presentation. The first two rows of the orchestra were always reserved for our white friends, and our leading colored citizens sat right behind them—with an empty row intervening, of course.

Mr. Ed Smith, our local undertaker, invariably occupied a box to the left of the house and wore his cutaway coat and striped breeches. This distinctive garb was usually reserved for those rare occasions when he officiated at the funerals of our most prominent colored citizens. Mr. Thaddeus Long, our colored mailman, once rented a tuxedo and bought a box too. But nobody paid him much mind. We knew he was just showing off.

The title of our play never varied. It was always Prince Charming and the Sleeping Beauty, but no two presentations were ever the same. Miss H. Belle LaPrade, our sixth-grade teacher, rewrote the script every season, and it was never like anything you read in the storybooks.

Miss LaPrade called it "a modern morality play[1] of conflict between the forces of good and evil." And the forces of evil, of course, always came off second best.

The Booker T. Washington Colored Grammar School was in a state of ferment from Christmas until February, for this was the period when parts were assigned. First there was the selection of the Good Fairies and the Evil Fairies. This was very important, because the Good Fairies wore white costumes and the Evil Fairies black. And strangely enough most of the Good Fairies usually turned out to be extremely light in complexion, with straight hair and white folks' features. On rare occasions a dark-skinned girl might be lucky enough to be a Good Fairy, but not one with a speaking part.

There never was any doubt about Prince

---

1. **morality play:** a drama intended to teach people right from wrong.

185

Teaching Strategies

VOCABULARY PREVIEW
These vocabulary words are defined at the bottom of the selection pages on which they appear.

distinctive standing out from others

elite group seen as the best

expire to die

impromptu on the spur of the moment

inconsolable brokenhearted

intervening coming between

pigmentation skin color

rationalize to make excuses for

sneering having a mocking smile

vanquish to conquer

LIMITED ENGLISH PROFICIENCY

■ Use the Reader's Guidesheet, *Unit Two Resource Book,* page 38.

■ Be sure students realize that *Negro* and *colored* are outdated terms that many African Americans now consider insulting. Watch for slang or terms that may be unfamiliar: *fettle (condition), brain (hit), scrap (fight).*

★ Text annotations marked with a red star (5, 9, 11) may be helpful for students with limited English proficiency.

TEXT ANNOTATIONS

1. HISTORICAL SIDELIGHT
Segregated schools—separate schools for blacks and whites—did not become illegal until 1954. The narrator's school is named for Booker T. Washington (1856–1915), an influential black educator who founded Tuskegee Institute, a vocational school for African Americans in Alabama. Mention that the initial T. in his name stands for Taliaferro, the name of the street in "The War of the Wall" (page 26).

2. ACTIVE READING: Review
How does the selection of Good Fairies and Evil Fairies mirror the racial segregation in Hopkinsville? *(Possible response: Just as the best seats are reserved for whites, the best parts in the play are given to lighter-skinned students.)*

Guided Reading for Less-Proficient Students

These questions can help guide students through the reading. Ask each question at the point of the selection where the capital letter and arrow appear in the margin. In addition, you may wish to use appropriate Active Reading annotations.

A. Which children are chosen to play Good Fairies? *(light-skinned students)* Which play the Evil Fairies? *(dark-skinned students)* Summarizing

B. How does the narrator know he will never be chosen for the part of Prince Charming? *(Light-skinned boys always get the part, and the narrator is dark-skinned.)* Recalling

C. What role in the drama does the narrator always have to play? *(Head Evil Fairy)* Recalling

Continued on page 186

PORCH NO. 2   1947   Philip Guston
Munson-Williams-Proctor Institute, Utica, New York.

Charming and the Sleeping Beauty. They were always light-skinned. And though nobody ever discussed those things openly, it was an accepted fact that a lack of pigmentation was a decided advantage in the Prince Charming and Sleeping Beauty sweepstakes.

And therein lay my personal tragedy. I made the best grades in my class; I was the leading debater and the scion[2] of a respected family in the community. But I could never be Prince Charming, because I was black.

In fact, every year when they started casting our grand dramatic offering, my family started pricing black cheesecloth at Franklin's Department Store. For they knew that I would be leading the forces of darkness and skulking back in the shadows—waiting to be vanquished in the third act.

Mamma had experience with this sort of thing. All my brothers had finished Booker T. before me.

Not that I was alone in my disappointment. Many of my classmates felt it too. I probably just took it more to heart. Rat Joiner, for instance, could rationalize the situation. Rat was not only black; he lived on Billy Goat Hill.[3] But Rat summed it up like this:

"If you black, you black."

I should have been able to regard the matter calmly too. For our grand dramatic offering was only a reflection of our daily community life in Hopkinsville. The yallers[4] had the best of everything. They held most of the teaching jobs in Booker T. Washington Colored Grammar School. They were the Negro doctors, the lawyers, the insurance men. They even had a "Blue Vein Society,"[5] and if your dark skin obscured your throbbing pulse, you were hardly a member of the elite.

Yet I was inconsolable the first time they turned me down for Prince Charming. That was the year they picked Roger Jackson. Roger was not only dumb; he stuttered. But he was light enough to pass for white, and that was apparently sufficient.

In all fairness, however, it must be admitted that Roger had other qualifications. His

---

2. scion (sī′ ən): a descendant.
3. Billy Goat Hill: the name of a very poor section of town.
4. yallers: *dialect,* black people with light brown, tan, or yellowish skin.
5. Blue Vein Society: the upper class, sometimes called blue bloods.

Words to Know and Use	**pigmentation** (pig mən tā′ shən) *n.* a skin color **vanquish** (vaŋ′ kwish) *v.* to conquer, defeat **rationalize** (rash′ ən əl īz′) *v.* to explain or make excuses for **elite** (ā lēt′) *n.* a group regarded as the best **inconsolable** (in′ kən sōl′ ə bəl) *adj.* brokenhearted; not able to be comforted

186

Guided Reading for Less-Proficient Students

Continued from page 185

D. Why is the narrator especially jealous of Leonardius? *(Leonardius, as Prince Charming, gets to kiss Sleeping Beauty—Sarah Williams, a girl with whom the narrator is in love.) Recalling*

E. What is supposed to happen at the end of the play? *(Prince Charming is supposed to conquer the Head Evil Fairy with his sword.) Recalling*

F. Why does the narrator feel that punching Leonardius was "an act of self-defense"? *(He was sure that Leonardius was about to hit him with his sword.) Recalling*

G. Why is the curtain brought down before the end of the play? *(A fight breaks out among the actors.) Summarizing* father owned the only colored saloon in town and was quite a power in local politics. In fact, Mr. Clinton Jackson had a lot to say about just who taught in the Booker T. Washington Colored Grammar School. So it was understandable that Roger should have been picked for Prince Charming.

My real heartbreak, however, came the year they picked Sarah Williams for Sleeping Beauty. I had been in love with Sarah since kindergarten. She had soft light hair, bluish-gray eyes, and a dimple which stayed in her left cheek whether she was smiling or not.

Of course Sarah never encouraged me much. She never answered any of my fervent love letters, and Rat was very scornful of my one-sided love affairs. "As long as she don't call you a black baboon," he sneered, "you'll keep on hanging around."

After Sarah was chosen for Sleeping Beauty, I went out for the Prince Charming role with all my heart. If I had declaimed boldly in previous contests, I was matchless now. If I had bothered Mamma with rehearsals at home before, I pestered her to death this time. Yes, and I purloined[6] my sister's can of Palmer's Skin Success.[7]

I knew the Prince's role from start to finish, having played the Head Evil Fairy opposite it for two seasons. And Prince Charming was one character whose lines Miss LaPrade never varied much in her many versions. But although I never admitted it, even to myself, I knew I was doomed from the start. They gave the part to Leonardius Wright. Leonardius, of course, was yaller.

The teachers sensed my resentment. They were almost apologetic. They pointed out that I had been such a splendid Head Evil Fairy for two seasons that it would be a crime to let anybody else try the role. They reminded me that Mamma wouldn't have to buy any more cheesecloth because I could use my same old costume. They insisted that the Head Evil Fairy was even more important than Prince Charming because he was the one who cast the spell on Sleeping Beauty. So what could I do but accept?

I had never liked Leonardius Wright. He was a goody-goody, and even Mamma was always throwing him up to me. But, above all, he too was in love with Sarah Williams. And now he got a chance to kiss Sarah every day in rehearsing the awakening scene.

Well, the show must go on, even for little black boys. So I threw my soul into my part and made the Head Evil Fairy a character to be remembered. When I drew back from the couch of Sleeping Beauty and slunk away into the shadows at the approach of Prince Charming, my facial expression was indeed something to behold. When I was vanquished by the shining sword of Prince Charming in the last act, I was a little hammy perhaps—but terrific!

The attendance at our grand dramatic offering that year was the best in its history. Even the white folks overflowed the two rows reserved for them, and a few were forced to sit in the intervening one. This created a delicate situation, but everybody tactfully ignored it.

When the curtain went up on the last act, the audience was in fine fettle. Everything

---

6. **purloined:** stole.
7. **Palmer's Skin Success:** a product that is supposed to lighten the skin of black people.

THE REVOLT OF THE EVIL FAIRIES   187

Looking at Style

10. LITERARY CONCEPT: Conflict

Have students note the words that exaggerate the conflict between good and evil and make it humorous—the narrator "slunk from the shadows," the narrator "challenged" Leonardius to "mortal combat"; Leonardius has a "shining sword."

11. VOCABULARY: Slang

Make sure students understand that the author is punning on two slang meanings of *yellow*—"light-colored" and "cowardly." ★

Art Note

Shifting Embrace by Philomena Williamson shows both chaos and deception. Beneath the two main subjects are other figures who wear masks. In this painting, everyone is either in turmoil or pretending to be someone else. *What situations in "The Revolt of the Evil Fairies" capture the spirit of this painting?*

12. LITERARY CONCEPT: Humor

Ask students to **visualize** this all-out fight between the actors. Ask them what humorous scenes this section reminds them of. *(Possible response: slapstick comedy, cartoons, barroom brawl scenes in Westerns)* Ask why Rat joined in. *(Possible response: It was an excuse for him to fight.)*

13. ACTIVE READING: Evaluate

Ask students if they think the narrator lost his fight when Leonardius "vanquished" him. *(Possible responses: Yes, because in the end he did what the teacher wanted; no, because he got the satisfaction of hitting Leonardius.)*

ENCOURAGING INDEPENDENT READING

Ludell, novel by Brenda Wilkinson

The Soul Brothers and Sister Lou, novel by Kristin Hunter

South Town, novel by Lorenz Graham

had gone well for me too—except for one spot in the second act. That was where Leonardius unexpectedly rapped me over the head with his sword as I slunk off into the shadows. That was not in the script, but Miss LaPrade quieted me down by saying it made a nice touch anyway. Rat said Leonardius did it on purpose.

The third act went on smoothly, though, until we came to the vanquishing scene. That was where I slunk from the shadows for the last time and challenged Prince Charming to mortal combat. The hero reached for his shining sword—a bit unsportsmanlike, I always thought, since Miss LaPrade consistently left the Head Evil Fairy unarmed—and then it happened!

Later I protested loudly—but in vain—that it was a case of self-defense. I pointed out that Leonardius had a mean look in his eye. I cited the impromptu rapping he had given my head in the second act. But nobody would listen. They just wouldn't believe that Leonardius really intended to brain me when he reached for his sword.

Anyway, he didn't succeed. For the minute I saw that evil gleam in his eye—or was it my own?—I cut loose with a right to the chin, and Prince Charming dropped his shining sword and staggered back. His astonishment lasted only a minute, though, for he lowered his head and came charging in, fists flailing. There was nothing yellow about Leonardius but his skin.

The audience thought the scrap was something new Miss LaPrade had written in. They might have kept on thinking so if

SHIFTING EMBRACE 1990 Philemona Williamson Collection of Mr. and Mrs. Clarence Otis. Photo by Manu Sassoonian. Courtesy, June Kelly Gallery, New York .

Miss LaPrade hadn't been screaming so hysterically from the sidelines. And if Rat Joiner hadn't decided that this was as good a time as any to settle old scores. So he turned around and took a sock at the male Good Fairy nearest him.

When the curtain rang down, the forces of Good and Evil were locked in combat. And Sleeping Beauty was wide awake and streaking for the wings.

They rang the curtain back up fifteen minutes later, and we finished the play. I lay down and expired according to specifications, but Prince Charming will probably remember my sneering corpse to his dying day. They wouldn't let me appear in the grand dramatic offering at all the next year. But I didn't care. I couldn't have been Prince Charming anyway. ❧

Words to Know and Use	**impromptu** (im prämp′ tōō′) *adj.* without preparation; on the spur of the moment
	expire (ek spīr′) *v.* to die
	sneering (snir′ iŋ) *adj.* having a mocking smile **sneer** *v.*

188

Comprehension Check

1. What play did the school present every year? *(an adaptation of Sleeping Beauty)*

2. Why did the narrator especially want to be Prince Charming this particular year? *(He was in love with the girl who played Sleeping Beauty.)*

3. Why didn't the narrator get the role of Prince Charming? *(His skin was too dark.)*

4. What role did the narrator play? *(Head Evil Fairy)*

5. What was the "revolt" and how did it start? *(The actors playing the Evil Fairies fought with the actors playing the Good Fairies. The narrator started the fight by punching Leonardius.)*

Responding to Reading

First Impressions

1. What event in this story affected you the most? Jot down your thoughts in a notebook or journal.

Second Thoughts

2. Do you think the narrator is justified in his rebellion during the third act? Give reasons for your answer.

3. Name all the causes of the chain of events in this story. Was any one cause more important than the others? Explain.

   Think about
   • Leonardius's actions
   • the attitudes of the teachers and townspeople

4. The narrator and his friend Rat Joiner have different attitudes about their situation. Which character would you resemble if you were in the story? Why?

5. Do you think the author intended the story to be funny? Explain your opinion.

Broader Connections

6. Were you surprised about the discrimination within the African-American community in the story? Do you think that attitude still exists? Share your opinion.

Literary Concept: Conflict

Conflict is a struggle between opposing forces that forms the basis for the plot of a story. **External conflict** is a struggle between a character and an outside force, such as another character, society, or nature. **Internal conflict** occurs when a character has to struggle within himself or herself, as when making a decision or resolving a problem. With whom or what does the narrator of this story have conflict? Are his conflicts internal, external, or both?

Concept Review: Climax What is the climax, or turning point, of this story?

THE REVOLT OF THE EVIL FAIRIES   189

Literary Concept: Conflict

Students will likely point out that the narrator's biggest conflict is an external one with Leonardius, since they actually come to blows. Others may say that the narrator's biggest struggle is with the society he lives in, because the community supports discrimination. The issue of skin color also causes internal conflict for the narrator—it causes him to feel angry and hurt.

Concept Review: Climax The climax of the story comes during the final act of the play, when the narrator departs from the script and hits Leonardius, starting the revolt.

Writing Options

The Writing Options are designed to meet varied student interests and abilities. Have each student choose one writing activity to complete

Journal Update Invite students to write about whether they think skin-color discrimination exists in their school or community today.

Links to
Writer's Craft

Writing Option 4 is an exercise in narrative writing. For more practice in narrative writing, see *The Writer's Craft*, Grade 7, "Narrative and Literary Writing," pages 70–90.

Vocabulary Practice
Answers to Exercise

1. sneering	6. impromptu
2. pigmentation	7. inconsolable
3. intervening	8. rationalize
4. vanquish	9. expire
5. distinctive	10. elite

For Alternative Learning Styles

In pairs, students can take turns putting the vocabulary words into questions such as the following: "How would you invite people to an impromptu party?" or "How could a cup of coffee cause a secret agent to expire?" The partner may answer with words or actions or both.

Closure

Point out to students that there is a lot of table-turning in "The Revolt of the Evil Fairies." The narrator is supposed to be an Evil Fairy, but he is actually fighting against discrimination. Even though he gets in trouble for being a bad kid, he is basically a good kid showing the reader how bad the adults are.

---

*W*riting Options

1. This story is told from one character's point of view. Rewrite the **climax** of the story from Leonardius's point of view.

2. What if Sarah, Leonardius, and the narrator had met after the play? Write the **conversation** they might have had among themselves.

3. Skim "The Noble Experiment," on page 143. Then compare and contrast the personalities of Jackie Robinson and the narrator of this story. Would the narrator of this story have ever been chosen for the "noble experiment"? Write your **opinion** and give reasons.

4. The school play in this story did not go quite according to the script. Write an **account** of a performance in which you participated that, like the one in the story, unexpectedly changed from what was planned.

*V*ocabulary Practice

Exercise On your paper, write the word from the list that best completes the meaning of each sentence below.

1. The narrator's __?__ expression showed contempt, not respect, for Leonardius.

2. Those children of lighter __?__ were chosen to be Good Fairies.

3. In the __?__ years since this episode, schools have become integrated.

4. In most "Sleeping Beauty" productions, Prince Charming is able to __?__ the Evil Fairies.

5. The __?__ nature of this performance could not be denied; it was unique.

6. Rat Joiner would have happily joined in any __?__ fight; he was always ready.

7. Sobbing, Sarah was __?__ about her ruined acting debut.

8. The teacher tried to __?__ the narrator's role by saying that he already had the costume.

9. In the last scene, the Head Evil Fairy is supposed to __?__.

10. Many of the town's most important citizens, the __?__, attended the annual play.

> **Words to Know and Use**
>
> ---
>
> distinctive
> elite
> expire
> impromptu
> inconsolable
> intervening
> pigmentation
> rationalize
> sneering
> vanquish

The Spelling Connection

Spelling Prefixes and Base Words A prefix such as **re, de, ad, ex, in, con, sub, pre, per,** or **pro** can be added directly to the beginning of a base word to change its meaning. Adding a prefix does not change the spelling of the base word.
Example: con + sequence = **con**sequence
Base Words and Prefixes from the Selection
re + wrote = **re**wrote   **de** + claimed = **de**claimed
in + tend = **in**tend   **ad** + vantage = **ad**vantage
in + consolable = **in**consolable

Other Prefixes and Base Words

exact	**re**commend	**de**serve	**de**part
conquest	**con**sequence	**pre**diction	**ex**claim
suburban	**sub**division	**pro**long	**per**form

Exercise Match up spelling words with definitions.

1. very accurate; just right

2. revised

3. a foretelling of what may happen

4. a more favorable position; anything that helps

*O*ptions for Learning (Multimodal/Cross-Curricular Activities)

1 • Speak from the Heart Suppose you were the narrator of this story. Plan, practice, and give a speech to your class, explaining how you feel about being discriminated against because of your dark skin color.

2 • Plays for Little Folks Write your own stage play for young children based on "Sleeping Beauty" or another fairy tale. Make the dialogue and the stage directions easy enough for third or fourth graders to follow.

3 • Booker T. and W. E. B. In a small group, divide yourselves into two research teams. One team should research Booker T. Washington to learn about his accomplishments and what he stood for. The other team should research W. E. B. Du Bois. Find out how the two men differed in their outlooks. Both teams can share their information with the rest of the class.

 FACT FINDER HISTORY

What Supreme Court case abolished segregation in public schools?

*T*ed Poston
1906–1974

Theodore Roosevelt was President when Ted Poston was born in Hopkinsville, Kentucky, and named Theodore Roosevelt Augustus Major Poston. Poston began his writing career as a teenager working on his family's newspaper, which was forced to close when it became too controversial. After college, Poston worked for black-owned newspapers in Pittsburgh and New York City. When he applied for a job with the *New York Post* in 1937, only two black journalists had ever worked for a white-owned daily newspaper in New York.

Poston was told that the job was his if he could find a front-page story for the next day's paper. He did, and he stayed at the *Post* until 1972.

Poston faced danger reporting events concerning race relations in the South. During the 1955 bus boycotts in Montgomery, Alabama, his boss in New York asked him to call every night to prove that he was alive. He won the Heywood Broun Award of the American Newspaper Guild and several other awards in the 1950s for those reports. Poston also wrote short stories, some autobiographical, about barriers faced by African Americans.

THE REVOLT OF THE EVIL FAIRIES   191

Cross-Curricular Projects

History A group of volunteers can research segregation in the United States in the early 1900s and do a joint presentation in which each student presents a different aspect of segregation, such as segregation in schools, restaurants, movie theaters, or the armed forces.

Art Interested students could work together to create a mural that explores the ongoing struggle between good and evil in the world around them.

Music Invite interested students to form a group and write a song about prejudice and how to fight it. The group can model its songs on popular tunes by Irving Berlin, Duke Ellington, George and Ira Gershwin, W. C. Handy, or other songwriters of the early 1900s.

Objectives

- To understand and analyze a short story

- To examine the use of exaggeration and sarcasm in humor

- To enrich reading by predicting, evaluating, and reviewing

- To express understanding of the story through a choice of writing forms, including a letter, a feature article, a comparison-and-contrast essay, and a pen-portrait

Prereading/Motivation

Examine What You Know

Discussion Prompts If you could meet any character from a movie, book, or TV show, whom would you choose? Why would you like to meet that character? How is that character like or different from the real people you know?

Expand Your Knowledge

Additional Background Cameroon is home to some 200 ethnic groups. The country's economy depends largely on agriculture. Although the chief cities, Douala and Yaoundé, have modern office buildings and apartments, many people in the small rural villages live in clay and wood huts.

Thematic Link— Turning the Tables

Jamie Nutbeam turns the tables on Angelica Tonks by inventing a relative who is more fascinating than the "wonderfully interesting" Tonkses. However, the tables are turned on Jamie when his fictional aunt unexpectedly takes on a life of her own.

Fiction

*A*unt *M*illicent

MARY STEELE

*E*xamine What You Know (Prior Knowledge)

A character in this story says, "The most interesting characters in the world are usually the made-up ones." Think about adventurous characters in movies and books and compare them with real people you know or know about. Do you agree or disagree with the statement? Discuss your thoughts with your class, giving examples to support your opinion.

*E*xpand Your Knowledge (Building Background)

Although the **setting** of this story is Australia, the mysterious character of Aunt Millicent finds adventure almost halfway around the world in Cameroon, on the west coast of Africa. Originally Cameroon was called the Cameroons, because one part was ruled by France and the other by Great Britain. The Cameroons became independent in the early 1960s, and in 1972 the two countries united to become the United Republic of Cameroon. Lake Chad, at the northern tip of Cameroon, is a lake that grows and shrinks in the rainy and dry seasons.

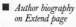

*W*rite Before You Read (Journal Writing)

If you were able to choose an exciting adventure for yourself, what would you do? Where would you go? Whom would you take with you? In your journal or notebook, write notes to describe the most exciting adventure that you personally would enjoy.

■ *Author biography on Extend page*

MORE JOURNAL WRITING IDEAS

■ Use the title and the boldfaced sentences on pages 200 and 202 to predict what this story might be about.

■ Describe the most interesting person you know.

COLLABORATIVE LEARNING OPTIONS

Opportunities for collaborative learning include Broader Connections (p. 208), Options for Learning 1, 2, and 4 (p. 210), and Cross-Curricular Projects (p. 210).

ADDITIONAL RESOURCES

Unit Two Resource Book
Reader's Guidesheet, p. 46
Reading Skills, p. 47
Literature Skills, p. 48
Vocabulary Connections, p. 49
Spelling Connections, p. 50
Comprehension and Vocabulary Check Tests, p. 51
Selection Test, pp. 52–53

Aunt Millicent

MARY STEELE

I, said Angelica Tonks, grandly, "have eight uncles and eleven aunts."

Angelica Tonks had more of most things than anyone else. She held the class record for pairs of fashion sneakers and Derwent pencil sets, and her pocket-money supply was endless. Now, it seemed, she also had the largest uncle-and-aunt collection in town. Her classmates squirmed and made faces at each other. *Awful* Angelica Tonks.

Mr. Wilfred Starling dusted the chalk from his bony hands and sighed. "Well, Angelica, aren't you a lucky one to have nineteen uncles and aunts. You'll just have to choose the most interesting one to write about, won't you?"

"But they're *all* interesting," objected Angelica. "The Tonks family is a wonderfully interesting family, you know. It will be terribly hard to choose just one."

There were more squirms. The class was fed up with the wonderfully interesting Tonks family. In fact, Mr. Wilfred Starling nearly screamed. He just managed to swallow his exasperation, which sank down to form a hard bubble in his stomach. Straightening his thin shoulders, he said, "Right; everyone, copy down this week's homework assignment from the board. And remember, Angelica, a pen portrait of just one aunt or uncle is all I want. Just *one*." *Please not a whole gallery of tedious and terrible Tonkses,* he thought to himself.   ◀ A

The class began to write. Jamie Nutbeam, sitting behind Angelica, leaned forward and hissed, "If the rest of your family is so *wonderfully interesting,* they must be a big improvement on you, Honky![1] And, anyway, I bet the aunt I write about will beat any of yours!"

"I bet she won't," Angelica hissed back. "She'll be so *boring.* What's her name, this boring aunt?"

Jamie finished copying and put down his pen. "Aunt Millicent, and she's pretty special."

"Millicent!" scoffed Angelica. "What a name! No one's called Millicent these days!"

"QUIET, you two!" barked Mr. Starling, massaging his stomach, "and start tidying up, everyone—it's time for the bell." *Oh bliss,* he thought.

As the classroom emptied, Jamie lingered behind.

---

1. Honky: a nickname which when combined with her last name, *Tonks,* makes *Honky Tonks,* a term for noisy nightclubs.

Words to Know and Use	**exasperation** (eg zas′ pər ā′ shən) *n.* annoyance; irritation **tedious** (tē′ dē əs) *adj.* boring; dull

193

Teaching Strategies

VOCABULARY PREVIEW

These vocabulary words are defined at the bottom of the selection pages on which they appear.

baseless without foundation in fact

capsize to be overturned

enterprising adventurous

exasperation irritation

exotic strange; unusual

hoax a trick or deception

intrepid very brave

prolific producing many children

tedious boring

wielding handling and using

LIMITED ENGLISH PROFICIENCY

■ Use the Reader's Guidesheet, *Unit Two Resource Book,* page 46.

■ Certain British terms and expressions in the story may be unfamiliar to students. You may wish to read these aloud and explain their meanings.

★ Text annotations marked with a red star (1, 6, 8, 10, 12, 14, 16, 19, 23, 26, 29, 30, 37, 38) may be particularly helpful for students with limited English proficiency.

TEXT ANNOTATIONS

1. CULTURAL SIDELIGHT
Explain to students that Australia was once a British colony and that many Australians are of British descent. As a result, the English spoken in Australia contains many British terms, such as Derwent colored pencils. ★

2. LANGUAGE: Nicknames
Tell students that in the nickname "Honky" Tonks, onomatopoeia and rhyme are used to indicate that Angelica is noisy—she "honks." *Honky* is not used in Australia as an unflattering term for whites.

3. LITERARY CONCEPT: Humor
Ask students what is funny in this paragraph. *(Possible responses: the contrast between what Mr. Starling says and thinks, the fact that a teacher is glad class is over)*

Guided Reading for Less-Proficient Students

These questions can help guide students through the reading. Ask each question at the point of the selection where the capital letter and arrow appear in the margin. In addition, you may wish to use appropriate Active Reading annotations.

A. Why does the class dislike Angelica Tonks? *(She brags about her possessions and family.)* Summarizing

B. Why does Jamie make up an imaginary person? *(His assignment is to write about an aunt or uncle, but he has no aunts or uncles.)* Summarizing

C. How do Jamie's parents react to his plan to invent an aunt? *(They think it's fun and help him.)* Summarizing

D. What details about Aunt Millicent do the Nutbeams invent? *(She is Dr. Nutbeam's sister and an explorer, an expert surveyor working for a foreign government in the Cameroons.)* Summarizing

Continued on page 194

"What is it, Jamie?" asked Mr. Starling wearily, piling his books and papers together and trying not to burp.

"Well, the trouble is I haven't any aunts or uncles to do a portrait of," said Jamie, turning rather red, "so is it all right if I make **B** ▶ one up? An aunt?"

Oh, I see! Well, in that case . . . yes, perfectly all right," replied Mr. Starling. He gazed rather sadly out the window. "The most inter-**4** esting characters in the world are usually the made-up ones, you know, Jamie. Think of Sherlock Holmes and Alice and Dr. Who and Indiana Jones . . ."

Jamie interrupted. "Does anyone need to know I've made her up? This aunt?"

"Well, *I* won't say anything," promised Mr. Starling. "It's for you to make her seem real so we all believe in her. You go home and see what you can dream up."

"She has a name already," Jamie called back as he left the room. "She's Aunt Millicent."

Aunt Millicent Nutbeam! The hard bubble in Mr. Starling's stomach began to melt away.

That evening, Jamie Nutbeam said to his family at large, "Did you know that awful Angelica Tonks has eight uncles and eleven aunts?"

"Well, everybody knows that they're a big family," replied his mother.

"Prolific, I'd call it," grunted Jamie's father from behind his newspaper.

5 "Yes, dear—prolific. Now, Mrs. Tonks was a Miss Blizzard," continued Mrs. Nutbeam,

"and there are lots of Blizzards around here as well as Tonkses, all related, no doubt. But fancy nineteen! Who told you there were nineteen, Jamie?"

"She did—old Honky Tonks herself. She told the whole class *and* Mr. Starling—boast-**6** ing away as usual. She's a *pill*." Jamie was jotting things on paper as he talked. "We have to write a pen portrait of an aunt or uncle for homework, and Honky can't decide which one to do because they're all so *wonderfully interesting*, she says. Urk!" He paused and then added, "I'm doing Aunt Millicent."

Jamie's father peered over the top of his newspaper. "Aunt who?"

"Who's Aunt Millicent?" demanded Jamie's sister, Nerissa.

"You haven't got an Aunt Millicent," said his mother. "You haven't any aunts at all, or uncles, for that matter."

"I *know* I haven't," Jamie snapped. "It's *hopeless* belonging to a nuclear family![2] It's unfair—I mean, awful Honky has nineteen **7** aunts and uncles, and Nerissa and I haven't got any, not one." Jamie ground the pencil between his teeth.

"You won't have any teeth either, if you munch pencils like that," remarked his father, who was a dentist.

Jamie glowered, spitting out wet splinters.

"Anyway, he's right," announced Nerissa. "It would be great to have even one aunt or

---
2. **nuclear family:** a mother, a father, and their children living together in one house.

| Words to Know and Use | **prolific** (prō lif′ ik) *adj.* producing many children |

194

Guided Reading for Less-Proficient Students

Continued from page 193

E. How does Grandma help to make Aunt Millicent seem real? *(She makes up details about Millicent's childhood; she decides to knit socks for Millicent.)* Summarizing

F. How does Jamie's portrait affect most of the class? *(They want to learn more about Millicent; they are excited about becoming explorers themselves.)* Summarizing

G. What does Jamie's story inspire the Nutbeams to do? *(Mrs. Nutbeam brings home exotic items; Nerissa dreams about the jungle; Grandma knits socks for Millicent; all learn about the Cameroons.)* Summarizing

H. What problem related to Aunt Millicent is developing for the Nutbeams? *(People believe that Millicent is real; they are so interested in her that they are asking awkward questions.)* Inferring uncle. Then we might have some cousins, too. Everyone else has cousins. Angelica Tonks probably has about a hundred and twenty-seven."

"Well, I'm sorry," sighed Mrs. Nutbeam, "but your father and I are both 'onlys,' and there's nothing we can do about that, is there? Not a thing! Now, what's all this about an Aunt Millicent?"

"Oh, it's OK," grumbled her son. "Mr. Starling said to write about *an* aunt or uncle, not exactly *my* aunt or uncle. He says I can invent one."

"Will you explain that she's not real?" asked Nerissa, doubtfully.

"Mr. Starling says I don't have to, and he's not going to tell. He says I have to make people believe that she *is* real. Anyway, I don't want Honky Tonks to know that she's made-up, because Aunt Millicent is going to be amazing—much better than any of those boring Tonkses. It's time Honky was taken down a peg or two."

8

9

predict

How will Jamie's Aunt Millicent project turn out?

Dr. Nutbeam quite understood how Jamie felt. From time to time Angelica Tonks visited his dentist's chair. She would brag about her "perfect" teeth if there was nothing to be fixed, but if she needed a filling, her shrieks of "agony" would upset everyone in the waiting room, and Mrs. Tonks would call Dr. Nutbeam a *brute*. He was often tempted to give Angelica a general anesthetic[3] and post her home in a large jiffy bag.

Now he folded his newspaper; Jamie's project sounded rather fun. "Right, Jamie," he said, "tell us about Aunt Millicent and let

us get some facts straight. Is she my sister, or Mum's? We must get that settled to start with."

10

"I can't decide," frowned Jamie. "What do you think?"

"She'd better be your sister, dear," said Mrs. Nutbeam calmly to her husband. "I grew up here and everyone knows I was an only child, but you came from another town. You're more mysterious."

◄ C

Dr. Nutbeam looked pleased. "Mm . . . mm. That's nice . . . having a sister, I mean. Is she younger than me?"

"No, older," said Jamie.

"Where does she live?" asked Nerissa. "Has she a family of her own? Lots of cousins for us?"

"No way—she hasn't time for all that sort of thing. And she doesn't live anywhere in particular."

Mrs. Nutbeam looked puzzled. "What *do* you mean, dear? What does Auntie Millicent do, exactly?"

"She's an explorer," said Jamie, proudly. "She works for foreign governments, and she's terribly busy—flat out."

There was something of a pause. Then Dr. Nutbeam said, "Ah," and stroked his bald patch. "That explains why we haven't seen her for so long."

11

"What does she explore?" demanded Nerissa. "Is there anything left in the world to look for?"

Jamie was beginning to feel a bit rushed.

---

3. **general anesthetic** (an' es thet' ik): a drug or gas used to cause a person to fall into a deep sleep.

---

8. VOCABULARY: Idiom
Ask students what "taken down a peg or two" might mean. Help them use **prior knowledge** and **context clues** to figure out that the phrase means "made less proud or vain." Invite students to think of other idioms that are similar in meaning. *(Possible responses: "put in one's place," "had the wind taken out of one's sails," "brought back to earth")* ★

9. ACTIVE READING: Predict
How will Jamie's Aunt Millicent project turn out? *(Possible responses: He'll get away with it because he has a great imagination; his plan will fail because someone is bound to find out that Aunt Millicent is not real.)*

10. LANGUAGE: Briticisms
Point out that British people often use the term *mum* for "mother." It is the British equivalent of the American *mom*. ★

11. LITERARY CONCEPT: Humor
Ask students what is surprising and humorous about this dialogue. *(Possible responses: the way Dr. Nutbeam talks about the imaginary Millicent as though she were real, the way all the Nutbeams "get into" the idea of Millicent)*

Guided Reading for Less-Proficient Students

Continued from page 194

I. Why does Jamie feel he should "kill off" his aunt? *(He's afraid people will discover that Millicent doesn't really exist.)* Recalling

J. Why do people lose interest in Aunt Millicent? *(They think that because of her marriage and retirement she is no longer special.)* Recalling

EXOTIC LANDSCAPE   1910   Henri Rousseau (1844-1910) Oil on canvas, 51 3/4 x 64 inches. Norton Simon Foundation, Pasadena, California.

196   UNIT TWO   TURNING THE TABLES

"Well, I'm not sure yet, but foreign governments need people like her to search for water in deserts and rich mineral deposits and endangered species and things . . . you know."

Nerissa lay on the floor with her eyes closed and began to imagine her new aunt slashing a path through tangled jungle vines, searching for a rare species of dark blue frog. The mosquitoes were savage. The leeches were huge and bloated. Aunt Millicent's machete was razor sharp . . .

"This is all very unexpected," murmured Mrs. Nutbeam, "to have a sister-in-law who is an explorer, I mean. I wonder how you get started in that sort of career?" Her own job as an assistant in an antique and curio shop suddenly seemed rather drab.

Dr. Nutbeam was staring at the wall. In his mind's eye he clearly saw his sister on a swaying rope suspension bridge above a terrifying ravine. She was leading a band of native bearers to the other side. How much more adventurous, he thought, than drilling little holes in people's teeth. He wrenched his gaze back to Jamie and asked, "Do we know what Millie is actually exploring at present?"

Jamie munched his pencil for a moment and then said, "She's in Africa, somewhere near the middle, but I'm not sure where, exactly."

"In the middle of Africa, is she?" echoed Dr. Nutbeam. "Mm . . . then it wouldn't surprise me if she were in the Cameroons. There's a lot of dense forest in the Cameroons, you know."

"I thought Cameroons were things to eat," frowned Nerissa. "Sort of coconut biscuits."

"No, no, dear, those are macaroons," said her mother.

"*They're* bad for your teeth, too," remarked her father, absently, "like eating pencils."

Jamie fetched the atlas and found a map of Africa. His father stood behind him, peering at it. "There it is, in the middle on the left-hand side, just under the bump."

"It's called Cameroon here," Jamie said. "Just one of them."

"Well, there's East Cameroon and West Cameroon, see," pointed his father, "and sometimes you lump them together and call them Cameroons. Look—here's the equator just to the south, so it must be pretty hot and steamy at sea level."

"Poor Millicent," sighed Mrs. Nutbeam. "I do hope her feet don't swell in the heat, with all that walking."

Jamie examined the map closely. "That's peculiar—the north border of the Cameroons seems to be floating in a big lake . . . um, Lake Chad . . . it looks all swampy, with funny dotted lines and things. I bet that bit needs exploring. They've probably lost their border in the mud, and Aunt Millicent could be on an expedition to find it."

"Is she all by herself?" asked Nerissa. "I'd be scared in a place like that."

"Of course she's not by herself," snorted Jamie. "She works for a foreign government, don't forget, and she'd have a whole support team of porters and cooks and scientists and things."

"She must be an expert at something herself, don't you think?" suggested Mrs. Nutbeam. "I would imagine that she's a surveyor."

"Yes, she'd use one of those instruments

◄ D

12. VOCABULARY: Clipped Words
Have students use **context clues** to figure out the meaning of *curio*. As an additional hint, tell them that the word is a clipped, or shortened, form of a word they already know. See if students can guess the word. Then explain that a *curiosity*, or *curio*, is a rare or unusual item. ★

13. ACTIVE READING: Question
Ask students why they think each member of the Nutbeam family is so eager to help create Jamie's fictitious aunt. If necessary, help students by reading the following example of a think-aloud, or model one of your own.

Think-Aloud Script Why are all the Nutbeams so willing to help Jamie pull off his trick? I know that Dr. and Mrs. Nutbeam have no brothers or sisters. Maybe they wish they really had siblings. Also, they both think their jobs are boring. So the parents may be happy to help create Millicent as a way to make their own lives more exciting. Nerissa may enjoy the idea of Aunt Millicent as a role model of an adventurous adult female. It's also pretty clear that Angelica Tonks annoys the whole family, so helping Jamie fool her seems OK.

14. VOCABULARY: Scientific Terms
Help students pronounce the word *theodolite* (thē äd′ ō līt′). Explain that surveyors use theodolites to make accurate measurements of angles on a piece of land. Urge volunteers to find a picture of the instrument in a dictionary or an encyclopedia and display it for the class. ★

15. LITERARY CONCEPT: Humor
Have students discuss how the author makes the character of Grandma amusing. (Possible responses: Grandma worries about an imaginary daughter's health; she plans to knit socks for, and even invents character flaws of, someone who doesn't exist.)

16. VOCABULARY: Idiom
Ask students what they think Grandma means when she says that woolen socks "breathe." Help students **infer** that air can pass through the thick wool. ★

17. GEOGRAPHICAL SIDELIGHT
At one time, numerous wild animals roamed southern Cameroon, but many have been killed off by hunters and farmers. However, monkeys, elephants, giraffes, and antelope can still be found in wildlife preserves in northern Cameroon.

---

you look through, on legs," added Nerissa.

14 "You mean a theodolite, dimwit," answered her brother.

"She'd certainly need one of those if she's measuring angles and distances and drawing maps," agreed Dr. Nutbeam. "My word, what a clever old sister I have!"

"I wonder if she was good at geography at school?" said Nerissa.

"Well, you'll be able to ask Grandma tomorrow. She's coming for her winter visit, remember?"

"Oh help! What'll Grandma *say?*" gasped Jamie. "Do you think she'll mind? I mean—we've invented a daughter for her without asking!"

"I shouldn't think she'd mind," said his mother. "We'll break the news to her carefully and see how she takes it."

Grandma Nutbeam, as it turned out, was delighted.

"How exciting!" she exclaimed. "I always wanted a daughter, and it's been very lonely since Grandpa died. Now I'll have a new interest! Just show me on the map where Millicent is at the moment, please, dear."

Jamie pointed to the dotted lines in swampy Lake Chad near the top end of the Cameroons, and Grandma stared in astonishment.

"Gracious heaven! What an extraordinary place to go to, the silly girl! I hope she's remembered her quinine tablets.[4] **15** Millicent was never very good at looking after herself, you know. Let me see—I think I'll get some wool tomorrow and knit her some good stout hiking socks."

Jamie blinked. "There's no need to do that, Grandma. She's not really real, you know."

"Well, she'll be more real to me if I make her some socks," Grandma declared.

"Wouldn't they be rather hot in the Cameroons?" objected Nerissa. "It's awfully near the equator, don't forget."

"Woolen socks are best in any climate," **16** said Grandma firmly. "They breathe."

"Now, Mother," interrupted Dr. Nutbeam, "you can tell us what Millicent was like as a girl. I can't remember her very well, as she was so much older than me, but I have a feeling that she ran away from home a lot."

Grandma pondered a moment. "Now that you mention it, she did. She did indeed. I thought we'd have to chain her up sometimes! We lived near the edge of town, you'll remember, and Millie would look out toward the paddocks[5] and hills and say that she wanted to know what was over the horizon, or where the birds were flying to, or where the clouds came from behind the hills. We never knew where she'd be off to next—but she certainly ended up in the right job! I'm so glad she became an explorer. If I were a bit younger and had better feet, I might even go and join her. It would be most interesting to see the Cameroons. It's **17** full of monkeys, I believe."

"Was Aunt Millicent good at geography at school?" Nerissa remembered to ask.

"Let me think—yes, she must have been because one year she won a prize for it, and the prize was a book called *Lives of the Great Explorers.*" ◄ **E**

"Well, there you are," remarked Mrs.

---

4. **quinine** (kwī′ nīn′) **tablets:** pills taken to treat malaria.

5. **paddocks:** in Australia, fields surrounded by a fence.

Looking at Style

To discuss an aspect of Steele's writing style in "Aunt Millicent," read the following sentences:

- "I bet she won't," Angelica *hissed* back. (p. 193)
- "Millicent!" *scoffed* Angelica. (p. 193)
- "QUIET, you two," *barked* Mr. Starling. (p. 193)
- "Prolific, I'd call it," *grunted* Jamie's father. (p. 194)
- "I know I haven't," Jamie *snapped*. (p. 194)

Have students note the italicized verb in each sentence. Then ask the following questions:

1. Why do you think Steele uses these verbs instead of the using word *said* each time?
2. What other words does the author use in the story instead of *said?*
3. What other words can you think of to replace the word *said?* Write sentences using your own colorful verbs.

Nutbeam. "That's probably how it all started."

Next day, Grandma Nutbeam began to knit a pair of explorer's socks. She decided on khaki with dark blue stripes around the top.

18

evaluate

How do you like Jamie's family?

Angelica Tonks had found it so difficult to select one of the nineteen aunts and uncles that her pen portrait was left until the very last minute and then scrawled out in a great hurry. She had finally chosen Aunt Daisy Blizzard, Mrs. Tonks's eldest sister.

Mr. Wilfred Starling asked Angelica to read her portrait to the class first, to get it over with. As he had expected and as Jamie Nutbeam had hoped, Angelica's aunt sounded anything but wonderfully interesting. She had always lived on the same street, her favorite color was deep purple and she grew African violets on the bathroom shelf, but that was about all.

Many of the other portraits weren't much better, although there was one uncle who had fallen into Lake Burley Griffin and been rescued by a passing Member of Parliament. Someone else's aunt had competed in a penny-farthing bicycle race in northern Tasmania, only to capsize and sprain both her knees; and there was a great-uncle who had been present at the opening of the Sydney Harbor Bridge in 1932 but couldn't remember it at all as he'd been asleep in his pram[6] at the time.

Mr. Starling saved Jamie's portrait until last, hoping for the best. Jamie cleared his throat nervously and began:

"I have never met Aunt Millicent, and no one in my family knows her very well as she hasn't been in Australia for a long time. This is because Aunt Millicent is an explorer . . . "

Mr. Wilfred Starling had been hoping for a bright spot in his day, and Aunt Millicent Nutbeam was it. He smiled happily when Jamie explained how Millicent had gained her early training as an explorer by regularly running away from home. He sighed with pleasure as Jamie described the swampy region of Lake Chad, where Millicent was searching through the mud and papyrus[7] for the northern border of the Cameroons. He positively beamed when he heard that Grandma Nutbeam was knitting explorer's socks for her daughter.

The rest of the class sat spellbound as Jamie read on, except for Angelica Tonks, whose scowl grew darker by the minute. Jamie had barely finished his portrait when her hand was waving furiously.

Mr. Starling's beam faded. "What *is* it, Angelica?"

"I don't believe it. Women don't go exploring! I think Jamie's made it all up! He's a cheat!"

Mr. Starling's stomach lurched, but before he had time to say anything, the

---

6. **pram:** a British term for a baby carriage.
7. **papyrus** (pə pī′ rəs): tall water plant.

19
20
21

Words to Know and Use	**capsize** (kap′ sīz′) *v.* to be overturned or upset

199

18. ACTIVE READING: Evaluate
How do you like Jamie's family?
(Possible responses: They are a lot of fun; they make good jokes; I like the way they share their ideas; they are a really weird bunch; they don't seem very serious about life; they don't seem real.)

19. LANGUAGE: Australian Terms
Some names, expressions, and references here may be unfamiliar to students. Parliament is similar to the U.S. Congress, and a Member of Parliament is elected to represent the people of an area, like a U.S. representative or senator. A penny-farthing was a type of bicycle popular in the late nineteenth century, with a large front wheel and a small rear wheel. It was so called because its wheels differed in size like penny and farthing coins. Tasmania is an island state of Australia, south of the mainland, and Sydney is an Australian city. *Pram* is a shortened form of *perambulator*, the British term for a baby carriage. ★

20. LITERARY CONCEPT: Characterization
Mention that the author finds several ways to describe Mr. Starling's mood in this passage. Challenge students to find the phrases she uses. *("smiled happily," "sighed with pleasure," "positively beamed")*

21. ACTIVE READING: Review
Ask students why they think Angelica is scowling. *(Possible responses: She is jealous of Jamie; she doesn't believe that Jamie is telling the truth.)*

Illustration by David Tamura.

other girls in the class rose up in a passion and rounded on Angelica.

"Who *says* women don't go exploring?"

"Women can do anything they want to these days, Angelica Tonks! Don't you know that?"

"I'd really like to be an explorer or something—maybe a test pilot."

Who says women don't go exploring?

"Well, *I'd* like to be a diver and explore the ocean floor and have a good look at the *Titanic.*"

"What does your aunt wear when she's at work?"

"What color are her new socks?"

The boys began to join in.

"Can your aunt really use a machete?"

"How many languages can she speak?"

"Does she always carry a gun? I bet she's a crack shot!"

"How does a theodolite work?"

The clamor was so great that hardly anyone heard the bell. Angelica Tonks heard it and vanished in a sulk. Mr. Starling heard it and happily gathered up his books. He gave Jamie a secret wink as he left the room.

The end of the assignment was not the end of Aunt Millicent. At school, the careers teacher ran some special sessions on "Challenging Occupations for Women" after he had been stormed by the girls from Jamie's class for information about becoming test pilots, mobile-crane drivers, buffalo hunters and ocean-floor mappers. The science teacher was asked to explain the workings of a theodolite to the class.

At home, Aunt Millicent settled happily into the Nutbeam family, who all followed her adventures with great interest. Dr. Nutbeam brought home library books about the Cameroons and Central Africa. Jamie

◀ F

22

roared his way through one called *The Bafut Beagles*. Mrs. Nutbeam rummaged through an old storeroom at the curio shop and began to collect exotic objects. She brought home a brace of hunting spears from Kenya, which she hung on the family-room wall.

"Just the sort of souvenir Millicent could have sent us," she explained. "See—those marks on the blades are very probably dried bloodstains."

23 Another time she unwrapped a stuffed mongoose, announcing that Auntie had sent this from India on one of her earlier trips.

Jamie and Nerissa stroked it. "What a funny animal," said Nerissa. "Like a weasel."

Grandma was knitting her way down the second sock leg. "That funny animal is a very brave creature," she admonished, tapping the mongoose with her knitting needle. "I'll always remember Kipling's story of Rikki-tikki-tavi and how he fought that dreadful king cobra. Brrr!"

24 "Who won?" asked Jamie.

"You could read it yourself and find out, young man," said Grandma, starting to knit a new row. "I expect Millicent has met a few cobras in her time."

Nerissa had splendid dreams nearly every night. Aunt Millicent strode through most of them, wielding her machete or shouldering her theodolite. Sometimes Nerissa found herself wading through swirling rivers or swinging on jungle vines like a gibbon.[8] Jamie was often there, too, or some of her school friends, or Grandma followed by a mongoose on a lead. Once, Mrs. Nutbeam speared a giant toad, which exploded and woke Nerissa up. In another dream, Nerissa's father was polishing the fangs of a grinning crocodile, which lay back in the dentist's chair with its long tail tucked neatly under the sterilizer. It looked slightly like Mrs. Tonks.

Mrs. Nutbeam brought home still more curios: a bamboo flute and a small tom-tom, which Jamie and Nerissa soon learned to play. Mysterious drumbeats and thin flutey tunes drifted along the street from the Nutbeams' house. School friends came to beat the tom-tom and to stroke the mongoose and to see how the explorer's socks were growing. ◄ G

"Will you be sending them off soon, to the Cameroons?" they asked Grandma, who was turning the heel of the second sock.

"I think I'll make another pair, perhaps even three pairs," replied Grandma. "I might just as well send a large parcel as a small one."

"Yes, and then Aunt Millie will have spare pairs of socks she can wash," said Nerissa. "Socks must get very smelly near the equator."

25 Word of Millicent Nutbeam, intrepid explorer, began to spread through the town. Children told their families about the spears, the tom-tom, the mongoose and the khaki socks. Not every small town could claim to be connected to a famous international explorer—it was exciting news.

---

8. **gibbon:** a small ape.

23. SCIENCE SIDELIGHT
Some students may be unfamiliar with mongooses. Have students turn to the picture of a mongoose on page 322 of this book. Explain that a mongoose is a small, thin, carnivorous mammal related to minks, otters, and weasels and known for its ability to kill rodents and snakes. ★

24. LITERARY SIDELIGHT
Point out that the story to which Grandma refers, "Rikki-tikki-tavi" by Rudyard Kipling, begins on page 323 of this book. It is one of many stories in *The Jungle Book*, which is based on Kipling's experiences in India.

25. ACTIVE READING: Predict
Ask students to predict what might happen now that news of Millicent is quickly spreading through town. What problems might Millicent's popularity cause for the Nutbeams? Might it help the Nutbeams? How? *(Any response is valid.)*

Words to Know and Use	**exotic** (eg zät' ik) *adj.* strange; unusual
	wielding (wēld' in) *adj.* handling and using **wield** *v.*
	intrepid (in trep' id) *adj.* very brave

201

26. LANGUAGE: Briticisms
Students might not be familiar with the British use of the term *surgery* to refer to a doctor's office. Ask students to tell what this word means in American English. ("an operation") ★

27. LITERARY CONCEPT: Humor
Ask students how the author makes this scene funny. Point out that Mrs. Tonks has come to talk to Dr. Nutbeam but is unable to say anything because he has filled her mouth with instruments. She has had the tables turned on her.

28. ACTIVE READING: Connect
Ask students what advice they might offer Mrs. Nutbeam at this point. If they were Mrs. Nutbeam, what would they tell people who asked about Aunt Millicent? Would they continue to cover for Jamie, or would they confess? Why?

29. VOCABULARY: Idiom
Discuss the expression "found herself on slippery ground." Have students use **prior knowledge** and **context clues** to discover that the phrase means "found herself in a dangerous or uncertain situation." Ask students to suggest other expressions that have a similar meaning. (Possible responses: "was skating on thin ice," "was out on a limb," "was walking a tightrope") ★

Angelica Tonks, however, told her mother that she didn't believe Jamie's aunt was an explorer at all. "I bet he just invented that to make his aunt seem more interesting than all the rest," she scoffed.

Mrs. Tonks sniffed a good deal and then decided it was time to have a dental checkup. "I'll get to the bottom of that Millicent Nutbeam, you mark my words," she told Angelica, as she telephoned Dr. Nutbeam's surgery for an appointment.

"Well, well—good morning, Mrs. Tonks," said Dr. Nutbeam, a few days later. "We haven't seen you for a while! Just lie right back in the chair, please, and relax!"

Mrs. Tonks lay back, but she didn't relax one bit. Her eyes were sharp and suspicious. "Good morning, Dr. Nutbeam. How is the family?" she inquired. "And how is your sister?"

Dr. Nutbeam pulled on his rubber gloves. "My sister? Which one? . . . Er, probe, please, nurse."

Before he could say "Open wide," Mrs. Tonks snapped, "Your sister the so-called explorer. Huh! The one in the Cameroons."

"Ah, *that* sister. You mean Millicent . . . now, just open wider and turn this way a little. Yes, our Millie, she does work so hard . . . oops, there's a beaut cavity! A real crater!" He crammed six plugs of cotton wool around Mrs. Tonks's gums. "My word, what a lot of saliva! We'll have some suction, please, nurse, and just wipe that dribble from the patient's chin." He continued to poke and scrape Mrs. Tonks's molars, none too gently. "Ah, here's another trouble spot. Mm . . . have you ever been to the Cameroons, Mrs. Tonks?"

Mrs. Tonks's eyes glared. She tried to shake her head, but could only gurgle, "Argggg . . ."

"No, I didn't think you had. Such a fascinating place!" Dr. Nutbeam turned on the squealing high-speed drill and bored into her decaying tooth, spraying water all over her chin.

When he had told his family about this encounter with Mrs. Tonks, his wife complained, "It's all very well for you. *You* can just cram people's mouths full of wadding and metal contraptions and suction tubes if they start asking awkward questions, but what am I supposed to do?"

People are asking to see photos of Millicent.

The truth was that increasing numbers of townsfolk were calling at the antique shop where Mrs. Nutbeam worked. They were eager to know more about Millicent Nutbeam and her adventurous life. They felt proud of her.

"It's getting quite tricky," Mrs. Nutbeam explained. "People are asking to see photos of Millicent and wanting us to talk at the elderly citizens' club about her. This aunt is becoming an embarrassment. I wish people weren't so curious. Sometimes I don't know what to say!"

Grandma found herself on slippery ground, too, when she met the postman at the gate.

"Morning," he said, sorting through his mailbag. "You must be Jamie's grandmother, then."

Speaking . . . Listening . . . Viewing

Speaking/Listening To further explore the topic of humor, invite volunteers to tell jokes, or tell a few yourself, while the class listens. Have students identify what makes each funny. Exaggeration? Sarcasm? Absurdity? A pun?

Question: Why do elephants wear green beanies?

Answer: So they can walk across pool tables without being seen.

Technique: This joke works on the ask-a-silly-question principle—a large dose of absurdity.

Question: Why did the elephant cross the road?

Answer: Because he was stapled to a chicken.

Technique: Here the humor also hinges on the absurd and the grotesque—as well as on an allusion to another, more famous joke.

PORTRAIT OF MADAME BÉNARD 1930 Edouard Vuillard
Musée National d'Art Moderne, Paris. Giraudon/Art Resource, New York.

Art Note
The French painter Édouard Vuillard (1868–1940) spent the last years of his career painting portraits. His *Portrait of Madame Bénard* places the subject in her own living room, where she clearly feels most at home. *What words would you use to describe Madame Bénard? Why do you think this painting was chosen to accompany "Aunt Millicent"?*

30. LANGUAGE: Briticisms
Ask students to use **context clues** to infer what the expression "gone round the twist" means. Bring out the idea that it means "gone crazy" or "gone mad." Call attention to the clue "Mad, I call it" several lines later. Have students offer equivalent idioms they may know, such as "gone off her rocker," "gone off the deep end," or "lost her marbles." ★

"Yes, I am," Grandma replied, rather surprised.

"Mother of the explorer, eh?"

"Gracious!" exclaimed Grandma. "Fancy you knowing about that!"

"Oh, my girl Julie has told us all about it. She's in Jamie's class at school. Funny thing—Julie's gone round the twist since she heard about all that exploring business. Says she wants to buy a camel and ride it around Australia, and one of her friends is going to apply for a job on an oil rig. I ask you!"

"Well, that's nice," said Grandma, soothingly. "Girls are so enterprising these days."

"Huh! Mad, I call it." The postman held out a bundle of letters. "Here you are. Now,

30

Words to Know and Use	**enterprising** (ent' ər prī' ziŋ) *adj.* adventurous; energetic

203

31. ACTIVE READING: Review
Discuss the excuses that Grandma gives the postman. Ask students how convincing they seem. Which of the two excuses seems more believable? Have students think of other excuses Grandma might have given for not receiving more mail from Millicent.

32. LITERARY CONCEPT: Characterization
Have students describe the way Jamie's mood has changed since he first invented Aunt Millicent. What details in the passage indicate that Jamie is now upset? *(Possible responses: He speaks in a demanding way; he growls.)*

33. LITERARY CONCEPT: Theme
Remind students that the title of this subunit is "Turning the Tables." Discuss how this theme now applies to the story. How have the tables been turned on the Nutbeams? *(Possible responses: Jamie invented Aunt Millicent, but now it appears she has taken over; the Nutbeams were afraid the plan wouldn't work, but now it's working too well.)*

34. GEOGRAPHICAL SIDELIGHT
Invite students who are familiar with the Andes to explain that they are a mountain range that runs the length of western South America. Ask volunteers to show the exact location of the Andes or of Peru on a globe or wall map. Point out that the Andes are the longest chain of mountains in the world, stretching for 4,500 miles from Cape Horn to Panama.

that's *another* funny thing—the Nutbeams don't get much foreign mail, come to think of it. You'd think the explorer would write to them more often, her being in the traveling line."

Grandma breathed deeply. "Oh, it's not easy, you know, writing letters when you're exploring. For one thing, there's never a decent light in the tent at night—and besides, there's hardly ever a post office to hand when you need it. She glanced through the letters. "Goodness! There's one from South America . . . Peru."

"That's what made me wonder. Is it from her?" asked the postman, eagerly.

Her? Ah . . . Millicent. I don't know. It's for Dr. Nutbeam, my son, and it's typed. Anyway, as far as we know, Millicent is still in the Cameroons, although we've not had word for some time."

"She could have moved on, couldn't she?" suggested the postman. "Peru, eh? Oh well, I'd better move on, too. G'day to you!"

At school, Julie, the postman's daughter, said to Jamie, "Why has your auntie gone to South America? What's she exploring now?"

"Who said she's gone to South America?" demanded Jamie. He felt he was losing control of Aunt Millicent.

"My dad said there was a letter from her in Peru," replied Julie.

"Well, no one told *me*," growled Jamie.

At home he announced, "Julie is telling everybody that our Aunt Millicent is in Peru! What's she talking about? What's happening?"

Grandma stopped knitting. "Julie. Is that the name of the postman's girl?"

"Yes—her dad said there was a letter for us from Auntie in Peru, or somewhere mad."

"Oh, I remember—he asked me about it," said Grandma.

"Well . . . what did you *say?*" wailed Jamie.

"I just said I didn't know who the letter was from and that I thought Millicent was still in the Cameroons, but that we hadn't heard for a while where she was. That's all."

"The letter from Peru," chuckled Dr. Nutbeam, "is about the World Dental Conference on plaque, which is being held next year in Lima. It has nothing to do with Millicent."

"Well of *course* it hasn't," spluttered Jamie. "She doesn't exist!"

"But Jamie, in a funny sort of way she *does* exist," said Mrs. Nutbeam.

His father grinned. "My sister is quite a girl! She's begun to live a life of her own!"

"That's the trouble," said Jamie. "She seems to be doing things we don't know about."

While they were talking, the telephone rang. Dr. Nutbeam was no longer grinning when he came back from answering it. "That was Frank Figgis from the local paper."

"Frank, the editor?" asked Mrs. Nutbeam. "What did he want?"

"He wants to do a full-page feature on our Millicent," groaned her husband. "He's heard that she's about to set out on a climbing expedition in the Andes! Up some peak that has never yet been conquered!"

"What nonsense!" snapped Grandma. "She's too old for that sort of thing."

"It's just a rumor!" shouted Jamie. "Who said she's going to the Andes? *I* didn't say she was going there. She's still in the Cameroons!"

"Calm down, dear," said his mother, "and

let's hear what Dad said to Frank Figgis."

Dr. Nutbeam was rubbing his head. "I stalled for time–I said we'd not heard she was in the Andes but that we'd make inquiries and let him know. Whatever happens, Millicent mustn't get into print. We'll all be up on a charge of false pretenses[9] or something!"

Jamie snorted. "Well, if she's climbing an Ande, it might be best if she fell off and was never seen again."

35
36

review   Is Jamie's Aunt Millicent getting out of control?

Nerissa shrieked, *"No! She mustn't–she's our only aunt, and we've only just got her!"*

Mrs. Nutbeam sighed. "Listen, Jamie, perhaps the time has come to own up that Aunt Millicent is not real."

"We can't do that!" wailed Jamie. "Everyone would think we're loony . . . and that Grandma's absolutely bonkers, knitting socks for an aunt who isn't there. And what about the mongoose? Anyway, I *can't* let Honky Tonks find out now–she'd never stop crowing, and she'd be more awful than ever."

Jamie decided to lay the whole problem of Aunt Millicent Nutbeam before Mr. Starling, right up to her unexpected expedition to the Andes and Mr. Figgis's plan to write a full-page feature about her for the local paper. He finished by saying, "I think I might have to kill her off."

"That'd be a shame," sighed Mr. Starling. "She's quite a lady, your aunt!"

"It would be pretty easy to get rid of her," Jamie went on. "In her sort of job she could sink into a quicksand, or be trampled by a herd of elephants, or something."

Mr. Starling shook his head violently. "No, no–it would only make things worse if she died a bloodcurdling death like that. No one would be likely to forget her if she was squashed flat by a stampeding elephant. She'd become more interesting than ever!"

"Well, she could die of something boring, like pneumonia," said Jamie. "Or . . . will I have to own up that she isn't real?"

"Do you want to own up?"

"Not really. I'd feel stupid, and I specially don't want Angelica Tonks to know I invented an aunt."

Mr. Starling quite understood. "I see! Anyway, a lot of people would be sad to discover that Millicent Nutbeam was a <u>hoax</u>. The girls in your class, for example–she means a lot to them."

"What'll I do then?"

"If you want people to lose interest in her, you'll just have to make her less interesting. I think she should retire from exploring, for a start."

"Aw, gee!" Jamie felt very disappointed. "I suppose so. I'll see what they think at home."

"What he means," said Dr. Nutbeam, when Jamie had repeated Mr. Starling's

---

9. false pretenses: a legal term that means to lie or purposely mislead.

37

| *Words to Know and Use* | **hoax** (hōks) *n.* a trick or deception |

205

35. LITERARY CONCEPT: Humor
Ask students what might be considered humorous in Jamie's comment. *(Possible responses: Jamie's reference to "an Ande" is funny because the Andes are always referred to in the plural—one doesn't say "he was in Colorado climbing a Rocky"; it is amusing that he's so eager to kill Millicent off.)*

36. ACTIVE READING: Review
Is Jamie's Aunt Millicent getting out of control? *(Possible responses: Yes, because now people want to see her and rumors about her are all over town; no, because the Nutbeams can still make up anything they want to and no one can prove that Millicent doesn't exist.)*

37. VOCABULARY: Idiom
If students are unfamiliar with the expression "own up," have them use **context clues** to figure out that it means "admit" or "confess." ★

advice, "is that it's time my dear sister Millicent settled down."

"I quite agree with that," remarked Grandma, who was up to the sixth sock foot. "She's not as young as she was, and it's high time she had some normal home life. I think she should get married, even though she's getting on a bit. Perhaps to a widower."

"That sounds terribly boring," yawned Nerissa.

"Well, that's what we need," said Jamie, "something terribly boring to make people lose interest."

Grandma sniffed. "In my day it would have been called a happy ending."

"Well, I suppose it's a happier ending than being squashed by an elephant," conceded Jamie.

"How about marrying her to a retired accountant who used to work for a cardboard-box company?" suggested his father. "That sounds pretty dull."

"Good heavens, it's all rather sudden!" said Mrs. Nutbeam. "Last time we heard of her she was climbing the Andes!"

"No, she *wasn't*." At last Jamie felt he had hold of Aunt Millicent again. "That South American stuff was just a rumor. The postman started it because of the letter from Peru, and then the story just grew!"

Dr. Nutbeam nodded. "Stories seem to have a habit of doing that, and so do rumors! But we can easily squash this one about the Andes. I'll just explain about the World Dental Conference on plaque. I even have the letter to prove it."

Illustration by Steve Johnson with Lou Fancher.

Dr. Nutbeam called Frank Figgis on the phone. He explained about the letter from Peru and about the ridiculous rumor which the postman had started. "In your profession, Frank," he added sternly, "you should be much more careful than to listen to <u>baseless</u> rumor. It could get you into all sorts of trouble! In any case, Millicent is giving up exploring to marry a retired accountant. She's had enough."

Frank Figgis was fast losing interest. "I see—well, sometime when she's in Australia, we could do an interview about her former life . . . maybe."

"Maybe, although she has no immediate plans to return here. I believe she and her husband are going to settle down in England—somewhere on the seafront, like Bognor."

Jamie passed on the same information to

Words to Know and Use	**baseless** (bās' lis) *adj.* having no foundation in fact

his classmates. The girls were shocked.

"She's what?"

"Getting married to an *accountant?*"

"She can't be!"

"How boring for her!"

"Where in the world is Bognor? Is there really such a place?"

Angelica Tonks smiled like a smug pussy-cat. "See! Your Aunt Millicent is just like any other old aunt, after all!"

Jamie caught Mr. Starling's eye. It winked.

Aunt Millicent Nutbeam retired, not to Bognor but to live quietly with her family. Nerissa still had wonderful dreams. Dr. Nutbeam still brought home books about far-off places. The bloodstained spears remained on the wall and the mongoose on the shelf. Jamie and Nerissa still played the tom-tom and the bamboo flute.

Grandma Nutbeam's holiday came to an end, and she packed up to return home. She left a parcel for Jamie. When he opened it, he found three pairs of khaki socks with dark blue stripes and a card which said:

Dear Jamie,
Aunt Millicent won't have any use for these now that she has settled down, so you might as well have them for school camps. Isn't it lucky that they are just your size!
With love from Grandma.

40. **ACTIVE READING:** Connect
Ask students if they agree that marrying and settling down is boring. If they were Aunt Millicent, would they choose to marry, or would they rather continue to explore? Have them explain their opinions.

41. **LITERARY CONCEPT:** Characterization
Ask students if they feel that it is just a coincidence that the socks fit Jamie. If it isn't, what does this show about Grandma's character? *(Possible responses: She was going to give the socks to Jamie all along; she knew that Millicent would have to go sometime; she used the story as an excuse to do something nice for her grandson; she wants Jamie to be adventurous like his fictional aunt.)*

ENCOURAGING INDEPENDENT READING

Dear Lovey Hart: I Am Desperate, novel by Ellen Conford

Family Reunion, novel by Caroline Cooney

The Heroic Life of Al Capsella, novel by J. Clarke

Landing on Marvin Gardens, novel by Rona Zable

Comprehension Check

1. What assignment does Mr. Starling give the class? *(to write a pen-portrait of an aunt or uncle)*

2. Why is the assignment a problem for Jamie? *(He has no aunts or uncles.)*

3. How does Jamie get around his problem? *(He invents an aunt to write about.)*

4. Who helps Jamie think of details about his aunt? *(his mother, father, sister, and grandmother)*

5. Where is Aunt Millicent supposedly exploring? *(the Cameroons)*

6. Why do people think Millicent is in Peru? *(A letter from Peru arrives, and a rumor starts.)*

7. How does the family make people lose interest in Millicent? *(by having her marry and retire)*

8. What does Grandma give Jamie at the end? *(the socks she had knitted for Aunt Millicent)*

Student Response

Responding to Reading

1. Any response is valid.

2. **Possible responses:** The people feel so bored with their lives that anyone with a colorful life fascinates them; they are impressed and inspired by a woman with so many accomplishments.

3. **Possible responses:** Good results: Jamie's pen-portrait impresses the class and annoys Angelica Tonks; Jamie's family enjoys having a new "relative"; everyone is inspired to learn about many new things, from foreign countries to interesting careers. Bad results: Millicent gets out of the family's control; the family has to keep telling people more and more complicated stories.

4. **Possible responses:** Jamie's family is wonderful because they are supportive of him and become involved in his project; they are odd people who let Jamie make up an untrue story that takes over their lives; they are typical people with typical jobs and interests; they are not typical because they have such good imaginations and get so involved in Jamie's Aunt Millicent project.

5. Any response is valid. Students may decide that the characters are popular because they are ordinary and people identify with them, or because they are larger than life, strange, or fascinating.

Challenge Question

The characters in the story think that Millicent's life is glamorous. What is the "down side" of a career like hers? *(Possible responses: danger, loneliness, lack of comfort and convenience, physical hardship, lack of "civilization")*

Literary Concept: Humor

Examples of exaggeration: Mr. Starling feels like screaming at Angelica and thinks having class end will be "bliss"; Dr. Nutbeam says that chewing pencils will leave Jamie toothless; Nerissa says that Angelica probably has "a hundred and twenty-seven" cousins. Examples of sarcasm: Jamie calls the Tonkses "wonderfully interesting" when he really means the opposite; Mrs. Tonks asks Dr. Nutbeam how Millicent is when she doesn't even believe in her. Other

Responding to Reading

First Impressions

1. Who is your favorite character in this story? Why? Jot down your thoughts in your journal.

Second Thoughts

2. Why do you think the imaginary Aunt Millicent becomes so popular with Jamie's family and with the people in the town?

3. What good and bad results does Jamie's story have?

4. What do you think of Jamie's family? Are they a typical family? Explain your opinion.

Broader Connections

5. Even though they know she is imaginary, Jamie's family enjoys Aunt Millicent and her adventures. In small groups, discuss your favorite fictional characters from books or movies. Why do you think these kinds of characters are popular with so many people?

Literary Concept: Humor

One of the techniques that writers use to create humor is **exaggeration,** or an extreme overstating of an idea. Dr. Nutbeam exaggerates when he thinks that he would like to anesthetize Angelica and send her home in a jiffy bag.

Another way to create humor is by using **sarcasm,** which is criticism hidden by humor. A sarcastic remark seems complimentary but is really meant to criticize. Mr. Starling uses sarcasm when he says, "Well, Angelica, aren't you a lucky one to have nineteen uncles and aunts." Actually, the teacher finds the Tonkses "tedious and terrible."

Skim the story to find other examples of exaggeration and sarcasm. Then see if you can find others ways in which humor is created in this selection.

examples of humor: the characters' names, contrasts between what people say and what they think, the unexpected eagerness with which everyone believes in the fantasy and elaborates it

Writing Options

1. How might Aunt Millicent feel if she knew that her amazing adventures were a topic of town gossip? Use your imagination and what you know from the story to write a **letter** from her to one of the townspeople.

2. Write an **article** for the full-page feature Frank Figgis planned about Aunt Millicent. It may be about her childhood, her work in Cameroon, or her travels.

3. Both Jamie and the narrator of "The Revolt of the Evil Fairies" faced a problem. **Compare and contrast** how each deals with his problem.

4. Write your own **pen-portrait** of a real or imaginary aunt or uncle. If your relative is imaginary, use the notes about the adventure you described in your journal to spice up the character's life.

Vocabulary Practice

Exercise Decide whether the boldfaced word in each sentence below is used correctly or incorrectly. Write *Correct* or *Incorrect* on your paper, and give your reason for each answer.

1. The townspeople took pride in Aunt Millicent's **intrepid** adventures in far-off parts of the world.

2. When Jamie tried the **hoax**, he wondered if it would taste as good as his last piece.

3. Girls in Jamie's school hoped for the excitement of a **tedious** career like Aunt Millicent's.

4. Jamie might have felt **exasperation** when his good idea got out of hand.

5. Jamie created Aunt Millicent because his real family was so **exotic.**

6. It was easy to picture Millicent **wielding** her long, sharp knife in the jungle.

7. Aunt Millicent would hate to have her boat **capsize** in the swampy waters of Lake Chad.

8. Grandma Nutbeam was not **prolific** because she had only one son.

9. Grandma Nutbeam called only the most easily embarrassed girls **enterprising.**

10. The story about Millicent's going to Peru was **baseless.**

> *Words to Know and Use*
>
> **baseless**
> **capsize**
> **enterprising**
> **exasperation**
> **exotic**
> **hoax**
> **intrepid**
> **prolific**
> **tedious**
> **wielding**

Writing Options

The Writing Options are designed to meet varied student interests and abilities. Have each student choose one activity to complete.

Journal Update Have students write about their idea of a challenging occupation or a place they would like to visit.

Links to Writer's Craft

Writing Option 4 is an exercise in descriptive writing. For more practice, see *The Writer's Craft,* Grade 7, "Observation and Description," pages 49–69.

Vocabulary Practice

Answers to Exercise

1. Correct

2. Incorrect; a hoax is a trick.

3. Incorrect; *tedious* means "boring."

4. Correct

5. Incorrect; *exotic* means "strange" or "unusual."

6. Correct

7. Correct

8. Correct

9. Incorrect; *enterprising* means "energetic" or "courageous."

10. Correct

For Alternative Learning Styles

Have students work in small groups to tell an adventure story that contains all the vocabulary words. Have each student contribute one sentence, using one vocabulary word in that sentence.

Closure

In a comical way, the tables are turned on the Nutbeams as their fictitious relative gains a life of her own. Encourage students to look for table turning as they watch situation comedies on television.

The Spelling Connection

The Letters *qu* When *qu* is pronounced like *k*, it can appear in the middle or at the end of a word. At the end of a word, the spelling *que* is used. When *qu* is pronounced like *kw*, it can appear at the beginning of a word or within a word.

Examples: bou**quet**   ban**quet**   **qu**iet   bou**tique**

qu Words from the Selection

anti**que**   **qu**ickly   s**qu**irmed   in**qu**ired
pla**que**   **qu**inine   e**qu**ator

Other *qu* Words

techni**que**   **qu**ite   a**qu**arium
eti**quette**   **qu**arrel   s**qu**irrel

Exercise Find *qu* words to match the clues.

1. a fish tank
2. wiggled
3. proper behavior
4. a film on teeth
5. a valuable old item
6. a method
7. rapidly
8. a small shop
9. asked
10. a line around the earth

Extending the Lesson

Options for Learning

These activities suit a variety of learning styles and modes of expression.

Collaborative Learning Activities
See Options 1, 2, and 4

1. Your Turn Remind students that a story should include a conflict—internal or external—involving one or more characters.

2. Fabulous Females Students might look in magazines for articles about outstanding women or research the lives of women who first ventured into traditionally male professions. They may also interview working women they know.

3. A Cartography Career? Students may copy a map from an atlas. Suggest they use colored pencils to differentiate the various features they are including.

4. Play Time Have students look back at *The Monsters Are Due on Maple Street* on page 158 to see the form that is followed for writing dialogue and stage directions in a script.

FACT FINDER SOCIAL STUDIES

Students can use a recent almanac or encyclopedia to find that Cameroon's population is estimated to be about 13 million as of 1993.

Mary Steele

■ **More About the Author** Most of Steele's jobs have involved books—she has been an English teacher, an editor, and a librarian. Some of her favorite activities are beachcombing, bush walking, singing, and solving crossword puzzles.

■ **Other Works** Novel: *Mollyroots' Rib at Misery Pond*

Options for Learning (Multimodal/Cross-Curricular Activities)

1 • Your Turn In small groups or as a class, compose the further adventures of Aunt Millicent. Try brainstorming before you start, as Jamie's family did. One student can begin with a sentence or episode, then each student can add a new part to the story.

2 • Fabulous Females As Jamie's grandmother says, "Girls are so enterprising these days." Women work far out in space, deep in the ocean, and most places in between. Research a woman who has an unusual, exciting career. Share your findings with your class.

3 • A Cartography Career? Try your hand as a cartographer. Draw a topographical map of Cameroon, indicating wetlands, dry areas, jungles, and rivers. Include the countries and bodies of water that border Cameroon. Show on your map where Aunt Millicent worked.

4 • Play Time Rewrite an episode of the story as a play. Include dialogue and stage directions. Then invite classmates to join you in performing the play for the rest of your class.

FACT FINDER SOCIAL STUDIES

What is the population of Cameroon?

Mary Steele
1930–

Mary Steele has lived in Australia all of her life. She grew up surrounded by pets: a flock of ducks, canaries, finches, a peacock, a cockatoo, and a parakeet. Two of her favorite authors are E. B. White and Roald Dahl.

Steele likes to write for young people "because they are curious and full of fun, and their imaginations still work." She rewrites stories several times before she is satisfied. "By the time I've finished," she says, "the characters seem like old friends or part of the family."

In 1986, her book *Arkwright* was named the Australian Junior Book of the Year. In 1989 she was asked, as one of Australia's sixteen leading children's writers, to write a story on the theme of "dream time." She wrote "Aunt Millicent."

Cross-Curricular Projects

Geography Suggest that a small group of volunteers create a travel brochure entitled "Explorers' Adventures." They may design adventurous trips to three parts of the world, describing each area's people, geography, plants, and animals and telling why going there would be an exciting adventure.

Science Encourage students to learn about theodolites—How do they work? what are they used for? For the class, invite a surveyor to display a theodolite and give a presentation.

Music Interested students may write an original song entitled "The Ballad of Aunt Millicent," telling all about her adventures up to her marriage and retirement. Students may record their song or perform it live for the class.

Math Challenge students to invent math problems based on Aunt Millicent's adventures. (Example: If Aunt Millicent traveled from Cameroon to Peru and back, how far did she travel?) Partners can solve each other's problems by using maps and rulers.

Fiction

Gentleman of Río en Medio

JUAN A. A. SEDILLO (hwän, se dě' yô)

Examine What You Know (Prior Knowledge)

Owning a piece of property gives people certain rights. Do property owners have responsibilities as well, or may they do anything they want to with what is theirs? As a class, discuss these rights and responsibilities. Have one class member take notes, separating your ideas into two categories. One should list the rights of property owners. The other should list their responsibilities.

Expand Your Knowledge (Building Background)

Land ownership is an important issue in this story. Although the story is fictional, the setting—a small Hispanic farming community called Río en Medio—actually exists. Located in the mountains above Santa Fe, New Mexico, Río en Medio consists of a few scattered adobe (sunbaked-brick) ranch houses along a river that is often dry. Since there is little good land, only a few crops and fruit trees grow on terraced mountainsides. Río en Medio is a close-knit community where members of extended families depend on one another for survival. Hispanic people have lived there for generations, and some families even trace their origins to the Spanish settlers of the sixteenth and seventeenth centuries.

Write Before You Read (Journal Writing)

■ *Author biography in Reader's Handbook*

Imagine that you owned a piece of land. Would you allow people in the community to use it? Would the way people used it affect your decision? Write your responses in your journal. As you read, compare your ideas with those of the characters in this story.

Objectives

■ To understand and analyze a short story

■ To examine the use of a first-person narrator in a short story

■ To enrich reading by inferring character traits

■ To express understanding of the story through a choice of writing forms, including an opinion and a letter

Prereading/Motivation

Examine What You Know

Discussion Prompts Do landowners have a right to expect their neighbors to keep property in good condition? Are landowners entitled to privacy on their land? How much privacy should they be allowed?

Expand Your Knowledge

Additional Background The population of New Mexico is 38 percent Hispanic American and 9 percent Native American. The area was a territory of Spain, and then Mexico, until annexation by the United States in 1846. It became a state in 1912. Spanish is spoken widely in the state and is the dominant language in several areas.

Thematic Link— Turning the Tables

The Americans realize that the gentleman of Río en Medio is entitled to additional money for his property, but he adheres to his personal code of honor and declines. Later, the tables are turned and the gentleman's code requires that he respect the unwritten rights of the children, which cost the Americans a handsome price.

MORE JOURNAL WRITING IDEAS

■ Imagine that you bought property from people who had lived on the property for many years. How would you feel about their returning to visit?

■ What special feelings do you have about land or about plants and trees?

COLLABORATIVE LEARNING OPTIONS

Opportunities for collaborative learning include Examine What You Know, Broader Connections, and the Literary Concept.

ADDITIONAL RESOURCES

Unit Two Resource Book
Reader's Guidesheet, p. 54
Reading Skills, p. 55
Literature Skills, p. 56
Vocabulary Connections, p. 57
Spelling Connections, p. 58
Comprehension Check Test, p. 59
Selection Test, pp. 60–61

Teaching Strategies

VOCABULARY PREVIEW

The focus of vocabulary study for this selection is context clues. See *Unit Two Resource Book*, Vocabulary Connections, page 57.

LIMITED ENGLISH PROFICIENCY

■ Use the Reader's Guidesheet, *Unit Two Resource Book*, page 54.

■ Several Spanish words and phrases are included in the story. You may want to call attention to the footnotes that define their meanings and give pronunciations for students.

★ The text annotation marked with a red star (1) may be particularly helpful for students with limited English proficiency.

TEXT ANNOTATIONS

1. VOCABULARY
You may wish to pronounce the title for students and point out that *río en medio* means "river in the middle," which refers to the geography of the village. ★

2. ACTIVE READING: Review
What details in the opening paragraph hint that history and heritage may be important to the old man? *(His people have lived on the land and worked the land for hundreds of years.)*

3. LITERARY CONCEPT: Characterization
Ask students what they know so far about the gentleman of Río en Medio. *(Although poor, he has dignity; he is patient; he is proud of his family.)*

4. LITERARY CONCEPT: Point of View
Ask students whether this story is told from a first-person or third-person point of view *(first-person)* Have them explain their reasoning. *(The first-person pronouns I and we indicate a first-person narrator.)*

Gentleman of Río en Medio[1]

JUAN A. A. SEDILLO

It took months of negotiation to come to an understanding with the old man. He was in no hurry. What he had the most of was time. He lived up in Río en Medio[1], where his people had been for hundreds of years. He tilled the same land they had tilled. His house was small and wretched, but quaint. The little creek ran through his land. His orchard was gnarled and beautiful.

The day of the sale he came into the office. His coat was old, green and faded. I thought of Senator Catron,[2] who had been such a power with these people up there in the mountains. Perhaps it was one of his old Prince Alberts.[3] He also wore gloves. They were old and torn, and his fingertips showed through them. He carried a cane, but it was only the skeleton of a worn-out umbrella. Behind him walked one of his innumerable kin—a dark young man with eyes like a gazelle.

The old man bowed to all of us in the room. Then he removed his hat and gloves, slowly and carefully. Chaplin[4] once did that in a picture, in a bank—he was the janitor. Then he handed his things to the boy, who stood obediently behind the old man's chair.

There was a great deal of conversation, about rain and about his family. He was very proud of his large family. Finally we got down to business. Yes, he would sell, as he had agreed, for twelve hundred dollars, in cash. We would buy, and the money was ready. "Don[5] Anselmo," I said to him in Spanish, "we have made a discovery. You remember that we sent that surveyor, that engineer, up there to survey your land so as to make the deed. Well, he finds that you own more than eight acres. He tells us that your land extends across the river and that you own almost twice as much as you thought." He didn't know that. "And now, Don Anselmo," I added, "these Americans are *buena gente*,[6] they are good people, and they are willing to pay you for the additional land as well, at the same rate per acre, so that instead of twelve hundred dollars you will get almost twice as much, and the money is here for you."

◄ A

---

1. **Río en Medio:** (rē' ð en mā' dyô) *Spanish.*
2. **Senator Catron** (ka' trən): Thomas Benton Catron, U.S. senator from New Mexico, 1912–1917.
3. **Prince Alberts:** long, double-breasted dress coats.
4. **Chaplin:** Charlie Chaplin, a famous comedian and star of silent films.
5. **Don** (dôn) *Spanish:* a title of respect, much like *Sir* in English.
6. ***buena gente*** (bwe' nä hen' tä) *Spanish:* good people.

212   UNIT TWO   TURNING THE TABLES

Guided Reading for Less-Proficient Students

These questions can help guide students through the reading. Ask each question at the point of the selection where the capital letter and arrow appear in the margin. In addition, you may wish to use appropriate Active Reading annotations.

A. What surprising news does the narrator have for Don Anselmo about his property? *(He owns more land than expected, so the buyers are willing to pay almost twice as much as planned.)* Recalling

B. How does Don Anselmo react to the offer of more money? *(He is insulted and refuses to accept it.)* Recalling

C. What annoys the new owners? *(Village children continually play on their property.)* Recalling

D. According to Don Anselmo, who owns the trees? *(the children of the village)* Recalling

E. How do the new owners get the trees back from the children? *(They pay each individual for his or her tree.)* Recalling

SPRINGTIME   W. Victor Higgins   Courtesy, Gerald Peters Gallery, Santa Fe, New Mexico.

Art Note

W. Victor Higgins was born in Indiana in 1884 and studied painting in Chicago, then Europe. When he moved to Taos, New Mexico, he found a world that suited his artistic ideas. *Springtime* shows an adobe house of the Southwest, screened by lacelike trees and threatened by an approaching storm. *Why do you think this painting was chosen to illustrate the story?*

5. ACTIVE READING: Evaluate
Ask students why the old man is so upset by the prospect of making more money. *(Possible responses: He feels that the Americans' offer of more money does not show respect; a man of honor never goes back on an agreement.)*

6. LITERARY CONCEPT: Character
What is more important to the old man than money? *(Possible responses: his sense of honor; his family; his pride)*

The old man hung his head for a moment in thought. Then he stood up and stared at me. "Friend," he said, "I do not like to have you speak to me in that manner." I kept still and let him have his say. "I know these Americans are good people, and that is why I have agreed to sell to them. But I do not care to be insulted. I have agreed to sell my house and land for twelve hundred dollars and that is the price."

I argued with him, but it was useless.

Finally he signed the deed and took the money but refused to take more than the amount agreed upon. Then he shook hands all around, put on his ragged gloves, took his stick, and walked out with the boy behind him.

A month later my friends had moved into Río en Medio. They had replastered the old adobe house, pruned the trees, patched the fence, and moved in for the summer. One day they came back to the office to com-

7. ACTIVE READING: Review

Ask students to think of adjectives that describe the way the children act at the orchard. *(playful, possessive, good-natured)* What does this say about their intentions? *(Possible responses: The children do not seem to intend any harm; they only want to play and have fun.)*

8. ACTIVE READING: Review

Ask students why the narrator calls on Don Anselmo to help solve the problem of the children. *(Possible responses: He is the most respected man in the village; he is the property's original owner.)*

9. LITERARY CONCEPT: Contrast

Ask students to describe the differences between the narrator's view of the problem and Don Anselmo's view. *(Possible responses: The narrator has a logical view based on respect for the law. Don Anselmo's view is shaped by his family ties and by customs of his community.)*

10. ACTIVE READING: Evaluate

Ask if students think it was right that the Americans bought each tree separately. *(Possible responses: Yes, the Americans paid as a way of being good neighbors and showing respect for the traditions of Río en Medio, even though they have no legal obligation to do so; no, the Americans should not have to pay any more money—they bought the property legally and should not have to abide by other people's customs.)*

---

7 ▸

C ▸

plain. The children of the village were over-running their property. They came every day and played under the trees, built little play fences around them, and took blossoms. When they were spoken to, they only laughed and talked back good-naturedly in Spanish.

I sent a messenger up to the mountains for Don Anselmo. It took a week to arrange another meeting. When he arrived, he repeated his previous preliminary performance. He wore the same faded cutaway,[7] carried the same stick, and was accompanied by the boy again. He shook hands all around, sat down with the boy behind his chair, and talked about the weather. Finally I broached the subject. "Don Anselmo, about the ranch you sold to these people. They are good people and want to be your friends and neighbors always. When you sold to them, you signed a document, a deed, and in that deed you agreed to several things. One thing was that they were to have the complete possession of the property. Now, Don Anselmo, it seems that every day the children of the village overrun the orchard and spend most of their time there. We would like to know if you, as the most respected man in the village, could not stop them from doing so in order that these people may enjoy their new home more in peace."

8

Don Anselmo stood up. "We have all learned to love these Americans," he said, "because they are good people and good neighbors. I sold them my property because I knew they were good people, but I did not

sell them the trees in the orchard."

This was bad. "Don Anselmo," I pleaded, "when one signs a deed and sells real property, one sells also everything that grows on the land, and those trees, every one of them, are on the land and inside the boundaries of what you sold."

"Yes, I admit that," he said. "You know," he added, "I am the oldest man in the village. Almost everyone there is my relative, and all the children of Río en Medio are my *sobrinos* and *nietos*,[8] my descendants. Every time a child has been born in Río en Medio since I took possession of that house from my mother, I have planted a tree for that child. The trees in that orchard are not mine, *Señor*; they belong to the children of the village. Every person in Río en Medio born since the railroad came to Santa Fe owns a tree in that orchard. I did not sell the trees because I could not. They are not mine."

9

D ◂

There was nothing we could do. Legally we owned the trees, but the old man had been so generous, refusing what amounted to a fortune for him. It took most of the following winter to buy the trees, individually, from the descendants of Don Anselmo in the valley of Río en Medio. ❧

10

E ◂

---

7. **cutaway**: man's formal daytime coat.
8. *sobrinos* and *nietos* (sō brē′ nôs; nyā′ tôs) *Spanish*: nephews and nieces; grandchildren.

Comprehension Check

1. To whom does the old man sell his land? *(Americans)*

2. What do the new owners offer the gentleman when they discover the property extends farther than they thought? *(more money)*

3. How does the gentleman respond to the new offer? *(He is insulted and refuses it.)*

4. What problem do the new owners have after they move in? *(Village children constantly play on their property.)*

5. Why do the village children think they have a right to play in the orchard? *(The gentleman planted a tree for each child when he or she was born.)*

6. How do the new owners solve their problem? *(They pay each individual for his or her tree.)*

Bums in the Attic
from The House on Mango Street

SANDRA CISNEROS

I want a house on a hill like the ones with the gardens where Papa works. We go on Sundays, Papa's day off. I used to go. I don't anymore. You don't like to go out with us, Papa says. Getting too old? Getting too stuck-up, says Nenny. I don't tell them I am ashamed—all of us staring out the window like the hungry. I am tired of looking at what we can't have. When we win the lottery . . . Mama begins, and then I stop listening.

People who live on hills sleep so close to the stars they forget those of us who live too much on earth. They don't look down at all except to be content to live on hills. They have nothing to do with last week's garbage or fear of rats. Night comes. Nothing wakes them but the wind.

One day I'll own my own house, but I won't forget who I am or where I came from. Passing bums will ask, Can I come in? I'll offer them the attic, ask them to stay, because I know how it is to be without a house.

Some days after dinner, guests and I will sit in front of a fire. Floorboards will squeak upstairs. The attic grumble.

Rats? they'll ask.

Bums, I'll say, and I'll be happy.

HODGKIN'S HOUSE, CAPE ANN, MASSACHUSETTS   1928   Edward Hopper
Private collection. Courtesy, Hirschl and Adler Galleries, New York.

This piece is a reflection on the ideas in the main selection and is suggested for students' independent reading. Optional discussion questions follow.

1. What is the narrator's view of her family? *(Possible responses: She's ashamed of being poor; she feels embarrassed by them in public; she is tired of wishing for a better life for everyone, especially since it seems nearly impossible to reach.)*

2. How would the narrator turn the tables on her own fate? *(Possible responses: One day she hopes to have her own fine house; she plans to live differently than other rich people; she will be generous and kind to the poor.)*

3. What would the narrator in this story think of Don Anselmo's outlook? *(Possible responses: The narrator would identify with Don Anselmo's sensitivity for other people in his community; the narrator might put more emphasis on the value of a lovely house than Don Anselmo does.)*

Art Note
The lonely dignity of *Hodgkin's House, Cape Anne, Massachusetts* is typical of the melancholy art of the American artist Edward Hopper (1882–1967). In this painting of an elegant home, there is a quiet beauty, yet there is also a feeling of desolation. In Hopper's world nothing is so perfect that it does not take on the tones of sadness and loneliness. *Would you want to live in this house? Why or why not?*

ENCOURAGING INDEPENDENT READING

Student Response

Responding to Reading

1. Any response is valid.

2. Possible responses: Don Anselmo turned the tables on the Americans. He sold them his property, but he did not consider the orchard to be his, so they had to buy each tree separately. The community also turned the tables on the Americans. The community's concept of property won out in the end and earned money for many of its people.

3. Possible responses: Some students may claim they would make different choices than Don Anselmo and accept additional money for the land they own. Others may support him for adhering to his own code of beliefs, in which land and property are shared with family members.

4. Possible responses: The narrator of "Bums in the Attic" and Don Anselmo both believe in sharing their property with others. The old man shares his orchard with his descendants; the narrator will share her home with bums.

5. Any response is valid.

Challenge Question

Do you think Don Anselmo planned from the very beginning that the children would be paid for their trees? Explain. (Possible responses: Yes, he would want to help his young descendants and is careful to sell to buyers who are good people, so he probably expected them to honor his wishes; no, he may never even have thought about the trees since he never regarded them as his.)

Literary Concept: Narrator

This narrator is thoughtful, observant, and patient. As he negotiates between the two parties, he attempts to understand their different views. Although he seems to represent the law, he shows respect for Don Anselmo's values and views, and he speaks to him in Spanish.

Responding to Reading

First Impressions

1. Jot down words and phrases to describe Don Anselmo.

Second Thoughts

2. In your opinion, who turned the tables on whom in this story? Explain.

3. Do you agree with Don Anselmo's understanding of his rights and responsibilities as a landowner?

   Think about
   • why he refuses to accept more money for his land
   • why he feels the trees belong to the children
   • the ideas you wrote about earlier concerning land ownership

4. Read "Bums in the Attic," on page 215. How does the narrator's attitude toward ownership compare with Don Anselmo's?

Broader Connections

5. Do you think people such as Don Anselmo exist in the real world? Give examples of people you know to explain your opinion.

Literary Concept: Narrator

A **narrator** is a person who tells a story. A first-person narrator is usually a character in the story. He or she uses the pronoun I or we in telling the story. How would you describe the narrator of this story? How do you think he feels about Don Anselmo? Use evidence from the story to support your answer.

Writing Options

1. If you owned a tree in Don Anselmo's orchard, would you sell it to the Americans? Write your **opinion** and explain your reasoning.

2. Suppose the Americans were really angry about the children's use of their orchard. Write an angry **letter** to the citizens of Río en Medio, informing them that they have no right to be on the property.

Writing Options

The Writing Options are designed to meet varied student interests and abilities. Have each student choose one writing activity to complete.

Journal Update Encourage students to recall problems that they or someone they know has experienced with neighbors. Were the neighbors able to work things out by themselves? Were other people, such as the police, called in? What did students learn from these incidents?

Closure

Don Anselmo turns the tables on the American buyers so that he can fulfill his own sense of responsibility to his community and its traditions. Ask students to think about how other "table turners"—the narrator in "Revolt of the Evil Fairies" and Jamie Nutbeam in "Aunt Millicent"—would have judged Don Anselmo's actions. Would Jamie admire Don Anselmo's sense of family? Would the narrator in "Evil Fairies" respect his independence?

Poetry

old age sticks
E. E. CUMMINGS

The *Rebel*
MARI EVANS

*E*xamine What You Know   (Prior Knowledge)

Do you know someone who is controversial—someone who argues or says things that cause a dispute? With classmates, brainstorm a list of reasons that might explain why some people "cause so much trouble." Then list examples of people who might be labeled controversial.

*E*xpand Your Knowledge
(Building Background)

Early in this century, many well-known U.S. poets (including E. E. Cummings) rebelled against using traditional forms of poetry to express their images and ideas. These controversial new poets felt that the poetry written in the past was stiff and artificial. They believed that by breaking traditional poetic rules, poetry could sound more like personal thought and feeling. Cummings, for example, divided words into parts; used spaces, capital letters, and punctuation marks in new ways; invented new words; and gave old words new meanings. Many poets today, like Mari Evans, still write in this style.

*E*nrich Your Reading   (Reading Skill)

Reading Modern Poetry   Because modern poets often break lines or words into unfamiliar patterns, some modern poetry may seem confusing at first glance. Read and reread the poems slowly. In "old age sticks," decide whose words are *inside* the parentheses, and whose words are *outside* them. In "The Rebel," look for differences between the speaker and other people.

■ *Author biographies on Extend page*

OLD AGE STICKS / THE REBEL   217

Objectives

■ To understand and analyze two poems written in free verse

■ To enrich reading by examining modern poetry

■ To express understanding of the poems through a choice of writing forms, including a free-verse poem and a letter

Prereading/Motivation

Examine What You Know

Discussion Prompts   When people cause trouble, do they more often harm themselves or others? Is causing trouble ever a good thing to do? Why?

Expand Your Knowledge

Additional Background   The new poets wanted their poetry to sound more like everyday speech than like the high-flown language of earlier poetry. Many also insisted that poetry be based on ordinary life and personal experience instead of on the feelings and exploits of extraordinary or ideal people such as the heroes of the Light Brigade. Although some poets still use traditional poetic forms and subjects, most contemporary poetry is intended to be more intimate and immediate.

Enrich Your Reading

For Alternative Learning Styles   To exercise oral language skills, invite volunteers to read each poem aloud. Guide them to stress certain words or to pause in places that will help to make the poem more like everyday speech. This will also make the poems easier to understand.

JOURNAL WRITING IDEAS

■ Write about a time when you or someone else caused trouble and what happened as a result.

■ Discuss whether you prefer to express your feelings in poetry or prose, and why.

■ If you were to rebel, whom or what would you rebel against? Explain.

COLLABORATIVE LEARNING OPTIONS

Opportunities for collaborative learning include Options for Learning 1 and 2 (p. 221) and Cross-Curricular Projects (p. 221).

ADDITIONAL RESOURCES

Unit Two Resource Book
Reader's Guidesheet, p. 62
Reading Skills, p. 63
Literature Skills, p. 64
Vocabulary Connections, p. 65
Spelling Connections, p. 66
Comprehension Check Test, p. 67
Selection Test, p. 68

Technology and Enrichment

 Audiocassette Tape 1, Side 1

Thematic Link— Turning the Tables

In "old age sticks," youth turns the tables on repressive old age, but the tables are turned again when youth itself grows old. The speaker in "The Rebel," after a lifetime of troublemaking, envisions people at her funeral who suspect that she has turned the tables on them by only pretending to be dead.

old age sticks/THE REBEL **Teacher's Edition**   **217**

VOCABULARY PREVIEW

The focus of vocabulary study for this selection is using familiar words to understand new words. See *Unit Two Resource Book*, Vocabulary Connections, page 65

LIMITED ENGLISH PROFICIENCY

■ Use the Reader's Guidesheet, *Unit Two Resource Book*, page 62.

■ Because modern styles are employed in these poems, you may wish to read each poem aloud in order to clarify meaning.

★ The text annotation marked with a red star (2) may be particularly helpful for students with limited English proficiency.

TEXT ANNOTATIONS

1. ACTIVE READING: Question
Ask students what is unusual about the first stanza. *(Possible responses: lines of only two or three words; no formal sentences; unusual capitalization and punctuation, especially parentheses; use of ampersand)*

2. LITERARY CONCEPT: Free Verse
Help **clarify** for students the fairly straightforward meaning "hidden" inside parentheses and alongside ampersands: "Old age sticks up Keep Off signs and youth yanks them down. Old age cries No Trespassing and youth laughs." ★

Responding to Reading

1. Any response is valid.

2. **Possible responses:** Youth rebels against old age but can't prevent itself from getting old too; despite its warnings, old age can't stop youth from being rebellious.

3. **Possible responses:** Yes, because youths tend to rebel against adults; yes, because youths think they are different but will eventually become like those they rebel against; no, because youths are not as opposed to adults or as rebellious as the poet suggests.

4. **Possible responses:** I would have praised him for his bold new style; I would have criticized him for being too hard to understand.

old age sticks

E. E. CUMMINGS

1
old age sticks
up Keep
Off
signs)&

A ▶
5   youth yanks them
down(old
age
cries No

2
Tres)&(pas)
10 youth laughs
B ▶
(sing
old age

scolds Forbid
den Stop
15 Must
n't Don't

&)youth goes
right on
gr
20 owing old   ◀ C

---

*R*esponding to Reading

First Impressions of "old age sticks"

1. What words and phrases from the poem stand out in your mind? Jot these down in your journal.

Second Thoughts on "old age sticks"

2. What do you think the last stanza means?

3. Do you agree with the ideas the poet expresses about old age and youth? Explain.

4. If you had been a critic in the 1920s reviewing Cummings's controversial new poetry, would you have criticized or praised him? Why?

218   UNIT TWO   TURNING THE TABLES

Guided Reading for Less-Proficient Students

These questions can help guide students through the reading. Ask each question at the point of the selection where the capital letter and arrow appear in the margin. In addition, you may wish to use appropriate Active Reading annotations.

A. What does youth do to the Keep Off signs that old age puts up? *(yanks them down)* Recalling

B. How does youth react when old age warns it not to trespass? *(Youth laughs.)* Recalling

C. What does youth keep doing? *(growing old)* Recalling

D. What event does the speaker in "The Rebel" imagine? *(her own funeral)* Recalling

E. What does the speaker expect curiosity seekers to do at her funeral? *(to wonder if she is dead or just causing trouble)* Recalling

3 | The *Rebel*

MARI EVANS

When I
die
I'm sure
I will have a
5 Big Funeral . . .   ◄ D
Curiosity
seekers . . .
coming to see
if I
10 am really   4
Dead . . .
or just
trying to make
Trouble . . .   ◄ E

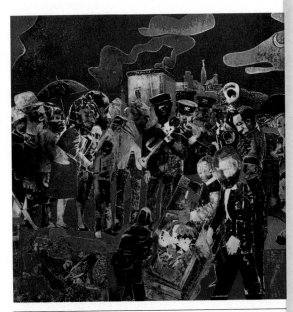

NEW ORLEANS FAREWELL   1974   Romare Bearden
Courtesy, The Estate of Romare Bearden and
George and Joyce Wein Collection.

THE REBEL   219

3. ACTIVE READING: Predict
Ask students to predict what a poem with this title might be about.

4. ACTIVE READING: Review
Ask students why people go to funerals. *(Possible responses: to show sympathy for the family or respect for the dead)* Then ask what is unusual about the motives of those who go to the speaker's funeral. *(Possible responses: They go because they're curious, not out of sympathy or respect.)*

ENCOURAGING INDEPENDENT READING

I Am a Black Woman, poems by Mari Evans

No Thanks, poems by E. E. Cummings

Tulips and Chimneys, poems by E. E. Cummings

Where Is All the Music? poems by Mari Evans

Comprehension Check

✓ 1. Between whom is the conflict in "old age sticks"? *(old and young people)*

2. How does youth react to the rules and warnings given by old age? *(Youth laughs and ignores them.)*

3. What does youth keep on doing in spite of old age? *(growing old)*

4. What event does the speaker in "The Rebel" discuss? *(her funeral)*

5. Why does the speaker think most people will attend? *(They'll be curious to see if she's really dead or just tricking them.)*

Student Response

Responding to Reading

1. Any response is valid.

2. Possible responses: She seems to have a wide reputation as a rebel or troublemaker; she is the kind of individual who surprises people.

3. Possible responses: "Big Funeral" might indicate a particular kind of highly public ceremony, such as a funeral for a famous or an infamous person; "Curiosity" may suggest that the speaker herself or himself is a curiosity; "Dead" may be for emphasis, *really* dead, as opposed to only causing trouble; "Trouble" could mean that the speaker wants to cause or has already caused an uproar in the community.

Comparing the Poems

4. Possible responses: Youth and the rebel both cause controversy. They are alike in that they are perceived by others as threatening and upsetting. They are different in that the rebel is a single individual who has done something controversial, whereas youth is apparently only behaving according to nature, with all other youths.

5. Possible responses: Despite its disdain for old age, youth cannot help but grow old itself, so time turns the tables on youth. The speaker of "The Rebel" turns the tables on enemies by making them wonder even at the funeral if he or she is really dead; the speaker is so rebellious that he or she might turn the tables even on death itself.

Literary Concept: Free Verse

The line lengths in these free verse poems are much shorter than those in traditional poems. Punctuation and capitalization are used very differently in free verse; complete sentences and regular grammar are often not used. The poems sound as if someone is thinking out loud or speaking naturally.

Writing Options

The Writing Options are designed to meet varied student interests and abilities. Have each student choose one writing activity to complete.

Responding to Reading

First Impressions of "The Rebel"

1. What is your impression of the speaker? Jot down your thoughts in your notebook or journal.

Second Thoughts on "The Rebel"

2. What do you learn about the speaker from this poem? Give evidence from the poem for your answer.

   Think about
   • why the speaker believes she will have a "Big Funeral"
   • what kind of person attracts "Curiosity seekers"

3. Note which words are capitalized in the poem. Why do you think Evans did this?

Comparing the Poems

4. Who causes controversy in the two poems? Explain how those people are alike and how they are different.

5. In what way do you think the tables are turned in these poems?

Literary Concept: Free Verse

Poetry without regular rhyme, rhythm, or line length is called **free verse.** When you read these two poems aloud, you will notice the absence of regular rhyme and rhythm. What other differences do you notice between these poems and more traditional poems, like "The Charge of the Light Brigade" on page 86?

Writing Options

1. Look at your list of controversial people. Write a **free-verse poem** about a person from your list or a controversial event. You may want to experiment with a variety of nontraditional forms as Evans and Cummings do.

2. As a youth, what would you say to old age? Write a **letter** stating your complaints, praise, or other feelings you might have about old people in general or about the process of aging.

Closure

Conflicts between generations appear in several of the selections in this subunit. Encourage students to interview people of various ages, from teenagers to the elderly, to discover reasons for these conflicts. As youth matures, and adults grow older, the tables turn naturally. Challenge students to name other ways generations turn the tables on each other.

Options for Learning (Multimodal/Cross-Curricular Activities)

1 • **Oral Interpretation** Choose either poem to read aloud. Try emphasizing different words and varying your voice tones. Read the poem to your classmates, and let them compare your interpretation with the interpretations of other readers.

2 • **Free-Thinking Poets** Look through poetry books for other poems that have forms different from those of traditional poems. Share the most interesting with your class.

Mari Evans

Mari Evans writes poetry, political articles, theater pieces, literary criticism, and short stories. She has received many honors, including a National Endowment for the Arts Creative Writing Award.

After college, Evans wrote for a weekly paper owned by African Americans. She has also worked as a research associate, a director of publications, and an editor. She has taught at Indiana, Northwestern, Purdue, and Cornell Universities and produced and directed a TV series, *The Black Experience.*

Evans learned, from Langston Hughes among others, that writing is a craft that "one learns by doing." She revises endlessly, and even regards a printed poem as still in process.

E. **E. Cummings** 1894-1962

E. E. Cummings wrote a poem every day from the time he was eight until he was twenty-two. Critics either loved or hated his poetry from the time his first book, *Tulips and Chimneys,* was published in 1923. Cummings won many honors and prizes for poetry. At Harvard University he helped start a poetry society.

During World War I, Cummings volunteered as an ambulance driver in France. Later, however, he was imprisoned in a French prisoner-of-war camp, mainly because he refused to say he hated the Germans. He wrote a novel about his experiences and then joined the U.S. Army. After World War I, Cummings studied painting in Paris. There he established a routine he followed most of his life: painting in the afternoon and writing poetry and plays at night. In 1930 he was drawn to the lively artistic and intellectual life of New York's Greenwich Village, where he settled.

Options for Learning
These activities suit a variety of learning styles and modes of expression

Collaborative Learning Options
See Options 1 and 2.

1. Oral Interpretation Suggest that students practice with a tape recorder, trying different interpretations before choosing one to perform.

2. Free-Thinking Poets Besides poetry anthologies in the school or local library, students may also look in magazines that publish poetry, such as *Poetry, The Atlantic,* or *The New Yorker.*

Mari Evans

■ **More About the Author** Evans says that she chose to be a poet at the age of ten, when she read Langston Hughes's *The Weary Blues* and thought, "Why, he's writing about me!" She later met and worked with Hughes. Her work has been translated into six languages. Her birthdate does not appear here because she refuses to reveal her age.

■ **Other Works** Poetry: *A Dark and Splendid Mass;* Play: *River of My Song*

■ **Awards** Indiana University Writers' Conference award, Black Academy of Arts and Letters poetry award, both for *I Am a Black Woman*

E .E. Cummings

■ **More About the Author** Cummings's avoidance of capital letters began when he was at Harvard, when some of his work accidentally was published with erroneous capitalization. He liked how it looked so much that he used nonstandard capitalization in other poems.

■ **Other Works** Poetry: *The Complete Poems, 1913–1962;* Play: *him;* Journal: *The Enormous Room*

■ **Awards** National Book Award special citation for *Poems: 1923–1954;* Bollingen Prize in Poetry, 1957.

Cross-Curricular Projects

Art Ask students to cut out magazine pictures that depict youth and old age and to paste them on a large sheet of paper to create a collage. Students should then caption each picture and title the collage.

Math Have students research life expectancy statistics for men and women in the United States over the past century. Ask students to create a bar or line graph showing the changes in average life expectancy.

Social Studies Ask volunteers to research and report on the funeral customs of different peoples of the world, including ethnic and religious groups.

Music Have students choose appropriate music to accompany their reading a modern poem aloud to the class. Later, invite readers to explain why they selected the music they did and to describe how it affected the mood of the poem.

Objectives

- To understand and analyze an excerpt from an autobiography

- To understand and appreciate the use of dialect

- To enrich reading by making predictions

- To express understanding of the work through a choice of writing forms, including a ballad, a persuasive essay, a memo, and a story

Prereading/Motivation

Examine What You Know

Discussion Prompts What inspired these pranks? How did you or the other students feel while doing them and afterwards? Did these pranks have any long-lasting consequences? What made these adventures or misadventures especially memorable?

Expand Your Knowledge

Additional Background Students in preparatory schools were expected to go on to attend public schools. Public schools in Great Britain, which are equivalent to grades 7–12 in U.S. schools, are actually privately funded. These exclusive schools, some of which are centuries old, serve only 6 percent of British children, most of them boys, and have been the training ground for members of Parliament and leaders in every field. Roald Dahl later attended Rexton Public School, which proved much stricter than the Llandaff preparatory school.

Thematic Link— Turning the Tables

Roald and his friends decide to get even with the filthy, mean-spirited owner of a candy store by playing a prank on her. They briefly revel in their glory until fear and the adult authorities turn the tables on them.

Nonfiction

from Boy
Tales of Childhood
ROALD DAHL (rōō' äl däl)

Examine What You Know
(Prior Knowledge)
Childhood pranks take many forms—funny or not so funny, harmless or harmful. In small groups, describe your own pranks or ones you have heard about, and explain what the results of the pranks were.

Expand Your Knowledge
(Building Background)
Roald Dahl, a well-known author of books for young people, was also the author of many real-life schoolboy pranks. This selection from his **autobiography** begins when he is seven and a student at Llandaff Cathedral School in Wales. This school was what the British call a preparatory school, designed to prepare students for an eventual university education. Students had to pay tuition and were given rigorous academic training. These schools, many of which still operate today, were very costly; those who attended them usually had prestige and privilege. The headmaster and teachers were very strict, and any boys caught playing pranks could look forward to corporal punishment—that is, a beating.

Write Before You Read   (Journal Writing)
Below are ten terms that relate to this selection. Use these clues and your imagination to predict, in one or two paragraphs, what might happen in the selection. After you read, compare your predictions with the actual events.

1. boys	5. filthy fingers	9. glory
2. sweet jars	6. dead mouse	10. headmaster
3. small treasures	7. loose floorboard	
4. Mrs. Pratchett	8. prank	

- *Author biography on Extend page*

MORE JOURNAL WRITING IDEAS

- Does the idea of getting even with someone make a prank more fun? Explain.

- Do you enjoy taking part in pranks or hearing about them, or do you tend to disapprove of them? Why?

COLLABORATIVE LEARNING OPTIONS
Opportunities for collaborative learning include Examine What You Know (p. 222), Options for Learning 1, 3, and 4 (p. 236), and Cross-Curricular Projects (p. 236).

ADDITIONAL RESOURCES
Unit Two Resource Book
Reader's Guidesheet, p. 69
Reading Skills, p. 70
Literature Skills, p. 71
Vocabulary Connections, p. 72
Spelling Connections, p. 73
Comprehension and Vocabulary Check Tests, p. 74
Selection Test, pp. 75–76

from Boy
Tales of Childhood

ROALD DAHL

The Bicycle and the Sweetshop

When I was seven my mother decided I should leave kindergarten and go to a proper boy's school. By good fortune, there existed a well-known preparatory school for boys about a mile from our house. It was called Llandaff Cathedral School, and it stood right under the shadow of Llandaff cathedral. Like the cathedral, the school is still there and still flourishing.

But here again, I can remember very little about the two years I attended Llandaff Cathedral School, between the ages of seven and nine. Only two moments remain clearly in my mind. The first lasted not more than five seconds, but I will never forget it.

It was my first term, and I was walking home alone across the village green after school when suddenly one of the senior twelve-year-old boys came riding full speed down the road on his bicycle about twenty yards away from me. The road was on a hill and the boy was going down the slope; and as he flashed by, he started backpedaling very quickly so that the freewheeling mechanism of his bike made a loud whirring sound. At the same time, he took his hands off the handlebars and folded them casually across his chest. I stopped dead and stared after him. How wonderful he was! How swift and brave and graceful in his long trousers with bicycle clips around them and his scarlet schoolcap at a jaunty angle on his head! One day, I told myself, one glorious day I will have a bike like that, and I will wear long trousers with bicycle clips, and my school cap will sit jaunty on my head, and I will go whizzing down the hill pedaling backwards with no hands on the handlebars!

I promise you that if somebody had caught me by the shoulder at that moment and said to me, "What is your greatest wish in life little boy? What is your absolute ambition? To be a doctor? A fine musician? A painter? A writer? Or the Lord Chancellor?" I would have answered without hesitation that my only ambition, my hope, my longing was to have a bike like that and to go whizzing down the hill with no hands on the handlebars. It would be fabulous. It made me tremble just to think about it.

◄ A

My second and only other memory of Llandaff Cathedral School is extremely

| Words to Know and Use | **flourish** (flur′ ish) *v.* to thrive; grow vigorously |

223

Guided Reading for Less-Proficient Students

These questions can help guide students through the reading. Ask each question at the point of the selection where the capital letter and arrow appear in the margin. In addition, you may wish to use appropriate Active Reading annotations.

A. What have you learned about the main character? *(He is a boy about seven, a new student at a preparatory school; he admires an older boy who rides a bike without holding the handlebars.)* Summarizing

B. Where do Roald and his friends stop on the way to and from school? *(the sweetshop)* Recalling

C. Who is the owner of the sweetshop and how does she treat the boys? *(a nasty old woman, who treats the boys with suspicion)* Recalling

D. What is the most disgusting thing about Mrs. Pratchett? *(her filthy hands)* Recalling

Continued on page 224

Teaching Strategies

VOCABULARY PREVIEW
These vocabulary words are defined at the bottom of the selection pages on which they appear.

cauldron a large kettle

flourish to thrive; grow vigorously

glimmer to give off a dim light

loathsome disgusting

malignant wishing or causing evil

sullen gloomy

venom hatred

LIMITED ENGLISH PROFICIENCY
■ Use the Reader's Guidesheet, *Unit Two Resource Book,* page 69.

■ In this selection, Mrs. Pratchett speaks in a dialect. You may want to read certain passages aloud to help students.

★ Text annotations marked with a red star (3, 8, 11, 13, 14, 16, 21, 22, 24) may be particularly helpful for students with limited English proficiency.

TEXT ANNOTATIONS
1. LITERARY CONCEPT: Autobiography
Dahl's father had died of pneumonia a few years before. His mother, who was Norwegian, was attempting to fulfill a promise made to her husband, also Norwegian, that their children would be educated in Great Britain. Dahl's father believed British schools superior to Norwegian ones.

2. ACTIVE READING: Connect
Invite students to share similar experiences in their own lives. Who inspired their deepest admiration and greatest ambitions when they were seven years old? *(Any response is valid.)*

3. CULTURAL SIDELIGHT
The Lord Chancellor, a leader in Parliament, presides over the House of Lords and is a member of the cabinet. The House of Lords reviews laws passed by the House of Commons and serves as Great Britain's highest court of appeals. ★

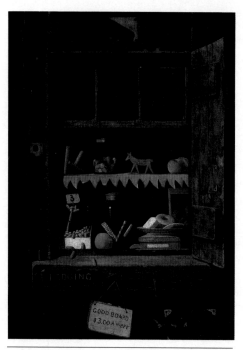

THE POOR MAN'S STORE 1885 John Frederick Peto
Museum of Fine Arts, Boston. Gift of Maxim Karolik to the M. and M. Karolik Collection of American Paintings, 1815-1865.

bizarre. It happened a little over a year later, when I was just nine. By then I had made some friends, and when I walked to school in the mornings, I would start out alone but would pick up four other boys of my own age along the way. After school was over, the same four boys and I would set out together across the village green and through the village itself, heading for home. On the way to school and on the way back, we always passed the sweetshop. No we

didn't; we never passed it. We always stopped. We lingered outside its rather small window, gazing in at the big glass jars full of Bull's-eyes and Old-fashioned Humbugs and Strawberry Bonbons and Glacier Mints and Acid Drops and Pear Drops and Lemon Drops and all the rest of them. Each of us received sixpence[1] a week for pocket money, and whenever there was any money in our pockets, we would all troop in together to buy a pennyworth of this or that. My own favorites were Sherbet Suckers and Licorice Bootlaces.

One of the other boys, whose name was Thwaites, told me I should never eat Licorice Bootlaces. Thwaites's father, who was a doctor, had said that they were made from rats' blood. The father had given his young son a lecture about Licorice Bootlaces when he had caught him eating one in bed. "Every rat catcher in the country," the father had said, "takes his rats to the Licorice Bootlace Factory, and the manager pays tuppence[2] for each rat. Many a rat catcher has become a millionaire by selling his dead rats to the factory."

"But how do they turn the rats into licorice?" the young Thwaites had asked his father.

"They wait until they've got ten thousand rats," the father had answered, "then they dump them all into a huge shiny steel <u>cauldron</u> and boil them up for several hours. Two men stir the bubbling cauldron with

---

1. **sixpence** (siks' pəns): in England, six pennies.
2. **tuppence** (tup' əns): in England, two pennies.

Words to Know and Use | **cauldron** (kôl' drən) *n.* a large kettle

224

long poles, and in the end they have a thick, steaming rat stew. After that, a cruncher is lowered into the cauldron to crunch the bones, and what's left is a pulpy substance called rat mash."

"Yes, but how do they turn that into Licorice Bootlaces, Daddy?" the young Thwaites had asked, and this question, according to Thwaites, had caused his father to pause and think for a few moments before he answered it. At last he had said, "The two men who were doing the stirring with the long poles now put on their Wellington boots[3] and climb into the cauldron and shovel the hot rat mash out onto a concrete floor. Then they run a steamroller over it several times to flatten it out. What is left looks rather like a gigantic black pancake, and all they have to do after that is to wait for it to cool and to harden so they can cut it up into strips to make the Bootlaces. Don't ever eat them," the father had said. "If you do, you'll get ratitis."

"What is ratitis, Daddy?" young Thwaites had asked.

"All the rats that the rat catchers catch are poisoned with rat poison," the father had said. "It's the rat poison that gives you ratitis."

"Yes, but what happens to you when you catch it?" young Thwaites had asked.

"Your teeth become very sharp and pointed," the father had answered. "And a short stumpy tail grows out of your back just above your bottom. There is no cure for ratitis. I ought to know. I'm a doctor."

We all enjoyed Thwaites's story, and we made him tell it to us many times on our walks to and from school. But it didn't stop any of us except Thwaites from buying Licorice Bootlaces. At two for a penny they were the best value in the shop. A Bootlace, in case you haven't had the pleasure of handling one, is not round. It's like a flat black tape about half an inch wide. You buy it rolled up in a coil, and in those days it used to be so long that when you unrolled it and held one end at arm's length above your head, the other end touched the ground.

Sherbet Suckers were also two a penny. Each Sucker consisted of a yellow cardboard tube filled with sherbet powder, and there was a hollow licorice straw sticking out of it. (Rat's blood again, young Thwaites would warn us, pointing at the licorice straw.) You sucked the sherbet up through the straw, and when it was finished, you ate the licorice. They were delicious, those Sherbet Suckers. The sherbet fizzed in your mouth, and if you knew how to do it, you could make white froth come out of your nostrils and pretend you were throwing a fit.

Gobstoppers, costing a penny each, were enormous hard, round balls the size of small tomatoes. One Gobstopper would provide about an hour's worth of nonstop sucking, and if you took it out of your mouth and inspected it every five minutes or so, you would find it had changed color. There was something fascinating about the way it went from pink to blue to green to yellow. We used to wonder how in the world the Gobstopper Factory managed to achieve this magic. "How *does* it happen?" we would ask each other. "How *can* they make it keep changing color?"

---

3. **Wellington boots:** high, rubber boots.

6

7

226

8. VOCABULARY: Context Clues

Challenge students to find the word that names a kind of anesthetic and the phrases that are clues to what an anesthetic is. (*chloroform; "could put you to sleep for hours at a stretch"*) Have students confirm the meanings of *anesthetic* and *chloroform* by looking up their definitions. ★

9. LITERARY CONCEPT:
Characterization

Ask students to describe the kind of person Thwaites is. (*Possible responses: Thwaites is clever, imaginative, and articulate—a good storyteller; he enjoys gory details, is never at a loss for ideas, and sees himself as an expert.*)

10. ACTIVE READING: Evaluate

Ask students if they think the author has described the boys realistically. (*Possible responses: Yes, Roald and his friends are like real children—they are curious and mischievous, have vivid imaginations, enjoy disgusting things, and dislike bossy adults; no, the boys are exaggerated—their reactions are too extreme and their stories too elaborate to be realistic.*)

11. LITERARY CONCEPT: Dialect

Some students may have difficulty understanding Mrs. Pratchett's speech. First, ask a volunteer to explain the idiom "fork out" and to suggest another idiom with the same meaning. (*Possible responses: "to hand over some money"; "pay out"*) Then read the passage aloud. ★

"It's your spit that does it," young Thwaites proclaimed. As the son of a doctor, he considered himself to be an authority on all things that had to do with the body. He could tell us about scabs and when they were ready to be picked off. He knew why a black eye was blue and why blood was red. "It's your spit that makes a Gobstopper change color," he kept insisting. When we asked him to elaborate on this theory, he answered, "You wouldn't understand it if I did tell you."

Pear Drops were exciting because they had a dangerous taste. They smelled of nail varnish, and they froze the back of your throat. All of us were warned against eating them, and the result was that we ate them more than ever.

Then there was a hard brown lozenge called the Tonsil Tickler. The Tonsil Tickler tasted and smelled very strongly of chloroform. We had not the slightest doubt that these things were saturated in the dreaded anesthetic which, as Thwaites had many times pointed out to us, could put you to sleep for hours at a stretch. "If my father has to saw off somebody's leg," he said, "he pours chloroform onto a pad, and the person sniffs it and goes to sleep, and my father saws his leg off without him even feeling it."

"But why do they put it into sweets and sell them to us?" we asked him.

You might think a question like this would have baffled Thwaites. But Thwaites was never baffled. "My father says Tonsil Ticklers were invented for dangerous prisoners in jail," he said. "They give them one with each meal, and the chloroform makes them sleepy and stops them rioting."

"Yes," we said, "but why sell them to children?"

"It's a plot," Thwaites said. "A grown-up plot to keep us quiet."

The sweetshop in Llandaff in the year 1923 was the very center of our lives. To us, it was what a bar is to a drunk or a church is to a bishop. Without it, there would have been little to live for. But it had one terrible drawback, this sweetshop. The woman who owned it was a horror. We hated her, and we had good reason for doing so.

> ## We hated her, and we had good reason for doing so.

Her name was Mrs. Pratchett. She was a small skinny old hag with a moustache on her upper lip and a mouth as sour as a green gooseberry. She never smiled. She never welcomed us when we went in, and the only times she spoke were when she said things like, "I'm watchin' you, so keep yer thievin' fingers off them chocolates!" Or "I don't want you in 'ere just to look around! Either you *forks* out or you *gets* out!"

But by far the most <u>loathsome</u> thing about Mrs. Pratchett was the filth that clung around her. Her apron was gray and greasy. Her blouse had bits of breakfast all over it, toast crumbs and tea stains and splotches of dried egg yolk. It was her hands, however, that disturbed us most. They were disgust-

Words to Know and Use	**loathsome** (lōth′ səm) *adj.* deserving of hate; disgusting

---

Looking at Style

Have students read the following descriptions by Roald Dahl, then answer the questions and complete the directions that follow.

■ She was a small skinny old hag with a moustache on her upper lip and a mouth as sour as a green gooseberry. (p. 226)

■ Her blouse had bits of breakfast all over it, toast crumbs and tea stains and splotches of dried egg yolk. (p. 226)

1. What do these descriptions have in common?

2. What impression do you form of Mrs. Pratchett as a result of the details that Dahl uses to describe her?

3. Describe a person whom you know, using details of his or her physical appearance. The details should suggest your favorable or unfavorable impression of the person .

ing. They were black with dirt and grime. They looked as though they had been putting lumps of coal on the fire all day long. And do not forget, please, that it was these very hands and fingers that she plunged into the sweet-jars when we asked for a pennyworth of Treacle Toffee or Wine Gums or Nut Clusters or whatever. There were precious few health laws in those days, and nobody, least of all Mrs. Pratchett, ever thought of using a little shovel for getting out the sweets as they do today. The mere sight of her grimy right hand with its black fingernails digging an ounce of Chocolate Fudge out of a jar would have caused a starving tramp to go running from the shop. But not us. Sweets were our lifeblood. We would have put up with far worse than that to get them. So we simply stood and watched in <u>sullen</u> silence while this disgusting old woman stirred around inside the jars with her foul fingers.

The other thing we hated Mrs. Pratchett for was her meanness. Unless you spent a whole sixpence all in one go, she wouldn't give you a bag. Instead you got your sweets twisted up in a small piece of newspaper which she tore off a pile of old *Daily Mirrors* lying on the counter.

So you can well understand that we had it in for Mrs. Pratchett in a big way, but we didn't quite know what to do about it. Many schemes were put forward, but none of them was any good. None of them, that is, until suddenly, one memorable afternoon, we found the dead mouse.

The Great Mouse Plot

My four friends and I had come across a loose floorboard at the back of the classroom, and when we prized it up with the blade of a pocketknife, we discovered a big hollow space underneath. This, we decided, would be our secret hiding place for sweets and other small treasures such as conkers[4] and monkey nuts and birds' eggs. Every afternoon, when the last lesson was over, the five of us would wait until the classroom had emptied, then we would lift up the floorboard and examine our secret hoard, perhaps adding to it or taking something away.

One day, when we lifted it up, we found a dead mouse lying among our treasures. It was an exciting discovery. Thwaites took it out by its tail and waved it in front of our faces. "What shall we do with it?" he cried.

"It stinks!" someone shouted. "Throw it out of the window quick!"

"Hold on a tick," I said. "Don't throw it away."

Thwaites hesitated. They all looked at me.

When writing about oneself, one must strive to be truthful. Truth is more important than modesty. I must tell you, therefore, that it was I and I alone who had the idea for the great and daring Mouse Plot. We all have our moments of brilliance and glory, and this was mine.

"Why don't we," I said, "slip it into one of

---

4. conkers: horse chestnuts threaded on a string used in a boys' game in England.

| *Words to Know and Use* | **sullen** (sul' ən) *adj.* gloomy; acting moody |

227

12. ACTIVE READING: Connect
Have students tell how they would react to Mrs. Pratchett's filthiness. Would they be able to eat candy she picked out for them? *(Any response is valid.)*

13. VOCABULARY: Multiple Meanings
Have students use context clues to define *meanness* in this paragraph. *("stinginess," "cheapness")* Invite students to share other meanings of this word. *("cruelty," "selfishness")* ★

14. VOCABULARY: Idioms
Challenge students to define *tick* on the basis of **context clues** and use their **prior knowledge** to speculate about the origin of this idiom. *("a moment"; from the ticktock of a clock)* Point out other idioms on this page—such as "all in one go", and "had it in for"—and have students use context clues to determine their meanings. *("all at once"; "wanted to harm or get even with")* ★

15. ACTIVE READING: Question
Ask students what other motivation the boys might have for suggesting that Roald be the one to put the mouse in the jar. (Possible responses: If they are caught, he will be blamed; they're afraid to take the risk.)

16. LANGUAGE: Briticisms
Point out the boys' compliment "Well done you!" and ask how it is different from what Americans would say. (Americans would not use the pronoun at the end.) ★

Mrs. Pratchett's jars of sweets? Then when she puts her dirty hand in to grab a handful, she'll grab a stinky dead mouse instead."

The other four stared at me in wonder. Then, as the sheer genius of the plot began to sink in, they all started grinning. They slapped me on the back. They cheered me and danced around the classroom. "We'll do it today!" they cried. "We'll do it on the way home! *You* had the idea," they said to me, "so *you* can be the one to put the mouse in the jar."

Thwaites handed me the mouse. I put it into my trouser pocket. Then the five of us left the school, crossed the village green and headed for the sweetshop. We were tremendously jazzed up. We felt like a gang of desperados setting out to rob a train or blow up the sheriff's office.

"Make sure you put it into a jar which is used often," somebody said.

"I'm putting it in Gobstoppers," I said. "The Gobstopper jar is never behind the counter."

"I've got a penny," Thwaites said, "so I'll ask for one Sherbet Sucker and one Bootlace. And while she turns away to get them, you slip the mouse in quickly with the Gobstoppers."

Thus everything was arranged. We were strutting a little as we entered the shop. We were the victors now, and Mrs. Pratchett was the victim. She stood behind the counter, and her small <u>malignant</u> pig-eyes watched us suspiciously as we came forward.

"One Sherbet Sucker, please," Thwaites said to her, holding out his penny.

I kept to the rear of the group, and when I saw Mrs. Pratchett turn her head away for a couple of seconds to fish a Sherbet Sucker out of the box, I lifted the heavy glass lid of the Gobstopper jar and dropped the mouse in. Then I replaced the lid as silently as possible. My heart was thumping like mad, and my hands had gone all sweaty.

"And one Bootlace, please," I heard Thwaites saying. When I turned around, I saw Mrs. Pratchett holding out the Bootlace in her filthy fingers.

"I don't want all the lot of you troopin' in 'ere if only one of you is buyin'," she screamed at us. "Now beat it! Go on, get out!"

As soon as we were outside, we broke into a run. "Did you do it?" they shouted at me.

"Of course I did!" I said.

"Well done you!" they cried. "What a super show!"

I felt like a hero. I *was* a hero. It was marvelous to be so popular.

Mr. Coombes

The flush of triumph over the dead mouse was carried forward to the next morning as we all met again to walk to school.

"Let's go in and see if it's still in the jar," somebody said as we approached the sweetshop.

"Don't," Thwaites said firmly. "It's too

Words to Know and Use	**malignant** (mə lig′ nənt) *adj.* wishing or causing evil; very harmful

dangerous. Walk past as though nothing has happened."

As we came level with the shop, we saw a cardboard notice hanging on the door.

We stopped and stared. We had never known the sweetshop to be closed at this time in the morning, even on Sundays.

"What's happened?" we asked each other. "What's going on?"

We pressed our faces against the window and looked inside. Mrs. Pratchett was nowhere to be seen.

"Look!" I cried. "The Gobstopper jar's gone! It's not on the shelf! There's a gap where it used to be!"

"It's on the floor!" someone said. "It's smashed to bits, and there's Gobstoppers everywhere!"

"There's the mouse!" someone else shouted.

We could see it all, the huge glass jar smashed to smithereens with the dead mouse lying in the wreckage and hundreds of many-colored Gobstoppers littering the floor.

G ▶

"She got such a shock when she grabbed hold of the mouse that she dropped everything," somebody was saying.

"But why didn't she sweep it all up and open the shop?" I asked.

Nobody answered me.

We turned away and walked toward the school. All of a sudden we had begun to feel slightly uncomfortable. There was something not quite right about the shop being closed. Even Thwaites was unable to offer a reasonable explanation. We became silent. There was a faint scent of danger in the air now. Each one of us had caught a whiff of it. Alarm bells were beginning to ring faintly in our ears.

17

After a while, Thwaites broke the silence. "She must have got one heck of a shock," he said. He paused. We all looked at him, wondering what wisdom the great medical authority was going to come out with next.

"After all," he went on, "to catch hold of a dead mouse when you're expecting to catch hold of a Gobstopper must be a pretty frightening experience. Don't you agree?"

Nobody answered him.

"Well now," Thwaites went on, "when an old person like Mrs. Pratchett suddenly gets a very big shock, I suppose you know what happens next?"

"What?" we said. "What happens?"

"You ask my father," Thwaites said. "He'll tell you."

"You tell us," we said.

"It gives her a heart attack," Thwaites announced. "Her heart stops beating, and

18

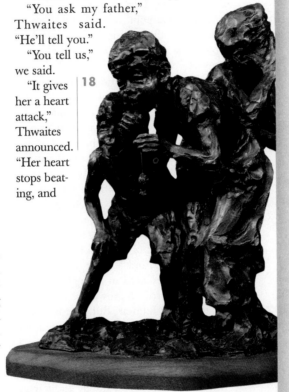

Autobiography
Ask how the author adds to the suspense in this section. (Possible response: He uses sensory details to make the danger seem real—details that appeal to the sense of smell; like "scent of danger", and "whiff," and details that appeal to the sense of hearing, like "alarm bells,"and "ring.")

Art Note

"I think that most artists have a constant drive to create but are plagued with the frustration of interruptions," says the artist Terry Mimnaugh (1954–). This handicap does not seem to have interfered with her inspiration, especially in *The Apprentice*, a bronze sculpture that seems to burst with life. The heavy metal does not limit the vitality of the figures. *Which form of art do you find more interesting—painting or sculpture? Why?*

18. SCIENCE SIDELIGHT

A heart attack is caused by a blockage in a coronary artery, interfering with the flow of blood to the heart. Thwaites's point that a great shock can bring on a heart attack is a valid one. Such a shock, however, can lead to a heart attack only in a person whose arteries are already diseased.

19. ACTIVE READING: Review
Ask students how they think Roald feels now. *(Possible responses: He is very frightened; he believes that Thwaites's theory may be correct.)*

20. ACTIVE READING: Connect
Ask students whether Dahl's statement about how children perceive adults matches their own memories of childhood. *(Any response is valid.)*

21. VOCABULARY: Idiom
Have students use context clues and prior knowledge to figure out the meaning of "was for the high jump." *("was about to receive a severe punishment")* ★

19

she's dead in five seconds."

For a moment or two my own heart stopped beating. Thwaites pointed a finger at me and said darkly, "I'm afraid you've killed her."

I'm afraid you've killed her.

"*Me?*" I cried. "Why just *me?*"

H ▶ "It was *your* idea," he said. "And what's more, *you* put the mouse in."

All of a sudden, I was a murderer.

At exactly that point, we heard the school bell ringing in the distance, and we had to gallop the rest of the way so as not to be late for prayers.

Prayers were held in the Assembly Hall. We all perched in rows on wooden benches, while the teachers sat up on the platform in armchairs, facing us. The five of us scrambled into our places just as the Headmaster marched in, followed by the rest of the staff.

The Headmaster is the only teacher at Llandaff Cathedral School that I can remember, and for a reason you will soon discover, I can remember him very clearly indeed. His name was Mr. Coombes, and I have a picture in my mind of a giant of a man with a face like a ham and a mass of rusty-colored hair that sprouted in a tangle all over the top of his head. All grown-ups appear as **20** giants to small children. But Headmasters (and policemen) are the biggest giants of all and acquire a marvelously exaggerated stature. It is possible that Mr. Coombes was a perfectly normal being, but in my memory he was a giant, a tweed-suited giant who

always wore a black gown[5] over his tweeds and a waistcoat under his jacket.

Mr. Coombes now proceeded to mumble through the same old prayers we had every day, but this morning, when the last amen had been spoken, he did not turn and lead his group rapidly out of the hall as usual. He remained standing before us, and it was clear he had an announcement to make.

"The whole school is to go out and line up around the playground immediately," he said. "Leave your books behind. And no talking."

Mr. Coombes was looking grim. His hammy pink face had taken on that dangerous scowl which only appeared when he was extremely cross and somebody was for the high jump. I sat there small and frightened among the rows and rows of other boys, and to me at that moment the Headmaster, with his black gown draped over his shoulders, was like a judge at a murder trial.

"He's after the killer," Thwaites whispered to me.

I began to shiver.

"I'll bet the police are here already," Thwaites went on. "And the Black Maria's[6] waiting outside."

As we made our way out to the playground, my whole stomach began to feel as though it was slowly filling up with swirling water. *I am only eight years old,* I told myself. *No little boy of eight has ever murdered anyone. It's not possible.*

Out in the playground on this warm,

21

---

5. **black gown:** a robe much like those worn by graduating students.
6. **Black Maria:** a police patrol wagon.

22. VOCABULARY: Briticisms
Invite students to use context clues and their own experience to define the word *form* in this passage. *("a grade in a British school")* ★

23. ACTIVE READING: Evaluate
Ask students if they think Roald is relieved mainly because Mrs. Pratchett is not dead or because he will not be punished for her murder. *(Possible responses: He wanted to scare her, not hurt her, so he is relieved to learn that she's all right; he was really concerned about himself all along, imagining his own punishment for her murder; he is probably relieved for both reasons.)*

© Superstock.

cloudy September morning, the Deputy Headmaster was shouting, "Line up in forms! Sixth Form over there! Fifth Form next to them! Spread out! Spread out! Get on with it! Stop talking all of you!"

Thwaites and I and my other three friends were in the Second Form, the lowest but one, and we lined up against the red-brick wall of the playground shoulder to shoulder. I can remember that when every boy in the school was in his place, the line stretched right around the four sides of the playground—about one hundred small boys altogether, aged between six and twelve, all of us wearing identical gray shorts and gray blazers and gray stockings and black shoes.

"Stop that *talking!*" shouted the Deputy Head. "I want absolute silence!"

But why for heaven's sake were we in the playground at all? I wondered. And why were we lined up like this? It had never happened before.

I half expected to see two policemen come bounding out of the school to grab me by the arms and put handcuffs on my wrists.

A single door led out from the school onto the playground. Suddenly it swung open and through it, like the angel of death, strode Mr. Coombes, huge and bulky in his tweed suit and black gown, and beside him, believe it or not, right beside him trotted the tiny figure of Mrs. Pratchett herself!

Mrs. Pratchett was alive!

The relief was tremendous.

"She's alive!" I whispered to Thwaites standing next to me. "I didn't kill her!" Thwaites ignored me.

"We'll start over here," Mr. Coombes was

Speaking . . . Listening . . . Viewing

Speaking/Listening Tell students that physical punishment was common in British schools. Ask them to consider whether this type of discipline is appropriate, how it affects children, and how well it works.

Create listening circles. In each circle, a student should start round one by expressing his or her opinion. The student on the speaker's right should respond to his or her comments, either agreeing or disagreeing, and giving reasons for the response. This process is repeated until everyone in the circle has had a turn. No interruptions are allowed. (Note: You might start the discussion by expressing a controversial opinion in support of corporal punishment.)

In round two, a speaker may respond to any previous opinion. A speaker might begin by saying, "I'd like to comment on something that ——— said earlier. I disagree with his comment that . . ." The speaker should then call on someone in the group—other than the preceding speaker—to speak next.

saying to Mrs. Pratchett. He grasped her by one of her skinny arms and led her over to where the Sixth Form was standing. Then, still keeping hold of her arm, he proceeded to lead her at a brisk walk down the line of boys. It was like someone inspecting the troops.

"What on earth are they doing?" I whispered.

Thwaites didn't answer me. I glanced at him. He had gone rather pale.

"Too big," I heard Mrs. Pratchett saying. "Much too big. It's none of this lot. Let's 'ave a look at some of them titchy ones."

Mr. Coombes increased his pace. "We'd better go all the way around," he said. He seemed in a hurry to get it over with now, and I could see Mrs. Pratchett's skinny goat's legs trotting to keep up with him. They had already inspected one side of the playground where the Sixth Form and half the Fifth Form were standing. We watched them moving down the second side . . . then the third side.

"Still too big," I heard Mrs. Pratchett croaking. "Much too big! Smaller than these! Much smaller! Where's them nasty little ones?"

They were coming closer to us now . . . closer and closer.

They were starting on the fourth side . . .

Every boy in our form was watching Mr. Coombes and Mrs. Pratchett as they came walking down the line toward us.

"Nasty, cheeky lot, these little'uns!" I heard Mrs. Pratchett muttering. "They comes into my shop, and they thinks they can do whatever they well likes!"

Mr. Coombes made no reply to this.

"They nick things when I ain't lookin'," she went on. "They put their grubby 'ands all over everything, and they've got no manners. I don't mind girls. I never 'ave no trouble with girls, but boys is 'ideous and 'orrible! I don't 'ave to tell *you* that, 'Eadmaster, do I?"

"These are the smaller ones," Mr. Coombes said.

I could see Mrs. Pratchett's piggy little eyes staring hard at the face of each boy she passed.

Suddenly she let out a high-pitched yell and pointed a dirty finger straight at Thwaites. "That's 'im!" she yelled. "That's one of 'em! I'd know 'im a mile away, the scummy little bounder!"

The entire school turned to look at Thwaites. "W-what have *I* done?" he stuttered, appealing to Mr. Coombes.

"Shut up," Mr. Coombes said.

Mrs. Pratchett's eyes flicked over and settled on my own face. I looked down and studied the black asphalt surface of the playground.

"'Ere's another of 'em!" I heard her yelling. "That one there!" She was pointing at me now.

"You're quite sure?" Mr. Coombes said.

"Of course I'm sure!" she cried. "I never forgets a face, least of all when it's as sly as that! 'Ee's one of 'em all right! There was five altogether! Now where's them other three?"

The other three, as I knew very well, were coming up next.

Mrs. Pratchett's face was <u>glimmering</u> with <u>venom</u> as her eyes traveled beyond me down the line.

"There they are!" she cried out, stabbing the air with her finger. "'*Im* . . . and '*im* . . . and '*im!* That's the five of 'em all right! We don't need to look no farther than this, 'Eadmaster! They're all 'ere, the nasty, dirty little pigs! You've got their names, 'ave you?"

"I've got their names, Mrs. Pratchett," Mr. Coombes told her. "I'm much obliged to you."

"And I'm much obliged to *you*, 'Eadmaster," she answered.

As Mr. Coombes led her away across the playground, we heard her saying, "Right in the jar of Gobstoppers it was! A stinkin' dead mouse which I will never forget as long as I live!"

"You have my deepest sympathy," Mr. Coombes was muttering.

"Talk about shocks!" she went on "When my fingers caught 'old of that nasty, soggy, stinkin' dead mouse, . . . " Her voice trailed away as Mr. Coombes led her quickly through the door into the school building. ❧

Editor's Note: After being identified by Mrs. Pratchett in the schoolyard lineup, Roald and his friends were ordered into the headmaster's office. There they received a caning (beating) from Mr. Coombes, while Mrs. Pratchett watched. When Roald's mother saw her son's bruises, she promised to send him to school in England. The following year, Roald went to boarding school.

ENCOURAGING INDEPENDENT READING

Annie John, short stories by Jamaica Kincaid

In My Place, an autobiography by Charlayne Hunter-Gault

Long Ago in Oregon, autobiographical poems by Claudia Lewis

The Lost Garden, a memoir by Laurence Yep

Words to Know and Use	**glimmer** (glim′ ər) *v.* to give off a flickering dim light **venom** (ven′ əm) *n.* bitterness; hatred

233

Comprehension Check

1. What is Roald Dahl's first and most pleasant memory of Llandaff Cathedral School? (*seeing a boy ride a bicycle without holding the handlebars*)

2. What is the one drawback of the sweetshop? (*the owner, Mrs. Pratchett*)

3. Who invents the scheme to get even with Mrs. Pratchett? (*Roald*)

4. What does Roald do to upset her? (*He puts a dead mouse in a jar of candy.*)

5. What does Thwaites tell Roald the frightening trick did to Mrs. Pratchett? (*killed her*)

6. How do Roald and his friends get caught? (*Mrs. Pratchett identifies them in the schoolyard.*)

Student Response

Responding to Reading

1. Any response is valid.

2. Possible responses: Yes, because the pleasure the boys got from upsetting Mrs. Pratchett outweighed the embarrassment and pain of being found out and beaten; no, because the boys' revenge was outweighed by the horror and fear that Roald felt when he thought he had killed Mrs. Pratchett and by the pain of his punishment.

3. Possible responses: She is a slovenly, unpleasant person who is suspicious and quarrelsome and who treats children, especially boys, badly; she is worn out by the difficulties of running her shop and policing children, some of whom take advantage of her.

4. Any response is valid.

5. Possible responses: The pleasure with which he tells the story seems to indicate that Dahl feels that the prank was worth the punishment; his negative depictions of Mrs. Pratchett seem to indicate that he still sympathizes with the children and not with her.

6. Possible responses: The prank was acceptable, since no real harm was done; the punishment, not the prank, went too far—Mrs. Pratchett had a scare, but the boys were physically injured. The prank did go too far—Mrs. Pratchett didn't deserve such a fright, and the boys didn't deserve the beating.

Challenge Question

On the basis of this selection, what kinds of stories would you expect to find in Roald Dahl's library? *(Possible responses: violent stories, monster stories, stories in which adults are the enemy, funny stories, stories about kids who get in trouble, revenge stories)*

---

*R*esponding to Reading

First Impressions

1. What part of this selection did you enjoy most? Write your reaction in your journal or on a sheet of paper.

Second Thoughts

2. Was the boys' revenge worth their punishment?

3. What do you think of Mrs. Pratchett?

   Think about
   - how she treats the boys
   - the problems of owning a shop in which many customers are children

4. What parts of this selection remind you of experiences you had when you were younger?

   Think about
   - the terror Dahl felt when he thought he'd killed Mrs Pratchett
   - feelings about the candy or the store
   - stories you heard that were similar to the rat-mash story
   - pranks you discussed before reading

5. How do you think the grown-up Dahl feels about the prank he played in order to get even with Mrs. Pratchett? Why?

Broader Connections

6. Is a prank like the one in this story acceptable or not? In other words, how far is too far?

*L*iterary Concept: Dialect

You remember that **dialect** is the type of language spoken by a group of people in a particular region. Dialect includes both expressions and pronunciation. In our country, a southern drawl and a western twang are both dialects. Writers sometimes try to record these special accents on paper so that the reader will have a better idea of how the characters might sound. In *Boy*, Roald Dahl imitates Mrs. Pratchett's British working-class accent by dropping the beginning *h* from words like *here: 'ere.* Find other ways he represents her dialect. Then read some of her speeches aloud.

Literary Concept: Dialect

In addition to dropping initial *h*'s, Mrs. Pratchett drops the initial *th* in such words as *them ('em),* drops the *g*'s from such words as *thieving (thievin'),* and sometimes adds a final *s* to plural verbs—for example, she says, "They *comes* into my shop, and they *thinks* they can do whatever they well *likes!*" Mrs. Pratchett also uses a variety of dialectal expressions, such as "titchy ones" and "nick."

Writing Options

1. A **ballad** is a song or poem that tells a story. Use the events of this selection to write "The Ballad of the Dead Mouse."

2. From the selections in this subunit, choose a character who you think would fit in with Roald Dahl's gang of friends. Write a **persuasive essay** convincing Dahl to accept this person as part of his group.

3. Imagine that you are the local health inspector. Write a **memo** to the Board of Health after you inspect Mrs. Pratchett's sweetshop.

4. In rat-mash style, create a gruesome **story** about how your favorite kind of candy is made. Include a description of the candy, using Dahl's description on pages 224–225 as a model.

Vocabulary Practice

Exercise A On your paper write the word from the list that best completes the meaning of the sentence.

1. The hatred that Mrs. Pratchett feels toward the boys is like ____.

2. The boys think Mrs. Pratchett is ____ because of her disgusting clothes and filthy hands.

3. The huge container for cooking rat-mash is called a ____.

4. Children help candy stores ____ even when the shopkeepers are disagreeable.

5. When Mrs. Pratchett screams at them, the boys become quiet and ____.

6. A flickering ____ of hope shines from Dahl's eyes when he sees that Mrs. Pratchett is alive.

7. It is obvious from the ____ look in Mrs. Pratchett's eyes that she wants a severe punishment for the boys.

Exercise B Find the three adjectives in the list of words. Write a synonym for each.

> **Words to Know and Use**
>
> cauldron
> flourish
> glimmer
> loathsome
> malignant
> sullen
> venom

Writing Options

The Writing Options are designed to meet varied student interests and abilities. Have each student choose one writing activity to complete.

Journal Update Suggest that students write about differences between their school and the British preparatory school that the author attended.

Links to Writer's Craft

Writing Option 4 is an exercise in narrative writing. For more practice, see *The Writer's Craft*, Grade 7, "Narrative and Literary Writing," pages 70–92.

Vocabulary Practice

Answers to Exercise A

1. venom
2. loathsome
3. cauldron
4. flourish
5. sullen
6. glimmer
7. malignant

Answers to Exercise B

loathsome—disgusting

malignant—harmful

sullen—resentful

For Alternative Learning Styles
Ask students to create an impromptu round-robin story, using each of the vocabulary words. Students can take turns adding details to the story, using a vocabulary word in each sentence.

Closure

Recall for students Dahl's picture of himself as a "small and frightened" boy confronted by the "giant" headmaster. Ask students if this picture of a child's world reflects their experience. Invite students to debate whether young children are helpless against unfair adults or have their own ways to turn the tables on the adult world.

The Spelling Connection

Silent Letters A few consonants are silent in certain combinations, such as *gn, kn, mb, lm, wh, sw, wr, ph,* and *lk.*

Examples: who se   w rapped   sa l mon

Silent Letters in Words from the Selection

walk   wrists   wreckage
talking   pocketknife   crumbs

Other Words with Silent Letters

whole	written	knives
stalk	folklore	knocked
sword	answer	sign

Exercise Make up a folk tale about Johnny Appleseed, Paul Bunyan, Dick Tracy, or another folk hero. Try to think of a heroic or humorous tale. Include at least these spelling words: *sign, answer, wrists, talking,* and *stalk.*

Extending the Lesson

Options for Learning

These activities suit a variety of learning styles and modes of expression.

Collaborative Learning Activities
See Options 1, 3, and 4.

Options for Learning

1. **Jawbreakers and Licorice** If students have difficulty obtaining manufacturing information, they might consult confectionary cookbooks to find out how other candies are made.

2. **Clean Up Pratchett** Students might contact a county public-health service or the community public-health department for information about health codes.

3. **British Public Schools** Information is available in books about Great Britain and encyclopedias.

4. **Meet Roald** If several students read the autobiography, suggest that they share anecdotes with the class in a round table discussion.

 FACT FINDER SOCIAL STUDIES
Students can use an encyclopedia or a dictionary to find that there were twelve tuppence and a penny in a crown.

Roald Dahl

■ **More About the Author** Dahl claimed that conspiring against adults was the key to his success in writing for children. When criticized for the antisocial behavior in his stories, Dahl remarked, "I never get any protests from children. All you get are giggles of mirth and squirms of delight. I know what children like."

■ **Other Works** Novels: *Charlie and the Great Glass Elevator, The BFG, The Witches, Danny the Champion of the World, Fantastic Mr. Fox;* screenplays: *Chitty Chitty Bang Bang, Willy Wonka and the Chocolate Factory;* short story collection: *The Wonderful Story of Henry Sugar and Six More*

■ **Awards** Edgar Allan Poe awards from the Mystery Writers of America in 1954 and 1959

Options for Learning (Multimodal/Cross-Cultural Activities)

1 • **Jawbreakers and Licorice** Gobstoppers and Licorice Bootlaces are British names for candy that is also sold in the United States. From a candy manufacturer or another source, find out how jawbreakers or licorice is really made. Share your information with the class.

2 • **Clean Up Pratchett** Find out about health codes in your area that would have forced Mrs. Pratchett to clean up her store. You might interview a candy store owner to find out what the government requires in the way of cleanliness and packaging.

3 • **British Public Schools** How do British public schools differ from U.S. public schools? Do research in a library, or ask someone who attended a British public school to describe his or her school days. List differences on a chart to display in class.

4 • **Meet Roald** Read *Boy: Tales of Childhood,* from which this piece was taken, to enjoy more tales of Dahl's youth. Share some of his adventures with the class.

 FACT FINDER SOCIAL STUDIES
In Great Britain, how many tuppence were in a crown?

Roald Dahl
1916–1990

Roald Dahl became a writer even though his school reports said, "I have never met a boy who so persistently writes the exact opposite of what he means. He seems incapable of marshaling his thoughts on paper," and "Vocabulary negligible, sentences malconstructed. He reminds me of a camel."

He is most famous for his twenty children's books, which some critics complain are too violent. Children love them. His first children's book was *The Gremlins* (a word he invented), about tiny people who cause mysterious malfunctions in airplanes. Two of his best known children's books are *James and the Giant Peach* and *Charlie and the Chocolate Factory.* Dahl once said, "Had I not had children of my own, I would have never written books for children, nor would I have been capable of doing so."

Cross-Curricular Projects

Science/Health Ask students to prepare a TV news report about the controversy over sugar's effects on people. Suggest that they use a magazine or an encyclopedia for information. Their report should tell how sugar is used by the body, whether one kind of sugar is better for us than another, and how much is too much.

Social Studies/Geography Have students create a travel guide to Wales, with a map showing Llandaff.

Social Studies Why are gruesome stories so appealing to children? Students might interview each other and some adults as well for answers.

Art/Drama Have students create a costume or mask for an actor playing Mrs. Pratchett. Then have them dramatize a scene.

NARRATIVE WRITING

Think about a television show or a movie you really like. Why does it hook you and keep your interest? Chances are that it involves a dramatic twist like the ones in the selections in this subunit; for example, a change of fortune, an unexpected reversal of power, or a "loser" managing to come out on top. Since people enjoy these kinds of plots, such stories—whether fiction or nonfiction—are often turned into dramas. Plays, films, and television shows are all types of drama. A drama, like a story, is a kind of narrative writing. In this workshop you'll choose a story and rewrite it as a drama.

USE NARRATIVE WRITING FOR

stories
ballads
plays
skits
biographies

Here is one writer's PASSkey to this assignment.

GUIDED ASSIGNMENT: FROM STORY TO DRAMA

Choose a selection you have read and rewrite it as a drama for the stage.

PURPOSE: To dramatize a narrative

AUDIENCE: Other students

SUBJECT: Selection from this book

STRUCTURE: Stage drama

```
                The Painter
                by Denny Fox

based on "The War of the Wall" by Toni Cade Bambara

                Characters

Tina .........cousins, age   Frieda .......twins, age
Lou          thirteen        Hattie        eight
Painter ......muralist       Mama .........Tina's mom
Side Pocket ..pool shark      Daddy ........Tina's dad
Mr. Eubanks ..barber         Mrs. Morris ..twins' mom

  Scene 1: A spring morning in the 1970s. On a
  street in a Southern town are a barber shop, a
  stretch of high, marked-up wall, and a pool
```

◀ **STUDENT MODEL**
Before you write, read the first scene of one student's drama.

◀ A brief description of characters and setting is provided before the play begins.

WRITER'S WORKSHOP   237

ADDITIONAL RESOURCES

Unit Two Resource Book
Writer's Workshop Worksheet, p. 77
Writer's Workshop: Peer and Self-Evaluation, p. 78
Writer's Workshop: Assessment Guidelines, p. 79

Technology and Enrichment
Elaboration, Revision, and Proofreading
   Transparencies 9–12
Writer's Databank Software: File 5,
   Word Usage
Fine Art Transparency 4, Worksheet 10

Links to
Writer's Craft

For more about narrative writing, see *The Writer's Craft*, Grade 7, "Narrative and Literary Writing," pages 70–85.

Objectives

■ To understand the relationship between a story and a drama

■ To retell a story as a drama, using stage directions and dialogue

■ To draft, revise, edit, and share narrative writing in dramatic form

Teaching Strategies

DISCUSSING THE ASSIGNMENT

Begin by putting a Venn diagram on the board (large intersecting circles) and labeling its parts Story, Play, and Both. Ask students how stories and plays are alike and different. In the intersecting part of the circles, under *Both*, elicit that both have characters, a setting, a plot, and a conflict. In the story circle, elicit that stories include description and narration and are meant to be read. The play circle should indicate that plays have stage directions and are meant to be performed. Later, students may use the diagram as they begin planning their own drama.

Next, point out the PASSkey for the Guided Assignment and ask the class to note how the student model reflects its parts. Note that students' PASSkeys may be different from this one, but that listing their own purpose, audience, subject, and structure will help them keep their writing on track.

If you wish, you may give students the option of writing about something else that is important to them, such as those topics listed under Alternative Writing and Research Topics on the bottom of page 238.

ANALYZING THE MODEL

Read aloud the introductory material on page 237, and then have volunteers read the parts of the characters in the scene on page 238. Then ask the class to turn to pages 27–33 and note some of the changes that Denny Fox had to make when he recast the story as a drama. *(Some story narration became dialogue, and many story details were omitted because they were not absolutely necessary to the plot.)*

Questions such as the following may help the class further analyze the model. Students may work with partners or in small groups to make their analysis and later reconvene to share ideas with the class.

■ Of what importance is the text material that appears before the speaking parts begin?

■ Why do you think the stage directions are underlined and placed in parentheses?

■ Why can't all the dialogue be taken word for word from the original story?

■ Compare the ending of Scene 1 in the drama with the same section of the story. How are they alike? How are they different?

Prewrite and Explore

Direct students to choose a selection to adapt from Unit 1 or 2. You may want them to check their selections with you in case any choices should simply prove too difficult to recast.

This may be a good opportunity for your students to work collaboratively in small groups to produce one drama per group. They can divide up according to the drama they choose, or you might assign groups yourself. Point out the side notes on page 239, Working Together, that give tips for sharing the work.

Point out, too, that although students don't have to use the graphic shown on page 239 to plan each scene, they should draw up some kind of graphic organizer.

Stage directions (underlined and in parentheses) guide the actors. ▶

Dialogue replaces the short story's description and narration. ▶

A direct quotation is taken from the story. ▶

The dialogue leads into more action, which is described in stage directions. ▶

The first scene draws viewers in by setting up a conflict. ▶

hall with a gumball machine in front. A ladder leans against the wall. Nearby, a woman in overalls stirs a bucket of paint. Her car sits at the curb. Tina and Lou approach.

TINA (<u>noticing the painter</u>). What's <u>she</u> doing?

LOU. Hey, she can't paint that wall! It's ours!

TINA. Yeah! We've been pitching pennies there since we were kids. And we've got important stuff carved on it.

LOU. Yeah—even Jimmy Lyons's name. That's all we've got to remember him by now. Remember how he used to take us fishing?

TINA. You think I'm ever going to forget him? I wish he'd never had to go fight in Vietnam.

LOU. I still can't believe he's dead. (<u>The cousins have reached the painter.</u>)

TINA (<u>angrily</u>). Quit messing with our wall!

PAINTER (<u>absent-mindedly, not looking at the children</u>). The barber gave me permission.

LOU (<u>exchanging a look with Tina and slouching against the painter's car</u>). Listen. If you lean close, you'll get a whiff of bubble gum and kids' sweat. And that'll tell you something—that this wall belongs to the kids of Taliaferro Street.

TINA (<u>moving toward the ladder as the painter climbs it</u>). You think you can just ignore us? And climb on up with your paint bucket? You're not even from around here—you've got New York plates on your old clunky car! (<u>Tina grabs the ladder, about to shake it.</u>)

LOU (<u>alarmed, pulling Tina away</u>). Hey, don't! Come on—we're already late for school. (<u>Tina and Lou walk away.</u>)

Alternative Writing and Research Topics

Narrative Writing Have you ever turned the tables on someone and then discovered that your revenge was perfect and well-deserved? Write a drama to tell what happened.

Opinion Essay In both "The Revolt of the Evil Fairies" and *Boy* the main character gets his revenge but pays for it physically. Is revenge worth the pain and the intense effort it requires? Write an explanation of your views on revenge.

Poetry Do you admire the main character in the poem "The Rebel"? In a poem of your own, explain why or why not.

Research Report Research a famous rebel. It might be someone from ancient history such as Spartacus, someone from American history such as Nat Turner, or a contemporary figure like Sinead O'Connor. Write a report about this rebel.

Prewrite and Explore

1 Choose your material To choose a piece to dramatize, skim the selections you have already read. You need a piece that you like and that means something to you. You also need a piece that tells a story. You may use fiction, nonfiction, or poetry. The strongest dramas will come from stories with action that you can see in your mind and with characters you can relate to.

2 Get the big picture Plays are divided into scenes, which change when the time or place of the action changes. To plan the scenes in your play, you can start with a list of the main events in the story you've chosen. Each event can become a scene. You may later choose to leave out a scene or invent a new one, to tell the story clearly in play form.

After you've listed the events, you're ready to gather information.

◀ **WORK TOGETHER**
Does your favorite story seem too long or complicated? Try asking others to join you in a group effort.

◀ **WORK TOGETHER**
Try working as a group to list scenes. Then each member might plan and write one scene.

GATHERING INFORMATION

Each scene you write must reflect the setting, the characters' personalities, and the action. Therefore, you'll need to start with a detailed plan for each scene. Scene charts like the one Denny Fox used can help you gather details.

SCENE 1
Summary: The cousins notice the painter.

Setting	Characters	Action
Small-town business district, quiet morning, kids walking to school past a marked-up wall	Tina—impulsive, bossy Lou—quiet, thoughtful Painter— artsy-looking, focusing on her task, ignoring surroundings	Painter prepares to do a mural on wall. Cousins recall the wall's importance to them, then heckle the painter.

◀ **STUDENT MODEL**

This assignment is especially good for ESL students to complete. Because they are being asked to recast something already in print as opposed to writing something original, students can feel free to use some of the language from the story they choose in their new dramatic versions. Show students which parts of the original story can be used directly and which might need to be changed to a different format. Suggest that they work with partners whose first language is English.

Cooperative Writing

For students who choose to write cooperatively, stress that the better the group works together, the better their drama will be. The group should make their graphic together and plan what segment of the play each student will do individually. They should also come to agreement on how each segment should look. After they finish their individual parts, they should come back together to synthesize their segments and make a whole out of the parts. Encourage them to make the drama uniform in style. After they present their drama, you can give individual as well as group grades.

Draft and Discover

As they draft their dramas, remind students to let the characters tell the story.

Modeling Show students how to do this on the board or overhead projector. You might start with this passage from *Boy* on page 227.

> The other thing we hated Mrs. Pratchett for was her meanness. Unless you spent a whole sixpence all in one go, she wouldn't give you a bag. Instead you got your sweets twisted up in a small piece of newspaper which she tore off a pile of old *Daily Mirrors* lying on the counter.
>
> So you can well understand that we had it in for Mrs. Pratchett in a big way, but we didn't quite know what to do about it.

With students, rewrite the passage in dramatic version:

Roald *(wrinkling his nose)*. So Mrs. Pratchett has dirty hands. You know what bothers me almost as much?

Thwaites. What?

Roald *(looking disgusted)*. She won't even give us a paper sack to carry our sweets in! *(exasperated)* How can anyone be that cheap?

Thwaites *(angry)*. Right! And who wants his pear drops all twisted up in a corner of yesterday's *Daily Mirror*? Yuck!

Roald *(demanding justice)*. I say we get even with Mrs. Patchett!

Thwaites *(throwing up his hands in frustration)*. Sure! But how?

Revise Your Writing

Urge students to test their work for elements that contribute to realistic speech: sentence fragments, slang, interruptions, and use of regional dialects if appropriate. If students have added any dialogue of their own, have them check to be sure it suits each character. If they've added a narrator, suggest that they delete most dialogue that introduces characters and sets the scene—information that a narrator can do better anyway!

Finally, remind students to use the Revision Questions to evaluate their work.

Draft and Discover

STAGE DIRECTIONS
Use stage directions to (1) show the action, (2) describe facial expressions, tone of voice, or movements, and (3) describe setting and props.

1 Set the format When you follow standard drama format, starting your draft is easy. First, list your cast of characters, perhaps with a brief description of each. Next, for each scene, write a short paragraph that describes the setting. To guide actors, include stage directions, underlined and in parentheses, with your dialogue. You can look at *The Monsters Are Due on Maple Street* or the stage directions in *Funny Boy* (Unit 5) to see how this format works. Review the Elements of Drama on pages 155–156 for additional help.

WORKING TOGETHER
For help with dialogue, try improvising your scene with a small group. One group member can take notes.

2 Get into character In a short story, the author narrates the action and describes the characters. For your drama, you will invent dialogue to replace narration and description. Try imagining what each character might say in the scenes you have set up. Your scene charts will help. You can use—or ignore—any dialogue in the original story. Make sure your dialogue sounds like real speech and is not artificial. Use it to show characters' personalities and concerns. If you think a character might say something that's not in the original story, go ahead and write it. It may help bring the character to life.

Revise Your Writing

1 Focus on action Your scene charts show the action you planned for each scene. Now you need to make sure that your dialogue clearly explains the action as well as the reasons for the action. If it does not, revise to include references to the action. For example, you might have characters anticipate an action, discuss it, or respond to it. You can also use your stage directions to specify the action.

COMPUTER TIP
Save, then copy your drama. As you tinker with scenes, try out changes on the copy.

2 Adjust the scenes Now that you have a draft, you should also have a firmer sense of what your play is about. Review each scene, asking yourself what it contributes to your play's message. Adding, changing, or even cutting scenes can help you focus your drama. You might even decide to add a narrator, as in *The Monsters Are Due on Maple Street*.

3 Talk through it Try reading your draft aloud with friends, each taking one or more parts. Afterwards, you can use the revision questions on the next page.

CONFERENCING TIP

As you conference with individual writers or small groups for this workshop, you may wish to focus on

- making dialogue realistic
- making sure the plot moves forward
- subject/verb agreement

Proofread

Proofread for errors in grammar, spelling, capitalization, and punctuation. Pay special attention to subject-verb agreement.

THE EDITOR'S EYE: AGREEMENT

A verb must agree with its subject in number.

Singular subjects need singular verbs. Plural subjects need plural verbs.

Problem   <u>One</u> of the cousins <u>talk</u> angrily to the painter.

Revised   <u>One</u> of the cousins <u>talks</u> angrily to the painter.

NEED MORE HELP?
See the Language Workshop on pages 242–244 and pages 759–761 of the Language Handbook.

Publish and Present

On with the Show   With the help of friends, present your drama as a dramatic reading. If time permits, have the group present your drama as a stage play, with props, costumes, and so on.

DRAMATIC READING TIPS
See the Speaking and Listening Workshop on page 245.

Reflect on Your Writing

Briefly answer the following questions. Put the answers with your drama, and add it to your portfolio.

FOR YOUR PORTFOLIO

1. What new things did you discover about the story as you dramatized it?
2. Is drama easy or hard for you to write?

Proofread

Note that The Editor's Eye feature previews the content in the Language Workshop that follows. The brief review in the feature may be enough for students, or you may choose to teach the Language Workshop, pages 242–244, before they proofread.

TEACHING TIP: PROOFREADING

Dramas are likely to pose format problems. Encourage students to proofread each of the following items one at a time: introductory material, dialogue, character identification, and stage directions.

Use these models as needed to reinforce the Editor's Eye feature:

1. One of the people on the street (<u>is</u>, are) angry with the painter.

2. All of the observers (was, <u>were</u>) anxious about her painting.

3. When they saw the finished wall, everyone (<u>was</u>, were) stunned.

4. The painter and her paints, however, (was, <u>were</u>) gone.

5. Each one of us (want, <u>wants</u>) to thank her.

Publish and Present

If presenting each drama seems too time-consuming, try binding them into a book and keeping them until an opportunity arises to present them, perhaps in a school talent show.

Reflect on Your Writing

You may choose to have students answer the following questions in addition to or instead of those in their text:

■ Does my dialogue sound like real speech? How can I improve it?

■ What was easy and hard about working with a group?

Closure

Suggest that students each read one published drama and compare/contrast the techniques they used with those used by the dramatist.

Assessment Guidelines

These guidelines may help you assess student writing:

Content
■ A story is recast as a drama.
■ The drama gives a complete and accurate picture of the action.

Style
■ The dialogue is appropriate to characters.
■ The dialogue is natural-sounding.

Usage and Mechanics
■ Standard grammar is used, but the drama veers into slang/dialect as necessary.
■ Subject-verb agreement is correct.
■ The drama follows rules for formatting, spelling, capitalization, and punctuation.

See also *Unit Resource Book Two*, page 80.

Objectives

- To identify the subjects of sentences
- To use subjects and verbs that agree in number

Teaching Strategies

Review with students the concepts of singular and plural and the importance of making subjects and verbs agree. Have them read the review of subject-verb agreement on page 242, and work with them on the first two models on that page.

Now point out the third set of models next to the Reminder on page 242. Remind students that the subject is the actor in the sentence. It is sometimes easier to find the simple subject if they find the verb first. For example, in the sample sentence "One of the neighbors is afraid," they should ask *who is afraid? One* is the subject. In the next sample sentence, they should ask *who discuss their lawns? The men* is the subject.

Work through Exercise 1 orally, emphasizing this strategy with sentences 1, 2, 7, and 8.

Answers to Exercise 1

1. object, zooms
2. group, comes
3. people, discover
4. cars, are

SUBJECT—VERB AGREEMENT

A verb and its subject must agree in number.

In drama, every word counts, and audiences listen carefully. Errors in subject-verb agreement can make dialogue sound jarring and unreal. Such errors can distract an audience.

Nouns and verbs have **number**—that is, they can be **singular** (one thing or action) or **plural** (two or more things or actions). When we say ▶ that a subject and verb **agree** in number, we mean that they are both singular or both plural.

> The <u>phone</u> (singular) <u>is</u> (singular) dead.
> The <u>phones</u> (plural) <u>are</u> (plural) dead.

You can usually decide whether a subject and verb agree by saying the sentence to yourself.

> The <u>boy</u> (singular) <u>talks</u> (singular) about space creatures.
> The <u>boys</u> (plural) <u>talk</u> (plural) about space creatures.

Often a phrase appears between the subject and the verb. The simple subject is never part of such a phrase. Don't mistake the noun ▶ in the phrase for the subject. Make the verb agree with the simple subject.

> <u>One</u> (of the neighbors) <u>is</u> afraid.
> The <u>men</u> (on the block) <u>discuss</u> their lawns.

GRAMMAR TIP
An *s* at the end of a verb shows that the verb is singular—just the opposite of what it shows for nouns!

REMINDER
The **simple subject** is the key word in the subject that tells whom or what the sentence is about.

Exercise 1   Concept Check   Write the simple subject of each sentence. Then write the verb form that agrees with the subject.

1. A bright object with strange markings (zooms, zoom) over Maple Street.
2. A group of neighbors (comes, come) out to watch.
3. Gradually, people (discovers, discover) mysterious problems.
4. Even their cars (is, are) not working.

242   UNIT TWO   TURNING THE TABLES

ADDITIONAL RESOURCES
Unit Two Resource Book
Language Workshop Practice, p. 80

Technology and Enrichment

Grammar and Usage Copy Masters, pp. 8–13
Grammar Test Generator

Links to
Writer's Craft

For more about subject-verb agreement, see *The Writer's Craft,* Grade 7, "Understanding Subject and Verb Agreement," pages 577–595.

5. In the confusion, a boy carrying comic books (mentions, mention) space invaders.
6. Then one man's car (starts, start) by itself.
7. His neighbors from Maple Street quickly (grows, grow) suspicious of him.
8. One of the people (accuses, accuse) him of being an alien.
9. I (was, were) fascinated by this play.
10. By reading it, you (gets, get) insights into the way mobs act.

Compound Subjects

Compound subjects are two or more subjects sharing the same verb. Compound subjects joined with *and* take a plural verb.

> <u>Steve</u> and his <u>friend</u> <u>stay</u> calm.

When compound subjects are joined with *or* or *nor,* the verb agrees in number with the subject that is closer to the verb.

> Either <u>Tommy</u> or his <u>mother</u> <u>buys</u> comic books.
> A <u>meteor</u> or <u>sunspots</u> <u>cause</u> power failure.

Verbs in Questions

In most sentences, the subject comes before the verb. However, in questions, part or all of the verb comes first. The subject and verb must still agree in number.

> <u>Does</u> <u>Les</u> <u>stare</u> at the sky every night?
> Why <u>is</u> <u>he</u> so different?
> Where <u>does</u> <u>Les</u> really <u>live</u>?

Verbs in Sentences that Start with There and Here

When *there* or *here* begins a sentence, look for the subject later in the sentence. Then check for agreement with the verb.

> There <u>are</u> <u>clues</u> in Tommy's comic book.
> There <u>is</u> a <u>moral</u> to this story.
> Here <u>is</u> one <u>explanation</u> for the disaster.

CAUTION
Don't be fooled by the contractions *there's, here's,* and *where's.* All three are singular and agree only with singular subjects. There <u>are</u> (not *there's*) no <u>batteries</u> left. Here <u>are</u> (not *here's*) some <u>suggestions</u>. Where <u>are</u> (not *where's*) Tommy's <u>parents</u>?

5. boy, mentions
6. car, starts
7. neighbors, grow
8. One, accuses
9. I, was
10. you, get

Next, review the last three types of troublesome sentences on page 243. Point out to students that in sentences beginning with *here* or *there, here* and *there* are not subjects. Tell students that in such sentences they should again ask *who* or *what* is performing the action.

Last, point out the "Caution" in the margin, and practice it briefly.

PRACTICE, PRACTICE, PRACTICE

Provide these sentences to reinforce what the class just learned. Students may work in groups and do the practice orally, or they may write the sentences and compare their answers with partners. Have students read the sentences aloud using the correct verb or verb part and identify each subject. (The correct verbs are underlined.)

1. Roald and Thwaites (<u>like</u>, likes) sweets. *(Roald, Thwaites)*

2. Either Thwaites or his father (have warned, <u>has warned</u>) the boys about licorice bootlaces. *(Thwaites, father)*

3. Here (is, <u>are</u>) the licorice bootlaces. *(bootlaces)*

4. Do these candies (<u>look</u>, looks) like blood? *(candies)*

5. (Do, <u>Does</u>) Roald really believe the story about rats' blood? *(Roald)*

Grammar Games: Time to Agree

Have small groups of students choose a piece of literature—part of a short story, a few verses from a narrative poem, a news story, or a scene from a play. Then have each group copy the piece, leaving out complete and simple subjects in one place and complete and simple predicates in others. Tell them to replace missing sentence parts with long blank lines.

Have groups exchange their work and challenge each other to rewrite their passages. Groups need not replace the missing sentence parts exactly, but a coherent passage must result, and—most important—all the subjects and verbs must agree. The group whose rewrite is the most entertaining and most free from errors is the winner. Note: Groups can make the new passage funny or tragic or overly dramatic just for effect. Display the originals and the new versions next to each other on a bulletin board.

Answers to Exercise 2

1. mowers/radios, refuse
2. man/friend, try
3. Sally/Steve, feels
4. reasons, are
5. anyone, Doesn't (believe)
6. neighbors, are
7. Myra/Ethel, defend
8. Tommy/child, screams
9. forms, There are
10. aliens, do (go)

Answers to Exercise 3

Scene 2: Sunday evening, April 14, 1912. In the radio room of the *Titanic*, in the North Atlantic, two radio operators talk. Jack, in his headphones, <u>sits</u> at the radio; Harold <u>stretches</u> out on a sofa.

Harold. I'm beat. Those rich passengers from first class sure <u>don't</u> give us much rest, do they?

Jack. Well, to them, the radio is a new toy. Passengers <u>want</u> to play with it by sending messages. That lady with the diamonds <u>comes</u> in here every two hours. She and her father in New York <u>seem</u> worried about each other. *(New messages <u>come</u> in over the headphones.)*

Harold. We're doing a good job, anyway. The captain and the first mate <u>say</u> so. *(as Jack writes a message)* What's the news?

Jack *(sounding bored).* <u>There are</u> more icebergs ahead. Either the captain or the helmsman <u>needs</u> to know. Can you take the messages up?

Harold *(tiredly).* Sure. I'll bring back coffee and doughnuts.

Answers to Exercise 4

Subjects and verbs will vary.

Exercise 2   Concept Check   Write the simple or compound subject in each sentence. Then write the verb that agrees in number.

1. Even lawn mowers and transistor radios (refuses, refuse) to work.
2. A man and his friend (tries, try) to quiet the crowd.
3. Neither Sally nor Steve (feels, feel) right about watching Les.
4. There (is, are) good reasons why Les scans the sky at night.
5. (Doesn't, Don't) anyone believe him?
6. (Is, Are) the neighbors desperate enough to attack Les?
7. Myra and Ethel (defends, defend) their husbands.
8. Either Tommy or another child (screams, scream).
9. (There's, There are) two shadowy forms watching from a distance.
10. Where (does, do) the aliens go next?

Exercise 3   Revision Skill   Rewrite the following portion of a drama, correcting errors in subject-verb agreement.

Scene 2: Sunday evening, April 14, 1912. In the radio room of the *Titanic,* in the North Atlantic, two radio operators talk. Jack, in his headphones, sit at the radio; Harold stretch out on a sofa.

Harold. I'm beat. Those rich passengers from first class sure doesn't give us much rest, do they?

Jack. Well, to them, the radio is a new toy. Passengers wants to play with it by sending messages. That lady with the diamonds come in here every two hours. She and her father in New York seems worried about each other. *(New messages comes in over the headphones.)*

Harold. We're doing a good job, anyway. The captain and the first mate says so. *(as Jack writes a message)* What's the news?

Jack *(sounding bored).* There's more icebergs ahead. Either the captain or the helmsman need to know. Can you take the messages up?

Harold *(tiredly).* Sure. I'll bring back coffee and doughnuts.

Exercise 4   Revising Your Writing   Reread the drama you wrote for the Writer's Workshop on pages 237–241. Lightly underline the subject and verb of each sentence and check to be sure that subjects and verbs agree in number. Correct any errors you find.

LANGUAGE HANDBOOK
For review and practice: Section 8, Subject-Verb Agreement, pages 259–261.

Closure

Remind students that subject-verb agreement may make the difference between clarity and confusion in their writing. Explain that agreement is especially crucial when they write drama, because in this format the audience cannot refer back to the written word in order to clarify understanding.

Additional Practice

Choose the correct form.
1. The painter with all the buckets and brushes (stand, <u>stands</u>) near the wall.
2. Quietly (<u>she</u>, they) studies it.
3. Children and adults both (<u>wonder</u>, wonders) what she will paint.
4. "Here (<u>is</u>, are) your bucket," says Tina.
5. This wall with all its scratches and dents (<u>is</u>, are) important to the people.
6. What (change, <u>changes</u>) in this landmark are planned?
7. Neither Lou nor the other observers (has, <u>have</u>) any idea.
8. Soon the mural with its brilliant colors (<u>is</u>, are) finished.
9. (Isn't, <u>Aren't</u>) Tina and Lou ashamed for annoying that wonderful painter?
10. Tina and I both (<u>love</u>, loves) the mural now.

SPEAKING AND LISTENING
WORKSHOP

DRAMATIC READING SKILLS

Dramas, like the one you wrote in the Writer's Workshop, are created to be performed. A **dramatic reading** is one kind of performance. In a dramatic reading, actors sit or stand on a bare stage and hold scripts. They must keep the audience's attention without props, scenery, or costumes. The techniques they use can help you when you read your own drama aloud.

1. Prepare Read your material—aloud, if possible—several times beforehand. Know the high points: the flashes of humor, excitement, or tension.

2. Project Speak up! Hold your head, and the script, *up* as you read. Don't shout, but aim your voice outward, to the very back of the room. To emphasize humor, try a slight increase in the volume of your voice. To show tension, try raising the volume, then dropping it.

3. Create You may be able to come up with a special tone of voice, or a special way of pronouncing words, that fits your character. Match this voice to the character's personality.

4. Pause Nothing shouts like silence. At the exciting points in the drama, you may tend to rush through your lines. Pause instead. The people in the audience will hold their breath with you.

5. Think Don't drone along on automatic pilot. Think about what other characters say, and react as if you were really the character. Also think about what you're saying. How does your character feel? How can you show it?

6. Move Use your whole body. Your hands and face can express your emotions. Body language, including your posture and movements, also express emotions. For example, a quick double take can convey humor. Your posture also affects your voice—both its tone and its volume.

◀ REMINDER
....
There's only one time *not* to pause: when another character has just stopped speaking and it's your turn to begin. Then, don't let it drag—jump right in.

Exercise 1 Choose a sentence you like from one of the works in this unit. Read it aloud several times, practicing the six tips above.

Exercise 2 With a small group, participate in a reading of the drama you wrote for the Writer's Workshop on page 237. Try out various interpretations of key dialogue before you begin.

Objective

■ To use appropriate tones and gestures in a dramatic reading

Teaching Strategies

Have students turn to pages 52 and 53 and review the "tall tale" that Jean Little told in "Little by Little." Then ask volunteers to read aloud the strategies on page 245. As each is read, discuss with the class how they might use the strategy with the passage.

APPLYING THE STRATEGIES

Next have students form four groups who will work together to apply the strategies to the Jean Little passage. (Because Jean does most of the talking, students will have to divide the passage to give each member a turn.) Point out that the purpose of the exercise is to see which group can present the passage most effectively and dramatically.

After each group has responded, encourage class members to tell what they liked about the interpretation. Then ask the actors which strategy they consider most effective and which they most enjoyed applying.

Answers to Exercise 1
Have students choose a passage other than the one in the Jean Little piece, and evaluate their applications in their journals.

Answers to Exercise 2
Encourage students to form new groups for their dramas, perhaps only reading part of each one to apply the strategies.

ADDITIONAL RESOURCES
Unit Two Resource Book
Speaking and Listening Workshop Practice, p. 81

Objectives

■ To extend the study of the unit theme, "Scales of Justice," to novels and other longer works

■ To read independently for personal enrichment and enjoyment

ROLL OF THUNDER, HEAR MY CRY

Study Focus

■ Historical setting as it relates to racial prejudice and poverty

■ African-American children as victims in society

■ Themes of persecution and survival

About Mildred D. Taylor

Born in Jackson, Mississippi, in 1943, Taylor draws on family narratives and her own experiences to create memorable stories. Her writing reflects racial pride while educating readers in African-American struggles of the past and present.

■ **Other Works** Novels: *The Friendship, The Gold Cadillac, Mississippi Bridge, Let the Circle Be Unbroken*

 ■ **Awards** Newbery Medal, 1977, for *Roll of Thunder, Hear My Cry;* Christopher Award, 1988, for The *Gold Cadillac;* Coretta Scott King Book Award, 1990, for *The Road to Memphis*

Reading on Your Own

Suggested Novels for Unit Two

The novels introduced on these pages allow you to explore the unit theme, "Scales of Justice," in more depth and in different ways.

ROLL OF THUNDER, HEAR MY CRY

MILDRED D. TAYLOR ©1976

During the Depression, when many people lost their jobs, life was especially difficult for African Americans. Roll of Thunder, Hear My Cry is a historical novel about a family who must struggle to overcome both prejudice and poverty in rural Mississippi. The story contains both terrifying and humorous incidents. As you draw close to the Logan family, you will watch them keep their spirits up in the face of discrimination. You may become angry at the injustice of the poor treatment received by the black school that the Logan children attend. However, you will enjoy the Logan children's occasional tipping of the scales of justice in their favor. As you read, put yourself in the children's place and ask yourself the following questions:

• How would you react if a school bus deliberately splashed dirty water on you?

• How would you feel if your whole school were treated as second-class?

• What might you do to turn the tables on mean spirited people without getting in trouble?

MILDRED D. TAYLOR

Roll of Thunder, Hear My Cry

246

Guide for Teaching

A study guide for the paired novels **Where the Lilies Bloom** and *Roll of Thunder, Hear My Cry* is available from McDougal, Littell. See the Teacher's Resource File for ordering information.

BROTHER EAGLE, SISTER SKY: A MESSAGE FROM CHIEF SEATTLE

SUSAN JEFFERS ©1991

Based on a letter that Chief Seattle supposedly wrote to the President of the United States around 1855, *Brother Eagle, Sister Sky: A Message From Chief Seattle* explains Native American beliefs about the earth and the way people should treat it. Chief Seattle clearly explains his belief that the earth does not belong to people but people belong to the earth and must care for it and cherish it. His letter will make you think hard about how we modern Americans treat our environment. As you read, you might consider the following questions:

• Do you agree with Chief Seattle's view of people's relationship with nature?

• If you had a conversation with Chief Seattle, what concerns would you talk about?

• How would Chief Seattle make himself heard today?

MANIAC MAGEE

JERRY SPINELLI ©1990

Enjoy the humorous adventures of Maniac Magee, a very different sort of boy hero. Besides being able to run faster and hit more home runs than anybody else, Maniac can also settle problems between angry gangs of kids. In fact, his exploits are so unbelievable that other kids write jump-rope rhymes about them. Maniac Magee acts according to his own scales of justice—with humorous and positive results. As you smile over his strange ways of dealing with problems, think about the following questions:

• What would it be like to be better at all sports than anyone you know?

• If you were a superhero, what real problems would you solve?

• Would you be happy if everyone shared Maniac Magee's unusual way of thinking?

Other Recommended Books

Jack Tales by Richard Chase (©1943). This enjoyable collection of folk tales from the southern Appalachians is filled with stories about justice, turning the tables, and victims and victors.

Stepping on the Cracks by Mary Downing Hahn (©1991). This historical novel, set in Maryland during World War II, deals with a deserter from the army and a group of young friends who decide to take care of him. In this story courage of all kinds is tested.

The Black Americans: A History in Their Own Words, 1619-1983 by Milton Meltzer (©1984). This fascinating book is a collection of letters, speeches, articles, and other documents written by African Americans. It includes testimonies from slaves and free men and women, both famous and unknown.

Sing Down the Moon by Scott O'Dell (©1970). In this historical novel, a Navaho girl is involved in the three-hundred-mile journey known as the Long Walk, from Canyon de Chelly to Fort Sumner. The heroine escapes from the fort and returns to her canyon, where she discovers that survival of the spirit is just as important as physical survival.

247

■ **Awards** Newbery Medal, ALA Award, 1991, Boston Globe/Horn Book Award, 1990, all for *Maniac Magee*.

BROTHER EAGLE, SISTER SKY: A MESSAGE FROM CHIEF SEATTLE

Study Focus

■ Native Americans as victims and victors

■ contrast between Native Americans' and whites' attitudes toward land

■ Chief Seattle's concerns with ecology and the environment

About Susan Jeffers

Jeffers is a highly respected artist known for her distinctive pen-and-ink drawings. She specializes in outdoor landscapes. She says, "I live and work . . . in a small house on a lake. Around me are the woods and animals that I love to draw." Her work reflects a deep love and respect for nature.

■ **Other Works** (as illustrator): Stories: *Thumbelina, Snow White and the Seven Dwarfs, Black Beauty;* poems: *The Song of Hiawatha,* "Stopping by Woods on a Snowy Evening," "The Midnight Farm"

■ **Awards** Caldecott Honor Award, 1974, for *Three Jovial Huntsmen;* Golden Kite Award and Society of Children's Book Writers, 1988, for *Forest of Dreams*.

MANIAC MAGEE

Study Focus

■ Maniac's turning the tables and revealing his own scales of justice

■ Use of humor and exaggeration

■ Story as an example of realistic fiction

About Jerry Spinelli

Spinelli's work is marked by his unflagging and quirky sense of humor. He creates witty books filled with imaginative events. Asked where he gets his ideas, Spinelli said, "From you. You're the funny ones. You're the fascinating ones. You're the elusive and inspiring and promising and heroic and maddening ones."

■ **Other Works** Novels: *Space Station Seventh Grade, Dump Days, Night of the Whale, There's A Girl in My Hammerlock, Fourth Grade Rats*.

Subunit One: Driven by Dreams

	SELECTION	DIFFICULTY LEVEL	READING SKILLS	LITERATURE SKILLS	WRITING OPTIONS	VOCABULARY WORDS/SKILLS
Fiction	*The Smallest Dragonboy* Anne McCaffrey Pages 251–267	Challenge	Fantasy	Suspense	Handbook Dialogue Notes	consensus imperative contemptuous indifference desolation obscure dissipate replenish evasion sloth
Poetry	*Wishes* Georgia Douglas Johnson *Dream Deferred* Langston Hughes *Formula* Ana Maria Iza Pages 268–272	Average	Understanding poetry Figurative language	Imagery Simile	Poem Thematic connection	Word attack Skill: connotations
Nonfiction	*Eleanor Roosevelt* William Jay Jacobs Pages 273–285	Average	Understanding nonfiction	Biography Conflict	Advice column Summary Conversation Job description	brooding combatant compassionate priority prominent

WRITER'S WORKSHOP   Pages 286–290 ································

Mode	Guided Assignment	Writing Skills	Proofreading Focus
Informative	Magazine article	Creating questions Using facts and figures Catchy beginning	Avoiding run-on sentences

OPTIONS FOR LEARNING	SPELLING SKILLS	COMMUNITY AND PARENT RESOURCE SUGGESTIONS	AUDIOVISUAL RESOURCES

Book cover
Glossary
Illustration
Retelling
	ous/us and *ize/ise* suffixes	Invite a librarian or bookstore owner to discuss the popularity of fantasy novels in the young adult market.	*Literature & Language* Audiocassette Tape 2, side 1.
			Dragon Song. Dragon Singer. Dragon Drums.
			  Audiocassettes. Recorded Books, 1992.
			  A reading of three of Anne McCaffrey's books.

	Proofreading for Spelling	Invite an expert on dreams, a dream interpreter, or a psychologist to talk about the importance of dreaming.	*Langston Hughes.* Video or filmstrip. American School Publishers, 1990. Explores Hughes's life and includes selections from his finest work. *Langston Hughes.* Filmstrip. Eye Gate Media, 1989. (15 min.) An inspiring profile of the writer.
Collage Panel discussion Poster Interview	Words with silent *gh*	Invite elderly citizens who have memories of the days of Eleanor Roosevelt to share their memories with the class. Ask a doctor to discuss polio.	*Conversations with Great Americans: Industrial Era and Modern.* Computer software. Focus Media. Provides an interactive look at history through the eyes of Eleanor Roosevelt and others. *Eleanor Roosevelt.* Video. Coronet, 1991. (26 min.) Profiles the First Lady with eye-opening visuals of her early life, the White House years, and her career after Franklin Roosevelt's death.

LANGUAGE WORKSHOP Pages 291–293 ⦙⦙⦙⦙⦙⦙⦙⦙

Grammar Concept	Skill Focus
Complete sentences	Avoiding fragments and run-ons

RELATED SKILLS WORKSHOP Page 294 ⦙⦙⦙⦙⦙

Language Strand	Skill Focus
Reading	Skimming Scanning

Subunit Two: Fight to the Finish

	SELECTION	DIFFICULTY LEVEL	READING SKILLS	LITERATURE SKILLS	WRITING OPTIONS	VOCABULARY WORDS/SKILLS	
Fiction	*Old Sly Eye* Russell Gordon Carter Pages 296–303	Challenge	Problem-solving	Character	New ending Notice	abruptly elude endure grope ponder	
Nonfiction	*Nadja on My Way* Nadja Salerno- Sonnenberg Pages 304–315	Average	Making connections	Style Internal conflict	Essay Chant Letter Comparison	audition deliberate evict gruff immerse	inevitable obsessed preliminaries prodigy subconsciously
Poetry	*The Women's 400 Meters* Lillian Morrison *To James* Frank Horne Pages 316–321	Average	Recognizing the speaker	Theme	Response to advice Poem	Word Attack Skill: context clues	
Fiction	*Rikki-tikki-tavi* Rudyard Kipling Pages 322–338	Average	Personification	Minor characters Setting	Lyrics Summary	cower cultivated immensely revive veranda	

WRITER'S WORKSHOP   Pages 339–343 ··

Mode	Guided Assignment	Writing Skills	Proofreading Focus
Informative and persuasive	Problem-solution editorial	Freewriting Supporting with facts Persuasion Transitions	Homonyms

OPTIONS FOR LEARNING	SPELLING SKILLS	COMMUNITY AND PARENT RESOURCE SUGGESTIONS	AUDIOVISUAL RESOURCES
	the assimilated prefix *ad*	Take a field trip to a zoo and observe panthers' behavior. Invite a member of a historical society to discuss life in colonial New England.	
Recording of Nadja Collage Interviews Mandala	*com/con* and *im/in* prefixes	Invite a violinist or professional musician to perform for the class and to discuss the business of music. Take students on a field trip to a symphony.	*It Ain't Necessarily So,* CD by Capitol Records, CDC7, 54576-2 *Nadja Salerno-Sonnenberg,* CD by Angel Records, CDC7, 49276-2
Textured picture Interview	Proofreading for Spelling	Invite a track coach to discuss running competition. Take students to a track meet.	
Research cobras Comic book Radio Reading Panel discussion	Silent *e* words and suffixes	Invite students' adult relatives from India to share their culture with the class.	*The Jungle Books.* 10 audiocassettes. Recorded Books, 1992. (13 hrs.) All of Kipling's *Jungle Books,* including "Rikki-tikki-tavi." *Rikki-tikki-tavi.* Video. Guidance Associates. (26 min.) Story is narrated by Orson Welles in this award-winning live-action video.

LANGUAGE WORKSHOP Pages 344–346 . . . .

Grammar Concept	Skill Focus
Words often confused	Homonyms Spelling

RELATED SKILLS WORKSHOP Page 347 . . . . . .

Language Strand	Skill Focus
Reading	Language of persuasion

Reading on Your Own

Novels, thematically connected to Unit Three, suggested for independent reading during or after completion of the unit (pages 348–349)

The Hobbit   J. R. R. Tolkien
The Gift of the Girl Who Couldn't Hear   Susan Shreve
Anpao: An American Indian Odyssey   Jamake Highwater

Cooperative Project Unit Three: REACHING FOR THE STARS

A Space Colony of the Future

> *Such a colony would give human beings a chance to begin again . . .*

1 Project Preview

This project challenges students to extend what they have learned about the unit theme, "Reaching for the Stars." In task groups of five to six, students will work collaboratively to design a space colony on an imaginary planet.

Each group will plan one aspect of colony life. Groups may choose from topics such as transportation, farming, architecture, entertainment, and law. By exploring such topics, students will also be exploring the needs and problems of our own world and be thinking of possible solutions.

As a culminating experience, students will hold a Future Fair, where each group will present its vision of life on a new world.

This project can be shortened or extended, depending on the needs, interests, and abilities of your class and the time available.

OBJECTIVES
■ To create a plan for one aspect of life on a space colony
■ To research current problems related to the group's chosen topic
■ To design a presentation and display of the group's plan

MATERIALS
■ large sheets of drawing paper or a flip chart
■ if available, brochures or pamphlets describing model communities
■ tables, art supplies, video and audio equipment for student presentations and displays

2 Implementing the Project

Introduction
Ask students to imagine that they are part of a team of earth inhabitants who have been chosen to travel through space and to start a new colony on a remote planet. Tell them to assume that this new planet is identical in every way to earth, except that the new planet has no other human inhabitants. The colonists can expect to find the same atmosphere, landscape, temperatures, plants, animals, minerals, and resources. Their task for the next several days will be to help design a plan for living on this new world. Collectively, they will be creating a type of model community for the future.

Alternative You may wish to introduce one complication on the new planet, such as a creature that feeds on human beings or a poisonous ocean.

Opening Discussion
Lead the class in a discussion of how life might be different on a space colony. Point out that such a colony would give human beings a chance to begin again and to avoid the mistakes made on earth. Encourage students to stretch their imaginations and to explore diverse ways of thinking.

As the discussion proceeds, keep a running list on the board of all the issues that arise. For homework, ask students to think about one issue that most interests them. You may wish to assign a short writing topic, "If we could start all over, . . ." to solicit ideas on how a space colony might deal with that issue.

Choosing Topics
On the next day, ask each student to discuss his or her chosen topic or to read aloud his or her writing. Invite other students to share their ideas on that topic as well. As each issue is discussed, keep track of students' ideas by using simple charts on large sheets of drawing paper like the one in the next column. You may find it useful to contrast life on the space colony with life on earth.

When discussion begins to wane, ask students to decide which topics would be the most interesting for this project.

Assigning Groups
If feasible, allow students to choose their own topics and organize the groups accordingly, with five or six students in a group.

Here are some possibilities for group projects:

Architecture One group might create a brochure or pamphlet with drawings of the colony's buildings. The pamphlet might include drawings of family residences, office buildings, and public facilities, as well as descriptions of these buildings and their distinctive features.

TRANSPORTATION

Space Colony
■ solar-powered, airborne vehicles for ground travel
■ airways, with computer-defined boundaries, for commuter traffic
■ personal, affordable rockets for long-distance travel

Earth
■ fossil-fuel-burning vehicles (cars, trains, buses)—damage environment
■ crowded, dangerous highways, expensive to maintain
■ expensive plane travel

Laws of the Land One group might devise a plan for governing the space colony, perhaps creating a simple constitution, detailing the form of government and the rights and obligations of citizens.

Transportation A group that focuses on this topic might create models of futuristic vehicles or posters showing the colony's means of transportation.

Entertainment One group might devise new forms of entertainment for the space colony. The group might think of new technologies for motion pictures, music, spectator sports, or computer games.

Gathering and Analyzing Information

Encourage each group to be flexible and creative in assigning responsibilities for the project. The groups should try to draw on the interests and unique abilities of each group member. For example, one group member may do library research while another might build a demonstration model or design a poster. While some library research may prove helpful, it is not a requirement for every group. For this assignment, thoughtful discussion and creative thinking are the most important ingredients.

Groups might begin the project by thinking about current problems and proposed solutions related to their topic. For example, a group dealing with transportation might identify major problems, such as the pollutants from fossil fuel. They might use this information to think of new forms of transportation that do not use fossil fuels.

With the help of a librarian, you can also identify articles or science fiction movies that might spur thinking. You might consider inviting community residents to share their ideas of how the future might look. For example, a car mechanic or dealer might discuss the cars of the future and their environmental impact; an architect or contractor can discuss how buildings of the future might be made.

Groups should meet periodically (perhaps every other day) to discuss the information they find, exchange ideas, and formulate their plans.

Move from group to group to monitor and facilitate progress.

You may find it useful to use a tape recorder to record group discussions. During each day of group work, place a recorder in the middle of each group, moving the recorder to a different group each day. This strategy will help keep groups on task and can later serve as an informal means of assessment.

Preparing the Presentation

Encourage students to move to the next phase—preparing the presentation—as soon as it seems reasonable to do so. Make sure that groups divide the work fairly and that each individual understands what is required.

Schedule a day for the class Future Fair, allowing enough time for parents, visitors, and other classes to make plans to attend. Explain that each group will present its ideas on the day of the fair. Invite the entire class to come up with a name for the occasion, such as Space Pilgrims, A New America, The World of Tomorrow, or A Galaxy Gala.

Presentation

Set up display stations in different locations around the room or perhaps in the school vestibule. Each group can be given an allotted time in which to explain its ideas. Groups may use posters, models, brochures, handouts, illustrations, or other means to attract interest and explain concepts. Individuals in the group may take turns presenting their ideas, or one presenter may speak for the group. Consider inviting a reporter from the local news media to cover the event.

3 Project Assessment

Group Assessment

Groups may be given a single grade on the basis of preparation, presentation, and content. To assess preparation, you can review tape recordings of group sessions or ask to see notes and other records of student work. In addition, you can also ask students in each group to write a brief report of what was accomplished and the work that was done. To assess presentation, you can evaluate the materials and oral explanations given on the day of the Future Fair. Consider such factors as the ambitiousness and creativity of the project, the clarity and attractiveness of the group's materials, and the quality of the group's ideas.

Individual Assessment

If you wish to give individual grades as well, you can adapt some of the suggestions given above for evaluating preparation. Individual students can write a short self-evaluation in which they explain what they contributed to the project and what they learned. You may also ask students to keep a project log that describes the work that was done each day. Written reports from group members can also help you to determine which students did the most to contribute to the projects.

If some groups did not cooperate fully and share the work load, you may also wish to assign individual grades for each student's role in the presentation. This may motivate some students to take a more active role in future group projects.

For the Portfolio

Students can include copies of any written materials created for the project in their portfolios. In addition, you can take photographs of displays and audiotape or videotape any presentations.

4 Team-Teaching Options

Social Studies

Discuss how the founders of our country created our governmental system and how they tried to correct injustices or imbalances that had existed under the British system. Discuss some of the major problems they faced in designing a new form of government.

Math

Create an alternative system of exchange (perhaps a method of bartering) that might replace or simplify our current monetary system.

Art

Create drawings or displays that capture various aspects of life on a space colony of the future.

Science

Study the history of space travel and the modern inventions that came out of the U. S. space program. Explore the likelihood that other planets could sustain life.

Unit Preview

In Unit Three, "Reaching for the Stars," students will examine how dreams and determination motivate individuals to achieve. The unit contains two subunits:

- Subunit 1: "Driven by Dreams"
- Subunit 2: "Fight to the Finish"

Connections to Unit Six

Unit Six, "Themes in World Folklore," contains literature from the oral tradition that connects with the themes in Unit Three. You may wish to begin or end Unit Three with selections from Unit Six that relate to the theme "Reaching for the Stars":

ADDITIONAL RESOURCES

Unit Three Resource Book
Unit Test, pp. 64–67

Technology and Enrichment
Family and Community Involvement
   Source Book, pp. 12–14

About the Art

The Starry Night, by Vincent van Gogh (1853–1890), is one of the Dutch artist's most famous oil paintings. Completed in 1889, when van Gogh was in the midst of a severe mental crisis, the work shows a turbulent, whirling night sky. The earth below appears tranquil in comparison with the unsettled heavens. The intense colors are thickly applied to the canvas with short, sharp brush strokes that convey a tormented personal vision of nature. *Van Gogh said that he was "driven by dreams." How do you think this painting illustrates his statement?*

REACHING FOR THE STARS

If there is no

struggle, there

is no progress.

Frederick Douglass

THE STARRY NIGHT 1889 Vincent van Gogh
Oil on canvas, 29 x 35 1/4 inches (73.3 x 92.1 cm).
Collection of The Museum of Modern Art, New
York. Acquired through the Lillie B. Bliss Bequest.
Photograph © 1992 The Museum of Modern Art,
New York.

249

Discussion Questions

To help students probe connections between the fine art, the quotation, and the unit theme, have them consider the following questions:

1. What does the phrase "reaching for the stars" mean to you? *(Possible responses: setting a lofty goal, aspiring to greatness)*

2. How does the idea expressed in the quotation relate to reaching for the stars? *(Possible responses: The quotation emphasizes that struggle is involved in reaching for a lofty goal; it focuses on the need for action, since things left alone may stagnate or decay.)*

3. How does the art relate to the unit title? *(Possible responses: It shows a sky filled with stars that one might try to "reach"; it conveys the heavens' lofty grandeur.)*

4. How does the art relate to the quotation? *(Possible responses: It suggests a struggle in the turbulent skies; it depicts the turmoil out of which may come progress and peace on earth.)*

5. On the basis of the quotation and the art, what kinds of selections do you imagine this unit will contain? *(Possible responses: selections about individuals who struggle to achieve, selections about people with high-minded goals and dreams)*

About the Quoted Author

Frederick Douglass was born a slave sometime around the year 1817. At the age of eight, he was taken to Baltimore to work for a new master. Motivated by the desire for a better life, Douglass spent twelve years educating himself. Eventually he fled to Massachusetts to escape slavery. A speech he gave on freedom at an 1841 antislavery meeting marked the beginning of his work as a vocal opponent of racial and religious discrimination. Having bought his own freedom, he worked to help other slaves win their freedom as well. He conferred often with President Lincoln on the problem of slavery.

Have students read the introduction to Subunit 1, "Driven by Dreams." Ask them to explain how being driven by dreams relates to reaching for the stars. How do a person's dreams carry him or her upward? At what times are dreams and stars usually seen? How might a star's light symbolize a dream?

INTEGRATING THE LANGUAGE ARTS

The literary selections in this subunit focus on the theme "Driven by Dreams." Reading skills, literature skills, writing options, language study, vocabulary, and spelling skills are all based on these literary selections.

Writer's Workshop After reading several selections that deal with individuals driven by dreams, students will use informative writing to compose a magazine article about a person who has pursued a dream.

Language Workshop The Language Workshop deals with avoiding sentence fragments and run-ons. In informing others about people they admire, students will see the importance of writing in complete sentences.

Reader's Workshop The Reader's Workshop presents techniques for skimming and scanning, which students can use as they do research for their articles.

FOR ADDITIONAL CHALLENGE

The following selections offer challenge in the exploration of the subunit theme:

"All You've Ever Wanted," short story by Joan Aiken

Earth Shine, nonfiction by Anne Morrow Lindbergh

Madame Curie, biography by Eve Curie

The Sword in the Stone, novel by T. H. White

ADDITIONAL RESOURCES

Technology and Enrichment
Family and Community Involvement Source Book, p. 12

Guidelines for Reading and Literature Assessment, Observation Assessment Forms

DRIVEN BY DREAMS

Stars have always inspired people to dream, to stretch beyond themselves. We "reach for a star" when we set a high goal or fight a good fight, when we let our imagination soar or tap hidden strengths. There are billions of real stars, but none are as bright as the stars we create for ourselves with our dreams and goals.

In *Driven by Dreams,* you will read about dreamers of all kinds, from a boy fighting for glory to a woman who worked for people who had no one else to speak for them. Their struggles to achieve their dreams may inspire you to work hard to achieve your own dreams.

250   UNIT THREE   DRIVEN BY DREAMS

Observation Assessment

Observing how students respond to the text, to the classroom instruction, and to peers is an important part of an assessment program. The following suggestions and the form in the *Guidelines for Reading and Literature Assessment* booklet can be used to implement observation assessment.

■ **Reading Behavior** As students work through the subunit, assess how they establish a context for reading. See how effectively they use elements such as selection titles, headings, quotations in large type, and illustrations to help them understand the purpose and meaning of the selections. Also evaluate how they use context clues to understand the meanings of unfamiliar vocabulary words. Throughout the subunit, look for growth in their ability to use context as an aid to understanding.

Fiction

The *Smallest Dragonboy*

ANNE McCAFFREY

Examine What You Know (Prior Knowledge)

Think about a time when you wanted something so much that you could hardly think about anything else. What did you desire? What obstacles were in your way? In your journal or notebook, describe the situation.

Expand Your Knowledge (Building Background)

The main character of this story, which takes place on the imaginary planet Pern, has his heart set on becoming a dragonrider. The dragonriders of Pern are brave warriors who ride fire-breathing dragons to protect their planet from deadly plant spores. These spores, called Thread because of their shape, fall from the sky on regular occasions. If Thread are allowed to reach Pern's soil, they will destroy all living things.

Newborn dragons, hatched from huge eggs, choose their young riders through a silent communication known as Impression. An Impression allows a dragon and its rider to read each other's mind, thus creating a lifelong partnership based on trust and love.

The people of Pern live in cave colonies called *weyrs*. This particular story takes place in Benden Weyr, a colony of dragonriders located in the Benden Mountains of Pern.

Enrich Your Reading (Reading Skill)

Fantasy   This story is a **fantasy,** a story set in an imaginary world in which characters wish for things that are impossible in the real world. As you read, you will be presented with detailed information about life on Pern. At various places, you will find questions to help you review this information. Keep in mind that you do not have to understand all the details to enjoy the story.

■ *Author biography on Extend page*

THE SMALLEST DRAGONBOY   251

JOURNAL WRITING IDEAS
■ What do you think a "dragonboy" might be?

■ Describe dragons that you have read about in stories or that you have seen in movies. Were they good or evil?

■ Has an older boy or girl ever tried to bully you? Why do you think some people are bullies?

COLLABORATIVE LEARNING OPTIONS
Opportunities for collaborative learning include Options for Learning 2, 3, and 4 (p. 267), and Cross-Curricular Projects (p. 267).

ADDITIONAL RESOURCES
Unit Three Resource Book
Reader's Guidesheet, p. 1
Reading Skills, p. 2
Literature Skills, p. 3
Vocabulary Connections, p. 4
Spelling Connections, p. 5
Comprehension and Vocabulary Check Tests, p. 6
Selection Test, pp. 7–8

Technology and Enrichment
🎧 Audiocassette Tape 2, Side 1

Objectives

■ To understand and analyze a short story

■ To examine how an author creates suspense

■ To recognize elements of a fantasy

■ To express understanding of the story through a choice of writing forms, including a handbook, a dialogue, notes for a news story, and a character sketch

Prereading/Motivation

Examine What You Know

Discussion Prompts Have you ever waited impatiently for a special day to come—or put all your energy into achieving a goal? What stood between you and what you wanted?

Expand Your Knowledge

Additional Background In McCaffrey's fantasy world, Pern is the third planet of the sun Rukbat in the Sagittarian Sector. Humans settled the planet and later used their knowledge of genetic engineering to alter a native animal into a new species that resembled Earth's legendary dragons. The dragons can both fly and teleport themselves, or transport themselves by thinking of where they want to go. Dragonriders are a separate group in the society of Pern—they live in their own colonies apart from craftspeople and others.

Enrich Your Reading

For Alternative Learning Styles Visual learners might create a comic book based on the plot of the story.

Thematic Link— Driven by Dreams

Keevan's one dream is to Impress, or be chosen by, a dragon and become a dragonrider. Driven by that dream, he bravely struggles to prove his worth in spite of his youth, his competitors, and physical pain.

VOCABULARY PREVIEW

These vocabulary words are defined at the bottom of the selection pages on which they appear.

consensus general agreement

contemptuous scornful

desolation misery

dissipate gradually disappear

evasion act of avoiding

imperative necessary

indifference lack of concern

obscured hidden from view

replenished resupplied

sloth laziness

LIMITED ENGLISH PROFICIENCY

■ Use the Reader's Guidesheet, *Unit Three Resource Book*, page 1.

■ Help students use context clues and prior knowledge to guess the meanings of terms the author has invented for this fantasy.

★ Text annotations marked with a red star (3, 5, 8, 12, 14, 16, 17, 18, 27, 30, 37) may be particularly helpful for students with limited English proficiency.

TEXT ANNOTATIONS

1. ACTIVE READING: Predict
Based on the problems mentioned in these two paragraphs, ask students to predict important conflicts that Keevan will face in the story. *(Possible responses: His small size will put him at a disadvantage with his peers; the oldest boy, Beterli, will give him an especially hard time.)*

2. LITERARY CONCEPT: Fantasy
Invite volunteers to list things about life on Pern that are different from life on Earth. *(The people on Pern ride dragons; people and dragons communicate telepathically; evil Thread falls from the sky; people live in caves.)*

The *Smallest* Dragonboy

ANNE McCAFFREY

Although Keevan lengthened his walking stride as far as his legs would stretch, he couldn't quite keep up with the other candidates. He knew he would be teased again.

Just as he knew many other things that his foster mother told him he ought not to know, Keevan knew that Beterli, the most senior of the boys, set that spanking pace just to embarrass him, the smallest dragonboy. Keevan would arrive, tail fork-end of the group, breathless, chest heaving, and maybe get a stern look from the instructing wingsecond.

Dragonriders, even if they were still only hopeful candidates for the glowing eggs which were hardening on the hot sands of the Hatching Ground cavern, were expected to be punctual and prepared. Sloth was not tolerated by the weyrleader of Benden Weyr. A good record was especially important now. It was very near hatching time, when the baby dragons would crack their mottled[1] shells and stagger forth to choose their lifetime companions. The very thought of that glorious moment made Keevan's breath catch in his throat. To be chosen—to be a dragonrider! To sit astride the neck of the winged beast with the jeweled eyes; to

be his friend in telepathic communion[2] with him for life; to be his companion in good times and fighting extremes; to fly effortlessly over the lands of Pern! Or, thrillingly, *between* to any point anywhere on the world! Flying *between* was done on dragonback or not at all, and it was dangerous.

Keevan glanced upward, past the black mouths of the weyr caves in which grown dragons and their chosen riders lived, toward the Star Stones that crowned the ridge of the old volcano that was Benden Weyr. On the height, the blue watch-dragon, his rider mounted on his neck, stretched the great transparent pinions[3] that carried him on the winds of Pern to fight the evil Thread that fell at certain times from the sky. The many-faceted rainbow jewels of his eyes glistened momentarily in the greeny sun. He folded his great wings to his back, and the watch-pair resumed their statuesque pose of alertness.

Then the enticing view was obscured as Keevan passed into the Hatching Ground

---

1. **mottled** (mät′ ′ld): spotted or streaked with different colors.
2. **telepathic communion**: a close relationship in which ideas and feelings are communicated between two minds without talking.
3. **pinions** (pin′ yənz): wings.

| *Words to Know and Use* | **sloth** (slōth) *n.* laziness |
| | **obscured** (əb skyʊʊrd′) *adj.* hidden from view **obscure** *v.* |

Guided Reading for Less-Proficient Students

These questions can help students through the reading. Ask each question at the point of the selection where the capital letter and arrow appear in the margin. In addition, you may wish to use appropriate Active Reading annotations.

A. How does a candidate become a dragonrider? *(The candidate must be chosen by a newly hatched dragon.)* Recalling

B. How are Keevan and Beterli opposites? *(Keevan is

the youngest and smallest candidate while Beterli is the oldest and much larger.)* Inferring

C. Why are bronze dragons so special? *(They are the biggest dragons; they father all the new dragons; their riders can become weyrleaders.)* Recalling

D. Why is this Impression so important to Beterli? *(He has been passed over eight times; if he is not chosen this time, he'll be too old to be a dragonrider.)* Inferring

Continued on page 253

PANORAMA OF MACHU PICCHU 1978 Susan Shatter Private collection, Courtesy, Fischbach Gallery, New York.

Art Note
High in the Andes Mountains of Peru is a peak called Machu Picchu. On top of this peak, an ancient city of the Incas was built. The ruin and isolation of this city in the high peaks of the Andes is what Susan Shatter (1943–) has portrayed in her painting *Panorama of Machu Picchu*. How does this representation of an ancient, "lost" city capture the feeling of the setting of "The Smallest Dragonboy"?

3 cavern. The sands underfoot were hot, even through heavy wher-hide boots. How the boot maker had protested having to sew so small! Keevan was forced to wonder again why being small was reprehensible.[4] People were always calling him "babe" and shooing him away as being "too small" or "too young" for this or that. Keevan was con-
4 stantly working, twice as hard as any other boy his age, to prove himself capable. What if his muscles weren't as big as Beterli's? They were just as hard. And if he couldn't overpower anyone in a wrestling match, he
B ▶ could outdistance everyone in a footrace.

"Maybe if you run fast enough," Beterli had jeered on the occasion when Keevan had been goaded to boast of his swiftness, "you could catch a dragon. That's the only way you'll make a dragonrider!"

"You just wait and see, Beterli, you just wait," Keevan had replied. He would have

liked to wipe the contemptuous smile from Beterli's face, but the guy didn't fight fair even when the wingsecond was watching. "No one knows what Impresses a dragon!"

"They've got to be able to *find* you first, babe!"

Yes, being the smallest candidate was not an enviable position. It was therefore imperative that Keevan Impress a dragon in his first hatching. That would wipe the smile off every face in the cavern and accord him the respect due any dragonrider, even the smallest one.

Besides, no one knew exactly what Impressed the baby dragons as they struggled from their shells in search of their lifetime partners.
5

---

4. **reprehensible:** deserving of blame; bad.

Words to Know and Use	**contemptuous** (kən temp′ choo əs) *adj.* lacking respect; scornful **imperative** (im per′ ə tiv) *adj.* absolutely necessary

253

3. VOCABULARY: Definitions
Invite students to tell what *wher-hide* might be. *(Possible response: leather made from the skin of a wher—an animal of Pern)* Explain that the author has created some unique vocabulary to make her imaginary world more believable. Have students list some examples they have encountered so far and speculate on their meanings. *(Possible responses: watch-dragon, a dragon that acts as a guard, watching for Threads; wingsecond, an instructor of dragonboys; weyrleader, leader of a dwelling called a weyr)* ★

4. LITERARY CONCEPT: Characterization
Invite volunteers to make an inference about the kind of person Keevan is. *(Possible response: He is highly motivated to achieve, perhaps because he feels he must compensate for his small size.)*

5. ACTIVE READING: Question
Ask students to tell what the word *impress* means ordinarily. *(to influence positively, persuade, or make a mark on.)* Ask them to explain what it means on Pern. *(to be chosen by a dragon to be its lifetime partner)* Invite students to speculate on why the verb is written with a capital letter. *(Possible response: The capital shows that Impressing is an important ritual on Pern.)* ★

Guided Reading for Less-Proficient Students

Continued from page 252

E. What is the disagreement at dinner about? *(whether the youngest and oldest candidates should have a chance to become dragonriders)* Summarizing

F. What is the "news" that Beterli is suggesting to Keevan? *(The younger candidates have been dropped from the Impression.)* Inferring

G. Why might both Keevan and Beterli miss the Impression? *(Beterli has been disqualified for hurting Keevan; Keevan has a broken skull and leg.)* Recalling

H. What does Keevan do when he realizes that Impression has begun? *(He drags himself out of bed, dresses, and begins to hobble down to the Hatching Ground.)* Recalling

Continued on page 254

6. ACTIVE READING: Review
What is Keevan hoping for? *(Possible response: Keevan hopes that at his first hatching he will be able to Impress a dragon, thereby silencing those who say he is too young or too small to be a dragonrider.)*

7. LITERARY CONCEPT: Fantasy
Invite students to speculate on why the author has given the Pern characters such unusual names. *(Possible response: The unfamiliar names remind us that this is a fantasy story, a story set in a different time and world.)* Guide students in reaching a consensus on how to pronounce the names.

8. VOCABULARY: Definitions
Elicit the meanings of these words related to the dragon eggs: *hatching* ("breaking out of a shell"); *striations* and *stretch marks* ("lines on the egg made by the dragon moving inside"); and *clutch* ("a group of eggs"). What does "the extent of the striations" say about the nearness of Impression time? *(Possible response: More lines show that the baby dragons are putting more pressure on the walls of the eggs and are getting closer to breaking out.)* ★

9. LITERARY CONCEPT: Suspense
Ask students how the wingsecond's words build the reader's interest in the final outcome of the story. *(Possible response: From his words, we know that almost half of the candidates will be disappointed at the hatching, and we wonder if young Keevan has a chance.)*

6

review What is Keevan hoping for?

"I like to believe that dragons see into a man's heart," Keevan's foster mother, Mende, told him. "If they find goodness, honesty, a flexible mind, patience, courage—and you've that in quantity, dear Keevan—that's what dragons look for. I've seen many a well-grown lad left standing on the sands, Hatching Day, in favor of someone not so strong or tall or handsome. And if my memory serves me" (which it usually did—Mende knew every word of every Harper's tale worth telling, although Keevan did not interrupt her to say so), "I don't believe that F'lar, our weyrleader, was all that tall when bronze Mnementh chose him. And Mnementh was the only bronze dragon of that hatching."

Dreams of Impressing a bronze were beyond Keevan's boldest reflections, although that goal dominated the thoughts of every other hopeful candidate. Green dragons were small and fast and more numerous. There was more prestige to Impressing a blue or a brown than a green. Being practical, Keevan seldom dreamed as high as a big fighting brown, like Canth, F'nor's fine fellow, the biggest brown on all Pern. But to fly a bronze? Bronzes were almost as big as the queen, and only they took the air when a queen flew at mating

7

C ▶ time. A bronze rider could aspire to become weyrleader! Well, Keevan would console himself, brown riders could aspire to become wingseconds, and that wasn't bad. He'd even settle for a green dragon; they were small, but so was he. No matter! He simply had to Impress a dragon his first time in the Hatching Ground. Then no one

in the weyr would taunt him anymore for being so small.

"Shells," thought Keevan now, "but the sands are hot!"

"Impression time is imminent,[5] candidates," the wingsecond was saying as everyone crowded respectfully close to him. "See the extent of the striations on this promising egg." The stretch marks *were* larger than yesterday.

8

Everyone leaned forward and nodded thoughtfully. That particular egg was the one Beterli had marked as his own, and no other candidate dared, on pain of being beaten by Beterli on the first opportunity, to approach it. The egg was marked by a large yellowish splotch in the shape of a dragon backwinging to land, talons outstretched to grasp rock. Everyone knew that bronze eggs bore distinctive markings. And naturally, Beterli, who'd been presented at eight Impressions already and was the biggest of the candidates, had chosen it.

*S*ome of you may be disappointed on the great day.

"I'd say that the great opening day is almost upon us," the wingsecond went on, and then his face assumed a grave expression. "As we well know, there are only forty eggs and seventy-two candidates. Some of you may be disappointed on the great day. That doesn't necessarily mean you aren't dragonrider material, just that *the* dragon for

9

---

5. **imminent:** about to happen.

254   UNIT THREE   DRIVEN BY DREAMS

---

you hasn't been shelled. You'll have other hatchings, and it's no disgrace to be left behind an Impression or two. Or more."

Keevan was positive that the wingsecond's eyes rested on Beterli, who'd been stood off at so many Impressions already. Keevan tried to squinch down so the wingsecond wouldn't notice him. Keevan had been reminded too often that he was eligible to be a candidate by one day only. He, of all the hopefuls, was most likely to be left standing on the great day. One more reason why he simply had to Impress at his first hatching.

10

review | Why is Keevan afraid that he won't Impress a dragon?

"Now move about among the eggs," the wingsecond said. "Touch them. We don't know that it does any good, but it certainly doesn't do any harm."

Some of the boys laughed nervously, but everyone immediately began to circulate among the eggs. Beterli stepped up officiously to "his" egg, daring anyone to come near it. Keevan smiled, because he had already touched it . . . every inspection day . . . as the others were leaving the Hatching Ground, when no one could see him crouch and stroke it.

Keevan had an egg he concentrated on, too, one drawn slightly to the far side of the others. The shell bore a soft greenish-blue tinge with a faint creamy swirl design. The consensus was that this egg contained a mere green, so Keevan was rarely bothered by rivals. He was somewhat perturbed then to see Beterli wandering over to him.

"I don't know why you're allowed in this Impression, Keevan. There are enough of us without a babe," Beterli said, shaking his head.

"I'm of age." Keevan kept his voice level, telling himself not to be bothered by mere words.

"Yah!" Beterli made a show of standing on his toe tips. "You can't even see over an egg. Hatching Day, you better get in front or the dragons won't see you at all. 'Course, you could get run down that way in the mad scramble. Oh, I forget, you can run fast, can't you?"

"You'd better make sure a dragon sees *you* this time, Beterli," Keevan replied. "You're almost overage, aren't you?" ◄ D

Beterli flushed and took a step forward, hand half raised. Keevan stood his ground, but if Beterli advanced one more step, he would call the wingsecond. No one fought on the Hatching Ground. Surely Beterli knew that much.

11

Fortunately, at that moment the wingsecond called the boys together and led them from the Hatching Ground to start on evening chores.

There were "glows" to be replenished in the main kitchen caverns and sleeping cubicles, the major hallways, and the queen's apartment. Firestone sacks had to be filled against Thread attack, and black rock brought to the kitchen hearths. The boys fell to their chores, tantalized by the odors

12

| Words to Know and Use | **consensus** (kən sen' səs) *n.* an opinion shared by most; general agreement
replenished (ri plen' ishd) *adj.* added to; resupplied **replenish** *v.* |

255

---

10. ACTIVE READING: Review
Why is Keevan afraid that he won't Impress a dragon? (*Possible responses: Since there are thirty-two more candidates than eggs, many boys will be disappointed; being the youngest and smallest, Keevan fears he will be passed over.*)

11. LITERARY CONCEPT: Conflict
By taunting Keevan, Beterli creates an external conflict between himself and Keevan. Ask students if they think Beterli has an internal conflict that leads him to tease Keevan. (*Possible responses: Keevan's youth might remind Beterli that he is almost too old to Impress a dragon; Beterli has tried before and failed.*)

12. VOCABULARY: Context Clues
Invite students to speculate on the meaning of *glows* ("lamps"), *firestone sacks* ("bags of ammunition against Thread"), and *black rock* ("fuel used in hearths for cooking or heating"). Ask them what clues the author gives to help readers define these made-up terms. (*Possible responses: She tells where the items are used; the terms contain familiar words that suggest what the items look like or what purpose they serve.*) ★

Looking at Style

Read these descriptions to students, having them listen for visual details:

■ The many-faceted rainbow jewels of his eyes glistened momentarily in the greeny sun. (p. 252)

■ The egg was marked by a large yellowish splotch in the shape of a dragon backwinging to land, talons outstretched to grasp rock. Everyone knew that bronze eggs bore distinctive markings. (p. 254)

Discuss the following questions and activity.

1. What colors are mentioned? What other visual details are given?

2. How important are the details in allowing the reader to visualize the objects? What if the details were omitted?

3. Look closely at an object. Describe its color, shape, and markings so that others can visualize it.

THE WHITE DRAGON   ©1992   Michael Whelan.

of roasting meat. The population of the weyr began to assemble for the evening meal, and the dragonriders came in from the Feeding Ground or their sweep checks.

It was the time of day Keevan liked best. Once the chores were done, before dinner was served, a fellow could often get close to the dragonriders and listen to their talk. Tonight Keevan's father, K'last, was at the main dragonrider table. It puzzled Keevan how his father, a brown rider and a tall man, could *be* his father—because he, Keevan, was

so small. It obviously never puzzled K'last when he deigned[6] to notice his small son: "In a few more turns, you'll be as tall as I am—or taller!"

K'last was pouring Benden drink all around the table. The dragonriders were relaxing. There'd be no Thread attack for three more days, and they'd be in the mood

---

6. **deigned** (dānd): lowered oneself to do something beneath one's dignity.

to tell tall tales, better than Harper yarns, about impossible maneuvers they'd done a-dragonback. When Thread attack was closer, their talk would change to a discussion of tactics of evasion, of going *between*, how long to suspend there until the burning but fragile Thread would freeze and crack and fall harmlessly off dragon and man. They would dispute the exact moment to feed firestone to the dragon so he'd have the best flame ready to sear Thread midair and render it harmless to ground—and man—below. There was such a lot to know and understand about being a dragonrider that sometimes Keevan was overwhelmed. How would he ever be able to remember everything he ought to know at the right moment? He couldn't dare ask such a question; this would only have given additional weight to the notion that he was too young yet to be a dragonrider.

"Having older candidates makes good sense," L'vel was saying, as Keevan settled down near the table. "Why waste four to five years of a dragon's fighting prime until his rider grows up enough to stand the rigors?" L'vel had Impressed a blue of Ramoth's first clutch. Most of the candidates thought L'vel was marvelous because he spoke up in front of the older riders, who awed them. "That was well enough in the Interval when you didn't need to mount the full weyr complement[7] to fight Thread. But not now. Not with more eligible candidates than ever. Let the babes wait."

"Any boy who is over twelve turns has the right to stand in the Hatching Ground," K'last replied, a slight smile on his face. He never argued or got angry. Keevan wished he were more like his father. And oh, how he wished he were a brown rider! "Only a dragon . . . each particular dragon . . . knows what he wants in a rider. We certainly can't tell. Time and again the theorists"—and K'last's smile deepened as his eyes swept those at the table—"are surprised by dragon choice. *They* never seem to make mistakes, however."

Now, K'last, just look at the roster of this Impression. Seventy-two boys and only forty eggs. Drop off the twelve youngest, and there's still a good field for the hatchlings to choose from. Shells! There are a couple of weyrlings unable to see over a wher egg, much less a dragon! And years before they can ride Thread."

"True enough, but the weyr is scarcely under fighting strength, and if the youngest Impress, they'll be old enough to fight when the oldest of our current dragons go *between* from senility."

"Half the weyrbred lads have already been through several Impressions," one of the bronze riders said then. "I'd say drop some of *them* off this time. Give the untried a chance."

"There's nothing wrong in presenting a clutch with as wide a choice as possible," said the weyrleader, who had joined the table with Lessa, the weyrwoman.

---

7. **complement:** the entire group.

| *Words to Know and Use* | **evasion** (ē vā′ zhən) *n.* the act of avoiding or escaping from |

257

15. ACTIVE READING: Evaluate For Alternative Learning Styles Ask two volunteers to read the dialogue between L'vel and K'last that begins here and ends after four paragraphs. Then ask other students which character has the strongest argument. Have them explain their reasoning. *(Any response is valid.)*

16. VOCABULARY: Interjection Explain to students that *Shells!* is an interjection, or an exclamation that shows strong feelings. Ask students if they think the word *shells* refers to something on Pern. *(Possible response: It could refer to the shells of dragon eggs.)* ★

Speaking . . . Listening . . . Viewing

Viewing *Star Wars*, the 1977 blockbuster science fiction film directed by George Lucas, contains many of the same themes as "The Smallest Dragonboy." Treat students to a screening of this film, available from Fox Video. Before they watch, invite them to look for answers to these questions:

1. As Keevan strives to become a dragonrider, he learns his society's traditions. What does Luke Skywalker aspire to become in *Star Wars*? What traditions does he learn?

2. Who in *Star Wars* are the equivalents of dragonriders, and what evil do they fight?

3. Keevan is often humiliated by Beterli, an older and bigger boy. In *Star Wars*, who treats Luke like Beterli treats Keevan?

4. Keevan is humbled because of his size, yet in the end he surpasses all his fellow candidates by Impressing a bronze dragon. How does Luke rise from his humble beginnings to become a hero?

17

"Has there ever been a case," she said, smiling in her odd way at the riders, "where a hatchling didn't choose?"

Her suggestion was almost heretical and drew astonished gasps from everyone, including the boys.

F'lar laughed. "You say the most outrageous things, Lessa."

"Well, *has* there ever been a case where a dragon didn't choose?"

"Can't say as I recall one," K'last replied.

"Then we continue in this tradition," Lessa said firmly, as if that ended the matter.

But it didn't. The argument ranged from one table to the other all through dinner, with some favoring a weeding out of the candidates to the most likely, lopping off those who were very young or who had had multiple opportunities to Impress. All the candidates were in a swivet,[8] though such a departure from tradition would be to the advantage of many. As the evening progressed, more riders were favoring eliminating the youngest and those who'd passed four or more Impressions unchosen. Keevan felt he could bear such a dictum[9] only if Beterli was also eliminated. But this seemed

18

less likely than that Keevan would be tuffed out, since the weyr's need was for fighting dragons and riders.

19

review What are the adults arguing about?

By the time the evening meal was over, no decision had been reached, although the weyrleader had promised to give the matter due consideration.

He might have slept on the problem, but few of the candidates did. Tempers were uncertain in the sleeping caverns next morn-

KEEVAN.   Illustration by Robin Wood.

ing as the boys were routed out of their beds to carry water and black rock and cover the "glows." Mende had to call Keevan to order twice for clumsiness.

"Whatever is the matter with you, boy?" she demanded in exasperation when he tipped black rock short of the bin and sooted up the hearth.

"They're going to keep me from this Impression."

"What?" Mende stared at him. "Who?"

"You heard them talking at dinner last night. They're going to tuff the babes from the hatching."

20

---

8. **swivet:** a state of annoyance.
9. **dictum:** a pronouncement made with authority.

Mende regarded him a moment longer before touching his arm gently. "There's lots of talk around a supper table, Keevan. And it cools as soon as the supper. I've heard the same nonsense before every hatching, but nothing is ever changed."

"There's always a first time," Keevan answered, copying one of her own phrases.

"That'll be enough of that, Keevan. Finish your job. If the clutch does hatch today, we'll need full rock bins for the feast, and you won't be around to do the filling. All my fosterlings make dragonriders."

"The first time?" Keevan was bold enough to ask as he scooted off with the rockbarrow.

Perhaps, Keevan thought later, if he hadn't been on that chore just when Beterli was also fetching black rock, things might have turned out differently. But he had dutifully trundled the barrow to the outdoor bunker for another load just as Beterli arrived on a similar errand.

"Heard the news, babe?" asked Beterli. He was grinning from ear to ear, and he put an unnecessary emphasis on the final insulting word.

"The eggs are cracking?" Keevan all but dropped the loaded shovel. Several anxieties flicked through his mind then: He was black with rock dust—would he have time to wash before donning the white tunic of candidacy? And if the eggs were hatching, why hadn't the candidates been recalled by the wingsecond?

"Naw! Guess again!" Beterli was much too pleased with himself.

With a sinking heart Keevan knew what the news must be, and he could only stare with intense <u>desolation</u> at the older boy.

"C'mon! Guess, babe!"

"I've no time for guessing games," Keevan managed to say with <u>indifference</u>. He began to shovel black rock into his barrow as fast as he could.

"I said, 'Guess.'" Beterli grabbed the shovel.

"And I said I'd no time for guessing games."

Beterli wrenched the shovel from Keevan's hands. "Guess!"

"I'll have the shovel back, Beterli." Keevan straightened up, but he didn't come up to Beterli's bulky shoulder. From somewhere, other boys appeared, some with barrows, some mysteriously alerted to the prospect of a confrontation among their numbers.

He must've been dropped from the candidacy.

"Babes don't give orders to candidates around here, babe!"

Someone sniggered, and Keevan knew, incredibly, that he must've been dropped from the candidacy.

He yanked the shovel from Beterli's loosened grasp. Snarling, the older boy tried to regain possession, but Keevan clung with all his strength to the handle, dragged back and forth as the stronger boy jerked the shovel about.

With a sudden, unexpected movement,

◀ F

21

22

23

24

| Words to Know and Use | **desolation** (des′ ə lā′ shən) *n.* feeling of loneliness and misery
 indifference (in dif′ ər əns) *n.* a lack of interest or concern |

259

Beterli rammed the handle into Keevan's chest, knocking him over the barrow handles. Keevan felt a sharp, painful jab behind his left ear, an unbearable pain in his right shin, and then a painless nothingness.

Mende's angry voice roused him, and startled, he tried to throw back the covers, thinking he'd overslept. But he couldn't move, so firmly was he tucked into his bed. And then the constriction of a bandage on his head and the dull sickishness in his leg brought back recent occurrences.

"Hatching?" he cried.

No, lovey," said Mende, and her voice was suddenly very kind, her hand cool and gentle on his forehead. "Though there's some as won't be at any hatching again." Her voice took on a stern edge.

Keevan looked beyond her to see the weyrwoman, who was frowning with irritation.

"Keevan, will you tell me what occurred at the black-rock bunker?" Lessa asked, but her voice wasn't angry.

He remembered Beterli now and the quarrel over the shovel and . . . what had Mende said about some not being at any hatching? Much as he hated Beterli, he couldn't bring himself to tattle on Beterli and force him out of candidacy.

"Come, lad," and a note of impatience crept into the weyrwoman's voice. "I merely want to know what happened from you, too. Mende said she sent you for black rock. Beterli—and every weyrling in the cavern—seems to have been on the same errand. What happened?"

"Beterli took the shovel. I hadn't finished with it."

"There's more than one shovel. What did he *say* to you?"

"He'd heard the news."

"What news?" The weyrwoman was suddenly amused.

"That . . . that . . . there'd been changes."

"Is that what he said?"

"Not exactly."

"What did he say? C'mon, lad. I've heard from everyone else, you know."

"He said for me to guess the news."

"And you fell for that old gag?" The weyrwoman's irritation returned.

"Consider all the talk last night at supper, Lessa," said Mende. "Of course the boy would think he'd been eliminated."

"In effect, he is, with a broken skull and leg." She touched his arm, a rare gesture of sympathy in her. "Be that as it may, Keevan, you'll have other Impressions. Beterli will not. There are certain rules that must be observed by all candidates, and his conduct proves him unacceptable to the weyr."

She smiled at Mende and then left.

How will what happened to Keevan affect his candidacy? *predict*

"I'm still a candidate?" Keevan asked urgently.

"Well, you are and you aren't, lovey," his foster mother said. "Is the numb weed working?" she asked, and when he nodded, she said, "You just rest. I'll bring you some nice broth."

At any other time in his life, Keevan would have relished such cosseting,[10] but he lay there worrying. Beterli had been dismissed. Would the others think it was his

---

10. **cosseting:** pampering.

fault? But everyone was there! Beterli provoked the fight. His worry increased, because although he heard excited comings and goings in the passageway, no one tweaked back the curtain across the sleeping alcove he shared with five other boys. Surely one of them would have to come in sometime. No, they were all avoiding him. And something else was wrong. Only he didn't know what.

Mende returned with broth and beachberry bread.

"Why doesn't anyone come see me, Mende? I haven't done anything wrong, have I? I didn't ask to have Beterli tuffed out."

Mende soothed him, saying everyone was busy with noontime chores and no one was mad at him. They were giving him a chance to rest in quiet. The numb weed made him drowsy, and her words were fair enough. He permitted his fears to dissipate. Until he heard the humming. It started low, too low to be heard. Rather he felt it in the broken shinbone and his sore head. And thought, at first, it was an effect of the numb weed. Then the hum grew, augmented by additional sources. Two things registered suddenly in Keevan's groggy mind: The only white candidate's robe still on the pegs in the chamber was his; and dragons hummed when a clutch was being laid or being hatched. Impression! And he was flat abed.

Bitter, bitter disappointment turned the warm broth sour in his belly. Even the small voice telling him that he'd have other opportunities failed to alleviate[11] his crushing depression. *This* was the Impression that mattered! This was his chance to show *everyone* from Mende to K'last to L'vel and even the weyrleaders that he, Keevan, was worthy of being a dragonrider.

He twisted in bed, fighting against the tears that threatened to choke him. Dragonmen don't cry! Dragonmen learn to live with pain. . . .

Pain? The leg didn't actually pain him as he rolled about on his bedding. His head felt sort of stiff from the tightness of the bandage. He sat up, an effort in itself since the numb weed made exertion difficult. He touched the splinted leg, but the knee was unhampered. He had no feeling in his bone, really. He swung himself carefully to the side of his bed and slowly stood. The room wanted to swim about him. He closed his eyes, which made the dizziness worse, and he had to clutch the bedpost.

Gingerly he took a step. The broken leg dragged. It hurt in spite of the numb weed, but what was pain to a dragonman?

No one had said he couldn't go to the Impression. "You are and you aren't," were Mende's exact words.

Clinging to the bedpost, he jerked off his bed shirt. Stretching his arm to the utmost, he jerked his white candidate's tunic from the peg. Jamming first one arm and then the other into the holes, he pulled it over his head. Too bad about the belt. He couldn't wait. He hobbled to the door, hung on to

---

11. **alleviate:** to lessen; decrease.

261

29. ACTIVE READING: Predict
Invite students to predict what else was wrong, taking into account the "excited comings and goings in the passageway." (*Possible response: The hatching has begun and the excited candidates are hurrying to the Hatching Ground.*)

30. LITERARY CONCEPT: Fantasy
Ask students what they think *broth, beachberry bread,* and *numb weed* are. (*Possible responses: Broth is a liquid in which meat or other food has been cooked; beachberry bread is bread made with berries; numb weed is an herb that kills pain.*) Have them tell which items are realistic (*broth and bread*) and which are fantasy (*beachberry and numb weed*). ★

31. ACTIVE READING: Connect
Have you ever wanted to do something so badly that you ignored your own physical pain? Tell what happened. If you were Keevan, would you go to the Impression with a broken leg and cracked skull? (*Any response is valid.*)

the curtain to steady himself. The weight on his leg was unwieldy. He'd not get very far without something to lean on. Down by the bathing pool was one of the long crook-necked poles used to retrieve clothes from the hot washing troughs. But it was down there, and he was on the level above. And there was no one nearby to come to his aid. Everyone would be in the Hatching Ground right now, eagerly waiting for the first egg to crack.

The humming increased in volume and tempo, an urgency to which Keevan responded, knowing that his time was all too limited if he was to join the ranks of the hopeful boys standing about the cracking eggs. But if he hurried down the ramp, he'd fall flat on his face.

He could, of course, go flat on his rear end, the way crawling children did. He sat down, the jar sending a stab of pain through his leg and up to the wound on the back of his head. Gritting his teeth and blinking away the tears, Keevan scrabbled down the ramp. He had to wait a moment at the bottom to catch his breath. He got to one knee, the injured leg straight out in front of him. Somehow he managed to push himself erect, though the room wanted to tip over his ears. It wasn't far to the crooked stick, but it seemed an age before he had it in his hand.

Then the humming stopped!

Then the humming stopped!

Keevan cried out and began to hobble frantically across the cavern, out to the bowl of the weyr. Never had the distance between the living caverns and the Hatching Ground seemed so great. Never had the weyr been so silent, breathless. As if the multitude of people and dragons watching the hatching held every breath in suspense. Not even the wind muttered down the steep sides of the bowl. The only sounds to break the stillness were Keevan's ragged breathing and the thump-thud of his stick on the hard-packed ground. Sometimes he had to hop twice on his good leg to maintain his balance. Twice he fell into the sand and had to pull himself up on the stick, his white tunic no longer spotless. Once he jarred himself so badly he couldn't get up immediately.

Then he heard the first exhalation of the crowd, the ooohs, the muted cheer, the susurrus[12] of excited whispers. An egg had cracked, and the dragon had chosen his rider. Desperation increased Keevan's hobble. Would he never reach the arching mouth of the Hatching Ground?

Another cheer and an excited spate of applause spurred Keevan to greater effort. If he didn't get there in moments, there'd be no unpaired hatchling left. Then he was actually staggering into the Hatching Ground, the sands hot on his bare feet.

No one noticed his entrance or his halting progress. And Keevan could see nothing but the backs of the white-robed candidates, seventy of them ringing the area around the eggs. Then one side would surge forward or back, and there'd be a cheer. Another dragon had been Impressed. Suddenly a large gap appeared in the white human wall, and Keevan had his first sight of the eggs. There didn't seem to be *any* left uncracked, and he

---

12. **susurrus** (sə sʉr′ əs): a murmuring or rustling sound.

262   UNIT THREE   DRIVEN BY DREAMS

could see the lucky boys standing beside wobble-legged dragons. He could hear the unmistakable plaintive crooning of hatchlings and their squawks of protest as they'd fall awkwardly in the sand.

Suddenly he wished that he hadn't left his bed, that he'd stayed away from the Hatching Ground. Now everyone would see his ignominious[13] failure. He scrambled now as desperately to reach the shadowy walls of the Hatching Ground as he had struggled to cross the bowl. He mustn't be seen.

He didn't notice, therefore, that the shifting group of boys remaining had begun to drift in his direction. The hard pace he had set himself and his cruel disappointment took their double toll on Keevan. He tripped and collapsed sobbing to the warm sands. He didn't see the consternation[14] in the watching weyrfolk above the Hatching Ground, nor did he hear the excited whispers of speculation. He didn't know that the weyrleader and weyrwoman had dropped to the arena and were making their way toward the knot of boys slowly moving in the direction of the archway.

"Never seen anything like it," the weyrleader was saying. "Only thirty-nine riders chosen. And the bronze trying to leave the Hatching Ground without making Impression!"

"A case in point of what I said last night," the weyrwoman replied, "where a hatch-

Photograph used with permission of Windstone Editions © 1988,1992. No copying permitted.

ling makes no choice because the right boy isn't there."

"There's only Beterli and K'last's young one missing. And there's a full wing of likely boys to choose from. . . ."

"None acceptable, apparently. Where is the creature going? He's not heading for the entrance after all. Oh, what have we there, in the shadows?" ◀ I

Keevan heard with dismay the sound of voices nearing him. He tried to burrow into the sand. The mere thought of how he would be teased and taunted now was unbearable.

Don't worry! Please don't worry! The thought was urgent, but not his own. | 35

Someone kicked sand over Keevan and butted roughly against him.

"Go away. Leave me alone!" he cried.

Why? was the injured-sounding question inserted into his mind. There was no voice, no tone, but the question was there, perfectly clear, in his head.

Incredulous, Keevan lifted his head and stared into the glowing jeweled eyes of a small bronze dragon. His wings were wet; the tips hung drooping to the sand. And he sagged in the middle on his unsteady legs, although he was making a great effort to keep erect. | 36

Keevan dragged himself to his knees, oblivious[15] to the pain of his leg. He wasn't

---

13. **ignominious** (ig′ nə min′ ē əs): shameful; disgraceful.
14. **consternation**: concern; fear.
15. **oblivious**: unaware of; not paying attention to.

35. ACTIVE READING: Question
Ask students what the source of this thought could be, if it isn't Keevan's. *(Possible response: It could be a dragon's thought—dragons communicate telepathically with their riders.)*

36. LITERARY CONCEPT: Theme
When students understand that Keevan has Impressed the bronze dragon, have them suggest what theme, or main message, the story presents. *(Possible responses: By acting bravely and boldly, people can fulfill their dreams and goals; people must aim high, and never underestimate themselves.)*

37. VOCABULARY: Context Clues
Have students use context clues to infer that the word *draconic* means "of or having to do with a dragon." ★

38. ACTIVE READING: Question
Have students speculate on why Keevan's name is suddenly spelled and pronounced *K'van*. Hint: Have them recall the names of other dragonriders —K'last and L'vel. *(Possible response: Upon Impressing a dragon, a candidate's name changes to reflect his new status. The vowels in the first syllable of the name are replaced with an apostrophe.)* Students can confirm or correct their speculations in the next few lines.

39. ACTIVE READING: Predict
Ask volunteers to predict what type of future K'van and Heath will have together. *(Any response is valid. Some students may predict that K'van will become weyrleader, since his bronze dragon makes him eligible.)*

ENCOURAGING INDEPENDENT READING

Dragonsong, novel by Anne McCaffrey

The Hero and the Crown, novel by Robin McKinley

Howl's Moving Castle, novel by Diana Wynne Jones

A Wizard of Earthsea, novel by Ursula K. LeGuin

---

37 even aware that he was ringed by the boys passed over, while thirty-one pairs of resentful eyes watched him Impress the dragon. The weyrleaders looked on, amused and surprised at the draconic choice, which could not be forced. Could not be questioned. Could not be changed.

J ▶ *Why?* asked the dragon again. *Don't you like me?* His eyes whirled with anxiety, and his tone was so piteous that Keevan staggered forward and threw his arms around the dragon's neck, stroking his eye ridges, patting the damp, soft hide, opening the fragile-looking wings to dry them, and assuring the hatchling wordlessly over and over again that he was the most perfect, most beautiful, most beloved dragon in the entire weyr, in all the weyrs of Pern.

38 "What's his name, K'van?" asked Lessa, smiling warmly at the new dragonrider. K'van stared up at her for a long moment. Lessa would know as soon as he did. Lessa was the only person who could "receive" from all dragons, not only her own Ramoth.

Then he gave her a radiant smile, recognizing the traditional shortening of his name that raised him forever to the rank of dragonrider.

My name is Heath, thought the dragon mildly and hiccuped in sudden urgency. *I'm hungry.*

"Dragons are born hungry," said Lessa, laughing. "F'lar, give the boy a hand. He can barely manage his own legs, much less a dragon's."

K'van remembered his stick and drew himself up. "We'll be just fine, thank you."

"You may be the smallest dragonrider ever, young K'van, but you're the bravest," said F'lar.

And Heath agreed! Pride and joy so leaped in both chests that K'van wondered if his heart would burst right out of his body. He looped an arm around Heath's neck, and the pair—the smallest dragonboy and the hatchling who wouldn't choose anybody else—walked out of the Hatching Ground together forever. ❧ **39**

264   UNIT THREE   DRIVEN BY DREAMS

Comprehension Check

1. What do dragonriders and their dragons fight against? *(Thread)*

2. What is Keevan's size and age in comparison to the other candidates? *(He is the smallest and the youngest.)*

3. Why is this Beterli's last chance to be a dragonrider? *(He has already tried to Impress eight times and is almost overage.)*

4. How is Keevan hurt? *(In a fight with Beterli, his skull and leg are broken.)*

5. What happens to Beterli after his fight with Keevan? *(He is disqualified from Impression.)*

6. What sound does Keevan hear that lets him know the Impression is about to begin? *(humming)*

7. How does Keevan get to the Hatching Ground? *(He drags himself there despite his pain.)*

8. What kind of dragon does Keevan Impress? *(a bronze)*

*R*esponding to Reading

First Impressions

1. What were your feelings during the Impression? Jot down your response in your journal or notebook.

Second Thoughts

2. How does Keevan prove himself worthy of the bronze dragon?

3. Why do you think Beterli and Keevan have such a powerful effect on each other?

4. What human qualities seem to be most valued by the people of Pern?

> **Think about**
> - what dragons look for in humans
> - why Beterli is disqualified
> - the difficulties and dangers of life on Pern

5. Would you like to live on Pern? Why or why not?

Broader Connections

6. People often cheer for underdogs, competitors like Keevan who are not expected to win. What other underdogs do you know about? What makes their success satisfying? How are they like Keevan?

*L*iterary Concept: Suspense

Suspense is the excitement or tension that readers feel as they become involved in a story. Suspense is usually caused by uncertainty about what will happen next. One way writers achieve suspense is by adding complications. For example, the dinner discussion adds the complication that Keevan might be too young to be a candidate.

Work with a partner to see how McCaffrey creates suspense. Create a line graph to track the suspense. On the horizontal line, list important events in the plot, such as "*Beterli fights Keevan.*" On the vertical line, make a suspense scale by listing the numbers 1 (least suspenseful) to 10 (most suspenseful). Then place a dot on the graph above each event and across from the number that shows your level of suspense. After finishing, draw a line that connects the dots. Compare your graph to others in the class.

THE SMALLEST DRAGONBOY   265

Student Response

Responding to Reading

1. Any response is valid.

2. **Possible responses:** Keevan follows the rules, has the qualities of honesty, patience, and courage that may appeal to dragons, works harder than other boys, and endures great pain to be Impressed; despite his broken leg and skull, Keevan still manages to reach the Hatching Ground without help.

3. **Possible responses:** Each reminds the other of his shortcomings. Keevan's youth may be threatening to Beterli because it reminds him that he is almost overage and has repeatedly failed to Impress. Beterli's age and size may make Keevan aware of his own smallness, and Beterli's insulting remarks may embarrass Keevan as well as increase his self-doubt.

4. **Possible responses:** Goodness, honesty, patience, courage, and loyalty are valued most by the people of Pern. Beterli was disqualified for his cruelty and his failure to obey the rules.

5. Any response is valid.

6. Any response is valid. Students might cite Jackie Robinson and Jean Little as examples from selections in this book. Both show great determination in the face of adversity; Robinson was courageous.

Challenge Question

Would the plot and characters of this story work as well in a different setting? If so, what details of the plot would need to change? *(Possible responses: Yes, the basic story could work in other settings; the goals of the boys would be different, the contest and dangers would be different, Beterli would be disqualified for a different reason. No, the setting is too important a part of the fantasy; changing the setting would ruin the story.)*

Literary Concept: Suspense

Possible events listed on graphs:

Keevan and Beterli argue during dragonrider training.

Adults argue at dinner.

Beterli fights Keevan.

Keevan wakes up injured.

Keevan limps to Hatching Ground.

Keevan arrives at Impression.

Keevan Impresses Heath.

Writing Options

The Writing Options are designed to meet varied student interests and abilities. Have each student choose one writing activity to complete.

Journal Update Invite students to add to their journal entries for "The Smallest Dragonboy." They might discuss whether they have been given a different impression of dragons in this story, or whether they would like to read more fantasy.

Links to Writer's Craft

Writing Option 4 is an exercise in descriptive writing. For more practice, see *The Writer's Craft,* Grade 7, "Observation and Description," pages 48–67.

Vocabulary Practice

Answers to Exercise

1. replenish   6. contemptuous
2. imperative   7. indifference
3. evasion   8. obscure
4. sloth   9. dissipate
5. consensus   10. desolation

For Alternative Learning Styles

For more practice with the words, invite students to think of antonyms for as many of the new vocabulary words as possible. Another option is to have students use the words to make up and recite original sentences about their everyday lives.

Closure

Keevan is truly driven by his dream. Ask students to think of him in terms of their own world. Do they know people like him? Do they think that being driven to achieve is usually positive or negative? Lead a short discussion about the idea of kids and adults being so goal-oriented that other things are shoved aside.

Writing Options

1. Review the story to find rules and instructions for dragonrider candidates. Use what you find to write a **handbook** for candidates.

2. Write a **dialogue** of a talk show that has Keevan, you, and one other literary character as guests. The topic: Overcoming the obstacles to your dreams. Be sure to include your own dreams and the obstacles standing in your way.

3. Write **notes** that a reporter at the hatching ground might have made. Describe the sights and sounds of the hatching.

4. Lessa is the only character who can "receive" from all dragons. Review the story and write a **character sketch** of her. Include information about her job, her powers, and her personality.

Vocabulary Practice

Exercise   On your paper, write the vocabulary word that most closely matches the meaning of the boldfaced word or phrase in each sentence.

1. To **renew** the food supply of the dragons takes hard work.
2. It is **essential** that Thread be stopped from destroying Pern.
3. **Avoidance** is difficult when Thread falls from the sky.
4. Dragonrider candidates must avoid **laziness.**
5. The dragonriders did not reach an **agreement** during their dinner discussion.
6. Beterli showed a **disrespectful** attitude toward Keevan.
7. Keevan tried to show his **lack of concern** about the dinner discussion.
8. The morning mist could **hide** the view of the Hatching Ground.
9. The crowd of candidates will **scatter** after the last hatching.
10. Beterli probably felt **great sadness** when he realized he would not be a candidate.

> *Words to Know and Use*
>
> consensus
> contemptuous
> desolation
> dissipate
> evasion
> imperative
> indifference
> obscure
> replenish
> sloth

The Spelling Connection

Spelling Patterns: *ous/us* and *ize/ise* The suffix **ous,** meaning "full of" or "having certain characteristics," can be added to words to form adjectives. The suffix **ize,** meaning "to make or become," is added to words to form verbs. Both **us** and **ise** are parts of words; they are not suffixes.

Examples: industry + **ous** = industri**ous**
critic + **ize** = critic**ize**

ous/us and *ize/ise* Words from the Selection
marvel**ous**   offici**ous**   consens**us**

outrage**ous** ignomini**ous** surpr**ise**

Other *ous/us* **and** *ize/ise* **Words**
courage**ous** circ**us** real**ize** desp**ise**
adventur**ous** geni**us** apolog**ize** exerc**ise**

Exercise Pick words that fit the definitions.

adjectives	nouns	verbs
wonderful	workout	understand
daring	animal show	say you're sorry
meddlesome	bright person	find fault

Options for Learning (Multimodal/Cross-Curricular Activities)

1 • A Book by Its Cover Design an eye-catching bookcover for "The Smallest Dragonboy." Your cover should include a front and back side, as well as inside flaps that summarize the story and the author's life.

2 • Pern Tour Guide Create a glossary of Pern terms from the story to help first-time visitors. You might use one of the many reference books about Pern, such as *The Dragonlover's Guide to Pern*, by Jody Lynn Nye with Anne McCaffrey, to help you. Make up definitions and create illustrations to help visitors.

3 • Thread Alert Scan some of McCaffrey's Pern novels to find a description of a Thread attack. Then draw an illustration or give an oral report to describe the event.

4 • Dragon, Dragon Find a myth, folk tale, or legend from another country about dragons, and retell the story to your class. Describe the dragons so that your classmates can compare them to the dragons in Pern.

 FACT FINDER MATHEMATICS

In the hatching described in the story, what percentage of the candidates Impressed dragons?

Anne McCaffrey
1926—

The inspiration for "The Smallest Dragonboy" came from Anne McCaffrey's brother, Kevin. When Kevin was twelve, a bone disease forced him to keep his arm in a painful cast. His bravery inspired his sister to write about a boy who overcomes pain.

McCaffrey writes her novels and short stories at Dragonhold, her name for her home in County Wicklow, Ireland. Born in Cambridge, Massachusetts, McCaffrey's writing career began in the United States, where she has spent most of her life.

Nicknamed "the Dragon Lady" by fans, her best-known books are *Dragonflight, Dragonsong,* and *Dragonsinger.* These stories are set in Pern, a world with its own history, geography, and culture.

McCaffrey tries to give all her books a scientific basis. While writing, she talks to experts in many areas. McCaffrey is the first woman to have won a Hugo Award for science fiction.

She encourages "anyone to write—to dream up their own special world—as an escape or an exercise in imagination."

THE SMALLEST DRAGONBOY   267

Options for Learning
These activities suit a variety of learning styles and modes of expression.

Collaborative Learning Activities
See Options 2, 3, and 4.

1. A Book by Its Cover Encourage students to get ideas by looking at the covers of fantasy novels by Anne McCaffrey and other writers. Covers should provoke interest but not give away the ending.

2. Pern Tour Guide Suggest that students look at the glossary in this book and other texts to understand what should be included in their own glossary.

3. Thread Alert To help students get started, tell them that Thread attacks as a rain of organisms that eat everything but stone, metal, and water.

4. Dragon, Dragon Encourage students to find legends and tales from different parts of the world, such as Europe and Asia.

 FACT FINDER MATHEMATICS
On page 257, L'vel noted that there were seventy-two boys on the roster and only forty eggs. Later, however, Beterli was disqualified, so forty of seventy-one boys, or about 56 percent, were Impressed at this hatching.

Anne McCaffrey

■ **More About the Author** Anne McCaffrey's novels address themes about love, growing up, and adjusting to change—themes that readers can identify with.

■ **Other Works** *Dragonquest, The White Dragon, Dragondrums, Moreta: Dragonlady of Pern, Nerilka's Story, Dragonsdawn, The Renegades of Pern, All the Weyrs of Pern*

 ■ **Awards** In addition to her 1967 Hugo Award for *Dragonflight,* McCaffrey has won numerous other awards, including an E. E. Smith Award for fantasy, an ALA notable book citation, and a Hornbook Fanfare Citation.

Cross-Curricular Projects

Social Studies Like the knights of the Middle Ages and the samurai of feudal Japan, the dragonriders of Pern are members of a warrior society. Have students compare and contrast the experiences of the dragonriders and dragonboys with the training and preparation of a knight or samurai.

Science Suggest that students do research on the eggs of reptiles (the type of animal that dragons are frequently likened to). Ask them to find out the size of a clutch, incubation period, egg size, and color. Have them compare their findings to the information about dragon eggs in the story.

Science/Language Arts The fantasy dragons of Pern communicate with their riders by telepathy. Hold a student debate on whether or not telepathy is possible in the real world. Ask students to do some library research to prepare for the debate. Tell them that telepathy is a form of ESP, or extrasensory perception.

Objectives

■ To understand and analyze three poems

■ To understand the use of imagery and to review the concepts of simile and metaphor

■ To recognize implied meanings conveyed by imagery and figurative language

■ To express understanding of the poems through a choice of writing forms, including a poem and a thematic connection

Prereading/Motivation

Examine What You Know

Discussion Prompts Which of your daydreams do you think might really come true some day? Which can't come true? What could you do to make your fondest daydreams become realities?

Expand Your Knowledge

Additional Background In some ways daydreams are related to night dreams. Both are a form of release from the tensions, problems, and conflicts of everyday life. Many psychologists study daydreams and night dreams as a way of furthering their understanding of mental health and the workings of the mind.

Enrich Your Reading

For Alternative Learning Styles You may wish to have students close their eyes and listen as you read the poems aloud. Tell students to visualize the images by concentrating on what they can see, hear, smell, taste, and feel.

Thematic Link— Driven by Dreams

Each poem touches on a different aspect of dreaming. "Wishes" reveals the speaker's dreams and desires; "Dream Deferred" ponders the fate of an unfulfilled dream; "Formula" tells what is needed for dreaming.

Poetry   *Wishes*   *Dream Deferred*   *Formula*

GEORGIA DOUGLAS   LANGSTON HUGHES   ANA MARIA IZA
JOHNSON

Examine What You Know (Prior Knowledge)

Daydreams can be pleasant fantasies, wishes for a better life, or ways of setting goals. What types of daydreams do you have? Complete a spider word web like the one below. Name some of your daydreams on the spider's "legs." On the lines coming out of the legs, write details about your dreams.

My Daydreams

Professional Dancer — dance troupe / New York stage / wildly popular

Expand Your Knowledge (Building Background)

Daydreams are the key to the three poems you will read next. Psychologists say that daydreams are important for mental health. Daydreams offer harmless ways of expressing wishes, fears, and hopes. They release tension and relieve boredom. They are also a way of rehearsing for the future.

Enrich Your Reading (Reading Skill)

Understanding Poetry You may not understand everything in these poems all at once. The meanings are hinted at, not stated directly. Your imagination will help you follow those hints. As you read, let ideas and images freely surface in your mind. Look for **imagery,** or language that appeals to the senses, and **figurative language,** or language that describes things in new ways. Be ready to see, hear, and feel things the way the poet wants you to imagine them.

■ *Author biographies in Reader's Handbook*

JOURNAL WRITING IDEAS

■ Write your own definition of *dream* and *daydream,* including an example of each.

■ List the benefits and dangers of daydreaming.

■ Make notes about an interesting or unusual dream you had.

COLLABORATIVE LEARNING OPTIONS

Opportunities for collaborative learning include discussion of questions 2–5 on page 272.

ADDITIONAL RESOURCES

Unit Three Resource Book
Reader's Guidesheet, p. 9
Reading Skills, p. 10
Literature Skills, p. 11
Vocabulary Connections, p. 12
Spelling Connections, p. 13
Comprehension Check Test, p. 14
Selection Test, p. 15

Technology and Enrichment
Thinking Skills Transparency 3

Wishes

GEORGIA DOUGLAS JOHNSON

I'm tired of pacing the petty round of the ring of the thing I know— ◀ A
I want to stand on the daylight's edge and see where the sunsets go.

I want to sail on a swallow's tail and peep through the sky's blue glass. | 1
I want to see if the dreams in me shall perish or come to pass. ◀ B

5   I want to look through the moon's pale crook and gaze on the moon-man's face. | 2
I want to keep all the tears I weep and sail to some unknown place. ◀ C

---

*R*esponding to Reading

First Impressions of "Wishes"

1. What images came to mind as you read this poem? Describe them briefly in your journal or notebook.

Second Thoughts on "Wishes"

2. What do the wishes in the poem reveal about the speaker and her dreams?

3. Are the wishes expressed in the poem anything like your own daydreams? Explain.

4. The **mood** of a poem is the feeling it creates in the reader. How would you describe the mood of this poem? Cite lines or phrases that help establish the mood.

WISHES 269

Guided Reading for Less-Proficient Students

These questions can help guide students through the reading. Ask each question at the point of the selection where the capital letter and arrow appear in the margin. In addition, you may want to use appropriate Active Reading annotations.

A. How does the speaker feel about doing the same thing every day? *(She is bored with it.)* Inferring

B. What would the speaker like to know about her future? *(She wants to know whether or not her dreams will come true.)* Recalling

C. Where would the speaker like to travel? *(She would like to go to a faraway and unexplored place.)* Summarizing

Continued on page 270

Teaching Strategies

VOCABULARY PREVIEW
The focus of the vocabulary study for these selections is connotations. See *Unit Three Resource Book*, Vocabulary Connections, page 12.

LIMITED ENGLISH PROFICIENCY

■ Use Reader's Guidesheet, *Unit Three Resource Book*, page 9.

■ Help set the stage for the poems by explaining each speaker's role. In "Wishes" the speaker is telling the reader what she wants; in "Dream Deferred" the speaker is asking the reader questions; in "Formula" the speaker is giving the reader instructions.

★ Text annotations marked with a red star (2, 3) may be particularly helpful for students with limited English proficiency.

TEXT ANNOTATIONS
1. ACTIVE READING: Question
Remind students that figurative language describes things in new ways. Ask them what the phrase "peep through the sky's blue glass" suggests. *(Possible responses: to see what's beyond the earth's atmosphere; to see beyond surface appearances; to explore the new and unfamiliar)*

2. VOCABULARY: Multiple Meanings
Have students use context clues and prior knowledge to understand that *crook* here means "curved shape," not "thief." ★

Responding to Reading
1. Any response is valid.

2. Possible responses: The speaker feels bored and wants excitement; she is curious about the world's wonders; she's a dreamer who wants to escape the routines of everyday life; she has a bold imagination, but she doesn't seem very practical.

3. Any response is valid.

4. Possible responses: The mood is adventurous ("I want to stand on the daylight's edge and see where the sunsets go"); the mood is playful ("I want to sail on a swallow's tail"); the mood is sad ("I want to keep all the tears I weep").

3. VOCABULARY: Word Meanings

Students may be unfamiliar with the words *deferred* and *fester*. Have them look the words up in a dictionary to figure out the meanings intended here. (*Deferred* means "put off till later" and *fester* means "fill with pus" or "become irritated.") Have students make up their own sentences using these words. ★

4. LITERARY CONCEPT: Imagery

Have students discuss the images that appear in their mind as they read the poem. Which images appeal to sight? to smell? to taste? to touch? to hearing? (*Possible responses: sight—a dried raisin, a running sore; touch—a heavy load; taste—a syrupy sweet; smell—rotten meat; hearing—explode.*)

Responding to Reading

1. Any response is valid.

2. **Possible responses:** It means having to wait for something you want badly; it means that you may never get what you want; it means probable disappointment. Examples will reflect each student's experience.

3. **Possible responses:** When dreams do not come true, bad things can happen; dreams that are delayed turn lifeless or ugly or even violent; people can't wait forever for their dreams to be fulfilled.

Dream Deferred

LANGSTON HUGHES

What happens to a dream deferred:
Does it dry up
3 like a raisin in the sun?
Or fester like a sore—
5 And then run?
Does it stink like rotten meat?
Or crust and sugar over—
D ▶ like a syrupy sweet?

4 Maybe it just sags
10 like a heavy load.

E ▶ *Or does it explode?*

*R*esponding to Reading

First Impressions of "Dream Deferred"

1. What are you left thinking about at the end of this poem?

Second Thoughts on "Dream Deferred"

2. What does the phrase "dream deferred" mean to you? Give examples of your own or someone else's deferred dreams.

3. What do you think is the **theme** of the poem?
  Think about
  • the kinds of comparisons that are made throughout the poem
  • the emphasis given to the last line

270   UNIT THREE   DRIVEN BY DREAMS

Guided Reading for Less-Proficient Students

Continued from page 269

D. What does the speaker suggest might happen to a dream deferred? (*It might "dry up"; it might "fester like a sore"; it might "stink like rotten meat"; it might "crust and sugar over."*) Recalling

E. What do you think happens when a dream explodes? (*Possible responses: People may become violent; the dreamer is left without hope; lives may be damaged or even destroyed.*) Inferring

F. What makes dreaming an easy thing to do? (*You need no permission, no special preparation, and no money to dream.*) Summarizing

G. What brings a dream to an end? (*"a blow upon the soul"*) Recalling

Formula

ANA MARIA IZA
Translated by Ron Connally

To dream,
  you don't have to ask permission,
5 nor cry out,
  nor humble yourself,
5 nor put on lipstick;
  it's enough to close your eyes halfway
  and feel distant.
  Perhaps the night dreams
6 that it is no longer night;
10 the fish, that they are boats;
  the boats, fish;
  the water, crystal.
  To dream . . .
  is a simple thing;
15 it doesn't cost a cent,
  you need only to turn your back
  on the hours that pass
  and cover over pain,
  your ears,
20 your eyes
  and stay so,
  stay . . .
7 until we are awakened
G by a blow upon the soul.

RECLINING WOMAN   1978   Will Barnet © 1992
Will Barnet/VAGA New York.

Art Note

Will Barnet (1911–) was born in Beverly, Massachusetts, a seaport and an industrial town. His simple and thoughtful paintings are strongly influenced by Japanese prints. In *Reclining Woman*, the classic grace of a sleeping woman is contrasted with the upright forms of tree trunks. The quietness of sleep is reinforced by the peaceful dove in the tree. *Do you think the woman looks contented? How can you tell?*

5. LITERARY CONCEPT: Contrast
Point out that all of these activities involve people other than oneself. You "ask permission" from another person; you "humble yourself" before another; you "cry out" for another to hear; you "put on lipstick" for someone else to see. What does this suggest about dreaming? *(Possible responses: Dreaming is completely private; you dream only for yourself; you don't need anyone's help to dream.)*

6. ACTIVE READING: Review
Ask students what the night, the fish, the boats, and the water have in common. *(They dream of being something other than themselves.)* Discuss what the poet may be suggesting about the nature of people's dreams. *(Possible response: People dream of leading different lives, which look better to them than their own lives.)*

7. LITERARY CONCEPT: Imagery
Have students describe what they picture as they read the last two lines of the poem. *(Possible responses: an attack of some kind; a person being forcefully awakened; an interruption such as a noise or a voice that stops the dreaming)* Ask who or what could be striking a blow upon the soul. *(Any response is valid.)*

ENCOURAGING INDEPENDENT READING

The Dream Keeper, poems by Langston Hughes

"Roadways," poem by John Masefield

"Success Is Counted Sweetest," poem by Emily Dickinson

Comprehension Check

1. In "Wishes" why does the speaker want to "sail to some unknown place"? *(She's bored and unhappy with her life; she wants adventure.)*

2. In "Dream Deferred" to what is a dream drying up compared? *(a raisin in the sun)*

3. At the end of the poem, what does the speaker wonder about a dream deferred? *(if it will explode)*

4. In "Formula" what is it the speaker says you need no permission and no money to do? *(to dream)*

Student Response

Responding to Reading

1. Any response is valid.

2. **Possible responses:** It is sad because dreams end when we wake; it is frightening because a "blow upon the soul" sounds ominous; it is hopeful because dreaming provides an escape from the pains of life.

3. **Possible responses:** The speaker's formula is correct because dreaming totally depends on the dreamer; the formula is not clear and has too many confusing images.

4. Any response is valid.

5. **Possible responses:** "Wishes"—dreamy, escapist, fanciful, sad; "Dream Deferred"—angry, reflective, frustrated; "Formula"—playful, instructive, imaginative, depressing. Students may draw upon virtually any line as evidence of mood. You may wish to point out that even experts often disagree what a poem's mood is.

Literary Concept: Imagery

Possible responses: Sight—daylight's edge, sky's blue glass, moon-man's face, sunsets, raisin drying, running sore; sound—a dream exploding; smell—rotten meat; taste—a syrupy sweet; touch—a heavy load, lipstick.

Concept Review: Simile A dream like a dried raisin, a festering sore, rotten meat, a syrupy sweet, or a heavy load.

Writing Options

The Writing Options are designed to meet varied student interests and abilities. Have each student choose one writing activity to complete.

Journal Update Some people think our dreams reveal significant information about our real selves; others think dreams are meaningless. Have students write their own opinions in their journals.

Responding to Reading

First Impressions of "Formula"

1. How did this poem affect you? Jot down your thoughts.

Second Thoughts on "Formula"

2. Do you think the ending of the poem is hopeful, sad, or something else? Explain.

3. What is your opinion of the speaker's formula for dreaming?

Comparing the Poems

4. Which poem meant the most to you or came the closest to describing your own dreams? Explain.

5. How do the moods of the three poems differ? Give evidence from each poem to support your answer.

Literary Concept: Imagery

You know that **imagery** is language that appeals to the senses. Most images are visual; they create mental pictures in the reader's mind. "Wishes," for example, describes a desire "to sail on a swallow's tail," causing readers to picture a swallow in flight. Other images appeal to senses of touch, smell, taste, or sound. In order to see how poets use imagery, create a chart listing the five senses. Then find images in the three poems to fill in as much of the chart as you can. Some images may appeal to two senses.

Concept Review: Simile   Find two similes in "Dream Deferred."

Writing Options

1. You described some of your dreams before you read. Now write a **poem** about your dreams. Choose a form that best fits your ideas and feelings.

2. Find a poem that fits the theme of "Driven by Dreams." Copy it and write a **thematic connection,** or an explanation of why the poem fits the theme.

Closure

Ask students which poem might have the greatest appeal for Keevan from "The Smallest Dragonboy." If needed, point out that "Wishes" might appeal to Keevan's desire to do something extraordinary in his life. "Dream Deferred" might speak to Keevan's fear that his dream might never be realized. "Formula" might appeal to Keevan's wish for a different type of existence.

Nonfiction

Eleanor Roosevelt
WILLIAM JAY JACOBS

Examine What You Know (Prior Knowledge)

You may know that Eleanor Roosevelt was the wife of the United States' thirty-second President, Franklin Delano Roosevelt. She was also one of the most famous American women of this century. What do you know about these two famous people? Share your knowledge in a class discussion.

Expand Your Knowledge (Building Background)

As you will learn, Eleanor Roosevelt was much more than the wife of a president. Her life spanned a period of dramatic changes in the United States and the world. The time line below shows some events that occurred during her lifetime.

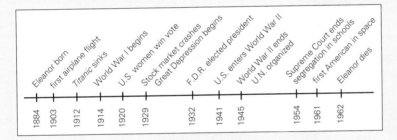

Write Before You Read (Journal Writing)

Many people become involved in political and social issues because, like Eleanor Roosevelt, they dream of a better world. What issues do you care about? What dreams do you have for your community, your nation, or the world? List these issues and dreams in your notebook or journal.

■ *Author biography on Extend page*

ELEANOR ROOSEVELT   273

Objectives

■ To understand and analyze a biography

■ To examine style in biography and to review the concept of conflict

■ To enrich reading by empathizing with the subject of a biography

■ To express understanding of the selection through a choice of writing forms, including an advice column, a summary, a conversation, and a job description

Prereading/Motivation

Examine What You Know

Discussion Prompts What made Eleanor Roosevelt or Franklin D. Roosevelt famous? What problems did Franklin Roosevelt face during his presidency? How did Eleanor help him?

Expand Your Knowledge

Additional Background The years between 1884 and 1962 were full of historic events. During Eleanor's life the United States went through the Spanish-American War, two world wars, and the Korean War. The U.S. economy crashed, and relations between working people and their employers changed forever. Born only fifteen years after the completion of the transcontinental railroad, Eleanor saw the invention of the radio, the television, the automobile, and the airplane. This new technology made U.S. citizens the most mobile and informed people in the world. Also during this time, women and African Americans courageously and insistently demanded their rights as citizens. Through it all, Eleanor Roosevelt was there, helping to bring about positive changes for millions of people.

MORE JOURNAL WRITING IDEAS
■ Can an unhappy childhood affect someone's life in positive ways? Explain.

■ Do you think a shy person can become a leader? Give reasons to support your answer.

COLLABORATIVE LEARNING OPTIONS
Opportunities for collaborative learning include Options for Learning 2 and 4 (p. 285), and Cross-Curricular Projects (p. 285).

ADDITIONAL RESOURCES
Unit Three Resource Book
Reader's Guidesheet, p. 16
Reading Skills, p. 17
Literature Skills, p. 18
Vocabulary Connections, p. 19
Spelling Connections, p. 20
Comprehension and Vocabulary Check Tests, p. 21
Selection Test, pp. 22–23

Technology and Enrichment
Active Reading Transparencies 13–14; Worksheets

Thematic Link—
Driven by Dreams

Although her childhood was darkened by tragedy and disappointment, Eleanor Roosevelt conquered her fears. Driven by dreams of a better world, she used her talents and energies to fight for human rights everywhere.

Eleanor Roosevelt

WILLIAM JAY JACOBS

Eleanor Roosevelt was the wife of President Franklin Delano Roosevelt. But Eleanor was much more than just a president's wife, an echo of her husband's career.

Sad and lonely as a child, Eleanor was called "Granny" by her mother because of her seriousness. People teased her about her looks and called her the "ugly duckling." . . .

Yet despite all of the disappointments, the bitterness, the misery she experienced, Eleanor Roosevelt refused to give up. Instead she turned her unhappiness and pain to strength. She devoted her life to helping others. Today she is remembered as one of America's greatest women.

Eleanor was born in a fine townhouse in Manhattan. Her family also owned an elegant mansion along the Hudson River, where they spent weekends and summers. As

a child Eleanor went to fashionable parties. A servant took care of her and taught her to speak French. Her mother, the beautiful Anna Hall Roosevelt, wore magnificent jewels and fine clothing. Her father, Elliott Roosevelt, had his own hunting lodge and liked to sail and to play tennis and polo. Elliott, who loved Eleanor dearly, was the younger brother of Theodore Roosevelt, who in 1901 became President of the United States. The Roosevelt family, one of America's oldest, wealthiest families, was respected and admired.

To the outside world it might have seemed that Eleanor had everything that any child could want—everything that could make her happy. But she was not happy. Instead her childhood was very sad.

Almost from the day of her birth, October 11, 1884, people noticed that she was an unattractive child. As she grew older, she could not help but notice her mother's extraordinary beauty, as well as the beauty of her aunts and cousins. Eleanor

Photo of Eleanor Roosevelt's family: *left,* brothers Elliott and Hall; *center,* Eleanor's father; *right,* Eleanor at age six. UPI/Bettmann.

was plain looking, ordinary, even, as some called her, homely. For a time she had to wear a bulky brace on her back to straighten her crooked spine.

Her parents had wanted a boy.

4 When Eleanor was born, her parents had wanted a boy. They were scarcely able to hide their disappointment. Later, with the arrival of two boys, Elliott and Hall, Eleanor watched her mother hold the boys on her lap and lovingly stroke their hair, while for Eleanor there seemed only coolness, distance.

5 Feeling unwanted, Eleanor became shy and withdrawn. She also developed many fears. She was afraid of the dark, afraid of animals, afraid of other children, afraid of being scolded, afraid of strangers, afraid that people would not like her. She was a frightened, lonely little girl.

B ▶

The one joy in the early years of her life was her father, who always seemed to care for her, love her. He used to dance with her, to pick her up and throw her into the air while she laughed and laughed. He called her "little golden hair" or "darling little Nell."

Then, when she was six, her father left. An alcoholic, he went to live in a sanitarium[1] in Virginia in an attempt to deal with his drinking problem. Eleanor missed him greatly.

6 Next her mother became ill with painful headaches. Sometimes for hours at a time, Eleanor would sit holding her mother's head in her lap and stroking her forehead. Nothing else seemed to relieve the pain. At those times Eleanor often remembered how her mother had teased her about her looks and called her "Granny." But even at the age of seven, Eleanor was glad to be helping someone, glad to be needed—and noticed.

The next year, when Eleanor was eight, her mother, the beautiful Anna, died. Afterward her brother Elliott suddenly caught diphtheria[2] and he, too, died. Eleanor and her baby brother, Hall, were taken to live with their grandmother in Manhattan.

A few months later another tragedy struck. Elliott Roosevelt, Eleanor's father, also died. Within eighteen months Eleanor had lost her mother, a brother, and her dear father. . . .

7
◀ C

Few things in life came easily for Eleanor, but the first few years after her father's death proved exceptionally hard. Grandmother Hall's dark and gloomy townhouse had no place for children to play. The family ate meals in silence. Every morning Eleanor and Hall were expected to take cold baths for their health. Eleanor had to work at better posture by walking with her arms behind her back, clamped over a walking stick.

Instead of making new friends, Eleanor often sat alone in her room and read. For many months after her father's death, she pretended that he was still alive. She made him the hero of stories she wrote for school. Sometimes, alone and unhappy, she just cried.

Some of her few moments of happiness came from visiting her uncle, Theodore

---

1. **sanitarium:** an institution for the care of people with a specific disease or other health problem.
2. **diphtheria** (dif thir′ ē ə): a serious infectious disease.

4. LITERARY CONCEPT: Conflict
Ask students what conflicts affected Eleanor Roosevelt's early life. (*She was unattractive, whereas her mother, cousins, and aunts were beautiful; she was a girl, but her parents had wanted a boy.*)

5. VOCABULARY: Context Clues
Have students use **context clues** to determine the meaning of the word *withdrawn* here. ("*detached from others,*" "*isolated,*" "*solitary*") ★

6. LITERARY CONCEPT:
Characterization
Ask what Eleanor's stroking her mother's head reveals about Eleanor. (*Possible responses: Even as a child she was kind and compassionate; she wanted to help others; she forgave her mother for not showing her love.*)

7. EDITORIAL NOTE
Because of space limitations, two paragraphs of the original text have been omitted here. The paragraphs elaborate on the close relationship between Eleanor and her father and the advice he had given her in letters.

Guided Reading for Less-Proficient Students

Continued from page 274

E. With whom did Eleanor fall in love? (*her fifth cousin, Franklin Delano Roosevelt*) Recalling

F. In what ways did Eleanor change when Franklin got polio? (*She stood up to her mother-in-law, and she became involved in politics.*) Summarizing

G. How was Eleanor a link between the president and the public? (*She traveled and told Franklin what people were thinking; she saw how people were suf-* fering and urged him to help them.) Summarizing

H. What did Mrs. Roosevelt fight hardest to change? (*racial and religious prejudice*) Recalling

I. After Franklin died, what did President Truman ask Eleanor to do? (*become a delegate to the new United Nations*) Recalling

J. Why was Eleanor Roosevelt remembered as the "First Lady of the World"? (*She worked for human rights all over the world.*) Recalling

Roosevelt, in Oyster Bay, Long Island. A visit with Uncle Ted meant playing games and romping outdoors with the many Roosevelt children.

Once Uncle Ted threw her into the water to teach her how to swim, but when she started to sink, he had to rescue her. Often he would read to the children old Norse tales and poetry. It was at Sagamore Hill, Uncle Ted's home, that Eleanor first learned how much fun it could be to read books aloud.

For most of the time, Eleanor's life was grim. Although her parents had left plenty of money for her upbringing, she had only two dresses to wear to school. Once she spilled ink on one of them, and since the other was in the wash, she had to wear the dress with large ink stains on it to school the next day. It was not that Grandmother Hall was stingy. Rather, she was old and often confused. Nor did she show much warmth or love for Eleanor and her brother. Usually she just neglected them.

Just before Eleanor turned fifteen, Grandmother Hall decided to send her to boarding school in England. The school she chose was Allenswood, a private academy for girls located on the outskirts of London.

It was at Allenswood that Eleanor, still thinking of herself as an "ugly duckling," first dared to believe that one day she might be able to become a swan.

At Allenswood she worked to toughen herself physically. Every day she did exercises in the morning and took a cold shower. Although she did not like competitive team sports, as a matter of self-discipline she tried out for field hockey. Not only did she make the team but, because she played so hard, also won the respect of her teammates.

They called her by her family nickname, "Totty," and showed their affection for her by putting books and flowers in her room, as was the custom at Allenswood. Never before had she experienced the pleasure of having schoolmates actually admire her rather than tease her.

At Allenswood, too, she began to look after her health. She finally broke the habit of chewing her fingernails. She learned to eat nutritious foods, to get plenty of sleep, and to take a brisk walk every morning, no matter how miserable the weather. . . .

Eleanor was growing up, and the joy of young womanhood had begun to transform her personality.

In 1902, nearly eighteen years old, she left Allenswood, not returning for her fourth year there. Grandmother Hall insisted that, instead, she must be introduced to society as a debutante—to go to dances and parties and begin to take her place in the social world with other wealthy young women.

Away from Allenswood, Eleanor's old uncertainty about her looks came back again. She saw herself as too tall, too thin, too plain. She worried about her buckteeth, which she thought made her look horselike. The old teasing began again, especially on the part of Uncle Ted's daughter, "Princess" Alice Roosevelt, who seemed to take pleasure in making Eleanor feel uncomfortable.

Eleanor, as always, did as she was told. She went to all of the parties and dances. But she also began working with poor children at the Rivington Street Settlement House on New York's Lower East Side. She taught the girls gymnastic exercises. She took children to museums and to musical performances. She tried to get the parents interested in politics in order to get better schools and cleaner, safer streets.

Meanwhile, Eleanor's life reached a turning point. She fell in love! The young man was her fifth cousin, Franklin Delano Roosevelt.

E ▶

Eleanor and Franklin had known each other since childhood. Franklin recalled how once he had carried her piggyback in the nursery. When she was fourteen, he had danced with her at a party. Then, shortly after her return from Allenswood, they had met by chance on a train. They talked and almost at once realized how much they liked each other.

For a time they met secretly. Then they attended parties together. Franklin—tall, strong, handsome—saw her as a person he could trust. He knew that she would not try to dominate him.

But did he really love her? Would he always? She wrote to him, quoting a poem she knew: "'Unless you can swear, *For life, for death!*' Oh, never call it loving!'"

Franklin promised that his love was indeed "for life," and Eleanor agreed to marry him. It was the autumn of 1903. He was twenty-one. She was nineteen.

On March 17, 1905, Eleanor and Franklin were married. "Uncle Ted," by then President of the United States, was there to "give the bride away.". . .

In May 1906 the couple's first child was born. During the next nine years Eleanor gave birth to five more babies, one of whom died in infancy. Still timid, shy, afraid of making mistakes, she found herself so busy that there was little time to think of her own drawbacks.

Still, looking back later on the early years of her marriage, Eleanor knew that she should have been a stronger person, especially in the handling of Franklin's mother, or, as they both called her, "Mamma." Too often Mamma made the decisions about such things as where they would live, how their home would be furnished, how the children would be disciplined. Eleanor and Franklin let her pay for things they could not afford—extra servants, vacations, doctor bills, clothing. She offered, and they accepted.

Before long, trouble developed in the relationship between Eleanor and Franklin. Serious, shy, easily embarrassed, Eleanor could not share Franklin's interests in golf and tennis. He enjoyed light talk and flirting with women. She could not be lighthearted. So she stayed on the sidelines. Instead of losing her temper, she bottled up her anger and did not talk to him at all. As he used to say, she "clammed up." Her silence only made things worse, because it puzzled him. Faced with her coldness, her brooding silence, he only grew angrier and more distant.

Meanwhile, Franklin's career in politics advanced rapidly. In 1910 he was elected to the New York State Senate. In 1913 President Wilson appointed him Assistant Secretary of the Navy—a powerful position in the national government, which required the Roosevelts to move to Washington, D.C.

In 1917 the United States entered World War I as an active combatant. Like many socially prominent women, Eleanor threw

12

13

14

Words to Know and Use	**brooding** (brood′ iŋ) *adj.* full of worry; troubled **brood** *v.* **combatant** (kəm bat′ 'nt) *n.* fighter **prominent** (präm′ ə nənt) *adj.* well-known; widely recognized

277

herself into the war effort. Sometimes she worked fifteen or sixteen hours a day. She made sandwiches for soldiers passing through the nation's capital. She knitted sweaters. She used Franklin's influence to **15** get the Red Cross to build a recreation room for soldiers who had been shell-shocked in combat. . . .

In 1920 the Democratic Party chose Franklin as its candidate for Vice-President of the United States. Even though the Republicans won the election, Roosevelt became a well-known figure in national politics. All the time, Eleanor stood by his side, smiling, doing what was expected of her as a candidate's wife.

She did what was expected—and much more—in the summer of 1921 when disaster struck the Roosevelt family. While on vacation Franklin suddenly fell ill with infantile paralysis—polio—the horrible disease that each year used to kill or cripple thousands of children, and many adults as well. When Franklin became a victim of polio, nobody knew what caused the disease or how to cure it.

Franklin lived, but the lower part of his body remained paralyzed. For the rest of his life, he never again had the use of his legs. He had to be lifted and carried from place to place. He had to wear heavy steel braces from his waist to the heels of his shoes.

His mother, as well as many of his advisers, urged him to give up politics, to live the life of a country gentleman on the Roosevelt estate at Hyde Park, New York. This time, **16** Eleanor, calm and strong, stood up for her ideas. She argued that he should not be treated like a sick person, tucked away in

Franklin Delano Roosevelt reading victory telegram on election night, November 1932. © N.Y. Daily News, used by permission.

the country, inactive, just waiting for death to come.

Franklin agreed. Slowly he recovered his health. His energy returned. In 1928 he was elected governor of New York. Then, just four years later, he was elected President of the United States.

Meanwhile, Eleanor had changed. To keep Franklin in the public eye while he was recovering, she had gotten involved in politics herself. It was, she thought, her "duty." From childhood she had been taught "to do the thing that has to be done, the way it has to be done, when it has to be done."

With the help of Franklin's adviser Louis Howe, she made fund-raising speeches for the Democratic Party all around New York State. She helped in the work of the League of Women Voters, the Consumer's League, and the Foreign Policy Association. After becoming interested in the problems of working women, she gave time to the Women's Trade Union League (WTUL).

It was through the WTUL that she met a group of remarkable women—women doing exciting work that made a difference in the world. They taught Eleanor about life in the slums. They awakened her hopes that something could be done to improve the condition of the poor. She dropped out of the "fashionable" society of her wealthy friends and joined the world of reform—social change.

For hours at a time, Eleanor and her reformer friends talked with Franklin. They showed him the need for new laws: laws to get children out of the factories and into schools; laws to cut down the long hours that women worked; laws to get fair wages for all workers.

By the time that Franklin was sworn in as president, the nation was facing its deepest depression. One out of every four Americans was out of work, out of hope. At mealtimes people stood in lines in front of soup kitchens for something to eat. . . .

Eleanor worked in the charity kitchens, ladling out soup. She visited slums. She criss-crossed the country learning about the suffering of coal miners, shipyard workers, migrant farm workers, students, housewives—Americans caught up in the paralysis of the Great Depression. Since Franklin himself remained crippled, she became his eyes and ears, informing him of what the American people were really thinking and feeling.

Eleanor also was the president's conscience, personally urging on him some of the most compassionate, forward-looking laws of his presidency, including, for example, the National Youth Administration (NYA), which provided money to allow impoverished young people to stay in school.

She lectured widely, wrote a regularly syndicated[3] newspaper column, "My Day," and spoke frequently on the radio. She fought for equal pay for women in industry. Like no other First Lady up to that time, she became a link between the president and the American public. ◄ G

Above all she fought against racial and religious prejudice. When Eleanor learned that the DAR (Daughters of the American Revolution) would not allow the great black singer Marian Anderson to perform in their auditorium in Washington, D.C., she resigned from the organization. Then she arranged to have Miss Anderson sing in front of the Lincoln Memorial.

Similarly, when she entered a hall where, as often happened in those days, blacks and whites were seated in separate sections, she made it a point to sit with the blacks. Her example marked an important step in making the rights of blacks a matter of national priority. ◄ H

---
3. **syndicated:** sold to many newspapers for publication.

Words to Know and Use	**compassionate** (kəm pash' ən it) adj. showing concern or sympathy **priority** (prī ôr' ə tē) n. something that must receive attention first

279

Speaking . . . Listening . . . Viewing

Viewing Students may enjoy a film or video about Eleanor Roosevelt, such as the following:

- *The Eleanor Roosevelt Story* (1966), Commonwealth United
- *Eleanor Roosevelt: First Lady of the World* (1985), Rights Group

Use the following questions for discussion:

1. Were you surprised by anything you saw? Has your view of Eleanor Roosevelt changed?

2. What kind of information did you get that you didn't get from reading the biography? How did this affect your feelings about Eleanor?

3. Which picture or pictures revealed the most about her character? What did you see that helped you to understand the kind of person she was?

A direct quote from Eleanor has been omitted because of space limitations. The passage reads:

"As Eleanor later declared, 'I think that sometimes I acted as his conscience. I urged him to take the harder path when he would have preferred the easier way. In that sense, I acted on occasion as a spur, even though the spurring was not always wanted or welcome.

"'Of course,' said Eleanor, 'I loved him and I miss him.'"

23. ACTIVE READING: Review
Ask students how for Eleanor the period after Franklin's death was like her time at Allenswood. *(Possible response: At both times Eleanor found new strengths, new interests, and a new way of life.)*

24. ACTIVE READING: Connect
Have students brainstorm some reasons critics might have had for claiming that Eleanor Roosevelt was unqualified to be a delegate to the United Nations. *(Possible responses: She had never held an official government position; she did not have a college education; she was a woman, and at that time few women held important positions.)*

25. EDITORIAL NOTE
Sentences discussing Eleanor's work in the United Nations have been omitted because of space limitations.

26. HISTORICAL SIDELIGHT
Eleanor Roosevelt was unanimously elected to chair the committee that wrote the declaration, which has remained the standard for measuring how well a nation lives up to the principles of the UN charter and has had a great influence on the way laws, treaties, and constitutions are written throughout the world.

On December 7, 1941, Japanese forces launched a surprise attack on the American naval base at Pearl Harbor, Hawaii, as well as on other American installations in the Pacific. The United States entered World War II, fighting not only against Japan but against the brutal dictators who then controlled Germany and Italy.

Eleanor helped the Red Cross raise money. She gave blood, sold war bonds. But she also did the unexpected. In 1943, for example, she visited barracks and hospitals on islands throughout the South Pacific. When she visited a hospital, she stopped at every bed. To each soldier she said something special, something that a mother might say. Often, after she left, even battle-hardened men had tears in their eyes. Admiral Nimitz, who originally thought such visits would be a nuisance, became one of her strongest admirers. Nobody else, he said, had done so much to help raise the spirits of the men.

By spring 1945 the end of the war in Europe seemed near. Then, on April 12, a phone call brought Eleanor the news that Franklin Roosevelt, who had gone to Warm Springs, Georgia, for a rest, was dead. . . .

After Franklin's funeral, every day that Eleanor was home at Hyde Park, without fail, she placed flowers on his grave. Then she would stand very still beside him there.

With Franklin dead, Eleanor Roosevelt might have dropped out of the public eye, might have been remembered in the history books only as a footnote to the president's program of social reforms. Instead she found new strengths within herself, new ways to live a useful, interesting life—and to help others. Now, moreover, her successes were her own, not the result of being the president's wife.

In December 1945 President Harry S Truman invited her to be one of the American delegates going to London to begin the work of the United Nations. Eleanor hesitated, but the president insisted. He said that the nation needed her; it was her duty. After that, Eleanor agreed.

In the beginning some of her fellow delegates from the United States considered her unqualified for the position, but after seeing her in action, they changed their minds.

It was Eleanor Roosevelt who, almost single-handedly, pushed through the United Nations General Assembly a resolution giving refugees from World War II the right *not* to return to their native lands if they did not wish to. . . .

Next Mrs. Roosevelt helped draft the United Nations Declaration of Human Rights. The Soviets wanted the declaration to list the duties people owed to their countries. Again Eleanor insisted that the United Nations should stand for individual freedom—the rights of people to free speech, freedom of religion, and such human needs as health care and education. In December 1948, with the Soviet Union and its allies refusing to vote, the Declaration of Human Rights won approval of the UN General Assembly by a vote of forty-eight to zero.

Even after retiring from her post at the UN, Mrs. Roosevelt continued to travel. In places around the world she dined with presidents and kings. But she also visited tenement slums[4] in Bombay, India; factories

---

4. **tenement slums:** parts of a city where poor people live in crowded, shabby buildings.

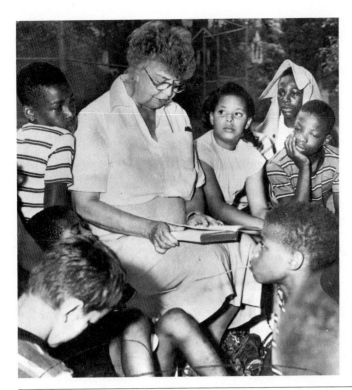

Eleanor Roosevelt reading to children during a picnic at Hyde Park, New York, July 1952. AP/Wide World Photos.

27. EDITORIAL NOTE
Because of space limitations, two paragraphs have been omitted here. They describe Eleanor's other good works and Clare Boothe Luce's opinion of her.

in Yugoslavia; farms in Lebanon and Israel.

Everywhere, she met people who were eager to greet her. Although as a child she had been brought up to be formal and distant, she had grown to feel at ease with people. They wanted to touch her, to hug her, to kiss her.

Eleanor's doctor had been telling her to slow down, but that was hard for her. She continued to write her newspaper column, "My Day," and to appear on television. She still began working at seven-thirty in the morning and often continued until well past midnight. . . .

Gradually, however, she was forced to withdraw from some of her activities, to spend more time at home.

On November 7, 1962, at the age of seventy-eight, Eleanor died in her sleep. She was buried in the rose garden at Hyde Park, alongside her husband.

Adlai Stevenson, the American ambassador to the United Nations, remembered her as "the First Lady of the World," as the person—male or female—most effective in working for the cause of human rights. As Stevenson declared, "She would rather light a candle than curse the darkness."

And perhaps, in sum, that is what the struggle for human rights is all about. ❧

Comprehension Check

1. When Eleanor was a child, how did she and others rate her appearance? *(as unattractive, "homely")*

2. Who raised Eleanor after her parents died? *(her grandmother)*

3. What was a positive turning point in Eleanor's life as a young woman? *(going to boarding school)*

4. Why was Eleanor called Franklin Roosevelt's eyes and ears during his presidency? *(His paralysis kept him in Washington, so she traveled and told him what she saw and heard.)*

5. For what groups did Eleanor fight to make improvements? *(underdogs—women, the poor, African Americans, mistreated people around the world)*

6. For what world organization did Eleanor work after Franklin died? *(the United Nations)*

This excerpt from Eleanor Roosevelt's autobiography is a reflection on the ideas in the main selection. Optional discussion questions follow.

1. What did Eleanor most want as a child? *(approval and love)*

2. What does Eleanor see as her faults? *(being too afraid of doing something wrong, being too "hide-bound" by her sense of duty)*

3. What quality did Eleanor Roosevelt gain in middle age that helped her become successful? *(courage)*

4. Compare and contrast this part of Eleanor's autobiography with Jacobs's biography. Which is more personal? *(the autobiography)* Which do you prefer? *(Any response is valid.)*

ENCOURAGING INDEPENDENT READING

The Autobiography of Eleanor Roosevelt

Eleanor Roosevelt, biography by Karen McAuley

Eleanor Roosevelt's My Day: Her Acclaimed Columns, 1936–1945, edited by Rochelle Chadakoff

"Life Was Meant to Be Lived": A Centenary Portrait of Eleanor Roosevelt, by Joseph Lash

INSIGHT

from The Autobiography of Eleanor Roosevelt

ELEANOR ROOSEVELT

In the beginning, because I felt, as only a young girl can feel it, all the pain of being an ugly duckling, I was not only timid, I was afraid. Afraid of almost everything, I think: of mice, of the dark, of imaginary dangers, of my own inadequacy. My chief objective, as a girl, was to do my duty. This had been drilled into me as far back as I could remember. Not my duty as I saw it, but my duty as laid down for me by other people. It never occurred to me to revolt. Anyhow, my one overwhelming need in those days was to be approved, to be loved, and I did whatever was required of me, hoping it would bring me nearer to the approval and love I so much wanted.

As a young woman, my sense of duty remained as strict and rigid as it had been when I was a girl, but it had changed its focus. My husband and my children became the center of my life, and their needs were my new duty. I am afraid now that I approached this new obligation much as I had my childhood duties. I was still timid, still afraid of doing something wrong, of making mistakes, of not living up to the standards required by my mother-in-law, of failing to do what was expected of me.

As a result, I was so hidebound by duty that I became too critical, too much of a disciplinarian. I was so concerned with bringing up my children properly that I was not wise enough just to love them. Now, looking back, I think I would rather spoil a child a little and have more fun out of it.

It was not until I reached middle age that I had the courage to develop interests of my own, outside of my duties to my family. In the beginning, it seems to me now, I had no goal beyond the interests themselves, in learning about people and conditions and the world outside our own United States. Almost at once I began to discover that interest leads to interest, knowledge leads to more knowledge, the capacity for understanding grows with the effort to understand.

From that time on, though I have had many problems, though I have known the grief and the loneliness that are the lot of most human beings, though I have had to make and still have to make endless adjustments, I have never been bored, never found the days long enough for the range of activities with which I wanted to fill them. And, having learned to stare down fear, I long ago reached the point where there is no living person whom I fear, and few challenges that I am not willing to face.

Responding to Reading

First Impressions

1. What words and phrases would you use to describe Eleanor Roosevelt? Record them in your journal or notebook.

Second Thoughts

2. Which feelings or experiences from Eleanor's childhood are similar to your own?

3. Which of Eleanor Roosevelt's accomplishments do you find most impressive? Why?

4. Why do you think Eleanor was able to overcome her fears?

> **Think about**
> - her feelings about herself
> - her goals and values
> - what she says in her autobiography

5. Do you think Eleanor's strong sense of duty helped or hurt her? Explain.

Broader Connections

6. Think about the organizations and issues Eleanor Roosevelt worked for during her lifetime. If she were alive today, which national and world issues would concern her? Explain your answer.

Literary Concept: Biography

A **biography** is the story of a person's life, written by another person. Biographies can vary in style. Some biographies are carefully balanced, showing both the strengths and the weaknesses of the subject. Other biographies are more one-sided, either praising the subject or finding fault. How would you describe the style of Jacobs's biography? What details in the selection support your ideas?

Concept Review: Conflict   Name the most important conflicts Eleanor faced, both external and internal.

ELEANOR ROOSEVELT   283

Responding to Reading

1. Any response is valid.

2. Any response is valid. Encourage students to explain similarities.

3. Possible responses: her work for human rights at the United Nations, her bravery and outspokenness in the fight for racial equality, her work for women and the poor, her role as a first lady and political activist

4. Possible responses: because she received love and affection from friends, because she saw people in real need and knew she could not help if she were fearful, because she had been trained to do her duty, because she desired to make real changes in the world, because she was forced to face her fears during personal crises, because others depended on her for strength

5. Possible responses: Eleanor's sense of duty helped her by giving her energy and focus when life was difficult; it hurt her by causing her to repress her own ideas; it hurt her by making her focus so much on other people and world problems that she neglected her personal life.

6. Possible responses: She would probably continue to work for human rights and against persecution, racism, hunger, and poverty throughout the world; she would likely help people with AIDS, the homeless, and victims of drug abuse.

Challenge Question

If Eleanor could read Jacobs's biography of her, what might her reaction be? *(Possible responses: She might like it; she might agree with the presentation of her childhood; her modesty might make her think that he praised her too much; she might want the writing to be more objective and less emotional.)*

Literary Concept: Biography and Conflict

Biography   Students may find this biography balanced in its portrait of Eleanor's strengths and weaknesses as a young person but more one-sided in its positive picture of her as an adult and public figure. Examples of her feelings of inferiority and weakness are conveyed in the accounts of her childhood and marriage, but Jacobs seems to have only praise for her political work.

Conflict   Eleanor's internal conflicts included her feelings of ugliness, her sense of not being loved, and her avoidance of social relationships. Her external conflicts included her struggle for independence from her domineering mother-in-law, some conflicts with her husband, her struggle against racism, and her struggle against those who would deny human rights.

Writing Options

The Writing Options are designed to meet varied student interests and abilities. Have each student choose one writing activity to complete.

Journal Update Invite students to add to their journal entries about "Eleanor Roosevelt." Suggest that they write about what they would like to ask or tell Eleanor Roosevelt if she were alive.

Links to
Writer's Craft

Writing Option 4 is an exercise in description. For more practice in descriptive writing, see *The Writer's Craft,* Grade 7, "Observation and Description," pages 49–69.

Vocabulary Practice

Answers to Exercise

1. compassionate; she cared about helping others, not about receiving attention.

2. No; she was energetic and worked hard for human rights.

3. Yes; she fought hard for human rights.

4. No; a brooding visitor would be unable to cheer them up.

5. brooding and compassionate

For Alternative Learning Styles
Allow students to browse through newspapers and magazines to see if they can find the vocabulary words in articles and can locate pictures that illustrate the meanings of the words.

Closure

Eleanor Roosevelt was an extraordinary woman who had great dreams for the entire human race and did what she could to make them come true. At the same time, she fought and conquered her personal demons and fears. Ask students to explore how the speakers in the poems "Wishes" and "Formula" might be speaking for Eleanor. Then urge them to find other poems that might be speaking about her life and dreams.

Writing Options

1. Write an **advice column** from Eleanor Roosevelt to a teenager who wants to overcome a lack of self-confidence. Use examples from her own life in your letter.

2. Write a **summary** of what you learned about Eleanor Roosevelt in this selection. At the end of your summary, list three things you would like to know more about.

3. Eleanor called herself "the President's conscience." Look back at the list you made of your own dreams for a better world. Decide which issue Eleanor would care about most, and then write the **conversation** she might have with her husband about solving that problem.

4. Write a **job description** of Eleanor's role as First Lady. Describe her activities and responsibilities.

Vocabulary Practice

Exercise On your paper, respond to each of the following questions.

1. Would Eleanor have preferred to be called **compassionate** or **prominent?** Why?

2. Were comfort and relaxation a main **priority** in Eleanor's life? How can you tell?

3. Can Eleanor be considered a **combatant** for social justice? Why or why not?

4. Would wounded soldiers enjoy talking to a **brooding** visitor? Why or why not?

5. Which two adjectives from the vocabulary list describe personality traits?

Words to Know and Use

**brooding
combatant
compassionate
priority
prominent**

The Spelling Connection

Spelling Patterns: *ought, ight,* and *eigh* in Words with Silent *gh* The letters **gh** are usually silent in the familiar letter combinations **ough, ight,** and **eigh.**
Examples: br**ough**t s**igh**t w**eigh**

Words from the Selection with Silent *gh*
might	light	through
frightened	although	brought
lighthearted	thought	
rights	fought	

Other Words with Silent *gh*
ought	slight	height
throughout	delightful	neighborhood
doughnut	sightseeing	eightieth

Exercise Fill in the blanks with **gh** words.

Coretta Scott King studied music and ___ have become a famous musician, but she joined her husband in his work for civil ___. At the ___ of protest demonstrations, she was always there. ___ her life, she has ___ for justice.

*O*ptions for Learning (Multimodal/Cross-Curricular Activities)

1 • The Time of Her Life Make a collage to create a visual impression of Eleanor Roosevelt's life. Look through biographies of Eleanor and through newspapers and magazines of her time. Pick out photographs, drawings, cartoons, advertisements, and other visual items. Make copies of what you find and use them for your collage. Display your work in your classroom.

2 • In Her Footsteps Eleanor Roosevelt has been a role model for many women. Conduct a panel discussion about whether or not she should be a role model for women today. The panelists should represent a variety of viewpoints.

3 • Battle of the First Ladies Research the wife of a president who served after Franklin Roosevelt. Compare and contrast this First Lady with Eleanor Roosevelt. Make a poster that shows similarities and differences to share with your class.

4 • The Hot Seat Eleanor Roosevelt was extremely controversial in her day. With a classmate, act out an interview with her. Prepare questions ahead of time that reflect the split in public opinion about her actions. If needed, research the answers. The interview should capture Eleanor's personality and beliefs.

 FACT FINDER HISTORY

During what years was Eleanor Roosevelt a delegate to the United Nations General Assembly?

*W*illiam Jay Jacobs
1933

Jacobs's admiration for Eleanor Roosevelt goes back a long way. "As a child, Franklin Roosevelt was my hero, my model of personal courage. Like Roosevelt, I had polio. . . . The more I learned about Eleanor Roosevelt, the more I saw her as a woman of courage. She turned her pain to strength." Jacobs believes young people need historical role models who faced tests and persisted.

Jacobs has written many biographies for young people, including biographies of Hernando Cortes, Edgar Allan Poe, Abraham Lincoln, and Winston Churchill. His book *Mother, Aunt Susan and Me: The First Fight for Women's Rights* won several awards.

In addition to being a writer, Jacobs has taught history and social studies since 1975 in the Darien, Connecticut, public schools. Before then, he taught at several colleges and universities.

ELEANOR ROOSEVELT   285

Cross-Curricular Projects

Science In small groups, students may research and report on technology that developed during Eleanor's lifetime. Have the class vote to decide which technological change most affected her ability to achieve her goals.

History Ask volunteers to research the movements and organizations Eleanor Roosevelt supported. Then have students create either print or radio advertisements to attract new members to these groups.

Science/Health Have volunteers research how polio affected Americans' health in the 1940s and 1950s and what happened to nearly eliminate the disease.

Extending the Lesson

These activities suit a variety of learning styles and modes of expression.

Collaborative Learning Options
See Options 2 and 4.

Options for Learning

1. The Time of Her Life Provide large sheets of paper. Suggest the titles listed under Encouraging Independent Reading (p. 282) for research.

2. In Her Footsteps Have students meet in small groups to brainstorm and choose viewpoints. Suggest they gather more facts to support their ideas and develop their arguments.

3. Battle of the First Ladies Books about the White House and the first ladies, as well as biographies and back issues of magazines and newspapers, will be helpful.

4. The Hot Seat Suggest that interested students research actual criticism of Eleanor in period magazines and newspapers.

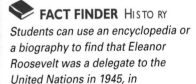 **FACT FINDER** HISTORY

Students can use an encyclopedia or a biography to find that Eleanor Roosevelt was a delegate to the United Nations in 1945, in 1949–1952, and in 1961.

William Jay Jacobs

■ **More About the Author** Jacobs believes that by writing biographies he is "able to reach a very special audience: young people searching for models, trying to understand themselves." He says, "My primary task, perhaps, is to introduce them to that great reservoir of recorded history from which our civilization has drawn inspiration."

■ **Other Works** Nonfiction: *Search for Freedom: America and Its People, Women in American History*; biographies: *Hannibal: An African Hero, Roger Williams, Stalin, Truman*

 ■ **Awards** Notable Children's Books in Social Studies selection, National Council for the Social Studies and Children's Book Council; Best Children's Books of 1979 selection, Child Study Association; Fulbright fellowship, 1980

Objectives

- To understand the purpose and characteristics of a magazine article
- To interview and write about someone who has pursued a dream
- To organize and write a factual article, using appropriate transitions
- To draft, revise, edit, and share informative writing

Teaching Strategies

DISCUSSING THE ASSIGNMENT

Share with students that magazine articles are examples of informative writing, a type of writing that presents and explains facts. Call on volunteers to tell how magazine articles they have read are examples of informative writing.

Have students study the PASSkey, and be sure they understand the purpose, audience, subject, and structure it suggests. Point out that it is not necessary for the subject of their article to have achieved a dream—but he or she should at least have chased after one. Also tell students that their PASSkeys may differ from the one in the text. If you wish, you may give students the option of writing about something else that is important to them, such as those suggested under Alternative Writing and Research Topics on the bottom of page 287.

ANALYZING THE MODEL

Have a volunteer read aloud the student model on pages 286-287. Ask students to give examples of the facts that Liz Herrera's article contains. *(Possible responses: Irene Grainge is a visually impaired track runner; others tried to discourage her from running; she practiced daily; she has never placed first in an event, but she has never come in lower than third.)* Then ask students how they think Herrera learned all her facts, and how they came to that conclusion. *(Possible response: observation and probably an interview, because there are too many details and too many good comments by the runner for this to have been a second- or third-hand story)*

WRITER'S WORKSHOP

INFORMATIVE WRITING

USE INFORMATIVE WRITING FOR
news articles
magazine articles
summaries
job descriptions
reports
comparison-contrast
  papers
essays

This subunit is full of dreamers, both imaginary and real. Your own experience tells you how powerful dreams can be. In this workshop you'll write a magazine article about a real person who has pursued a dream. You'll use **informative writing,** or writing that explains facts. Yet you'll also use your creativity to help you choose facts that create the impression you want. With creative choices, you can show how well you understand a person driven by dreams.

Here is one writer's PASSkey to this assignment.

GUIDED ASSIGNMENT: MAGAZINE ARTICLE

Write a magazine article about a person who has pursued a dream.

PURPOSE: To inform
AUDIENCE: Classmates and other students
SUBJECT: A person who pursued a dream
STRUCTURE: A magazine article

STUDENT MODEL
The opening hooks readers' curiosity.

The writer clearly states Irene's dream.

> **A Winner**
> **by Liz Herrera**
>
> At school track meets, you can always pick out Irene Grainge. She's the one who sets her starting blocks by bending down so low that her nose touches the track. She's not goofing around. She's trying to find the right distance from the starting line to set the blocks. "I'm not blind," Irene jokes. "I just can't see."
>
> Irene was born with an incurable eye disease. Her vision was almost gone by the time she was ten. On eye charts, she can read only the big E. She can see colors and shapes, but she can't make out details unless they're right in front of her nose. Still, she's dreamed of competing as a runner since she was five and watched her first Olympics on television.

286   UNIT THREE   DRIVEN BY DREAMS

ADDITIONAL RESOURCES

Unit Three Resource Book
Writer's Workshop Worksheet, p. 24
Writer's Workshop: Peer and Self-Evaluation, p. 25
Writer's Workshop: Assessment Guidelines, p. 26

Technology and Enrichment

Elaboration, Revision, and Proofreading
  Transparencies 5–8

Writer's Databank Software: File 12, Writing
  Introductions

Links to
Writer's Craft

For more about informative writing, see *The Writer's Craft,* Grade 7, "Informative Writing: Explaining What," pages 116–129, and "Observation and Description, Character Sketch" pages 48–66.

When Irene wanted to go out for track, the gym teachers thought she shouldn't. Irene didn't argue. Instead, she had her brother walk her around the track so that she could get her bearings. Then she started running laps. Every lunch period, before she ate, she ran. Sometimes a friend ran with her. Often Irene ran alone. She didn't miss a day. After two months the coach gave in and let her enter a meet.

Now Irene competes in the fifty-yard dash, the hundred-yard dash, and the four-hundred-meter relay. She's also practicing for the hurdles. Each day, repeating "Step, step, step, jump" to herself, she clears a row of barriers she can hardly see.

So far, Irene has never placed first in an event. However, she's never placed below third either. Her personal best gets a little better at each meet. People sometimes make fun of her when she puts her face against the blocks. She doesn't mind. "I'm doing what I love," she says. "I just feel lucky." To those who don't know her, Irene's actions may look weird. To those who know her, she looks like a winner.

◄ Irene's story is told in chronological order.

◄ Facts and figures help readers understand.

◄ The writer includes a quote from Irene.

◄ The writer's opinion appears only briefly, at the end.

Prewrite and Explore

1 **Find the dreamers**   Try brainstorming about dreamers you've known. For example, you may know someone who has started a wildlife shelter or helped a troubled child. You might also ask an older relative to tell you about dreamers in your family. You may know of politicians, entertainers, or sports figures who have been inspired by dreams. List as many names as you can think of. Remember, your article need not be about someone famous—or even about someone who succeeds. With dreams, it's the trying that matters most.

2 **Get ready to roll**   Scan your list of dreamers for the one you'd like to focus on. Then you can use the ideas on the next page to gather facts for your article.

NEED MORE IDEAS?
Try flipping through magazines and newspapers. Look for stories about people you admire.

◄ **ASK FOR HELP**
Want a good source of facts about famous people? Ask a librarian to help you find a biographical dictionary.

To analyze the model further, form students into four groups. Have two groups discuss the Set 1 questions and the two other groups the Set 2 questions.

Set 1

■ What is good about the introduction?

■ Why is it important for Liz to explain her subject's dream at the beginning of the article?

■ What strategy does Liz use to make the runner so believable and likable?

Set 2

■ Why might Liz have used Irene's humorous comment in her very first paragraph?

■ How does Liz organize her work? What other methods of organization might also work for this kind of writing?

■ What kind of conclusion has Liz written? Why is it appropriate?

Afterward, have all four groups share what they discussed. If time permits, have the class talk about other formats Liz might have used to present her story.

Prewrite and Explore

Before students begin thinking of people to write about, suggest that they brainstorm the kinds of dreamers they might consider. For example, they might want to write about heroes, people who help the homeless, animal lovers, people who dream of saving the environment, and so on. Then have students make a list of those in their chosen categories whose stories would make interesting articles.

Alternate Writing and Research Topics

Informative Article The scene in "The Smallest Dragonboy" in which Keevan "impresses" Heath is very much like what people describe as "bonding." Make some notes and then write an article about a subject who bonds with an unusual animal.

Poetry Write a poem that expresses Keevan's happiness at being chosen by a dragon.

Research Interview In "Eleanor Roosevelt," we learn that someone as important as a first lady could suffer from feelings of fear, shyness, and unattractiveness. Research another famous person who had similar problems, and write an interview you might have had with him or her.

Share with students that the graphic organizer on page 288 is an appropriate one to use for an interview. Point out, however, that there are other kinds just as good, and if they'd rather interview someone using a list of ideas or a set of note cards, that is fine.

Draft and Discover

As students draft, encourage them to begin with the best quotations or the most impressive facts from their interviews. Since an introductory "grabber" like Liz Herrera's can be added later, this suggestion lets students begin where they feel most confident.

TEACHING TIP: CHALLENGE

Strong writers might try using their articles to compare and contrast their contemporary dreamers with similar dreamers from some past era. Although students can't interview the latter, they can read letters, diaries, and biographies to capture their subjects' dreams. The challenge for students lies not only in working with two subjects, but also in organizing their writing to give both subjects equal treatment.

TEACHING TIP: COMPUTER

Students who draft on computers might consider keying all their interview questions and answers into a separate document or into a Notes section of their working document to be retrieved as necessary. In this way students can monitor the flow of their articles without worrying about where the quotations will go until they're ready to use them.

IN OTHER CLASSES
A similar list of questions based on what you know can help you gather information for reports in science and social studies.

► **STUDENT MODEL**

TIPS FOR INTERVIEWS
• Ask permission beforehand to tape or take notes.
• Tell the person what you know—but listen more than you talk.
• Share your responses as you listen.
• If the person starts a new topic, follow it. You can always come back to your list.

GATHERING INFORMATION

You might review your own memories, ask to look through your subject's scrapbooks, or interview your subject or someone close to him or her. Using a list of questions will help. (If your subject is a famous person you can't contact, a list of questions can guide your research in magazines and books.) What questions you use will depend on what you already know and what you think will interest your readers. Notice how Liz used a list to develop her questions for an interview.

Who is my subject? What is he or she like?
Irene: upbeat, fast runner, determined. Vision problems—not sure what they are. Ask Irene for details.

What is the dream? How did it start?
Dream: to run track. Don't know how it started. Ask Irene.

How has the person pursued it?
On track team, but joined late. Why? Ask.

What obstacles have come up, and how has the person handled them?
Obstacle: can't see how far to set starting blocks, so she scrunches down so close her nose touches. Others? Ask.

What has the dream meant to the subject?
What does it mean to me?
To me: I admire her. She works a lot, doesn't get much glory. I think she's a hero for trying. To her? Ask how she feels about it.

3 **Get the scoop**   You might use written notes, audiotape, or videotape to record an interview. Be sure to record the date and the place of the interview too. If you use written sources, take notes. Include titles, authors, and page numbers in your notes so that you can check back easily if you need to.

Managing the Paper Load

To minimize corrections later, circulate among students, quickly skimming their works in progress and questioning them on organization and other drafting strategies. You'll want to be sure students have their organization plan well formulated here—or at least by the time they revise.

Draft and Discover

1 Jump in   Don't worry yet about an introduction. It's fine to start in the middle. You'll find a lot to say if you start with the part of the person's story that impresses you most. For example, you might start by describing the person's response to a tough obstacle. Then see where your writing leads. Be sure to write in the third person (*she, he,* or *they*), not in the first person (*I* or *we*).

2 Use your notes   When you run out of words, go back to your notes or tapes. Use them to fill in details you forgot and to remind you of other areas you want to cover. Because this is informative writing, you need to downplay your opinions and focus on facts. Load your draft with details, figures, and specifics. To make your writing even more authentic, use quotes from your subject.

◄ **GRAMMAR TIP**
Use pronouns carefully. Word your sentences so that it's always clear who's being discussed.

Revise Your Writing

1 Shape and smooth it   At this point your draft is probably in sections. Now you can choose a means of organization. You might tell the person's story in chronological order or start at the present and work backward. You might describe the dream, then explain how the person pursued it, and finally explain what the pursuit has meant to the dreamer. Transitions like *at first, now, later,* and *in 1990* can help you join sections smoothly.

2 Add a hook   After your article has taken shape, look again at the beginning. Try adding an unusual statement, a catchy quote, or a vivid description. Then use the revision questions below.

Revision Questions

For You	For a Peer Reader
1. Have I made the dream as clear as possible?	1. Which part of my article holds your attention best?
2. Would more facts or figures make my article more specific?	2. Were you ever unsure who was being talked about?
3. Does my opinion appear only at the end if at all?	3. How would you sum up this person's dream?

Revise Your Writing

At this stage students should be encouraged to check their PASSkeys to see whether their purpose and audience are the same or have changed along the way. Advise them to do another PASSkey if anything is different.

Next, if they haven't already done so, have students write their introductions and conclusions. Suggest that they use a quotation in both places if possible, and be sure they've given an opinion of their dreamer in at least one place.

As students revise their articles, circulate around the room noting their use (or lack) of transitions. Point out the importance of words such as *before, then, during, after,* and *meanwhile* for chronological order; *because, if, then, as a result,* and *therefore* for cause-and-effect order; and *first, second, more important,* and *most important* for order of importance. If students need reminders about specific kinds of transitions, refer them to page 698 in the Writer's Handbook.

Modeling You might use an overhead projector to model the use of transitions. Write three or four sentences about what you've done in the last hour, without transitions. Then, with students, add simple time order transitions or cause and effect transitions. Point out how the transition words relate the sentences to one another and make them cohesive.

Finally, encourage students to use the Revision Questions.

CONFERENCING TIP

As you conference with individual writers for this workshop, you may wish to focus on

■ use of transitions

■ statements of opinion

■ introductory paragraphs

Cooperative Writing: Revising

Form the class into small groups of four or five to work on their introductions and conclusions. Encourage group members to help one another refine and improve these sections and to share ideas on the kinds of material to use there.

After everyone has finished writing, group members should listen to the final version of each grabber and conclusion, offering suggestions on content and style.

Proofread

Note that The Editor's Eye feature previews the content in the Language Workshop that follows. You may choose to teach the Language Workshop, pages 291–293, before having students proofread.

Use the following sentences as needed for reinforcement. Possible corrections are listed for each one.

1. At first Irene had no racing skills she just liked to run. (At first Irene had no racing skills. She just liked to run.)

2. "I'm not blind I just can't see," said Irene. ("I'm not blind. I just can't see," said Irene.)

3. Irene has not yet won a race it's just a matter of time until she does. (Irene has not yet won a race. It's just a matter of time until she does.)

4. What kind of inspiration does she offer us she's pursued her dream—and caught it. (What kind of inspiration does she offer us? She's pursued her dream—and caught it.)

Publish and Present

As the magazine is taking shape, have one or two students draw up a title page, a copyright page, and a table of contents. If possible, arrange to have the cover reinforced and laminated, since the magazine will probably be a popular item that is handled frequently.

Reflect on Your Writing

You may choose to have students answer the following questions in addition to or instead of those in their text:

■ How well did I make use of my interview information? What might I have done differently?

■ Did I choose my subject well? Next time would I choose someone else to write about?

Closure

Now that students have written an article complete with statistics and quotations, encourage them to note how these features are handled in published articles.

> **COMPUTER TIP**
> To catch run-ons in your writing, scroll backwards. Read each sentence aloud, starting at the bottom of the screen and working up.

> **NEED MORE HELP?**
> See the Language Workshop on pages 291–293 and pages 718–720 of the Language Handbook.

FOR YOUR PORTFOLIO ▶

Proofread carefully, and correct any errors in grammar, spelling, capitalization, and punctuation. Watch for run-ons.

THE EDITOR'S EYE: RUN-ON SENTENCES

Avoid run-on sentences—two or more sentences written incorrectly as one.

Two complete sentences must be separated with a period. When you forget the period, the result is a run-on sentence. You can catch run-ons easily when you proofread. To repair them, end each sentence with a period, and begin each with a capital letter.

Problem	Often Irene ran alone she didn't miss a day.
Revised	Often Irene ran alone. She didn't miss a day.

Publish and Present

Here is a class project that will let you share your work with others.

A Magazine of Dreamers Combine the class's articles into a magazine. Choose a title, and design a cover that indicates what's inside. Each student might be responsible for supplying photos or drawings for his or her article and for choosing one or two lines of the article to highlight in large type, as in published magazines.

Reflect on Your Writing

Write brief answers to the questions below. Put your answers in your portfolio with your article.

1. Now that you have written this article, do you admire the person more or less? Why?

2. As you wrote about someone else's dream, what insights did you gain about your own dreams?

Assessment Guidelines

These guidelines may help you assess student writing:

Content
■ The article informs the reader about someone with a dream.
■ The first paragraph effectively draws the audience's attention.
■ The writer's opinion is stated and supported.
■ The closing paragraph provides a satisfactory conclusion.

Style
■ Facts are organized logically and effectively.
■ Transitions are specific and effective.
■ Language is appropriate to the subject matter.

Usage and Mechanics
■ Standard grammar and usage is evident.
■ Quotations are punctuated correctly.

See also *Unit Resource Book Three,* page 26.

LANGUAGE WORKSHOP

AVOIDING FRAGMENTS AND RUN-ONS

> A group of words that is only part of a sentence is a **sentence fragment**. A **run-on sentence** is two or more sentences written incorrectly as one.

Sentence Fragments

When you're deeply involved in *what* you're writing, you may pay less attention to *how* you're writing. You may not notice that you're writing fragments instead of sentences.

When we talk, sentence fragments are natural, so in written dialogue or drama, fragments are fine. Fragments are also acceptable in journals, since personal writing is like talking. In other kinds of writing, however, fragments leave readers guessing.

You know that a complete sentence has two main parts: a subject and a predicate. To repair a fragment, first decide what's missing. Then add the missing part.

Fragment	Elliott Roosevelt's only daughter. (What about his only daughter? The predicate is missing.)
Sentence	Elliott Roosevelt's only daughter was born in 1884.
Fragment	Had many fears. (Who had many fears? The subject is missing.)
Sentence	Young Eleanor Roosevelt had many fears.
Fragment	Feeling homely and shy. (Who did what while feeling homely and shy? Both subject and predicate are missing.)
Sentence	Feeling homely and shy, Eleanor became withdrawn.

Notice that words ending in *-ing* are not necessarily verbs. An *-ing* word is part of a verb only when used with a form of *to be* (*is, was, has been, could be,* and so forth).

PROOFREADING TIP

The proofreading stage is a good time to catch fragments. A peer editor may be able to spot them more easily than you can.

◄ REMINDER

The **predicate** tells what the subject *does* or *is.*

Objectives

■ To recognize and correct sentence fragments and run-on sentences

Teaching Strategies

SENTENCE FRAGMENTS

Have students read page 291, noting the characteristics of sentence fragments and studying the ways to correct them. Then provide the following fragments for students to correct in oral practice. Possible answers are provided.

1. The smallest dragonboy. *(The smallest dragonboy wished for a dragon of his own.)*

2. Grew up with dragons. *(The children of the weyr grew up with dragons.)*

3. With a loud, brisk hum. *(The young dragons hatched with a loud, brisk hum.)*

4. Although young, hoped to be worthy of a dragon. *(Although young, Keevan hoped to worthy of a dragon.)*

5. Jabbing the shovel into Keevan's chest. *(Jabbing the shovel into Keevan's chest, Beterli knocked him to the ground.)*

6. A broken skull and leg. *(With a broken skull and leg, how could Keevan attend the Hatching?)*

7. Worthy of a bronze dragon. *(Never in all his life did Keevan think himself worthy of a bronze dragon.)*

After the oral practice, have students work in small groups to complete Exercises 1 and 2.

ADDITIONAL RESOURCES
Unit Three Resource Book
Language Workshop Practice, p. 27

Technology and Enrichment
Grammar and Usage Copy Masters 15, 16

Links to
Writer's Craft

For more about avoiding fragments and run-ons, see *The Writer's Craft,* Grade 7, "Correcting Problem Sentences," pages 294–298.

Answers to Exercise 1

Added words to complete fragments will vary.

1. F—was very favorable
2. F—She
3. F—Eleanor became withdrawn
4. S
5. F—Eleanor
6. S
7. F—She spent many years
8. S
9. F—She became
10. F—Even after her husband's death, she

Answers to Exercise 2

1. Both word groups lack nouns or pronouns that explain who or what. Since they don't have subjects, neither makes a complete thought. "The choice of the baby dragons could not be questioned. Their choices could not be changed."

2. The fragments sound like two rules that can never be altered. The paragraph would lack that decisiveness if the fragments were changed.

3. Other examples of fragments: "To be chosen—to be a dragonrider!" and the next six lines on page 252; these exclamations show the build up of emotion in Keevan. Other responses include "Too bad about the belt," (p. 261, a character's thought); "Never seen anything like it. Only thirty-nine riders chosen. And the bronze trying to leave without making Impression." and "None acceptable, apparently." (p. 263, characters are talking in fragments, quite common in dialogue)

Correcting Run-on Sentences

Introduce the problem of run-ons and the comma splice on page 292. Then provide the following sentences for oral practice.

1. Eleanor married Franklin she was only nineteen at the time. (*Eleanor married Franklin. She was only nineteen at the time.*)

2. Later Franklin became President, Eleanor stood by him. (*Later Franklin became President. Eleanor stood by him.*)

Exercise 1 Concept Check   Write *S* for each complete sentence. Write *F* for each fragment. Then add words to make each fragment a sentence.

1. The article about Eleanor Roosevelt.
2. Was born into a wealthy family.
3. Noticing her mother's coldness toward her.
4. She feared the dark.
5. Was married at nineteen and raised five children.
6. An illness paralyzed her husband's legs.
7. Learning about human rights.
8. Eleanor blossomed.
9. A powerful public speaker.
10. Continued to help the world's needy people.

> BREAKING THE RULES ▶

Exercise 2 Looking at Style   Professional writers sometimes use fragments on purpose. For example, in "The Smallest Dragonboy" (page 251), Anne McCaffrey writes that leaders were surprised at one baby dragon's choice, which could not be forced. Then she adds, "Could not be questioned. Could not be changed."

1. Explain why the two word groups quoted are fragments. Which part is missing? How would you make each a complete sentence?

2. How would McCaffrey's paragraph sound if the two fragments were complete sentences?

3. Find two other examples of fragments in "The Smallest Dragonboy." Why do you think a professional like McCaffrey would choose to use these fragments?

Run-on Sentences

Like fragments, run-on sentences can occur when you're more involved with ideas than with form. In one kind of run-on, sentences are strung together with no punctuation. In another kind, sentences are joined with only a comma; this error is called a **comma splice.** To repair run-ons, end each complete sentence with a period. Then start the next sentence with a capital letter.

> SAY IT ALOUD ▶
>
> Reading your work aloud may help you spot run-on sentences. Notice where you pause to end each complete thought. Have you placed a period there?

Run-on	Eleanor had to wear a back brace her mother teased her by calling her Granny.
Run-on	Eleanor had to wear a back brace, her mother teased her by calling her Granny.
Correct	Eleanor had to wear a back brace. Her mother teased her by calling her Granny.

Grammar Games: Story Challenge

Have students form two teams. Explain that they will retell the story "The Smallest Dragonboy" with sentence fragments and run-on sentences and their corrections.

The first student from Team 1 and Team 2 meet in the center of the classroom. The Team 1 player begins by describing or telling something from the first part of the story using a sentence fragment or a run-on. The Team 2 player must correct the sentence

to everyone's satisfaction. Then the next two students come up, but this time the Team 2 player gives the incorrect sentence and the Team 1 player corrects it. Play continues, and the story moves forward with each round. At the end of the story, the team with the most correct sentences wins. Note that this challenge game can also be played in writing on two overhead projectors.

Exercise 3 Concept Check   On your paper, correct these run-ons.

1. Elliott Roosevelt was the younger brother of Theodore Roosevelt, Elliott loved his daughter Eleanor dearly.

2. As a child, Eleanor lived in luxury she was taught French and cared for by servants.

3. When Eleanor was only eight her mother died then within eighteen months her father and brother died too.

4. Eleanor made her first real friends at an English boarding school, they called her Totty and admired her spirit.

5. At eighteen Eleanor began working to help children in New York slums about this time she and Franklin Roosevelt fell in love.

6. Franklin entered politics, in 1920 he ran for vice-president.

7. After several years an illness left Franklin unable to walk, then Eleanor entered politics herself.

8. Franklin was elected president in 1932, Eleanor traveled around the country seeing the effects of poverty and prejudice.

9. She learned of the need for social change she also convinced Franklin to work for change.

10. In 1945 Eleanor Roosevelt was made a delegate to the United Nations there she continued to fight for human rights.

Exercise 4 Proofreading Skill   Working in small groups, correct each fragment and each run-on in the following paragraph.

Eleanor Roosevelt saw the world change in amazing ways during her lifetime. Born just over a hundred years ago. She was nineteen when the Wright brothers flew the first airplane at Kitty Hawk, she was seventy-six when Alan Shepard became the first American in space. She saw the beginning and the end of both world wars. The tragedies of the Great Depression. The victory of the Supreme Court decision against segregation. Eleanor's own life was another kind of victory. She overcame her own sorrows and fears she became a tireless fighter for human rights.

Exercise 5 Revising Your Writing   Proofread the article you wrote for the Writer's Workshop on pages 286–290. Correct any fragments and run-ons you find. Then do the same with the other pieces in your portfolio.

◀ **HINT** . . . .
Try having one group member read the paragraph aloud.

LANGUAGE HANDBOOK . . . .
For review and practice: Section 2, Understanding Sentences, pages 717–720.

---

3. Eleanor traveled across the country she saw the need for social change. (*Eleanor traveled across the country. She saw the need for social change.*)

Work with students as a class to correct the run-ons in Exercise 3.

Answers to Exercise 3
Brief forms of corrections follow.

1. of Theodore Roosevelt. Elliott

2. in luxury. She

3. her mother died. Then

4. boarding school. They

5. New York slums. About this time

6. politics. In 1920

7. unable to walk. Then Eleanor

8. in 1932. Eleanor traveled

9. for social change. She also convinced

10. United Nations. There

Answers to Exercise 4
Possible corrections are given.

Eleanor Roosevelt saw the world change in amazing ways during her lifetime. Born just over a hundred years ago, she was nineteen when the Wright brothers flew the first airplane at Kitty Hawk. She was seventy-six when Alan Shepard became the first American in space. She saw the beginning and the end of both world wars, the tragedies of the Great Depression, and the victory of the Supreme Court decision against segregation. Eleanor's own life was another kind of victory. She overcame her sorrows and fears. She became a tireless fighter for human rights.

Answers to Exercise 5
Student responses will vary.

Additional Practice

Identify and correct the fragments and run-ons.

1. Though small, a good heart. (F—*Though small, Keevan had a good heart.*)

2. The best runner in the weyr. (F—*Keevan was the best runner in the weyr.*)

3. The dragonriders fought the evil Thread they were protectors of their world. (R—*The dragonriders fought the evil Thread. They were protectors of their world.*)

4. In spite of the insults of Beterli, Keevan, the smallest dragonboy. (F—*In spite of the insults of Beterli, Keevan, the smallest dragonboy, grew stronger each day.*)

5. Soon Beterli was no longer a candidate, Keevan was the youngest dragonrider. (R—*Soon Beterli was no longer a candidate. Keevan was the youngest dragonrider.*)

Closure

Remind students that their magazine articles will be easier to understand if they find and correct sentence fragments and run-ons. Point out, however, that if their subject spoke in fragments, students should leave them alone, since they are quoted material. Suggest that students note other types of writing in which fragments are acceptable and those in which they are not.

Objectives

- To understand the value of skimming and scanning

- To practice skimming and scanning for information

Teaching Strategies

Study with students the top half of page 294. Then ask them to do the following activities quickly and give their answers orally:

1. Scan page 104 in this text. What do you notice? *(large blue quote, footnotes, blue box at bottom)*

2. Skim page 122 to find out what page the poem "What Do We Do with a Variation?" is found on. *(129)*

3. What subjects are discussed on pages 780–781 in this book? *(semicolon, colon, and hyphen)*

4. Scan page 661 to find books that Laurence Yep wrote. *(Dragonwings, Child of the Owl, Sea Glass)*

TEACHING TIP: LEP

Although LEP students may already have this skill using their first languages, their ability may not be evident with English. Have them skim and scan in English texts at least once a day.

Answers to Exercise
Step 1: the title cluster at the top of page 144, the large capital letters I and W, the footnotes, the boxed words at the bottom of page 145

Step 2: She preferred to spoil them a little rather than discipline them too much.

Step 3: As a young person, Eleanor was frightened and concerned with doing her duty, but as she grew older she gained courage and developed interests of her own.

READER'S WORKSHOP

SKIMMING AND SCANNING

IN OTHER CLASSES
Before you start reading a science or social studies chapter, skim it to get the big picture.

When you read to find information, skimming and scanning can help. These techniques make both research and studying easier.

Skimming is reading quickly to find the main idea or to get an overview. When you skim, you read only the title, the headings, the words in special type, and the first sentence of each paragraph. You also take time to read charts, graphs, and time lines.

Scanning is searching for a particular fact or definition. When you scan, your eyes sweep across a page, looking for key words that may lead you to the information you want.

TEST-TAKING TIP
In open-book tests, scan your book for specific facts or figures.

You can use a folded piece of paper to train yourself to scan. Choose a textbook page you've already read. Put the edge of the folded paper below the first line of the page. Then move the paper quickly down the page. Look for a fact you know is there. When you come to key words about the fact, remove the paper. Read that section more slowly to find what you need.

Exercise   Follow these directions step by step.

Step 1   Try skimming the first two pages of "The Noble Experiment" (pages 144–145). What are three things that especially stand out? Write your answers on your paper.

Step 2   Using a folded piece of paper, scan the excerpt from Eleanor Roosevelt's autobiography on page 282. Search for an answer to the following question:

How did Eleanor Roosevelt feel about spoiling children?

Write your answer.

TEST-TAKING TIP
Take a minute to skim a test before you start it. The overview will help you decide how much time to spend on each part.

Step 3   Skim the excerpt from Eleanor Roosevelt's autobiography, reading the first sentence of each paragraph. Then write a sentence summing up the main idea of the excerpt.

ADDITIONAL RESOURCES
Unit Three Resource Book
Reader's Workshop Practice, p. 28

Additional Practice

Answer the following questions by skimming and scanning material from this text.

1. Scan to find the name of the author of "Formula" on page 250. *(Ana Maria Iza)*

2. Skim to find the passage in "Eleanor Roosevelt" describing Eleanor's personal response to segregation laws. *(second column, last paragraph, p. 279)*

3. Scan to find the name of K'van's dragon in "The Smallest Dragonboy." *(Heath)*

FIGHT TO THE FINISH

An Olympic runner refuses to give up, despite her twisted ankle, and she hobbles to the finish line. A child fighting a deadly disease greets visitors with a smile. An old soldier boldly leads a charge from which he may never return.

Some people never quit. When the challenge is greatest, they dig deep within themselves for courage or grit. They stretch their powers, whether mental or physical, to the limit. They put everything on the line.

As you read these selections, look for the qualities that enable these characters to fight to the finish. Think about how you would handle the dangers and difficulties they face.

Observation Assessment

Observing how students respond to the text, to the classroom instruction, and to peers is an important part of an assessment program. The following suggestions and the form in the *Guidelines for Reading and Literature Assessment* booklet can be used to implement observation assessment.

■ Writing Behavior As students work through this subunit, assess how they develop and present their ideas in writing. Encourage them to give thought to the arrangement of ideas and to distinguish main ideas from supporting details. See how effectively they are able to create a smooth and logical flow of ideas. As they work through the subunit, look for growth in their ability to present written ideas in a clear, orderly fashion.

Subunit Preview

Have students read the introduction to Subunit 2, "Fight to the Finish." Ask them to explain how fighting to the finish relates to reaching for the stars. How is determination a factor in both? In what ways does attaining a lofty goal involve struggling to the end?

INTEGRATING THE LANGUAGE ARTS

The literary selections in this subunit focus on the theme "Fight to the Finish." Reading skills, literature skills, writing options, language study, vocabulary, and spelling skills are all based on these literary selections.

Writer's Workshop After reading several selections that deal with individuals who struggle to overcome problems, students will write to inform readers about a problem and to persuade readers to accept a solution.

Language Workshop The Language Workshop deals with words often confused or misspelled. Students will see that using the correct words and spelling them correctly can improve their ability to persuade readers.

Reader's Workshop The Reader's Workshop in this subunit focuses on the language of persuasion. Students will learn how to use logical and correct reasoning in the presentation of their ideas.

FOR ADDITIONAL CHALLENGE

The following selections offer extra challenge in the exploration of the subunit theme:

"The Wish," short story by Roald Dahl

"Coyote Kills the Giant," folk tale told by Richard Erdoes and Alfonso Ortiz

Profiles in Courage, biographies by John F. Kennedy

ADDITIONAL RESOURCES

Technology and Enrichment
Family and Community Involvement Source Book, p. 13

Guidelines for Reading and Literature Assessment, Observation Assessment Forms

Objectives

- To understand and analyze a short story
- To examine character
- To enrich reading by identifying problems and solutions
- To express understanding of the story through a choice of writing forms, including a new ending and a notice

Prereading/Motivation

Examine What You Know

Discussion Prompts In a tough situation, do you tend to panic, freeze, or be calm? Have you ever been surprised by someone else's reaction?

Expand Your Knowledge

Additional Background In the spring of 1675, New Hampshire, which included part of what is now Maine, was part of the Massachusetts Bay Colony. Relations between white settlers in New England and local Native Americans had been unsettled since the Pequot War of 1637. Then, in June 1675, the killing of three Wampanoag and a raid on a colonial settlement triggered King Philip's War (or Metacomet's Rebellion), which lasted through August 1676.

Enrich Your Reading

Possible problems for chart:
Panther has killed calf; panther gets away; panther is in cabin with Alben; Alben has no weapons in loft; family will return without knowing danger.

Possible solutions for chart:
Alben shoots at panther; Alben climbs up to loft; Alben uses blanket as protection; Alben grabs gun, runs outside, and shoots panther.

**Thematic Link—
Fight to the Finish**

Alben Hastings and a panther fight to the finish for survival. Alben's victory ultimately depends on his courage, intelligence, pride, and sense of responsibility to his family.

Fiction

Old Sly Eye

RUSSELL GORDON CARTER

Examine What You Know (Prior Knowledge)

Have you ever been in a situation where you had nothing to count on but your own resources? Perhaps it was some sort of emergency or danger. Maybe you had to face someone or something at school. In a class discussion, describe a time when you or someone you've heard of or read about faced a great difficulty all alone. How did you or the other person react? What lessons might have been learned from the experience?

Expand Your Knowledge (Building Background)

Self-reliance was a necessary quality for the early settlers of the American colonies. They, like the main **character** in the following story, struggled to gather or grow enough to eat and to survive the killing cold of New England winters. Because they faced the constant threat of Indian raids, wild animals, and war with the French, most settlers, including young boys, kept their guns close at hand, even while eating or attending church.

Enrich Your Reading (Reading Skill)

Problem Solving The conflict in a story is usually a problem or a set of related problems that the characters must solve. The main character of this story, Alben, must face a very dangerous series of problems all by himself. As you read or when you finish, identify Alben's problems and solutions by making a chart like the one started below. You can then evaluate Alben's problem-solving abilities and understand how the conflict is resolved.

■ *Author biography in Reader's Handbook*

Problem	Solution
Alben hears loud noises in the barn.	He goes to investigate.

JOURNAL WRITING IDEAS

■ Would you like to have been an early settler in America? Why or why not?

■ In what ways do you rely on yourself? on others?

■ Do you enjoy reading pioneer stories or seeing them on television? Why or why not?

COLLABORATIVE LEARNING OPTIONS

Opportunities for collaborative learning include Enrich Your Reading, First Impressions (p. 303), and the For Alternative Learning Styles activity for Vocabulary Practice (p. 303).

ADDITIONAL RESOURCES

Unit Three Resource Book
Reader's Guidesheet, p. 29
Reading Skills, p. 30
Literature Skills, p. 31
Vocabulary Connections, p. 32
Spelling Connections, p. 33
Comprehension and Vocabulary Check Tests, p. 34
Selection Test, p. 35

Old Sly Eye

RUSSELL GORDON CARTER

It was a May evening in the year 1675. Alone in his father's log house on the northern edge of Dover township in the province of New Hampshire, Alben Hastings lit the lantern and opened his worn copy of *The Pilgrim's Progress*. Suddenly a loud commotion sounded in the direction of the barn—mad squeals and frightened bellowings and the hollow thudding of hoofs. Leaping erect, he seized his musket and, lantern in hand, went racing outside.

He was within a dozen yards of the barn, the wind singing in his ears, when the moon rolled from beneath a formation of ragged clouds, and he checked himself abruptly. There beside the shed lay the recently born calf, and over it crouched a big catlike creature, its solitary eye gleaming, its great round tufted tail weaving savagely to and fro—a panther.

Dropping the lantern, Alben raised the musket and fired, only to see the creature leap sidewise, apparently unhurt. The next instant it swept past him and vanished in the deep shadows.

A ▶ The boy clenched his teeth. "Old Sly Eye!" he muttered angrily, and his thoughts went swiftly back to the morning two weeks earlier when his father had set forth with Mr. Stephen Wainright on a prolonged trapping expedition beyond the Piscataqua.

"Yes, my lad," John Hastings had said then, "I know how much you would like to come along, but 'tis your duty to stay behind and look after your mother and sister. And mind ye keep a good watch over the livestock! I wouldn't want to come home and find Old Sly Eye had done to us what he's done to others."

Alben strode to where the calf was lying. It wasn't his fault that Old Sly Eye had somehow managed to break into the barn, for his father himself had said the barn was reasonably secure against varmints. The calf lay motionless—there was no question that it was dead. Within the barn the cow and the two oxen were still stamping about and letting out occasional bellows, but the boy was not so much concerned with them; they were safe and unhurt.

As Alben continued to stare at the calf, he thought of other plunderings within the township—cattle and swine slain by the big one-eyed panther that often killed for the mere sake of killing. Ever since the previous autumn, Old Sly Eye had eluded the bullets and traps of the angry settlers—and tonight

---

Words to Know and Use

abruptly (ə brupt′ lē) *adv.* suddenly
elude (ē lood′) *v.* to avoid or get away from by being sly or quick

297

Continued on page 298

BLACK HOUSE   1984   Jennifer Bartlett   The St. Louis Art Museum, Purchase: Eliza McMillan Purchase Fund.

he, Alben Hastings, had had an easy shot at close range and had failed to bring the beast down!

Well, regrets wouldn't help. Since the calf was dead, it would serve as food, and therefore the thing for him to do was to hang it on a tree or against the barn, high enough so that nothing could get at it. At the cabin—up in the loft where he and his father were accustomed to sleep—there was a coil of rope he could use. Returning to the lantern, which had gone out, he picked it up and started at a slow walk for the house.

In the south, silver-edged clouds were racing past the moon. He wondered what the hour might be. Perhaps his mother and Rebecca would soon be coming home from the Wainright cabin, a mile or so to the west. They had gone over to help care for old Mrs. Wainright, who had fallen and broken a leg.

The door to the log house was swinging and creaking on its hinges, and as he shouldered his way inside, the wind caught it and thrust it shut behind him. Striding to the fireplace, he groped for the powder horn and bag of shot on the high mantel and reloaded the musket.

On the frontier a loaded musket sometimes meant the difference between life and death. After he had set it down, resting the muzzle against the wall, he crossed the hard-packed earthen floor to the ladder leading to the loft. It would be as black as midnight up there, but there was no need to bother with flint and steel.[1] He knew exactly where the rope was hanging.

B ▶

With quick, sure steps he started up the ladder, but as his hands closed on the top rung, he felt his heart tighten and his throat go suddenly dry. Something was in the loft—something heavy enough to cause the boards to creak! He was about to back downward when there was a snarl and a rush of padded feet, and the next instant a heavy body thudded against his shoulder and then hurtled past him, knocking the ladder violently sidewise. With a desperate lunge Alben clutched at the edge of the loft, and for several seconds after the ladder had crashed to the floor, he clung there, his legs dangling. Then he succeeded in swinging himself upward.

C ▶

Old Sly Eye! Crouching on the edge of the high platform, Alben felt the tumultuous pounding of his heart as he stared downward into blackness. The panther was over near the door; he could hear it crooning and snarling. He could hear the occasional thump and swish of its long, heavy tail against the wall. Presently it moved, and he had a partial glimpse of it in a narrow band of moonlight slanting through the opening in the shutter across the south window. He saw its solitary gleaming eye, the other lost perhaps in an encounter with another panther. Then it vanished again in the blackness, and now he could hear it going around and around the room, hissing and muttering, and making other catlike sounds deep within its throat.

Why had Old Sly Eye entered the house? Alben asked himself the question while he was groping about for something with which to defend himself. Was it in hope of finding another victim? Panthers as a rule kept away from humans, yet Old Sly Eye was no ordinary panther. Or was it perhaps curiosity that had prompted the creature to enter the partly open door? The boy could not be sure. He knew only that the panther was down there, unable to get out, and that he himself was in danger.

The loft held no weapon or heavy object that could be used as a weapon. In his two hands he held the rope. It was a stout new half-inch Portsmouth rope, more than a score of feet long—but what good was it? As he finally tossed it aside, he thought longingly of his loaded musket down near the fireplace.

The panther continued to move here and there, now and again passing through the band of moonlight. Every little while it would snarl in a way that made Alben shiver, and once he thought he heard it sharpening its claws on one of the logs. Or was it trying to reach the loft? The logs that formed the walls were unevenly placed—it might come slithering upward. And he was utterly defenseless, lacking even a knife.

---

1. **flint and steel:** tools used to start a fire. Flint is a hard rock that when struck on steel produces a spark.

| Words to Know and Use | **grope** (grōp) v. to touch or feel about in search of something |

5. ACTIVE READING: Predict
Ask students for their predictions about what will occur next in the story. (Any response is valid.)

6. ACTIVE READING: Question
Ask students why they think Old Sly Eye has entered the house. Encourage them to **infer** an answer on the basis of their knowledge about the panther's past actions and the encounter between the cat and Alben. If necessary, help students by reading the following example of a think-aloud, or model one of your own.

Think-Aloud Script I wonder why the panther entered the house? Alben thinks it might have entered to search for another victim. But he also knows that panthers usually stay away from humans. I know the panther has killed cattle and pigs in the township, and it killed the calf. I can't believe that it would go into a house where there were no animals unless something were wrong. It's acting out of character. I'm going to infer that it is acting strangely because it is sick or wounded.

7. ACTIVE READING: Review
Ask students what factors are causing Alben to be in danger. (Possible responses: The panther can climb and leap and might be able to reach the loft and hurt Alben; the panther is trapped in the room, and there is no exit for Alben except through that room; Alben has no weapon.)

299

Looking at Style

To start a discussion about the author's writing style in "Old Sly Eye," read these sentences aloud:

■ . . . He could hear it [the panther] crooning and snarling. He could hear the occasional thump and swish of its long, heavy tail against the wall.

■ He could hear it going around and around the room, hissing and muttering, and making other catlike sounds deep within its throat.

■ Every little while it would snarl in a way that made Alben shiver, and once he thought he heard it sharpening its claws.

Discuss the following points with students:
1. What effect do the descriptions of the panther's sounds have on readers?
2. Find descriptions of how the panther looked and smelled. List all the verbs, adjectives, and nouns that help the reader visualize the panther.

OLD SLY EYE **Teacher's Edition** **299**

8. LITERARY CONCEPT: Sensory Details

Ask students to identify details that appeal to the sense of touch in this paragraph and the previous one and to explain the purpose of these details. *(Possible responses: "a feeling of icy water cascading down his spine"; "Perspiration bathed his face and neck and armpits"; "cold hands clutching one of the posts"; "lips drawn tightly across his teeth"; "sent a chill through him." The details make Alben's fear seem more real.)*

9. ACTIVE READING: Evaluate

Ask students to evaluate the plan that Alben creates to solve the problem of how to elude Old Sly Eye. Will it work? Why or why not? *(Any response is valid.)*

10. LITERARY CONCEPT: Suspense

Ask students to identify details that add to the suspense here. *(Possible responses: darkness, "resounded to a frightful scream," teeth chattering, "bound like a ghost," snarling)*

11. VOCABULARY: Multiple Meanings

Choose a volunteer to explain the meaning of *stout* in this sentence. *("sturdy or substantial")* Invite other volunteers to give different meanings of *stout.* *("bold or brave," "bulky in figure," "firm," "powerful or forceful")* ★

Suddenly, with a feeling of icy water cascading down his spine, he remembered his mother and sister. Why had he not thought of them before? They, perhaps more than himself, were the ones who were in danger! Even at that moment they might be approaching the house. They would open the door and then . . .

8 Perspiration bathed his face and neck and armpits. With cold hands clutching one of the posts, he stared downward, lips drawn tightly across his teeth. What could he do to warn them? Of course, if he should hear them coming he would shout; yet even so, Rebecca might think he was joking. He remembered with regret some of the jokes he had played in the past. But it was possible that they might reach the door before he heard them. The thought of the two of them unsuspectingly entering the cabin sent a chill through him. "I must do something!"

D ▶ he said to himself.

Yes, but what? He was a virtual prisoner in the loft. There were no windows, and the only way to get down was either to jump or slide down the rope secured to a post. In either case the panther would be waiting for him. Again he thought of his musket. Was there any way he could reach it, perhaps with the aid of the rope? No, the weapon was too far away.

9 The more he pondered, the more he became convinced that the only thing to do would be to go down the rope and then make a rush for the door. It would perhaps take three seconds to go down the rope and another three seconds to reach the door—but during that time Old Sly Eye was not likely

to be sitting quietly on his haunches! Alben drew his sleeve across his moist forehead. He was strong and active, but what chance would he have in a barehanded struggle with a powerful panther? Nevertheless, there seemed no other way.

Knotting an end of the rope securely round a post, he gathered up the rest of it, ready to toss it downward. His eyes had by now grown more accustomed to the darkness, and he thought he could make out the panther directly below him. He let the rope drop, and an instant later the house resounded to a frightful scream that set his teeth to chattering. He saw the creature bound like a ghost through the band of moonlight, and then heard it snarling over near the door.

10

While he waited, listening, he fancied he heard distant voices, as if his mother and sister coming through the forest might be talking to each other—or was it merely the sound of the wind? Raising his own voice, he shouted, "Mother! Rebecca! Keep away, there's a panther in the house!" There was no response. He waited a minute or two and then shouted again. Still there was no response. He had the sudden unhappy feeling that perhaps no one could hear him outside the stout log house—that no matter how much he might shout, it would do no good.

11

The night was silent now save for occasional gusts of wind and the snarling of the panther and the thumping of its tail against the door. Supposing the door should suddenly open and Rebecca should call, "Alben,

---

Words to Know and Use | **ponder** (pän′ dər) *v.* to think deeply; carefully consider are you asleep?" Then the panther would leap and strike—and then . . .

It was more than he could <u>endure</u>! He must risk his life. He mustn't remain idle another moment. But if only he had a weapon of some sort—anything, even a short stick with which he could thrust! Maybe he could find a stick. He would make another search. It would take only a few seconds.

A s he was feeling about in the darkness, his hands encountered the blankets that on cold nights he and his father used for sleeping. There they were, neatly folded against the wall. With a quick exclamation he seized one and shook it out. Here was something perhaps better than a stick! The blanket was **12** thick and heavy—at least it would protect his face.

Holding it loosely over his left arm, he seated himself on the edge of the loft, ready to descend. The panther was still over by the door, and he imagined it waiting for him, teeth bared, claws prepared to strike and to rip. Again he thought of the musket. If only he could get his hands on it!

Still holding the blanket loosely over his left arm, he started downward. His feet had hardly touched the floor when a nerve-shattering scream filled the house and a glistening body flashed toward him through the band of moonlight. Crouching, he flung the blanket out protectingly almost at the same **E ▶** instant the snarling panther was upon him.

Perhaps for half a minute it seemed that he and the panther and the blanket were all hopelessly entangled. He could feel the

LORD OF THE RIMROCK 1988 Leon Parson Print from National Wildlife Galleries, Fort Myers, Florida.

rough wool against his face. He could feel the weight of the creature upon him and smell the strong unpleasant odor of it. Then needlelike claws, caught in the folds of wool, were raking his back and shoulders. Lashing out with hands and feet, Alben tried desperately to free himself. A corner of the blanket covered his head. He reached upward, tore it loose, then rolled sidewise, all the while kicking and struggling.

Suddenly he was free! Rolling twice over, he sprang to his feet. The musket over there by the fireplace! Darting across the room, he snatched it up.

At that moment, above the snarls of the **13** panther still with claws entangled in the blanket, he heard voices outside. It was not the wind; it was not his fancy—the voices

Words to Know and Use | **endure** (en door') *v.* to withstand; put up with; tolerate

301

12. ACTIVE READING: Question
Ask students why they think the blanket may be "better than a stick." (*Possible response: The blanket can be used as a shield, whereas a stick would be unlikely to hurt the cat much.*)

Art Note

Leon Parson was born in Provo, Utah. Of his eight brothers and sisters, five became artists. Parson now lives close to Yellowstone and Grand Teton national parks and so is familiar with scenes like that depicted in *Lord of the Rimrock*. In this painting, the cougar, or yellow panther, steps carefully down from the rimrock, or rock at the edge of a plateau. *Choose three adjectives to describe this animal. Choose three adverbs to describe how the animal moves. Could these words also describe Old Sly Eye?*

13. ACTIVE READING: Connect
If you were Alben, what would you do at this point in the story? Why? (*Any response is valid.*)

14. LITERARY CONCEPT: Metaphor
Ask students to identify the metaphor in the first part of this sentence. *("tongue of flame")* What two things are being compared? *(a tongue and the fire coming out of a rifle)* If necessary, explain that firearms emit flame, produced by the explosion of the gunpowder, from their barrels when fired.

15. ACTIVE READING: Evaluate
Have students give their opinions of Alben's words to his family. Ask if his response is believable. *(Possible responses: Alben's modesty is believable because it seems in keeping with the maturity of his character; Alben's modesty and low-key response is unbelievable, since he has just finished a fight that almost killed him.)*

ENCOURAGING INDEPENDENT READING

April Morning, novel by Howard Fast

Everyday Life in Early America, nonfiction by David Freeman Hawke

The Light in the Forest, novel by Conrad Richter

New Hampshire, nonfiction by Sylvia McNair

Sarah Bishop, novel by Scott O'Dell

---

were real. With musket raised, he hesitated. Should he risk a shot in the darkness? If he were to miss, it might be fatal, not merely to himself but also to his mother and sister. No, he must not miss! Racing to the door, he flung it wide and leaped outside into the night.

His mother and Rebecca were crossing the clearing from the western edge of the woods. Catching sight of him in the moonlight, the girl shouted, "Alben, what are you doing?"

He paid no heed to her. He was half a score of yards now from the open door of the cabin, musket raised, jaws set. The seconds passed while he waited, listening to the thumping of his heart.

"Alben!" This time it was his mother. "What's wrong?"

At that moment a great tawny, glistening shape appeared in the doorway, its solitary eye gleaming. It swung its head first to the right and then to the left. It raised its voice in a prolonged scream. Then spying the boy, it came bounding forward.

A tongue of flame flashed from the musket, and the crash sent the echoes flying.

They continued to tremble across the moon-lit clearing while the panther lay twitching on the grass.

Alben strode to where it was lying. Dead, he said to himself. As dead as the calf! But there were two bullet marks on the panther, one on the throat and the other on the side of the small narrow head, close to one of the rounded ears! Suddenly he understood. His first shot had not missed, after all! Probably it was that first bullet, momentarily bewildering the creature, which had caused it to seek shelter in the house.

"Alben, Alben! Oh, Alben!"

He turned to confront the others. Both were talking to him at once. "Your shirt, 'tis torn to shreds! And you are bleeding! Oh, Alben, are you badly hurt? Tell us what happened!"

He took a deep breath and then smiled. It was easy enough to smile now! "Not so very much happened," he replied slowly. "Yes, I know I'm a bit scratched an' torn, but after all, nobody could expect to fight Old Sly Eye barehanded and not get himself hurt a little!" And then while they gazed at him, wide-eyed, he told them the whole story. ❧

Comprehension Check

1. Who is Old Sly Eye? *(a dangerous panther)*

2. Why does Alben first shoot at Old Sly Eye? *(The panther has killed one of the Hastings's calves.)*

3. What surprise does Alben find in the loft? *(The panther is there.)*

4. Why is Alben worried about his mother and sister? *(They are on their way home, unaware of the danger, and could be attacked by the panther.)*

5. What "weapon" does Alben use when he cannot reach his musket? *(a blanket)*

6. What happens to Old Sly Eye at the end? *(Alben shoots and kills him.)*

*R*esponding to Reading

First Impressions

1. Do you think this story would make a good television program or movie? Share your opinion with your classmates.

Second Thoughts

2. Why do you think Alben is able to win the fight with Old Sly Eye?

   Think about
   - his motivation for killing the panther
   - his previous training in self-reliance
   - his personal qualities

3. Look back at your chart describing how Alben solves his problems. Think of other solutions he could have tried.

4. Do you think this story could have really happened? Explain.

*W*riting Options

1. Write a **new ending** for the story. Begin with Alben in the loft. What might he discover instead of a blanket that would change the story?

2. Write a **notice** (that might begin "Be it known to all that . . . "), to be posted in the territory, describing Alben's heroic achievement.

*V*ocabulary Practice

Exercise   Analogies   An **analogy** contains two pairs of related words. The second pair is related in the same way as the first pair, as in this example: TALL : SHORT; pretty : ugly. *Tall* and *short* are opposites; *pretty* and *ugly* are also opposites. In each item below, determine how the words in the first pair are related. Then decide which vocabulary word best completes the second pair.

Words to Know and Use
abruptly
elude
endure
grope
ponder

1. QUIETLY : SILENTLY; _____ : suddenly
2. TRY : SUCCEED; _____ : seize
3. SEARCH : FIND; _____ : decide
4. NICE : PLEASANT; _____ : tolerate
5. WHISPER : SHOUT; _____ : confront

OLD SLY EYE   303

Student Response

Responding to Reading

1. Any response is valid.

2. Possible responses: Alben is able to win because of his maturity, sense of responsibility, courage, and ability to think clearly under pressure; he knows he must succeed in order to protect his mother, his sister, and himself; his experiences of living on the harsh frontier have prepared him for survival.

3. Any response is valid. Have students suggest specific solutions. For example, he could have left the calf on the ground and shot the panther if it reappeared.

4. Possible responses: Yes, the events are perfectly possible during the time in which they are set; no, in reality a boy could not defeat a panther with a blanket, so the whole story is unlikely.

Writing Options

The Writing Options are designed to meet varied student interests and abilities. Have each student choose one writing activity to complete.

Journal Update Invite students to answer this question in their journals: What dangers in today's world might be similar to the danger of wild animals in Alben's day?

Vocabulary Practice

Answers to Exercise
1. abruptly (synonyms)
2. grope (action, goal)
3. ponder (action, goal)
4. endure (synonyms)
5. elude (antonyms)

Closure

Tell students that "a fight to the finish" can mean "kill or be killed"—that is, it involves matching all of one's wits and strength against a fearful enemy. Invite students to compare this kind of conflict and the conflicts that take place in the world of sports. Ask students to listen to sports broadcasts to notice how sports events are portrayed as life-and-death struggles.

The Spelling Connection

The Assimilated Prefix *ad* When the last letter of a prefix changes to match the first letter of a root, the prefix is said to become assimilated. The prefix **ad** becomes **ac** before **c**, **af** before **f**, **ap** before **p**, **as** before **s**, and **at** before **t**.

Example: ad + proved = approved

Assimilated *ad* in Words from the Selection
ad + customed = accustomed
ad + proaching = approaching

Other Words with Assimilated *ad*

account	affection	affluence
appeal	assemble	assistance
attract	attention	

Exercise Write a word that has the same root, but with the prefix *ad*.

1. discount
2. reproaching
3. influence

4. repeal
5. distract
6. resistance

Objectives

- To understand and analyze an auto-biographical excerpt

- To examine an author's style and to review the concept of internal conflict

- To enrich reading by making connections

- To express understanding of the selection through a choice of writing forms, including an essay, a chant, a letter, and a comparison

Prereading/Motivation

Examine What You Know

Discussion Prompts In what ways do you compete in school, at home, in sports, and in your social life? Is competition always good for people? When could it be bad?

Expand Your Knowledge

Additional Background Music students at Juilliard select a major—voice, conducting, any orchestral or keyboard instrument, composition, or piano accompaniment—and go on to train privately with a teacher. Students study such subjects as music theory, music history, and ear training; they must also perform regularly as part of their preparation for concert careers.

Enrich Your Reading

For Alternative Learning Styles Nadja's story is filled with the pressure of performance. To help students connect with Nadja, ask them to remember a time when they worried about performing in a play or athletic event, or even about reading aloud.

Thematic Link—Fight to the Finish

When Nadja Salerno-Sonnenberg enters an international violin competition in 1981, she is fighting both internal conflicts and ambitious rivals in her quest for first prize. Although she frequently feels like giving up, she fights her own fears to the finish—and wins a life in professional music.

Nonfiction *from* ## Nadja on My Way
NADJA SALERNO-SONNENBERG

Examine What You Know (Prior Knowledge)

Competition plays a big part in almost everyone's life. With a partner, brainstorm the types of competition you and your friends experience. Then, on a chart like the one below, list the "highs" or good things about competition and also the "lows" or things you don't like.

	Highs	
	Lows	

Expand Your Knowledge (Building Background)

From the time they are little, thousands of talented young people struggle to succeed in the highly competitive field of classical music. The very best of them gain acceptance to schools that specialize in the performing arts, such as the Juilliard School in New York City. There, young musicians spend years of dedication and hard work perfecting their skills. Older students audition for the right to participate in national and international competitions. Those students talented enough to win a major competition are almost guaranteed a successful international career as a concert musician.

Enrich Your Reading (Reading Skill)

Making Connections Every reader connects with a literary work in a different way. What you like or don't like depends a great deal on how much you already know and care about a particular subject. Nadja Salerno-Sonnenberg describes her competitive spirit in this selection. As you read, think about how your feelings about competition connect with Nadja's.

■ *Author biography on Extend page*

JOURNAL WRITING IDEAS

■ Use the title and the photographs to predict what this selection might be about.

■ How do you react to competition? What competitive situations affect you most?

■ What are your thoughts and feelings about playing a musical instrument?

COLLABORATIVE LEARNING OPTIONS

Opportunities for collaborative learning include Examine What You Know, Options for Learning 1-4 (p. 315), and Cross-Curricular Projects (p. 315).

ADDITIONAL RESOURCES

Unit Three Resource Book
Reader's Guidesheet, p. 36
Reading Skills, p. 37
Literature Skills, p. 38
Vocabulary Connections, p. 39
Spelling Connections, p. 40
Comprehension and Vocabulary Check Tests, p. 41
Selection Test, pp. 42–43

from *Nadja on My Way*

NADJA SALERNO-SONNENBERG

1 Back when my mother first put the violin under my chin, I didn't just accept it because I was a wimp . . . I never listened to authority easily. I fought my mother and I fought my teachers a lot. But I did listen to logic easily. Why would Mama want me to play the violin if it were bad for me? I trusted her love, so playing the violin must be good. . . .

Nadja holding violin. © Janette Beckman.

I never questioned why I was playing the violin. At the age of twelve, I wasn't thinking about my life. At the age of sixteen, I cared about the Yankees. I was falling in love and wondering what I should do with my hair.

A life as a musician didn't seem particularly noble at that age, but playing violin was something I could do, so I did it. The 2 older I got, the better I got. And the better I got, the harder it would be to quit and become something useful.

During my first year of college at Juilliard, I resolved to work out my technical problems with Miss DeLay [Nadja's violin teacher]. I just took it for granted that I would keep getting better. I never thought I might reach the limit of my talent or end up not good enough to make it. 3

But I began to see that I hadn't even begun to work. There were college players my age and younger who could blow me out of the room. All of them were intensely ambitious about making a career, and I finally realized a career is what I wanted too. At the same time, though, I began to 4 feel I'd come to that realization too late. . . . The big question wouldn't go away. Would I be good enough to make it? Could I make a living as a violinist? The more I thought about it, the worse things got.

VOCABULARY PREVIEW

These vocabulary words are defined at the bottom of the selection pages on which they appear.

audition a test of skill or ability

deliberate to consider carefully

evicted forced to move

gruff rough and husky

immerse to involve oneself completely

inevitable unavoidable

obsessed preoccupied

preliminary an early part of a competition

prodigy of a child genius

subconsciously without being aware

LIMITED ENGLISH PROFICIENCY

■ Use the Reader's Guidesheet, *Unit Three Resource Book*, page 36.

■ You may clarify idioms and musical references.

★ Text annotations marked with a red star (3, 9, 11, 16, 18) may be particularly helpful for students with limited English proficiency.

TEXT ANNOTATIONS

1. EDITORIAL NOTE
The phrase "as you probably know by now" has been omitted at the end of this sentence. A sentence omitted at the end of the following paragraph reads "Maybe I wasn't the kid who was Mr. Spock, but that's logical enough for me."

2. LITERARY CONCEPT: Irony
What is humorous or ironic about Nadja's remark? *(Possible response: Her suggestion that playing the violin is not useful contrasts ironically with the fact that she has been training to be a violinist her whole life.)*

3. VOCABULARY: Idioms
Help students with the idioms *"took it for granted," "make it," "blow me out of the room."* ("did not question," "succeed," and "play much better than I.") ★

4. EDITORIAL NOTE
A lengthy digression telling how Nadja earned money by playing in an orchestra has been omitted for space.

Guided Reading for Less-Proficient Students

These questions can help guide students through the reading. Ask each question at the point of the selection where the capital letter and arrow appear in the margin. In addition, you may wish to use appropriate Active Reading annotations.

A. Why does Nadja's violin playing change after she begins studying at Juilliard? *(She loses confidence; as a result her playing worsens and eventually she stops playing.)* Clarifying

B. What is Nadja afraid of? *(doing her very best but still failing; not being as good as other players)* Recalling

C. Why does Nadja sign up for the Naumburg competition? *(to prove that she hasn't given up on herself as a violinist, to find out if she can succeed)* Recalling

Continued on page 306

5. ACTIVE READING: Question
Ask students why they think Nadja suddenly can't play the musical piece. (Possible response: *She becomes self-conscious and focuses on her uncertainty rather than on the music.*)

6. LITERARY CONCEPT: Conflict
Ask students to describe Nadja's struggle with herself at this point in the narrative. (Possible response: *For the first time, Nadja has become aware of other gifted musicians around her, and she has become self-conscious and insecure. She struggles between her desire to succeed and her fear of failure.*)

7. EDITORIAL NOTE
Two paragraphs have been omitted here because of space limitations. They referred to Nadja's failure in ballet as a child.

8. ACTIVE READING: Evaluate
Ask students if they think Miss DeLay's response to Nadja's behavior is helpful to Nadja, and why or why not. (Possible responses: *Yes, because she is forcing Nadja to make a decision; no, because after all, it was Miss DeLay who let her begin coming to her lessons without her violin; no, because Nadja might quit for good.*)

A piece such as the *Carmen Fantasy* (a violin transcription[1] of Bizet's opera by Sarasate) is very hard technically. I played it easily when I didn't know how hard it was. Then I turned eighteen and thought, "My God, that piece is really difficult! How did I ever play it?"

And as I realized it was hard, I couldn't play it at all. Never mind that I played it just fine yesterday.

I started realizing how difficult it was to play thirds.[2] The lower my self-confidence sunk, the more I thought, "How did I ever do any of this before?"

By the time I was halfway through being nineteen, I couldn't play a G-major scale in tune. I was a cripple on the instrument. It got to the point where I didn't even want to hear myself play because I sounded so bad. It was torture. I stopped playing the violin for seven long months: the worst period of my life.

I couldn't play anymore, and my life was over.

I was used to success, to the prodigy label in newspapers, and now I felt like a failure. A has-been. I couldn't play anymore, and my life was over. I felt like a bum, that I should go hang out on the Bowery.[3]

I started showing up for my lesson without my fiddle. Thank God, Miss DeLay understood, and we spent the lesson time talking about music, life, and my problems.

Everything I was going through boiled down to fear. Fear of trying and failing. To measure up against all those wonderfully talented players at Juilliard, I would have to commit myself as never before. And if I disciplined myself to really work, and gave the violin my all, and *failed* . . . I would have to deal with it forever.

If you go to an audition and don't really try, if you're not really prepared, if you didn't work as hard as you could have and you don't win, you have an excuse.

"Honest," you can say, "if I had worked harder, I would have won." But nothing is harder than saying, "I gave it my all and it wasn't good enough."

Even having nothing to do with music, that's a really hard thing for anybody to face. It's very hard to give everything you have and then hear someone say, "Sorry. Do something else." . . .

Not long after I turned twenty, one week, like every week, I went to see Miss DeLay.

This time, Miss DeLay looked at me and said, "Listen, if you don't bring your violin next week, I'm throwing you out of my class."

And I laughed. I thought she and I were such good friends she would never do that.

Miss DeLay rose from the couch and, in a very calm way, said, "I'm not kidding. If

---

1. **transcription:** a musical arrangement made so a musical piece can be played on a particular instrument.
2. **thirds:** chords composed of three notes, each two degrees apart on a musical scale.
3. **Bowery:** a run-down area of New York City.

Words to Know and Use	**prodigy** (präd′ ə jē) *adj.* of a child with extraordinary talent or genius **audition** (ô dish′ ən) *n.* a test of skill or ability, usually of a musician or actor; a tryout

---

Guided Reading for Less-Proficient Students

Continued from page 305

D. How do you know that Nadja is trying her best to win the competition? (*She practices all day every day; she avoids everyone she knows; she thinks about nothing but her music.*) Summarizing

E. Why does Nadja save her best piece for the finals? (*She hopes that she can pass the semifinals with her weak piece and win the finals with her best piece.*) Inferring

F. How does Nadja feel now that the competition is over? (*tremendously relieved, happy again*) Recalling

G. After winning the competition, what does Nadja realize? (*that playing the violin will be her life work*) Recalling you're going to waste your talent, I don't want to be part of it. This has gone on long enough."

Then she walked out of the room.

I went home in deep shock. I was petrified. Should I quit? Could I lose Miss DeLay as a teacher and friend? There was one person I could talk to, my oldest friend, Cecile Licad.

Cecile had stayed at Curtis after I left and then moved on to the Institute for Young Musicians in Vermont. But we had stayed best buddies and, over the years, had played many recitals together—from New Rochelle to Manila. Thankfully, Cecile was living nearby in New York just then, and I called her immediately.

"Cecile," I said, "what am I going to do?"

Cecile hardly ever speaks, but when she does, it's usually wise for you to listen.

There was a pause, and then she said in her wonderful gruff voice, "Don't give up."

Three words. That was it.

"Okay, Cecile. I won't."

Now I just needed to prove it.

The 1981 Walter W. Naumburg International Violin Competition was coming up in two months. I was in no shape for a competition. I hadn't touched the violin for more than half a year. I had no idea if I could touch the violin now without feeling sick. If I could even manage to get into the finals of the competition, it would be a miracle.

The winner would receive three thousand dollars and solo recitals at the Library of Congress, Lincoln Center's Alice Tully Hall, and the Ambassador Auditorium in Pasadena. There would also be performances with the Chicago Symphony, the American Symphony Orchestra in Carnegie Hall, and with orchestras in Detroit, Buffalo, Aspen, and Los Angeles.

I put my name down for the audition.

Despite all the fear, all the self-doubt, I needed to take a shot. I needed to see what I was made of.

I wanted to live. Even as an honest failure.

I wanted to live. Even as an honest failure.

From the day I signed up for the Naumburg competition, everything changed. I had made a decision to start again, to save my life, and that meant a 360-degree turnaround.

I immersed myself in practicing. An enormous amount of work had to be done in two months. I went from not practicing at all to thirteen hours a day.

My fingers were like linguine.[4] I spent two weeks just playing scales. If I thought I sounded bad before, now I sounded worse than awful.

At the time, I lived on 72nd Street, close to West End Avenue. I had an efficiency apartment with a window the size of a shoebox. I didn't do my laundry; I left my apartment only to walk to Juilliard—and not on Broadway like everyone else. I walked

---

4. **linguine** (lin̄ gwē′ nē): thin, flat noodles.

Words to Know and Use

gruff (gruf) *adj.* rough and husky
immerse (im mʉrs′) *v.* to involve oneself completely

12. ACTIVE READING: Review
Ask students to explain why Nadja's behavior changes so radically after she enters the competition. *(Possible responses: She is totally concentrated on her music; everything—from social life to food—comes second to the violin; she is terrified of failing and is taking it out on herself.)*

13. ACTIVE READING: Evaluate
Have students evaluate Nadja's statement about her own preparedness. Given her state of mind at the time, do they think her perception is accurate? *(Any response is valid.)*

up Amsterdam Avenue because I didn't want to see anybody, didn't want to bump into anybody, didn't want anyone to ask what I was doing.

I stopped going to classes and became a hermit. I even talked Miss DeLay into giving my lesson at night.

My eating habits were awful. I lived on fried sausages, a pint of peanut butter/chocolate ice cream, and a gallon of Coca-Cola every day. That's all I ate for eight weeks.

I was nuts. I was completely <u>obsessed</u> with getting back into shape, with doing well in this competition. If I could, people would know I was still on earth. Not to count me out; to stop asking, "Whatever happened to Nadja?"

The last week before the Naumburg auditions, I couldn't touch the violin. I had worked and worked and worked and worked, and then I just couldn't work anymore.

I certainly could have used it. I wasn't as prepared as I should have been. But I simply had to say, "Nadja, you've dedicated yourself to this thing. Ready or not, do your best."

Fifty violinists from around the world auditioned for the competition on May 25, 26, and 27, 1981. Those that made it past the <u>preliminaries</u> would go on to the semifinals. Those that passed that stage would go to the finals. In years past, one violinist was chosen as winner and two received second and third place.

On May 26, the day of my audition, I went to the Merkin Concert Hall at 67th Street and Broadway. I waited, played for twenty minutes, and went home. I couldn't tell whether the preliminary judges were impressed or not. I'd find out the next evening.

Maybe <u>subconsciously</u> I was trying to keep busy; that night, when I fried the sausages, I accidentally set my apartment on fire. I grabbed my cat and my violin and ran out the door. The fire was put out, but everything in my place was wrecked.

Fortunately, the phone was OK, and on the evening of May 27, I had the news from Lucy Rowan Mann of Naumburg. Thirteen of us had made it.

Talk about mixed emotions. I was thrilled to be among the thirteen, a group that

Violin teacher Dorothy DeLay coaches Nadja, 1980.
Photograph by Charles Abbott.

Words to Know and Use	**obsessed** (əb sest´) *adj.* greatly preoccupied with something **obsess** *v.* **preliminary** (prē lim´ ə ner´ ē) *n.* a match or competition before the main contest; *plural*—**preliminaries** **subconsciously** (sub kän´ shəs lē) *adv.* without being fully aware

included established violinists, some of whom had already made records. But it also meant I had to play the next day in the semifinals of the competition.

Everyone entering the competition had been given two lists of concertos.[5] One was a list of standard repertory[6] pieces. The other list was twentieth-century repertory. For our big competition piece, we were to choose from each list and play a movement from one in the semifinals and a movement from the other in the finals—if we made it that far.

From the standard repertory list, I chose the Tchaikovsky[7] Concerto. I had been playing the Tchaik for three years, so it was a good piece for me.

From the twentieth-century list, I chose the Prokofiev[8] G-minor Concerto. I had never played it onstage before.

My goal had been just passing the auditions, but now my thought pattern began to change. If I wanted a sliver of a chance of advancing again, my brain said, "Play your strong piece first."

Logically, I should play the Tchaikovsky in the semifinals just to make it to the next stage. Who cared if that left me with a piece I probably wouldn't play as well in the finals of the competition? It'd be a miracle to get that far.

There wouldn't be more than seven violinists chosen for the final round, and if I were in the top seven of an international group, that was plenty good enough.

The semifinals were held on May 28 in Merkin Concert Hall. You were to play for thirty minutes: your big piece first, then the judges would ask to hear another.

There was a panel of eight judges. They had a piece of paper with my choices of the Tchaikovsky and the Prokofiev in front of them. "Which would you like to play?" they asked.

I said meekly, "Prokofiev."

My brain and all the logic in the world had said play your strong piece. My heart said, "Go for it all. Play your weak piece now, save Tchaikovsky for the finals."

Maybe I don't listen to logic so easily after all.

I was so tense, I was beyond shaking.

My good friend, the pianist Sandra Rivers, had been chosen as accompanist for the competition. She knew I was nervous. There had been a very short time to prepare; I was sure there'd be memory slips, that I'd blank out in the middle and the judges would throw me out. My hands were like ice.

The first eight measures of the Prokofiev don't have accompaniment. The violin starts the piece alone. So I started playing.

I got through the first movement, and Sandra said later my face was white as snow. She said I was so tense, I was beyond shaking. Just a solid brick.

It was the best I'd ever played it. No memory slips at all. Technically, musically, it was there.

---

5. **concertos** (kən cher′ tōz): musical compositions for one or more solo instruments and an orchestra.
6. **repertory** (rep′ ər tôr′ ē): a group of musical works a musician is expected to know how to play.
7. **Tchaikovsky** (chī kôf′ skē): Peter Ilich Tchaikovsky (1840–1893), a famous Russian composer.
8. **Prokofiev** (prō kôf′ ē ef′): Sergey Prokofiev (1891–1953), a noted modern Russian composer.

14

15

◄ **E**

16

14. ACTIVE READING: Evaluate
Have students evaluate Nadja's strategy. In their opinion, is her logic sound? (Possible responses: Yes, she should go with whichever of the pieces makes her feel most confident right now; no, if she uses her best piece now it would be like admitting she isn't going to win in the finals.)

15. LITERARY CONCEPT: Conflict
Ask students to identify the conflict between Nadja's brain and her heart. (Her brain says to play her strong piece now, while her heart hopes that she can make it to the finals and play the piece there.)

16. VOCABULARY: Technical Terms
Some students may have difficulty understanding Salerno-Sonnenberg's use of the musical terms measures and first movement. If necessary, explain to students that a measure is a grouping of musical beats and that a movement is a section of a lengthy work, such as a symphony or sonata.

For Alternative Learning Styles Ask a music student to show students how measures are indicated in musical notation. ★

Looking at Style

These ideas may be helpful for discussing Nadja's writing style in "Nadja on My Way."

Have students read the following passage, noting the italicized phrases:

She said I was so tense, I was beyond shaking. *Just a solid brick.*

It was the best I'd ever played it. *No memory slips at all.*

Then discuss the following questions and activity:

1. Why do you think the author uses sentence fragments rather than complete sentences?

2. Replace the sentence fragments with complete sentences. How do the meaning and the feeling of the passage change?

3. Write your own paragraph about something you've done. Include sentence fragments.

17. LITERARY CONCEPT: Conflict
Ask students whether a person's inner struggles can be seen or sensed by others. Encourage students to make connections between their own experiences and this passage of the selection. Have them identify the detail that shows the external expression of Nadja's inner feelings. ("*the blood was just rushing back into my face*")

18. VOCABULARY: Idioms
Some students may have difficulty understanding the idioms "*a shot in the arm*" and "*the last straw.*" Explain that the idioms mean "a boost" and "an event that pushes one beyond the limit of endurance." Point out the contrast between what Nadja said she needed and the two disastrous events that happened to her. ★

19. ACTIVE READING: Evaluate
Ask students whether they think Nadja really hates her competitor or is exaggerating. Then ask whether they think that winning a competition is worth the destruction of a friendship. (*Any response is valid.*)

20. ACTIVE READING: Connect
Ask students what Nadja's behavior indicates about her state of mind. (*Possible response: Her destruction of her special concert gown shows how heavy the pressure was; she was so relieved she just didn't care.*)

I finished it thinking, "Have I sold my soul for this? Is the devil going to visit me at midnight? How come it went so well?"

I didn't know why, but often I do my best under the worst of circumstances. I don't know if it's guts or a determination not to disappoint people. Who knows what it is, but it came through for me, and I thank God for that.

As the first movement ended, the judges said, "Thank you." Then they asked for the *Carmen Fantasy*.

I turned and asked Sandy for an A, to retune, and later she said the blood was just rushing back into my face.

I whispered, "Sandy, I made it. I did it."

"Yeah," she whispered back, kiddingly, "too bad you didn't screw up. Maybe next time."

At that point I didn't care if I did make the finals because I had played the Prokofiev so well. I was so proud of myself for coming through.

I needed a shot in the arm; that afternoon I got <u>evicted</u>. While I was at Merkin, my moped[9] had blown up. For my landlord, that was the last straw.

What good news. I was completely broke and didn't have the next month's rent anyway. The landlord wanted me out that day. I said, "Please, can I have two days? I might get into the finals; can I please go through this first?"

I talked him into it and got back to my place in time for the phone call. "Congratulations, Nadja," they said. "You have made the finals."

I had achieved the ridiculously unlikely,

and I had saved my best piece. Yet part of me was sorry. I wanted it to be over already. In the three days from the preliminaries to the semifinals, I lost eight pounds. I was so tired of the pressure.

There was a fellow who advanced to the finals with me, an old, good friend since pre-college. Competition against friends is <u>inevitable</u> in music, but I never saw competition push a friendship out the window so quickly. By the day of the finals, I hated him and he hated me. Pressure was that intense.

The finals were held on May 29 at Carnegie Hall and open to the public. I was the fourth violinist of the morning, then there was a lunch break, and three more violinists in the afternoon.

I played my Tchaikovsky, Saint-Saëns's *Havanaise*, and Ravel's *Tzigane* for the judges: managers, famous violinists, teachers, and critics. I went on stage at five past eleven and finished at noon. Those fifty-five minutes seemed like three days.

I was so relieved when I finished playing; I was finished! It's impossible to say how happy I was to see the dressing room. I destroyed my gown tearing it off, changed, and went out for lunch with my friends.

It was like coming back from the grave. We laughed and joked, and I got caught up on *General Hospital*. I was calm but thrilled it was over. I made it to the finals, that's it, I'm done.

◄ F

---

9. **moped** (mō′ ped′): a motorized bicycle.

Words to Know and Use	**evicted** (ē vikt′ ′d) *v.* to be forced to move from a rented house or apartment **inevitable** (in ev′ i tə bəl) *adj.* sure to happen; unavoidable

310

Speaking . . . Listening . . . Viewing

Listening To reinforce aural learning skills, play any available recording that features solo violin—if possible, one of Nadja Salerno-Sonnenberg's recordings. Invite students to respond to the music by creating a list of words and phrases that conveys the emotions and images evoked by the music. Two

CD's that would be appropriate are *It Ain't Necessarily So* (Capitol Records, CDC7 S45762) and *Nadja Salerno-Sonnenberg* (Angel Records, CDC7 49272).

As I returned to Carnegie Hall to hear the other violinists, I realized I'd made a big mistake: they might ask for recalls. A recall is when they can't decide between two people and they want you to play again. It's been done; it's done all the time in competitions. No way was I in shape to go onstage and play again.

In the late afternoon, the competition was over. Everybody had finished playing. Quite luckily—no recalls.

The judges <u>deliberated</u> for an hour. The tension in the air was unbelievable. All the violinists were sitting with their little circle of friends. I had my few friends around me, but no one was saying much now.

Finally, the Naumburg Foundation president—founder and first violinist of the Juilliard String Quartet and that year's presenter—Robert Mann came on stage.

"It's always so difficult to choose . . ." he began.

Every year we hold this competition," Robert Mann said. "And in the past, we've awarded three prizes. This year we've elected to only have one prize, the first prize."

My heart sank. Nothing for me. Not even Miss Congeniality.

"We have found," Mann went on, "that second place usually brings great dismay to the artist because he or she feels like a loser. We don't want anyone here to feel like a loser. Every finalist will receive five hundred dollars except the winner, who will receive three thousand dollars."

And then he repeated how difficult it was

to choose, how well everyone had played . . . dah, dah, dah.

I was looking down at the floor.

"The winner is . . ."

And he said my name.

A friend next to me said, "Nadja, I think you won!"

I went numb. My friends pulled me up and pointed me toward the stage. It was a long walk because I had slipped into a seat in the back.

Sitting up in front was my old friend. I would have to walk right past him and I was dreading it, but before I could, he got up and stopped me.

He threw his arms around me, and I threw my arms around him. I kept telling him how sorry I was. I was holding him and started to cry, saying, "I'm sorry, I'm sorry, I'm sorry." I didn't want to lose, but I really didn't want him to lose either. And he was holding me and saying, "Don't be sorry. I'm so proud of you." It was over, and we would be friends again.

I took my bow, then ran to Juilliard. Ten blocks uptown, one block west, to give Miss DeLay the news. She could be proud of me now, too.

Suddenly, everything was clear. Playing the violin is what I'd do with my life. ◄ **G** Heaven handed me a prize: "You've been through a lot, kid. Here's an international competition."

Everything had changed when I prepared for the Naumburg, and now everything changed again. I bought a gown at Saks that cost as much as a season ticket at Yankee Stadium (I kept thinking I could find some-

21

22

23

21. ACTIVE READING: Evaluate
Encourage students to offer their opinions on how competition makes people feel. Do they agree that people who finish in second and third place feel like losers? Do they think that abolishing these categories is a good idea? Why or why not? *(Any response is valid.)*

22. ACTIVE READING: Connect
Ask students what would be their thoughts and feelings at this moment if they were Nadja. *(Any response is valid.)*

23. LITERARY CONCEPT: Conflict
Ask students what conflicting emotions Nadja is feeling at this point. *(Possible responses: joy, guilt, regret, relief, shame, love)* Encourage students to discuss how it is possible for a person to feel more than one emotion at a time. Why does this happen? How can people handle these emotions?

Words to Know and Use | **deliberate** (di lib′ ər āt′) *v.* to carefully consider

311

Nadja rehearsing with conductor James Levine for a performance at The Ravinia Festival, Highland Park, Illinois, 1987.

thing as good for five dollars at a garage sale). I made my first recording–Fauré and Prokofiev sonatas with Sandra Rivers on the Musicmasters label. Between September 1981 and May 1982, I played a hundred concerts in America, made one trip to Europe, then two months of summer festivals. And people asked me back.

There was a great deal of anxiety playing in Europe for the first time. American musicians have their nationality to overcome. When you play Beethoven in Germany, no matter what, they're going to hate you. The audience has come to hear the American violinist who dares to play Beethoven.

My first time in Germany, walking onstage and feeling the vibes, I would rather have been a fire hydrant on Broadway. But I was able to rely on my self-confidence to pull me through.

Self-confidence onstage doesn't mean a lack of nerves backstage. The stakes had increased. This wasn't practice anymore; this was my life. I'd stare into a dressing-room mirror and say, "Nadja, people have bought tickets, hired baby sitters; you've got to calm down; go out there and prove yourself."

Every night I'd prove myself again. My life work had truly begun. 🍃

24

Comprehension Check

1. Why does Nadja stop playing the violin? *(She loses her confidence and is afraid of failure.)*

2. After seven months of not playing the violin, why does Nadja suddenly begin to practice thirteen hours a day? *(She has entered the Naumburg competition.)*

3. What big decision about what to play in the finals does Nadja face? *(whether to save her weakest or her strongest piece of music for the finals)*

4. What is the outcome of the conflict between Nadja and the friend she lost because of their competition? *(They make up after Nadja wins.)*

5. What is Nadja's life work? *(performing on the violin)*

Responding to Reading

First Impressions

1. As you think about Nadja, what words or phrases come to mind? Jot them down in your journal.

Second Thoughts

2. How well does Nadja fit your image of a classical musician? Explain.

3. What were the "highs" and "lows" of Nadja's decision to compete in the Naumburg International Violin Competition?

   Think about
   - her lifestyle when she decided to resume playing
   - how she felt before, during, and after the competition

4. Think about how Miss DeLay handled Nadja. Would you have dealt with Nadja in the same way? Why or why not?

5. What do you think Nadja would have done if she had fought to the finish but lost the competition?

Broader Connections

6. In some middle schools, competition has been made much less important. Tryouts for teams, bands, and other activities have been eliminated. Anyone who wants to join a team or club may do so and can participate as much as anyone else. Based on Nadja's experiences and your own, do you think this is a good idea? Explain your opinion.

Literary Concept: Style

The **style** of a piece of literature refers to the way it is written. Style does not describe *what* is said, but rather *how* it is said. Style includes sentence length, word choice, tone, use of dialogue, and imagery. Nadja's writing style is informal and conversational, as if she were talking directly to the reader. How does her style differ from that in the selections "Eleanor Roosevelt" or "Homeless"?

Concept Review: Internal Conflict Remember that internal conflict involves struggles or problems that a character faces within herself or himself. Describe Nadja's internal conflicts.

NADJA ON MY WAY   313

Literary Concept: Style

Ann Quindlen's and William Jay Jacobs's styles are more formal and mature—less spontaneous—than Nadja's. Nadja's use of sentence fragments, slang, idioms, and dialogue gives her writing a friendly, confiding tone. By contrast, "Homeless" and "Eleanor Roosevelt" are written in standard English. Their complex, grammatically correct sentences convey a more serious tone.

Concept Review: Internal Conflict Nadja fears failing, yet she is extremely ambitious. She struggles with self-consciousness and lack of confidence, as well as with the challenge of doing her best and risking the realization that she might not have "what it takes."

Student Response

Responding to Reading

1. Any response is valid.

2. **Possible responses:** Nadja does not fit the image of a classical musician because she is young, casual, and emotional; Nadja fits the image because she is completely dedicated to her music.

3. **Possible responses:** Highs—winning the Naumburg competition, making up with her friend after the competition; lows—becoming obsessed with practice, being almost evicted, hating her friend, being so scared of competing

4. **Possible responses:** Yes, because Nadja needed to be forced to make a decision; yes, because Nadja was acting spoiled; no, because Miss DeLay could have driven a very talented player away from the violin.

5. **Possible responses:** She would have continued to play but would not have been a star; she would have worked even harder to prepare for the next competition; she would have stopped playing the violin altogether.

6. **Possible responses:** Teams or clubs that let anyone in don't develop people's skills or talents; competition is good, since it makes people try their best. Groups that let anybody join are just being fair to everyone; competition makes people feel bad and hate one another.

Challenge Question

Prodigies like Nadja must practice every day for hours, even when they are very young. Many experts feel that this training puts too much pressure on children, yet most of the world's best performers are products of this kind of training. Do you think parents should demand so much of their children? *(Any response backed by reasons is valid.)*

Writing Options

The Writing Options are designed to meet varied student interests and abilities. Have each student choose one writing activity to complete.

Journal Update Invite students to write about any new insights they have about competition. Does it have advantages and disadvantages that they had not realized before?

Links to Writer's Craft

Writing Option 4 is an exercise in informative writing. For more practice, see *The Writer's Craft,* Grade 7, "Informative Writing: Explaining *What*," pages 117–137.

Vocabulary Practice

Answers to Exercise

1. obsessed
2. prodigy
3. subconsciously
4. evict
5. audition
6. deliberate
7. gruff
8. preliminaries
9. immerse
10. inevitable

For Alternative Learning Styles

Encourage students to draw or paint visual representations of the words *audition, evict, prodigy,* and *deliberate.* Interested students might attempt more abstract representations of *gruff* and *obsessed.*

Closure

Tell students that Nadja uses her talent and ambition to push toward her goal. Then ask students to compare Nadja with two other fighters they have read about—Jackie Robinson and Eleanor Roosevelt. Elicit from students that each was able to conquer inner doubts and fears by binding herself or himself to a dream.

Writing Options

1. Write a short **essay** about whether you would you be willing to go through what Nadja did in order to succeed.

2. Using Nadja's experiences as a guide, compose a pep club **chant** that the Juilliard cheerleaders could shout to boost the competitive spirit of the students.

3. Imagine you are Nadja and write a **letter** to your mother explaining why you haven't picked up your violin for seven months.

4. Listen to a recording of classical violin music. Then listen to your favorite rock music recording. Write a **comparison** of the two pieces of music, including a description of the feelings both recordings give you.

Vocabulary Practice

Exercise On your paper, write the word from the list that best completes the meaning of each sentence.

1. Because the violinist was __?__ with winning, she practiced thirteen hours a day.

2. She did not want to lose the __?__ reputation that she earned at the age of four.

3. She could play her music almost __?__, neither thinking nor looking at the notes.

4. The landlord wanted to __?__ her because of her constant practicing.

5. She was nervous before the __?__ for a position with the local symphony.

6. Before making a decision, the judges had to __?__ over her performance for an hour.

7. Finally the oldest judge, in a raspy, __?__ voice, announced that the young woman had made the finals.

8. Having passed the __?__ with flying colors, she prepared herself for the semifinals.

9. For the next week she would __?__ herself in her music.

10. Because of her talent and hard work, it seemed __?__ that she would become a violinist for a major orchestra.

Words to Know and Use
audition
deliberate
evict
gruff
immerse
inevitable
obsessed
preliminaries
prodigy
subconsciously

The Spelling Connection

Spelling Pattern: *com/con* and *im/in* Prefixes The prefixes **com** and **im** are joined to roots or base words that begin with *m, p,* or *b.* The spellings **con** and **in** are used before most other letters.

Example: con + nection = **con**nection

Words from the Selection with *com/con* and *im/in*

confidence   congratulations   concerto   competition
intensely   congeniality   commit   competition
immediately impressed   immersed   impossible

Other *com/con* and *im/in* Words

continent   consume   common   communicate
inspection   innumerable   immature   immobile

Exercise Complete each alphabetized group with a word that has the same prefix.

1. concerto, congratulations, congress, ___
2. command, commit, ___, communicate
3. included, ___, inspection, intensely
4. immature, ___, immobile, impossible

Options for Learning (Multimodal/Cross-Curricular Activities)

1 • Listen to Nadja Find a recording of Nadja's music or one of the pieces she mentions in the selection. Play the recording in class, and discuss your feelings about the music with classmates.

2 • Emotional Performance When Nadja performs, she throws herself completely into her work; her face mirrors what she feels as she plays. Look through magazines for pictures of performers, whether they are in music, sports, chess, or other fields. Find pictures that show extreme emotions. Copy the pictures and create a collage, which you can title and share with your class.

3 • Competitor Talk Interview artists, athletes, or others who compete regularly. Before the interview, prepare a list of questions for the competitors. Tape your interviews, summarize your findings, and play interesting segments as part of an oral report on the subject of competition.

4 • Make a Mandala In art, a mandala is a circular design containing images that are intended to be a symbol for a person, idea, or place. Make a mandala showing Nadja's personality. You may make the mandala flat, using paints and other colors, or three-dimensional, by gluing on objects that represent Nadja's personality.

 FACT FINDER MUSIC

Who was Antonio Stradivari and what was his biggest contribution to music?

Nadja Salerno-Sonnenberg
1961–

Although Nadja was born in Rome, her family moved to New Jersey when she was eight so that she could study at the nearby Curtis Institute of Music in Philadelphia. Although she and her mother were abandoned by both her natural father and stepfather, Nadja says that her mother kept prodding her to play the violin. "I studied the violin because I was forced to. I'm naturally lazy—not disciplined at all. So my mother made me practice." Since winning the Naumburg Competition in 1981, she has played with many of the major orchestras of the world including the Chicago, New York, and London symphonies.

Nadja is known as a rebel with an unusual style. When she plays, instead of a traditional black dress, she wears purple or electric blue pants, a blouse, and boots. During her performances she makes faces and moans. This has no effect on her playing, however. Nadja gives about one hundred performances a year.

Extending the Lesson

Options for Learning
These activities suit a variety of learning styles and modes of expression.

Collaborative Learning Activities
See Options 1–4.

1. **Listen to Nadja** Local libraries will have recordings, tapes, or CD's.

2. **Emotional Performance** Students may find photographs in *Musician, American Theater, Sports Illustrated,* or *Dance* magazine.

3. **Competitor Talk** Encourage students to make written requests to interview local competitors.

4. **Make a Mandala** Encourage students making three-dimensional art to experiment with different materials. Be sure to let students display their mandalas in the classroom.

 FACT FINDER MUSIC

Students can use a general encyclopedia or an encyclopedia of music to find out that "Stradivarius" is the Latin form of the surname of Antonio Stradivari, an Italian who is generally considered the greatest violin maker in history.

Nadja Salerno-Sonnenberg
■ **More About the Author** Nadja Salerno-Sonnenberg has continued to perform in concert halls around the world and to record with leading orchestras. In 1990 she recorded a performance of Antonio Vivaldi's *The Four Seasons,* a group of four concertos.

Cross-Curricular Projects

Math Have students research the Juilliard School's admission statistics for a recent year. Students might make a chart showing how the number of applications to each department relates to the corresponding numbers of acceptances and graduates.

Science Have students research the craft of violin making. Students might find out what types of wood are considered most desirable and what other materials are used.

Art Encourage students to find and bring in paintings about music and musicians. Ask students to compare the painting styles of artists from different times.

Music Have students research the life histories of other famous musicians—including jazz and folk performers—concentrating on autobiographies if possible. Invite them to give reports comparing their performers with Nadja.

Objectives

- To analyze and understand poetry
- To understand and appreciate the use of imagery
- To enrich reading by recognizing the speaker in poems
- To express understanding of the selections through a choice of writing forms, including a personal response and a poem

Prereading/Motivation

Examine What You Know

Discussion Prompts What makes a good runner? How important is winning to someone running a race? Are there any benefits to running if you lose? What is your opinion of competitive running?

Expand Your Knowledge

Additional Background The first indoor track meet in the United States was held in 1868 and sponsored by the New York Athletic Club; the organization had just built the first outdoor cinder running track. In the late 1800s the sport of track and field as we know it became popular in colleges. Almost fifty years later, high school students began competing in track and field.

Enrich Your Reading

For Alternative Learning Styles Invite students to take turns reading the poems aloud. For the first poem, students may imagine that they are radio or television commentators capturing the feel of a race for their audience. For the second poem, they may play the part of a coach discussing a recent victory with a star runner.

Thematic Link— Fight to the Finish

These two poems about races convey the excitement of competition. The first poem describes runners' jittery anticipation before a race and the race's explosive start. The second describes a sprint from start to finish, with the race becoming a metaphor for life itself.

Poetry

The Women's 400 Meters

LILLIAN MORRISON

To James

FRANK HORNE

Examine What You Know (Prior Knowledge)

Think about the running events that you have seen or that you have run yourself. Then, visualize the emotions on the runners' faces as they cross the finish line. What motivates people to make such an effort? What are the rewards for running a race? With your class, discuss why people might choose to participate in races, and whether or not you think the activity is worth the hours of practice and stress, both physical and mental, that it requires.

Expand Your Knowledge (Building Background)

The runners described in the following poems are competing in a track meet. Older tracks were covered with cinders—black bits of burnt wood or coal ashes that gave traction to a runner's feet. At the starting line, runners dug starting holes in the cinders to give their feet something to push off from when they leaped forward at the start. Newer tracks have a rubberized asphalt or other synthetic surface. Sprinters now may use metal starting blocks. Whether old or new, most tracks are 400 meters around and a pistol is still fired to signal the start.

Enrich Your Reading (Reading Skill)

Recognizing the Speaker In poetry, the voice that "talks" to the reader is called the **speaker.** The speaker in a poem is similar to the narrator in a work of fiction. The speaker may reflect the thoughts and feelings of the poet, but sometimes a poet creates a speaker with a separate identity. As you read the next two poems, ask yourself what you know or might guess about the speaker.

■ *Author biographies on Extend page*

JOURNAL WRITING IDEAS

- List all the words that come to mind when you think about running a race.

- Describe the most exciting athletic event you ever watched.

COLLABORATIVE LEARNING OPTIONS

Opportunities for collaborative learning include Options for Learning 1 and 2 (p. 321) and Cross-Curricular Projects (p. 321).

ADDITIONAL RESOURCES

Unit Three Resource Book
Reader's Guidesheet, p. 44
Reading Skills, p. 45
Literature Skills, p. 46
Vocabulary Connections, p. 47
Spelling Connections, p. 48
Comprehension Check Test, p. 49
Selection Test, p. 50

The Women's 400 Meters

LILLIAN MORRISON

Skittish,
they flex knees, drum heels and
shiver at the starting line

1
◄ A

waiting the gun
5 to pour them over the stretch
like a breaking wave.

2
◄ B

Bang! they're off
careening down the lanes,
each chased by her own bright tiger.   **◄ C**

Responding to Reading

First Impressions of "The Women's 400 Meters"

1. Write a few words or phrases that describe your impressions of the runners in the poem.

Second Thoughts on "The Women's 400 Meters"

2. Why do you think the poem describes only the beginning of the race?

3. Based on the poem and your own experience, what might the runners be thinking as they await the start?

4. What do you think the last line of the poem means?

Teaching Strategies

VOCABULARY PREVIEW

The focus of vocabulary study for this selection is context clues. See *Unit Three Resource Book*, Vocabulary Connections, p. 47.

LIMITED ENGLISH PROFICIENCY

■ Use the Reader's Guidesheet, *Unit Three Resource Book*, page 44.

★ Text annotations marked with a red star (1, 4) may be particularly helpful for students with limited English proficiency.

TEXT ANNOTATIONS

1. ACTIVE READING: Review
Have students point out the verbs in the first stanza. *(flex, drum, shiver)* Ask how these words help readers to picture the runners at the starting line. *(Possible responses: We see their nervousness; these small, specific movements show how they feel as well as how they act.)* ★

2. LITERARY CONCEPT: Simile
Ask students what things are being compared here. *(The runners are being compared to a breaking wave.)* Ask what such a comparison is called and what word helps readers recognize it. *(a simile; like signals a simile.)*

Responding to Reading

1. Any response is valid.

2. Possible responses: The nervous anticipation at the beginning of a race is exciting; the poet wants to focus on the runners' strong desire and their anticipation of the race, not on who wins.

3. Possible responses: The runners might be trying to plan out their strategy for the race; they might be trying to overcome nervousness or fears; they might be imagining victory.

4. Possible responses: The women or girls are running very fast, as if chased by wild animals; each runner is pushed ahead by her personal ambition, dream, or even fear.

Guided Reading for Less-Proficient Students

These questions can help guide students through the reading. Ask each question at the point of the selections where the capital letter and arrow appear in the margin. In addition, you may wish to use appropriate Active Reading annotations.

A. Whom or what is the speaker describing in the first stanza? *(runners at the starting line)* Clarifying

B. What are the runners waiting for? *(the sound of the starting gun)* Inferring

C. What happens in the last stanza of the poem? *(The starting gun is fired and the runners dash off.)* Inferring

D. What is the speaker remembering with James? *(James's last race)* Recalling

E. How did the speaker feel when James won? *(great, fantastic)* Inferring

Continued on page 318

3. ACTIVE READING: Question
Ask students why the speaker begins the poem with a series of questions. *(Possible responses: The speaker wants the runner to remember the exact details of his previous victory; the questions are a way of getting the runner to recall the great effort needed for victory.)*

4. VOCABULARY: Context Clues
Have students use **context clues** and prior knowledge to figure out that *sinews* means "muscles" or "tendons." Ask students why the speaker's sinews would tighten. *(Possible responses: He or she is feeling the tension of the race; he or she experiencing what James is feeling.)* ★

5. LITERARY CONCEPT: Speaker
Ask students what "my thrill / Of a thousand races" suggests about the speaker. *(Possible responses: The speaker has seen or experienced many, many races; perhaps he or she was also a runner; perhaps he or she is a coach.)*

To James

FRANK HORNE

© 1979   Robert M. Cunningham from U.S. Postal Service Olympic stamp album.

Do you remember
How you won
That last race . . . ?
How you flung your body
5 At the start . . .
How your spikes
Ripped the cinders
In the stretch . . .
How you catapulted
10 Through the tape . . .
Do you remember . . . ?
Don't you think
I lurched with you
Out of those starting holes . . . ?
15 Don't you think
My sinews tightened
At those first
Few strides . . .
And when you flew into the stretch
20 Was not all my thrill
Of a thousand races
In your blood . . . ?
At your final drive
Through the finish line
25 Did not my shout

◀ D

3

4

5

Guided Reading for Less-Proficient Students

Continued from page 317

F. What advice about life does the speaker give James? *(He should live his life as if it were a race; he should always try his hardest.)*

Tell of the
Triumphant ecstasy
Of victory . . . ? ◄ E
Live
30 As I have taught you │ 6
To run, Boy—
It's a short dash
Dig your starting holes
Deep and firm
35 Lurch out of them
Into the straightaway
With all the power │ 7
That is in you.
Look straight ahead
40 To the finish line
Think only of the goal
Run straight
Run high
Run hard
45 Save nothing
And finish
With an ecstatic burst
That carries you │ 8
Hurtling
50 Through the tape
To victory. . . . ◄ F

TO JAMES   319

6. LITERARY CONCEPT: Speaker
Ask students what has just been revealed about the speaker. (Possible responses: The speaker taught James to run; perhaps the speaker is James's coach or a parent or friend.)

7. ACTIVE READING: Review
Ask students in what ways James can apply the lessons of racing to his own life. If necessary, help students by reading the following example of a think-aloud, or model one of your own.

Think-Aloud Script The speaker tells James to live as he has been taught to run. The first thing he needs to do is to prepare himself for the race of life. He has to dig "deep and firm" starting holes. I guess that means that the race hasn't started yet; maybe youth is a time of preparing for the race of life. Then the speaker tells James to start strong, to "lurch" out of the starting blocks "With all the power / That is in you." Whatever he does in life, he must try his hardest. Also, he should never lose sight of his goal.

8. ACTIVE READING: Evaluate
Ask what the speaker's advice to "save nothing" means. ("Don't hold anything back" or "Give the race all you've got") Then ask if students think this is good advice. Have them explain their reasoning. (Possible responses: This is good advice because if you give all your energy, you will do the best you can and have the pleasure of being completely involved; this is good advice only if James has sound goals; this may be bad advice if James decides to go after goals that aren't good for him.)

ENCOURAGING INDEPENDENT READING

Hosannah the Home Run!, poems about sports selected by Alice Fleming

Jesse Owens, nonfiction by Tony Gentry

Speed, novel by R. Knudson

Track and Field for Young Champions, nonfiction by Robert J. Antonacci and Gene Schoor

Comprehension Check

✓ 1. What part of a race is described in "The Women's 400 Meters?" *(the beginning)*

2. According to the poem, what "chases" each of the runners? *(a bright tiger)*

3. In "To James," who taught James how to run? *(the speaker, who may be his coach or parent)*

4. To what does the speaker want James to apply the lessons learned in racing? *(to his own life)*

5. What does the speaker want for James at the end? *(victory or success in life)*

Student Response

Responding to Reading

1. Any response is valid.

2. **Possible responses:** The speaker is very involved in James's racing, as indicated in lines 15–28. He or she is probably James's coach or might be a parent or an adult friend, as revealed in lines 29–31; the speaker also cares a great deal about James personally— lines 29—51 are advice for James's life.

3. **Possible responses:** Life is like a race, and you should give it everything you've got; you will succeed only if you constantly push yourself and work hard.

4. **Possible responses:** Yes, because Nadja's own life has shown that hard work can bring victory; yes, because Nadja believes in putting everything into what she does; no, because she knows that giving your best might not be enough and that losing may make you feel like a failure.

5. **Possible responses:** The speakers would disagree, since the speaker in Morrison's poem doesn't focus on winning at all, suggesting that it may not be important, whereas Horne's poem describes victory as all-important. The speakers would agree; even though the Morrison poem doesn't discuss victory, you know that all the runners are trying their hardest to win.

6. Any response is valid.

7. **Possible responses:** The cheers and excitement of spectators are thrilling and supportive, pushing athletes and performers to greater achievements; spectators put pressure on athletes and performers and make them nervous.

Writing Options

The Writing Options are designed to meet varied student interests and abilities. Have each student choose one writing activity to complete.

Journal Update Have students review their journal entries for "The Women's 400 Meters" and "To James." Then ask them to write an evaluation of these poems. Which one do they think is better, and why? How has the poem changed their understanding of running, racing, or coaching?

R*esponding to Reading*

First Impressions of "To James"

1. What do you think of the speaker of this poem? Jot down your ideas in your journal or notebook.

Second Thoughts on "To James"

2. What do you think is the speaker's relationship to James? Explain your reasoning, based on details from the poem.

3. In your opinion, what is the **theme** of this poem?

4. Do you think the author of *Nadja on My Way* would agree with the speaker's advice? Explain.

Comparing the Poems

5. Do you think the speakers of the two poems would agree or disagree about the subject of winning? Explain.

6. Which poem comes closer to your idea of what runners might think and experience during a race?

Broader Connections

7. Both poems are told from the point of view of a spectator. What effect do you think spectators have on athletes or performers?

W*riting Options*

1. Based on your own feelings about running, as you wrote them in your journal, write your **response** to the advice given by the speaker in "To James."

2. Think of a time when you were a spectator at an event. Write a **poem** that describes the scene and expresses what you felt while watching the event.

Closure

Ask students to think about what the runners in these poems have in common with Alben in "Old Sly Eye" and with Nadja Salerno-Sonnenberg. Remind students that the qualities needed for success in athletic competition, such as concentration, discipline, and persistence, often serve people in other areas of life. Invite students to name things besides athletic competition that can be considered "fights to the finish." Tell them to be on the lookout for people, such as celebrities and politicians, who use the language of racing or fighting to describe their goals and ambitions.

Options for Learning (Multimodal/Cross-Curricular Activities)

1 • Art of Racing Try making a textured picture to depict the race in either poem. Glue fabric or any other materials you wish on cardboard or heavy paper to illustrate the scene. Incorporate details from the poem in your artwork, and try to convey the emotions that either the runners or the spectators feel.

2 • Road to Victory Interview a track coach or a high school runner to find out how runners prepare for meets. Find out how much practice is required, what kinds of training procedures are used, and how much time is spent in training. Share your findings with your class.

Lillian Morrison 1917–

Lillian Morrison has made a career of writing books for young people. Born in New Jersey, she graduated from Columbia University with a degree in library science. Morrison then began work with the New York Public Library. She served as the young-adult librarian and later as the coordinator of young-adult services.

Morrison's love of sports is so great that she wrote an entire collection of poems about sports, called *Sprints and Distances*. As Morrison says, "I am drawn to athletes, dancers, drummers, jazz musicians, who . . . symbolize for us something joyous, ordered, and possible in life." Morrison's poetry has appeared in a number of books and in such magazines as *Prairie Schooner, Sports Illustrated*, and *Atlantic Monthly*.

Frank S. Horne 1899–1974

Born and raised in Brooklyn, New York, Frank Horne graduated from the City College of New York. While there, he became an outstanding track star.

Horne then left New York to earn a master's degree and a doctorate in optometry. A few years later he was struck by what he called a "mean illness" that caused some loss of the use of his legs. Moving to a warmer climate, Horne began teaching at a high school in Georgia. As the track coach, he led his runners to several championships. Horne's poem "To James" is based on these experiences. The poem appeared as part of a collection of poems written as "letters" to others. In 1936 Horne stopped teaching and became a public housing specialist for the federal government in Washington, D.C.

Extending the Lesson

Options for Learning

These activities suit a variety of learning styles and modes of expression.

Collaborative Learning Activites
See Options 1 and 2.

1. **Art of Racing** Encourage students to gather and share a variety of materials, such as photos cut from old magazines, paints, glitter, thread, and wire. Suggest that they invent ways of conveying energy and movement in their pictures. Display the finished works and allow time for discussion.

2. **Road to Victory** Students might do some preliminary research to make their questions effective. Have them make charts or illustrations to enhance their oral presentations.

Lillian Morrison and Frank Horne

■ **Other Works by Morrison** Poetry: *The Sidewalk Racer and Other Poems of Sports and Motion, Overheard in a Bubble Chamber and Other Science Poems, The Break Dance Kids: Poems of Sport, Motion, and Locomotion; Rhythm Road: Poems to Move To*

■ **Other Works by Horne** Poetry: *Haverstraw*

 ■ **Awards** Frank Horne received the second prize for poetry in the *Crisis* Amy Springarn Contest, 1925, and the James J. and Jane Hoey Award for Inter-Racial Justice from the Catholic Inter-Racial Council of New York, Inc.

Cross-Curricular Projects

Science/Health Ask students to find out about the health risks that runners face. Suggest that they research current periodicals or interview health professionals specializing in sports medicine. What are the most common running injuries, and what can be done about them? Have students prepare a question-and-answer brochure to share their findings.

Math Invite students to research the records for the 400-meter run. Tell them to find the current U.S. and world records for both women and men. Students may also want to find the records for high school athletes in their state. They can report their findings in the form of a bar graph.

Physical Education/History Ask small groups of students to research the history of track and field and to create time lines to share their findings. Then discuss the time lines. Which are most informative? easiest to read? most appealing? What makes an effective time line?

Objectives

- To understand and analyze a short story

- To understand the function of minor characters and to review the concept of setting

- To enrich reading by recognizing the use of personification

- To express understanding of the story through a choice of writing forms, including lyrics, a summary, a battle scene, and an informative report

Prereading/Motivation

Examine What You Know

Discussion Prompts When natural enemies meet, what happens? Why do you think some animals are natural enemies? Are the enemies you listed equally matched, or do some of the animals have an advantage over their enemies?

Expand Your Knowledge

Additional Background The mongoose can kill snakes, rats, and mice. It also eats young birds and birds' eggs. It is a fierce animal but can be tamed. The cobra uses its poison either by biting or by spitting it. When squirted in the eyes, the poison can blind a human being if it is not washed out immediately. Cobras eat frogs, birds, fish, and small mammals.

Enrich Your Reading

For Alternative Learning Styles To reinforce oral language skills, invite volunteers to read some of the dialogue aloud after they finish the selection. Tell students to try to capture the distinct personality of their characters.

Thematic Link— Fight to the Finish

Rikki-tikki-tavi is a courageous and determined mongoose who fights two deadly cobras, thus saving the lives of an English family living in colonial India. Rikki-tikki will not quit until his victory is complete, though he risks his own life in the process.

Fiction

Rikki-tikki-tavi

RUDYARD KIPLING

Examine What You Know (Prior Knowledge)

Natural enemies fight or fear each other by instinct. What natural enemies can you name from the animal kingdom? Think about common enemies such as dogs and cats as well as more exotic animals you may have heard or read about. With a partner, brainstorm a list of natural enemies. Combine your ideas with those of your classmates.

Expand Your Knowledge (Building Background)

If you lived in India, you would almost certainly mention the mongoose and the cobra as a pair of natural enemies—a pair that will fight to the death. The mongoose, growing only as long as sixteen inches, seems hardly a match for the poisonous cobra, a snake that averages six feet in length and six inches in diameter. You will learn more about these animals in this story, which is set in India during the late 1800s. At that time the British ruled India. British families lived in open, airy houses called bungalows—one-story homes with big windows and large shaded porches to protect the inhabitants from the hot sun. Because of the heavy seasonal rains, vines and creepers covered every outside wall, and bushes could grow to be as big as an average-sized American garage. The jungle grew so close to the bungalows that it was not uncommon to find snakes, insects, or wild animals near or even in these homes.

Enrich Your Reading (Reading Skill)

■ *Author biography on Extend page*

Personification In the story, you will see what Kipling imagines that animals think, feel, and say about each other. Kipling creates in each animal a distinct human personality. Giving human qualities to an object, animal, or idea is called **personification**. As you read, think of people you know who have personalities similar to the ones Kipling gives his animal characters.

JOURNAL WRITING IDEAS

■ Use the title, the pictures, and the quotations in large print to predict what this story might be about.
■ Describe a real or fictional animal with a distinct personality.
■ Suppose you had to write a story about an animal that shared your personality. Which animal would you choose and why?

COLLABORATIVE LEARNING OPTIONS

Opportunities for collaborative learning include Examine What You Know, Options for Learning 2, 3, and 4 (p. 338), and Cross-Curricular Projects (p. 338).

ADDITIONAL RESOURCES

Unit Three Resource Book
Reader's Guidesheet, p. 51
Reading Skills, p. 52
Literature Skills, p. 53
Vocabulary Connections, p. 54
Spelling Connections, p. 55
Comprehension and Vocabulary Check Tests, p. 56
Selection Test, pp. 57–58

Rikki-tikki-tavi

RUDYARD KIPLING

This is the story of the great war that Rikki-tikki-tavi fought single-handed, through the bathrooms of the big bungalow in Segowlee cantonment.[1] Darzee the Tailorbird helped him, and Chuchundra the Muskrat, who never comes out into the middle of the floor, but always creeps around by the wall, gave him advice, but Rikki-tikki did the real fighting.

He was a mongoose, rather like a little cat in his fur and his tail, but quite like a weasel in his head and his habits. His eyes and the end of his restless nose were pink. He could scratch himself anywhere he pleased with any leg, front or back, that he chose to use. He could fluff up his tail till it looked like a bottle brush, and his war cry as he scuttled through the long grass was *Rikk-tikk-tikki-tikki-tchk!*

One day, a high summer flood washed him out of the burrow where he lived with his father and mother, and carried him, kicking and clucking, down a roadside ditch. He found a little wisp of grass floating there, and clung to it till he lost his senses. When he revived, he was lying in the hot sun on the middle of a garden path, very draggled indeed, and a small boy was saying, "Here's a dead mongoose. Let's have a funeral."

"No," said his mother, "let's take him in and dry him. Perhaps he isn't really dead."

They took him into the house, and a big man picked him up between his finger and thumb and said he was not dead but half choked. So they wrapped him in cotton wool, and warmed him over a little fire, and he opened his eyes and sneezed.

"Now," said the big man (he was an Englishman who had just moved into the bungalow), "don't frighten him, and we'll see what he'll do."

It is the hardest thing in the world to frighten a

Bronze cobra about 1919 Jean Dunand The Metropolitan Museum of Art, Rogers Fund, 1970.

1. **cantonment:** a place where soldiers are lodged.

| Words to Know and Use | **revive** (ri vīv') v. to regain consciousness; wake up |

323

Teaching Strategies

VOCABULARY PREVIEW
These vocabulary words are defined at the bottom of the selection pages on which they appear.

cower to crouch in fear

cultivated planted

immensely very much

revive to regain consciousness

veranda a long open porch

LIMITED ENGLISH PROFICIENCY
■ Use the Reader's Guidesheet, *Unit Three Resource Book,* page 51.

■ The story contains Indian names that you may wish to read aloud.

★ Text annotations marked with a red star (3, 6, 8, 14, 22, 28) may be particularly helpful for students with limited English proficiency.

TEXT ANNOTATIONS

1. LITERARY CONCEPT: Personification
Point out that Kipling describes Rikki-tikki as a warrior in a "great war," as if he were human. Ask students why Kipling doesn't mention Rikki's enemies here. *(Possible responses: This is Rikki-tikki's story; the author wants to get us interested in Rikki-tikki first.)*

2. CULTURAL SIDELIGHT
India's annual rainy season lasts from mid-June through September. Rivers often flood the land, destroying crops and houses.

Art Note
In this bronze and gold statue, the artist Jean Dunand (1877–1942) emphasizes the sinuousness and tension of the cobra as it rises to a striking position. With its hood flattened, the cobra is clearly about to hurl itself at an enemy. *What words would you use to describe a cobra? Could the same words be used to describe this statue?*

Guided Reading for Less-Proficient Students

These questions can help guide students through the reading. Ask each question at the point of the selection where the capital letter and arrow appear in the margin. In addition, you may wish to use appropriate Active Reading annotations.

A. How does Rikki-tikki come to be at the bungalow? *(He is washed there in a flood.)* Recalling

B. What kind of character is Rikki-tikki? *(He is playful, curious, and restless.)* Summarizing

C. Why is Nag the cobra worried about Rikki-tikki? *(Nag knows that mongooses can kill cobras, so that he and his family are in danger.)* Summarizing

D. Why are the cobras able to escape from Rikki? *(He doesn't chase them because he's not sure he can beat two cobras at the same time; because of his youth, Rikki misses his chance to kill Nagaina.)* Summarizing

Continued on page 324

Teacher Notes (left margin)

3. ACTIVE READING: Review
Have students discuss the ways in which Kipling makes Rikki-tikki seem like a human being in this passage. *(Possible responses: Rikki-tikki is curious; his family has a motto; he makes his own decisions, as if capable of thought.)* If necessary, ask a volunteer to explain what "eaten up from nose to tail with curiosity" means. *(very curious about everything)* ★

4. LITERARY CONCEPT: Characterization
Remind students that we often learn about characters through their actions. Discuss what Rikki-tikki's actions in this passage show about his character. *(They all point to his curiosity.)*

5. ACTIVE READING: Predict
Teddy's mother fears that the mongoose may cause trouble, while his father feels that it will prevent trouble. Ask students to predict what may happen as a result of Rikki-tikki's moving into the bungalow. *(Any response is valid.)*

---

mongoose, because he is eaten up from nose to tail with curiosity. The motto of all the mongoose family is "Run and find out," and Rikki-tikki was a true mongoose. He looked at the cotton wool, decided that it was not good to eat, ran all around the table, sat up and put his fur in order, scratched himself, and jumped on the small boy's shoulder.

The motto of all the mongoose family is "Run and find out."

"Don't be frightened, Teddy," said his father. "That's his way of making friends."

"Ouch! He's tickling under my chin," said Teddy.

Rikki-tikki looked down between the boy's collar and neck, snuffed at his ear, and climbed down to the floor, where he sat rubbing his nose.

"Good gracious," said Teddy's mother, "and that's a wild creature! I suppose he's so tame because we've been kind to him."

"All mongooses are like that," said her husband. "If Teddy doesn't pick him up by the tail, or try to put him in a cage, he'll run in and out of the house all day long. Let's give him something to eat."

They gave him a little piece of raw meat. Rikki-tikki liked it immensely; and when it was finished, he went out into the veranda and sat in the sunshine and fluffed up his fur to make it dry to the roots. Then he felt better.

"There are more things to find out about

in this house," he said to himself, "than all my family could find out in all their lives. I shall certainly stay and find out."

He spent all that day roaming over the house. He nearly drowned himself in the bathtubs, put his nose into the ink on a writing table, and burned it on the end of the big man's cigar, for he climbed up in the big man's lap to see how writing was done. At nightfall he ran into Teddy's nursery to watch how kerosene lamps were lighted, and when Teddy went to bed, Rikki-tikki climbed up too. But he was a restless companion, because he had to get up and attend to every noise all through the night, and find out what made it. Teddy's mother and father came in, the last thing, to look at their boy, and Rikki-tikki was awake on the pillow.

"I don't like that," said Teddy's mother. "He may bite the child."

"He'll do no such thing," said the father. "Teddy is safer with that little beast than if he had a bloodhound to watch him. If a snake came into the nursery now—"

But Teddy's mother wouldn't think of anything so awful.

Early in the morning Rikki-tikki came to early breakfast in the veranda, riding on Teddy's shoulder, and they gave him banana and some boiled egg. He sat on all their laps one after the other, because every well-brought-up mongoose always hopes to be a house mongoose some day and have rooms to run about in; and Rikki-tikki's mother (she used to live in the general's house at Segowlee) had carefully told Rikki what to

| Words to Know and Use | **immensely** (im mens′ lē) *adv.* very much; enormously |
| | **veranda** (və ran′ də) *n.* a long open porch, usually with a roof |

324

Guided Reading for Less-Proficient Students

Continued from page 323

E. Why is Rikki concerned with keeping up his strength and quickness after killing Karait? *(He knows that other enemies, including the cobras, still lurk in the garden.)* Inferring

F. What do you think Chuchundra is trying to warn Rikki-tikki about? *(He wants Rikki to know that Nag is nearby.)* Inferring

G. What plan does Rikki have for attacking Nag in the bathroom? *(He plans to jump on Nag while he is asleep, biting his head and breaking his back.)* Summarizing

H. Why is Rikki-tikki concerned about Nagaina's eggs? *(If they hatch, there will be new cobras to battle in the garden.)* Inferring

Continued on page 325

do if ever he came across white men.

Then Rikki-tikki went out into the garden to see what was to be seen. It was a large garden, only half cultivated, with bushes, as big as summerhouses, of Marshal Niel roses, lime and orange trees, clumps of bamboos, and thickets of high grass. Rikki-tikki licked his lips. "This is a splendid hunting ground," he said, and his tail grew bottle-brushy at the thought of it; and he scuttled up and down the garden, snuffing here and there till he heard very sorrowful voices in a thornbush. It was Darzee the Tailorbird and his wife. They had made a beautiful nest by pulling two big leaves together and stitching them up the edges with fibers, and had filled the hollow with cotton and downy fluff. The nest swayed to and fro, as they sat on the rim and cried.

"What is the matter?" asked Rikki-tikki.

"We are very miserable," said Darzee. "One of our babies fell out of the nest yesterday and Nag ate him."

"H'm," said Rikki-tikki, "that is very sad—but I am a stranger here. Who is Nag?"

Darzee and his wife only cowered down in the nest without answering, for from the thick grass at the foot of the bush there came a low hiss—a horrid cold sound that made Rikki-tikki jump back two clear feet. Then inch by inch out of the grass rose up the head and spread hood of Nag, the big black cobra, and he was five feet long from tongue to tail. When he had lifted one-third of himself clear of the ground, he stayed balancing to and fro exactly as a dandelion tuft balances in the wind, and he looked at Rikki-tikki with the wicked snake's eyes that never change their expression, whatever the snake may be thinking of.

"Who is Nag?" said he. "I am Nag. The great God Brahm[2] put his mark upon all our people, when the first cobra spread his hood to keep the sun off Brahm as he slept. Look, and be afraid!"

He spread out his hood more than ever, and Rikki-tikki saw the spectacle mark on the back of it that looks exactly like the eye part of a hook-and-eye fastening. He was afraid for the minute, but it is impossible for a mongoose to stay frightened for any length of time; and though Rikki-tikki had never met a live cobra before, his mother had fed him on dead ones, and he knew that all a grown mongoose's business in life was to fight and eat snakes. Nag knew that too and, at the bottom of his cold heart, he was afraid.

"Well," said Rikki-tikki, and his tail began to fluff up again, "marks or no marks, do you think it is right for you to eat fledglings out of a nest?"

Nag was thinking to himself, and watching the least little movement in the grass behind Rikki-tikki. He knew that mongooses in the garden meant death sooner or later for him and his family, but he wanted to get Rikki-tikki off his guard. So he dropped his head a little, and put it on one side. ◄ C

"Let us talk," he said. "You eat eggs. Why

---

2. **Brahm:** another name for *Brahma,* creator of the universe in the Hindu religion.

Words to Know and Use	**cultivated** (kul′ tə vāt′ id) *adj* . planted or prepared for planting, as opposed to wild **cultivate** *v.* **cower** (kou′ ər) *v.* to crouch or shrink down in fear

325

6. VOCABULARY: Context Clues
Students may be unfamiliar with a tailor-bird. Have them use **context clues** to guess what kind of bird it is. Explain that a tailorbird is a small Asiatic or African bird that stitches leaves together to hold and camouflage its nest. ★

7. LITERARY CONCEPT: Conflict
Remind students that external conflict can be a struggle of one character against another, whereas internal conflict involves a character's inner struggles. Ask them how both types of conflict appear at this point in the story. *(Possible responses: Rikki-tikki faces an external conflict with Nag; both Nag and Rikki-tikki face the internal conflict of overcoming their fear as they prepare for battle.)*

8. VOCABULARY: Context Clues
Have students use **context clues** to figure out the meaning of the word *fledglings.* Remind them that Darzee and his wife's complaint that Nag ate one of their babies supports the idea that fledglings are young birds. The term can also refer to a young or inexperienced person. ★

Guided Reading for Less-Proficient Students

Continued from page 324

I. How does Darzee's wife help Rikki-tikki with his plan? *(She distracts Nagaina by pretending to be lame, giving Rikki time to get to the melon bed.)* Summarizing

J. Why does Nagaina want to kill the people? *(She wants revenge for her husband's death.)* Recalling

K. Why does Rikki follow Nagaina into her hole? *(If he doesn't, her egg will hatch, and she and her baby will still be a threat.)* Inferring

L. What prevents Rikki-tikki from growing too proud, even after killing all the cobras? *(He has become more mature through his experiences, and he knows he must always be on guard against other dangers.)* Analyzing

9. ACTIVE READING: Review
What problems does Rikki face?
(Possible responses: He faces two enemies, Nag and Nagaina, who are
working together against him; he is
young and inexperienced as a fighter;
he is fighting in unfamiliar territory.)

10. ACTIVE READING: Evaluate
Have students discuss how well prepared they think Rikki-tikki is for a show-
down with Nag or Nagaina. (Possible
responses: Rikki-tikki is well prepared,
as shown by Nag's fear of him and
Rikki-tikki's escape from Nagaina's
attack. Rikki-tikki is not well prepared,
because he did not know how to kill
Nagaina when he had the chance; he
is young and has much to learn.)

11. LITERARY CONCEPT: Suspense
Ask students to identify the details that
build suspense in this part of the story.
(Possible response: The narrator mentions that Karait's bite is as dangerous
as a cobra's, that fighting Karait is riski-
er than fighting Nag, and that Rikki
does not know the technique for biting
Karait.)

should not I eat birds?"

"Behind you! Look behind you!" sang Darzee.

Rikki-tikki knew better than to waste time in staring. He jumped up in the air as high as he could go, and just under him whizzed by the head of Nagaina, Nag's wicked wife. She had crept up behind him as he was talking, to make an end of him. He heard her savage hiss as the stroke missed. He came down almost across her back, and if he had been an old mongoose, he would have known that then was the time to break her back with one bite; but he was afraid of the terrible lashing return stroke of the cobra. He bit, indeed, but did not bite long enough; and he jumped clear of the whisking tail, leaving Nagaina torn and angry.

"Wicked, wicked Darzee!" said Nag, lashing up as high as he could reach toward the nest in the thornbush. But Darzee had built it out of reach of snakes, and it only swayed to and fro.

Rikki-tikki felt his eyes growing red and hot (when a mongoose's eyes grow red, he is angry); and he sat back on his tail and hind legs like a little kangaroo, and looked all around him, and chattered with rage. But Nag and Nagaina had disappeared into the grass. When a snake misses its stroke, it never says anything or gives any sign of what it means to do next. Rikki-tikki did not care to follow them, for he did not feel sure that he could manage two snakes at once. So he trotted off to the gravel path near the house, and sat down to think. It was a serious matter for him.

D ▶

review What problems does Rikki face?

If you read the old books of natural history, you will find they say that when the mongoose fights the snake and happens to get bitten, he runs off and eats some herb that cures him. That is not true. The victory is only a matter of quickness of eye and quickness of foot—snake's blow against mongoose's jump—and as no eye can follow the motion of a snake's head when it strikes, this makes things much more wonderful than any magic herb. Rikki-tikki knew he was a young mongoose, and it made him all the more pleased to think that he had managed to escape a blow from behind.

It gave him confidence in himself, and when Teddy came running down the path, Rikki-tikki was ready to be petted. But just as Teddy was stopping, something wriggled a little in the dust, and a tiny voice said: "Be careful. I am Death!" It was Karait, the dusty brown snakeling that lies for choice on the dusty earth; and his bite is as dangerous as the cobra's. But he is so small that nobody thinks of him, and so he does the more harm to people.

Rikki-tikki's eyes grew red again, and he danced up to Karait with the peculiar rocking, swaying motion that he had inherited from his family. It looks very funny, but it is so perfectly balanced a gait that you can fly off from it at any angle you please, and in dealing with snakes this is an advantage.

If Rikki-tikki had only known, he was doing a much more dangerous thing than fighting Nag; for Karait is so small, and can turn so quickly, that unless Rikki bit him close to the back of the head, he would get the return stroke in his eye or his lip. But Rikki did not know. His eyes were all red,

Speaking . . . Listening . . . Viewing

Listening Play a recording of "Rikki-tikki-tavi," such as that made by Anthony Quayle (Caedmon, CDL 51257)

After playing the recording, ask the following questions:

1. Did the recording help you to understand the characters and their motivations better?

2. Did you find it easier to read the selection yourself or to listen to the recording? Explain.

3. What was your reaction to the way the narrator made each character's voice sound different?

DEBER DHOORA DEE, KUMAON, INDIA, WITH ITS WELL AND DEODARS (CEDRUS DEODARA)   Marianne North   © 1992
The Trustees of the Royal Botanic Gardens, Kew, U.K.

and he rocked back and forth, looking for a good place to hold. Karait struck out. Rikki jumped sideways and tried to run in, but the wicked little dusty gray head lashed within a fraction of his shoulder, and he had to jump over the body, and the head followed his heels close.

Teddy shouted to the house, "Oh, look here! Our mongoose is killing a snake." And Rikki-tikki heard a scream from Teddy's mother. His father ran out with a stick, but by the time he came up, Karait had lunged out once too far, and Rikki-tikki had sprung, jumped on the snake's back, dropped his head far between his forelegs, bitten as high up the back as he could get hold, and rolled away.

That bite paralyzed Karait, and Rikki-tikki was just going to eat him up from the tail, after the custom of his family at dinner, when he remembered that a full meal makes a slow mongoose; and if he wanted all his strength and quickness ready, he must keep himself thin. He went away for a dust bath under the castor-oil bushes, while Teddy's father beat the dead Karait.   ◄ E

Looking at Style

To discuss Kipling's writing style, read the following sentences aloud or write them on the board, drawing special attention to the similes.

■ He was a mongoose, rather *like a little cat in his fur and his tail,* but quite *like a weasel in his head and his habits.* (p. 323)

■ He could fluff up his tail till it looked *like a bottle brush.* (p. 323)

■ Rikki-tikki saw the spectacle mark . . . that looks exactly *like the eye part of a hook-and-eye fastening.* (p. 325)

Ask the following questions:

1. What comparison or comparisons does Kipling make in each sentence?

2. Do the comparisons make it easier for you to visualize the things he describes? Why or why not?

3. Do you like the way that Kipling uses similes? Why or why not?

12. ACTIVE READING: Review

Why is Rikki amused by the fuss? (Possible responses: Since fighting snakes is the normal job of a mongoose, Rikki is amused by all the attention given his battle; Rikki doesn't understand what is going on, but he enjoys watching the reactions of the family.)

13. LITERARY CONCEPT: Personification

Rikki refuses to eat or drink to excess, and he is determined to stay fierce and warlike. Ask students what this behavior says about Rikki's character. (Possible responses: Like a good warrior, Rikki doesn't let anything get in the way of his duty; Rikki is already maturing; he has the discipline needed for battle.)

14. VOCABULARY: Animal Names

Ask volunteers to describe a muskrat. Explain that it is a furry brown rodent that lives much of its life in water. Muskrats, as their name implies, are relatives of the rat. Show students a picture of a muskrat in a dictionary or an encyclopedia. ★

15. LITERARY CONCEPT: Minor Characters

Ask students what function Chuchundra has in this part of the story, even though he is not a main character. (He indirectly warns Rikki about Nag.) Have students discuss how Chuchundra's character contrasts with Rikki's. (Possible response: Chuchundra is timid and helpless, whereas Rikki is courageous and independent.)

"What is the use of that?" thought Rikki-tikki. "I have settled it all."

And then Teddy's mother picked him up from the dust and hugged him, crying that he had saved Teddy from death; and Teddy's father said that he was a providence,[3] and Teddy looked on with big scared eyes. Rikki-tikki was rather amused at all the fuss, which, of course, he did not understand. Teddy's mother might just as well have petted Teddy for playing in the dust. Rikki was thoroughly enjoying himself.

review   Why is Rikki amused by the fuss?

That night at dinner, walking to and fro among the wineglasses on the table, he might have stuffed himself three times over with nice things. But he remembered Nag and Nagaina, and though it was very pleasant to be patted and petted by Teddy's mother, and to sit on Teddy's shoulder, his eyes would get red from time to time, and he would go off into his long war cry of *"Rikk-tikk-tikki-tikki-tchk!"*

Teddy carried him off to bed and insisted on Rikki-tikki sleeping under his chin. Rikki-tikki was too well bred to bite or scratch, but as soon as Teddy was asleep, he went off for his nightly walk around the house; and in the dark he ran up against Chuchundra the Muskrat, creeping around by the wall. Chuchundra is a brokenhearted little beast. He whimpers and cheeps all the night, trying to make up his mind to run into the middle of the room. But he never gets there.

"Don't kill me," said Chuchundra, almost weeping. "Rikki-tikki, don't kill me!"

"Do you think a snake-killer kills muskrats?" said Rikki-tikki scornfully.

"Those who kill snakes get killed by snakes," said Chuchundra, more sorrowfully than ever. "And how am I to be sure that Nag won't mistake me for you some dark night?"

"There's not the least danger," said Rikki-tikki. "But Nag is in the garden, and I know you don't go there."

"My cousin Chua the Rat told me—" said Chuchundra, and then stopped.

"Told you what?"

"H'sh! Nag is everywhere, Rikki-tikki. You should have talked to Chua in the garden."

"I didn't—so you must tell me. Quick, Chuchundra, or I'll bite you!"

Chuchundra sat down and cried till the tears rolled off his whiskers. "I am a very poor man," he sobbed. "I never had spirit enough to run out into the middle of the room. H'sh! I mustn't tell you anything. Can't you *hear*, Rikki-tikki?"

Rikki-tikki listened. The house was as still as still, but he thought he could just catch the faintest *scratch-scratch* in the world—a noise as faint as that of a wasp walking on a windowpane—the dry scratch of a snake's scales on brickwork.

"That's Nag or Nagaina," he said to himself, "and he is crawling into the bathroom sluice.[4] You're right, Chuchundra; I should have talked to Chua."

---

3. **providence:** a blessing; something good given by God.

4. **bathroom sluice:** a passageway fitted with a gate or other device that controls the water flow out of a bathtub.

He stole off to Teddy's bathroom, but there was nothing there, and then to Teddy's mother's bathroom. At the bottom of the smooth plaster wall there was a brick pulled out to make a sluice for the bath water, and as Rikki-tikki stole in by the masonry curb where the bath is put, he heard Nag and Nagaina whispering together outside in the moonlight.

"When the house is emptied of people," said Nagaina to her husband, "*he* will have to go away, and then the garden will be our own again. Go in quietly, and remember that the big man who killed Karait is the first one to bite. Then come out and tell me, and we will hunt for Rikki-tikki together."

"But are you sure that there is anything to be gained by killing the people?" said Nag.

"Everything. When there were no people in the bungalow, did we have any mongoose in the garden? So long as the bungalow is empty, we are king and queen of the garden; and remember that as soon as our eggs in the melon bed hatch (as they may tomorrow), our children will need room and quiet."

"I had not thought of that," said Nag. "I will go, but there is no need that we should hunt for Rikki-tikki afterward. I will kill the big man and his wife, and the child if I can, and come away quietly. Then the bungalow will be empty, and Rikki-tikki will go."

Rikki-tikki tingled all over with rage and hatred at this, and then Nag's head came through the sluice, and his five feet of cold body followed it. Angry as he was, Rikki-tikki was very frightened as he saw the size of the big cobra. Nag coiled himself up, raised his head, and looked into the bathroom in the dark, and Rikki could see his eyes glitter.

"Now, if I kill him here, Nagaina will know; and if I fight him on the open floor, the odds are in his favor. What am I to do?" said Rikki-tikki-tavi.

Nag waved to and fro, and then Rikki-tikki heard him drinking from the biggest water jar that was used to fill the bath. "That is good," said the snake. "Now, when Karait was killed, the big man had a stick. He may have that stick still, but when he comes in to bathe in the morning, he will not have a stick. I shall wait here till he comes. Nagaina—do you hear me?—I shall wait here in the cool till daytime."

There was no answer from outside, so Rikki-tikki knew Nagaina had gone away. Nag coiled himself down, coil by coil, around the bulge at the bottom of the water jar, and Rikki-tikki stayed still as death. After an hour he began to move, muscle by muscle, toward the jar. Nag was asleep, and Rikki-tikki looked at his big back, wondering which would be the best place for a good hold. "If I don't break his back at the first jump," said Rikki, "he can still fight. And if he fights—O Rikki!" He looked at the thickness of the neck below the hood, but that was too much for him; and a bite near the tail would only make Nag savage.

"It must be the head," he said at last; "the head above the hood. And, when I am once there, I must not let go."

Then he jumped. The head was lying a little clear of the water jar, under the curve of it; and, as his teeth met, Rikki braced his back against the bulge of the red earthenware to hold down the head. This gave him just one second's purchase, and he made the most of it. Then he was battered to and fro

16

17

18

◀ G

16. HISTORICAL SIDELIGHT
In the late 1800s, when this story takes place, homes in India did not have indoor plumbing with water faucets and drains for bathtubs. A tub had to be filled with water from a jar. The dirty water was drained through a sluice, or passageway, in the wall.

17. ACTIVE READING: Predict
Have students predict whether Rikki will attack Nag now or later. Encourage them to base their predictions on what they already know about Rikki from the story. (Any response is valid.)

18. LITERARY CONCEPT: Suspense
Ask students to identify in this passage phrases that contain repeated words. ("coil by coil," "muscle by muscle") Have students tell how the repetition in these phrases affects readers. (Possible responses: The repetition helps readers visualize the action; by slowing the action, it builds suspense about what will happen.)

Multicultural Connections

When this story was written around the turn of the century, Great Britain ruled India as a colony. In one way or another, India was ruled by the British for over two hundred years. Though the Indians had a longer history of civilization than the British, they were denied the right to govern themselves.

Rudyard Kipling was a staunch defender of the right of the British to rule other peoples, especially people of color. In one of his poems he urged the British to "Take up the White Man's burden . . . To serve your captives' need."

Ask students how they would feel about Kipling's story if they were natives of India. Would they want to read a story written by a man who defended the rights of the British to rule their country?

as a rat is shaken by a dog—to and fro on the floor, up and down, and around in great circles; but his eyes were red, and he held on as the body cart-whipped over the floor, upsetting the tin dipper and the soap dish and the flesh brush, and banged against the tin side of the bath.

As he held, he closed his jaws tighter and tighter, for he made sure he would be banged to death; and, for the honor of his family, he preferred to be found with his teeth locked. He was dizzy, aching, and felt shaken to pieces when something went off like a thunderclap just behind him. A hot wind knocked him senseless, and red fire singed his fur. The big man had been awakened by the noise, and had fired both barrels of a shotgun into Nag just behind the hood.

review   **19**   What happened in the fight?

Rikki-tikki held on with his eyes shut, for now he was quite sure he was dead. But the head did not move, and the big man picked him up and said, "It's the mongoose again, Alice. The little chap has saved *our* lives now."

Then Teddy's mother came in with a very white face, and saw what was left of Nag, and Rikki-tikki dragged himself to Teddy's bedroom and spent half the rest of the night shaking himself tenderly to find out whether he really was broken into forty pieces, as he fancied.

When morning came, he was very stiff, but well pleased with his doings. "Now I have Nagaina to settle with, and she will be worse than five Nags; and there's no know-

ing when the eggs she spoke of will hatch. Goodness! I must go and see Darzee," he said.

Without waiting for breakfast, Rikki-tikki ran to the thornbush where Darzee was singing a song of triumph at the top of his voice. The news of Nag's death was all over the garden, for the sweeper had thrown the body on the rubbish heap.

"Oh, you stupid tuft of feathers!" said Rikki-tikki angrily. "Is this the time to sing?"

"Nag is dead—is dead—is dead!" sang Darzee. "The valiant Rikki-tikki caught him by the head and held fast. The big man brought the bang stick, and Nag fell in two pieces! He will never eat my babies again."

"All that's true enough. But where's Nagaina?" said Rikki-tikki, looking carefully around him.

"Nagaina came to the bathroom sluice and called for Nag," Darzee went on, "and Nag came out on the end of a stick—the sweeper picked him up on the end of a stick and threw him upon the rubbish heap. Let us sing about the great, the red-eyed Rikki-tikki!" And Darzee filled his throat and sang.

"If I could get up to your nest, I'd roll your babies out!" said Rikki-tikki. "You don't know when to do the right thing at the right time. You're safe enough in your nest there, but it's war for me down here. Stop singing a minute, Darzee."

What danger does Rikki still face?   **review**   **21**

"For the great, the beautiful Rikki-tikki's sake I will stop," said Darzee. "What is it, O Killer of the terrible Nag?"

"Where is Nagaina, for the third time?"

"On the rubbish heap by the stables,

mourning for Nag. Great is Rikki-tikki with the white teeth."

"Bother my white teeth! Have you ever heard where she keeps her eggs?"

"In the melon bed, on the end nearest the wall, where the sun strikes nearly all day. She hid them there weeks ago."

"And you never thought it worthwhile to tell me? The end nearest the wall, you said?"

"Rikki-tikki, you are not going to eat her eggs?"

"Not eat exactly, no. Darzee, if you have a grain of sense you will fly off to the stables and pretend that your wing is broken, and let Nagaina chase you away to this bush. I must get to the melon bed, and if I went there now, she'd see me."

Darzee was a feather-brained little fellow who could never hold more than one idea at a time in his head. And just because he knew that Nagaina's children were born in eggs like his own, he didn't think at first that it was fair to kill them. But his wife was a sensible bird, and she knew that cobra's eggs meant young cobras later on. So she flew off from the nest, and left Darzee to keep the babies warm, and continue his song about the death of Nag. Darzee was very like a man in some ways.

She fluttered in front of Nagaina by the rubbish heap and cried out, "Oh, my wing is broken! The boy in the house threw a stone at me and broke it." Then she fluttered more desperately than ever.

Nagaina lifted up her head and hissed. "You warned Rikki-tikki when I would have killed him. Indeed and truly, you've chosen a bad place to be lame in." And she moved toward Darzee's wife, slipping along over the dust.

"The boy broke it with a stone!" shrieked Darzee's wife.

"Well! It may be some consolation to you when you're dead to know that I shall settle accounts with the boy. My husband lies on the rubbish heap this morning, but before night the boy in the house will lie very still. What is the use of running away? I am sure to catch you. Little fool, look at me!"

Darzee's wife knew better than to do *that*, for a bird who looks at a snake's eyes gets so frightened that she cannot move. Darzee's wife fluttered on, piping sorrowfully, and never leaving the ground, and Nagaina quickened her pace.

Rikki-tikki heard them going up the path from the stables, and he raced for the end of the melon patch near the wall. There, in the warm litter above the melons, very cunningly hidden, he found twenty-five eggs, about the size of a bantam's[5] eggs, but with whitish skins instead of shells.

"I was not a day too soon," he said, for he could see the baby cobras curled up inside the skin, and he knew that the minute they were hatched they could each kill a man or a mongoose. He bit off the tops of the eggs as fast as he could, taking care to crush the young cobras, and turned over the litter from time to time to see whether he had missed any. At last there were only three eggs left, and Rikki-tikki began to chuckle to himself, when he heard Darzee's wife screaming.

"Rikki-tikki, I led Nagaina toward the house, and she has gone into the veranda

_____
5. **bantam's**: of a breed of small hen.

22. VOCABULARY: Slang
Ask students what the word *bother* usually means. ("to annoy or disturb") Then ask whether that meaning of the word seems to fit in the context of this sentence. See if students can use **context clues** to figure out that here *bother* means "never mind" or "forget about." ★

23. LITERARY CONCEPT: Minor Characters
Ask students to describe the difference between Darzee and his wife. (*Possible responses: Darzee is scatter-brained, whereas his wife is sensible; Darzee is weak, but his wife is strong.*)

24. LITERARY CONCEPT: Plot
Ask students to explain why Rikki-tikki must crush the eggs so quickly. (*Possible responses: They are about to hatch; Nagaina may return at any minute.*) Encourage students to explain why Kipling may have chosen to include this race against time in the story. (*Possible responses: It builds suspense; it creates interest in what will happen next.*)

Art Note

Claude Monet (1840–1926) is regarded as one of the most important French impressionists. Throughout his artistic career he explored the effects of changing light on color at different times of day and during different seasons. In many of his works, the play of light and color is more important than the subject matter. *Corner of an Apartment* shows a boy and a woman surrounded by tropical plants in the shadows of a large, mysterious apartment. The large plants lend a junglelike atmosphere to the room. The people seem entirely lost in the depths of this apartment. *In what way does this scene reflect the setting of "Rikki-tikki-tavi"?*

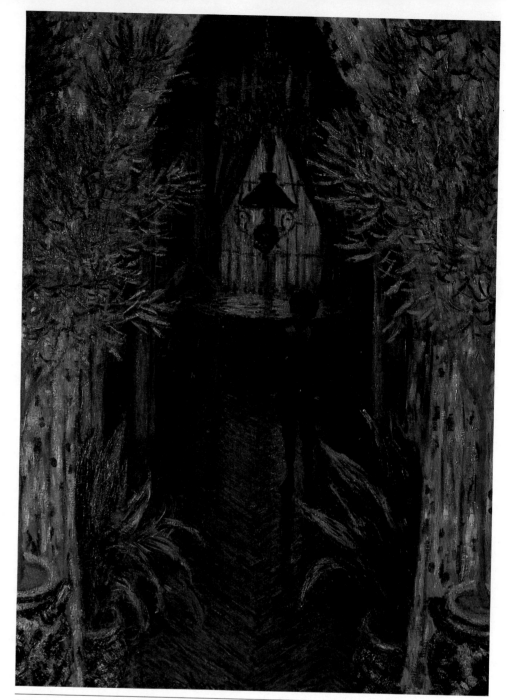

CORNER OF AN APARTMENT 1875 Claude Monet Musée d'Orsay, Paris. Giraudon/Art Resource, New York.

332   UNIT THREE   FIGHT TO THE FINISH

and—oh, come quickly—she means killing!"

Rikki-tikki smashed two eggs, and tumbled backward down the melon bed with the third egg in his mouth, and scuttled to the veranda as hard as he could put foot to the ground. Teddy and his mother and father were there at early breakfast, but Rikki-tikki saw that they were not eating anything. They sat stone-still, and their faces were white. Nagaina was coiled up on the matting by Teddy's chair, within easy striking distance of Teddy's bare leg; and she was swaying to and fro, singing a song of triumph.

"Son of the big man that killed Nag," she hissed, "stay still. I am not ready yet. Wait a little. Keep very still, all you three! If you move, I strike; and if you do not move, I strike. Oh, foolish people, who killed my Nag!"

Teddy's eyes were fixed on his father, and all his father could do was to whisper, "Sit still, Teddy. You mustn't move. Teddy, keep still."

Then Rikki-tikki came up and cried, "Turn around, Nagaina. Turn and fight!"

"All in good time," she said, without moving her eyes. "I will settle my account with you presently. Look at your friends, Rikki-tikki. They are still and white. They are afraid. They dare not move, and if you come a step nearer, I strike."

"Look at your eggs," said Rikki-tikki, "in the melon bed near the wall. Go and look, Nagaina!"

The big snake turned half around, and saw the egg on the veranda. "Ah-h! Give it to me," she said.

Rikki-tikki put his paws on each side of the egg, and his eyes were blood-red. "What price for a snake's egg? For a young cobra? For a young king cobra? For the last—the very last of the brood? The ants are eating all the others down by the melon bed."

What price for a snake's egg? For a young cobra?

Nagaina spun clear around, forgetting everything for the sake of the one egg. Rikki-tikki saw Teddy's father shoot out a big hand, catch Teddy by the shoulder, and drag him across the little table with the teacups, safe and out of reach of Nagaina.

"Tricked! Tricked! Tricked! *Rikk-tck-tck!*" chuckled Rikki-tikki. "The boy is safe, and it was I—I—I that caught Nag by the hood last night in the bathroom." Then he began to jump up and down, all four feet together, his head close to the floor. "He threw me to and fro, but he could not shake me off. He was dead before the big man blew him in two. I did it! *Rikki-tikki-tck-tck!* Come then, Nagaina. Come and fight with me. You shall not be a widow long."

Nagaina saw that she had lost her chance of killing Teddy, and the egg lay between Rikki-tikki's paws. "Give me the egg, Rikki-tikki. Give me the last of my eggs, and I will go away and never come back," she said, lowering her hood.

"Yes, you will go away, and you will never come back. For you will go to the rubbish heap with Nag. Fight, widow! The big man has gone for his gun. Fight!"

Rikki-tikki was bounding all round Nagaina, keeping just out of reach of her

25

J ▶

26

27

25. ACTIVE READING: Connect
Ask students how they would respond if they discovered a cobra at the breakfast table. *(Any response is valid.)*

26. ACTIVE READING: Review
Invite students to explain why Rikki is bragging to Nagaina now. *(Possible responses: He is drawing attention away from the family and making Nagaina think of him as her enemy; he is trying to provoke Nagaina into a fight.)*

27. ACTIVE READING: Evaluate
Ask students what they think of Rikki's insistence on destroying Nagaina's children and of Nagaina's devotion to her eggs. Do they feel any sympathy for Nagaina or her unborn children? *(Any response is valid.)*

28. LITERARY CONCEPT: Simile
Call attention to Kipling's use of similes in this passage. Have students explain the meaning of each expression. *(Possible responses: "flew like an arrow" means "moved swiftly"; "goes like a whiplash flicked across a horse's neck" means "travels very rapidly.")* Some students may need to break the compound word into two simple words to understand what a whiplash is.* ★

29. ACTIVE READING: Question
Ask students why they think following a cobra into its hole is considered unwise. *(Possible responses: In the hole it is too dark to see the cobra's actions; the cobra is thinner and can maneuver itself better than a mongoose.)*

30. LITERARY CONCEPT:
Characterization
Ask students what Darzee's song tells readers about his character. *(Possible responses: He is a pessimist; he exaggerates; he is impulsive about forming opinions; his mood changes quickly.)*

stroke, his little eyes like hot coals. Nagaina gathered herself together and flung out at him. Rikki-tikki jumped up and backward. Again and again and again she struck, and each time her head came with a whack on the matting of the veranda, and she gathered herself together like a watch spring. Then Rikki-tikki danced in a circle to get behind her, and Nagaina spun around to keep her head to his head, so that the rustle of her tail on the matting sounded like dry leaves blown along by the wind.

He had forgotten the egg. It still lay on the veranda, and Nagaina came nearer and nearer to it, till at last, while Rikki-tikki was drawing breath, she caught it in her mouth, turned to the veranda steps, and flew like an arrow down the path, with Rikki-tikki behind her. When the cobra runs for her life, she goes like a whiplash flicked across a horse's neck. Rikki-tikki knew that he must catch her, or all the trouble would begin again.

She headed straight for the long grass by the thornbush, and as he was running, Rikki-tikki heard Darzee still singing his foolish little song of triumph. But Darzee's wife was wiser. She flew off her nest as Nagaina came along, and flapped her wings about Nagaina's head. If Darzee had helped her, they might have turned her, but Nagaina only lowered her hood and went on. Still, the instant's delay brought Rikki-tikki up to her, and as she plunged into the rat hole where she and Nag used to live, his little white teeth were clenched on her tail, and he went down with her—and very few mongooses, however wise and old they may be, care to follow a cobra into its hole.

It was dark in the hole; and Rikki-tikki never knew when it might open out and give Nagaina room to turn and strike at him. He held on savagely, and stuck out his feet to act as brakes on the dark slope of the hot, moist earth. ◄ K

*V*ery few mongooses . . . care to follow a cobra into its hole.

Then the grass by the mouth of the hole stopped waving, and Darzee said, "It is all over with Rikki-tikki! We must sing his death song. Valiant Rikki-tikki is dead! For Nagaina will surely kill him underground."

So he sang a very mournful song that he made up on the spur of the minute; and just as he got to the most touching part, the grass quivered again, and Rikki-tikki, covered with dirt, dragged himself out of the hole leg by leg, licking his whiskers. Darzee stopped with a little shout. Rikki-tikki shook some of the dust out of his fur and sneezed. "It is all over," he said. "The widow will never come out again." And the red ants that live between the grass stems heard him, and began to troop down one after another to see if he had spoken the truth.

Rikki-tikki curled himself up in the grass and slept where he was—slept and slept till it was late in the afternoon, for he had done a hard day's work.

"Now," he said, when he awoke, "I will go back to the house. Tell the Coppersmith, Darzee, and he will tell the garden that Nagaina is dead."

The Coppersmith is a bird who makes a

noise exactly like the beating of a little hammer on a copper pot. The reason he is always making it is that he is the town crier to every Indian garden, and tells all the news to everybody who cares to listen. As Rikki-tikki went up the path, he heard his "attention" notes like a tiny dinner gong, and then the steady *"Ding-dong-tock!* Nag is dead—*dong!* Nagaina is dead! *Ding-dong-tock!"* That set all the birds in the garden singing, and the frogs croaking, for Nag and Nagaina used to eat frogs as well as little birds.

When Rikki got to the house, Teddy and Teddy's mother (she looked very white still, for she had been fainting) and Teddy's father came out and almost cried over him; and that night he ate all that was given him till he could eat no more, and went to bed on Teddy's shoulder, where Teddy's mother saw him when she came to look late at night.

"He saved our lives and Teddy's life," she said to her husband. "Just think, he saved all our lives."

Rikki-tikki woke up with a jump, for the mongooses are light sleepers.

"Oh, it's you," said he. "What are you bothering for? All the cobras are dead. And if they weren't, I'm here."

Rikki-tikki had a right to be proud of himself. But he did not grow too proud, and he kept that garden as a mongoose should keep it, with tooth and jump and spring and bite, till never a cobra dared show its head inside the walls. ❧ ◀ L

31. LITERARY CONCEPT:
Characterization
Ask students what the animals in the garden think of Rikki. *(Possible response: They think he is a hero, a mighty champion.)*

ENCOURAGING INDEPENDENT READING
The Jungle Book, short stories by Rudyard Kipling

Just So Stories, short stories by Rudyard Kipling

Kim, novel by Rudyard Kipling

The Lives and Times of Archy and Mehitabel, fiction by Don Marquis

Comprehension Check

1. What do all mongooses have in common? *(They are curious; they fight snakes.)*

2. Why does Nagaina feel that Teddy's family must be killed? *(so Rikki will leave)*

3. What does Rikki do when Nag enters the bungalow? *(He waits for Nag to fall asleep, then attacks him.)*

4. What does Rikki do to trick Nagaina into leaving Teddy alone? *(He shows her the last egg and gets her to chase him.)*

5. Where does Rikki's final battle with Nagaina take place? *(in her rat hole, her home)*

6. What is the result of the battle? *(Rikki kills Nagaina and breaks the last egg.)*

Student Response

Responding to Reading

1. Any response is valid.

2. **Possible responses:** He is young, determined, and courageous. He is also clever and good at seeing the strengths and weaknesses of his ene-mies. For example, he plans a masterful surprise attack on Nag in the bathroom, distracts Nagaina from the family by drawing attention to himself and her egg, and has the foresight to destroy Nagaina's eggs.

3. **Possible responses:** He fights to pro-tect the family, since he is fond of them; he acts only from instinct, since it is a mongoose's nature to battle snakes.

4. **Possible responses:** Darzee and Chuchundra lack intelligence and are afraid; the snakes have too much pride; Rikki is somewhat naive at first; Rikki is vain about his abilities.

5. **Possible responses:** Personification makes it easier for readers to care about what happens; it adds both humor and heroism to the story; it increases our enjoyment.

6. Any response is valid.

Challenge Question

Some critics charge that "Rikki-tikki-tavi" encourages prejudice. The characters who are most "Indian"—Darzee and Chuchundra—are shown as weak, fearful, and stupid, whereas the hero, Rikki, has the best qualities of an English school-boy. Do you think these critics are right? *(Possible responses: Yes, Rikki does seem more English than Indian; the other male animals seem either stupid or evil. No, this is just a story about animals; it doesn't make sense to find preju-dice in a harmless story.)*

Literary Concept: Minor Characters

Darzee warns Rikki about Nagaina and by his stupidity makes Rikki seem clever; Darzee's wife distracts Nagaina; Karait is used to show how tough Rikki is; Teddy's father helps Rikki during his bat-tle with Nag; Teddy's vulnerability makes Rikki more heroic.

---

*R*esponding to Reading

First Impressions

1. How did you feel about Rikki by the end of the story? Jot down your reaction in your notebook or journal.

Second Thoughts

2. What abilities or qualities enable Rikki to fight the cobras to the finish?

   Think about
   - the battle with Nag in the bathroom
   - Nagaina's threatened attack on the family at breakfast

3. Do you think Rikki fights Nag and Nagaina to protect Teddy and his parents, or does he act only from instinct? Explain your answer.

4. What human weaknesses are shown in the animal characters?

5. What do you think the use of **personification** adds to the story?

Broader Connections

6. "Rikki-tikki-tavi" is considered by many to be a **classic** story—one that is read and enjoyed by many generations. Why do you think this story is a classic?

---

*L*iterary Concept: Minor Characters

Characters that play a small role in the plot are called **minor characters.** An author often uses them to keep the plot moving, or to provide a contrast to a main character. For example, Chuchundra advances the plot (when he tells Rikki where Nag is) and contrasts with Rikki (Chuchundra is a coward). How do other minor characters function in the story?

Concept Review: Setting   Compile a list of details that Kipling uses in the story to establish the setting.

Concept Review: Setting Details include the Indian names of places and animals and the description of the vegetation growing in the garden.

Writing Options

1. In the story, Darzee sings a song about Rikki killing Nag. Write the **lyrics** of that song, beginning with the words quoted in the story.

2. Most, but not all, of the characters in the story consider Rikki to be a hero. Write a **summary** of the story from Nagaina's point of view.

3. Choosing a pair from the list you prepared earlier, write a **battle scene** between natural enemies. Use details, as Kipling did, to make the battle exciting and easy to follow.

4. Skim the story for details about the habits of a mongoose. Check in an encyclopedia for additional information. Combine them to write an **informative report** about mongooses.

Vocabulary Practice

Exercise On a separate sheet of paper, write the letter of the situation that best demonstrates the meaning of the boldfaced word.

1. **revive**
   a. a package sent to a faraway country
   b. a drowning victim brought back to life
   c. a teacher writing a lesson on the board

2. **veranda**
   a. a couple having tea on the porch
   b. a young lady reading in the park
   c. a child sitting quietly in a classroom

3. **cower**
   a. an animal trembling in fear
   b. a bird singing a song
   c. a snake slithering through the grass

4. **cultivated**
   a. a table covered with breakfast dishes
   b. a garden planted with flowers
   c. a bungalow filled with people

5. **immensely**
   a. an extremely happy lottery winner
   b. a slightly bored audience
   c. a contented, sleepy young boy

> **Words to Know and Use**
>
> cower
> cultivated
> immensely
> revive
> veranda

Writing Options

The Writing Options are designed to meet varied student interests and abilities. Have each student choose one writing activity to complete.

Journal Update Invite students to list several reasons why they would advise friends or family members to read "Rikki-tikki-tavi." If students did not enjoy the story, have them list ways they think it could have been improved.

Links to Writer's Craft

Writing Option 4 is an exercise in informative writing. For more practice, see *The Writer's Craft,* Grade 7, "Informative Writing: Reports," pages 187–213.

Vocabulary Practice

Answers to Exercise

1. b

2. a

3. a

4. b

5. a

For Alternative Learning Styles

Invite students to create newspaper headlines that contain the vocabulary words. The headlines may or may not relate to events in this story. (Example: "Doctors Revive Man Who Falls Off Roof") Encourage students to share their headlines with the class.

Closure

Discuss how Rikki's battles are similar to or different from the battles in other selections in this subunit. For example, like Alben in "Old Sly Eye," Rikki must fight against an old, experienced enemy; like Nadja, Rikki must show absolute control and self-discipline in order to succeed; like the runners in the poems, Rikki must exert himself to the fullest at every stage of his battle. Ask students which of these "competitors" they most enjoyed reading about and why.

The Spelling Connection

Silent -e Words and Suffixes When a suffix that begins with a consonant is added to a word that ends in silent **e**, the silent **e** is usually kept.
Example: sincere/sincer**ity**/sincere**ly**

Silent -e Words from the Selection
settle/sett**ling**/settle**ment**
live/li**ving**/live**ly**
sense/sen**sing**/sense**less**
safe/safe**ly**/safe**ty**

Other Words with Silent e's and Suffixes
since**rely** secu**rely** clo**sely**
waste**ful** hope**ful** care**ful**
forgive**ness** like**ness** amaze**ment**

Exercise Match definitions with listed words.
1. full of life
2. without meaning
3. a close similarity
4. characterized by close attention
5. great wonder

Extending the Lesson

Options for Learning

These activities suit a variety of learning styles and modes of expression.

Collaborative Learning Activities
See Options 2, 3, and 4.

1. The Deadly Cobra Besides using encyclopedias and books, students might use the *Readers' Guide to Periodical Literature* to find recent articles about cobras.

2. Comic Creation Encourage students to decide, before they begin drawing, how many panels will appear and what each one will show. You may want to make comic books available to familiarize students with this type of art and its storytelling techniques.

3. Radio Rikki It may help students to listen first to a radio version or a recording of another story.

4. Disney's Version Disney movies are often available in local libraries.

 FACT FINDER SOCIAL STUDIES
Students can use an encyclopedia to find that mongooses belong to the family Viverridae (which also includes civets).

Joseph Rudyard Kipling

■ **More About the Author** Kipling believed it was the duty of Great Britain to spread its culture around the world, and much of his writing glorifies the British Empire. Although his reputation as a writer has faded somewhat over the years, he is generally regarded as a master of the short adventure story.

■ **Other Works** Novel: *The Light That Failed*; short stories: *Plain Tales from the Hills*; poems: "Gunga Din," "The Road to Mandalay"

■ **Awards** Nobel Prize for Literature, 1907

Options for Learning (Multimodal/Cross-Curricular Activities)

1 • The Deadly Cobra Create a display about cobras. Do research to find out about their habitat and habits. Include such facts as how many people are killed by cobras in an average year, whether there is an antidote for cobra venom, and whether cobras can really be hypnotized by snake charmers.

2 • Comic Creation Make a comic-book version of part of this story. Reread the story to determine the important scenes you want to use. Select dialogue for the talk balloons in your comic. Illustrate your scenes and then share your book with younger audiences.

3 • Radio Rikki Stage a radio reading of the story. Assign students to perform the parts of the characters and the narrator and to supply sound effects. Rehearse, then tape your performance for other classes.

4 • Disney's Version Disney cartoons and movies also personify animals. In fact, the Disney studios have animated several of Kipling's stories. Watch one of the animated versions. Then have a panel discussion analyzing the Disney version and comparing how Kipling and the Disney studios personify animals.

 FACT FINDER SCIENCE
To what animal family do mongooses belong?

Joseph Rudyard Kipling
1865–1936

Though educated in England, Kipling was born in India, where his father was a school principal. Kipling loved to read as a child, and his first job was as a journalist on a British newspaper in India. His stories about his Indian travels made him wildly popular, and when he returned to London in 1889 he was already famous.

When he had children of his own, Kipling turned to writing children's stories. His first collection, *The Jungle Books,* was about an Indian boy who was raised by wolves. Between chapters about the boy, Kipling inserted other stories. "Rikki-tikki-tavi" is one of these.

Kipling received numerous honors and awards for his work. In 1907 he became the first Englishman to win the Nobel Prize for Literature. He is buried in London in Poet's Corner of Westminster Abbey, near Shakespeare.

Cross-Curricular Projects

Science Have students research the climate, landscape, and vegetation of India. Invite students to share their information with the class.

Art Invite students to choose or create their own illustration for the story. Students may wish to render the garden or any of the action scenes in the story.

Social Studies Have students investigate India's long struggle for independence from Great Britain. Ask them to construct a time line listing key people, dates, and events.

Language Arts Ask students to imagine they interviewed Rikki-tikki after his final battle. What questions would they ask him? What answers might he give? Have students write an interview with Rikki and then perform it with a partner for the rest of the class.

WRITER'S WORKSHOP

INFORMATIVE AND PERSUASIVE WRITING

In this subunit, you've met fighters—characters who stood up to difficult problems, even life-and-death struggles, and found solutions. In this workshop, you will propose your own solution to a real-life problem. You will also stand up for your ideas, convincing readers that your solution is worthwhile. You will write a **guest editorial.** Newspapers, newsmagazines, and television news programs often include guest editorials, which offer the views of people who are not on the regular staff. For this assignment, you will combine two types of writing. You will use **informative** writing to explain your ideas, and you will use **persuasive** writing to convince readers to accept those ideas.

COMBINE
INFORMATIVE AND
PERSUASIVE WRITING
FOR
advertisements
editorials
campaign pamphlets
letters to lawmakers
speeches
fund-raising appeals
letters of complaint

Here is one writer's PASSkey to this assignment.

GUIDED ASSIGNMENT: PROBLEM-SOLUTION

Write an editorial that explains a problem, proposes a solution for the problem, and persuades readers to accept that solution.

PURPOSE: To inform and persuade

AUDIENCE: Readers of the school newspaper

SUBJECT: A problem

STRUCTURE: Guest editorial

Solving the Money Blues
by Jason Harkness

Doug is in seventh grade. His brother Darrell is in tenth. Both boys need money for things like clothes, sports equipment, after-school treats, and entertainment. Both get allowances, but Darrell gets more because he's older. Also, Darrell has a part-time job at a taco shop. What does Doug have? He has a money problem.

Many middle school students are like Doug. We need money as much as high school students do. Yet we have fewer ways to earn it. Legally, most of us are too young to hold

◄ STUDENT MODEL

◄ An anecdote grabs readers' attention.

◄ The second paragraph explains the problem, using facts and details.

WRITER'S WORKSHOP   339

ADDITIONAL RESOURCES
Unit Three Resource Book
Writer's Workshop Worksheet, p. 59
Writer's Workshop: Peer and Self-Evaluation, p. 60
Writer's Workshop: Assessment Guidelines, p. 61

Technology and Enrichment
◆ Writer's Databank Software: File 6,
   Commonly Misspelled Words
▲ Thinking Skills Transparency 5
   Elaboration, Revision, and Proofreading
   Transparencies 21–24
   Fine Art Transparency Pack

Links to
Writer's Craft

For more about informative/persuasive writing, see *The Writer's Craft,* Grade 7, "Persuasion," pages 138–151 and pages 270–274, "Using Transitions."

Objectives

■ To combine informative and persuasive writing in a problem-solving effort

■ To draft, revise, edit, and share informative and persuasive writing

Teaching Strategies

DISCUSSING THE ASSIGNMENT

Have students read the first paragraph and the Guided Assignment on page 339. Point out that students will be writing an editorial. Hand out examples of newspaper and magazine editorials (or show them on the overhead) and ask students why and how this type of writing differs from modes such as straight informative and narrative. Lead them to see how persuasion is used and encourage them to imitate the tone and language of these models when they write their own problem-solution editorial. Call attention to the model PASSkey, noting that the assignment combines two different kinds of writing.

If students would rather do another type of writing, you may give them the option to do so. Encourage them, however, to make a PASSkey that will guide them as they write. The Alternative Writing and Research Topics at the bottom of the next page offer some possibilities.

ANALYZING THE MODEL

Have a volunteer read aloud the student model on pages 339–340.

Point out that Jason decided to break his editorial into four paragraphs. Ask students to identify the purpose or function of each paragraph.

Additional discussion questions about the model could include the following:

■ Why do you think Jason divided his editorial into four paragraphs?

■ Are there any "holes" or weak spots in Jason's argument?

■ What specific persuasive language does Jason use to close his editorial? Does it convince you?

■ What other kind of ending might Jason have used? Would it have been as effective as the ending he chose? Explain.

Prewrite and Explore

Encourage students to get feedback from peers on their solutions. Now is the time to discover whether solutions are valid and logical or whether more brainstorming is needed. At this point students should also determine what kind of facts, statistics, etc. they will need to back up their statements and do the appropriate research.

The third paragraph offers a solution. ▶

The writer anticipates a possible objection and answers it. ▶

Facts and an example stress the benefits of the solution. ▶

Persuasive language makes the conclusion strong. ▶

jobs. The only ways a seventh grader can earn money are paper routes, odd jobs, and babysitting. There aren't enough paper routes for everyone. Odd jobs don't provide steady money. Babysitting is our best chance, and some of us do get regular babysitting jobs. However, we risk losing them if we ever say no because of illness or other plans.

We probably can't change the employment laws any time soon. But there is a simple thing we can do to ease our money problems. We can start working in groups. Imagine five friends forming a group that does babysitting, pet care, or yardwork. They would have more customers than any of them had alone. They could back each other up too. If one of them was sick or had plans, another could fill in.

Some people might think that sharing work means less money for individuals. However, the opposite is true. For example, my cousins and their friends have had a successful babysitting group for over a year. Their customers never have to make more than one call to get a sitter. They know all the students are reliable, charge the same rate, and go by the same rules. My cousins earn the money they need and still have free time. Their success shows how well a group can work. Isn't the idea worth a try? We have nothing to lose—except our money problems.

Prewrite and Explore

WRITER'S CHOICE
Try finishing this sentence: *If I ruled the world, I'd . . .* What would you change? What would you fix?

1 **Look for problems** What really makes you mad? What bugs you in small ways, day after day? Try freewriting to recall all the things that have bothered you recently. You may recall large or small things from home or school. Newspapers, magazines, or television may have alerted you to issues in your community, the country, or the world. After freewriting, underline each problem you came up with.

Alternative Writing and Research Topics

Informative Article Competition in music is less obvious to the public than competition in sports, but it is just as fierce. Write an informational article about a less well-known but equally fierce competition in a field such as art, dance, science, or scholarship.

Personal Narrative Write about a time when you or someone you know "fought to the finish."

Poetry Do you have a "bright tiger" that follows you, always urging you to do your best or to do more and more? Write a poem using the idea in "The Women's 400 Meters" but changing the focus to something other than sports.

Research Report Read more about the cobra and the mongoose. In a report compare the facts with the fiction in "Rikki-tikki-tavi." How accurate is the story?

2 Collect your thoughts Any problem that matters to you and that you have ideas about will make a good topic. A focused **freewriting** is a good way to explore a problem. In this freewriting, you can concentrate on one problem, its causes and effects, and your questions and feelings about it.

3 Shape a solution Once you've explored a problem, you can focus on your solution. Brainstorming with friends can help now. As you work, think about your audience. Are you aiming at readers of a school newspaper, readers of a national magazine, or viewers of local or national television? What do they already know, and what will you need to explain to them? You might research facts and figures about the problem and your solution. Filling out a box chart like the one Jason used, below, is one way to shape your ideas.

◀ **REMINDER** · · · · · · · · ·

Freewriting is continuous writing for a short time—writing whatever comes into your head. It is brainstorming on paper.

◀ **STUDENT MODEL** · · · ·

GATHERING INFORMATION

Problem	Solution		
Middle school kids have a hard time earning money	Work in groups		
Causes	**Effects**	**How it works**	**Advantages**
Need money for extras	Stuck with odd jobs	Share customers and jobs	More customers and jobs
Low allowances	No steady income	Fill in for each other	Free time when needed

◀ **COMPUTER TIP** · · · ·

Above your draft, make four headings, one for each of your four sections. As you get new ideas or find new facts, file them under the appropriate headings.

Draft and Discover

1 Write in sections A problem-solution paper can have four main sections: an introduction that identifies the problem, a part that examines the problem in detail, a part that explains your solution, and a conclusion that tells why your solution is the right one. You can start with whichever section you're most interested in. You might try developing each section as one paragraph.

2 Deal with objections To "sell" your solution to readers, you can't ignore objections they might have. Mention one or two objections. Then explain why your solution is good in spite of them.

Here is an organizer that might help students who don't use the one on page 341.

Introduction	paragraph 2
catch reader's attention—use anecdote???	explain the problem
paragraph 3	*Conclusion:*
explain solution—note objections??	urge my readers to use my solution

Tell students who use the organizer above to write specific information in each box to replace the general ideas there now.

Draft and Discover

Modeling To show students how to disarm objections to their solutions, try the following plan. First, tell students about a problem *you* might like to write about. Put the problem on the board and draw three columns under it. In the first column, write a possible solution to the problem. In the second column, write an objection someone might have to this solution. In the third column, write what you might say to "counter" the objection.

TEACHING TIP: CHALLENGE

Encourage advanced writers to seek the opinions of knowledgeable people to help find a solution for their problem. These students may do research or interview adults and other students. Have students weave quotations from their sources into their editorials, supporting both their statement of the problem and its solution.

CONFERENCING TIP

As you conference with individual writers for this workshop, you may wish to focus on

- elaboration with facts and figures
- effective use of persuasive language
- correct spelling of "sound-alike" words

Revise Your Writing

Remind students to use the Revision Questions on page 342. Here are some additional questions students could ask themselves as they revise:

■ Is my introduction interesting enough to make others want to read more?

■ Does each paragraph deal with only one main idea?

■ Do the paragraphs follow one another logically?

■ Have I thought about and addressed possible objections to my plan?

Proofread

Note that The Editor's Eye feature previews the content in the Language Workshop that follows. If students do not need extra help with words often confused or misspelled, the brief review in the feature may be enough for them. If either the class or individual students might benefit from additional work, you may choose to teach the Language Workshop, pages 344–346, before having students proofread.

TEACHING TIP: PROOFREADING WITH COMPUTERS

Many students are probably aware that computers can check spelling and certain grammatical errors. Emphasize however, that students still need to proofread their papers because most spelling programs will not catch incorrect homophones/homonyms or typographical errors that produce an actual, though inappropriate, word. Also, most programs will not identify fragments or errors in capitalization. You may wish to have students consult the Writer's Databank Software to check commonly misspelled words.

TEACHING TIP: SELF-ASSESSMENT

Remind students that self-assessment can take place at any time during the school year. Have them compare their latest compositions with earlier work from their portfolios. Ask how they think their work has improved. In what areas do they need more work?

1 Review the problem First, try focusing on the sections of your draft that deal with the problem. Your main goal here is to explain the problem clearly, and in detail. You might want to open with an anecdote or a surprising statistic to introduce the problem and get readers interested. Then, be sure to show readers why the problem is important. You also might explain the causes of the problem. This knowledge will help readers see why your solution would be effective.

2 Adjust the solution Your view of the problem may have changed as you wrote. Make sure the solution still fits. You also can make sure you've dealt with readers' possible objections.

3 End strongly As you "sell" your solution, you'll need to be persuasive. This means choosing facts that show the strengths of your solution and explaining logically why your solution will work. Your conclusion may include a call to action, urging readers to do something or to change their ways of thinking.

4 Build bridges As you rework your draft, notice how the four sections of your paper are connected. Ask yourself which thoughts lead from one section to the next. Then look for words and phrases that could make these thought-bridges clearer to your readers. Words and phrases that help readers make connections from one paragraph to the next are called **transitions.** You might ask a peer to read your final draft for sense and smoothness.

THINKING SKILLS
For more about using logic and persuasion, see the Reader's Workshop on page 347.

IN OTHER CLASSES
In social studies, try looking at current or historical events as solutions to problems. Ask yourself which problems an event solved, and how it solved them.

Revision Questions

For You	For a Peer Reader
1. Have I shown why the problem is important to me?	1. Have I given enough information to clearly explain the problem?
2. Have I included enough facts to help readers understand the problem and the solution?	2. What is your opinion of my solution?
3. Have I used clear logic to convince readers?	3. How could I make my conclusion more persuasive?

342   UNIT THREE   FIGHT TO THE FINISH

Read your paper carefully, repairing any grammar, capitalization, punctuation, or spelling errors you find. Pay special attention to words that are easily confused.

THE EDITOR'S EYE: WORDS OFTEN CONFUSED

Homonyms are words that sound alike, but have different spellings and different meanings. Double-check these words when you write.

Be careful with *there*, *they're*, and *their*.

The word *there* is an adverb: Put the books *there*.

The word *they're* is a contraction of *they are: They're* late again.

The word *their* is a possessive pronoun: They brought *their* books.

Problem *There* success shows how well a group can work.

Revised *Their* success shows how well a group can work.

Publish and Present

Mail It Off   With your teacher's help, find the address of a local or national newspaper, magazine, or television news program. Submit a copy of your editorial and include a short cover letter.

Reflect on Your Writing

Write short answers to the following questions. Attach your answers to your editorial, and add it to your portfolio.

1. Now that you've finished your editorial, how has your view of the problem changed?
2. What did you enjoy about working with persuasion? What was hardest for you?

NEED MORE HELP?
. . . .
See the Language Workshop on pages 344–346.

◄ 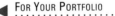 FOR YOUR PORTFOLIO
. . . .

Use these models as needed to reinforce the Editor's Eye feature.

1. Young teenagers often have a problem with (there, they're, <u>their</u>) money.

2. The problem is that (there, <u>they're</u>, their) often short of it.

3. Older teens can earn (there, they're, <u>their</u>) spending money at stores and fast-food places.

4. Young teens, however, can only go (<u>there</u>, they're, their) to buy, not to work.

5. Eventually, (there, <u>they're</u>, their) going to have to come up with a good source of funds.

Publish and Present

Writing for the Community Encourage students who intend to submit their editorials to a newspaper or television show to find out first what the rules are for submission of unsolicited manuscripts. This may save hurt feelings later if the material is neither used nor returned.

Reflect on Your Writing

You may wish to have students answer the following questions in addition to or instead of those in their texts:

■ Did I present my problem clearly and my solution persuasively?

■ What did I learn from this assignment?

Closure

Suggest that when students see examples of informative and persuasive writing in newspapers and magazines, they pay special attention to the structure and the persuasive language of the writer. Encourage students to copy or cut out the editorials they like best and tape them in their journals for future reference.

Assessment Guidelines

These guidelines may help you assess student writing:

Content
■ The problem and solution are clear and logical.
■ The problem and solution are elaborated with facts and figures.
■ Possible objections are anticipated and addressed.

Style
■ Language is persuasive without resorting to questionable or empty propaganda techniques.

■ Transitions are smooth and logical.

Usage and Mechanics
■ Homonyms are used correctly.

■ Errors in capitalization and punctuation are avoided.

See also *Unit Three Resource Book,* page 61.

Objective

■ To use homonyms correctly in writing

Teaching Strategies

HOMONYMS

Remind students that homonyms are words that sound alike but that have different meanings and spellings. Go over the sets of homonyms with the class, pointing out spelling and usage and trying to fashion mnemonic devices to help students distinguish among them.

TEACHING TIP: LEP

Since the apostrophe does not exist in many other languages, it may be necessary to stress to ESL students the difference between it and the comma. Remind these students, too, that contractions are simply "speaking shortcuts." Until these students become comfortable with contractions, keep reminding them of the missing letters and stressing the meaning of each contraction.

MORE MNEMONICS

Here are a few mnemonic devices to add to the ones in the text sidenotes. Encourage students to invent some of their own.

■ *lose, loose*

Because *loose* has an extra o, there is more room in it, and it doesn't fit tightly.

■ *there, they're, their*

The word *here*, which names a place, is inside the word *there*, which names another place.

■ *to, too, two*

Twins always come in *twos*.

WORDS OFTEN CONFUSED OR MISSPELLED

> Do not confuse words that are homonyms or that are similar in sound or appearance.

Misspelled and misused words make your writing less convincing. Oddly, simple words can be the trickiest. **Homonyms** are words that have the same sound but have different spellings and different meanings, such as *here* and *hear*. Other word pairs are confused because they are similar in sound or appearance, such as *lose* and *loose*.

The word **capital** means "excellent, very serious, or most important." It also means "a seat of government."

The word **capitol** means "a building in which a state legislature meets."

The **Capitol** is the building in Washington, D.C., in which the U.S. Congress meets.

> The *capital* of New Hampshire is Concord.
> New Hampshire's legislature meets in the *capitol* building.
> The Senate meets in the *Capitol* building in Washington, D.C.

SPELLING TIP
Remember—you h*ear* with your *ear*.

► **hear** means "to listen to" or "to take notice of."
here means "in this place."

> Alben could *hear* the panther snarling in the darkness.
> "Why did Old Sly Eye come in *here?*" he wondered.

SPELLING TIP
Possessive forms of pronouns (*yours, his, hers, its, theirs, ours, whose*) NEVER have apostrophes.

its is a possessive pronoun meaning "belonging to it."
► **it's** is a contraction for *it is* or *it has*.

> The panther had lost one of *its* eyes years before.
> "*It's* killed the calf," Alben thought. "Will it kill me?"

lose means "to mislay" or "to suffer the loss of something."
loose means "unfastened, slack, or free."

> Alben tried not to *lose* his composure.
> He remembered the *loose* rope hanging in the corner.

ADDITIONAL RESOURCES
Unit Three Resource Book
Language Workshop Practice, p. 62

Technology and Enrichment
Grammar Test Generator

 Writer's Databank Software: File 6, Commonly Misspelled Words

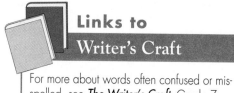

Links to
Writer's Craft

For more about words often confused or misspelled, see **The Writer's Craft**, Grade 7, "Using the Right Word," pages 673–676.

"I couldn't save *our* calf," he thought grimly.
"Now my mother and sister *are* in danger as well."

peace means "quiet" or "freedom from disagreements."
piece means "a section or part of something."

Wishing for *peace* and safety, Alben tried to decide what to do.
He didn't even have a *piece* of wood to use as a weapon.

principle means "a standard, a rule of behavior, or a basic truth."
principal means "of central importance" or "the head of a school."

Alben's family made it a *principle* to help their neighbors.
Protecting his mother and sister was Alben's *principal* goal.

quite means "really or truly" or "to a considerable degree."
quiet means "noiseless, peaceful, or motionless" or "silence or stillness."

Alben knew that Old Sly Eye was *quite* dangerous.
In the *quiet* darkness, he heard the panther moving about.

there means "in that place."
their means "belonging to them."
they're is a contraction for *they are*.

"Old Sly Eye is *there* by the door," he thought.
"My mother and sister are probably on *their* way home."
"*They're* going to be here soon. I must act," he decided.

to means "toward" or "in the direction of." It also can be joined to the base form of a verb, as in *to sing* or *to become*.
too means "also." It can also mean "excessively," as in *too hot*.
two is the number 2.

He would jump from the loft *to* the floor.
"Will Old Sly Eye kill me *too?*" he asked himself.
He heard the voices of *two* people approaching the cabin.

weather means "atmospheric conditions, such as temperature and cloudiness."
whether is a word that helps to express choice or alternative.

The blankets were folded when the *weather* grew warmer.
Alben wasn't sure *whether* or not a blanket would protect him.

◀ **SPELLING TIP** ‥‥‥‥‥‥
Remember—you can take a *piece* of *pie*.

◀ **SPELLING TIP** ‥‥‥‥‥‥
Remember—it's smart to make the princi*pal* your *pal*.

PRACTICE, PRACTICE, PRACTICE

Use the following sentences for additional practice. (Correct responses are underlined.)

1. (Hear, <u>Here</u>) is my problem.

2. I need a (peace, <u>piece</u>) of good advice.

3. I have (<u>quite</u>, quiet) a nice part-time job doing yard work.

4. Of course I don't want to (<u>lose</u>, loose) it.

5. But (its, <u>it's</u>) just not a job that pays well.

6. (<u>There</u>, Their, They're) are three birthdays in my family next month.

7. I have to get enough money for presents, but (<u>who's</u>, whose) going to give it to me?

8. Last week (<u>our</u>, are) (<u>principal</u>, principle) told me about a baby-sitting job.

9. But it would be (to, two, <u>too</u>) hard for me (<u>to</u>, two, too) have (to, <u>two</u>, too) jobs.

10. I don't know (weather, <u>whether</u>) to laugh or cry.

For Alternative Learning Styles Visual learners might enjoy making "cue cards" for everyone to use. Each card would have a funny drawing and caption that suggests the meaning of a homonym, which is printed in bold letters. The idea is to have students think of the drawing whenever they see the word.

Grammar Games: Homonym Challenge

Assemble students into groups and challenge each group to write one or more paragraphs in which they use correctly all of the homonyms from the workshop. When groups are finished, have them trade papers and check each other's work. Assign one point for each homonym used correctly. The group with the most points wins.

Answers to Exercise 1

1. are
2. too, to
3. whose
4. whether
5. piece
6. here
7. lose
8. their
9. quiet
10. You're

Answers to Exercise 2

Have you ever had a chance to <u>hear</u> Nadja Salerno-Sonnenberg perform? <u>It's</u> an experience I'll never forget. Wearing a big, <u>loose</u> shirt and tight pants, she looks <u>a lot</u> like a punk <u>who's</u> wandered into a classical concert. She takes up her violin, and the hall becomes absolutely <u>quiet</u>. As she plays, she twists and bends so much that I wonder <u>whether</u> she'll fall. Yet her playing is smooth as water. "It sounds <u>too</u> good to be real," my friend whispers. After Nadja finishes, my friend and I clap until our hands get sore. Around us, people jump to <u>their</u> feet, shouting, "Encore, encore!" Nadja grins and does a little strut-dance, then begins playing one final <u>piece</u>.

Answers to Exercise 3

Check a few student papers to gauge whether these corrections have been made.

Closure

Remind students that the points made in the Language Workshop should help as they proofread their editorials—and their writing assignments in other classes. You may wish to have students summarize what they've learned by giving specific examples of situations in which they need to know the difference between *whose* and *who's*, and *there*, *they're* and *their*.

346 UNIT THREE **Fight to the Finish**

SPELLING TIP
A lot is always two words! This overused phrase is NEVER written as one word.

PROOFREADING TIP
Use scanning (see page 294) to spot tricky words in proofreading. Try scanning backwards, starting with the last word in your paper.

▶ Alben knew a lot of men *whose* shots had missed the cat. "Now I'm another one *who's* missed Old Sly Eye," he thought.

Exercise 1 Concept Check Write the correct word from the choices in parentheses.

1. "Where (our, are) my mother and sister?" Alben wondered.
2. In the cabin, it was (to, too, two) dark (to, too, two) see.
3. Then Alben knew (who's, whose) voices he had heard outside.
4. He had to decide (weather, whether) to risk a shot.
5. The panther had torn a (piece, peace) out of his shirt.
6. "Don't come over (hear, here)—stay back!" he shouted.
7. If Alben missed, he might (lose, loose) his life.
8. Now he could see (there, their, they're) frightened faces in the moonlight.
9. The roar of the musket shattered the (quite, quiet) night.
10. "Oh, Alben! (Your, You're) hurt!" his mother cried.

Exercise 2 Proofreading Skill Rewrite the following paragraph, correcting the ten misspelled or misused words.

Have you ever had a chance to here Nadja Salerno-Sonnenberg perform? Its an experience I'll never forget. Wearing a big, lose shirt and tight pants, she looks alot like a punk whose wandered into a classical concert. She takes up her violin, and the hall becomes absolutely quite. As she plays, she twists and bends so much that I wonder weather she'll fall. Yet her playing is smooth as water. "It sounds to good to be real," my friend whispers. After Nadja finishes, my friend and I clap until our hands get sore. Around us, people jump to they're feet, shouting, "Encore, encore!" Nadja grins and does a little strut-dance, then begins playing one final peace.

Exercise 3 Revising Your Writing Reread the problem-solution paper you wrote for the Writer's Workshop on pages 339–343. When you find any of the commonly confused words covered in this lesson, check their spelling. Then do the same for the other papers in your portfolio.

346 UNIT THREE FIGHT TO THE FINISH

Additional Practice

Complete the following sentences with the correct word from each set in parentheses. (Correct words are underlined.)

1. (Its, <u>It's</u>) a beautiful day, isn't it?
2. Can you (<u>hear</u>, here) the birds?
3. (Its, <u>It's</u>) so (quite, <u>quiet</u>) (hear, <u>here</u>), and the (<u>weather</u>, whether) is lovely!
4. What was that sound over (<u>there</u>, their, they're)?
5. Oh, (its, <u>it's</u>) just a robin or (to, too, <u>two</u>) reacting to (<u>our</u>, are) presence.

6. Look! (<u>There</u>, Their, They're) is a bluejay. Can you (<u>hear</u>, here) it singing?
7. Yes, but let's walk on before we disturb (<u>its</u>, it's) nest.
8. Guess what? We're about (<u>to</u>, too, two) (<u>lose</u>, loose) (<u>our</u>, are) way!
9. No, not (<u>quite</u>, quiet). (<u>Our</u>, Are) compass is still pointing east.
10. Do you know (weather, <u>whether</u>) we have (<u>to</u>, too, two) walk west to get home?

READER'S WORKSHOP

THE LANGUAGE OF PERSUASION

As a writer, you have two main ways to persuade. You can use emotion, and you can use logic. **Logic** is correct reasoning. Incorrect, or **faulty,** reasoning weakens persuasive writing. Learn to recognize and avoid the kinds of faulty reasoning listed below.

Incorrect Generalization   A **generalization** is a broad statement about a number of people or things, such as "Cobras are venomous." Some generalizations are true. However, words like *none, all, every, always,* or *never* can make some generalizations too broad to be true. "None of today's kids are physically fit" is an example of a generalization that is too broad. Data aren't available on *every* young person's physical fitness. Also, the terms *kids* and *physically fit* don't refer to measurable things like ages or specific physical abilities. Help keep your generalizations accurate with words like *few, most, many, sometimes, often,* or *seldom* and with specific facts that can be proved.

Either/Or   Sometimes a writer suggests that there are only two choices, when actually there are many. "If we don't give seventh-graders more homework, they'll do badly on state tests" illustrates either/or reasoning. There's more than one way to raise test scores.

Bandwagon   A statement like "Join the crowd! Support my plan!" appeals to people's desire to belong—to jump on the bandwagon. This is an indirect and unfair use of emotion, and it is not logical.

Snob Appeal   This technique appeals indirectly to another emotion—the desire to be special. Statements like "Only the brightest people see the wisdom of this idea" rely on snob appeal.

Exercise 1   Concept Check   Identify each of the four types of faulty reasoning used in the paragraph below.

(1) Everyone would be better off if we used my recycling plan. (2) So don't be left out—join the effort. (3) Those who truly have foresight will appreciate this plan most of all. (4) If we don't start doing as I suggest, we'll soon be buried in our own litter.

Exercise 2   Revising Your Writing   Reread your problem-solution paper, checking for faulty reasoning. Make any needed revisions.

ADDITIONAL RESOURCES
Unit Three Resource Book
Reader's Workshop Practice, p. 63

Objective

■ To learn how to recognize and avoid faulty reasoning

Teaching Strategies

Remind students that every time they hear a commercial or read an advertisement, someone is trying to persuade them to buy something or to use a service. Have students read the examples of faulty reasoning on page 347 and identify the clues that reveal the fallacy in each one.

Suggest that students check their understanding of fallacies by figuring out what needs to be done to each example to make it a valid, logical statement. For example, in the bandwagon fallacy "Join the crowd! Support my plan!" students would have to list specific benefits of the speaker's plan before they could support it.

Answers to Exercise 1
1. incorrect generalization
2. bandwagon
3. snob appeal
4. either-or

Answers to Exercise 2
Have students flag suspected examples of fallacies in their work and exchange papers with peer readers to corroborate them.

Additional Practice

Identify the kind of faulty reasoning in each example.

1. Either we win this game or our team is washed up for good. *(either-or)*

2. The weather report is always wrong. *(incorrect generalization)*

3. Only people with intelligence buy Suds cleanser. Are you one of them? *(snob appeal)*

4. Join the millions of Americans who already own Wobbly washers. Buy one today! *(bandwagon)*

Objectives

■ To extend the study of the unit theme, "Reaching for the Stars," to novels and other longer works

■ To read independently for personal enrichment and enjoyment

THE HOBBIT

Study Focus
■ Fantasy setting of Middle Earth

■ A character's courage in pursuing his dreams

■ Conflict between good and evil

About J.R.R. Tolkien

Tolkien is one of the best-known and most prolific writers of books for young people and adults. Critics have found religious and moral messages in his work, though Tolkien claimed he wrote only to entertain. In addition to fantasy, Tolkien wrote many scholarly works on medieval language and literature.

■ **Other Works** Novels: *The Lord of the Rings, Farmer Giles of Ham;* stories: *Unfinished Tales of Numenor and Middle-Earth*

■ **Awards** Children's Spring Book Festival Award, 1983, for *The Hobbit;* International Fantasy Award, 1957, for *The Lord of the Rings;* Benson Medal, Royal Society of Literature, 1966.

Reading on Your Own

Suggested Novels for Unit Three

The novels introduced on these pages allow you to explore the unit theme, "Reaching for the Stars," in more depth and in different ways.

THE HOBBIT
J.R.R. TOLKIEN ©1938

This exciting fantasy is the story of a hero's struggle to win a dragon's treasure. As you follow the adventures of Bilbo, the wizard Gandalf, and twelve dwarfs, you will be plunged into a different world—the world of Middle Earth. Follow Bilbo as he leaves the safety of his home, crosses the Misty Mountains, proceeds through Mirkwood, and finally reaches the Lonely Mountain, home of the terrible Smaug. Find out how Bilbo and his friends battle the forces of evil, fight a dragon, and make personal sacrifices for the good of the community. As you are drawn into their quest, see if you can . . .

• become involved with the characters of a whole new land, called Middle Earth

• imagine the frightening and unfamiliar setting of the Lonely Mountain

• recognize how the heroes of this fantasy are like heroes in real life

THE GIFT OF THE GIRL WHO COULDN'T HEAR

SUSAN SHREVE ©1991

This novel is about dreams and the courage it takes to make those dreams come true. It is the story of a seventh grader who changes from a smart, friendly, self-confident teenager to someone who is insecure and bad-tempered. Thirteen-year-old Eliza has had a dream that has focused her life since she was in the third grade. She is an excellent singer and has dreamed of singing the lead in the seventh-grade musical. Now, all of a sudden, she loses her confidence and self-esteem. Consequently, she refuses to try out for the musical. It is her best friend, Lucy—a deaf girl—who teaches Eliza a valuable lesson and shows her the meaning of true courage. As you read, ask yourself the following questions:

• How can a girl who cannot hear teach Eliza a lesson about music?

The Gift of the Girl Who Couldn't Hear

Susan Shreve

• Who do you believe has more courage, Eliza or Lucy?

• How can people find the courage required to achieve their dreams?

ANPAO: AN AMERICAN INDIAN ODYSSEY

JAMAKE HIGHWATER ©1977

In this novel a number of Native American tales are combined as the hero, Anpao, goes on a quest to learn about his heritage. Driven by his dream, Anpao experiences terrible struggles and battles as he travels through the past in search of his destiny. Along the way he meets remarkable beings and becomes a participant in many of the myths and legends handed down in Native American oral history. His journey through the cultures and customs of many different tribes allows him to understand the great diversity of Native American lifestyles and experiences. As you read, think about the following questions:

• Which of the Native American beliefs and customs appeal most to you?

• What would it be like to journey through the past to relive some of your ancestors' lives?

ANPAO
JAMAKE HIGHWATER

• Will Anpao be able to succeed in spite of the dangers he faces?

Other Recommended Books

The Dream Catcher by Monica Hughes (©1987). In this science fiction novel a fifteen-year-old girl in a futuristic society is involved in a political rescue as she strives to free people from the control of a giant computer that has taken over their minds.

The Hero and the Crown by Robin McKinley (©1984). In this fantasy a girl goes on a difficult quest for the magical objects that will restore power to her kingdom. Along the way she must battle dragons and an evil magician.

The Mouse Rap by Walter Dean Myers (©1990). In this contemporary realistic novel a group of fourteen-year-old friends from Harlem have numerous adventures, including a search for a treasure hidden in the days of Al Capone.

Park's Quest by Katherine Paterson (©1988). An eleven-year-old boy has a dream and a quest in this realistic novel. He wants to learn about his father, who died in Vietnam. As he travels and meets various people, he makes discoveries about both his family and himself.

349

■ **Awards** Newbery Honor Book, 1978, for *Anpao: An American Indian Odyssey;* Notable Children's Book Award, 1984, for *Legend Days*

THE GIFT OF THE GIRL WHO COULDN'T HEAR

Study Focus

■ Contrasts and similarities between characters

■ Themes of friendship and perseverance

■ A character's inner conflicts

About Susan Shreve

Having a father who was a crime reporter meant growing up "in a house full of stories," according to Shreve. At age nine she was writing for a neighborhood theater. She admits, "I write the kind of books I liked to read as a child—stories that could happen, often with a rebellious hero because that's the sort of child I was."

■ **Other Works** Novels: *The Masquerade, How I Saved the World on Purpose, Lucy Forever and Miss Rosetree.*

 ■ **Awards** ALA Best Book for Young Adults, 1980, for *The Masquerade;* Notable Children's Trade Book in social studies, 1980, for *Family Secrets: Five Very Important Stories*

ANPAO: AN AMERICAN INDIAN ODYSSEY

Study Focus

■ Historical setting with mythical characters

■ Use of figurative language and symbolism

■ Native Americans' struggle to create and preserve a beautiful land

About Jamake Highwater

Highwater is a prominent commentator on Native American culture. He has retold many myths and tales. Says Highwater, "I have always preferred the night and the shadow side of existence, because I believe that the unknown is knowable and that the real effort of the artist is to describe the fragile place where the inner and outer worlds meet."

■ **Other Works** Nonfiction: *Song from the Earth: American Indian Painting; Fodor's Indian America;* novels: *Journey to the Sky; The Sun, He Dies;* poetry: *Moonsong Lullaby*

Overview

Subunit One: Tests of Conscience

SELECTION	DIFFICULTY LEVEL	READING SKILLS	LITERATURE SKILLS	WRITING OPTIONS	VOCABULARY WORDS/SKILLS	
Fiction *The Christmas Hunt* Borden Deal Pages 353–367	Easy	Predicting	Foreshadowing	Personal experience Summary Explanation Persuasive	brashness clamor cringe heft inadequate	irate mimicry refuse stricken tactic
Poetry *If I Can Stop One Heart from Breaking* Emily Dickinson *Bitter Cold, Living in the Village* Po Chu-i Pages 368–372	Average	Making comparisons	Imagery	Essay Poem	Word Attack Skill: context clues	
Nonfiction *America the Not-so-Beautiful* Andrew A. Rooney Pages 373–376	Average	Fact and opinion	Persuasive writing Exaggeration Personal examples	Analysis Letter	Word Attack Skill: base words	
Nonfiction *The Endless Steppe* Esther Hautzig Pages 377–387	Challenge	Historical setting	Description External conflict	Comparison Survival guidebook Sermon House listing	acquisition allot archive dexterously etiquette	morbidly pilfering preoccupation superfluous transformation

WRITER'S WORKSHOP Pages 388–392

Mode	Guided Assignment	Writing Skills	Proofreading Focus
Persuasive writing	Speech to persuade	Using the *Readers' Guide* Persuasive Techniques Organization Persuasive Speech	Indefinite pronouns

OPTIONS FOR LEARNING	SPELLING SKILLS	COMMUNITY AND PARENT RESOURCE SUGGESTIONS	AUDIOVISUAL RESOURCES
Discussion Oral presentation Art Role-playing	the prefix *ex-*	Invite a hunter to explain how hunting dogs perform.	*Old Yeller.* 16mm film or video. Walt Disney Educational Media. From the book by Fred Gipson. The touching story of the alliance between a mongrel and a young boy.
	Proofreading for Spelling	Invite a local poet to discuss poetry writing with the class.	*A Brighter Garden: Poems of Emily Dickinson.* Video. Spoken Arts, 1991. (15 min.) A collection of Dickinson's seasonal poems; each season is explored in a blend of music, art, and poetry. *Emily Dickinson: A Certain Slant of Light.* 16mm film or video. International Film Bureau, 1984. (29 min.) Julie Harris discusses the poet's life.
	More silent *-e* words and suffixes	Take a field trip to a recycling center or landfill project. Invite an EPA official or sanitation engineer to talk to the class.	*One Earth: An Environmental Overview.* Filmstrip. National Geographic, 1991. Highlights environmental issues around the world.
Research Stalin Oral report Travel brochure Diorama	Prepositional prefixes	Invite an immigrant from Russia to discuss Siberia with the class. Invite a World War II refugee to talk about his or her experiences.	*Literature & Language* Audiocassette Tape 2, side 1

LANGUAGE WORKSHOP Pages 393–395 • • • • • • • • •

Grammar Concept	Skill Focus
Pronoun problems	Indefinite pronouns *Who* and *whom*

RELATED SKILLS WORKSHOP Page 396 • • • • •

Language Strand	Skill Focus
Speaking and Listening	Critical listening

Subunit Two: Bonds of the Heart

	SELECTION	DIFFICULTY LEVEL	READING SKILLS	LITERATURE SKILLS	WRITING OPTIONS	VOCABULARY WORDS/SKILLS
Fiction	*A Crush* Cynthia Rylant Pages 398–407	Average	Character development	Third-person point of view	Learning log Personal narrative Story Speech	cherish discreetly impaled suitor swarthy
Poetry	*The Highwayman* Alfred Noyes Pages 408–414	Challenge	Narrative poetry	Onomatopoeia Rhyme Rhythm	Summary Epitaph	Word Attack Skill: the suffixes *-ly* and *-ness*
Poetry	*Graduation Morning* Pat Mora *There Is No Word for Goodbye* Mary TallMountain Pages 415–419	Average	Understanding cultural context	Repetition	Thesaurus entry Poem	Word Attack Skill: the prefix *a-*
Drama	*Driving Miss Daisy* Alfred Uhry Pages 420–456	Average	Reading a screenplay	Foil Climax	Director's notes Memo Scene Persuasive letter	appalling perpetual competence recoil demolish reprisal derivation sniping dubiously upholstery

W*RITER'S* WORKSHOP Pages 457–461 ··

Mode	Guided Assignment	Writing Skills	Proofreading Focus
Writing about literature	Character analysis	Generalizations Organization Thesis statements Sentence rhythm	Sentence combining

OPTIONS FOR LEARNING	SPELLING SKILLS	COMMUNITY AND PARENT RESOURCE SUGGESTIONS	AUDIOVISUAL RESOURCES
Pictures Research tattoos Musical theme Research Special Olympics	Words from French	Invite a worker at a group home for the mentally retarded to discuss how the home helps its residents. Invite a tattoo artist to discuss his or her work.	*Meet the Newbery Author: Cynthia Rylant.* Video. American School Publishers, 1990. (10 min.) A revealing portrait of the author in her home. *Welcome Home, Jellybean.* 16mm or video. Cynthia Cherbak Productions/MTI, 1992. (30 min.) Based on Marlene Fanta Shyer's book; the story of a mother's determination to bring her institutionalized daughter home despite her family's unwillingness.
	More compound words	Invite a local actor to read "The Highwayman" to the class.	*Literature & Language* Audiocassette Tape 2, side 1 *Parnassus: Famous Poems that Tell Great Stories.* Audiocassette. Decca Records. Tennyson's "The Charge of the Light Brigade" and Noyes' "The Highwayman" are included.
	Proofreading for Spelling	Ask an expert in languages, Native American languages if possible, to share knowledge of concept words in various languages.	*Maricela.* Films Incorporated Video, 1986. (62 min.) From the WonderWorks series. Maricela's mother, formerly a schoolteacher in El Salvador, is now a domestic for a wealthy American family. Maricela finds herself torn between life at home and the demands of her new world.
Movie critique Time line Perform a scene Research groups	Greek combining forms	Take students on a field trip to a theater. Invite a parent who was a civil rights activist to discuss the movement.	*Driving Miss Daisy.* Video. Warner Home Video, Inc., 1989. (99 min.) The award-winning feature film stars Jessica Tandy as Miss Daisy and Morgan Freeman as Hoke.

LANGUAGE WORKSHOP Pages 462–464 · · · · · · · · ·

Grammar Concept	Skill Focus
Sentence Combining	Combining parts Adding words

RELATED SKILLS WORKSHOP Page 465 · · · · ·

Language Strand	Skill Focus
Vocabulary	Denotation and Connotation

Reading on Your Own

Novels thematically connected to Unit Four, suggested for independent reading during or after completion of the unit (pages 466–467)

The Flawed Glass by Ian Strachan
One-Eyed Cat by Paula Fox
The Clay Marble by Minfong Ho

Video Pen Pals

Students will create entertaining videos that capture their unique personalities and the special flavor of life at their school.

1 Project Preview

As the unit title, "Person to Person," suggests, people are social creatures. This unit project invites students to make personal connections with students in another school. Students will work together in small groups to create a videotape, or videotapes, to portray themselves and their school. They will exchange videos with a classroom in a partner school, one chosen by the teacher or a school administrator. If desired, the project may culminate in a field trip to the partner school.

OBJECTIVES
- To find out interesting and unique things about your fellow students and your school
- To plan and produce a videotape that portrays the students in your class and life at your school
- To exchange videotapes with students in another school

MATERIALS
- One or more video cameras and a recorder, or camcorders
- One or more videocassettes

2 Implementing the Project

At the beginning, find out what channels you need to work through in order to arrange this project. You will probably need the approval of your school administration and the administration of the cooperating school. Allow plenty of time to make the preliminary arrangements.

Try to choose a school that is different from yours in some interesting ways. For example, if your school is in an urban area, you might team up with a suburban or rural school. You might team up with a school in a different geographic region or one with a different ethnic or socioeconomic mix of students.

Once you have found a classroom willing to participate, make sure that the other teacher fully understands this project. You may wish to check with one another and trade ideas at various stages of the project.

ARRANGING FOR VIDEOTAPING

You may want to contact someone who can help you with the videotaping procedures for the project, especially if you are not very familiar with the process. Your school may have a media resource person, a librarian, or a teacher's assistant who can lend a hand. A parent with a flexible work schedule might also be willing to donate time to the project.

If your school does not have video equipment, you may be able to borrow equipment from a parent or a local merchant. The project can be adapted to the availability of equipment. Each group might have its own video camera or camcorder and produce a separate video. Alternatively, a single camera might be passed from group to group, with the groups taping their segments on the same videocassette.

INTRODUCING THE PROJECT

Explain to students that they will be working in small groups to plan and produce a videotape about themselves and their school. Give them some information about their partner school and tell them that the purpose of the videos is to establish person-to-person links with students at the partner school.

To spur interest, you can ask students to watch television programs intended for young people that follow a video magazine format. Often, these shows consist of interviews with young people who are doing interesting things and short features on high schools or middle schools that are involved in unique projects. Use these programs to discuss the possibilities for filming and producing your own videos.

In discussion, ask students how they could present themselves in a way that will interest strangers. How could they create entertaining videos that capture their unique personalities and the special flavor of life at their school?

As a way to personalize the project, you might draft a group letter of introduction to the other class. You could solicit suggestions from your students and compose the letter on the board or on oversized paper. When the letter is complete, it can be copied onto stationery and mailed.

Also, individual students might be invited to participate in a "pen pal"

adjunct to this project. Students could be given extra credit for corresponding with a partner at the other school. The letters could be sent in a packet periodically or through a computer networking system.

GROUP INVESTIGATIONS

Divide students into groups of four to five, making an effort to achieve maximum diversity in each group. For the next several days, the groups will work as teams of investigative reporters, gathering information about group members and the school. Encourage students to conduct informal interviews with group members, other students, and teachers; to take note of any newsworthy events or projects; and to look for creative ways of capturing their subjects on video. As students are gathering information, hold class meetings to check on their progress and to offer help and advice. Each group should try to find its own distinctive way of gathering and presenting information, giving free rein to imagination.

Remind students that this project has two main objectives: to capture the personalities of group members on camera and to capture the unique qualities of the school. Some groups may find it necessary to separate these two tasks; others may find ways of blending the two.

CREATING A PROJECT DESCRIPTION

After students have gathered information and done some preliminary planning, have each group prepare a one-page description of its project. In this way you can steer groups away from duplication and help them to keep their projects manageable. Confer with each group about what they plan to do. You may also have the descriptions read aloud and invite all students to offer suggestions or to raise questions.

Here are some possible project forms.

Option 1: Video Montage   Groups could create a montage (a rapid succession of visual images) with an accompanying sound track. The montage could portray aspects of everyday life at school, perhaps featuring shots of group members involved in various school activities.

The montage will require careful planning. If the group does not have the equipment or knowledge to edit videos it will have to take a series of shots, turning the camera and recorder on and off as required.

Option 2: School News   Groups could create a newscast or a series of short features about themselves and their school. The newscast can focus on interesting events, unusual characters, student opinion, or other topics.

Option 3: Music Narrative   Students can create their own music video, one that tells a story about themselves and their school. You may wish to approve the choice of music ahead of time to ensure its suitability for an academic environment. Students may create original music or use a tape of a popular recording.

Option 4: Hot Topics   Students could interview one another or present a panel discussion about some controversial topic, for instance, music censorship, prejudice, or the rights of teenagers. These topics might also be discussed in the format of a talk show in which a host interviews both guests and audience members.

PRODUCTION

When students are ready to begin taping, be prepared for a little mayhem. To make the process go as smoothly as possible, you may wish to schedule separate taping sessions for each group, giving the rest of the class other work to complete during taping. While the groups are taping, you will need to serve as a facilitator, a problem solver, and a coach to keep students on track and to minimize disruptions.

You will probably want to set time limits both for the finished tape (perhaps ten to fifteen minutes) and the actual filming.

If the groups will be coordinating their efforts to produce a single tape, you will need to allow extra time for cooperation among the groups. For the production of a single tape, it is especially important to avoid duplication. Groups may also need your assistance to develop continuity between the segments, .

You may wish to set aside class time to help students develop some form of credits for their tapes. Each group might create a name and a logo for their production company (such as the roaring lion of MGM productions). Credit could be given to group members by filming a poster board with their names printed on it.

PRESENTATION

The project could culminate in a screening party that features a single tape or multiple tapes, depending on how you shaped the project. You might invite administrators, the other class, or any other interested people from the community for a viewing of the tape. Popcorn and soft drinks might be welcomed by all viewers.

3 *Project Assessment*

Evaluate each group's video by using the following criteria:
1. Does the video show evidence of thoughtful planning and preparation on the part of group members?
2. Does the video capture the personalities of group members and the flavor of life at your school?
3. Are the visual images appropriately matched with a sound track?
4. Is the information presented in a creative and appealing way?

Provide each group with brief written comments and confer with the groups to explain how you assigned their grades for the project.

As another means of grading, you could also ask each student to write a project evaluation, noting what each group member contributed to the final product and discussing problems that arose during the project.

For the Portfolio

Keep master copies of all the videos in your classroom or school library for future reference. Include a copy of your written assessment in each student's portfolio. At the end of the year, you might share the videos with teachers from the next grade level.

4 *Team-Teaching Options*

Social Studies

Have students study the progress of information technology in the twentieth century, including radio, movie newsreels, television, rapid satellite transmissions, computer networking, and other advances. Have them give a summary of how such technology has affected people's daily lives.

Art

Allow students to design a promotional poster for the video or videos produced by your class.

Science

Have students study the scientific principles involved in video recording and discuss how this technology has revolutionized the television industry.

Music

Encourage students to create an audiotape featuring segments of the songs that are most popular among students in your school. Alternatively, they could create an audiotape of a school choir or other performance group and send the tape along with the video to the partner school.

Unit Preview

In Unit Four, "Person to Person," students will explore how human beings act and react with one another in emotional situations. The unit contains two subunits:

- Subunit 1: "Tests of Conscience"
- Subunit 2: "Bonds of the Heart"

Connections to Unit Six

Unit Six, "Themes in World Folklore," contains literature from the oral tradition that connects with the themes in Unit Four. You may wish to begin or end Unit Four with selections from Unit Six that relate to the theme "Person to Person":

- "Prometheus," p. 633
- "Where the Girl Saved Her Brother," p. 636
- "How Odin Lost His Eye," p. 640

ADDITIONAL RESOURCES

Unit Four Resource Book
Unit Test, pp. 71–74

Technology and Enrichment
Family and Community Involvement
    Source Book, pp. 15–17

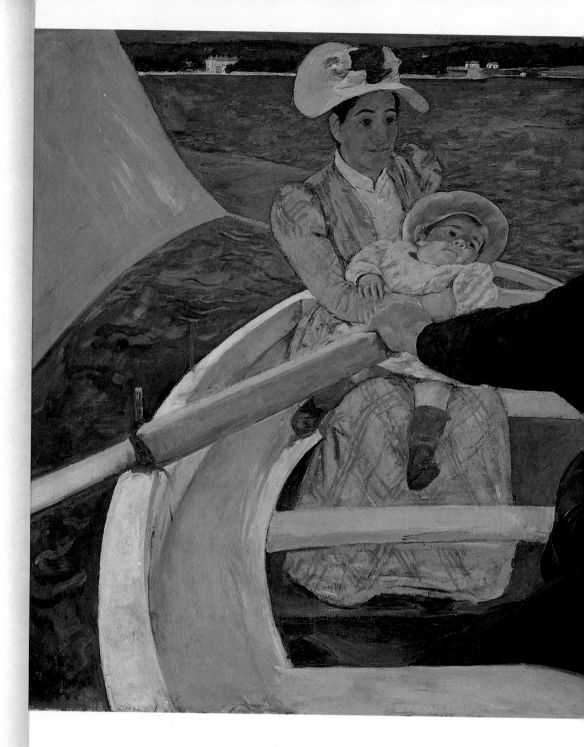

About the Art

Mary Cassatt (1845–1926) is one of America's best-known painters. She spent years in Paris where she was influenced by impressionism and such masters as Renoir, Manet, Cézanne, and Degas. Cassatt is most famous for her appealing paintings of mothers and children. The lines in *The Boating Party*—the sail, oar, sides of the boat—force the viewer's eye to the mother and child. *Study the woman's expression. How does she feel about the boat ride? about the man rowing?*

PERSON
TO
PERSON

. . . .

*C*an I ever know you

Or you know me?

Sara Teasdale

THE BOATING PARTY 1893–94
Mary Cassatt   National Gallery of Art,
Washington, D.C. Chester Dale Collection.

351

Discussion Questions

To help students probe connections between the fine art, the quotation, and the unit theme, have them consider the following questions:

1. What does the phrase "person to person" suggest to you? *(Possible responses: a very close, personal relationship; a private talk or confrontation between two people)*

2. How does the quotation relate to the theme of "person to person"? *(Possible response: People never know one another completely, no matter how close they are.)*

3. Do you agree with the quotation? Why or why not? *(Possible responses: Yes, because you can never really get inside another person's mind; no, if a person is honest with you, you can know them.)*

4. How does the art relate to the theme of "person to person"? *(Possible responses: The people in the boat seem to have a close relationship; woman and child are both looking at the man lovingly.)*

5. Based on the quotation and the art, what kinds of selections do you predict this unit will offer? *(Possible response: selections about close relationships between people; selections about encounters between people; selections that reveal the characters' true selves)*

About the Quoted Author

Sara Teasdale was born in St. Louis, Missouri, in 1884. Growing up, she found herself keenly sensitive to the beauty of nature and often wove the theme of nature into her work. Many of her other poems are about love and death. Often the speakers in her poems are women who face death or desertion by a loved one. They view their fate sadly but not cynically. In addition to being a writer, Teasdale was an editor of several volumes of poems.

Subunit Preview

Have students read the introduction to Subunit 1, "Tests of Conscience." Ask them to explain how tests of conscience apply to personal relationships. Can students think of times when they have had to choose between being concerned about their own comfort or wishes and doing what was right for someone else? Have they ever sacrificed something for another person?

INTEGRATING THE LANGUAGE ARTS

Every selection in this subunit focuses on the theme "Tests of Conscience." Reading skills, literature skills, writing options, language study, vocabulary, and spelling skills are all based on these literary selections.

Writer's Workshop After reading selections that deal with tests of conscience, students will use persuasive writing to try to move readers to take action on a matter of conscience.

Language Workshop The Language Workshop in this subunit focuses on using indefinite and interrogative pronouns correctly. Students will see that using correct pronouns can increase their effectiveness in persuasive writing.

Speaking and Listening Workshop The Speaking and Listening Workshop in this subunit is about listening critically. In order to evaluate a persuasive speech, students must learn to listen closely to the speaker's key arguments.

FOR ADDITIONAL CHALLENGE

The following selections explore the subunit theme further:

A Christmas Carol, novella by Charles Dickens

"Mother to Son," poem by Langston Hughes

The Adventures of Huckleberry Finn, novel by Mark Twain

ADDITIONAL RESOURCES

Family and Community Involvement Source Book, p. 15

Guidelines for Reading and Literature Assessment: Observation Assessment Forms

People are social—we live together and need each other. The ties that join one person to another—whether based on love, friendship, necessity, or duty—are strong and, at times, demanding. These ties require us to give and receive, to make decisions, to be unselfish, sometimes even to make sacrifices.

Our personal relationships often depend on treating each other fairly and with compassion. Our consciences tell us what is right and fair. Daily, we are confronted with situations in which we have to decide if we will do the *right* thing or do the thing that will please us personally, which is often the more selfish, easier path to follow.

This group of selections presents situations that offer choices. The characters must decide whether or not to listen to their consciences. As you imagine yourself in each situation, decide which path you would choose.

352   UNIT FOUR   TESTS OF CONSCIENCE

Observation Assessment

Observing how students respond to the text, to the classroom instruction, and to peers is an important part of an assessment program. The following suggestions and the form in the *Guidelines for Reading and Literature Assessment* booklet can be used to implement observation assessment.

■ **Reading Behavior** As students work through the subunit, assess their engagement with the text. Note how well readers integrate new ideas with prior knowledge and experiences. Also note how well they are able to identify external and internal conflict in the development of plot. Evaluate students' sensitivity to the author's purpose and style. Most importantly, see how well students are able to express opinions, judgments, or insights about the text. Throughout the unit, watch for growth in each student's ability to become actively involved in the reading process.

Fiction

The Christmas Hunt

BORDEN DEAL

Examine What You Know (Prior Knowledge)

In many places in the United States, hunting is a common pastime, and for some people it is an occupation. What do you know about hunting? For what reasons do people hunt? What are your feelings about hunting? Write your ideas about hunting in your journal or notebook.

Expand Your Knowledge (Building Background)

The following story is about hunting quail, small game birds that can legally be shot. Bird hunters frequently have trained bird dogs. These dogs instinctively stop quartering, or searching, a field when they smell the birds' scent on the ground. The dogs freeze, lift a front paw, and point their nose toward the birds. On command they flush the quail, or scare the birds into the air, and then the hunters fire. The dogs, which are trained not to eat the fallen birds, find and bring the birds back to the hunters. Bird dogs are sometimes entered in competitive field trials, in which they are judged on their ability to obey orders, search a field, smell out game birds, and retrieve the birds without damaging them.

Enrich Your Reading (Reading Skill)

Predicting Based on the material on this page, the title, large blue quotes, and pictures, what do you predict this story will be about? As you read, look for clues in the main character's behavior and speech to predict what will happen next and how the story will end. Be aware that your expectations will probably change as you are reading. Copy the chart below onto a separate sheet of paper and track your changing expectations.

■ *Author biography on Extend page*

Event in the story	Prediction
1. Tom asks father to take him on hunt	Father will refuse
2.	

THE CHRISTMAS HUNT   353

JOURNAL WRITING IDEAS

■ Write about a time when you were considered too young to do something you wanted to do.

■ Have you ever felt as if you had to prove something to someone? What happened?

COLLABORATIVE LEARNING OPTIONS

Opportunities for collaborative learning include Options for Learning 1–4 (p. 367) and Cross-Curricular Projects (p. 367).

ADDITIONAL RESOURCES

Unit Four Resource Book
Reader's Guidesheet, p. 1
Reading Skills, p. 2
Literature Skills, p. 3
Vocabulary Connections, p. 4
Spelling Connections, p. 5
Comprehension and Vocabulary Check Tests, p. 6
Selection Test, pp. 7–8

Objectives

■ To understand and analyze a short story

■ To examine the use of foreshadowing

■ To enrich reading by using the strategy of predicting

■ To express understanding of the story through a choice of writing forms, including a personal experience, a summary, an explanation, and a persuasive essay

Prereading/Motivation

Examine What You Know

Discussion Prompts What kinds of animals are hunted in this country? Do most people hunt mainly for sport or for food? What must a person know about the woods and about wild game to be a safe and effective hunter?

Expand Your Knowledge

Additional Background There are several types of sporting dogs—each with its own method of aiding game-bird hunters. Spaniels are used to flush birds from their hiding places. Pointers and setters stand rigidly and point their noses and bodies in the direction of birds. Retrievers fetch the birds that hunters have shot.

For Alternative Learning Styles Find pictures of bird dogs, such as the German shorthaired pointer, in an encyclopedia or a reference book about dogs, and show them to students.

Enrich Your Reading

After students finish reading, have them look over their charts to see how their predictions changed during the course of their reading.

Thematic Link— Tests of Conscience

After he recklessly wounds his father's prized hunting dog, the ten-year-old narrator passes a test of conscience by owning up to his mistake and voluntarily giving up something he values.

VOCABULARY PREVIEW

These vocabulary words are defined at the bottom of the selection pages on which they appear.

brashness recklessness

clamor a loud noise; uproar

cringe to shrink back

heft to lift something

inadequate not enough

irate angry

mimicry an act of imitation

refuge a safe place

stricken wounded

tactic a strategy

LIMITED ENGLISH PROFICIENCY

■ Use the Reader's Guidesheet, *Unit Four Resource Book*, page 1.

■ To clarify difficult vocabulary, you may wish to have students retell selected passages in their own words.

★ Text annotations marked with a red star (2, 4, 5, 7, 27) may be particularly helpful for students with limited English proficiency.

TEXT ANNOTATIONS

1. LITERARY CONCEPT: Point of View
Ask students to identify the story's point of view and to describe the narrator. *(The point of view is first person; the narrator is a ten-year-old.)*

2. VOCABULARY: Definition
Some students may have difficulty with the word *pursed*. Help them use **context clues** or **prior knowledge** to determine that the word means "puckered" or "drawn tightly together." Ask what the mother might be thinking to cause her to purse her lips. *(Possible response: She sees through her husband's sweet-talking and realizes that feeding the crowd will be a lot of work.)* ★

3. ACTIVE READING: Connect
Invite students to share any problems they have had in getting adults to take them seriously. Ask what strategies they find most effective in gaining the attention of adults. *(Any response is valid.)*

The Christmas Hunt

BORDEN DEAL

It should have been the best Christmas of them all, that year at Dog Run. It started out to be, anyway. I was so excited, watching my father talking on the telephone, that I couldn't stand still. For I was ten years old, and I had never been on a quail shoot in my whole life. I wanted to go on the big Christmas Day hunt even more than I wanted that bicycle I was supposed to get. And I really needed the bicycle to cover with speed and ease the two miles I had to walk to school.

The Christmas Day hunt was always the biggest and best of the season. It was almost like a field trial; only the best hunters and the finest dogs were invited by my father. All my life I had been hearing tales of past Christmas Day hunts. And now I knew with a great ten-year-old certainty that I was old enough to go.

My father hung up the phone and turned around, grinning. "That was Walter," he said. "There'll be ten of them this year. And Walter is bringing his new dog. If all he claims for that dog is true—"

"Papa," I said.

"Lord," my mother said. "That'll be a houseful to feed."

My father put his arm around her shoulders, hugging her. "Oh, you know you like it," he said. "They come as much for your cooking as they do for the hunting, I think."

My mother pursed her lips in the way she had and then smiled. "Wild turkey," she said. "You think you could shoot me four or five nice fat wild turkeys?"

I wanted to jump up and down to attract attention. But that was kid stuff, a tactic for the five-year-olds, though I had to admit it was effective. But I was ten. So I said, "Papa."

My father laughed. "I think I can," he said. "I'll put in a couple of mornings trying."

"Papa," I said desperately.

"Wild turkey stuffed with wild rice," my mother said quickly, thoughtfully, in her planning voice. "Giblet gravy, mashed potatoes, maybe a nice potato salad—"

"If I don't fail on the turkeys," my father said.

"Papa!" I said.

My father turned to me. "Come on, Tom," he said. "We've got to feed those dogs."

That's the way parents are, even when you're ten years old. They can talk right on

Words to Know and Use	**tactic** (tak' tik) *n.* a method used to accomplish something; a strategy

354

Guided Reading for Less-Proficient Students

These questions can help guide students through the reading. Ask each question at the point of the selection where the capital letter and arrow appear in the margin. In addition, you may wish to use appropriate Active Reading annotations.

A. What two things does the narrator desire? *(He wants a bicycle, and he wants even more to go on the Christmas Day hunt.)* Recalling

B. How is Calypso Baby special among the dogs that Tom's father owns? *(She is the best bird dog in*

that part of the country and Tom's father's personal dog.) Recalling

C. What is Tom planning to do? *(He is going hunting by himself.)* Recalling

D. Why does Tom nearly begin to cry? *(Possible responses: He has failed to shoot, and the birds are gone; he has made mistakes; he has not lived up to his image of himself.)* Recalling

Continued on page 355

and never hear a word you say. I ran after my father as he left the kitchen, hoping for a chance to get my words in edgewise. But my father was walking fast, and already the clamor of the bird dogs was rising up to cover any speech I might want to make.

Already the clamor of the bird dogs was rising.

The dogs were standing on the wire fence in long, dappled rows, their voices lifted in greeting. Even in my urgent need I had to stop and admire them. There's nothing prettier in the whole world than a good bird dog. There's a nobleness to its head, an intelligence in its eyes, that no other animal has. Just looking at them sent a shiver down my backbone, and the thought of shooting birds over them—well, the shiver just wasn't in my backbone now; I was shaking all over.

All of the dogs except one were in the same big run. But my father kept Calypso Baby in her own regal pen. I went to her and looked into her soft brown eyes. She stood up tall on the fence, her strong, lithe body stretched to its full height, as tall as I was.

"Hello, Baby," I whispered, and she wagged her tail. "You gonna find me some birds this Christmas, Baby? You gonna hunt for me like you do for Papa?"

She lolled her tongue, laughing at me. We were old friends. Calypso Baby was the finest bird dog in that part of the country. My father owned a number of dogs and kept and trained others for his town friends. But Calypso Baby was his personal dog, the one that he took to the field trials, the one he shot over in the big Christmas Day hunt held at Dog Run.

My father was bringing the sack of feed from the shed. I put out my hand, holding it against the wire so Calypso Baby could lick my fingers.

"This year," I whispered to her. "This year I'm going." I left Calypso Baby, went with determination toward my father. "Papa," I said, in a voice not to be denied this time.

My father was busy opening the sack of dog food.

"Papa," I said firmly, "I want to talk to you." It was the tone and the words my father used often toward me, so much of mimicry that my father looked down at me in surprise, at last giving me his attention.

"What is it?" he said. "What do you want?"

"Papa, I'm ten years old," I said.

My father laughed. "Well, what of it?" he said. "Next year you'll be eleven. And the next year twelve."

"I'm old enough to go on the Christmas hunt," I said.

Incredibly, my father laughed. "At ten?" he said. "I'm afraid not."

I stood, stricken. "But—" I said.

"No," my father said, in the voice that meant No, and no more talking about it. He hoisted the sack of feed and took it into the wire dog pen, the bird dogs crowding around him, rearing up on him in their eagerness.

Words to Know and Use	**clamor** (klam' ər) *n.* a loud noise; uproar **mimicry** (mim' ik rē) *n.* an act of imitation **stricken** (strik' ən) *adj.* suddenly affected by pain; wounded

355

4. VOCABULARY: Idiom
Some students may be unfamiliar with the idiom "get my words in edgewise." Help those students use **context clues** or **prior knowledge** to determine that the phrase means "to say something during a moment when another person is silent."

For Alternative Learning Styles Choose a volunteer to demonstrate how a card or a piece of paper can be slipped into a narrow opening "edgewise." ★

5. VOCABULARY: Technical Terms
In the second full paragraph on this page, *run* means "an enclosure in which dogs can feed or exercise." As used in the name Dog Run, however, the word means "a track or path frequented by animals." The term *shoot over* is used twice on the page; it describes the act of using a dog to find birds during a hunt. ★

6. ACTIVE READING: Predict
Ask students for their predictions about how Tom will respond to his father's decision. What do they think will happen next? *(Any response is valid.)*

Guided Reading for Less-Proficient Students

Continued from page 354

E. What factors cause Tom to accidentally shoot Calypso Baby? *(He is angry at his failures, fearful that the dog does not respect him, physically tired, and frustrated; and in the crucial moments before pulling the trigger, he hurries.)* Summarizing
F. How does Tom's father react to the news of Calypso Baby's injury? *(He says he will talk to Tom later, then tends to the dog.)* Summarizing
G. What does Tom decide his punishment should be? *(He should not be given a bicycle for Christmas.)* Summarizing
H. Why does Tom's father give him a puppy? *(Possible responses: He is impressed with Tom's sacrifice; he wants Tom and the puppy to learn to hunt together; he wants to help Tom make up for his mistake.)* Recalling/Analyzing
I. When will Tom be allowed to go on the Christmas Day hunt? *(when both he and the puppy have grown up)* Recalling

THE CHRISTMAS HUNT **Teacher's Edition** **355**

"Well, come on and help me," my father said impatiently. "I've got a lot of things to do."

Usually I enjoyed the daily feeding of the dogs. But not today; I went through the motions dumbly, silently, not paying any attention to the fine bird dogs crowding around me. I cleaned the watering troughs with my usual care, but my heart was not in it.

After the feeding was over, I scuffed stubbornly about my other tasks and then went up to my room, not even coming down when my father came home at dusk excited with the two wild turkeys he had shot. I could hear him talking to my mother in the kitchen, and the ring of their voices had already the feel of Christmas, a hunting cheer that made them brighter, livelier, than usual. But none of the cheer and the pleasure came into me, even though Christmas was almost upon us and yesterday had been

THE EYES HAVE IT   Andrew Chapman   Courtesy of the artist.

the last day of school.

That night I hunted. In my dreams I was out ahead of all the other men and dogs, Calypso Baby quartering the field in her busy way, doing it so beautifully I ached inside to watch her. All the men and dogs stopped their own hunting to watch us, as though it were a field trial. When Calypso Baby pointed, I raised the twelve-gauge[1] shotgun, moved in on her on the ready, and Calypso Baby flushed the birds in her fine, steady way. They came up in an explosive whir, and I had the gun to my shoulder, squeezing off the shot just the way I'd been told to do. Three quail dropped like stones out of the covey,[2] and I swung the gun, following a single. I brought down the single with the second barrel, and Calypso Baby was already bringing the first bird to me in her soft, unbruising mouth. I knelt to pat her for a moment, and Baby whipped her tail to tell me how fine a shot I was, how much she liked for me to be the one shooting over her today.

Soon there was another covey, and I did even better on this one, and then another and another, and nobody was hunting at all, not even my father, who was laughing and grinning at the other men, knowing this was his boy, Tom, and his dog, Calypso Baby, and just full of pride with it all. When it was over, the men crowded around and patted me on the shoulder, hefting the full game

7

8

---

1. **twelve-gauge** (gāj): having the widest barrel in common use.
2. **covey** (kuv′ ē): a small flock.

Words to Know and Use	**heft** (heft) *v.* to lift something to see how heavy it is

356

bag in admiration, and then there was my father's face close before me, saying, "I was wrong, son, when I said a ten-year-old boy isn't old enough to go bird hunting with the best of us."

Then I was awake, and my father, dressed in his hunting clothes, was shaking me, and it was morning. I looked up dazedly into his face, unable to shake off the dream, and I knew what it was I had to do. I had to show my father. Only then would he believe.

"Are you awake?" my father said. "You'll have to change the water for the dogs. I'm going to see if I can get some more turkeys this morning."

"All right," I said. "I'm awake now."

My father left. I got up and ate breakfast in the kitchen, close to the warm stove. I didn't say anything to my mother about my plans. I went out and watered the dogs as soon as the sun was up, but I didn't take the time, as I usually did, to play with them.

"Me and you are going hunting," I told Calypso Baby as I changed her water. She jumped and quivered all over, knowing the word as well as I did.

I went back into the house, listening for my mother. She was upstairs, making the beds. I went into the spare room where my father kept all the hunting gear. I was trembling, remembering the dream, as I went to the gun rack and touched the cold steel of the double-barreled twelve-gauge. But I knew it would be very heavy for me. I took the single-barrel instead, though I knew that pretty near ruined my chances for a second shot unless I could reload very quickly.

I picked up a full shell[3] bag and hung it under my left arm. I found a game bag and hung it under my right arm. The strap was too long, and the bag dangled emptily to my knees, banging against me as I walked. I tied a knot in the strap so the bag would rest comfortably on my right hip. The gun was heavy in my hands as I walked into the hallway, listening for my mother. She was still upstairs.

"Mamma, I'm gone," I shouted up to her. "I'll be back in a little while." That was so she wouldn't be looking for me.

"All right," she called. "Don't wander far off. Your father will be back in an hour or two and might have something for you to do."

I hurried out of the house, straight to Calypso Baby's pen. I did not look up, afraid that my mother might be watching out of the window. That was a danger I could do nothing about, so I just ignored it. I opened the gate to Baby's pen, and she came out, circling and cavorting.

"Come on, Baby," I whispered. "Find me some birds now. Find me a whole lot of birds."

We started off, circling the barn so we would not be seen from the house and going straight away in its shadow as far as we could. Beyond the pasture we crossed a cornfield, Calypso Baby arrowing straight for the patch of sedge grass beyond. Her tail was whiplike in its thrash, her head high as she plunged toward her work, and I had to hurry to keep up. The gun was clumsy in

---

3. **shell:** a shotgun cartridge.

10. ACTIVE READING: Review
Ask students to contrast Tom's dream with this short scene at the gun rack. (Possible response: In his dream Tom confidently shoots many birds with a double-barreled twelve-gauge shotgun, but here he nervously selects a single-barreled gun in recognition of his small size.)

11. ACTIVE READING: Evaluate
Have students evaluate Tom's plan to hunt alone with Calypso Baby. Given his father's previous response to Tom's request to hunt and Tom's behavior toward his mother as he leaves the house, do students think Tom's plan is a good one? Why or why not? (Any response is valid.)

12. ACTIVE READING: Predict
Have students contrast this passage, in which the narrator states that he did not even remember to raise the gun to his shoulder, with his statement in the first few lines of this page that he "knew all about hunting." Ask what the narrator's performance here hints about how this hunting expedition will turn out. *(Possible responses: It will be a disaster; the boy will not succeed; he may do all right in spite of his lack of knowledge.)*

13. ACTIVE READING: Question
Ask students if they think that the dog actually looked up at Tom with "contempt." *(Possible responses: The dog really is contemptuous of Tom's inexperience; because of Tom's shame, frustration, and regret, he may only imagine that there is contempt in the dog's eyes.)*

my hands, and the two bags banged against my hips. But I remembered not to run with the gun, remembered to keep the breech[4] open until I was ready to shoot. I knew all about hunting; I just hadn't had a chance to practice what I knew. When I came home with a bag full of fine birds, my father would have to admit that I knew how to hunt, that I was old enough for the big Christmas Day hunt when all the great hunters came out from town for the biggest day of the season.

When I ducked through the barbed-wire fence, Calypso Baby was waiting for me, standing a few steps into the sedge grass, her head up watching me alertly. Her whole body quivered with her eagerness to be off. I swept my arm in the gesture I had seen my father use so many times, and Calypso Baby plunged instantly into the grass. She was a fast worker, quartering back and forth with an economical use of her energy. She could cover a field in half the time it took any other dog. The first field was empty, and we passed on to the second one. Somehow Calypso Baby knew that birds were here. She steadied down, hunting slowly, more thoroughly.

Then, startling me though I had been expecting it, she froze into a point, one foot up, her tail straight back, her head flat with the line of her backbone. I froze too. I couldn't move; I couldn't even remember to breech the gun and raise it to my shoulder. I stood as still as the dog, all of my knowledge flown out of my head, and yet far back under the panic, I knew that the birds weren't going to hold. They were going to

rise in just a moment. Calypso Baby, surprised at my inaction, broke her point to look at me in inquiry. Her head turned toward me, and she asked the question as plain as my father's voice: *Well, what are you going to do about these fine birds I found for you?*

I could move then. I took a step or two, fumblingly breeched the gun, raised it to my shoulder. The birds rose of their own accord in a sudden wild drum of sound. I yanked at the trigger, unconsciously bracing myself against the blast and the recoil. Nothing happened. Nothing at all happened. I tugged at the trigger wildly, furiously, but it was too late and the birds were gone.

I lowered the gun, looking down at it in bewilderment. I had forgotten to release the safety. I wanted to cry at my own stupidity. I could feel the tears standing in my eyes. This was not at all like my dream of last night, when I and the dog and the birds had all been so perfect.

Calypso Baby walked back to me and looked up into my face. I could read the puzzled contempt in her eyes. She lay down at my feet, putting her muzzle on her paws. I looked down at her, ashamed of myself and knowing that she was ashamed. She demanded perfection, just as my father did.

"It was my fault, Baby," I told her. I leaned over and patted her on the head. "You didn't do anything wrong. It was me."

I started off then, looking back at the bird dog. She did not follow me. "Come on," I told her. "Hunt."

She got up slowly and went out ahead of me again. But she worked in a puzzled manner, checking back to me frequently.

---

4. **breech:** the back part of a gun barrel.

She no longer had the joy, the confidence, with which she had started out.

"Come on, Baby," I coaxed her. "Hunt, Baby. Hunt."

We crossed into another field, low grass this time, and when we found the covey, there was very little time for setting myself. Calypso Baby pointed suddenly. I jerked the gun to my shoulder, remembering the safety this time, and then Calypso Baby flushed the birds. They rose up before me, and I pulled the trigger, hearing the blast of the gun, feeling the shock of it into my shoulder knocking me back a step.

But not even one bird dropped like a fateful stone out of the covey. The covey had gone off low and hard on an angle to the left, and I had completely missed the shot, aiming straight ahead instead of swinging with the birds. Calypso Baby did not even attempt to point singles. She dropped her head and her tail and started away from me, going back toward the house.

I ran after her, calling her, crying now but with anger rather than hurt. Baby would never like me again. She would hold me in the indifference she felt toward any person who was not a bird hunter. She would tolerate me as she tolerated my mother and the men who came out with shiny new hunting clothes and walked all over the land talking about how the dogs didn't hold the birds properly so you could get a decent shot.

I couldn't be one of those. I ran after the dog, calling her, until at last she suffered me to come near. I knelt, fondling her head, talking to her, begging her for another chance.

"I'll get some birds next time," I told her. "You just watch. You hear?"

At last, reluctantly, she consented to hunt again. I followed her, my hands gripping the heavy gun, determined this time. I knew it was my last chance; she would not give me another. I could not miss this time.

We hunted for an hour before we found another covey of birds. I was tired, the gun and the frustration heavier with every step. But, holding only last night's dream in my mind, I refused to quit. At last Calypso Baby froze into a beautiful point. I could feel myself sweating, my teeth gritted hard. I had to bring down a bird this time.

I had to bring down a bird this time.

It seemed to be perfect. I had plenty of time, but I hurried anyway, just to be sure. Then the birds were rising in a tight cluster, and I was pulling the trigger before I had the heavy gun lined up—and in the midst of the thundering blast, I heard Calypso Baby yell with pain as the random shot tore into her hip.

I threw down the gun and ran toward her, seeing the blood streaking down her leg as she staggered away from me, whimpering. I knelt, trying to coax her to me, but she was afraid. I was crying, feeling the full weight of the disaster. I had committed the worst crime of any bird hunter; I had shot my own dog.

Calypso Baby was trying to hide in a clump of bushes. She snapped at me in her fear when I reached in after her, but I did not feel the pain in my hand. I knelt over her, looking at the shredded hip. It was a

14. LITERARY CONCEPT: Similes
Have students find the simile in this sentence ("like a fateful stone") and then find a similar simile in Tom's dream on page 356. Ask students why they think Deal repeats the figure of speech. (The simile on page 356—"three quail dropped like stones"—describes how Tom successfully shoots birds in his dream. Deal may repeat the simile here to underscore the contrast between Tom's fantasy of success and the reality of his failure.)

15. ACTIVE READING: Predict
Ask students for their predictions about how Tom's "last chance" to shoot a bird will turn out. (Any response is valid.)

16. LITERARY CONCEPT: Plot
Ask students how Tom's decision to hunt by himself with Calypso Baby and his accidental shooting of the dog build the conflict in the plot. (Possible response: His hunting with Calypso Baby is done without the knowledge or permission of his parents, and this secrecy creates the potential for conflict between Tom and his parents. Now a fiercer conflict between Tom and his father—over the shooting of his father's "personal dog"—seems inevitable.)

Looking at Style

To discuss Deal's writing style, read students the following sentences, emphasizing the italicized words.

■ I pulled the trigger, *hearing the blast of the gun, feeling the shock of it.* (p. 359)

■ I ran after the dog, *calling her,* until at last she suffered me to come near. (p. 359)

Point out to students that *hearing, feeling,* and *calling* are present participles used as adjectives modifying the pronoun *I.* Ask students what effect the use of present participles rather than verbs in the past tense has on the sentences. Encourage students to recognize that Deal's use of present participles helps the reader share Tom's emotions rather than just observing his actions.

terrible wound. I could see only blood and raw flesh. I snatched off the empty hunting bag I had donned so optimistically, the shell bag, and took off my coat. I wrapped her in the coat and picked her up in my arms. She was very heavy, hurting, whining with each jolting step as I ran toward the house.

I came into the yard doubled over with the catch in my side from the running, and my legs were trembling. My father was sitting on the back porch with three wild turkeys beside him, cleaning his gun. He jumped to his feet when he saw the wounded dog.

"What happened?" he said. "Did some fool hunter shoot her?"

I stopped, standing before my father and holding the wounded dog. I looked into his angry face. They were the most terrible words I had ever had to say. "I shot her, Papa," I said.

My father stood very still. I did not know what would happen. I had never done anything so bad in my whole life, and I could not even guess how my father would react. The only thing justified would be to wipe me off the face of the earth with one <u>irate</u> gesture of his hand.

I gulped, trying to move the pain in my throat out of the way of the words. "I took her out bird hunting," I said. "I wanted to show you—if I got a full bag of birds, I thought you'd let me go on the Christmas Day hunt—"

"I'll talk to you later," my father said grimly, taking the dog from me and starting into the kitchen. "I've got to try to save this dog's life now."

I started into the kitchen behind my father. He turned. "Where's the gun you shot her with?" he said.

"I—left it."

"Don't leave it lying out there in the field," my father said in a stern voice.

I wanted very badly to go into the kitchen, find out that the dog would live. But I turned, instead, and went back the way I had come, walking with my head down, feeling shrunken inside myself. I had overreached. I had risen up today full of pride beyond my ability, and in the stubbornness of the pride, I had been blind until the terrible accident had opened my eyes so that I could see myself clearly—too clearly. I found the gun, the two bags, where I had dropped them. I picked them up without looking at the smear of blood where Calypso had lain. I went back to the house slowly, not wanting to face it, reluctant to see the damage I had wrought.

When I came into the kitchen, my father had the dog stretched out on the kitchen table. My mother stood by his side with bandages and ointment in her hands. The wound was cleaned of the bird shot and dirt and blood. Calypso Baby whined when she saw me, and I felt my heart <u>cringe</u> with the rejection.

My father looked at me across the dog. The anger was gone out of him; his voice was slow and searching and not to be denied. "Now I want to know why you took my gun and my dog without permission," he said.

"David," my mother said to him.

| Words to Know and Use | **irate** (ī rāt′) *adj.* angry |
| | **cringe** (krinj) *v.* to shrink back from something unpleasant |

17
18
◄ F
19

My father ignored her, kept his eyes hard on my face. I knew it wouldn't do any good to look toward my mother. This was between me and my father, and there was no refuge for me anywhere in the world. I didn't want a refuge. I knew I had to face not only my father but myself.

"I—I wanted to go on the Christmas Day hunt," I said again. "I thought if I—" I stopped. It was all that I had to say. It seemed pretty flimsy to me now.

You understand what you've done?

My father looked down at the dog. I was surprised at the lack of anger in him. I could read only sadness in his voice. "She may be ruined for hunting," he said. "Even if the wound heals good, if she doesn't lose the use of her leg, she may be gun-shy for the rest of her life. At best, I'll never be able to show her in field trials again. You understand what you've done?"

"Yes, sir," I said. I wanted to cry. But that would not help, any more than anger from my father would help.

"You see now why I said you weren't old enough?" my father said. "You've got to be trained for hunting, just like a dog is trained. Suppose other men had been out there; suppose you had shot a human being?"

"David!" my mother said.

My father turned angrily toward her. "He's got to learn!" he said. "There's too many people in this world trying to do things without learning how to do them first. I don't want my boy to be one of them."

"Papa," I said. "I'm—I'm sorry. I wouldn't have hurt Calypso Baby for anything in the world."

I'm not going to punish you," my father said. He looked down at the dog. "This is too bad for a whipping to settle. But I want you to think about today. I don't want you to put it out of your mind. You knew that when the time came ripe for it, I intended to teach you, take you out like I'd take a puppy, and hunt with you. After a while, you could hunt by yourself. Then if you were good enough—and only if you were good enough—you could go on the Christmas Day hunt. The Christmas Day hunt is the place you come to, not the place you start out from. Do you understand?"

"Yes, sir," I said. I would have been glad to settle for a whipping. But I knew that a mere dusting of the breeches would be inadequate for my brashness, my overconfidence, for the hurt I had given not only to the fine bird dog but also to my father—and to myself.

"You've got to take special care of Calypso Baby," my father said. "Maybe if you take care of her yourself while she's hurt, she'll decide to be your friend again."

I looked at the dog, and I could feel the need of her confidence and trust. "Yes, sir," I said. Then I said humbly, "I hope she will be friends with me again."

361

20. LITERARY CONCEPT: Characterization

Ask students what not wanting a "refuge" reveals about Tom. *(Possible responses: He is a responsible young man who can face the consequences of his actions; he is too willing to let his father make the rules and to submit to his father's punishment.)*

21. ACTIVE READING: Connect

If you were Tom, how would you feel at this moment in the story? *(Any response is valid.)*

22. ACTIVE READING: Question

What does Tom's father mean when he says that the Christmas Day hunt is "the place you come to, not the place you start out from"? *(Possible response: He means that it is a privilege to participate in the Christmas Day hunt, and a person must earn that privilege.)*

23. ACTIVE READING: Evaluating

Ask students to evaluate the reasoning behind Tom's father's insistence that Tom "take special care of Calypso Baby." Is this the best way to respond to the situation, or would punishing Tom be better? Why? *(Any response is valid.)*

24. ACTIVE READING: Review

Ask students to **infer** the reason why Tom feels better. Encourage them to base their answer on what they know about Tom's hopes for Christmas, his actions with the gun, and his father's failure to punish him. If necessary, help students by reading the following example of a think-aloud, or model one of your own.

Think-Aloud Script I wonder why Tom feels better at this point. He says he feels a loss inside him, yet he feels better too. I remember that at the beginning of the story Tom wants a bicycle for Christmas. I also know from his actions and his words in the scenes after his shooting of Calypso Baby that he feels ashamed and regretful. Although his father and mother have not punished him, I think Tom feels that he needs punishment, so he decides to take responsibility for punishing himself. Doing so allows him to feel better without necessarily filling the loss he feels inside. He has lost the bicycle—but he has done the right thing in his own eyes.

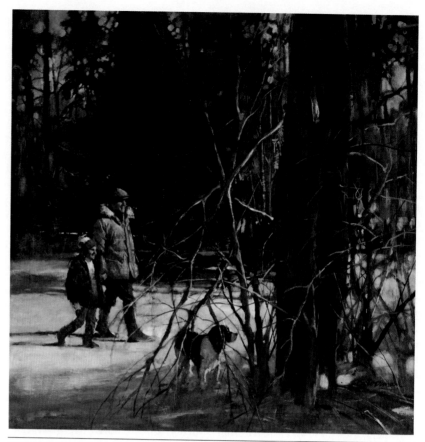

WOODLAND WALK © 1989 Burt Silverman.

I went toward the hall, needing to be alone in my room. I stopped at the kitchen doorway, looking back at my father and mother watching me. I had to say it in a hurry if I was going to say it at all.

"Papa," I said, the words rushing softly in my throat, threatening to gag there before I could get them out. "I—I don't think I deserve that bicycle this Christmas. I don't deserve it at all."

My father nodded his head. "All right, son," he said gravely. "This is your own punishment for yourself."

"Yes," I said, forcing the word, the loss empty inside me, and yet feeling better too. I turned and ran out of the room and up the stairs.

Christmas came, but without any help from me at all. I went to bed on Christmas Eve heavy with the knowledge that tomorrow morning there would be no shiny new bicycle under the tree; there would be no

Christmas Day hunt for me. I couldn't prevent myself from waking up at the usual excited time, but I made myself turn over and go back to sleep. When I did, reluctantly, go downstairs, the Christmas tree did not excite me, nor the usual gifts I received every year: the heavy sweater, the gloves, the scarf, the two new pairs of blue jeans. I just wouldn't let myself think about the bicycle.

After my father had gone outside, my mother hugged me to her in a sudden rush of affection. "He would have given you the bicycle anyway," she said, "if you hadn't told him you didn't want it."

I looked up at her. "I didn't deserve it," I said. "Maybe next year I will."

She surprised me then by holding me and crying. I heard the first car arrive outside, the voices of the men excited with the promise of hunting. My mother stood up and said briskly, "Well, this is not getting that big dinner cooked," and went into the kitchen without looking back.

I went out on the front porch. It was perfect quail-hunting weather, cold but not too cold, with a smoky haze lying over the earth. The dogs knew that today was for hunting. I could hear them from around behind the house, standing on the wire fence in broad-shouldered rows, their voices yelping and calling. All except Calypso Baby. All except me.

I stood aside, watching the men arrive in their cars, my father greeting them. Their breaths hung cloudy in the air, and they moved with a sharp movement to their bodies. These were the best hunters in the whole countryside, and today would be a great comradeship and competition. Any man invited on this hunt could be proud of the invitation alone.

I felt almost remote as I watched, as I went with them around the side of the house to the dogs. They all went to examine Calypso Baby, and I felt a freezing inside; but my father only said, "She got shot by accident," and did not tell the whole terrible story.

Then my father looked at his watch and said, "Let's wait for a few more minutes. Walter ought to be here soon. Hate to start without him."

One of the men called, "Here he comes now," and Walter drove up in his battered car.

"Come here, son," my father said, speaking to me for the first time this morning, and I went reluctantly to his side. I was afraid it was coming now, the whole story, and all the men would look at me in the same way that Calypso Baby had after I had shot her.

My father drew me to the side of Walter's car, reached in, and brought out a basket. "You wanted a bicycle," he said. "Then you decided yourself you should wait. Because you made the decision yourself, I decided you were old enough for this."

I looked at the bird-dog puppy in the basket. All of a sudden Christmas burst inside me like a skyrocket, out of the place where I had kept it suppressed all this time.

"Papa," I said. "Papa—"

"Take him," my father said.

I reached into the basket and took out the puppy. The puppy licked my chin with his harsh, warm tongue. He was long, gangly, his feet and head too big for his body—but absolutely beautiful.

25. ACTIVE READING: Question
Why do you think Tom's mother cries at this moment? (Possible responses: She is sorry about the events that have occurred; she is pleased that Tom is brave and mature enough to make the decision he did; she is moved by her son's growing up so soon.)

26. LITERARY CONCEPT:
Characterization
Ask students to describe how Tom's father's words and actions add to readers' understanding of the father. (Possible responses: Tom's father respects his son for what he has done, and his gift shows both his respect and his kindness; he's making up for his earlier neglect of Tom.)

27. VOCABULARY: Definition
Some students may have difficulty with the word gangly. If necessary, help those students use their **prior knowledge** of puppies and **context clues** to determine that the term means "loosely and awkwardly built." ★

28. ACTIVE READING: Evaluate
Ask students if they think Tom deserves his father's gift, and why or why not. (Possible responses: He deserves the dog because he has shown bravery and integrity by telling the truth and sacrificing something he wanted; he doesn't deserve the dog because he shouldn't be rewarded for simply doing what is right and because he hasn't yet shown he can responsibly care for a dog.)

29. ACTIVE READING: Question
Ask students what they think the "great deal" Tom learns while training Calypso Boy might consist of. Encourage them to consider both practical aspects of hunting and qualities of responsibility. (Any response is valid.)

ENCOURAGING INDEPENDENT READING

National Velvet, novel by Enid Bagnold

Old Yeller, novel by Fred Gipson

The Red Pony, novel by John Steinbeck

Where the Red Fern Grows, novel by Wilson Rawls

28

My father knelt beside me, one hand on the puppy. "I told Walter to bring me the finest bird-dog puppy he could find," he said. "He's kin to Calypso Baby. He's got good blood."

"Thank you, Papa," I said in a choking voice. "I—I'd rather have him than the bicycle. I'll name him Calypso Boy, I'll—"

"When this puppy is ready for birds, we'll train him," my father said. "While we train the puppy, we'll train you too. When the time comes, you can both go on the Christmas Day hunt—if you're good **H** ▶ enough."

"We'll be good enough," I said. "Both of us will be good enough."

"I hope so," my father said. He stood up and looked at the men standing around us, all of them smiling down at me and Calypso Boy. "Let's go," he said. "Those birds are going to get tired of waiting on us."

They laughed and hollered, and the dogs moiled and sounded[5] in the excitement as they were let out of the pen. They fanned out across the pasture, each man or two men taking a dog. I stood watching, holding the puppy warm in my arms. I looked at

Calypso Baby, standing crippled in her pen looking longingly after the hunters. I went over and spoke to her. She whined; then for the first time since the accident, she wagged her tail at me.

I looked down at the puppy in my arms. "We'll be going," I told him, as he licked at my chin. "One of these days, when you're a dog and I'm a man, we'll be right out there with the best of them." ◀ I

It was three years more before I got to go on my first Christmas hunt. Papa had been right, of course. In the time between, I had learned a great deal myself while training **29** Calypso Boy to hunt. With the good blood in him, he turned out to be a great bird dog—second only, I guess, to Calypso Baby, who recovered well from her wound and was Papa's dog the day Calypso Boy and I made our first Christmas hunt.

But of all the Christmases, before and since, I guess I remember best the one when Calypso Baby was hurt—and Calypso Boy first came to me. ❧

---

5. **moiled and sounded:** ran about and howled.

Comprehension Check

1. What does Tom ask his father to allow him to do? (go on the Christmas Day hunt)

2. What does Tom decide to do without telling his father or mother? (He decides to take Calypso Baby quail hunting by himself.)

3. What disaster befalls Tom on his hunt? (He shoots and wounds Calypso Baby.)

4. What does Tom give up to punish himself? (a bicycle)

5. What Christmas present does Tom receive instead? (a new puppy, Calypso Boy)

Responding to Reading

First Impressions

1. What were your feelings at the end of the story? Jot them down in your notebook or journal.

Second Thoughts

2. Do you think Tom should have received a puppy at the end of the story? Explain your opinion.

3. How would you evaluate the way Tom's father treated him?

Think about
- the father's behavior before the accident
- his reaction when he learned Tom had shot Calypso Baby
- his actions on Christmas Day

4. Why is the Christmas Day hunt so important to Tom?

5. How do you think this experience has changed Tom? Base your answer on the story and your own experiences.

Broader Connections

6. Alben, the hero of "Old Sly Eye," and Tom both use guns. How are the two boys different? What might Alben say to Tom?

Literary Concept: Foreshadowing

When writers hint at a future event in a story, they are using a technique called **foreshadowing.** Deal uses foreshadowing in the first two sentences of this story. When Tom says "It should have been the best Christmas of them all. . . . It started out to be, anyway," you get a clue that this Christmas did not turn out the way Tom had expected. Review the story to find two more clues that foreshadow what happened. Then look back at your prediction chart and see if your predictions reflected any of those clues.

THE CHRISTMAS HUNT   365

Literary Concept: Foreshadowing

Possible responses: "The gun was heavy in my hands as I walked into the hallway . . ." (p. 357); "The gun was clumsy in my hands . . ." (p. 357–358); "This was not at all like my dream of last night" (p. 358); "I knew it was my last chance . . ." (p. 359); "It seemed to be perfect. I had plenty of time . . . sure" (p. 359).

Student Response

Responding to Reading

1. Any response is valid.

2. Possible responses: Yes, because he acts maturely when he gives up the bicycle; yes, because having a puppy will teach him responsibility; no, because his wrongdoing is more serious than his sacrifice.

3. Possible responses: Except at the story's beginning, when Tom's father ignores Tom, he treats Tom fairly and generously; if he had paid more attention to Tom in the beginning, the hunting accident might not have happened; he is too easy on Tom after what Tom does.

4. Possible responses: The hunt is an exciting occasion; participating in the hunt symbolizes becoming a man; it is a way of winning his father's respect and a way of getting attention.

5. Possible responses: Tom now understands something about rules and about patience—his father had good reasons for not allowing him to hunt, and Tom's patience will allow him to learn the skills necessary to join in the hunt; it has taught him that telling the truth, acting selflessly, and taking responsibility is the best course for him to pursue.

6. Possible responses: Alben is deft and confident with his weapon, but Tom is unskilled and unsure; Alben thinks of his family, whereas Tom thinks of himself. Alben might encourage Tom to learn to shoot a rifle correctly; he might tell Tom to think of others first; he would approve of Tom's taking responsibility for his wrongdoing.

Challenge Question

Identify the conflicts that Tom faces in this story. (Possible responses: external conflicts with his father and Calypso Baby, internal conflicts about his inability to live up to his dream and about his shooting of the dog)

THE CHRISTMAS HUNT **Teacher's Edition**   **365**

Writing Options

The Writing Options are designed to meet varied student interests and abilities. Have each student choose one writing activity to complete.

Journal Update Invite students to write about what they think it takes to turn a boy into a man or a girl into a woman. Ask if they consider a 13-year-old an adult.

Links to Writer's Craft

Writing Option 4 is an exercise in persuasive writing. For more practice, see *The Writer's Craft,* Grade 7, "Persuasion," pages 139–163.

Vocabulary Practice

Answers to Exercise

1. b	6. c
2. d	7. d
3. c	8. d
4. b	9. a
5. a	10. d

For Alternative Learning Styles
Encourage students to use their voices and bodies to act out the words *brashness, clamor, cringe, heft, irate,* and *stricken.*

Closure

Ask students if they think any characters besides Tom face a test of conscience in this story. Ask them to think of other characters they have read about this year who face a test of conscience. Direct their thoughts to characters in Unit 2.

Writing Options

1. Did you ever do something that bothered your conscience? Write about a **personal experience** that might be compared to Tom's. Include your feelings at the time and the outcome of your actions.

2. Imagine that you are a psychologist analyzing Tom's hunting dream. Write a **summary** of the dream, describe what it shows about Tom, and indicate why it's in the story.

3. Tom's father says, "The Christmas Day hunt is the place you come to, not the place you start out from." Write an **explanation** of what he means.

4. Look at the journal entry you wrote about hunting. Use these notes, as well as what you learned from the story, to write a **persuasive essay** arguing for or against hunting.

Vocabulary Practice

Exercise On your paper write the letter of the word or phrase that best completes the sentences below.

1. If Tom heard a **clamor,** the noise would be (a) musical (b) loud (c) soothing (d) soft.

2. If Tom's father had been **irate,** he might have (a) praised (b) laughed at (c) cried with (d) shouted at Tom.

3. Since Tom was **stricken** by his father's refusal, he looked (a) excited (b) eager (c) dejected (d) confident.

4. When Tom used **mimicry** in his talk with his father, he was (a) questioning (b) imitating (c) yelling (d) explaining.

5. If the men were to **heft** the bag, they could determine its (a) weight (b) odor (c) age (d) color.

6. If quail are in a **refuge,** they are probably (a) dead (b) frightened (c) safe (d) exposed.

7. If Tom has learned a lesson about **brashness,** he will avoid (a) fear (b) cowardliness (c) anticipation (d) recklessness.

8. If Tom's punishment was **inadequate,** it was (a) just right (b) too quick (c) appropriate (d) not sufficient.

9. To persuade his father, Tom developed a **tactic,** or (a) strategy (b) question (c) gift (d) game.

10. Calypso Baby's rejection of Tom made Tom **cringe,** or (a) cry (b) fight (c) reach out (d) draw back.

> **Words to Know and Use**
>
> brashness
> clamor
> cringe
> heft
> inadequate
> irate
> mimicry
> refuge
> stricken
> tactic

The Spelling Connection

Spelling Pattern: The Prefix *ex* The prefix *ex* remains *ex* before a root that begins with a vowel or with **p, t,** or **c.** However, **ex** changes to **ef** before roots that begin with **f** and changes to **e** before most other consonants.
Examples: **ex** + terior = **ex**terior
ex + levate = **e**levate
The Prefix *ex* in Words from the Selection
ex**cited**   ex**plosive**   ex**amine**
ex**cept**   **ef**fective

Other Words with the Prefix *ex*
ex**cuse**   ex**tremely**   **ef**fort
ex**pert**   ex**tinct**   **e**volve
Exercise Fill in the blanks with spelling words.
A guide dog needs __ instruction before it can help a blind person. A dog must learn to be calm and not get __ while walking along and crossing busy streets. It takes a great deal of __ to make a dog __. A dog is trained to obey commands __ when they would lead to danger.

*O*ptions for Learning (Multimodal/Cross-Curricular Activities)

1 • Fifty Lashes? Whether you agree or disagree with the way Tom's father handled him, what punishment might he have used? Discuss the father's actions with your parents, counselor, or classmates. Then describe another way he could have dealt with the situation.

2 • History's Canine Hunters Dogs have helped humans hunt for many centuries. Research the history of hunting dogs in books about dogs and in encyclopedias. Give an oral presentation with visual aids.

3 • Feelings in Art Think about the setting, sounds, and colors, as well as Tom's feelings, when he shoots Calypso Baby. Then choose an art form to express his feelings. Share your art with your classmates.

4 • Nobody Heard Mother Tom's mother twice started to say something while Tom's father spoke to Tom about the shooting, but she never finished her sentences. With another student, role-play the conversation that might have occurred between Tom's parents after Tom left the kitchen.

 FACT FINDER SCIENCE
How large are most adult quail?

*B*orden Deal
1922–1985

Borden Deal once said that his characters "live and work in real time in real places." Much of his work is set in the South, which Deal knew well. Born in Pontotoc, Mississippi, Deal worked on his father's cotton farm during the Great Depression. After graduating from the University of Alabama, he wrote advertisements before beginning his own full-time writing career.

Deal's novels and short stories have been translated into more than twenty languages and adapted for the stage, movies, radio, and television. More than one hundred of Deal's stories, poems, and reviews have been published in magazines. Several stories were included in *Best American Short Stories, Best Detective Stories of the Year*, and *The Wonderful World of Dogs*.

THE CHRISTMAS HUNT   367

Cross-Curricular Projects

Social Studies Interested students may research hunting traditions and restrictions in various societies. Their reports might contain information on animals ranging from pheasants in the United States to elephants in eastern Africa.

Science Suggest that students prepare a report on various breeds of dogs and their characteristics. Encourage students to include appropriate illustrations.

Art Have volunteers collect pictures of hunting scenes. Encourage them to discuss the different attitudes toward hunting displayed by various artists.

Music Tom's feelings change a great deal during the course of the story. Encourage students to select musical recordings that express his varying emotions.

EXPLORE

Objectives

- To understand and analyze two poems
- To examine the use of imagery
- To enrich reading by making comparisons
- To express understanding of the poems through a choice of writing forms, including an essay and a poem

Prereading/Motivation

Examine What You Know

Discussion Prompts What situations make you feel compassionate toward others? Is there a difference between compassion and pity? Explain.

Expand Your Knowledge

Additional Background Both Po Chü-i and Emily Dickinson lived during periods of great poetic activity. Po lived and wrote during the Tang Dynasty (618–907)—a period of extraordinary cultural, scientific, and political energy in China, during which poetry flourished. Emily Dickinson belonged to a generation of writers—many of them New Englanders like herself—who came to dominate the U.S. literary scene in the 1800s. Poe, Melville, Hawthorne, Emerson, and Thoreau emerged during this rich period in U.S. culture.

Thematic Link— Tests of Conscience

In each of these poems, the conscience of the speaker demands that action be taken to relieve suffering people. Dickinson's speaker in "If I Can Stop One Heart from Breaking" may pass the test, but the speaker in Po Chü-i's "Bitter Cold, Living in the Village" is stricken by guilt for not acting as his conscience demands.

Poetry

If I Can Stop One Heart from Breaking

EMILY DICKINSON

Bitter Cold, Living in the Village

PO CHÜ-I (bō' chü' ē')

Examine What You Know   (Prior Knowledge)

Compassion means both a feeling of sorrow for the suffering of others and the urge to help them. You probably know people who are very sensitive to the suffering of others—you may be such a person yourself. Do you think most people feel compassion, or do most not care about others? Can people switch their feelings of compassion on and off? Do enough people act on their compassion to help relieve the suffering of others? Discuss your ideas with a small group of students. Then compare your group's conclusions with the speakers' feelings in these poems.

Expand Your Knowledge   (Building Background)

Eleven hundred years and twelve thousand miles separated Po Chü-i and Emily Dickinson. Po lived in China from 772 to 846. Dickinson lived in Massachusetts during the mid-1800s. Their personalities were as different as the times they lived in. Po was a popular and sought-after officer of the imperial court, a man who worked in large cities and traveled widely. Dickinson was a shy girl from a small town, who after a failed romance retired to her father's home and lived there for the rest of her life. Yet both wrote about the same universal ideas that have fascinated poets over the centuries and across cultures: love, grief, compassion, and death.

Write Before You Read   (Journal Writing)

In your journal, write about a person or persons for whom you have felt compassion. What caused your feelings? Did you help the person?

■ *Author biographies on Extend page*

368   UNIT FOUR   TESTS OF CONSCIENCE

MORE JOURNAL WRITING IDEAS

■ Have you ever felt that you needed someone else's compassion? What were the circumstances?

■ Have you ever been angered by people who did not show compassion? Write about the incident.

COLLABORATIVE LEARNING OPTIONS

Opportunities for collaborative learning include Options for Learning 1 and 2 (p. 372) and Cross-Curricular Projects (p. 372).

ADDITIONAL RESOURCES

Unit Four Resource Book
Reader's Guidesheet, p. 9
Reading Skills, p. 10
Literature Skills, p. 11
Vocabulary Connections, p. 12
Spelling Connections, p. 13
Comprehension Check Test, p. 14
Selection Test, p. 15

If I Can Stop One Heart from Breaking

EMILY DICKINSON

> If I can stop one Heart from breaking
> I shall not live in vain
> 1 | If I can ease one Life the Aching
> A ▶ | Or cool one Pain
>
> 5 | Or help one fainting Robin
> 2 | Unto his Nest again
> B ▶ | I shall not live in Vain.

Responding to Reading

First Impressions of "If I Can Stop One Heart from Breaking"

1. What is your reaction to the speaker in this poem? Explain your answer.

Second Thoughts on "If I Can Stop One Heart from Breaking"

2. Why do you think the speaker says it is enough to help only one heart or one robin?

3. What effect does Dickinson's unusual capitalization have on the poem?

Guided Reading for Less-Proficient Students

These questions can help guide students through the reading. Ask each question at the point of the selection where the capital letter and arrow appear in the margin. In addition, you may wish to use appropriate Active Reading annotations.

A. What does the speaker think one should do in life? *(help those who are suffering)* Recalling

B. What does the speaker mean by "I shall not live in Vain"? *(that his or her life will be worthwhile)* Clarifying

C. Why are the villagers in need? *(They are cold and hungry, and a heavy snow has fallen.)* Recalling

D. What does the speaker do when the winter is harsh? *(He shuts his gate tightly and covers himself with fur, wool, and silk.)* Summarizing

---

Teaching Strategies

VOCABULARY PREVIEW

The focus of vocabulary study for these selections is context clues. See *Unit Four Resource Book*, Vocabulary Connections, p. 12.

LIMITED ENGLISH PROFICIENCY

■ Use Reader's Guidesheet, *Unit Four Resource Book*, page 9.

★ The text annotation marked with a red star (4) may be particularly helpful for students with limited English proficiency.

TEXT ANNOTATIONS

1. LITERARY CONCEPT: Style
Have students describe the effect of the simple words, short lines, and easy rhymes. *(Possible response: The speaker's thoughts come across to the reader clearly and simply, as in everyday speech.)*

2. ACTIVE READING: Review
Ask students if they think the speaker looks for birds to help or if the robin might stand for something else. *(Possible responses: The robin is a symbol of any person or creature in need; the assumption is that a person who will help such a small creature will help anyone.)*

Responding to Reading

1. Any response is valid.

2. **Possible responses:** The speaker believes that instead of focusing on many, he or she would do better to focus on helping just one person or creature at a time; the speaker feels that the important thing is how well, not how often, he or she can help; the speaker feels discouraged or depressed and is hoping to do at least one good thing in his or her life.

3. **Possible responses:** Because the reader pauses at the capitalized words, they are felt to be more important; capital letters make words seem more grand, noble, or beautiful.

Bitter Cold, Living in the Village

PO CHÜ-I

3 In the twelfth month of this Eighth Year,
On the fifth day, a heavy snow fell.
Bamboos and cypress all perished from the freeze.
How much worse for people without warm clothes!

5 As I looked around the village,
Of ten families, eight or nine were in need.
The north wind was sharper than the sword,
And homespun cloth could hardly cover one's body.
4 Only brambles were burnt for firewood,
C ▶ 10 And sadly people sat at night to wait for dawn.

From this I know that when winter is harsh,
The farmers suffer most.
Looking at myself, during these days—
How I'd shut tight the gate of my thatched hall,
15 Cover myself with fur, wool, and silk,
D ▶ Sitting or lying down, I had ample warmth.
I was lucky to be spared cold or hunger,
Neither did I have to labor in the field.

5 Thinking of that, how can I not feel ashamed?
20 I ask myself what kind of man am I.

HERDSMEN IN SNOW STORM   Zeng Shanqing
Courtesy, The Chinese Cultural Institute, San Francisco.

Comprehension Check

✓ 1. In Dickinson's poem, does the speaker express a desire to help all suffering people? *(No, the speaker says that it would be enough to help just one.)*

2. What living things does Dickinson's speaker wish to help? *(people who hurt, a robin)*

3. What causes all the hardships in Po Chü-i's poem? *(a snowstorm, poverty)*

4. Why isn't the speaker suffering the same hardships? *(He has plenty of clothing and a warm house.)*

5. Why is the speaker critical of himself? *(He is well-off, but he hasn't helped his needy neighbors.)*

*R*esponding to Reading

First Impressions of "Bitter Cold, Living in the Village"

1. What might you say to the speaker if you met him? Jot down your thoughts on a sheet of paper.

Second Thoughts on "Bitter Cold, Living in the Village"

2. In your opinion, should the speaker feel ashamed? Why or why not?

3. Which image showing the contrast between the speaker and the villagers is the most memorable?

4. Do you think the speaker's twinge of conscience has changed him permanently? Explain your answer, using your earlier discussion about compassion, as well as evidence from the poem.

Comparing the Poems

5. Do you think one speaker is more or less compassionate than the other one? Explain.

6. If only one of these poems about compassion could be in this text, which one would you choose? Why?

Broader Connections

7. Dickinson focuses her compassion on individuals; Po focuses his compassion on a group. Do you think it is more useful to help an individual, or is it more efficient to work with a group or organization that helps many people?

*W*riting Options

1. Imagine that you need help. Which speaker would you ask? Write a short **essay** explaining your choice.

2. Write a **poem** about feeling compassion for other people. You might use the example you wrote about in Write Before You Read to express your ideas about compassion. Before writing, consider whether a poem with rhyme and rhythm or a poem with free verse will best suit your ideas.

Student Response

Responding to Reading

1. Any response is valid.

2. **Possible responses:** The speaker should feel ashamed because he hasn't even tried to help his neighbors; the speaker shouldn't feel ashamed about being comfortable but should find a way to share his good fortune; the speaker has nothing to be ashamed of, since he can't help a whole village.

3. Any response is valid.

4. **Possible responses:** The speaker has not been changed permanently, since in the poem he asks himself a question but does not answer it or say how he will change; the speaker's close attention to what happens around him and his pained tone in the last two lines show that he has been changed for good.

5. Any response is valid.

6. Any response is valid. Encourage students to compare and contrast the poems when giving their reasons.

7. Any response is valid. Encourage students to give examples.

Writing Options

The Writing Options are designed to meet varied student interests and abilities. Have each student choose one writing activity to complete.

Journal Update Have students review their journal entries for the poems and add to them by creating images and comparisons that show the effects of weather on people.

Closure

Ask students to consider how the test of conscience of a speaker from a far-off time and place relates to our world today. Lead a class discussion focused on the question, Are people whose basic needs have been met obliged to help those who lack food, warmth, and shelter?

Extending the Lesson

Options for Learning

These activities suit a variety of learning styles and modes of expression.

Collaborative Learning Activities
See Options 1 and 2.

1. **How People Help** Students may be able to find information on nationwide or worldwide charities in an almanac or a recent encyclopedia. Phone directories may help students identify local charities.

2. **Poetry Festival** Poems by Dickinson are included in many anthologies, as well as in collections of her work. Some of Po Chü-i's works may be found in anthologies of Chinese literature.

Emily Dickinson

■ **More About the Author** In Amherst, people called Emily Dickinson "The Myth" because no one ever saw her. In fact, the last time she left her home was in 1864—twenty-two years before her death. Eventually, she almost never left her upstairs room, though she sent beautiful notes, and sometimes poems, to family and friends. She took to wearing only white clothing and is said to have given sweets and cookies to neighborhood children by lowering them from her window in a basket.

Po Chü-i

■ **More About the Author** To understand Po's wish that even peasant women be able to enjoy his poetry, one must know that in his era few such women were taught to read. Thus, he meant that he wanted his work to be clear enough to be understood and remembered by anyone who heard it. Po Chü-i's poetry is still widely read. His most famous works are the poems "The Song of Everlasting Regret" and "The Lute Song."

Options for Learning (Multimodal/Cross-Curricular Activities)

1 • How People Help Research charities that help the unfortunate. Find out the total amount of money that is donated each year to charities. How much time is volunteered? What charities operate in your town? Share your discoveries with the class in an oral report.

2 • Poetry Festival At the library or bookstore, locate more poetry by Emily Dickinson, Po Chü-i, or your favorite poet. In a class poetry reading, read your favorite poem. You might choose appropriate music to accompany your reading.

Emily Dickinson 1830–1886

Emily Dickinson was born in Amherst, Massachusetts, the daughter of a U.S. Congressman. After a happy childhood, she attended college for a year. Back home in Amherst, she filled her days with domestic chores, while at night she wrote poems about nature, life, and death. After a failed love affair, she lived a solitary life, visiting only close friends and relatives, and frequently writing love poetry.

Whenever Dickinson completed a poem, she sewed it into a small booklet and put it in her bottom bureau drawer. Though she sometimes shared a poem with her family or close friends, no one knew until her death that 1,755 poems were hidden in her room. In 1955, sixty-nine years after her death, all of her poems were published in one volume. Unknown during her lifetime, Emily Dickinson is now famous worldwide.

Po Chü-i 772–846

Po Chü-i was China's earliest popular poet. He wrote more than 2,800 poems, some of which were copied on inn and monastery walls by those who appreciated his work. Po Chü-i took his craft and his audience seriously; it is said that he continually revised and simplified his poems until even an unschooled peasant woman could enjoy them.

Although Po is now most famous for his long narrative poetry, he had hoped to be remembered for a group of fifty poems about social evils.

Writing poetry was only part of Po's life. He passed the imperial government's civil service exam when he was only eighteen, and he held many important posts in his career as a loyal and responsible servant of the Emperor.

372   UNIT FOUR   TESTS OF CONSCIENCE

Cross-Curricular Projects

Geography Have volunteers prepare a report on the climate of China, dealing with all parts of that large and various country. Tell them to include data on temperature, precipitation, and other climatic features. Urge them to use graphic aids to present their findings.

Art Invite interested students to prepare paintings or other artworks to illustrate either poem. Students might focus on a single image from a poem or present a broader vision of its subject.

Science Assign partners to research and present a report on the health hazards of freezing temperatures and the conditions that cause frostbite and hypothermia. Suggest that they explain and demonstrate ways to guard against cold-weather hazards, as well as first aid to use in an emergency.

Social Studies Ask interested students to study current affairs and, on a map of the world and a separate map of the United States, indicate the areas in which people are most needy.

Nonfiction

America the Not-so-Beautiful

ANDREW A. ROONEY

Examine What You Know (Prior Knowledge)

What have you thrown away in the last twenty-four hours—cereal boxes, paper napkins, plastic yogurt cups, pop cans, lunch bags, shampoo bottles, school papers, ballpoint pens? Make a list. Combine your list with those of your classmates to get a class total. What does the class trash-o-meter tell you?

Expand Your Knowledge (Building Background)

Every day, people in the United States throw out 438,000 tons of garbage, which would fill 63,000 trucks. Of this amount, 150,000 tons consists of packaging material, 43,000 tons is food, and the remainder consists of every other imaginable waste. Yearly, we throw away 350 million plastic cigarette lighters, 1½ billion ballpoint pens, 200 million tires, 13 million tons of newspaper, and 34 million Christmas trees.

Where does our trash go? Most of it goes into landfills, which are filling up as waste increases. The world's largest landfill, Fresh Kills, on New York's Staten Island, is the size of 16,000 baseball diamonds. It is so large that astronauts reported seeing only two man-made objects from space with their naked eyes: the Great Wall of China and the Fresh Kills dump.

Enrich Your Reading (Reading Skill)

Fact and Opinion Writers use facts and opinions to persuade readers to accept their point of view. A **fact** is a statement that can be proved to be true, such as "The Fresh Kills landfill in New York is the world's largest landfill." You can check an almanac or a book of statistics to prove or disprove this statement. In contrast, an **opinion** is a person's belief and cannot be proved. "Most New Yorkers don't care enough about the environment" is an opinion. There are no statistics to prove this statement. As you read this essay, decide which statements are facts and which are opinions.

■ *Author biography in Reader's Handbook*

AMERICA THE NOT-SO-BEAUTIFUL 373

Objectives

■ To understand and analyze an essay

■ To examine persuasive writing techniques

■ To enrich reading by distinguishing between fact and opinion

■ To express understanding of the essay through a choice of writing forms, including an analysis and a letter

Prereading/Motivation

Examine What You Know

Suggest that students look at the contents of the wastebasket in their classroom, the trash cans in the cafeteria, the wastebaskets and garbage cans at their homes, and any recycling bins they have at home or at school. Some might want to do a trash inventory of their own family for a week.

Expand Your Knowledge

Additional Background The first significant U.S. antipollution legislation was enacted in 1899, but few efforts to combat pollution were made for more than half a century. In the 1960s, books like Rachel Carson's *Silent Spring* raised public awareness of the dangers of pesticides. In the 1970s, events such as Earth Day showed that pollution had become a truly national concern.

Enrich Your Reading

Remind students that words like "I think" and "I believe" signal opinions. Some opinions are harder to identify because they are stated as facts; they frequently involve generalizations such as "Everybody knows that . . ." Point out that the statements in Expand Your Knowledge are facts; the statistics can be checked.

JOURNAL WRITING IDEAS

■ What steps can we take to reduce the amount of material we throw away each day?

■ Have you ever visited a dump or an incinerator? What sensory details would you use to describe the setting and atmosphere of the place?

COLLABORATIVE LEARNING OPTIONS

Opportunities for collaborative learning include Examine What You Know and the Literary Concept (p. 376).

ADDITIONAL RESOURCES

Unit Four Resource Book
Reader's Guidesheet, p. 16
Reading Skills, p. 17
Literature Skills, p. 18
Vocabulary Connections, p. 19
Spelling Connections, p. 20
Comprehension Check Test, p. 21
Selection Test, p. 22

Thematic Link—
Tests of Conscience

Andy Rooney shows us that tests of conscience are not always dramatic; people may face such tests every day in small ways. He challenges readers to examine their consciences for reactions to the world's trash crisis.

America the Not-so-Beautiful

ANDREW A. ROONEY

Next to saving stuff I don't need, the thing I like to do best is throw it away. My idea of a good time is to load up the back of the car with junk on a Saturday morning and take it to the dump. There's something satisfying about discarding almost anything.

Throwing things out is the American way. We don't know how to fix anything, and anyone who does know how is too busy to come, so we throw it away and buy a new one. Our economy depends on us doing that. The trouble with throwing things away is, there is no "away" left.

Sometime around the year 500 B.C., the Greeks in Athens passed a law prohibiting people from throwing their garbage in the street. This Greek law was the first recognition by civilized people that throwing things away was a problem. Now, as the population explodes and people take up more room on Earth, there's less room for everything else.

The more civilized a country is, the worse the trash problem is. Poor countries don't have the same problem because they don't have much to discard. Prosperity in the United States is based on using things up as fast as we can, throwing away what's left, and buying new ones.

We've been doing that for so many years that (1) we've run out of places to throw things because houses have been built where the dump was and (2) some of the things we're throwing away are poisoning the Earth and will eventually poison all of us and all living things.

Ten years ago most people thought nothing of dumping an old bottle of weed or insect killer in a pile of dirt in the back yard or down the drain in the street, just to get rid of it. The big companies in America had the same feeling, on a bigger scale. For years the chemical companies dumped their poisonous wastes in the rivers behind the mills, or they put it in fifty-gallon drums in the vacant lots, with all the old, rusting machinery in it, up behind the plants. The drums rusted out in ten years and dumped their poison into the ground. It rained, the poisons seeped into the underground streams and poisoned everything for miles around. Some of the manufacturers who did this weren't even evil. They were dumb and irresponsible. Others were evil because they knew how dangerous it was but didn't want to spend the money to do it right.

The problem is staggering. I often think of it when I go in a hardware store or a Sears, Roebuck and see shelves full of poison. You know that, one way or another, it's all going to end up in the Earth or in our rivers and lakes.

4 I have two pint bottles of insecticide with 5 percent DDT in them in my own garage that I don't know what to do with. I bought them years ago when I didn't realize how bad they were. Now I'm stuck with them.

5 The people of the city of New York throw away nine times their weight in garbage and junk every year. Assuming other cities come close to that, how long will it be before we trash the whole Earth?

Of all household waste, 30 percent of the weight and 50 percent of the volume is the packaging that stuff comes in.

Not only that, but Americans spend more for the packaging of food than all our farmers together make in income growing it. That's some statistic.

Trash collectors are a lot more independent than they used to be because we've got more trash than they've got places to put it. They have their own schedules and their own holidays. Some cities try to get in good with their trash collectors or garbage men by calling them "sanitation engineers." Anything just so long as they pick it up and take it away.

We often call the dump "the landfill" now, too. I never understood why land has to be filled, but that's what it's called. If you're a little valley just outside town, you have to be careful or first thing you know you'll be getting "filled."

If 5 billion people had been living on Earth for the past thousand years as they have been in the past year, the planet would be nothing but one giant landfill, and we'd have turned America the beautiful into one huge landfill.

6 The best solution may be for all of us to pack up, board a spaceship, and move out. If Mars is habitable, everyone on Earth can abandon this planet we've trashed, move to Mars, and start trashing that. It'll buy us some time. ✤

◀ C

---

4. ACTIVE READING: Question
Ask students what they think Rooney should do with his bottles of insecticide. *(Possible response: He might phone an Environmental Protection Agency office to find out where he could take them for proper disposal.)*

5. LITERARY CONCEPT: Persuasion
Elicit from students that these paragraphs contain facts rather than opinions. Encourage students to discuss how this information influences their thinking about the trash problem.

For Alternative Learning Styles Help students understand these facts by showing them unopened packages of such products as deodorants, potato chips, and toys, then discussing how much of the weight and volume is actual product and how much is packaging.

6. LITERARY CONCEPT: Humor
Point out to students that some authors cloak serious ideas in humor. Ask what is absurd in this paragraph and what serious idea Rooney is trying to convey. *(Possible responses: The idea of all of us going to Mars is absurd; the serious idea is that we are making the earth a mess by producing so much trash.)*

ENCOURAGING INDEPENDENT READING

A Few Minutes with Andy Rooney, nonfiction by Andy Rooney

Pieces of My Mind, nonfiction by Andy Rooney

The Silent Spring, nonfiction by Rachel Carson

Comprehension Check

1. Besides saving stuff, what does Rooney like to do? *(throw stuff away)*

2. In what way have large manufacturers contributed to the nation's waste problem? *(They have discarded poisonous waste materials irresponsibly.)*

3. What do Americans spend more money on—food or the packaging it comes in? *(the packaging)*

4. Where does Rooney suggest people move? *(Mars)*

Student Response

Responding to Reading

1. Any response is valid.

2. **Possible responses:** toxic waste, because it poisons land and water for so many years; the landfill problem, because we can't live safely on top of our own garbage

3. **Possible responses:** People who can buy a lot of new things are seen as successful; our economy won't grow unless people buy more and more things; companies make money by selling new things to people.

4. **Possible responses:** worse, since there are now new warnings about toxic waste, the ozone layer, and acid rain; better, since more people, both in the United States and around the world, are concerned about environmental problems; the same, since even though the situation may have improved in some places, it has probably gotten worse in others.

Literary Concept: Persuasive Writing

Example of fact: "Of all household waste, 30 percent of the weight and 50 percent of the volume is the packaging that stuff comes in"; example of opinion: "Some of the manufacturers who did this weren't even evil. They were dumb and irresponsible"; example of exaggeration: "We don't know how to fix anything, and anyone who does know how is too busy to come"; personal example: "My idea of a good time is to load up the back of the car with junk on a Saturday morning and take it to the dump."

Writing Options

The Writing Options are designed to meet varied student interests and abilities. Have each student choose one writing activity to complete.

Journal Update Have students write statements of fact and opinion, exaggerations, and personal examples dealing with the environment where they live.

Responding to Reading

First Impressions

1. What feelings does Rooney's article trigger in you? Describe them briefly in your journal.

Second Thoughts

2. In your opinion, which of the problems Rooney discusses is the most serious? Why?

3. Rooney says, "Prosperity in the United States is based on using things up as fast as we can, throwing away what's left, and buying new ones." Explain what he means by this and give your opinion.

4. Rooney's article was published in 1989. Based on your observations, is our trash crisis now better, the same, or worse than he reports?

Literary Concept: Persuasive Writing

In a persuasive essay such as "America the Not-so-Beautiful," writers use **facts** and **opinions** to convince readers to accept their viewpoint. Another persuasive writing technique is **exaggeration,** or making an extreme statement that startles the reader. For example, Rooney suggests that a solution to Earth's trash problem is to "move to Mars and start trashing that." A third technique is the use of **personal examples.** These make the issue real, as in Rooney's anecdote about the insecticide in his garage. Work with a partner to find other examples of these persuasive techniques in the article.

Writing Options

1. Review the list you created earlier of "thrown-away" articles. How many of the articles could have been reused or recycled? Could you have used permanent articles such as glasses instead of disposable ones such as paper cups? Write an **analysis** of your trash habits.

2. With his article, Rooney is trying to awaken the conscience of the nation, and he blames companies as well as individuals. Think of one group that you blame for the trash problem. Write a **letter** to that group with a specific suggestion that will help solve the problem.

376   UNIT FOUR   TESTS OF CONSCIENCE

Closure

Point out to students that a single person like Andy Rooney can make a difference by persuading people to face up to a test of conscience. Urge students to think about other ways in which an author can nudge the conscience of a reader.

Objectives

- To understand and analyze a memoir

- To examine the use of description and to review the concept of external conflict

- To enrich reading by understanding a historical setting

- To express understanding of the selection through a choice of writing forms, including a comparison, a guidebook, a sermon, and an advertisement

Nonfiction

from *The Endless Steppe*
Growing Up in Siberia

ESTHER RUDOMIN HAUTZIG

Examine What You Know (Prior Knowledge)

In many places around the world, people are being forced out of their homelands for political or economic reasons. Imagine what it would be like to suddenly be sent against your will to somewhere far away. How would you cope with the shock and the adjustments you would have to make to a totally unfamiliar location? In your journal or notebook, describe the kinds of feelings you think you might have in such a situation.

Expand Your Knowledge (Building Background)

In 1941, the family in this selection was sent from their home in Poland to Siberia, 2,500 miles away. Banishing criminals and political prisoners, such as this family, to the harsh, barren plains, or steppes, of Siberia was a common practice of the Russian government from the time of the czars. The vast, empty landscape and the long, brutal winters made Siberia the perfect natural prison. There was no way to escape and nowhere to escape to. In the 1930s and 1940s during Josef Stalin's leadership, ten million Soviet peasants, in addition to millions of others who opposed Soviet government policies, were sent to Siberia and forced to do manual labor. Many never returned.

Enrich Your Reading (Reading Skill)

Historical Setting You know that the setting is the time and place in which the action happens. In nonfiction pieces set in the past, however, the setting includes more than just a physical description of the location. It also involves the customs and beliefs of the times. As you read, notice how the physical setting, as well as the values and customs, influences the people in the selection.

■ *Author biography on Extend page*

THE ENDLESS STEPPE 377

Prereading/Motivation

Examine What You Know

Discussion Prompts Did you ever have to change schools or move to a new neighborhood? How did you feel? Suppose you were forced to move to a different country. How might you feel?

Expand Your Knowledge

Additional Background Much of Siberia is covered with ice and snow six months of the year. Temperatures in some places drop as low as -90 degrees Fahrenheit. These conditions, plus Siberia's size—greater than that of the United States—explain why the Russian government used it as a prison and why the name *Siberia* has come to symbolize remote exile.

Enrich Your Reading

For Alternative Learning Styles To illustrate the historical setting of this memoir, bring in pictures showing Eastern European life in the 1940s or earlier and have students pick out details that are not seen in the United States today—clothes, hairstyles, modes of transportation, and so on.

JOURNAL WRITING IDEAS

■ What might you find in a book about growing up in your region? Jot down your ideas.

■ A steppe is a harsh, treeless plain. What feelings does the phrase "endless steppe" give you?

COLLABORATIVE LEARNING OPTIONS

Opportunities for collaborative learning include Multicultural Connections (p. 382), Options for Learning 1, 2, and 3 (p. 387), and Cross-Curricular Projects (p. 387).

ADDITIONAL RESOURCES

Unit Four Resource Book
Reader's Guidesheet, p. 23
Reading Skills, p. 24
Literature Skills, p. 25
Vocabulary Connections, p. 26
Spelling Connections, p. 27
Comprehension and Vocabulary Check Tests, p. 28
Selection Test, pp. 29–30

Technology and Enrichment
Audiocassette Tape 2, Side 1

Thematic Link— Tests of Conscience

The narrator and her family face a test of conscience when they have to share their home with a beggar who is reputed to be a thief. They meet the test by treating the man with courtesy and respect. This treatment gives him dignity and makes him rise beyond their expectations.

VOCABULARY PREVIEW

These vocabulary words are defined at the bottom of the selection pages on which they appear.

acquisition the act of getting something

allot to give out as a share

archive a storehouse for records

dexterously skillfully

etiquette good manners

morbidly in a gloomy, depressed way

pilfering stealing

preoccupation a state of being engrossed

superfluous unnecessary; excess

transformation a change

LIMITED ENGLISH PROFICIENCY

■ Use Reader's Guidesheet, *Unit Four Resource Book,* page 23.

■ Many sentences in this selection are long and present challenging syntax. Help students identify the simple subjects and the verbs in long sentences.

★ Text annotations marked with a red star (2, 3, 11, 15) may be particularly helpful for students with limited English proficiency.

TEXT ANNOTATIONS

1. LITERARY CONCEPT: Imagery
Discuss why the author uses the word *thin* to describe the Siberian spring. Have students brainstorm images and ideas that the word brings to their minds. *(Possible responses: Thin might mean "not very warm or bright"; it might refer to gray and rainy days or to a cold wind.)*

2. LITERARY CONCEPT: Figurative Language
Point out that the author creates a vivid picture of the Siberian mud by using a simile and a metaphor. Ask students to identify each. *(metaphor: "the steppe became an ocean of mud"; simile: "like walking through knee-deep molasses")* ★

3. VOCABULARY: Definition
If necessary, explain that a derrick is a kind of crane used for lifting and moving heavy objects. ★

from # The Endless Steppe

Growing Up in Siberia

ESTHER RUDOMIN HAUTZIG

1   The spring came, the rather thin spring of the Siberian steppe.

2   But it is impossible to have any thoughts of the thin Siberian spring without first recalling the thick mud. What with the spring rains and the thaw, the steppe became an ocean of mud, and to walk through it was like walking through knee-deep molasses. If one was not lucky enough to own a pair of *sapogy,* the handsome knee-high leather boots that the well-to-do wore, if one had nothing but the same old pair of school oxfords, or even *pimy* boots, along with the energy needed to pull a foot up from the bottom of this mud, one also more often than not had to stop to hunt for the shoe left behind. Whatever one wore, the object developed a crust of mud that had to be broken off after each excursion. While I may have found some of this fun, my mother did not; her trips to and from the bakery in the mud required more energy than she had. She said that time and again, exhausted, she would stand still, with both legs buried in the mud, thinking that only a derrick would be able to hoist her out.

3   Mud or no mud, Siberia notwithstanding, with the spring I was happy. I had a friend to whisper and gossip with; I played tag and hopscotch—which a less muddy patch in the schoolyard permitted—and along with the other girls, I watched the boys' preoccupation with their pigeons. Raising pigeons was one of their favorite pastimes, and luring the birds away from each other apparently its major objective.

Svetlana and I studied together and complemented[1] each other: she helped me with my Russian grammar and spelling, and I helped her with ideas for themes. Although I always enjoyed school, going to school in Siberia became for me a daily trip to paradise. The return trip to the hut was not. The last day of school for me was a sad day.

As soon as school was over, we began to work on our potato crop for the coming winter.

The government had allotted individual plots of land on the outskirts of the village, and one bought tiny potatoes to sow, with the expectation that they would produce a new crop.

This was not a foregone conclusion[2] with

---

1. **complemented:** worked together to make a complete whole
2. **foregone conclusion:** something sure to occur

Words to Know and Use	**preoccupation** (prē äk′ yŏŏ pā′ shən) *n.* a state of being wrapped up or engrossed in something	
	allot (ə lät′) *v.* to give out as a share or portion	

378

Continued on page 379

that unyielding earth. Very early in the morning, we would go out with shovels and sacks of potatoes to fight, cajole[3], and work this land. Whatever was produced here would belong to us, which was worth remembering as our backs ached and our skin blistered in the sun. And what was produced, what little, *did* belong to us. There was no pilfering in the unprotected, unguarded potato plots. Considering the empty bellies, this degree of honesty was astonishing.

With summer upon us, the hut became unbearably stifling, the vermin[4] unbearably populous, and all tempers reacted accordingly—our landladies', the little boy's, and ours. After all, ten human beings were inhabiting this wretched little oven.

Father decided to investigate the possibility of finding us new quarters.

On the north side of the village, there were some dilapidated[5] and unoccupied huts. Unoccupied with reason: there was no heating of any kind, no floors, and no glass in the windows. But they were empty. Father went to the village housing chief and asked if we might enjoy the privilege of occupying one of these huts.

About this time, factories were beginning to be built in Rubtsovsk—among them a huge tractor factory—and with them came a large migration from European Russia of engineers, technicians of all sorts, and workers. In order to house these people, large

Esther Hautzig in Siberia at age thirteen. Photo copy by Peter Schaaf.

new buildings were erected near the factories and alongside the huts. The district where they existed became known as the *novostroyka*, meaning new buildings. To me, these buildings were the ultimate in beauty and comfort. They were painted white and yellow and light green, and there were floors in them; and some apartments even had bathrooms, but these were only for the chiefs of the factories.

Miraculously, we were permitted to move into one of the empty huts, and we were to be alone at last!

The Kaftals elected to stay on with the sisters. Inevitably, seven people who had been virtually[6] bedfellows ended up getting on one another's nerves.

As for me, the wretched little hut became my dream house. Every day, after working in the potato patch, I went there and cleaned it as best I could. We also picked up manure, mixed it with clay, and either replaced some of the old square blocks in the walls or repaired others. Father got some whitewash at the construction job, and we covered the walls with it. And someplace or other we found glass for the windows.

Before we could cover the floor with fresh clay, we had to dig a cold cellar. Since it

---

3. **cajole** (kə jōl'): to coax, usually by flattering.
4. **vermin:** bugs or small animals that are pests.
5. **dilapidated:** run down; shabby; falling apart.
6. **virtually:** practically; in effect.

Words to Know and Use	**pilfering** (pil' fər iŋ) *n.* stealing **pilfer** *v.*

379

4. ACTIVE READING: Question
Ask students why they think there is no stealing even though food is so precious. *(Possible responses: Everyone knows how hard it is to grow food and therefore cannot be so cruel as to steal it; the exiles have a basic respect for others in the same situation; they have pride; people could figure out who is a thief.)*

5. LITERARY CONCEPT: Historical Setting
Explain that the village housing chief is a figure typical of the Communist bureaucracy of the Soviet Union. Have students **scan** for other details that clarify the historical setting. *(Possible responses: the government-assigned farmland; the engineers from European Russia; the new apartment buildings; the factory chiefs.)*

6. HISTORICAL SIDELIGHT
When Germany invaded the Soviet Union in 1941, Josef Stalin ordered hundreds of Soviet industries moved to Siberia, beyond the Nazis' reach. Factories were probably being erected in Esther's village for this reason.

7. ACTIVE READING: Connect
Ask students what they think of Esther's reactions to the "wretched little hut." Have them discuss why their attitude may differ from Esther's. *(Possible responses: The hut, Esther's "dream house," seems crude, lacking bathrooms, glass in the windows, and flooring; Esther is impressed, but only because her living conditions have been so much worse.)*

Guided Reading for Less-Proficient Students

Continued from page 378

D. Why is Esther unhappy about having to share her hut with Vanya? *(Vanya is a one-legged beggar; people say he steals; beggars have always horrified Esther.)* Recalling

E. What does Vanya do that impresses the Rudomins? *(He speaks politely and uses the language of an educated person; he tries not to intrude on or bother the family.)* Recalling

F. How does Ivan Petrovich change? How does Esther's view of him change? *(He begins to behave with dignity; she comes to see him as a human being like all the others on the steppe.)* Summarizing

8. ACTIVE READING: Question
Ask students what Esther may be referring to when she mentions unwelcome hints. *(Possible response: the nosiness and interference of the people with whom she and her family shared their previous hut.)*

9. LITERARY CONCEPT:
Informational Writing
Remind students that literary nonfiction often informs while it entertains. Ask them what information in Esther's account of her life might also appear in a history or social studies book. *(Possible response: details about the cold cellar and the bania, which provide specific information about the daily life of the time; these were familiar parts of life before refrigerators and indoor plumbing became common.)*

10. ACTIVE READING: Review
Why is Esther's memory of the flowers so important to Grandmother? *(Possible responses: Esther's memory will keep the past alive after Grandmother is dead; by making sure that Esther remembers the flowers, Grandmother is also making sure that Esther remembers her grandfather; Grandmother wants Esther to know her family roots.)*

would be impossible to keep the potatoes from freezing in an outdoor cellar, we dug one in the middle of our room. Father found some split logs lying around the *novostroyka* and covered the hole with them. Since the rounded logs were also still covered with bark, they gave our floor an odd look, but no matter: we had our own home and our own stove, an outdoor summer one that Father had constructed of bricks, where we could cook our own little flour cakes and our own soup without lining up to do so— and without any helpful and unhelpful, welcome and unwelcome, hints as to their preparation.

That spring Mother had learned that there was such a marvelous thing as a public bath, a *bania*, in the village, and to get there became her dearest wish. What if we did eat a little less for a week or two to save up for such a treat? Wouldn't it be heavenly to feel *clean* before we moved to our own home?

The *bania* was in a small building with two entrances, one for men and one for women. We found that Mother was not the only woman with a passion for cleanliness: the line was long; the wait would be a couple of hours at least. We waited.

There were two rooms in the *bania;* one had stone benches and faucets along the walls, the other was a steam room, a rather crude sauna where one used twigs in the Finnish fashion to clean oneself and stir up one's circulation.

We were assigned a cubbyhole for our clothes, and since we were to use the room with the faucets, we were given a basin and a piece of pumice.[7] We filled our basins at a faucet, sat down on a stone bench, and

scrubbed away. The water was *hot*. Mother was entranced. Now we were quite ready to move.

Outside the hut, there was a small piece of land that no one seemed to be using. With our potatoes and some tomato plants and corn seed given to us by Svetlana, we would turn it into a vegetable patch. ◄ C

The plans Grandmother and I were making for this garden inevitably recalled Grandfather and our garden in Vilna. As her eyes filled with tears, Grandmother tested my memory. Did I remember what Grandfather had said about the irises? and the pansies? Did I remember the lilac tree?

Yes, I remembered everything. I remembered exactly where Grandfather had said to plant each flower. I remembered the prize of fifty groshes[8] that each week was given to the child whose flowers looked best. Yes, I remembered.

"Good!" Grandmother raised her head; she was proud of me. I had passed the test. "And you will never forget?" No, I would never forget. "Good!" Now my memory was to be honored, she seemed to say; it was to become the <u>archive</u> of her beloved past.

Why is Esther's memory of the flowers so important to Grandmother?

review   **10**

Could we plant some flowers? I wanted to know. Grandmother was a realist who lived in the future as well as the past; no, we could not; we needed every inch for growing food.

In this world of scarcity, the <u>acquisition</u> of

---

7. **pumice** (pum' is): light volcanic rock used for rubbing away dirt.
8. **groshes** (grôsh' əz): a form of *groszy*, Polish coins of small value.

Words to Know and Use

archive (är' kīv) *n.* a storehouse for records of the past
acquisition (ak' wə zish' ən) *n.* the act of getting something

the most trivial or seemingly useless object was a topic for conversation. So Svetlana told me that her father had gotten a large quantity of hospital gauze.[9] (How and why I did not know or care to ask.) She asked me if I wanted some. I assured her I did; I would use it for curtains.

"White hospital gauze for curtains, Esther?"

"You will see," I said mysteriously.

I began to save onion peelings and asked Svetlana to do the same. In school, we had learned that onion peelings when boiled in water exuded a yellow pigment which could be used as dye. Svetlana had either forgotten this or else had no need to remember such things. She wondered what I was up to, but I told her it was a secret.

When I had gathered a big pile of onion peel, I boiled it until the water was a pot of pale yellow dye. I dunked the gauze in this, let it stay for several hours, and to my delight it worked. The gauze was now a pretty yellow. I stretched it out and dried it in the sun, and then I made our curtains. There were no curtain rods to be had, so we tacked them on with little nails, and my pride in the result was very great. Everyone agreed that the curtains were very pretty and just what this hut needed.

The hut was heaven. We ate when we wanted to, slept when we wanted to; at night we would sit outside and gaze at the Siberian sky where there was always something to see; we would sit there quietly, quietly. Even Mother seemed to regain some of her old zest for life.

It was too good to be true to last.

One day the village housing chief came to our hut when I was alone and told me that the next day we were to have a tenant, whether we wanted one or not.

"Who is it going to be?" I asked.

"Vanya, the bum."

"Vanya, the bum? . . . " I was horrified.

---

9. **gauze** (gôz): a thin open-weaved fabric used as bandages.

A typical Siberian mud hut (1929). Sovfoto.

11. VOCABULARY: Definitions
Ask students to use **context clues** to determine the meanings of the words *exuded* ("gave forth") and *pigment* ("a coloring"). ★

12. LITERARY CONCEPT: Characterization
Ask students what they learn about Esther as a person from the curtains she makes. (Possible responses: She's clever, inventive, and resourceful; she has a positive attitude.)

13. ACTIVE READING: Review
Ask students why Esther's mother has "regained some of her old zest for life." (Possible responses: The curtains cheer her up; she's had a bath; she and her family have a home of their own; she has some peaceful moments.)

14. ACTIVE READING: Predict
Ask students what sort of person they think Vanya the bum will be. (Any response is valid, as long as students recognize that Esther's anxiety is understandable.)

Looking at Style

Ask volunteers to read the following passages aloud while other students listen for repetition.

■ Yes, *I remembered* everything. *I remembered* exactly where Grandfather had said to plant each flower. *I remembered* the prize of fifty groshes that each week was given to the child whose flowers looked best. Yes, *I remembered*. (p. 380)

■ We ate *when we wanted to*, slept *when we wanted to* . . . (p. 381)

■ Soon he began to wash himself, which pleased us more than it is polite to say. *And* to comb his beard. *And* to carry himself with dignity. (p. 384)

Discuss the effect of these repetitions. Ask,

1. How does repetition help to emphasize and clarify a point? How does it create drama?

2. How does the rhythm of repetition affect readers?

15. VOCABULARY: Idiom
Explain that *beggar* refers not merely to a person who begs, but to any extremely poor person. The word is no longer much used in the United States. The word *bum* is also rarely used today to refer to the indigent. Ask students what words are commonly used instead of *beggar* or *bum* in the United States today. *(Possible responses: panhandler, homeless person, street person)* ★

16. ACTIVE READING: Connect
How would it feel to have a beggar move in with you? *(Any response is valid.)*

17. LITERARY CONCEPT: Theme
Esther's mother's lecture points to the central issue in this episode. Ask students what Mrs. Rudomin is concerned about. *(Possible response: She may feel that every human being deserves respect and courtesy; she may feel that her family is prejudging Vanya, not giving him a chance.)*

> ## 18. CULTURAL SIDELIGHT
> "Vanya" is an affectionate nickname for "Ivan." Although such nicknames are traditional in Russia, they are used only among close friends and family members. A mere acquaintance is disrespectful if he or she uses this kind of nickname. Point out to students that Ivan at first calls himself Vanya, suggesting that his life as a bum has eroded his self-respect.

15

I had been taught never to call anyone names, but everyone called this one-legged man "Vanya the bum." He was the village beggar, and people said he stole. Now this bum was going to live with us? In Vilna, there had been many beggars. Whenever I saw them, I was morbidly affected. Where did they eat? Did they ever bathe at all? And, most important, where did they go at night? Where did they sleep? Thinking

D ▶ about them, I used to shudder.

Now one was going to live with us.

16

connect How would it feel to have a beggar move in with you?

When I gave the news to my parents, they were no less stunned than I was.

"Vanya, the bum? . . ." Father asked.

I assured him that I had heard correctly.

Mother coughed. A signal to father that she disapproved of his language. Vanya was not to be called a bum. The lecture that followed seemed to me—and perhaps to Father too—untimely, like correcting the grammar of someone who is trying to tell you the

17 house is on fire. The lecture continued: Vanya was not to be called Vanya either. He must have a proper name. We were to introduce ourselves as usual, etc. Perhaps this man has a *worthy* reason for begging? Don't you *agree*, Samuel?

Father not only agreed but, having been rebuked,[10] went on to remind me that we must not judge people by their appearance, etc., etc.

Fidgeting from foot to foot, I listened to everything they had to say; but as far as I

was concerned, Vanya the bum was coming to live with us, and I was not only terrified but revolted.

Perhaps the village housing chief would have a change of heart, I thought to myself.

The next evening, Vanya the bum stood at our open door.

"May I come in?"

"Of course you may." Mother stood up.

"Good evening." Father went toward Vanya.

"Good . . . evening." Vanya's response was tentative.

Regardless of all these amenities,[11] this tall, bone-thin specter in filthy clothes, with dark bushy hair and a matted beard, was still a bum to me. But I felt Mother's eyes on me.

"Good evening," I said, going forward but keeping my hands rigidly at my sides. "My name is Esther Rudomin. What's yours?"

"Vanya."

His deeply sunken eyes darted from Mother to Father and back to me.

"My name is Ivan Petrovich, my child," he amended, and there was a tiny spark in his eyes.

"Welcome to our house, Ivan Petrovich," my father said.

For the first time, Grandmother, who had been watching this scene more or less huddled in her bed, spoke up. "Welcome," she murmured.

---

10. rebuked: blamed; scolded in a sharp way.
11. amenities: courteous acts and pleasant manners of polite social behavior.

Words to Know and Use	**morbidly** (môr′ bid lē) *adv.* in a gloomy, depressed way

18

Multicultural Connections

The Rudomins do the polite thing and call their new housemate Ivan Petrovich. An outsider to Russian culture, however, might not know that etiquette was even involved in the choice between "Vanya" and "Ivan Petrovich." Emphasize to students that etiquette varies from culture to culture. Often, what one culture considers extremely impolite—belching at a meal, for example—may be just what etiquette demands in another culture.

Invite students to list practices or habits that they believe to be polite but which may have no significance or may even seem impolite in other cultures. If different cultural backgrounds are represented in your classroom, have students compare their lists to see which etiquette rules the cultures have in common.

"Thank you, thank you. Where may I put down my stick? And this bag?" The bag was a tattered, dusty bundle.

No one had given this matter a thought.

In a tiny room with a hole in its center and three of its corners already occupied by beds, the obvious answer was the fourth corner. But the intention had been to build the winter stove in that corner.

*T*he transformation from village bum to Ivan Petrovich did not take place overnight—

"So we will make the stove smaller," Mother said, answering our unspoken words, and pointed to the corner. "Maybe we can get some wood for a *nari*, like ours."

"Oh, please—don't worry about me. I'll be very comfortable just as it is." He smiled a little sardonically.[12] "I beg your pardon for this intrusion. Your privacy—"

I could see that my parents and my grandmother were as impressed as I was at his language and his accent: this was no illiterate.

Using his stick dexterously, he hobbled off to his corner on his one leg. There, he stretched out on the floor with his head on his bundle and said that he would rest.

It was an awkward moment. It was still early; what were we to do now? Just sit and watch this stranger rest?

"Please," he said with his eyes closed, "the child can sing and play and do anything she likes. When I am tired, I sleep; and when I sleep, I sleep the sleep of the dead."

"Thank you," I said.

And I meant it. Living with a bum was going to be more agreeable than living with our former landladies, who were forever hushing me and the little boy.

The transformation from village bum to Ivan Petrovich did not take place overnight—either in my mind or in reality. At first he remained a shadowy figure from the dark world of the homeless, the friendless, the outcast. He left very early each morning, and when he came home at night, he went directly to his corner—not that there was anyplace else to go. He talked very little, munched on bits of food he had picked up, and went to sleep. But before he ate, he always offered me anything he had brought—a fresh carrot, perhaps, or a beet. My parents always offered food in return, but he always refused. I, on the other hand, used to accept a bit of carrot or beet because I didn't want to hurt his feelings. Recently, Mother had amended her view of the etiquette for accepting precious food: When some was offered, you took a tiny bit if you thought they did not have enough, but that you took; it was only polite to do so.

After a few weeks had gone by, the transformation began: he started to eat with us, sharing whatever he had brought. If we cooked potatoes, we added his carrot to it

———————————
12. **sardonically:** in a mocking or bitter way.

19. ACTIVE READING: Evaluate
Ask students for their reactions to Vanya now. (Possible responses: He seems nice; I'm glad he is polite and pleasant; if he is educated, I wonder where he came from and what happened to him; I don't know about him—maybe they shouldn't trust him.)

Words to Know and Use	**dexterously** (deks' tər əs lē) *adv.* skillfully **transformation** (trans' fər mā' shən) *n.* a change **etiquette** (et' i kit) *n.* the proper way to behave toward others; good manners

383

20. LITERARY CONCEPT: Historical Setting

Point out to students that Ivan Petrovich's history is like that of many people in the Soviet Union during Stalin's regime. Ask students what effect Ivan's story has on the reader. *(Possible response: It makes the narrative more serious and real; it reminds the reader that this is not just a story and that the Rudomins are still in danger.)*

21. ACTIVE READING: Review

Ask students to identify the **cause** and the **effect** of the change in Ivan Petrovich. *(Possible response: The cause is the family's courteous treatment of Ivan Petrovich as if he were their equal. The effect is an increase in his self-respect, shown by his taking care of his appearance and walking and acting with dignity.)*

22. ACTIVE READING: Review

Ask students to discuss the effect Ivan Petrovich has on Esther. *(Possible response: She learns that the way a person is treated determines how the person acts and views him or herself; she may never be quite so ready to prejudge a person again.)*

ENCOURAGING INDEPENDENT READING

Siberia, nonfiction by Madelyn Klein Anderson

Summer of My German Soldier, novel by Bette Greene

---

and called it a vegetable stew. If it was a white beet, we boiled it until we could spread it on bread instead of jam.

20 Then he began to talk. Ivan Petrovich was a shoemaker from the Ukraine, a man who knew his craft and who had read many books. But once he had talked too much or too carelessly or had been misunderstood. He never did know why he had been sent to prison in Siberia; such a piece of information had been considered superfluous. And when he had been released, he had only one leg left and made his way from village to village begging.

Soon he began to wash himself, which pleased us more than it is polite to say. And to comb his beard. And to carry himself with dignity. He became Ivan Petrovich—for the time being at least. **21**

When he first came to our house, we were the object of much curiosity: What is it like to have a bum in your house? Does he steal? How do you talk to a bum? How does he talk to you? Doesn't it make you shudder?

But as Ivan Petrovich came to regard himself differently, so did the villagers: he became much less a bum and much more just another human being cast off on the great Siberian steppe. **◄ F**

One day he disappeared. He left as usual early one morning, and that was the last **22** that any of us ever saw of Ivan Petrovich, formerly known as Vanya the bum. ❧

Words to Know and Use   **superfluous** (sə pʉr′ flo͞o əs) *adj.* unnecessary; not important

---

Comprehension Check

1. Where are the Rudomins living when the selection begins? *(in Siberia, in a hut with several other people)*

2. Where do they move in the course of the memoir? *(to a hut that had been broken-down and empty)*

3. What treat do Esther and her mother enjoy before the move? *(a visit to a bania, or bathhouse)*

4. How does Esther improve the hut? *(She makes curtains from hospital gauze.)*

5. Who moves into the hut with Esther's family? *(Vanya the bum, a one-legged beggar)*

6. How does the family treat the beggar? *(They are courteous to him.)*

7. How does Vanya change after he moves in? *(He cleans himself up and becomes more dignified.)*

Responding to Reading

First Impressions

1. What were your thoughts as you finished reading this piece? Jot them down in your journal or notebook.

Second Thoughts

2. How do you think the family felt when Ivan Petrovich left?

3. Why did the family's treatment of Vanya help transform him into Ivan?

4. How were Esther and her family able to keep their dignity in such a terrible setting?

5. Of the hardships Esther and her family faced, which would be the most difficult for you? Explain.

Broader Connections

6. If each family in the United States took in a "bum" like Ivan, do you think the homeless problem would be solved?

Literary Concept: Description

Writers use **description** to help readers get a mental picture of a scene, an event, or a character. Skim the second paragraph of the selection in which Hautzig describes the mud of Siberia. How does this description explain the kinds of things that became important to Esther and her mother later in the selection?

Concept Review: External Conflict With what external forces do Esther and her family struggle in this account?

THE ENDLESS STEPPE 385

Responding to Reading

1. **Any response is valid.**

2. **Possible responses:** disappointed, regretful, or worried, because by this time they had come to like Ivan Petrovich; relieved, because they had more room; insulted, because he didn't even say goodbye, even though they had been kind to him

3. **Possible responses:** The Rudomins' treatment of him restored his self-respect after all of his suffering; people live up to others' expectations of them.

4. **Possible responses:** They drew strength from one another; Esther's parents insisted on ethical standards of behavior; they never stopped working to improve their lives, even though they could set only very small goals.

5. **Any response is valid.** Encourage students to describe hardships they have faced and to compare their experiences with Esther's.

6. **Possible responses:** Yes, there are far more families with homes than people who are homeless; no, new people keep becoming homeless, so any solution would have to solve the causes of homelessness.

Challenge Question

Esther Hautzig writes about her own family in this piece. What is her opinion of her family members, and how does she convey it? *(Possible responses: She admires the strength and dignity of her family members very much; rather than stating her opinion, she conveys it by describing their words and actions in a respectful manner.)*

Literary Concept: Description
The description of the mud in the springtime shows how hard and dirty life was in Siberia. It helps to explain why a hot bath was so important to Esther's mother and why Esther and her family worked hard to decorate and equip their new home.

Concept Review: External Conflict
The external forces with which Esther and her family struggle include the harsh Siberian environment, state officials, and annoying housemates.

Writing Options

The Writing Options are designed to meet varied student interests and abilities. Have each student choose one writing activity to complete.

Journal Update Have students review their journal entries for *The Endless Steppe*. Encourage them to add new insights and ideas about the importance of looking beyond appearances and stereotypes.

Links to Writer's Craft

Writing Option 4 is an exercise in persuasive writing. For more practice, see *The Writer's Craft*, Grade 7, "Persuasion," pages 140-163.

VOCABULARY PRACTICE

Answers to Exercise

1. Antonyms	6. Antonyms
2. Antonyms	7. Synonyms
3. Synonyms	8. Antonyms
4. Synonyms	9. Synonyms
5. Antonyms	10. Synonyms

For Alternative Learning Styles

In groups, students may demonstrate meanings while others guess the words. For example, they might tie their shoes *dexterously*, might *morbidly* discuss a horror movie; might point out storage files in the classroom as *archives*, and so on.

Closure

Point out to students that Esther has her conscience tested when she must decide how to treat a needy human being. The courtesy she and her family extend to Vanya not only helps restore his dignity but also shows that their own dignity is intact despite the hardships of life on the steppe. Let students discuss other real-life situations they know about —whether from news reports or personal experience—in which people are tested by a decision about how to treat others.

Writing Options

1. Write a **comparison** of this selection and "Homeless" (page 44). Consider the behavior of Ann and Vanya, as well as the beliefs of Quindlen and the Rudomins.

2. Esther and her family adjusted as best they could to their new environment. Based on what they did, write a Siberian **survival guidebook**. Give tips on how to make a home, decorate, find food, cook, and even entertain. You may invent details and descriptions.

3. Imagine that Ivan left the village to become a wandering preacher. Write his **sermon** telling people how one family's treatment of him helped change his life.

4. Suppose the Rudomins decided to sell the hut. Write the **house listing** (real estate ad) describing the house. Begin with a summarizing phrase such as "Home for sale, cheap," and include important details about the house and grounds.

Vocabulary Practice

Exercise On a separate sheet of paper, write *Synonyms* or *Antonyms* to show whether each pair of words mean the same thing or the opposite.

1. morbidly : cheerfully
2. superfluous : necessary
3. transformation : change
4. allot : distribute
5. pilfering : donation
6. acquisition : loss
7. etiquette : manners
8. dexterously : clumsily
9. preoccupation : concentration
10. archive : storehouse

> **Words to Know and Use**
>
> acquisition
> allot
> archive
> dexterously
> etiquette
> morbidly
> pilfering
> preoccupation
> superfluous
> transformation

The Spelling Connection

Prepositional Prefixes A preposition is placed before a word to show that word's relation to another word in a sentence. Prefixes like **super, sub, pre, post, fore,** and **trans** often have the meanings of prepositions.
Example: **sub** + terranean = **sub**terranean

Prepositional-Prefix Words from the Selection
foregone   **pre**paration
preoccupation   **super**fluous
transformation

Other Words with Prepositional Prefixes
transparent	**fore**warned	**post**script
submerge	**super**sonic	**post**pone

Exercise Fit spelling words to the meanings.
1. to put off for later
2. a state of being absorbed
3. the act of getting ready
4. an addition to something already written
5. more than necessary

Options for Learning (Multimodal/Cross-Curricular Activities)

1 • **Treacherous Times** Research the dictatorship of Joseph Stalin during the 1930s and 1940s in the Soviet Union. Why did Stalin banish so many people? What happened to those he banished? Share your findings with the class.

2 • **Not Just History** In many places in the world today, people are being banished from their homelands for various reasons—race or ethnic background, religion, political beliefs, and so on. Research one area from which refugees are streaming today, and, in an oral report, compare the lives of the exiles to that of the Rudomins.

3 • **Passport to Siberia** Design and write a travel brochure for modern Siberia. Find pictures and information in *National Geographic* or other magazines. Recommend places to go and sights to see. Include a brief history of Siberia.

4 • **Model Maker** Build a diorama of the Rudomins' hut after their makeover. Use details from the story and your imagination. Display your model in class.

 FACT FINDER SOCIAL STUDIES

What is the population of Siberia today?

---

*E*sther Rudomin Hautzig
1930–

Esther Hautzig and her family traveled six weeks in a cattle car to Siberia, where her mother was assigned to work in a mine, and her father was drafted into the Soviet army. Her grandfather died in a slave labor camp.

After World War II, Esther immigrated to America. She lived with an uncle in Brooklyn, finished high school, and attended college. "I had always dreamt of becoming a writer," Hautzig says, "though that didn't necessarily mean becoming a published author!" Her first three books were how-to books about cooking without a stove, making inexpensive gifts, and home decorating with little money, skills she learned in Siberia. "I think I'm frugal because I didn't have (anything). I don't believe in waste, and I believed in recycling maybe before the word had been invented."

The Endless Steppe was rejected by several publishers as an adult book. Published as a children's book, it won seven awards and was translated into eight languages.

Hautzig says, "I never pass street people without remembering Vanya the bum. I have to look them in the eye, wish them a good day, and treat them as human beings who are down on their luck."

Cross-Curricular Projects

Art Ask volunteers to draw or paint portraits of Ivan Petrovich, based on Esther's description. Students can make a gallery of their portraits and discuss their different interpretations.

Home Arts/Science Suggest that students follow in Esther's footsteps by experimenting with ways to make dyes out of vegetables. Then have them use their dyes to produce items to ornament their homes or persons.

History Interested students can research how Soviet communism ended. They may wish to read news accounts of the 1991 coup against Mikhail Gorbachev and the events that followed. Suggest that students present their findings in the form of a radio play.

Objectives

■ To understand the elements of a persuasive speech

■ To write a persuasive speech that advocates action

■ To draft, revise, edit, and share persuasive writing

Teaching Strategies

DISCUSSING THE ASSIGNMENT

Have students read the first paragraph on page 388 and be sure they understand that the purpose of persuasive writing is to convince others to think or act in a certain way. Ask volunteers to give examples of persuasive writing. Call students' attention to the model and explain that the student who wrote it was concerned about homeless people and tried to get others concerned. Have students read the Guided Assignment on page 388, and ask them to note the purpose, audience, subject, and structure of the PASSkey. Point out to students that during their writing their PASSkey might change. If you wish, you may give students the option of doing a different assignment. The Alternative Writing and Research Topics on page 389 offer some good choices.

ANALYZING THE MODEL

Have a volunteer read aloud the student model on pages 388-389. Ask students whether they think Margo's argument, or case for supporting the homeless shelter, was convincing. *(Possible response: Yes; she avoids any show of emotion yet makes a very good case for her beliefs. She states her point of view, supports it with valid and logical reasons, and ends by calling on her audience to act.)*

WRITER'S WORKSHOP

PERSUASIVE WRITING

USE PERSUASIVE WRITING FOR
advertisements
letters to the editor
persuasive speeches
debates
personal requests
editorials

The pieces in this subunit stir our consciences. They make us think about the way things ought to be. When you write to persuade, you start with something that is bothering you and think of a way it can be fixed. You express your opinions, and you try to get others to agree. In many cases, persuasive writing is also meant to move people to action. In this workshop, you'll use persuasion as you write a speech.

> Here is one writer's PASSkey to this assignment.

GUIDED ASSIGNMENT: SPEECH TO PERSUADE

Write a speech that persuades listeners to take some kind of action on an issue you care about.

PURPOSE: To persuade
AUDIENCE: Classmates
SUBJECT: A shelter for the homeless
STRUCTURE: Speech

STUDENT MODEL
The writer starts by stating the issue and her position.

▶

Facts and statistics back up the writer's reasons.

▶

Support the Shelter
by Margo Bachman

Next month, our city will vote on creating a shelter for the homeless. The plan calls for the city to lease the old Fitzroy Hotel building downtown. Homeless people could have rooms and bathrooms and share the kitchens that will be installed on each floor. People could stay up to one month. I think everyone should do his or her best to help this plan succeed.

I support the shelter for several reasons. First, the plan is practical. The building was a hotel, so it's already set up to house a lot of people. It has seventy-five rooms. Second, the plan is low-cost. The owner would lease the Fitzroy to the city for only a thousand dollars

388 UNIT FOUR TESTS OF CONSCIENCE

ADDITIONAL RESOURCES

Unit Four Resource Book
Writer's Workshop Worksheet, p. 31
Writer's Workshop: Peer and Self-Evaluation, p. 32
Writer's Workshop: Assessment Guidelines, p. 33

Technology and Enrichment
 Elaboration, Revision, and Proofreading Transparencies 21–24

 Writer's Databank Software: File 3, Ideas for Writing

 Fine Art Transparency Pack

Links to Writer's Craft

For more about persuasive writing, see *The Writer's Craft*, Grade 7, "Persuasion," pages 138–151, and "Audience," pages 233–234.

a month. The city would pay the rent with the
money it makes on restaurant taxes. The cost of
adding kitchens would also be low because the
Rotary Club has offered free materials.

Most importantly, setting up a shelter just
seems like the right thing to do. Our city has
hundreds of homeless families today. So many
new families are homeless because the whole
country is having money problems. Last year,
over fifty thousand businesses closed, and
hundreds of thousands of people lost their
jobs. Families could no longer afford their
homes. Many moved in with relatives, but when
the relatives could no longer afford to help
them, they became homeless. I think it's our
duty to help people who have experienced this
bad luck.

Some people think a shelter will encourage
the homeless to stay homeless. I think the
short stays allowed in the shelter would
prevent that problem. During that worry-free
month, people can look for jobs and figure out
what they will do next.

As kids, we won't vote on the shelter, but we
still have voices. We can talk to adults and
hand out leaflets. There's a lot of unhappiness
in the world, and we can't do much about it.
Here's something we <u>can</u> do. Let's do it.

◀ The writer stresses her most important reason.

◀ The writer uses logic to answer an opposing argument.

◀ The writer states what she wants listeners to do, ending with a strong appeal.

Now you can start on your own speech.

Prewrite and Explore

1 **Take your pick** To find a topic, try brainstorming with a few
classmates. Your group might use headings like *world,
country, community, school, parents,* and *friends.* Under each heading,
group members can list things that upset them or that need fixing. Your
friends' ideas may spark new ideas in you. Afterwards, scan the lists for
the issues you care most about. Any issue that has two sides will make
a good speech topic.

To help students understand the parts of
a persuasive speech and how they
work together, ask the class these questions about the model. You may wish to
have students work in groups, two questions to a group, and later have them
share what they've discussed.

Questions for Group A
■ What reasons does Margo give for
supporting the homeless shelter? Are
they good enough to convince people
to vote for it? Explain.

■ How do you know that Margo's supporting evidence is solid?

Questions for Group B
■ In what order does Margo present the
parts of her argument? What facts and
statistics does she use to support each
part?

■ Does Margo's argument convince you
to support the city's plan? Explain how
she accomplishes this. If not, explain
why and tell what she might have done
to persuade you.

Prewrite and Explore

Point out to students that the issue they
will address most successfully is the one
which they feel most strongly about. Tell
them that their issue need not be one of
national importance; in fact, it may be
a problem confined to their own neighborhoods. Suggest that they ask themselves what issue nags at them every
day or is always in the back of their
minds. As an alternative to brainstorming with partners to find an issue, suggest to students that they freewrite in
their journals.

Alternative Writing and Research Topics

Persuasive Essay When Tom went out hunting in
spite of his father's wishes, tragedy followed. Has
anything like that ever happened to you? Write an
essay that persuades young people to follow the
rules—despite a terrible temptation to break them!
Personal Writing How do you feel when you see a
homeless person? Do you have a strong desire to
help, yet face frustration because you don't know
what to do? Describe your feelings and frustrations in
a short composition.

Opinion Essay Andy Rooney's essay takes a lighthearted approach to a very serious problem. Using
Rooney's essay as a model, write your opinion of a
different American crisis.

Research Report Research what happened to one
group of people during World War II. For example,
research the Polish Jews, Danes, Latvians, or Chinese.
Summarize your findings in a written report.

Whatever issue each student decides upon, encourage all to make notes and graphic organizers to guide them as they write. You may wish to refer to the Thinking Skills Transparency Pack for ideas on graphic organizers that students might use. Point out to students the importance of researching facts and statistics to support the stands they have chosen. Remind them, however, never to copy the exact words of their sources unless they give full credit to the source. Call attention to page 390 where the use of the *Readers' Guide* is explained.

Modeling Often students end up using only encyclopedias for research because they don't know how to access other sources of information. In small groups, with the help of the librarian, show students how you look up a subject in the *Readers' Guide.* Explain that you want to write a speech about the health care system or some other topic currently in the news. Have students watch you look up the subject in the *Readers' Guide* and then find the cited magazine articles. If your library has a computerized or microfiche guide to magazine articles, show students how to use it.

TEACHING TIP: CHALLENGE

Strong writers and students whose research skills are already quite sophisticated might enjoy the challenge of supporting a difficult or unpopular cause. For example, in certain parts of the United States, leaders in the timber industry and environmentalists are often at odds with one another. Generally, the industrialists are popular because they provide jobs, while the environmentalists are unpopular because they would cost jobs. Challenge your advanced students to find an unpopular cause and defend it.

2 Set your direction Before you go any further, try writing one sentence that sums up your position or opinion. If you can list reasons for your position, jot them down too. When you know your position, you can start gathering information.

GATHERING INFORMATION

The more accurate and current your facts and statistics, the stronger your speech. Magazines provide current facts. You can use the *Readers' Guide to Periodical Literature* in your public library to find out which magazines have the information you need. Usually the *Readers' Guide* is in the reference section of the library.

USING THE *READERS' GUIDE*

Start by looking up your subject. For example, Margo looked up "Homeless." She found quite a few articles within subtitles under "Homeless." Here is what she saw under the subtitle "Housing":

> **HOMELESS**
> Housing
> Gimme shelter [Los Angeles Mission] B. Streisand. il *U.S. News & World Report* 112:17 F 3 '92
> Homelessness is a housing problem [New York City study by Marybeth Shinn] *Health* (San Francisco, Calif.: 1992) 6:15 F/Mr '92
> The Wright shelter [housing for the homeless in Mari County, Calif. originally designed by F. L. Wright] M. M. Soviero. il *Popular Science* 240:58+ Ja '92

The many abbreviations in the *Readers' Guide* are explained in the front of the guide. The diagram below shows one entry.

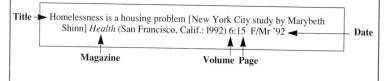

NOTETAKING
For help in taking notes, see the Research and Report Writing Section in the Writer's Handbook.

▶ Once you have found the listing for an article that might be useful to you, copy the name and date of the magazine and the page numbers. Go to the magazine room, and ask the librarian for the issue of the magazine you want. Often, magazines are bound in large volumes, so keep your date and page numbers with you. When you find the article, skim it to see if it will help you. If so, take notes, including bibliography notes.

Paragraphs at Work

Remind students that in persuasive writing they state an opinion and back it up with convincing reasons. They can help the audience by mentioning each reason and its supporting evidence in a separate paragraph. Other reminders:

■ Explain each reason in a topic sentence.

■ Be sure that all the evidence sentences in a paragraph support the reason being explained. Take out any evidence that doesn't belong there.

■ Write separate paragraphs also for the introduction and the conclusion.

■ State the most important reason last.

■ Tie the paragraphs together with appropriate and effective transitions. Refer students to page 698 in the Writer's Handbook for transitions to use in order-of-importance compositions.

3 Target your audience Persuasion works best when it's geared to a specific audience. Make notes about your audience: their ages, their main concerns, their knowledge and viewpoint about your issue. Think of opposing views they might have. Try to guess which kinds of evidence might convince them.

Draft and Discover

1 Start drafting You might start with a paragraph that sums up the issue and states your position. If your audience isn't familiar with the issue, explain it as clearly and briefly as possible.

2 Speak your mind Write about the reasons for your position. Check your notes for facts and statistics that back up your reasons. As you write, bear in mind the main arguments your listeners might raise. You can mention and then counter these arguments.

3 Talk action Come right out and say what you want your listeners to do. For example, you may want them to write letters, volunteer, or give money. Decide exactly what you want, and express it in one or more sentences. This is your call to action.

◀ **WRITER'S CHOICE**
Keep an open mind as you research your issue. You may change your mind! It's OK to switch sides before— or after—you start to draft.

Revise Your Writing

1 Sort it out As you reread your draft, think about organization. You might try this type of plan:

Paragraph 1: Summary of issue and your position statement
Paragraph 2: Reasons and supporting evidence
Paragraph 3: Opposing arguments and your answer to them
Paragraph 4: Your call to action

◀ **PARAGRAPHING**
You might choose to write a new paragraph for each reason.

2 Use strategy Three strategies can help you convince your listeners. First, back up each point with facts and statistics. Second, appeal to logic: use reasoning that makes sense. Third, appeal to emotion: choose words that create the feelings you want.

3 Practice out loud Try reading your speech to a partner, who can help you revise the weaker areas.

◀ **VOCABULARY TIP**
How can you use words to create feelings? See the Denotation and Connotation Workshop on page 465.

Draft and Discover

No matter where in their speech students begin drafting, encourage them to think about the placement of the points they will make and the facts that support them. One strategy to keep in mind is this: an audience remembers best the point that it hears last. Therefore, students should strive to make their last point the most important and the most persuasive. Note that this is what Margo did in the model.

Another helpful strategy to remember is to tailor the talk to the audience. If they were speaking to their classmates, students advocating a change in school policy might use some slang and emphasize student benefits. However, if they were addressing the board of education, their language and tone would be more formal, and the evidence would probably emphasize the benefits to the community rather than to the students. Point out that in both cases the message is the same; all that changes is the style of delivery and the emphasis.

Revise Your Writing

Since their written compositions will eventually be presented as speeches, students might consider these points as they revise:

■ **Address listeners directly** Use the pronouns *you* or *we* to help listeners feel that they must somehow respond to the speech.

■ **Take advantage of sound devices** For example, alliteration or the repetition of key points can be very effective.

■ **Practice before a small group** Have speakers and listeners alike note words and phrases to stress. Sometimes a sentence will be more effective in inverted order. Listeners might suggest that evidence sentences be rearranged within paragraphs to make a stronger argument.

Before students go on to Proofread, remind them to use the Revision Questions on page 392.

Cooperative Writing

Form the class into small groups of four or five to work together on developing their speeches. Encourage students to help each other refine and improve ideas and arguments and to share information about resources.

After students have drafted their speeches, direct them to practice delivering them to the group. The group should respond constructively to help speakers improve organization, word choice, and delivery.

CONFERENCING TIP

As you conference with individual writers for this workshop, you may wish to focus on

■ sensible and solid reasoning

■ organization and order of arguments

■ emotional statements

■ use of indefinite pronouns

Proofread

The Editor's Eye feature previews the content in the Language Workshop that follows. If students do not need extra help with indefinite pronouns, the brief review in The Editor's Eye may be enough for them. If the class or individual students might benefit from additional work, you may choose to teach the Language Workshop, pages 393-395, before students proofread.

Be sure students check punctuation carefully, since it offers excellent clues for the speaker. A comma in the right place, for example, signals the speaker to pause, or to raise or lower the voice.

Use the following models for extra reinforcement of the Editor's Eye topic:

1. Just about everyone (feel, <u>feels</u>) sorry for homeless people.

2. Any homeless person would love to have a place of (<u>his or her</u>, their) own.

3. Everybody (deserve, <u>deserves</u>) food and shelter.

4. Many of the homeless will turn (his or her, <u>their</u>) lives around.

Publish and Present

Writing for the Community You may wish to have the class select the three or four best student persuaders and have them speak at the next home and school meeting. Not only would this showcase your curriculum, but it would also indicate to parents and other teachers the concerns of seventh-grade students.

Reflect on Your Writing

You may wish to have students answer the following questions in addition to or instead of those in their texts:

■ After I gave my speech, how did I feel about speaking to a group?

■ Did I have enough good reasons and facts to be convincing?

Closure

Have students watch and listen closely to televised political speeches. Ask them to note their evaluations in their journals.

Revision Questions

For You	For a Peer Reader
1. Do I state the issue clearly and show its importance?	1. What main message does my speech leave you with?
2. Is my reasoning logical? Do I offer enough evidence?	2. Which part works best to persuade you?
3. What words would help me strengthen my persuasion?	3. Can you think of important arguments I ignored?

Proofread

Check your grammar and mechanics carefully, and correct any errors you find. Pay special attention to indefinite pronouns.

THE EDITOR'S EYE: INDEFINITE PRONOUNS

An indefinite pronoun is a pronoun that does not refer to a particular person, place, or thing.

Words like *everyone* and *anybody* are indefinite pronouns. Personal pronouns used with them must agree in number.

Problem   I think *everyone* should do *their* best.

Correct   I think *everyone* should do *his or her* best.

> **NEED MORE HELP?**
> See the Language Workshop on pages 393–395.

> **SPEAKING AND LISTENING TIP**
> Practice reading your speech aloud several times in advance. If you stumble at the same places each time, try changing your wording.

> **FOR YOUR PORTFOLIO**

Publish and Present

▶ **Classroom Soapbox**   Deliver your speech to your class. Use effective speaking skills: make eye contact with your listeners, speak at a normal rate, and project your voice toward the back wall of the room.

Reflect on Your Writing

▶ Add your answers to the questions below to your portfolio.

1. When you first read your speech aloud, what surprised you most?

2. Did you find it harder to appeal to logic or to emotion? Why?

Assessment Guidelines

These guidelines may help you assess student writing:

Content

■ The introduction states the issue and the speaker's stand on it.

■ The middle paragraphs give reasons for the speaker's stand and provide facts to support it.

■ The conclusion restates the speaker's argument and calls on the audience for action.

Style

■ The tone and diction shows an awareness of audience.

■ Transitions make clear the flow of the argument.

Usage and Mechanics

■ Indefinite pronouns are used correctly.

■ The speaker makes use of punctuation clues to vary his or her speed and diction.

See also *Unit Four Resource Book*, page 33.

LANGUAGE WORKSHOP

PRONOUN PROBLEMS

Indefinite Pronouns

You remember that a pronoun takes the place of a noun or another pronoun. You probably also remember that personal pronouns, such as *he, she,* or *they,* refer to specific people, places, or things. Indefinite pronouns are different. An indefinite pronoun does not refer to any specific person, place, or thing. Study the indefinite pronouns below. Notice which are singular and which are plural.

INDEFINITE PRONOUNS				
Singular	another	anybody	anyone	anything	each
	either	everybody	everyone	everything	one
	neither	nobody	somebody	someone	no one
Plural	both	few	many	several	

With singular indefinite pronouns, use singular personal pronouns. With plural indefinite pronouns, use plural personal pronouns.

Singular

> In Siberia, the girls waded through mud so deep that *one* lost *her* shoe.
>
> *Each* of the boys hoped *he* could raise a champion racing pigeon.
>
> *Nobody* neglected *his or her* potato plot during the brief summer.

Plural

> In the hot, flea-infested huts, *few* could control *their* tempers.
>
> *Many* knew Vanya the bum, but *they* didn't know his story.

Don't be confused if a phrase appears between the indefinite pronoun and the personal pronoun.

◄ **HIS OR HER?** . . . .
When the person referred to could be either male or female, use "he or she," "him or her," or "his or her(s)."

ADDITIONAL RESOURCES
Unit Four Resource Book
Language Workshop Practice, p. 34
Grammar and Usage Copy Masters, pp. 38–40

Links to Writer's Craft

For more about pronoun problems, see *The Writer's Craft,* Grade 7, "Using Pronouns," pages 432–442.

Objectives

- To distinguish between singular and plural indefinite pronouns
- To use indefinite pronouns correctly
- To use *who* and *whom* correctly

Teaching Strategies

Indefinite Pronouns

Students may have difficulty associating words such as *everyone* and *everything* with singular usage. Help them to understand the difference between several people acting together as one person, and several people acting individually. Give students these examples, and suggest that they write them in their journals.

Singular indefinite pronoun:
- Everyone agrees with the committee's decision. (Here a group is acting together as one person. Suggest that students visualize a crowd shouting together in agreement.)

Plural indefinite pronoun:
- Many agree with the decision. (Here the people are acting individually. Suggest that students visualize a crowd in which scattered people are shouting "Yes!" and scattered people are shouting "No!")

Indefinite pronoun and verb separated by a phrase:
- One of my favorite speeches is President Kennedy's inaugural address. (Here the subject is *one,* not *speeches.* Have students mentally omit the phrase to see which verb to use.)

Provide the following practice for students.

1. No one (want, <u>wants</u>) to listen to speeches all day.

2. However, someone in our class (use, <u>uses</u>) (<u>his or her</u>, their) lunch period for listening to televised political speeches.

3. Speaking of speeches, few (is, <u>are</u>) really entertaining.

4. However, several of the most famous speeches (is, <u>are</u>) good to know.

5. Each of them (offer, <u>offers</u>) a message to remember forever.

Answers to Exercise 1

1. he or she

2. him or her

3. his or her

4. their

5. their

6. his or her

7. its

8. his or her

9. his or her

10. their

Interrogative Pronouns Who and Whom

Although students usually don't have a problem using *who* as a subject and *whom* as an object, some do feel silly saying "To whom did you give the book?" To make students more comfortable with the formal-sounding use of *whom*, you may want to give them some opportunities to use the word orally, figuring that the more they use it, the less strange it will sound to them. For example, you might have students work in groups to write short stories or skits set in very formal places (consulates, exclusive country clubs, high-society functions). Later, have the stories read and the skits performed while the audience critiques the speakers' use of *who* and *whom*.

Answers to Exercise 2

1. Who

2. whom

3. whom

| Incorrect | Each of the girls studied *their* lessons. (The personal pronoun should agree with *each*, not with *girls*.) |
| Correct | Each of the girls studied *her* lessons. |

Exercise 1   Concept Check   For each indefinite pronoun, choose the correct personal pronoun. Write your choices on your paper.

1. In Esther's hut, everyone shared what (he or she, they) had.
2. No one wanted Vanya the bum to live with (him or her, them).
3. Couldn't anybody have a home of (his or her, their) own?
4. Many of the villagers had (his or her, their) own reasons for not trusting Vanya.
5. Several told (his or her, their) friends that Vanya was a thief.
6. Could anyone hide (his or her, their) surprise at Vanya's story?
7. He endured many hardships, and each left (its, their) mark.
8. Long ago, one of Vanya's neighbors had spread (his or her, their) opinion that this honest, well-educated man was a traitor.
9. Soon, as everybody watched from (his or her, their) window, Vanya was removed and sent to prison in Siberia.
10. Esther liked and respected Vanya; both enjoyed (his or her, their) time together.

Who and Whom

When *who* and *whom* are used to ask questions, they are called interrogative pronouns. *Who* is used for the subject form and *whom* is the object form.

Who found the ruined hut? (*Who* is the subject of *found*.)

Whom did you invite to dinner? (*Whom* is the direct object. The subject is *you*, and the verb is *did invite*.)

From *whom* did you hear the news? (*Whom* is the object of the preposition *from*.)

REMINDER
To find the subject and verb of a question more easily, change the question into a statement: *You did hear the news from whom.*

Exercise 2   Concept Check   In each sentence below, choose the correct interrogative pronoun.

1. (Who, Whom) told Esther how to make dye from onion peels?
2. From (who, whom) did she get the material for her curtains?
3. In school, (who, whom) did Esther like best?

Grammar Games: Whodunit?

Prepare a sheet of cardboard with a spinner, and then write the indefinite pronouns and the words *who* and *whom* in a circle around it. Group the class into two teams, and tell them that they will construct a mystery story using the target words on the cardboard.

Have players from both teams alternately spin and use their target words in sentences, gradually composing an oral mystery story. Players who use their words incorrectly are out, as are those whose sentences do not advance the mystery. (Note that players don't have to memorize the story, but they have to pay enough attention to know what has already happened when their turn comes.) The last three sets of players on each team receive the dubious honor of bringing the mystery to a close and tying up all the narrative "loose ends." The team with the most players remaining at the end of the game wins.

4. (Who, Whom) reminded Esther of her grandmother's flower garden?

5. (Who, Whom) did Mrs. Rudomin tell about the public baths?

6. With (who, whom) did the Rudomins sit and watch the stars?

7. To (who, whom) did Esther tell the news about Vanya?

8. (Who, Whom) decided how the family would treat Vanya?

9. (Who, Whom) did Vanya blame for his misfortunes?

10. (Who, Whom) knows why Vanya left the Rudomins?

Exercise 3 Proofreading Skill   Correct the pronoun problems in the following paragraph. Look for problems with indefinite pronouns and personal pronouns, and with the use of *who* and *whom*.

> Growing up on the Siberian steppe was hard. No one had enough room for their belongings, or even enough food. Everyone had to find ways to keep their self-respect. Esther's family noticed a ruined hut and moved in. Each of the family members used their talents to make the hut a home. Whom would have expected Esther to make bright curtains in such a place? Few could believe his or her eyes when Mr. Rudomin found glass for the windows. Who did the village leader send to live with the family then? He sent someone with almost nothing to call their own. It seemed that all of the family were being punished for his or her pride.

Exercise 4 Revise Your Writing   Reread the persuasive speech you wrote for the Writer's Workshop on pages 388–392. Then follow the steps below.

1. Lightly underline each indefinite pronoun you have used. Label each **S** (singular) or **P** (plural).

2. Correct any agreement problems involving indefinite pronouns and personal pronouns.

3. Lightly circle the words *who* and *whom* each time you find them.

4. Correct any problems involving the use of *who* and *whom*.

LANGUAGE HANDBOOK
. . . .
For review and practice: Section 5, Using Pronouns, pages 736–737, 738–739; Section 8, Subject-Verb Agreement, page 762.

4. Who

5. Whom

6. whom

7. whom

8. Who

9. Whom

10. Who

Answers to Exercise 3

Growing up on the Siberian steppe was hard. No one had enough room for <u>his or her</u> belongings, or even enough food. Everyone had to find ways to keep <u>his or her</u> self-respect. Esther's family noticed a ruined hut and moved in. Each of the family members used <u>his or her</u> talents to make the hut a home. <u>Who</u> would have expected Esther to make bright curtains in such a place? Few could believe <u>their</u> eyes when Mr. Rudomin found glass for the windows. <u>Whom</u> did the village leader send to live with the family then? He sent someone with almost nothing to call <u>his</u> own. It seemed that all of the family were being punished for <u>their</u> pride.

Answers to Exercise 4
Check students' papers randomly to note whether directions have been followed.

Closure

Have students note that using such grammatical structures as indefinite pronouns correctly is one sign of a literate speaker and writer. Encourage the class to use these structures in writing and speaking whenever possible, and consciously pair the correct verbs and modifiers with them.

Additional Practice

Choose the correct verb. (Answers are underlined.)

1. One of the most interesting stories in the world of fashion (<u>is</u>, are) the history of jeans.

2. Almost everyone (consider, <u>considers</u>) jeans an American garment.

3. Yet almost everything about jeans (<u>has</u>, have) a tie to other cultures.

4. For example, nobody (seem, <u>seems</u>) surprised at the names of French designers on today's jeans.

5. Furthermore, one of Italy's cities, Genoa, (claim, <u>claims</u>) fame for the name *jeans*.

6. Another, the French city of Nimes, (lend, <u>lends</u>) its name to denim.

7. Everybody (expect, <u>expects</u>) jeans to be functional and comfortable.

8. No one (want, <u>wants</u>) seams to break or pockets to rip.

Teaching Strategies

Share with students that critical listening begins before a speaker even gets up to speak. Approaching the speaker with an open and inquisitive mind will prepare students for listening intelligently.

Have a volunteer read the strategies for critical listening before, during, and after hearing a speaker. Ask students to name any personal strategies or guides that they use to help them listen well. In addition to the strategies in the text, the following may also be of use to students:

■ When listening to a topic in current events, have students ask themselves what might have been left out of the report and whether there is another side to the story.

■ When listening to a news report, especially to a report of late-breaking news, tell students not to accept every detail they hear. Remind them that when late-breaking news occurs, many "facts" have not yet been verified.

■ When listening to a persuasive speech or report, advise students not to be swayed by "emotional" language or editorializing. A speaker editorializes when he or she allows personal opinions to influence word choice.

Answers to Exercise
Ask to see students' evaluations of their listening skills.

ADDITIONAL RESOURCES
Unit Four Resource Book
Speaking and Listening Workshop
    Practice, p. 35

SPEAKING AND LISTENING
WORKSHOP

CRITICAL LISTENING

Critical listening doesn't mean finding fault. Instead, it means listening carefully and thinking about what you hear. You use critical listening skills before, during, and after any presentation, speech, class lecture, and even when watching television.

Before You Listen

1. Keep an open mind   Don't prejudge the speaker. Instead, think about the speaker's purpose. Try to predict what he or she might focus on.

2. Prepare yourself   Go over what you already know about the speaker's topic. Then think of some questions or areas you'd like to see discussed.

While You Listen

3. Look interested   Be kind to the speaker. Return his or her eye contact, and make it clear that you're paying attention. If you chat with neighbors, the speaker may get thrown off track.

▶ **4. Concentrate**   Don't just let the words flow over you—pick up on the speaker's strategies. Is he or she relying on logic, emotion, or both? Does the speaker's reasoning make sense? Does he or she supply enough facts and statistics, or does he or she use mostly opinions?

5. Process key ideas   Catch the speaker's key words and ideas, perhaps jotting them down. Then, mentally, put them in your own words. Do they still make sense? Do they have the same impact?

After You Listen

6. Ask questions   Repeat the speaker's words in your questions, so that you check your understanding as you get answers.

7. Sum up and evaluate   What does the speaker want you to do, and why? Are you convinced? Why or why not?

Exercise   Follow Steps 1–6 above as you listen to a classmate give his or her persuasive speech. Then write answers to the questions in Step 7. Finally, write an evaluation of your own listening.

HELP!
For tips on spotting faulty reasoning, see the Reader's Workshop on page 347.

IN OTHER CLASSES
In math class, try mentally putting key ideas and instructions into your own words to check your understanding and remember what you hear.

Additional Practice

Write what is wrong with the critical listening behaviors noted below. (Responses are given.)

1. Alessandro accepts anything a speaker says as truth. *(Speakers can be wrong about some facts.)*

2. Margaret looks around the classroom while a speaker is talking. According to her, "I can listen and look around at the same time." *(Looking at the speaker helps students to concentrate on his or her words. It also helps to keep the speaker on track.)*

BONDS OF THE HEART

When people form close relationships, anything may happen. The bonds they establish may bring unexpected joy, comic irritation, heartfelt love, or even heroic sacrifice. Sometimes, their bonds can endure all hardships, even surviving separation or death. At other times, bonds strain to the breaking point.

In the following selections you will read about very different links between people. The characters range from a man who falls instantly in love to an old woman who takes years to let down her guard. As you read, think about how these relationships compare to your own.

Subunit Preview

Invite students to read the introduction to Subunit 2, "Bonds of the Heart." Encourage them to identify the kinds of person-to-person relationships that involve close bonds or ties, such as those between parent and child, siblings, husband and wife or friends. Why are such relationships often demanding?

INTEGRATING THE LANGUAGE ARTS

The literary selections in this subunit focus on the theme of "Bonds of the Heart." Reading skills, literature skills, writing options, language study, vocabulary, and spelling skills are all based on these literary selections.

Writer's Workshop After reading several selections that deal with bonds of the heart, students will write an analysis of a character from one of these works.

Language Workshop The Language Workshop in this subunit deals with sentence combining. Students will discover how joining sentences and sentence parts can help them connect their thoughts and make their writing more interesting.

Vocabulary Workshop The Vocabulary Workshop in this subunit deals with denotation and connotation. Students will see how words' connotations can suggest positive or negative qualities.

FOR ADDITIONAL CHALLENGE

The following selections offer extra challenge in the exploration of the subunit theme:

After the Rain, novel by Norma Mazer

Face to Face: A Collection of Stories by Celebrated Soviet and American Writers, edited by Anatoly Aleksin and Thomas Pettepiece

ADDITIONAL RESOURCES

Family and Community Involvement Source Book, p. 16
Guidelines for Reading and Literature Assessment: Observation Assessment Forms

Observation Assessment

Observing how students respond to the text, to the classroom instruction, and to peers is an important part of an assessment program. The following suggestions and the form in the *Guidelines for Reading and Literature Assessment* booklet can be used to implement observation assessment.

■ Group Interaction As students work through this subunit, assess how they interact in collaboration with others. Note how frequently they engage in speaking and listening activities, and how often they initiate discussion, dialogue, or debate about the meaning of the text. Evaluate how well they provide positive support for their peers in exchange of ideas. Assess how well students share goals, values, and practices with others. Note if they play several roles, such as performer, audience member, leader, and supporter.

Objectives

■ To understand and analyze a short story

■ To identify characteristics of the third-person point of view and to review the concept of minor characters

■ To enrich reading by distinguishing between static and dynamic characters

■ To express understanding of the story through a choice of writing forms, including a learning log, a personal narrative, a story, and a speech

Prereading/Motivation

Examine What You Know

Discussion Prompts What image do you have of the mentally retarded? What advice would you give to someone who feels uncomfortable around retarded people?

Expand Your Knowledge

Additional Background Most forms of mental retardation are caused by chromosomal defects. Although IQ tests were once believed to be the best measures of retardation, today assessments of physical and social skills and emotional maturity are also used.

Enrich Your Reading

Have students make a character chart, listing the name of each character as he or she is introduced. Ask them to identify under each name any points in the story where that character changes and to describe the causes of the changes.

Thematic Link—
Bonds of the Heart

When jars of fresh flowers start appearing in the window of Stan's Hardware, people in town suspect that someone has a crush on Dolores. Dolores's admirer turns out to be Ernie, whose bonds of the heart transform him and others.

Fiction   A *Crush*
CYNTHIA RYLANT

Examine What You Know   (Prior Knowledge)

How do you react toward people who are mentally retarded? Are you uncomfortable or frightened? Do you feel pity or curiosity or compassion? Or do you just see them as human beings? Discuss with your classmates how people of normal intelligence often react to mentally retarded people, and whether you think such reactions are justified.

Expand Your Knowledge   (Building Background)

The most common standard by which people's intelligence is compared is a number called IQ, or intelligence quotient. IQ is measured by tests. While the average person has an IQ of 90 to 109, people with an IQ below 70 are considered mentally retarded. Retarded people, such as one of the characters you will meet in this story, are classified by the degree of their retardation as mildly, moderately, severely, or profoundly retarded. Today, about three percent of the people in the United States are considered retarded. In the past, many of the retarded were put into institutions. Today, however, most mentally handicapped people live within the community, either in group homes or with their families.

Enrich Your Reading   (Reading Skill)

■ *Author biography on Extend page*

Character Development   In the following story, some characters change and grow while others remain the same. A **static character** is one who changes little, if at all, from the beginning of a story to the end. A **dynamic character** changes significantly. As you read the next story, decide which characters are static and which are dynamic.

398   UNIT FOUR   BONDS OF THE HEART

JOURNAL WRITING IDEAS

■ If you had a crush on someone, would you reveal it? How?

■ On what occasions do people give each other fresh flowers? Would you enjoy receiving fresh flowers? Explain.

COLLABORATIVE LEARNING OPTIONS

Opportunities for collaborative learning include annotation 5 (p. 400), Speaking . . . Listening . . . Viewing (p. 402), Vocabulary Practice (p. 406), Options for Learning 2 and 3 (p. 407), and Cross-Curricular Projects (p. 407).

ADDITIONAL RESOURCES

Unit Four Resource Book
Reader's Guidesheet, p. 36
Reading Skills, p. 37
Literature Skills, p. 38
Vocabulary Connections, p. 39
Spelling Connections, p. 40
Comprehension and Vocabulary Check Tests, p. 41
Selection Test, pp. 42–43

A *Crush*

CYNTHIA RYLANT

When the windows of Stan's Hardware started filling up with flowers, everyone in town knew something had happened. Excess flowers usually mean death, but since these were all real flowers bearing the aroma of nature instead of floral preservative, and since they stood bunched in clear Mason jars instead of impaled on Styrofoam crosses, everyone knew nobody had died. So they all figured somebody had a crush and kept quiet.

A ▶

There wasn't really a Stan of Stan's Hardware. Dick Wilcox was the owner, and since he'd never liked his own name, he gave his store half the name of his childhood hero, Stan Laurel in the movies. Dick had been married for twenty-seven years. Once, his wife Helen had dropped a German chocolate cake on his head at a Lion's Club dance, so Dick and Helen were not likely candidates for the honest expression of the flowers in those clear Mason jars lining the windows of Stan's Hardware, and speculation had to move on to Dolores.

1

Dolores was the assistant manager at Stan's and had worked there for twenty years, since high school. She knew the store like a mother knows her baby, so Dick—who had trouble keeping up with things like prices and new brands of drywall compound—tried to keep himself busy in the back and give Dolores the run of the floor. This worked fine because the carpenters and plumbers and painters in town trusted Dolores and took her advice to heart. They also liked her tattoo.

2

Dolores was the only woman in town with a tattoo.

Dolores was the only woman in town with a tattoo. On the days she went sleeveless, one could see it on the taut brown skin of her upper arm: "Howl at the Moon." The picture was of a baying coyote, which must have been a dark gray in its early days but which had faded to the color of the spackling paste Dolores stocked in the third aisle. Nobody had gotten out of Dolores the true story behind the tattoo. Some of the men who came in liked to show off their own, and they'd roll up their sleeves or pull open their shirts, exhibiting bald eagles and rattlesnakes and Confederate flags, and they'd

Words to Know and Use | **impaled** (im pāld') *adj.* pierced through **impale** *v.*

399

Teaching Strategies

VOCABULARY PREVIEW

These vocabulary words are defined at the bottom of the selection pages on which they appear.

cherish to treasure

discreetly tactfully

impaled pierced through

suitor a man seeking a woman's love

swarthy having darkish skin

LIMITED ENGLISH PROFICIENCY

■ Use the Reader's Guidesheet, *Unit Four Resource Book,* page 36.

★ Text annotations marked with a red star (2, 5) may be particularly helpful for students with limited English proficiency.

TEXT ANNOTATIONS

1. ACTIVE READING: Review
Ask students why Dick is ruled out as the receiver of the anonymous flowers. *(Possible responses: He's been married for twenty-seven years; neither he nor his wife seems romantic.)*

2. VOCABULARY: Specialized Vocabulary
Some students may be unfamiliar with the names of materials stocked in hardware stores, such as "dry wall compound" here and "spackling paste" in the next paragraph. If necessary, identify these for students as names of materials and tools someone might use in building or repairing a house. ★

Guided Reading for Less-Proficient Students

These questions can help guide students through the reading. Ask each question at the point of the selection where the capital letter and arrow appear in the margin. In addition, you may wish to use appropriate Active Reading annotations.

A. What appears in the windows of Stan's Hardware that makes everybody think someone has a crush? *(bouquets of fresh flowers)* Recalling

B. What makes some women in town think Dolores doesn't want love? *(She doesn't wear makeup or dress attractively.)* Recalling

C. Where has Ernie spent most of his life and why? *(in his house; he is retarded and his mother has kept him in)* Inferring

D. How does Ernie get his packets of seeds? *(They come to his house by mistake.)* Recalling

Continued on page 400

3. **ACTIVE READING: Question**
Invite students to speculate about why Dolores does not tell anyone the origin of her tattoo. *(Possible responses: She is embarrassed about how she got it; it means too much to her to discuss with anyone; she thinks it's no one's business but her own.)*

4. **ACTIVE READING: Evaluate**
Ask students whether they think the people in town have good reasons for thinking that Dolores is not likely to attract a man. *(Any response is valid.)*

5. **VOCABULARY: Specialized Vocabulary**
Some students may not be familiar with the fashion and cosmetic references here. Ask those who know their meanings to explain the terms "blunt cut," "silk-blend blouse," "Liz Claiborne skirt," "beige foundation," and "gray liner."

For Alternative Learning Styles Have small groups of students find advertisements in fashion magazines to illustrate the terms' meanings. ★

6. **LITERARY CONCEPT: Suspense**
Ask students why this part of the story is suspenseful. What makes them want to keep reading? *(Possible responses: The narrator says a man loves Dolores but does not provide any details about him; the narrator lists all the things the man does not know about Dolores but doesn't explain why he loves her, so readers become curious about him.)*

try to coax out of Dolores the history of her coyote. All of the men had gotten their tattoos when they were in the service, drunk on weekend leave and full of the spitfire of young soldiers. Dolores had never been in the service, and she'd never seen weekend leave, and there wasn't a tattoo parlor anywhere near. They couldn't figure why or where any half-sober woman would have a howling coyote ground into the soft skin of her upper arm. But Dolores wasn't telling.

That the flowers in Stan's front window had anything to do with Dolores seemed completely improbable. As far as anyone knew, Dolores had never been in love, nor had anyone ever been in love with her. Some believed it was the tattoo, of course, or the fine, dark hair coating Dolores's upper lip which kept <u>suitors</u> away. Some felt it was because Dolores was just more of a man than most of the men in town, and fellows couldn't figure out how to court someone who knew more about the carburetor of a car or the backside of a washing machine than they did. Others thought Dolores simply didn't want love. This was a popular theory among the women in town who sold Avon and Mary Kay cosmetics. Whenever one of them ran into the hardware for a package of light bulbs or some batteries, she would mentally pluck every one of

the black hairs above Dolores's lip. Then she'd wash that grease out of Dolores's hair, give her a good blunt cut, dress her in a decent silk-blend blouse with a nice Liz Claiborne skirt from the Sports line, and, finally, tone down that <u>swarthy</u>, longshoreman look of Dolores's with a concealing beige foundation,[1] some frosted peach lipstick, and a good gray liner for the eyes.

Dolores simply didn't want love, the Avon lady would think as she walked back to her car carrying her little bag of batteries. If she did, she'd fix herself up.

The man who was in love with Dolores and who brought her zinnias and cornflowers and nasturtiums and marigolds and asters and four-o'clocks in clear Mason jars did not know any of this. He did not know that men showed Dolores their tattoos. He did not know that Dolores understood how to use and to sell a belt sander. He did not know that Dolores needed some concealing beige foundation so she could get someone to love her. The man who brought flowers to Dolores on Wednesdays when the hardware opened its doors at 7:00 A.M. didn't care who Dolores had ever been or what anyone had ever thought of her. He loved her, and he wanted to bring her flowers.

Ernie had lived in this town all of his life and had never before met Dolores. He was thirty-three years old, and for thirty-one of those years he had lived at home with his mother in a small dark house on the edge of

---

1. **concealing beige foundation:** a cosmetic that covers skin flaws.

Words to Know and Use	**suitor** (sōōt' ər) *n.* a man seeking a woman's love **swarthy** (swôrth' ē) *adj.* having darkish skin

400

Guided Reading for Less-Proficient Students

Continued from page 399

E. Why does Ernie move into the group home? *(His mother has died and he cannot live alone.)* Recalling

F. What finally draws Ernie outside? *(his love of plants; seeing Jack plant seeds)* Recalling

G. What inspires Ernie to plant his flower seeds? *(falling in love with Dolores)* Recalling

H. What happens when Ernie leaves the flowers for Dolores? *(Dolores smells them and puts them in the window; watching her makes Ernie and Jack happy.)* Recalling

I. At the end, how does Jack show he understands Ernie? *(by making him an indoor garden)* Inferring town near Beckwith's Orchards. Ernie had been a beautiful baby, with a shock of shining black hair and large blue eyes and a round, wise face. But as he had grown, it had become clearer and clearer that though he was indeed a perfectly beautiful child, his mind had not developed with the same perfection. Ernie would not be able to speak in sentences until he was six years old. He would not be able to count the apples in a bowl until he was eight. By the time he was ten, he could sing a simple song. At age twelve, he understood what a joke was. And when he was twenty, something he saw on television made him cry.

Ernie's mother kept him in the house with her because it was easier, so Ernie knew nothing of the world except this house. They lived, the two of them, in tiny dark rooms always illuminated by the glow of a television set, Ernie's bags of Oreos and Nutter Butters littering the floor, his baseball cards scattered across the sofa, his heavy winter coat thrown over the arm of a chair so he could wear it whenever he wanted, and his box of Burpee seed packages sitting in the middle of the kitchen table.

These Ernie <u>cherished</u>. The seeds had been delivered to his home by mistake. One day a woman wearing a brown uniform had pulled up in a brown truck, walked quickly to the front porch of Ernie's house, set a box down, and with a couple of toots of her horn, driven off again. Ernie had watched her through the curtains and, when she was gone, had ventured onto the porch and shyly, cautiously, picked up the box. His mother checked it when he carried it inside.

The box didn't have their name on it, but the brown truck was gone, so whatever was in the box was theirs to keep. Ernie pulled off the heavy tape, his fingers trembling, and found inside the box more little packages of seeds than he could count. He lifted them out, one by one, and examined the beautiful photographs of flowers on each. His mother was not interested, had returned to the television, but Ernie sat down at the kitchen table and quietly looked at each package for a long time, his fingers running across the slick paper and outlining the shapes of zinnias and cornflowers and nasturtiums and marigolds and asters and four-o'clocks, his eyes drawing up their colors.

Two months later Ernie's mother died. A neighbor found her at the mailbox beside the road. People from the county courthouse came out to get Ernie, and as they ushered him from the home he would never see again, he picked up the box of seed packages from his kitchen table and passed through the doorway.

7. ACTIVE READING: Review
Ask students what the house Ernie shares with his mother suggests about his mother and his life. (Possible responses: Ernie's mother might be depressed or ashamed to have a retarded son; she doesn't have the energy or skills to take him outside; Ernie's life is limited and boring.)

8. LITERARY CONCEPT: Character
Invite students to draw conclusions about Ernie from what they have read thus far. (Ernie seems like a young child; he leaves his belongings all over; he's crazy about cookies; he is shy and nervous about going outside.)

9. LITERARY CONCEPT: Imagery
Have students explain what the author's description of Ernie's eyes "drawing up" the colors from the pictures on the seed packets suggests. (Possible responses: that Ernie is taking them in like a sponge or a thirsty plant; that the packets fascinate Ernie)

Words to Know and Use	**cherish** (cher′ ish) *v.* to hold dear; treasure

401

10. ACTIVE READING: Review
Discuss with students how Ernie's life changes at the group home. *(He starts learning how to do things for himself, such as simple cooking, cleaning, and caring for plants.)*

11. ACTIVE READING: Question
Ask students why Ernie is afraid to go into the garden. If necessary, help students by reading the following example of a think-aloud, or model one of your own.

Think-Aloud Script Why is Ernie so afraid to go into the garden? I know that his mother always kept him in the house with her, so he didn't go out for years. When he did go out on his mother's porch to get the box of seeds, the author used the word *ventured*, as if Ernie's going outside were an adventure. If going onto the porch of his old home was scary, going into the garden of the group home would be even scarier.

12. ACTIVE READING: Review
Ask students what Ernie's disbelief about the vegetables suggests about the way his mind works. *(Possible response: Ernie can't believe in something he hasn't seen.)*

Eventually Ernie was moved to a large white house near the main street of town. This house was called a group home, because in it lived a group of people who, like Ernie, could not live on their own. There were six of them. Each had his own room. When Ernie was shown the room that would be his, he put the box of Burpee seeds—which he had kept with him since his mother's death—on the little table beside the bed, and then he sat down on the bed and cried.

E ▶

Ernie cried every day for nearly a month. And then he stopped. He dried his tears, and he learned how to bake refrigerator biscuits and how to dust mop and what to do if the indoor plants looked brown.

10

Ernie loved watering the indoor plants, and it was this pleasure which finally drew him outside. One of the young men who worked at the group home—a college student named Jack—grew a large garden in the back of the house. It was full of tomato vines and the large yellow blossoms of healthy squash. During his first summer at the house, Ernie would stand at the kitchen window, watching Jack and sometimes a resident of the home move among the vegetables. Ernie was curious, but too afraid to go into the garden.

11

Then one day when Ernie was watching through the window, he noticed that Jack was ripping open several slick little packages and emptying them into the ground. Ernie panicked and ran to his room. But the box of Burpee seeds was still there on his table, untouched. He grabbed it, slid it under his bed, then went back through the house and out into the garden as if he had done this every day of his life.

He stood beside Jack, watching him empty seed packages into the soft black soil, and as the packages were emptied, Ernie asked for them, holding out his hand, his eyes on the photographs of red radishes and purple eggplant. Jack handed the empty packages over with a smile and with that gesture became Ernie's first friend.

◀ F

12

Jack tried to explain to Ernie that the seeds would grow into vegetables, but Ernie could not believe this until he saw it come true. And when it did, he looked all the more intently at the packages of zinnias and cornflowers and the rest hidden beneath his bed. He thought more deeply about them, but he could not carry them to the garden. He could not let the garden have his seeds.

That was the first year in the large white house.

The second year, Ernie saw Dolores, and after that he thought of nothing else but her and of the photographs of flowers beneath his bed.

Love is such a mystery.

Jack had decided to take Ernie downtown for breakfast every Wednesday morning to ease him into the world outside that of the group home. They left very early, at 5:45 A.M., so there would be few people and almost no traffic to frighten Ernie and make him beg for his room. Jack and Ernie drove to the Big Boy restaurant which sat across the street from Stan's Hardware. There they ate eggs and bacon and French toast among those whose work demanded rising before the sun: bus drivers, policemen, nurses, millworkers. Their first time in the Big Boy,

Speaking . . . Listening . . . Viewing

Viewing Call attention to the fact that although Ernie never speaks in the story, his feelings are made clear in other ways. Ask students to suggest ways in which feelings can be communicated nonverbally. *(Possible responses: by body language, by facial expression, by actions)* To demonstrate the concept of nonverbal communication, have students watch about five minutes of a videotaped TV show or movie with the sound turned off.

As they watch, have students call out what they think the actors are feeling or saying. Then replay the tape with sound to contrast students' ideas with the actual dialogue. These questions may aid discussion:

1. What body language did the actors use?

2. What facial expressions conveyed feelings?

3. Were there particular actions that gave you clues to how the characters were feeling?

Ernie was too nervous to eat. The second time, he could eat, but he couldn't look up. The third time, he not only ate everything on his plate, but he lifted his head and he looked out the window of the Big Boy restaurant toward Stan's Hardware across the street. There he saw a dark-haired woman in jeans and a black T-shirt unlocking the front door of the building, and that was the moment Ernie started loving Dolores and thinking about giving up his seeds to the soft black soil of Jack's garden.

Love is such a mystery, and when it strikes the heart of one as mysterious as Ernie himself, it can hardly be spoken of. Ernie could not explain to Jack why he went directly to his room later that morning, pulled the box of Burpee seeds from under his bed, then grabbed Jack's hand in the kitchen and walked with him to the garden, where Ernie had come to believe things would grow. Ernie handed the packets of seeds one by one to Jack, who stood in silent admiration of the lovely photographs before asking Ernie several times, "Are you sure you want to plant these?" Ernie was sure. It didn't take him very long, and when the seeds all lay under the moist black earth, Ernie carried his empty packages inside the house and spent the rest of the day spreading them across his bed in different arrangements.

That was in June. For the next several Wednesdays at 7:00 A.M., Ernie watched every movement of the dark-haired woman behind the lighted windows of Stan's Hardware. Jack watched Ernie watch Dolores and discreetly said nothing.

When Ernie's flowers began growing in

Illustration by Patty Dryden.

July, Ernie spent most of his time in the garden. He would watch the garden for hours, as if he expected it suddenly to move or to impress him with a quick trick. The fragile green stems of his flowers stood uncertainly in the soil, like baby colts on their first legs, but the young plants performed no magic for Ernie's eyes. They saved their shows for the middle of the night and next day surprised Ernie with tender small blooms in all the colors the photographs had promised.

The flowers grew fast and hardy, and one early Wednesday morning, when they looked as big and bright as their pictures on the empty packages, Ernie pulled a glass

Words to Know and Use	**discreetly** (di skrēt′ lē) *adv.* in a polite way; tactfully

403

13. ACTIVE READING: Review
Ask students to **infer** what qualities Jack has that enable him to be a good friend to Ernie. *(Possible responses: patience, an ability to notice and appreciate small changes, gentleness, respect for Ernie's feelings, a willingness to try new things one at a time)*

14. ACTIVE READING: Connect
Ask students whether they share the narrator's sense of wonder at how mysterious love is. *(Any response is valid.)*

Art Note
The giving of flowers is treated by Patty Dryden as a spontaneous, almost magical act. In her brisk strokes we see a man about to offer the flowers that are hidden behind his back—while the flowers themselves seem to burst into passionate flames. The viewer's gaze is drawn forcefully to the flowers, which tell us more about the man than his face would. *Explain how the artist makes sure that the viewer will focus on the flowers. Then write a title for this painting.*

15. ACTIVE READING: Review
Ask students what this passage suggests about how Ernie thinks. *(Possible responses: Ernie does not know how slowly plants grow; he expects the plants to change suddenly; he's afraid he'll miss something.)*

Looking at Style

Point out that Cynthia Rylant sometimes focuses on a significant detail that tells something about a character and also leaves a sharp visual image in the mind. Have students reread the passage about Dolores's tattoo on pages 399–400 and discuss the significance of that detail with these questions:

1. What does the tattoo tell about Dolores?

2. What does the tattoo show about her relationships with people?

3. What visual detail would you associate with Ernie?

16. ACTIVE READING: Evaluate
Ask students to discuss how giving flowers affects Ernie and what he expects in return. *(Possible responses: Just giving them to Dolores makes him happy; he expects nothing in return.)* Ask if they think most men would be content just to give flowers without identifying themselves or expecting something in return. *(Any response is valid.)*

17. LITERARY CONCEPT: Theme
Encourage students to explain what theme is suggested by the changes in Dick's and Dolores's behavior. *(Possible responses: Love changes people; love brightens our lives; being appreciated makes a person appreciate others.)*

18. ACTIVE READING: Review
Ask students what they have learned from Ernie and Jack about mentally retarded people and their friends. *(Possible responses: Mentally retarded people can do many things, and they have strong interests and feelings; people need to understand their feelings and encourage them to expand their worlds.)*

ENCOURAGING INDEPENDENT READING

The Broken Boy, novel by Karen Ackerman

Mental Retardation, nonfiction by Robert E. Dunbar

canning jar off a dusty shelf in the basement of his house. He washed the jar, half filled it with water, then carried it to the garden where he placed in it one of every kind of flower he had grown. He met Jack at the car and rode off to the Big Boy with the jar of flowers held tight between his small hands. Jack told him it was a beautiful bouquet.

When they reached the door of the Big Boy, Ernie stopped and pulled at Jack's arm, pointing to the building across the street. "OK," Jack said, and he led Ernie to the front door of Stan's Hardware. It was 6:00 A.M., and the building was still dark. Ernie set the clear Mason jar full of flowers under the sign that read "Closed," then he smiled at Jack and followed him back across the street to get breakfast.

When Dolores arrived at seven and picked up the jar of zinnias and cornflowers and nasturtiums and marigolds and asters and four-o'clocks, Ernie and Jack were watching her from a booth in the Big Boy. Each had a wide smile on his face as Dolores put her nose to the flowers. Ernie giggled. They watched the lights of the hardware store come up and saw Dolores place the clear Mason jar on the ledge of the front window. They drove home still smiling.

All the rest of that summer, Ernie left a jar of flowers every Wednesday morning at the front door of Stan's Hardware. Neither Dick Wilcox nor Dolores could figure out why the flowers kept coming, and each of them assumed somebody had a crush on the

other. But the flowers had an effect on them anyway. Dick started spending more time out on the floor making conversation with the customers, while Dolores stopped wearing T-shirts to work and instead wore crisp white blouses with the sleeves rolled back off her wrists. Occasionally she put on a bracelet.

By summer's end Jack and Ernie had become very good friends, and when the flowers in the garden behind their house began to wither, and Ernie's face began to grow gray as he watched them, Jack brought home one bright day in late September a great long box. Ernie followed Jack as he carried it down to the basement and watched as Jack pulled a long glass tube from the box and attached this tube to the wall above a table. When Jack plugged in the tube's electric cord, a soft lavender light washed the room.

"Sunshine," said Jack.

Then he went back to his car for a smaller box. He carried this down to the basement where Ernie still stood staring at the strange light. Jack handed Ernie the small box, and when Ernie opened it, he found more little packages of seeds than he could count, with new kinds of photographs on the slick paper.

"Violets," Jack said, pointing to one of them.

Then he and Ernie went outside to get some dirt.

Comprehension Check

1. Why does the idea that the flowers are for Dolores seem improbable? *(Dolores has never seemed interested in love.)*

2. What is Ernie's most cherished possession? *(his seed packets)*

3. How do Ernie and Jack become friends? *(Jack gives Ernie some empty seeds packets .)*

4. When does Ernie fall in love with Dolores? *(when he first sees her)*

5. What does Ernie start thinking about after he sees Dolores? *(planting his flower seeds)*

6. What does Ernie do with his flowers? *(He leaves them in front of the hardware store for Dolores.)*

7. How do the flowers affect Dolores and Dick? *(Dolores dresses up a bit, and Dick is friendlier.)*

*R*esponding to Reading

First Impressions

1. How did the story make you feel? Describe your reaction in your journal or notebook.

Second Thoughts

2. What are the effects of Ernie's crush?

> **Think about**
> • the changes in Ernie
> • the changes in other characters

3. How do you think Dolores would react if she found out who was sending her flowers? Explain your opinion.

> **Think about**
> • what you know about her personality
> • the differences between Dolores and Ernie

4. Think about your previous discussion about retarded people. Have your feelings changed after reading the story? Why or why not?

Broader Connections

5. Do you have a friend, neighbor, or relative who is mentally disabled? How does the character of Ernie compare with the retarded person you know? How does the care received by Ernie compare with the care received by the person you know?

*L*iterary Concept: Third-Person Point of View

In a story told from a **third-person point of view,** the narrator is outside of the action, not one of the characters. This kind of narrator uses pronouns such as *he* and *she* to tell the story. A third-person narrative can be either omniscient or limited. If the story is told from an **omniscient,** or all-knowing, point of view, the narrator reports the thoughts of more than one character. In the **limited** point of view, the narrator tells what only one character thinks and feels. Is the third-person point of view in "A Crush" omniscient or limited? Why?

Concept Review: Minor Character   Jack is a minor character in this story. What does he contribute to the plot? Is he dynamic or static?

A CRUSH   405

Responding to Reading

1. Any response is valid.

2. **Possible responses:** Ernie's crush inspires him to plant his seeds and makes him happier; it gives him the courage to try new things; it makes the townspeople curious; it makes Dolores care about her appearance and Dick become more sociable with his customers.

3. **Possible responses:** She might be shocked or embarrassed or wish that he were someone else; she might understand and appreciate his admiration and be kind to Ernie, since she seems to treat people well.

4. Any response is valid.

5. Any response is valid.

Challenge Question

What might Ernie's seeds stand for or symbolize in this story? *(Possible responses: The seeds may symbolize Ernie's potential for growth; the seeds may symbolize the possibility of beauty or wonder.)*

Literary Concept: Third-Person Point of View

This story is told from a third-person omniscient point of view. The narrator tells us the thoughts and feelings of all the characters and gives details about their lives in the past.

Concept Review: Minor Character Jack introduces Ernie to gardening and brings him to town, where he sees Dolores; he is Ernie's friend and teacher. Jack is a static character; he does not change throughout the story.

Writing Options

The Writing Options are designed to meet varied student interests and abilities. Have each student choose one writing activity to complete.

Journal Update Invite students to add to their journal entries about "A Crush" by writing about one of these topics:

1. Predict a change that may happen "after" the story—when Ernie meets Dolores, for example.

2. Cynthia Rylant has said that she likes to write about people who don't get any attention and make them "shine with their beauty." Choose one of the characters and describe his or her inner beauty.

Links to
Writer's Craft

Writing Option 4 is an exercise in persuasive writing. For more practice, see **The Writer's Craft,** Grade 7, "Persuasion," pages 139–163.

Vocabulary Practice

Answers to Exercise

1. discreetly

2. swarthy

3. cherish

4. suitor

5. impaled

For Alternative Learning Styles
Have small groups of students brainstorm synonyms for each vocabulary word. Then have them use a thesaurus to add additional synonyms to their lists. Alternatively, have students write an analogy for each word, such as "Cherish is to despise as hot is to cold."

Closure

Tell students that, in the selections in this subunit, bonds of the heart change people's lives. Then elicit from students that a crush can range from a passion for a movie star to the start of a lasting love or friendship.

Writing Options

1. Assume that Jack is working in the group home as part of his college studies. Write an entry from his **learning log**—his personal learning diary—in which he discusses what he has learned from and about Ernie.

2. Write a **personal narrative** about a time when you had a crush on someone. Your narrative can be humorous or serious.

3. Everyone in town is curious about Dolores's tattoo. Write a **story** that explains how, when, where, and why she got her coyote tattoo.

4. How would you feel if in your neighborhood someone wanted to build a group home for retarded people? Write a **speech** you might deliver at a town meeting that explains your opinion.

Vocabulary Practice

Exercise On a separate sheet of paper, write the word from the list that best completes the meaning of the sentence.

1. While eating breakfast, Ernie __?__ watched the hardware store so that other people would not notice his interest.

2. Dolores had dark eyes and a __?__ complexion.

3. To love someone without reservation is to __?__ him or her.

4. If Ernie decided to try to convince Dolores to marry him, he would have been her __?__.

5. Empty seed packets, __?__ on sticks in the garden, showed which flowers were planted in each row.

> **Words to Know and Use**
>
> cherish
> discreetly
> impaled
> suitor
> swarthy

The Spelling Connection

Words from French Many words in the English language come from French. Some French letter patterns appear in words commonly used in English: *eur, eau,* silent final *t,* and silent final *ue.*

Examples: gour**met**   chauff**eur**   chat**eau**

French Words from the Selection

bou**quet**   restauran**t**   bei**ge**

Other French Words

amat**eur**   bur**eau**   ber**et**   lea**gue**
grand**eur**   plat**eau**   ball**et**   va**gue**

Exercise Replace wrong words with rhyming words.
1. I met Deborah in *buffet* class.
2. Nice young men always bring a girl a *toupee.*
3. Fold your clothes and put them in the *plateau.*
4. I've joined a club called the Junior *Fatigue.*
5. Why don't you wear a *ballet* on your head?

Options for Learning (Multimodal/Cross-Curricular Activities)

1 • Avon Calling Imagine that some women in town take it upon themselves to change Dolores's appearance. Draw or paint before-and-after pictures of Dolores, similar to those sometimes found in popular women's magazines.

2 • A Tale of Tattoo Research the history of tattoos. How are they created? What countries or cultures are known for tattoos? Why are they worn? What are unusual examples? Present your findings, with pictures if possible. In addition, you may want to design a tattoo for Ernie and Jack.

3 • Mood Music Imagine that you are making a movie version of this story. Choose a piece of music, either classical or popular, to use as the movie's musical theme. Explain your choice to the class.

4 • Special Olympics The Special Olympics was created not only to allow mentally handicapped people to participate in athletic activities, but also to help change the general public's attitude toward retarded people. Find out who started these games and when and how they work, both in the United States and internationally.

 FACT FINDER HEALTH

At what age would Ernie have spoken in sentences if he had been a normal child?

Cynthia Rylant
1954–

In the town of Kent, Ohio, where Cynthia Rylant lives, a strange small man sometimes brings flowers in Mason jars to waitresses at a little diner. He became the inspiration for Ernie. Beside the diner is a hardware store. "That's where my imagination found Dolores," reports Rylant.

Rylant grew up in the mountains of West Virginia. She lived with her grandparents for four years while her mother studied nursing. Later, she shared an apartment with her mother. She wrote her first book, *When I Was Young in the Mountains,* in one night. Nevertheless, she says, "It took me about seven years to feel like a writer."

Rylant has achieved success in many forms of writing: picture books for children, young-adult novels, short stories, and poetry. One of her recent books, *A Fine White Dust,* was named a Newbery Honor Book. Her award-winning book of poetry is called *Waiting to Waltz: A Childhood.*

A CRUSH   407

Cross-Curricular Projects

Science/Math If the season is suitable and the materials are available, students may wish to grow their own flowers. Before they begin, have them research which plants will grow in the available conditions. Have students make a graph showing how long each type of plant takes to germinate, grow to maturity, and flower.

Art Invite students to draw, paint, or otherwise create artistic representations of the flowers named in this story. Urge them to make each species recognizable and to suggest some of the power and meaning the flowers had for characters in the story.

Psychology Have teams of students find out more about group homes for the mentally retarded. Urge them to visit, if possible, a group home to interview the staff and residents. Have students share their findings in a panel discussion.

Objectives

- To analyze a narrative poem

- To understand the use of ono-matopoeia and to review the concepts of rhyme and rhythm

- To enrich reading by appreciating the narrative elements of a poem

- To express understanding of the selection through a choice of writing forms, including a summary and an epitaph

Prereading/Motivation

Examine What You Know

Discussion Prompts Would you donate a kidney to a loved one if the operation risked your own health? Under what circumstances, if any, would you give all your money to a friend? Do you think people who make great sacrifices for love are noble or foolish?

Expand Your Knowledge

Additional Background As British roads improved during the late 1600s, stagecoaches began running regularly. They often made stops at inns, which had stables to accommodate the horses. Since poor people rarely traveled and police forces did not yet exist, the passengers in stagecoaches were excellent targets for thieves.

Enrich Your Reading

For Alternative Learning Styles You might want to play a recording of a dramatic reading of this poem. Tell students to listen closely to find out what happens to the main characters.

Thematic Link— Bonds of the Heart

Romantic bonds cause both a brave young beauty and a dashing thief to lose their lives for each other. People say that on windy winter nights they can still hear the highwayman returning to see his love—a testimony to the power of the bonds of the heart.

Poetry

The *Highwayman*
ALFRED NOYES

*E*xamine What You Know
(Prior Knowledge)

What kinds of sacrifices would you be willing to make for someone you love? Rate each of the items below on a scale of 1 to 5. Discuss your responses with your classmates.

What would you sacrifice for love?				
Completely unwilling				Very willing
1	2	3	4	5
Money				
Personal property				
Personal goals				
Safety				
Freedom				
Life				

*E*xpand Your Knowledge (Building Background)

This poem about two lovers is set in eighteenth-century England. One of the lovers is a highwayman—a thief on horseback. Highwaymen were usually young and daring men who streaked through the night, skillfully racing their horses down dark and lonely country roads. They stole jewels and money from the rich who traveled by stagecoach. Some of them, like Robin Hood, gave what they stole to the poor. Redcoats—the same English soldiers who fought against American colonists—defended citizens from these raiders of the night.

*E*nrich Your Reading (Reading Skill)

■ *Author biography in Reader's Handbook*

Narrative Poetry Like fiction, narrative poetry tells a story. Unlike fiction, however, narrative poems are written in lines and stanzas. They rely on sound devices such as rhyme and rhythm and are meant to be read aloud. As you read, think about why the writer told the story of "The Highwayman" in the form of a poem.

JOURNAL WRITING IDEAS

■ What handsome or romantic outlaws have you encountered in films or on television? Do you find such outlaws appealing? Why or why not?

■ Describe a real-life sacrifice for love that you have heard about.

■ Do you believe that love can overcome all obstacles? Give reasons to support your opinion.

COLLABORATIVE LEARNING OPTIONS

Opportunities for collaborative learning include Examine What You Know and the Literary Concept (p. 414).

ADDITIONAL RESOURCES

Unit Four Resource Book
Reader's Guidesheet, p. 44
Reading Skills, p. 45
Literature Skills, p. 46
Vocabulary Connections, p. 47
Spelling Connections, p. 48
Comprehension Check Test, p. 49
Selection Test, p. 50

Technology and Enrichment
🎧 Audiocassette Tape 2, Side 1

The Highwayman

ALFRED NOYES

Part 1

1
The wind was a torrent of darkness among the gusty trees,
The moon was a ghostly galleon[1] tossed upon cloudy seas,
The road was a ribbon of moonlight over the purple moor,[2]
And the highwayman came riding—
5   Riding—riding—
The highwayman came riding, up to the old inn door.

2
He'd a French cocked hat on his forehead, a bunch of lace at his chin,
A coat of the claret[3] velvet, and breeches of brown doeskin.
They fitted with never a wrinkle. His boots were up to the thigh.
10 And he rode with a jeweled twinkle.
    His pistol butts a-twinkle.

3 His rapier hilt[4] a-twinkle, under the jeweled sky.

4
Over the cobbles[5] he clattered and clashed in the dark innyard
He tapped with his whip on the shutters, but all was locked and barred.
15 He whistled a tune to the window, and who should be waiting there
But the landlord's black-eyed daughter,
    Bess, the landlord's daughter,

A ▶ Plaiting[6] a dark red love knot into her long black hair.

---

1. **galleon** (gal' ē ən): a large sailing ship.
2. **moor:** a stretch of open, rolling wasteland, usually covered with heather.
3. **claret:** dark red, like the color of red wine.
4. **rapier** (rā' pē ər) **hilt:** sword handle.
5. **cobbles:** rounded stones used for paving roads.
6. **plaiting:** braiding.

THE HIGHWAYMAN   409

Original illustration by Charles Mikolaycak for "The Highwayman." Courtesy of the Kerlan Collection at the University of Minnesota. Used with permission of the illustrator and Lothrop, Lee and Shepard Publishers.

And dark in the dark old innyard a stable wicket[7] creaked
20 Where Tim the ostler[8] listened. His face was white and peaked.
5 His eyes were hollows of madness, his hair like moldy hay,
   But he loved the landlord's daughter,
      The landlord's red-lipped daughter,
   Dumb as a dog he listened, and he heard the robber say—

25 "One kiss, my bonny sweetheart, I'm after a prize tonight,
   But I shall be back with the yellow gold before the morning light;
6 Yet, if they press me sharply, and harry me through the day,
   Then look for me by moonlight,
      Watch for me by moonlight,
B ▶ 30 I'll come to thee by moonlight, though hell should bar the way."

---

7. **wicket:** a small door or gate.
8. **ostler** (äs′ ler): an inn employee who cares for guests' horses.

410   UNIT FOUR   BONDS OF THE HEART

Guided Reading for Less Proficient Students

(Continued from page 409)

F. Why does the highwayman return, and what happens to him when he does? *(He returns because he hears of Bess's death, and he is shot by the soldiers.)* Summarizing

G. According to the last two stanzas, what happens on windy and moonlit winter nights? *(The ghosts of the highwayman and Bess meet again at the inn.)* Recalling

He rose upright in the stirrups. He scarce could reach her hand,
7 But she loosened her hair in the casement.[9] His face burnt like a brand
As the black cascade of perfume came tumbling over his breast;
And he kissed its waves in the moonlight,
35   (Oh, sweet black waves in the moonlight!)
Then he tugged at his rein in the moonlight, and galloped away to the west.

Part 2

He did not come in the dawning. He did not come at noon;
And out of the tawny sunset, before the rise of the moon,
When the road was a gypsy's ribbon, looping the purple moor,
40 A redcoat troop came marching–
8   Marching–marching–
C ▶ King George's men came marching, up to the old inn door.

They said no word to the landlord. They drank his ale instead.
But they gagged his daughter, and bound her, to the foot of her narrow bed.
45 Two of them knelt at her casement, with muskets at their side!
There was death at every window;
9   And hell at one dark window;
For Bess could see, through her casement, the road that *he* would ride.

They had tied her up to attention, with many a sniggering jest.
50 They had bound a musket beside her, with the muzzle beneath her breast!
"Now keep good watch!" and they kissed her. She heard the doomed man
    say–
Look for me by moonlight;
    Watch for me by moonlight;
D ▶ *I'll come to thee by moonlight, though hell should bar the way!*

55 She twisted her hands behind her; but all the knots held good!
She writhed her hands till her fingers were wet with sweat or blood!
They stretched and strained in the darkness, and the hours crawled by like
    years,
Till, now, on the stroke of midnight,
    Cold, on the stroke of midnight,
10 60 The tip of one finger touched it! The trigger at least was hers!

---

9. casement: a window frame with side hinges.

THE HIGHWAYMAN   411

7. LITERARY CONCEPT: Simile
Ask students what is meant by the speaker's saying that the highwayman's face "burnt like a brand." *(The highwayman's face was flushed; it was hot and red like a torch.)* Why is his face "burning"? *(Possible response: He is filled with passion at the sight and smell of Bess's hair.)* ★

8. LITERARY CONCEPT: Repetition
Point out the repetition of the word *marching,* and have students identify the effect of repeating this word. *(Possible responses: The repetition imitates the rhythmic steps of soldiers on the march; the repetition emphasizes the soldiers' power and persistence.)*

9. ACTIVE READING: Question
Choose volunteers to explain the meaning of lines 46–48. *(Possible responses: "There was death at every window" means that armed soldiers are stationed at each window; "hell at one dark window" refers to Bess's terrible suffering as she watches the road that will lead her beloved into a deathtrap.)*

10. ACTIVE READING: Predict
Invite students to predict what Bess will do after reaching the musket's trigger. If necessary, help them by reading the following example of a think-aloud, or model one of your own.

Think-Aloud Script Bess knows that the highwayman is coming back to see her, but she cannot warn him that the soldiers are waiting for him. They have tied her up with a musket—perhaps to taunt her or to make sure she won't try to escape. Bess probably wants to fire the gun as a warning to her beloved.

Speaking . . . Listening . . . Viewing

Viewing In the PBS production of *Anne of Green Gables,* Anne Shirley gives a dramatic reading of "The Highwayman." Play a videotape of this scene for the class.

Speaking/Listening Invite students to find other examples of narrative poems in the library. Have students recite their favorite narrative poems to the class. Possibilities include the following:

"The Village Blacksmith" and "Paul Revere's Ride" by Henry Wadsworth Longfellow

"The Lady of Shalott" by Alfred, Lord Tennyson

"Ballad of Birmingham" by Dudley Randall

THE HIGHWAYMAN **Teacher's Edition**   **411**

11. LITERARY CONCEPT: Repetition
Ask students to identify phrases that are repeated in this stanza *("she would not," "in the moonlight")* What is the effect of such repetition? *(Possible responses: It adds to the suspense; it stresses the importance of what is happening; it helps to show how determined Bess is.)*

12. ACTIVE READING: Review
Ask students to explain what information is conveyed by *"Tlot-tlot; tlot-tlot."* *(Possible responses: The highwayman's horse is galloping down the road; Bess's worst fear is being realized—the highwayman is falling into the trap.)*

Art Note

The noted illustrator Charles Mikolaycak is a New York artist who has won a number of awards for his work. He is noted for his attention to detail and for being able to involve the viewer in his pictures through movement and the grace of his human figures. His work is often filled with delicate patterns and flowing lines. *How do the visual images created by the illustrator reflect the poetic images in "The Highwayman"? Consider both the lines and the colors of the illustrations when you answer.*

The tip of one finger touched it. She strove no more for the rest.
Up, she stood to attention, with the muzzle beneath her breast.
11 She would not risk their hearing; she would not strive again;
For the road lay bare in the moonlight;
65   Blank and bare in the moonlight;
And the blood in her veins, in the moonlight, throbbed to her love's refrain.

12 *Tlot-tlot; tlot-tlot!* Had they heard it? The horse hoofs ringing clear;
Tlot-tlot, tlot-tlot, in the distance? Were they deaf that they did not hear?
Down the ribbon of moonlight, over the brow of the hill.
70   The highwayman came riding—
            Riding—riding—
The redcoats looked to their priming![10] She stood up, straight and still.

---

10. priming: the explosive used to set off a firearm.

Original illustration by Charles Mikolaycak for "The Highwayman." Courtesy of the Kerlan Collection at the University of Minnesota. Used with permission of the illustrator and Lothrop, Lee and Shepard Publishers.

Looking at Style

Read aloud lines 97–102 of the poem, asking students to notice whether Noyes uses any three-syllable words. Then ask the following questions:

1. Why do you think Noyes relies so heavily on one-syllable and two-syllable words here?

2. Do you think short words slow down the oral reading of a poem, or do they speed it up?

3. Could Noyes have created the same type of

pounding rhythm if he used many long and fancy words? Explain.

4. Do you think Noyes would have been good at creating tongue twisters? Why or why not?

Tlot-tlot, in the frosty silence! *Tlot-tlot*, in the echoing night!
Nearer he came and nearer. Her face was like a light.
75　Her eyes grew wide for a moment; she drew one last deep breath,
Then her finger moved in the moonlight,
　　Her musket shattered the moonlight,
Shattered her breast in the moonlight and warned him—with her death.

He turned. He spurred to the west; he did not know who stood
80　Bowed, with her head o'er the musket, drenched with her own blood!
Not till the dawn he heard it, his face grew gray to hear
How Bess, the landlord's daughter,
　　The landlord's black-eyed daughter,
Had watched for her love in the moonlight, and died in the darkness there.

85　Back, he spurred like a madman, shouting a curse to the sky,
With the white road smoking behind him and his rapier brandished high.
Blood-red were his spurs in the golden noon; wine-red his velvet coat;
When they shot him down on the highway,
　　Down like a dog on the highway,
90　And he lay in his blood on the highway, with a bunch of lace at his throat.

And still of a winter's night, they say, when the wind is in the trees,
When the moon is a ghostly galleon tossed upon cloudy seas,
When the road is a ribbon of moonlight over the purple moor,
A highwayman comes riding—
95　　*Riding—riding—*
A highwayman comes riding, up to the old inn door.

Over the cobbles he clatters and clangs in the dark innyard;
He taps with his whip on the shutters, but all is locked and barred.
He whistles a tune to the window, and who should be waiting there
100　*But the landlord's black-eyed daughter,*
　　Bess, the landlord's daughter,
Plaiting a dark red love knot into her long black hair.

---

13. ACTIVE READING: Connect
Ask students to describe their opinions of Bess and her sacrifice. (*Possible responses: She's a tragic figure who deserves our pity and respect; she's foolish to sacrifice her life for a robber; she's just wasted her life for a man who's probably going to die too.*)

14. ACTIVE READING:
Connect/Review
Ask students how the visual image of the bunch of lace at the bloody corpse's throat makes them feel. (*Any response is valid.*) Then ask students why Noyes mentions it at this point in the poem. (*Possible responses: to provide a striking contrast with the ugliness of the highwayman lying dead in his own blood, to contrast the romance of his life with his "dying like a dog")*

15. LITERARY CONCEPT: Theme
Ask students what the last two stanzas suggest the theme of this narrative poem to be. (*Possible responses: that love is immortal, that nothing can stop true love)*

ENCOURAGING INDEPENDENT READING

The Poet's Tales: A New Book of Story Poems, selected by William Cole

---

Comprehension Check

1. In what part of the day do most of the events in this poem take place? *(in the night)*

2. Who are the lovers in the poem? *(Bess and the highwayman)*

3. How do you think King George's soldiers know where to find the highwayman? *(Tim must have told them.)*

4. Why does Bess shoot herself? *(to warn the high-wayman away)*

5. Why does the highwayman return towards the inn? *(He has heard that Bess has died.)*

6. What do we learn about the lovers at the end of the poem? *(The lovers are reunited after death; they continue to meet at the inn.)*

Student Response

Responding to Reading

1. Any response is valid.

2. Possible responses: Bess is heroic because she takes her own life so that her sweetheart might live; the highwayman is heroic because he returns to avenge Bess's death despite danger; neither character is heroic—Bess wastes her life for a romantic ideal, and the highwayman is simply a handsome criminal.

3. Possible responses: The redcoats are unnecessarily cruel to Bess; their actions are worse than those of the highwayman; the redcoats are just doing their duty as soldiers, using Bess as a means of capturing the highwayman; the redcoats go beyond the call of duty by making Bess a prisoner; they are responsible for her death.

Literary Concept: Onomatopoeia

Examples of onomatopoeia include *clattered, clashed, tapped, creaked, sniggering, tlot-tlot,* and *clangs.* These words help the reader to "hear" the action of the poem. They contribute to the suspense and make the poem more interesting, both to hear and to read.

Concept Review: Rhyme and Rhythm Rhyming words include *trees and seas, moor and door, innyard and barred,* and *there and hair.* Students' marks for rhythm will vary, depending on how they read the poem. In general, there are six beats in each of the longer lines and two or three beats in each of the shorter lines. The rhyming words at the ends of lines make the poem musical and give it a ringing, almost echoing sound; the rolling rhythms imitate the rhythms of a galloping horse. If the poem were in free verse, it would lose much of its excitement and tension.

Responding to Reading

First Impressions

1. What images will you remember from this poem? Describe them briefly in your journal or notebook.

Second Thoughts

2. Do you think either Bess or the highwayman is heroic? Explain.
   Think about
   - the sacrifice each made
   - your own views about love and sacrifice
   - the reasons for their entrapment and death

3. What is your opinion of the actions of the redcoats?
   Think about
   - their duty to capture outlaws
   - the trap that they set up
   - their treatment of Bess

Literary Concept: Onomatopoeia

The use of words that imitate sounds is called **onomatopoeia.** *Tick-tock,* for example, imitates the sound of a clock. What examples of onomatopoeia can you find in the poem? What do these sound effects add to the poem?

Concept Review: Rhyme and Rhythm Read aloud the last two stanzas. Then make a copy of the stanzas, marking the beats, or the syllables that receive emphasis. Draw lines that connect rhyming words at the ends of lines. Discuss how the rhythm and rhyme affect your enjoyment of the poem. How would the effect be different if the poem had been written in free verse?

Writing Options

1. Write a **summary** of the story from the viewpoint of the landlord, the ostler, or a redcoat soldier.

2. An **epitaph** is a written tribute to a dead person. Write an epitaph for either the highwayman or Bess.

414   UNIT FOUR   BONDS OF THE HEART

Writing Options

The Writing Options are designed to meet varied student interests and abilities. Have each student choose one writing activity to complete.

Journal Update Suggest that students write about whether the poem reminds them of any other stories about sacrifices for love. They could also answer these questions: If a singer recorded a song based on this poem, would young people find it romantic? Why or why not?

Closure

Like Ernie in "A Crush," the highwayman and Bess have a secret love that changes their lives completely. Unlike Ernie, these two characters must face death itself as the price of love. Bess makes the ultimate sacrifice—her life—and the highwayman loses his life in a hopeless quest for vengeance. Ask students which of the three characters best reflects their own ideals of love.

Objectives

- To understand and analyze two poems
- To analyze the use of repetition in poetry
- To enrich reading by understanding cultural contexts
- To express understanding of the poems through a choice of writing forms, including a thesaurus entry and a poem or a character sketch

Poetry

Graduation Morning
PAT MORA

There Is No Word for Goodbye
MARY TALLMOUNTAIN

Examine What You Know (Prior Knowledge)

Think about the crossroads in your life—times when one part of your life ends and a new part begins. For example, the transition from elementary to middle school would be a crossroad, as would saying goodbye to a best friend who is moving. What feelings and thoughts do such situations bring about? Why is it sometimes so hard to say goodbye to the old and hello to the new? In your journal, describe your thoughts at such times.

Expand Your Knowledge
(Building Background)

The following poems portray two young people who are moving on to new chapters in their lives. The first poem is set near the Rio Grande, the boundary between Texas and Mexico. In this border area, customs and traditions from the United States and Mexico blend together. Many residents on both sides of the river speak two languages, English and Spanish. A number of Mexican citizens, like the woman in this poem, work in Texas and return at night to their homes in Mexico.

The second poem describes a farewell scene between two Native Americans. They are Athabaskans, the name given to various tribes in northern Canada—including the Sarsis, the Beavers, and the Chipewyans—who speak the Athabaskan language. Though their numbers are now small, the Athabaskans have a long, proud history.

Enrich Your Reading (Reading Skill)

Understanding Cultural Contexts   The scenes presented in these two poems reflect how crossroads or passages are experienced in different cultures. As you read, look for details about each culture. Then think about the ways in which the poems are similar, despite the differences in the cultures.

- *Author biographies in Reader's Handbook*

GRADUATION MORNING/THERE IS NO WORD FOR GOODBYE   415

Prereading/Motivation

Examine What You Know

Discussion Prompts What are some of the common crossroads in a young person's life? How can you make a difficult transition easier to handle?

Expand Your Knowledge

Additional Background Towns and cities along the Rio Grande in Texas are typically a blend of English- and Spanish-speaking cultures. In some areas more than half of the population speaks Spanish. Signs of Mexican influence are everywhere, from bilingual menus in restaurants to bilingual programs in schools.

The Athabaskans live in the semi-Arctic region of Canada. Many live on reservations where the traditions and customs of the past are preserved and handed down to new generations.

Enrich Your Reading

Invite students from different cultures to describe how their native cultures influence their life today.

Thematic Link— Bonds of the Heart

In "Graduation Morning" the woman and the boy exhibit a strong emotional bond that developed while the boy was growing up. In "There Is No Word for Goodbye" the speaker and her aunt share a close bond that cannot be limited by distance or time.

JOURNAL WRITING IDEAS

- Describe a time when you had to say goodbye to someone or something in your life.
- Write about a crossroad you anticipate reaching in the future and how you plan to handle it.

COLLABORATIVE LEARNING OPTIONS

Opportunities for collaborative learning include Enrich Your Reading (p. 415) and Writing Option 1 (p. 419).

ADDITIONAL RESOURCES
Unit Four Resource Book
Reader's Guidesheet, p. 51
Reading Skills, p. 52
Literature Skills, p. 53
Vocabulary Connections, p. 54
Spelling Connections, p. 55
Comprehension Check Test, p. 56
Selection Test, p. 57

VOCABULARY PREVIEW

The focus of vocabulary study for this selection is the prefix *a-*. See *Unit Four Resource Book*, Vocabulary Connections, page 54.

LIMITED ENGLISH PROFICIENCY

■ Use the Reader's Guidesheet, *Unit Four Resource Book*, page 51.

■ You may wish to read each poem aloud, encouraging students to visualize the images as they listen.

★ Text annotations marked with a red star (2, 5, 8) may be helpful for students with limited English proficiency.

TEXT ANNOTATIONS

1. ACTIVE READING: Review
Have students find details that suggest that the woman in the poem is Mexican. *(Possible responses: She calls the boy by a Spanish nickname; she offers him Mexican candy; her skin is brown.)*

2. ACTIVE READING: Review
Ask students to tell what they learn in this stanza about the relationship between the woman and the boy. *(Possible responses: The woman has known him since he was a young boy; she cared for him and cleaned his mother's house; he loved to see her; they had a very close relationship.)* ★

3. LITERARY CONCEPT: Characterization
Ask students what they learn about the boy here. *(Possible responses: He looks for her in the audience at graduation; he wants her to share this important moment in his life; he cares about her.)*

4. LITERARY CONCEPT: Figurative Language
Ask students what is unusual about the expression "her eyes stroke his face." *(Hands, not eyes, usually stroke; eyes can't really stroke.)* Point out that *luceros* refers to the woman's eyes here, not her nickname for the boy. Discuss what the poet may be suggesting in this description of the woman. *(Possible responses: The woman's eyes reflect her love for the boy; her eyes are like stars because of the affection they reveal; she's happy because he looked for her.)*

Graduation Morning

PAT MORA

for Anthony

> She called him *Lucero*,[1] morning star,
> snared him with sweet coffee, pennies,
> Mexican milk candy, brown bony hugs.

> Through the years she'd cross the Rio
> Grande to clean his mother's home. "*Lucero,
> mi*[2] *lucero*," she'd cry, when she'd see him
> running toward her in the morning,
> when she pulled stubborn cactus thorns
> from his small hands, when she found him
> hiding in the creosote.[3]

> Though she's small and thin,
> black sweater, black scarf,
> the boy in the white graduation robe
> easily finds her at the back of the cathedral,
> finds her amid the swirl of sparkling clothes,
> finds her eyes.

> Tears slide down her wrinkled cheeks.
> Her eyes, *luceros*, stroke his face.

---

1. lucero (loō se′ rŏ) *Spanish.*
2. mi (mē) *Spanish:* my.
3. creosote (krē′ ə sōt′): short for *creosote bush*, a bush found in the Southwest.

Responding to Reading

First Impression of "Graduation Morning"

1. What images do you form of the woman and the boy in this poem? Briefly describe them in your journal or notebook.

Second Thoughts on "Graduation Morning"

2. Why do you think the housekeeper and the boy feel such a strong bond between them?

3. What feelings do you think the housekeeper has at this crossroads in the boy's life?

4. Why do you think the poem focuses on the housekeeper rather than the boy's parents?

Responding to Reading

1. Any response is valid.

2. Possible responses: They have known each other for many years; the woman is like a mother to him; she has always been affectionate and has given him many small gifts.

3. Possible responses: She is proud that he is graduating; she may be sad because she is losing him; she probably is thinking about all that has happened over the years; she is happy that he still cares about her.

4. Possible responses: The housekeeper's presence at the graduation is unusual—it makes an interesting topic for a poem. A poem about his parents' reaction would probably be less interesting. This poem is not so much about the boy's graduation as it is about the special relationship between him and the housekeeper.

There Is No Word for Goodbye

MARY TALLMOUNTAIN

Sokoya,[1] I said, looking through
    the net of wrinkles into
    wise black pools
    of her eyes.

5 What do you say in Athabaskan
    when you leave each other?
    What is the word
    for goodbye?

  A shade of feeling rippled
10   the wind-tanned skin.
    Ah, nothing, she said,
    watching the river flash.

  She looked at me close.
    We just say, Tlaa.[2] That means,
15   See you.
    We never leave each other.
    When does your mouth
    say goodbye to your heart?

---

1. **sokoya** (sə koi′ yə): aunt on mother's side.
2. **tlaa** (tlä).

---

5. LITERARY CONCEPT: Metaphor
Remind students that a metaphor is a comparison that does not use the words *like* or *as*. What are the aunt's wrinkles compared to? *(a net)* What are her eyes compared to? *(black pools)* What do these metaphors suggest about the aunt? *(Possible responses: she's old and wise; her niece values her opinion)* ★

6. ACTIVE READING: Evaluate
The speaker says that the aunt displays a "shade of feeling." Ask students to discuss what this feeling might be. *(Possible responses: She might be sad that her niece doesn't know more about her own people or their language; the niece may be leaving her; she might be pained by memories of other people leaving her.)*

7. ACTIVE READING: Question
What does the aunt mean by asking, "When does your mouth say goodbye to your heart"? *(Possible responses: She implies that her niece is as dear to her as her heart; she and her niece are like two parts of a single body.)*

Multicultural Connections

When Cultures Meet The woman in "Graduation Morning" straddles two cultures. She works as a domestic in one country and lives in another country. Ask students to imagine that they are the woman in the poem. How might they feel about working for another family as a domestic? Would they feel separated by barriers of language and culture? Would they care about the family they worked for, or would they feel distanced from them?

Language A people's vocabulary is greatly affected by its culture and environment. As revealed in "There Is No Word for Goodbye," the Athabaskan language has no word for goodbye because the Athabaskans believe that people are never apart. Ask students to make a list of words they would keep or eliminate in their ideal culture.

8. VOCABULARY: Definition
If students are unfamiliar with the blue-bell, explain that it is a plant with small, blue, bell-shaped flowers. Then ask what a touch "light as a bluebell" might be. *(a very gentle touch)* ★

9. LITERARY CONCEPT: Repetition
Have students find all the places in the poem where the word *goodbye* is repeated. Discuss what effect the repetition has in the poem. *(Possible responses: the title and lines 8, 18, and 28; it emphasizes the idea that the niece is leaving; it keeps readers focused on the question the niece has asked her aunt.)*

ENCOURAGING INDEPENDENT READING

"To a Golden-Haired Girl in a Louisiana Town," poem by Vachel Lindsay

"To My Brother Miguel," poem by Cesar Vellejo

"She Dwelt Among the Untrodden Ways," poem by William Wordsworth

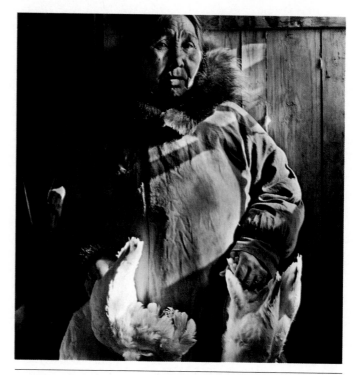

SHUGNAK, ALASKA 1974 Alex Harris Courtesy of the photographer.

> She touched me light
> 8 | as a bluebell.
> 20   You forget when you leave us,
>   You're so small then.
>   We don't use that word.
>
> We always think you're coming back,
>   but if you don't,
> 25   we'll see you some place else.
> 9 | You understand,
> E ▶   There is no word for goodbye.

418   UNIT FOUR   BONDS OF THE HEART

Comprehension Check

✓

1. How does the woman in "Graduation Morning" feel about the boy? *(She seems to love him; she has deep affection for him.)*

2. Why did the woman cross the Rio Grande every day? *(to work as a housekeeper and babysitter)*

3. Where are the woman and the boy? *(in a cathedral at the boy's graduation)*

4. In "There Is No Word for Goodbye" who is the speaker and with whom is she conversing? *(The speaker is a young Native American woman who is talking to her aunt.)*

5. What does the speaker ask her aunt? *(What is the word in our native language for goodbye?)*

6. Why does the aunt not tell the speaker the word to use in saying goodbye? *(Their language has no word for goodbye.)*

Responding to Reading

First Impressions of "There Is No Word for Goodbye"

1. How do you feel about the aunt's response to her niece's question? Describe your feelings in your journal or notebook.

Second Thoughts on "There Is No Word for Goodbye"

2. What can you infer about the bonds between the aunt and the niece?

3. In this poem, what do you learn about the Athabaskans and how they view one another?

   Think about
   • why they have "no word for goodbye"
   • what the aunt means by saying, "we'll see you some place else"

Comparing the Poems

4. Which poem comes closer to expressing your own feelings about crossroads in your life? Explain.

5. What similarities do you see between the two poems?

Literary Concept: Repetition

Repetition is the technique of using a sound, a word, a phrase, or a sentence over and over again for emphasis. In "Graduation Morning," the Spanish word *lucero,* or its plural form, appears four times. Why do you think the word is repeated so often? How is it used differently at the end of the poem?

Writing Options

1. Create a **thesaurus entry** for *goodbye.* A thesaurus entry lists words or phrases that can be used as synonyms for a given word. In your entry, include expressions that suggest meeting one another again. You may include foreign phrases or slang terms.

2. Write a **poem** or **character sketch** that describes an older person who has influenced your life.

Responding to Reading

1. Any response is valid.

2. Possible responses: They are very close to each other; it seems that they were separated when the speaker was younger ("You forget when you leave us, / You're so small then"), and the speaker is about to leave again.

3. Possible responses: They have very close family ties; they view family members as a part of themselves; they are a tightly knit community; they believe in an afterlife in which they will be together again.

4. Any response is valid.

5. Possible responses: Both deal with two people who must part with each other; both show two people who share strong feelings for each other; both focus on the small but significant details of human relationships.

Literary Concept: Repetition

Lucero may be repeated to emphasize the love that the woman feels for the boy, her "morning star." Its repetition shows that she is a caring person who uses language imaginatively. At the end, it is repeated to show that her eyes have become "morning stars."

Closure

Ask students to compare the bonds of the heart described in both poems. How do these bonds connect to their own ideas of love? How are their bonds similar to or different from those of characters in "A Crush" and "The Highwayman"? Which bonds seem strongest, and why?

Objectives

- To understand and analyze a drama
- To identify a foil and to review the concept of a climax
- To understand and follow a screenplay, including stage directions and dialect
- To express understanding of the drama through a choice of writing forms, including director's notes, a memo, a scene, and a persuasive letter

Prereading/Motivation

Examine What You Know

Discussion Prompts What challenges have Jews and African Americans faced? How has society changed as a result of its struggle to overcome these challenges?

Expand Your Knowledge

Additional Background Uhry himself was very surprised that the play was so successful. Produced by Richard and Lili Zanuck, the movie version was filmed at half its original budget. Jessica Tandy won an Oscar for Best Actress, and both Dan Aykroyd and Morgan Freeman were nominated for Oscars.

Enrich Your Reading

Encourage students to read individual words aloud as needed. Remind them that the words are often spelled phonetically. As often as necessary in the early part of the play, read lines of dialect aloud to them so they get the idea. If you have students read the play aloud, allow frequent changes of the lead parts of Daisy and Hoke. Scene changes can be good cast-switching places to allow more students to participate.

Thematic Link— Bonds of the Heart

Although their relationship begins unsteadily, Daisy and Hoke develop a powerful bond of love and trust. Daisy grows to cherish Hoke's decency and concern, while Hoke comes to appreciate Daisy's independence and spirit.

Drama

Driving Miss Daisy
ALFRED UHRY

Examine What You Know   (Prior Knowledge)

This drama, which takes place in the South between 1948 and 1973, is about a wealthy Jewish widow and the African-American chauffeur who works for her. Based on what you know, how do you think these characters would view one another? What problems might they encounter in their relationship? Share your ideas in a class discussion.

Expand Your Knowledge   (Building Background)

Few people would have expected this gentle drama about a relationship between two people to become such a success. *Driving Miss Daisy* opened in 1987 as a small production in New York City. It soon moved to Broadway and won the Pulitzer Prize in drama. You are about to read the original screenplay of the 1989 movie version of the play. The movie won four Academy Awards (Oscars), including the award for Best Picture.

Enrich Your Reading   (Reading Skill)

Reading a Screenplay   If you were to see the movie *Driving Miss Daisy*, you would understand where the action occurs just by watching. In the screenplay, changes in time and location are written. Each new scene is marked by a word or phrase in capital letters that tells where it takes place. Since the play spans many years, the year, if it has changed from the previous scene, is named next. Read all stage directions carefully so that you can keep track of when and where the action occurs.

If you were listening to the movie, you would have no trouble understanding the dialect spoken by the actors. In the script, the author shows dialect by omitting letters and respelling words. If you come to dialect that seems confusing, try reading it aloud. For example, Hoke says, "You doan' mean! Oscar say you need a driver for yo' family. What I be doin'?" Read the lines aloud and you will "hear" the meaning.

■ *Author biography on Extend page*

JOURNAL WRITING IDEAS

- Predict what Daisy will be like.
- If you were suddenly forced to rely on a stranger, what feelings might you experience?
- Write about a special moment that helped to strengthen your friendship with someone.

COLLABORATIVE LEARNING OPTIONS

Opportunities for collaborative learning include Options for Learning activities 1, 3, and 4 (p. 456) and Cross-Curricular Projects (p. 456).

ADDITIONAL RESOURCES

Unit Four Resource Book
Reader's Guidesheet, p. 58
Reading Skills, p. 59
Literature Skills, p. 60
Vocabulary Connections, p. 61
Spelling Connections, p. 62
Comprehension and Vocabulary Check Tests, p. 63
Selection Test, pp. 64–65

Driving Miss Daisy

ALFRED UHRY

CHARACTERS

Daisy Werthan

Boolie, her son

Florine, his wife

Hoke Colburn, chauffeur

Beulah, friend

Nonie, friend

Miriam, friend

Miss McClatchey, secretary

Oscar, porter

Idella, housekeeper

Katie Bell, cook

State Trooper

Second Trooper

Produce Man

PART 1

DAISY'S KITCHEN, August 1948. Daisy, who is seventy-two and energetic, enters. Idella, who is Daisy's age, is polishing silver.

Daisy. I'm gone to the market, Idella.

Idella. Mmmmm.

BACK YARD. Daisy is backing her car out of the garage. It suddenly shoots backward and stops, hanging over the edge of the neighbor's stone wall. Daisy gets out and slams the door, and the car drops into the neighbor's garden.

KITCHEN, later. Idella and Boolie are eating fried chicken.

Boolie. Mama!

Daisy *(off camera)*. No!

Boolie. Mama!

Daisy *(off camera)*. No!

Boolie. It's a miracle you're not laying in Emory Hospital—or decked out at the funeral parlor.

(Boolie goes into the pantry, where Daisy is transferring pickles from a large crock into jars.)

Daisy. The cucumbers are pretty this summer.

---

2. LITERARY CONCEPT: Dialect
Some students may have difficulty with the dialect that Idella uses. Help students understand that *yassum* means "Yes, ma'am." Explain that *off camera* means that Idella can be heard but not seen; the camera is focusing on Daisy. ★

3. ACTIVE READING: Review
Ask students to **infer** the tone of voice that Boolie uses in this passage and to explain why he speaks that way. *(Possible responses: He speaks sarcastically out of frustration with Daisy; he is trying to bully or coax her into agreeing with him.)*

4. VOCABULARY: Idiom
Ask students what "you're a doodle" might mean *("you're a silly person").* Then ask what tone Boolie probably uses with this statement. *(affectionate)* Point out how Daisy's reply contrasts greatly in tone with Boolie's affectionate teasing. ★

Boolie. Look at you! You didn't even break your glasses.

Daisy. It was the car's fault.

Boolie. Mama, you had the car in the wrong gear.

Daisy. I did not. *(calls to* Idella) Idella, you want a pickle with your lunch?

Idella *(off camera).* Not me.

Daisy. Well, I'm putting up a jar for you to take home to William, you hear?

2 | **Idella** *(off camera).* Yassum. Thank you. He love your pickles.

Daisy. That's because he has more sense than you do.

Boolie. You backed the car right into the Pollocks' yard!

Daisy. You should have let me keep my LaSalle. It never would have behaved this way.

Boolie. Mama, cars don't behave. They are behaved upon. The fact is that you, all by yourself, demolished that Packard.[1]

Daisy. Think what you want. I know the truth.

Boolie. The truth is you just cost the insurance company twenty-seven hundred dollars. You are a terrible risk. Nobody is going to issue you a policy after this.

Daisy. You're just saying that to be hateful.

3 | **Boolie.** OK. Yes. I'm making it all up. Every insurance company in America is lined up out there in the driveway, falling all over themselves to get you to sign up.

Daisy. If you're going to stand in my pantry and lie like a rug, well, I think it's time for you to go somewhere else.   ◀ **A**

Boolie. OK. I'd better get back to the office. Florine'll have a fit if I don't come home on time tonight.

Daisy. Y'all must have plans tonight.

Boolie. Going to the Ansleys for a dinner party.

Daisy. I see.

Boolie. You see what?

Daisy. This is her idea of heaven on earth, isn't it?

Boolie. What?

Daisy. Socializing with Episcopalians.

Boolie. You're a doodle, Mama. I'll stop by tomorrow evening.

Daisy. How do you know I'll be here? I'm certainly not dependent on you for company.   **4**

Boolie. Fine. I'll call first. But you know that we have got some real serious talking to do.

Daisy. No.

Boolie. Mama! *(Daisy starts singing and goes upstairs.)*

HALLWAY, next day. Daisy *is on the phone.*

---

1. **Packard:** name of a luxury American automobile, 1899–1958.

	Words to Know and Use	**demolish** (di mäl′ ish) *v.* to wreck; destroy

422

Guided Reading for Less-Proficient Students

(Continued from page 421)

E. How does Hoke react to Daisy's questions about his salary? *(He says it's none of her business.)* Recalling

F. How does Hoke finally get Daisy to allow him to drive her? *(He drives beside her as she walks until she gets in.)* Summarizing

G. On her first ride with Hoke, how does Daisy try to control him? *(by telling him how fast and where to drive and by taking the keys when she leaves)* Summarizing

H. Why does it bother Daisy to have people think she is rich and to see that she has a chauffeur? *(She doesn't like showing off; she still thinks of herself as being poor.)* Inferring

Continued on page 423

Daisy. Well, I need you now! I have to be at the beauty shop in half an hour! . . . No, I most certainly did not know you had to call a minimum of two hours ahead. I don't know why you call yourselves a taxi company if you can't provide taxi-cabs! *(She hangs up. Idella is nearby, dusting rag in hand.)*

5 **Idella.** You call your son at the mill, he send somebody to carry you.

Daisy. That won't be necessary. I'll fix my own hair.

Idella. Sometimes I think you ain't got the sense God gave a lemon! *(Daisy glares at her; Idella returns the glare.)*

6 *LIVING ROOM. Daisy and three friends are finishing a game of mah-jongg.*

Beulah. Well, it's not my day for mah-jongg. That's easy to see.

Daisy. I have to thank y'all for coming here again. I'm a real pariah[2] without my car.

Nonie. When are you getting your new one?

Daisy. I don't know. Boolie's being real pokey.

Miriam. Don't worry, sugar. I'll come after you for temple tomorrow. *(Idella enters with dishes of ice cream.)*

Beulah. Oh, it's your peach, Daisy. That's my favorite.

Daisy. Well then, try not to get your ciga-rette dirt in it.

FRONT HALL, later. Boolie and Florine enter. He is wearing jeans and a plaid shirt. She is wearing a denim skirt and a plaid blouse.

Boolie *(calling).* Mama? You there?

Florine *(calling).* Hey, Mother Werthan! It's just us! *(Daisy comes downstairs, a book in her hand.)*

Daisy. Why didn't you call?

Florine. We can't stay.

Daisy *(sizing up both of their outfits).* So I gather.

Boolie. The Millers are giving a hayride for their anniversary.

Florine. I had these made. Doesn't your baby look cute?

Daisy. That's not exactly the word I'd pick.

Boolie *(seeing her book).* Oh, I've been meaning to read that!

Daisy. Well, I'm sorry. I can't lend it to you. It's due back at the library tomorrow.

Boolie. You want me to return it for you?

Daisy. No, thank you. I will go to the library on the streetcar.

Boolie. Mama! Quit being so stubborn! You know perfectly well that we are going to have to—*(Florine puts a hand on his arm to hush him up.)*

Daisy. Go on now. You don't want to keep the horses waiting. *(Boolie looks exasper-ated.)*

LIBRARY. Daisy leaves the library holding two slim books and her purse. Miss Jensen, the librarian, hurries outside, carrying a hefty book.

Miss Jensen. Miz Werthan! Miz Werthan! Just a minute!

Daisy. Miss Jensen! What in the world?

---

2. **pariah** (pə rī′ ə): a person rejected by others; social outcast.

---

5. **LITERARY CONCEPT:** Dialect
Have students use **context clues** to fig-ure out that here the expression *to carry you* means "to drive you." ★

6. **CULTURAL SIDELIGHT**
Mah-jongg is an ancient Chinese game that is still played in many parts of the world. It is similar to rummy, except that 136 or 144 tiles engraved with Chinese symbols and pictures are used instead of cards.

7. **ACTIVE READING:** Review
Florine's words may be confusing to stu-dents. Call on a volunteer to explain this passage. *(Boolie and Florine are wearing matching farm outfits that she had someone make especially for the hayride. Florine is speaking to Daisy, Boolie's mother, when she calls Boolie "your baby.")*

Guided Reading for Less-Proficient Students

Continued from page 422

I. How does Daisy misjudge Hoke? *(She thinks he has stolen a can of her salmon, but he brings another can to replace the one he has eaten.)* Recalling

J. At the cemetery, how does Daisy help Hoke and how does she allow Hoke to help her? *(Discovering he can't read, she teaches him to recognize a name on a tombstone, and she allows him to carry her tools and take her arm.)* Summarizing

K. Why does Daisy dislike Florine? *(Daisy doesn't like Florine's showiness, her celebrating Christmas, her socializing with Christians, and her pulling away from Judaism.)* Summarizing

L. Why are Daisy and Hoke driving to Mobile? *(to attend her brother Walter's birthday party)* Recalling

(Continued on page 424)

8. ACTIVE READING: Review
Ask students to **infer** why Daisy is reluctant to take the book and refuses the extra peaches and watermelon. (*Possible response: She knows she can't carry them all and walk home.*)

9. LITERARY CONCEPT: Character
Have students tell what they learn about Boolie in this scene. (*Possible responses: He is a businessman; he owns a textile mill in Atlanta; he has to compete against other textile mills.*)

Miss Jensen. You forgot to ask for the Lincoln biography you reserved. I checked it out for you.

Daisy (*eyeing the book dubiously*). Well! Aren't you the sweet thing!

Miss Jensen. Why, you're just about my best customer! (*She hands Daisy the book.*)

Daisy. Thank you. (*She heads off.*)

PIGGLY WIGGLY MARKET. Daisy's shopping cart contains her three books, her purse, a bar of soap, one lamb chop, and a can of peas.

Produce Man. How many peaches for you today, Miz Werthan?

Daisy. Three, thank you.

Produce Man. You're not gonna be gettin' any better ones the rest of the summer. Lemme give you a few more.

Daisy. Just the three.

8 | **Produce Man.** How about a nice watermelon? (*Daisy shakes her head no and walks to the checkout counter.*)

DAISY'S DRIVEWAY. Daisy lugs her parcels slowly up the driveway.

BOOLIE'S OFFICE. Boolie's on the phone.

9 | **Boolie.** Well, I. W., you know as well as I do that Werthan Bag and Cotton isn't the only textile mill in Atlanta. If you want to get other bids . . . Oh, you did. . . . That's what Ideal bid, huh? . . . Okay. You ever do business with Ideal before? (*Miss*

Photographs from the Zanuck production of *Driving Miss Daisy*, starring Jessica Tandy, Morgan Freeman, and Dan Aykroyd. Warner Brothers, 1989.

McClatchey appears at the door. He raises his hand, telling her to wait.)

Miss McClatchey. It's important, Mr. Werthan.

Boolie (*on the phone*). Can you have lunch with me tomorrow? . . . Herrens all right? . . . Yes. Twelve-thirty. Love to Peggy and the children. (*He hangs up. To* Miss McClatchey.) What's wrong?

424

Words to Know and Use | **dubiously** (dōō' bē əs lē) *adv.* in a doubtful way; skeptically

---

Guided Reading for Less-Proficient Students

(Continued from page 423)

M. Why do you think the state troopers question Hoke and Daisy? *(They think Hoke might have stolen the car; they dislike blacks and Jews; they are harassing Hoke and Daisy.)* Inferring

N. How does Hoke stand up to Daisy on their trip to Mobile? *(He stops the car and leaves to relieve himself, even though she told him not to.)* Summarizing

O. Why does Daisy finally say something nice about Hoke? *(He has come to work even though there is an ice storm.)* Drawing Conclusions

P. What comparison does Hoke make when the temple is bombed? *(He compares it to his childhood memory of a black man being lynched.)* Recalling

(Continued on page 425)

Miss McClatchey. Oscar's stuck in the freight elevator.

FREIGHT ELEVATOR. The elevator is well above floor level, revealing only a pair of legs up to the knees. Boolie arrives.

Boolie. Oscar?

Oscar *(from inside the elevator).* Yassuh. Here I am.

Boolie. You all right?

Oscar. Nawsuh. I'm stuck.

Boolie. I know. Fiddle with the lever.

Oscar. It all fiddled out. I done everythin' I know how.

Boolie *(angry).* Call Bell Elevator, Miss McClatchey.

Miss McClatchey. I already did. They're backed up. But they'll be here around one.

Boolie. One! Did you tell them it's an emergency?

Miss McClatchey. You don't have to holler at me, Mr. Werthan. I didn't break the elevator. *(A crowd of workers has gathered.)*

Boolie. You got that stuff for Davison Paxon in there, Oscar?

Oscar. Wrapped and ready to go.

Boolie. I told them they'd have it yesterday. Call Bell back! *(Miss McClatchey goes off. We hear a voice from the crowd.)*

Hoke. Oscar! *(Boolie turns and sees Hoke, who is about sixty.)* You hear me, Oscar?

Oscar. I hear you.

Hoke. Is there a little doohickey up yonder where the gate suppose to close? Stickin' down a little?

Oscar. Wait a minute. Yeah. It right here.

Hoke. Well, reach up and mash on it. Mash it up till it catch.

Oscar. I done it. Now what?

Hoke. Well, just work the lever. *(The elevator comes down, and Oscar comes into view. The workers applaud.)*

Boolie *(to Hoke).* Excuse me, do you work here?

Oscar. Nawsuh, this Hoke.

Hoke. Pleased to see you, suh.

Boolie. Oh. Well, thank you. How did you know about the elevator?

Hoke. I used to drive for the Avondale Dairy, and they have a sorry old elevator worse then disheah.

Oscar. Don't you remember? Hoke the one I told you about.

Boolie. Oh, of course. *(He heads back to his office, and Hoke follows.)*

Hoke. Mist' Werthan. Y'all people Jewish, ain't you?

Boolie. Yes, we are. Why do you ask?

Hoke. Well, suh, I'd druther work for Jews. People always talkin' 'bout they stingy and they cheap, but don' say none of that 'round me.

Boolie. Good to know you feel that way.

Hoke. Yassuh. One time I workin' for this woman over near Little Five Points. What was that woman's name? I forget. Anyway, one day, she have all these old shirts and collars be on the bed, and she say, "They b'long to my daddy, and we fixin' to sell 'em to you for twenty-five cents apiece." *(pause)* Any fool can see the whole bunch together ain't worth a nickel.

---

10. LITERARY CONCEPT: Dialect
Some students may have difficulty with the dialect spoken by Oscar in this scene. Help them understand that *yassuh* means "yes, sir" and that *nawsuh* means "no, sir." Occasionally you may wish to have a volunteer rephrase the dialect into standard English. ★

11. LANGUAGE: Slang
If students are unfamiliar with the slang term *doohickey*, explain that it means "gadget." Invite students to offer other slang terms they may know that mean the same thing, such as *doodad*, *gizmo*, or *thingamajig*. ★

12. LITERARY CONCEPT: Dialect
Hoke and Oscar both speak in dialect. Help students understand that *disheah* is a way of saying "this one here." ★

13. LITERARY CONCEPT: Character
Discuss how Hoke's character is revealed through his actions and speech in this scene. Ask students to describe their first impressions of Hoke. *(Possible responses: He is competent, experienced and resourceful; he speaks in an honest, straightforward manner; he is an independent thinker.)*

Guided Reading for Less-Proficient Students

(Continued from page 424)

Q. What evidence in this scene supports Hoke's statement that things have not changed all that much? *(Hoke feels Daisy is too prejudiced to be seen with him socially; Hoke is still a chauffeur listening to Dr. King's speech on the car radio, while Daisy hears Dr. King at an elegant dinner.)* Summarizing

R. How does Daisy show her mind is wandering?

(She thinks she is still a schoolteacher; she looks for imaginary papers and stumbles around.) Clarifying

S. How is Hoke Daisy's friend in this scene? *(He encourages her, points out her blessings, and brings her back to reality.)* Summarizing

T. How does the ending of the drama show a bond of the heart between Daisy and Hoke? *(Hoke feeds Daisy pie and she is delighted.)* Analyzing

14 Anyway, them the people callin' Jews cheap. So I say, "Yassum, I think about it," and I get me another job as fast as I can. So then I go to work for Judge Harold Stone, another Jewish gentleman jes' like you.

Boolie. You drove for Judge Stone?

Hoke. Seven years to the day, nearabout. An' I be there still if he din' up and die. Miz Stone say, "Move on down to Savannah with me, Hoke," 'cause my wife dead by then, but I say, "No, thank you." I din' want to leave my granbabies.

Boolie. Judge Stone was a friend of my father's.

Hoke. You doan' mean! Oscar say you need a driver for yo' family. What I be doin'? Runnin' yo' children to school and yo' wife to the beauty parlor and like that?

Boolie. I don't have any children, but tell me—

Hoke. Thass a shame. My daughter bes' thing ever happen to me. But you a young man yet. I wouldn't worry none.

Boolie. I won't. Thank you. Hoke, what I'm looking for is somebody to drive my mother around.

Hoke. Excuse me for askin', suh, but how come she ain' hiring for herself?

Boolie. Well, it's a difficult situation.

Hoke. Mmmm hmmm. She done gone 'round the bend[3] a little? That'll happen when they get on.

Boolie. Oh, no. She's all there. Too much there is the problem. It just isn't safe for her to drive anymore. She knows it, but she won't admit it.

Hoke. Cahill! That woman in Little Five Points name Miz Frances Cahill! I leave her and go right to Judge Stone, and he the reason I happy to hear y'all Jews.

Boolie. Hoke, I want you to understand— my mother is a little high-strung. But the fact is you'd be working for me. She can say anything she likes, but she can't fire you. You understand?   15

Hoke. Doan' you worry none about it. I hold on no matter what way she run me. When I nothin' but a little boy down there on the farm above Macon where I come from, I used to wrastle hogs to the ground at killin' time. And ain' no hog got away from me yet.   16

Boolie. How does twenty dollars a week sound?

Hoke. Soun' like you done hire yo' mama a chauffeur.   ◄ B

Boolie *smiles with relief.*

DAISY'S FRONT HALL. Idella *is using a carpet sweeper.* Boolie *and* Hoke *enter.*

Boolie. How are you, Idella?

Idella. Livin'.

Boolie. Where's that vacuum cleaner I brought over here?

Idella. In the closet.

Boolie *(to* Hoke*).* She won't touch it.

Idella. I would if it didn' give me a shock every time I go near it.

---

3. **gone 'round the bend:** a phrase suggesting that someone has lost mental alertness or become senile.

Looking at Style

To discuss Alfred Uhry's style in *Driving Miss Daisy*, read the following examples of Hoke's dialogue:

■ An' I be there still if he din' up and die.

■ You doan' mean! Oscar say you need a driver for yo' family. What I be doin'? Runnin' yo' children to school and yo' wife to the beauty parlor and like that?

■ Excuse me for askin', suh, but how come she ain' hiring for herself?

Discuss Hoke's dialect with the class.

1. What does Hoke mean by such words as *din'* and *doan*? How would you express what he is saying?

2. What words do you notice in Hoke's dialogue on page 426 in which he drops the final sound? Which of his other expressions are not standard English?

3. How does this dialogue add realism to the drama and help to characterize Hoke? What does the difference in Hoke's and Boolie's speech suggest?

Boolie. It works for me.

Idella. Good. You clean up. I go down and run yo' office. (*Hoke laughs. Idella shoots him a look.*)

Boolie. Where's Mama?

Idella. Up yonder.

Boolie. I guess you know who this is.

Idella. Mmmm hmmm.

Boolie. I'll be right back, Hoke. (*He heads upstairs.*)

Idella (*to Hoke*). I wouldn't be in your shoes if the Sweet Lawd Jesus come down and ask me hisself!

DAISY'S BEDROOM. Daisy is at a desk, paying bills. Boolie enters.

Boolie. Good morning, Mama. (*She ignores him.*) All I'm asking is for you to come and say hello.

Daisy. Now you listen here. Unless they rewrote the Constitution and didn't tell me, I still have rights.

Boolie. Well, of course, Mama, but–

Daisy. What I do not want–and absolutely will not have–is some chauffeur sitting in my kitchen, gobbling up my food, running up my phone bill. Oh, I hate all that in my house.

Boolie. You have Idella.

Daisy. Idella is different. She's been coming to me since you were in the eighth grade, and we know how to stay out of each other's way. And even so, there are nicks and chips in my wedding china.

Boolie. Do you think Idella has a vendetta[4] against your wedding china?

Daisy. Stop being sassy. I was brought up to do for myself. On Forsythe Street we couldn't afford them. That's still the best way if you ask me!

Boolie. Them? Afford them? You sound like Governor Talmadge.

Daisy. Why, Boolie! What a thing to say! I'm not prejudiced! Aren't you ashamed?

Boolie. I got to get back to the mill. You might as well try to make the best of this, Mama. (*He leaves.*)

KITCHEN. Idella is rolling out biscuit dough. Hoke is sitting nearby.

Hoke. I knew a Miss Idella once, down there in Macon.

Idella. Doan' say.

Hoke. You talkin' about sing! I mean that woman had lungs! She'd a been a whole church choir by herself if they'd a let her. And fat, too! She about the size of that stove yonder. (*Idella laughs. Daisy enters.*)

Daisy. Don't talk to Idella. She's got work to do.

Hoke. Yassum.

GARDEN. Hoke, a trowel in hand, is kneeling by a bed of flowers. Daisy appears at a window. Hoke looks up.

Hoke. Looks like yo' zinnias could use a little tendin' to.

Daisy. You leave my flower bed alone.

---

4. **vendetta:** a bitter quarrel; effort to take revenge.

◀ C

19

17. LITERARY CONCEPT: Sarcasm
Ask students what makes Idella's comment funny. (*She reverses roles by putting Boolie in his place—if he can tell her how to do her job, she can tell him how to do his.*)

18. ACTIVE READING: Question
Ask students why they think Daisy is so strongly against having a chauffeur. If necessary, help them by reading the following example of a think-aloud, or model one of your own.

Think-Aloud Script Why does Daisy hate the idea of a chauffeur so much? She says he'll eat all her food and run up her phone bill. If Daisy were really worried about Hoke's eating or phone habits, she would just lay down the law to him and make sure her rules were followed. There must be another reason. Daisy wants to be independent. Maybe Daisy resists a chauffeur because she doesn't want to admit she can't be totally independent any more. She doesn't want to see herself as a helpless old woman who must depend on others. ★

19. HISTORICAL SIDELIGHT
Daisy's "them" refers to African Americans. In 1948, the year in which the play is set, Herman Talmadge was the governor of Georgia. Like many other Southern governors of his time, he was known for his prejudice toward African Americans.

Multicultural Connections

Tell students that the word *prejudice* comes from the Latin prefix *pre-*, meaning "before," and the Latin word *judicium*, meaning "judgment." Ask students to define what prejudice means. (*making a judgment before you have any facts; unreasonable dislike of a particular group, race, or religion*)

Discuss these questions with students:

1. What situation does Hoke describe on pages 425 and 426 that is an instance of prejudice? (*his former employers saying that Jews are cheap.*)

2. Read aloud Daisy's dialogue at the top of the second column of page 427, and discuss how her words are an example of prejudice. (*She calls an entire group of people "them" as though they are all alike and not individuals.*)

20. LITERARY CONCEPT: Dialect
Have a volunteer explain the meaning of *brung* (brought). Point out that it is another example of Hoke's dialect. Choose a volunteer to rephrase Hoke's words into standard English. *(I know that, but I brought this from home. I'll give the car a thorough polishing.)* ★

21. ACTIVE READING: Review
What has Daisy refused to let Hoke do so far? *(Possible responses: talk to Idella, tend Daisy's garden, look at her things, touch her, or drive her car.)* Ask students why they think she does this. *(Possible responses: She doesn't want to let go of her independence; she hopes if she doesn't use Hoke, Boolie will get rid of him; she may not trust Hoke.)*

Hoke. Yassum. You know, Miz Daisy, you got a nice place back beyond the garage ain't doin' nothin' but sittin' there. I could put you some butter beans and some Irish potatoes—

Daisy. If I want a vegetable garden, I'll plant it for myself.

Hoke. Well, anything else I kin do for you?

Daisy. Go back where you belong. *(She closes the window.)*

HALLWAY. Hoke is studying the pictures on the wall. Daisy appears.

Daisy. What are you doing there?

Hoke. I love a house with pictures. Make a home. Disheah you, ain't it?

Daisy. Yes.

Hoke. Look like you been a teacher or something.

Daisy. I don't like you nosing through my things. *(She leaves.)*

GARAGE. Hoke gets into the new car. Daisy enters the garage.

Daisy. What are you doing?

Hoke. Fixin' to back de car out.

Daisy. Why? I'm not going anywhere.

20 **Hoke.** I know that, but I brung disheah from home. *(He pulls a cloth from his coat.)* Give the car a good wipe off.

Daisy. What for? It's never been out of the garage.

Hoke. You tellin' me!

Daisy. I don't want you touching my car. You understand? *(He reluctantly gets out of the car.)*

Hoke. Yassum. I reckon I jes' set in the kitchen till five o'clock.

Daisy. That's your affair. *(Hoke goes toward the back door. Then Daisy attacks her flower bed.)*

SCREEN PORCH. Daisy is reading the morning paper. Hoke enters.

Hoke. Mornin', Miz Daisy.

Daisy. Good morning.

Hoke. Right cool in the night, wasn't it?

Daisy. I wouldn't know. I was asleep.

Hoke. Idella says we runnin' outta coffee and Dutch Cleanser.

Daisy. We are?

Idella is in the living room, working.

Idella. Yassum, and we low on silver polish, too.

Daisy. I know . . . and I'm fixin' to go to the Piggly Wiggly on the trolley. *(She gets up and walks toward the front hall.)*

Hoke. Now, Miz Daisy, how come you doan' let me drive you?

Daisy. No, thank you.

FRONT HALL. Daisy puts on her hat and gathers her gloves and purse.

Hoke. Ain' that what Mist' Werthan done hire me for?

Daisy. That's his problem.

Hoke. All right den. I find somethin' to do.

Daisy. You leave my things alone! *(She marches outside; Hoke follows.)*

Hoke. You know, that Oldsmobile ain't moved an inch from where Mist' Werthan rode it over here from Century Motors.

21

Seem like that insurance company done give you a whole new car for nothin'.

Daisy. That's your opinion.

Hoke. Yassum. And my other opinion is a fine rich Jewish lady like you doan' b'long draggin' up the steps of no bus luggin' no grocery bags. I come along and carry them fo' you.

Daisy. I don't need you. I don't want you. And I don't like you saying I'm rich.

Hoke. I won' say it no more then.

Daisy. Is that what you and Idella talk about in the kitchen? I hate being discussed behind my back in my own house! I was born on Forsythe Street, and, believe you me, I know the value of a penny. My brother Manny brought home a white cat one day, and Papa said we couldn't keep it because we couldn't afford to feed it. My sisters saved up money so I could go to school and be a teacher. We didn't have anything!

Hoke. Yassum, but look like you doin' all right now. *(Daisy glares at him, and he retreats to the house.)*

STREET. Daisy *is walking along the sidewalk. She notices that* Hoke *is driving slowly behind her.*

Daisy *(horrified)*. What are you doing?

Hoke. Tryin' to take you to the sto'. *(A neighbor, who is gardening in her front yard, looks surprised at this unusual spectacle.)*

Daisy *(to Hoke)*. Go away! I've ridden the trolley with groceries plenty of times.

Hoke. Yassum, but I feel bad takin' Mist' Werthan's money for doin' nothin'.

Daisy. How much does he pay you?

Hoke. That between him and me, Miz Daisy.

Daisy. Anything over seven dollars a week is robbery. Highway robbery.

Hoke. Specially when I doan' do nothin' but set on a stool in the kitchen all day long. *(Daisy notices another neighbor watching her through a window.)*

Daisy. All right, the Piggly Wiggly. And then home. Nowhere else.

Hoke. Yassum. *(He stops the car and hops out, but she quickly gets in before he can help her.* Hoke *gets back in.)*

Daisy. Wait. You don't know how to run this car.

Hoke. Ain' you jes' seen me do it? Anyway, disheah automatic. Any fool can run it.

Daisy. Any fool but me, apparently.

Hoke. Ain' no need to be so hard on yoseff now. You cain' drive, but you probably do alotta things I cain' do. It all work out.

Daisy. The idea! *(Hoke starts driving.)*

Hoke. I love the smell of a new car. Doan' you, Miz Daisy? *(no answer)*

Daisy. I'm nobody's fool, Hoke.

Hoke. Nome.

Daisy. I can see that speedometer as well as you can.

Hoke. I see dat.

Daisy. My husband taught me how to run a car.

Hoke. Yassum.

Daisy. So don't think for even a minute that you can—wait! You're speeding! I see it!

24 ◄ E

25

◄ F

22

23

22. ACTIVE READING: Question
Ask students why they think Daisy doesn't like Hoke to say she is rich. *(Possible responses: She doesn't see herself as rich; she is embarrassed about it and wants to pretend she is not; she identifies with being poor.)*

23. ACTIVE READING: Evaluate
Ask students what they think of Hoke's strategy to get Daisy to accept his driving. *(Possible responses: His method is indirect and sneaky; he's trying to embarrass her into accepting him; nothing else has worked and this might succeed.)*

24. LITERARY CONCEPT: Character
Discuss what Hoke's response to Daisy reveals about his character. *(Possible responses: He is sort of like Daisy—she won't talk about some things and he won't either; Hoke can be very friendly but also knows when to keep his mouth shut; he has a strong sense of dignity.)*

25. ACTIVE READING: Evaluate
Discuss the significance of this moment in the play. Point out that it is the first time that Daisy allows Hoke to do something for her, which also means she has begun to give up her independence. Ask students why they think Daisy decides to get into the car. *(Possible responses: She is embarrassed to have the neighbors see her; she feels that it is wasteful for Hoke to be paid for doing nothing; she is finally beginning to accept the idea of receiving help.)*

26. LITERARY CONCEPT: Humor
Remind students that two techniques for creating humor are exaggeration and sarcasm. Ask how both of these techniques are used here by Hoke and Daisy. *(Possible responses: Daisy's fears are exaggerated in that she wishes to move so slowly; Hoke sarcastically jokes that they may as well be walking.)*

27. LITERARY CONCEPT: Character
What does Daisy's insistence on taking Highland Avenue show about her? *(Possible responses: She is a creature of habit; she does not wish to change her ways so late in life; she will assert her will in small details since she has made the "major" concession of letting Hoke drive.)*

28. ACTIVE READING: Review
Point out that Hoke ends up going to the market his way, but when he and Daisy disagree on where to park the car, Hoke gives in to Daisy's wishes. What does this reveal about the nature of their relationship? *(Possible responses: Each character is beginning to compromise a little; the two are learning to accept and tolerate each other.)*

Hoke. We ain' goin' but nineteen miles an hour.

Daisy. I like to go under the speed limit.

Hoke. Yassum, but the speed limit thirty-five here.

Daisy. The slower you go, the more you save on gas.

Hoke. We barely moving. Might as well walk to the Piggly Wiggly.

Daisy. Is this your car?

Hoke. Nome.

Daisy. Do you pay for the gas?

Hoke. Nome.

Daisy. All right then. My son may think I'm losing my abilities, but I am still in control of what goes on in my car. Where are you going?

Hoke. To the grocery sto'.

Daisy. Then why didn't you turn on Highland Avenue?

Hoke. Piggly Wiggly ain't on Highland Avenue. It on Euclid.

Daisy. I know where it is, and I want to go to it the way I always go. On Highland Avenue.

Hoke. That three blocks out of the way, Miz Daisy.

Daisy. Go back! Go back this minute!

Hoke. We in the wrong lane. I cain' jes'—

Daisy. If you don't go back, I'll get out of this car and walk.

Hoke. We movin'! You cain' open the do'!

Daisy. This is wrong. Where are you taking me?

Hoke. The sto'.

Daisy. This is wrong. You have to go back to Highland Avenue.

Hoke. Mmmm. Hmmm.

Daisy. I have been driving to the Piggly Wiggly since they put it up and opened it for business! This isn't the way! Go back! Go back this minute!

Hoke. Yonder the Piggly Wiggly, Miz Daisy.

Daisy. Get ready to turn.

Hoke. Yassum.

Daisy. Look out! There's a little boy behind that shopping cart!

Hoke. I see dat.

Daisy. Pull in next to the blue car.

Hoke. We closer to the do' right here.

Daisy. I don't park in the sun! It fades the upholstery.

Hoke. Yassum. *(He parks the car as directed. Daisy quickly gets out, heads for the store, then stops.)*

Daisy. Wait a minute. Give me the keys.

Hoke. Yassum.

Daisy. Stay right here by the car. And you don't have to tell everybody my business.

Hoke. Nome. Don't forget the Dutch Cleanser now. *(She glares at him and enters the store. Hoke goes to a pay phone and dials a number.)*

Hoke. Hello? Miz McClatchey? Hoke Colburn here. Can I speak to him? . . . Mornin', Mist' Werthan. Guess where I'm at. . . . I jes' drove yo' mama to the sto'. . . . Oh, she flap around a little on the way. But she all right. She in the sto'. *(He sees Daisy in the store through the front window. She suddenly sees him.)*

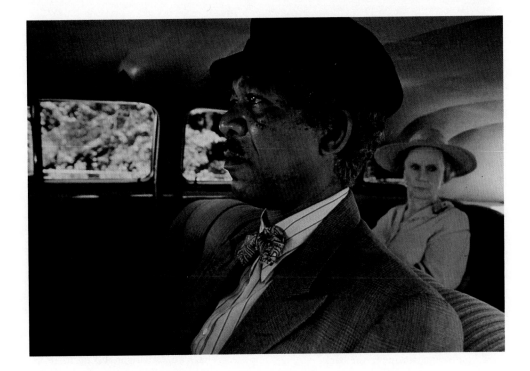

29. LITERARY CONCEPT: Humor
Ask students what Hoke means to imply by mentioning the creation of the world. *(Possible responses: Hoke is making a joke by suggesting that getting Miss Daisy to accept his help was almost as difficult as God's having to create the entire universe.)*

30. ACTIVE READING: Review
Call students' attention to the directions and ask them how much time has passed since the last scene and how they know. *(Possible response: about two months. The story opens in August 1948, and it is now autumn.)*

31. VOCABULARY: Idiom
Have students use **context clues** to understand that the expression *pitch a fit* means "throw a fit." ★

32. VOCABULARY: Definition
Explain to students unfamiliar with the term *temple* that it is a Jewish house of worship, or *synagogue*. ★

29 Uh oh. She done see me on the phone. She liable to throw a fit right there by the checkout. . . . Yassuh. Only took me six days. Same time it take the Lawd to make the worl'.

30 *DAISY'S HOUSE, autumn. A Werthan Company truck is parked outside.*

LIVING ROOM. Oscar *and his assistant,* Junior, *are removing slipcovers and rolling up rugs.* Hoke, *jacket off, is helping them.*

Oscar. How the old lady been treating you, Hoke?

31 **Hoke.** She know how to pitch a fit. I tell you that. *(*Oscar *and* Junior *laugh.* Daisy *enters, wearing a fur piece, a hat, and gloves.)*

Daisy. What's so funny?

Hoke. Nothin', Miz Daisy. We jes' carryin' on.

Daisy. Oscar and Junior have been doing my fall cleaning for fifteen years, and they never carried on before. Leave them alone.

Hoke. Yassum.

Daisy. And put your coat on. We're late.

Hoke. I be right there.

Daisy *(off camera).* Idella! I'm gone to temple!

32

Hoke *(as he leaves).* And I right behind her, Idella.

THE TEMPLE. The service is over, and people are leaving. Daisy, *who is with friends, sees* Hoke *standing beside her car, which is*

33. ACTIVE READING: Review
Ask students how Hoke's ideas about wealth **contrast** with Daisy's. *(He would be proud of being rich; she says it is vulgar to display wealth and does not want to admit that she's rich.)*

34. ACTIVE READING: Evaluate
Discuss the significance of Florine's comment about Daisy. What does it indicate about her feelings toward her mother-in-law? *(Possible responses: She resents the amount of time Boolie spends with his mother; she feels Daisy demands too much attention from Boolie.)*

parked right in front of the temple. Two other chauffeur-driven sedans are behind it. She hurries to the car and gets in by herself.

Daisy. I can get myself in. Just go. Hurry up out of here!

Hoke. Yassum. *(Bewildered, he gets in the car and starts driving.)*

Daisy. I didn't say speed. I said get me away from here.

Hoke. Somethin' wrong back yonder?

Daisy. No.

Hoke. Somethin' I done?

Daisy. No. *(a beat)* Yes.

Hoke. I ain' done nothin'!

Daisy. You had the car parked right in front of the temple! Like I was the queen of Romania! Everybody saw you! Didn't I tell you to wait for me in the back?

Hoke. I jes' tryin' to be nice. They two other chauffeurs right behind me.

Daisy. You made me look like a fool.

Hoke. You ain' no fool, Miz Daisy.

Daisy. Slow down. Miriam and Beulah and them, I could see what they were thinking.

Hoke. What that?

Daisy. That I'm trying to pretend I'm rich.

Hoke. You is rich, Miz Daisy!

Daisy. No, I'm not. And nobody can ever say I put on airs. On Forsythe Street we made many a meal off of grits[5] and gravy. I did without plenty of times, I can tell you.

Hoke. And now you doin' with. What so terrible in that?

Daisy. You! Why do I talk to you? You don't understand me.

Hoke. Nome, I don't. I truly don't. 'Cause if I ever was to get ahold of what you got, I be shakin' it around for everybody in the worl' to see.

Daisy. That's vulgar! Don't talk to me! *(Hoke mutters something under his breath.)* What? What did you say? I heard that!

Hoke. Miz Daisy, you needs a chauffeur, and I needs a job. Let's jes' leave it at dat. *(They eye each other warily in the rearview mirror.)*

BOOLIE'S FRONT HALL, early morning, winter. The phone rings. Boolie answers it.

Boolie. Good morning, Mama. What's the matter? . . . No, I don't always think something's the matter when you call. It's just that when you call so early in the morning. . . . What? . . . All right. I'll be there as soon as I can. *(He hangs up and enters the breakfast room.)* I better go on over there.

Florine. It's not healthy for you to rush like this in the morning.

Boolie. I eat too much anyway. And it sounds like she needs me.

Florine. When doesn't it? *(She smiles at him.)* Give Mother Werthan my love. *(He hurries out.)*

DAISY'S KITCHEN. Daisy, in a warm bathrobe, is pacing. Boolie enters.

Boolie. I didn't expect to find you in one piece.

Daisy. I wanted you to be here when he comes. I wanted you to hear it for yourself.

---

5. **grits:** short for *hominy grits,* a Southern dish made of coarsely ground dry corn.

Boolie. Hear what? What is going on?

Daisy. He's stealing from me.

Boolie. Hoke? Are you sure?

Daisy. I don't make empty accusations. I have proof!

Boolie. What proof?

Daisy. This! *(She pulls an empty can of salmon from her robe pocket.)* I found this hidden in the garbage pail under some coffee grounds.

Boolie. You mean he stole a can of salmon?

Daisy. I knew something was funny. They all take things, you know. So I counted.

Boolie. You counted?

Daisy. The silverware first and then the linen napkins, and then I went into the pantry. The first thing that caught my eye was a hole behind the corned beef. And I knew right away. There were only eight cans of salmon. I had nine. Three for a dollar on sale.

Boolie. Very clever, Mama. You made me miss my breakfast and be late for a meeting at the bank for a thirty-three-cent can of salmon. *(He pulls some bills from his pocket.)* Here. You want thirty-three cents? Here's a dollar! Here's ten dollars! Buy a pantry full of salmon.

Daisy. Why, Boolie! The idea! Waving money at me like I don't know what! I don't want the money. I want my things.

Boolie. One can of salmon?

Daisy. Well, it was mine! I leave him plenty of food every day, and I always tell him exactly what it is. They want something, they just take it. He'll never admit this. "Nome," he'll say. "I doan' know nothin'

'bout that." And I don't like it! I don't like living this way! I have no privacy!

Boolie. All right. I give up. You want to drive yourself again, you just go ahead and arrange it with the insurance company. Take your blessed trolley. Buy yourself a taxicab. Anything you want. Just leave me out of it.

Daisy. Boolie. . . . *(Hoke and Idella enter by the back door, and Idella goes off to the pantry.)*

Hoke. Mornin', Miz Daisy. I b'lieve it fixin' to clear up. 'Scuse me, Mist' Werthan. Y'all busy?

Boolie. Hoke, I think we have to have a talk.

Hoke. All right. Jes' lemme put my coat away. I be right back. *(He pulls a small paper bag from his pocket.)* Oh, Miz Daisy. Yestiddy when you out visitin', I ate a can o' your salmon. I know you say eat de leffover pork chops, but they stiff. Here, I done buy you another can. You want me to put it in the pantry?

Daisy. Yes, thank you, Hoke.

Hoke. I be right with you, Mist' Werthan. ◀ l
(He goes off to the pantry.)

Daisy *(trying for dignity).* Well, I got to get dressed now. 'Bye, son. *(She heads for the stairs.)*

CEMETERY, May 1951. *Daisy is planting verbena beside a headstone that reads "Sigmund Werthan." Hoke ambles over.*

Hoke. I jes' thinkin', Miz Daisy. We bin out heah to the cemetery three times dis month already.

Daisy. It's good to come in nice weather.

35. ACTIVE READING: Evaluate
Ask students to whom Daisy is referring when she says "they all take things." *(to African-American servants)* Ask if Daisy's statement reflects prejudice and why. *(Possible response: Yes, she is saying that all African-American servants steal.)*

36. LITERARY CONCEPT: Character
What do Daisy's actions in the pantry reveal about her character? *(Possible responses: She keeps track of everything in her house; she wants everything in her house in an exact order; she is very aware of what things cost.)*

37. LITERARY CONCEPT: Character
What does Hoke's action of replacing the salmon reveal about his character? *(Possible responses: He is a very honest person; he, like Daisy, attends to details.)*

38. ACTIVE READING: Evaluate
Ask students how they think Daisy feels after Hoke replaces the can. *(Possible responses: embarrassed for accusing Hoke of stealing and for making such a fuss with Boolie; she may be embarrassed to hear that the pork chops she left for Hoke were too dry.)* Ask how students think Boolie feels. *(Possible responses: amused; relieved)*

Hoke. Yassum. Mist' Sig's grave mighty well tended. I b'lieve you the best widow in the state of Georgia.

Daisy. Boolie's always pestering me to let the staff out here tend to this plot. Perpetual care they call it.

Hoke. Well, doan' do it. It right to have somebody from the family looking after you.

Daisy. I'll certainly never have that. Boolie will have me in perpetual care before I'm cold.

Hoke. Go on 'way from here!

Daisy. Hoke, put that pot of azaleas on Leo Bauer's grave.

Hoke. Miz Rose Bauer's husband?

Daisy. That's right. She asked me to bring it out here for her.

Hoke. Yassum. Where the grave at?

Daisy. I'm not exactly sure. But I know it's over that way. *(points)* You'll see the headstone. Bauer.

Hoke *(vaguely)*. Yassum.

Daisy. What's the matter?

Hoke. Nothin' the matter. *(He goes to the car, gets the azaleas, and comes back.)* Miz Daisy . . .

Daisy. I told you, it's over there. It says Bauer on the headstone.

Hoke. Now, how do that look?

Daisy. What are you talking about?

Hoke. I'm talkin' 'bout I cain' read.

Daisy. What?

Hoke. I cain' read.

Daisy. That's ridiculous. Anybody can read.

Hoke. Nome. Not me.

Daisy. Then how come I see you looking at the paper all the time?

Hoke. Thass it. Jes' lookin'. I dope out what's happenin' from the pictures best I can.

Daisy. You know your letters, don't you?

Hoke. My ABC's? Yassum, pretty good. I jes' cain' read.

Daisy. Stop saying that. It's making me mad. If you know your letters, you can read. You just don't know you can read. I taught some of the stupidest children God ever put on the face of the earth, and all of them could read enough to find a name on a tombstone. The name is Bauer. Buh buh buh buh buh Bauer. What does that buh letter sound like?

Hoke. Sound like a B.

Daisy. Of course. Buh Bauer. Er er er er. BauER. That's the last part. What letter sounds like er?

Hoke. An R?

Daisy. So the first letter is a . . .

Hoke. B.

Daisy. And the last letter is an . . .

Hoke. R.

Daisy. B-R. B-R. B-R. Buh-err. Buh-err. It even sounds like Bauer.

Hoke. Thass it?

Words to Know and Use	**perpetual** (pər pech' ōō əl) *adj.* endless; lasting forever

Daisy. That's it. Now go on over there and look for a headstone with a B at the beginning and an R at the end, and that will be Bauer.

Hoke. We ain' goin' worry 'bout what come in the middle?

Daisy. Not right now. This will be enough for you to find it. Go on now.

Hoke. Yassum.

Daisy. And don't come back here telling me you can't do it. Because you can. *(Hoke carries the potted azaleas past a number of* headstones. *Then, there it is—BAUER. He silently mouths the Buh and the Er and places the azaleas gently by the headstone. Then he returns to* Daisy.*)*

Hoke. Miz Daisy . . .

Daisy. Yes?

Hoke. I sure 'preciate this, Miz Daisy.

Daisy. Don't be ridiculous! I didn't do anything. Now, let's get all this back to the car. I'm burning up out here. *(He gathers up her digging tools and takes her elbow as they walk to the car.)* ◀ J

43

Responding to Reading

First Impressions of Part 1

1. What are your impressions of Daisy and Hoke so far? Write your thoughts in your journal or notebook.

Second Thoughts on Part 1

2. How would you describe Daisy's attitude toward Hoke in the first part of the play?

3. What is your opinion of how Hoke handles Miss Daisy?

   Think about
   • Daisy's reactions to Hoke and the other characters
   • what Boolie expects from Hoke

4. Daisy often reacts to situations with anger and impatience. Why do you think she does this?

5. Why do you think Daisy and Hoke have different attitudes about Daisy's being rich?

Reading On

In the next section of the play, watch to see how Hoke and Daisy's relationship grows. Also take note of Boolie and Florine. What kind of people are they?

---

43. ACTIVE READING: Evaluate
Ask students if they like the way Daisy speaks to Hoke here. Why or why not? *(Possible responses: Yes, she is admirable because she gives Hoke the confidence he needs to succeed; no, she scolds Hoke as if he were a child.)*

Responding to Reading

1. Any response is valid.

2. **Possible responses:** Daisy is annoyed and short-tempered with Hoke and is rude to him; Daisy at first distrusts Hoke but later softens her attitude toward him and allows him to help her.

3. **Possible responses:** Hoke deals with Daisy's antagonistic attitude with skill, patience, and understanding; Hoke has more patience with Daisy than Boolie expects; he lets Daisy insult him too much and allows her to act out her prejudice.

4. **Possible responses:** She resents having to rely on someone else to get around; she resents her loss of privacy and independence, and the constant threat of changes in her routine; she maintains her authority by getting angry.

5. **Possible responses:** Daisy sees her wealth in contrast with her youthful poverty, whereas Hoke cannot imagine getting past his own poverty; Daisy is still insecure about her wealth while Hoke is realistic about it.

1. ACTIVE READING: Review
Ask students about the setting at the beginning of Part 2. (It is Christmas morning, 1953, at Boolie's home.) How much time has passed since the beginning of the story? (five years) Have students **predict** how Daisy and Hoke's relationship may have changed during that period of time.

2. ACTIVE READING: Review
Have students find similarities in the way Florine and Daisy treat Boolie. (Possible responses: Both demand Boolie's attention; both speak to him in a bossy way.)

3. ACTIVE READING: Question
Ask students why Katie Bell may not have written down her instructions. (Possible responses: She may not know how to write; Florine may not have told her; Florine is blaming her for what she herself forgot; she may have her own way of doing things.) How does this relationship compare to Daisy and Hoke's? (Any response is valid.)

4. LITERARY CONCEPT: Conflict
Have students describe the conflict between Boolie and Florine. (Possible responses: Florine is jealous of Daisy; Boolie doesn't like Florine making critical remarks about his mother; Florine can tell Daisy doesn't like her so she takes it out on Boolie.)

PART 2

1 *BOOLIE'S DEN, Christmas morning, 1953. Boolie is going through a pile of long-playing Christmas records, none of them particularly religious. Through the open door we see a huge Christmas tree.*

Florine *(off camera)*. Of course I told you! *(We hear a muffled voice rising in protest.)* **2** Now, how can I be expected to buy it if you don't write it down? *(more of the muffled voice)* Boolie! I need you!

Boolie. Be right there! *(He enters the kitchen. Florine is staring at a large bowl full of sliced oranges and bananas.)*

Florine *(to the new cook)*. I told you. I told you a million times, Katie Bell. Write it down.

Katie Bell. Yassum.

Florine. More I cannot do. *(to Boolie)* We're out of coconut.

Boolie *(the peacemaker)*. I'm sure we can manage, Katie Bell.

Katie Bell. I tole her.

3 **Florine.** But you didn't write it down! I don't need to stand around and listen to excuses on Christmas Day. Maybe you can figure out how to serve ambrosia to fifty people without coconut. I give up. *(She leaves.)*

Boolie *(to Katie Bell)*. I'll call Mama. She has the whole Piggly Wiggly in her pantry. *(He goes to the phone and dials.)* Mama? Merry Christmas. Listen, do Florine a favor, all right? . . . You got a package of coconut in your pantry? . . .

Would you bring it when you come? . . . Many thanks. See you anon,[6] Mama. Ho ho ho! *(He hangs up and bounds upstairs.)* Honey! Hey, honey! *(He enters the master bedroom.)* Florine! Florine!

Florine *(from her large closet)*. In here.

Boolie. Your ambrosia's saved. Mama's got the coconut!

Florine. I knew she was good for something.

Boolie. Florine! I told you I don't like all this sniping at Mama. She's an old lady for goodness' sake! *(Florine's eyes flash, and she starts to speak, then changes her mind and kisses Boolie seductively.)* **4**

Florine. I think your mama woulda liked it if you'da married some little old bookworm.

Boolie. Mmmm. Hmmm.

DAISY'S CAR, night, passing suburban houses with outdoor Christmas decorations. Hoke is driving. Daisy is not in a festive mood.

Hoke. Ooooooh, look at them lit-up decorations!

Daisy. Everybody's giving the Georgia Power Company a merry Christmas.

Hoke. Miz Florine's got 'em all beat with the lights. 'Specially now they got that new house.

Daisy. That silly Santa Claus winking on the front door!

---

6. **anon:** soon.

Words to Know and Use | **sniping** (snīp' iŋ) *n*. attacking someone in a sly or deceitful way **snipe** *v*.

Hoke. I bet she have the biggest tree in Atlanta. Where she get 'em so large?

Daisy. Absurd. If I had a nose like Florine's, I wouldn't go around saying "Merry Christmas" to anybody.

Hoke. I enjoy Christmas at they house.

Daisy. I don't wonder. You're the only Christian in the place.

Hoke. 'Cept they got that new cook.

Daisy. Florine never could keep help. Of course, it's none of my affair.

Hoke. Nome.

Daisy. Too much running around, if you ask me. The Garden Club this and the Junior League that! But she'd die before she'd fix a glass of iced tea for the Temple Sisterhood!

Hoke. Yassum. You right.

Daisy. I just hope she doesn't take it in her head to sing this year. *(She imitates.)* Glo-o-o-o-o-o-o-o-o-o-o-o-o-ria! She sounds as if she has a bone stuck in her throat.

Hoke. You done say a mouthful, Miz Daisy.

Daisy. You didn't have to come. Boolie would have run me out.

Hoke. I know dat.

Daisy. Then why did you?

Hoke. That my business. *(Hoke turns the car into Boolie's driveway, passing a facsimile of Rudolph the Red-Nosed Reindeer.)* Well, looka there. Look what Miz Florine done.

Daisy. Oh, my Lord! If her grandfather, old man Freitag, could see this! What is it you say? I bet he'd jump up out of his grave and snatch her baldheaded. *(Hoke gets out and goes to open the passenger door.)*

Hoke. Go on 'way from here, Miz Daisy! Jump up and snatch her baldheaded!

Daisy. Wait a minute. *(She takes a small package wrapped in brown paper from her purse.)* This isn't a Christmas present.

Hoke. Nome.

Daisy. You know I don't give Christmas presents.

Hoke. Yassum.

Daisy. I just happened to run across it this morning. Go on. Open it. *(He unwraps the present.)*

Hoke. Ain' nobody never give me no book. *(He reads, not without difficulty.)* "Handwriting Copy Book—Grade Five."

Daisy. I always taught out of these.

5. **ACTIVE READING: Question**
What does Daisy mean by her comment? *(She is making reference to an old stereotype about Jews having big noses. Daisy means that Florine looks and is Jewish and should not be celebrating a Christian holiday.)*

6. **ACTIVE READING: Evaluate**
Ask students to explain Daisy's objection to Florine. *(Florine seems to be denying her Jewishness.)* Then invite them to give other explanations for Florine's behavior. *(Possible responses: She simply prefers the members and activities of the Garden Club and Junior League over those of the Temple Sisterhood; she wants to avoid Daisy; she is a social climber; she is helping her husband's business by socializing.)*

7. **VOCABULARY: Idiom**
Ask volunteers to think of other idioms that give the same meaning as "jump up out of his grave and snatch her baldheaded." *(Possible responses: "roll over in his grave"; "be fit to be tied")* Point out that Daisy is using Hoke's idiom; ask how this shows a change in their relationship. *(Possible response: She has learned to appreciate him and the way he expresses himself.)* ★

8. **ACTIVE READING: Evaluate**
Daisy says that her gift to Hoke is not a Christmas present. Ask students why they think Daisy stresses this point so much. *(Possible responses: After disapproving of Florine's celebrating Christmas, it would seem hypocritical for Daisy to celebrate as well; she doesn't want to admit she likes Hoke well enough to give him a present.)*

Hoke. Yassum.

Daisy. It's faded, but it works. If you practice, you'll write nicely.

Hoke. Yassum.

Daisy. But you have to practice. I taught Mayor Hartsfield out of this same book.

Hoke *(very touched).* Thank you, Miz Daisy.

Daisy. It's not a Christmas present.

Hoke. Nome.

Daisy. Jews haven't any business giving Christmas presents. And you don't have to go yapping about this to Boolie and Florine.

Hoke. This strictly between you and me.

Florine *(off camera).* Merry Christmas, Mother Werthan! *(They turn and see Boolie and Florine at the doorway.)*

Hoke. They done seen us.

9 **Daisy.** I hope I don't spit up. *(He helps her up the steps toward the house.)*

DAISY'S CAR, spring, 1955. Hoke is driving. Boolie is with him.

10 **Hoke.** You know, yo' mama done watch over dis machine like a chicken hawk. One day we park in front of de dry cleaner up yonder at de Plaza, and dis white man—look like some kind of lawyer, banker, dress up real fine—he done lay his satchel up on our hood while he open up his trunk, you know, and what he want to do that for? 'Fore I could stop her, yo' mama jump out de back do' and run that man every which way. She wicked 'bout her paint job. *(He stops the car at Mitchell Motors. He and Boolie get out.)*

Boolie. Did Mama tell you this new car has air conditioning?

Hoke. She say she doan' like no air cool. Say it give her the neck ache. *(They walk toward a new 1955 Cadillac.)*

Boolie. You know how Mama fought me, but it's time for a trade. I bet you will miss the old one, though.

Hoke. Not me. Unh unh.

Boolie. Oh, come on. Aren't you a little sorry to see it go?

Hoke. It ain' goin' nowhere. I done bought it.

Boolie. You didn't!

Hoke. Already made the deal with Mist' Red Mitchell inside yonder.

Boolie. For how much?

Hoke. Dat for him and me to know.

11

Boolie. Why didn't you just buy it from Mama? You'd have saved money.

Hoke. Yo' mama in my business enough as it is. I ain' studyin' makin' no monthly car payments to her. Disheah mine the regular way.

Boolie. It's a good car, all right. I guess nobody knows that better than you.

Hoke. Bes' ever come off the line. And dis new one, Miz Daisy doan' take to it, I let her ride in disheah now an' again.

Boolie. Mighty nice of you.

Hoke. Well, we all doin' what we can.

Boolie. You want to drive the new one home?

Hoke. No, suh.

Boolie. Why not?

Hoke. 'Cause I doan' want you gettin' them nasty ashes all over my upholstery.

DAISY'S KITCHEN, June 1957. Idella, in her eighties and looking worn, is taking fried chicken out of a skillet. Daisy enters.

Daisy. That's not enough chicken.

Idella. How much you an' Hoke plannin' to eat?

Daisy. I like to give them leftovers when I get there.

Idella. You will, 'less you make a pig of yos-eff.

Daisy. Did you put mustard in those eggs?

Idella. I always put mustard in my stuffed eggs.

Daisy. Spicy things make me sick.

Idella. You go upstairs and see 'bout your packing. *(Daisy starts out, then stops.)*

Daisy. Don't put the peaches in the icebox. I hate cold peaches.

Idella. Yassum. *(Daisy leaves.)* Act like I ain' never made a picnic in my life.

DAISY'S DRIVEWAY. Daisy drags a heavy suitcase out to the garage and returns to the house. Then she comes out with the picnic lunch and a wrapped gift. Hoke pulls up in his car and gets out.

Daisy *(extremely irritated).* It's three after seven!

Hoke. Yassum. You say we leavin' at fifteen to eight.

Daisy. At the latest, I said.

Hoke. Now what bizness you got, draggin' disheah out de house by yoseff?

Daisy. Who was here to help me?

Hoke. Miz Daisy, it doan' take me more 'an five minutes to load up de trunk of dis car.

Daisy. I hate doing things at the last minute.

Hoke. What you talkin' 'bout? You ready to go for the las' week and a half! *(He picks up the present.)*

Daisy. Don't touch that.

Hoke. Ain' it wrap pretty! Dat Mist' Walter's present?

Daisy. Yes. It's fragile. I'll hold it on the seat with me. *(As Hoke loads the trunk, Boolie pulls up in his car and gets out.)* Well, you nearly missed us.

Boolie. I thought you were leaving at quarter of.

Hoke. She takin' on.

Daisy. Be still.

Boolie *(holding out a gift).* Florine sent this for Uncle Walter. *(Daisy recoils from it.)* Well, it's not a snake, Mama. I think it's note paper.

Daisy. How appropriate. Uncle Walter can't see.

Boolie. Maybe it's soap.

Daisy. How nice that you show such an interest in your uncle's ninetieth birthday.

Boolie. Don't start up, Mama. I cannot go to Mobile with you. I have to go to New York tonight for the convention.

Daisy. The convention starts Monday. And I know what else I know.

12

13

14

◀ **L**

Words to Know and Use | **upholstery** (up hōl' stər ē) *n.* the soft fabric covering furniture
recoil (ri koil') *v.* to draw back from something distasteful or painful

439

---

12. ACTIVE READING: Review
Ask students what they can **infer** about the setting and about Daisy from the stage directions. *(Possible responses: Two years have passed since the last scene. We know that Daisy is also in her eighties, since she and Idella are the same age.)*

13. VOCABULARY: Idiom
Have students explain the meaning of the expression *takin' on.* *(Possible responses: making a fuss; getting upset)* Ask students to recall another idiom that Hoke used to express a similar idea about Miss Daisy. *(pitch a fit, p. 431)* ★

14. LITERARY CONCEPT: Humor
Ask students how Daisy uses sarcasm as a way of being critical here. *(Possible responses: She says, "How appropriate" when she really means "how inappropriate"; she compliments Boolie on showing an interest when she knows he has no idea what the gift is.)*

15

Boolie. Just leave Florine out of it. She wrote away for those tickets eight months ago.

Daisy. I'm sure *My Fair Lady* is more important than your own flesh and blood.

Boolie. Mama! I can't talk to you when you're like this. *(Daisy gets into the car.)*

Daisy. They expect us for a late supper in Mobile.

Boolie. You'll be there. *(He takes Hoke out of Daisy's hearing.)*

Daisy. I know they'll fix crab. All that trouble.

Boolie *(to Hoke)*. I don't know how you'll stand all day in the car.

Hoke. She doan' mean nothin'. She jes' worked up.

16

Boolie. Here's fifty dollars in case you run into trouble. Don't show it to Mama. You've got your map?

Hoke. She got it in wid her. Study ever' inch of the way.

Boolie. I'll be at the Ambassador Hotel in New York. On Park Avenue.

Daisy. It's seven-sixteen.

Boolie. You ought to have a job on the radio announcing the time.

Daisy. I want to miss the rush hour.

Boolie. Congratulate Uncle Walter for me. And kiss everybody in Mobile. *(Hoke gets in the car and starts the engine.)*

Daisy. Did you have the air condition checked? I told you to have the air condition checked.

Hoke. Yassum, I had the air condition checked, but I don't know what for. You doan' never allow me to turn it on.

Daisy. Hush up. *(The car moves down the driveway.)*

COUNTRY ROADSIDE. Daisy and Hoke are eating lunch, relaxed.

Hoke. Idella stuff eggs good.

Daisy. You stuff yourself good. *(They eat in peaceful silence.)* I was thinking about the first time I ever went to Mobile. It was Walter's wedding. 1888.

Hoke. 1888! You weren't nothing but a little child!

Daisy. I was twelve. We went on the train. And I was so excited. I'd never been in a wedding party, and I'd never seen the ocean. Papa said it was the Gulf of

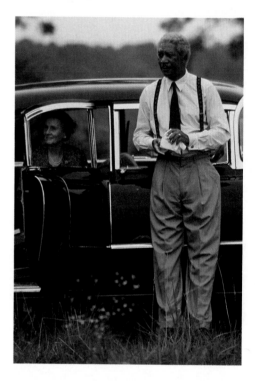

Mexico and not the ocean. I asked Papa if it was all right to dip my hand in the water. He laughed because I was so timid. And then I tasted the salt water on my fingers. Isn't it silly to remember that?

Hoke. No sillier than most of what folks remember. *(A state patrol car pulls up. Two troopers are in the front seat.)*

Trooper *(to Hoke)*. Hey, boy! *(Hoke looks at him evenly.)* What do you think you're doing with this car?

Daisy *(calm, but angry)*. This is my car, officer.

Trooper *(gets out and walks over)*. Yes, ma'am. Can I see the registration, please? *(to Hoke)* And your license, boy. *(Hoke produces the registration and the license. The trooper studies both. To Daisy.)* What's this name? Wetheran?

Daisy. Werthan.

Trooper. Werthan. Never heard that one before. What kind of name is that?

Daisy. It's of German <u>derivation</u>.

Trooper. German derivation. Unh hunh. *(He hands the papers back to Hoke and waves him on. The Cadillac goes off down the road. The trooper gets back in the patrol car.)* An old nigger and an old Jew[7] woman takin' off down the road together. Now that is one sorry sight.

Second Trooper. I'll tell you one sorrier. They're sittin' in a Cadillac, and I'm sittin' here next to you. *(The first trooper guns the car off in the other direction.)*

M ▶ *DAISY'S CAR, passing cotton fields.*

Hoke. You talkin' 'bout first time before. I tell you 'bout the first time I ever leave the state of Georgia?

Daisy. When was that?

Hoke. A few minutes back.

Daisy. Go on!

Hoke. Thass right. First time. My daughter, she married to a Pullman porter, and she all the time goin'—Detroit, New York, St. Louis—and I say, "Well, that very nice, Tommie Lee, but I jes' doan' feel the need." So dis it, Miz Daisy, and I got to tell you, Alabama ain' lookin' like much so far.

Daisy. It's nicer the other side of Montgomery.

Hoke. If you say so. Pass me up one of them peaches, please, ma'am.

Daisy. Oh, no!

Hoke. What happen?

Daisy. That sign said Phenix City—thirty miles. We're not supposed to go to Phenix City. We're going the wrong way!

Hoke. Maybe you done read it wrong.

Daisy. I didn't. Stop the car! Stop the car! *(Hoke swerves off the road. Daisy wrestles with the map.)* Here! You took the wrong turn at Opelika! *(He takes the map.)*

Hoke. You took it wid me. And you readin' the map!

Daisy. I'm such a fool! I didn't have any business coming in the car by myself with just you. I should have come on the train.

---

7. nigger . . . Jew: *slang. Nigger* is an insulting name for an African American. *Jew* (as in this case) may also be derogatory, depending on the speaker's intent.

Words to Know and Use | **derivation** (der′ ə vā′ shən) *n.* origin; source

441

17. VOCABULARY: Pejorative Term
Help students understand that the word *boy* is a derogatory term when used by white people to refer to an African American male. It implies a superior and intimidating attitude on the part of the speaker. ★

18. ACTIVE READING: Evaluate
Point out to students that the trooper is insulting both Hoke and Daisy by calling them derogatory names based on their race and religion. Ask students how they feel when they read these offensive terms, and how often they still hear them. Ask why they think the author included words with such negative connotations. *(Responses will vary.)* Then ask students what their impressions are of the state troopers. *(Possible responses: They are prejudiced against African Americans and Jews; they don't like to see a white woman and a black man riding together.)*

19. CULTURAL SIDELIGHT
If students are unfamiliar with the term *Pullman porter*, explain that a Pullman is a railroad car with small private rooms. A porter is a railroad employee who takes care of passengers on the train. For many years, most Pullman porters were African American.

I'd be safe there. I just should have come on the train.

Hoke. Yassum. You sho' shoulda'.

DAISY'S CAR, traveling at night. Daisy *and* Hoke *are tired.*

Daisy. They've fixed crab for me! Minnie always fixes crab! They go to so much trouble! It's all ruined by now!

Hoke. We got to pull over, Miz Daisy.

Daisy. Is something wrong with the car?

Hoke. Nome. I got to be 'scused.

Daisy. What?

Hoke. I got to make water.

Daisy. You should have thought of that back at the Standard Oil station.

20 **Hoke.** Colored cain' use the toilet at no Standard Oil. You know dat.

Daisy. Well, there's no time to stop. We'll be in Mobile soon. You can wait.

Hoke. Yassum. *(a beat)* Nome. *(He stops the car.)*

Daisy. I told you to wait!

21 **Hoke.** Yassum. I hear you. How you think I feel havin' to ax you when can I make water like I some dog?

Daisy. Why, Hoke! I'd be ashamed!

22 **Hoke.** I ain' no dog and I ain' no chile and I ain' just a back of the neck you look at while you going wherever you want to go. I a man, nearly seventy-two years old, and I know when my bladder full, and I gettin' out dis car and goin' off down the road like I got to do. And I'm takin' the car key this time. And that's the end of it! *(He gets out of the car and slams the door.*

Daisy *sits still for a moment, then rolls down the window.)*

Daisy. Hoke! *(silence)* Hoke! *(silence)* Hoke! *(She starts to get out of the car—when a man appears in the shadowy dark. She is frightened.)*

Hoke. You all right in there, Miz Daisy?

Daisy *(relieved, but quickly her old snappish self).* Of course I am!

◄ N

WALTER'S LIVING ROOM, the next evening. Walter, *old and blind, is in a chair surrounded by relatives.* Daisy *is talking to* Boolie *by phone.*

Daisy *(on the phone).* Uncle Walter appreciates your call. I don't think he can come to the phone. . . .

BOOLIE'S HOTEL ROOM.

Boolie *(on phone).* Fine. How is Hoke?

WALTER'S LIVING ROOM.

Daisy *(on phone).* What do you mean? How should he be? *(Uncle Walter's daughter enters with a birthday cake, and the singing of "Happy Birthday" starts.)* I have to hang up, Boolie. . . . I'll tell him. . . . Yes, we will. . . . All right. You, too. 'Bye. *(Daisy looks at* Walter *with love and pride.* Hoke *and* Katie Bell *enter from the kitchen.* Hoke *nods gravely at* Daisy. *She nods back gratefully.)*

23

BOOLIE'S OFFICE, 1962. Hoke *enters.*

Boolie *(to* Hoke*).* To what do I owe this honor?

Hoke. We got to talk, Mr. Werthan.

Boolie. What is it?

442   UNIT FOUR   BONDS OF THE HEART

Multicultural Connections

Hoke makes reference to one aspect of segregation in the 1950s: separate bathrooms for blacks and whites. Segregation also was practiced in schools, hotels, buses, movie theaters, restaurants, and even at drinking fountains. Ask students to imagine they were an African American living in the South in the 1950s. Would they behave as Hoke does? How might Hoke's attitude and behavior in the 1950s be different from the attitude of an African American of the 1990s?

Hoke. It Mist' Sinclair Harris.

Boolie. My cousin Sinclair?

Hoke. His wife.

Boolie. Jeanette?

Hoke. The one talk funny.

Boolie. She's from Canton, Ohio.

Hoke. Yassuh. She's tryin' to hire me.

Boolie. What?

Hoke. She say, "How are they treating you, Hoke?" You know how she soun', like her nose stuff up. And I say, "Fine, Miz Harris," and she say, "Well, if you was lookin' for a change, you know where to call." I thought you want to know 'bout it.

Boolie. I'll be . . .

Hoke. Ain' she a mess? *(a pause)* She say name yo' sal'ry.

Boolie. I see. And did you?

Hoke. Did I what?

Boolie. Name your salary.

Hoke. Now, what you think I am? I ain' studyin' workin' for no trashy somethin' like her.

Boolie. But she got you thinking, didn't she?

Hoke. You might could say dat.

Boolie. Well, how does sixty-five dollars a week sound?

Hoke. Sounds pretty good. Course, seventy-five sounds better.

Boolie. So it does. Beginning this week.

Hoke. Das mighty nice of you, Mist' Werthan. I 'preciate it. Mist' Werthan, you ever had people fightin' over you?

Boolie. No.

Hoke. Well, I tell you. It feel good. *(He smiles and walks happily out of the office.)*

DAISY'S LIVING ROOM, May 1963. Daisy *is playing mah-jongg with* Beulah, Miriam, *and another woman.*

Miriam *(putting a tile on the table).* Six bams.

Beulah. Mah-jongg!

Miriam. You are the luckiest thing, Beulah!

Daisy. 'Scuse me a second. *(She goes to the kitchen.* Hoke *and* Idella *are watching a soap opera on a black-and-white TV set.* Idella, *now old and frail, is shelling peas.)*

Daisy. I don't know how y'all can look at that.

Hoke. You see it a few times, you get in it.

Daisy. Both of your brains are fixing to evaporate. You can bring in the cake now, Hoke.

Hoke. Yassum.

Daisy. Don't make a mess with those peas, Idella.

Idella. Do I ever? *(Daisy leaves.* Hoke *puts napkins, forks, and plates on a tray that holds a cake.)*

Hoke *(nodding toward the soap opera).* Ain't the blonde one got a lotta hair? How do she make it so shiny?

Idella. Washes it in my-naise. *(He looks dubious.)* Yes, she do. It was in *Life* magazine.

Hoke. Don' seem human, do it? *(He picks up the tray and goes out. The camera focuses on the soap opera. Then* Hoke *comes back.)* What happen? Linda up to somethin', ain' she? *(no answer)* Idella?

24. LITERARY CONCEPT: Dialect
Ask students what Hoke means when he says, *I ain' studyin' workin' for no trashy somethin' like her.* Allow them to suggest other ways to state the same idea. *(Possible responses: "I'm not planning to work for someone as unrefined as she is." "I'm not considering working for anyone so rude.")* ★

25. LITERARY CONCEPT: Character
Invite students to tell what Hoke's conversation with Boolie indicates about Hoke's character. *(Possible responses: He has cleverly engineered this conversation to get himself a raise; just as he has become more assertive with Daisy, he is also more assertive with Boolie; he is unafraid to ask for what he feels he deserves; he knows how to negotiate.)*

26. VOCABULARY: Dialect
Ask students what word Idella means when she says *my-naise (mayonnaise).* Also see if they remember the meaning of *dubious,* originally explained on page 424. ★

27

27. LITERARY CONCEPT: Plot

Ask students to **infer** what has happened. *(Idella has died; Daisy's family and Hoke are attending her funeral.)* Ask why this scene at the church is significant in showing changes in Daisy's character. *(Possible responses: Daisy is attending the funeral of her servant as if Idella had been a friend or equal; previously Daisy would never have attended a black church; Hoke is sitting with the family.)*

28. VOCABULARY: Special Terms

Help students understand the references in this passage: *funny papers* (comics), *Krispy Kreme* (a store), and *Lawd* (dialect for Lord). ★

29. ACTIVE READING: Review

Ask students why Daisy is surprised to see Hoke. *(Possible response: The weather is bad.)* Ask how Daisy feels about this. *(Possible response: touched, very grateful)*

(We hear a bowl hit the floor and see peas rolling on the linoleum.) Idella! Idella!

27 *A BAPTIST CHURCH. The congregation is black, except for Daisy, Boolie, and Florine, who sit in the rear. Hoke is sitting with them.*

DAISY'S KITCHEN, two months later. Daisy is frying chicken. Hoke enters and watches her.

Hoke. You fixin' to ruin it?

Daisy. What are you talking about?

Hoke. You got de skillet turn up too high, and de chicken too close together.

Daisy. Mind your business.

Hoke. It's yo' chicken. *(He leaves the kitchen. Daisy turns the flame down.)*

DAISY'S DINING ROOM. Daisy is seated at the table. Hoke enters and puts in front of her a plate of fried chicken, stewed okra, and rice.

Daisy. Thank you, Hoke. *(He goes into the kitchen and begins to eat the same meal at the kitchen table.)*

DAISY'S YARD, July 1963. Daisy and Hoke are working side by side in a vegetable garden.

DAISY'S LIVING ROOM, winter, 1964. While an ice storm rages outside, Daisy tries to read by candlelight. She hears the back door open and close.

Daisy *(alarmed)*. Who is it?

Hoke *(off camera)*. Mornin', Miz Daisy.

Daisy. Oh, Hoke. *(Hoke enters, wearing an overcoat and galoshes and carrying a small paper bag.)* What in the world?

Hoke. I learn to drive on ice when I deliver milk for the Avondale Dairy. Ain' much to it. Other folks bangin' into each other like they in the funny papers, though. Oh, I stop at the Krispy Kreme. Lawd knows you got to have yo' coffee in the mornin'.

Daisy *(touched)*. How sweet of you, Hoke! *(He hands her a cup of coffee and sips his own.)*

Hoke. We ain' had no good coffee 'roun heah since Idella pass.

Daisy. Mmmm. Hmmm. I can fix her biscuits, and we both know how to make her fried chicken. But nobody can make Idella's coffee. I wonder how she did it.

Hoke. I doan' know. *(They sip silently for a moment, deep in thought.)*

Daisy. Idella was lucky.

Hoke. Yassum. I 'spec she was. *(He starts out of the room.)*

Daisy. Where are you going?

Hoke. Take off my overshoes.

Daisy. I didn't think you'd come today.

Hoke. It ain' my day off, is it?

Daisy. Well, I don't know what you can do around here except keep me company.

Hoke. I can light us a fire. *(He goes into the kitchen.)*

Daisy. Eat anything you want out of the ice-box. It'll all spoil anyway.

Hoke *(off camera)*. Yassum.

Daisy. And wipe up what you tracked onto the kitchen floor.

28

29

Hoke (*off camera*). Now, Miz Daisy, what you think I am? A mess? (*The phone rings.*)

Daisy (*on her way to the phone*). Yes. That's exactly what I think you are.

Hoke (*off camera*). All right den. All right.

HALLWAY. Daisy *answers the phone.*

Daisy. Hello?

BOOLIE'S DEN. Intercut between Daisy *and* Boolie *during this conversation.*

Boolie. I'll be out after you as soon as I can get down the driveway.

Daisy. Stay where you are, Boolie. Hoke is here with me.

Boolie. How did he manage that?

Daisy. He's very handy. I'm fine. I don't need a thing in the world.

Boolie. Hello? (*to Florine*) I must have the wrong number. I never heard Mama saying loving things about Hoke before.

Daisy. I didn't say I love him. I said he was handy.

Boolie. Uh hunh.

Daisy. Honestly, Boolie. Are you trying to irritate me in the middle of an ice storm? (*She hangs up.*)

30

◀ ○

Responding to Reading

First Impressions of Part 2

1. Have your feelings about Hoke or Daisy changed? Jot down your thoughts in your journal or notebook.

Second Thoughts on Part 2

2. How has Hoke and Daisy's relationship changed?

> **Think about**
> • Daisy's gift to Hoke
> • their trip to Mobile

3. How would you describe Boolie's relationship with his mother? Use examples from the play to explain your answer.

4. Why do you think Daisy and Florine resent each other?

Reading On

The play has now entered the 1960s, a time when African Americans campaigned for their rights in the face of sometimes violent resistance. As you read, look for signs of how the society is changing and how each character responds to these changes.

30. ACTIVE READING: Question
Why does Daisy stress that she never said she loved Hoke? (*Possible responses: She is too stubborn to admit that she is fond of him; she is too proud to reveal her feelings; she won't give Boolie the satisfaction of admitting that Hoke is valuable to her.*)

Responding to Reading

1. Any response is valid.

2. **Possible responses:** Daisy is much fonder of Hoke and relies on him much more; Hoke takes less nonsense from Daisy and speaks his mind more often; they are becoming friends and are more respectful toward each other.

3. **Possible responses:** Daisy relies a little less on Boolie now that she has Hoke; she is critical of Boolie, as when he does not attend his uncle's birthday party, but she seems to love him. Boolie accepts his mother's failings with humor; he loves her and worries about her, as when he would have come in the storm, and he teases her, as on the phone.

4. **Possible responses:** Daisy resents Florine's showiness, her eagerness to join secular organizations, and her pulling away from Judaism; Florine resents Daisy's constant demands on Boolie's time and Daisy's contempt for Florine.

PART 3

TRAFFIC JAM, September 1964. Daisy is in her car. Hoke, walking against the halted traffic, reaches the car.

Daisy. Well, what is it? What took so long?

Hoke. Couldn't help it. Big mess up yonder.

Daisy. What's the matter? I might as well not go to temple at all now!

Hoke. You cain' go to temple today, Miz Daisy.

Daisy. Why not? What in the world is the matter with you?

Hoke. Somebody done bomb the temple.

Daisy. What? Bomb the temple?

Hoke. Yassum. Dat why we stuck here so long.

Daisy. I don't believe it.

Hoke. Dat what the police tell me up yonder. Say it happen about a half hour ago.

Daisy. Oh, no! Well, was anybody there? Were people hurt?

Hoke. Din' say.

Daisy. Who would do such a thing?

Hoke. You know good as me. Always be the same ones.

Daisy. Well, it's a mistake. I'm sure they meant to bomb one of the Conservative synagogues or the Orthodox one. The temple is Reform. Everybody knows that.

Hoke. It doan' matter to them people. A Jew is a Jew to them folks. Jes' like light or dark, we all the same nigger. *(Daisy dabs her eyes with a Kleenex.)* I know jes' how you feel, Miz Daisy. Back down there above Macon on the farm—I 'bout ten or 'leven years old—and one day my frien' Porter, his daddy hangin' from a tree. And the day befo', he laughin' and pitchin' horseshoes wid us. And den he hangin' up yonder wid his hands tie behind his back an' the flies all over him. I threw up right where I was standin'. You go on and cry.

Daisy. I'm not crying. *(collecting herself)* Why did you tell me that story?

Hoke. I doan' know. Seem like disheah mess put me in mind of it.

Daisy. The temple has nothing to do with that!

Hoke. So you say.

Daisy. You don't even know what happened. How do you know that policeman was telling the truth?

Hoke. Now, why would a policeman go and lie 'bout a thing like dat?

Daisy. Well, you never get things right anyway.

Hoke. Miz Daisy, somebody done bomb dat place, and you know it, too.

Daisy. Go on. Just go on now. I don't want to hear any more about it.

Hoke. You de boss.

Daisy. Stop talking to me!

THE COMMERCE CLUB, summer, 1966. A dozen businessmen are seated at a long table. Boolie is at one end, flanked by Florine and Daisy. One man, who is standing and holding a large silver bowl, beckons to Boolie. Boolie rises and takes the trophy.

Boolie. Thank you, Wellborn. And thank you all. I am deeply grateful to be chosen 1966 Man of the Year by the Atlanta Business Council—an honor I've seen bestowed upon some mighty fine fellas and which I certainly never expected to come to me. I'm afraid the loss here *(touching his hair)* and the gain here *(patting his belly)* have given me an air of competence I don't possess. But I'll tell you, I sure wish my father and my grandfather could see this. Seventy-two years ago they leased an old mill out on the Decatur Road with two looms in operation. They managed to grow with Atlanta, and to this day, we of Werthan Industries believe we want what Atlanta wants. This award proves we must be right. Thank you. *(applause)*

DAISY'S FRONT HALL, fall, 1966. Daisy is dialing the phone.

5 **Daisy.** Hidey, Miss McClatchey. . . . You always recognize my voice. What a shame a wonderful girl like you never married. Miss McClatchey, is my son in? . . . Oh,

6 no, no, no. Please tell him I bought the tickets for the UJA banquet. . . . And don't worry. My cousin Tillie in Chattanooga married for the first time at fifty-seven. 'Bye. *(She hangs up.)*

BEDROOM. Daisy is at her desk, paying bills. Boolie enters.

Boolie. How are you feeling, Mama?

Daisy. Not a good question to ask somebody nearly ninety.

Boolie. Well, you look fine.

Daisy. It's my ageless appeal.

Boolie. Miss McClatchey gave me your message.

Daisy. Florine's invited, too.

Boolie. Thank you very much.

Daisy. I guess Hoke should drive us. There'll be a crowd.

Boolie. Mama, we have to talk about this. You know, I believe Martin Luther King has done some mighty fine things.

Daisy. Boolie, if you don't want to go, why don't you just come right out and say so?

Boolie. I want to go. You know how I feel about him.

Daisy. Of course, but Florine—

Boolie. Florine has nothing to do with it. I still have to conduct business in this town.

Daisy. I see. You will go out of business if you attend the King dinner.

Boolie. Not exactly. But a lot of men I do business with wouldn't like it. They might snicker a little and call me Martin Luther Werthan behind my back. Maybe I wouldn't hear about certain meetings at the Commerce Club. Jack Raphael, over at Ideal Mills, he's a New York Jew instead of a Georgia Jew, and the really smart ones come from New York, don't they? So some of the boys might start throwing business to Jack instead of to old Martin Luther Werthan. I don't know. Maybe it wouldn't happen, but that's the way it works. If we don't use those seats, somebody else will.

Daisy. I'm not supposed to go, either?

---

5. LITERARY CONCEPT: Dialect
Some students may be confused by Daisy's use of the word *hidey*. Explain that it is a Southern dialect, similar to the Western expression *howdy*. It is Daisy's friendly way of saying hello. ★

6. VOCABULARY: Abbreviation
Explain that UJA stands for United Jewish Appeal, an organization in the United States that raises funds to help Jews around the world. The banquet's purpose is to raise money for UJA. ★

7. HISTORICAL SIDELIGHT
Have students share what they know about Dr. Martin Luther King, Jr. If necessary, explain that he was an Atlanta minister who led marches and protests in the 1950s and 1960s to gain civil rights for African Americans. In the play, King is being honored at the UJA dinner for his work.

8. ACTIVE READING: Evaluate
Have students explain why Boolie will not go to the King dinner. *(Possible response: He is afraid his business associates will disapprove.)* Ask students whether they think Boolie is correct in thinking he will lose business by attending the dinner, and if that justifies his not going. *(Any response is valid.)*

9. LITERARY CONCEPT: Characterization
Ask students how Boolie's words point out the changes in both his and Daisy's attitudes. (Possible responses: He shows the prejudice that she denies having; his caution brings out her independent spirit.)

10. ACTIVE READING: Connect
Ask students who they believe is right about the mailbox, Hoke or Daisy. Encourage them to describe what they believe each character is feeling and why he or she is arguing. (Any response is valid.)

11. ACTIVE READING: Question
Why does Daisy assume that Hoke knows Martin Luther King? (Possible responses: because both Hoke and King are African Americans; she may think there are not many African Americans in Atlanta and that they all know one another.) Discuss what this indicates about her character. Is she prejudiced? ignorant? naive? (Any response is valid.)

Boolie. Mama, you can do whatever you want.

Daisy. Thanks for your permission.

Boolie. Can I ask you something? When did you get so fired up about Martin Luther King? Time was, I'd have heard a different story.

Daisy. Why, Boolie! I've never been prejudiced, and you know it!

Boolie. OK. Why didn't you ask Hoke to go to the dinner with you?

Daisy. Hoke? Don't be ridiculous! He wouldn't go!

Boolie. Ask him and see.

KITCHEN. Hoke *sits at the table, squinting at the paper through thick glasses.* Daisy *enters.*

Daisy. All right. *(They go out and get in the car.* Hoke *drives down the driveway, almost hitting the mailbox.)* I don't know why you still drive. You can't see.

Hoke. Yassum, I can.

Daisy. You didn't see that mailbox.

Hoke. How do you know what I din' see?

Daisy. It nearly poked through my window. This car is all scratched up.

Hoke. Ain' no sucha thing.

Daisy. How would you know? You can't see. What a shame. It's a brand-new car, too.

Hoke. You done had this car two years come March.

MAIN THOROUGHFARE.

Daisy. You forgot to turn.

Hoke. Ain' this dinner at the Biltmo'?

Daisy. You know it is.

Hoke. Biltmo' this way.

Daisy. You know so much!

Hoke. Yassum. I do.

Daisy. I've lived in Atlanta all my life.

Hoke. And ain' run a car in twenty years.

Daisy. Boolie said the silliest thing the other day.

Hoke. That right? *(a long beat)* Well, what did he say?

Daisy. Well, he was talking about Martin Luther King. *(a beat)* I guess you know him, don't you?

Hoke. Martin Luther King? Nome.

Daisy. I was sure you did. But you've heard him preach?

Hoke. Same way as you, over the TV.

Daisy. I think he's wonderful.

Hoke. Yassum. *(a long beat)* What you getting at, Miz Daisy?

Daisy. Well, it's so silly! Boolie said you wanted to go to this dinner with me. Did you tell him that?

Hoke. Nome.

Daisy. I didn't think so. You can hear him whenever you want.

Hoke. You want the front do' or the side do' to the Biltmo'?

Daisy. You pick. Isn't it wonderful the way things are changing?

BILTMORE HOTEL. Hoke *stops the car by the front entrance. He turns in his seat to face* Daisy.

Hoke. What you think I am, Miz Daisy?

Daisy. What do you mean?

Hoke. You think I some old somethin' sittin' up here doan' know nothin' 'bout how to do?

Daisy. I don't know what you're talking about.

Hoke. Invitation to disheah dinner come in the mail a month ago. Did be you want me to go wid you, how come you wait till we in the car and on the way to ask me?

Daisy. What? All I said was that Boolie said you wanted to go.

Hoke. Mmmm. Hmmm.

Daisy. Well, my stars! Aren't you a big baby!

12

Hoke. Ne'er mind baby. Next time you ask me someplace, ask me regular.

Daisy. You don't have to carry on so much!

Hoke. Thass all. Less drop it.

Daisy. Honestly!

13

Hoke. You talkin' 'bout things change. They ain' change all dat much. (*He opens his door.*) I hep you to the do'.

Daisy. Thank you, Hoke. I can help myself. (*Daisy gets out and enters the hotel. Hoke makes no effort to help her.*)

HOTEL BALLROOM. The room is filled with people sitting at tables, listening to Dr. King.

Dr. King (*off camera*). . . . Segregation has placed the whole South socially, educationally, and economically behind the rest of the nation. Yet there are in the white South millions of people of good will whose voices are yet unheard, whose course is yet unclear, and whose courageous acts are yet unseen. . . .

DAISY'S CAR. Hoke is listening to the speech on the radio.

Dr. King (*off camera*). These persons are often silent today because of fear—fear of social, political, and economic <u>reprisals</u>. In the name of human dignity, and for the cause of democracy, these millions are called upon to gird their courage, to speak out, to offer leadership that is needed.

14

HOTEL BALLROOM.

Dr. King (*off camera*). If the people of good will of the white South fail to act now, history will have to record that the greatest tragedy of this period of social transition was not the vitriolic[8] words and the violent actions of the bad people, but the <u>appalling</u> silence and the indifference of the good people.

◀ Q

DAISY'S KITCHEN, March 1970. Hoke enters the back door.

Hoke (*calling*). Mornin', Miz Daisy. (*no answer*) Miz Daisy? (*He goes into the dining room, where all the drawers in the sideboard are open. He goes into the front hall.*) Miz Daisy?

Daisy (*off camera*). Hoke! Is that Hoke?

---

8. **vitriolic:** (vi′ trē äl′ ik) harsh and biting.

Words to Know and Use	**reprisal** (ri prī′ zəl) *n.* an injury done in response to an injury received; retaliation **appalling** (ə pôl′ iŋ) *adj.* horrifying; dreadful **appall** *v.*

449

12. ACTIVE READING: Connect
Discuss Hoke's feelings about Daisy's invitation. Ask students why he is upset about the way Daisy invites him to the dinner. Ask, "If you were Hoke, would you feel hurt or insulted? Why or why not?" *(Any response is valid.)*

13. ACTIVE READING: Review
Ask students why Hoke says that things aren't changing that much. *(Possible responses: He thinks Daisy didn't ask him to the dinner because he is black; he means that even if things are changing, people are still prejudiced.)*

14. ACTIVE READING: Evaluate
Ask students which characters in the play Dr. King's remarks might apply to. *(Possible responses: Boolie, who fears losing money if he attends the dinner; Daisy, who didn't ask Hoke to the dinner until the last minute.)*

Speaking . . . Listening . . . Viewing

Listening/Viewing Have students watch Dr. Martin Luther King, Jr.'s famous "I Have a Dream" speech in *A Day to Remember: August 28, 1963* (PBS Video) or another of his taped speeches. Ask students to think about the following questions as they watch and to jot down their ideas on paper. Later, have students share their thoughts in a class discussion.

1. What was Dr. King's main message in the speech?

2. What details and facts did he use to support his main ideas?

3. How effective did you feel Dr. King was in delivering his speech? Why?

4. What parts of the speech did you feel were most memorable? What made them so?

15. VOCABULARY: Word Parts
If students do not know the word *disarray*, have them divide the word into its parts to find the prefix *dis-*, meaning "the opposite of," and *array*, meaning "order." ★

16. VOCABULARY: Definition
If students do not know the word *totters*, help them understand its meaning of "walks unsteadily." Ask students how Daisy has changed since the last scene. *(Possible response: Her hair is messy, she thinks she's still a teacher, she walks unsteadily.)* ★

17. ACTIVE READING: Review
Ask students to explain what has happened to Daisy. As necessary, help them understand that Daisy is experiencing a condition that occurs in elderly people, when their minds suddenly take them back to an earlier time in their lives.

15 **Hoke.** Yassum. You all right? (Daisy *makes her way slowly downstairs. Her hair is in disarray.*)

Daisy. Hoke? Hoke?

Hoke. Yassum.

Daisy. Where did you put my papers?

Hoke. What papers, Miz Daisy?

Daisy. My papers! I had them all corrected last night, and I put them in the front so I wouldn't forget them on my way to school. What did you do with them? (*She goes unsteadily into the den. Hoke follows.*)

Hoke. School? What you talkin' 'bout? (Daisy *rifling through drawers.*)

Daisy. The children will be so disappointed if I don't give them their homework back. I always give it back the next day. That's why they like me.

Hoke. You talkin' outta yo' head!

Daisy. Why aren't you helping me?

Hoke. What you want me to do, Miz Daisy?

Daisy. Find those papers! I told you. It's all right if you moved them. I won't be mad with you. But I've got to get to school now. I'll be late, and who will take care of my class? Oh, I do everything wrong. **16** (*She totters into the living room. Hoke follows her.*)

Hoke. Set down. You 'bout to fall and hurt yoseff.

Daisy. It doesn't matter. It's all my fault. I didn't do right. It's so awful!

Hoke. Now you lissen heah. Ain' nothin' awful 'cep the way you carryin' on.

Daisy. I'm so sorry. It's all my fault. I can't find the papers, and the children are waiting.

Hoke. No, they ain'. You ain' no teacher no mo'.

Daisy. It doesn't make any difference.

Hoke. Miz Daisy, ain' nothin' the matter wid you.

Daisy. You don't know! You don't know! What's the difference?

Hoke. Your mind done took a turn this **17** mornin'. Thass all. (*She has now worked her way to the front hall. Hoke dials a number quickly.*)

Hoke (*into the phone*). Lemme have 'im, Miz McClatchey.

Daisy. Go on. Just go on now.

BOOLIE'S OFFICE.

Boolie (*into the phone*). What can I do for you this morning? (*Intercut between* Boolie *and* Hoke *during this conversation.*)

Hoke. It yo' mama.

Boolie. What's the matter?

Hoke. She worked up.

Boolie. Why should today be different from any other day?

Hoke. No, this ain' the same. (Daisy *pulls a drawer out of the commode,*[9] *and it crashes to the floor.*)

Boolie. I'll be right there. ◀ R

---

9. **commode:** a chest of drawers; bureau.

STAIRCASE. Daisy *starts upstairs.* Hoke *follows her.*

Hoke. You snap right back if you jes' let yoseff.

Daisy. I can't! I can't!

Hoke. You a lucky ole woman! You know dat?

Daisy. No! No! It's all a mess now. And I can't do anything about it. *(She goes into Boolie's old bedroom.* Hoke *settles her in a chair.)*

Hoke. You rich, you well fo' yo' time, and you got people care 'bout what happen to you.

Daisy. I'm being trouble. Oh, I don't want to be trouble to anybody.

Hoke. You want somethin' to cry 'bout, I take you to the state home, show you what layin' out dere in de halls. An' I bet none of them take on as bad as yo' doin'.

Daisy *(less agitated, but still confused).* I'm sorry. I'm so sorry. Those poor children in my class.

Hoke. You keep dis up, I promise, Mist' Werthan call the doctor on you, and dat doctor gon' take you in the insane asylum 'fore you know what hit you. Dat de way you want it to be?

Daisy *(in her normal voice).* Hoke, do you still have that Oldsmobile?

Hoke. From when I firs' come here? Go on, Miz Daisy. Dat thing been in the junkyard fifteen years or mo'. I drivin' yo' next to las' car now; '65 Cadillac, runnin' fine as wine.

Daisy. You ought not to be driving anything, the way you see.

Hoke. How you know the way I see, 'less you lookin' outta my eyes?

Daisy. Hoke?

Hoke. Yassum?

Daisy. You're my best friend.

Hoke. Come on, Miz Daisy. You jes'—

Daisy. No. Really. You are. You are. *(She takes his hand.)*

Hoke. Yassum.

18. ACTIVE READING: Review
Have students explain what Hoke means by "the state home." Make sure they understand that he is referring to a state-run institution where mentally ill people are cared for. ★

19. ACTIVE READING: Review
Ask students what indications are given that Daisy is coming back to normal. *(Possible responses: Her voice is normal, she mentions Hoke's old Oldsmobile.)*

20. LITERARY CONCEPT: Climax
Ask students to discuss the significance of Daisy's comment. *(Possible responses: Daisy finally admits her feelings for Hoke; her character undergoes a major change at this point; admitting how she feels about Hoke shows how vulnerable she feels.)*

21

LIVING ROOM, November 1973. The furniture is gone. Boolie, *now sixty-five, is checking a moving carton.* Hoke, *now eighty-five, shuffles into the room.*

Hoke. Mornin', Mist' Werthan.

Boolie. Hey, Hoke! Good to see you! You didn't drive yourself out here?

Hoke. No, suh. I doan' drive no mo'. My granddaughter run me out.

Boolie. Is she old enough to drive?

Hoke. Michelle thirty-seven. Teach biology at Spelman College.

Boolie. I never knew that.

Hoke. Yassuh.

22

Boolie. I've taken most of what I want out of the house. Is there anything you'd like before the Goodwill comes?

Hoke. My place full to bustin' now.

Boolie. It feels funny to sell the house while Mama's still alive.

Hoke. I 'gree.

Boolie. But she hasn't been inside the door for two years now. I suppose you don't get out to see Mama very much.

Hoke. No, suh, I doan'. It hard—not drivin'. Dat place ain' on no bus line. I goes in a taxicab sometimes.

Boolie. I'm sure she appreciates it.

Hoke. Some days she better than others. Who ain't? *(Boolie takes Hoke's arm as they head for the back door.)*

NURSING HOME, sun porch. Daisy *is sitting in a sunny corner, her walker close by. She is* ninety-seven years old and very fragile. Boolie *and* Hoke *appear.*

Boolie. Happy Thanksgiving, Mama. Look who I brought.

Hoke. Mornin', Miz Daisy. *(She nods.)* You keepin' yoseff busy? *(no response)*

Boolie. She certainly is. She goes to jewelry making—how many times a week, is it, Mama? She makes all kinds of things. Pins and bracelets. She's a regular Tiffany's.[10]

Hoke. Ain't that somethin'? *(Daisy seems far away.)*

Boolie. Hoke, you know I thought of you the other morning on the expressway. I saw an Avondale milk truck.

Hoke. You doan' say.

Boolie. A big monster of a thing; must've had sixteen wheels. I wonder how you'd have liked driving that around.

Daisy *(suddenly).* Hoke came to see me, not you.

23

Hoke. This is one of her good days.

Boolie. Florine says to wish you a happy Thanksgiving. She's in Washington, you know. *(no response)* You remember, Mama. She's a Republican National Committee woman now.

Daisy. Good Lord! *(Hoke laughs. Boolie grins.)* Boolie!

Boolie. What is it, Mama?

Daisy. Go charm the nurses.

---

10. **Tiffany's:** name of a well-known expensive jewelry store.

24

Boolie (*to* Hoke). She wants you all to herself. You're a doodle, Mama. (*He leaves. Daisy dozes for a minute. Then she looks at Hoke.*)

Daisy. Boolie payin' you still?

Hoke. Every week.

Daisy. How much?

25 **Hoke.** That between me an' him, Miz Daisy.

Daisy. Highway robbery. (*She closes her eyes, then opens them.*) How are you?

Hoke. Doin' the bes' I can.

Daisy. Me, too.

Hoke. Well, thass all there is to it, then. (*She nods, smiles. He sees an untouched slice of pumpkin pie on the table beside her.*) Looka here. You ain' eat yo' Thanksgiving pie. (*She tries to pick up her fork. He gently takes it from her.*) Lemme help you wid it. (*He cuts a small piece of pie and carefully feeds it to her. She is delighted. It tastes good. He feeds her another. And another. The end.*) 🐦 ◀ T

24. ACTIVE READING: Review
Ask students if they recall when Boolie called his mother a "doodle" earlier in the play. (*See page 422, in the play's opening dialogue.*) Point out that by using the same expression here, the playwright has found a subtle way to tie the beginning and end of the play together.

25. LITERARY CONCEPT: Repetition
Point out that Hoke has made this same remark to Daisy and Boolie several times during the play. Ask students how this remark shows that some things about the characters have not changed. (*Possible response: Daisy still prods and pries, and Hoke still guards his dignity.*)

ENCOURAGING INDEPENDENT READING

Martin Luther King: The Peaceful Warrior, biography by Ed Clayton

Purlie Victorious, drama by Ossie Davis

A Raisin in the Sun, drama by Lorraine Hansberry

Comprehension Check

1. Why does Boolie demand that Daisy stop driving? (*She had an accident.*)
2. What does Boolie hire Hoke to do? (*drive Daisy where she wants to go*)
3. What happens to make Daisy think Hoke is a thief? (*She notices that a can of salmon is missing.*)
4. What does Daisy teach Hoke at the cemetery? (*how to find a name on a headstone*)
5. Whom do Hoke and Daisy encounter on their drive to Mobile? (*two prejudiced state policemen*)
6. Why doesn't Daisy need Boolie during the ice storm? (*Hoke has come to the house.*)
7. Why can't Daisy attend temple in Part 3? (*It has been bombed.*)
8. Why does Hoke reject Daisy's invitation to the King dinner? (*She asked him at the last minute.*)
9. Why does Boolie move Daisy out of her house? (*She cannot take care of herself anymore.*)
10. How does Hoke help Daisy at the nursing home? (*He talks to her and feeds her.*)

Student Response

Responding to Reading

1. Any response is valid.

2. **Possible responses:** It is ironic that Daisy, who rejected Hoke's help for so long, is now delighted to have it; Hoke, who is hired to drive Daisy, now cannot drive himself; Daisy and Hoke, whose relationship seems doubtful at first, end up being close; Hoke, who earlier had to eat in a separate room, now feeds Daisy.

3. **Possible responses:** They needed each other; their values and attitudes are actually quite similar; both care sincerely about others; they are both outsiders in white, gentile Southern society.

4. **Possible responses:** Yes, because he becomes both more assertive and more understanding; no, because he is patient, assertive, and understanding from the very beginning of the play.

5. **Possible responses:** She is prejudiced, as evidenced by her treatment of and remarks to Hoke, even as late in the play as the King dinner; she is not prejudiced, just narrow-minded because of the society she lives in; she is prejudiced to begin with, but, because of Hoke, she learns to be more tolerant.

6. **Possible responses:** Yes, he accepts Daisy's rudeness and insults without complaint; no, he adjusts to the way things were at the time but still stands up for his rights and dignity.

Literary Concept: Foil

Boolie is a foil who highlights Daisy's impatience, independence, and prejudiced attitudes; Florine is a foil who highlights Daisy's feelings about Jewish pride.

Concept Review: Climax

Possible responses: Hoke's rebuke about the UJA dinner invitation; Daisy's calling Hoke her best friend; the last scene, where we see Hoke's friendship with Daisy has outlasted his role as driver.

---

*R*esponding to Reading

First Impressions of Part 3

1. What are your feelings at the end of the play? Write down your response in your journal or notebook.

Second Thoughts on Part 3

2. Irony occurs when an outcome is the opposite of what might have been expected. What is ironic about the ending of the play?

> **Think about**
> • how you expected Daisy and Hoke to act before you read the play
> • the contrast between the play's ending and its opening

3. In your opinion, what caused Daisy and Hoke to form a bond of the heart?

4. Do you think Hoke changes during the course of the play? Explain.

5. Daisy says twice in the play, "I'm not prejudiced!" Do you agree with her statements, both at the beginning and at the end of the play? Explain, using examples from the play.

Broader Connections

6. The original Uncle Tom was a character from a famous antislavery novel, *Uncle Tom's Cabin.* As a slave, he humbly obeyed the will of his white masters. Morgan Freeman, the actor who played Hoke in the movie, was concerned that his character not be seen as an Uncle Tom. Does Hoke act like an Uncle Tom? Why or why not?

*L*iterary Concept: Foil

A **foil** is a character who provides a striking contrast to a main character. Foils help to draw attention to certain qualities in the main character. Which characters serve as foils to Daisy? What aspects of her personality do they highlight?

Concept Review: Climax Which scene do you consider to be the climax or turning point of the play?

Challenge Question

Why is it important to this drama that Daisy is Jewish and Hoke is an African American? *(Possible responses: Daisy and Hoke are drawn together in part because each is a member of a group that has suffered greatly because of bigotry; their differences bring out the theme that patience and caring rise above racial and religious boundaries.)*

Writing Options

1. Choose your favorite scene in the play. Write **director's notes** for that scene, advising the actors how they should play it and what qualities they should convey.

2. Imagine that the producer of the film suggested cutting the scene with the speech by Martin Luther King, Jr. As the writer, write a **memo** to the producer to explain the importance of that scene.

3. Choose another African American you have read about in this textbook. How would he or she have gotten along with Miss Daisy? Write a short dramatic **scene,** in play form, in which the two characters meet for the first time.

4. Do you think this play should be taught next year? Write a **persuasive letter** to your teacher, stating your opinion and supporting it with reasons.

Vocabulary Practice

Exercise   Choose the word from the list that best completes each sentence. Use each word only once. Write the answers on a separate sheet of paper.

1. The lynching of his friend's father upset Hoke; he found the action __?__.

2. If someone committed another act of violence to revenge the bombing, it would be a __?__.

3. Alone with Boolie, Florine showed her feelings toward her mother-in-law by __?__ at her.

4. Boolie was sure that Daisy would __?__ another car if she were allowed to drive.

5. Hoke took good care of the inside of the car, including the __?__.

6. Boolie felt better knowing that Daisy was in the car with a driver like Hoke who showed __?__.

7. Boolie responded __?__ to Daisy's claim that Hoke was a thief.

8. Daisy's reaction to any gifts from Florine was to __?__ from them.

9. Daisy could have bought __?__ care for her husband's grave but preferred to provide it herself.

10. Daisy told the state troopers that the __?__ of her name was German.

Words to Know and Use
appalling
competence
demolish
derivation
dubiously
perpetual
recoil
reprisal
sniping
upholstery

DRIVING MISS DAISY   455

The Spelling Connection

Greek Combining Forms Suffixes can be added to some Greek combining forms to make English nouns and adjectives. Also, two Greek combining forms can be joined like the two parts of a compound word. The spelling of a Greek combining form may change slightly when joined to other word parts. Example: psycho (mind) + logy (study) = psychology
Selection Words with Greek Combining Forms
tele (far off) + **phon** (sound) = telephone
bio (life) + **logy** (study) = biology

Other Words with Greek Combining Forms

arch = first	archaeology	archives
patri = father	patriarch	paternal
techni = skill	technology	technical
phobia = fear	hydrophobia	acrophobia

Exercise Find a word above to match each meaning.
1. first father
2. study of the beginnings
3. study of life
4. study of skills
5. sound from far off

Extending the Lesson

Options for Learning

These activities suit a variety of learning styles and modes of expression.

Collaborative Learning Activities
See Options 1, 3, and 4.

1. **At the Movies** Students may find the film at the library or a video store. Suggest that they take notes as they watch the movie.

2. **The March of Time** Students can find information in encyclopedias or books on American history, especially those dealing with the civil rights movement.

3. **That's Entertainment** Students need not memorize their lines but should be familiar with them, even with script in hand. One student may be the director for the scene.

4. **Friends and Foes** Students will find the *Readers' Guide to Periodical Literature* helpful when searching for magazine articles.

 FACT FINDER HISTORY

By consulting an encyclopedia or a recent history book, students can find out that Martin Luther King, Jr., was assassinated in 1968.

Alfred Uhry

■ **More About the Author** Uhry's career shows the importance of persistence. The first New York production for which he was the lyricist closed after one performance. Uhry felt frustrated having to compromise with other writers. The play he wrote by himself, *Driving Miss Daisy*, has been a tremendous success.

■ **Other Works** Musical play: *Here's Where I Belong*; screenplay: *Mystic Pizza* (coauthor).

 ■ **Awards** 1988 Pulitzer Prize for drama for *Driving Miss Daisy*.

*O*ptions for Learning (Multimodal/Cross-Curricular Activities)

1 • **At the Movies** Obtain a video of the movie *Driving Miss Daisy* to show in class or watch at home. Then have a panel discussion with others who have seen the film. Act as movie critics to discuss how well the movie matched your interpretations of the screenplay. For example, did Jessica Tandy portray Daisy as you had imagined her? Did Dan Aykroyd and Morgan Freeman portray Boolie and Hoke in the way you expected? Discuss all the differences that you noticed between the movie and the screenplay.

2 • **The March of Time** Research the progress that African Americans made from 1948–1973, the period of this play. On a large sheet of paper, make a time line showing major events in the struggle for racial equality.

3 • **That's Entertainment** As a class, select your favorite scene from the play. Then hold auditions for the parts by taking turns reading. After the parts are assigned, rehearse your scene and perform for the class.

4 • **Friends and Foes** Like Daisy and Hoke, Jews and African Americans have had a long and sometimes troubled relationship. Read through history books and current magazines to find out more about this subject. Report your findings to the class.

 FACT FINDER HISTORY

In what year was Martin Luther King, Jr., assassinated?

*A*lfred Uhry
1936–

If Alfred Uhry hadn't returned to his roots when he did, the world might never have known Hoke and Miss Daisy. Born in Atlanta, Georgia, Uhry began his career in drama in New York as a lyricist, or song writer, for musicals. In 1975, Uhry wrote both the script and song lyrics for a hit musical entitled *The Robber Bridegroom*. After this hit, however, success seemed to escape Uhry's grasp, and he returned to teaching at New York University.

In his words, "Something whispered in my ear that it was time to sit down and write a play." He remembered his grandmother, who had become a family legend because of her bad temper. She insisted on driving long after it was safe for her to do so, and eventually the family found her a black chauffeur. Thus, the idea for Miss Daisy was born.

Today, Uhry still writes in New York for both the theater and film industries.

Cross-Curricular Projects

Social Studies Have students research the progress that African Americans have made since 1973. Let them continue the time line they began in Option for Learning 2, adding the major events that have occurred between 1973 and the present.

Science Have students research the various kinds of illnesses, both mental or physical, that can affect the elderly. Tell them to learn about the symptoms, causes, effects, and possible cures or treatments. Have them share their findings with the class.

Art Suggest that interested students research clothing styles of the South in the late 1940s, the 1950s, and the 1960s. Then have them sketch costumes for characters in various scenes of the play. Explain that the costumes should reflect the setting, helping an audience to understand how much time has passed from one scene to the next.

Culture Students who are fans of classic cars may enjoy preparing displays of the LaSalle, Packard, Oldsmobile, and Cadillacs mentioned in the drama.

WRITER'S WORKSHOP

WRITING ABOUT LITERATURE

Think of some people you know well. You've probably seen them in many different situations. In *Driving Miss Daisy,* we get to know the characters in the same way. As we watch their relationships change over time, we see deeply into the characters themselves. One way to focus your insights about a character—and about a piece of literature—is to write a character analysis. When you **analyze** something, you break it down into its parts, examining each part separately. In a **character analysis,** you examine a character's traits. You look at the ways those traits work together, and you notice the effects they have.

USE LITERARY ANALYSIS FOR
book reviews
character analyses
essay exams
learning-log entries
study guides

GUIDED ASSIGNMENT: CHARACTER ANALYSIS

Write an analysis of a character in *Driving Miss Daisy.*

Here is one writer's PASSkey to this assignment.

PURPOSE: To write about literature
AUDIENCE: Classmates
SUBJECT: A character in "Charles"
STRUCTURE: A character analysis

The Monster
by Greg Chu

When I first read "Charles," by Shirley Jackson, I thought Laurie was a little monster. He disrupts his kindergarten, swears, and hits the teacher. The teacher tries to control him, but nothing works. At home, he's a "swaggering character" who often smarts off. He seems like a problem child. However, Laurie has two strengths. He's fair, and he's determined. His strengths just don't go over very well with his teacher.

On the first day of school, Laurie is "awfully fresh," and the teacher spanks him. After that, Laurie acts worse and worse. I

◀ **STUDENT MODEL**
Before you analyze a character in *Driving Miss Daisy,* read how one student analyzed a character in a story at the beginning of this book.

◀ The writer makes a generalization about the character.

WRITER'S WORKSHOP   457

ADDITIONAL RESOURCES
Unit Four Resource Book
Writer's Workshop Worksheet, p. 66
Writer's Workshop: Peer and Self-Evaluation, p. 67
Writer's Workshop: Assessment Guidelines, p. 68

Technology and Enrichment
Elaboration, Revision, and Proofreading
    Transparencies 25–28
Thinking Skills Transparency 7
Fine Art Transparency Pack
Writer's Databank Software: Files 7-10,
    Elaboration

Links to
Writer's Craft

For more about writing about literature, see *The Writer's Craft,* Grade 7, "Responding to Literature," pages 164-177, and pages 254–270, "Elaboration."

Objectives

■ To understand the elements of a character analysis

■ To use generalizations to write a thesis statement

■ To analyze a character in *Driving Miss Daisy*

■ To draft, revise, edit, and share writing about literature

Teaching Strategies

DISCUSSING THE ASSIGNMENT

Explain to students that perhaps without realizing it, they analyze things every day. Remind them that to analyze something simply means to study its parts and come to a conclusion about it. For example, if students like a certain song and someone asks them why, they might think about the words, the melody, the way the artist sings it, and maybe even the way it makes them feel. Then they can explain why they like it.

Now share with students that in this workshop they will analyze a character from literature. Have them read the first paragraph on page 457, and then discuss the Guided Assignment and its PASSkey. Be sure students understand the purpose, audience, subject, and structure for their writing. Clarify for them that the subject of Greg's writing is a character from "Charles," but the subject of their writing will be a character from *Driving Miss Daisy.* If you wish, you may give students the option of writing about something else that is important to them. The Alternative Writing and Research Topics on page 458 offer some good choices.

ANALYZING THE MODEL

You may want to read aloud the student model on page 457–458, pausing to point out the parts of the composition and the strategies the student author used. Remind students that they don't have to agree with Greg Chu's analysis of Laurie as long as the reasons and examples Greg has chosen support his belief. Ask students whether the examples Greg gave of Laurie's behavior support his generalization. *(Yes; he points out that Laurie is aware of what is fair and unfair. The examples he chooses from the story all support this view.)*

Remind students that they can use some familiar strategies to read and respond to the student model: question, connect, predict, review, and evaluate. The questions that follow may also be useful. Have students work with partners to discuss them, and afterward ask them to share their comments in a whole-class discussion.

■ Does Greg's analysis show Laurie as a positive or a negative character? How do you know?

■ What strategy does Greg use to support his analysis?

■ What transitions does Greg use? How do they pull the whole composition together?

■ Do you agree with Greg's analysis? Why or why not?

Prewrite and Explore

One way to begin a literary analysis is to think about the themes of the selection. Remind students that the theme of a work is the message the author wants to convey to the reader. Once students have determined the theme of *Driving Miss Daisy*, they can look at which characters exemplify it by virtue of their words, actions, and personality traits. This might make it easier for students to select a character and decide what they want to say about him or her.

TEACHING TIP: COMPUTER

Students who would like to analyze each character briefly before choosing one to write about might make a three-part chart of the character's traits. First, have students choose newspaper style, or column format, in setting up their format lines. Next, have them set up three columns, which allows a separate column for notes on each character. This gives students a quick overview of the characters' personalities and the ways in which their actions affect the story.

▶ The writer explores the character's motives.

really don't blame him. A teacher who spanks a kindergartner the first day she meets him, just because he mouths off, is pretty mean. On the second day Laurie hits the teacher. Of course that's wrong, but it may seem fair to Laurie. She hit him first, the day before.

As the weeks go by, Laurie's sense of fairness probably makes him see the teacher as a bully. She hits children, stands them in the corner, and washes out their mouths with soap. Laurie is determined not to be bullied. No matter how much she punishes him, he keeps acting up. His determination earns the children's respect. When the teacher tells them not to play with him, they ignore her. When she keeps him after school, they all stay with him.

The good side of Laurie's fairness comes out, too. One day, without being asked, Laurie does some chores for the teacher. The teacher calls him her "helper" and gives him an apple. After that he behaves better. In other words, as soon as the teacher stops being mean, Laurie tries harder to cooperate. He slips up at times, but nobody's perfect. Laurie's no angel, but he's not a problem child. He just ran into a problem teacher.

▶ Details from the story show what the writer means.

▶ The conclusion echoes the introduction, with a twist.

Now that you've read Greg's paper, it's time to begin your own.

Prewrite and Explore

1 Explore a character *Driving Miss Daisy* has three major characters: Daisy, Hoke, and Boolie. Start by choosing the one you understand best. Next, try brainstorming about the character's traits. You might jot down your feelings about the character, then list the traits that make you feel as you do.

2 Find an angle Here are three approaches to analyzing a character: (1) you can examine his or her strengths and weaknesses; (2) you can figure out his or her motives, or reasons for

---

Alternative Writing and Research Topics

Character Analysis Ernie's love for Dolores in "A Crush" caused changes in her world that Ernie never intended and never knew about. Write an analysis of someone, real or fictional, explaining how the person's strengths, weaknesses, or motives changed the world in which he or she lived.

Poetry Several kinds of love are expressed in this subunit, from good friendship to love expressed between a housekeeper and her employer's son.

Write a poem about love between two people. The love may be romance, friendship, dependence, or however you choose to define it through your poem.

Researching Films *Driving Miss Daisy* describes how love grows between two people of widely different backgrounds. Do some research on other films with the same theme, and write a paper describing briefly the three or four films you found most interesting.

doing things; (3) you can trace how and why the character changes. Try choosing one approach and using it to freewrite about the character you selected. After you finish, underline the parts of your freewriting that seem most important to you.

3 **Search the play** Whichever approach you choose, you'll need details and quotations from the play. Keeping your focus in mind, look back through the play. Look for examples of the ideas you are pointing out.

◀ WRITER'S CHOICE ....

You can mix two approaches. For instance, you might see how a character's strengths and weaknesses affect his or her motives.

GATHERING INFORMATION

Try making a chart based on your approach. For example, Greg focused on his character's motives. He made the chart below, and wrote in his ideas, then filled in details from the story.

Action	page	Possible motives	Details and quotes	page
is "awfully fresh" on first day	7	He's a smart aleck.	"swaggering character," smarts off at home	7 8, 9
hits teacher	8	getting even	She hit him first.	7
refuses to cooperate	8, 9 10, 11	Teacher's too mean.	She tries to turn kids against him.	8
			She washes out kids' mouths with soap.	10, 11

◀ STUDENT MODEL ....

4 **Generalize** Look over the details in your prewriting notes, and sum them up in two or more generalizations—broad statements—about your character. For example, scanning his notes, Greg noticed that Laurie seldom gave up. Greg wrote a generalization: *"Laurie is determined."* Then Greg noticed that Laurie often treated the teacher as she had treated him. Greg wrote *"Laurie is fair."*

◀ NEED MORE HELP? ....

For more about generalizations, see the Reader's Workshop on page 347.

Have students read all four subsections of Prewrite and Explore, pages 458–459. Even if they don't use the organizer in the text, encourage them to make graphics to guide them as they write.

Modeling You might show students another type of graphic organizer that shows a cause-and-effect chain of events. Show this chain on the board:

CAUSE: Miss Daisy wrecks her Packard.

EFFECT: Boolie buys her a new car and hires Hoke as chauffeur.

CAUSE: Boolie hires Hoke as chauffeur.

EFFECT: Miss Daisy begins to rely on Hoke.

CAUSE: Miss Daisy begins to rely on Hoke.

EFFECT: Miss Daisy and Hoke gradually become friends.

Be sure students understand that each effect becomes the cause of another effect.

Draft and Discover

One strategy for drafting is to set a five-minute rule. Students give themselves five minutes to solve any problem that arises; after five minutes they must move on. Such a "rule" helps keep ideas flowing.

Later, as students share their drafts, have readers react especially to the following: generalizations and the number and appropriateness of the details that support them; how well thesis statements reflect the main ideas and goals of the papers, and how well the writing is focused around the thesis statements.

TEACHING TIP: LEP

LEP students may have difficulty understanding what some of the lines mean. This may prove particularly troublesome when the lines are part of the evidence, details, and quotations they're using as they draft. If you can't help them directly, assign an advanced student to interpret for them and help make the connections they will need.

Revise Your Writing

As they begin revising, students might benefit from seeing how a classmate's character analysis is organized. Borrow a draft from one of your strongest writers (who may remain anonymous) and review it briefly with the class.

Students who have difficulty supporting generalizations might benefit from joining a group. Work with the group to identify the thesis statement of the paper mentioned above. Then model the process of finding supporting references, and show students how to incorporate them into a draft.

Note that The Editor's Eye feature previews the content in the Language Workshop that follows. If students do not need extra help in sentence combining, the brief review in The Editor's Eye may be enough for them. If the class or individual students might benefit from additional work, you may choose to teach the Language Workshop, pages 462–464, before having students proofread.

Draft and Discover

Draft and Discover

1 **Fill in the blanks**   One way to draft a character analysis is to write each of your generalizations at the top of a blank page. Then, beneath each generalization, write as much as you can to explain it. Include details and quotations from the play.

2 **Make connections**   After you've written about each generalization, you need to explain how they're connected. Maybe they show strengths or weaknesses, or shed light on motives. Write a sentence explaining the connections. This serves as your **thesis statement,** a sentence that tells the main idea and goal of your paper. Refer to your thesis statement often to keep your writing focused.

Revise Your Writing

1 **Find your organization**   You can start your analysis by naming your character and stating your thesis. Then you can write one or more paragraphs about each generalization, using details and quotations as support. To end your paper with flair, you might use a quotation from the play that illustrates your thesis. You might find a way to refer to the beginning of your paper, perhaps echoing a phrase.

2 **Listen to the rhythm**   If you've ever heard rap music, you know that sentences have rhythm. Read your sentences aloud to hear their rhythm. Which ones sound the way you want? To get more of that sound, try changing or combining other sentences.

· · · · **WRITER'S CHOICE**
You might prefer a narrative format, explaining your initial impression of the character, then telling how and why your views changed.

· · · · **NEED MORE HELP?**
See the Language Workshop on pages 462–464.

HE EDITOR'S EYE: SENTENCE COMBINING

Join two complete sentences with a comma and an appropriate conjunction.

When your sentences sound choppy, you can combine some of them. If two short sentences express similar ideas, join them with a comma and the conjunction *and*. If they express contrasting ideas, join them with a comma and *but*.

Problem   Laurie's no angel. He's not a problem child.

Combined   Laurie's no angel, **but** he's not a problem child.

Cooperative Writing

Have the class form small groups to work on sentence combining. Instruct each group member in turn to read from their drafts sentences that they consider choppy or awkward. The other students must use the strategy in The Editor's Eye to improve them. If the original sentences don't yield well to the strategy, however, group members should try to come up with new sentences to replace the originals.

CONFERENCING TIP

As you conference with individual writers for this workshop, you may wish to focus on

■ thesis statements and generalizations

■ elaboration using details and quotations

■ sentence-combining

3 **Try a peer reader** When you're ready, you can ask a friend to read your character analysis. Use the question lists below.

Proofread

Reread your paper, correcting errors in grammar and mechanics.

Publish and Present

Here is an idea for sharing your writing with others.

Critics' Forum Think of movie critics who discuss movies with each other on television. Since some of your classmates have also written about the character you chose, you can hold a similar discussion. First, form a group and read your papers aloud. Then respond to one another's interpretations. Say whether you agree or disagree, and explain why.

Reflect on Your Writing

Write brief answers to the questions below. Add them to your character analysis when you put it in your portfolio.

◀ FOR YOUR PORTFOLIO

1. What insights did you gain about the character you analyzed?
2. Has your opinion of the character changed? Why or why not?

Use the following models as needed for extra reinforcement of the Editor's Eye topic:

1. Boolie was Miss Daisy's son. He loved her very much. (*Boolie was Miss Daisy's son, and he loved her very much.*)

2. Miss Daisy was a difficult woman. She knew how to get her way. (*Miss Daisy was a difficult woman, and she knew how to get her way.*)

3. Hoke was always polite. He never let Miss Daisy take advantage of his good will. (*Hoke was always polite, but he never let Miss Daisy take advantage of his good will.*)

Proofread

Have students proofread their analyses, concentrating on punctuation of quotations from the play. Refer students to pages 784–785 of the *Language Handbook* for help.

Publish and Present

Besides the critics' forum, some students might stage an informal debate with those whose thesis statements oppose their own.

Reflect on Your Writing

You may wish to have students answer the following questions in addition to or instead of those in their texts:

■ What was the hardest part about writing a character analysis? How did I work through my difficulties?

■ How did peer comments help me to evaluate and revise my work?

Closure

Have students watch the movie review segment of a local news show and notice the kinds of comments the reviewers make about the characters. Suggest that students focus on the evidence each reviewer uses to support his or her opinion.

Assessment Guidelines

These guidelines may help you assess student writing:

Content
■ The introduction identifies the character and the selection and offers an opinion in the thesis statement.
■ Each generalization is supported with evidence from the play.
■ The conclusion effectively closes the analysis.

Style
■ Paragraphing is logical, and transitions provide coherence.
■ Choppy sentences have been transformed by sentence combining.

Usage and Mechanics
■ Errors in spelling, capitalization, and punctuation are avoided.
■ Subjects and verbs agree.

See *Unit Four Resource Book*, page 68.

Objectives

■ To learn strategies for combining sentences and sentence parts

■ To use combined sentences for variety in writing

Teaching Strategies

STRIVING FOR VARIETY

Explain to students that combining words, sentence parts, and complete sentences is one way to gain variety of expression. Remind them, however, that only related sentences can be combined. Use the exercises on this page to review with them the rules for combining with a comma and *and, but,* or *or.* In addition to the examples in the text, you may want to use the following sentences for oral practice.

1. Ernie has a crush on Dolores. Ernie brings her flowers every Wednesday. **(and)**

2. Dolores doesn't know who leaves the flowers. She displays them anyway. **(but)**

3. Do the flowers make Dolores feel more feminine? Do they just make her feel more cheerful? **(or)**

4. The flowers definitely make the store more attractive. They lure Dick out of the storeroom and into the store. **(and)**

5. Stan's Hardware has certainly undergone a change. Ernie knows nothing about it. **(but)**

LANGUAGE WORKSHOP

SENTENCE COMBINING

In writing, as in music, repeating one rhythm can get dull. You can vary your sentence rhythms and avoid too many short, choppy sentences by using the techniques below.

Combining Sentences

You can combine two sentences when their thoughts are related. For example, since the thoughts in these two sentences are related, the sentences can be combined:

> Everyone wonders how Dolores got her tattoo. She won't tell.
> Everyone wonders how Dolores got her tattoo, **but** she won't tell.

The thoughts in the following two sentences are not closely related, so the sentences should not be combined:

> Everyone wonders how Dolores got her tattoo. Tattoos can be removed with lasers.

····· REMINDER
If ideas are similar, use a comma and the word *and.* If ideas contrast, use a comma and the word *but.* If ideas are alternatives, use a comma and the word *or.*

► When two related sentences contain equally important ideas, you can join the sentences with a comma and a conjunction (*and, but,* or *or*).

> Dick owns Stan's Hardware. Dolores is the assistant manager.
> Dick owns Stan's Hardware, **and** Dolores is the assistant manager.

> Someone is bringing them flowers. They don't know who it is.
> Someone is bringing them flowers, **but** they don't know who it is.

> The flowers might be for Dick. They might be for Dolores.
> The flowers might be for Dick, **or** they might be for Dolores.

Combining Sentence Parts

Sometimes, instead of joining two entire sentences, you can combine only their subjects, verbs, or objects. In such cases, use conjunctions and leave out words or ideas that are repeated.

ADDITIONAL RESOURCES
Unit Four Resource Book
Language Workshop Practice, p. 69

Technology and Enrichment
Sentence Composing Copy Masters

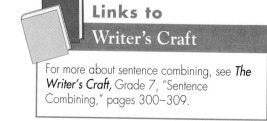

Links to
Writer's Craft

For more about sentence combining, see *The Writer's Craft,* Grade 7, "Sentence Combining," pages 300–309.

The jars hold marigolds. They also hold zinnias.
The jars hold marigolds **and** zinnias.

Ernie had seeds. He had never planted them, though.
Ernie had seeds **but** had never planted them.

◀ **PUNCTUATION NOTE**
....
When only sentence parts are joined, no comma is used before the conjunction.

Exercise 1   Concept Check   Rewrite each pair as one sentence. Use the conjunctions in parentheses. Eliminate italicized words.

1. Dolores understands hardware. The customers trust her. (**, and**)
2. Maybe Dolores hates makeup. Maybe she just doesn't care. (**, or**)
3. Ernie doesn't know Dolores. He has a crush on her. (**, but**)
4. Dolores can't figure out who's bringing the flowers. Dick *can't either*. (**and**)
5. Both are curious. *However, they both* say nothing. (**but**)
6. Each wonders if the other has a new friend. *Each thinks the other might have* a secret lover. (**or**)
7. As the weeks go by, Dolores starts dressing differently. *She also starts* wearing jewelry. (**and**)
8. Dolores never sees Ernie. He makes her happy. (**, but**)
9. Ernie learns to grow flowers outdoors. *He even learns to grow them* indoors. (**and**)
10. Jack is just a college student. *However,* he makes a big difference in Ernie's life. (**, but**)

Adding Words to Sentences

Sometimes the ideas in two sentences are not equally important. When you revise, you see that only one word (or word group) in one of the sentences adds new meaning. Add that part to the other sentence.

Dolores has a tattoo of a coyote. The coyote is howling.
Dolores has a tattoo of a **howling** coyote.

The flowers appear every Wednesday. They are on the doorstep.
The flowers appear **on the doorstep** every Wednesday.

You may need to change some words slightly. You might add *-ly, -ing, -ed,* or other endings.

In the sun, the zinnias seem to glow. They look bright.
In the sun, the zinnias seem to glow **brightly.**

Dolores picks up the flowers. She looks surprised.
Dolores, **looking surprised,** picks up the flowers.

◀ **PUNCTUATION NOTE**
....
When you add a word or word group, you may need to add one or more commas. For comma rules see Section 10, pages 775-776, of the Language Handbook.

Answers to Exercise 1

1. Dolores understands hardware, <u>and</u> the customers trust her.

2. Maybe Dolores hates makeup, <u>or</u> maybe she just doesn't care.

3. Ernie doesn't know Dolores, <u>but</u> he has a crush on her.

4. Dolores <u>and Dick</u> can't figure out who's bringing the flowers.

5. Both are curious <u>but say nothing</u>.

6. Each wonders if the other has a new friend <u>or a secret lover</u>.

7. As the weeks go by, Dolores starts dressing differently <u>and wearing jewelry</u>.

8. Dolores never sees Ernie, <u>but</u> he makes her happy.

9. Ernie learns to grow flowers outdoors <u>and indoors</u>.

10. Jack is just a college student, <u>but</u> he makes a big difference in Ernie's life.

Adding Words to Sentences

Now review the strategy of adding only single words or phrases to sentences. Point out that when the "borrowed" words become appositives or participial phrases in the new sentences, they should be set off with commas. Have students note the last model at the bottom of page 463. If they need a review of this usage, refer students to "Commas with Interrupters" on page 777 of the Language Handbook.

TEACHING TIP: LEP

Many LEP students may not understand how the forms of some English words change when sentences are combined. Here is an example.

The highwayman thought about the innkeeper's daughter. He rode across the moor.

Combined sentences The highwayman, thinking about the innkeeper's daughter, rode across the moor. Or, The highwayman, riding across the moor, thought about the innkeeper's daughter.

Encourage these students to focus on ideas rather than forms while they are writing. During revision, peers can help them determine the correct forms.

Grammar Games: Costume Combos

Tell students to imagine that they've been invited to a costume party where guests can win prizes for the most imaginative costumes. Then instruct them to write on strips of oak tag ten simple, short sentences about costumes that guests might wear.

Group the class into two or three teams, whose players will alternate to combine sentences correctly. Place half of the sentences face down on a desk, and you keep the other half. Hold up one of your sentences to face the first player. He or she selects at

random from the sentences on the desk and must combine them correctly or be out. Play continues, and the team with the most players left at the end of a stated time wins.

You can vary the game by cutting several sentence strips into sections and mixing them with the strips on the desk. That way, students can practice combining words and sentence parts as well as complete sentences.

Answers to Exercise 2

Possible sentences are given.

1. Colorful packets of seeds are Ernie's treasures.

2. Ernie lives in a group home with other retarded people.

3. One day he sees the hardware store through the restaurant window.

4. Ernie smiles shyly when he sees Dolores.

5. Jack, wanting to be Ernie's friend, shows him how to grow flowers.

6. Then Ernie secretly brings the flowers to Dolores.

7. Ernie blossoms just like his flowers.

8. Cynthia Rylant based the character of Ernie on a real person in her town.

9. Rylant may have known an independent woman like Dolores.

10. The real world is filled with imperfect people like Dolores and Ernie.

Answers to Exercise 3

A possible response is given.

Cynthia Rylant grew up in West Virginia. There she lived with her grandparents in the mountains. Her grandfather worked hard in the mines, and he came home covered with coal dust. Her grandmother cooked fried okra and corn bread. Cynthia treasures the memories of family evenings on the front porch. Most of all, she remembers the sparkling stars.

Answers to Exercise 4

Have students underline the sentence version they prefer.

Answers to Exercise 5

Check students' papers at random to see whether appropriate changes have been made.

Closure

Now that students have practiced sentence combining, have them go back to their character analyses and see if there are any short sentences they can combine. Suggest a check of previous papers as well.

WRITER'S CHOICE
Some words or word groups can fit in several places in a sentence. You can choose the placement that "feels" best to you.

Exercise 2 Concept Check To the first sentence of each pair below, add the italicized word or word group. Decide where it fits best. Make needed changes, and write your new sentence.

1. Packets of seeds are Ernie's treasures. The packets are *colorful*.

2. Ernie lives in a group home. He lives *with other retarded people*.

3. One day he sees the hardware store. He is looking *through the restaurant window*.

4. Ernie smiles when he sees Dolores. His smile is *shy*. (Use *-ly*.)

5. Jack shows him how to grow flowers. Jack helps him because he *wants to be Ernie's friend*. (Use *-ing*.)

6. Then Ernie brings the flowers to Dolores. He does this in *secret*. (Use *-ly*.)

7. Ernie blossoms. In this way, he is *just like his flowers*.

8. Cynthia Rylant based the character of Ernie on a real person. The person lived *in her town*.

9. Rylant may have known a woman like Dolores. Dolores was *independent*.

10. The real world is filled with people like Dolores and Ernie. These characters are *imperfect*, like real people.

Exercise 3 Revision Skill Revise the paragraph below, using techniques from this workshop. Then share your work with classmates.

Cynthia Rylant grew up in West Virginia. There she lived with her grandparents. They lived in the mountains. Her grandfather worked in the mines. He worked hard. He came home covered with dust. The dust was from coal. Her grandmother cooked fried okra. She also cooked corn bread. Cynthia remembers family evenings on the front porch. She treasures those memories. Most of all, she remembers the stars. They sparkled.

REVISING TIP
Like a musician, you can work by ear, trying out rhythms and patterns to find the ones you're most comfortable with.

Exercise 4 Looking at Style Look back at "A Crush" on page 398. Rewrite the first two sentences as several shorter sentences. Compare your sentences with the original. Which style do you prefer?

Exercise 5 Revising Your Writing Read the character analysis you wrote for the Writer's Workshop on pages 457–461. Use techniques from this workshop to vary the rhythms of your sentences and remove repetition.

Additional Practice

Combine the following sentences.

1. A snake slithered under the door. The snake was long. It was speckled.

2. The soup was full of vegetables, noodles, and savory broth. Steam rose from the soup.

3. She wore her gold medal. She was proud.

4. We leaped to our feet. We cheered.

5. The vase is valuable. It has a crack.

6. The poodle next door sleeps on pillows. The pillows are silk. The poodle is pampered.

7. The employee stood at the door of the office. He seemed hesitant to enter.

8. An army of ants moved silently through the jungle. The army moved steadily.

9. The raccoons wait at our back door. They are hungry. They wait every day.

VOCABULARY WORKSHOP

DENOTATION AND CONNOTATION

The dictionary gives definitions, or **denotations,** of words. As you know, some words have the same denotation. Words also have **connotations**—the ideas or feelings they suggest. No two words have exactly the same connotations—not even words with the same meaning. Connotations can be generally **positive** (suggesting pleasant feelings) or **negative** (suggesting unpleasant feelings). For example, *determined* has positive connotations, but *stubborn* has negative connotations. Some words are **neutral.** Words like *chair* and *talk* have neither positive nor negative connotations.

Exercise 1 First, write *Positive* or *Negative* to describe each italicized word's connotations. Be ready to discuss your reasons. Then, using a dictionary, write the word's denotation. If a word has multiple meanings, choose the one that fits the sentence best.

1. The *nag* and its rider galloped along the deserted road.
2. In the moonlight the road *glistened* like a band of silver.
3. The *ghostly* cry of an owl echoed over the moor.
4. *Sneering*, the horseman peered ahead.
5. He sat poised and *upright* in the saddle.

Exercise 2 The italicized words have positive connotations. Replace each with a synonym whose connotations are negative. You may use a dictionary or a thesaurus.

> On a *cool* evening the *highwayman* enters the courtyard of the inn. There at her window stands the landlord's *slender* daughter. He *murmurs* to her, then *slips* away into the *dusky* night. She will wait *eagerly* for his *promised* return.

Exercise 3 Read the paper you wrote for the Writer's Workshop on pages 457–461. Lightly underline all the words you used to describe the character, and evaluate their connotations. Insert words with more appropriate connotations where needed.

◀ **WORD PLAY**

Which would you rather have—a sly friend or a clever friend? a celebration or a bash? striking clothes or flashy clothes?

◀ **MULTIPLE MEANINGS**

Many words have more than one denotation—that is, they have multiple meanings. A word's context can help you figure out which meaning is intended. For more about context clues, see the Vocabulary Workshop on page 117.

VOCABULARY WORKSHOP 465

ADDITIONAL RESOURCES
Unit Four Resource Book
Vocabulary Workshop Practice, p. 70

Additional Practice

Write a description of the most beautiful countryside you can imagine. Then write the same description using precise words with negative connotations. Share your work with a partner.

Objectives

■ To differentiate among the connotations of words

■ To use words with appropriate shades of meaning for context

Teaching Strategies

Have students read the introductory paragraph on page 465. Explain that knowing whether a word has a positive or negative connotation and using it appropriately can help them improve their writing. Work through Exercises 1 and 2 orally, encouraging students to use the most expressive words they know.

Have students use the concept of positive and negative connotations to describe people and objects in their neighborhoods or towns. For instance, ask which candidate will win the next election, the one known as a "thrifty public servant" or the one called a "cheap bozo."

Answers to Exercise 1

1. nag—negative; horse

2. glistened—positive; sparkled

3. ghostly—negative; like a ghost

4. Sneering—negative; smiling with scorn or contempt

5. upright—positive; sitting up straight

Answers to Exercise 2
Possible responses are given.

On a frigid evening the robber enters the courtyard of the inn. There at her window stands the landlord's bony daughter. He mumbles to her, then slinks away into the gloomy night. She will wait impatiently for his supposed return.

Answer to Exercise 3
Check students' revisions.

Objectives

■ To extend the study of the unit theme, "Person to Person," to novels and other longer works

■ To read independently for personal enrichment and enjoyment

THE FLAWED GLASS

Study Focus
■ A character's struggle to communicate with others

■ Symbolism of the book's title

■ Bonds of the heart between two characters

About Ian Strachan

Strachan has worked in several media, including theater, radio, and television. In Strachan's media work, he has served in various capacities, such as actor, writer, and producer. Strachan currently works full-time writing children's books. He lives in England with his wife and children.

Reading on Your Own

Suggested Novels for Unit Four

The novels introduced on these pages all present difficult challenges in personal relationships and reflect the Unit theme "Person to Person."

THE FLAWED GLASS
IAN STRACHAN ©1990

Shona MacLeod has such a severe physical handicap that she can hardly speak and walking is difficult for her. She is very intelligent and understands everything that goes on around her, but she cannot respond. Shona's world is so limited that she thinks of herself as being locked in a tower, waiting for a rescuer. Life on her island off the coast of Scotland is simple, bleak, and backwards. Because she is cut off from personal relationships with others, even her own family does not know what Shona can achieve. When a young American boy comes to the island, Shona learns with joy that he is someone who has the patience and insight to see past her difficulties and set her free. As you read, try to imagine . . .

• the pain and frustration of being unable to communicate

• how a computer might link Shona to other people

• how Shona would feel if she could save her family from disgrace

466

Guide for Teaching

A study guide for the paired novels *The Red Pony* and *The Clay Marble* is available from McDougal, Littell. See the Teacher's Resource File for ordering information.

ONE-EYED CAT

PAULA FOX ©1974

Have you ever been tempted to do something forbidden? This is what Ned faces in *One-Eyed Cat.* When Ned's uncle gives Ned a BB gun, Ned's father forbids him to fire it until he is fourteen—three years away! Because he trusts Ned completely, his father stores the gun in the attic, where it remains an irresistible temptation. Ned grapples with an agonizing test of conscience as his secret and his guilt threaten to become more than he can handle. As you read, consider these questions:

- What are the consequences of Ned's firing the gun?

- What will Ned's silence cost him?

- How can Ned make amends to the victim of his shooting spree?

THE CLAY MARBLE

MINFONG HO ©1991

Twelve-year-old Dara and her family flee her peaceful village because there is no food; the land has been destroyed by war. With their belongings in an ox-cart, they head for a refugee camp on the border between Cambodia and Thailand. In this realistic novel, Dara struggles with personal relationships that have been changed by war. She watches her brother Sarun's personality change as he considers joining the army. Read to find answers to these questions:

- Can Dara and her family survive when the shelling begins again?

- Will Sarun join the army?

- Can Dara's family build a new life in a country still at war?

Other Recommended Books

On My Honor by Marion Dane Bauer (©1987). In this contemporary novel, Joel discovers the consequences of disobedience when his best friend drowns in a river. Can Joel tell anyone what really happened?

A Fine White Dust by Cynthia Rylant (©1986). In this realistic novel, a boy struggles to live up to his religious faith in spite of his parents' apathy and his best friend's atheism.

Treasure Island by Robert Louis Stevenson (©1883). This classic adventure tale tests both a boy's courage and his loyalty to a friendly pirate he meets on a search for buried treasure.

So Far from the Bamboo Grove by Yoko Kawashima Watkins (©1986). In this historical novel based on the author's childhood, a Japanese girl and her mother and sister flee Korea in the face of war.

467

ONE-EYED CAT

Study Focus

- A test of conscience involving the firing of a gun

- A character's struggle with guilt and remorse

- Vivid, descriptive language

About Paula Fox

Fox has a great respect for other authors and their writing. She has said, "It is the work of other writers and the examples of their lives that provide the deepest encouragement and the most abiding inspiration." Of her own work, Fox has said, "Writing is tremendously hard work. There is nothing more satisfying, but it is work all the same."

- **Other Works** Novels: *A Likely Place, Portrait of Ivan, Poor George, The Stone-Faced Boy, How Many Miles to Babylon?*

- **Awards** Newbery Medal, 1974, for *The Slave Dancer;* American Book Award, 1983, for *A Place Apart;* Newbery Honor book, 1985, for *One-Eyed Cat.*

THE CLAY MARBLE

Study Focus

- Realistic settings of Cambodia and Thailand

- A character's struggle with relationships

- A family's bonds of the heart

About Minfong Ho

Born in Burma, Ho worked as a manual laborer in a plywood factory before he became a journalist, lecturer, and author. Ho has said, "There is so much, so much beauty and so much pain in the world around me which I want to write about—because I want to share it. Hopefully, young readers in America will understand better, through some of my stories, the youth around me in Asia."

- **Other Works** Novels: *Rice Without Rain, Sing to the Dawn;* journalism: "Hsin Nu-Ren," column in the Singapore *Sunday Times*

Overview

Unit Five: A QUESTION OF IDENTITY

Subunit One: Declarations of Independence

	SELECTION	DIFFICULTY LEVEL	READING SKILLS	LITERATURE SKILLS	WRITING OPTIONS	VOCABULARY WORDS/SKILLS
Nonfiction	*The Autobiography of Malcolm X* Malcolm X with Alex Haley Pages 471–478	Average	Making inferences	Allusion Motivation	Personal memoir Poem Compare/contrast Persuasive speech	articulate emulate feign painstaking rehabilitation
Poetry	*Without Commercials* Alice Walker Pages 479–483	Average	Reading stanzas	Tone Theme	Essay Rebuttal	Word Attack Skill: the prefix *im-*
Fiction	*A Man Who Had No Eyes* MacKinlay Kantor Pages 484-488	Challenge	Stereotypes	Irony	Dialogue Speech	Word Attack Skill: Latin roots
Drama	*Funny Boy* Allan Burns Pages 489–511	Average	Stage directions	Exposition Humor	Humor column Character analysis Letter of advice Scenario	alienate girth amiably insolent bemused militant engrossed relinquish flippant reverie

WRITER'S WORKSHOP Pages 512–516 ································

Mode	Guided Assignment	Writing Skills	Proofreading Focus
Writing about Literature/Persuasion	Advertising poster	Summarizing Visual elements Persuasive language	Verb tenses

OPTIONS FOR LEARNING	SPELLING SKILLS	COMMUNITY AND PARENT RESOURCE SUGGESTIONS	AUDIOVISUAL RESOURCES
Book list Statistics Literacy information Oral report	Final *y* and suffixes	Invite literacy volunteers to discuss how they teach people to read. Ask a Black Muslim to share beliefs and history.	*Malcolm X.* Video. Library Video Co., 1992. (30 min.) Dramatically paced; probes deeply into the life of Malcolm X.
	More *com/con, im/in* prefixes	Ask a plastic surgeon to discuss his or her business with the class.	*Literature & Language* Audiocassette Tape 2, side 1. *Alice Walker.* Audiocassette. American Audio Prose Library. (46 min.) In this interview, Walker elaborates on themes from her work.
	Proofreading for Spelling	Contact the Society for the Blind or the local Lions club to have a volunteer discuss what blind people have accomplished and how they have overcome problems.	*Literature & Language* Audiocassette Tape 2, side 2.
Act a scene Skit Sketch clothing Storyboard	Assimilated prefixes	Take students on a field trip to see a dramatic production by a high school or community acting troupe.	

LANGUAGE WORKSHOP Pages 517–519 . . . .

Grammar Concept	Skill Focus
Verb tenses	Understanding tenses Avoiding unnecessary tense shifts

RELATED SKILLS WORKSHOP Page 520 . . . . . .

Language Strand	Skill Focus
Reading	Fact and Opinion

Subunit Two: Doors of Understanding

	SELECTION	DIFFICULTY LEVEL	READING SKILLS	LITERATURE SKILLS	WRITING OPTIONS	VOCABULARY WORDS/SKILLS	
Fiction	*Last Cover* Paul Annixter Pages 522–533	Easy	Context clues	Flashback Narrator	Advertising flyer Letter Comparison/ contrast	bleak confound essence harried intricate	invalid passive sanction sanctuary wily
Poetry	*A Minor Bird* Robert Frost *The Time We Climbed Snake Mountain* Leslie Marmon Silko Pages 534–537	Average	Comparing/ contrasting	Imagery	Bill of rights Poem	Word Attack Skill: multiple meanings	
Nonfiction	*Primary Lessons* Judith Ortiz Cofer Pages 538–548	Challenge	Identifying an opinion	Title Description	Memo Notes Opinion Report	adaptation adhere chaos hierarchy incomprehensible	minimize niche predecessor relish rote
Nonfiction	*Oh Broom, Get to Work* Yoshiko Uchida Pages 549–556	Average	Predicting	Setting	Plot capsule Character sketch	alumnus communing cryptic deity divulge expediency morose occult	pallid precept seminary solace sorcery strident zeal
Fiction	*The Medicine Bag* Virginia Driving Hawk Sneve Pages 557–568	Average	Making connections	Internal conflict Exposition	Dialogue Song lyric Comparison/contrast Booklet	confines descendant fatigue reluctantly unseemly	

WRITER'S WORKSHOP   Pages 569–573

Mode	Guided Assignment	Writing Skills		Proofreading Focus
Informative	Research report	Finding sources Taking notes Outlining	Transitions Bibliography	Proofreading

OPTIONS FOR LEARNING	SPELLING SKILLS	COMMUNITY AND PARENT RESOURCE SUGGESTIONS	AUDIOVISUAL RESOURCES
Drawing Map Oral book report Poster	Doubling final consonants	Take the class to visit an art museum. Invite a farmer to discuss problems that wildlife cause on a farm. Ask an artist to work in front of the class.	
	Proofreading for Spelling	Invite a bird-watcher to talk to the class.	*The Afterglow: A Tribute to Robert Frost.* 16mm film or video. Pyramid, 1990. (35 min.) Burgess Meredith speaks Frost's words while walking in the countryside surrounding Frost's Vermont cabin. *American Indian Poetry.* Video. Great Plains Instructional Television Library. (30 min.) Poetry written by members of the Paiute, Sioux, Zuni, and other tribes.
Diagram Debate Map Report	Latin word parts	Invite someone who attended school in Puerto Rico to talk to the class. Ask those who have gone to a school of a different language to discuss their experiences.	*Literature & Language* Audiocassette Tape 2, side 2.
	Paired prefixes	Invite immigrants to discuss their experiences for the class.	
Radio news show Poll Interview Medicine bag	Pronunciation problems	Take students to visit a museum in order to see Native American artifacts. If possible, visit a reservation.	*The Taos Pueblo.* Video. Bullfrog Films, 1987. A day spent at a thousand-year-old pueblo in New Mexico.

LANGUAGE WORKSHOP Pages 574–576 ∎∎∎∎∎∎∎∎∎

Grammar Concept	Skill Focus
Proofreading Skills	Punctuation Capitalization Grammar and usage

RELATED SKILLS WORKSHOP Page 577 ∎∎∎∎∎∎

Language Strand	Skill Focus
Reading	Main ideas, supporting details

Reading on Your Own

Novels, thematically connected to Unit Five, suggested for independent reading during or after completion of the unit (pages 578–579)

The House of Dies Drear by Virginia Hamilton
Risk N' Roses by Jan Slepian
The Adventures of Tom Sawyer by Mark Twain

Cooperative Project — Unit Five: A Question of Identity

A Dramatization

1 Project Preview

In this unit project, students will explore the topic of personal identity by working in small groups to produce and perform original skits. The dramatizations can be based on elements of the *Funny Boy* episode of *Room 222* or on other dramas or situation comedies that the class has read or seen on television. As an alternative, groups may create their own dramas from scratch. All skits will be performed for a live audience; you may also wish to videotape them. The skits may be humorous, serious, or a mixture of both. All students should be encouraged to perform in some capacity, though acting responsibilities may be balanced with other duties in the project.

OBJECTIVES
■ To explore the theme of identity in relation to characters in a dramatic script
■ To plan, prepare, and present a skit, either an extension or parody of an existing drama or a totally original production
■ To develop listening and viewing skills by watching and evaluating the performances of others

MATERIALS
■ a variety of costumes and props, as needed
■ a video camera and recorder or a camcorder (optional)

2 Implementing the Project

WARM-UP ACTIVITY
Explain to students that many dramas and situation comedies deal with issues of identity. In *Funny Boy*, for instance, the main character, Harvey, learns that he does not have to play the role of class clown to gain acceptance. Harvey learns to accept himself and to stop putting on an act for the benefit of others. Ask students to think of other examples of television shows in which main characters learn lessons about themselves. Point out how often characters in TV sitcoms learn lessons "the hard way," with hilarious results. Ask students to think about why problems of coming to terms with one's identity or personality are so common in television shows.

INTRODUCING THE PROJECT
Tell students that this project challenges them to create and perform scenes that explore issues of identity. Their group can create a new scene for *Funny Boy*, use another situation comedy or a serious drama as a starting point, or create a scene from scratch. Each group will have creative control of its project, from planning to performance.

ASSIGNING GROUPS
Divide students into groups of five or six. You might want to aim for a good mix of shy and outgoing students. Students who are comfortable in front of an audience might play the major roles, but all students should be encouraged to perform.

Ask groups to think about possible situations for their skits. Explain that this is an opportunity for them to write humor if they want to. Share the following suggestions with your students to stimulate thinking. (Although these suggestions refer to *Funny Boy*, students may use other dramas if they desire.)

Futurizing Create a skit that takes place sometime after the action in *Funny Boy*. For example, you could show Harvey coming back to his school as a teacher, much to Mr. Walters's dismay. You might present Harvey finally succeeding in winning the attention of Marge, the girl pasting copy in the school newspaper office, or show what happens to Harvey after he loses weight.

Spinoff Series Create a scene from a new television series featuring one or more of the characters from *Room 222*. Perhaps Alice Johnson, the student teacher, is given a class of her own; perhaps Harvey becomes the star of his own show.

Updating Rewrite part of *Funny Boy* as though it were taking place right now. Recast the dialogue or the situation to give the play a contemporary feel.

New Scene Write a new scene for *Funny Boy*, one that might logically have taken place. You might, for example, show Harvey in Mr. Walters's class or show the newspaper workers discussing Harvey in his absence.

Inner Voice Take one of the scenes in *Funny Boy* and add what Harvey is thinking as he speaks his lines. When the scene is acted out, one student can play Harvey while another plays the part of his inner voice.

To illustrate this idea, here is part of a scene based on the passage in which Harvey jokes with a group of girls about going to *Hello Dolly* (page 496):

Harvey. The reason I've got two tickets is that I take up two seats.
Inner Voice. Why did I say a stupid thing like that? It's not bad enough that I'm fat; I have to go around pointing it out to everybody!

CREATING THE SCRIPT
After students know what they need to do, give them time to brainstorm. At first, students should think of as many different ideas as they can; later, they can evaluate the ideas and modify them.

Once a group has decided on an idea, it can divide responsibilities for the project. Some students may be given writing jobs, while others may be responsible for props, costumes, and so on. All students, however, need to be given a voice at each stage of production. Caution groups that they will need to be flexible, especially when they run into difficulties. In many cases, groups will need to revise their plans and assignments along the way.

In some groups, the writing of dialogue will proceed smoothly. Other groups will have more trouble. You may wish to use the following strategies with groups who need help.

Improvised Writing Have students improvise different versions of their scene while a tape recorder is running or someone is taking notes. After the group has decided on the best version, its members can refer to the tape or the notes to create a final script.

On-Stage Revising Have students write a rough draft or outline of their script and then act out the scene. They should stop to add or change lines whenever necessary. A scribe can take notes as group members suggest revisions. A neat copy of the final version can be photocopied to give to all members of the group.

Extemporizing If students are more comfortable with improvisation than with writing, you may allow them to perform without a written script. Have students write an outline of the plot and then practice the scene several times, creating the dialogue extemporaneously. In their performance the group members should present a well-rehearsed, polished scene.

As students work on their scripts and rehearse, remind them what it means to stay in character. Whether they are writing a script or acting out a role, they must always make sure that each character dresses, acts, and talks in a way that is in keeping with that character's identity.

Remind students that any humor they write should be kept in good taste!

COSTUMES AND PROPS

Explain that the props and costumes used in a production can be helpful in developing characters. Near the end of *Funny Boy*, for example, Harvey is shown in dress clothes, which suggest a change in his attitude about himself. Earlier in the play, just before Harvey's first appearance, the stage directions suggest that Pete Dixon be shown with a pipe, which might stand for patience or thoughtfulness.

Students should have no problem creating costumes and props from everyday items at home. However, if you choose a Readers Theater format, costumes and props can be suggested rather than real. For example, all students might wear black slacks and T-shirts, with each adding one item of clothing, perhaps a cap or a scarf, to suggest a quality of his or her character.

PERFORMANCE

Each group's performance should be presented to the entire class. Students can memorize their lines, work with scripts, or improvise. If the productions are successful, you might wish to schedule performances for parents or other classrooms. If you have no stage or theater facilities available, consider placing students on stools or chairs in a Readers Theater format, where the students can give dramatic readings without stage movement.

If you decide to videotape the performances, try to enlist the help of a volunteer to handle the taping while you manage the classroom "theater."

3 Project Assessment

Group Assessment
Evaluate the group performances, using the following criteria:

Script Is the dialogue well-written and believable? Does the plot flow smoothly and hold the interest of the audience?

Characterization Are the characters interesting and believable? Do they talk and behave in appropriate ways?

Poise and Polish Do the actors seem to be well rehearsed? Are the props and costumes (if any) appropriate for the characters and action?

You may wish to provide each group with a written evaluation based on these criteria. In addition, you should have each student write comments on at least one group's performance. For example, after thoroughly discussing the criteria, you might ask five students to evaluate the first group's performance, another five students to evaluate the second group's, and so on.

To make sure that students are taking the task seriously, give them some credit for writing the evaluations. Eventually, the names of student evaluators can be cut off the top of the comment sheets, and their comments can be handed to the groups along with your evaluation.

Individual Assessment
You may also wish to give each student an individual grade. To do so, allow five minutes at the end of each day so that every student can make a detailed record of all that he or she has done to contribute to the project. Time spent outside of class in making costumes and props and in writing and rehearsing can be noted, in addition to the work done during class.

Have periodic conferences with individual students to keep track of progress. Also, meet with each group occasionally to see that the work is being divided equitably and that all students are doing their share of the work. At the end of the project, you can assign grades for individual effort, based on your conferences with students and their records of their own work.

For the Portfolio
In each student's portfolio include a copy of your written evaluation, as well as the student's project log (record of work). If video or audio recordings of the performances have been made, keep the tapes in your classroom library, and make a note in each portfolio about the existence of the tapes.

4 Team-Teaching Options

Social Studies
Help students explore the impact that television had on life in the United States when it became popular in the 1950s. Popular magazines from that era, such as *Life* and *Look*, may provide a useful starting point.

Mathematics
Discuss the techniques of polling that are used to measure the popularity of current television shows. Explain the concepts of statistical sampling and audience share.

Art
Explore the various ways in which a painter can communicate an identity for his or her subject. Compare portraits by famous artists in terms of such techniques as the use of line, light, color, perspective, and texture.

Unit Preview

In Unit Five, "A Question of Identity," students will explore how individuals see themselves and how they express individuality. This unit contains two sub-units:

■ Subunit 1: "Declarations of Independence"

■ Subunit 2: "Doors of Understanding"

Connections to Unit Six

Unit Six, "Themes in World Folklore," contains literature from the oral tradition that connects with the themes in Unit Five. You may wish to begin or end Unit Five with selections from Unit Six that relate to the theme "A Question of Identity":

■ "Echo and Narcissus," p. 646

■ "The Emperor's New Clothes," p. 648

■ "The Fatal Flower," p. 653

ADDITIONAL RESOURCES
Unit Five Resource Book
Unit Test, pages 79–82

Technology and Enrichment
Family and Community Involvement
  Source Book, pp. 18–20

About the Art

Jesús Guerrero Galván (1910–1973) studied art in Texas before he returned to Mexico to teach art. *I and My Future* shows a young person, perhaps the artist, studying a portrait of himself as an adult. Note that though the face is soft and youthful, the hand and arm are as mature as the face in the painting. *How do you connect this painting with the unit theme?*

A QUESTION OF IDENTITY

....

The person portrayed

and the portrait

are two entirely

different things.

José Ortega y Gasset

YO Y MI FUTURO (I and my future)
1951   Jesús Guerrero Galván Collection,
Pascual Gutierrez Roldan.

469

About the Quoted Author

Born in Madrid, Spain, in 1883, José Ortega y Gasset became a noted philosopher. *Meditations on Quixote*, published in 1914, presented ideas that foreshadowed the existential philosophies that appeared some ten years later. Ortega was deeply influenced by the German philosopher Nietzsche, as evidenced in Ortega's best-known book, *The Revolt of the Masses*, written in 1930.

Invite students to read the introduction to Subunit 1, "Declarations of Independence." Ask them to explain how declarations of independence relate to identity. Ask students how they show their own individuality. Discuss why a person would want to show himself or herself as different from others.

Suggest that students read the subunit table of contents. Have them comment on the titles and authors, predicting which selections they will like best.

INTEGRATING THE LANGUAGE ARTS

Every selection in this subunit focuses on the theme "Declarations of Independence." Reading skills, literature skills, writing options, language study, vocabulary, and spelling are all based on these literary selections.

Writer's Workshop After reading several selections that deal with declarations of independence, students will use persuasive writing to try to convince others to read the students' favorite books.

Language Workshop The Language Workshop in this subunit deals with verb tenses. Students will learn that using correct verb tenses can help make their writing persuasive.

Reader's Workshop The Reader's Workshop in this subunit discusses fact and opinion. As they read, students will learn to judge whether opinions are strongly supported by facts.

FOR ADDITIONAL CHALLENGE

The following selections offer extra challenge in the exploration of the subunit theme.

Growing Up, autobiography by Russell Baker

Homesick, autobiography by Jean Fritz

"Summer School," essay by Gary Soto

ADDITIONAL RESOURCES

Technology and Enrichment
Family and Community Involvement Source Book, p. 18

Guidelines for Reading and Literature Assessment: Observation Assessment Forms

DECLARATIONS OF INDEPENDENCE

Each of us likes to express our individuality in a different way. For some of us, it may be the clothes we choose to wear or the way we fix our hair. Others express their unique personality through their behavior. Still others express who they are by standing up for their beliefs on important social issues.

No matter how we show our individuality, that expression is a statement of our freedom from the influence of others. In these selections, note the different ways people express their own special beliefs about themselves. See if you can determine each person's unique "declaration of independence."

Observation Assessment

Observing how students respond to the text, to the classroom instruction, and to peers is an important part of an assessment program. The following suggestions and the form in each *Guidelines for Reading and Literature Assessment* booklet can be used to implement observation assessment.

■ **Reading Behavior** As students read the subunit, assess how well they connect reading with other language arts skills. Evaluate to what degree they understand that developing reading skills can also improve their skills in writing, speaking, and listening. Also see how well they understand that reading literature can help them read and understand materials in other subject areas as well. Determine whether students feel encouraged to read for enjoyment outside of school. Throughout the subunit, look for growth in students' appreciation of reading as a means of helping themselves in all subject areas.

Nonfiction

from The Autobiography of Malcolm X

MALCOLM X *with* ALEX HALEY

E*xamine What You Know*   (Prior Knowledge)

You are about to read a section from the autobiography of the African-American leader Malcolm X. On the diagram below, Malcolm X's life has been divided into four parts. Brainstorm each of these categories to see what you and your classmates already know about Malcolm X. As you read, see if any of your ideas change.

Childhood	**X**	Imprisonment
Civil Rights		Death

E*xpand Your Knowledge*   (Building Background)

Malcolm Little was born in Omaha, Nebraska, in 1925. His father was murdered when Malcolm was only six. Problems throughout his youth reached a climax when Malcolm was arrested in 1942 and sentenced to ten years in prison for burglary.

Prison became a turning point for Malcolm. In prison he joined the Black Muslims, a black religious group. He changed his name to represent what he was leaving behind: "Ex-smoker. Ex-drinker. Ex-Christian. Ex-Slave." His controversial career began upon his release from prison, when he became a Black Muslim minister. A powerful public speaker, Malcolm X preached that in order to achieve independence, African Americans should live and work completely apart from white people. Malcolm X believed that violence was acceptable in the fight for civil rights. Later, he came to believe in the possibility of brotherhood among all people. He was assassinated in 1965.

W*rite Before You Read*   (Journal Writing)

■ *Author biography on Extend page*

Suppose that, like Malcolm X, you faced ten years of confinement. How would you plan to spend your time? In your journal, describe what your thoughts might be if you faced such a sentence.

THE AUTOBIOGRAPHY OF MALCOLM X   471

Objectives

■ To understand and analyze an excerpt from an autobiography

■ To examine the use of allusion and to review the concept of motivation

■ To enrich reading by making inferences

■ To express understanding of the story through a choice of writing forms, including a personal memoir, a poem, a comparison/contrast, and a persuasive speech

Prereading/Motivation

Examine What You Know

Discussion Prompts With what decade is Malcolm X associated? For what is he famous? What do you know about the feature film *Malcolm X?*

Expand Your Knowledge

Additional Background When Malcolm was a boy in Lansing, Michigan, his home was burned down by the Ku Klux Klan. After his conviction for burglary, Malcolm spent seven years in prison. When Malcolm joined the Nation of Islam, or Black Muslims, they were led by Elijah Muhammad, who preached that blacks are superior to whites; the group has since changed its name to the American Muslim Mission, and it now preaches the equality of races.

Thematic Link— Declarations of Independence

In this excerpt from *The Autobiography of Malcolm X,* Malcolm describes how when he was in prison, a dictionary helped him learn to read and write effectively. He explains how literacy made him a "truly free" man.

MORE JOURNAL WRITING IDEAS

■ Look at the painting on page 473. Then write about your earliest experiences in a library.

■ Invent for yourself a new name that describes something about you. Explain its meaning.

■ Which of the books you have read has had the greatest effect on your life? Explain.

COLLABORATIVE LEARNING OPTIONS

Opportunities for collaborative learning include Examine What You Know and Options for Learning 1, 2, and 4 (p. 478).

ADDITIONAL RESOURCES

Unit Five Resource Book
Reader's Guidesheet, p. 1
Reading Skills, p. 2
Literature Skills, p. 3
Vocabulary Connections, p. 4
Spelling Connections, p. 5
Comprehension and Vocabulary Check Tests, p. 6
Selection Test, pp. 7–8

VOCABULARY PREVIEW

These vocabulary words are defined at the bottom of the selection pages on which they appear.

articulate able to express oneself clearly

emulate to imitate

feign to pretend

painstaking very careful

rehabilitation the restoring of an ability to lead a useful life

LIMITED ENGLISH PROFICIENCY

■ Use the Reader's Guidesheet, *Unit Five Resource Book,* page 1.

★ Text annotations marked with a red star (1, 2) may be particularly helpful for students with limited English proficiency.

TEXT ANNOTATIONS

1. VOCABULARY: Slang
Have students "translate" this sentence into Standard English. *(Possible response: "Excuse me, sir, let me speak to you about a man named Elijah Muhammad.")* Ask students how Malcolm feels about relying on slang to communicate his ideas in writing. *(Possible responses: He thinks that slang is inappropriate; he wants to write in a way that will impress people.)* ★

2. VOCABULARY: Idioms
Ask a volunteer to explain why Malcolm says that many of the words in books "might as well have been in Chinese." *(Possible responses: He is a poor reader; he finds the English words as difficult to understand as a foreign language.)* Then ask students what Malcolm means by describing himself as "still going through only book-reading motions." *(He is reading books but not understanding them.)* ★

3. ACTIVE READING: Review
Ask students to explain what has motivated Malcolm X to request a dictionary, tablets, and pencils. *(Possible responses: He wants to write to Elijah Muhammad; he wants to have the knowledge that Bimbi has; he wants to read with understanding, increase his vocabulary, and improve his penmanship.)*

from # The Autobiography of Malcolm X

MALCOLM X
with **Alex Haley**

It was because of my letters that I happened to stumble upon starting to acquire some kind of a homemade education.

I became increasingly frustrated at not being able to express what I wanted to convey in letters that I wrote, especially those to Mr. Elijah Muhammad.[1] In the street, I had been the most <u>articulate</u> hustler out there—I had commanded attention when I said something. But now, trying to write simple English, I not only wasn't articulate, I wasn't even functional. How would I sound writing in slang, the way I would *say* it, something such as, "Look, daddy, let me pull your coat about a cat, Elijah Muhammad—"

Many who today hear me somewhere in person or on television, or those who read something I've said, will think I went to school far beyond the eighth grade. This impression is due entirely to my prison studies.

It had really begun back in the Charlestown Prison, when Bimbi[2] first made me feel envy of his stock of knowledge.

Bimbi had always taken charge of any conversation he was in, and I had tried to <u>emulate</u> him. But every book I picked up had few sentences which didn't contain anywhere from one to nearly all of the words that might as well have been in Chinese. When I just skipped those words, of course, I really ended up with little idea of what the book said. So I had come to the Norfolk Prison Colony still going through only book-reading motions. Pretty soon, I would have quit even these motions, unless I had received the motivation that I did.

I saw that the best thing I could do was get hold of a dictionary—to study, to learn some words. I was lucky enough to reason also that I should try to improve my penmanship. It was sad. I couldn't even write in a straight line. It was both ideas together that moved me to request a dictionary along with some tablets and pencils from the Norfolk Prison Colony school.

---

1. **Elijah Muhammad** (e li′ jə moo ham′ əd): 1897–1975; leader of the Black Muslim movement in the United States.
2. **Bimbi:** a fellow inmate.

Words to Know and Use	**articulate** (är tik′ yoo lit) *adj.* able to express oneself clearly in words **emulate** (em′ yoo lāt′) *v.* to imitate or copy

Guided Reading for Less-Proficient Students

These questions can help guide students through the reading. Ask each question at the point of the selection where the capital letter and arrow appear in the margin. In addition, you may wish to use appropriate Active Reading annotations.

A. How well could Malcolm read and write before coming to prison? *(very poorly)* Recalling

B. How does Malcolm teach himself to read? *(He copies the dictionary, learning not only the words but also information about a variety of subjects.)* Summarizing

C. What benefits does Malcolm get from reading? *(Possible responses: Reading helps him discover a "new world"; it fills up his free time; it allows him to forget that he is in prison; it helps him to feel free.)* Clarifying

Continued on page 473

THE LIBRARIES ARE APPRECIATED 1943 Jacob Lawrence Philadelphia Museum of Art, Louis E. Stern Collection.

I spent two days just riffling uncertainly through the dictionary's pages. I'd never realized so many words existed! I didn't know *which* words I needed to learn. Finally, just to start some kind of action, I began copying.

I'd never realized so many words existed!

In my slow, painstaking, ragged handwriting, I copied into my tablet everything printed on that first page, down to the punctuation marks.

I believe it took me a day. Then, aloud, I read back to myself everything I'd written on the tablet. Over and over, aloud to myself, I read my own handwriting.

I woke up the next morning, thinking about those words—immensely proud to realize that not only had I written so much at one time, but I'd written words that I never knew were in the world. Moreover, with a little effort, I also could remember what many of these words meant. I reviewed the words whose meanings I didn't remember. Funny thing, from the dictionary's first page right now, that *aardvark* springs to my mind. The dictionary had a picture of it, a long-tailed, long-eared,

| Words to Know and Use | **painstaking** (pānz′ tāk′ iŋ) *adj.* very careful |

473

Art Note

Jacob Lawrence was born in 1917 in Atlantic City, New Jersey. In 1930, when he moved to New York City with his family, he began studying art. His distinctive paintings, which focus mainly on the African-American experience, have been popular with both critics and the public. He was the first African-American artist to be honored with a one-man show at the Museum of Modern Art in New York City. In *The Libraries Are Appreciated* he expresses the tranquillity of public libraries and the enjoyment people find in them. This work is typical of Lawrence's style, which features highly stylized figures and shapes, flat primary colors, and sharp contrasts. *What role did libraries play in Malcolm X's life?*

4. ACTIVE READING: Evaluating Challenge students to evaluate Malcolm X's method of teaching himself. Is copying every mark on a dictionary page and repeatedly reading the copy aloud a useful exercise? Why or why not? *(Any response is valid.)*

5. LITERARY CONCEPT: Character Ask students what Malcolm's study habits reveal about his personality. *(Possible responses: He is persistent; he does not easily give up; he's very disciplined.)*

Guided Reading for Less-Proficient Students

Continued from page 472

D. In what ways does Malcolm X take advantage of the Norfolk Prison Colony's educational facilities? *(He borrows many books from the prison library and attends classes and debates.)* Recalling

6. ACTIVE READING: Question
Have students draw on their own experiences to explain how "the dictionary is like a miniature encyclopedia." *(Possible response: A dictionary contains information about many subjects, including places, people, and events.)*

7. LITERARY CONCEPT: Theme
Ask students to explain how reading can open up new worlds. *(Possible responses: By reading, a person can learn about other countries, other times, and other people; reading exposes people to new thoughts and takes them beyond the limits of their surroundings.)*

8. LITERARY CONCEPT: Motivation
Ask students to explain the connection between the emphasis on rehabilitation in the prison and the "sizable number of well-read inmates." *(Possible responses: The prison officials want the convicts to improve themselves; the convicts may be trying to impress the officials so that their sentences will be reduced.)*

burrowing African mammal, which lives off termites caught by sticking out its tongue as an anteater does for ants.

I was so fascinated that I went on—I copied the dictionary's next page. And the same experience came when I studied that. With every succeeding page, I also learned of people and places and events from history. Actually, the dictionary is like a miniature encyclopedia. Finally, the dictionary's A section had filled a whole tablet—and I went on into the B's. That was the way I started copying what eventually became the entire dictionary. It went a lot faster after so much practice helped me to pick up handwriting speed. Between what I wrote in my tablet and writing letters, during the rest of my time in prison, I would guess, I wrote a million words.

B ▶

I never had been so truly free in my life.

I suppose it was inevitable that as my word base broadened, I could for the first time pick up a book and read and now begin to understand what the book was saying. Anyone who has read a great deal can imagine the new world that opened. Let me tell you something: from then until I left that prison, in every free moment I had, if I was not reading in the library, I was reading on my bunk. You couldn't have gotten me out of books with a wedge.[3] Between Mr. Muhammad's teachings, my correspondence, my visitors—usually Ella and

Reginald[4]—and my reading of books, months passed without my even thinking about being imprisoned. In fact, up to then, I never had been so truly free in my life. **◀ C**

The Norfolk Prison Colony's library was in the school building. A variety of classes was taught there by instructors who came from such places as Harvard and Boston universities. The weekly debates between inmate teams were also held in the school building. You would be astonished to know how worked up convict debaters and audiences would get over subjects like "Should Babies Be Fed Milk?"

Available on the prison library's shelves were books on just about every general subject. Much of the big private collection that Parkhurst[5] had willed to the prison was still in crates and boxes in the back of the library—thousands of old books. Some of them looked ancient: covers faded, old-time parchment-looking binding. Parkhurst, I've mentioned, seemed to have been principally interested in history and religion. He had the money and the special interest to have a lot of books that you wouldn't have in general circulation. Any college library would have been lucky to get that collection.

As you can imagine, especially in a prison where there was heavy emphasis on <u>rehabilitation</u>, an inmate was smiled upon if he demonstrated an unusually intense interest in books. There was a sizable number of **8**

---
3. **wedge:** a tapered piece of wood or metal used for splitting wood or rock.
4. **Ella and Reginald:** Malcolm's sister and brother.
5. **Parkhurst:** a millionaire interested in the education and training of prisoners.

Words to Know and Use	**rehabilitation** (rē' hə bil' ə tā' shən) *n.* the restoring of a person's ability to lead a useful life

474

Multicultural Connections

You may wish to read aloud this passage from *The Autobiography of Malcolm X:*

■ The teachings of Mr. Muhammad stressed [that] when white men had written history books, the black man simply had been left out. . . . When my class . . . had studied seventh-grade United States history back in Macon, the history of the Negro had been covered in one paragraph. . . . I took special pains to hunt in the library for books that would inform me on details about black history.

These questions may be useful for discussion:
1. Why is it important for people to know the history of their ancestors?
2. What have you learned about the history of your own ancestors from textbooks?
3. How has the study of history changed since Malcolm X was in school?
4. From what sources other than textbooks have you learned about the past? What have you learned in history classes about other cultures?

well-read inmates, especially the popular debaters. Some were said by many to be practically walking encyclopedias. They were almost celebrities. No university would ask any student to devour literature as I did when this new world opened to me, of being able to read and *understand*.

I read more in my room than in the library itself. An inmate who was known to read a lot could check out more than the permitted maximum number of books. I preferred reading in the total isolation of my own room.

9

D ▶

When I had progressed to really serious reading, every night at about ten I would be outraged with the "lights out." It always seemed to catch me right in the middle of something engrossing.

Fortunately, right outside my door was a corridor light that cast a glow into my room. The glow was enough to read by, once my eyes adjusted to it. So when "lights out" came, I would sit on the floor where I could continue reading in that glow.

At one-hour intervals the night guards paced past every room. Each time I heard the approaching footsteps, I jumped into bed and feigned sleep. And as soon as the guard passed, I got back out of bed onto the floor area of that light-glow, where I would read for another fifty-eight minutes—until the guard approached again. That went on until three or four every morning. Three or four hours of sleep a night was enough for me. Often in the years in the streets, I had slept less than that. ❧

INSIGHT

Aardvark
JULIA FIELDS

Since
   Malcolm died
   That old aardvark
   has got a sort of fame
   for himself—
   I mean, of late, when I read
   The dictionary the first
   Thing I see
   Is that animal staring at me.
And then
   I think of Malcolm—
   How he read
   in the prisons
   And on the planes
   And everywhere
   And how he wrote
   About old Aardvark.
Looks like Malcolm X helped
Bring attention to a lot of things
We never thought about before.

| Words to Know and Use | **feign** (fān) *v.* to pretend |

475

9. ACTIVE READING: Connect
Ask students why Malcolm may prefer reading in the total isolation of his own room. *(Any response is valid.)*

INSIGHT

This poem is a reflection on the ideas in the main selection and is suggested for students' independent reading. Optional discussion questions follow.

1. Of the thousands of words he copied from the dictionary, Malcolm describes only "aardvark" in detail. What purpose does this single example serve in his autobiography? *(Possible responses: It is one of the first words in the dictionary, so it represents the beginning of Malcolm's self-education; it's an unusual word, one that draws attention to the unusual way that Malcolm learned to read.)*

2. What purpose does the aardvark serve in this poem? *(Possible response: It is a symbol of Malcolm's role in focusing attention on problems and issues that had been ignored or neglected.)*

3. How do you think the speaker of the poem regards Malcolm X? *(Possible responses: as a hero and leader, with fondness and respect)*

4. In what way is Malcolm like an aardvark? *(Possible responses: He paved the way for new understandings; he was unusual and fascinating, like an aardvark.)*

ENCOURAGING INDEPENDENT READING

Malcolm X, biography by Arnold Adoff

Malcolm X Talks to Young People, nonfiction by Malcolm X

Now Is Your Time! The African-American Struggle for Freedom, nonfiction by Walter Dean Myers

Roll of Thunder, Hear My Cry, novel by Mildred Taylor

Comprehension Check

✓ 1. Why does Malcolm X request a dictionary, tablets, and pencils from the Norfolk Prison Colony school? *(He wants to learn to read and write properly.)*

2. In what specific way does he use these three tools? *(He copies the dictionary page by page in his own hand.)*

3. What allows Malcolm X to feel "truly free" in prison? *(learning to read and write well)*

Student Response

Responding to Reading

1. Any response is valid.

2. Possible responses: He was a highly motivated and disciplined person, who loved learning and self-improvement; he was intelligent and courageous; he was a criminal who did his best to turn his life around.

3. Possible responses: an improvement in Malcolm's vocabulary, giving him the ability to read a wide range of books; an improvement in his self-esteem and confidence; his gaining knowledge of many subjects

4. Possible responses: Reading gave Malcolm a sense of power and independence; not being able to read well had severely limited him; he felt free because he could escape prison mentally and because reading expanded his knowledge and imagination.

5. Possible response: Malcolm X educated people about matters they may not have thought deeply about before, especially racial injustice.

6. Any response is valid.

Challenge Question

Challenge students to explain why the prison debates were important to the inmates. (Possible responses: The debates provided an opportunity for a free exchange of ideas and expression of emotions; they gave prisoners an opportunity to be part of a team; a debate is exciting because it is a verbal battle between opponents.)

Literary Concept: Allusion

The poem alludes to the passage in *The Autobiography of Malcolm X* where Malcolm describes learning the meaning of *aardvark* as a result of copying the first page of the dictionary.

Concept Review: Motivation

His motivation shifted from envy of his friend to pride in his success, fascination with what he discovers through books, and the sense of freedom that he gains from reading.

Responding to Reading

First Impressions

1. What are your feelings about Malcolm X's accomplishments? Write your response in your journal.

Second Thoughts

2. Based on this excerpt, how would you describe Malcolm X?

3. What do you think was the most important result of Malcolm X's copying pages from the dictionary? Why?

4. Malcolm X says that when he learned to read he "had never been so truly free" in his life. What do you think he meant by this?

5. Read or reread "Aardvark" on page 475. What do you think the last three lines might mean?

Broader Connections

6. Malcolm X was an eighth-grade dropout. If he had stayed in school, do you think he would have developed the same desire to learn that he did in prison? What steps do you think schools and the community could take to instill in students a greater desire for learning?

Literary Concept: Allusion

An **allusion** is a reference to another work of literature or to a familiar person, place, or event. Usually the reader must understand the allusion in order to understand the work in which it appears. How does the poem "Aardvark" use allusion?

Concept Review: Motivation   Malcolm X states that his original motivation for wanting to improve his reading was envy of his friend Bimbi. Did his motivation for reading change after he completed copying the dictionary?

Writing Options

1. Malcolm X was very frustrated when he could not communicate his ideas and feelings in writing. Write a **personal memoir** about a time when you experienced a similar frustration.

2. Write a **poem** about an instance in your life in which you declared your independence.

3. Consider the actions Malcolm X took in this excerpt and the change he caused in himself. **Compare and contrast** his actions and motivations with those of Jackie Robinson, Jean Little, or Eleanor Roosevelt.

4. Write a **persuasive speech** that Malcolm X might give about literacy—the ability to read and write.

Vocabulary Practice

Exercise Analogies Determine the relationship between the first pair of words. Then decide which vocabulary word best completes the second pair in order to express a similar relationship.

1. FOLLOW : INSTRUCTIONS ::_____: hero
2. GRACEFUL : DANCER ::_____: speaker
3. LOUD : QUIET ::_____: careless
4. RECOVERY : HOSPITAL ::_____: prison
5. WISH : HOPE ::_____: pretend

> *Words to Know and Use*
>
> ---
>
> **articulate**
> **emulate**
> **feign**
> **painstaking**
> **rehabilitation**

Writing Options

The Writing Options are designed to meet varied student interests and abilities. Have each student choose one writing activity to complete.

Journal Update Invite students to review their journal entries for this selection and to write about books that have affected them powerfully, as Malcolm's reading affected him.

Links to Writer's Craft

Writing Option 4 is an exercise in persuasive writing. For more practice, see *The Writer's Craft,* Grade 7, "Persuasion," pages 138–163.

Vocabulary Practice

Answers to Exercise

1. emulate
2. articulate
3. painstaking
4. rehabilitation
5. feign

For Alternative Learning Styles

Suggest that students study the vocabulary words by emulating Malcolm X's method of learning—copying the dictionary entry for each word, down to the punctuation marks. After they complete all five entries, discuss what they learned by such a process.

The Spelling Connection

Final y Words and Suffixes When a suffix is added to a word with a final **y** preceded by a vowel, the **y** is kept; when the **y** is preceded by a consonant, the **y** changes to **i.** The **y** never changes before **ing.**
Examples: empty empties emptied emptying
Words from the Selection with Final y and Suffixes

convey	conveys	conveyed	conveying
copy	copies	copied	copying
try	tries	tried	trying
study	studies	studied	studying

Other Words with Final y and Suffixes

display	displays	displayed	displaying
reply	replies	replied	replying
essay	essays	essayist	

Exercise Correct the form of each underlined word.
1. The class was *study* rehabilitated people.
2. Students *try* to create a few *display.*
3. Some wrote *essay* and *copy* them neatly.
4. Their work *convey* what people really can do.

Extending the Lesson

Options for Learning

These activities suit a variety of learning styles and modes of expression.

Collaborative Learning Activities
See Options 1, 2, and 4.

1. **Recommended Reading** You might wish to allow students time to browse in a library before working on their lists.

2. **So Many Words, So Little Time** Students might enjoy working on this activity in pairs. One student could give the data about a dictionary page aloud as the other student records it. Then the partners could switch roles.

3. **Reading Power** Students might check in a local or school library for listings of regional human-service organizations. A reference librarian may also be able to help them.

4. **Say It Loud** Students can find information on Malcolm X in an encyclopedia, in books about African-American heroes, and in magazine and newspaper articles about the film *Malcolm X*.

FACT FINDER SOCIAL STUDIES

Students can use their state's annual budget reports to determine per-pupil and per-prisoner expenditures.

Malcolm X

■ **More About the Author** In late 1963, Malcolm X traveled to Mecca in Saudi Arabia, where he experienced a religious conversion and adopted the orthodox Muslim belief in the equality of the races. He returned to the United States, established the Organization of Afro-American Unity, and preached against racism for the rest of his life.

■ **Other Works** *Malcolm X Talks to Young People; Malcolm X Speaks; Malcolm X: Speeches at Harvard*

Closure

The excerpt from his autobiography shows how Malcolm X found an inner freedom. Have students discuss in small groups why Malcolm X should or should not be a role model for today's young people.

Options for Learning (Multimodal/Cross-Curricular Activities)

1 • Recommended Reading Suppose that you were being sent away for ten years and could select only ten books to take with you. In small groups, decide which books would be the most valuable to have. Compare your lists.

2 • So Many Words, So Little Time Let any dictionary fall open and carefully read one page. Jot down how many entries were on the page, how many were new to you, and how many historical facts were given. Share your results.

3 • Reading Power Write to either a local or national literacy program for information about illiteracy. Find out how many people can't read, how reading is taught to adults, and how learning to read affects them.

4 • Say It Loud Malcolm X urged African Americans to make use of what he called Black Power. Do research to find out what Malcolm believed African Americans should do to improve their lives. Make an oral report on your findings.

FACT FINDER SOCIAL STUDIES

Find out how much money your state spends per year to jail a criminal and how much the state spends per year to educate a child.

Malcolm X
1925–1965

In prison, Malcolm X began to follow the teachings of Elijah Muhammad and the Nation of Islam, also known as the Black Muslims. After his release he became a minister for this group and soon became more famous than Elijah Muhammad. Malcolm X preached in favor of black power and black nationalism, opposing white oppression and integration. However, because of a dispute within the faith, Malcolm was expelled from the group. He then traveled to Africa where he became a follower of traditional Islam.

In 1965 Malcolm X founded the Organization of Afro-American Unity to bring publicity to the plight of African Americans. He and Alex Haley, who later wrote *Roots*, worked together on Malcolm's autobiography. While preparing to speak in Harlem on February 21, 1965, he was assassinated. Three men, two of whom were Black Muslims, were convicted of his murder and sentenced to life in prison. His autobiography was published after his death.

Cross-Curricular Projects

Art Invite students to create portraits of Malcolm X in any medium they choose. Some students might assemble a collage of photographs; others may prefer to work from their own imaginations.

Social Studies Have volunteers research the history of the Nation of Islam (Black Muslims). How did the organization begin, and how has it changed over the years?

Social Studies Ask interested students to compare and contrast Malcolm X and Martin Luther King, Jr., in terms of their views on race relations.

Geography Have volunteers prepare a map that shows the places where Malcolm X lived and traveled.

Poetry

Without Commercials

ALICE WALKER

Examine What You Know   (Prior Knowledge)

The world around us is full of ads for weight-loss programs, hair products, fitness programs, cosmetics, contact lenses, tanning salons, and plastic surgery. It often seems that no one is happy with the way he or she looks. How do you feel about your own appearance? How important are your looks to your view of yourself? In your journal or notebook, write down your feelings.

Expand Your Knowledge   (Building Background)

Each year thousands of people are so unhappy about their looks that they decide to change them. Some changes are related to ethnic characteristics. For example, many Caucasians go to tanning salons or

spend hours in the sun to darken their skin. Some African Americans bleach their skin to lighten it. Some Asians have surgery to remove the fold in their upper eyelids. Each year over half a million people in the United States have cosmetic surgery of some kind. Cosmetic surgeons flatten ears that stick out. They also perform face lifts, forehead lifts, thigh lifts, hair transplants, nose reshapings, and tummy tucks. The fees for such operations are often high. A nose reshaping alone may cost as much as six thousand dollars.

Enrich Your Reading   (Reading Skill)

■ *Author biography on Extend page*

Reading Stanzas   A group of lines that forms a unit in poetry is called a **stanza.** A stanza is comparable to a paragraph in prose. Like a paragraph, each stanza may present its own unique images. All stanzas in a poem, however, usually relate to a central idea or overall theme. In the following poem, notice how the stanzas help organize the speaker's advice about appearances.

WITHOUT COMMERCIALS   479

Objectives

■ To understand and analyze a poem

■ To examine an author's tone and to review the concept of theme

■ To enrich reading by understanding the organization of stanzas

■ To express understanding of the poem through a choice of writing forms, including an essay and a rebuttal

Prereading/Motivation

Examine What You Know

Discussion Prompts In what ways does appearance affect a person's life? Why are so many people dissatisfied with their looks?

Expand Your Knowledge

Additional Background Two-thirds of all plastic surgery performed in the United States is done for medical reasons. The other third is cosmetic surgery, intended only to improve a person's appearance.

Enrich Your Reading

Ask five volunteers to read one stanza each of the poem. After each stanza has been read, have students describe its main idea.

Thematic Link— Declarations of Independence

Alice Walker asks four different groups of people to declare their independence from society's standards of personal beauty and to celebrate their own look.

JOURNAL WRITING IDEAS
■ Use the title and illustration to predict what this poem might be about.

■ What do you think makes people good-looking? Does someone's personality affect his or her looks?

COLLABORATIVE LEARNING OPTIONS
Opportunities for collaborative learning include Options for Learning 1, 2, and 4 (p. 483) and Cross-Curricular Projects (p. 483).

ADDITIONAL RESOURCES
Unit Five Resource Book
Reader's Guidesheet, p. 9
Reading Skills, p. 10
Literature Skills, p. 11
Vocabulary Connections, p. 12
Spelling Connections, p. 13
Comprehension Check Test, p. 14
Selection Test, p. 15

Technology and Enrichment
Audiocassette Tape 2, Side 1

VOCABULARY PREVIEW

The focus of vocabulary study for this selection is the prefix *im-*. See *Unit Five Resource Book*, page 12.

LIMITED ENGLISH PROFICIENCY

■ Use the Reader's Guidesheet, *Unit Five Resource Book*, page 9.

■ Walker's use of figurative language may be challenging for some students. To help clarify meanings, you may wish to have students put some of the expressions into their own words.

★ The text annotation marked with a red star (6) may be particularly helpful for students with limited English proficiency.

TEXT ANNOTATIONS

1. ACTIVE READING: Question
Ask students to describe the speaker's attitude in the poem's opening lines. What words provide clues about that attitude? *(Possible responses: The speaker is firm, commanding, scolding, inspiring. Clues include "Listen" and "stop.")*

2. ACTIVE READING: Review
Ask students to **infer** what group of people the speaker is talking to in this stanza and to explain how they know. *(Possible response: to white people who tan themselves; clues are references to white and tanning)*

3. ACTIVE READING: Question
What might the speaker mean by the term unfolding? *(Possible response: It might refer to an Asian person having surgery to remove inner eyefolds.)*

4. ACTIVE READING: Connect
Ask students to explain what it is that the speaker wants people to stop doing in this stanza. *(Possible response: having surgery to make their noses smaller)*

Without Commercials

ALICE WALKER

1
Listen,
stop tanning yourself
and talking about
fishbelly
A ▶ 5 white.
The color white
is not bad at all.
There are white mornings
that bring us days.
10 Or, if you must,
2 tan only because
it makes you happy
to be brown,
to be able to see
15 for a summer
the whole world's
darker
face
reflected
20 in your own.

*

Stop unfolding
your eyes.
3 Your eyes are
beautiful.
B ▶ 25 Sometimes
seeing you in the street
the fold zany
and unexpected
I want to kiss
30 them

and usually
it is only
old
gorgeous
35 black people's eyes
I want
to kiss.

* *

Stop trimming
your nose. **4**
40 When you
diminish
your nose
your songs
become little
45 tinny, muted
and snub.
Better you should **◀ C**
have a nose
impertinent
50 as a flower,
sensitive
as a root;
wise, elegant,
serious and deep.

Guided Reading for Less-Proficient Students

These questions can help guide students through the reading. Ask each question at the point of the selection where the capital letter and arrow appear in the margin. In addition, you may wish to use appropriate Active Reading annotations.

A. What advice does the speaker give to white people? *(Stop tanning yourself.)* Recalling

B. Why does the speaker say people should stop worrying about extra folds of skin in their eyes? *(Their eyes are beautiful as they are.)* Recalling

C. What does the speaker say happens when people have their noses made smaller? *(Their songs do not sound as nice.)* Inferring

D. According to the speaker, what should be the only reasons for dark-skinned people to lighten their skin? *(They wish to be brown; it can make them happy to see the world's lighter faces reflected in their own.)* Recalling

E. To whom does the speaker compare the audience? *(Adam and Eve)* Recalling

55 A nose that
   sniffs
   the essence
   of Earth. And knows
   the message
60 of every
   leaf.

   * * *

   Stop bleaching
   your skin
   and talking
65 about
   so much black
   is not beautiful
   The color black
   is not bad
70 at all.
   There are black nights
   that rock
   us
   in dreams.
75 Or, if you must,
   bleach only
   because it pleases you
   to be brown,
   to be able to see
80 for as long
   as you can bear it
   the whole world's
   lighter face
   reflected

5

D ▶ 85 in your own.

   * * * *

   As for me,
   I have learned
   to worship
   the sun
90 again.

   To affirm
   the adventures
   of hair.

   For we are all
95 *splendid*
   descendants
   of Wilderness,
   Eden:
   needing only
100 to see
   each other
   without
   commercials
   to believe.

6

105 Copied skillfully
   as Adam.

   Original

7

   as Eve.

◀ E

ECHOES OF HARLEM   1980   Faith Ringgold and Willi Posey.   Collection, Philip
Morris Companies.   Courtesy, Bernice Steinbaum Gallery, New York.

5. LITERARY CONCEPT: Repetition
Ask students what lines in this stanza almost repeat or are parallel to lines from the first stanza. *(Lines 68–70 almost repeat lines 6–7; line 71 parallels line 8; lines 82–85 almost repeat lines 16–20.)* Ask how repetition ties together the ideas presented in the stanzas. *(Possible response: It shows that people at both ends of the skin color spectrum are discontent with their color.)*

6. ACTIVE READING: Review
What idea or message about life does the speaker suggest by referring to all human beings as "descendants of Wilderness, / Eden"? *(Possible responses: All human beings share a common heritage; the speaker suggests that we ought to copy our ancestors' pride in their natural appearance.)* ★

7. ACTIVE READING: Question
Challenge students to figure out why Adam is "copied" and Eve is "original." *(Possible responses: Adam is said to have been made in God's image— copied; Eve was not made in anyone's image—original.)*

Art Note

Echoes of Harlem is a quilt by Faith Ringgold and Willi Posey (1907–1981). Completed in 1980, it is made of hand-painted cotton fabric. Its portrayal of many faces in different angles offers an unusual composite of people who have lived in Harlem. *What impression do you receive from this large quilt and its many faces?*

ENCOURAGING INDEPENDENT READING

All the Colors of the Race, poetry by Arnold Adoff

Ego Tripping and Other Poems for Young People, poetry by Nikki Giovanni

Here I Am! An Anthology of Poems Written by Young People in Some of America's Minority Groups, edited by Virginia Baron

In Search of Our Mother's Gardens, nonfiction by Alice Walker

Comprehension Check

1. According to the speaker, why do some people tan? *(They think their skin is too white.)*

2. What does the speaker want to do to eyes with folds and old black people's eyes? *(kiss them)*

3. What must people stop doing to their noses? *(having their noses made smaller)*

4. According to the speaker, what do some black people do because they feel "so much black/is not beautiful"? *(bleach their skin)*

5. To whom does the speaker compare everyone? *(Adam and Eve)*

Student Response

Responding to Reading

1. Any response is valid.

2. Possible responses: the same, because in all four stanzas the speaker encourages people to accept rather than change their appearance; different, because the speaker says changing your skin color a little bit is all right, but the speaker believes that nobody should have cosmetic surgery.

3. Possible responses: to enjoy the natural beauty in other people and in ourselves; to stop being influenced by how advertisers define beauty. The speaker wants people to stop changing their natural looks; Adam and Eve were splendid as created.

4. Any response is valid.

Literary Concept: Tone

Possible responses: Walker's tone is firm, imperative, accusing, impassioned, insistent, demanding, and loving.

Concept Review: Theme

Possible responses: People should love and enjoy their own unique appearance; people should free themselves from society's negative messages.

Writing Options

The Writing Options are designed to meet varied student interests and abilities. Have each student choose one writing activity to complete.

Journal Update Invite students to write in their journals whether reading "Without Commercials" has affected their feelings about their own attractiveness.

Closure

Encourage students to determine what negative messages are presented in TV commercials about products that affect people's appearance. Ask students to imagine what Walker would say about each commercial.

---

*R*esponding to Reading

First Impressions

1. Which part of this poem did you find most meaningful? Why?

Second Thoughts

2. Each of the first four **stanzas** addresses a concern that different people have about their appearance. Do you think the speaker's advice to each group is the same or different? Explain.

3. What do you think it means to see people "without commercials"?
   Think about
   • what the speaker wants people to stop doing
   • why Adam, Eve, and Eden are mentioned

4. Do you agree with the speaker of this poem? Explain.

*L*iterary Concept: Tone

A writer's attitude toward his or her subject is called **tone**. For example, a writer's tone may be angry, bitter, admiring, or humorous, depending on how he or she feels about the subject. You can figure out the tone from the word choice and the kinds of statements the writer makes. How would you describe Walker's tone in this poem?

Concept Review: Theme   What theme, or message about life, do you think Walker presents in "Without Commercials"?

*W*riting Options

1. Write a short **essay** on why you think this poem is in a subunit called Declarations of Independence.

2. Suppose you were a plastic surgeon or you owned a cosmetic company. What would you say to Walker? Write a **rebuttal** in which you defend the right of individuals to change their appearance.

Options for Learning (Multimodal/Cross-Curricular Activities)

1 • A Matter of Looks Stage a debate on whether people should spend large amounts of time and money on personal appearance. Set up two teams. Each team may do a survey of other students' opinions and do library research. Then hold your debate for your classmates.

2 • The Old You! Think of a new product that will immediately undo all the changes people have made in their appearances. Create a television commercial for your product. If possible, add music and videotape your commercial.

3 • With Commercials In a week's time period, notice how many television commercials encourage people to change their appearance. Keep a running list of the day, time, product, and appearance change suggested. Post your list on a bulletin board to share with others.

4 • Cosmetic Surgery Research one type of cosmetic surgery such as those mentioned on the Explore page. If possible, find out from a plastic surgeon what is involved in the operation and its cost. Share the information with your classmates.

 FACT FINDER HISTORY

Who were the first people to use cosmetics?

Alice Walker
1944-

Alice Walker has always been a person with strong beliefs. She was born in Eatonton, Georgia, to sharecropper parents. As one of eight children, Walker felt different from others and spent much time alone reading. She wrote her first poems when she was eight years old.

As an adult, Walker worked in the civil rights movement in the 1960s and then moved to California to begin the most famous of her nine books, *The Color Purple*. The novel won a Pulitzer Prize and the National Book Award, and it was made into a movie.

Walker still acts on her strong opinions. She is now a vegetarian, works for animal rights, and has even been arrested while protesting the development of nuclear weapons.

Cross-Curricular Projects

Science/Health Have volunteers prepare a report on health issues involving cosmetics. Students might research information on products for the hair and the skin, as well as such items as whitening toothpaste and nail polish.

History Suggest that students research fashions popular in the 1960s, when the phrase "Black is beautiful" and the Black Power movement were current.

Art Invite interested students to use newspaper and magazine images in a collage expressing Walker's message.

Music Encourage students to set Walker's poem to music, either by singing it to an original tune, conveying its emotions by performing an instrumental piece, or reading it aloud over appropriate background music.

Objectives

- To understand and analyze a short story
- To examine the use of irony
- To enrich reading by understanding stereotypes
- To express understanding of the story through a choice of writing forms, including a dialogue and a speech

Prereading/Motivation

Examine What You Know

Discussion Prompts When you imagine a blind person, what picture do you create in your mind? Is the person happy or sad? strong or weak? How would you feel if you bumped into this person on a sidewalk? What would you do and say?

Expand Your Knowledge

Additional Background Blows to the eye and chemical burns, along with explosions, firearms, and other sources of particles that enter the eye, cause most eye injuries. Many serious eye injuries occur during sports activities.

Enrich Your Reading

For Alternative Learning Styles Ask students to choose one of the following groups and draw a picture of a person who is typical of that group: college students, the poor, the rich, farmers, rock musicians. Point out that a stereotype is an unfair idea of a group's typical characteristics. Suggest that the drawings are stereotypical—they imply that all members of a group look a certain way.

Thematic Link— Declarations of Independence

Kantor plays with stereotypes of the blind as Mr. Parsons reacts to a blind peddler. At the end the reader discovers that Parsons himself is blind. His successful life is his declaration of independence from his disability, in contrast to the peddler's submission to his handicap.

Fiction

A Man Who Had No Eyes

MacKinlay Kantor

Examine What You Know (Prior Knowledge)

Blindness is a key element in the selection you are about to read. How do you respond to people who cannot see? What feelings do you have? Do you ever try to help them in any way? Finish the statements below and share your reactions with your classmates.

When I Meet a Blind Person . . .		
I feel . . .	I want to . . .	I never . . .

Expand Your Knowledge
(Building Background)

Over twenty million people in the world are partially or totally blind; half a million of these are U.S. citizens. The most common cause of blindness is disease, mainly diabetes. The second leading cause is accidental injury. Approximately one thousand people a day experience eye injuries in the workplace. Such eye injuries cost business and industry over five hundred million dollars a year, yet ninety percent of these injuries could be prevented if workers wore protective eyewear.

Enrich Your Reading (Reading Skill)

Stereotype A broad and unfair generalization about a particular group of people is called a **stereotype**. People often form stereotypes about racial, religious, political, or social groups. Occasionally people form stereotypes about those with disabilities such as blindness. In any case, stereotypes do not allow for individual differences within a group. As you read the next selection, ask yourself if it presents any stereotypes about blind people.

- *Author biography in Reader's Handbook*

584   UNIT FIVE   DECLARATIONS OF INDEPENDENCE

JOURNAL WRITING IDEAS

- List activities that you take for granted but a blind person cannot do—for example, looking at the stars, reading a sign, and riding a bicycle.

- List your five senses. Which do you use most? Which do you think a blind person uses most?

COLLABORATIVE LEARNING OPTIONS

Opportunities for collaborative learning include Examine What You Know and Closure (p. 488).

ADDITIONAL RESOURCES

Unit Five Resource Book
Reader's Guidesheet, p. 16
Reading Skills, p. 17
Literature Skills, p. 18
Vocabulary Connections, p. 19
Spelling Connections, p. 20
Comprehension Check Test, p. 21
Selection Test, p. 22

Technology and Enrichment
Audiocassette Tape 2, Side 2

A Man Who Had No Eyes

MacKINLAY KANTOR

A beggar was coming down the avenue just as Mr. Parsons emerged from his hotel.

He was a blind beggar, carrying the traditional battered cane and thumping his way before him with the cautious, half-furtive effort of the sightless. He was a shaggy, thick-necked fellow; his coat was greasy about the lapels and pockets, and his hand splayed over the cane's crook with a futile sort of clinging. He wore a black pouch slung over his shoulder. Apparently he had something to sell.

The air was rich with spring; sun was warm and yellowed on the asphalt. Mr. Parsons, standing there in front of his hotel and noting the *clack-clack* approach of the sightless man, felt a sudden and foolish sort of pity for all blind creatures.

And, thought Mr. Parsons, he was very glad to be alive. A few years ago he had been little more than a skilled laborer; now he was successful, respected, admired. . . . Insurance. . . . And he had done it alone, unaided, struggling beneath handicaps. . . . And he was still young. The blue air of spring, fresh from its memories of windy pools and lush shrubbery, could thrill him with eagerness.

He took a step forward just as the tap-tapping blind man passed him by. Quickly the shabby fellow turned.

"Listen, guv'nor. Just a minute of your time."

Mr. Parsons said, "It's late. I have an appointment. Do you want me to give you something?"

"I ain't no beggar, guv'nor. You bet I ain't. I got a handy little article here"—he fumbled until he could press a small object into Mr. Parsons's hand—"that I sell. One buck. Best cigarette lighter made."

Mr. Parsons stood there, somewhat annoyed and embarrassed. He was a handsome figure with his immaculate gray suit and gray hat and Malacca stick. Of course the man with the cigarette lighters could not see him. . . . "But I don't smoke," he said.

"Listen. I bet you know plenty people who smoke. Nice little present," wheedled the man. "And mister, you wouldn't mind helping a poor guy out?" He clung to Mr. Parsons's sleeve.

Mr. Parsons sighed and felt in his vest pocket. He brought out two half dollars and pressed them into the man's hand. "Certainly. I'll help you out. As you say, I can give it to someone. Maybe the elevator boy would—" He hesitated, not wishing to

---

VOCABULARY PREVIEW

The focus of vocabulary study for this selection is Latin roots. See *Unit Five Resource Book*, Vocabulary Connections, p. 19.

LIMITED ENGLISH PROFICIENCY

■ Use the Reader's Guidesheet, *Unit Five Resource Book*, page 16.

■ Dialect and slang in the story may be challenging to some students. Suggest that students read passages aloud to clarify meanings.

★ The text annotation marked with a red star (2) may be particularly helpful for students with limited English proficiency.

TEXT ANNOTATIONS

1. ACTIVE READING: Connect
Ask students how they would feel if they saw this blind man walking toward them. *(Possible responses: sad, sympathetic, nervous, helpless, repulsed)*

2. VOCABULARY: Slang
Some students may have difficulty with the slang terms *ain't*, *guv'nor*, and *buck*. Have volunteers provide their meanings. *("am not," "governor" or "sir," "dollar")*. Point out that *guv'nor* is a term of respect, like *sir*. Indicate that "I got" is nonstandard and ask for the correct usage. *("I have")* ★

3. LITERARY CONCEPT: Stereotypes
Ask students to respond to the way the peddler and Mr. Parsons are portrayed. Do they seem to fit the stereotypes of a blind beggar and a businessman? *(Possible responses: The peddler is sneaky, desperate, pitiful, and poor; Mr. Parsons is impatient, successful, and decisive. The peddler seems to fit the stereotype of a panhandler, begging for money and pity; Mr. Parsons seems to be a typical businessperson—hardworking, well-dressed, successful, wealthy.)*

Guided Reading for Less-Proficient Students

These questions can help guide students through the reading. Ask each question at the point of the selection where the capital letter and arrow appear in the margin. In addition, you may wish to use appropriate Active Reading annotations.

A. How would you describe the two men in the story? *(One is a blind, dirty peddler thumping his way with a cane. The other is Mr. Parsons, a successful, optimistic young man in the insurance business.)* Summarizing

B. How did the peddler become blind? *(He was in a chemical-factory explosion.)* Recalling
C. What does the peddler hope to get by telling his story to Mr. Parsons? *(more money)* Inferring
D. How is the peddler's story untrue? *(The peddler was not trampled; it was he who climbed over Mr. Parsons to escape the fire.)* Recalling
E. What does Mr. Parsons reveal about himself at the end? *(He is blind.)* Drawing conclusions

4. ACTIVE READING: Question
Ask what the phrase "an insane sort of pride" suggests about the peddler's attitude toward his disability. *(Possible responses: He seems almost proud to be a victim; he probably tells people about how he was blinded.)*

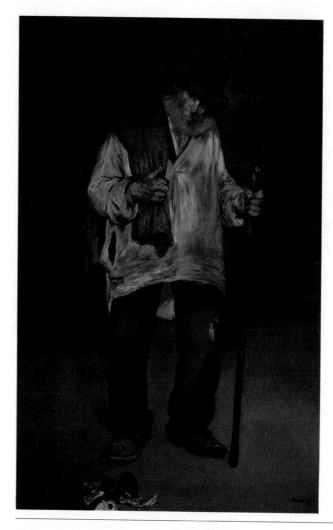

THE RAGPICKER   about 1865-69
Edouard Manet (1832-1883)   Oil on canvas,
76 3/4 x 51 1/4 inches.   Norton Simon
Foundation, Pasadena, California.

be boorish and inquisitive, even with a blind peddler. "Have you lost your sight entirely?"

The shabby man pocketed the two half dollars. "Fourteen years, guv'nor." Then he added, with an insane sort of pride, "Westbury, sir. I was one of 'em."

"Westbury," repeated Mr. Parsons. "Ah, yes. The chemical explosion. . . . The papers haven't mentioned it for years. But at the time it was supposed to be one of the greatest disasters in−"

"They've all forgot about it." The fellow shifted his feet wearily. "I tell you, guv'nor, a man who was in it don't forget about it. Last thing I ever saw was C shop going up in one grand smudge and gas pouring in at all the busted windows."

B ▶

Mr. Parsons coughed, but the blind peddler was caught up with the train of his one dramatic reminiscence. And also, he was thinking that there might be more half dollars in Mr. Parsons's pocket.

"Just think about it, guv'nor. There was a hundred and eight people killed, about two hundred injured, and over fifty of them lost their eyes. Blind as bats—" He groped forward until his dirty hand rested against Mr. Parsons's coat. "I tell you, sir, there wasn't nothing worse than that in the war. If I had lost my eyes in the war, OK. I would have been well took care of. But I was just a workman, working for what was in it. And I got it. You're so right I got it, while the capitalists were making their dough! They was insured, don't worry about that. They—"

5

"Insured," repeated his listener. "Yes. That's what I sell—"

"You want to know how I lost my eyes?" cried the man. "Well, here it is!" His words fell with the bitter and studied drama of a story often told, and told for money. "I was there in C shop, last of all the folks rushing out. Out in the air there was a chance, even with buildings exploding right and left. A lot of guys made it safe out the door and got away. And just when I was about there, crawling along between those big vats, a guy behind me grabs my leg. He says, 'Let me past, you—!' Maybe he was nuts. I dunno. I try to forgive him in my heart, guv'nor. But he was bigger than me. He hauls me back and climbs right over me! Tramples me into the dirt. And he gets out, and I lie there with all that poison gas pouring down on all sides of me, and flame and stuff. . . ." He swallowed—a studied sob—and stood dumbly expectant. He could imagine the next words: *Tough luck, my man. Awfully tough. Now I want to—*

◀ C

"That's the story, guv'nor."

The spring wind shrilled past them, damp and quivering.

"Not quite," said Mr. Parsons.

The blind peddler shivered crazily. "Not quite? What do you mean, you—?"

"The story is true," Mr. Parsons said, "except that it was the other way around."

"Other way around?" He croaked unamiably. "Say, guv'nor—"

"I was in C shop," said Mr. Parsons. "It was the other way around. You were the fellow who hauled back on me and climbed over me. You were bigger than I was, Markwardt."

6

◀ D

The blind man stood for a long time, swallowing hoarsely. He gulped: "Parsons. I thought you—" And then he screamed fiendishly: "Yes. Maybe so. Maybe so. But I'm blind! I'm blind, and you've been standing here letting me spout to you, and laughing at me every minute! I'm blind!"

People in the street turned to stare at him.

"You got away, but I'm blind! Do you hear! I'm—"

"Well," said Mr. Parsons, "don't make such a row about it, Markwardt. So am I." 🙠

7

◀ E

A MAN WHO HAD NO EYES   487

5. ACTIVE READING: Review
Ask students how the peddler has reacted emotionally to the accident that blinded him. What details help make his attitude clear? (*He feels bitter, cheated, and victimized; he blames the factory owners; he resents not being provided for, as a wounded soldier would have been. Details include his complaints, his self-pity, and his near hysteria.*)

6. ACTIVE READING: Review
Ask students how Markwardt must feel when he realizes who has been listening to his story. (*Possible response: ashamed, embarrassed, and frightened that this is the man he pushed aside to save himself*)

7. ACTIVE READING: Evaluate
Ask students why they think Parsons hadn't revealed his blindness sooner. (*Possible responses: Blindness is not an important part of his self-image; he's too proud to tell strangers he is blind; he thought the blind beggar wouldn't be able to tell; he already recognized Markwardt's voice.*)

ENCOURAGING INDEPENDENT READING

Emma and I, autobiography by Sheila Hocken

Story of My Life, autobiography by Helen Keller

If You Could See What I Hear, autobiography by Tom Sullivan

Comprehension Check

✓ 1. How is Mr. Parsons different from the blind peddler? (*He's well-dressed, successful, busy, and wealthy, whereas the peddler is shabby and pitiful.*)

2. What story does the peddler tell Mr. Parsons in hopes of getting more money? (*how he was blinded in a chemical explosion*)

3. How does Mr. Parsons know that the blind peddler's story is untrue? (*He was there and was Markwardt's victim.*)

4. What do Mr. Parsons and the blind peddler have in common besides the episode at the chemical factory? (*They are both blind.*)

Student Response

Response to Reading

1. Any response is valid.

2. **Possible responses:** He is courageous and determined, able to overcome obstacles, self-confident and optimistic, kind and soft-spoken; he feels superior to the peddler.

3. **Possible responses:** Yes, because he is in bad shape, selling lighters on the street; no, because he is a selfish liar and he wallows in his blindness instead of overcoming it.

4. **Possible response:** The author suggests that Markwardt thinks of Parsons as a stereotypical businessman and Parsons views Markwardt as a stereotypical blind man. The author uses these stereotypes to trick the reader and show that blind people can be good and bad, just like other people.

5. **Possible responses:** He is never described as looking at anything; he notices the peddler by the sound of his cane; he has a cane too; he thinks of his struggles against handicaps.

Challenge Question

In light of the ending, to whom do you think the title refers? *(Possible responses: It refers to both Markwardt and Parsons, since both are blind; it refers just to Markwardt, since Parsons is able to "see" himself and his situation clearly.)*

Literary Concept: Irony

Hoping to coax money from Parsons, Markwardt describes being blinded in an accident when a man trampled over him, blocking his escape. Ironically, however, it is Parsons who was the victim and Markwardt the attacker. Irony is also produced when Markwardt learns that Parsons, the successful businessman, is blind himself.

Responding to Reading

First Impressions

1. What was your reaction to the end of the story? Write your response in your journal or notebook.

Second Thoughts

2. What is your opinion of Mr. Parsons?
   Think about
   • his occupation and outlook on life
   • how his revelation at the end affects your thinking

3. Do you feel sympathy for Markwardt? Why or why not?

4. How does the author use **stereotypes** in this story?
   Think about
   • what the **characters** think about each other
   • the ideas about blind people that you discussed before reading

5. Look back at the story now that you know the end of the plot. What clues might have told you that Mr. Parsons is blind?

Literary Concept: Irony

Irony occurs when there is a big difference between what is expected to happen and what actually happens. For example, when you are certain that you failed a test but receive an A on it, the situation is ironic. What irony exists in "A Man Who Had No Eyes"?

Writing Options

1. The story ends with Mr. Parsons telling Markwardt that he is blind. Write the next few lines of **dialogue** that might take place between the two men.

2. Suppose that Mr. Parsons were honored at an insurance company banquet. Write an **introductory speech** in which you praise him for his accomplishments and independence in spite of his disability.

Writing Options

The Writing Options are designed to meet varied student interests and abilities. Have each student choose one writing activity to complete.

Journal Update Let students tune in to senses other than sight. Let them blindfold themselves. Then make some sounds by, for example, ringing a bell, tapping a pencil and opening and closing a door. Walk around the classroom, handing students objects to feel. Introduce some smells. Then invite students to write about their sensory impressions.

Closure

To demonstrate the great variety of ways to assert one's independence, ask students to choose partners and brainstorm a list of heroes—real or fictional—who have gained their independence in admirable and unusual ways.

Drama

Funny Boy
ALLAN BURNS

Examine What You Know (Prior Knowledge)

What kinds of jokes or stories does your favorite comedian tell? Does this comedian rely on sarcastic wit, or does he or she use sounds and movement to imitate funny situations? As a class, think of comedians and people you know who use the various kinds of humor described below. Then look for some of these kinds of humor in *Funny Boy*.

sarcastic, dry humor

comic impressions

jokes on current events

daily living, family life stories

FUNNY

pokes fun at self

slapstick comedy

lightning-fast comebacks

language, play on words

Expand Your Knowledge (Building Background)

Funny Boy is from a popular television series entitled *Room 222*. The show, which appeared on ABC from 1969 to 1973, was set in Walt Whitman High School. Each week the half-hour segments explored, with some humor, many situations that real students and teachers faced and continue to face today. For example, the series dealt with racial integration, drug abuse, and teenage pregnancy.

Enrich Your Reading (Reading Skill)

Stage Directions At the beginning of each scene, this play offers two kinds of stage directions. The directions for the television version include camera directions, like those given in *The Monsters Are Due on Maple Street* (page 157). *Funny Boy* also includes directions labeled *For the stage*, which would be used for a stage version of the play. As you read, notice how the action has been adapted for both kinds of performances.

■ *Author biography on Extend page*

Objectives

■ To understand and analyze a drama

■ To identify exposition and to review the concept of humor

■ To enrich reading by understanding the purposes of stage directions

■ To express understanding of the selection through a choice of writing forms, including a humor column, a character analysis, a letter, and a scenario

Prereading/Motivation

Examine What You Know

Discussion Prompts Can you describe one of your favorite comedian's routines? What makes it so funny?

Expand Your Knowledge

Additional Background With its topical, believable stories and setting in an integrated urban high school, *Room 222* was a departure from typical 1960s sitcoms. Its central characters were Pete Dixon, the black teacher who taught history in room 222; Mr. Kaufman, the Jewish principal; and Alice Johnson, a white student teacher. It won an Emmy Award for outstanding new series of 1969–1970.

Enrich Your Reading

For Alternative Learning Styles Interested students can easily act out parts of this drama, especially since most of the play takes place in classrooms. Other students may prefer to sketch sets for a stage production of the drama.

Thematic Link—Declarations of Independence

Harvey Butcher—friendless, overweight, and disruptive—depends on his joking and clowning to win people over. He uses humor to hide his true feelings until he is finally able to declare his independence by accepting himself and letting others begin to know the real Harvey.

JOURNAL WRITING IDEAS

■ Describe a time when you said or did something that made people laugh. How did you feel?

■ Did you ever have a teacher who helped you in a special way? Relate the experience.

COLLABORATIVE LEARNING OPTIONS

Opportunities for collaborative learning include Speaking . . . Listening . . . Viewing (p. 499), Options for Learning 1, 2, and 4 (p. 511), and Cross-Curricular Projects (p. 511).

ADDITIONAL RESOURCES

Unit Five Resource Book
Reader's Guidesheet, p. 23
Reading Skills, p. 24
Literature Skills, p. 25
Vocabulary Connections, p. 26
Spelling Connections, p. 27
Comprehension and Vocabulary Check Tests, p. 28
Selection Test, pp. 29–30

VOCABULARY PREVIEW

These vocabulary words are defined at the bottom of the selection pages on which they appear.

alienate to cause to be unfriendly

amiably agreeably

bemused confused

engrossed completely occupied

flippant lacking in seriousness

girth the distance around something

insolent disrespectful

militant a person fighting for a cause

relinquish to give up

reverie a daydream

LIMITED ENGLISH PROFICIENCY

■ Use the Reader's Guidesheet, *Unit Five Resource Book*, page 23.

■ You may wish to explain to students some of the puns and idioms in this selection.

★ Text annotations marked with a red star (3, 6, 8, 9, 13, 15, 20, 21, 34, 39) may be particularly helpful for students with limited English proficiency.

TEXT ANNOTATIONS

1. ACTIVE READING: Predict
Invite students to use the cast of characters to make some predictions about what will happen in the play. (*Possible responses: Events will take place in a teachers' cafeteria and in a restaurant; a history class might be a big part of the story, since two history teachers have roles; some action will involve the school paper.*)

2. LITERARY CONCEPT: Stage Directions
For Alternative Learning Styles Ask volunteers to sketch the stage set on the chalkboard. Note that there are three acting areas on the stage—the classroom on the right, the faculty room on the left, and a center area that is used for various settings. Keep the sketch on the board throughout the reading of the play and have volunteers redraw the center area when appropriate.

Funny Boy

ALLAN BURNS

CHARACTERS

Pete Dixon, history teacher

Liz McIntyre, guidance counselor

Seymour Kaufman, principal

Alice Johnson, student teacher

Gordon Walters, history teacher

Bill Cruickshank, newspaper advisor

Waiter, in the restaurant

Serving Lady, in the teachers' cafeteria

Students

Richie

Harvey Butcher

JoEllen

Carl

Neil Kovack

Boy at Banquet

Marge

Al

Patty

Suzy

Richie's Date

Nonspeaking Parts

Four girls in Quad

Students on the Newspaper Staff

1

Exterior of Whitman High School. It is early, before school opens, and there is almost no activity. Interior shot of the teachers' cafeteria. Pete Dixon is eating breakfast and marking papers. Liz McIntyre comes up to the table carrying a tray. On the tray is a small plate containing half a grapefruit.

2

For the stage: The stage is divided into three acting areas. At the right are several rows of classroom chairs—the kind with a writing surface on the right arm—set diagonally facing the center of the back wall. There may be three or four chairs to a row. Facing them, also set diagonally, is a teacher's desk and chair. The teacher will be more or less facing the audience, and the students visible mostly in profile. The walls and the door to the classroom are imaginary.

At left is a group of armchairs, a divan, coffee table and stand with coffee urn and paper cups. This area represents the faculty room.

490   UNIT FIVE   DECLARATIONS OF INDEPENDENCE

Guided Reading for Less-Proficient Students

These questions can help guide students through the reading. Ask each question at the point of the selection where the capital letter and arrow appear in the margin. In addition, you may wish to use appropriate Active Reading annotations.

A. Why might Harvey Butcher be expelled? (*He's disruptive, loud, and rude.*) Recalling
B. What does the principal decide to do about Harvey? (*give him one more chance by moving him*

to Pete's American history class) Recalling
C. How does Harvey behave on his first day in Pete's class? (*He comes late, clowns around, and makes jokes.*) Summarizing
D. How successful is Harvey when he tries to be sociable? (*Girls enjoy his humor but otherwise ignore him; Harvey pokes fun at himself but has no real conversation with others.*) Analyzing

Continued on page 491

The center area will be used for various settings, with slight rearrangement of furniture in view of the audience during the play.

There is no opening or closing curtain. At the start of the play, the center area is occupied by a cafeteria table and some chairs. When the play begins, the house lights go down, and Pete Dixon *takes his place at the table. He begins his business of eating breakfast and marking papers and is joined by* Liz McIntyre.

Liz. Good morning, Pete.

Pete. Hi, Liz. Eating light, I see.

Liz. It's my new diet: half a grapefruit every time you're hungry. *(sits down)* You eat about thirty grapefruits a day.

Pete. Is this the Mayo Clinic Diet or the Weight Watchers Diet?

Liz. I think it's the Grapefruit Growers' Diet.

(Suddenly Mr. Kaufman *looms over their table, carrying a tray loaded with food.)*

Kaufman *(sourly)*. Good morning, Breakfast Clubbers.

Liz. Hi, Mr. Kaufman . . . join us.

Kaufman. Thank you. *(He sits down, eyes the trayful of food, sighs, picks up his glass of juice, and starts to take a sip of it.)*

Kaufman. I hope you all had a pleasant weekend, because it's going to be a terrible week.

Pete. Why do you say that?

Kaufman. I say that because there's a hair in my orange juice. Any time there's a hair in your orange juice the first thing Monday morning, it's going to be a terrible week. *(Making a face, he sets the glass aside,* picks up a spoon, and starts sugaring his coffee. A highly agitated . . . teacher, Mr. Walters, comes up to the table.)

Walters. Mr. Kaufman, I've got to talk to you.

Kaufman. See?

Walters *(nods to* Liz *and* Pete*)*. Miss McIntyre . . . Mr. Dixon. *(back to* Kaufman*)* I am *not* going to go through another week trying to teach a history class with Harvey Butcher in it! Either he goes or I do!

*(*Kaufman *looks at him like it's a tough choice.)*

Kaufman *(glumly)*. Sit down, Mr. Walters.

*(*Walters *sits, almost quivering with annoyance and agitation. It is obvious that he is not one of* Kaufman's *favorite people.)*

Kaufman. Would you care for a glass of juice? *(He indicates the glass with the hair in it.* Pete *and* Liz *stifle smiles.)*

Walters. Thank you, I've had mine already.

Kaufman. Miss McIntyre, are you familiar with Harvey Butcher?

Liz. I'm afraid I am. I've had him in a dozen times for counseling, but I can't get through to him.

Walters. Nobody can.

Pete. I don't believe that.

Walters. That's because you don't know him. He's not in *your* American history class.

*(*Alice Johnson *comes bouncing up to the table, full of her usual enthusiasm. She is carrying a Coke and a doughnut.)*

Alice. Good morning, everybody!

---

3. LITERARY CONCEPT: Humor
Point out that the Mayo Clinic and Weight Watchers have devised weight-reduction diets. Ask why Liz's response is humorous. *(Possible responses: In a quick comeback Liz implies that grapefruit farmers are making a lot of money from all the grapefruit she's eating.)* ★

4. ACTIVE READING: Review
In addition to the statement that Walters "is not one of Kaufman's favorite people," what clues in the stage directions reveal the principal's dislike of Walters? *(Kaufman hesitates when Walters threatens to quit; he "glumly" invites Walters to sit down; he offers Walters the orange juice with a hair in it.)*

5. LITERARY CONCEPT:
Characterization
Ask students what they can **infer** about Pete Dixon from this brief exchange. *(Possible responses: Dixon does not give up on students; he believes he can get through to even the most difficult students.)*

Guided Reading for Less-Proficient Students

Continued from page 490

E. What good effects does Harvey's essay on Benjamin Franklin have? *(Harvey receives a good grade; students and teachers like his humor; because of the essay, Pete Dixon is able to get Harvey the chance to write a humor column.)* Summarizing

F. How has writing the humor column changed Harvey's behavior? *(He gets in trouble much less; he is more serious in class.)* Summarizing

G. Why is the dinner a problem for Harvey? *(He is having trouble getting a date.)* Inferring

H. What surprising announcement does Harvey make? *(He is quitting the paper.)* Recalling

I. What advice does Pete Dixon give Harvey? *(He tells Harvey to give people a chance to become close to him and see him for who he really is.)* Summarizing

Continued on page 492

6. VOCABULARY: Jargon

Refer students to page 93 of this book to review the concept of jargon. Explain that "Readjustment Opportunity" and "Social Adjustment," are examples of administrative jargon. Ask students why Pete feels that these terms are phony. *(Possible response: They make expelling a student sound positive and constructive when it's really just a way to get rid of a troublemaker.)* ★

7. ACTIVE READING: Evaluate

Ask students if they agree with Alice that a school can't give up on a kid, or if they agree with Mr. Kaufman that it is sometimes necessary to expel students. *(Any response is valid.)*

8. VOCABULARY: Idiom

Some students may be unfamiliar with the term "dirty look." Ask a volunteer to define it. *("a look that conveys displeasure with someone; a frown or glare")* Ask why Pete gives Alice a dirty look. *(Possible response: She, only a student teacher, is volunteering him to teach a very difficult student.)* ★

(Liz and Pete greet her with smiles, and Mr. Walters looks annoyed that she is interrupting his business. They shake hands. Alice's is by far the firmer of the two grips.)

Kaufman. Miss McIntyre, do you think we should consider "Ro-ing" Harvey Butcher?

Liz. Yes, I'm afraid I do.

Walters. So do I!

Alice. What's "Ro-ing"?

Liz. RO is the new term for SA.

Alice. SA?

Pete *(disdainful of the term)*. Social Adjustment.

6 **Liz.** RO stands for Readjustment Opportunity.

Pete. Which is just another phony way of saying—

Kaufman. —We're gonna throw him out.

Liz *(to Alice)*. *Transfer* him to another school. Sometimes the shock of being uprooted and thrust into a new environment straightens a kid out.

Pete. But most times it doesn't. It's really admitting we've given up on the kid.

Alice. We can't give up on a kid.

7 **Kaufman.** Occasionally we *do* give up on a kid.

Walters. And if anybody deserves being given up on, it's Harvey Butcher.

Pete. What's his problem?

Walters. If you knew him, you wouldn't have to ask. He's disruptive, insolent, loud, and rude. ◄ A

Kaufman. He's going to get a gold pin for perfect attendance in the Detention Room.

Pete. So what's to be accomplished by sending him to another school? What if he doesn't straighten out there? What then?

Liz. He gets expelled permanently.

Walters. Mr. Dixon, you wouldn't be so ready to stand up for him if he was in *your* history class.

Alice *(her back is up)*. We could handle him in our class, couldn't we, Mr. Dixon?

Pete *(embarrassed)*. Alice, I don't think this is any of our business.

Kaufman *(cuts him off)*. Just hold on a second. I think Miss Johnson has the beginnings of an interesting idea here . . .

(Alice looks pleased.)

Kaufman. Mr. Walters, you want to get rid of Butcher?

Walters. By all means.

Kaufman. And Mr. Dixon would like to give him one more chance. Is that right, Mr. Dixon?

Alice. Right.

(Pete gives her a fast dirty look.)

Kaufman. Well, I'm sure Harvey Butcher's schedule can be rearranged so that he can be in *your* American history class.

Pete *(ironically)*. Don't go to any trouble on my account.

8

| Words to Know and Use | **insolent** (in′ sə lənt) *adj.* boldly showing no respect |

492

Guided Reading for Less-Proficient Students

Continued from page 491

J. How do the other students respond to Harvey when he comes to the dinner alone? *(They welcome him; they say they're glad to see him.)* Recalling

Kaufman. No trouble at all.

(Alice gives Pete a triumphant grin.)

B ▶ Pete (flat). Thank you.

9 | *Dissolve to: Interior of Room 222,* Pete Dixon's *classroom. Close shot of the blackboard. Written on the board in chalk are the following questions: (1) How would Benjamin Franklin fit into present-day America? (2) Describe the problems of the opposing factions at the Constitutional Convention.*

Camera pulls back to a full shot of the class quietly taking the test. Pete *is sitting at his desk, working on some papers. Various shots catching the students in a variety of attitudes as they work on the test:* Richie, Jason, *and others.* Pete *glances at his watch.*

10 | *For the stage: At the end of the last scene, the faculty exit, two stagehands remove the cafeteria table and chairs from the center, and students slide unobtrusively into their seats in the classroom stage right. These actions, and all the others in the play, take place in view of the audience.* Pete Dixon, *instead of exiting with the other faculty, waits for a moment in the center, possibly puts a pipe in his pocket, then crosses to the classroom, pantomimes opening an imaginary door, and sits at his desk. A moment of silence.*

Pete. You have fifteen more minutes.

(They go back to work. Suddenly, the silence is broken by the sound of someone running outside in the hallway. Everyone looks up as the heavy footsteps pass the door, then slow down and come back and slide heavily up to the door. Everyone's attention is riveted on the door, and Pete is beginning to rise from behind his desk when the door is suddenly thrown open and Harvey Butcher bursts in. Harvey is a seventeen-year-old homely, fat boy with a perpetually cherubic expression on his face. He stands in the doorway for a moment, panting exaggeratedly, and the class begins to laugh.)

Pete. Come on in. Don't stand there.

(Harvey nods and starts in, pretending to trip over a nonexistent doorstep, stumbling halfway across the room and dropping his books. The class roars. Harvey smiles pleasantly at Pete, then takes his hand and pumps it.)

11

Harvey. Hello, there, sir—my name is Harvey Butcher and I want to tell you it's an honor and a pleasure to be in your history class, Mr. Mason.

Pete. *Dixon.*

Harvey (points at him, as if to say "You're right!"). Dixon. Well, of course. You can see why I made the mistake. Mason—Dixon . . .

(The class laughs. Pete looks annoyed at Harvey, who bends down and starts walking around stiff-legged, picking up his books, to continued laughter.)

Pete (biting it off). The class is taking a test.

(Harvey, still bent over, looks up, his face a mask of wide-eyed innocence, and pretends to notice the class for the first time.)

Harvey. Oh. (pause, then to class) Best of luck, everyone!

(They laugh again.)

Pete (to class warningly). You've got twelve minutes left.

12. ACTIVE READING: Connect
Ask students what kind of impression Harvey has made on Mr. Dixon. *(Possible response: probably a bad one since Pete seems annoyed by Harvey's antics)* Then ask, What impression has he made on you? Do you like him or dislike him? Why? *(Any response is valid.)*

PORTRAIT OF MOISE KISLING   1916
Amedeo Modigliani   Musée d'Art Moderne,
Villeneuve d'Asq, Donation of Genevieve and
Jean Masurel.

(*The class quickly resumes taking the test.* Harvey, *with* Pete's *cool assistance, finishes picking up his books.*)

Harvey (*stage whisper*). I'm sorry, sir. I did want to make an impression on you.

Pete. Oh, you have. Now just sit down until the bell.

(Harvey *nods and heads down the aisle, making a funny face that* Pete *can't see. There are three empty seats, and* Harvey *stops, as if*

12

unable to decide which one to take, then turns to Pete *questioningly as he points to each of the empty desks.)*

Pete. Take any desk you like.

(Harvey nods, then puts down his books and starts to pick a desk up.)

Pete. What do you think you're doing?

Harvey. You said I could take any one I like. I like this one. *(puts it down)* On second thought, I like that one. *(He starts to pick up another desk, but* Pete *stands up and heads down the aisle.)*

Pete. All right, that's enough.

(Harvey, as if expecting this, nods amiably, *picks up his books, and heads for the* door.)

Pete. Where are you going?

Harvey. To the Detention Room. I thought I'd volunteer and save you the trouble. *(He waves and exits.* Pete *looks after him in amazement, then turns to* Alice.)

Pete. Miss Johnson, take over.

Alice *(rising).* Right. *(She heads for the door.)*

Pete. I mean take over the class.

Alice. Oh.

(Interior of the corridor. Harvey Butcher *is partway down the hall as* Pete *comes out of Room 222, closing the door behind him.)*

Pete. *Mr.* Butcher.

(Harvey stops and turns.)

Harvey. Sir?

(Pete stands there, his hands on his hips, making Harvey *come back to him.* Harvey *walks slowly back, and we can sense him sizing* Pete *up.)*

Harvey. They'll be expecting me in the Detention Room. If I don't show up, they'll think something's happened to me.

Pete. You can send them a note telling them that you're being held prisoner by Mr. Mason in Room 222.

(Harvey looks at Pete, *bemused.)*

Pete. I want to know why you came to class thirty minutes late. I know you've got a good explanation.

Harvey. I do? I'd sure like to hear it, then.

Pete. I'll tell you what—you go back in the classroom and think up a good excuse that will satisfy both of us. You can make up the test during lunch.

(Pete opens the door and motions him in. Interior shot of Room 222 as the door opens and Harvey *reenters, followed by* Pete. Harvey, *as he enters, grasps his own collar from behind, like he's being carried in by the scruff of the neck, and wears a* hangdog *expression that gets an immediate laugh from the class.* Pete *just watches,* deadpan,[1] *as* Harvey, *still holding his collar, goes down the aisle and deposits himself in an empty seat with a large thud. Close-up of* Alice *and* Pete *as she* relinquishes *the chair behind the desk to him.)* ◄ C

_____

1. **deadpan:** with a face that shows no emotion.

495

13. LITERARY CONCEPT: Humor
Ask students how Harvey is making a play on words. *(Harvey plays on the double meaning of "Take any desk you like"; Pete means "Sit at any desk you like," but Harvey pretends to think that take means "carry away.")* ★

14. ACTIVE READING: Evaluate
Ask students if they think Harvey should be punished for being late and disruptive. *(Possible responses: Yes, because he has broken the rules; no, because detention or whatever would just be more of the same for him and nothing would change.)*

15. VOCABULARY: Definition
For Alternative Learning Styles You may wish to have a pair of students demonstrate the meaning of *hangdog* by having them role-play Pete and Harvey in this scene. Then elicit a definition of *hangdog* from the class. *("guilty-looking," "ashamed")* ★

496

16. CULTURAL SIDELIGHT
Jackie Gleason (1916–1987) was a plump comedian whose two most popular television series were *The Jackie Gleason Show*, a variety show, and *The Honeymooners*, a situation comedy. As the "Poor Soul," Gleason wore shabby clothes and evoked sympathy with his shy, childlike manner. In his "away-we-go" routine, Gleason would cry, "And a-WAY we GO!" before rushing into the wings of the stage.

17. LITERARY CONCEPT: Humor
Challenge students to identify the various kinds of humor that Harvey uses in this scene. (*Possible responses: He uses exaggeration when he says he takes up two seats; he uses sarcasm in his remark about the girls' "fascinating" conversation, since they aren't saying anything; he combines a comic impression with slapstick in his "away-we-go" getaway.*)

18. LITERARY CONCEPT: Character
What has the scene with the group of girls and the scene with JoEllen revealed about Harvey? (*Possible responses: He isn't popular; he can't relax and talk naturally with his classmates; he uses humor to cover up his discomfort with people; he likes JoEllen.*)

Alice (*whispers encouragingly*). I think you're starting to make progress with him!

(*Pete regards her with an expression of disbelief.*)

Exterior of school quadrangle that afternoon. Small knots of students cluster around, lingering after school, chatting, horsing around, laughing. Several couples sit quietly, holding hands, saying little. Harvey Butcher comes out of the building, looking around, then crosses to a group of girls and, doing a Jackie Gleason "Poor Soul,"[2] walks up to them. He takes a pair of tickets out of his pocket and holds them up.

16

For the stage: The quadrangle is suggested by the action center stage, where some boys may be tossing a football; other students are sitting on benches which they have brought in.

Harvey. I've got two tickets for *Hello Dolly* Friday night.

(*No one shows the slightest interest in the fact.*)

Harvey. The reason I've got two tickets is that I take up two seats.

(*The girls laugh. Harvey stands there, as if waiting for someone to say something that will include him in their conversation, but no one does.*)

17

Harvey. Boy, you gotta be fast to keep up with all this fascinating conversation!

(*He turns and does an "away-we-go!" getaway.[3] As soon as he does, the group of girls clusters back together, chattering away. This fact is not lost on Harvey. He looks around the quadrangle for a friendly face. A shot of*

JoEllen, *an extremely fresh-faced, pretty girl. JoEllen is standing alone, books cradled in her arms, waiting for someone. Harvey comes up to her. We are acutely aware of Harvey's lack of physical attractiveness when he isn't acting funny—and around JoEllen he doesn't act funny.*)

Harvey. Hi, JoEllen.

JoEllen. Hi, Harvey.

Harvey. How did things go in Walters's history class without me today?

JoEllen (*smiles*). It sure was quiet. We missed you.

Harvey. I bet Walters didn't. (*enthusiastically*) Boy, remember the time ole Walters came into class late—

(*Carl, a good-looking boy, joins them. He ignores Harvey.*)

Carl. Let's go, JoEllen. Everybody's waiting.

JoEllen. OK. (*starts off, then stops, remembering Harvey*) So long, Harv. We'll sure miss you in history. (*She runs after Carl.*)

Harvey (*to self*). Sure you will.

(*Close shot of Harvey. He's embarrassed, fearing other students may have witnessed the previous scene. Liz and Pete approach.*)

18

Liz. Hello, Harvey.

Harvey (*coming on strong*). Hi folks . . . Look, I'd like to stay and spend a little time with you people, but I have to

---

2. **Jackie Gleason "Poor Soul":** refers to a timid, long-suffering character created by the comedian Jackie Gleason in the 1950s.

3. **"away-we-go!" getaway:** refers to Jackie Gleason's exaggerated movements when leaving a stage.

Looking at Style

To discuss Allan Burns's writing style in *Funny Boy*, call attention to such dialogue as this:

■ **Harvey.** Boy, you gotta be fast to keep up with all this fascinating conversation!
■ **Harvey.** Boy, remember the time ole Walters came into class late—
■ **JoEllen.** So long, Harv. We'll sure miss you in history.
■ **Harvey.** Sure you will.

Use these activities for discussing Burns's style:

1. What unusual spellings do you notice? What incorrect usage?
2. How long are the sentences? What interjection is used? What nickname?
3. Is this dialogue realistic? In what ways is it like the speech in a typical high school?
4. Write some dialogue that reflects the way you and your classmates speak.

spread myself around, you know—I'm very big around here. I'm very big around *everywhere,* here . . . here . . . and here . . . *(indicating his girth)* Oh well, everybody loves a fat boy, right? *(He spins and walks quickly away, doing a stiff-legged funny walk.)*

Liz. Works hard at it, doesn't he?

Pete *(thoughtfully)*. He's got energy all right. I'd sure like to do something with it.

(Close shot of Pete *watching* Harvey *go, thinking.)*

Interior of Room 222, next day. Pete *is going around the room, passing out the graded essay tests. The students react typically.* Pete *finishes passing them out and heads back to the front of the room.*

For the stage: At the end of the last scene, the actors exit, taking benches and props with them, and students slide quietly into their classroom seats at right as Pete *enters with the tests.*

Harvey *(raising hand)*. Hey, where's *my* test? Did you burn it?

(The class laughs, and Pete *grins.)*

Pete. No, I thought I'd give everybody a treat this morning and read yours aloud. *(picks it up)* On second thought, why don't you read it yourself?

(The class applauds and cheers. Harvey *modestly accedes to their wishes and goes to the head of the class, throwing kisses and bowing. He takes the paper* Pete *is holding out to him.)*

Harvey *(reacts)*. What's this—a B minus? This paper is an F if I ever saw one—and I've seen quite a few.

(laughter.)

Pete *(smiles)*. Sorry to bring up your average, Harvey, but the grade stands. Read, please. *(to class)* As you recall, the question was to show how Benjamin Franklin would fit into today's society. *(He nods to* Harvey.)

Harvey *(reads)*. Fade in The Loan Department of the Liberty Bell Savings and Loan. The vice-president glances up from his desk and sees a man with shoulder-length hair and rectangular glasses standing at the counter. *(pantomimes pushing down intercom button.)* "I thought I said no hippies in here."

(The class laughs.)

Harvey. He's my next appointment? OK, send him in—but have the guard keep an eye on him. *(pantomimes watching* Franklin *come in, then shakes hands)* Welcome to Liberty Bell, Mr. Franklin. That's a nice kite you're carrying. Is there any particular reason you've got that key tied to the string? *(pause)* You're waiting for the next thunderstorm so you can go out and fly it. *(pantomimes pushing down intercom again)* Have the guard move down this way in case I need him. *(laughter from class)* Well, Mr. Franklin, what can we do for you? *(pause)* You're applying for a loan so you can keep publishing your almanac? May I have your application form, please? *(looks at it)* "Printer,

19. LITERARY CONCEPT: Humor
Both Harvey and Pete use irony to be funny in this exchange. Ask students to explain how. *(Possible responses: Harvey knows that his classmates will laugh when he says his paper deserves an F instead of a B minus, because this behavior is totally unexpected from a student. Similarly, it is humorous for Pete to apologize for bringing up Harvey's average, since teachers are expected to want their students to improve.)*

20. CULTURAL SIDELIGHT
Hippies were young people in the 1960s who rejected middle-class values and lifestyles. They defied dress codes, grew their hair long, and often wore glasses with steel rims or no rims; thus, they looked somewhat like Benjamin Franklin. ★

21. HISTORICAL SIDELIGHT
In his famous 1752 experiment, Benjamin Franklin proved that lightning was electric. During a thunderstorm, Franklin flew a kite with a key attached to the end of the string. Lightning struck the kite and traveled down the string to the key, where it created a spark. This experiment led Franklin to invent the lightning rod. Franklin published *Poor Richard's Almanack,* a yearly publication that was famous for such sayings as "A penny saved is a penny earned." ★

Words to Know and Use | **girth** (gᵘrth) *n.* the distance around something

497

22. LITERARY CONCEPT: Drama
Ask students how the action of the play is carried over from the preceding scene to the next one. *(Possible response: After the students in the classroom laugh over Harvey's paper, the teachers in the faculty room are shown laughing over the same paper.)*

23. ACTIVE READING: Evaluate
Have students review Walters's and Pete's argument. Then ask them who they think is right, and why. *(Any response is valid.)*

writer, inventor, philosopher, statesman, and scientist." *(pause)* Can't you hold a *job*, Mr. Franklin?

(The class roars its appreciation.)

Cut to: Interior of teachers' lounge. Pete is reading aloud from Harvey's paper as Alice, Liz, Mr. Walters, and Bill Cruickshank listen. Laughter.

For the stage: The laughter in the classroom scene, stage right, continues as the laughter in the faculty room, stage left, begins. Pete Dixon leaves the classroom and joins the group in the faculty room. Then the students disappear from the classroom as Pete reads from Harvey's paper.

Pete. You say you write wise sayings? Let's see. *(reads)* "A penny saved is a penny earned." *(pause)* Make that "A *dollar* saved is a dollar earned . . . at Liberty Bell Savings and Loan," and we've got a deal.

(They all laugh.)

Liz. That's funny. I like it.

Walters *(smiling)*. Who in the world wrote that? It's very good.

Pete *(pause)*. Harvey Butcher.

(Walters's smile fades. Alice mugs[4] at him triumphantly. He grabs the paper out of Pete's hand and looks at it.)

Walters *(accusingly)*. You gave him a B minus.

Pete. Why not?

Walters *(sputtering)*. Well, *because . . .* that's not a proper essay! He's ridiculing the assignment.

(Bill Cruickshank reaches out and takes the paper from him and peruses it.)

Pete *(shrugs)*. He's got most of the facts in there. It shows as much thought as some of the essays I gave A's. To write that, he had to know the subject.

Walters *(huffily)*. Well, it's *your* business if you want to encourage that sort of thing.

(Alice looks apoplectic,[5] but Pete smiles and shakes his head as Walters fussily begins correcting papers. Pete turns to Cruickshank, who is still reading Harvey's essay.)

Pete. What do you think, Bill?

Cruickshank. If I were this kid's creative writing teacher, I'd give him an A.

(Alice wrinkles her nose in Walters's direction.)

Pete. I'm glad to hear you say that. I'd like you to offer him a job on the school paper.

Cruickshank *(taken aback)*. Now wait a minute . . .

Pete. Your paper hasn't had a humor column for three years. Harvey Butcher could do one for you.

Cruickshank. Uh uh. I'm having enough problems *without* any humor column.

Liz. What kind of problems?

Cruickshank. Once there was a time when the kids who ran the high school newspaper were cooperative, proadministration types who wrote daring editorials about things like school spirit and litterbugs.

---

4. **mugs**: makes a face at.
5. **apoplectic** (ap′ ə plek′ tik): red-faced and speechless with anger.

PORTRAIT OF HENRI LAURENS   1915   Amedeo Modigliani   Private collection.

Speaking . . . Listening . . . Viewing

Viewing Show students one or more of these videos to help them grasp the different types of humor listed on page 489:

- ■ "Who's on First?" from *The Best of Abbott and Costello Live* (Warner Home Video)
- ■ an episode of *I Love Lucy* (Fox Video)
- ■ an episode of *The Honeymooners* (MPI Home Video)

You may wish to hold a class discussion that focuses on the following questions:

1. What kinds of humor did you see in each performance? Describe your favorites.

2. What special abilities or skills did each comedian need in the performances you've seen?

3. Was there anything old-fashioned about the language or the subject matter? Explain.

24. ACTIVE READING: Connect
Invite students to share their personal experiences and opinions of how a teacher's attitude toward students can make a difference in the students' performance.

25. LANGUAGE: Nonstandard English
Have students find examples of Richie's and Neil's nonstandard language *("This here is Neil"; "gotta")* and slang. *("outta sight")* Ask students what this informal language adds to the drama. *(Possible responses: It makes the dialogue and characters seem realistic; the slang sets the drama in a particular time and place.)* Have students suggest a current equivalent for "outta sight."

26. LITERARY CONCEPT: Character
Have students contrast Richie with Neil Kovack, the editor. *(Possible responses: Richie loves Harvey's humor, but Neil remains unresponsive; Richie is happy-go-lucky, whereas Neil is serious and responsible and may be challenging Harvey to prove himself.)*

But now . . . *now* I've got the rebels, the <u>militants</u>, the free-speechers. I spend most of my time trying to find dirty words they conceal in the backgrounds of the drawings.

Pete *(grinning).* You missed a beauty last week.

Cruickshank. Thanks for reminding me. They crossed me up and made it so big I missed it with my magnifying glass.

Pete *(holding up* Harvey's *paper).* Bill, the kid who wrote this needs help. He's gonna get thrown out of this school unless he shapes up—but he doesn't figure there's anything to shape up *for.* I want to give him something. That column.

Walters *(looks up from his papers).* He isn't worth the trouble, believe me.

Cruickshank *(looks at* Walters, *then at* Pete*).* OK, I'll do it.

Pete *(smiles).* Hey, I must be more persuasive than I thought!

Cruickshank. It wasn't you that sold me. *(nods toward* Walters*)* It was him.

Interior of The Whitman Blue and Gold *office. Richie is introducing* Harvey *around. As* Cruickshank *noted, the staffers are, for the most part, an anarchistic-looking[6] bunch.* Neil Kovack, *an intense-looking type with long hair, comes up with some pages of copy. He looks inquiringly at* Harvey.

For the stage: This scene takes place in center stage. The characters, perhaps assisted by one or two stagehands, will bring in their own props—*bulletin board, table, chairs, typewriter, painting easel.*

Richie. Hey, Neil, this is Harvey Butcher. This here is Neil Kovack, our editor. *(to* Neil*)* Wait'll you read this man's stuff—he's outta sight!

Neil *(nods).* Think of a name for your column. I gotta have a masthead[7] made up.

Harvey. A name. How about "Fred"?

(Richie breaks up.)

Neil. Take any desk that's empty. I need five hundred words minimum from you by Thursday.

Harvey. I'd better get to work, then—I only *know* four hundred words.

(Richie cracks up again, but Neil *doesn't.)*

Harvey *(to* Richie*).* Stick around, Baby—I think I'm gonna need your support. *(He crosses to an empty desk with a typewriter on it. A fairly cute girl is standing at a table a few feet away doing paste-up work[8] using rubber cement and a brush. Harvey keeps looking at her as he arranges his gear, hoping to catch her eye. He finally does, but she just looks at him blankly.)*

Harvey. I've been watching you work.

Marge. So?

---

6. anarchistic-looking (an′ ər kis′ tik): looking like people who rebel against authority and the rules of society.
7. masthead: here, the headline that appears above each installment of a newspaper column.
8. paste-up work: the arranging and glueing of text, artwork, and photographs onto sheets of paper as a guide for a printer.

Words to Know and Use
militant (mil′ i tənt) *n.* a person fighting for a cause

Harvey (*trying to kid her*). Well, it's a pleasure to watch someone who does their job really well. I mean, the graceful way you dip your brush into that gunk and then . . . (*pantomimes*) . . . stroke it on. It's beautiful.

(*The girl stares at him hostilely. This is a person with no sense of humor. Harvey realizes she's not digging him, which makes him try too hard.*)

Harvey. Who taught you that backhand? Pancho Gonzales?[9]

Marge. You know, we have a lot of work to do around here. We don't need any clowns. (*She plops her brush angrily into the jar of glue and walks away.*)

27 **Harvey.** I wasn't trying—(*He looks after her helplessly, realizing he's <u>alienated</u> her for keeps, a look of misery on his face. Neil strolls over to him.*)

Neil (*notes Harvey's expression*). For a humor columnist, you certainly don't look very happy.

28 **Harvey.** That's the way it is with us funny guys sometimes—all the laughter and gaiety is *inside*. (*He picks up some typing paper and begins to wind it into his typewriter sadly. Fade out.*)

Fade in: Interior of Mr. Kaufman's *office.* Mr. Kaufman *is reading* The Whitman Blue and Gold *and wearing a strange expression [for him]: a smile. Not only that, he is chuckling.* Pete Dixon *sticks his head in the open door.*

For the stage: This scene takes place stage left in the faculty lounge.

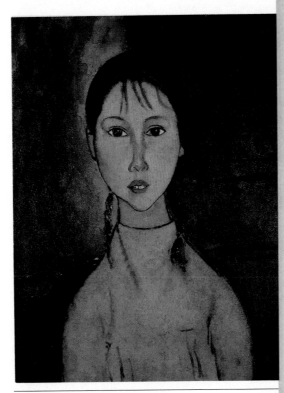

GIRL WITH PIGTAILS 1918 Amedeo Modigliani
The Nagoya City Art Museum.

Pete. You got a minute for the junior class advisor?

(*Kaufman waves him in but continues to read, smiling.*)

Kaufman. Did you read this Butcher kid's column in *The Blue and Gold?*

Pete (*nods*). Pretty funny stuff.

---

9. **Pancho Gonzales** (pän′ chō gən zä′ ləz) Richard Alonzo Gonzales, a U.S. professional tennis player who dominated the sport in the 1950s.

501

27. LITERARY CONCEPT: Drama
Have students discuss the importance of this dialogue between Marge and Harvey. (*Possible responses: It reminds us that Harvey has big problems relating to people; it suggests that his troubles aren't over.*)

28. LITERARY CONCEPT: Irony
Call on volunteers to explain why Harvey's statement here is ironic. (*Possible response: Harvey says his happiness is on the inside, but inside he is really unhappy.*)

29. ACTIVE READING: Review
Ask students to **infer** what has happened since the last scene ended. (*Possible response: The article Harvey was just starting to work on in the last scene has been published in the paper, and it's making Kaufman chuckle.*)

Art Note

This study, *Girl with Pigtails*, is more realistic than most Modigliani portraits. The brush strokes are unusually smooth and finished, and the colors are soft. In this painting the artist captured a fleeting expression on the face of a girl; the expression is serious, yet young and innocent. *Compare this portrait with the one on page 504. How are they alike? different?*

LITERARY CONCEPT: Humor
Ask students what kind of humor Harvey uses in the excerpt from his column that Kaufman reads. If necessary, refer students to page 489. *(Possible responses: dry, sarcastic humor; a joke on current events in the form of the bad lunchroom food; a comic impression in the style of a wire-service news report)*

31. ACTIVE READING: Review
Ask students to **infer** what the principal has found hidden in the drawing. *(a dirty word)*

For Alternative Learning Styles Invite volunteers to use the stage directions to pantomime Kaufman's discovery and reaction.

32. LITERARY CONCEPT: Character
Call on individuals to tell what this scene reveals about Harvey. How is he changing? *(Possible responses: He is becoming more responsible; the newspaper column is an outlet for his humor, so he takes his classwork more seriously.)*

30

Kaufman. Listen to this. *(reads)* "Dateline: Whitman High School, October third. Militant students took over the school cafeteria today but gave up when the dietician threatened to serve them lunch . . ."

Pete *(smiling)*. Now, that's what I call social satire.

Kaufman. That's what *I* call public service. Pete, I'm happy to report that Harvey's attendance in the Detention Room has dropped off about seventy-five percent.

Pete. I'm glad to hear it. Maybe he just needed a nudge in the right direction. *(pause)* I came in to get your OK to have another Junior Class Achievement Dinner. I want to take the juniors who work on *The Blue and Gold* this time.

Kaufman. I don't know, Pete. Those things are getting expensive.

Pete. Look, you let me take the juniors on the football team . . . the basketball team . . . the class officers and club presidents. The kids on the paper work just as hard.

Kaufman. Maybe you could have it here . . . use the teachers' cafeteria.

Pete. This is supposed to be a reward, not a punishment.

Kaufman. You could tell 'em you're going to have it in the cafeteria and then call it off at the last minute. That would seem like a reward, wouldn't it? *(pause)* Go ahead . . . just don't spend too much.

(Pete grins and exits as Kaufman picks up the issue of the school paper and resumes reading, smiling and chuckling. On the side of the paper facing the camera, there is a large editorial-type drawing, very detailed. Kaufman finishes reading Harvey's column, still smil-

ing, and turns the paper over so that he is looking at the drawing. He stares at it for a minute, then the smile fades from his lips. He picks up a pair of reading glasses and, holding them like a magnifying glass, scans the drawing, prepared for the worst. The expression on his face tells us when he has found it. In fact, it's even worse than he expected.)

31

Interior of Room 222. Pete *is roaming around the room, throwing questions.*

For the stage: This scene takes place in the classroom, stage right.

Pete. What do you mean President Washington was unpopular? Wasn't he called the father of our country?

Al. Yes, but there sure were a lot of people who didn't agree with him, like what he said in his farewell address.

Pete. Well, what did he say . . . Harvey?

Harvey. Well . . . *(pause)* Mainly he spoke about partisanship[10] in America, sectionalism, we should avoid foreign entanglements.

(The class registers disappointment at Harvey's answer.)

32

Harvey *(to class at large)*. In case you're all wondering why the straight answer, I don't have time for the funny stuff anymore. I mean, I'm not gonna give you any of my material free when I can use it in my column.

◀ **F**

(The bell rings, and the class starts to break.)

Pete. Read Chapter Sixteen tonight.

---

10. partisanship (pärt′ i zən ship′): support of a particular idea or political party.

(As they file out, Harvey passes Pete's desk.)

Pete. Funny column yesterday. Even Mr. Kaufman liked it.

Harvey. I guess I'm gonna have to aim a little higher, then. *(He starts to go.)*

Pete. Harvey?

(Harvey turns.)

Pete. We're having a dinner Friday for the juniors on *The Blue and Gold* staff. Maybe you can make it.

Harvey *(pleased)*. Sure. Sure, I'd like that.

Pete. It's at Emilio's Restaurant. Bring a date if you want.

33

(Harvey's face suddenly clouds over.)

Harvey *(numbly)*. A date . . .

Interior of school cafeteria. Harvey *is sitting alone at a rectangular table for eight. A sort of average-looking girl named* Patty Muller *comes up to the other end of the table carrying a tray.*

For the stage: At the end of the last scene, Pete Dixon *exits, leaving* Harvey *alone in the classroom.* Harvey *remains, absorbed in thought. Meanwhile, stagehands are setting the center stage for the next scene. They bring in a table and chairs and a tray with* Harvey's *lunch. When the stage is ready,* Harvey *moves to the table and begins to eat.* Patty Muller *enters.*

Patty *(indicating chair)*. Is this seat taken?

Harvey *(putting her on)*. I've been saving it for you.

(Patty nods and takes her lunch off the tray, puts the tray on the stacker, then sits down

and starts to eat. As she eats her lunch at the other end of the table, she takes out a copy of The Blue and Gold *and reads. Close shot of* Harvey, *looking at her furtively. He screws up enough courage to brazen it out.)*

34

Harvey. You're in Mr. Dixon's first-period history, aren't you?

Patty *(looks up, surprised)*. Yes.

Harvey. So am I.

Patty. I know. You're Harvey Butcher.

Harvey *(points at her)*. Patty Muller.

Patty *(nods)*. You're very funny in class.

(Harvey grins deprecatingly[11] and shrugs. There is a small, awkward silence. Small beads of perspiration appear on Harvey's *forehead.)*

35

Patty *(indicating newspaper)*. Your new column is hysterical. I mean, everybody is talking about how funny it is.

Harvey. Thank you. *(long pause, then haltingly)* Mr. Dixon is having a dinner for the juniors who are on the staff of the paper and I was wondering—

(Another girl, Suzy, comes up with her tray and plops down next to Patty.*)*

Suzy. Hi, Patty, did Norman get around to asking you to the party Friday?

Patty. *Finally.* I was sure I was gonna end up sitting home Friday night with nothing to do.

(Harvey quickly resumes eating his lunch.)

---

11. deprecatingly (dep′ rə kāt′ iŋ lē): in a way that mocks himself.

33. ACTIVE READING: Predict
Ask students to predict how this new complication—Harvey's needing a date—will be resolved. *(Any response is valid.)*

34. VOCABULARY: Definitions
Have students use **context clues** and **prior knowledge** to determine that *furtively* means "secretly," *screws up enough courage* means "gathers courage with difficulty," and *brazen it out* means "behave boldly while concealing one's shame or fear." ★

35. ACTIVE READING: Connect
Ask students to describe the nervousness they feel when trying to make a new friend or inviting someone to a party or special event.

PORTRAIT OF BEATRICE   1916   Amedeo Modigliani
Private collection.

Interior of a phone booth that afternoon. Harvey *is perspiring profusely as he dials the phone with fear-numbed fingers. After two rings, he nearly hangs up but forces himself not to. After a pause, we hear a phone being answered.*

For the stage: The booth is imaginary, and Harvey *makes his calls in pantomime down right near the footlights. Meanwhile, other actors and stagehands will be changing the set center stage, removing the cafeteria table and replacing the equipment for the newspaper office. The movement behind* Harvey *must be* carefully timed so that none of his telephone dialogue will be lost. In pantomime, Harvey inserts a coin in the imaginary telephone and dials.*

Harvey. Hello, Connie . . . this is Harvey Butcher. *(pause)* In your third-period English class . . . *(pause)* I'm the funny guy. *(another pause)* . . . Kind of heavy. *(pause)* Uh, Connie . . . I'll tell you why I'm calling. You see, Mr. Dixon is taking the juniors on the staff of *The Blue and Gold* to dinner on Friday and . . . uh . . . well, what I was wondering is . . . if you're not doing anything Friday night— what? *(He listens, then:)* Oh. Well, sure . . . I mean, hair does have to be washed, doesn't it? Bye. *(Harvey is on the phone again.)*

Harvey *(into phone, very fast)*. Hello, Darlene Frank of Claymore Avenue? This is "The Question Man"—answer this question correctly and win a fabulous prize! Ready? All right then, here's the question: Do you have a date Friday night? *(pause)* No? Then you win . . . Miss Frank . . . an all-expenses-paid night on the town with Harvey Butcher, the well-known columnist for *The Whitman Blue and Gold.* How about that? *(pause)* Yeah, this is Harvey. Can you make it? *(listens, nodding)* Your hair . . . I understand. *(faking brightness)* Well, in that case, Darlene, you don't win the big prize, but we're sending you a consolation prize of a bottle of shampoo.

Interior of The Blue and Gold *office. The usual "getting-out-the-paper" activity is in progress as* Harvey *enters. He is very high-*

strung and hypertense and wears some sort of a manic grin.

For the stage: The action takes place center stage in the area prepared during the last scene.

39

Harvey. Hello, fellow staffers of *The Daily Planet!* Clark Kent here . . . mild-mannered humor columnist . . . who is, in reality . . . *(puffs out chest and holds out arms in Superman pose)* . . . Superfat! *(He lets out his breath, and his stomach swells over his belt. He gets a couple of laughs, but everybody goes back to work. Harvey cannot stop; he goes pacing around the room.)*

Harvey. Has anyone seen Lois Lane? Ah, there you are! *(He crosses to the humorless girl doing paste-up.)*

Harvey. I'm terribly sorry, Lois—I know you've had your heart set on me taking you to that banquet Friday night, but I've got to wash my hair.

(The girl looks at him oddly. Neil Kovack comes up.)

Neil. I need this week's column from you, Harvey.

Harvey. Ah, yes! My column. *(He opens his notebook and hands Neil some pages.)*

H ▶ Harvey. Here it is, little editor—and I hope you enjoy it, because it's my last one. *(He pats Neil on the shoulder and heads for the door. When he reaches the threshold, he strikes a Superman-taking-off pose.)*

Harvey. Up, up . . . and away! *(His arms extended, he does a flying leap out the door.)*

Interior of Room 222. Pete is sitting at his desk grading papers when Harvey suddenly appears in the open door. Pete looks up.

For the stage: At the end of the last scene, the news staff (except Harvey) exit, taking their equipment with them and leaving the center stage bare. Harvey, after his "Up, up . . . and away!" walks slowly toward the footlights, engrossed in thought. Meanwhile, Pete Dixon has taken his place at his desk in the classroom. Harvey enters the area. When Harvey and Pete exit from the classroom later in the scene, they move to center stage.

Harvey. Brace yourself, Mr. Dixon; your big dinner Friday night is going to be a major bomb.

Pete. Oh?

Harvey. That's right. I'm not going to be there.

Pete. Why not?

Harvey. Because I'm not on *The Blue and Gold* anymore. I just quit. *(He exits. Pete gets up and follows him out the door. Interior shot of the corridor. Except for Harvey, it is deserted when Pete comes out of the room.)*

40

Pete. Harvey? *(He goes after him quickly. Harvey stops, turns, and looks at Pete innocently.)*

Pete. Why?

Words to Know and Use | **engrossed** (en grōst′) *adj.* completely occupied; absorbed **engross** *v.*

505

---

39. ACTIVE READING: Review
Ask a volunteer to explain the Superman references. *(The Daily Planet is a newspaper in the comic book; Superman masquerades as Clark Kent, a "mild-mannered" reporter; Lois Lane is his girlfriend.)* ★

40. ACTIVE READING: Review
Urge students to explain why Harvey tells Pete Dixon of his decision. *(Possible responses: Harvey is being courteous, since Dixon got him on the paper and invited him to the dinner; Harvey hopes that Pete will talk him out of quitting.)* Then have students give their opinions of Harvey's quitting the paper. Is it a childish thing to do, or is it reasonable? *(Any response is valid.)*

41. LITERARY CONCEPT: Character
Ask students why Pete refuses to smile at Harvey's joke. What does his not smiling show about him? *(Possible responses: Pete is concerned; Pete is annoyed that he got Harvey the job and now Harvey's quitting; Pete wants Harvey to be serious instead of just laughing trouble off.)*

42. LITERARY CONCEPT: Climax
Ask students why Harvey's crying could be the climax of the play. *(Possible responses: It is the most emotional moment; Harvey's feelings of rejection have reached a crisis; Harvey is being honest about his feelings for the first time.)*

43. LITERARY CONCEPT: Theme
Suggest that volunteers state Pete's advice as a theme of the play. *(Possible response: If we accept and like ourselves, other people will accept and like us too.)*

Harvey. Look, I quit, that's all. What's the difference whether I write a crummy column or not?

(Pete *looks at him, trying to read his mood.*)

Pete. Why come and tell me, then—if it doesn't make any difference?

Harvey. I just thought you had a right to know, since it was your idea in the first place.

Pete. What happened, Harvey?

Harvey. Nothing happened. Why are you trying to make a big deal out of it?

Pete. I'm not—I'm just interested in knowing why this sudden change of attitude.

Harvey. Well, you see, it's this way—I've been offered this better job, see . . . Humor editor for *The National Geographic.* (Pete *doesn't smile.*) Oh, come on, sir . . . that deserves at least a little smile, doesn't it? Just a teeny little . . . *(With his fingers he pushes the corner of his own mouth into a smile.)*

Pete. You can still come Friday night if you want to. I figure the columns you've written are worth the price of dinner for two.

Harvey. Ah, well, you see . . . now that's another problem. I haven't been able to find the girl to bring to that affair who measures up to my own incredibly high standards.

Pete *(understanding).* You don't have to bring a date, Harvey.

Harvey. You're not suggesting, sir . . . Mr. Dixon, sir . . . that I haven't been able to get a date, are you, sir?

Pete. Harvey, it just isn't necessary . . .

Harvey *(cuts in).* Isn't necessary? Of course it's necessary! I don't want you going around with the impression that I can't get a date! Fat people *do* date, sir. You see, that's one of the great things about a school the size of Whitman—no matter how fat and homely you are, there's always somebody bad enough to go out with you. *(He's trying to make the whole thing sound funny and flippant, but his tear ducts betray him. Harvey turns his head so that Pete can't see the tears.)*

Pete. Harvey.

Harvey. Mr. Dixon . . . *please* . . . (Harvey *stands there, humiliated, wiping away the tears, unable to face* Pete.)

Harvey. I'm *not* gonna be the only one there without a date!

Pete *(gently).* Hey . . . would it really be so bad?

(His back still turned. Harvey *nods his head emphatically.*)

Pete. Isn't what you're doing to yourself worse? Isn't *this* worse?

(Harvey *says nothing.*)

Pete. Harvey, give yourself a chance. *(pause)* Try accepting yourself as you are . . . and maybe other people will.

Harvey. Easy to say.

Pete *(with the heat of conviction).* I *know* it's not easy. But it's up to you. Anybody tries to make contact . . . you give 'em a joke . . . you make 'em laugh . . . but you

---

don't let anybody get close . . . (pause) Try giving people a chance. Let 'em know who you really are!

(Shot of Harvey's face as Pete stands behind him trying to reach him. The camera moves in for a close shot.)

Interior of banquet room, Friday night. The junior-class members of The Blue and Gold staff and their dates are noisily assembled in a typical banquet room in a small Italian restaurant. Pete and Liz are sitting together at one end of the table. A boy, Neil, is staring at the menu as a waiter awaits his order.

For the stage: In center stage, actors and stagehands bring on a large restaurant table with chairs and settings for nine people. There is an empty seat next to Marge. When the table is ready, the actors take their seats.

Neil. What's this? Veal piccolini?

Waiter. That's thin slices of veal sauteed in Marsala wine . . . covered with prosciutto ham and mozzarella cheese.

Neil (shakes his head). I don't like veal.

(Camera pans to Richie and his date. Richie is staring at the menu.)

Richie (to date). What's a sweetbread?

Richie's Date. Beats me.

Richie. Hey, Mr. Dixon. What's a sweetbread?

Pete. A sweetbread? Well, it's a . . . (tries to describe it with his hands) . . . they're . . . (to Liz) What's a sweetbread?

Liz (no hesitation). Sweetbreads are the thymus glands of a young calf.

(A disgusted look crosses everyone's face.)

Richie. I think I'll have a pizza. (suddenly looks up) Hey, look who's here!

(Angle shot of doorway. Harvey Butcher is standing there a bit self-consciously. Everyone turns and looks and sees Harvey. He is greeted with laughs and cheers and assorted cries of "Harvey!" . . . "Hey, man" . . . "We didn't think you were coming," and so on. Harvey is all dressed up and looks about ninety-five percent better than we have ever seen him look. Grinning, he grabs an extra chair and pushes it toward the table as room is made for him. Close-up of Harvey. As he sits down, he glances down the table toward Pete. Pete catches Harvey's glance and gives him a smile of encouragement. As Harvey sits there, looking around, slightly ill at ease, everyone is expectant, waiting for him to say something funny.)

Boy's Voice. Hey, Harvey . . . how come you're late?

(A couple of laughs, anticipating his answer . . . Harvey looks around at the faces . . .)

Harvey (long pause). I almost didn't come at all . . . because I couldn't get a date.

(Camera moves to Pete and Liz. Pete turns and looks at Harvey; Liz looks pained by his candid admission. Shot of various students as they react to Harvey's admission, not with pity or embarrassment, but with a sort of respect for his honesty . . .)

Harvey. But somebody told me I should . . . (He glances over at Pete.) I really wanted to come anyway . . . I like doing the column . . . and I like being on the staff . . . with everybody . . . so I decided to come tonight . . .

44

ENCOURAGING INDEPENDENT READING

The Cat Ate My Gymsuit, novel by Paula Danziger

One Fat Summer, novel by Robert Lipsyte

Popcorn Days and Buttermilk Nights, novel by Gary Paulsen.

(The room is very quiet . . . All the kids watching Harvey *. . .)*

45 **Marge.** We're glad you did . . .

(Others join in agreeing. Shot of Harvey *looking at* Pete. *Fade out.)*

J ▶ *Fade in: Interior of teachers' cafeteria, Monday noon.* Mr. Kaufman *is just taking a tray near the end of the line as* Pete *comes up behind him.*

46 *For the stage: This scene may be omitted. For television, it is a kind of wind-up scene which may follow the final commercial. For the purposes of the drama itself, the play ends satisfactorily with* The Blue and Gold *banquet. If the scene is used, all of the actors but* Pete Dixon *exit, and* Dixon *joins* Mr. Kaufman *stage left in the faculty room, where a small cafeteria table has been set up.*

Pete. I had a message you wanted to see me.

Kaufman. I got the bill from your Emilio's Restaurant for your Junior Class Achievement orgy. I wanted to go over a few things with you. *(He takes a bill out of his pocket as he and* Pete *inch forward in the line along the steam table.)*

Kaufman. Which one of the students had the double martini?

Pete *(grins).* That was for the waiter. Believe me, he needed it.

Kaufman *(consulting bill).* How many in your party altogether?

Pete. Let's see . . . fifteen students, Liz, and myself.

Kaufman. Seventeen. You got charged for eighteen dinners.

Pete. Harvey Butcher had two.

*(Kaufman *nods as if this makes sense and puts the bill back in his pocket. He takes a jello salad on a single leaf of lettuce.)*

Kaufman. How was the food?

Pete. Good. I had veal scallopini and mushrooms.

*(Kaufman's *eyes glaze slightly as he lapses into a sort of glutton's* reverie. *He is snapped back to reality by the voice of the serving lady behind the steam table.)*

Serving Lady. Tuna surprise or franks and beans, Mr. Kaufman?

Kaufman. No surprises for me today, thanks.

Serving Lady. Franks and beans, then?

*(Kaufman *nods glumly, and she slaps the rubbery frankfurter and soggy beans on a plate and hands it to him.)*

Kaufman *(to* Pete*).* The next time you decide to have another one of your achievement dinners . . .

Pete. Yes?

Kaufman. Please take me with you. *(He picks up his tray and ambles disconsolately off, and we fade out.)* ❧

Words to Know and Use	**reverie** (rev' ər ē) *n.* a daydream

508

Comprehension Check

1. Why is Harvey nearly thrown out of Whitman? *(He is loud and disruptive in class.)*
2. How does Pete learn that Harvey is a funny writer? *(He writes a funny essay about Ben Franklin.)*
3. What job does Mr. Dixon get for Harvey? *(writing a humor column for the school newspaper)*
4. Is Harvey any good at this job? *(Yes, his newspaper columns are very funny.)*
5. Why is Harvey nervous about the dinner? *(He's afraid he won't be able to get a date.)*
6. Why does Harvey suddenly quit his job on *The Blue and Gold?* *(He is embarrassed that he can't get a date; he doesn't want to go to the dinner alone.)*
7. What happens to Harvey at the end? *(He shows up at the dinner without a date, and everyone welcomes him.)*

*R*esponding to Reading

First Impressions

1. How do you feel about Harvey? Write your response in your journal or notebook.

Second Thoughts

2. In your opinion, what are Harvey's biggest strengths and his biggest weaknesses?

3. How much do you think Harvey has changed by the end of the play? Explain your opinion.

   Think about
   • whether he has accepted himself as he is
   • how he uses humor
   • how Pete Dixon helps him

4. How would you react to Harvey if he were in your class?

5. Do you think *Funny Boy* is realistic in its portrayal of students and teachers? Explain.

Broader Connections

6. After reading this play, do you think you would enjoy being a teacher? Why or why not?

*L*iterary Concept: Exposition

The part of the play that provides background information and introduces the characters, setting, and plot is called the **exposition**. Where in *Funny Boy* is the exposition, and what does it explain?

Concept Review: Humor Consider your prereading discussion about humor. How many examples of different kinds of humor can you find in the play?

Concept Review: Humor Among the different types of humor in the play are slapstick (Harvey's first entrance into the classroom), plays on words (Harvey's pun on two meanings of *take*), exaggeration (Harvey's claim that he needs two seats at a play), sarcasm (Harvey's description of a painful silence as a fascinating conversation), irony (Harvey's saying that a funny guy's happiness is on the inside when he is actually unhappy), satire (Harvey's treating the cafeteria food as a weapon that would stop a militant takeover), and comic impersonations (Harvey's impersonations of Jackie Gleason and Superman).

Responding to Reading

1. Any response is valid.

2. **Possible responses:** Harvey's biggest strengths are his sense of humor and his intelligence; his weaknesses include his lack of confidence, his poor self-image, and his inability to relate to his peers except as a clown.

3. **Possible responses:** Harvey has changed a great deal. By using the column as a channel for his humor, he has become more serious in class; and because of his relationship with Pete Dixon, he has begun to confront his own feelings and accept himself.

4. **Possible responses** may include feelings of acceptance, pity, contempt, and appreciation.

5. **Possible responses:** Yes, because both students and teachers really behave like those in the play; yes, because every class has a clown and teachers vary in their dedication; no, because Pete Dixon is too perfect and Harvey's turnaround is not true to life; no, because it's a television show and the problem, unlike problems in real life, has to be resolved by the end.

6. Any response is valid.

Challenge Question

What message does *Funny Boy* convey about what it means to be yourself? *(Possible responses: Being yourself means being honest with others and not hiding your feelings; it means accepting yourself as you are; it means finding a way to use your talents constructively so that you can be productive and happy.)*

Literary Concept: Exposition

The exposition occurs in the opening scene in the faculty room. This scene introduces the main characters—Harvey Butcher and Pete Dixon—and establishes Harvey's conflict with himself and others as the central problem of the plot.

Writing Options

The Writing Options are designed to meet varied student interests and abilities. Have students choose one writing activity to complete.

Journal Update: Invite students to review and update their journal entries for *Funny Boy.* Suggest that they discuss a time when they have felt the way that Harvey feels.

Links to Writer's Craft

Writing Option 4 is an exercise in narrative writing. For more practice, see *The Writer's Craft,* Grade 7, "Narrative and Literary Writing," pages 71–93.

Vocabulary Practice

Answers to Exercise

1. Antonyms	6. Synonyms
2. Synonyms	7. Synonyms
3. Antonyms	8. Antonyms
4. Synonyms	9. Synonyms
5. Antonyms	10. Synonyms

For Alternative Learning Styles

Have student partners make up questions and answers containing the vocabulary words. One partner should ask a question for the other partner to answer, with each partner using a sentence that contains at least one vocabulary word. Example: "How did the militant annoy people?" "With his insolent remarks."

Closure

Point out that Harvey Butcher, like the people described in "Without Commercials," at first rejects himself. Later he declares his independence by accepting himself. Have students discuss ideas about "looking good."

Writing Options

1. Harvey wrote the humor column for his school newspaper. Write your own **humor column** about something going on at your school.

2. Write a **character analysis** of either Harvey or Pete. Be sure to describe their characteristics, strengths, and weaknesses.

3. Based on what you learned about them during the play, write a **letter of advice** to Mr. Walters, Mr. Kaufman, or Alice.

4. Write a **scenario,** or quick plot summary, of the next episode of the series featuring Harvey.

Vocabulary Exercise

Exercise   On a separate sheet of paper, identify each pair of words as *Synonyms* or *Antonyms.*

1. flippant—serious
2. girth—circumference
3. amiably—disagreeably
4. bemused—confused
5. alienate—befriend
6. engrossed—absorbed
7. insolent—disrespectful
8. relinquish—keep
9. militant—agitator
10. reverie—daydream

> *Words to Know and Use*
>
> **alienate**
> **amiably**
> **bemused**
> **engrossed**
> **flippant**
> **girth**
> **insolent**
> **militant**
> **relinquish**
> **reverie**

The Spelling Connection

Assimilated Prefixes   When the last letter of a prefix changes to match the first letter of a root word, the prefix is said to be assimilated. Prefixes that change are: **ob, sub, com, ad,** and **in.**
Example: **ad** + similated = **as**similated
              (to)   (similar)   (made similar to)

Words from the Selection with Assimilated Prefixes

application	**ap**plying	**ap**preciation
appointment	**sup**port	**op**portunity

Other Words with Assimilated Prefixes

correspond	**ir**regular	**op**pose
correction	**ir**rigation	**op**ponent

Exercise   Unscramble the letters to make words. *Hint:* Look for doubled letters.

1. ptpurso	5. lagippyn
2. npopnteo	6. tilpnacoipa
3. eronriccto	7. garurriel
4. sepoop	8. girroiinat

Options for Learning (Multimodal/Cross-Curricular Activities)

1 • Act Funny With other students, choose a scene from *Funny Boy* to perform. Pay close attention to the stage directions in order to set the scene properly. If you have a camcorder available, try the television version of the play and videotape it to show to the class; otherwise, perform the stage version.

2 • Historic Humor For his test, Harvey wrote a humorous sketch that thrust Benjamin Franklin into today's world. With classmates, take another historical figure and create a humorous skit in which that person encounters problems typical of today's society. Practice and perform your skit for the class.

3 • Hip Threads This episode was first broadcast around 1970. Research magazines from this time to discover what students wore then. Sketch or wear appropriate clothing and hairstyles of the period. Explain these styles to the class.

4 • Sketch a Scene A storyboard includes a series of rough sketches of a drama's important scenes. Choose a scene from this play and draw a storyboard of the action. Share your storyboard with others.

 FACT FINDER HISTORY

Harvey jokes about the Mason-Dixon line. What was it?

A*llan P. Burns*
1935-

The screenplay *Funny Boy* is only one example of the award-winning career Allan Burns has had in television and film. Born in Baltimore, Burns has lived and attended school in Hawaii and Oregon.

Burns began writing and producing television series right after college. His writing talent was first recognized in 1968 when he won an Emmy Award for the show *He and She.* He won a Writers Guild Award for *Funny Boy* as the Best Comedy Script in

1970. With producer and director James L. Brooks, he created and produced the very popular television series *The Mary Tyler Moore Show, Rhoda,* and *Lou Grant.* During these years, Burns won five more Emmy Awards for writing and producing.

In the late 1970s, Burns extended his writing talents to movie scripts. He received an Oscar nomination for his screenplay for the 1979 movie *A Little Romance.* Burns presently lives in southern California with his wife, who is also a writer.

Cross-Curricular Projects

Social Studies Ask interested students to find out about methods of discipline in schools and options for students who are expelled. Suggest that they talk to a principal or a guidance counselor about the effectiveness of different methods.

Math At the beginning, Harvey has "perfect attendance in the Detention Room." Assume that this means he earns a detention once a day. Harvey's attendance drops off about 75 percent. Ask students to figure out how many days a month he still has detention.

Performing Arts Hold an open-mike session to allow funny boys and girls to try out their comic routines. Volunteers for this activity should write their material carefully, rehearse, and commit the routine to memory.

Health Characters in this play often meet in the school cafeteria and talk about the cafeteria's food. Suggest that students interview your school's dietitian to find out about the nutritional guidelines used when planning and preparing meals.

Extending the Lesson

Options for Learning

These activities suit a variety of learning styles and modes of expression.

Collaborative Learning Activities
See Options 1, 2, and 4.

1. Act Funny Small groups of students should choose different scenes and perform them in the order they occur in the play.

2. Historic Humor Direct students to their social studies textbooks to find historical figures.

3. Hip Threads To follow up this activity, you might schedule a Hippie Day in which students wear 1960s-style clothing to class.

4. Sketch a Scene Show students a real storyboard or a comic book to give them an idea of how to convey their scene in pictures.

 FACT FINDER HISTORY
Established by the surveyors Charles Mason and Jeremiah Dixon in 1767, the Mason-Dixon line was long considered the dividing line between the North and the South. It is the boundary line that separates Maryland from Pennsylvania.

Allan P. Burns

■ **More About the Author** Burns was the head writer of two television series, *He and She* and *Get Smart.* He was also the creator of and a writer for the series *Eisenhower and Lutz* and *The Duck Factory.*

■ **Other Works** Screenplays: *Butch and Sundance: The Early Days, I Won't Dance, Just the Way You Are, Just Between Friends*

 ■ **Awards** Emmy Awards for comedy series writing for *He and She* and *The Mary Tyler Moore Show;* Emmy Awards for comedy series production for *The Mary Tyler Moore Show;* Writer's Guild Award for television comedy for *Room 222*

Objectives

■ To create an advertising poster

■ To use persuasive strategies to write about a favorite book

■ To draft, revise, edit, and share writing about literature

Teaching Strategies

DISCUSSING THE ASSIGNMENT

Have students imagine that a relative of theirs has just invented a new and completely different kind of video game, and she wants them to help market it to young people. Ask students to think about how they would advertise the game. For example, if they were to make a poster, what would it say to convince people to buy the game? Discuss with students some of the persuasive strategies that advertisers use. Then ask what characteristics of the video game they would emphasize to encourage people to buy it. Finally, talk about the kinds of visuals that would "hook" people their age.

Ask a volunteer to read the introductory paragraph and the Guided Assignment and PASSkey on page 512. Then give students a few minutes to study the model poster. Be sure students understand that they are combining two kinds of writing in this assignment. They are writing about literature in a persuasive way. If you wish, you may give students the option of writing something else. Suggestions can be found on page 514 under Alternative Writing and Research Topics.

ANALYZING THE MODEL

As students study the poster, give them time to react to it and discuss the things they like best about it. Ask whether they like the "promotional copy" above the book's title and whether they think it catches people's attention. Have students comment on the persuasive language used by the student author in the summary. Call on volunteers to tell specifically what words or phrases they find particularly effective and why. Ask how the poster appeals to them visually.

Writer's WORKSHOP

WRITING ABOUT LITERATURE/PERSUASION

As a group, you have shared and discussed the literary selections that have been presented in this book. Now it's time for you to share a book of your own choosing with your classmates. For this assignment you will create an advertising poster that promotes your favorite book. Your goal will be to "sell" your book to your classmates—to interest them enough in your book to make them want to read it. You will combine writing about literature with persuasive writing. Just like other kinds of advertisements, your advertisement will also contain visual images to capture your audience's attention and help promote the book.

> Here is one writer's PASSkey to this assignment.

GUIDED ASSIGNMENT: ADVERTISING POSTER

Create an advertising poster that promotes your favorite book.

PURPOSE: To persuade others to read a book

AUDIENCE: Classmates

SUBJECT: A favorite book

STRUCTURE: Poster

Prewrite and Explore

1 **Find the good parts**   You can choose any book that you enjoy and would like to write about. If you skim it again, you'll recall the parts you like best. You might jot words and phrases to remind yourself which parts these are and what you like about them.

2 **Look at possibilities**   Book covers and jacket flaps, back covers of paperbacks, posters in bookstore windows, supermarket book displays, and magazines are all good places to find examples of book advertisements. Notice the visual elements—the illustrations, the design, the style and size of lettering—as well as the verbal elements of the advertisements. Study the student model on the facing page to see another example of a book advertisement.

ADDITIONAL RESOURCES

Unit Five Resource Book
Writer's Workshop Worksheet, p. 31
Writer's Workshop: Peer and Self-Evaluation, p. 32
Writer's Workshop: Assessment Guidelines, p. 33

Technology and Enrichment
Elaboration, Revision, and Proofreading
   Transparencies 11–14
Fine Arts Transparency Pack

 Writer's Databank Software: File 5,
   Word Usage

Links to
Writer's Craft

For more about persuasive writing, see *The Writer's Craft,* Grade 7, "Persuasion," pages 138–151, and pages 226–230, "Using Graphic Devices for Writing."

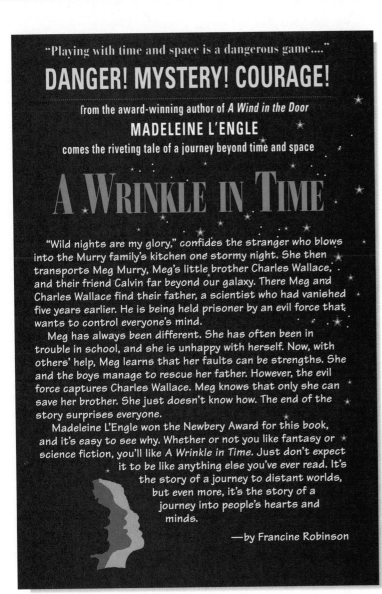

◄ The writer quotes an exciting line from the book.

◄ Descriptive language captures readers' interest.

◄ The writer explains the main conflicts in the plot.

◄ The writer mentions the author's credentials.

◄ Persuasive language urges the audience to read the book.

Prewrite and Explore

First, help the class choose their books. If students keep a reading log, suggest that they look through it for comments and quotations they may have jotted there. You might have them think about books they've enjoyed and freewrite about one or two.

Once students have a title, encourage them to make the first sketch of their posters. Suggest that they refer to the model and note that the large letters of the promotional copy balance the large block of small print that follows. Even the size of the top copy varies to hold the interest of the reader and to keep the poster balanced visually. You may want to read with students the notes in the Gathering Information box on page 514. If students would prefer a different kind of graphic organizer, you might suggest clustering, a tree diagram, or a story map.

Alternative Writing and Research Topics

Advertising Poster Suppose your class were putting on the play *Funny Boy*. Make a poster that not only advertises the performance but gives the audience a preview of the story.

Personal Letter Malcolm X made his personal declaration of independence while he was in prison. Write a letter that Malcolm X might have sent to his family, explaining what he has learned from his prison experience.

Poetry Alice Walker wants people to accept themselves the way they are. Use her poem as a model for an advice poem of your own.

Research Biography Harvey Butcher was a sad student wearing a happy face—until one teacher took an interest in him. Do some research, either by interviewing or by reading short biographies in the library, to find out about other teachers who have changed their students' lives. Write a short biography of one of the teachers.

Draft and Discover

Share with students that it may take time and several changes to find the mix of quotations, art, promotional copy, and book excerpts they want to use. Suggest that students try to keep the same tone for each quote and paragraph they choose. If a book is adventurous, for example, all the copy might suggest adventure. If it is a fantasy, each head, piece of art, and summary passage should call out "FANTASY!"

As students draft, circulate around the room to observe and offer suggestions. Encourage students who are having difficulties to meet with you for brief problem-solving conferences at any time during the drafting process.

For Alternative Learning Styles

This assignment is a good opportunity for artistic students to shine. Encourage them to be creative in both their visual elements and their layouts. Emphasize, however, that visuals are not enough; the poster needs to contain information about the book.

TEACHING TIP: CHALLENGE

Challenge your advanced students to choose a book of short stories or poems and highlight two items on their posters. The challenge lies in finding a common ground to unite the two titles and then in coming up with art and attention-getting copy applicable to both selections.

3 Sketch a plan and gather material Taking off from what you've seen, you can plan your poster. Then you can gather the information that you will include on it. Keep in mind that although most posters do not contain extended sections of text, yours will.

GATHERING INFORMATION

Try closing your eyes for a minute to visualize your poster. Then sketch out your plan, with notes about what goes where. Think of things that will appeal to your classmates: attention-grabbing art and lettering, surprising quotes and details from the book, facts about the author, an idea of the plot, "teaser" words and phrases. Look at Francine's plan for her text below.

<u>quotes and details</u>: "Playing with time and space is a dangerous game." "Wild nights are my glory." Stranger blows in during storm, transports them to distant galaxy.

<u>teasers</u>: courage, danger, mystery, riveting

<u>about the author</u>: Also wrote <u>A Wind in the Door.</u> Won Newbery Medal.

<u>conflict summary</u>: Meg and others rescue her father; she must rescue Charles Wallace.

<u>how it's unique</u>: Meg's not like a hero. She's in trouble a lot, unpopular. Also, not the usual space stuff. More about people.

Draft and Discover

> **WRITER'S CHOICE**
> If you get an idea that's not in your sketch, don't be afraid to try it. It may be just the touch you need.

1 Get into gear To get yourself going, write a short paragraph tracing key action in your book. If your book is nonfiction, write an overview of its main ideas. Include enough detail to give readers a taste of the book—but leave them wanting more.

2 Sell it To persuade your audience, you need to appeal to their logic as well as their emotions. The best way to appeal to logic is to present facts as clearly as possible. Your facts include information about the book and the author. Your opinion is supported by those facts. You can appeal to emotions through the words that express your own enthusiasm and the visuals you choose.

CONFERENCING TIP

As you conference with individual writers for this workshop, you may wish to focus on

- the synopsis or overview of the book
- persuasive language
- the layout of the poster

3 Make it shine You can use your own photos, drawings, or paintings to underscore your words, or you can cut pictures from magazines. As you select or plan your pictures, think about the impact they will have on your audience. Be creative—the more fun you have designing your poster, the better your audience will respond.

Revise Your Writing

1 Lay it out Now you can arrange your material as it will appear in your poster. Work with it until it satisfies you. Don't forget that it's fine to break up your writing into sections between art elements, to enclose some sections in boxes, and to vary your lettering.

2 Check your wording This is a good time to look at the words you've used. Try focusing on verbs. For example, Malcolm X doesn't write that he *read* literature but that he *devoured* literature. Francine Robinson doesn't write that the stranger *comes* in but that she *blows* in. Could you replace any ordinary verbs with ones that create more vivid images? Could you replace any with verbs whose connotations—emotional overtones—reflect your feelings better?

3 Work with a peer Using the lists of questions below, you and a peer can take turns responding to each other's posters.

Revision Questions	
For You	**For a Peer Reader**
1. Have I given a good idea of the content of the book?	1. Which part of my poster caught your interest first?
2. Have I chosen words and visuals that strengthen each other?	2. What do you think you'd like about this book?
3. Would any changes generate more excitement about the book?	3. How might I increase the impact of my wording or design?

◀ **COMPUTER TIP**
You may be able to add computer graphics to your written text. Try different sizes and fonts for your lettering.

◀ **IN OTHER CLASSES**
In art class you can try similar ways of fusing visual elements with words. For example, you might include written material in a collage.

◀ **NEED MORE HELP?**
See the Vocabulary Workshop on denotation and connotation, page 465.

Revise Your Writing

Have students read the first subsection under Revise Your Writing. Suggest that they photocopy their lettering, visual elements, and copy in different sizes. They can then rearrange pieces and decide what sizes look best as they experiment with different layouts.

After students read the second revising suggestion, you might have the class generate a list of exciting verbs. For example, you could write ordinary verbs like *read, come, see,* and *feel,* on the board and have students brainstorm, or check a thesaurus, for synonyms.

Modeling Remind students that advertising is supposed to excite the reader or viewer about the product. Write on the board a statement like "This is the best book I ever read." With their help, rewrite the sentence as many ways as you can to make it less trite and more specific. For example, "This book woke me up to a new world of adventure," "This book made me yearn to visit Africa," and so on.

Note that the Editor's Eye feature on page 516 previews the content in the Language Workshop that follows. If students don't need extra help with verb tenses, the brief review in The Editor's Eye may be enough for them. You may choose to teach the Language Workshop, pages 517–519, before having students proofread.

Use these models as reinforcement of The Editor's Eye topic:

1. The Murrys use a tesseract when they went to Camazotz.

2. Charles Wallace's mind was captured, and Meg stops her search.

3. When they find Mr. Murry, he was unreachable.

4. Then Meg finds Mrs. Who's glasses and will decide to use them.

5. Will the glasses get them out of Camazotz and sent them back to Earth?

Proofread

Have students proofread their poster copy, watching for correct punctuation of quotations as well as shifts in verb tense. Explain that verb tenses don't have to be the same throughout their poster copy as long as the shifts they do make are necessary to its meaning.

TEACHING TIP: LEP

LEP students may have difficulty with verb tenses. Work with them individually to proofread their papers. Have them read each sentence aloud, and focus their attention on the time of the action.

Publish and Present

Break students into two groups and let one group give their pitch while the others go "shopping." Then switch so that both groups can give their pitches.

Writing for the Community Ask both the school and public librarians to display the posters after your fair. Some posters might be displayed in the school corridors so that other readers may enjoy them.

Reflect on Your Writing

You may wish to use these questions instead of or in addition to those in the text.

■ Is advertising something I enjoy doing?

■ Which part of this assignment did I prefer—designing the visuals or writing copy?

Closure

Now that students have completed their posters, suggest that they remain on the lookout for others that promote similar items (movies, educational toys, and music). Ask them to examine both the promotional copy and the persuasive language used in the text. Encourage students to bring in copies if possible.

THE EDITOR'S EYE: VERB TENSES

Avoid unnecessary shifts in verb tense.

Verbs change form, or **tense,** to show changes in time. In some of your sentences and paragraphs, all the action occurs in the same time period. Then you need to keep all your verbs in the same tense.

Problem	He is being held prisoner by an evil force that wanted to control everyone's mind.
Revised	He is being held prisoner by an evil force that wants to control everyone's mind.
Also Correct	He was being held prisoner by an evil force that wanted to control everyone's mind.

NEED MORE HELP?
See the Language Workshop on pages 517–519.

Proofread

Check your poster carefully, correcting errors in spelling, punctuation, and grammar. Pay special attention to verb tenses.

Publish and Present

Here is a suggestion for promoting your book to your classmates.

Book Share Fair Find an area in your classroom where you can display your poster and stand next to it to give a "sales pitch." As your classmates walk by, use your poster and try to talk them into reading your book. List titles and authors of books that your classmates convince you to read as well!

Reflect on Your Writing

FOR YOUR PORTFOLIO
Write your answers to the questions below. Attach them to your poster when you place it in your portfolio.

1. How did you feel when you saw others' responses to your poster?
2. What did you enjoy most about designing your poster?

Assessment Guidelines

These guidelines may help you assess student writing:

Content

■ The promotional copy identifies the book and includes quotations to "hook" the reader.
■ The text gives a good idea of the book's content.
■ The artwork complements and echoes the tone of the copy.

Style

■ The copy evinces a balance between vivid description and logical persuasion.
■ The copy is inviting and easy to read.
■ The book is summarized in the student's own words.

Usage and Mechanics

■ Errors in spelling, capitalization, and punctuation are avoided.
■ Shifts in verb tense are few and necessary.

See *Unit Five Resource Book,* page 33.

LANGUAGE WORKSHOP

VERB TENSES

As you know, verbs tell about actions or states of being. Verbs also tell about time. All verbs change form, or **tense,** to show changes in time. When you write, be sure your tense changes make sense. Otherwise your readers will end up wondering what happened when.

Verb tenses are formed from the **principal parts** of verbs: the **present,** the **past,** the **present participle,** and the **past participle.** These basic forms may be combined with helping verbs such as *will* and *have.* The chart below shows time spans that verb tenses cover.

Tense	Example	Use
• **Present**	she walks	for action that is happening now
• **Past**	she walked	for action that was completed in the past
• **Future**	she will walk	for action that will happen in the future
• **Present Perfect**	she has walked	for action that began in the past and continues into the present, or for action completed at an indefinite time in the past
• **Past Perfect**	she had walked	for action in the past that was completed before another action in the past

◀ **GRAMMAR TIP**
Verb-tense changes are made in three ways: the addition of an ending: *walk, walked;* a change in spelling: *bring, brought;* a change in helping verbs: *has walked, will walk.*

Exercise 1 Concept Review Make two columns. Label the first *Verbs* and the second *Verb Tenses.* In the first, write each verb in the sentences below. In the second, write the tense of each verb.

1. Finally, spring has arrived.
2. In his expensive suit, the businessman feels proud.
3. A beggar has stopped the successful businessman.
4. The businessman asks about the beggar's story.

◀ **REMINDER**
An adverb, such as *not, always,* or *usually,* sometimes comes between parts of a verb. It is not part of the verb.

ADDITIONAL RESOURCES
Unit Five Resource Book
Language Workshop Practice, p. 34

Technology and Enrichment
Grammar and Usage Copy Masters, pages 46–53

Links to
Writer's Craft

For more about verb tenses, see *The Writer's Craft,* Grade 7, "Using Verbs," pages 472–480.

Objective

■ To use verb tenses correctly in writing

■ To limit shifts in verb tenses to those necessary for clarity

■ To understand why shifts in verb tense may confuse a reader

Teaching Strategies

Remind students that in addition to signaling the time of verbs, tenses help to clarify the action. That is, by the tenses that writers choose, they make the order of events clear and thus support coherence.

Have students review the five verb tenses shown on page 517 and note the example and use of each one. Work through Exercise 1 orally with students to be sure they understand the reason for each choice of tense.

For Alternative Learning Styles
Visual learners might be encouraged to make time lines showing how the tenses progress from farthest in the past, through the present, and into the future. To make it interesting, have them choose a topic and write related sentences about it using their time lines. For example,

Past Perfect Mavis *had attended* Reggie's party the previous week and *had seen* Rochelle's new hairdo.

Present Perfect Mavis *has* always *wanted* a hairdo like that.

Past So Mavis *copied* the color, cut, and style of Rochelle's hair.

Present Now Mavis *takes* off the styling cap and *looks* at her work.

Future Maybe someday Mavis *will love* her greenish-blonde curls.

Answers to Exercise 1

Verbs	Verb Tenses
1. has arrived	present perfect
2. feels	present
3. has stopped	present perfect
4. asks	present

5. injured   past
6. will see   future
7. had gone   past perfect
8. exploded   past
9. burned   past
10. will remember   future

Avoiding Unnecessary Shifts in Tense

Read with students the boxed rule and the explanation for shifts in verb tense on page 518. Clarify the reference to a chain of events by explaining that as used here, the term refers to two actions, but not necessarily in the sense that one caused the other.

Advise students to be careful about gauging the correctness of tense shifts "by ear." A safer and more correct strategy is simply to ask themselves which action happened first, or farther back in time. Have students identify the tense of this verb and then work forward to decide which tense to use for the action that happened later. If students need more practice in avoiding tense shifts, refer them to pages 743–744 of the Writer's Handbook and page 33 of the Unit Five Resource Book. Note that it doesn't matter where the two verbs appear in the sentence; all students have to do is figure out which action logically had to take place first.

Answers to Exercise 2
(Responses may vary.)

1. Alex Haley <u>helped</u> Malcolm X with an autobiography, and later Haley <u>became</u> famous for his own book *Roots*.

2. Malcolm X <u>wrote</u> most of his own material, but Haley <u>helped</u> him to shape it.

3. Haley <u>researched</u> *Roots* for years and even <u>traveled</u> to West Africa for information.

5. An accident injured the beggar fourteen years ago.
6. Because of the accident he will never see again.
7. The beggar had gone to work as usual on the day of the accident.
8. The factory exploded into an inferno of burning chemicals.
9. To his horror, the chemicals burned him badly.
10. He will always remember the sight of the factory in flames.

Avoiding Unnecessary Shifts in Tense

> Use the same tense to show two or more actions that occur in the same time period.

In some of your writing, all the action in a sentence or a paragraph takes place in one time period. To show this kind of consistent action, use the same tense for all the verbs in the sentence or paragraph.

Incorrect   Malcolm X *stays* in his cell and *studied*.
Correct   Malcolm X *stays* in his cell and *studies*.
Correct   Malcolm X *stayed* in his cell and *studied*.

You do need to change tenses when you write about a chain of events. For example, the sentence below tells about two actions in the past. One, however, finished before the other. Notice how the change in verb tense reflects the flow of time.

The day *ended* (past), and Malcolm X *had copied* (past perfect) the entire first page of the dictionary.

When you proofread, check the verb tenses you've used. Make sure that you haven't shifted—changed—tenses without reason. Often you can tell "by ear" whether a tense shift makes sense.

ASK FOR HELP
When you are unsure about tense shifts in your writing, ask a peer to read the passage for clarity.

Exercise 2 Concept Review   Rewrite each sentence to correct shifts in verb tense.

1. Alex Haley helped Malcolm X with an autobiography, and later Haley becomes famous for his own book *Roots*.
2. Malcolm X writes most of his own material, but Haley had helped him to shape it.
3. Haley researches *Roots* for years and even traveled to West Africa in search of information.

Grammar Games: Verb Tense Tango

Make (or have students help you make) 8 1/2 x 11 "Bingo" cards with the letters T A N G O at the top where B I N G O would ordinarily be. And instead of numbers under the letters, each square should have a simple sentence printed inside. Cards should contain sentences with a variety of tenses. The game is played just like Bingo, and you are the caller. If you say A, *past perfect*, students who have a sentence under the letter A with the verb in the past perfect tense can put a marker on that square. The first student who completes a row horizontally, vertically, or diagonally wins. Keep some kind of tally to know which tenses you call for which letters. A sheet of paper on which you note your calls as you make them should suffice.

4. There he will visit villages and has learned more about his heritage.

5. Certain mysterious words and stories had been in his family for generations, and he discovers their meanings.

Exercise 3 Proofreading Skill
Work in groups to revise the paragraph below. Look carefully at each verb in italics, and decide how to correct unneeded tense shifts. Write the corrected paragraph.

Malcolm X's autobiography *tells* about his childhood struggles with poverty and hunger. Bright but indifferent, he *dropped* out of school. The unfairness of his life *makes* him angry. As a teenager, he *sells* drugs and *burglarized* houses. His life *will spiral* out of control, and his prison sentence *has* almost *seemed* like a relief to him. In prison he *will concentrate* for the first time on learning. He *improves* his shaky reading and writing skills. The more he *reads* and *wrote*, the more clearly he *had thought*. Finally he *has regained* control of his life. Once freed, Malcolm X *becomes* a powerful figure in the fight against inequality.

Exercise 4 Looking at Style
Reread the second paragraph of the excerpt from *The Autobiography of Malcolm X* on page 472. How do the changing verb tenses show the different periods of time discussed in the paragraph?

Exercise 5 Revising Your Writing
Reread your advertising poster, and lightly underline each verb you used. Check your tenses carefully. Be sure your tense shifts make sense, and correct any that do not.

LANGUAGE HANDBOOK
. . . .
For review and practice: Section 6, Using Verbs, pages 743–746.

4. There he <u>visited</u> villages and <u>learned</u> more about his heritage.

5. Certain mysterious words and stories <u>had been</u> in his family for generations, and he <u>discovered</u> their meanings.

Answers to Exercise 3
Malcolm X's autobiography <u>told</u> about his childhood struggles with poverty and hunger. Bright but indifferent, he <u>dropped</u> out of school. The unfairness of his life <u>made</u> him angry. As a teenager, he <u>sold</u> drugs and <u>burglarized</u> houses. His life <u>spiraled</u> out of control, and his prison sentence almost <u>seemed</u> like a relief to him. In prison he <u>concentrated</u> for the first time on learning. He <u>improved</u> his shaky reading and writing skills. The more he <u>read</u> and <u>wrote</u>, the more clearly he <u>thought</u>. Finally he <u>regained</u> control of his life. Once freed, Malcolm X <u>became</u> a powerful figure in the fight against inequality.

Answers to Exercise 4
At the time he wrote his autobiography, Malcolm X was already out of prison and working for his cause, so all the verbs are in some form of the past tense. He used the past perfect tense to refer to his early life on the streets because this period is the farthest in the past. For the other periods of his life he used the simple past tense, with a brief exception—the word *now* and the conditional past tense—to describe the moment he realized he was not an articulate writer.

Answers to Exercise 5
Check students' posters for correct shifts in verb tense.

Closure

Now that students have learned how to avoid making unnecessary shifts in verb tense, have them check their earlier work for this kind of error. Ask them, too, to be aware of this problem in the future whenever they revise their own work or act as peer reader for any of their classmates.

Additional Practice

Revise the following paragraphs to correct any confusing shifts in tense. *(Answers follow each paragraph.)*

In the eighteenth and nineteenth centuries, many people <u>keep</u> commonplace books, in which they <u>jot</u> down interesting passages from their reading. Both Benjamin Franklin and Thomas Jefferson <u>were keeping</u> such books. They sometimes <u>will quote</u> passages from these books in their own writings. *(kept, jotted, kept, quoted)*

Today few people <u>kept</u> commonplace books. It <u>was</u>, however, a practice worth reviving. Sometimes writers <u>will be collecting</u> passages for commonplace books over a period of many years. In time, their collections <u>numbered</u> thousands of passages. Then, when they <u>needed</u> a writing idea, they simply <u>browsed</u> through their commonplace books. As a source of interesting quotes, a commonplace book <u>had made</u> any writer's work more fun to read. *(keep, is, collect, number, need, browse, makes)*

Objectives

- To distinguish between facts and opinions
- To identify judgment words

Teaching Strategies

Review the difference between facts and opinions by reading aloud the boxed definitions and the paragraph on page 520. Remind students that in many kinds of writing, facts are mixed with opinions, and that the authors of such writing often do not make it clear which are which. Emphasize to students the importance of reading carefully so as not to mistake an author's opinions for facts.

Next, call attention to the judgment words at the center of the page. If students have not done so themselves, add to that list these words and phrases that signal opinions: *think, feel, may, might, probably, perhaps, in my judgment, if you ask me,* and *as I see it.* After discussing these additions with students, caution them that not every opinion is signaled in such a way. Again, stress the importance of careful reading.

Answers to Exercise

1. F; a collection of Alice Walker's work

2. O; silly

3. F; biography

4. O; no, greater

5. O; should

6. F; TV schedule; contact network

7. F; contact Writer's Guild

8. O; excellent

9. O; few, more important

10. F; read autobiography

ADDITIONAL RESOURCES

Unit Five Resource Book
Reader's Workshop Practice, p. 35

FACT AND OPINION

A **fact** is a statement that can be proved. An **opinion** cannot be proved.

Fact   *Funny Boy* was written by Allan Burns.
Opinion   *Funny Boy* is a hilarious play.

You could prove the first statement by looking in a reference book or by asking Allan Burns himself. The second statement, however, expresses what a person thinks—it is an opinion, not a fact. In some kinds of writing, such as news reports, sticking to facts is crucial. In others, such as editorials, reviews, and advertisements, opinions are important. However, opinions must be supported by facts.

Opinions often contain **judgment words**—words that express personal feelings. See if you can add any judgment words to the list below.

wonderful	horrible	ridiculous	great	silly
awful	boring	excellent	terrible	

WRITING TIP
Although judgment words sometimes signal faulty logic, a well-supported opinion can strengthen an appeal to emotion.

▶ When you read and write, notice which statements are facts and which are opinions. Ask yourself whether enough facts are presented to support the opinions.

Exercise   For each sentence below, write *F* for a fact or *O* for an opinion. If the sentence is a fact, write a way it could be proved. If the sentence is an opinion, list any judgment words you find in it.

1. Alice Walker wrote a poem called "Without Commercials."
2. It's silly for people to try to change the way they look.
3. Alice Walker was the daughter of sharecroppers.
4. No U.S. poet is greater than Alice Walker.
5. People should accept themselves as they are.
6. *Funny Boy* was an episode of the television series *Room 222.*
7. Allan Burns won a Writer's Guild Award for *Funny Boy.*
8. Allan Burns is an excellent writer.
9. Few things are more important than the ability to read.
10. A love of reading made Malcolm X aware of new ideas.

NEED HELP?
For more about appeals to emotion and faulty logic, see the Reader's Workshop on page 347.

520   UNIT FIVE   DECLARATIONS OF INDEPENDENCE

Additional Practice

Have students select a topic of particular interest to them and write several paragraphs that contain facts and opinions. Then tell students to trade papers and identify the facts and opinions in them. In addition, have students identify any judgment words the papers contain.

DOORS OF UNDERSTANDING

Doors have often been used as metaphors to describe the workings of the mind and heart. We open the door to new ideas and new relationships, but close it to people we do not like. An open door suggests an inviting attitude; a closed door implies "Do not disturb!"

In this group of selections, you will meet fictional characters and real people who pass through various doors of understanding. Some of the doors are opened freely. Others have to be pushed open, at times against great resistance.

As you read, decide which doors are being opened—or closed—and what is learned as a result.

Subunit Preview

Assign students to read the introduction to Subunit 2, "Doors of Understanding." Ask them to explain how doors of understanding relate to identity. What kinds of understanding do people have about themselves? Does understanding oneself help a person to understand others better?

INTEGRATING THE LANGUAGE ARTS

Every selection in this subunit focuses on the theme "Doors of Understanding." Reading skills, literature skills, writing options, language study, vocabulary, and spelling are all based on these literary selections.

Writer's Workshop After reading several selections that deal with doors of understanding, students will use informative writing to better their understanding of another culture by writing a report on an interesting custom of its people.

Language Workshop The Language Workshop in this subunit deals with proofreading skills. Students will see that proofreading their own work and correcting mistakes will help readers to better understand their ideas.

Reader's Workshop The Reader's Workshop in this subunit focuses on main ideas and supporting details. Students will learn to improve their understanding of reading materials by identifying main ideas and supporting details.

FOR ADDITIONAL CHALLENGE

The following selections offer extra challenge in the exploration of the subunit theme.

Hatchet, novel by Gary Paulsen

Jacob Have I Loved, novel by Katherine Paterson

ADDITIONAL RESOURCES

Technology and Enrichment
Family and Community Involvement Source Book, p. 19

Guidelines for Reading and Literature Assessment: Observation Assessment Forms

---

Observation Assessment

Observing how students respond to the text, to the classroom instruction, and to peers is an important part of an assessment program. The following suggestions and the form in each *Guidelines for Reading and Literature Assessment* booklet can be used to implement observation assessment.

■ **Writing Behavior** As students work through the subunit, assess how well they engage in personal writing as a means of expression. Determine to what degree they write well-constructed, cohesive pieces that are appropriate to the genre. Also evaluate how much they draw on personal knowledge and experiences in composing text. Note how well students' creative writing reveals a strong sense of voice, personal style, and originality. Evaluate students' willingness to follow appropriate conventions of spelling, grammar, and usage. How well does their writing exhibit grammatical structure appropriate to their purposes, and how rich and varied is their vocabulary?

Objectives

- To understand and analyze a short story

- To examine the use of flashback and review the concept of a narrator

- To enrich reading by using context clues to understand unfamiliar words

- To express understanding of the story through a choice of writing forms, including an advertising flyer, a letter, a comparison/contrast, and a feature article

Examine What You Know

Discussion Prompts What pets do you have or would you like to have? What is the best thing about having a pet? What are some of the challenges? What do pets need from people? What benefits do people get from pets?

Expand Your Knowledge

Additional Background Fox hunting for sport began in England in the 1700s. The group of hunters on horseback is called *the field* and is led by a *master of foxhounds*. The *pack* of hounds is managed by a person called a *huntsman*. Many hunters participate for sport alone and do not kill the fox after it is captured.

Enrich Your Reading

For Alternative Learning Styles
When students encounter an unfamiliar word, have them read the sentence and its surrounding sentences aloud, saying "blank" in place of the word. Have them think of words they know that would make sense in the blank.

Thematic Link—
Doors of Understanding

Although Colin seems different from his brother and his father, his drawing of the hidden fox opens doors of understanding—and appreciation—between his father and him.

Fiction

Last Cover

PAUL ANNIXTER

Examine What You Know (Prior Knowledge)

Do you know someone who feels an especially strong attachment to his or her pet? Why do you think some people develop such close ties with animals? What can a pet offer that another human cannot? Discuss your ideas about pets with your classmates.

Expand Your Knowledge (Building Background)

In this story two boys who live near the woods adopt a red fox as their pet. The red fox is the most common fox in the world. Red foxes are clever and quick. They are excellent hunters who feed on anything from rodents to the carcasses of large animals. A fox and its mate may travel thirty miles to find a hunting territory, which may be the size of seventy city blocks. In turn, foxes are often hunted for their fur, for sport, or because their raids on chicken houses are a nuisance to farmers.

In a fox hunt, dogs are used to find the fox in its hiding place. When found, the cries of the dogs signal the fox's location to the hunters on horseback, who follow the dogs.

Enrich Your Reading (Reading Skill)

Context Clues As you read "Last Cover," you may come across unfamiliar words or phrases. Often you can discover their meaning if you make use of context clues—words or sentences around a term that help explain its meaning. Use a chart like the one below to record unfamiliar words and phrases, their context clues, and probable meanings.

Word or Phrase	Context Clues	Probable Meaning
kit	tiny, pet fox Colin and I raised	a baby fox
pine		
pranking		

■ *Author biography on Extend page*

JOURNAL WRITING IDEAS

■ How is your personality different from the personalities of your brothers or sisters? Write about these differences.

■ Describe a pet or your favorite animal.

■ Write about a time when you felt a close bond of understanding with a friend or relative.

COLLABORATIVE LEARNING OPTIONS

Opportunities for collaborative learning include Options for Learning 3 and 4 (p. 533) and Cross-Curricular Projects (p. 533).

ADDITIONAL RESOURCES

Unit Five Resource Book
Reader's Guidesheet, p. 36
Reading Skills, p. 37
Literature Skills, p. 38
Vocabulary Connections, p. 39
Spelling Connections, p. 40
Comprehension and Vocabulary Check Tests, p. 41
Selection Test, pp. 42–43

Last Cover

PAUL ANNIXTER

I'm not sure I can tell you what you want to know about my brother; but everything about the pet fox is important, so I'll tell all that from the beginning.

It goes back to a winter afternoon after I'd hunted the woods all day for a sign of our lost pet. I remember the way my mother looked up as I came into the kitchen. Without my speaking, she knew what had happened. For six hours I had walked, reading signs, looking for a delicate print in the damp soil or even a hair that might have told of a red fox passing that way—but I had found nothing.

"Did you go up in the foothills?" Mom asked.

I nodded. My face was stiff from held-back tears. My brother, Colin, who was going on twelve, got it all from one look at me and went into a heartbroken, almost silent, crying.

Three weeks before, Bandit, the pet fox Colin and I had raised from a tiny kit, had disappeared, and not even a rumor had been heard of him since.

"He'd have had to go off soon anyway," Mom comforted. "A big, lolloping fellow like him, he's got to live his life same as us. But he may come back. That fox set a lot of store by you boys in spite of his wild ways."

"He set a lot of store by our food, anyway," Father said. He sat in a chair by the kitchen window, mending a piece of harness. "We'll be seeing a lot more of that fellow, never fear. That fox learned to pine for table scraps and young chickens. He was getting to be an egg thief, too, and he's not likely to forget that."

"That was only pranking when he was little," Colin said desperately.

From the first, the tame fox had made tension in the family. It was Father who said we'd better name him Bandit, after he'd made away with his first young chicken.

"Maybe you know," Father said shortly. "But when an animal turns to egg sucking, he's usually incurable. He'd better not come pranking around my chicken run again." ◄ **A**

It was late February, and I remember the <u>bleak</u>, dead cold that had set in, cold that was a rare thing for our Carolina hills. Flocks of sparrows and snowbirds had appeared, to peck hungrily at all that the pigs and chickens didn't eat.

"This one's a killer," Father would say of a morning, looking out at the whitened barn roof. "This one will make the shoats[1] squeal."

A fire snapped all day in our cookstove and another in the stone fireplace in the living room, but still the farmhouse was never

---

1. **shoats** (shōts): young pigs.

Words to Know and Use | **bleak** (blēk) *adj.* harsh and dreary

523

523

Teaching Strategies

VOCABULARY PREVIEW
These vocabulary words are defined at the bottom of the selection pages on which they appear.

bleak harsh and dreary

confound to bewilder

essence a basic nature

harried worried

intricate elaborately detailed

invalid a sickly or disabled person

passive inactive; lacking in energy

sanction to approve

sanctuary shelter; protection

wily crafty

LIMITED ENGLISH PROFICIENCY
■ Use the Reader's Guidesheet, *Unit Five Resource Book*, p. 36.

■ The characters in this story speak in a dialect. You may wish to read passages aloud to clarify meanings.

★ Text annotations marked with a red star (2, 3, 4, 8, 9, 16) may be particularly helpful for students with limited English proficiency.

TEXT ANNOTATIONS
1. LITERARY CONCEPT: Point of View
Ask students how they can tell the story is being told from a first-person point of view. *(The narrator uses the pronouns* I *and* my*)* Discuss how first-person narration might affect the telling of the story. *(Possible responses: Only one character's thoughts will be revealed; things will be presented as one person saw them.)*

2. LANGUAGE: Compound Words
Have students use word parts to figure out that *foothills* are hills near the foot, or bottom, of a mountain. ★

3. VOCABULARY: Idiom
The idiom "set a lot of store by" is used here and in the preceding sentence. Ask students to use **context clues** and **prior knowledge** to figure out its meaning. *("thought very highly of")* Ask what "pine for" might mean. *("desire")* ★

Guided Reading for Less-Proficient Students

These questions can help guide students through the reading. Ask each question at the point of the selection where the capital letter and arrow appear in the margin. In addition, you may wish to use appropriate Active Reading annotations.

A. How do different views of Bandit cause tension in the family? *(The boys' view of Bandit as a pet conflicts with their father's anger at the fox for eating chickens.)* Summarizing

B. How does Father feel about Colin's interest in art? *(He feels that it is childish and interferes with Colin's doing more important work.)* Inferring

C. How does Bandit come to be Colin's "whole life"? *(The fox cub is very special—it is intelligent, wild, and different; and Colin feels very close to it.)* Summarizing

Continued on page 524

4. VOCABULARY: Context Clues
Ask students to find the **context clue** that defines "sleepers" here. ("animals that . . . hole up and stay hid") Then ask students to use context clues to discover what "woods lore" means. ("knowledge of the woods") ★

5. ACTIVE READING: Connect
Ask students how they feel about the narrator's assessment. Do they agree that ordinary people are tough and strong? How do they think the narrator feels about himself and about Colin? Encourage students to share their thoughts about special and ordinary people. (Any response is valid.)

6. LITERARY CONCEPT: Conflict
Ask students what conflict is evident here. (Colin's mother and father disagree about the importance of his artistic talents.)

warm. The leafless woods were bleak and empty, and I spoke of that to Father when I came back from my search.

"It's always a sad time in the woods when the seven sleepers are under cover," he said.

"What sleepers are they?" I asked. Father was full of woods lore.

"Why, all the animals that have got sense enough to hole up and stay hid in weather like this. Let's see, how was it the old rhyme named them?

Surly bear and sooty bat,
Brown chuck and masked coon
Chippy-munk and sly skunk,
And all the mouses
'Cept in men's houses.

"And man would have joined them and made it eight, Granther Yeary always said, if he'd had a little more sense."

"I was wondering if the red fox mightn't make it eight," Mom said.

Father shook his head. "Late winter's a high time for foxes. Time when they're out deviling, not sleeping."

My chest felt hollow. I wanted to cry like Colin over our lost fox, but at fourteen a boy doesn't cry. Colin had squatted down on the floor and got out his small hammer and nails to start another new frame for a new picture. Maybe then he'd make a drawing for the frame and be able to forget his misery. It had been that way with him since he was five.

I thought of the new dress Mom had brought home a few days before in a heavy cardboard box. That box cover would be fine for Colin to draw on. I spoke of it, and Mom's glance thanked me as she went to

get it. She and I worried a lot about Colin. He was small for his age, delicate and blond, his hair much lighter and softer than mine, his eyes deep and wide and blue. He was often sick, and I knew the fear Mom had that he might be predestined.[2] I'm just ordinary, like Father. I'm the sort of stuff that can take it—tough and strong—but Colin was always sort of special.

Mom lighted the lamp. Colin began cutting his white cardboard carefully, fitting it into his frame. Father's sharp glance turned on him now and again.

"There goes the boy making another frame before there's a picture for it," he said. "It's too much like cutting out a man's suit for a fellow that's, say, twelve years old. Who knows whether he'll grow into it?"

Mom was into him then, quick. "Not a single frame of Colin's has ever gone to waste. The boy has real talent, Sumter, and it's time you realized it."

"Of course he has," Father said. "All kids have 'em. But they get over 'em."

"It isn't the pox[3] we're talking of," Mom sniffed.

"In a way it is. Ever since you started talking up Colin's art, I've had an <u>invalid</u> for help around the place."

Father wasn't as hard as he made out, I knew, but he had to hold a balance against all Mom's frothing.[4] For him the thing was the land and all that pertained to it. I was follow-

---

2. **predestined** (prē des′ tind): describing someone whose fate is decided beforehand, by God; in this case, chosen for an early death.
3. **pox**: a contagious disease causing skin eruptions.
4. **frothing** (frôth′ iŋ): light, meaningless talking.

Words to Know and Use	**invalid** (in′ və lid) n. a sickly or disabled person

---

Guided Reading for Less-Proficient Students

Continued from page 523

D. Why do the boys keep their continuing bond with Bandit a secret from their father? (They fear he will kill Bandit for taking chickens.) Inferring

E. How does Father feel about the hunt for Bandit? (He thinks the method of hunting is unsportsmanlike and refuses to participate, but he knows that Bandit is a menace who must be stopped.) Recalling

F. What two discoveries does the narrator make by the pool? (Bandit's hiding place and the essence of his brother) Recalling

G. What happens to Bandit? (He is killed by a hunter who happens to be passing by.) Recalling

H. Why does Father change his mind about Colin's art at the end of the story? (Colin's picture of Bandit's hiding place has impressed him.) Inferring

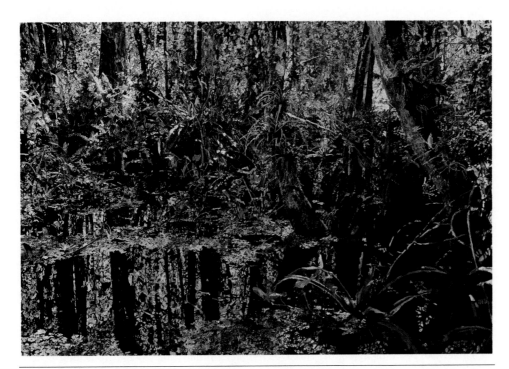

CORKSCREW BOG   1987   William Nichols   Courtesy, OK Harris Works of Art, New York.

Art Note

Landscape painters often impose their own visions on the world before them. In *Corkscrew Bog*, William Nichols realistically portrays a Florida wetland as a tangled confusion of light, shadow, and reflection. One can almost hear the noises and smell the odors of the bog. *Why would this scene be a perfect place for a fox to live?*

7. ACTIVE READING: Evaluate
Ask students why Colin's father seems to be so critical of Colin's art. *(Possible responses: He wants his son to follow the family tradition of devotion to the land; he is a practical man who sees no value in art.)* Encourage students to share their own opinions of Colin's interest and his father's response to it. *(Any response is valid.)*

8. LANGUAGE: Dialect
Some students may be confused by the dialect in this passage, such as "made out to scorn" and "white-livered." If necessary, explain that the first means "acted as if he scorned," and the second means "weak" or "cowardly." ★

7 ing in Father's footsteps, true to form, but Colin threatened to break the family tradition with his leaning toward art, with Mom "aiding and abetting[5] him," as Father liked to put it. For the past two years she had had dreams of my brother becoming a real artist and going away to the city to study.

It wasn't that Father had no understanding of such things. I could remember, through the years, Colin lying on his stomach in the front room making pencil sketches and how a good drawing would catch Father's eye halfway across the room; and how he would sometimes gather up two or three of them to study, frowning and muttering, one hand in his beard, while a great pride rose in Colin, and in me too. Most of Colin's drawings were of the woods and wild things, and there Father was a master critic. He made out to scorn what seemed to him a passive "white-livered" interpretation of nature through brush and pencil instead of rod and rifle. 8

---

5. aiding and abetting: helping and urging.

Words to Know and Use	**passive** (pas' iv) *adj.* inactive, but receiving action; lacking in energy or willpower

525

Speaking . . . Listening . . . Viewing

Viewing The following films may be useful for prompting discussion about life with wild animals.
■ *Rascal*, based on the book by Sterling North. A young boy assumes responsibility for a feisty baby raccoon. MCI/Coronet Film & Video, HD-67554.
■ *Canines: Pets and Predators*. Wolves, coyotes, jackals, foxes, and dogs are examined. Britannica Video, 3678-065.

After students see one of the movies, discuss with them questions such as the following:

1. How do the animals compare with Bandit? In what ways are they similar or different?

2. Did you feel closer to the animals in the movie or to Bandit? Why?

3. How do the animals affect people's lives? Are the animals portrayed as helpers or as threats?

4. What difficulties might filmmakers encounter in using animals as stars?

9. VOCABULARY: Context Clues
If students are unfamiliar with the word *vixen*, have them use the **context clue** "she-fox" to figure out that a vixen is a female fox. ★

10. ACTIVE READING: Question
Have students identify when the incident being described takes place. *(a year and a half before the present)* Encourage them to identify the point where this incident from the past ends. *(It ends after the first full paragraph in the second column of this page.)*

11. LITERARY CONCEPT: Character
Ask students what they think Father's advice indicates about him. *(Possible responses: He doesn't believe in being soft with anyone, including the fox and his son; he believes that things can't change and shouldn't change—that you can't make a dog out of a fox or an artist out of a farm boy.)*

12. LITERARY CONCEPT: Point of View
Remind students that in first-person narration, the story is told from only one character's viewpoint. Ask how the narrator's view of Colin differs from his father's. *(Possible response: The narrator sees Colin as more in touch with nature than his father does.)*

At supper that night, Colin could scarcely eat. Ever since he'd been able to walk, my brother had had a growing love of wild things; but Bandit had been like his very own, a gift of the woods. One afternoon a year and a half before, Father and Laban Small had been running a vixen through the hills with their dogs. With the last of her strength, the she-fox had made for her den, not far from our house. The dogs had overtaken her and killed her just before she reached it. When Father and Laban came up, they'd found Colin crouched nearby, holding her cub in his arms.

The fox became Colin's whole life.

Father had been for killing the cub, which was still too young to shift for itself, but Colin's grief had brought Mom into it. We'd taken the young fox into the kitchen, all of us, except Father, gone a bit silly over the little thing. Colin had held it in his arms and fed it warm milk from a spoon.

"Watch out with all your soft ways," Father had warned, standing in the doorway. "You'll make too much of him. Remember, you can't make a dog out of a fox. Half of that little critter has to love, but the other half is a wild hunter. You boys will mean a whole lot to him while he's kit, but there'll come a day when you won't mean a thing to him, and he'll leave you shorn."[6]

For two weeks after that, Colin had nursed the cub, weaning it from milk to bits of meat. For a year they were always together. The cub grew fast. It was soon following Colin and me about the barnyard. It turned out to be a patch fox, with a saddle of darker fur across its shoulders.

I haven't the words to tell you what the fox meant to us. It was far more wonderful owning him than owning any dog. There was something rare and secret, like the spirit of the woods, about him; and back of his calm, straw-gold eyes was the sense of a brain the equal of a man's. The fox became Colin's whole life.

Each day, going and coming from school, Colin and I took long side trips through the woods, looking for Bandit. Wild things' memories were short, we knew; we'd have to find him soon, or the old bond would be broken.

Ever since I was ten, I'd been allowed to hunt with Father, so I was good at reading signs. But, in a way, Colin knew more about the woods and wild things than Father or me. What came to me from long observation Colin seemed to know by instinct.

It was Colin who felt out, like an Indian, the stretch of woods where Bandit had his den, who found the first slim, small fox-print in the damp earth. And then, on an afternoon in March, we saw him. I remember the day well, the racing clouds, the wind rattling the tops of the pine trees and swaying the Spanish moss. Bandit had just come out of a clump of laurel; in the maze of leaves behind him, we caught a glimpse of a slim red vixen, so we knew he had found a mate. She melted from sight like a shadow, but Bandit turned to watch us, his mouth open, his tongue lolling as he smiled his old foxy smile. On his thin chops, I saw a tell-tale chicken feather.

---

6. shorn: cut off, like hair; forsaken.

Colin moved silently forward, his movements so quiet and casual he seemed to be standing still. He called Bandit's name, and the fox held his ground, drawn to us with all his senses. For a few moments he let Colin actually put an arm about him. It was then I knew that he loved us still, for all of Father's warnings. He really loved us back, with a fierce, secret love no tame thing ever gave. But the urge of his life just then was toward his new mate. Suddenly, he whirled about and disappeared in the laurels.

Colin looked at me with glowing eyes. "We haven't really lost him, Stan. When he gets through with his spring sparking,[7] he may come back. But we've got to show ourselves to him a lot, so he won't forget."

"It's a go," I said.

"Promise not to say a word to Father," Colin said, and I agreed. For I knew by the chicken feather that Bandit had been up to no good.

A week later the woods were budding, and the thickets were rustling with all manner of wild things scurrying on the love scent. Colin managed to get a glimpse of Bandit every few days. He couldn't get close though, for the spring running was a lot more important to a fox than any human beings were.

Every now and then Colin got out his framed box cover and looked at it, but he never drew anything on it; he never even picked up his pencil. I remember wondering if what Father had said about framing a picture before you had one had spoiled something for him.

I was helping Father with the planting now, but Colin managed to be in the woods every day. By degrees, he learned Bandit's range, where he drank and rested and where he was likely to be according to the time of day. One day he told me how he had petted Bandit again and how they had walked together a long way in the woods. All this time we had kept his secret from Father.

As summer came on, Bandit began to live up to the prediction Father had made. Accustomed to human beings, he moved without fear about the scattered farms of the region, raiding barns and hen runs that other foxes wouldn't have dared go near. And he taught his wild mate to do the same. Almost every night they got into some poultry house, and by late June, Bandit was not only killing chickens and ducks but feeding on eggs and young chicks whenever he got the chance.

*B*andit was not only killing chickens and ducks but feeding on eggs.

Stories of his doings came to us from many sources, for he was still easily recognized by the dark patch on his shoulders. Many a farmer took a shot at him as he fled, and some of them set out on his trail with dogs, but they always returned home without even sighting him. Bandit was familiar with all the dogs in the region, and he knew a hundred tricks to confound them. He got

---

7. **spring sparking:** an old slang term referring to the mating period of certain animals.

Words to Know and Use | **confound** (kən found′) *v.* to bewilder; confuse

527

◀ D

13. ACTIVE READING: Evaluate
Point out that it is very unusual for a wild fox to allow a person to touch it. Encourage students to discuss the fox's behavior and the boys' reaction to it. Ask why Colin feels that the boys haven't really lost Bandit. *(Any response is valid.)*

14. ACTIVE READING: Predict
Ask students what prediction they would make about Bandit's future at this point. *(Possible responses: The boys will capture him and keep him safe; Bandit will be killed by a farmer.)*

Speaking . . . Listening . . . Viewing

Speaking A traditional fox hunt has strict rules. For example, only the dogs may kill the fox, so the hunters carry no weapons. Many hunt clubs even prefer to keep the fox alive because the same fox may be run season after season. It is the chase, not the kill, that is important.

Ask students to stage a mock debate between members of a hunt club and animal-rights activists about the following: *Resolved, that fox hunting is cruel even when the fox is not killed.*

Urge students in the audience to listen critically, following the guidelines below, to carefully evaluate the ability of each side to make its case.

■ Decide whose argument is the stronger. Take notes, and score the positive points on each side.

■ Note the speakers' delivery. Can they be easily understood? Are their arguments clear and well stated? Do they stick to the point?

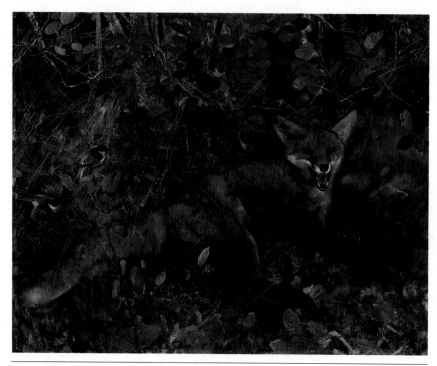

FOXES 1886 Bruno Liljefors The Gothenburg Art Gallery, Göteborg, Sweden.

a reputation that year beyond that of any fox our hills had known. His confidence grew, and he gave up wild hunting altogether and lived entirely off the poultry farmers. By September, the hill farmers banded together to hunt him down.

It was Father who brought home that news one night. All time-honored rules of the fox chase were to be broken in this hunt; if the dogs couldn't bring Bandit down, he was to be shot on sight. I was stricken and furious. I remember the misery of Colin's face in the lamplight. Father, who took pride in all the ritual of the hunt, had refused to be a party to such an affair, though in justice he could do nothing but sanction any sort of hunt; for Bandit, as old Sam Wetherwax put it, had been "purely getting in the Lord's hair."

The hunt began next morning, and it was the biggest turnout our hills had known. There were at least twenty mounted men in the party and as many dogs. Father and I were working in the lower field as they

15

◄ E

Words to Know and Use | **sanction** (saŋk′ shən) *v.* to give approval for

528

passed along the river road. Most of the hunters carried rifles, and they looked ugly.

Twice during the morning I went up to the house to find Colin, but he was nowhere around. As we worked, Father and I could follow the progress of the hunt by the distant hound music on the breeze. We could tell just where the hunters first caught sight of the fox and where Bandit was leading the dogs during the first hour. We knew as well as if we'd seen it how Bandit roused another fox along Turkey Branch and forced it to run for him and how the dogs swept after it for twenty minutes before they sensed their mistake.

Noon came, and Colin had not come in to eat. After dinner Father didn't go back to the field. He moped about, listening to the hound talk. He didn't like what was on any more than I did, and now and again I caught his smile of satisfaction when we heard the broken, angry notes of the hunting horn, telling that the dogs had lost the trail or had run another fox.

I was restless, and I went up into the hills in midafternoon. I ranged the woods for miles, thinking all the time of Colin. Time lost all meaning for me, and the short day was nearing an end when I heard the horn talking again, telling that the fox had put over another trick. All day he had deviled the dogs and mocked the hunters. This new trick and the coming night would work to save him. I was wildly glad as I moved down toward Turkey Branch and stood listening for a time by the deep, shaded pool where for years we boys had gone swimming, sailed boats, and dreamed summer dreams.

Suddenly, out of the corner of my eye, I saw the sharp ears and thin, pointed mask of a fox—in the water almost beneath me. It was Bandit, craftily submerged there, all but his head resting in the cool water of the pool and the shadow of the two big beeches that spread above it. He must have run forty miles or more since morning. And he must have hidden in this place before. His knowing, crafty mask blended perfectly with the shadows and a mass of drift and branches that had collected by the bank of the pool. He was so still that a pair of thrushes flew up from the spot as I came up, not knowing he was there.

Bandit's bright, <u>harried</u> eyes were looking right at me. But I did not look at him direct. Some woods instinct, swifter than thought, kept me from it. So he and I met as in another world, indirectly, with feeling but without sign or greeting.

Suddenly I saw that Colin was standing almost beside me. Silently as a water snake, he had come out of the bushes and stood there. Our eyes met, and a quick and secret smile passed between us. It was a rare moment in which I really "met" my brother, when something of his <u>essence</u> flowed into me, and I knew all of him. I've never lost it since.

My eyes still turned from the fox, my heart pounding, I moved quietly away, and Colin moved with me. We whistled softly as we went, pretending to busy ourselves along the bank of the stream. There was magic in it, as if by will we wove a web of protection

529

16
17
18
◀ F

16. LITERARY CONCEPT: Figurative Language
If students are confused by the term "hound music," explain that during a fox hunt the hounds howl, or *bay*, as they chase the fox, creating a kind of "music." ★

17. LITERARY CONCEPT: Setting
Invite students to describe Bandit's hiding place in sensory language. *(Possible responses: cool, shady, wet, shadowy)*

18. ACTIVE READING: Question
Ask students why they think the narrator does not look directly into Bandit's eyes. If necessary, help students by reading the following example of a think-aloud, or model one of your own.

Think-Aloud Script Why does Stan avoid looking into Bandit's eyes when he discovers the fox hiding? I can tell that Stan thinks Bandit is in a good hiding place because Stan says that Bandit was "craftily submerged" and that he "blended perfectly." Perhaps Stan is afraid that if Bandit knows he has been seen, he'll run. Another possibility occurs to me: I know that sometimes a dog challenges another dog by staring at it. Maybe foxes do that too. Maybe Stan's "woods instinct" tells him that right now Bandit is scared and might mistake Stan for an enemy.

Looking at Style

Have students read these sentences:
- Ever since he'd been able to walk, my brother had had a growing love of wild things; but Bandit had been like his very own, a gift of the woods. (p. 526)
- Wild things' memories were short, we knew; we'd have to find him soon, or the old bond would be broken. (p. 526)
- Every now and then Colin got out his framed box cover and looked at it, but he never drew anything on it; he never even picked up his pencil. (p. 527)

Then discuss the following questions and activity:

1. Why might Annixter have used semicolons rather than periods to separate complete statements? How connected are the ideas in the statements?

2. What would be the difference if each statement were a separate sentence? When reading, do you pause longer at a period than at a semicolon?

3. Using semicolons, write sentences about nature.

19. LITERARY CONCEPT: Irony
Remind students that irony involves the unexpected. Ask them how Bandit's death is ironic. (Possible responses: Bandit is killed by chance rather than by the organized hunt; after all the suspense, Bandit's death is presented suddenly, almost offhandedly.)

20. ACTIVE READING: Review
Ask students to think about similarities between this story and "The Christmas Hunt" (page 353). (Possible responses: Both deal with hunting and with people's relationships with animals; both have rural settings; both have boys in conflict with their fathers; both end with fathers supporting their sons.)

ENCOURAGING INDEPENDENT READING

The Devil of the Woods, short stories by Paul Annixter

Trumpeter: The Story of a Swan, novel by Jane and Paul Annixter

The Yearling, novel by Marjorie Kinnan Rawlings

about the fox, a ring-pass-not that none might penetrate. It was so, too, we felt, in the brain of Bandit, and that doubled the charm. To us he was still our little pet that we had carried about in our arms on countless summer afternoons.

Two hundred yards upstream, we stopped beside slim, fresh tracks in the mud where Bandit had entered the branch. The tracks angled upstream. But in the water the <u>wily</u> creature had turned down.

We climbed the far bank to wait, and Colin told me how Bandit's secret had been his secret ever since an afternoon three months before, when he'd watched the fox swim downstream to hide in the deep pool. Today he'd waited on the bank, feeling that Bandit, hard pressed by the dogs, might again seek the pool for <u>sanctuary</u>.

We looked back once as we turned homeward. He still had not moved. We didn't know until later that he was killed that same night, by a chance hunter, as he crept out from his hiding place.

That evening Colin worked a long time on his framed box cover that had lain about the house untouched all summer. He kept at it all the next day too. I had never seen him work so hard. I seemed to sense in the air the feeling he was putting into it, how he was *believing* his picture into being. It was

19

G ▶

evening before he finished it. Without a word he handed it to Father. Mom and I went and looked over his shoulder.

It was a delicate and <u>intricate</u> pencil drawing of the deep branch pool; and there was Bandit's head, and watching, fear-filled eyes hiding there amid the leaves and shadows, woven craftily into the maze of twigs and branches as if by nature's art itself. Hardly a fox there at all, but the place where he was—or should have been. I recognized it instantly, but Mom gave a sort of incredulous sniff.

"I'll declare," she said, "it's mazy as a puzzle. It just looks like a lot of sticks and leaves to me."

Long minutes of study passed before Father's eye picked out the picture's secret, as few men's could have done. I laid that to Father's being a born hunter. That was a picture that might have been done especially for him. In fact, I guess it was.

Finally he turned to Colin with his deep, slow smile. "So that's how Bandit fooled them all," he said. He sat holding the picture with a sort of tenderness for a long time, while we glowed in the warmth of the shared secret. That was Colin's moment. Colin's art stopped being a pox to Father right there. And later, when the time came for Colin to go to art school, it was Father who was his solid backer. ❧

20

◀ H

Words to Know and Use	**wily** (wīl' ē) *adj.* crafty; sly **sanctuary** (saŋk' chōō er' ē) *n.* shelter; protection **intricate** (in' tri kit) *adj.* elaborately detailed

530

Comprehension Check

1. Why are the two boys upset at the beginning of the story? (*Their pet fox has disappeared.*)

2. What special interest does Colin pursue at home? (*art, drawing pictures*)

3. What secret do the boys keep from their father? (*They know where Bandit is.*)

4. Why do farmers dislike Bandit? (*He kills their chickens and ducks and feeds on eggs.*)

5. Where do the boys find Bandit hiding during the hunt? (*in a pool of water*)

6. What finally happens to Bandit? (*He is killed by a chance hunter.*)

7. What picture does Colin draw at the end of the story? (*Bandit in his hiding place*)

8. What effect does the drawing have on Colin's father? (*He finally appreciates Colin and his artistic ability.*)

Responding to Reading

First Impressions

1. What were your thoughts at the end of the story? Describe your reaction in your journal.

Second Thoughts

2. In your opinion, why are the doors of understanding opened between Colin and his father?

Think about
- why the father changes his mind about Colin's art
- what Colin and his father have in common

3. Why do you think Bandit is so important to the two boys?

Think about
- how a wild animal is different from a tamed one
- your previous discussion of what pets do for people

4. Which family member do you think shows the most understanding of Colin? Explain your opinion.

5. Why do you think Colin leaves the framed box cover blank for the entire summer?

6. What do you think the title of the story means?

Broader Connections

7. Based on this story and your own experience, do you think people should raise wild animals as pets? Do you think wild animals should be raised in zoos? Give reasons for your answers.

Literary Concept: Flashback

The events in a story's plot usually occur in the order in which they happen. Sometimes, however, writers interrupt the flow of events to describe an episode that happened before the beginning of the story. This is called a **flashback.** Find a flashback in "Last Cover." What does the flashback contribute to your understanding of the story?

Concept Review: Narrator How does the narrator's opinion of his brother come through in his story?

LAST COVER 531

Responding to Reading

1. Any response is valid.

2. **Possible responses:** Colin's father recognizes that he and his son share a knowledge and love of the woods; he finally recognizes Colin's talent and great love of nature.

3. **Possible responses:** They rescued him from death; they see the fox as a friend, almost an equal; they identify with his wildness; because he is wild, his love is a special gift.

4. **Possible responses:** his brother, since he almost reads Colin's mind at times; his mother, because she recognizes his talent as an artist

5. **Possible responses:** He is waiting for the right moment to draw something significant; he is too upset to draw; his father's comments discourage him; he is working mentally on an idea that he is not ready to draw.

6. **Possible responses:** Bandit's secret hiding place in the pool is the last cover he takes to hide from the hunters; Colin's drawing on the box cover is the one that finally wins his father's admiration and approval.

7. Any response is valid.

Challenge Question

How is Stan's relationship to Colin similar to Colin's relationship to Bandit? *(Possible responses: Stan is very protective of Colin, as Colin is of Bandit; Stan admires Colin greatly for his instinctual knowledge of the woods, and Colin admires Bandit for the same reason; both Colin and Bandit are a little bit wild and spooky.)*

Literary Concept: Flashback

The flashback describes how Bandit "became Colin's whole life." It helps to explain why the fox is such a special pet to the boy.

Concept Review: Narrator It comes through in his thoughts—he admires Colin's artistic ability and love of nature, and he worries about his brother's sensitivity. It comes through in his actions—he suggests the box cover for Colin's drawing, and he wanders in the woods, halfway searching for Colin.

Writing Options

The Writing Options are designed to meet varied student interests and abilities. Have each student choose one writing activity to complete.

Journal Update Invite students to write their thoughts about art or hunting after reading "Last Cover."

Links to
Writer's Craft

Writing Option 4 is an exercise in informative writing. For more practice, see *The Writer's Craft,* Grade 7, "Informative Writing: Explaining *What,*" pages 117–137.

Vocabulary Practice

Answers to Exercise

1. sanctuary
2. sanction
3. wily
4. bleak
5. invalid
6. confound
7. passive
8. essence
9. harried
10. intricate

For Alternative Learning Styles

Have students describe imaginary scenarios to partners, leading up to blanks that stand for the vocabulary words—for example, "Last June I caught a cold from my sister, which developed into a fever and a cough. I spent three weeks in bed, feeling like an *blank.*" The partner then tries to guess the appropriate vocabulary word. *(invalid)*

Closure

Have students discuss all the doors of understanding that are opened by the end of the story. Then invite students to imagine and describe a sequel to the story. They might address these questions: What becomes of Colin and his art? Do the boys get another pet? How do Colin and his father get along?

Writing Options

1. Imagine that Colin is holding his first exhibition of paintings. Write an **advertising flyer** about his art and background to get people to come to his exhibition.

2. Imagine that you are a neighbor of the two brothers. Write a **letter** to the local paper in which you voice your approval or disapproval of the fox hunt.

3. Write a **comparison-contrast paper** that explains the differences and the similarities between the two brothers.

4. Find out more about fox hunts. Write a **feature article** to report your findings and to explain what happens on the hunt.

Vocabulary Practice

Exercise On your paper, write the word from the list that is most closely related to the meaning of the boldfaced word or phrase.

1. Bandit found **safety** in his hiding place.

2. The boys' father did not **encourage** the idea of keeping a wild fox as a pet.

3. Like all foxes, Bandit proved himself to be a **clever** trickster.

4. The winter proved to be **cheerless** and bitterly cold.

5. Colin's avoidance of chores led his father to compare him to a **sickly, bedridden person.**

6. The fox was able to **confuse** the dogs during the hunt.

7. A person who is **lacking in spirit or force** would not please Colin's father.

8. To understand Colin's **true character,** his father needed to understand his art.

9. The farmers were **troubled** by Bandit's constant attacks on their livestock.

10. Colin's picture showed **complex** use of details.

> **Words to Know and Use**
>
> bleak
> confound
> essence
> harried
> intricate
> invalid
> passive
> sanction
> sanctuary
> wily

The Spelling Connection

Spelling Pattern: Doubling Final Consonants In a multisyllabic word, the final consonant is doubled before a suffix only when the final syllable is accented, as in *admit, admitted.* When the final consonant is not accented, the final consonant is not doubled, as in *visit, visited.*

Words from the Selection with and Without Doubling

beginning   forgetting   remembered   scattered

Other Words with and Without Doubling

transmitted   omitting   transferred
preferred   differed   entered

Exercise Use spelling words to fill in the blanks.

The famous artist John James Audubon is __ for his paintings and drawings of birds. His genius at painting was not recognized in the __ . In 1803, Audubon first __ the United States. His father wanted him to learn farm management, but Audubon __ to paint.

*O*ptions for Learning   (Multimodal/Cross-Curricular Activities)

1 • **Nature's Art**   Colin created an intricate pencil drawing of Bandit's hiding place. Using a different medium, such as paint, chalk, ink, fabric, clay, or whatever you choose, create your own interpretation of the scene he presented. Before you begin, skim the story to find relevant details.

2 • **The Lay of the Land**   Skim "Last Cover" and list the sites where the action takes place. Use this information and your imagination to make a map of the area.

3 • **Call of the Wild**   Read *Call of the Wild* by Jack London, *Rascal* by Sterling North, *Born Free* by Joy Adamson, or another book of your choice about taming wild animals. Give an oral book report in which you draw comparisons to Bandit's response toward taming.

4 • **Fox Facts**   Find out about any foxes that live in your area. Then create a poster that provides interesting facts about these foxes, including pictures if possible.

 FACT FINDER SCIENCE

Name a hibernating animal that is not among the seven mentioned in the father's rhyme.

---

*P*aul Annixter
1894–1985

Paul Annixter is a pen name that Howard A. Sturtzel used for the more than five hundred short stories he published. Most of these stories are about wildlife.

When he was nine, Sturtzel and his mother were left alone, having to earn a living for themselves and his paralyzed grandmother. Sturtzel sold newspapers and candy and later worked as a hotel bellhop. When he was sixteen, he traveled across the United States and Canada, living the life of a hobo.

Eventually, Sturtzel settled a timber claim in northern Minnesota, where he lived alone for one and a half years and began to write.

After attending college, he married the daughter of his favorite writer and tutor, Will Levington Comfort. He and his wife Jane worked together to produce more than twenty novels for young people, including *The Phantom Stallion* (1961) and *Windigo* (1963). "Where one may have a weakness," he said of himself and his wife, "the other is apt to have a strength."

LAST COVER   533

Cross-Curricular Projects

Science Have volunteers form groups and encourage each group to learn about one type of fox: the red fox, the gray fox, the arctic fox, the bat-eared fox, and so on. Then have them work together on a chart that presents the animals' similarities and differences.

Math Invite interested students to find statistics on the ten most popular pets in the United States or the world. Ask them to present their findings in a bar graph.

Extending the Lesson

Options for Learning

These activities suit a variety of learning styles and modes of expression.

Collaborative Learning Activities
See Options 3 and 4.

1. Nature's Art For inspiration, students may look at nature photos, books of art reproductions, or Sierra Club publications.

2. The Lay of the Land Encourage students to compile a list of symbols for such features as Bandit's pool and the foothills where Stan searches for him.

3. Call of the Wild Students will find the card catalog helpful when searching for a book to read. Suggest they look under "Animals" or "Wild Animals."

4. Fox Facts Students might get facts from a local zoo, an animal-rights group, or an environmental organization.

 FACT FINDER SCIENCE
Students could look in an encyclopedia or a book about animals to find that hibernators include hamsters, frogs, snakes, turtles, ground squirrels, and hedgehogs.

Paul Annixter

■ **More About the Author** As early as the age of eight, Sturtzel wrote pieces on the life and death of a cattail and the life story of an acorn. About his life in Minnesota, he said, "I think there is no better forcing ground for a writer than a timber claim, particularly one that is a long way from anywhere at all. By the time you get to talking to yourself in short pithy sentences, you'll be writing, if there's any of it in you."

■ **Other Works** Novels: *Buffalo Chief* ; short story collections: *Brought to Cover*, *Pride of Lions*.

Objectives

- To understand and analyze two poems
- To examine the imagery of a poem
- To enrich reading by comparing and contrasting
- To express understanding of the poems through a choice of writing forms, including a bill of rights and a poem

Prereading/Motivation

Examine What You Know

Discussion Prompts Do you have different feelings about different types of animals? Which animals do you feel are most and least important to people? Why?

Expand Your Knowledge

Additional Background Frost's poems are especially identified with Vermont and New Hampshire, states whose official birds are the hermit thrush and the purple finch. In New Mexico many types of snakes abound, including poisonous rattlesnakes and coral snakes.

Thematic Link— Doors of Understanding

In "A Minor Bird," the speaker regrets closing a door of understanding to a wild bird. In "The Time We Climbed Snake Mountain," the speaker opens a door of understanding by showing respect for a yellow snake.

Poetry   ^A *Minor Bird*
ROBERT FROST

The Time We Climbed
Snake Mountain
LESLIE MARMON SILKO

Examine What You Know   (Prior Knowledge)

Are you the sort of person who feels responsibility toward animals? Or do you feel that the needs of animals should be secondary to those of humans? Rate yourself on the following scale and compare your views to those of your classmates.

	Animal Attitude Scale				
	Strongly disagree			Strongly agree	
	1	2	3	4	5
I like being around animals.					
I feel a strong link to animals.					
People should be judged by how they treat animals.					
Animals have rights that people abuse.					

Expand Your Knowledge   (Building Background)

These poems show two speakers' responses to animals found in their natural environments. Those environments, or settings, are very different. Robert Frost's poem, like most of his poetry, is set in the isolated New England countryside where Frost lived and worked. Leslie Marmon Silko's poem is set in the West, where the speaker is part of a mountain-climbing expedition. Silko lives on the Laguna Pueblo Reservation in mountainous New Mexico. Her writing often reflects the experiences and beliefs of her Native American culture.

Write Before You Read   (Journal Writing)

■ *Author biographies in Reader's Handbook*

In your journal or notebook, write about a personal experience you have had that involved an animal.

534   UNIT FIVE   DOORS OF UNDERSTANDING

MORE JOURNAL WRITING IDEAS

■ List animals you dislike or fear, and explain why you feel as you do.

■ Describe a person you consider to be an animal lover.

COLLABORATIVE LEARNING OPTIONS

Opportunities for collaborative learning include Examine What You Know and Writing Option 1 (p. 537).

ADDITIONAL RESOURCES

Unit Five Resource Book
Reader's Guidesheet, p. 44
Reading Skills, p. 45
Literature Skills, p. 46
Vocabulary Connections, p. 47
Spelling Connections, p. 48
Comprehension Check Test, p. 49
Selection Test, p. 50

A Minor Bird ⎮ 1

ROBERT FROST

I have wished a bird would fly away,
And not sing by my house all day;

Have clapped my hands at him from the door
When it seemed as if I could bear no more. ◀ A

5   The fault must partly have been in me.
The bird was not to blame for his key. ⎮ 2

And of course there must be something wrong
In wanting to silence any song. ◀ B

Responding to Reading

First Impressions of "A Minor Bird"

1. What did you think about the speaker as you read this poem?
   Describe your thoughts in your journal or notebook.

Second Thoughts on "A Minor Bird"

2. How do you think the speaker judges himself? Do you agree with
   him? Explain your opinion.

3. Based on your own experiences, do you find the speaker's irritation
   with the bird to be a normal response? Explain.

4. Explain what you think the title of the poem means.

A MINOR BIRD   535

Teaching Strategies

VOCABULARY PREVIEW

The focus of vocabulary study for this selection is the prefix *im-*. See *Unit Five Resource Book*, Vocabulary Connections, page 49.

LIMITED ENGLISH PROFICIENCY

■ Use the Reader's Guidesheet, *Unit Five Resource Book*, page 44.

■ Since both poems contain rich imagery, you may wish to have students listen as you read the poems aloud before they read on their own.

★ Text annotations marked with a red star (1, 2) may be particularly helpful to students with limited English proficiency.

TEXT ANNOTATIONS

1. ACTIVE READING: Review
Be sure students understand that "minor bird" does not refer to a type of bird, like a robin or sparrow. Tell them not to confuse the title with "myna bird." ★

2. VOCABULARY: Multiple Meanings
Ask students what the word *key* means in the poem. Have them use **context clues** to determine that here it refers to a set of musical tones. Have students suggest other meanings of *key*. (*Possible responses: "an instrument that unlocks a door"; "the answer to a problem"; "an important or essential person or thing"; "an explanation of symbols and abbreviations"*) ★

Responding to Reading

1. Any response is valid.

2. Possible responses: He judges himself to be lacking in patience, intolerant, too hasty, and unfair.

3. Any response is valid.

4. Possible responses: The speaker thinks that the bird is of little importance, or minor; the speaker is referring to the minor key of the bird's song.

Guided Reading for Less-Proficient Students

These questions can help guide students through the reading. Ask each question at the point of the selection where the capital letter and arrow appear in the margin. In addition, you may wish to use appropriate Active Reading annotations.

A. Why do you think the speaker does not wish to hear the bird's song? (*He or she may find it distracting or annoying.*) Inferring

B. How does the speaker respond to his or her own irritation? (*by blaming himself or herself*) Inferring

C. Why does the speaker need "good places" for his or her hands? (*in order to get a secure grip on firm rock while climbing the mountain*) Clarifying

D. To whom does the speaker say the mountain belongs? (*the snake*) Recalling

The Time We Climbed Snake Mountain

LESLIE MARMON SILKO

Seeing good places
    for my hands
3 I grab the warm parts of the cliff
C ▶   and I feel the mountain as I climb.
5 Somewhere   around here
    yellow spotted snake is sleeping   on his rock
      in the sun.

So
    please, I tell them
10   watch out,
don't step on the spotted yellow snake
      he lives here.
4
D ▶ The mountain is his.

THE MOUNTAIN, NEW MEXICO
1931 Georgia O'Keeffe
Oil on canvas, 30 x 36 inches.
Collection of the Whitney Museum of Art, New York. Photograph by Sheldon C. Collins, New Jersey.

Comprehension Check

1. What does the speaker of "A Minor Bird" find unbearable? *(the singing of a bird)*

2. What does the speaker think there is something wrong with? *(wanting to silence a bird)*

3. What is the speaker of the second poem doing? *(climbing a mountain)*

4. What does the speaker warn his or her companions against? *(stepping on the spotted yellow snake)*

Responding to Reading

First Impressions of "The Time We Climbed Snake Mountain"

1. What mental pictures did you form while reading this poem? Describe them in your journal or notebook.

Second Thoughts on "The Time We Climbed Snake Mountain"

2. What does the poem reveal about the speaker's attitude toward the snake?

3. Do you agree or disagree with the speaker's claim that the mountain belongs to the snake? Explain your opinion.

Comparing the Poems

4. Do you think both poems share a common theme? Give reasons for your answer.

5. In your opinion, how would each speaker respond to the Animal Attitude Scale? Compare and contrast their ratings to your own.

6. Which of the two poems do you think would mean more to Colin in "Last Cover"? Explain your choice.

Broader Connections

7. In recent years, animal rights activists have taken action on various issues, ranging from the killing of animals for fur to the use of animals in scientific experiments. What is your opinion of the animal rights movement? How do you think the speakers in the two poems would react to it?

Writing Options

1. Work with a partner to come up with an animal **bill of rights.** List what you believe are the most important rights.

2. Write a **poem** that reflects your feelings and ideas about a particular animal, such as a snake or bird.

Student Response

Responding to Reading

1. Any response is valid.

2. **Possible responses:** The speaker respects the snake; she considers the snake's rights equal to her own.

3. Any response is valid.

4. **Possible responses:** Yes, because they both express a respect for animals; no, because the first poem focuses on a person's response to an animal, whereas the second focuses on the equality of animals and people.

5. Any response is valid.

6. **Possible responses:** "A Minor Bird" would mean more, because it deals with regret; "The Time . . ." would mean more because of the speaker's respect for nature.

7. **Any response is valid.** Students may conclude that the speaker in the second poem would be more likely to advocate animal rights than the speaker in the first poem.

Writing Options

The Writing Options are designed to meet varied student interests and abilities. Have each student choose one writing activity to complete.

Journal Update Ask students to review and add to their journal entries for these two poems. Suggest that they contrast the attitudes many people have toward birds and snakes.

Closure

Have students listen at home to the sounds of birds and other animals, such as dogs, cats, frogs, and crickets. Ask them to take notes on the different sounds they hear, answering the following questions:

■ What sounds, exactly, did each animal make?

■ How did the sounds make you feel? Relaxed? Annoyed? Distracted? Happy?

■ Do you think you would mind the animal's sound outside your home all day? Why or why not?

Objectives

■ To understand and analyze a personal essay

■ To explore the meaning of a title and to find examples of effective description

■ To enrich reading by identifying an author's opinions

■ To express understanding of the essay through a choice of writing forms, including a memo, notes for an autobiography, an opinion, and a short report

Prereading/Motivation

Examine What You Know

Discussion Prompts What was the name of your first teacher? Can you describe his or her looks? What did you do all day at school back then? Do you remember any of your classmates? What else do you recall?

Expand Your Knowledge

Additional Background After Spain surrendered Puerto Rico to the United States, the island became essentially a U.S. colony. Until 1947, the governor was appointed by the United States rather than elected by the Puerto Rican people. Though Puerto Ricans became citizens of the United States in 1917, the country did not become a self-governing commonwealth until 1952. It has a constitution of its own that is based on the U.S. Constitution.

Enrich Your Reading

Refer students to the definitions of *Fact and Opinion* in the Reader's Handbook on page 682, and make sure that they understand the difference between them.

Thematic Link— Doors of Understanding

The narrator looks back on her first experiences of school and on the doors of understanding that were opened or closed there. She describes her encounters with teachers who judged others in terms of status and wealth, and she reflects upon a school system that tried to force Spanish-speaking students to learn English by rote.

Nonfiction

Primary Lessons
from Silent Dancing
JUDITH ORTIZ COFER

Examine What You Know (Prior Knowledge)

Think about your first experiences with formal schooling, which probably took place in kindergarten or first grade. Looking back, how would you rate your first teacher and school? If you could change anything about your first classroom experience, what would it be? Write your thoughts in your journal or notebook.

Expand Your Knowledge (Building Background)

Judith Ortiz Cofer, a poet and novelist, shares her earliest memories of school in this essay from her collection *Silent Dancing: A Partial Remembrance of a Puerto Rican Childhood.* At the age of six, Cofer moved from Paterson, New Jersey, back to her birthplace, Puerto Rico, along with her mother and brother. They lived in her grandmother's house while her father, a member of the U.S. Navy, was stationed in Europe. Later, the family reunited in Paterson when his ship returned to New York. The family's cycle of moving from the mainland to Puerto Rico and back continued for over twenty years.

Cofer's homeland, Puerto Rico, is an island in the Caribbean Sea about a thousand miles southeast of Florida. Puerto Rico is a commonwealth; its people are U.S. citizens with limited rights. For example, they have no voting representative in Congress, and they cannot vote in U.S. presidential elections. The island has a mixture of ethnic groups, the largest being Spanish and African. First claimed for Spain by Christopher Columbus in 1493, Puerto Rico remained a Spanish colony until 1898, when the United States took possession after winning the Spanish-American war.

Enrich Your Reading (Reading Skill)

■ *Author biography on Extend page*

Identifying an Opinion As you read, determine Cofer's opinions about her school in Puerto Rico and the school system as a whole.

538 UNIT FIVE DOORS OF UNDERSTANDING

JOURNAL WRITING IDEAS

■ List feelings and ideas suggested by the phrases "primary lessons" and "silent dancing."

■ Examine the map. Write about what you think you might find in these places if you traveled there.

COLLABORATIVE LEARNING OPTIONS

Opportunities for collaborative learning include Writing Option 4 (p. 547). Options for Learning activities 1, 2, and 4 (p. 548), and Cross-Curricular Projects (p. 548).

ADDITIONAL RESOURCES

Unit Five Resource Book
Reader's Guidesheet, p. 51
Reading Skills, p. 52
Literature Skills, p. 53
Vocabulary Connections, p. 54
Spelling Connections, p. 55
Comprehension and Vocabulary Check Tests, p. 56
Selection Test, pp. 57–58

Technology and Enrichment
 Audiocassette Tape 2, Side 2

Primary Lessons

from Silent Dancing

JUDITH ORTIZ COFER

My mother walked me to my first day at school at La Escuela Segundo Ruiz Belvis, named after the Puerto Rican patriot born in our town. I remember yellow cement with green trim. All the classrooms had been painted these colors to identify them as government property. This was true all over the Island. Everything was color-coded, including the children, who wore uniforms from first through twelfth grade. We were a midget army in white and brown, led by the hand to our battleground. From practically every house in our barrio[1] emerged a crisply ironed uniform inhabited by the savage creatures we had become over a summer of running wild in the sun.

At my grandmother's house, where we were staying until my father returned to Brooklyn Yard in New York and sent for us, it had been complete <u>chaos</u>, with several children to get ready for school. My mother had pulled my hair harder than usual while braiding it, and I had dissolved into a pool of total self-pity. I wanted to stay home with her and Mamá, to continue listening to stories in the late afternoon, to drink *café con leche*[2] with them, and to play rough games with my many cousins. I wanted to continue living the dream of summer afternoons in Puerto Rico, and if I could not have it, then I wanted to go back to Paterson, New Jersey, back to where I imagined our apartment waited, peaceful and cool, for the three of us to return to our former lives. Our gypsy lifestyle[3] had convinced me, at age six, that one part of life stops and waits for you while you live another for a while—and if you don't like the present, you can always return to the past. Buttoning me into my stiff blouse while I tried to squirm away from her, my mother attempted to explain to me that I was a big girl now and should try to understand that, like all the other children my age, I had to go to school.

"What about him?" I yelled, pointing at my brother who was lounging on the tile floor of our bedroom in his pajamas, playing quietly with a toy car.

"He's too young to go to school; you

---

1. **barrio** (bär′ ē ō): a neighborhood in a Latin American city.
2. *café con leche* (kä fā′ kôn le′ chā) *Spanish:* coffee with milk.
3. **gypsy lifestyle:** a way of life in which one continually moves from place to place.

Words to Know and Use	**chaos** (kā′ äs′) *n.* a state of disorder and confusion

539

Teaching Strategies

VOCABULARY PREVIEW

These vocabulary words are defined at the bottom of the selection pages on which they appear.

adaptation a thing changed to suit conditions

adhere to be loyal

chaos a state of disorder

hierarchy a group organized by rank

incomprehensible not understandable

minimize to reduce to smallest amount

niche a person's place in society

predecessor one who comes before

relish to enjoy

rote memorization without understanding

LIMITED ENGLISH PROFICIENCY

■ Use the Reader's Guidesheet, *Unit Five Resource Book,* Page 51.

■ Be sure students understand Cofer's uses of figurative language and idioms. Phrases such as "a midget army," "I lived in a bubble," "batch of offspring," and "the grocer was swamped" may need clarification.

★ Text annotations marked with a red star (2, 4, 6, 8, 12, 19) may be particularly helpful for students with limited English proficiency.

TEXT ANNOTATIONS

1. VOCABULARY: Foreign Words
If you have Spanish-speaking students, have them pronounce Spanish words in the story for the class.

2. LITERARY CONCEPT: Metaphor
Encourage students to explain why the children were "a midget army" being led to the "battleground." *(Possible responses: The children in uniforms were like small soldiers; the classroom was the battleground.)* ★

3. ACTIVE READING: Connect
Have you ever felt that you wanted to return to a place and time from the past? Why did you feel that way? *(Any response is valid.)*

Guided Reading for Less-Proficient Students

These questions can help guide students through the reading. Ask each question at the point of the selection where the capital letter and arrow appear in the margin. In addition, you may wish to use appropriate Active Reading annotations.

A. Where is the author living, and why is this day important? *(She is living temporarily with her mother and grandmother in Puerto Rico; today is the first day of school.)* Summarizing

B. Why is the author so unwilling to go to school? *(She doesn't want to give up her childhood freedom; she likes being home during the day.)* Recalling

C. What is Cofer's opinion of the way English was taught at her school? *(She thinks the method was not logical because students didn't understand the words; she doesn't think that students should be forced to learn English.)* Summarizing/Inferring

Continued on page 540

4. ACTIVE READING: Review
Students may be confused by the fact that *Mama* obviously isn't the author's mother. Have them **scan** the essay for earlier **context clues** to **infer** that Mama is Cofer's grandmother. ★

5. ACTIVE READING: Review
Ask students to **infer** what the author really meant when she said she didn't speak Spanish. *(Possible responses: She thought of herself as an "ordinary American kid," that is, one who speaks English; she regarded Spanish as a "secret language" that is spoken only at home or in private.)*

6. VOCABULARY: Idiom
Explain that a *strait* is a narrow channel, often difficult to navigate, that connects two larger bodies of water. Help students use this definition and **context clues** to **infer** Cofer's meaning. *(Possible response: Her cousins were in the same situation as she was; like the author, they too were herded to school.)* ★

7. LITERARY CONCEPT: Opinion
Ask students whether this sentence is a fact or an opinion. *(Possible response: This sentence reflects the author's opinion; other children might have looked forward to returning to school in September.)*

4   know that. Now stay still." My mother pinned me between her thighs to button my skirt, as she had learned to do from Mamá, from whose grip it was impossible to escape.

"It's not fair, it's not fair. I can't go to school here. I don't speak Spanish." It was my final argument, and it failed miserably because I was shouting my defiance in the language I claimed not to speak. Only I knew what I meant by saying in Spanish that I did not speak Spanish. I had spent my early childhood in the United States, where I lived in a bubble created by my Puerto Rican parents in a home where two cultures and languages became one. I learned to listen to the English from the television with one ear while I heard my mother and father speaking in Spanish with the other. I thought I was an ordinary American kid—

5   like the children on the shows I watched—and that everyone's parents spoke a secret second language at home. When we came to Puerto Rico right before I started first grade, I switched easily to Spanish. It was the language of fun, of summertime games. But school—that was a different matter.

I made one last desperate effort to make my mother see reason: "Father will be very angry. You know that he wants us to speak good English." My mother, of course, ignored me as she dressed my little brother in his play clothes. I could not believe her indifference to my father's wishes. She was usually so careful about our safety and the many other areas that he was forever reminding her about in his letters. But I was right, and she knew it. Our father spoke to us in English as much as possible, and he corrected my pronunciation constantly—not "jes" but "y-es." Y-es, sir. How could she send me to school to learn Spanish when we

would be returning to Paterson in just a few months?

But, of course, what I feared was not language but loss of freedom. At school there would be no playing, no stories, only lessons. It would not matter if I did not understand a word, and I would not be allowed to make up my own definitions. I would have to learn silence. I would have to keep my wild imagination in check. Feeling locked into my stiffly starched uniform, I only sensed all this. I guess most children can intuit[4] their loss of childhood's freedom on that first day of school. It is separation anxiety[5] too, but mother is just the guardian of the "playground" of our early childhood. ◄ B

6   The sight of my cousins in similar straits comforted me. We were marched down the hill of our barrio where Mamá's robin's-egg-blue house stood at the top. I must have glanced back at it with yearning. Mamá's house—a place built for children—where anything that could be broken had already been broken by my grandmother's early batch of offspring (they ranged in age from my mother's oldest sisters to my uncle, who was six months older than me). Her house had long since been made childproof. It had been a

7   perfect summer place. And now it was September—the cruelest month for a child.

La Mrs., as all the teachers were called, waited for her class of first graders at the door of the yellow and green classroom. She too wore a uniform: it was a blue skirt and a white blouse. This teacher wore black high

---

4. **intuit** (in tōō′ it): to understand without conscious thought.
5. **separation anxiety** (aŋ zī′ ə tē): the emotional disturbance caused by being separated from a parent.

Guided Reading for Less-Proficient Students

Continued from page 539

D. Why did the author become a teacher's pet? *(Her family had status; she had lived in New York; her father was in the navy, and he had a name associated with land and money.)* Recalling

E. What do you know about Lorenzo? *(He was poor, black, bright, talented, and eager to please the teachers.)* Recalling

F. Why did the teachers choose Cofer to host the PTA show instead of Lorenzo? *(They thought Lorenzo wouldn't have enough money for a suit, and he was black; they chose the author because her family had status; her knowledge of English would impress the superintendent.)* Summarizing

Art Note
Born in 1922 in Cataño, Puerto Rico, Julio Rosado del Valle has studied art at schools in his homeland, in Italy, and in the United States. *Saro & Aita*, a work from 1949, shows a mother and daughter, with the mother in a pose of protection. The angular body of the mother seems a source of strength and support. *Compare this portrait with the one on page 499.*

Multicultural Connections

Migration Puerto Ricans migrated to New York City and other cities on the East Coast in large numbers after World War II. Most, however, retained strong ties to the island and sometimes traveled back and forth, as Cofer's family did. Ask students how they would feel if their family migrated to a new land where a different language was spoken. What problems do they think they would encounter? Would they return to their former residence to visit? Why or why not?

Titles and Special Names Puerto Rican children use *La Mrs.* or *El Mister* ("the Mrs." or "the Mister") to refer to their teachers. Ask bilingual children in your class what special titles are used in their native language to honor people in various professions. Then guide students in comparing English titles with those used in other languages and cultures.

8. VOCABULARY: Jargon
Explain that the phrase "standard issue" is in quotes because it is military jargon. Have students use the dictionary definitions of *standard* and *issue* to figure out that together they mean "that which is given out to everybody and is all the same." Then ask why Cofer uses a military term to describe her teacher's clothes. *(Possible response: Uniforms remind her of the military; school seemed rigid, formal, and disciplined.)* ★

9. ACTIVE READING: Review
Ask students why they think it was easy for the teacher to persuade her students that changing her shoes was a "privilege." *(Possible responses: The children wanted to please the teacher; they believed that changing her shoes is a privilege because they had been taught to believe and respect teachers.)*

10. LANGUAGE: Onomatopoeia
Point out that most languages have words that imitate the sounds of animals, as illustrated by these examples in English and Spanish. Ask students why the Puerto Rican children had a difficult time accepting the English word to describe a rooster's crowing. *(Possible responses: It seemed like a mistake to them; they were so used to the Spanish word that it seemed as if no other term was accurate.)*

11. ACTIVE READING: Review
Why weren't the Spanish-speaking children able to learn English? *(They weren't really taught English; they were simply bombarded with English words and told to memorize the words.)*

8 heels with her "standard issue." I remember this detail because when we were all seated in rows, she called on one little girl and pointed to the back of the room where there were shelves. She told the girl to bring her a shoe box from the bottom shelf. Then, when the box had been placed in her hands, she did something unusual. She had the little girl kneel at her feet and take the pointy high heels off her feet and replace them with a pair of satin slippers from the shoe box. She told the group that every one of us would have a chance to do this if we behaved in her class. Though confused about the prize, I soon felt caught up in the **9** competition to bring *La Mrs.* her slippers in the morning. Children fought over the privilege.

Our first lesson was English. In Puerto Rico, every child has to take twelve years of English to graduate from school. It is the law. In my parents' school days, all subjects were taught in English. The U.S. Department of Education had specified that as a United States territory, the Island had to be "Americanized," and to accomplish this task, it was necessary for the Spanish language to be replaced in one generation through the teaching of English in all schools. My father began his school day by saluting the flag of the United States and singing "America" and "The Star-Spangled Banner" by <u>rote</u>, without understanding a word of what he was saying. The logic behind this system was that though the children did not understand the English words, they would remember the rhythms. Even the games the teacher's manuals required them to play

became absurd adaptations. "Here We Go Round the Mulberry Bush" became "Here We Go Round the Mango Tree." I have heard about the confusion caused by the use of a primer[6] in which the sounds of animals were featured. The children were forced to accept that a rooster says *cock-a-doodle-doo* when they knew perfectly well from hearing their own roosters each morning that in Puerto Rico a rooster says *cocorocó*. Even the vocabulary of their pets was changed; there are still family stories circulating about the bewilderment of a first grader coming home to try to teach his dog to speak in English. The policy of assimilation by immersion[7] failed on the Island. Teachers <u>adhered</u> to it on paper, substituting their own materials for the texts, but no one took their English home. In due time, the program was <u>minimized</u> to the one class in English per day that I encountered when I took my seat in *La Mrs.*'s first-grade class. **10**

◄ **C**
11

Why aren't the Spanish-speaking children able to learn English?

review

Catching us all by surprise, she stood very straight and tall in front of us and began to sing in English:

Pollito–Chicken
Gallina–Hen
Lápiz–Pencil
Y Pluma–Pen.

---

6. **primer** (prim′ ər): a schoolbook for teaching reading.
7. **assimilation by immersion** (ə sim′ ə lā′ shən, im mʉr′ shən): learning a language by being exposed to it all the time.

Words to Know and Use	**rote** (rōt) *n.* memorization without understanding **adaptation** (ad′ əp tā′ shən) *n.* a thing changed to suit new conditions **adhere** (ad hir′) *v.* to be loyal **minimize** (min′ ə mīz′) *v.* to reduce to the smallest possible amount

542

"Repeat after me, children: Pollito—Chicken," she commanded in her heavily accented English that only I understood, being the only child in the room who had ever been exposed to the language. But I too remained silent. No use making waves or showing off. Patiently *La Mrs.* sang her song and gestured for us to join in. At some point it must have dawned on the class that this silly routine was likely to go on all day if we did not "repeat after her." It was not her fault that she had to follow the rule in her teacher's manual stating that she must teach English *in* English, and that she must not translate but merely repeat her lesson in English until the children "begin to respond" more or less "unconsciously." This was one of the vestiges[8] of the regimen followed by her predecessors in the last generation. To this day I can recite "Pollito—Chicken" mindlessly, never once pausing to visualize chicks, hens, pencils, or pens.

I soon found myself crowned "teacher's pet" without much effort on my part. I was a privileged child in her eyes simply because I lived in "Nueva York" and because my father was in the navy. His name was an old one in our pueblo, associated with once-upon-a-time landed people and long-gone money. Status is judged by unique standards in a culture where, by definition, everyone is a second-class citizen. Remembrance of past glory is as good as titles and money. Old families living in decrepit old houses rank over factory workers living in modern comfort in cement boxes—all the same. The professions raise a person out of the dreaded "sameness" into a niche of status, so that teachers, nurses, and everyone who went to school for a job were given the honorifics[9] of *El Míster* or *La Mrs.* by the common folks, people who were likely to be making more money in American factories than the poorly paid educators and government workers.

What kinds of people are respected in this society?

review

My first impressions of the hierarchy began with my teacher's shoe-changing ceremony and the exaggerated respect she received from our parents. *La Mrs.* was always right, and adults scrambled to meet her requirements. She wanted all our schoolbooks covered in the brown paper now used for paper bags (used at that time by the grocer to wrap meats and other foods). That first week of school, the grocer was swamped with requests for paper, which he gave away to the women. That week and the next, he wrapped produce in newspapers. All school projects became family projects. It was considered disrespectful at Mamá's house to do homework in privacy. Between the hours when we came home from school and dinner time, the table was shared by all of us working together, with the women hovering in the background. The teachers communicated directly with the mothers, and it was a matriarchy[10] of far-

---

8. **vestiges** (ves′ tij əz): traces of something that is now gone.
9. **honorifics** (än′ ər if′ iks): titles or words used to show respect.
10. **matriarchy** (mā′ trē är′ kē): a social group in which women rule.

Words to Know and Use	**predecessor** (pred′ ə ses′ ər) *n.* a person who comes before **niche** (nich) *n.* the place a person occupies in society **hierarchy** (hī′ ər är′ kē) *n.* a group of people organized according to rank or authority

543

12. VOCABULARY: Idiom
For Alternative Learning Styles
To help students understand what "making waves" means, ask them to visualize themselves in a small rowboat in the middle of a big lake. How would they feel about someone "making waves"? *(Possible response: A person who makes waves is a troublemaker, someone who "rocks the boat" and makes people uncomfortable or afraid.)* ★

13. LITERARY CONCEPT: Opinion
Cofer says that the teacher was not to blame for her method of teaching. According to Cofer, who was to blame? If necessary, help students by reading the following example of a think-aloud, or model one of your own.

Think-Aloud Script The author says about *La Mrs.*, "It was not her fault that she had to follow the rule in her teacher's manual." Whose fault was it? Maybe the fault lay with the people who wrote the teacher's manual, which Cofer seems to be quoting in this sentence. I wonder if this manual was written by the same government agency that made the schools teach English by rote? Maybe Cofer is blaming the government or the people in charge of the schools who are putting its policy into effect. Cofer seems to be very critical of this teaching method.

14. ACTIVE READING: Review
What kinds of people are respected in this society? *(Possible responses: descendants of people who had land and money; "professionals," or people who went to school to learn a job; people in the military; government workers)*

15. ACTIVE READING: Predict
Ask students to predict who would be shown greater favor by the teacher, the author or Lorenzo, and to explain their reasoning. *(Possible response: The teacher would always favor the author because of her status; Lorenzo may have fallen from favor because of his lower social status)*

16. LITERARY CONCEPT: Description
Ask students what impression this description gives of Lorenzo as a person. Ask them to cite particularly effective phrases and details. *(Possible responses: Lorenzo seems small, lively, eager, and almost comic in his appearance. Details include "unmindful of the giggles," "jumped up to erase the board" and "baggy pants rode down as . . . he strained up.")*

QUEBRADILLAS   Luis G. Cajiga   Courtesy, Instituto de Cultura Puertorriqueno, San Juan, Puerto Rico.

reaching power and influence.

There was a black boy in my first-grade classroom who was also the teacher's pet but for a different reason than I: I did not have to do anything to win her favor; he would do anything to win a smile. He was as black as the cauldron that Mamá used for cooking stew, and his hair was curled into tight little balls on his head—*pasitas*,[11] like little raisins glued to his skull, my mother had said. There had been some talk at Mamá's house about this boy; Lorenzo was his name. I later gathered that he was the grandson of my father's nanny. Lorenzo lived with Teresa, his grandmother, having been left in her care when his mother took off for "Los Nueva Yores" shortly after his birth. And they were poor. Everyone could see that his pants were too big for him—hand-me-downs—and his shoe soles were as thin as paper. Lorenzo seemed unmindful of the giggles he caused when he jumped up to erase the board for *La Mrs.* and his baggy pants rode down to his thin hips as he strained up to get every stray mark. He

---

11. *pasitas* (pä sē′ täs) *Spanish:* small raisins.

Looking at Style

To discuss Cofer's writing style in "Primary Lessons," read the following excerpts from pages 539–540 aloud to the class or write them on the board, stressing the italicized words.
- "I had dissolved into *a pool of total self-pity*."
- Our *gypsy lifestyle* had convinced me"
- "I had spent my early childhood in the United States, where I *lived in a bubble*"
- "mother is just the *guardian of the 'playground'* of our early childhood."

Discuss these questions with students:

1. What does the author mean by each of these figurative expressions?

2. What images or mental pictures come to mind with each expression?

3. In your opinion, do such expressions make the writing more interesting? Why or why not?

seemed to <u>relish</u> playing the little clown when she asked him to come to the front of the room and sing his phonetic[12] version of "o-bootifool, forpashios-keeis," leading the class in our <u>incomprehensible</u> tribute to the American flag. He was a bright, loving child, with a talent for song and mimicry that everyone commented on. He should have been chosen to host the PTA show that year instead of me.

At recess one day, I came back to the empty classroom to get something. My cup? My nickel for a drink from the kiosk[13] man? I don't remember. But I remember the conversation my teacher was having with another teacher. I remember because it concerned me and because I memorized it so that I could ask my mother to explain what it meant.

"He is a funny *negrito*,[14] and, like a parrot, he can repeat anything you teach him. But his mamá must not have the money to buy him a suit."

"I kept Rafaelito's First Communion suit; I bet Lorenzo could fit in it. It's white with a bow tie," the other teacher said.

"But Marisa," laughed my teacher, "in that suit Lorenzo would look like a fly drowned in a glass of milk."

Both women laughed. They had not seen me crouched at the back of the room, digging into my school bag. My name came up then.

"What about the Ortiz girl? They have money."

"I'll talk to her mother today. The superintendent, *El Americano* from San Juan, is coming down for the show. How about if we have her say her lines in both Spanish and English."

The conversation ends there for me. My mother took me to Mayagüez and bought me a frilly pink dress and two crinoline petticoats[15] to wear underneath so that I looked like a pink and white parachute with toothpick legs sticking out. I learned my lines, "*Padres, maestros,* Mr. Leonard, *bienvenidos*[16]/Parents, teachers, Mr. Leonard, welcome . . ." My first public appearance. I took no pleasure in it. The words were formal and empty. I had simply memorized them. My dress pinched me at the neck and arms and made me itch all over.

I had asked my mother what it meant to be a *"mosca en un vaso de leche,"* a fly in a glass of milk. She had laughed at the image, explaining that it meant being "different," but that it wasn't something I needed to worry about. 🍃

---

12. **phonetic** (fō net' ik): based on the way words are pronounced.
13. **kiosk** (kē' äsk'): an open stand where things are sold.
14. *negrito* (ne grē' tō) *Spanish:* a small black boy.
15. **crinoline petticoats** (krin' ə lin'): underskirts of coarse, stiff cloth that make a skirt stand out.
16. *Padres, maestros . . . bienvenidos* (pä' dres, mä es' trōs, byem ve nē' dōs) *Spanish.*

Words to Know and Use	**relish** (rel' ish) *v.* to enjoy **incomprehensible** (in' käm' prē hen' sə bəl) *adj.* not capable of being understood

545

---

17. ACTIVE READING: Review
Ask students which words from the song "America the Beautiful" Lorenzo was trying to sing. ("*Oh, beautiful, for spacious skies . . .* ") Why didn't Lorenzo seem to understand the words? (*He had memorized English words, but he didn't know their meanings or pronunciations; his lack of understanding was a result of the school's method of teaching.*) ★

18. CULTURAL SIDELIGHT
Race relations in Puerto Rico have historically been less strained than on the mainland of the United States. Most Puerto Ricans have Europeans, Africans, and Arawak (the indigenous people of the island) among their ancestors. People belonging to the upper classes, however, are still predominantly of pure Spanish ancestry. This may have a bearing on the prejudice the teachers exhibit.

19. ACTIVE READING: Review
Ask students how people in the audience might have responded to the author's use of both Spanish and English. (*Possible responses: they were probably impressed; they might have assumed that she had learned English at school; her speech might have been seen as evidence of the school's success.*)

20. ACTIVE READING: Evaluate
Ask students what they think of the mother's response to the phrase meaning "a fly in a glass of milk." (*Possible response: The mother seems to have the same prejudice as the teachers.*)

ENCOURAGING INDEPENDENT READING

Candita's Choice, novel by Mina Lewiton

Danza!, novel by Lynn Hall

The Puerto Ricans in America, nonfiction by Ronald J. Larsen

The War Between the Classes, novel by Gloria D. Miklowitz

Comprehension Check

1. Where was the author living when she started school? (*in Puerto Rico*)

2. What two languages did the author speak? (*English and Spanish*)

3. What strange "privilege" did *La Mrs.* give to a well-behaved child? (*She let the child change her shoes for her.*)

4. What was the purpose of the song the teacher sang? (*It was supposed to help students learn English.*)

5. How did the parents treat teachers in Puerto Rico? (*with great respect*)

6. What did Lorenzo's clothes show about him? (*He was poor.*)

7. Why was the author chosen to host the PTA show instead of Lorenzo? (*He was poor and black; her family had status.*)

PRIMARY LESSONS **Teacher's Edition** **545**

Student Response

Responding to Reading

1. Any response is valid.

2. Possible responses: Yes; she speaks fondly of her home life there; no, she focuses on the rigid ideas and prejudices she saw in Puerto Rico.

3. Possible responses: She thinks the government forced the school to teach things students didn't need to learn, using techniques that didn't work; she thinks her teacher abused her authority over the children, failed to reward deserving students, and was respected by parents for the wrong reasons. Students may judge Cofer's assessment as fair or unfair, but they should give reasons for their judgment.

4. Possible responses: School opened a door of understanding for the author by enabling her to see the injustice done to Lorenzo and others like him; school also allowed her to realize her community's emphasis on status and money; school closes a door on the freedom of Cofer's early childhood and on her innocence.

5. Any response is valid.

6. Possible responses: All instruction should be in English because learning English makes it easier for people to fit in and get ahead in the United States; bilingual education is better because students may need to learn certain new concepts in their native language in order to fully grasp them. Also, bilingual education helps students to appreciate their own culture and language.

Challenge Question

What do you think was the author's main purpose in writing "Primary Lessons"? (Possible responses: to trace the growth of her own ideas; to criticize certain evils she sees in society; to express her opinion of education in Puerto Rico)

Responding to Reading

First Impressions

1. What is your first impression of the author? Jot down your reaction in your journal or notebook.

Second Thoughts

2. Do you think Cofer is proud of her Puerto Rican heritage? Explain.

3. What is Cofer's opinion of the school and its methods of instruction? Do you think she is being fair?

   Think about
   - your opinion of the way English was taught
   - your reaction to the teacher's shoe-changing ceremony
   - why the community supported the school

4. What doors of understanding are opened—or closed—as a result of Cofer's school experience?

5. How is Cofer's first experience with school similar to or different from your own first experience?

Broader Connections

6. Some people believe that all instruction in U.S. schools should be in English. Others believe that non-English-speaking students should be taught first in their native language (a method called bilingual education). Which method makes more sense to you? Consider Cofer's experience in your response.

Literary Concept: Title

Often, the title of a selection hints at the main idea, or theme. Why do you think Cofer titled this essay "Primary Lessons"? What are the different meanings of the title?

Concept Review: Description Find at least two sentences in the essay that you think provide good descriptions. What makes these descriptions effective?

Literary Concept: Title

The title can refer to lessons learned in primary school and to basic lessons about life. At school, Cofer learned these hard lessons: people often have to live by rigid or inflexible rules, people are unfairly separated into classes, and adults don't always deserve the respect given them.

Concept Review: Description Cofer's descriptions rely on precise details and inventive images. Possible examples: "Everyone could see that his pants were too big for him . . . and his shoe soles were as thin as paper." "I looked like a pink and white parachute with toothpick legs sticking out."

Writing Options

1. Imagine that you are an advisor to the superintendent of schools in this selection. Write a **memo** to him, giving your advice on how to improve Cofer's school.

2. Write **notes** for a chapter in your own autobiography about your first experience at school. What were your "primary lessons"?

3. Write your own **opinion** of the teachers' decision to have the narrator host the PTA show.

4. With a partner, research bilingual education in the United States. Find out about the arguments for and against it. Write a **short report** to share your findings.

Vocabulary Practice

Exercise A Write the letter of the word that is most nearly *opposite* in meaning to the capitalized word.

1. RELISH: (a) enjoy (b) dislike (c) favor (d) please (e) annoy

2. CHAOS: (a) order (b) confusion (c) noise (d) loudness (e) silence

3. ADHERE: (a) support (b) speak (c) betray (d) multiply (e) stick

4. MINIMIZE: (a) reduce (b) restrict (c) increase (d) fail (e) loosen

5. INCOMPREHENSIBLE: (a) mysterious (b) silly (c) large (d) understandable (e) chaotic

> **Words to Know and Use**
>
> adaptation
> adhere
> chaos
> hierarchy
> incomprehensible
> minimize
> niche
> predecessor
> relish
> rote

Exercise B Write the letter of the word that is *least* like the other words in the set.

1. (a) grandparent (b) ancestor (c) predecessor (d) friend

2. (a) place (b) position (c) niche (d) absence

3. (a) hierarchy (b) order (c) structure (d) disorder

4. (a) permanence (b) adaptation (c) alteration (d) change

5. (a) rote (b) repetition (c) routine (d) creativity

PRIMARY LESSONS   547

The Spelling Connection

Spelling Pattern: Latin Word Parts Suffixes can be added to Latin roots to make complete words. Use the meaning of a root to infer the meaning of an unfamiliar word.

Example: grad (by steps) gradual

Words with Latin Roots from the Selection

circ (around)	circulate
mater (mother)	matriarchy
sim (like)	assimilation
stat (stand)	status

Other Words with Latin Roots

manufacture	anniversary	universal
pedestrian	century	unanimous
quarter	magnify	

Exercise Fill in the blanks with spelling words.

1. __ describes one's position in society.
2. To __ is to go around and around.
3. A __ is a society is ruled by women.
4. Blending into society is called __

Writing Options

The Writing Options are designed to meet varied student interests and abilities. Have each student choose one writing activity to complete.

Journal Update Invite students to review their journal entries for "Primary Lessons." Has Cofer's essay reminded them of any further episodes from their early years at school or stirred up any forgotten feelings?

Links to Writer's Craft

Writing Option 4 is an exercise in report writing. For more practice, see *The Writer's Craft*, Grade 7, "Informative Writing: Reports," pages 187–205.

Vocabulary Practice

Answers to Exercise A

1. b	4. c
2. a	5. d
3. c	

Answers to Exercise B

1. d	4. a
2. d	5. d
3. d	

For Alternative Learning Styles

Ask students to choose partners. Have each pair write or draw an example that suggests the meaning of each vocabulary word. For example, they might write a nonsense sentence to suggest the word *incomprehensible* or draw a ladder to suggest *hierarchy*. Have pairs exchange their examples and try to guess the words of other pairs.

Closure

Sometimes doors of understanding can be closed as well as opened by one's school experience. Cofer learned the hard way that her school closed doors to students whose families lacked status or wealth. She also learned that some teaching methods got in the way of knowledge. What might Colin from "Last Cover" have felt about her school and its strict emphasis on uniformity?

PRIMARY LESSONS **Teacher's Edition** **547**

Extending the Lesson

Options for Learning

These activities suit a variety of learning styles and modes of expression.

Collaborative Learning Activities
See Options 1, 2, and 4.

1. **Who's on Top?** Students may wish to survey townspeople or classmates to determine the hierarchy in their community. In many communities, class divisions are also marked by geographical boundaries, such as railroad tracks and parks. Students may find such geographical divisions useful in understanding local class divisions.

2. **A Fifty-first State** Students can find information in encyclopedias, news magazines, or books about Puerto Rico.

3. **Migration Map** Provide maps or an atlas for students. Paterson is in northeast New Jersey, north of Newark. (The distance is about 1,500 miles.)

4. **Primary Focus** Suggest that students interview relatives and then friends, acquaintances, and teachers.

 FACT FINDER SOCIAL STUDIES

Students can use an almanac to find the latest U.S. Bureau of the Census estimate on the number of Puerto Ricans living in the mainland United States. The 1990 Census reported 2,727,754.

Judith Ortiz Cofer

■ **More About the Author** As a writer, Judith Ortiz Cofer has devoted herself mainly to poetry. She sees her bilingual background as one reason why the power and variety of language interest her. "My family," she notes, "is one of the main topics of my poetry . . . . In tracing their lives, I discover more about mine."

■ **Other Works** Poetry: *Peregrina, Terms of Survival*

■ **Awards** National Endowment for the Arts fellowship in poetry, 1989; Scholar of English Speaking Union at Oxford University, 1977; fellow of Fine Arts Council of Florida, 1980; Bread-loaf Writer's Conference, scholar, 1981; John Atherton Scholar in Poetry, 1982.

Options for Learning (Multimodal/Cross-Curricular Activities)

1 • Who's on Top? Cofer describes the hierarchy of her Puerto Rican town. Create a chart or diagram that shows the hierarchy in your community. Which people and which jobs are most valued? Which are least valued? Present your chart to the class.

2 • A Fifty-first State Some people would like to see Puerto Rico become a state. In a group of four, research the pros and cons of this issue. Then stage a debate, with two people arguing for statehood and two taking the opposing side.

3 • Migration Map Draw or copy a map and trace the route between Puerto Rico and Paterson, New Jersey. Estimate how many miles separate the two locations.

4 • Primary Focus Schools have changed since Cofer was in primary school. Interview other adults, especially any who attended school outside the United States, to find out about their primary-school experiences. Share their experiences with your class, and contrast these experiences with those in your own community.

 FACT FINDER SOCIAL STUDIES

About how many Puerto Ricans live in the mainland United States?

Judith Ortiz Cofer
1952–

As a child, Judith Cofer grew up in two different worlds, her native Puerto Rico and Paterson, New Jersey. Cofer's two homes, which shifted according to her father's assignments in the U.S. Navy, both contributed to her writing.

In Puerto Rico, she listened to her grandmother's stories in Spanish under a giant mango tree, surrounded by the women and children of her extended family. It was there, Cofer says, "that I first began to feel the power of words."

In Paterson she spent a great deal of time by herself, building up "an arsenal of [English] words by becoming an insatiable reader of books." She also served as her mother's interpreter.

Cofer left her two worlds to attend college. She later taught at the Universities of Miami and Georgia and at Macon College before receiving a poetry fellowship from the National Endowment for the Arts in 1989. Cofer's poems, essays, and reviews appear in literary magazines and anthologies. A novel, *The Line of the Sun*, was nominated for a Pulitzer Prize. She now lives in Georgia.

Cross-Curricular Projects

Math Ask students to suppose that Cofer's classroom has the same number of students as theirs and that the school year was 180 days long. If all the students have an equal chance to change the teacher's shoes, how many times would each one perform this service in the course of the year?

Music Interested students can listen to recordings or tapes of Puerto Rican music and compare it to the music of other Caribbean islands, such as Jamaica and Trinidad. They can then write a music review describing the similarities and differences.

Social Studies Have students make posters of distinguished Puerto Ricans, past and present, for a Puerto Rican Hall of Fame. Candidates may include Luis Munoz Marin, Roberto Clemente, Tito Puente, Herman Badillo, Piri Thomas, and Rita Moreno.

Language Arts Ask students to put themselves in Cofer's place at the PTA show. If they could give any speech they wanted, what would they say? Have them write the speech and deliver it to the class.

Nonfiction

Oh Broom, Get to Work

YOSHIKO UCHIDA (yō′ shē kō yōō chē′ dä)

Examine What You Know (Prior Knowledge)

This selection describes how a young girl tries to rid her household of a frequent guest whom she does not like. How would you deal with an unwanted guest? With your classmates, come up with creative solutions to this problem.

Expand Your Knowledge (Building Background)

As a young girl, Yoshiko Uchida, a novelist and writer of children's books, found herself constantly in the company of household guests. Her parents, both born and educated in Japan, had settled in Berkeley, California, near her father's workplace in San Francisco. Graduates of Japan's Doshisha University, her parents often opened their home to Japanese students who came to the United States to study religion at the University of California at Berkeley or the Pacific School of Religion.

These students were engaged in graduate work, the advanced courses taken by those who have already received a college or university degree. Their studies, made more difficult by living in a foreign and unwelcoming land, were in preparation for Christian ministry.

Write Before You Read (Journal Writing)

Think of times when you have tried to avoid someone's company—without letting him or her know what you were doing. What strategies did you employ to avoid spending time with that person? Did your strategies succeed without hurting that person's feelings? Write about your experience in your journal or notebook.

■ Author biography in Reader's Handbook

OH BROOM, GET TO WORK 549

VOCABULARY PREVIEW

These vocabulary words are defined at the bottom of the selection pages on which they appear.

alumnus a graduate of a school

communing talking privately

cryptic puzzling

deity a god; a divine being

divulge to reveal

expediency suitability for a purpose

morose gloomy

occult supernatural

pallid pale

precepts rule of conduct

seminary a school for training ministers, priests, or rabbis

solace comfort

sorcery magic

strident having a harsh sound

zeal enthusiasm

LIMITED ENGLISH PROFICIENCY

■ Use the Reader's Guidesheet, *Unit Five Resource Book*, page 59.

★ Text annotations marked with a red star (2, 4, 11, 17) may be particularly helpful for students with limited English proficiency.

TEXT ANNOTATIONS

1. LITERARY CONCEPT: Description
Ask students to point out details that create a vivid image of Mr. Okada. *(Possible responses: "thin hatless stranger," "sad, sullen eyes that peered from a pallid face")*

2. ACTIVE READING: Review
Discuss the phrase *redeem his presence.* Explain that one meaning of *redeem* is "to make up for." Have students **reread** the preceding paragraph to help them **infer** Uchida's meaning. *(Door-to-door peddlers carried valises; if the stranger carried a valise, it would redeem, or justify, his being at the door.)* ★

Oh Broom, Get to Work

YOSHIKO UCHIDA

Of the many visitors who came to our home in Berkeley during my childhood, I remember Mr. Okada because I disliked him most and because he was the target of the only successful bit of Oriental sorcery I ever practiced.

I first met Mr. Okada one cold and rainy afternoon when I answered the hesitant twinge of our front doorbell. I opened the door to find a thin, hatless stranger in a shabby overcoat, holding a carefully furled black umbrella still trickling water from its ferrule.[1]

I looked at him silently and waited for him to speak, but he only returned my silence, staring at me with sad, sullen eyes that peered from a pallid face. I had never seen him before and thought he might be another peddler my mother had befriended. I knew the Watkins Man, whose small black bag divulged thick, creamy chocolate bars and slim bottles of vanilla and lemon extract. I also knew the Real Silk Lady, who came calling with stockings and silk underwear stuffed inside her sample case.

I looked now to see if this stranger carried a valise,[2] but he had nothing to redeem his presence on a gloomy afternoon besides his enormous sopping umbrella.

Seeing that I was not about to break the silence or to let him in, he cleared his throat and spoke in a soft voice, totally unbecoming a man, I thought. "Is your mama at home?" he asked.

I had been cautioned against unlatching the screen door to strangers and kept my hand pressed firmly on the hook. "Wait a minute, I'll call her," I said, and took the added precaution of closing the door noisily in his face.

"There's a funny-looking man at the door," I called to my mother in the kitchen, and with only that cryptic description to enlighten her, she hurried to see who had come.

I heard her open the door and then quickly unlatch the screen. *"Mah,* Okada-san,"[3] she said. "Such a miserable day. *Dozo,*[4] please, do come in." And taking his umbrella, she quickly urged him toward the seat by the fire. "I am so sorry my daughter kept you waiting in the rain," she apologized.

---

1. **ferrule** (fer′ əl): a metal band protecting the end of an umbrella.
2. **valise** (və lēs′): a small suitcase or traveling bag.
3. *mah, Okada-san* (mä o kä dä sän) *Japanese:* The word *mah* expresses surprise. The word ending *-san* is added to a person's name as a polite form of address.
4. **dozo** (dō zō) *Japanese:* please.

Words to Know and Use	**sorcery** (sôr′ sər ē) *n.* magic **pallid** (pal′ id) *adj.* pale; lacking normal color **divulge** (də vulj′) *v.* to reveal **cryptic** (krip′ tik) *adj.* puzzling; mysterious

---

Guided Reading for Less-Proficient Students

These questions can help guide students through the reading. Ask each question at the point of the selection where the capital letter and arrow appear in the margin. In addition, you may wish to use appropriate Active Reading annotations.

A. Who is the stranger who comes to the door? *(a Japanese seminary student named Mr. Okada)* Recalling

B. Why does Mr. Okada frequently come to

Yoshiko's home? *(Possible responses: Her parents invite many lonely, homesick Japanese students to visit; Mr. Okada is lonely.)* Recalling

C. In Yoshiko's eyes, what are Mr. Okada's faults? *(He is gloomy and hardly ever speaks; he comes to the house too often and stays too long; he once embarrassed her in front of guests.)* Summarizing

Continued on page 551

I hated having my mother apologize on my behalf. "Why didn't he tell me he was your friend?" I asked the moment he left. "I thought he was a peddler. Besides, he looks like he has TB."[5]

At supper that night, Mother told how she had met Mr. Okada, a seminary student from Japan, at a recent WCTU[6] meeting in Mrs. Toda's home. My mother went to the monthly meetings of this organization partly because she believed in its precepts but mostly because its president, Mrs. Toda, was one of our dearest friends and neighbors. Whenever Mother sought to withdraw from its membership, she was drawn back not only by the covey of Japanese ladies who discussed temperance over steaming cups of green tea but by Mrs. Toda, whose quiet zeal she could not escape. It seemed incredible that a man could be trapped into attending one of these meetings.

"You mean he was the only man there?" I asked.

"He's just come from Japan, and he's terribly lonely."

"Poor fellow," my father interjected.

"But you mean he was really the only man there?" I persisted.

When my mother confirmed this fact, my opinion of Mr. Okada fell to new and terrible depths.

"What a sad case," I said, and believed at the time that I had dismissed him from further thought.

Lonely and homesick people were not unknown to me by any means. Living just across the bay from San Francisco where ships from the Orient deposited their store of lonely students and travelers, our family

was a ready source of solace. My parents were graduates of a well-known university in Japan, and it seemed that every alumnus arriving in California came directly to our home as though reporting in to an alumni office. They came in growing numbers over the years, to do graduate work at the university or at the divinity school, and whenever they longed to unburden themselves in their native tongue or sip a bowl of steaming bean-curd soup, they found both a willing ear and a generous table at our home.

On every major holiday my parents would call the seminary and invite the dozen or more students from Japan who had nowhere to go. Reeking of pomade,[7] polished and stiff in their squeaky shoes and their Sunday suits, they would crowd into our house and consume vast quantities of baked ham, roast turkey, or sukiyaki.[8]

Mr. Okada was always included in these groups and never failed to accept an invitation. Although the other men came in groups of three or four, he always came alone. He was often the first to arrive, offering only a shy smile as he stepped inside, and he usually sat on the hassock[9] beside the fireplace. On chilly days when an oak log sputtered in the fireplace, he would

---

5. TB: tuberculosis, a wasting disease of the lungs.
6. WCTU: Woman's Christian Temperance Union, an organization known for its fight against abuse of alcohol.
7. pomade (päm ād'): a scented hair oil.
8. sukiyaki (sōō' kē yä' kē): a Japanese dish of meat and vegetables, cooked in soy sauce.
9. hassock: a thick, soft cushion used as a low seat or a footstool.

Words to Know and Use	**seminary** (sem' ə ner' ē) *n.* a school where people are trained to become ministers, priests, or rabbis **precept** (prē' sept') *n.* a rule of conduct **zeal** (zēl) *n.* enthusiasm; eagerness **solace** (säl' is) *n.* comfort **alumnus** (ə lum' nəs) *n.* a graduate of a particular school; *plural*—**alumni** (ə lum' nī')

551

3. CULTURAL SIDELIGHT
Among the clues that suggest this episode is set in the past are *peddlers* and *TB*. Peddlers, who were prevalent in years past, are rarely seen today. TB, or tuberculosis, a very contagious disease, was once widespread in the United States.

4. VOCABULARY: Definition
Tell students that the general definition of *temperance* is "self-restraint" or "moderation," and point out the footnote that identifies the WCTU. In the time period of the story, *temperance* usually meant "total abstinence from alcohol." ★

5. CULTURAL SIDELIGHT
The Uchidas and their guests are Christians, which made them unusual for that time. Most Japanese people practiced Shintoism or Buddhism. In fact, Christianity was banned in Japan for hundreds of years. This might shed a special light on why the Uchidas' student guests are lonely and isolated.

6. LITERARY CONCEPT: Setting
Ask students to note details on this page that build a picture of the Japanese community in Berkeley. (*Possible responses: The green tea, bean-curd soup, sukiyaki, and conversation are Japanese, but baked ham, roast turkey, and the WCTU are American. The world in which Yoshiko lives seems to be a mix of two cultures.*)

Guided Reading for Less-Proficient Students

Continued from page 550

D. Why is Yoshiko particularly unhappy with Mr. Okada on the day she visits Mrs. Toda? (*She wants her mother to help her hold a funeral for a dead bird, but Mr. Okada is visiting.*) Summarizing

E. What is Mrs. Toda's advice? (*She thinks Yoshiko should try an old Japanese superstition—standing a*

broom upside down with a dust cloth on its sweeping end.) Recalling

F. Why does Mr. Okada leave? (*Possible responses: He knows what effect the upside-down broom is supposed to have; upon seeing the broom, he realizes he is not wanted.*) Drawing conclusions

7. ACTIVE READING: Connect
Ask students if they have ever been pressured into performing in public against their will. Invite them to share their experiences, and ask them how they would feel if they were in the narrator's place. *(Any response is valid.)*

8. ACTIVE READING: Review
Point out that although the narrator and main character are the same person, they don't see things quite the same way. Ask students how the attitudes of the narrator differ from those of the main character. If necessary, help students by reading the following example of a think-aloud, or model your own.

Think-Aloud Script How can I tell that the narrator is an adult now? I bet if the little girl were telling the story, she would say, "It was all Mr. Okada's fault, he's so creepy," but the narrator says, "I blamed it entirely on Mr. Okada, whose attempt to be sociable had only resulted in my humiliation." That's a pretty adult point of view. I don't think the little girl would have thought of that.

9. ACTIVE READING: Evaluate
Ask students for their judgment of Mr. Okada. *(Possible responses: He's clumsy; he's insensitive; he's trying to be nice but doesn't know how; he's very lonely; he's shy; he should get a life of his own; he may be poor since he often stays for dinner.)*

Illustration by Gary Mele.

lean toward it, neck thrust forward, hands outstretched, as though communing with some spirit in the fire. He seldom spoke more than four or five sentences during an entire evening, and then usually in a voice so low they were lost in the chatter and laughter that filled the room.

The one time he spoke up with some force was to suggest that I play the piano for the assembled group. Pretending that I hadn't heard him, I carefully inspected a spot on my shoe. But the men urged me on with encouraging words, and finally they began to clap. I wanted to pitch Mr. Okada into the fire for forcing me into the kind of performance I detested, but I knew the thing

7

had to be done. I got off to a fumbling start of "The Skylark" and had to stop in the middle to get the music from inside the piano bench and then begin again. It was a miserable show, and I blamed it entirely on Mr. Okada, whose attempt to be sociable had only resulted in my humiliation.

As the months went by, Mr. Okada not only accepted every invitation, he began to come uninvited. He had a distasteful habit of coming in the late afternoon and staying until my mother had to prepare supper and, consequently, felt obliged to ask him to stay.

One afternoon I had run all the way home with a stiff-feathered creature in my hands. "Mama, I found a dead sparrow," I shouted as I burst indoors. "Come help me bury it."

But I found my mother busy entertaining Mr. Okada in the living room. She sat calmly knitting a pair of black wool socks, and seated across from her, pale and morose in a rumpled sweat shirt and a baggy pair of pants, was Mr. Okada.

"Come in, Yo-chan,"[10] my mother called to me, but seeing Mr. Okada, I turned and fled.

I wrapped the small, stiff bird in a piece of red silk and laid it inside an empty candy box lined with foil. Then I buried it carefully in a hole which I dug beneath the flowering peach in our back yard. A chill tingled down my spine as I shaped the earth into a burial mound, and I hurried back inside

8

◀ **C**

9

---

10. Yo-chan (yō chän): the first part of the author's name, with the word ending *-chan*, a Japanese form often used when speaking to a child.

Words to Know and Use

communing (kə myōōn´ iŋ) *adj.* talking together privately **commune** *v.*
morose (mə rōs´) *adj.* in low spirits; gloomy

552

Looking at Style

Use the following to focus attention on style.

■ She sat calmly knitting a pair of black wool socks and / seated across from her, / *pale* and *morose* / in a *rumpled* sweat shirt / and a *baggy* pair of pants, / was Mr. Okada.

Discuss the sentence with students:

1. Direct attention to the italicized words and ask: Why did Uchida include these words? How do they help you visualize the characters and scene?

2. Read the sentence aloud, pausing at each slash. Ask: Why do you think the author uses a string of descriptive phrases to describe Mr. Okada? How does this string of phrases leading up to "Mr. Okada" help you imagine the effect of his presence?

3. Have students write a similar sentence about a teacher facing a group of students. Have them use a string of phrases to describe the students.

hoping that by now my mother might be free.

This time I found her in the kitchen getting the tea things from the cupboard. She was placing the cups on small wooden coasters and arranging them with the pot on her best cherry-wood tray.

"Oh, Mama," I wailed, "you're not giving him tea, are you? He'll never go home if you do."

But my mother just gave me a quick smile and told me she couldn't send him away without a cup of hot tea. I knew she was right. After all, she even served tea to the Real Silk Lady after viewing her wares.

"Did you bury your little bird?" she asked gently.

But the thought of Mr. Okada staying on for supper had already swept aside the sweet-sad dream of a bird funeral.

I ran outside simmering with frustration and decided to go see Mrs. Toda. I swung through the narrow wooden gate to their back yard and found Mr. Toda sitting in his canvas chair, wearing an old green eyeshade and dozing beneath its protective celluloid[11]. He started as I banged the gate shut, and shouted a loud welcome as though I were just as deaf as he.

"Come to see us at last, have you?" he shouted, although I had been there just two days before. "Would you like to see my carp?" he asked generously. If I had even expressed a halfhearted desire, he would have roused himself creakily and ruffled the murky depths of the pool with his stiff fingers to let me see his speckled gray carp flash to the surface.

But today I had no time for carp. I had to unburden myself to someone, and Mrs. Toda, since she had introduced Mr. Okada to my mother in the first place, seemed an excellent person on whom to fling my misery.

I let myself in from the back door and found the kitchen filled with the smell of nutmeg and spices sprinkled over hot custard. I sniffed happily.

"Sah, sah,[12] you are just in time," Mrs. Toda clucked, and quickly placed before me a large green cup of custard, still warm and steaming. By the time I had spooned up the last mouthful of slippery sweetness, my tale of woe was not quite so <u>strident</u>. Still, I had few kind thoughts.

"I hate and despise that horrible Mr. Okada," I blurted out.

"Mah! Tell me, what has he done?"

With Mrs. Toda's sympathetic sighs to urge me on, I quickly told her how often he came uninvited; how he came late and always stayed for supper; how I couldn't talk to Mama while he sat there; and finally, as his most unforgivable sin, I added, "And he never says anything. He just sits—like a mushroom!"

"Ah, he is a troublesome one," Mrs. Toda agreed. "And your poor mama busy with so many callers."

---

11. **celluloid:** (sel' yo͞o loid') a tough plastic.
12. **sah, sah:** (sä sä) *Japanese:* well, well.

13

◀ D

Words to Know and Use | **strident** (strīd' 'nt) *adj.* having a harsh sound

553

10. ACTIVE READING: Question
If readers have forgotten at this point who Mrs. Toda is, suggest that they **scan** earlier text to discover that she is a neighbor, a close friend, and the woman through whom Mr. Okada met the Uchidas.

11. LANGUAGE: Homonyms
Point out that here the word *started* doesn't mean "began"—it means Mr. Toda jumped when the gate banged, his reaction to being startled.

For Alternative Learning Styles
If necessary, **demonstrate** Mr. Toda's reaction. ★

12. CULTURAL SIDELIGHT
Mr. Toda's feelings about his carp are not a personal eccentricity. The carp is a special symbol in Japanese culture, representing strength, long life, and determination.

13. ACTIVE READING: Predict
Ask students how they think Mrs. Toda is going to react when she finds out what Yoshiko's problem is. (*Possible responses: She'll tell Yoshiko to quit being silly; she'll go over and call Mr. Okada away so Yoshiko can be with her mother; she'll reveal something about Mr. Okada that will change Yoshiko's attitude.*)

SHADOWS ON THE DOOR 1968 Jiro Takamatsu Collection of the Tokyo Metropolitan Museum.

She pursed her lips as she pondered the shape and size of my problem. Then she licked the remnants of custard from her fingertips, wiping them carefully on one corner of her big white apron.

The two of us sat at the round table in her kitchen as the last of the afternoon sun slanted in from the window. I studied the full, curved bins of her worktable, where Mrs. Toda stored her supplies of rice and flour. She studied her pet canary as it hopped restlessly in its golden cage.

"What can we do?" she murmured. Then, suddenly, she brightened. "I have an idea," she said, chuckling at the wickedness of it. "Now listen carefully and do exactly as I tell you."

"What? Tell me," I urged.

"The next time Mr. Okada comes, get your mama's broom and set it upside down on its handle."

She looked to see if I understood. I nodded.

"And then put a dust cloth over the sweeping end."

"And then?"

"Then, just wait for him to leave."

"That's all? Will it really make him go?"

Mrs. Toda nodded. "It is an old Japanese superstition. I've tried it once or twice myself."

"And did it work for you?"

"Always," she said confidently.

I didn't wait to hear any more. If Mr. Okada was still sitting in our living room, I might just have time before Mama had to start supper.

I ran home, went to the crack at the door, and looked into the living room from the kitchen. Mr. Okada was still there. He was staring moodily into his teacup, and my mother was patiently knitting, waiting for him to say something or take his leave.

I flung open the broom closet and quickly set up my silent oblation[13] to Mrs. Toda's antisocial deity. "Oh broom," I whispered. "Get to work!"

In the next fifteen minutes I made dozens of trips between the broom closet and the crack at the door. Still, Mr. Okada sat. Finally, I decided that the broom couldn't exert its occult powers over anything while shut up inside a closet. It would have to be moved as close to Mr. Okada as possible without my actually marching into the living room with it. I decided to set it up at the crack of the door. This obstructed my own

view, but I was willing to put up with this small inconvenience for the sake of expediency. Stooping down low to cast my own evil eye on Mr. Okada as well, I caught a narrow glimpse of him, looking now in my direction.

"Oh broom," I muttered, "get to work!"

In a very few minutes Mr. Okada rose, bowed to my mother, and thanked her for the tea. "I must go now," he said.

"You will not stay to supper then?" she asked.

"Thank you, no," he murmured. And he was gone.

"Mama! Mama!" I shouted as I plummeted into the living room. "I did it! It worked. I got rid of him for you. It really worked!"

My mother didn't know what I was talking about. I knew she was puzzled by Mr. Okada's unexpected departure, but I knew she was not displeased.

I danced around and around the living room, freed at last from Mr. Okada's murky presence. Overwhelmed with my new-found powers and filled with joy over my small triumph, it never once occurred to me that the crack at the door afforded a view into the kitchen as well as out or that poor Mr. Okada might have known a few old Japanese superstitions himself. 🙠

---

13. **oblation** (ə blā′ shən): a sacrifice to a god.

Words to Know and Use	**deity** (dē′ ə tē) *n.* a god; a divine being **occult** (ə kult′) *adj.* supernatural **expediency** (ek spē′ dē ən sē) *n.* suitability for the purpose at hand

555

16. ACTIVE READING: Predict
Now that students know Mrs. Toda's plan, ask them if they think it will work. (Any response is valid.)

17. VOCABULARY: Definition
Although the word *mood* can refer to both good and bad moods, the word *moodily* refers to a specific mood. Encourage students to use context clues to **infer** the word's meaning. (*in a gloomy, depressed manner.*) ★

18. ACTIVE READING: Review
Ask students to explain why Mr. Okada left. (*Possible responses: He saw the broom and knows the superstition; he realizes Yoshiko wants him to go.*)

ENCOURAGING INDEPENDENT READING

The Eternal Spring of Mr. Ito, novel by Sheila Garrigue

The Dancing Kettle, folk tales retold by Yoshiko Uchida

Comprehension Check

1. Who is the unwelcome visitor in this story? (*Mr. Okada*)

2. Why does he first come to the Uchidas' house? (*The Uchidas invite him; he is lonely.*)

3. What things does Mr. Okada do that annoy Yoshiko? (*He asks her to play the piano for the group; he comes uninvited and stays too long; he says little; he takes her mother's attention.*)

4. What does Mrs. Toda suggest to solve the problem? (*She suggests Yoshiko try an old Japanese superstition—turn a broom upside down and cover it with a cloth, which causes unwelcome guests to leave.*)

5. When does Mr. Okada finally leave? (*when Yoshiko sets the broom up by the door*)

Student Response

Responding to Reading

1. Any response is valid.

2. Possible responses: Yes, he was just shy and lonely, he deserved sympathy; no, he needed to rely on himself rather than to expect the Uchidas to keep him from being lonely all the time.

3. Possible responses: Mrs. Toda feels guilty because she introduced Mr. Okada to the Uchidas; Yoshiko's mother feels more sympathy for these lonely people far from home.

4. Possible responses: She was right to be polite and kind; she should have told Mr. Okada he was being a pest; she should have helped Mr. Okada make other friends; she should have spent more time with her daughter.

5. Possible responses: Yes, she says it worked for her; no, she just wants to cheer up Yoshiko and give her something to do; no, but Yoshiko's broom activity might give Mr. Okada a hint that he's overstayed his welcome.

Writing Options

The Writing Options are designed to meet varied student interests and abilities. Have each student choose one activity to complete.

Journal Update Describe a personal experience related to a superstition.

Vocabulary Practice

Answers to Exercise

1. morose	9. cryptic
2. alumnus	10. deity
3. seminary	11. communing
4. zeal	12. occult
5. precept	13. sorcery
6. strident	14. solace
7. expediency	15. pallid
8. divulge	

Closure

Discuss the unspoken understandings that pass between people when they are socializing. Ask how visitors should know when to drop by, when to wait for an invitation, and when to go home.

Responding to Reading

First Impressions

1. Jot down your first impression of the narrator in your journal.

Second Thoughts

2. Do you think the narrator was too hard on Mr. Okada? Explain.

3. Why do you think Mrs. Toda shows more sympathy to the narrator than the narrator's mother does?

4. What is your opinion of how the mother handled Mr. Okada's visits? Should she have done anything differently?

5. Do you think Mrs. Toda really believes in the broom superstition?

Writing Options

1. What if this selection were adapted for a television comedy? Write a **plot capsule** for a television magazine.

2. Write a **character sketch** of the narrator from Mr. Okada's viewpoint. Describe how he sees her and what he thinks of her.

Vocabulary Practice

Exercise Replace each numbered word or phrase with the word from the list that is closest in meaning. Use each word once.

1. He is a **(1) depressed (2) graduate** of a **(3) religious college.**

2. Sal showed **(4) great enthusiasm** by shouting a **(5) rule of conduct** in a **(6) shrill** voice.

3. For the sake of **(7) getting the job done efficiently,** she will **(8) reveal** a **(9) puzzling** clue to the identity of the **(10) god.**

4. Some, **(11) talking privately** with **(12) supernatural** spirits, use **(13) magic.**

5. Give **(14) comfort** to your **(15) pale** friend.

> *Words to Know and Use*
>
> alumnus
> communing
> cryptic
> deity
> divulge
> expediency
> morose
> occult
> pallid
> precept
> seminary
> solace
> sorcery
> strident
> zeal

The Spelling Connection

Spelling Pattern: Paired Prefixes Different prefixes can be added to the same base words. Sometimes the last letter of the prefix is changed to become the same as the first letter of the base.

Examples: sub + ceed = succeed
ex + ceed = exceed

Words from the Selection with Paired Prefixes

ad + sume = assume	con + sume = consume
sub + press = suppress	ex + press = express
ad + cept = accept	pre + cept = precept

Other Words with Paired Prefixes

com + lapse = collapse	re + lapse = relapse
ad + tend = attend	pre + tend = pretend
dis + solved = dissolved	re + solved = resolved

Exercise Use two spelling words with the same base word for each sentence.

1. I *take it for granted* you will *eat* your lunch.
2. We *agree* to the *rule.*
3. A *cave-in* might cause a *setback.*
4. Don't *make believe* you'll *be there* at church.

Fiction

The *Medicine Bag*

VIRGINIA DRIVING HAWK SNEVE

Examine What You Know (Prior Knowledge)

Most people in the United States can trace their roots to one or several ethnic groups. Their ethnic heritage may lead to a country in Africa, Europe, or Latin America, or perhaps to a Native American people. How important is your ethnic background to you? Do you take pride in your ethnic heritage, or are you unconcerned about it? Do you know what your ethnic heritage is? Jot down your thoughts in your journal or notebook.

Expand Your Knowledge (Building Background)

The narrator in this story traces part of his heritage to the Sioux, a Native American people. The Sioux are North American Plains Indians who gained fame for their skill in hunting and battle (their chiefs included Sitting Bull and Crazy Horse).

During the 1800s the Sioux gradually lost their land—and their independence—to white settlers. After being defeated by the U.S. Army, the Sioux were herded onto reservations where they were forced to change their way of living and where many of their customs gradually died out. Today most of the Sioux still live on reservations in North and South Dakota, Montana, and Nebraska. Their lives are far different from those of their ancestors, and many of them live in poverty. The great-grandfather in this story comes from the Rosebud Reservation in South Dakota, where eighteen thousand Sioux live.

Site of Sioux ceremonial Sun Dance near Rosebud, South Dakota.

Enrich Your Reading (Reading Skill)

Making Connections As you read, think about how the narrator's experiences with his relatives and friends compare with your own. Try to remember situations from your own life that may help you understand the narrator's feelings.

■ *Author biography on Extend page*

THE MEDICINE BAG 557

JOURNAL WRITING IDEAS

■ Have you ever felt embarrassed by a family member? Why? How were your feelings resolved?

■ Does your family have any heirlooms that have been passed down through the generations? Write about them.

COLLABORATIVE LEARNING OPTIONS

Opportunities for collaborative learning include Options for Learning activities 1 and 2 (p. 568) and Cross-Curricular Projects (p. 568).

ADDITIONAL RESOURCES

Unit Five Resource Book
Reader's Guidesheet, p. 66
Reading Skills, p. 67
Literature Skills, p. 68
Vocabulary Connections, p. 69
Spelling Connections, p. 70
Comprehension and Vocabulary Check Tests, p. 71
Selection Test, pp. 72–73

Objectives

■ To understand and analyze a short story

■ To examine internal conflict and to review the concept of exposition

■ To enrich reading by having students make connections between the story and their own lives

■ To express understanding of the story through a choice of writing forms, including a dialogue, a song lyric, a comparison-and-contrast paper, and a booklet

Examine What You Know

Discussion Prompts How does your family feel about its ethnic heritage? Does your family celebrate any ethnic holidays? In what ways do different people show they value their ethnic heritage?

Expand Your Knowledge

Additional Background There are approximately 2,000,000 Native Americans in the United States today, and fewer than 400,000 of them live on reservations. In South Dakota—including part of the Black Hills as well as on various reservations—there are about 50,000 Sioux, or Dakota, people.

Enrich Your Reading

As a way for students to connect before they read, have them discuss their feelings toward their own grandparents or older relatives. Ask how many have mixed feelings toward the old people in their lives.

Thematic Link— Doors of Understanding

In this story a man understands his great-grandson's anxieties about their shared Sioux heritage. This understanding, together with the man's bestowal of a traditional Sioux gift, allows the boy to embrace his heritage and keep a door of understanding open to his past.

The *Medicine Bag*

VIRGINIA DRIVING HAWK SNEVE

My kid sister Cheryl and I always bragged about our Sioux grandpa, Joe Iron Shell. Our friends, who had always lived in the city and knew about Indians only from movies and TV, were impressed by our stories. Maybe we exaggerated and made Grandpa and the reservation sound glamorous, but when we'd return home to Iowa after our yearly summer visit to Grandpa, we always had some exciting tale to tell.

We always had some authentic Sioux article to show our listeners. One year Cheryl had new moccasins that Grandpa had made. On another visit he gave me a small, round, flat rawhide drum that was decorated with a painting of a warrior riding a horse. He taught me a real Sioux chant to sing while I beat the drum with a leather-covered stick that had a feather on the end. Man, that really made an impression.

We never showed our friends Grandpa's picture. Not that we were ashamed of him, but because we knew that the glamorous tales we told didn't go with the real thing. Our friends would have laughed at the picture because Grandpa wasn't tall and stately like TV Indians. His hair wasn't in braids but hung in stringy gray strands on his neck, and he was old. He was our great-grandfather, and he didn't live in a tepee but all by himself in a part log, part tar-paper shack on the Rosebud Reservation in South Dakota. So when Grandpa came to visit us, I was so ashamed and embarrassed I could've died.

There are a lot of yippy poodles and other fancy little dogs in our neighborhood, but they usually barked singly at the mailman from the safety of their own yards. Now it sounded as if a whole pack of mutts were barking together in one place.

I got up and walked to the curb to see what the commotion was. About a block away I saw a crowd of little kids yelling, with the dogs yipping and growling around someone who was walking down the middle of the street.

I watched the group as it slowly came closer and saw that in the center of the strange procession was a man wearing a tall black hat. He'd pause now and then to peer at something in his hand and then at the houses on either side of the street. I felt cold and hot at the same time as I recognized the man. "Oh, no!" I whispered. "It's Grandpa!"

I stood on the curb, unable to move, even though I wanted to run and hide. Then I got mad when I saw how the yippy dogs were growling and nipping at the old man's baggy pant legs and how wearily he poked them away with his cane. "Stupid mutts," I said as I ran to rescue Grandpa.

When I kicked and hollered at the dogs to get away, they put their tails between

Continued on page 559

their legs and scattered. The kids ran to the curb where they watched me and the old man.

"Grandpa," I said and felt pretty dumb when my voice cracked. I reached for his beat-up old tin suitcase, which was tied shut with a rope. But he set it down right in the street and shook my hand.

"Hau, Takoza, Grandchild," he greeted me formally in Sioux.

All I could do was stand there with the whole neighborhood watching and shake the hand of the leather-brown old man. I saw how his gray hair straggled from under his big black hat, which had a drooping feather in its crown. His rumpled black suit hung like a sack over his stooped frame. As he shook my hand, his coat fell open to expose a bright red satin shirt with a beaded bolo tie under the collar. His get-up wasn't out of place on the reservation, but it sure was here, and I wanted to sink right through the pavement.

"Hi," I muttered with my head down. I tried to pull my hand away when I felt his bony hand trembling and looked up to see fatigue in his face. I felt like crying. I couldn't think of anything to say, so I picked up Grandpa's suitcase, took his arm, and guided him up the driveway to our house.

Mom was standing on the steps. I don't know how long she'd been watching, but her hand was over her mouth, and she looked as if she couldn't believe what she saw. Then she ran to us.

"Grandpa," she gasped. "How in the world did you get here?"

CHESTER MEDICINE CROW IN HIS RESERVATION HAT 1973 © James Bama   Courtesy, Big Horn Gallery, Cody, Wyoming.

She checked her move to embrace Grandpa, and I remembered that such a display of affection is unseemly to the Sioux and would embarrass him.

"Hau, Marie," he said as he shook Mom's hand. She smiled and took his other arm.

As we supported him up the steps, the door banged open and Cheryl came bursting out of the house. She was all smiles and

Words to Know and Use	**fatigue** (fə tēg′) *n.* extreme weariness or exhaustion **unseemly** (un sēm′ lē) *adj.* not decent or proper

559

6. LITERARY CONCEPT:
Foreshadowing
Ask students what Grandpa's collapse
might foreshadow in the story. (Possible
response: It could foreshadow his illness
or death.)

7. LITERARY CONCEPT: Character
Ask students what they can infer about
the narrator's character from his suggestion and his behavior with his great-
grandfather. (Possible responses: The
narrator stays cool during an emergency; his willingness to undress
Grandpa when he doesn't want to
gives the impression that Martin is
mature and responsible.)

8. LITERARY CONCEPT: Character
Ask students to describe what
Grandpa's actions tell them about his
character. (Possible responses: He
seems to be determined, courageous,
and fearless; he is a man who knows
what he wants.)

was so obviously glad to see Grandpa that I
was ashamed of how I felt.

"Grandpa!" she yelled happily. "You came
to see us!"

Grandpa smiled, and Mom and I let go of
him as he stretched out his arms to my ten-
year-old sister, who was still young enough
to be hugged.

"*Wicincala,* little girl," he greeted her and
then collapsed.

He had fainted. Mom and I carried him
into her sewing room, where we had a spare
bed.

After we had Grandpa on the bed, Mom
stood there helplessly patting his shoulder.

"Shouldn't we call the doctor, Mom?" I
suggested, since she didn't seem to know
what to do.

"Yes," she agreed with a sigh. "You make
Grandpa comfortable, Martin."

I reluctantly moved to the bed. I knew
Grandpa wouldn't want to have Mom
undress him, but I didn't want to, either. He
was so skinny and frail that his coat slipped
off easily. When I loosened his tie and
opened his shirt collar, I felt a small leather
pouch that hung from a thong around his
neck. I left it alone and moved to remove his
boots. The scuffed old cowboy boots were
tight, and he moaned as I put pressure on
his legs to jerk them off.

I put the boots on the floor and saw why
they fit so tight. Each one was stuffed with
money. I looked at the bills that lined the
boots and started to ask about them, but
Grandpa's eyes were closed again.

Mom came back with a basin of water.
"The doctor thinks Grandpa is suffering
from heat exhaustion," she explained as she
bathed Grandpa's face. Mom gave a big
sigh, "*Oh, hinh,* Martin. How do you suppose he got here?"

We found out after the doctor's visit.
Grandpa was angrily sitting up in bed while
Mom tried to feed him some soup.

"Tonight you let Marie feed you, Grandpa," spoke my dad, who had gotten home
from work just as the doctor was leaving.
"You're not really sick," he said as he gently
pushed Grandpa back against the pillows.
"The doctor said you just got too tired and
hot after your long trip."

Grandpa relaxed, and between sips
of soup, he told us of his journey.
Soon after our visit to him,
Grandpa decided that he would
like to see where his only living descendants
lived and what our home was like. Besides,
he admitted sheepishly, he was lonesome
after we left.

I knew that everybody felt as guilty as I
did—especially Mom. Mom was all Grandpa
had left. So even after she married my dad,
who's a white man and teaches in the college in our city, and after Cheryl and I were
born, Mom made sure that every summer
we spent a week with Grandpa.

I never thought that Grandpa would be
lonely after our visits, and none of us
noticed how old and weak he had become.
But Grandpa knew, and so he came to us.
He had ridden on buses for two and a half
days. When he arrived in the city, tired and
stiff from sitting so long, he set out, walking,
to find us.

Words to Know and Use	**reluctantly** (ri luk′ tənt lē) *adv.* unwillingly **descendant** (dē sen′ dənt) *n.* an immediate or remote offspring of a person

He had stopped to rest on the steps of some building downtown, and a policeman found him. The cop, according to Grandpa, was a good man who took him to the bus stop and waited until the bus came and told the driver to let Grandpa out at Bell View Drive. After Grandpa got off the bus, he started walking again. But he couldn't see the house numbers on the other side when he walked on the sidewalk, so he walked in the middle of the street. That's when all the little kids and dogs followed him.

I knew everybody felt as bad as I did. Yet I was so proud of this eighty-six-year-old man who had never been away from the reservation, having the courage to travel so far alone.

"You found the money in my boots?" he asked Mom.

"Martin did," she answered, and roused herself to scold. "Grandpa, you shouldn't have carried so much money. What if someone had stolen it from you?"

Grandpa laughed. "I would've known if anyone had tried to take the boots off my feet. The money is what I've saved for a long time—a hundred dollars—for my funeral. But you take it now to buy groceries so that I won't be a burden to you while I am here."

"That won't be necessary, Grandpa," Dad said. "We are honored to have you with us, and you will never be a burden. I am only sorry that we never thought to bring you home with us this summer and spare you the discomfort of a long trip."

Grandpa was pleased. "Thank you," he answered. "But do not feel bad that you didn't bring me with you, for I would not have come then. It was not time." He said this in such a way that no one could argue

with him. To Grandpa and the Sioux, he once told me, a thing would be done when it was the right time to do it, and that's the way it was.

"Also," Grandpa went on, looking at me, "I have come because it is soon time for Martin to have the medicine bag."

We all knew what that meant. Grandpa thought he was going to die, and he had to follow the tradition of his family to pass the medicine bag, along with its history, to the oldest male child.

"Even though the boy," he said, still looking at me, "bears a white man's name, the medicine bag will be his."

I didn't know what to say. I had the same hot and cold feeling that I had when I first saw Grandpa in the street. The medicine bag was the dirty leather pouch I had found around his neck. "I could never wear such a thing," I almost said aloud. I thought of having my friends see it in gym class or at the swimming pool and could imagine the smart things they would say. But I just swallowed hard and took a step toward the bed. I knew I would have to take it.

But Grandpa was tired. "Not now, Martin," he said, waving his hand in dismissal. "It is not time. Now I will sleep." ◄ D

So that's how Grandpa came to be with us for two months. My friends kept asking to come see the old man, but I put them off. I told myself that I didn't want them laughing at Grandpa. But even as I made excuses, I knew it wasn't Grandpa that I was afraid they'd laugh at.

Nothing bothered Cheryl about bringing her friends to see Grandpa. Every day after school started, there'd be a crew of giggling

12. ACTIVE READING: Evaluate

Ask students if they believe that Martin is right to feel worried that his friends will laugh at his great-grandfather or at himself. (Possible responses: Yes, Hank's remark could mean that Martin's friends see Grandpa as some sort of freak and will judge him harshly; no, because the way Cheryl's friends react suggests that everyone will be impressed with Grandpa.)

13. VOCABULARY: Definitions

Some students may be unfamiliar with words that describe Grandpa's clothing: *fringed*, *moccasins*, and *strands*. If possible, display a picture of moccasins, point out fringes on someone's clothing, and show strands of a student's hair. ★

14. ACTIVE READING: Question

Do you think Martin shows his feelings easily, or is Grandpa just perceptive? (Possible responses: Martin's face getting hot and cold suggests he is showing embarrassment and anxiety; Martin's great-grandfather seems to know a good deal about human nature.)

little girls or round-eyed little boys crowded around the old man on the patio, where he'd gotten in the habit of sitting every afternoon.

Grandpa would smile in his gentle way and patiently answer their questions, or he'd tell them stories of brave warriors, ghosts, and animals; and the kids listened in awed silence. Those little guys thought Grandpa was great.

I was so proud of him and amazed at how respectfully quiet my buddies were.

Finally, one day after school, my friends came home with me because nothing I said stopped them. "We're going to see the great Indian of Bell View Drive," said Hank, who was supposed to be my best friend. "My brother has seen him three times, so he oughta be well enough to see us."

When we got to my house, Grandpa was sitting on the patio. He had on his red shirt, but today he also wore a fringed leather vest that was decorated with beads. Instead of his usual cowboy boots, he had solidly beaded moccasins on his feet that stuck out of his black trousers. Of course, he had his old black hat on—he was seldom without it. But it had been brushed, and the feather in the beaded headband was proudly erect, its tip a brighter white. His hair lay in silver strands over the red shirt collar.

I stared just as my friends did, and I heard one of them murmur, "Wow!"

Grandpa looked up, and when his eyes met mine, they twinkled as if he were laughing inside. He nodded to me, and my face got all hot. I could tell that he had known all along I was afraid he'd embarrass me in front of my friends.

"*Hau, hoksilas,* boys," he greeted and held out his hand.

My buddies passed in a single file and shook his hand as I introduced them. They were so polite I almost laughed. "How, there, Grandpa," and even a "How-do-you-do, sir."

"You look fine, Grandpa," I said as the guys sat on the lawn chairs or on the patio floor.

"*Hanh,* yes," he agreed. "When I woke up this morning, it seemed the right time to dress in the good clothes. I knew that my grandson would be bringing his friends."

"You guys want some lemonade or something?" I offered. No one answered. They were listening to Grandpa as he started telling how he'd killed the deer from which his vest was made.

Grandpa did most of the talking while my friends were there. I was so proud of him and amazed at how respectfully quiet my buddies were. Mom had to chase them home at supper time. As they left, they shook Grandpa's hand again and said to me,

"Martin, he's really great!"

"Yeah, man! Don't blame you for keeping him to yourself."

"Can we come back?"

But after they left, Mom said, "No more visitors for a while, Martin. Grandpa won't admit it, but his strength hasn't returned. He likes having company, but it tires him."

That evening Grandpa called me to his room before he went to sleep. "Tomorrow," he said, "when you come home, it will be time to give you the medicine bag."

I felt a hard squeeze from where my heart is supposed to be and was scared, but I answered, "OK, Grandpa."

All night I had weird dreams about thunder and lightning on a high hill. From a distance I heard the slow beat of a drum. When I woke up in the morning, I felt as if I hadn't slept at all. At school it seemed as if the day would never end, and when it finally did, I ran home.

Grandpa was in his room, sitting on the bed. The shades were down, and the place was dim and cool. I sat on the floor in front of Grandpa, but he didn't even look at me. After what seemed a long time, he spoke.

"I sent your mother and sister away. What you will hear today is only for a man's ears. What you will receive is only for a man's hands." He fell silent, and I felt shivers down my back.

F ▶ "My father in his early manhood," Grandpa began, "made a vision quest to find a spirit guide for his life. You cannot understand how it was in that time when the great Teton Sioux were first made to stay on the reservation. There was a strong need **15** for guidance from *Wakantanka*, the Great Spirit. But too many of the young men were filled with despair and hatred. They thought it was hopeless to search for a vision when the glorious life was gone and only the hated <u>confines</u> of a reservation lay ahead. But my father held to the old ways.

"He carefully prepared for his quest with a purifying sweat bath, and then he went alone to a high butte[1] top to fast and pray. After three days he received his sacred dream—in which he found, after long searching, the white man's iron. He did not understand his vision of finding something belonging to the white people, for in that time they were the enemy. When he came down from the butte to cleanse himself at the stream below, he found the remains of a campfire and the broken shell of an iron kettle. This was a sign that reinforced his dream. He took a piece of the iron for his medicine bag, which he had made of elk skin years before, to prepare for his quest.

"He returned to his village, where he told his dream to the wise old men of the tribe. They gave him the name Iron Shell, but neither did they understand the meaning of the dream. The first Iron Shell kept the piece of iron with him at all times and believed it gave him protection from the evils of those unhappy days.

"Then a terrible thing happened to Iron Shell. He and several other young men were taken from their homes by the soldiers and sent far away to a white man's boarding school. He was angry and lonesome for his parents and the young girl he had wed before he was taken away. At first Iron Shell resisted the teacher's attempts to change him, and he did not try to learn. One day it was his turn to work in the school's blacksmith shop. As he walked into the place, he

---

1. **butte** (byo͞ot): a flat-topped hill rising from flatland.

15. CULTURAL SIDELIGHT
Nearly all Native American peoples' religious faith connects human beings to all other living things. Some Native American peoples believe that the spirits of all people join to form a single spiritual force. This force has the power to direct and influence lives. The Sioux word for this force is *Wakantanka;* the Iroquois word is *Orenda;* the Algonquians call it *Manitou.*

16. CULTURAL SIDELIGHT
Vision quests were vital rites of passage for Plains Indians. Both male and female teenagers sought supernatural visions by traveling to a remote location where they fasted, reflected, and encountered a spiritual being. The spiritual being taught the person prayers and songs and told them what objects to gather and carry as a charm. The youth, who was to carry these sacred objects in a "medicine bag," could call on this guardian throughout life.

17. ACTIVE READING: Connect
Ask students if they believe people's dreams are meaningful. Have they ever had a dream that affected their lives in some way? *(Any response is valid.)*

Words to Know and Use | **confines** (kän' fīnz') *n.* limits; boundaries

563

Small beaded pouch   about 1915   Private collection.
Photo by Benson L. Lanford and Robert W. Gilmore.

564   UNIT FIVE   DOORS OF UNDERSTANDING

knew that his medicine had brought him there to learn and work with the white man's iron.

"Iron Shell became a blacksmith and worked at the trade when he returned to the reservation. All of his life he treasured the medicine bag. When he was old and I was a man, he gave it to me, for no one made the vision quest any more."

Grandpa quit talking, and I stared in disbelief as he covered his face with his hands. His shoulders were shaking with quiet sobs, and I looked away until he began to speak again.

"I kept the bag until my son, your mother's father, was a man and had to leave us to fight in the war across the ocean. I gave him the bag, for I believed it would protect him in battle, but he did not take it with him. He was afraid that he would lose it. He died in a faraway place."

Again Grandpa was still, and I felt his grief around me.

"My son," he went on after clearing his throat, "had only a daughter, and it is not proper for her to know of these things."

He unbuttoned his shirt, pulled out the leather pouch, and lifted it over his head. He held it in his hand, turning it over and over as if memorizing how it looked.

"In the bag," he said as he opened it and removed two objects, "is the broken shell of the iron kettle, a pebble from the butte, and a piece of the sacred sage." He held the pouch upside down and dust drifted down.

"After the bag is yours, you must put a piece of prairie sage within and never open it again until you pass it on to your son." He replaced the pebble and the piece of iron and tied the bag.

18

19
◄ G

I stood up, somehow knowing I should. Grandpa slowly rose from the bed and stood upright in front of me holding the bag before my face. I closed my eyes and waited for him to slip it over my head. But he spoke.

"No, you need not wear it." He placed the soft leather bag in my right hand and closed my other hand over it. "It would not be right to wear it in this time and place where no one will understand. Put it safely away until you are again on the reservation. Wear it then, when you replace the sacred sage."

Grandpa turned and sat again on the bed. Wearily he leaned his head against the pillow. "Go," he said. "I will sleep now."

"Thank you, Grandpa," I said softly, and left with the bag in my hands.

That night Mom and Dad took Grandpa to the hospital. Two weeks later I stood alone on the lonely prairie of the reservation and put the sacred sage in my medicine bag. 🐾

20
◄ H

20. LITERARY CONCEPT: Theme
How does Martin's placing the sacred sage in the medicine bag suggest the meaning of the story? (Possible responses: It suggests that Martin has accepted his Sioux heritage; Martin will keep the link between generations alive; he has accepted the trust from his great-grandfather and will pass it on to his descendants.)

I N S I G H T

Looking North to Taos

RUDY BANTISTA

I saw the pueblo beneath the blue
mountain, the older
buildings crumbling,
melting into mud. I watched
the old men, their heads
hidden beneath blankets,
and I wondered.

I have heard the round dance songs
from a thousand miles away,
have held the record cover in my
hands and seen the young boys
pictured on the back, their braids
long, their smiles not showing.
And I have wondered.

I sit still in the cool grass
toward evening,
legs crossed and tongue silent,
thinking as I look into the
dancing supper fires, "Am I
an Indian?" And I wonder.

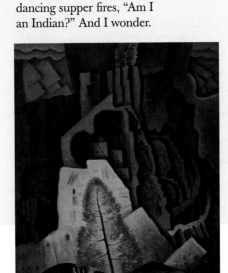

CLIFF DWELLINGS NO. 3   1927
Raymond Jonson   Collection of Jonson Gallery
of the University of New Mexico, Albuquerque.

THE MEDICINE BAG   565

INSIGHT
This poem is a reflection on the ideas in the main selection and is suggested for students' independent reading. Optional discussion questions follow.

1. How is the subject matter in this poem like that in "The Medicine Bag"? (Both works concern individuals who are not certain about their place in Native American society.)

2. Why do you think the speaker is uncertain if he is "an Indian"? (Possible responses: The speaker's life is so different from what he or she is seeing that he or she may not be able to feel a part of it all, whatever his or her heritage.)

Art Note
Oregon-born Raymond Jonson (1891–1982) studied art in Portland and Chicago. Then, in 1924, he moved to Santa Fe, New Mexico, where he found that the rugged landscape inspired him anew. The patterns of the ancient cliffs and ruins in Cliff Dwellings No. 3 (1927) seem to preview the geometric style of modernism. Is this landscape inviting or forbidding? Why?

ENCOURAGING INDEPENDENT READING

American Indian Myths and Legends, edited by Richard Erdoes and Alfonso Ortiz

The Ways of My Grandmothers, stories and myths by Beverly Hungry Wolf

Comprehension Check

✓ 1. Where do the narrator and his family live, and where does the narrator's great-grandfather live? (Martin and his family live in a city in Iowa, and Grandpa lives on a Sioux reservation in South Dakota.)

2. What mixed feelings does Martin have about Grandpa? (He loves him but is embarrassed by him; he is both proud and ashamed of him.)

3. What condition is Grandpa in? (old and frail)

4. How do Martin's friends react when they finally meet Grandpa? (They are fascinated and impressed.)

5. What gift does Grandpa give Martin, and when is Martin to wear it? (He gives Martin the medicine bag and tells him to wear it on the reservation.)

Student Response

Responding to Reading

1. Any response is valid.

2. **Possible responses:** Martin learns he is proud of his great-grandfather as well as his Sioux heritage; that the tradition of the medicine bag means a lot to him and connects him to his roots.

3. **Possible responses:** Yes, Grandpa is admirable because of his bravery and his determination to pass on Sioux traditions; no, Grandpa is clinging too much to the past and is embarrassing.

4. Any response is valid.

5. **Possible responses:** Yes, both have mixed feelings about accepting their Native American heritage; no, by the end of the story Martin has developed pride in his heritage while the speaker of the poem still feels confusion.

6. **Possible response:** They face poverty, exclusion, and the problems of being confined to a reservation; many leave the reservation and integrate themselves into mainstream society, thereby dropping the customs that make them unique.

Challenge Question

Grandpa tells Martin that in the bag are "the broken shell of the iron kettle, a pebble from the butte, and a piece of the sacred sage." What do you think these objects symbolize? *(Possible responses: The shell may symbolize work, the coming of modern times, or a link between white and Sioux cultures; the pebble may symbolize the Sioux's ties to the land or their home; the sage may symbolize spirituality or living things.)*

Responding to Reading

First Impressions

1. What thoughts went through your mind at the end of the story? Describe them in your journal or notebook.

Second Thoughts

2. What doors of understanding were opened for the narrator as a result of Grandpa's actions?

   Think about
   - how his opinion of Grandpa changes
   - why he put the sacred sage in his medicine bag

3. Do you admire Grandpa? Explain why or why not.

4. What connections were you able to make between your own experiences and the narrator's experiences?

5. Do the narrator in "The Medicine Bag" and the speaker in "Looking North to Taos" have similar feelings about their Native American heritage? Explain your answer.

Broader Connections

6. What difficulties do you think Native Americans face in the effort to continue their traditions? Use "The Medicine Bag" and your own knowledge as examples.

Literary Concept: Internal Conflict

An **internal conflict** occurs when a character has a struggle within himself or herself. Explain the internal conflict that the narrator faces. Is the conflict resolved? How?

Concept Review: Exposition The exposition introduces the setting, the main characters, and the conflict. What do you learn about the narrator's internal conflict from the exposition?

Literary Concept: Internal Conflict

Possible responses: Martin feels internal conflict about his buddies' possible reaction to his great-grandfather and about whether he wants the medicine bag. The first conflict is resolved when he and his friends are thoroughly impressed with Grandpa; the second is resolved when Martin accepts the medicine bag and knows he need not wear it all the time.

Concept Review: Exposition Martin has presented a glamorous image of his Sioux heritage but has not shown his friends the real picture; Martin feels love and tenderness for Grandpa but is also ashamed of him.

Writing Options

1. Imagine that the narrator grows up and has a son of his own. Write a **dialogue** about the time when he passes the medicine bag to his son.

2. Write a **song lyric** to tell the story of Grandpa and his gift. The lyric should also convey your own feelings about Grandpa.

3. Write a **comparison and contrast paper** that explains the similarities and differences between Grandpa and the "TV Indians" described on page 558.

4. Research the details of a vision quest, which can be found in books about the Sioux. Create a **booklet** to share your findings.

Vocabulary Practice

Exercise   Use your understanding of the boldfaced word to complete each of the following sentences. Write the letter of the word or phrase that best completes the sentence.

1. The narrator's **descendant** would be born (a) the same year as he was   (b) before him   (c) after him.

2. If the narrator greeted Grandpa **reluctantly,** his manner would show (a) excitement   (b) a lack of enthusiasm (c) bitter anger.

3. The **confines** of a reservation might be shown by (a) lines on a map   (b) photographs of daily life   (c) the tired faces of residents.

4. Grandpa would regard being hugged by his grown daughter as an **unseemly** display of affection because (a) he is too old for strong feelings   (b) the Sioux are not expected to show feelings toward adults openly   (c) he would be afraid of how it would look.

5. Grandpa's **fatigue** is most obvious when (a) he decides to take a bus trip   (b) he collapses   (c) he tells stories of his past glory.

> *Words to Know and Use*
>
> ---
>
> **confines**
> **descendant**
> **fatigue**
> **reluctantly**
> **unseemly**

Writing Options

The Writing Options are designed to meet varied student interests and abilities. Have each student choose one writing activity to complete.

Journal Update   Invite students to review their journal entries for "The Medicine Bag." What new insights might students add to their earlier writing about feeling ashamed of a loved one or about family mementos?

Links to Writer's Craft

Writing Option 4 is an exercise in informative writing. For more practice, see *The Writer's Craft,* Grade 7, "Informative Writing," pages 116–137.

Vocabulary Practice

Answers to Exercise
1. c
2. b
3. a
4. b
5. b

For Alternative Learning Styles

Encourage students to draw visual representations of one or more of the vocabulary words. Some students might portray something they find *unseemly;* still others might draw a family tree in which they place their own names and those of other *descendants* of their ancestors.

The Spelling Connection

Spelling Pattern: Pronunciation Problems   Difficulties in spelling can be caused by silent letters, unstressed middle vowels, or silent consonants when words are pronounced. They can also result from syllables not being pronounced.

Examples: several   whistle   postpone

Words with Such Problems from the Selection
respectfully   suffering   happily
funeral   groceries   recognized

Other Words with Pronunciation Problems
interest   privilege   favorite
terrify   rustle   handsome

Exercise   Match the definitions below with spelling words. Then write a short paragraph about one of your relatives. Include at least four spelling words.

1. preferred   3. concern   5. joyfully
2. good-looking   4. special right   6. frighten

Extending the Lesson

Options for Learning

These activities suit a variety of learning styles and modes of expression.

Collaborative Learning Activities
See Options 1 and 2.

1. **Native American Update** Suggest that students check recent encyclopedias, periodicals, and newspaper articles.

2. **Ethnic Profile** Encourage students to consult with their parents or other family members.

3. **Keeping the Past** Remind students to prepare a list of questions in advance and to listen carefully to the interviewee. With the interviewee's permission, students might tape the interview.

4. **Your Own Medicine Bag** Encourage students to take the time to think about which objects reflect their true feelings.

FACT FINDER GEOGRAPHY

Students can use an atlas to determine that the Little White River and the Keya Paha River run through the Rosebud Reservation.

Virginia Driving Hawk Sneve

■ **More About the Author** A member of the Rosebud Sioux people, Virginia Driving Hawk Sneve has worked to promote Native American issues on the Corporation for Public Broadcasting and has contributed stories, book reviews, and articles to many anthologies and magazines.

■ **Other Works** Novels: *Betrayed, When Thunders Spoke, High Elk's Treasure, Jimmy Yellow Hawk, The Chichi Hoohoo Bogeyman;* poetry: edited *Dancing Teepees,* a collection of poetry by Native American youth

Closure

Ask students how both Martin and Grandpa open "doors of understanding" for each other. Invite students to discuss how not pressuring someone can help him or her through an important life change or difficult time.

Options for Learning (Multimodal/Cross-Curricular Activities)

1 • Native American Update With a partner, investigate living conditions among modern Native Americans. What special problems and challenges do they face? What is being done to help them? Report your findings, using the format of a radio news show.

2 • Ethnic Profile As an extension of your prereading activities, work in a small group to conduct an ethnic poll in your class. Identify the different ethnic heritages in your classroom, and find out how important each student's ethnic background is to him or her. Your poll can take the form of a questionnaire or of individual interviews. When the poll is completed, give an oral report on the results.

3 • Keeping the Past Interview one of your grandparents or someone else's grandparent. Find out what objects or mementos hold a special meaning in his or her life and why. Report your findings to the class.

4 • Your Own Medicine Bag Choose three or four ordinary objects that you think represent your life or your destiny. Then make a bag for them, complete with a string or rope. Explain the significance of the objects to the class.

 FACT FINDER GEOGRAPHY

What two large rivers run through the Rosebud Reservation in South Dakota?

Virginia Driving Hawk Sneve
1933–

Virginia Driving Hawk Sneve grew up in a family she describes as "secure, warm, and loving" on the Sioux Rosebud Reservation in South Dakota. "I never realized that I was an Indian," she reports, "until I went to college at South Dakota State University. It was a shock to realize I was different. People expected me not to speak English well and to wear feathers and beads."

Sneve began to write as a way of correcting people's misconceptions of Native Americans. Her first book, *Jimmy Yellow Hawk,* was awarded the Interracial Council for Minority Books for Children Award. The award gave her the confidence to continue writing. Since then, she has gone on to write eleven more books. "The Medicine Bag" is based on the experience of a friend whose grandmother left her reservation for the first time to visit her family in Minneapolis.

Sneve writes in the summer and works as a counselor at Rapid City Central High School in South Dakota during the school year.

568 UNIT FIVE DOORS OF UNDERSTANDING

Cross-Curricular Projects

Music Have students research traditional Native American music, especially that of Plains peoples such as the Sioux. Students may be able to find recordings of the type of music the Sioux perform at religious festivals and other celebrations.

History Have students research the history of the Native American reservations. Encourage students to include information on the early schools, laws, government, population, and social conditions.

Art Invite students to present a festival of Native American arts. If possible, have them show some actual objects as well as photographs. Urge them to explain the objects' meanings, as well as to describe their materials and how they were made.

Science Encourage students to research and report on what archaeologists have learned about Native American cultures. Have students report on methods archaeologists use as well as on their findings.

WRITER'S WORKSHOP

INFORMATIVE WRITING

Doors of understanding open when we learn about the customs of others. In this subunit you've read about traditions in Puerto Rico, a superstition from Japan, and customs of the Sioux. Now you can deepen your understanding as you **research**—use outside sources to locate information about—a custom that interests you. You'll use **informative** writing—writing that explains facts and ideas—to prepare a brief report about the custom you've chosen.

USE INFORMATIVE WRITING FOR

reports
histories
biographies
instructions
explanations
analyses

GUIDED ASSIGNMENT: RESEARCH REPORT

Write an informative report about an interesting custom of a specific group of people.

Here is one writer's PASSkey to this assignment.

P URPOSE: To inform
A UDIENCE: Classmates, teachers, and friends
S UBJECT: An interesting custom
S TRUCTURE: Research report

The Prophet's Birthday
by Michael Deddeh

A new star shone in the sky the night he was born. Angels gathered, and his mother received a gift of gold. These tales commemorate Maulid-an-Nabi, the birthday of the prophet Muhammad. Muslims in Lebanon especially enjoy celebrating this traditional holiday.

Muhammad believed in generosity. He was born in the Arabian city of Mecca, around A.D. 570. As he grew up, the things that happened to poorer people upset him. He went into the mountains to meditate about the problem. There, in a vision, an angel said Muhammad was to be God's prophet. The angel gave Muhammad messages, which were later

◀ **STUDENT MODEL**
Before you write, read how one student responded to the assignment.

◀ The custom and people are identified in the introduction.

Objectives

■ To understand the purpose and characteristics of a research report

■ To make an outline and use it to write the report

■ To make a bibliography of sources used to document research

■ To draft, revise, edit, and share informative writing

Teaching Strategies

DISCUSSING THE ASSIGNMENT

Have students read the first paragraph on page 569 and be sure they understand that the purposes of informative writing are to inform and explain. Then discuss with students the role of research in obtaining the facts and ideas they will include in their reports. Tell them that although their research will consist mostly of library sources, such as books and magazine articles, it may also include information from interviews they conduct with people who are knowledgeable about the customs that are the subjects of their reports.

Next have students read the Guided Assignment and PASSkey for the research report. If students wish to write about another topic that interests them, you might give them the suggestions that appear on page 560 under Alternative Writing and Research Topics.

ANALYZING THE MODEL

Have a volunteer read aloud the model on pages 569–570. Ask students to identify the custom Michael Deddeh chose for his report and some of the details he gives to describe it. Then point out the bibliography at the end, and have students note the format in which Michael listed his sources.

ADDITIONAL RESOURCES

Unit Five Resource Book
Writer's Workshop Worksheet, p. 74
Writer's Workshop: Peer and Self-Evaluation, p. 75
Writer's Workshop: Assessment Guidelines, p. 76

Technology and Enrichment
Elaboration, Revision, and Proofreading Transparencies 29–34

Fine Art Transparency Pack

Writer's Databank Software: File 11, Outline Template

Links to
Writer's Craft

For more about informative writing, see *The Writer's Craft,* Grade 7, "Informative Writing: Reports," pages 186–205, and pages 278–280, "Writing Conclusions."

To analyze the model further, form students into four groups. Ask two groups to study the kind of organization Michael used and to identify the main idea of each paragraph. Have the other two groups analyze the style of the research report and note the kinds of details that make it interesting. Afterward, have all four groups share what they learned. If time permits, discuss with the class other kinds of information Michael might have included in his report.

Prewrite and Explore

Before students begin their library research, they may want to review how to use the library, what materials are available for research, and how to take notes. Refer them to the section entitled "Research and Report Writing" on pages 702–705 of the Writer's Handbook.

In addition to looking up a specific religion in an encyclopedia, suggest to students that they look up a specific country. These articles, too, may have headings for customs and celebrations.

Bring up the subject of plagiarism before students begin to take notes. Point out the sidenote on the bottom of page 572. Caution students that unless they use specific material in direct quotations, they should be especially careful even when taking notes. One good strategy to avoid inadvertent plagiarism is to have students close source books briefly and take notes in their own words.

Modeling Show students how you want them to do a bibliography. Point out that the bibliography information needs to be taken at the time they take notes so that they don't have to go back and find the source later. Using an encyclopedia or other reference book, go through the process of finding and recording the bibliography information on the board with them.

The transitions *later, over the years,* and *now* keep readers oriented in time. ►

A topic sentence states the main idea of the paragraph. ►

Details support the main idea. ►

The conclusion sums up feelings about the custom. ►

recorded in the Koran, a holy book. The Koran says people should give to the poor. Over the years Muhammad had more visions and founded a new religion, Islam. Muslims around the world now celebrate his birthday in September.

In Lebanon, Maulid-an-Nabi brings nine days of fun and generosity in honor of Muhammad. There are parades and fairs. People give gifts and food to the needy. Families invite friends to share huge meals that start with tabbouleh, a salad of chopped mint, parsley, onions, tomatoes, and cooked wheat. Next comes roast chicken with a special stuffing of ground lamb, rice, and spices. For dessert, there is baklava, a pastry with honey and pine nuts. Later in the evenings, people tell the story of Muhammad's birth.

The story says that a bright star appeared over Mecca on that night long ago. Seven thousand angels brought a beautiful gift: a golden bowl of dew for Muhammad's mother to bathe him in. This story shows the spirit of happiness and generosity that Lebanese Muslims feel on the prophet's birthday.

Bibliography

Adams, Charles J. "Islam." The World Book Encyclopedia. 1990 ed.

Dooley, Leticia. Customs Around the World. New York: Grove, 1982.

Khoury, C. "September in Lebanon." Junior Scholastic Sept. 1992: 19-21.

Now that you've read Michael's paper, it's time to begin your own.

Prewrite and Explore

1 **Browse around** If you need a writing idea, a trip to the library can help you find customs to write about. Since many customs are based on religious beliefs, you might locate an encyclopedia and look up a specific religion, such as Judaism, Hinduism, or Buddhism.

Alternative Writing and Research Topics

Research Report In "Last Cover" Stan and Colin cannot bear to let their pet fox return to the woods. Research other wild animals that humans have rescued and cared for. Find out whether any of these animals have been tamed, and, if so, how their caretakers live with them.

Personal Memoir "Primary Lessons" tells of the first serious lesson the author learned in school. Write your own memoir concerning a lesson about life that you learned sometime in your school career.

Informative Report "Oh Broom, Get to Work" describes an old Japanese superstition. Interview people about superstitions they know. Choose two common ones and try to find out their origins. Write your findings in a report.

The article you find may have headings for customs and celebrations. You also might browse through books shelved under the Dewey Decimal number 394. These deal with customs and traditions. As you browse, you can make a list of customs that interest you.

2 **Make a choice and research it** From your list, choose the custom that interests you most. Skim books and articles that might contain information on your topic. When you come to facts and details you can use, slow down and take notes on index cards.

3 **Take notes** Begin by recording information about each reference source you use: title, author (if named), name of article (for magazines and encyclopedias), date. This information will be used in the bibliography at the end of your report. Then begin taking notes about your topic, using one note card for each fact or idea that you might want to use in your report. When you take notes, don't copy. Write the ideas in your own words. If you want to record specific words from your source, put them in quotation marks.

4 **Get organized** After you gather information, you will be ready to organize it. If you scan your notes, you'll see that most of them relate to a few main ideas. Try grouping your note cards according to these main ideas. You might make an outline of your main ideas and details.

ORGANIZING INFORMATION

When you make an outline, you arrange ideas in a logical order. The main idea of each note-card group can become a main heading in your outline. The supporting facts on each note card can become subheadings. Study the portion of Michael's outline below.

```
The Prophet's Birthday
  I. Introduction
 II. Muhammad's belief in generosity
     A. Sympathy for the suffering of the poor
     B. Koran's commandment to help the needy
III. Fun and treats on Muhammad's birthday
     A. Parades and fairs
     B. Gifts to the poor
     C. Family feasts
     D. Storytelling
```

◀ **WRITER'S CHOICE**
Customs can be associated with holidays, seasons, coming of age, marriage, birth, and death.

◀ **REMINDER**
Try using the *Readers' Guide* to locate magazine articles about your topic.

◀ **WRITER'S CHOICE**
What if a card doesn't relate to any of your main ideas? You may want to use it as a starting point for researching a new idea, or you may decide not to use it at all.

◀ **STUDENT MODEL**

◀ **IN OTHER CLASSES**
In social studies you can use outlining to organize class notes and information from your textbook when you study for essay tests.

TEACHING TIP: LEP
Students originally from other countries might want to report on a custom from their native lands. In this case, since they already know more details than many books can offer, suggest that they research the history of the custom.

Encourage all students to make an outline to guide them as they write. Have them mark main ideas with a colored marker or pen. If students have too many main ideas, suggest that they limit themselves to the three for which they have the best details.

Next, tell students to organize their outlines. Have them begin with roman numerals *I* and *V*, labeling them *Introduction* and *Conclusion* respectively, and leaving plenty of space in between. Instruct students to add the roman numerals *II, III, and IV* between *I* and *V*, and list after each numeral one of the main ideas they've color-coded in their notes. Last, have students write under each main idea the details associated with it. At this point students' outlines are all but complete. Later they can jot down ideas for their introductions and conclusions, and arrange the details under each main idea in the order in which they will use them.

Cooperative Writing

The reports that middle school students write often sound almost exactly like the encyclopedia entry they used. Point out to them that while rearranging or substituting a few words prevents plagiarism, the material still sounds like it came from the source. In order to help them make their writing their own, have them work in small groups to revise sentences and paragraphs. Encourage one student to read aloud a paragraph; then the whole group can make suggestions for putting it in student language rather than encyclopedia language.

Draft and Discover

Encourage students to follow their outlines as they write. Just knowing that everything is organized and that at each point they will see what comes next may make even reluctant writers feel in control of the assignment.

Next, remind students not to forget their audience. Since they may be using unfamiliar terms to describe customs, have them provide a definition for each one. A good strategy is to work definitions into the text using descriptive phrases such as the following:

During Holi, *a springtime holiday in India,* it is the custom for people to go from house to house sprinkling colored water on everyone they meet.

Another useful strategy is to have students begin drafting with paragraphs II, III, and IV. Once these are written, the conclusion may follow naturally, and students can concentrate on unique openings for their introductions.

TEACHING TIP: CHALLENGE

You might challenge advanced writers to write about a custom that is found in two different cultures. Suggest that they compare and contrast the way it is observed in the two cultures. Have them show its origin and meaning in each culture and explain why differences in the way of its observance exist.

CONFERENCING TIP

As you conference with individual writers for this workshop, you may wish to focus on

■ rephrasing factual material in the student's own words

■ a satisfying introduction and conclusion

■ bibliography form

Revise Your Writing

Students might ask their peer reviewers to comment on these items:

■ the effectiveness of their introductions to "hook" readers and move easily to paragraph II;

■ the effectiveness of conclusions to provide a satisfying ending;

■ the correctness in content and form of their bibliographies.

572   UNIT FIVE **Doors of Understanding**

Draft and Discover

NEED MORE HELP?
For more about topic sentences and supporting details, see the Reader's Workshop on page 577.

1 Use your outline to plan paragraphs   Your outline is a blueprint for paragraphs. Each main heading suggests a topic sentence, and subheadings suggest the details that will complete a paragraph. Don't, however, let your outline stop your thinking. As you write, you may get good ideas that aren't part of your outline. It's fine to include them. If you want to stop writing and do more research first, go ahead.

COMPUTER TIP
Some computer programs have a split-screen feature. You can use it to keep your outline on the screen for reference as you draft.

2 Use transitions   In your outline, numbers and letters show how ideas relate. When you turn your outline into an essay, you need to replace the numbers and letters with **transitions**—words and phrases that show relationships of time, space, or logic.

3 Name your sources   At the end of your draft, add a list of the sources you used. This list, referred to as either a **bibliography** or **works cited,** backs up your facts and lets readers find more information if they want to. For bibliography guidelines, see Research and Report Writing in the Writer's Handbook.

Revise Your Writing

WRITING TIP
Remember, you can do more research at any time.

1 Adjust the focus   As you reread your draft, decide your main feeling about the custom. With that focus in mind, you can fine-tune the organization of your report. You may decide to insert key words, rearrange paragraphs, add more details to some parts, or omit parts. Next, write a short introduction, perhaps using attention-catching details related to your focus.

2 Wrap it up   Your conclusion may be a brief paragraph summing up the main ideas in your report, emphasizing the importance of the custom, or describing your feelings about it.

IT'S THE LAW!
Plagiarism, the use of someone else's words as if they were your own, is against the law. Even when you've named your sources, be sure to state ideas in your own words.

3 Listen for smoothness   You do not want your report to sound like an encyclopedia article. Instead, your sentences should reflect your own writing voice. They should flow naturally. Consider combining sentences or sentence parts to smooth out choppy places. When you're ready, ask a peer to read your draft. Use the checklists below.

Paragraphs at Work

If students have made outlines following the suggestions on the previous page, and if in doing so they understand the relationship between main ideas (color-coded notes) and details (points that explain or elaborate on the main ideas), they might not find paragraphing a problem.

Nevertheless, for "insurance," you may want to write the following suggestions on the chalkboard to assist students as they draft.

■ Cover each main idea of your outline in a separate paragraph.

■ Make sure that the main idea of each paragraph is clear by stating it in a topic sentence.

■ Use transitions to show the connections between paragraphs.

■ Write an interesting introduction and a satisfying conclusion.

Revision Questions

For You	For a Peer Reader
1. Have I included the details I found most interesting?	1. Which parts of my report are most vivid to you?
2. Could I add transitions to help my readers stay oriented?	2. Do all parts of my report reflect my own writing voice?
3. Could I combine sentences to make my report smoother?	3. What did you learn from my report?

Proofread

Check your report carefully for errors in grammar and mechanics.

THE EDITOR'S EYE: PROOFREADING

To proofread for spelling errors, start at the end of your paper and work toward the beginning. Proofreading symbols make it easy to note needed changes.

Problem Muhammad beleived in generousity.

Revised Muhammad believed in generosity.

◄ **NEED MORE HELP?**
See the Language Workshop on pages 574-576.

Publish and Present

Custom Fair With your teacher's help, plan a custom fair. Class members can bring appropriate illustrations, costumes, objects, or foods to display with their reports.

Reflect on Your Writing

Answer the following questions on a separate sheet of paper, then add the paper to your report. Place your report in your portfolio.

◄ **FOR YOUR PORTFOLIO**

1. If you had more time, what would you change in your report?
2. Did you prefer the research or the writing?

Proofread

Note that The Editor's Eye feature previews the content in the Language Workshop that follows. If the class or individual students might benefit from additional work, you may choose to teach the Language Workshop, pages 574–576, before having students proofread.

Write these sentences on the board for practice. Have one student use proofreading marks and the other rewrite the sentence correctly.

1. People of india have many Customs in cooking and eating food. *(The people of India have many customs regarding the cooking and eating of food.)*

2. In northern India they prepare small many dishes of Food rather then a few large ones *(In northern India they prepare many small dishes of food rather than a few large ones.)*

Publish and Present

For the Custom Fair, suggest that students show how something is made. For example, they might use a series of photos to show how clothing is put together, or demonstrate cooking a particular dish. Videotape the fair and keep the tape in the classroom library.

Reflect on Your Writing

You may choose to have students answer these questions in addition to or instead of those in the text:

■ How could I make my report sound more like my writing rather than like an encyclopedia?

■ In what parts of the report did I do my best work?

Closure

Now that students have written a research report, encourage them to watch researched television shows such as *60 Minutes* to observe how they explore a topic and reach a conclusion.

Assessment Guidelines

These guidelines may help you assess student writing.

Content

■ The introduction states the topic of the paper and hooks the reader.

■ The report develops the topic by providing ideas in a logical sequence.

■ Each idea is supported by examples and concrete details.

■ The closing paragraph comes to a satisfactory conclusion.

Style

■ Ideas are expressed in the writer's own words, except for direct quotations.

■ All quotations are documented correctly.

■ Transitions are specific and effective.

Usage and Mechanics

■ Quotations are punctuated correctly.

■ Paraphrasing is correct and effective.

See also *Unit Five Resource Book*, page 75.

Objective

■ To use proofreading symbols to correct errors in mechanics and usage

Teaching Strategies

Have students study the proofreading checklist on page 574 and review the proofreading symbols on page 575. Then provide the following models for chalkboard practice. Have students use colored chalk to make the proofreading symbols on these sentences.

1. In Purto Rico judith learned about school work and prejødice.

2. she and her family was thought off as rich.

3. Judith became a teacher's pet because she spooke english well?

4. Judith dosnt understand how animals can speak in so many languages!

5. In the Purto Rico of Judith's childood, people were juged by thier ancestory.

6. An old family name was as good a statys cymbal as money or titles.

7. In judiths first-grade class was a black child named Lorenzo.

8. He was a good child who tryed hard to please the teacher.

9. Lorenzo was past up for an oner at the end of the school year because he didnt have a good sut to wear.

10. Judith did not understand how not haveing a sut could cost him an oner.

After practicing on the chalkboard, have students work in small groups to complete Exercise 1 on page 576.

ADDITIONAL RESOURCES

Unit Five Resource Book
Language Workshop Practice, p. 77

Technology and Enrichment
Elaboration, Revision, and Proofreading Practice
  Transparencies 33, 34

PROOFREADING SKILLS

When you proofread, you focus on correcting errors. You look at grammar, spelling, punctuation, and capitalization. For a research report you also double-check your facts, dates, statistics, and source information.

When you proofread, you should have a dictionary handy so you can check the spelling of words you're not sure of. You may find it easier to proofread several times, looking for a different kind of problem each time. To avoid being distracted by content, begin proofreading at the end of your paper and work toward the beginning.

The list below shows nine common types of errors. Make a habit of double-checking those that crop up often in your writing.

COMPUTER TIP
Some software has a feature that checks spelling. It can be fooled by words that sound alike, so double-check these. (See the Language Workshop on pages 344–346.)

PUNCTUATION TIP
Watch out for unnecessary commas! Review the rules for using commas in the Language Handbook, pages 775–780. Then be sure to use commas only where they're needed.

PROOFREADING CHECKLIST

1. Do all my data (facts, statistics, and so on) match what I have in my notes?

2. Have I avoided sentence fragments and run-on sentences?

3. Do all my verbs agree with their subjects? Do my tense shifts make sense?

4. Do I use the correct subject and object forms of pronouns?

5. Each time I've joined two complete sentences, have I used a comma and an appropriate conjunction?

6. Is the first sentence in each of my paragraphs indented?

7. Do all sentences and proper nouns begin with capital letters?

8. Have I used commas, periods, and quotation marks correctly?

9. Have I checked my spelling, including words that sound alike?

---

574   UNIT FIVE   DOORS OF UNDERSTANDING

Links to
Writer's Craft

For more about proofreading, see *The Writer's Craft*, Grade 7, "Proofreading," pages 288–290.

Proofreading Symbols

The following symbols can remind you of changes to make when you recopy your draft.

Symbol	Meaning	Example
∧	Add letters or words.	1) He walked. *(slowly)*
⊙	Add a period.	2) He walked slowly⊙
≡	Capitalize a letter.	3) His name was m̲uhammad.
◡	Close up space.	4) They serve fruit cakes.
∧	Add a comma.	5) On his way backˏ he stopped.
/	Make a capital letter lowercase.	6) He looked at the S̸hrine.
¶	Begin a new paragraph.	7) at night. ¶ Usually, the journey
∼	Switch the positions of letters or words.	8) He never has been wrong.
ϑ	Take out letters or words.	9) We welcomed him gladly.

Michael used the symbols when he proofread his final paragraph.

The stor̸ey says that a bright s̸tar appeared over
m̲ecca on that night long ago. Seven thousand
ang̸les brought a beautiful gift: golden a bowl of dew
∧
for Muhammad's mother to bath̸e him in. This story
∧
shows the spirit of happiness and generoȗsity that
Lebanese Muslims feel on the prophet 's birthday.
∧

◀ STUDENT MODEL ⋯⋯⋯⋯

After you've proofread and marked a draft, you can recopy it, being sure to make all the corrections indicated. Then check the new copy—sometimes new errors creep in. A friend may be able to spot them more easily than you can at this point.

TEACHING TIP: LEP

Since rules for capitalization vary from language to language, you might want to work independently with students to be sure they understand the rules that govern capitalization in English. Here are a few rules of capitalization in other languages that differ from our own: Some languages, such as Arabic, Chinese, and Hebrew, make no distinction between capital letters and small ones. In German, all nouns are capitalized, but adjectives of nationality are not. In Spanish and French the words for *I*—*yo* and *je*—are not capitalized unless they begin a sentence.

Similarly, punctuation rules vary greatly from country to country. Since the apostrophe doesn't exist in many languages, you may need to clarify its use with ESL students—and be sure to differentiate it from the comma.

Although students grasp the use of end punctuation and most internal punctuation rather well, nearly everyone has some trouble with commas. You may want to do a brief review of these marks, concentrating on their use with introductory words, with interrupters, with compound sentences, and in a series. Explanations and practice sentences for these items can be found in the Language Handbook, pages 775–777.

LANGUAGE WORKSHOP   575

Grammar Games: What If???!!!

Have students form two teams. Explain that they may use their social studies texts to write a sentence to complete the question "What if . . ." They should use black markers and leave out all capital letters and punctuation. Sentences must in some way link with social studies, as in this example: "what if columbus discovered the allegheny monongahela and ohio rivers instead of the west indies" The first player on Team A holds up a sentence strip for the first player on Team B to read. The Team B player must rush over, take the sentence, "proofread" it with a colorful marker, and hold it up again—all within 15 seconds. If the proofreading is correct, the next student on Team B holds up a sentence for the next student on Team A, and play continues. Those who can't complete the proofreading correctly or in time are out. The team with the most students at the end of the game wins.

LANGUAGE WORKSHOP **Teacher's Edition**   **575**

Answers to Exercise 1

In Denmark the custom of wearing costumes on the last <u>M</u>onday before Lent <u>has</u> been popular for centuries. Schools are closed on this special day <u>c</u>alled Fastelavn. The night before Fastelavn, families buy or bake big, round rolls made with butter, sugar, raisins, <u>and</u> pieces of candied fruit peel. On the morning of Fastelavn, children dress in <u>their</u> masks and costumes and go from door to door as U.S. children do on Halloween night. They carry small money boxes. At each door they <u>sing</u> a traditional song, threatening to make misch<u>ie</u>f if they <u>are</u> not given sweet rolls to eat and money to put in their boxes. Later they use the money to buy candy, pastries, and soda. That evening everybody eats <u>his or her</u> fill at big family dinners. Long ago, this was a last feast before the long fasting period of Lent. Few Danes today still give up <u>their</u> favorite foods during Lent, <u>but</u> all Danish children still cele<u>b</u>rate Fastelavn.

Answers to Exercise 2

Ask students to use markers to make proofreading symbols on their papers. Check students' papers to see whether their errors have been corrected.

Answers to Exercise 3

Have students make these corrections as they did for Exercise 2. Then, as you check their portfolios, note whether all three questions have been adequately answered.

Closure

After this proofreading practice, bring to school (or have students bring in) an editorial page from the newspaper. Arm them with markers once again, and see how many corrections they can make on these "professional" pages. Because of space problems, students may make their symbols in the margins. Suggest that students practice regularly to keep their proofreading skills honed.

Exercise 1   Concept Check   Use the proofreading checklist to find mistakes in the paragraph below. (Hint: There are fourteen errors.) Then recopy the paragraph, correcting each error you found. Double-check your copy to be sure there are no new errors, and correct any you find.

In Denmark the custom of wearing costumes on the last monday before Lent have been popular for centuries. Schools are closed on this special day. Called Fastelavn. The night before Fastelavn, families buy or bake big, round rolls made with butter, sugar, raisons, pieces of candied fruit peel. On the morning of Fastelavn, children dress in they're masks and costumes and go from door to door as U.S. children do on Halloween night. They carry small money boxes. At each door they sang a traditonal song, threatening to make mischeif if they were not given sweet rolls to eat and money to put in their boxes. Later they use the money to buy candy, pastries, and soda. That evening, everybody eats their fill at big family dinners. Long ago, this was a last feast before the long fasting period of Lent. Few Danes today still give up his or her favorite foods during Lent, all Danish children still celabrate Fastelavn.

Exercise 2   Proofreading Your Writing   Using the checklist in this workshop, proofread the research report you wrote for the Writer's Workshop on pages 569–573. Use the proofreading symbols to mark errors. Then make a clean copy of your report, correcting your errors.

Exercise 3   Proofreading Your Writing   Using the proofreading checklist and symbols, proofread two other papers in your portfolio. Then answer the questions and follow the directions below.

1. In which of the nine problem areas did you find errors in your research report?
2. In the three papers you proofread, what is the total number of errors you found in each problem area?
3. Based on the number of errors you found in each area, list three areas you think you should focus on when proofreading your work in the future.

Additional Practice

Proofread these sentences.

1. to aquaint visitors with the new ostrich exibit the zoo has printed a special pamplet
2. at schduled times throughtout the day guides provide supplementry information
3. for example ostricks the worlds largest living birds are nearly eitht feet tall
4. before the new zeeland moas died out they were the only birds taller than ostricks
5. the extint elephant birds i beleive were the only birds heavyer than ostriches
6. by the time an ostrick is mature it can wiegh as much as 350 pounds
7. well with such wieght how do they fly visitors often ask
8. the anser ladies and gentlemen is that in fact they do not fly
9. if necesary an ostrick can move very fast on lan
10. over open ground in africa ostricks have been clocked at nearly fourty miles an hour

READER'S WORKSHOP

MAIN IDEAS AND SUPPORTING DETAILS

Informative writing deals with ideas. Each paragraph is a group of sentences about one idea—the **main idea.** Often the main idea of a paragraph is stated in a **topic sentence.** The other sentences contain **supporting details,** or details that relate to the main idea. When you revise reports and other informational pieces, you need to decide exactly what main idea each of your paragraphs is presenting. Then you will be able to figure out which kinds of details and transitions will strengthen the paragraph. Delete any sentences that don't refer to the main idea. Also, be sure to start a new paragraph when you begin to write about a new idea.

Writers often state the main idea at the beginning of a paragraph. The supporting details follow, explaining or illustrating the main idea. However, some paragraphs (such as this one) start with supporting details and build toward a main idea in the last sentence. The topic sentence, then, may come either first or last in a paragraph.

In some cases, a paragraph does not contain a topic sentence. The main idea is not stated directly; it is **implied,** or suggested, by the details in the paragraph. Writers use this technique to emphasize a main idea and to encourage readers to think about it for themselves.

◀ EXCEPTION
When a paragraph about one idea gets very long, you can give your readers a mental and visual rest by dividing it into two paragraphs.

◀ READING TIP
To understand an implied main idea, you must make an inference based on the details in the paragraph. For more about making inferences, see the Reader's Workshop on page 66.

Exercise 1   For each paragraph listed below, write the sentence that states the main idea and the sentences that contain supporting details. Be ready to explain your decisions.

1. Paragraph 7 of "Primary Lessons," on page 540.
2. Paragraph 11 of "The Medicine Bag," on page 559.

Exercise 2   Reread the last paragraph of "Primary Lessons," on page 545, and answer the questions below.

1. What details appear in the paragraph?
2. How would you state the main idea implied by the paragraph?
3. How might the effect of the paragraph have been different if the author had stated the main idea directly?

Exercise 3   Looking at Your Writing   Reread the report you wrote for the Writer's Workshop on pages 569–573. On a sheet of paper, write the main idea of each of your paragraphs. Then list the supporting details that develop each idea.

READER'S WORKSHOP   **577**

ADDITIONAL RESOURCES
Unit Five Resource Book
Reader's Workshop Practice, p. 78

Technology and Enrichment
Active Reading Transparencies 11–12

Additional Practice

Have students choose five paragraphs from the non-fiction selections in the unit and challenge partners to identify their main ideas and supporting details.

Objective

■ To understand main idea, topic sentence, and supporting details

Teaching Strategies

Have students read the three paragraphs on page 577. Help them understand the importance of knowing the main idea of each paragraph they write. Remind them that when they read in a content area such as social studies or science, looking for the main idea of each paragraph will help them better understand their reading and later provide a good means of review.

Answers to Exercise 1
(Shortened answers are given.)

1. The first sentence states the main idea, that the narrator felt the loss of her freedom when she had to go to school. The other sentences provide supporting details by explaining how school took it from her.

2. The last sentence states the main idea, that Grandpa's outfit was out of place in the narrator's neighborhood. The other sentences provide descriptive details about Grandpa's outfit and appearance.

Answers to Exercise 2
1. a saying or motto in Spanish and English and its meaning, the narrator's question to her mother, and her mother's laughing answer

2. Lorenzo is a victim of prejudice, no matter how gently it is spoken.

3. The paragraph would have lost its mystery. As it is, the reader feels a sense of discovery along with the narrator in figuring out the indirect insult independently.

Answers to Exercise 3
Check students' reports to see whether main ideas have been identified.

Objectives

■ To extend the study of the unit theme, "A Question of Identity," to novels and other longer works

■ To read independently for personal enrichment and enjoyment

THE HOUSE OF DIES DREAR

Study Focus

■ Unsolved mysteries of the past

■ Eerie mood of the story

■ A character's struggle with identity and understanding

About Virginia Hamilton

By her own admission, Hamilton has had "every source of occupation imaginable, from singer to bookkeeper." As a children's book author, she has distinguished herself by creating lively narratives with characters that reflect her own experiences and background. She says, "Black folk tales, I believe, allow us to share in the known, the remembered, and the imagined together as Americans sharing the same history."

■ **Other Works** Novels: *A White Romance; A Little Love; M. C. Higgins, the Great; Zeely; Jahdu*

 ■ **Awards** Edgar Allan Poe Award, 1969, for *The House of Dies Drear;* Newbery Honor Book, 1972, for *The Planet of Junior Brown;* Newbery Medal, 1975, for *M. C. Higgins, the Great*

Reading on Your Own

Suggested Novels for Unit Five

In the novels introduced on these pages, "A Question of Identity" arises for everyone—even the reader!

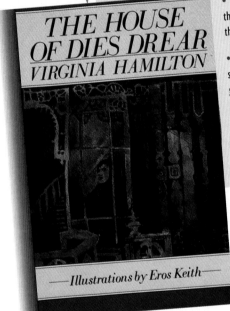

THE HOUSE OF DIES DREAR

VIRGINIA HAMILTON ©1968

Very odd things are happening in the old mansion called Drear House. Built before the Civil War, and once a stopping point on the Underground Railroad, the house has become a new home for a family named Small. However, it seems that someone is not happy that they have moved in. The secret passages behind every wall are filled with a strange sighing noise, and the ancient caretaker, Pluto, is rumored by the local people to be the devil himself! Share young Thomas Small's adventures as he tries to unravel questions of identity. As you read this mystery, think about these questions:

• Are ghosts causing the disturbances in the house?

• What secret is the strange little neighbor girl hiding?

• Could Thomas be running into hidden danger?

THE HOUSE OF DIES DREAR
VIRGINIA HAMILTON

—*Illustrations by Eros Keith*—

578

Guide for Teaching

A study guide for the paired novels *The House of Dies Drear* and *The Adventures of Tom Sawyer* is available from McDougal, Littell. See the Teacher's Resource File for ordering information.

RISK N' ROSES

JAN SLEPIAN ©1990

What would you do to become a member of the "in" crowd? Skip Berman's new idol Jean wants to find out. In this novel set in New York in the 1940s, Jean rules the playground, and her daring makes her extremely attractive and popular. However, she sets up dares as tests for Skip to join the group. When Skip's family embarrasses Skip in front of her new friend, Skip tries to declare her independence from them and ends up questioning her own identity. Jean's interest in Skip's handicapped sister, Angela, causes Skip to decide how far she will go to keep Jean's loyalty. As you read, ask yourself these questions:

- How outrageous will Jean's demands become?

- Will Skip be able to resist Jean's dares?

- Can Skip protect Angela?

THE ADVENTURES OF TOM SAWYER

MARK TWAIN © 1876

This timeless classic is about a young boy in Missouri before the Civil War. Tom Sawyer and his friends hide out on an island, intending to lead new lives as pirates even though their families and the town think that they have drowned. They return home when, unable to resist the temptation, they arrive at their own funerals! In further adventures, Tom and his sweetheart Becky are lost in a cave that holds a murderous secret. Read to find out . . .

- whether Tom's daring will prove to be disaster for his friends

- what Tom does when he becomes a witness to a murder

- how Tom rescues Becky from the cave

Other Recommended Books

Thunderwith by Libby Hathorn (© 1991). In this contemporary novel set in the Australian outback, a girl faces new and difficult relationships. After her mother's death, she must live with her father and his unfriendly wife and children. With the help of a dog, doors of understanding open.

Good Night, Mr. Tom by Michelle Magorian (© 1981). This historical novel is set in England during World War II, when children were being brought to the country to escape the bombing in London. An abused boy learns to live with a gruff but kindly old man.

Dogsong by Gary Paulsen (© 1985). In this contemporary realistic novel, a fourteen-year-old Eskimo boy searches for self-knowledge on a 1400-mile journey by dog sled, alone, across the tundra. On this long journey he finds his own song.

Waiting to Waltz: A Childhood by Cynthia Rylant (© 1984). This book of poetry follows the author's search for her own identity as she grows up in a small town in West Virginia.

579

RISK N' ROSES

Study Focus
- Significance of the Holocaust in relation to characters' identity
- Themes of prejudice and loyalty
- Characters' struggle for identity

About Jan Slepian

Intending to become a clinical psychologist, Slepian practiced speech therapy before becoming a children's book author. She sees writing as a form of self-discovery. She says, "I can see that my main concern seems to be with people who are out of the mainstream in some way."

- **Other Works** Novels: *The Alfred Summer, Lester's Turn, The Night of the Bozos, Getting On with It, Something Beyond Paradise*

- **Awards** ALA Notable Book, 1980, for *The Alfred Summer;* ALA Notable Book, 1983, for *The Night of the Bozos*

THE ADVENTURES OF TOM SAWYER

Study Focus
- Historical pre-Civil War setting
- Tom's donning a new identity
- Dialect and colloquial language

About Mark Twain

Considered by many to be America's greatest writer, Twain wrote dozens of popular novels, short stories, and essays. He based many of the characters in *Tom Sawyer* on family members and friends in Hannibal, Missouri, where he grew up. Twain gained world fame as a traveler, lecturer, and journalist.

- **Other Works** Novels: *The Adventures of Huckleberry Finn, The Prince and the Pauper, A Connecticut Yankee in King Arthur's Court;* stories: "The Celebrated Jumping Frog of Calaveras County," "The Man That Corrupted Hadleyburg"

- **Awards** Honorary M.A., Yale University, 1888; named to American Academy of Arts and Letters, 1904; Doctor of Literature, Oxford University, 1907

SELECTION	DIFFICULTY LEVEL	READING SKILLS	LITERATURE SKILLS	WRITING OPTIONS	VOCABULARY WORDS/SKILLS	
Links to Unit One *The Arrow and the Lamp* *Lazy Peter and His* *Three-Cornered Hat* *The Force of Luck* Pages 586–606	Average	Predicting	Myths Folk tales	Essay Letter of advice	benefactor spendthrift squander vilest wretched	

Links to Unit Two
The Wolf in Sheep's Clothing
The Travelers and the Purse
Anansi and His Visitor, Turtle
A Blind Man Catches a Bird
The Old Grandfather and His
   Little Grandson
Pages 607–617
	Easy	Making
		  connections
			Fables
			Setting
				Fable
				First-person
				  narrative
					Word Attack Skill:
					  the prefixes *re-* and *un-*	

Links to Unit Three *Phaëthon* *The People Could Fly* *Kelfala's Secret Something* Pages 618–631	Average	Understanding purpose	Symbol	Essay Article	abode acknowledge croon dissuade sear	
Links to Unit Four *Prometheus* *Where the Girl Saved Her Brother* *How Odin Lost His Eye* Pages 632–644	Average	Motivation	Hero/heroine Symbol	Myth Dialogue	aptitude endow explicit hover sustenance	
Links to Unit Five *Echo and Narcissus* *The Emperor's New Clothes* *The Fatal Flower* Pages 645–661	Average	Inference	Literary folk tales	Letter Testimonial	consultation diligence excessively exquisite realm	repulsive rogue sovereign stench vexed

WRITER'S WORKSHOPS Pages 662–667

Mode	Guided Assignment	Writing Skills		Proofreading Focus

Choice of modes:
  narrative, descriptive,
  informative,
  persuasive
	Choice of assignments: myth,
	story, comparison-contrast
	paper, script, report, pam-
	phlet, problem-solution
		Chronological order
		Using examples
		Transitions
			Dialogue
			Word choice
			Sensory details
				Varying sentence
				  beginnings

Self-Assessment	Portfolio review			

OPTIONS FOR LEARNING	SPELLING SKILLS	COMMUNITY AND PARENT RESOURCE SUGGESTIONS	AUDIOVISUAL RESOURCES
Oral summary Illustration	The suffixes -able and -ible	Invite a storyteller or immigrant to tell folk tales from other lands, particularly trickster tales.	*Aphrodite, Goddess of Love.* Video. Merit Audio Visual, 1992. A version of the Greek myth. *Greek Mythology.* Computer software. Teach Yourself by Computer Software, 1984. A tutorial program with graphics and animation presents Greek myths. *The Tricks of Life and Death by Olga Loya.* Olga Loya storyteller, 1989. Loya tells traditional Latin American tales in this bilingual collection.
Puppet show Dramatization	Proofreading for Spelling	Invite a student of African-American history to discuss the West African roots of African-American folk tales such as Brer Rabbit.	*Literature & Language* Audiocassette Tape2, side 2: "A Blind Man Catches a Bird." *Aesop's Fables.* Video. Churchill, 1991. (15 min.) Aesop's fables are presented with iconographic drawings and unique songs. *Anasi and the Spider.* Filmstrip. Weston Woods, 1974. The Ashanti tale adapted and illustrated by Gerald McDermott. *The Dancing Granny and Other African Tales.* Audiocassette. Caedmon, 1985. (45 min.) Ashley Bryan narrates trickster tales.
Myth creation Book jacket	Prefixes and roots	Invite grandparents to tell stories they were told as children.	*Heroes of Greek Myths.* Video or 4 filmstrips. Pied Piper. (45 min.) The set features Hercules, The Golden Fleece, Achilles, and Ulysses. *Meet the Newbery Author: Virginia Hamilton.* Video. American School Publishers, 1992. (26 min.) Hamilton shares tales of her family's history, including her grandfather's escape from slavery on the Underground Railroad.
Story illustration Oral report	Unstressed vowels	Invite a member of the local historical society to discuss the earliest Native American inhabitants of your region. Invite a local storyteller to tell some urban legends of your region.	*The Children of Odin: The Book of Northern Myths.* Audiocassette. Caedmon. Norse myths performed by Keir Dullea. *Keepers of the Animals: Native American Animal Stories.* 2 audiocassettes. Fulcrum Publishing, 1992. Twenty-four stories are told by Joseph Bruchac with Native American music between stories.
Product brochure Television ad	Adding suffixes	Ask a local bookseller or librarian to bring in a collection of children's books showing the wide variety of illustrations of folk tales and fables from around the world.	*Literature & Language* Audiocassette Tape 2, side 2: "Echo and Narcissus." *The Emperor's New Clothes.* 16mm film or video. Weston Woods, 1990. (8 min.) Brilliant color animation and jazzy music update the tale. *Tales of China and Tibet.* Audiocassette. Caedmon. Tales retold by I. C. Chang, performed by Siobhan McKenna.

LANGUAGE WORKSHOP Pages 668–670 . . . .

Grammar Concept	Skill Focus
Sentence variety	Sentence beginnings Sentence structure Sentence length

RELATED SKILLS WORKSHOP Page 671 . . . . . .

Language Strand	Skill Focus
Vocabulary	Greek roots

Cooperative Project Unit Six: THEMES IN WORLD FOLKLORE

A Storytelling Festival

Each group will plan a program of stories to be told by group members on the day of the festival.

1 Project Preview

This project is designed to give students direct experience in the art of storytelling. In small groups, students will prepare a series of tales, legends, myths, fables, or other stories to be presented at a storytelling festival. This festival can be held on one day in your classroom, or it can be expanded to involve other teachers and students in your school.

OBJECTIVES
- To learn about the importance and use of folklore and storytelling
- To work collaboratively with a small group to prepare a program of stories
- To develop speaking and listening skills by participating in a storytelling festival

MATERIALS
The following materials are optional.
- old clothing or other items to be used for costumes and props
- a roll of paper or cloth and art supplies for decorating presentation areas
- tape recorders, record players, and/or slide projectors

2 Implementing the Project

INTRODUCING THE PROJECT

To introduce the project, read aloud or narrate one or more of your favorite stories in the oral tradition. This might be a story that has been handed down in your family, an urban legend, a fairy tale, or a long joke. Explain that all such stories constitute folklore. If needed, review the explanation of folklore on pages 584 and 585 and ask students to name their own examples of folklore.

If possible, bring in some recordings of folklore, or invite a professional storyteller to visit your class. Many librarians would be happy to help you locate a storyteller. After listening to stories, talk about what goes into the art of storytelling and what keeps listeners engaged.

As homework, ask students to find one of their favorite stories. Encourage students to be creative in making their selections. Each student can either write a story down or commit it to memory.

When students return to class with their chosen stories, hold a storytelling circle. Rearrange the chairs or let the students sit on the floor. Then go around the circle until everyone has had a chance to tell or read his or her story.

Explain that this project will culminate in a storytelling festival. Each group will plan a program, or series of stories, to be told by group members on the day of the festival. Tell students that each group will be given an area of the room that they can decorate for their story program. Encourage students to begin thinking about clothing and other items that they might have at home and that would lend authenticity and interest to their presentation.

ASSIGNING GROUPS

To avoid having story programs with overlapping content, you can organize groups of five or six students according to themes or types of stories. Here are some possibilities: myths, folk tales, campfire stories, urban legends, ghost stories, ballads and narrative songs, tall tales, fables, tales from other countries, Native American tales, and fairy tales. You may also consider the following categories.

Retellings Students can find stories from everyday life and retell them in their own words. They may retell human interest stories from the media, stories from their own families, or stories about famous heroes or heroines.

Transformations Students could transform old stories by changing the format or story elements, as illustrated by these examples.
- modernize a selection from this unit by changing the setting and characters
- recast old nursery rhymes or fables by using characters from movies or television shows
- use your own school as the setting of a scary story
- tell a story from a different character's point of view, for example, "Cinderella" from an ugly stepsister's point of view
- change the ending of a familiar story
- make popular songs into stories

Topical Tales Students might also organize some of their stories by topics. "Wolf Tales," for instance, might be a combination of "The Three Little Pigs," "Little Red Riding Hood," "The Boy Who Cried Wolf," and other wolfish tales. "Frogs and Princes" could constitute stories such as "The Frog Prince," "The Frog Bride," and songs like "Frog Went A'Courtin'."

DESIGNING A STORY PROGRAM

After groups have been assigned, spend some time discussing what goes into a good story program. Talk about the importance of starting with a story that grabs the audience's attention. Suggest that students arrange their stories so that there is variety. A quiet story might be followed by one that is more exciting; a comic tale might be followed by a tragic one, and so on.

Set reasonable time limits for each group's program, depending on the desired length of the festival. Advise students that they will need to estimate the time of each story—a trial run would be helpful—so that they don't go past their limit. Remind students that the time limits are meant to give everybody a chance to perform.

GATHERING AND ANALYZING INFORMATION

Encourage students to find information that might give their presentation more authenticity. For example, groups telling Greek and Roman myths could find reproductions of art works that feature gods and goddesses; groups telling Native American tales might find information about the different tribes represented. Some groups might learn to imitate dialects from recordings; other groups might find information about the daily life of the people who originated the tales.

Each group should have about a week (perhaps more if time allows) to find and select its stories. If possible, schedule class library time so that students can work together to find materials.

Program Proposal

To keep the groups focused, ask them to write up a program proposal, answering the following questions:

What stories has your group chosen? (List stories in order of telling; give the title and identify the culture represented).

Will your group be using any costumes, props, or music in your program? If so, who will be responsible for these aspects of the program? What equipment, if any, is needed?

How do you plan to decorate your presentation area? Which group members will be responsible for which tasks?

Discuss each of these proposals with group members, offering advice or suggestions about the program order, the choice of stories, or any other important details.

Rehearsal

Allow a few days for rehearsal, making sure to visit each group as often as you can to discourage off-task behavior and to give feedback. If groups wish to enhance their stories, you may give them suggestions in the following areas.

Props Props should be used sparingly to suggest a character or situation. For example, an old man might carry a pipe, while a very young child might carry a rattle. A campfire might be suggested by colored paper for a fire and the placement of pillows in a circle around it. Students might also want to paint or decorate a special storyteller's chair or stool.

Costumes Help students to think of things that might be readily available. For example, a tall-tales group could wear lumberjack shirts, jeans, and suspenders. A group telling Roman myths might make old bedsheets into togas.

Music Groups may play recorded or live music between stories at the beginning of the program. Music should be appropriate to the subject.

Slides and Backdrops Slides could be shown during or between stories to set a mood. Groups could also make colorful backdrops of paper or cloth for their presentation areas.

As the rehearsal time draws to a close, ask each group to time its presentation. Programs that are too long or too short can be modified at this point. If you are inviting guests to the festival, you might want to hold a dress rehearsal.

Physical Arrangements

Make sure that each group has a designated area for the festival day. You might want to bring in portable room dividers or large pieces of cardboard and thumbtacks so that decorations aren't taped to the wall. If your classroom is small, consider holding the event in the cafeteria or gymnasium.

If parents or other guests are invited, your students could create a souvenir program, including the names of participants and the titles of their stories.

OPTIONS FOR PERFORMANCE

During the storytellings, students can sit on chairs or stools, or they can move around a bit. Invite groups to consider the following possibilities.

Pantomime While one student reads or tells a story, others could pantomime the action.

Puppetry Students could make hand puppets and act out their stories on a small stage.

Skits Students could act out scenes from stories or present them in a Readers Theater format.

Audience Participation Audience members might be invited to repeat key phrases from a story, such as " 'Let me in, let me in,' cried the BIG BAD WOLF." Groups that are comfortable with improvisation might stop a skit just before the conclusion and ask audience members to suggest an ending to improvise.

3 Project Assessment

Individual Work

Ask each group to keep a log with each student's name on a different page. Allow a few minutes at the end of each day of group work for each student to record his contribution in the log. All group members need to initial each entry to verify the work. Check these logs periodically to track student contributions and to identify any problems in task distribution. At the end of the project, grades for individual work can be assigned.

Presentation

After groups have finished their programs, give brief written comments or confer with each group about the following elements of their performance.

Content Were the stories interesting and appealing?

Organization Were the stories organized effectively? Did the presentation show evidence of careful planning?

Style Were the storytellers poised, comfortable, and lively in their performance?

For the Portfolio

Consider videotaping individual or group performances and including the tapes in students' portfolios or keeping them in your classroom library. Alternatively, you might put copies of your written comments in each student's portfolio.

4 Team-Teaching Options

Music

Study the musical characteristics of folk ballads and discuss the link between those characteristics (i.e., repetition, simplicity) and those of the oral tradition.

Art

Study the ways that different cultures have used myths and legends in the visual arts, perhaps focusing on famous or interesting examples.

Science

Contrast mythological explanations of natural phenomena with scientific explanations. Discuss whether or not mythology has anything in common with science.

Social Studies

Study the ways in which folklore reflects the values and attitudes of the culture from which it comes. You might compare and contrast two versions of the same fairy tale in terms of their cultural contexts.

Unit Preview

In Unit Six, "Themes in World Folklore," students will read a variety of myths, fables, folk tales, and legends from around the world. The unit contains five literature sections, each linked to a previous unit in the book:

■ Links to Unit One: A Matter of Perspective

■ Links to Unit Two: Scales of Justice

■ Links to Unit Three: Reaching for the Stars

■ Links to Unit Four: Person to Person

■ Links to Unit Five: A Question of Identity

Connections to Units One Through Five

The literature in Unit Six has been gathered from the oral traditions of many cultures. You may wish to begin or end Units One through Five with theme-related selections from Unit Six, or you may wish to have students read the Unit Six selections separately. In either case, students will find a rich variety of multicultural readings in Unit Six.

ADDITIONAL RESOURCES

Unit Six Resource Book
Unit Test, pp. 49–52

Technology and Enrichment
Family and Community Involvement
 Source Book, pp. 21–22

About the Art

Three Folk Musicians is the work of Romare Bearden (1914–1988). This colorful "patchwork" presentation combines collage and oil painting. Bearden has cut and torn paper images of parts of all kinds of people and clothing and combined them with layers of paint to create the musicians, who could be from anywhere. *Which parts of this picture are painted? Which are torn paper images? In your opinion, is this artwork a good choice for a unit on world folklore? Why or why not?*

THEMES IN WORLD FOLKLORE

These are the

stories that never,

never die, that are

carried like seed into

a new country.

Meridel Le Sueur

THREE FOLK MUSICIANS   1967
Romare Bearden   Courtesy, The Estate of
Romare Bearden and ACA Galleries, New York.

581

Discussion Questions

To help students probe connections between the fine art, the quotation, and the unit theme, have them consider the following questions:

1. What does the term *folklore* mean to you? *(Possible responses: stories that have been passed down from generation to generation; myths, legends, and stories from a particular people or culture; stories that were originally told orally and only later written down)*

2. How does the quotation apply to folklore? *(Possible responses: Folklore, since it is handed on from generation to generation, "never dies"; the folklore of a culture can travel with the people of the culture to countries around the world.)*

3. What qualities of stories help them live on for generations? *(Possible responses: appealing to all people, having lessons that apply to everyone)*

4. How does the art relate to the theme of world folklore? *(Possible responses: It shows folk musicians performing folk songs; the musicians' bodies are made of parts of people from all over the world; it suggests the passing on of culture and customs through music.)*

5. On the basis of the quotation and the art, what kinds of selections do you imagine this unit will contain? *(Possible response: popular folklore from many lands)*

About the Quoted Author

Meridel Le Sueur was born in 1900, the descendant of a temperance worker who had helped to found the state of Oklahoma. Le Sueur was greatly respected as a novelist in the 1930s, but in the 1950s Senator Joseph McCarthy branded her a "subversive" for her political views. Her reputation suffered until the 1970s, when her strong voice gained her renewed interest, especially among feminists. Le Sueur's work reflects strong social awareness and concern.

Encourage students to read the introduction to Unit Six. Show them how this unit is different from other units in the book.

Direct students to read through the entire table of contents. Then ask them what they learned about the folklore in this unit from the titles, the authors' names, and the descriptions. Stress these points:

■ The selections are a mix—myths, folk tales, fables, and legends.

■ The stories in each group are tied by theme to one another and to the selections in a previous unit.

■ The stories are multicultural, taken from around the world.

■ The stories are retold by a wide variety of authors.

Previewing the Pages

Have students preview one or more of the groups of selections by looking at the selections' titles and illustrations. Call attention to the small map that appears at the top of the first page of each story. Explain that the map shows the part of the world where that story originated. Also point out that in some selections there are pictures of artifacts from the cultures that produced the literature.

UNIT PREVIEW

The unit you are about to read is set apart from the other units in two ways.

Folklore All the selections in this unit are classified as folklore–traditional literature that was passed along by word of mouth before being written down. You will learn more about such literature in Elements of Folklore on pages 584–585.

Thematic Links to Previous Units The folklore in this unit is divided into five groups. The selections in each group relate to the theme of a previous unit in this book. For example, the first group of folklore selections extends the theme of Unit One, "A Matter of Perspective."

UNIT PREVIEW   583

Using the Selections

The selections in Unit Six may be read separately, or each group may be read in conjunction with the selections in the corresponding linked unit. The following are some suggestions for introducing the Unit Six literature in the classroom.

Separately

■ Have students read the selections in each group of Unit Six. Discuss the common theme in each group.

■ Talk about the ways in which the genres of myths, fables, folk tales, and legends are similar to and different from one another.

■ Discuss how the cultures responsible for the selections are reflected in the stories. Talk about regional or local customs and traditions suggested by the literature.

With the Linked Units

■ Have students read the selections in each group immediately before or after reading the selections in the linked unit. Discuss the characteristics shared by the selections' characters, plots, and themes.

■ Choose one or more selections from a Unit Six group to compare and contrast with a specific selection in the linked unit. Analyze the effects of the differences in time and setting between the folklore and the linked literature.

■ Look for a deeper understanding of the selections in Unit Six by comparing and contrasting them with more challenging stories in the linked units.

Elements of Folklore

This feature provides students with an opportunity to develop a vocabulary to use in reading and discussing folklore. The terms on these pages are discussed in depth in the selections that follow.

Objectives

■ To understand and appreciate folklore

■ To identify categories of folklore—myths, folk tales, fables, and legends

■ To recognize strategies for reading folklore

Motivation

Tell students that the word *folk* means "ordinary people" and *lore* means "knowledge." Stress that the folklore of a group of people includes not only their stories but also their arts and crafts, dances, games, superstitions, proverbs, holidays, and so on.

Invite volunteers to share examples from their community or heritage.

Teaching Strategies

Use these questions to prompt discussion of the first paragraph:

■ In our culture, what has replaced sitting around and listening to stories?

■ How is storytelling still practiced today?

■ Thousands of years ago there was no written language. How did people then preserve stories and customs of their culture?

Next, on the chalkboard, list the purposes of storytelling given in the second paragraph. Challenge students to identify examples of folk tales that fulfill these purposes. *(Possible responses: the King Arthur legend, Aesop's fables, frontier legends, fairy tales)*

Use the following prompts to develop students' understanding of the categories of folklore.

Elements of
FOLKLORE

Folklore can be defined as all the traditions, customs, and stories that are passed along by word of mouth in a culture. The stories of folklore have their beginnings in spoken language, not the written word. Because stories are passed along from teller to teller, generation to generation, their authorship cannot be traced to any one person. A single story may undergo frequent changes as each storyteller adds his or her special twist. Typically, folklore stories are collected and written down only after they have been told for many years, perhaps centuries. The stories you will read in this unit were not originated by the authors named but were retold or translated by them.

When storytellers weave their tales they offer more than entertainment. Their stories **keep the past alive,** introducing young people to the history, beliefs, and religion of their society. The stories **teach moral lessons** and **illustrate qualities that are valued by the society,** such as kindness and courage. They also **warn against negative qualities,** like greed and foolishness.

Very often, the same basic story appears in different cultures. For example, hundreds of versions of the Cinderella story have been found in places ranging from Canada to Africa to Japan. The similarities in these stories point to values that many cultures hold in common.

Folklore stories can be grouped into four major categories: **myths, folk tales, fables, and legends.**

Myths

Myths are stories that were created to answer basic questions about the world, the gods, and human life. Myths tell about events from the distant past and were considered truthful and often sacred by the societies that told them.

Many myths offer explanations of natural events. For example, you will read Greek myths that explain how deserts were formed and why voices sometimes echo. Almost all cultures have **creation myths,** which explain how the world came into being or how humans were created.

Myths usually tell about the adventures of gods or of human beings who come into contact with them. These gods and goddesses have extraordinary powers. The gods of ancient Greece, for instance, were all immortal—they could not die. Each god or goddess had his or her own special areas of power: Aphrodite governed love, Poseidon controlled the sea, Demeter ruled agriculture, and so on. Yet divine powers were not unlimited. Even Zeus, the ruler of the Greek gods, could not always get his way. In the myths of many cultures, the gods possess all the emotions and personality traits of human beings. Greek myths tell about the jealousy of Aphrodite and the impatience of Poseidon. In Norse mythology (the body of myths from Scandinavia), Thor is famous for his temper, and Loki is known for his trickery and deceit.

Myths Point out that myths are the earliest of all known stories. Many Greek myths, for example, were already old and familiar some 3,000 years ago. Have students tell what they know about the Greek gods and goddesses mentioned here (Zeus, Aphrodite, Poseidon, and Demeter) or their Roman counterparts (Jupiter, Venus, Neptune, and Ceres).

Point out to students that myths make exciting reading; they are filled with heroism, violence, trickery, humor, love triangles, and so on. They were adult stories, not children's stories, so in some ways they are like soap operas of the past. Students might especially enjoy reading Greek myths, Norse myths, African myths, and Native American myths.

Folk Tales

In contrast to myths, folk tales are not about the gods, nor are they about the origins of the world. Told primarily for entertainment, folk tales are not taken as truthful or factual by their audience.

The characters in folk tales are usually ordinary humans or animals that act like humans. Typically, the humans are peasants or other members of lowly classes; often, they are portrayed as having better values than the rich and powerful.

These tales are told in a simple style, sometimes with each character representing one human trait (greed, curiosity, kindness, and so on). Many folk tales feature a kind or cruel supernatural being, such as a giant or a fairy godmother. Magic and enchantment may play a key role in these stories.

The themes of folk tales are usually simple—the reward of good, the punishment of evil, the exposing of a fool. Some folk tales teach practical lessons for living; others illustrate moral truths or offer warnings about dangers to avoid.

Many folk tales are comical and poke fun at human weaknesses, such as the **trickster tales** found in most cultures. In a trickster tale a smart person or animal outwits or takes advantage of some fool.

Fables

Fables are very short tales that illustrate a clear, often directly stated, **moral**—a principle of right and wrong behavior. The characters are often animals that act like humans. Often these characters have human faults.

Legends

Legends are considered factual by those who tell them, and many have some basis in historical fact. For example, the legends surrounding King Arthur, Joan of Arc, and John Henry are based upon people who actually existed. These stories tend to be set in a past more recent than that of myths. Legends often include elements of magic and the supernatural.

Strategies for Reading Folklore

1. **Enjoy** the tale. These stories are fun because they are filled with action and adventure. As you read, imagine the stories being repeated through many generations.

2. **Think about the purpose** of the story. Is its purpose to explain a mystery of nature, to teach a lesson, or poke fun at human weaknesses?

3. **Look for values and customs** of the culture from which the story comes.

What is virtuous behavior, and how is it rewarded? What traits are admired and respected? Which are negative?

4. **Decide who holds the power** in the story. Do humans control their own fate, or are the gods or some supernatural power in charge?

5. **Compare** the story with others that you know about, perhaps from other cultures. What do the stories have in common?

Folk Tales Explain that one reason for the simple style of folk tales is that over the centuries oral storytellers tended to drop specific details of setting, plot, and character. Point out that folk tales dealing with supernatural beings are often called **fairy tales**. In regard to trickster tales, some students may be aware of tales featuring the tricksters Coyote, Anansi, and Brer Rabbit.

Fables Remind students of some familiar fables of Aesop, such as "The Ant and the Grasshopper" or "The Fox and the Grapes." You might want to suggest a moral, such as "Actions speak louder than words," and have students create a fable to illustrate it.

Legends Ask students if they are aware of any legends of their community or region. Such legends might describe the actions of a "larger-than-life" historical figure or events that purportedly occurred at a certain place. Have students retell the legends, noting which facts and details could be verified.

Strategies for Reading Folklore

Invite students to paraphrase the explanation of each of the strategies in this section. Have them look especially at strategy 4, helping them to recognize that many myths focus on power struggles between gods or between humans and gods.

Closure

Place the following word web on the board, and have students review what they have learned by listing details and ideas related to each term.

Objectives

- To understand and analyze folklore

- To examine elements of a myth and of folk tales

- To enrich reading by predicting

- To express understanding of the selections through a choice of writing forms, including an essay and a letter

Prereading/Motivation

Examine What You Know

Discussion Prompts Why do parents and children often have different points of view about curfews? Why do teachers and students have different points of view about grades or tests?

Expand Your Knowledge

Additional Background The human faults and virtues of the Greek gods and goddesses make their stories entertaining rather than terrifying. Although the Olympians have divine powers, magic as such is seldom a part of the myths about them. The world of the gods and goddesses is filled with beauty, which the Greeks valued highly.

The tricksters of Puerto Rican folklore have relatives in many other cultures. Although trickster tales reflect an admiration for cleverness, the tricksters themselves are not viewed as heroic but are seen for what they are—con artists.

That the roots of "The Force of Luck" are more Hispanic than Native American is shown by the presence of a miller, or grinder of grain. In a Mexican community, for example, a miller is often an important figure and a symbol of honest hard labor.

Thematic Link— A Matter of Perspective

In "The Arrow and the Lamp," Aphrodite, from her goddess's perspective, considers the mortal Psyche's beauty an offense. In "Lazy Peter and His Three-Cornered Hat," a trickster exploits the greedy farmer. In "The Force of Luck," events show that either luck or money rules human affairs—depending on your perspective.

A Matter of Perspective

Examine What You Know (Prior Knowledge)

The way you judge someone else depends on your perspective—where you are standing and what your own situation is. Folklore shows us that this truth has been understood by all peoples. In small groups discuss why people's perspectives cause their opinions to differ so greatly. For example, why does a farmer's point of view differ from a city dweller's? a poor person's from a rich person's?

Expand Your Knowledge (Building Background)

In each of the following tales, the perspectives of the characters are in sharp contrast. "The Arrow and the Lamp" is a Greek myth about Psyche (sī' kē), a mortal woman whose life is affected by how gods and goddesses view her. The Greeks believed that the gods controlled people's fates. Psyche angers Aphrodite (af' rə dīt' ē), the goddess of love, whose son Eros (er' äs') causes gods and mortals to fall in love. As you read, notice the "human" behavior of the gods and goddesses, and observe how the mortals respond to them.

Tricksters use the perspectives—and sometimes the weaknesses—of others to fool them. "Lazy Peter and His Three-Cornered Hat" is a typical trickster tale that comes from Puerto Rico. The folklore of Puerto Rico has roots in the Orient, Arabia, Spain, and West Africa. As you read about ordinary human characters in this tale, notice how each represents one point of view.

Your own perspective will determine your answer to the question posed in "The Force of Luck." This folk tale comes from the U.S. Southwest. Like tales from Puerto Rico, tales from the Southwest reflect a mixture of cultures, including Hispanic and Native American. Notice what values are upheld in this tale of a hard-working miller.

Write Before You Read (Journal Writing)

■ *Author biographies on Extend page*

Write about a time when your perspective on something was quite different from someone else's. Why were your viewpoints different? Did you ever end up agreeing?

MORE JOURNAL WRITING IDEAS

■ Describe a time when you were jealous. How did you deal with your feelings?

■ Have you ever played a terrible trick on someone? Describe the episode.

■ Do you believe in luck? Why or why not?

COLLABORATIVE LEARNING OPTIONS

Opportunities for collaborative learning include Examine What You Know, Options for Learning (p. 606), and Cross-Curricular Projects (p. 606).

ADDITIONAL RESOURCES

Unit Six Resource Book
Reader's Guidesheet, p. 1
Reading Skills, p. 2
Literature Skills, p. 3
Vocabulary Connections, p. 4
Spelling Connections, p. 5
Comprehension and Vocabulary Check Tests, p. 6
Selection Test, pp. 7–8

GREEK MYTH

The Arrow and the Lamp:
The Story of Psyche

Retold by MARGARET HODGES

Once a king and a queen had three daughters. All three were beautiful, but the youngest, Psyche, was different. Her sisters were content to know what they were told. Psyche always wanted to know more. She was so lovely that men called her a new Aphrodite, a young goddess of love and beauty, but no man dared to marry a goddess. So while the two older sisters found husbands and went away to live in their own homes, Psyche stayed on alone with her father and mother.

Now all might have been well if golden, sweet-smiling Aphrodite had not heard of Psyche. The goddess came up out of the sea to find out whether men were really leaving her temples empty and silent and throwing flowers in the streets where Psyche walked. And when Aphrodite saw that it was true, she no longer smiled. She was furious, and she said to herself, "This girl is mortal. Beautiful she may be, but like all mortals she will die, and until she dies, she must **A ▶** never have a happy day. I shall see to that."

Then she called her favorite child, Eros, and he came flying to her. This young god, as fair as his mother, had golden wings on which he moved swiftly and unseen on his mysterious errands, often doing mischief. He carried a golden bow and a quiver filled with arrows.

"Go to this girl, this Psyche," said Aphrodite. "Wound her with one of your arrows. Pour bitterness on her lips. Then find her the <u>vilest</u> husband in the world— mean, bad tempered, ugly—and make her fall in love with him."

There were two springs of water in Aphrodite's garden—one bitter, the other sweet. Carrying water from both springs, Eros flew off, invisible.

He found Psyche asleep. Her beauty moved him to pity, but, obeying his mother's command, he poured bitter water on her lips and touched her side with one of his arrows. Psyche felt the pain and opened her eyes. She could not see Eros, but as he looked into her eyes, the arrow trembled in his hand, and by chance he wounded himself. **◀ B** He poured a little of the sweet water on her forehead and flew away.

Still no lovers came to ask for Psyche's hand in marriage, so the king and the queen,

| Words to Know and Use | **vilest** (vīl' ist) *adj.* most horrible or unpleasant |

587

5. ACTIVE READING: Review
Psyche's response to the prophecy sheds some light on her perspective. Ask students what her response reveals about the way she views the gods. *(Possible responses: She accepts her fate and doesn't criticize Aphrodite, so she may believe that the goddess is right to be angry; she sees the gods as so powerful that people are helpless when faced with their punishment.)*

6. ACTIVE READING: Predict
Ask students whose voice they think Psyche hears in the night and what clues in the story have helped them guess the answer. *(Possible response: The voice is Eros', because the oracle said that Psyche wouldn't marry a mortal man but a creature with wings and because only a god could have such a palace.)*

guessing that their daughter had somehow angered one of the gods, asked an oracle[1] to look into the future and tell them what could be done to find a husband for her.

The oracle answered with frightening words: "Dress your daughter for her funeral. She will never marry a mortal man but will be the bride of a creature with wings, feared even by the gods. Take Psyche to the stony top of the mountain that looks down on your city, and leave her there alone to meet her fate."

When they heard this prophecy, all the people wept with Psyche's father and mother. But Psyche said, "Tears will not help me. I was doomed from the moment when you called me the new Aphrodite. It must be Aphrodite herself whom I have angered. Obey the oracle before the goddess punishes all of you. I alone must bear her anger."

Psyche led the way to the mountaintop and said good-bye to her weeping parents and the crowd of folk who had sadly followed her. When all were gone, she sat down, trembling and afraid, to wait. But no monster husband came. Instead, the warm west wind began to blow and, raising her gently in the air, carried her down the far side of the mountain to a green and flowering meadow in a hidden valley.

Psyche fell peacefully asleep in the soft grass. When she woke, she saw a grove of tall trees watered by a clear stream. In the grove stood a marvelous palace, its golden pillars topped with a roof of carved sandalwood and ivory.

She entered through the open doorway, wondering at the light that flashed from silver walls. Surely only a god could have made such a palace! Psyche passed from room to room, walking on floors made of precious stones, until she came to a marble pool filled with scented water.

Then a voice spoke to her: "Lady, all of this is yours. Ask for whatever you like." Unseen hands led her to the bath and afterward clothed her in a robe of fine silk. A table appeared, spread with delicious food, and Psyche ate and drank while invisible servants waited on her and the air was filled with the sound of sweet voices singing.

When darkness fell, Psyche found a bed ready for her and lay down to rest. But in the night she woke, feeling the presence of someone standing beside her bed, and she was full of fear. Then a voice said, "Do not be afraid, Psyche. I am the husband you have been waiting for. Trust me. No harm will come to you. Only do not try to see me." Psyche's husband stayed with her all night long, but before daylight he was gone.

For some months Psyche lived in the palace, surrounded by beauty and comfort. The unseen servants answered all her wishes, and when her unseen husband came at night, he was always kind. She began to long for the sound of his voice and very soon fell deeply in love with him. Still, the days seemed empty and she often felt lonely.

One night her husband said to her, "Psyche, your sisters are looking for you. If you hear them calling, do not answer."

Psyche promised to obey, but she wished more and more to see a face. The clear waters of the pool reflected only her own face, and the palace now seemed like a prison. At last her husband found her

---

1. **oracle:** in ancient Greece, a priest who consulted the gods in order to foretell the future

Guided Reading for Less-Proficient Students

Continued from page 587

E. Why does Psyche lose Eros? *(She looks at him.)* Summarizing

F. How does Psyche succeed in the tasks Aphrodite sets for her? *(Ants help her sort the grain; reeds tell her how to get the fleece; Zeus sends an eagle to help her get the water.)* Recalling

G. How are Psyche's trials finally brought to an end? *(Eros takes her to Mount Olympus, where Zeus and the other gods and goddesses make her immortal.)* Summarizing

LOVE AND THE MAIDEN John Roddam Spencer-Stanhope Private collection. Bridgeman/Art Resource, New York.

7. LANGUAGE: Word Choice
Discuss why *planting* is an effective word to use with *suspicions* here. *(Something that is planted gets bigger, branches out, and may take unexpected forms.)* ★

8. VOCABULARY: Idiom
Explain that "biding his time" means "waiting before doing something." Discuss why one might bide one's time. *(Possible responses: to wait for the best possible moment; to increase suspense)* ★

weeping and, taking her in his arms, said, "Well, my love, have your wish, even if it brings trouble. The west wind shall carry your sisters here." And Psyche thanked him with grateful kisses.

The next day she heard her sisters calling to her from the mountaintop, and she called back to them. Then the west wind carried them down into the valley, and when they found Psyche safe and well, they embraced her joyfully. But their joy turned to jealousy as she showed them her palace and they saw how she was dressed and waited on like a queen.

7 When Psyche confessed that she had never seen her husband, they spoiled her happiness by planting suspicions in her mind: "If your husband will not let you see him, he must be the monster that the oracle said you would marry. He is only biding his time until he is ready to kill you. Take our **8** advice. The next time he comes, have a lamp and a sharp knife hidden at your side. When he is asleep, light the lamp and look at him. If he is a monster, kill him while there is yet time."

The west wind carried the sisters away as safely as they had come, but Psyche was tormented by what they had said. At last she filled a little lamp with oil and found a sharp knife, both of which she hid beside her bed.

That night, when her husband was asleep, she lit the lamp and saw him—not a monster, but the most beautiful of beings, a fair and

THE ARROW AND THE LAMP 589

9. ACTIVE READING: Evaluate
Ask students if they think that Psyche's fate is quite fair. *(Possible responses: Yes, because Eros has asked her to trust him; yes, because she should have known that gods were involved somehow; no, because Eros hasn't told her what would happen if she tried to see him; no, because he's never given her a reason why she couldn't see him; no, she can't be expected to live forever with someone she can never see.)*

10. CULTURAL SIDELIGHT
In other myths and folk tales, such as the Greek myth of Orpheus and Eurydice and the Scandinavian folk tale "East of the Sun, West of the Moon," the main characters share Psyche's plight; they promise not to look at their beloved and lose the person the minute they do. Students may know other tales, such as "Pandora's Box," in which curiosity gets a character into deep trouble.

11. LITERARY CONCEPT: Myth
Remind students that in many myths, gods and goddesses are shown to have human weaknesses. Ask students what weaknesses Aphrodite shows here. *(Possible responses: jealousy, spitefulness, dishonesty)*

ROSES decorative panel 1909–1916 Ernest Quost
Musée d'Orsay, Paris.

graceful youth with golden wings, smiling even in his sleep. Psyche was moved by a deeper love than she had ever felt. She bent over her husband, and from the lamp a drop of oil, burning hot, fell on his shoulder. Stung by the pain, he opened his eyes and looked at her sternly. "Foolish Psyche," he said, "I knew how it would be. You could not trust me. You had to see for yourself. Now you will lose everything that I could give you, and I must lose you." Too late she knew who he was: Eros, the son of Aphrodite. There was a flash of golden wings and he was gone. The palace too was gone, and Psyche found herself alone again on the mountaintop.

Psyche was determined to find her lost husband, but although she walked all the roads of the world, she could not discover where he was. He had flown to one of his mother's many palaces, sick at heart and feverish with the burning pain of the oil from Psyche's lamp. Aphrodite was angrier than she had ever been. "You are meant to make mortals fall in love, not to fall in love yourself," she said. "However, you will soon be well and will forget all about that girl." She locked him into a chamber, and there he lay.

As Psyche searched for Eros, she came at last to a faraway river that flowed from a high waterfall. At the edge of the river stood a temple, and in its doorway she saw Aphrodite. She knelt at the feet of the goddess and begged Aphrodite to tell her where she could find Eros. But Aphrodite, jealous of her beauty, answered with a false smile, "I will give Eros back to you if you will do something for me." And when Psyche eagerly agreed, the goddess led her into the temple and showed her a room filled with a great heap of grains: corn and barley, poppy seed, lentils, and beans, all mixed together. "Anyone as ugly as you is fit only to work," Aphrodite said scornfully. "Sort all of these grains into separate piles, and have it done by evening."

When the goddess had left her, Psyche sat down and began to cry. The task was impossible. But as she sat there weeping, she saw a procession of little ants coming out of the earth and running to her rescue. They attacked the heap of grains and carried each kind to a separate pile, never stopping until the work was done. Then they vanished into the earth.

11

590   UNIT SIX THEMES IN WORLD FOLKLORE

When Aphrodite returned in the evening, she found Psyche sitting with folded hands. All the work was finished. "You do not deceive me, <u>wretched</u> girl," cried the goddess. "Someone has helped you. Tomorrow you must work alone, but your task is easy. Across the river is a field where golden sheep are grazing. Bring me a strand of their fleece."

At dawn Psyche went to the river and stepped into the water. But as she did so, she heard the whispering of the reeds that grew along the shore: "Psyche, the sheep are wild rams, as fierce as the sun's rays. They will batter you with their stony foreheads and pierce you with their sharp horns."

Psyche was ready to sink down into the river, despairing. But the reeds whispered, "Do not give up. Be patient. Things will change. Wait until the sun sinks. Then the rams sleep, and you can easily gather a strand of their golden fleece from the bushes along the edge of the field." Psyche obeyed, and in the evening gave the shining fleece to Aphrodite.

The goddess was enraged. She could not bear to find Psyche still alive. "Tomorrow you must work again," she said. She gave Psyche a crystal jar and pointed to the waterfall that plunged from the mountain peak. "That is where the river Styx comes from Hades, the land of death. Bring me water from the top of the waterfall," she ordered. She thought to herself, "The girl will never return. It is a just punishment for stealing my son's love."

Psyche made her way to the foot of the mountain and climbed the steep and rugged path—up, up, on and on, fearing every moment that she would fall and be dashed to pieces. At last she reached the topmost crag, a rough and slippery rock, and saw that the torrent of water poured out of a cavern guarded by dragons with unwinking eyes. Psyche heard the waters roaring, "Beware!" and stood as if turned to stone by fear. Then, from high in the air above her, there flew down an eagle, the messenger of Zeus, king of the gods. The eagle took the crystal jar in its claws and swooped past the dragons. It hovered at the top of the waterfall until the jar was filled to the brim, then brought it back to Psyche.

That night Aphrodite could hardly believe her eyes when she saw Psyche alive and well, bearing the jar of water in her hands. "I have obeyed all your commands," said Psyche. "I beg you to give me my husband."

"I have only one more task for you," said Aphrodite with a bitter smile. "If you accomplish this, Eros shall be yours forever. Go to the world of the dead and ask Queen Persephone to fill this box with some of her beauty." "For," she thought to herself, "no mortal comes back from Hades."

Psyche took the box. She knew now that Aphrodite wished nothing less than her death, and she climbed a high tower, ready to leap to the ground and so be taken at once to the land of the dead, never to return. But as she looked out from the top of the windy tower, a voice echoed from its walls: "Psyche, do not lose hope. There is a way to accomplish the last of your labors.

| *Words to Know and Use* | **wretched** (rech′ id) *adj.* deserving contempt; inferior |

591

12
13
◄ F
14

12. VOCABULARY: Definition
For Alternative Learning Styles Suggest that students draw a picture of a crag, showing how it differs from a slope, a peak, or a cliff. *(Pictures should show that a crag is a steep projection rising above its surroundings.)* ★

13. LITERARY CONCEPT: Myth
Ask students what helpers assist Psyche in performing the impossible tasks. *(ants, reeds, waters, and an eagle)* Ask what this unexpected help might imply about Psyche. *(Possible responses: Psyche has a god on her side; Psyche is beloved by all of nature; the gods really like Psyche.)*

14. ACTIVE READING: Predict
Ask students if they think Psyche will succeed in bringing back a box of Queen Persephone's beauty from the land of the dead. If she does succeed, will Aphrodite honor her promise? *(Any response is valid.)*

15. LITERARY CONCEPT: Myth
Point out that once again Psyche dis-
obeys the gods and is punished. Ask
students what conclusion they can draw
about the relationship between mortals
and the Greek gods. (Possible responses: The gods are all-powerful and cannot be disobeyed without consequences;
mortals are foolish to disobey them.)

16. ACTIVE READING: Evaluate
Ask students if they think Psyche has
earned her rewards. (Possible responses: Yes, by suffering and by showing
determination to win back her husband;
no, because she couldn't have completed Aphrodite's tasks without help and
she kept looking at things she was not
supposed to see.)

17. CULTURAL SIDELIGHT
You may wish to explain to students
at this point that for the Greeks, just
as Aphrodite was the goddess of
love and beauty, Psyche represented the human soul. In English, the
word *psyche* refers to the soul or the
mind, and *psychology* is the study
of the mind and mental processes.

Responding to Reading

1. Any response is valid.

2. **Possible responses:** Aphrodite is
powerful and immortal but also petty,
vain, and jealous; Psyche is too curious
and mistrustful but also brave and determined. Psyche's love for Eros makes her
devoted to him and strengthens her
resolve; Aphrodite, by contrast, just
seems to be possessive of Eros.

3. **Possible responses:** She brings them
some of Persephone's beauty; they
admire her courage; they feel sorry for
her; they know she really loves Eros;
Zeus wants her to join them.

4. **Possible responses:** to celebrate the
power of love, to show that love cannot
be separated from the soul, to reveal
the weakness of vanity and jealousy, to
promote steadfast courage, to explain
why bad things sometimes happen to
good people

Near at hand you will find a cave. A path
leads through it to the river Styx. Carry two
coins in your mouth to pay the ferryman
who will row you across the river to Hades
and back again. A three-headed dog guards
the palace of Hades. Take two barley cakes
for the dog. Give him one when you enter,
the other when you leave."

Psyche found the cave and followed the
dark path that led through it into the secret
places of the earth. When she came to the
river Styx, the ferryman took one of the
coins from her mouth and rowed her across.
When the fierce three-headed dog of Hades
barked at her, she silenced him with a barley
cake and went on to the jeweled palace of
Hades. There Queen Persephone came to
greet her. And when Psyche saw that gentle
face, she knew why even Aphrodite wanted
to have some of its beauty. The goddess
took the box and put something into it, saying in a voice both soft and kind, "Do not
open this, my child. It is not for you."

Gratefully, Psyche took the box and ran
from the palace. She gave her last cake to
the three-headed dog and her last coin to the
ferryman, and hurried up the path. But as
she stepped out under the open sky, she
thought, "My husband once said that I was

beautiful. He may no longer think so, after
all my labors. Perhaps I should keep a little
of Persephone's beauty for myself." She
opened the box. At once a deep sleep came
over her, and she lay as if dead.

But even from afar, Eros saw her. He had
recovered from his hurt, and his love for her
was so strong that he burst open the locked
door of his chamber and flew to her, tenderly
wiping away the spell of sleep. He closed the
box and gave it back to her. Then, with
Psyche in his arms, he flew upward. As they
neared the top of Mount Olympus, the
heavenly radiance shone brighter and
brighter, and in the center of the light
Psyche saw Zeus, the father of light. He
called Aphrodite and all the other gods and
goddesses together and spoke to them: "See
this mortal girl whom Eros loves. No mortal
can have Persephone's beauty, but Psyche
has brought some of that beauty to us. So
give her the food and drink of gods, and let
her be one of us, never to die, never to be
separated again from her love."

Finally, even Aphrodite said it should be
so. Then from Psyche's shoulders delicate
wings, like those of a butterfly, unfolded.
And mortals, seeing butterflies in summer
fields, remember Psyche and her love. ❧

Responding to Reading

1. Write your first reaction to this myth in your journal or notebook.

2. Compare the **characters** of Aphrodite and Psyche. Consider each
character's strengths and weaknesses and the way each loves Eros.

3. Why do you think the gods finally accept Psyche as Eros' wife?

4. In your opinion, why was this myth created? What purposes,
messages, and explanations might it have had for the early Greeks?

Lazy Peter and His Three-Cornered Hat

RICARDO E. ALEGRIA
Translated by Elizabeth Culbert

This is the story of Lazy Peter, a shameless rascal of a fellow who went from village to village making mischief.

One day Lazy Peter learned that a fair was being held in a certain village. He knew that a large crowd of country people would be there selling horses, cows, and other farm animals and that a large amount of money would change hands. Peter, as usual, needed money, but it was not his custom to work for it. So he set out for the village, wearing a red three-cornered hat.

The first thing he did was to stop at a stand and leave a big bag of money with the owner, asking him to keep it safely until he returned for it. Peter told the man that when he returned for the bag of money, one corner of his hat would be turned down, and that was how the owner of the stand would know him. The man promised to do this, and Peter thanked him. Then he went to the drugstore in the village and gave the druggist another bag of money, asking him to keep it until he returned with one corner of his hat turned up. The druggist agreed, and Peter left. He went to the church and asked the priest to keep another bag of money and to return it to him only when he came back with one corner of his hat twisted to the side. The priest said fine, he would do this.

Having disposed of three bags of money, Peter went to the edge of the village where the farmers were buying and selling horses and cattle. He stood and watched for a while until he decided that one of the farmers must be very rich indeed, for he had sold all of his horses and cows. Moreover, the man seemed to be a miser who was never satisfied but wanted always more and more money. This was Peter's man! He stopped beside him. It was raining, and instead of keeping his hat on to protect his head, he took it off and wrapped it carefully in his cape, as though it were very valuable. It puzzled the farmer to see Peter stand there with the rain falling on his head and his hat wrapped in his cape.

After a while he asked, "Why do you take better care of your hat than of your head?"

Peter saw that the farmer had swallowed the bait, and smiling to himself, he said that the hat was the most valuable thing in all the world and that was why he took care to protect it from the rain. The farmer's curiosity increased at this reply, and he asked Peter what was so valuable about a red three-cornered hat. Peter told him that the

---

TEXT ANNOTATIONS

1. VOCABULARY: Word Choice
"Shameless rascal" is a phrase seldom heard today, but its quaint, old-fashioned ring gives a certain air to the tale. Ask students for other words or phrases in this passage that have that same ring. (Possible responses: "fellow," "village," "making mischief")

2. LITERARY CONCEPT: Humor
Ask students what the writer means by the phrase "it was not his custom to work for it." (Possible responses: Peter is lazy; Peter gets his money in some underhanded way.) Ask why the writer uses the word custom to express this idea. (Possible responses: It makes Peter's laziness seem funny, as if it were just a lifestyle choice; it presents laziness as a cute shortcoming, part of Peter's charm.)

3. ACTIVE READING: Question
Ask students why Peter is so sure the farmer is his "man." What has made him pick out this particular fellow? (The man seems to be wealthy, stingy, and greedy.)

4. VOCABULARY: Idiom
Explain that the phrase "swallowed the bait" derives from fishing. Ask students what bait the farmer "swallows" and how Peter is like a fisherman. (Peter's hat is the bait; Peter has "hooked" the farmer by attracting his attention to the bait.) ★

Guided Reading for Less-Proficient Students

These questions can help guide students through the reading. Ask each question at the point of the selection where the capital letter and arrow appear in the margin. In addition, you may wish to use appropriate Active Reading annotations.

A. What steps has Peter taken so far in his plan? (He's left a bag of money with each of three men, asking that it be returned when he shows up with a corner of his hat turned a certain way.) Summarizing

B. Why does the farmer now want Peter's hat? (He's seen a man hand Peter a bag of money and thinks that the hat made him do it.) Summarizing

C. What happens when the farmer wears the hat? (No one gives him money; he gets upset.) Recalling

D. What is the outcome of Lazy Peter's trick? (The farmer tears up the hat, and Peter ends up with all the farmer's money.) Recalling hat worked for him; thanks to it, he never had to work for a living, because whenever he put the hat on with one of the corners turned over, people just handed him any money he asked for.

The farmer was amazed and very interested in what Peter said. As money-getting was his greatest ambition, he told Peter that he couldn't believe a word of it until he saw the hat work with his own eyes. Peter assured him that he could do this, for he, Peter, was hungry, and the hat was about to start working, since he had no money with which to buy food.

With this, Peter took out his three-cornered hat, turned one corner down, put it on his head, and told the farmer to come along and watch the hat work. Peter took the farmer to the stand. The minute the owner looked up, he handed over the bag of money Peter had left with him. The farmer stood with his mouth open in astonishment. He didn't know what to make of it. But of one thing he was sure—he had to have that hat!

Peter smiled and asked if he was satisfied, and the farmer said yes, he was. Then he asked Peter if he would sell the hat. This was just what Lazy Peter wanted, but he said no, he was not interested in selling the hat, because with it, he never had to work and he always had money. The farmer said he thought that was unsound reasoning because thieves could easily steal a hat, and wouldn't it be safer to invest in a farm with cattle? So they talked, and Peter pretended to be impressed with the farmer's arguments. Finally he said yes, he saw the point, and if the farmer would make him a good offer, he would sell the hat. The farmer, who

had made up his mind to have the hat at any price, offered a thousand pesos. Peter laughed aloud and said he could make as much as that by just putting his hat on two or three times.

As they continued haggling over the price, the farmer grew more and more determined to have that hat, until finally he offered all he had realized from the sale of his horses and cows—ten thousand pesos in gold. Peter still pretended not to be interested, but he chuckled to himself, thinking of the trick he was about to play on the farmer. All right, he said, it was a deal. Then the farmer grew cautious and told Peter that before he handed over the ten thousand pesos, he would like to see the hat work again. Peter said that was fair enough. He put on the hat with one of the corners turned up and went with the farmer to the drugstore. The moment the druggist saw the turned-up corner, he handed over the money Peter had left with him. At this the farmer was convinced and very eager to set the hat to work for himself. He took out a bag containing ten thousand pesos in gold and was about to hand it to Peter when he had a change of heart and thought better of it. He asked Peter please to excuse him, but he had to see the hat work just once more before he could part with his gold. Peter said that that was fair enough, but now he would have to ask the farmer to give him the fine horse he was riding as well as the ten thousand pesos in gold. The farmer's interest in the hat revived, and he said it was a bargain!

Lazy Peter put on his hat again, doubled over one of the corners, and told the farmer that since he still seemed to have doubts, this time he could watch the hat work in the

Looking at Style

Use these sentences to help focus students on elements of style in this folk tale:

■ Finally he said yes, he saw the point, and if the farmer would make him a good offer, he would sell the hat. (p. 594)

■ He asked Peter please to excuse him, but he had to see the hat work just once more before he could part with his gold. (p. 594)

Then discuss the following question and activity:

1. What similarities do you notice in the way the author presents the dialogue in these two cases?

2. Rewrite these passages, using direct quotations. Compare your rewrites with the original versions. Why do you think the author used the style that he did?

church. The farmer was delighted with this, his doubts were stilled, and he fairly beamed thinking of all the money he was going to make once that hat was his.

8

They entered the church. The priest was hearing confession, but when he saw Peter with his hat, he said, "Wait here, my son," and he went to the sacristy and returned with the bag of money Peter had left with him. Peter thanked the priest, then knelt and asked for a blessing before he left. The farmer had seen everything and was fully convinced of the hat's magic powers. As soon as they left the church, he gave Peter the ten thousand pesos in gold and told him to take the horse also. Peter tied the bag of pesos to the saddle, gave the hat to the farmer, begging him to take good care of it, spurred his horse, and galloped out of town.

9

As soon as he was alone, the farmer burst out laughing at the thought of the trick he had played on Lazy Peter. A hat such as this was priceless! He couldn't wait to try it. He

10

put it on with one corner turned up and entered the butcher shop.

The butcher looked at the hat, which was very handsome indeed, but said nothing. The farmer turned around, then walked up and down until the butcher asked him what he wanted. The farmer said he was waiting for the bag of money. The butcher laughed aloud and asked if he were crazy. The farmer thought that there must be something wrong with the way he had folded the hat. He took it off and doubled another corner down. But this had no effect on the butcher. So he decided to try it out some other place. He went to the mayor of the town.

The mayor, to be sure, looked at the hat but did nothing. The farmer grew desperate and decided to go to the druggist who had given Peter a bag of money. He entered and stood with the hat on. The druggist looked at him but did nothing.

The farmer became very nervous. He began to suspect that there was something very wrong. He shouted at the druggist, "Stop looking at me and hand over the bag of money!" ◄ C

8. VOCABULARY: Definition
By explaining that the words *sacred* and *sacristy* have the same root, lead students to **infer** that a sacristy is a special room in a church, where items used in religious services are kept. Tell students that these words contain the root of the Latin word *sacer*, meaning "holy," and ask them to name related words. *(sacrament, sacrifice)* ★

9. LITERARY CONCEPT: Character
Some characters have such strong traits that they seem like symbols. For example, Psyche could symbolize beauty and true love. Ask students what Lazy Peter and the farmer might symbolize. *(Possible responses: Peter might symbolize trickery; the farmer, foolishness and greed.)*

10. ACTIVE READING: Predict
Ask students what they think will happen to the farmer. *(Any response is valid.)*

Responding to Reading

1. Any response is valid.

2. **Possible responses:** The farmer is blinded by his own greed; Peter spots the farmer's weaknesses and exploits them.

3. **Possible responses:** no, because he is greedy and tries to cheat Peter out of what he thinks is a priceless item; yes, because losing everything he has is a worse fate than he deserves.

4. **Possible responses:** The farmer is tricked because he thinks he sees people giving Peter money for nothing; Peter sees that money is important to the farmer. In a sense, both Peter and the farmer have the same perspective— both want as much money as they can get with the least effort.

The druggist said he owed him nothing, and what bag of money was he talking about, anyway? As the farmer continued to shout about a bag of money and a magic hat, the druggist called the police. When they arrived, he told them that the farmer had gone out of his mind and kept demanding a bag of money. The police questioned the farmer, and he told them about the magic hat he had bought from Lazy Peter. When he heard the story, the druggist explained that Peter had left a bag of money, asking that it be returned when he appeared with a corner of his hat turned up. The owner of the stand and the priest told the same story. And I am telling you the farmer was so angry that he tore the hat to shreds and walked home. 🐾 ◄ **D**

Responding to Reading

1. Jot down your reaction to the story's ending.

2. In your opinion, why does Lazy Peter's trick work?

3. Do you feel sympathy for the farmer? Why or why not?

4. How do you think this tale fits the theme "A Matter of Perspective"? Before you answer, think about each character's point of view or attitude toward life.

HISPANIC FOLK TALE

The Force of Luck

RUDOLFO A. ANAYA

Once two wealthy friends got into a heated argument. One said that it was money which made a man prosperous, and the other maintained that it wasn't money, but luck, which made the man. They argued for some time and finally decided that if only they could find an honorable man, then perhaps they could prove their respective points of view.

One day while they were passing through a small village, they came upon a miller who was grinding corn and wheat. They paused to ask the man how he ran his business. The miller replied that he worked for a master and that he earned only four bits[1] a day, and with that he had to support a family of five.

The friends were surprised. "Do you mean to tell us you can maintain a family of five on only fifteen dollars a month?" one asked.

"I live modestly to make ends meet," the humble miller replied.

The two friends privately agreed that if they put this man to a test, perhaps they could resolve their argument.

"I am going to make you an offer," one of them said to the miller. "I will give you two hundred dollars, and you may do whatever you want with the money."

"But why would you give me this money when you've just met me?" the miller asked.

"Well, my good man, my friend and I have a long-standing argument. He contends that it is luck which elevates a man to high position, and I say it is money. By giving you this money, perhaps we can settle our argument. Here, take it, and do with it what you want!"

So the poor miller took the money and spent the rest of the day thinking about the strange meeting which had presented him with more money than he had ever seen. What could he possibly do with all this money? Be that as it may, he had the money in his pocket, and he could do with it whatever he wanted.

When the day's work was done, the miller decided the first thing he would do would be to buy food for his family. He took out ten dollars and wrapped the rest of the money in a cloth and put the bundle in his bag. Then he went to the market and bought supplies and a good piece of meat to take home.

On the way home he was attacked by a hawk that had smelled the meat which the miller carried. The miller fought off the bird, but in the struggle he lost the bundle of money. Before the miller knew what was

---

1. **four bits:** a slang term for fifty cents.

5. ACTIVE READING: Evaluate
Ask students to evaluate this statement. Should the miller have gone straight home and bought nothing? *(Possible responses: yes, because he could have put his money in a safe place and carried around only small amounts of it; no, because bad luck could have struck just as easily at his home; no, because there is no point in having money if you can't spend it.)*

6. LITERARY CONCEPT: Theme
Folk tales often contrast the noble poor with the greedy rich. Ask students if they think such a contrast is being drawn in this tale. *(Possible responses: Yes, because the rich men are using the honest miller as a pawn to settle a petty argument between themselves; no, because the rich men are honest with the miller and he needs the money the men give him.)*

7. VOCABULARY: Word Parts
If the word *earthenware* causes problems, have students break it down into its parts: *earth + -en + ware.* Then help students use their **prior knowledge** about word parts to determine that earthenware is made from earth, or clay. ★

happening, the hawk grabbed the bag and flew away with it. When he realized what had happened he fell into deep thought.

"Ah," he moaned, "wouldn't it have been better to let that hungry bird have the meat! I could have bought a lot more meat with the money he took. Alas, now I'm in the same poverty as before! And worse, because now those two men will say I am a thief! I should have thought carefully and bought nothing. Yes, I should have gone straight home, and this wouldn't have happened!"

So he gathered what was left of his provisions and continued home, and when he arrived he told his family the entire story.

When he was finished telling his story, his wife said, "It has been our lot to be poor, but have faith in God, and maybe someday our luck will change."

The next day the miller got up and went to work as usual. He wondered what the two men would say about his story. But since he had never been a man of money, he soon forgot the entire matter.

Three months after he had lost the money to the hawk, it happened that the two wealthy men returned to the village. As soon as they saw the miller, they approached him to ask if his luck had changed. When the miller saw them, he felt ashamed and afraid that they would think that he had squandered the money on worthless things. But he decided to tell them the truth, and as soon as they had greeted each other, he told his story. The men believed him. In fact, the one who insisted

that it was money and not luck which made a man prosper took out another two hundred dollars and gave it to the miller.

"Let's try again," he said, "and let's see what happens this time."

The miller didn't know what to think. "Kind sir, maybe it would be better if you put this money in the hands of another man," he said.

"No," the man insisted, "I want to give it to you because you are an honest man, and if we are going to settle our argument, you have to take the money!"

The miller thanked them and promised to do his best. Then, as soon as the two men left, he began to think what to do with the money so that it wouldn't disappear as it had the first time. The thing to do was to take the money straight home. He took out ten dollars, wrapped the rest in a cloth, and headed home.

When he arrived, his wife wasn't at home. At first he didn't know what to do with the money. He went to the pantry, where he had stored a large earthenware jar filled with bran. That was as safe a place as any to hide the money, he thought, so he emptied out the grain and put the bundle of money at the bottom of the jar, then covered it up with the grain. Satisfied that the money was safe, he returned to work.

That afternoon when he arrived home from work, he was greeted by his wife.

"Look, my husband, today I bought some good clay with which to whitewash[2] the entire house."

---

2. **whitewash:** to paint with a lime-and-water mixture.

Words to Know and Use	**squander** (skwän′ dər) *v.* to spend carelessly

598

Guided Reading for Less-Proficient Students

Continued from page 597

D. What does the man who believes in luck give the miller? *(a worthless piece of lead)* Recalling

E. How does the piece of lead bring the miller a lot of money? *(The miller gives it to his neighbor, a fisherman, to use as a weight. The fisherman pays him back with a fish, and in this fish the miller's wife finds a big diamond.)* Summarizing

F. How does the money he gets for the diamond change the miller's life? *(He uses the money to start his own mill, and his new business prospers, making him rich.)* Summarizing

G. What incidents prove that the miller was being honest with the two rich men all along? *(He finds the money the hawk stole and accidentally recovers the pot his wife gave away.)* Recalling

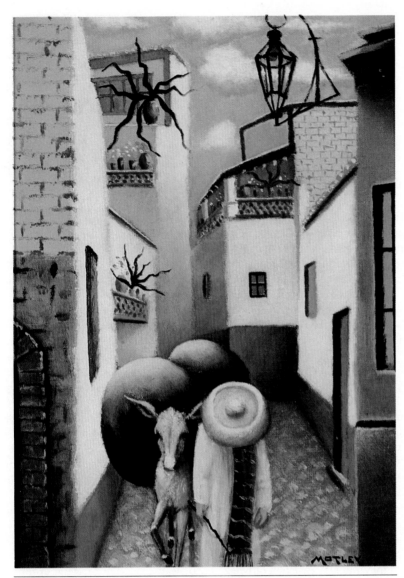

CALLEJON DEL BESO 1957 Archibald J. Motley, Jr. Kenkeleba House, New York.

"And how did you buy the clay if we don't have any money?" he asked.

"Well, the man who was selling the clay was willing to trade for jewelry, money, or anything of value," she said. "The only thing we had of value was the jar full of bran, so I traded it for the clay. Isn't it wonderful? I think we have enough clay to whitewash these two rooms!"

The man groaned and pulled his hair.

"Oh, you crazy woman! What have you done? We're ruined again!"

"But why?" she asked, unable to understand his anguish.

"Today I met the same two friends who gave me the two hundred dollars three months ago," he explained. "And after I told them how I lost the money, they gave me another two hundred. And I, to make sure the money was safe, came home and hid it inside the jar of bran—the same jar you have traded for dirt! Now we're as poor as we were before! And what am I going to tell the two men? They'll think I'm a liar and a thief for sure!"

C ▶

"Let them think what they want," his wife said calmly. "We will only have in our lives what the good Lord wants us to have. It is our lot to be poor until God wills it otherwise."

So the miller was consoled, and the next day he went to work as usual. Time came and went, and one day the two wealthy friends returned to ask the miller how he had done with the second two hundred dollars. When the poor miller saw them, he was afraid they would accuse him of being a liar and a spendthrift. But he decided to be

LA MOLENDERA   (The grinder)   Diego Rivera
Museo Nacional de Art, I.N.B.A. Mexico City.

truthful, and as soon as they had greeted each other, he told them what had happened to the money.

"That is why poor men remain honest," the man who had given him the money said. "Because they don't have money, they can't get into trouble. But I find your stories hard to believe. I think you gambled and lost the money. That's why you're telling us these wild stories."

"Either way," he continued, "I still believe that it is money and not luck which makes a man prosper."

"Well, you certainly didn't prove your point by giving the money to this poor miller," his friend reminded him. "Good evening, you luckless man," he said to the miller.

"Thank you, friends," the miller said.

"Oh, by the way, here is a worthless piece of lead I've been carrying around. Maybe you can use it for something," said the man

8

who believed in luck. Then the two men left, still debating their points of view on life.

Since the lead was practically worthless, the miller thought nothing of it and put it in his jacket pocket. He forgot all about it until he arrived home. When he threw his jacket on a chair, he heard a thump, and he remembered the piece of lead. He took it out of the pocket and threw it under the table. Later that night after the family had eaten and gone to bed, they heard a knock at the door.

"Who is it? What do you want?" the miller asked.

"It's me, your neighbor," a voice answered. The miller recognized the fisherman's wife. "My husband sent me to ask you if you have any lead you can spare. He is going fishing tomorrow, and he needs the lead to weight down the nets."

The miller remembered the lead he had thrown under the table. He got up, found it, and gave it to the woman.

"Thank you very much, neighbor," the woman said. "I promise you, the first fish my husband catches will be yours."

"Think nothing of it," the miller said and returned to bed. The next day he got up and went to work without thinking any more of the incident. But in the afternoon when he returned home, he found his wife cooking a big fish for dinner.

"Since when are we so well off we can afford fish for supper?" he asked his wife.

"Don't you remember that our neighbor promised us the first fish her husband caught?" his wife reminded him. "Well, this was the fish he caught the first time he threw his net. So it's ours, and it's a beauty. But you should have been here when I gutted him! I found a large piece of glass in his stomach!"

"And what did you do with it?"

"Oh, I gave it to the children to play with," she shrugged.

When the miller saw the piece of glass, he noticed it shone so brightly it appeared to illuminate the room, but because he knew nothing about jewels, he didn't realize its value and left it to the children. But the bright glass was such a novelty that the children were soon fighting over it and raising a terrible fuss.

Now it so happened that the miller and his wife had other neighbors, who were jewelers. The following morning when the miller had gone to work, the jeweler's wife visited the miller's wife to complain about all the noise her children had made.

"We couldn't get any sleep last night," she moaned.

"I know, and I'm sorry, but you know how it is with a large family," the miller's wife explained. "Yesterday we found a beautiful piece of glass, and I gave it to my youngest one to play with, and when the others tried to take it from him, he raised a storm."

The jeweler's wife took interest. "Won't you show me that piece of glass?" she asked.

"But of course. Here it is."

"Ah, yes, it's a pretty piece of glass. Where did you find it?"

"Our neighbor gave us a fish yesterday, and when I was cleaning it, I found the glass in its stomach."

"Why don't you let me take it home for just a moment. You see, I have one just like it, and I want to compare them."

Point out that in folk tales, events often happen in sets of three. The first two events, which are similar, set us up for the third one, which is different in some crucial way. Ask what example of this pattern they see so far in this story. *(Possible responses: The miller got three gifts from the rich men—two sums of money, which he lost, and some worthless lead. Maybe the lead will turn out to be valuable, or maybe he'll find that he can't get rid of it no matter how hard he tries.)*

10. VOCABULARY: Definitions
If students don't know what *illuminate* means, point out the **context clue** "shone so brightly" earlier in the sentence. Ask what something does when it shines very brightly. *(It lights up the area.)* ★

11. ACTIVE READING: Predict
Ask students what they think is going to happen to this piece of glass. *(Possible responses: If the jeweler's wife is so excited, it must be a jewel; the jeweler's wife will somehow steal it; she'll try to get it for nothing; she'll pay a lot of money for it.)*

Looking at Style

Ask for a volunteer to read this passage aloud:

"Yesterday we found a beautiful *piece of glass,* and I gave it to my youngest one to play with, and when the others tried to take it from him, he raised a storm."

The jeweler's wife took interest. "Won't you show me that *piece of glass?*" she asked.

"But of course. Here it is."

"Ah, yes, it's a pretty *piece of glass.* Where did you find it?" (p. 601)

Use these suggestions to stimulate discussion:
1. Do you think the repetition of "piece of glass" is boring, or do you think the repetition is serving some kind of purpose? Explain.
2. Reread the passage aloud to a group of your classmates, substituting a synonym every time "piece of glass" is repeated. Discuss whether or not the changes improve the passage.

"Yes, why not? Take it," answered the miller's wife.

So the jeweler's wife ran off with the glass to show it to her husband. When the jeweler saw the glass, he instantly knew it was one of the finest diamonds he had ever seen.

"It's a diamond!" he exclaimed.

"I thought so," his wife nodded eagerly. "What shall we do?"

"Go tell the neighbor we'll give her fifty dollars for it, but don't tell her it's a diamond!"

"No, no," his wife chuckled, "of course not." She ran to her neighbor's house. "Ah, yes, we have one exactly like this," she told the miller's wife. "My husband is willing to buy it for fifty dollars—only so we can have a pair, you understand."

"I can't sell it," the miller's wife answered. "You will have to wait until my husband returns from work."

That evening when the miller came home from work, his wife told him about the offer the jeweler had made for the piece of glass.

"But why would they offer fifty dollars for a worthless piece of glass?" the miller wondered aloud. Before his wife could answer, they were interrupted by the jeweler's wife.

"What do you say, neighbor, will you take fifty dollars for the glass?" she asked.

"No, that's not enough," the miller said cautiously. "Offer more."

"I'll give you fifty thousand!" the jeweler's wife blurted out.

"A little bit more," the miller replied.

"Impossible!" the jeweler's wife cried. "I can't offer any more without consulting my husband." She ran off to tell her husband how the bartering was going, and he told her he was prepared to pay a hundred thousand dollars to acquire the diamond.

He handed her seventy-five thousand dollars and said, "Take this and tell him that tomorrow, as soon as I open my shop, he'll have the rest."

When the miller heard the offer and saw the money he couldn't believe his eyes. He imagined the jeweler's wife was jesting with him, but it was a true offer, and he received the hundred thousand dollars for the diamond. The miller had never seen so much money, but he still didn't quite trust the jeweler.

"I don't know about this money," he confided to his wife. "Maybe the jeweler plans to accuse us of robbing him and thus get it back."

"Oh no," his wife assured him, "the money is ours. We sold the diamond fair and square—we didn't rob anyone."

"I think I'll still go to work tomorrow," the miller said. "Who knows, something might happen, and the money will disappear, then we would be without money and work. Then how would we live?"

So he went to work the next day, and all day he thought about how he could use the money. When he returned home that afternoon, his wife asked him what he had decided to do with their new fortune.

"I think I will start my own mill," he answered, "like the one I operate for my master. Once I set up my business we'll see how our luck changes."

The next day he set about buying everything he needed to establish his mill and to build a new home. Soon he had everything going.

Six months had passed, more or less, since he had seen the two men who had given him the four hundred dollars and the piece of lead. He was eager to see them again and to tell them how the piece of lead had changed his luck and made him wealthy.

Time passed and the miller prospered. His business grew, and he even built a summer cottage where he could take his family on vacation. He had many employees who worked for him. One day while he was at his store, he saw his two <u>benefactors</u> riding by. He rushed out into the street to greet them and ask them to come in. He was overjoyed to see them, and he was happy to see that they admired his store.

"Tell us the truth," the man who had given him the four hundred dollars said. "You used that money to set up this business."

The miller swore he hadn't, and he told them how he had given the piece of lead to his neighbor and how the fisherman had in return given him a fish with a very large diamond in its stomach. And he told them how he had sold the diamond.

"And that's how I acquired this business and many other things I want to show you," he said. "But it's time to eat. Let's eat first, then I'll show you everything I have now."

The men agreed, but one of them still doubted the miller's story. So they ate, and then the miller had three horses saddled, and they rode out to see his summer home. The cabin was on the other side of the river,

where the mountains were cool and beautiful. When they arrived the men admired the place very much. It was such a peaceful place that they rode all afternoon through the forest. During their ride they came upon a tall pine tree.

"What is that on top of the tree?" one of them asked.

"That's the nest of a hawk," the miller replied.

"I have never seen one; I would like to take a closer look at it!"

"Of course," the miller said, and he ordered a servant to climb the tree and bring down the nest so his friend could see how it was built. When the hawk's nest was on the ground they examined it carefully. They noticed that there was a cloth bag at the bottom of the nest. When the miller saw the bag, he immediately knew that it was the very same bag he had lost to the hawk which fought him for the piece of meat years ago.

"You won't believe me, friends, but this is the very same bag in which I put the first two hundred dollars you gave me," he told them.

"If it's the same bag," the man who had doubted him said, "then the money you said the hawk took should be there."

"No doubt about that," the miller said. "Let's see what we find."

The three of them examined the old, weather-beaten bag. Although it was full of holes and crumbling, when they tore it apart they found the money intact. The two men remembered what the miller had told them, and they agreed he was an honest and hon-

| Words to Know and Use | **benefactor** (ben´ ə fak´ tər) *n.* a person who provides money or help |

603

15

F ▶

16

15. LITERARY CONCEPT: Folk Tale
Ask students if they think this tale is saying that people should take risks to be successful in life or that they should be very cautious and conservative. Have them support their opinions with examples from the story. *(Possible responses: People should be cautious, as is shown by the miller's prospering when he uses his money for a steady, solid venture; people should take some risks, since trying to hide money away gets the miller into trouble and since his starting his own business is a sort of risk.)*

16. ACTIVE READING: Review
Ask students how the two rich men would explain the miller's success in life from their differing perspectives. *(Possible responses: The "luck man" would say that the miller just had good luck about the piece of lead and in having a jeweler as a neighbor; the "money man" would say that the miller's success came from the money he got for the diamond.)*

Speaking . . . Listening . . . Viewing

Viewing The following videos may be particularly useful for helping students understand more about how folklore reflects cultural values and concerns:

Students can learn more about the world of ancient Greece in *The Greeks,* a four-part video series that uses Greek myths as a starting point for an exploration of Greek culture. (Films Incorporated Video, 1987, 20 min. each)

Students will enjoy discussing similarities and differences between "The Arrow and the Lamp" and the tales in *Beauty and the Beast Stories,* a two-video set that presents folk tales of France, China, and the Inuit culture. (Britannica Video, 1992)

The traditional values of the Hispanic Southwest are portrayed in *Chicano from the Southwest,* in which a boy struggles to keep his traditions while growing up in the city. (Britannica Video, 1992) orable man. Still, the man who had given him the money wasn't satisfied. He wondered what had really happened to the second two hundred he had given the miller.

They spent the rest of the day riding in the mountains and returned very late to the house.

As he unsaddled their horses, the servant in charge of grooming and feeding the horses suddenly realized that he had no grain for them. He ran to the barn and checked, but there was no grain for the hungry horses. So he ran to the neighbor's granary, and there he was able to buy a large clay jar of bran. He carried the jar home and emptied the bran into a bucket to wet it before he fed it to the horses. When he got to the bottom of the jar, he noticed a large lump which turned out to be a rag-covered package. He examined it and felt something inside. He immediately went to give it to his master, who had been eating dinner.

"Master," he said, "look at this package which I found in an earthenware jar of grain which I just bought from our neighbor!"

The three men carefully unraveled the cloth and found the other one hundred and ninety dollars which the miller had told them he had lost. That is how the miller proved to his friends that he was truly an honest man.

And they had to decide for themselves whether it had been luck or money which had made the miller a wealthy man!

◄ G

17

Responding to Reading

1. What words or phrases would you use to describe the miller? Write them down in your journal or notebook.

2. Based on your own perspective and experience, who or what do you think is responsible for the miller's success? Why?

3. What values do you think this story teaches?

Comprehension Check

1. Who are Aphrodite and Eros? (*Aphrodite is the Greek goddess of love and beauty; Eros is her son.*)

2. Why does Eros leave Psyche? (*She looks at him even though he has told her not to.*)

3. What happens to Psyche in the end? (*Zeus makes her immortal so that she can live with Eros forever.*)

4. What does Lazy Peter give three people to hold for him? (*bags of money*)

5. Why does the farmer buy Lazy Peter's hat? (*He thinks the hat makes people give its wearer money.*)

6. What argument are the two wealthy men trying to settle when they meet the poor miller? (*whether luck or money brings prosperity*)

7. What do the wealthy men give the miller? (*two sums of money and a piece of lead*)

8. What does the miller's wife find in a fish's stomach? (*a diamond*)

Responding to Reading

Comparing the Selections

1. In which story do you think perspective most affects the plot?

2. Which character do you admire most? least? Explain.

Broader Connections

3. In the story of Psyche and in "The Force of Luck," the gods or fate determines the destinies of humans. Do you think that humans control their own destinies? Why or why not?

Literary Concepts: Myths and Folk Tales

In **myths** gods and goddesses have the same emotions and failings that humans possess. What specific human weaknesses are shown by the gods and goddesses in "The Arrow and the Lamp"?

Folk tales often teach lessons. What lesson do you think "Lazy Peter and His Three-Cornered Hat" teaches? Do you think "The Force of Luck" teaches a lesson? Why or why not?

Writing Options

1. Write a short **essay** on whether you believe luck or money is more important in achieving success.

2. Write a **letter of advice** that Lazy Peter might have sent Psyche.

Vocabulary Practice

Exercise   Which word best completes each sentence?

1. In the palace Psyche's __?__ was Eros.

2. The __?__ place that Psyche visited was the river Styx.

3. The farmer felt __?__ when he knew he had been tricked.

4. The miller did not want to seem like a __?__ who would __?__ money carelessly.

> *Words to Know and Use*
>
> **benefactor**
> **spendthrift**
> **squander**
> **vilest**
> **wretched**

LINKS TO UNIT ONE   605

Student Response

Responding to Reading

1. Possible responses: "The Arrow and the Lamp," because Aphrodite's perspective makes her angry and merciless, setting events in motion; "Lazy Peter and His Three-Cornered Hat," because the farmer's perspective makes him Peter's perfect sucker; "The Force of Luck," because the different perspectives of the wealthy men lead to an experiment that changes the miller's life

2. Any response is valid.

3. Any response is valid.

Challenge Question

How are the viewpoints of Psyche and the miller's wife similar? *(Possible responses: Both accept the idea that there are events they cannot control; both accept fate.)*

Literary Concepts: Myths and Folk Tales

Myths Possible responses: jealousy, vanity, cruelty, vindictiveness

Folk Tales "Lazy Peter . . ." may warn against greed, false impressions, and tunnel vision; "The Force of Luck" may teach the importance of making the most of money and lucky breaks through enterprise and work.

Writing Options

The Writing Options are designed to meet varied student interests and abilities. Have each student choose one writing activity to complete.

Journal Update Have students write about how perspective plays a part in their own lives.

Vocabulary Practice

Answers to Exercise
1. benefactor   3. wretched
2. vilest   4. spendthrift, squander

The Spelling Connection

The Suffixes *able* and *ible* The suffix *able* is commonly added to complete words; after *ce* or *ge*, the *e* is kept to protect the soft sound of *c* or *g*. The suffix *ible* is more commonly added to roots. The *i* in *ible* gives a preceding *g* a soft sound.

Examples: notice + **able** = notice**able**

Words from the Selections with *able* and *ible*

bear**able**	honor**able**	invis**ible**
impass**ible**	lik**able**	compar**able**
terr**ible**	change**able**	embrace**able**

Other Words with *able* and *ible*

| avail**able** | agree**able** | excit**able** |
| poss**ible** | manage**able** | |

Exercise Use a spelling word to answer each question.

1. Are myths likely to be true?
2. Why could Eros not be seen at times?
3. How might Psyche be described?
4. Does behaving decently seem like a key to luck?

Extending the Lesson

Options for Learning

These activities suit a variety of learning styles and modes of expression.

Collaborative Learning Activities
See Options 1 and 2.

1. **Tales of the Gods** Students can find myths in encyclopedias as well as in books of myths.

2. **Fool's Paradise** You may wish to provide large sheets of paper so that students can make "big books" to share with younger children.

Margaret Hodges

■ **More About the Author** Hodges appeared as a storyteller on the television program "Tell Me a Story" for eleven years.

■ **Other Works** Biographies: *Hopkins of the Mayflower, Lady Queen Anne;* folklore: *The Golden Deer; If You Had a Horse: Steeds of Myth and Legend*

 ■ **Awards** Caldecott Medal runner-up, *New York Times* outstanding juvenile book nomination

Ricardo Enrique Alegría

■ **More About the Author** The Indians of Puerto Rico are among Alegría's special interests.

■ **Other Works** Folk tales: *The Three Wishes;* nonfiction: *History of the Indians of Puerto Rico, Ball Courts and Ceremonial Plazas in the West Indies*

 ■ **Awards** Guggenheim Fellowship, National Trust for Historic Preservation award

Rudolfo A. Anaya

■ **More About the Author** Anaya has collected and published works of many other Chicano writers.

■ **Other Works** Novels: *Bless Me, Ultima; Heart of Aztlan; Tortuga;* short stories: *The Silence of the Llano*

 ■ **Awards** Premio Quinto Sol literary award, Before Columbus American Book Award

---

***O**ptions for Learning* (Multimodal/Cross-Curricular Activities)

1 • **Tales of the Gods** Find and read another Greek myth about Persephone, Aphrodite, Eros, or Zeus. Summarize the myth and share your summary with the class.

2 • **Fool's Paradise** Find a tale that describes a greedy fool like the farmer in "Lazy Peter and His Three-Cornered Hat." Illustrate the story as a comic book to share with your class.

Margaret Hodges 1911–

Though Margaret Hodges retired as a university professor in 1978, she has since published more than fifteen books. Hodges's many award-winning books fall into three categories: "real life stories based on the adventures and misadventures of my three sons"; retellings of folk tales and myths, such as *Hauntings: Ghosts and Ghouls from Around the World;* and biographies.

Ricardo Enrique Alegría 1921–

Ricardo Alegría is not only an avid collector of folk tales but also an anthropologist and historian. Alegría became a professor of history at the University of Puerto Rico. He has served as the director of the Institute of Puerto Rican Culture and the archaeological museum and research center at the University of Puerto Rico. He has written many books and articles on the history and folklore of Puerto Rico.

Rudolfo A. Anaya 1937–

Rudolfo Anaya says, "In New Mexico everyone tells stories; it is a creative pastime."

Anaya was born in Pastura, New Mexico. He has lived his entire life in New Mexico and now teaches at the University of New Mexico. He has given readings from his work throughout the Southwest and, in 1980, at the White House. Anaya has won many awards for his fiction and nonfiction, which draw on New Mexico's Hispanic past.

606 UNIT SIX THEMES IN WORLD FOLKLORE

Cross-Curricular Projects

Math Have students think of businesses they could start with $200 and ones they could start with $100,000.

Science If the miller and his wife had lived in Puerto Rico, what kind of fish might they have received from the fisherman? Have students gather information about Caribbean ocean life.

Music Have students listen to some narrative American folk songs. Encourage those who are musically inclined to write their own folk songs based on one or more of the tales.

Art Explain that Aphrodite (Venus) and Eros (Cupid) have been popular subjects for artists of Greece, Rome, and more modern societies. Have students find artistic representations of them.

Scales of Justice

Links to Unit Two

The Wolf in Sheep's Clothing	*The Travelers and the Purse* AESOP
Anansi and His Visitor, Turtle EDNA MASON KAULA	
A Blind Man Catches a Bird ALEXANDER MCCALL SMITH	
The Old Grandfather and His Little Grandson LEO TOLSTOY	

Examine What You Know (Prior Knowledge)

What is justice? How could you define *justice* in a way that would satisfy most people in the world? In small groups, work to come up with a definition of *justice*. Then share your definitions and decide which are the most accurate.

Expand Your Knowledge (Building Background)

The theme of justice appears in tales from all over the world. The first two selections you are about to read are fables thought to have been written by Aesop, a Greek slave who lived around the sixth century B.C. The third is an Ashanti fable featuring the tricky spider Anansi, who appears in many tales that originate in Africa. All three fables concern the simplest kind of justice between members of a community.

Justice is also an important theme in "A Blind Man Catches a Bird," from Zimbabwe, a country in southeastern Africa. The people of Zimbabwe represent many cultures and speak a variety of languages. This folk tale reflects the importance of storytelling as a great tradition and art in Africa.

The fifth selection, "The Old Grandfather and His Little Grandson," is a folk tale from Russia that has been told with slightly different twists in many countries. It too concerns simple justice. Leo Tolstoy was a wealthy aristocrat who became a leader of peasants, organizing famine-relief projects and working to educate the poor. Tolstoy collected many folk tales that he heard in peasant homes.

Write Before You Read (Journal Writing)

■ *Author biographies on Extend page and in Reader's Handbook*

Think of a real incident or a story you have heard that illustrates your group's definition of *justice*. In your journal, briefly describe the incident or story and explain how it relates to justice.

UNIT SIX THEMES IN WORLD FOLKLORE 607

Objectives

■ To understand and analyze folklore

■ To recognize the elements of fables and to review the concept of setting

■ To enrich reading by making connections between folklore and real life

■ To express understanding of the folklore through a choice of writing forms, including a fable and a first-person narrative

Prereading/Motivation

Examine What You Know

Discussion Prompts Why do people often disagree about what justice is? What areas of life do people most often disagree about? What are some examples of different ideas of justice?

Expand Your Knowledge

Additional Background Some experts believe that Aesop did not actually exist. They think the name was invented to provide an author for the beast fables of ancient Greece.

The Ashanti people live in Ghana, Togo, and the Ivory Coast. They are the largest ethnic group in Ghana. Though some live in cities, the great majority are farmers. In the 1700s and 1800s, the Ashanti Empire was a powerful West African state.

Zimbabwe was given its current name in 1980 when Great Britain officially recognized its independence. Prior to that, the country had been known as Rhodesia. For years, the country was the sight of fierce battles for independence as the black majority sought to gain basic rights of citizenship and economic power.

Thematic Link— Scales of Justice

In these five tales, a wolf, a traveler, a spider, a young man, and a peasant couple are brought to justice after they have behaved with deceit, greed, or selfishness.

MORE JOURNAL WRITING IDEAS

■ Describe an experience in which you felt you were the victim of an injustice. Who was responsible? How was the situation resolved?

■ Where did you learn about justice? Who influenced your views?

COLLABORATIVE LEARNING OPTIONS

Opportunities for collaborative learning include Examine What You Know, Options for Learning activities 1 and 2 (p. 617), and Cross-Curricular Projects (p. 617).

ADDITIONAL RESOURCES

Unit Six Resource Book
Reader's Guidesheet, p. 9
Reading Skills, p. 10
Literature Skills, p. 11
Vocabulary Connections, p. 12
Spelling Connections, p. 13
Comprehension Check Test, p. 14
Selection Test, pp. 15–16

Technology and Enrichment
Audiocassette Tape 2, Side 2: "A Blind Man . . ."

VOCABULARY PREVIEW

The focuses of vocabulary study for this selection are the prefixes *re-* and *un-*. See *Unit Six Resource Book,* Vocabulary Connections, p. 12.

LIMITED ENGLISH PROFICIENCY

■ Use the Reader's Guidesheet, *Unit Six Resource Book,* page 9.

★ The text annotation marked with a red star (Aesop's Fables: 1) may be particularly helpful for students with limited English proficiency.

Art Note

From anonymous thirteenth-century monks to the nineteenth-century French artist Grandville, many different artists have illustrated the fables of Aesop. In this modern work by Charles Santore, the artist has chosen to fill the canvas with woolly sheep with blank faces. The wolf, on the other hand, has been given a cunning, leering expression. *Does this portrayal of the wolf match your idea of the wolf in "The Wolf in Sheep's Clothing"?*

TEXT ANNOTATIONS

1. VOCABULARY: Definitions
This meaning of the word *fold* may be unfamiliar to some students. Have them use **prior knowledge** or **context clues** ("entered . . . with the flock") to determine that fold means "an enclosure for sheep." Encourage students to use context clues to realize that "mutton broth" is a soup made from the meat of sheep. ★

2. ACTIVE READING: Connect
Ask students what kind of person behaves like the "evildoer" in the story? *(Possible responses: a con artist, a crooked businessperson, a manipulative person)*

GREEK FABLES

Aesop's Fables

AESOP

Illustration by Charles Santore.

The Wolf in Sheep's Clothing

A certain wolf could not get enough to eat because of the watchfulness of the shepherds. But one night he found a sheep skin that had been cast aside and forgotten. The next day, dressed in the skin, the wolf strolled into the pasture with the sheep. Soon a little lamb was following him about and was quickly led away to slaughter.

That evening the wolf entered the fold with the flock. But it happened that the shepherd took a fancy for mutton broth that very evening and, picking up a knife, went to the fold. There the first he laid hands on and killed was the wolf.

The evildoer often comes to harm through his own deceit. ❧

The Travelers and the Purse

Two men were traveling in company along the road when one of them picked up a well-filled purse.

"How lucky I am!" he said. "I have found a purse. Judging by its weight it must be full of gold."

"Do not say, '*I* have found a purse,'" said his companion. "Say rather, '*We* have found a purse' and 'How lucky *we* are.' Travelers ought to share alike the fortunes or misfortunes of the road."

"No, no," replied the other angrily. "*I* found it and *I* am going to keep it."

Just then they heard a shout of "Stop, thief!" and looking around saw a mob of people armed with clubs coming down the road.

The man who had found the purse fell into a panic.

"We are lost if they find the purse on us," he cried.

"No, no," replied the other. "You would not say 'we' before, so now stick to your 'I.' Say '*I* am lost.'"

We cannot expect any one to share our misfortunes unless we are willing to share our good fortune also. ❧

Responding to Reading

1. What is your initial reaction to these two fables?

2. Do you think the man who found the purse in "The Travelers and the Purse" should have shared the gold? Why or why not?

3. Think about how you defined *justice* earlier. Which fable do you think more clearly illustrates that definition? Why?

4. In your opinion, are the morals at the end of these fables useful guides to living in today's world? Explain.

3. ACTIVE READING: Connect

Ask students what they would have done had they found a purse full of money while traveling with a companion. (*Any response is valid.*)

4. LITERARY CONCEPT: Fable

The moral is directly stated here. Ask students if they would draw the same lesson even if the moral were not directly stated. (*Possible responses: Yes, it's clear that the moral is about sharing both bad and good things; no, another moral could be drawn, perhaps one about people needing to stick together.*)

Responding to Reading

1. Any response is valid.

2. Possible responses: He should have shared the gold with his companion because they were making the journey together, and it would have been a generous thing to do; he shouldn't have to share the gold because he alone found the purse.

3. Any response is valid.

4. Possible responses: The morals are still useful because they are general and timeless—there will always be deceit, evildoers, misfortune, and good fortune; they are not useful because they are too old-fashioned and simplistic.

ASHANTI FABLE

Anansi and His Visitor, Turtle

EDNA MASON KAULA

It was almost time for Sun to sink to his resting place when Turtle, tired and dusty from hours of wandering, came to Anansi's house in the middle of a clearing in the woods. Turtle was hungry, and the appetizing aroma of freshly cooked fish and yams drew him to approach Anansi's door and to knock. Anansi jerked the door open. When he saw the tired stranger he was inwardly annoyed, but it was an unwritten law of his country that one must never, no never, refuse hospitality to a passerby.

Anansi smiled grimly and said, "Come in, come in, and share my dinner, Mr. Turtle."

A ▶

As Turtle stretched out one paw to help himself from the steaming platter, Anansi almost choked on a mouthful of food. In a shocked voice he said, "Turtle, I must remind you that in my country it is ill-mannered to come to the table without first washing. Please go to the stream at the foot of the hill and wash your dusty paws."

Turtle waddled down the hill and waded in the water for a while. He even washed

his face. By the time he had trudged back up the trail to Anansi's house, the platter of fish was half empty. Anansi was eating at a furious rate. **1**

Turtle stretched out one paw to help himself to food, but again Anansi stopped him. "Turtle, your paws are still dusty. Please, go wash them."

"It is the dust from the long trail up the hill," Turtle explained in a meek voice. Clearly, it was not Turtle's place to argue if he expected to share the delectable meal, **2** so he crawled down the hill a second time and rewashed his paws. Turtle was careful to walk on the grass beside the dusty trail on the climb back to Anansi's house. He hurried, for by now he was ravenous.

But, oh dear! Anansi had scraped the platter bare of fish and yams. "My, that was a good dinner," he said, wiping the last drop of gravy from his chin.

"Thank you for your wonderful hospitality, Anansi. Some day you must visit me." **3** And Turtle, in a huff, went on home. **◀ B**

Some months later Anansi visited Turtle. After creepy-crawling all day from one tall grass stem to the next, he found Turtle snoozing beside the river.

"Well, well," exclaimed Turtle. "So you have come to share my dinner. Make yourself comfortable, my dear Anansi, while I go below and prepare the food." He plunged into the river with a splash. Anansi was hungry. He paced the shoreline and watched for Turtle's reappearance.

At last, Turtle's head popped above the water. "Dinner is ready," he called as he bit into a huge clam. "Come on down." Then he disappeared from sight.

Anansi dived headfirst into the water, sank a few inches, then floated to the surface. His spindly legs and tiny body prevented him from sinking. He flipped and flapped his puny arms, tried swallow dives and belly-flops, but he could not reach the bed of the river.

Then that cunning spider schemed. He filled the pockets of his jacket with small round pebbles, dived into the river, and sank with a bump that landed him right at the dinner table. Before him was spread the most delicious meal he had ever seen. There were oysters and clams, mussels, slices of eel, and crabs. As a centerpiece, sprays of watercress rested against large pink shrimp. Anansi's eyes widened with pleasure, his stomach rumbled in anticipation.

Turtle, already seated at the table, swallowed a piece of eel, looked at Anansi and said, "Oh, Anansi, I must remind you that in my country it is ill-mannered to come to the table wearing a jacket. Please take it off."

Very slowly Anansi removed his jacket. Very slowly Anansi left the table. Without the weight of the pebbles to hold him down, he floated straight up through the green water and out of sight.

When you set out to outsmart another person to your own advantage, there is usually someone who can outsmart you.

5
◀ C

Responding to Reading

1. In your journal write your reaction to the end of this fable.

2. In your opinion, is Anansi or Turtle more responsible for the outcome of the fable? Explain.

3. What do you think this fable says about justice?

4. ACTIVE READING: Predict
Invite students to predict what hospitality Turtle will provide. *(Any response is valid.)*

5. LITERARY CONCEPT: Fable
In addition to the stated moral, what other purpose might this fable serve? *(Possible responses: entertainment; teaching a lesson about hospitality)* In what kind of place might it be especially important never to refuse hospitality to a passerby? *(Possible responses: in a harsh climate where food or water might be difficult to come by; in a place where traveling is dangerous or difficult)*

Responding to Reading

1. Any response is valid.

2. **Possible responses:** Turtle is more responsible because he gets even with Anansi and has the last laugh; Anansi is more responsible because it was his rude treatment of Turtle that started everything.

3. **Possible responses:** In the fable Turtle turns the tables on Anansi, which expresses the idea that others will treat us in the same way that we treat them.

1. ACTIVE READING: Connect
Ask students to draw on their own knowledge of blind people to explain why the blind man had "a great ability to interpret the noises made by animals." *(Possible responses: he has learned to depend on other senses besides sight; he gains his knowledge of the world primarily through hearing.)*

2. LITERARY CONCEPT:
Characterization
Ask students to explain what they learn about the two men's characters from their behavior in this scene. *(Possible responses: The blind man seems to be humble and trusting; the young man seems selfish and thoughtless.)*

ZIMBABWEAN FOLK TALE

A Blind Man Catches a Bird

ALEXANDER McCALL SMITH

A young man married a woman whose brother was blind. The young man was eager to get to know his new brother-in-law, and so he asked him if he would like to go hunting with him.

"I cannot see," the blind man said. "But you can help me see when we are out hunting together. We can go."

The young man led the blind man off into the bush. At first they followed a path that he knew, and it was easy for the blind man to tag on behind the other. After a while, though, they went off into thicker bush, where the trees grew closely together and there were many places for the animals to hide. The blind man now held onto the arm of his sighted brother-in-law and told him many things about the sounds that they heard around them. Because he had no sight, he had a great ability to interpret the noises made by animals in the bush.

"There are warthogs around," he would say. "I can hear their noises over there."

Or "That bird is preparing to fly. Listen to the sound of its wings unfolding."

To the brother-in-law, these sounds were meaningless, and he was most impressed at the blind man's ability to understand the bush although it must have been for him one great darkness.

They walked on for several hours, until they reached a place where they could set their traps. The blind man followed the other's advice and put his trap in a place where birds might come for water. The other man put his trap a short distance away, taking care to disguise it so that no bird would know that it was there. He did not bother to disguise the blind man's trap, as it was hot and he was eager to get home to his new wife. The blind man thought that he had disguised his trap, but he did not see that he had failed to do so and any bird could tell that there was a trap there.

They returned to their hunting place the next day. The blind man was excited at the prospect of having caught something, and the young man had to tell him to keep quiet, or he would scare all the animals away. Even before they reached the traps, the blind man was able to tell that they had caught something.

"I can hear birds," he said. "There are birds in the traps."

When he reached his trap, the young

612   UNIT SIX   THEMES IN WORLD FOLKLORE

Guided Reading for Less-Proficient Students

These questions can help guide students through the reading. Ask each question at the point of the selection where the capital letter and arrow appear in the margin. In addition, you may wish to use appropriate Active Reading annotations.

A. How are the two characters in the story helping each other? *(The young man is leading the blind man on a hunting trip, and the blind man is interpreting sounds for the young man.)* Recalling

B. What does the young man do after he discovers the pretty bird in the blind man's trap? *(He takes the prettier bird and gives the blind man the smaller bird.)* What does the blind man do with the small bird? *(He feels it, pockets it, and says nothing.)* Summarizing

C. Why is the young man ashamed? *(He realizes the blind man is aware of his trick.)* Inferring

D. How does the young man please the blind man? *(He gives the beautiful bird to the blind man.)* Recalling man saw that he had caught a small bird. He took it out of the trap and put it in a pouch that he had brought with him. Then the two of them walked toward the blind man's trap.

"There is a bird in it," he said to the blind man. "You have caught a bird too."

As he spoke, he felt himself filling with jealousy. The blind man's bird was marvelously colored, as if it had flown through a rainbow and been stained by the colors. The feathers from a bird such as that would make a fine present for his new wife, but the blind man had a wife too, and she would also want the feathers.

The young man bent down and took the blind man's bird from the trap. Then, quickly substituting his own bird, he passed it to the blind man and put the colored bird into his own pouch.

"Here is your bird," he said to the blind man. "You may put it in your pouch."

The blind man reached out for the bird and took it. He felt it for a moment, his fingers passing over the wings and the breast. Then, without saying anything, he put the bird into his pouch and they began the trip home. ◀ B

On their way home, the two men stopped to rest under a broad tree. As they sat there, they talked about many things. The young man was impressed with the wisdom of the blind man, who knew a great deal although he could see nothing at all.

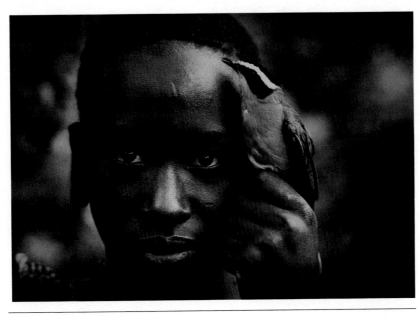

© 1991 by Robert Vavra.

4. ACTIVE READING: Connect
Ask students how they would respond to the young man's question. *(Any response is valid.)*

5. LITERARY CONCEPT: Fable
Ask students to explain the theme of this fable, as it is reflected in this concluding passage. *(Possible response: Honesty and fairness can repair a friendship that has been damaged by dishonesty and greed.)*

Responding to Reading

1. Any response is valid.

2. Possible responses: The blind man may have wanted to see what would happen next; he may have wanted the young man to "do the right thing" on his own.

3. Possible responses: to teach the young that honesty brings peace; to show how justice can operate on a personal level; to encourage people to respect each other's property.

"Why do people fight with one another?" he asked the blind man. It was a question which had always troubled him, and he wondered if the blind man could give him an answer.

The blind man said nothing for a few moments, but it was clear to the young man that he was thinking. Then the blind man raised his head, and it seemed to the young man as if the unseeing eyes were staring right into his soul. Quietly he gave his answer.

"Men fight because they do to each other what you have just done to me."

The words shocked the young man and made him ashamed. He tried to think of a response, but none came. Rising to his feet, he fetched his pouch, took out the brightly colored bird, and gave it back to the blind man.

The blind man took the bird, felt over it with his fingers, and smiled.

"Do you have any other questions for me?" he asked.

"Yes," said the young man. "How do men become friends after they have fought?"

The blind man smiled again.

"They do what you have just done," he said. "That's how they become friends again." ❧

Responding to Reading

1. What do you think is the most interesting part of this folk tale?

2. Why do you think the blind man keeps quiet when he first realizes that he has been cheated?

3. What purpose might this tale serve in African society?

The Old Grandfather and His Little Grandson

LEO TOLSTOY

The grandfather had become very old. His legs would not carry him, his eyes could not see, his ears could not hear, and he was toothless. When he ate, bits of food sometimes dropped out of his mouth. His son and his son's wife no longer allowed him to eat with them at the table. He had to eat his meals in the corner near the stove.

One day they gave him his food in a bowl. He tried to move the bowl closer; it fell to the floor and broke. His daughter-in-law scolded him. She told him that he spoiled everything in the house and broke their dishes, and she said that from now on he would get his food in a wooden dish. The old man sighed and said nothing.

A few days later, the old man's son and his wife were sitting in their hut, resting and watching their little boy playing on the floor. They saw him putting together something out of small pieces of wood. His father asked him, "What are you making, Misha?"

The little grandson said, "I'm making a wooden bucket. When you and Mamma get old, I'll feed you out of this wooden dish."

The young peasant and his wife looked at each other, and tears filled their eyes. They were ashamed because they had treated the old grandfather so meanly, and from that day they again let the old man eat with them at the table and took better care of him. ❧

Responding to Reading

1. What feelings did you have as you read this story?

2. Why do you think the couple treats the grandfather in the way that they do?

3. How do you think this tale involves "Scales of Justice"?

4. Do you think this tale is relevant today? Explain.

Comprehension Check

1. What does the wolf do to trick sheep? *(It wears a sheep skin.)*

2. According to Aesop, what must we share if we want others to share our misfortune? *(our good fortune)*

3. How does Anansi trick Turtle? *(He twice insists that Turtle go to the stream to wash his paws. While Turtle is gone, Anansi eats all the food.)*

4. Where does Turtle serve food when he tricks Anansi? *(underwater)*

5. How does the young man make the blind man his friend? *(He returns the bird he stole.)*

6. Whose action shames the couple into treating grandfather better? *(the grandson's)*

Student Response

Responding to Reading

1. Any response is valid.

2. Possible responses: the blind man's brother-in-law because he tried to take advantage of the blind man; the couple in Tolstoy's tale because they mistreated their own family member

3. Any response is valid.

Literary Concept: Fables

Anansi shows the human qualities of intelligence, selfishness, cunning, and greed; Turtle shows intelligence, vengefulness, cleverness, and humor; the wolf shows intelligence, slyness, and greed.

Concept Review: The setting of the thick African jungle is important in "A Blind Man Catches a Bird," but the story could happen in another setting if other types of animals were being hunted. The setting in "The Old Grandfather and His Little Grandson" is not very important because the fable could happen anywhere.

Writing Options

The Writing Options are designed to meet varied student interests and abilities. Have each student choose one writing activity to complete.

Journal Update Invite students to write about various animals that could be used as characters to illustrate particular human qualities in different settings, such as the seaside, rugged mountain country, the frozen north, and the prairie.

Responding to Reading

Comparing the Selections

1. In your opinion, do all of these stories reflect the idea of justice that you discussed before you read? Explain.

2. If you were a judge, which character would you punish most harshly? Explain your choice.

Broader Connections

3. Choose one of the simple truths demonstrated in these stories, and show how it applies to a situation in our nation or in the world today.

Literary Concept: Fables

A brief story written to teach a lesson about human nature is called a **fable.** The characters in fables are often animals that act and talk like humans. What human qualities do Anansi, Turtle, and the wolf in Aesop's fable show?

Concept Review: Setting How important is the setting in "A Blind Man Catches a Bird" and in "The Old Grandfather and His Little Grandson"? Could either story happen somewhere else?

Writing Options

1. Think of a lesson about life that you have learned. Write a **fable** that illustrates this lesson.

2. Write a **first-person narrative** about an experience you have had that illustrates the moral of one of these stories.

Options for Learning (Multimodal/Cross-Curricular Activities)

1 • **Telling Tales** Make puppets and use them to retell your favorite folk tale to young children. Practice with your classmates, and then arrange a folk-tale puppet show for a younger class.

2 • **Fable Follies** Locate a collection of fables, and in a small group, choose one to act out. Act out your fable for the class and have them guess the moral.

Aesop 620–560 B.C.

So little is known about Aesop that he might be a fable himself. Historians think he may have been an African slave who worked on the island of Samos. How many fables Aesop actually wrote remains a question.

His death even sounds like a folk tale. After Aesop insulted the people of Delphi, the story says, they secretly hid a golden bowl in his belongings as he prepared to leave. He was then arrested for theft and thrown off a cliff.

Alexander McCall Smith

Born in Zimbabwe, Alexander McCall Smith returned to his homeland after his education in Scotland. He recorded the stories of both old people and schoolchildren. These tales, he says, are "uniquely the

property of the people of Africa."

Smith has published several children's books, plays, and short stories. Many of the stories have been read on the radio in Britain, and one was made into an animated film.

Leo Tolstoy 1828–1910

Born to a wealthy family in Russia, the young Leo Tolstoy lived a life of luxury. He wrote his two most famous novels, *War and Peace* and *Anna Karenina*, while living on his large country estate. Later, however, Tolstoy began to question his

life. He no longer believed people were entitled to have as much land, money, and power as he had. Eventually, in his old age, he turned over his entire estate to his family and left. A few days later he died at a railroad station in a small town.

LINKS TO UNIT TWO   617

Options for Learning

These activities suit a variety of learning styles and modes of expression.

Collaborative Learning Activities
See Options 1 and 2.

1. Telling Tales Students might make puppets with papier-mâché heads and fabric bodies. They might decorate old socks or use pipe cleaners.

2. Fable Follies Encourage students to make decisions about what dialogue, physical movement, and props are necessary for a successful performance of the fable.

Aesop

■ **More About the Author** The scant information about Aesop comes from classical sources: Aristotle referred to Aesop as a public defender, and Plutarch wrote that the citizens of Athens erected a statue of Aesop.

Alexander McCall Smith

■ **More About the Author** Today Alexander McCall Smith is a Lecturer in Law at Edinburgh University. In addition to fiction, he writes law and medical books.

■ **Other Works** *Children of Wax: African Folk Tales*

Leo Tolstoy

■ **More About the Author** After writing his great novels and undergoing a religious conversion, Tolstoy tried to live simply and primitively. He made his own shoes and shirts and praised the virtues of physical labor.

■ **Other Works** Autobiographical novels: *Childhood, Boyhood, Youth;* Novel: *Resurrection;* Novella: *The Death of Ivan Ilyich*

Cross-Curricular Projects

Art Have students illustrate a fable they have read. They might work with paint, charcoal, colored pencils, pen and ink, or fabric. Encourage students to illustrate an important character or event in the story.

Science Have interested students prepare a research report on the real-life qualities of one of the animals featured in "The Wolf in Sheep's Clothing" or "Anansi and His Visitor, Turtle."

Social Studies Encourage students to find other fables from other cultures. Ask them to prepare a brief oral report comparing and contrasting two countries' treatment of the same animal, the same situation, or the same theme.

Music Have students find musical versions of fables or folk tales, such as "I Gave My Love a Cherry," "Hole in the Bucket," or "There Was an Old Woman Who Swallowed a Fly."

Closure

Divide the class into groups of five, and have each choose a different tale to read aloud as an ancient storyteller might have told it. Afterwards, have students discuss why these folk tales and fables have endured for generations. What is their lasting appeal?

Objectives

■ To understand and analyze a myth and folk tales

■ To recognize symbols in folklore

■ To enrich reading by understanding the purposes of folklore

■ To express understanding of the selections through a choice of writing forms, including an essay and an article

Prereading/Motivation

Examine What You Know

Discussion Prompts Who are your heroes? What difficulties did they have in achieving their dreams?

Expand Your Knowledge

Additional Background Apollo was dearly loved by the Greeks because he was handsome, eternally youthful, and wise. Only Zeus, his father, was worshiped more than Apollo. Apollo was unlucky in love; several myths tell of his failures. The Greeks consulted Apollo's oracle at Delphi to learn the future.

According to Hamilton, the idea of slaves flying to escape has been attributed to Gullah (Angolan) African slaves. Many slaves thought that those originally from Angola had special powers. Often in the tales of flying slaves, a magic hoe that works by itself is left in the field from which the slaves escape.

Traditionally, Kikuyu homesteads consisted of two circular log houses with thatched roofs. One was for females and small children; the other, for the older boys and their father. In the men's house, riddles and stories were told late into the night. These stories were an essential part of a boy's education, an oral passing on of history.

Thematic Link— Reaching for the Stars

In these stories very different characters reach for the stars. A mortal boy dares to drive a god's fiery chariot through the skies; slaves rediscover their ancient power and fly to freedom; a clever clown tries to trick a young woman into marrying him.

Reaching for the Stars

Links to Unit Three		
	Phaëthon	MOIRA KERR / JOHN BENNETT
	The People Could Fly	VIRGINIA HAMILTON
	Kelfala's Secret Something	ADJAI ROBINSON

Examine What You Know (Prior Knowledge)

A scientist works a lifetime to find the cure for a disease. A man who cannot read goes back to school. A woman runs for political office. Many people struggle against great odds to fulfill their dreams. In small groups discuss the different types of dreams people have and the obstacles that they must overcome to achieve those dreams. For every dream, think of at least one obstacle.

Expand Your Knowledge (Building Background)

A main character in the myth "Phaëthon" is a Greek god, Apollo. Handsome Apollo was the god of the sun, of music, and of healing. He and Clymene (klī' mə nē), a mortal woman, had a son named Phaëthon. In this myth Phaëthon dreams of riding gloriously through the heavens in his father's golden chariot.

The characters in the second story dream not of fame or glory but of freedom. "The People Could Fly" is an American slave tale. Because most slaves were not allowed to learn to read or write, much of their culture was passed down orally. To show this, the author has written her story in the **dialect** that slaves might have used. Tales such as this provided comfort and hope and preserved the history of the lives of slaves and the legends of their African homeland.

The third selection tells of yet another kind of dream. It is a folk tale of the Kikuyu people of Kenya in East Africa. The Kikuyus, Kenya's largest ethnic group, live mostly in the southern central part of the country, near the border of Tanzania. The Kikuyus in this story live near Mount Kilimanjaro, the highest mountain in Africa. Among the Kikuyus, the traditions and instructions of parents and elders are binding, almost like laws.

Write Before You Read (Journal Writing)

■ *Author biographies on Extend page*

Have you ever had a dream or goal that was frustrated when someone or something got in the way? In your journal describe your dream and explain how you fought for it.

MORE JOURNAL WRITING IDEAS

■ Think and write about what kinds of obstacles are the hardest to overcome—physical obstacles, mental obstacles, or obstacles put up by other people.

■ Speculate about what kinds of dreams American slaves and the son of Apollo might have.

COLLABORATIVE LEARNING OPTIONS

Opportunities for collaborative learning include Examine What You Know, Multicultural Connections (p. 621), Options for Learning 1 (p. 631), Cross-Curricular Projects (p. 631), and Closure (p. 631).

ADDITIONAL RESOURCES

Unit Six Resource Book
Reader's Guidesheet, p. 17
Reading Skills, p. 18
Literature Skills, p. 19
Vocabulary Connections, p. 20
Spelling Connections, p. 21
Comprehension and Vocabulary Check Tests, p. 22
Selection Test, pp. 23–24

GREEK MYTH

Phaëthon

MOIRA KERR / JOHN BENNETT

One day the fair youth Phaëthon, whose father was the sun god, Apollo, was taunted about his parentage by Epaphus[1], a youth of the same age whose father was the mighty Zeus.

Stung with shame, Phaëthon reported the insults to his mother, Clymene.

"I am unable to answer them. If my father is really a god, as you have told me, give me proof of my noble birth, and let me take my place in heaven."

Clymene was moved.

"It would not take you long to visit your father's dwelling place. If you wish to do so, go and question the sun himself, for Apollo is indeed your father."

Apollo's abode was a lofty palace of glittering gold and bronze. Its towering columns, supporting a roof of polished ivory, shone like fire. Its double doors reflected the light from their silver surfaces.

After climbing the steep approach, Clymene's son was ushered into the presence of his father, who was dressed in a purple robe and was sitting on a throne of shining emeralds. But Phaëthon could not approach too close, for he could not bear the blinding light.

"What do you want in this citadel[2],

Phaëthon, my son? Son, I call you, for you are one whom any parent would be proud to acknowledge."

"To prove that I am indeed your son, give me evidence."

"To remove any doubt from your mind, Phaëthon, make any request you wish, and you shall have it from me."

Instantly the lad asked to be allowed for one day to drive his father's sun chariot across the sky.

The words were scarcely spoken when Apollo regretted his oath. A mortal may, perhaps, break his word, but not so a god who had sworn by the waters of the Styx[3]. Apollo knew that the request meant death for a mortal, and he used every argument to dissuade his son from a venture that was suicide.

◀ A

"You cannot possibly keep the horses under control. I, a god, can scarcely manage them. Even Zeus himself couldn't drive the chariot. The heavens are dangerous. You will have to keep to the path, past the horns

---

1. **Epaphus** (ə paf′ əs): the son of Zeus and the mortal woman Io.
2. **citadel**: a fortress
3. **Styx** (stiks): in Greek mythology, the river around Hades across which dead souls are ferried.

Words to Know and Use	**abode** (ə bōd′) *n.* a home
	acknowledge (ak näl′ ij) *v.* to recognize the status or rights of
	dissuade (di swād′) *v.* to persuade not to do something

619

Guided Reading for Less-Proficient Students

4. ACTIVE READING: Connect
Ask students why young people do things that their parents believe they aren't ready for. Invite them to offer modern parallels to Phaëthon and Apollo's conflict. *(Possible responses: kids' arguing they are ready to date, to drive, to have a job, to stay out late)*

5. VOCABULARY: Unfamiliar Words
In Greek mythology, the Hours were goddesses who presided over the changes of the seasons. Students may need help in understanding some of the terms relating to horses. Explain that *yoke* means "to join animals together for pulling a wagon or chariot," that *steeds* are horses, and that a *harness* is an arrangement of straps by which horses are attached to a wagon or chariot. ★

6. LANGUAGE: Archaic Terms
Explain that *hither* and *thither* are adverbs meaning "to here" and "to there." They are used primarily in formal and literary contexts and may be becoming obsolete words. ★

From *Favorite Greek Myths* retold by Mary Pope Osborne, illustrated by Troy Howell. Illustrations copyright © 1989 by Troy Howell. Reprinted by permission of Scholastic, Inc.

of the hostile Bull, past the Thracian Archer and the paws of the raging Lion, past the Scorpion's cruel pincers and the clutching claws of the Crab.[4] Release me from my promise. Ask anything else and I shall grant it."

4
B ▶

But Phaëthon, full of confidence, would not change his mind, and the reluctant Apollo had the swift Hours yoke his team, lead the four fire-breathing steeds from the stable, and fasten on the jingling harness.

5

No sooner had the proud youth leaped into the chariot and taken the reins in his hands than the horses knew they had not the firm hands of their master to guide them. Feeling their burden was too light, off they raced, out of control. The lad was panic-stricken. He did not know the path, he did not even know the names of the horses, and he was not able to manage the horses, even had he known. He could only cling helplessly to the sides of the swaying chariot as it plunged hither and thither through the sky.

6

---

4. Bull, Thracian (thrā′ shən) **Archer, Lion, Scorpion, Crab:** the constellations known as Taurus, Sagittarius, Leo, Scorpio, and Cancer.

620 UNIT SIX THEMES IN WORLD FOLKLORE

For the first time, the cold stars of the Northern Plough grew hot, and the Serpent,[5] which lay close to the icy pole, was roused to fury as it sweltered in the heat. Phaëthon's terror mounted as he sighted the Scorpion and the other monstrous beasts sprawling over the face of the high heavens. Then the horses went plunging downward toward the earth. The heat of the sun's rays seared the ground, destroying vegetation and drying up rivers and seas. Great cities perished, and whole nations were reduced to ashes. So close did the chariot come to Africa that Libya became a desert.

Everywhere the ground gaped open, and great beams of light descended even to Tartarus,[6] frightening the king of the underworld and his queen. Three times did Poseidon try to emerge above the waters, but the fiery air was too much for him.

It was then that the alarmed Zeus had to interfere, or the whole world would have perished in flame. Mounting to the highest point of heaven, he let fly a powerful thunderbolt against the young charioteer, which dashed the luckless Phaëthon to earth.

His body fell into the Po River, and the Italian nymphs buried it on the bank. On a rock, they set this inscription:

"Here Phaëthon lies: his father's car he tried—
Though proved too weak, he greatly daring died."

---

5. **Northern Plough** (plou), **Serpent:** the constellations known as the Big Dipper and Draco.
6. **Tartarus** (tär′ tə rəs): in Greek mythology, another name for Hades, the world of the dead.

Responding to Reading

1. What adjectives would you use to describe Phaëthon? Jot them down in your journal.

2. In your opinion, who is most to blame for Phaëthon's death?

   Think about
   - the reason behind Phaëthon's requests
   - the roles of Apollo and Zeus in the story

3. What purposes do you think this myth served in Greek society? Before answering, review Elements of Folklore on pages 584–585.

Words to Know and Use	**sear** (sir) *v.* to burn the surface; scorch

621

7. ACTIVE READING: Review
Remind students that myths often were created to help explain natural occurrences in the world. Ask what natural phenomena might be explained by the events in this myth. (*Possible responses: a drought, a heat wave, the creation of the Sahara*)

8. CULTURAL SIDELIGHT
Help students locate the Po River in northern Italy, flowing eastward from the Alps into the Adriatic Sea. Explain that in mythology, nymphs are beautiful female nature spirits who live in rivers or trees. ★

9. LANGUAGE: Inverted Phrases
For Alternative Learning Styles Some students may be confused by the poetic technique of phrase inversion here. Present the poem as follows:

"Phaëthon lies here: he tried his father's car—
Though he proved too weak, he died daring greatly." ★

Responding to Reading

1. Any response is valid.

2. Possible responses: Apollo, because he allows his son to drive the chariot and because he has not publicly acknowledged his son; Zeus, because he kills Phaëthon; Epaphus, because he taunts Phaëthon; Phaëthon, because he insists on doing something he isn't ready for

3. Possible responses: explaining the daily course of the sun, explaining the presence of deserts, teaching a lesson about obedience to one's parents, warning against overconfidence and rashness

Multicultural Connections

The god Apollo is associated with the idea of the middle way, or moderation in all things. To the Greeks, harmony, balance, and justice were great virtues.

Have small groups of students find evidence of efforts by the ancient Greeks to achieve these goals. Encourage each group to choose a specific area to study, such as philosophy, architecture, education, medicine, government, or sports.

After they complete their research, have each group present their findings to the class. Encourage students to use photographs or other visual materials where appropriate to illustrate their ideas. Listening students may think of ways in which these Greek ideals have persisted into the modern world.

AFRICAN-AMERICAN FOLK TALE

The People Could Fly

VIRGINIA HAMILTON

1 They say the people could fly. Say that long ago in Africa, some of the people knew magic. And they would walk up on the air like climbin' up on a gate. And they flew like blackbirds over the fields. Black, shiny wings flappin' against the blue up there.

2 Then, many of the people were captured for Slavery. The ones that could fly shed their wings. They couldn't take their wings across the water on the slave ships. Too crowded, don't you know.

The folks were full of misery, then. Got sick with the up and down of the sea. So they forgot about flyin' when they could no longer breathe the sweet scent of Africa.

Say the people who could fly kept their power, although they shed their wings. They kept their secret magic in the land of slavery. They looked the same as the other people from Africa who had been coming over, who had dark skin. Say you couldn't tell anymore **A ▶** one who could fly from one who couldn't.

One such who could was an old man, call him Toby. And standin' tall, yet afraid, was a young woman who once had wings. Call her Sarah. Now Sarah carried a babe tied to her back. She trembled to be so hard worked and scorned.

3 The slaves labored in the fields from sunup to sundown. The owner of the slaves callin' himself their Master. Say he was a hard lump of clay. A hard, glinty coal. A hard rock pile, wouldn't be moved. His Overseer on horseback pointed out the slaves who were slowin' down. So the one called Driver cracked his whip over the slow ones to make them move faster. That whip was a slice-open cut of pain. So they did move faster. Had to.

Sarah hoed and chopped the row as the babe on her back slept.

Say the child grew hungry. That babe started up bawling too loud. Sarah couldn't stop to feed it. Couldn't stop to soothe and quiet it down. She let it cry. She didn't want to. She had no heart to <u>croon</u> to it. **4**

"Keep that thing quiet," called the Overseer. He pointed his finger at the babe. The woman scrunched low. The Driver cracked his whip across the babe anyhow. The babe hollered like any hurt child, and the woman fell to the earth.

The old man that was there, Toby, came and helped her to her feet.

"I must go soon," she told him.

"Soon," he said.

Sarah couldn't stand up straight any longer. She was too weak. The sun burned

---

Words to Know and Use | **croon** (krōōn) *v.* to sing softly

622

From *The People Could Fly: American Black Folktales* told by Virginia Hamilton and illustrated by Leo and Diane Dillon. Illustration copyright © 1985 by Leo and Diane Dillon. Reprinted by permission of Alfred A. Knopf, Inc.

Art Note

Leo and Diane Dillon often illustrate literary classics. This work for "The People Could Fly" gives the impression that flying is quite normal. Note how the people's bodies are angled to show the lifting, flying action. *What details do the Dillons emphasize in this work? Why do you think they do this?*

5. LITERARY CONCEPT: Metaphor
Ask students how Hamilton's description of the whip makes it seem alive. To what is the author comparing the whip? *(Possible responses: a vicious animal, the Overseer himself)*

6. LITERARY CONCEPT: Description
Ask students what this description suggests about the nature of the words of ancient Africa and their power. *(The words are magic; the words are secret.)* Invite students to discuss other traditional stories in which magic words have great powers.

her face. The babe cried and cried, "Pity me, oh, pity me," say it sounded like. Sarah was so sad and starvin', she sat down in the row.

"Get up, you black cow," called the Overseer. He pointed his hand, and the Driver's whip snarled around Sarah's legs. Her sack dress tore into rags. Her legs bled onto the earth. She couldn't get up.

Toby was there where there was no one to help her and the babe.

"Now, before it's too late," panted Sarah. "Now, Father!"

"Yes, Daughter, the time is come," Toby answered. "Go, as you know how to go!"

He raised his arms, holding them out to her. *"Kum . . . yali, kum buba tambe,"* and more magic words, said so quickly, they sounded like whispers and sighs.

The young woman lifted one foot on the air. Then the other. She flew clumsily at first, with the child now held tightly in her arms. Then she felt the magic, the African mystery. Say she rose just as free as a bird. As light as a feather.

The Overseer rode after her, hollerin'. Sarah flew over the fences. She flew over the woods. Tall trees could not snag her. Nor could the Overseer. She flew like an eagle now, until she was gone from sight. No one dared speak about it. Couldn't believe it. But it was, because they that was there saw that it was.

Say the next day was dead hot in the fields. A young man slave fell from the heat. The Driver come and whipped him. Toby come over and spoke words to the fallen one. The words of ancient Africa once heard are never remembered completely. The young man forgot them as soon as he heard them. They went way inside him. He got up and rolled over on the air. He rode it awhile. And he flew away.

Another and another fell from the heat. Toby was there. He cried out to the fallen and reached his arms out to them. *"Kum kunka yali, kum . . . tambe!"* Whispers and sighs. And they too rose on the air. They rode the hot breezes. The ones flyin' were black and shinin' sticks, wheelin' above the head of the Overseer. They crossed the rows, the fields, the fences, the streams, and were away.

"Seize the old man!" cried the Overseer. "I heard him say the magic *words*. Seize him!"

THE PEOPLE COULD FLY   623

Looking at Style

To discuss Hamilton's writing style in "The People Could Fly," have students read this paragraph:

Say the child grew hungry. That babe started up bawling too loud. Sarah couldn't stop to feed it. Couldn't stop to soothe and quiet it down. She let it cry. She didn't want to. She had no heart to croon to it. (p. 622)

Discuss the following questions and activity:

1. What does beginning a sentence with the word *say* seem to invite you to do? What other phrases might encourage you to use your imagination?

2. What idioms or colloquial phrases are used here? How do they affect this passage?

3. Have students write paragraphs that describe people working. Urge them to try to capture the sound of someone speaking. Have them act as storytellers and read their paragraphs aloud.

7. VOCABULARY: Unfamiliar Words
Ask students to explain the term *ring-sing*. Have them use **prior knowledge** and **context clues** to understand that it refers to moving around in a circle (ring) and singing together. ★

8. ACTIVE READING: Connect
Ask students how the last paragraph makes them feel. *(Possible responses: like the audience of a storyteller, like part of a long chain of storytellers and listeners)*

Responding to Reading

1. Any response is valid.

2. Possible responses: They need Toby to speak the magic words; it isn't the right time yet; they are not sure their magic will still work; they are just too tired and frightened; they don't want to leave the ones who can't fly.

3. Possible responses: Only some of the slaves remember the African magic that enables them to fly; only some have the courage to escape; some never learned how to fly.

4. Possible responses: No, because human flight is physically impossible; probably not, but flying in the story stands for rising above the oppression of slavery or escaping to freedom; yes, some may have believed that the story told of a time when anything was possible.

5. Possible responses: to give hope to those still held in slavery, to inspire future generations to continue the struggle for freedom, to make their listeners proud of their ancestors

The one callin' himself Master come runnin'. The Driver got his whip ready to curl around old Toby and tie him up. The slave owner took his hip gun from its place. He meant to kill old black Toby.

But Toby just laughed. Say he threw back his head and said, "Hee, hee! Don't you know who I am? Don't you know some of us in this field?" He said it to their faces. "We are ones who fly!"

And he sighed the ancient words that were a dark promise. He said them all around to the others in the field under the whip, ". . . *buba yali . . . buba tambe . . .*"

There was a great outcryin'. The bent backs straightened up. Old and young who were called slaves and could fly joined hands. Say like they would ring-sing. But they didn't shuffle in a circle. They didn't sing. They rose on the air. They flew in a flock that was black against the heavenly blue. Black crows or black shadows. It didn't matter, they went so high. Way above the plantation, way over the slavery land. Say they flew away to *Free-dom*.

And the old man, old Toby, flew behind them, takin' care of them. He wasn't cryin'. He wasn't laughin'. He was the seer. His gaze fell on the plantation where the slaves who could not fly waited.

"Take us with you!" Their looks spoke it, but they were afraid to shout it. Toby couldn't take them with him. Hadn't the time to teach them to fly. They must wait for a chance to run.

"Goodie-bye!" the old man called Toby spoke to them, poor souls! And he was flyin' gone.

So they say. The Overseer told it. The one called Master said it was a lie, a trick of the light. The Driver kept his mouth shut.

The slaves who could not fly told about the people who could fly to their children. When they were free. When they sat close before the fire in the free land, they told it. They did so love firelight and *Free-dom*, and tellin'.

They say that the children of the ones who could not fly told their children. And now, me, I have told it to you.

Responding to Reading

1. To what part of this story did you react most strongly? Why?

2. Why do you think the slaves who can fly take so long to do so?

3. Why do you think only some of the slaves in this story can achieve the dream of flying?

4. Do you think the storytellers who retold this story believed that people actually flew? Explain.

5. What reasons might slaves have had for telling this story?

KENYAN FOLK TALE

Kelfala's Secret Something

ADJAI ROBINSON

1 Listen, children, do you know the Gituyu? It is such an animal that in Kenya it is said that even the dogs will not eat its meat for supper, nor the hyena, nor even the wildcat—and never the poorest of people. That is tradition. This you must know.

But the story . . .

On the steep slopes of the Kilimanjaro stood a tiny village of very hardy people. Mountain climbers were they all, and their gardens of tea and pyrethrum[1] and coffee were as dear to their hearts as the cap of snow shielding the head of their father mountain. The men and women had strong hands and great mountain strides. They were a happy people with warm hearts. **2** And they were a people faithful to their traditions.

The young fellow, Kelfala, was one of these. Kelfala, the clown. People used to say that he was funny from the time he entered his mother's womb. He could make a thousand and one faces with his one fleshy face. His lips he could twist and curl, and even if you wanted to hiss, your hissing would turn to laughing. If you listened to Kelfala's stories, I tell you, you would see and hear all the animals in the forest in this one Kelfala. And he sprang surprises as fast as he spinned yarns, on everything around.

Kelfala, the clown, was like his grandfather before him. He was funny. He was clever. Oh, he was a charming darling. It seemed that nothing or no one could resist Kelfala. **◄ A**

No one, except the beautiful Wambuna. She would not even turn his way.

3 Before, as children, these two had played together, laughed together, teased together. But Wambuna had gone into the girl's society, as all girls of the village do. There, the old women had taught her how to wash and care for babies, how to prepare leaves and herbs for simple cures, how to sing the village songs, how to cook meats and yams and vegetables. Her roasted peanuts were always brown and tasty. And if you ate her sauces, you would lick your fingers as if you were going to bite them, too. Her graces were admired even by other young girls. And when she came out, she was **4** given the oath: that from that time on, if she talked to any man outside her family, she was bound to marry him. That was tradition. **◄ B**

Kelfala would sit in the bush and watch this darling Wambuna. Her skin was as

---

1. **pyrethrum** (pī reth′ rəm): a flowering plant that is used to make insecticide.

TEXT ANNOTATIONS

1. ACTIVE READING: Predict
Ask students why a storyteller might begin a tale this way. (Possible responses: to introduce an important idea or theme, to interest listeners or readers right away with a strange detail) Invite students to predict the role the Gituyu will play in this story. (Possible response: Someone will probably eat or be served a Gituyu.)

2. LITERARY CONCEPT: Repetition
Point out that Kikuyu cultural traditions were also mentioned at the end of the first paragraph. Have students explain what readers might infer from this repetition. (Possible responses: Traditions are important to the Kikuyu; the plot of the story depends on tradition.)

3. CULTURAL SIDELIGHT
In Kenya today, women generally accept the role of caretaker for their children. Some also work part time on large farms. Although the Kenyan government encourages women to become educated and join the work force, few choose to do so. The vast majority busy themselves with child care and farm labor. Invite students to discuss why this might be so.

4. ACTIVE READING: Connect
Ask students why people might have a tradition like this one. What purpose does it serve? (Possible responses: It keeps young men and women apart; it makes it difficult for young people to get to know one another and become romantically involved.) Have students speculate about how they would feel if they had to follow this tradition.

Guided Reading for Less-Proficient Students

These questions can help guide students through the reading. Ask each question at the point of the selection where the capital letter and arrow appear in the margin. In addition, you may wish to use appropriate Active Reading annotations.

A. What makes Kelfala such a popular individual? (He is able to make people laugh; he is an entertaining storyteller.) Summarizing

B. Why won't Wambuna talk to a man not of her family? (She would have to marry him.) Recalling

C. Why do the suitors say crazy things to Wambuna? (They are trying to make her speak to them.) Inferring

D. What does Kelfala expect to do with the "something" inside his sack? (win Wambuna) Drawing conclusions

Continued on page 626

5. LITERARY CONCEPT: Character
Ask students to describe what they learn about Wambuna's character from the narrator's description. (*Possible response: She is beautiful, cheerful, and proud.*) Ask students what similarities they can find in the characters of Kelfala and Wambuna. (*Possible responses: They are both charming in their own way; the narrator describes each of them as an irresistible "darling."*)

6. ACTIVE READING: Review
Ask how the narrator of this story tries to draw readers in and engage their sympathy for the characters and their problems. (*Possible responses: by addressing readers directly and asking them questions, by suggesting that readers would feel the way the characters do, by warning readers about what is important*) Ask which other story uses similar techniques. (*"The People Could Fly"*)

7. LITERARY CONCEPT: Character
Ask students why they think Kelfala behaves as he does. (*He wishes to win Wambuna by making her speak.*) What does this tell you about him? (*Possible responses: He is very self-confident; he is sure he can charm anyone.*)

8. ACTIVE READING: Predict
Invite students to predict what plan or secret Kelfala has in mind to win Wambuna. Encourage students to provide details based on what they already know about the characters and setting of the story.

smooth as a mirror. Her mahogany-brown arms swayed gracefully by her sides, keeping time with her swaying hips. When she laughed, she showed ivory-white teeth. And just a smile from Wambuna sent warm thrills through clownish Kelfala. Her head she carried erect, and the rings sat on her neck like rows of diamonds on a crown. The more Kelfala watched, the more he wanted Wambuna for his own.

But she had an endless stream of suitors. (If you could have seen her, you would not mind even being last, as long as you were in line.) Some of these young men went to her father to ask for Wambuna. That was tradition. But many had heard his loud "No-No" and tried to trick Wambuna, instead. But do you think she talked to the young men around? Well! You wait and see.

Always they paid their visits to her at the garden, always when the elders were having their rest from the hot midday sun.

"Wambuna, let me get you water from the stream."

"Ay'ee, Wambuna, I hit my toe against a stone. It is gushing out blood!"

"Wambuna, your plants are not growing at all. You are so lazy. Yambuyi's plants are better than yours, lazy you!"

"Wambuna, hear your father? He is snoring so hard under this hot sun, he has driven all the animals away!"

But Wambuna's lips were sealed, and all this teasing and coaxing only kept her lips tighter. She would not even raise her head to smile. She worked in silence, and if she talked at all, she only whispered kind things to her plants.

Now Kelfala joined the line, too. And—

tradition or not—he would not risk the father's "No-No." Why? He, Kelfala, the clown? Kelfala, who could coax words and laughter out of trees? He would get Wambuna to speak!

He tried his hippopotamus face, to get her to shout in fear. He turned into a leopard, springing into Wambuna's path when she was alone, so she would cry for help. He hid behind a clump of trees and became Wambuna's mother, asking questions and questions and questions that needed answers.

But Wambuna's lips were sealed.

The stream of suitors grew smaller, like the village stream itself, shrinking and shrinking in the dry season when the rains have stopped. But Kelfala did not give up. Finally, he confided in two friends that he had a something that would win Wambuna for him. A secret something. (He did not tell them what.)

For two weeks Kelfala and his two friends, Shortie Bumpie and Longie Tallie, trailed Wambuna and her family as they went to the farm. Then Kelfala's day came. They spied Wambuna going alone to the farm with her basket balanced on her head. He and Shortie Bumpie and Longie Tallie set out behind her, *kunye, kunye, kunye,* as if they were treading on hot coals. They stood behind the trees and bushes, unseen by anyone but themselves, and waited.

On this day, Kelfala had put on his best dress. But if you had seen him, you would think that he was the most unlikely suitor for a young girl. His dress was rags and tatters. He had rubbed grease all over his body, mud on his head, and funny chalk marks on his face. He also had painted his front teeth with red-black clay.

Guided Reading for Less-Proficient Students

Continued from page 625

E. Why does the Gituyu on Wambuna's fire make her speak? (*In Kenya, the Gituyu is considered unfit to eat; Wambuna is shocked.*) Inferring

F. How does Kelfala's plan fail? (*Wambuna speaks to all three men instead of Kelfala alone, so he cannot claim her for himself.*) Summarizing

9. ACTIVE READING: Review
Have students working in small groups
scan the story for details about the
Kikuyu world, culture, and beliefs. Have
each group present its deductions about
aspects of Kikuyu life.

10. LITERARY CONCEPT: Suspense
Have students describe how the author
builds suspense in this part of the story.
*(Possible responses: He reveals the
details of Kelfala's plan gradually,
keeping secret the meaning of Kelfala's
actions; he implies that soon Kelfala
and Wambuna will be married.)*

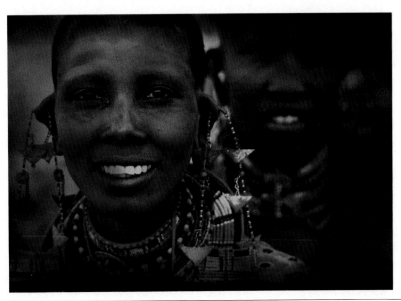

© 1991 by Robert
Vavra.

The birds were twitting happily as they caught worms on the dewy grass. Nearby, the stream was flowing by, its waters dazzling in the early morning sunlight. From time to time Kelfala opened his sack, touched his something, and smiled to himself.

Wambuna started working hard and fast. Indeed, she was racing the sun. By the time the sun got halfway on its journey, she hoped to have gotten to the end of hers. She only stopped her work for a moment, went to the stream with her calabash[2] for water, then returned and kindled a fire. She took some yams from her little basket, put them on the hot coals, and returned to her plants. She was weeding the new grasses on her tea beds.

Kelfala's opportunity had come. Soon, Kelfala, the clown, Kelfala, the funny one, would be married to the most beautiful, the most gentle, the mildest lady on Kilimanjaro. At least, that is what Kelfala thought.

Kelfala spied here, there, and everywhere from his hiding, stepped out into the open, and hopped and skipped to the fireplace. Out of his sack he pulled his something and placed it on the hot coals beside Wambuna's yams. Then he squatted on the largest fire stone and poled the red-hot coals. Shoving Wambuna's yams aside, he uttered a throaty chuckle, which he quickly trapped with his hands. He glanced again at the

---

2. **calabash** (kal′ ə bash′): the dried hollow shell of a gourd, used as a bowl.

Multicultural Connections

Marriage In some African and other societies, marriages are arranged by young people's parents. That's why some suitors ask Wambuna's father for her. Her only other option is to marry the first man outside her own family with whom she speaks.

Ask students how they might feel if they had to follow such traditions. Do arranged marriages have any advantages? What wisdom might be found in the Kikuyu tradition?

Homemaking In Kenyan society, women generally accept the traditional roles of cooking meals and raising children, while men leave the home to work. In modern U.S. society, many women work outside the home, arranging day care for their children.

Ask students how they might feel if they lived in Kenyan society. If they were parents, what advantages or disadvantages would there be? Would they prefer it to life in the United States? Why or why not?

fireplace, and like a cock ready to peck at the yams, he tittered quietly to himself. But again he quickly stopped himself.

But only for a moment, for suddenly more chuckles escaped, and Kelfala howled like a ruffled owl. He hooted the monkeys out of the tree tops. He rolled himself into a ball as he rolled and rolled with laughter. Kelfala, the laughing clown. He laughed and he laughed and he laughed.

Now, the bush came alive. Shortie Bumpie and Longie Tallie poked their heads out to see what was happening. At first they twitched their faces and cocked their ears. But as Kelfala rolled on and on, and the laughter rolled on and on, it dragged the two young men with it.

Wambuna—who had to poke her fire—tried to sneak past the hooting trio, but the loud roars quickly sank into *her* bones. Oh, how silly those three idle friends! Kelfala, that clown Kelfala! But as she watched them, her grin turned into a broad smile, *her* smile turned into a shy laugh, and without realizing it, she became one of the howling trio. She was all fits of laughter. Oh! How the tears ran down Wambuna's eyes.

All four laughed and laughed, laughed and laughed and laughed.

When all at once Kelfala stood, with arms akimbo[3] and stomach shot forward, and pointed to Wambuna's fireplace.

"A beautiful girl like you," he laughed, "proud as the cotton tree and the greatest cook in the village, you, you roast a Gituyu with your yams!"

Wambuna turned around.

There by the giant firestone, on the ashes, was Kelfala's something. A shrunken, old, burnt Gituyu!

Wambuna caught her breath, looked from Kelfala to his friends, and cried out between tears and laughter. "A Gituyu! It cannot be. It cannot . . ."

But at that Kelfala threw up his arms. "Aha! You have spoken to Kelfala. Kelfala, the great, Kelfala, the clown! Kelfala, the cunning one. Kelfala, the proud husband of a proud wife!"

The laughter was mine, see, I started it.

"Wait a minute, Kelfala," one of his friends said. "Kelfala, I tell you now, she doesn't belong to you."

"Oh no, you Shortie Bumpie? The trick was mine, see?" and with that, Kelfala hopped.

"The plan was mine, see?" and with that, Kelfala skipped.

"The secret was mine, see?" and with that, he jumped.

"The Gituyu was mine, see? My secret something! And the laughter was mine, see, I started it." And with that, he laughed and laughed and laughed. . . .

Wambuna stood, amazed, but she soon found support in Shortie Bumpie and Longie Tallie.

"I know that a man has had three wives, but never on this whole mountain has ever a woman shared three husbands," retorted Shortie Bumpie.

---

3. **akimbo** (ə kim′ bō) : with hands on hips and elbows bent outward.

"Yes, Kelfala, this girl either belongs to all of us . . . or none of us," cried the other friend.

You could see Kelfala's heart heaving.

"What did you say? You, Longie Tallie?" Wambuna lifted her eyes.

"Yes," Longie Tallie went on. "Wambuna laughed at you. She cried at you. She mumbled, she grumbled at you. She laughed-cried. She laughed-mumbled-cried at you. But she talked to all three of us!"

Wambuna pressed her lips together in a quiet, sly smile and looked into Kelfala's eyes. Then she walked back to her plants with her head raised up like a large pink rose in early spring.

15

Kelfala just looked, his head bowed like a weeping willow. But then he tapped his bag and grinned. "Today is only for today. There is still tomorrow. There will always be another secret."

16

That was tradition, too. 🐾

◄ F

Responding to Reading

1. Jot down your first impression of Kelfala.

2. Do you think Kelfala earns the right to fulfill his dream and marry Wambuna? Why or why not?

3. On the basis of this story, what qualities in men and women do you think the Kikuyu people value?

4. In what ways are Kelfala and Lazy Peter similar? How are they different?

Ask students what they think Wambuna has decided. (Possible responses: She doesn't have to marry any of them; they are too foolish for her; she really wants to marry Kelfala but is biding her time.)

16. LITERARY CONCEPT: Resolution
Ask students how Kelfala's final observation changes the end of the story. (Possible responses: It suggests that the story is not over, that he will try again and maybe win her next time; without this last remark, the story would have ended with Kelfala's defeat.)

Responding to Reading

1. Any response is valid.

2. Possible responses: Yes, because he is clever and charming and because he got her to speak; no, because he tricked her and because she did not speak only to him; no, because she doesn't want to marry him—after all, she could speak to him any time she wanted to.

3. Possible responses: In men, they value cleverness, persistence, and charm; in women, they value beauty, dignity, and hard work. In both, they value a sense of humor.

4. Possible responses: Kelfala and Lazy Peter both use cleverness and trickery to get what they want; both are ambitious schemers. Lazy Peter is more dishonest than Kelfala is; Kelfala is playful and good-humored, but Peter is not.

ENCOURAGING INDEPENDENT READING

Fourteen Hundred Cowries and Other African Tales, folk tales collected by Abayomi Fuja

The People Could Fly: American Black Folktales, retold by Virginia Hamilton

Gods, Heroes and Men of Ancient Greece, nonfiction by W. H. D. Rouse

---

✓ Comprehension Check

1. What favor does Phaëthon ask of Apollo? (to drive Apollo's sun chariot across the sky)

2. Why doesn't Apollo want to grant the request? (No one is capable of driving the chariot but Apollo)

3. How is Phaëthon finally stopped? (Zeus shoots him to earth with a thunderbolt.)

4. Who are the people who could fly? (slaves working in the fields; Africans brought here as slaves.)

5. How does Toby help the people? (He speaks magic words that enable them to fly away.)

6. What does Kelfala want? (to marry Wambuna)

7. How does Kelfala get Wambuna to speak? (He puts a Gituyu on her fire.)

8. Why doesn't Kelfala win Wambuna? (She speaks to three men, not to Kelfala alone.)

Student Response

Responding to Reading

1. Any response is valid.

2. Possible responses: "Phaëthon": to warn against overconfidence, to teach a lesson about obeying parents, to explain the origin of deserts; "The People Could Fly": to celebrate the spirit of freedom; to give hope to those still enslaved, to praise the strength and courage of slaves who escaped; "Kelfala's Secret Something": to teach Kenyan traditions, to entertain

3. Possible responses: Both are young men with high aspirations; both are persistent. Phaëthon's goal challenges authority, whereas Kelfala's goal is romantic and within accepted tradition; Phaëthon acts rashly but Kelfala plans carefully; Phaëthon is bold and direct, but Kelfala is wily and devious.

Challenge Question

How would you compare Phaëthon with Keevan in "The Smallest Dragonboy"? (Possible responses: Both set a high goal, but Keevan prepares and works to attain his, whereas Phaëthon wants an instant reward; Keevan is humble, but Phaëthon is conceited; each wants to be like his father.)

Literary Concept: Symbol

It might be a symbol of freedom, of escape from slavery, or of power to rise above oppression.

Writing Options

The Writing Options are designed to meet varied student interests and abilities. Have each student choose one writing activity to complete.

Journal Update Have students decide which of the stories would make the best movie and explain their choice.

Vocabulary Practice

Answers to Exercise

1. croon   4. dissuade
2. abode   5. sear
3. acknowledge

---

*R*esponding to Reading

Comparing the Selections

1. In your opinion, which of the characters' dreams should have been easiest to fulfill? Which should have been hardest? Why?

2. What do you think is the purpose of each story? How do the purposes differ?

3. How are Phaëthon and Kelfala alike and different?

*L*iterary Concept: Symbol

A **symbol** is a person, a thing, or an event that stands for something beyond itself, such as an idea or a group of people. For example, in Greek mythology, Zeus carries a thunderbolt, which is a symbol of his power. In "The People Could Fly," what might flying be a symbol of?

*W*riting Options

1. Think of a character in Unit 3 who tried to fulfill a dream. In a brief **essay,** contrast this character with Phaëthon.

2. Write an **article** for the *Kikuyu News*, headlined "Flash! Wambuna Speaks!" Then, using your imagination, tell the story of how Kelfala finally wins the right to marry Wambuna.

*V*ocabulary Practice

Exercise   Write the word from the list that is closest in meaning to the boldfaced word.

1. Her baby cried, but Sarah had no heart to **sing.**
2. Apollo's **home** was a palace of glittering gold.
3. He was happy to **admit** that Phaëthon was his son.
4. Apollo couldn't **discourage** his son from wanting to drive the chariot.
5. Phaëthon didn't mean to **burn** the earth.

> *Words to Know and Use*
>
> **abode**
> **acknowledge**
> **croon**
> **dissuade**
> **sear**

The Spelling Connection

Spelling Pattern: Prefixes and Roots A root, or fundamental word element, can be joined to many different prefixes. Changing the prefix forms a new word with a different meaning.

Examples: **con** + clude = **con**clude
              ex + clude = **ex**clude

Prefixes/Roots in Words from the Selections
evidence/**pro**vidence   **dis**suade/**per**suade
erect/**cor**rect   **sup**port/**re**port   resisted/insisted

Other Words with Prefixes and Roots

description   **pre**vention   **de**cision
inscription   **con**vention   **pre**cision

Exercise Fill in each blank with a spelling word.

The executives met in their annual __1__ to discuss environmental problems. One member read a __2__ that called for __3__, not just intervention after a crisis. "Let's make up our minds to __4__ problems quickly," __5__ a member. Everyone agreed to __6__ that __7__.

*O*ptions for Learning (Multimodal/Cross-Curricular Activities)

1 • Myth Maker   Create a myth to explain the origin of a natural occurrence, such as a volcano eruption. You may use Greek gods or gods you create. Share your myth with your classmates.

2 • Cover Art   Design a book jacket for a book containing one of these tales. Create an inviting illustration and share your drawing with the class.

---

*M*oira Kerr   1938–

Moira Kerr wrote her own versions of myths when her students did not enjoy the versions they were reading. She joined her artist friend John Bennett to create an illustrated book, *Myth.*

Born in Canada, Kerr taught for several years in Toronto. She now works in Oklahoma as a psychologist and is studying for her doctorate in ministry. "Much of my interest in life," Kerr says, "has been exploring the deep wisdom which lies within all of us."

*V*irginia Hamilton   1936–

Virginia Hamilton's future brightened when she received a college scholarship. Later, she began working on a children's story she had started in college, which became *Zeely,* her first book. In 1975 she became the first black writer to win the Newbery Medal, for her book *M. C. Higgins, the Great.* She speaks from her own family's experience when she writes about escaping slaves. Hamilton's great-grandmother is said to have been a conductor on the Underground Railroad.

*A*djai Robinson   1932–

Growing up in Sierra Leone, Adjai Robinson listened to storytellers recount wonderful tales. Later, he began to record folk tales and became a storyteller on the radio. Robinson came to the United States to lead workshops about African folklore and to attend Columbia University. In 1975 he moved to Nigeria to become principal education officer at the Nigeria Teachers Institute. Robinson has since published a number of children's books.

Cross-Curricular Projects

Science Have students do research on the sun—its temperature, diameter, and so forth—and on interesting sun-related subjects, such as solar energy and the solstice. Invite them to share their information with the class.

Music Have students research African American spirituals and songs of freedom. Hold a "music hour" in which some of these songs are played in class, with information given about each one. Students may also wish to compose their own freedom songs.

Home Arts Have students research Kikuyu cuisine and prepare a meal that Wambuna might have made, including meats, yams, vegetables, roasted peanuts, and sauces. Allow them to serve the meal in class.

Extending the Lesson

Options for Learning

These activities suit a variety of learning styles and modes of expression.

Collaborative Learning Activities
See Option 1.

1. Myth Maker Encourage students to read explanatory myths from several cultures before they make up their own.

2. Cover Art Suggest that students review their favorite book covers to get ideas about what elements their work should include.

Virginia Hamilton

■ **More About the Author** Hamilton has said that "the slaves . . . had no power, no weapons to aid them in overcoming their oppressors. So it was that they used the folklore they created . . . to give themselves comfort and strength through endless hard times."

■ **Other Works** Novels: *The Planet of Junior Brown, Jahdu, The House of Dies Drear*

 ■ **Awards** Coretta Scott King Award, Edgar Allan Poe Award, National Book Award

Adjai Robinson

■ **More About the Author** Robinson has said, "Each book that I have written for boys and girls is also a book I have written for myself . . . since, if I don't find the story exciting or interesting or funny . . . I don't think boys and girls will either."

■ **Other Works** Novels: *Femi and Old Grandaddie, Kasho and the Twin Flutes;* story collection: *Singing Tales of Africa*

Closure

In these stories, the characters' aspirations are made more meaningful by the obstacles that stand in their way. Point out to students how in the tales the practices and beliefs of the cultures in which they live create the obstacles that the characters must overcome.

Objectives

■ To understand and analyze myths and a legend

■ To analyze the qualities of a hero or heroine and to review the concept of symbolism

■ To enrich reading by understanding character motivation

■ To express understanding of the myths and legend through a choice of writing forms, including a myth and dialogue

Prereading/Motivation

Examine What You Know

Discussion Prompts What people in American history are remembered for their self-sacrifice? What legends are told about them? Do you remember hearing any of them as a child?

Expand Your Knowledge

Additional Background The heroic figures in the Greek and Norse myths have been celebrated in many ways. Prometheus is the hero of the Greek drama *Prometheus Bound* by Aeschylus, and the inspiration for artistic works by Beethoven, Goethe, and Shelley. Odin, whose Anglo-Saxon name is Woden, is the god for whom Wednesday (originally Woden's day) was named.

The Native American legend, "Where the Girl Saved Her Brother," provides a contemporary example of a legend that has its origin in an important historical event.

Thematic Link— Person to Person

Each main character shows a strong commitment to others. Prometheus cares so deeply about humans that he violates the will of Zeus to help them. Buffalo Calf Road Woman risks her life to save her brother in battle. Odin gives up an eye in order to help people on earth.

Person to Person

Links to Unit Four	*Prometheus* BERNARD EVSLIN
	Where the Girl Saved Her Brother RACHEL STRANGE OWL
	How Odin Lost His Eye CATHARINE F. SELLEW

*E*xamine What You Know (Prior Knowledge)

Almost every culture has myths and legends about people or gods who sacrifice themselves for others, or who risk doing so. Can you think of any myths or legends about great sacrifice? Why are such stories appealing or important? Discuss your ideas with your class.

*E*xpand Your Knowledge (Building Background)

"Prometheus" (prō mē′ thē əs) tells about the sacrifice made by a Greek god to serve humanity. Prometheus and his brother Epimetheus (ep′ ə mē′ thē əs) belonged to the oldest generation of gods, the giant Titans. They were the only two Titans who had sided with Zeus in his battle against his father Cronus (crō′ nəs), another Titan, to become supreme ruler. After his victory Zeus ordered Prometheus to create human beings. As you will see, Prometheus and Zeus disagreed about how to treat the humans.

"Where the Girl Saved Her Brother" describes a woman who risked her own life for her brother. This Native American legend is about the Battle of the Rosebud, which took place in southern Montana on June 17, 1876. This version is told by Rachel Strange Owl, a present-day Cheyenne. Such legends have been used as a way of passing along Native American history.

"How Odin Lost His Eye" is a myth that tells about the efforts of the mightiest Norse (Scandinavian) god to protect human beings. Odin lived with other Norse gods in a heavenly realm called Asgard. From his tall throne he watched over the humans whom he had created. Odin hoped to guard humans from his enemies, the evil frost giants, who roamed an icy realm called Jotunnheim.

*W*rite Before You Read (Journal Writing)

■ *Author biographies on Extend page*

What is the most memorable story of sacrifice for the good of others that you have heard? Summarize the story in a few sentences. As you read, compare that story with the selections.

632   UNIT SIX   THEMES IN WORLD FOLKLORE

MORE JOURNAL WRITING IDEAS

■ Write about a time you were asked to sacrifice something and tell how you felt about it.
■ Of all the people whom you know, who is the most concerned about others? Describe that person.

COLLABORATIVE LEARNING OPTIONS

Opportunities for collaborative learning include Literary Concept Review (p. 643), the vocabulary activity for Alternative Learning Styles (p. 643), Options for Learning activity 2 (p. 644), and Cross-Curricular Projects (p. 644).

ADDITIONAL RESOURCES

Unit Six Resource Book
Reader's Guidesheet, p. 25
Reading Skills, p. 26
Literature Skills, p. 27
Vocabulary Connections, p. 28
Spelling Connections, p. 29
Comprehension and Vocabulary Check Tests, p. 30
Selection Test, pp. 31–32

Prometheus

BERNARD EVSLIN

Prometheus was a young Titan, no great admirer of Zeus. Although he knew the great lord of the sky hated explicit questions, he did not hesitate to beard[1] him when there was something he wanted to know.

One morning he came to Zeus and said, "O Thunderer, I do not understand your design. You have caused the race of man to appear on earth, but you keep him in ignorance and darkness."

"Perhaps you had better leave the race of man to me," said Zeus. "What you call ignorance is innocence. What you call darkness is the shadow of my decree. Man is happy now. And he is so framed that he will remain happy unless someone persuades him that he is unhappy. Let us not speak of this again."

But Prometheus said, "Look at him. Look below. He crouches in caves. He is at the mercy of beast and weather. He eats his meat raw. If you mean something by this, enlighten me with your wisdom. Tell me why you refuse to give man the gift of fire."

Zeus answered, "Do you not know, Prometheus, that every gift brings a penalty? This is the way the Fates[2] weave destiny–by which gods also must abide.

Man does not have fire, true, nor the crafts which fire teaches. On the other hand, he does not know disease, warfare, old age, or that inward pest called worry. He is happy, I say, happy without fire. And so he shall remain."

"Happy as beasts are happy," said Prometheus. "Of what use to make a separate race called man and endow him with little fur, some wit, and a curious charm of unpredictability? If he must live like this, why separate him from the beasts at all?"

"He has another quality," said Zeus, "the capacity for worship. An aptitude for admiring our power, being puzzled by our riddles and amazed by our caprice.[3] That is why he was made."

"Would not fire, and the graces he can put on with fire, make him more interesting?"

"More interesting, perhaps, but infinitely more dangerous. For there is this in man too: a vaunting pride that needs little sustenance to make it swell to giant size. Improve his lot, and he will forget that

---

1. **beard**: to face up to.
2. **Fates**: in Greek mythology, the three goddesses who decide the course of people's lives.
3. **caprice** (kə prēs'): the quality of acting impulsively.

Words to Know and Use

explicit (eks plis' it) *adj.* plain; straightforward
endow (en dou') *v.* to provide with a quality or a talent
aptitude (ap' tə tood') *n.* a natural ability
sustenance (sus' tə nəns) *n.* nourishment; assistance

633

Teaching Strategies

VOCABULARY PREVIEW

These vocabulary words are defined at the bottom of the selection page on which they appear.

aptitude a natural ability

endow to provide with a quality

explicit straightforward

hover to fly over as if suspended

sustenance nourishment

LIMITED ENGLISH PROFICIENCY

■ Use the Reader's Guidesheet, *Unit Six Resource Book*, page 25.

■ The dialogue in "Prometheus" and "How Odin Lost His Eye" may sound unnatural to some students. You may wish to have them read the dialogue aloud to clarify meaning.

★ Text annotations marked with a red star ("Prometheus": 3, 5; "Where the Girl Saved Her Brother": 7) may be particularly helpful for students with limited English proficiency.

TEXT ANNOTATIONS

1. LITERARY CONCEPT: Symbol
Prometheus addresses Zeus as "Thunderer" because Zeus was originally a god of the sky, and one of his symbols was the thunderbolt. Ask students why they think thunder was chosen as a symbol for the king of the gods. *(Possible responses: because of its loudness and power; because people may have been in awe of thunder and lightning.)*

2. ACTIVE READING: Review
Why does Zeus believe that man is better off without the gift of fire? *(Possible responses: Man does not need fire because he is already happy without it; fire would bring penalties as well as benefits to man.)*

3. VOCABULARY: Definition
If students are unfamiliar with the word *vaunting*, help them use context clues or a dictionary to determine its meaning of "boasting or bragging." ★

Guided Reading for Less-Proficient Students

These questions can help guide students through the reading. Ask each question at the point of the selection where the capital letter and arrow appear in the margin. In addition, you may wish to use appropriate Active Reading annotations.

A. How do Zeus and Prometheus differ in their views of man? *(Zeus sees man as innocent and happy; Prometheus sees man as ignorant and in darkness.)* Recalling

B. Why does Prometheus want men to have fire? *(He*

knows it will help them if they use it properly.) Inferring

C. How has fire changed men's lives? *(Fire led to the development of farming, towns, industry, exploration, and war.)* Summarizing

D. What does Zeus predict men will do with fire? *(destroy themselves)* Recalling

E. Why does Zeus make Prometheus' punishment so severe? *(He has disobeyed Zeus and changed the course of human life.)* Inferring

PROMETHEUS CARRYING FIRE Jan Cossiers The Prado, Madrid Bridgeman/Art Resource, New York.

which makes him pleasing–his sense of worship, his humility. He will grow big and poisoned with pride and fancy himself a god, and before we know it, we shall see him storming Olympus. Enough, Prometheus! I have been patient with you, but do not try me too far. Go now and trouble me no more with your speculations."

Prometheus was not satisfied. All that night he lay awake making plans. Then he left his couch at dawn and, standing tiptoe on Olympus, stretched his arm to the eastern horizon where the first faint flames of the sun were flickering. In his hand he held

a reed filled with a dry fiber; he thrust it into the sunrise until a spark smoldered. Then he put the reed in his tunic and came down from the mountain.

At first men were frightened by the gift. It was so hot, so quick; it bit sharply when you touched it, and for pure spite made the shadows dance. They thanked Prometheus and asked him to take it away. But he took the haunch[4] of a newly killed deer and held it over the fire. And when the meat began to sear and sputter, filling the cave with its rich smells, the people felt themselves melting with hunger and flung themselves on the meat and devoured it greedily, burning their tongues.

"This that I have brought you is called 'fire,'" Prometheus said. "It is an ill-natured spirit, a little brother of the sun, but if you handle it carefully, it can change your whole life. It is very greedy; you must feed it twigs, but only until it becomes a proper size. Then you must stop, or it will eat everything in sight—and you too. If it escapes, use this magic: water. It fears the water spirit, and if you touch it with water, it will fly away until you need it again."

He left the fire burning in the first cave, with children staring at it wide-eyed, and then went to every cave in the land.

Then one day Zeus looked down from the mountain and was amazed. Everything had changed. Man had come out of his cave. Zeus saw woodmen's huts, farmhouses, villages, walled towns, even a castle or two. He saw men cooking their food, carrying torches to light their way at night. He saw forges blazing, men beating out

---

4. **haunch:** the hip and leg of an animal.

Speaking . . . Listening . . . Viewing

Listening Several musical compositions have been based on the myth of Prometheus. Have students listen to any of the following musical works:

■ *Prometheus*, a symphonic poem by Franz Liszt, 1850
■ *The Creatures of Prometheus*, a ballet with music by Ludwig van Beethoven, opus 43, 1801
■ *Prometheus, the Poem of Fire*, a symphonic poem by Aleksandr Scriabin, opus 60, 1908

After students listen to the composition, discuss the following questions:

1. What feelings did you experience while listening?

2. Did the music seem to fit the heroic subject matter? Why or why not?

3. Why do you think the story of Prometheus has appealed to so many artists?

ploughs, keels, swords, spears. They were making ships and raising white wings of sails and daring to use the fury of the winds for their journeys. They were wearing helmets, riding out in chariots to do battle, like the gods themselves.

Zeus was full of rage. He seized his largest thunderbolt. "So they want fire," he said to himself. "I'll give them fire—more than they can use. I'll turn their miserable little ball of earth into a cinder." But then another thought came to him, and he lowered his arm. "No," he said to himself, "I shall have vengeance—and entertainment too. Let them destroy themselves with their new skills. This will make a long, twisted game, interesting to watch. I'll attend to them later. My first business is with Prometheus."

He called his giant guards and had them seize Prometheus, drag him off to the Caucasus,[5] and there bind him to a mountain peak with great chains specially forged by Hephaestus[6]—chains which even a Titan in agony could not break. And when the friend of man was bound to the mountain, Zeus sent two vultures to <u>hover</u> about him forever, tearing at his belly and eating his liver.

Men knew a terrible thing was happening on the mountain, but they did not know what. But the wind shrieked like a giant in torment and sometimes like fierce birds.

Many centuries he lay there—until another hero was born brave enough to defy the gods. He climbed to the peak in the Caucasus and struck the shackles[7] from Prometheus and killed the vultures. His name was Heracles. 🐌

---

5. **Caucasus** (kô′ kə səs): a mountainous region in southeastern Europe, between the Black and Caspian seas.
6. **Hephaestus** (hē fes′ təs): in Greek mythology, the god of fire and metalworking.
7. **shackles**: metal bands for holding the ankles or wrists of a prisoner.

Responding to Reading

1. What were your first impressions of Zeus and Prometheus? In your journal write down words and phrases to describe them.

2. Prometheus views fire as a great gift, while Zeus focuses on the "penalty" that such a gift brings. In your opinion, which god makes the most sense in his views on human beings and fire?

   Think about
   • the changes that Prometheus' gift brings to people's lives
   • Zeus' dark predictions about humans
   • whether fire brings humans greater happiness

3. Prometheus knows that it is dangerous to anger Zeus. Why do you think he risks so much to help humans?

Words to Know and Use	**hover** (huv′ ər) *v.* to fly or flutter over a place as if suspended

635

7. ACTIVE READING: Review
What have men done since receiving the gift of fire? (Possible responses: Men have used it for cooking and for making tools and ships; they have used it to make weapons for war.)

8. LANGUAGE: Sexist Terms
Discuss the fact that throughout the myth the author refers to "man" and "men" when he really means "people" or "human beings." Explain that until recent times it was accepted practice for authors to use male terms to refer to people in general.

9. LITERARY CONCEPT: Hero
By using the phrase "another hero," the narrator implies that Prometheus is a hero for his actions. Ask students if they believe Prometheus is a hero or a villain for what he has done, and why. (Possible responses: He is a hero because he has given man a gift that may be very beneficial if used properly; he is a villain because he has made it possible for men to make war with one another.)

Responding to Reading

1. Any response is valid.

2. Possible responses: Zeus, because human beings use fire to make war; Prometheus, because fire gives human beings the potential for great accomplishments; Prometheus, because he gives humans knowledge.

3. Possible responses: He cares deeply about humans; he hates to see humans suffer and live in primitive ways, knowing they could be much more advanced than animals; humans are his creation, and he wants his work to be the best it can be.

2. LITERARY CONCEPT: Narrator
Ask students how the narrator's telling of the story reflects the Native Americans' point of view. *(Possible responses: She refers to reservations as "prisons"; she says that the white men wanted the Native Americans to give up their freedom and way of life; she implies that those who followed the orders were weak.)*

NATIVE AMERICAN LEGEND

Where the Girl Saved Her Brother

Told by RACHEL STRANGE OWL

Almost exactly a hundred years ago, in the summer of 1876, the two greatest battles between soldiers and Indians were fought on the plains of Montana. The first fight was called the Battle of the Rosebud. The second battle, which was fought a week later, was called the Battle of the Little Big Horn, where General Custer was defeated and killed. The Cheyennes call the Battle of the Rosebud the fight "Where the Girl Saved Her Brother." Let me tell you why.

But first let me explain what is meant when an Indian says, "I have counted coup." "Counting coup" is gaining war honors. The Indians think that it is easy to kill an enemy by shooting him from ambush. This brings no honor. It is not counting coup. But to ride up to an enemy, or walk up to him while he is still alive, unwounded and armed, and then to hit him with your feathered coup stick, or touch him with your hand, this brings honor and earns you eagle feathers. This is counting coup. To steal horses in a daring raid can also be counting coup. But one of the greatest honors is to be gained by dashing with your horse into the midst of your enemies to rescue a friend, surrounded and unhorsed, to

take him up behind you and gallop out again, saving his life by risking your own. That is counting coup indeed, counting big coup.

Well, a hundred years ago, the white men wanted the Indians to go into prisons called "reservations," to give up their freedom to roam and hunt buffalo, to give up being Indians. Some gave in tamely and went to live behind the barbed wire of the agencies, but others did not.

Those who went to the reservations to live like white men were called "friendlies." Those who would not go were called "hostiles." They were not hostile, really. They did not want to fight. All they wanted was to be left alone to live the Indian way, which was a good way. But the soldiers would not let them. They decided to make a great surround and catch all "hostiles," kill those who resisted, and bring the others back as prisoners to the agencies. Three columns of soldiers entered the last stretch of land left to the red man. They were led by Generals Crook, Custer, and Terry. Crook had the most men with him, about two thousand. He also had cannon and Indian scouts to guide him. At the Rosebud he met the united Sioux and Cheyenne warriors.

Guided Reading for Less-Proficient Students

These questions can help guide students through the reading. Ask each question at the point in the selection where the capital letter and arrow appear in the margin. In addition, you may wish to use appropriate Active Reading annotations.

A. Why does counting coup bring honor? *(It reveals a person's courage.)* Inferring

B. What problem do the Native Americans face? *(White men want to imprison them on reservations.)* Recalling

C. Why do the "hostiles" refuse to go to reservations? *(It means losing their land, their way of living, and their freedom; it means giving up their identity.)* Clarifying

D. How does Buffalo Calf Road Woman rescue her brother? *(She rides into the battle with a loud war cry, he jumps on her horse, and they ride away.)* Summarizing

E. What effect does her heroism have on the outcome of the battle? *(The enemy retreats.)* Recalling

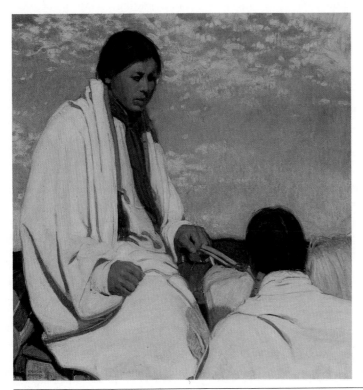

THE ENCOUNTER © 1920 Ernest Martin Hennings Courtesy, The Anschutz Collection, Denver.

3

The Indians had danced the sacred Sun Dance. The great Sioux chief Sitting Bull had been granted a vision telling him that the soldiers would be defeated. The warriors were in high spirits. Some men belonging to famous warrior societies had vowed to fight until they were killed, singing their death songs, throwing their lives away, as it was called. They painted their faces for war. They put on their finest outfits so that, if they were killed, their enemies should say, "This must have been a great fighter or chief. See how nobly he lies there."

The old chiefs instructed the young men how to act. The medicine men prepared the charms for the fighters, putting gopher dust on their hair, or painting their horses with hailstone designs. This was to render them invisible to their foes, or to make them bulletproof. Brave Wolf had the most admired medicine—a mounted hawk that he fastened to the back of his head. Brave Wolf always rode into battle blowing on his eaglebone

4

WHERE THE GIRL SAVED HER BROTHER 637

Multicultural Connections

Reservations The narrator of this legend expresses the view of many Native Americans when she describes the reservations as "prisons." Native Americans both past and present have resented white society forcing them off their land and altering their way of life.

Ask students how they might feel as a Sioux or Cheyenne in Montana in 1876. How would they have responded to the orders to move to a reservation? Why?

Government Policy In the 1800s, the U.S. government tried to justify moving Native Americans off their land. They claimed that they needed the land for expansion of the railroad and for pioneers settling in the area. Today, many Native American groups are demanding that their lands be returned to them.

Ask students to imagine they are U.S. officials today. Would they agree to the return of land or to other forms of compensation? Why or why not?

5. ACTIVE READING: Question
What do Crazy Horse's words indicate about his philosophy of war? *(Possible responses: He believes it is better to die a hero in battle than to live as a coward; he believes there are "good days" and "bad days" on which to fight, possibly determined by visions from the spirits.)*

6. ACTIVE READING: Review
Some students may be confused by the mention of white Crow scouts fighting on the side of the soldiers and against the other Native Americans. Remind them that the U.S. army generals used Native American scouts as guides. These scouts were looked upon as traitors by the other Native Americans.

7. VOCABULARY: Definitions
If students are unfamiliar with the words *trilling* and *undulating*, help them use **context clues** to understand that both words refer to "vibrating sounds."

For Alternative Learning Styles Invite a volunteer to make a trilling, undulating sound. ★

whistle—and once the fight started, the hawk came alive and whistled too.

Many proud tribes were there besides the Cheyenne—the Hunkpapa, the Minniconjou, the Oglala, the Burned Thighs, the Two Kettles—and many famous chiefs and brave warriors—Two Moons, White Bull, Dirty Moccasins, Little Hawk, Yellow Eagle, Lame White Man. Among the Sioux was the great Crazy Horse, and Sitting Bull—their holy man still weak from his flesh offerings made at the Sun Dance—and the fierce Rain-in-the-Face. Who can count them all, and what a fine sight they were!

Those who earned the right to wear war bonnets were singing, lifting them up. Three times they stopped in their singing, and the fourth time they put the bonnets on their heads, letting the streamers fly and trail behind them. How good it must have been to see this! What would I give to have been there!

5 Crazy Horse of the Oglala shouted his famous war cry, "A good day to die, and a good day to fight. Cowards to the rear, brave hearts—follow me!"

The fight started. Many brave deeds were done, many coups counted. The battle swayed to and fro. More than anybody else's, this was the Cheyenne's fight. This was their day. Among them was a brave young girl, Buffalo Calf Road Woman, who rode proudly at the side of her husband, Black Coyote. Her brother, Chief Comes-in-Sight, was in the battle too. She looked for him and at last saw him. His horse had been killed from under him. He was surrounded. Soldiers were aiming their rifles at him. Their white Crow scouts circled around him, waiting for an opportunity to count cheap coups upon him. But he fought them with bravery and skill. **6**

If their women fight like this, what will their warriors be like?

Buffalo Calf Road Woman uttered a shrill, high-pitched war cry. She raced her pony right into the midst of the battle, into the midst of the enemy. She made the spine-chilling, trilling, warbling sound of the Indian woman encouraging her man during a fight. Chief Comes-in-Sight jumped up on her horse behind his sister. Buffalo Calf Road Woman laughed with joy and with the excitement of battle. Buffalo Calf Road Woman sang while she was doing this. The soldiers were firing at her, and their Crow scouts were shooting arrows at her horse—but it moved too fast for her or Chief Comes-in-Sight to be hit. Then she turned her horse and raced up the hill from which the old chiefs and the medicine men watched the battle. The Sioux and Cheyenne saw what was being done. And then the white soldiers saw it too. They all stopped fighting and just looked at that brave girl saving her brother's life. The warriors raised their arms and set up a mighty shout—a long, trilling, undulating war cry that made one's hairs stand on end. And even some of the soldiers threw their caps in the air and shouted "Hurrah" in honor of Buffalo Calf Road Woman. **7**

The battle was still young. Not many men had been killed on either side, but the white general was thinking, "If their women fight

◀ D

like this, what will their warriors be like? Even if I win, I will lose half my men." And so General Crook retreated a hundred miles or so. He was to have joined up with Custer, Old Yellow Hair, but when Custer had to fight the same Cheyennes and Sioux again a week later, Crook was far away and Custer's army was wiped out. So Buffalo Calf Road Woman in a way contributed to the winning of that famous battle too.

Many who saw what she had done thought that she had counted the biggest coup—not taking life but giving it. That is why the Indians call the Battle of the Rosebud "Where the Girl Saved Her Brother."

The spot where Buffalo Calf Road Woman counted coup has long since been plowed under. A ranch now covers it. But the memory of her deed lives on—and will live on as long as there are Indians. This is not a fairy tale, but it is a legend. ❧

Responding to Reading

1. What was your favorite part of the story? Jot down your thoughts in your journal or notebook.

2. As you know, a legend may be based on a real person or event. What parts of this story could be true? What parts seem imaginary?

3. Why do you think the story of Buffalo Calf Road Woman continues to be told more than a hundred years after the event?

8. **LITERARY CONCEPT: Heroine**
Ask students what words they would use to describe Buffalo Calf Road Woman. *(Possible responses: brave, caring, self-sacrificing, loyal, fierce, proud.)*

Responding to Reading

1. Any response is valid.

2. **Possible responses:** True parts include the battle itself and details about its cause; imaginary parts may include specific details such as Brave Wolf's hawk coming alive and whistling in battle and General Crook's exact thoughts.

3. **Possible responses:** It is an inspirational legend that is sure to make Sioux and Cheyenne listeners feel proud of their heritage; Buffalo Calf Road Woman's story is interesting and very unusual; her courage and sacrifice provide a model to young people.

NORSE MYTH

How Odin Lost His Eye

CATHARINE F. SELLEW

1

Once when the world was still very young, Odin sat on his throne in the most beautiful palace in Asgard. His throne was so high that he could see over all three parts of the world from where he sat. On his head he wore a helmet shaped like an eagle. On his shoulders perched two black ravens called Memory and Thought. And at his feet crouched two snarling wolves.

The great king gazed thoughtfully down on the earth below him. He had made the green land that stretched out before his eyes. With the help of the other gods, he had made men and women who lived on that earth. And he felt truly like the All-father he was called.

A ▶

The fair elves had promised they would help his children of the earth. The elves were the tiny people who lived between heaven and earth. They were so small that they could flit about doing their work unseen. Odin knew that they were the artists who painted the flowers and made the beds for the streams. They took care of all the bees and the butterflies. And it was the elves who brought the gentle rain and sunshine to the earth.

Even the ugly dwarfs, who lived in the heart of the mountains, agreed to help.

They forged iron and metals, made tools and weapons. They dug gold and silver and beautiful jewels out of the earth. Sometimes they even cut the grain and ground the flour for the farmers on the earth.

All seemed to be going well. Odin found it hard to think of evil times. But he knew that the frost giants were only waiting for a chance to bring trouble to his children. They were the ones who brought cold and ice to the world and shook the earth in anger. They hated Odin and all the work of the gods.

And from high on his throne, Odin looked down beyond the earth, deep into the gloomy land of his enemies. He saw dark figures of huge men moving about. They looked like evil shadows. He, the king of the gods, must have more wisdom. It was not enough just to see his enemies. He must know more about them.

2

So Odin wrapped his tall figure in a blue cloak. Down from his throne he climbed. Down the broad rainbow bridge he strode, and across the green earth till he came to one of the roots of the great evergreen tree. There, close by the tree, was a well full of clear water. Its surface was so still it was like a mirror. In it one could see pictures of things that had happened and things that

---

Guided Reading for Less-Proficient Students

These questions can help guide students through the reading. Ask each question at the point of the selection where the capital letter and arrow appear in the margin. In addition, you may wish to use appropriate Active Reading annotations.

A. What is Odin's role in Asgard? *(He is the king who created the land and the people on earth.)* Recalling

B. Why does Odin wish to drink from the well? *(It will give him the knowledge to protect his people.)* Recalling

C. Why does Mimir require that Odin sacrifice an eye? *(Gazing into the mirror of life is a great gift and requires a great price.)* Inferring

D. What does Odin see when he gazes into the well? *(the past and the future; sorrow, death, joy, and a "glorious promise at the end")* Recalling were going to happen.

But beside the well sat an old man. His face was lined with the troubles of the world. His name was Mimir, which means "memory." No one, not even the great Odin, could see the pictures in the well unless he first drank some of its water. Only Mimir could give the magic drink.

"Aged Mimir," Odin said to the old man, "you who hold the knowledge of the past and future in your magic waters, let me have but one sip. Then I can know enough to protect the men and women of the earth
B ▶ from the hate of the giants."

Mimir looked kindly at Odin, but he did not smile. Although he spoke softly, his voice was so deep it reminded Odin of the distant roar of the ocean.

"The price of one drink from this well is not cheap," Mimir said. "And once you have drunk and gazed into the mirror of
3 life, you may wish you had not. For sorrow and death as well as joy are pictured there. Think again before you ask to drink."

But once the king of the gods had made up his mind, nothing could change it. He was not afraid to look upon sorrow and death.

"What is your price, aged Mimir?" Odin asked.

"You are great and good, Odin," answered Mimir. "You have worked hard to make the world. Only those who know hard work may drink from my well. However, that is not enough. What have you given up that is very dear to you? What have you sacrificed? The price of a drink must be a great sacrifice. Are you still willing to pay the price?"

What could the king of the gods sacrifice? What was most dear to him? Odin thought of his handsome son, Balder, whom he loved most in the world. To give up his son would be like giving up life and all that was wonderful around him. Odin stood silent before Mimir. Indeed that would be a high price!

Then Mimir spoke again. He had read Odin's thoughts.

"No, I am not asking for your dear son. The Fates say his life must be short, but he has time yet to live and bring happiness to the gods and the world. I ask for one of your eyes." ◀ **C**

© Hulton Deutsch.

5. LITERARY CONCEPT: Hero
Ask students how Odin's love of the human race is made apparent in this passage. *(Possible responses: He thinks of the people as his own children; he is willing to give up his eye "without another thought" and considers it a "small sacrifice.")*

6. LITERARY CONCEPT: Irony
Point out the irony of Odin's losing an eye in order to achieve a vision of the future. Ask students if they think the sacrifice was worth it. *(Any response is valid.)*

Responding to Reading

1. Any response is valid.

2. Possible responses: By having knowledge of the future, he would know what to expect and how to prepare himself; Odin sees the welfare of people as his responsibility, so he seeks knowledge.

3. Possible responses: It may be the ultimate defeat of the frost giants; it may be all people on earth living in peace and harmony.

4. Possible responses: The people who created the myth may have wanted to explain how the world began and the relationship between human beings and the most important god; they may have wanted to give humans hope and show them a comforting god.

ENCOURAGING INDEPENDENT READING

Adventures with the Gods, myths retold by Catharine F. Sellew

Heroes, Gods, and Monsters of the Greek Myths, myths retold by Bernard Evslin

Norse Gods and Giants, myths retold by Ingri and Edgar d'Aulaire

Once Upon a Totem, Native American legends retold by Christie Harris

---

5 Odin put his hands up to his bright blue eyes. Those two eyes had gazed across the world from his high throne in the shining city of the gods. His eyes had taught him what was good and beautiful, what was evil and ugly. But those eyes had also seen his children, the men and women of the earth, struggling against the hate of the giants. One eye was a small sacrifice to win knowledge of how to help them. And without another thought, Odin plucked out one of his blue eyes and handed it to Mimir.

Then Mimir smiled and gave Odin a horn full of the waters of his well.

"Drink deeply, brave king, so you may see all that you wish in the mirror of life."

Odin lifted the horn to his lips and drank. Then he knelt by the edge of the well and watched the pictures passing across its still and silent surface. When he stood up again, he sighed, for it was as Mimir had said. He had seen sorrow and death as well as joy. It was only the glorious promise at the end, that gave him courage to go on. ◄ D

So Odin, the great king of the gods, became one-eyed. If you can find Mimir's well, you will see Odin's blue eye resting on the bottom. It is there to remind men and women of the great sacrifice he made for them. ▪ 6

Responding to Reading

1. What was your reaction to Odin's sacrifice of his eye? Record your thoughts in your journal or notebook.

2. Odin wants to protect people from the frost giants. Why do you think he seeks knowledge instead of some other kind of help?
   Think about
   • what Odin might see in the well
   • how knowledge could help him

3. What do you think is the "glorious promise" that Odin sees in the well?

4. Why do you think this myth was first told? What message might its creators have wanted to share?

Comprehension Check

1. In "Prometheus," which two characters disagree about the way man should be treated? *(Prometheus and Zeus)*

2. What gift does Prometheus give to man? *(fire)*

3. What is Prometheus' punishment for his deed? *(He is chained to a mountain and vultures eat his liver.)*

4. In "Where the Girl Saved Her Brother," why do soldiers attack the Native Americans? *(The Native Americans refuse to go to reservations.)*

5. How does Buffalo Calf Road Woman save her brother? *(She rides into the battle on her pony and rescues her brother.)*

6. In "How Odin Lost His Eye," who are Odin's enemies? *(the frost giants)*

7. How can Odin gain more knowledge about his enemies? *(by drinking from the well of memory)*

8. What does Odin sacrifice to gain his knowledge? *(one of his eyes)*

Responding to Reading

Comparing the Selections

1. What do the two myths and the legend reveal about the traits or qualities that are admired in each society? Consider why each character is considered heroic.

2. Compare these three tales with the stories of sacrifice that you discussed before reading. What do all the stories have in common?

Broader Connections

3. Do you think humanity is making progress, as Prometheus believed we would; or is the human race going downhill, as Zeus predicted; or is humanity somewhere in the middle, as Odin seemed to believe?

Literary Concept: Hero/Heroine

A **hero** or **heroine** is a character whose actions win great admiration. In myths and legends the heroes represent the qualities that societies most admire. Which character do you consider most heroic—Prometheus, Odin, or Buffalo Calf Road Woman? Why?

Concept Review: Symbol What do you think fire symbolizes in "Prometheus"? Work with a partner to explore your ideas.

Writing Options

1. Write a **myth** about a modern Prometheus who wants to save humanity by giving it one more gift.

2. Write a **dialogue** between Prometheus, Odin, and Buffalo Calf Road Woman in which they discuss their frightening experiences.

Vocabulary Practice

Exercise Write a word from the list to fill in each blank.

Zeus had the power to __1__ humans with the ability, or __2__, to cook food for their own __3__. He might have chosen to give them __4__ instructions and to __5__ over them to make sure they used fire correctly.

> **Words to Know and Use**
> ——
> aptitude
> endow
> explicit
> hover
> sustenance

LINKS TO UNIT FOUR   643

Student Response

Responding to Reading

1. Possible responses: The Greek myth shows the importance of knowledge and progress; the Native American legend shows the importance of courage and family loyalty; the Norse myth shows the value of compassion and knowledge. All three show an appreciation of self-sacrifice.

2. Any response is valid.

3. Any response is valid.

Challenge Question

Promethean is an adjective used to describe someone who is courageously original, boldly creative, or life-bringing. Who in today's world would you describe as Promethean? *(Any response is valid.)*

Literary Concept: Hero/Heroine

Buffalo Calf Road Woman because she risks almost certain death to save her brother; Odin because what he does benefits all of humanity; Prometheus because he gave humans fire, and thus, knowledge.

Concept Review: Symbol *Possible responses:* knowledge or wisdom; human progress; civilization; creativity; skill.

Writing Options

The Writing Options are designed to meet varied student interests and abilities. Have each student choose one writing activity to complete.

Journal Update Have students write about a sacrifice they would make for someone or something they love.

Vocabulary Practice

Answers to Exercise
1. endow   4. explicit
2. aptitude   5. hover
3. sustenance

Closure

Ask students to explain why these selections accompany the "Person to Person" unit. How does each tale illustrate a "person to person" lesson?

The Spelling Connection

Spelling Pattern: Unstressed vowels Unstressed vowels can be hard to hear and identify. When you hear one, try changing the word's form, which may help you identify the vowel.

Example: human (unstressed *a*) humanity (stressed *a*)

Words with Unstressed Vowels from the Selections

medicine	medicinal (stressed form)
artist	artistic
courage	courageous

Other Words with Unstressed Vowels

emphasis	emphatic (stressed form)
fantasy	fantastic
hostile	hostility

Exercise Mark the accents in the following words. Then write a related form of the word.

1. angel   2. editor   3. geography
4. remedy   5. melody

Extending the Lesson

Options for Learning

These activities suit a variety of learning styles and modes of expression.

Collaborative Learning Activities
See Option 2.

1. Art for the Ages Students may wish to peruse books of great art to study the varying styles before choosing a style for their own work.

2. History Hunt Students can find information in encyclopedias and books about Native American history.

Bernard Evslin

■ More About the Author Evslin is a prolific author of books that retell myths and legends.

■ Other Works Myths: *The Trojan War, Adventures of Ulysses*; plays: *Step on a Crack, Geranium Hat.*

■ Awards National Book Award for *The Greek Hero*; NEA Award for best TV documentary on an educational theme, 1961; best TV film, 1959, for *Face of the Land*

Catharine F. Sellew

■ More About the Author After completing her studies at Wheaton College, Sellew began writing myths for young people.

■ Other Works Myths: *Adventures with the Giants, Adventures with the Gods, Adventures with the Heroes*; Bible stories: *Adventures with Abraham's Children.*

Options for Learning (Multimodal/Cross-Curricular Activities)

1 • Art for the Ages Illustrate one of the stories. Draw a series of sketches to illustrate the entire piece or draw a detailed version of one key scene.

2 • History Hunt Find out more about either the Battle of the Rosebud or the Battle of the Little Bighorn. Report your findings to the class.

Bernard Evslin 1922–

When Bernard Evslin's wife asked for advice on how to interest her students in mythology, he wrote his own version of a Greek myth. The students loved his story and asked for more, which Evslin supplied. He went on to write more than thirty books for young people, including *The Greek Gods and Heroes*. Over six million copies of his works are in print.

Evslin has also written award-winning television documentaries and two plays. One of his books, *The Green Hero*, was nominated for a National Book Award.

Rachel Strange Owl 1947–

Rachel Strange Owl, a Cheyenne Indian, lives on the Northern Cheyenne Lame Deer Reservation in Montana. In the early 1970s she told the legend "Where the Girl Saved Her Brother" to Richard Erdoes, a collector of Native American myths and legends. She first heard the story, which is based on actual events, from her mother.

Today, Strange Owl lives on the reservation with her husband and several of her seven children. She supervises artists who bead high-fashion clothes with Cheyenne and Cree designs.

Catharine F. Sellew 1922–1982

As a child, Catharine Sellew loved to listen as her mother read myths. Sellew later studied mythology and went on to publish her first collection of ancient Greek myths, *Adventures with the Gods*.

She then retold Norse myths in *Adventures with the Giants* and *Adventures with the Heroes*. She also retold stories from the Old Testament and wrote a novel for teenagers entitled *Torchlight*.

644 UNIT SIX THEMES IN WORLD FOLKLORE

Cross-Curricular Projects

Science Have students research the topic of fire. What are its elements? How is it created? What by-products does it make? How is it controlled? Have students share their information with the class.

Music Have students listen to recordings of traditional Native American songs and chants and discover the history behind each piece. Hold a class "music hour" in which the recordings are played and students tell what they know about the pieces.

Art Invite students to create a mural showing all the pictures that Odin viewed in the well. Pictures should reflect events that have happened in the past as well as events that students think may occur in the future. Let the artists discuss their work.

Drama Ask students to find another myth or Native American legend and to act out the story for classmates. A narrator may provide necessary information before or during the dramatic presentation. Productions can include costumes and props as well.

A Question of Identity

Links to Unit Five

Echo and Narcissus   MOIRA KERR / JOHN BENNETT
The Emperor's New Clothes   HANS CHRISTIAN ANDERSEN
The Fatal Flower   LAURENCE YEP

Examine What You Know   (Prior Knowledge)

Beauty is a key issue in a number of myths and folk tales. In many cases beauty is tied very closely to a character's identity. With a small group of classmates, list as many tales as you can—some of which may have been turned into animated movies—that deal with beauty. Compare your list with those of your classmates and discuss why beauty so often plays a role in such stories.

Expand Your Knowledge   (Building Background)

"Echo and Narcissus" tells the story of a Greek youth, Narcissus (när sis′ əs), who was famous for his beauty. The myth really begins with Zeus, who never lost his desire for pretty women, despite his marriage to Hera. Zeus often roamed the forests of the earth looking for nymphs—minor nature goddesses in the form of beautiful women. His jealous wife usually came looking for him, causing problems for anyone who got in her way. Hera never showed mercy to any nymph, including Echo.

"The Emperor's New Clothes" focuses not on beautiful faces but on beautiful clothes. This folk tale by Hans Christian Andersen of Denmark offers a humorous look at people's concern about their appearance.

"The Fatal Flower," a folk tale that originated in China, gives another view of beauty. Though the Chinese admire physical beauty, the desire for loveliness may be offset by the need to conform to society's roles. This thought is expressed by an old Chinese proverb, "The nail that sticks out gets hammered." Chinese immigrants to the United States told this tale to their children as a warning.

Write Before You Read   (Journal Writing)

Write your own proverb—a wise saying—about beauty. An example of such a proverb is "Beauty is only skin deep, but ugly goes to the bone." As you read, compare your proverb with the lessons of the stories.

■ *Author biographies on Extend page*

LINKS TO UNIT FIVE   645

Objectives

■ To understand and analyze a myth and folk tales

■ To distinguish between oral and literary folk tales

■ To enrich reading by inferring character traits

■ To express understanding of the selections through a choice of writing forms, including a letter and a testimonial

Prereading/Motivation

Examine What You Know

Discussion Prompts Think about characters from storybooks or Disney movies. Is the characters' beauty or ugliness important in the stories? Are their looks transformed? Does their appearance reflect their personality?

Expand Your Knowledge

Additional Background Ancient Greeks associated the beauty of flowers with the gods. "Echo and Narcissus" explains the origin of one such flower, the narcissus. Today the word *narcissism* is used to describe someone who loves himself excessively.

As a boy, Hans Christian Andersen was homely, awkward, and dreamy. For a time he was apprenticed to a weaver, and in "The Emperor's New Clothes" he used the knowledge that he gained.

With regard to "The Fatal Flower," Laurence Yep notes that early Chinese immigrants to the United States, because of ill treatment by whites, were forced to live as quietly as possible so as not to attract attention. In Chinese society of the past, boys were considered much more valuable than girls.

MORE JOURNAL WRITING IDEAS

■ Do you think beautiful people are happier than ordinary-looking people? Explain.

■ If someone asked you to identify and describe yourself, how would you answer?

COLLABORATIVE LEARNING OPTIONS

Opportunities for collaborative learning include Examine What You Know, Multicultural Connections (p. 651), Options for Learning (p. 661), and Cross-Curricular Projects (p. 661).

ADDITIONAL RESOURCES

Unit Six Resource Book
Reader's Guidesheet, p. 33
Reading Skills, p. 34
Literature Skills, p. 35
Vocabulary Connections, p.36
Spelling Connections, p.37
Comprehension and Vocabulary Check Tests, p.38
Selection Test, pp. 39–40

Technology and Enrichment

🎧 Audiocassette Tape 2, Side 2: "Echo and Narcissus"

Thematic Link— A Question of Identity

"Echo and Narcissus" presents two characters who lose their identities when the gods punish them. In "The Emperor's New Clothes," a trick forces the rulers to question their own abilities. In "The Fatal Flower," Gem learns that changing one's identity can have hidden consequences.

LINKS TO UNIT FIVE **Teacher's Edition**   **645**

VOCABULARY PREVIEW

These vocabulary words are defined at the bottom of the selection pages on which they appear.

consultation a meeting

diligence constant effort

excessively overly

exquisite beautiful; outstanding

realm a kingdom

repulsive offensive

rogue a rascal

sovereign a monarch

stench a strong, foul smell

vexed troubled

LIMITED ENGLISH PROFICIENCY

■ Use the Reader's Guidesheet, *Unit Six Resource Book*, page 33.

■ Help students understand the old-fashioned phrasing in the first two stories.

★ Text annotations marked with a red star ("Echo and Narcissus": 1; "The Emperor's New Clothes": 8, 11; "The Fatal Flower": 2, 5, 7, 12) may be particularly helpful for students with limited English proficiency.

TEXT ANNOTATIONS

1. LITERARY SIDELIGHT
Explain that nymphs are spirits thought to inhabit features of nature, such as trees and rivers. Although they looked like beautiful young women, the nymphs were minor goddesses who attended more important gods. ★

2. LITERARY CONCEPT: Theme
Ask students to explain how Hera's punishment affected Echo's identity. *(Possible responses: She lost her identity as a talker; she could only repeat others' words.)*

3. ACTIVE READING: Review
Call on a volunteer to explain the humor or cleverness of the dialogue between Echo and Narcissus. *(Possible responses: Echo's words have a sort of double meaning; although she is only echoing the last word or words of what Narcissus says, Echo's words seem to respond to his and express her desires.)*

646 UNIT SIX **Themes in World Folklore**

GREEK MYTH

Echo and Narcissus

MOIRA KERR / JOHN BENNETT

N ot many men, or even gods, were as handsome as young Narcissus. So fair was he that almost everyone who saw him fell in love with him that very moment.

One day, as Narcissus roamed the forests with his hunting companions, he was spied by the watchful eye of the nymph Echo. She had once been a great chatterer, ready to talk to any passerby on any subject at any time, and on several occasions she had detained the goddess Hera with hours of casual talk, just as Hera was on the point of stumbling upon Zeus with one of his illicit[1] loves. Eventually Hera grew so annoyed that she put a curse on Echo, and from that time on the unfortunate nymph could say nothing but the last few words that she had heard.

Trembling, Echo followed Narcissus through the trees. She longed to go closer to him, to gaze upon the beauty of his face, but she feared that he would laugh at her silly speech. Before long Narcissus wandered away from his companions, and when he realized he was lost, he called in panic, "Is there anybody here?"

"Here!" called Echo.

Mystified by this reply, Narcissus shouted, "Come!"

"Come!" shouted Echo.

Narcissus was convinced that someone was playing tricks on him.

"Why are you avoiding me?" he called. The only answer he heard was his own question repeated from the woods.

"Come here, and let us meet!" pleaded Narcissus.

"Let us meet!" Echo answered, delighted.

She overcame her shyness and crept from her hiding place to approach Narcissus. But he, satisfied now that he had solved the mystery of the voice, roughly pushed her away and ran.

"I would die before I would have you near me!" he shouted mockingly over his shoulder.

Helpless, Echo had to call after him, "I would have you near me!"

T he nymph was so embarrassed and ashamed that she hid herself in a dark cave and never came into the air and sunlight again. Her youth and beauty withered away, and her body became so shrunken and tiny that eventually she vanished altogether. All that was left was the pathetic voice which still roams the world, anxious to talk, yet able only to repeat what others say.

---

1. **illicit** (il lis′ it): against custom or law

These questions can help guide students through the reading. Ask each question at the point of the selection where the capital letter and arrow appear in the margin. In addition, you may wish to use appropriate Active Reading annotations.

A. What curse does Hera put on Echo? *(Echo can only repeat what she hears.)* Recalling

B. Why does Echo hide in a cave and wither away? *(She has been rejected by Narcissus.)* Summarizing

C. With whom does Narcissus fall in love? *(himself, his own reflection)* Summarizing

D. What finally happens to Narcissus? *(His body withers away, and he becomes a flower.)* Summarizing

Poor Echo was not the only one to be treated brutally by Narcissus. He had played with many hearts, and at last one of those he had scorned prayed to the gods that Narcissus would some day find himself scorned by one he loved. The prayer was heard and granted.

Tired and thirsty from his hunting, Narcissus threw himself down beside a still, clear pool to drink. As he leaned over the shining surface, he saw reflected the most beautiful face he had ever seen. His heart trembled at the sight, and he could not tear himself away from it—his own image.

For a long time Narcissus remained there beside the pool, never raising his eyes from the surface, and from time to time murmuring words of love. At last his body withered away and became the stem of a flower, and his head, the lovely gold and white blossom that still looks into quiet pools, and is called the narcissus. ❧

From *Favorite Greek Myths* retold by Mary Pope Osborne, illustrated by Troy Howell. Illustrations copyright © 1989 by Troy Howell. Reprinted by permission of Scholastic, Inc.

Art Note

In Troy Howell's representation of the vain Narcissus, the most prominent detail is the blond silky curls that frame Narcissus' face and suggest his amazing handsomeness. Have students compare Howell's treatment of the Phaëthon legend (p. 620) with this image of Narcissus to see how the artist has adapted his style to each subject. *Do you think the artist has represented the myth correctly? What is your opinion of Narcissus' appearance?*

Responding to Reading

1. Which character, Echo or Narcissus, made a bigger impression on you? Describe your thoughts in your journal or notebook.

2. Do you think the punishments given to Echo and Narcissus are fair?

   Think about
   - what each does to anger the gods
   - whether Echo or Narcissus deserves punishment
   - whether the punishments fit the offenses

3. How do you think Narcissus' identity is related to his appearance?

4. Myths can have more than one purpose. What are the purposes of this myth?

ECHO AND NARCISSUS   647

Responding to Reading

1. Any response is valid.

2. Possible responses: Yes, because the punishments make the offenders the victims of their own character flaws; no, because they amount to death sentences and never give Echo and Narcissus a chance to say they're sorry or to learn anything; Narcissus seems to deserve punishment more than Echo, since he was unkind to others but she was just too talkative.

3. Possible responses: Narcissus' identity is bound up with his appearance because his beauty is the one thing that everyone notices about him and that causes him to be cursed by the gods; his obsession with his beauty makes him lack compassion for others.

4. Possible responses: The myth warns against foolishness and idle chatter; it emphasizes the danger of being vain and conceited; it explains the origin of echoes and of the narcissus flower.

Looking at Style

Because Greek myths are among the oldest Western literature, authors who retell these myths often adopt an old-fashioned style, with long sentences and formal vocabulary. Read these sentences aloud:

■ So fair was he that almost everyone who saw him fell in love with him that very moment.

■ She longed to go closer to him, to gaze upon the beauty of his face . . .

■ "I would die before I would have you near me!" he shouted mockingly over his shoulder.

Ask students to do the following activities:

1. Identify formal words and phrases. How would you describe them? Do they seem old-fashioned? How does the order of the words make the sentences seem formal?

2. Rewrite the sentences in informal English, or use slang. Share your versions with the class.

1. LITERARY CONCEPT: Character
In what way is the Emperor like
Narcissus? (Possible response: He is
excessively concerned with his appearance; his obsession with his image
makes him neglect other aspects of life.)

2. LITERARY CONCEPT:
Foreshadowing
What clues suggest or foreshadow the
events to come? (Possible responses:
The men are referred to as "rogues,
calling themselves weavers"; the words
"gave out" suggest that they are just
spreading rumors, that their statement is
untrue.)

3. ACTIVE READING: Connect
Ask students to list some pros and cons
of being instantly able to tell who is
wise and who is foolish. (Any response
is valid.)

DANISH FOLK TALE

The Emperor's New Clothes

HANS CHRISTIAN ANDERSEN

Many years ago there was an Emperor who was so excessively fond of new clothes that he spent all his money in dress. He did not trouble himself in the least about his soldiers; nor did he care to go either to the theater or the chase, except for the opportunities they afforded him for displaying his new clothes. He had a different suit for each hour of the day; and as of any other king or emperor one is accustomed to say, "He is sitting in council," it was always said of him, "The Emperor is sitting in his wardrobe."[1]

Time passed away merrily in the large town which was his capital; strangers arrived every day at the court. One day two rogues, calling themselves weavers, made their appearance. They gave out that they knew how to weave stuffs of the most beautiful colors and elaborate patterns, the clothes manufactured from which should have the wonderful property of remaining invisible to everyone who was unfit for the office he held, or who was extraordinarily simple in character.

"These must indeed be splendid clothes!"

thought the Emperor. "Had I such a suit, I might at once find out what men in my realm are unfit for their office, and also be able to distinguish the wise from the foolish! This stuff must be woven for me immediately." And he caused large sums of money to be given to both the weavers, in order that they might begin their work directly.

So the two pretended weavers set up two looms and affected[2] to work very busily, though in reality they did nothing at all. They asked for the most delicate silk and the purest gold thread, put both into their own knapsacks, and then continued their pretended work at the empty looms until late at night.

"I should like to know how the weavers are getting on with my cloth," said the Emperor to himself, after some little time had elapsed. He was, however, rather embarrassed when he remembered that a simpleton, or one unfit for his office, would be unable to see the manufacture. To be

---

1. **wardrobe:** the place in which clothing is kept in a royal household.
2. **affected:** pretended.

Words to Know and Use	
excessively (ek ses′ iv lē) *adv.* overly; too much
rogue (rōg) *n.* a rascal
realm (relm) *n.* a kingdom

648

Guided Reading for Less-Proficient Students

These questions can help guide students through the reading. Ask each question at the point of the selection where the capital letter and arrow appear in the margin. In addition, you may wish to use appropriate Active Reading annotations.

A. What is the Emperor's main interest? (wearing fine clothes) Recalling

B. What special property do the weavers say their clothes will have? (Their clothes will be invisible to

incompetents and fools.) Recalling

C. How do the weavers make people believe they are really weaving cloth? (by pantomiming the weaving and talking about the colors and patterns as if they were real) Summarizing

D. Why do the Emperor and his courtiers praise the "clothes"? (They do not want people to think they are simple or unfit for office.) Summarizing

Continued on page 649

sure, he thought, he had nothing to risk in his own person, but yet he would prefer sending somebody else to bring him intelligence about the weavers and their work before he troubled himself in the affair. All the people throughout the city had heard of the wonderful property the cloth was to possess; and all were anxious to learn how wise, or how ignorant, their neighbors might prove to be.

"I will send my faithful old Minister to the weavers," said the Emperor at last, after some deliberation. "He will be best able to see how the cloth looks; he is a man of sense, and no one can be more suitable for his office than he is."

So the honest old Minister went into the hall, where the knaves[3] were working with all their might at their empty looms. "What can be the meaning of this?" thought the old man, opening his eyes very wide; "I cannot discover the least bit of thread on the looms!" However, he did not express his thoughts aloud.

The impostors requested him very courteously to be so good as to come nearer their looms, and then asked him whether the design pleased him and whether the colors were not very beautiful, at the same time pointing to the empty frames. The poor old Minister looked and looked; he could not discover anything on the looms for a very good reason: there was nothing there. "What!" thought he again. "Is it possible that I am a simpleton? I have never thought so myself, and at any rate if I am

so, no one must know it. Can it be that I am unfit for my office? No, that must not be said either. I will never confess that I could not see the stuff."

"Well, sir Minister!" said one of the knaves, still pretending to work. "You do not say whether the stuff pleases you."

"Oh, it is admirable!" replied the old Minister, looking at the loom through his spectacles. "This pattern, and the colors—yes, I will tell the Emperor without delay how very beautiful I think them."

"We shall be much obliged to you," said the impostors, and then they named the different colors and described the patterns of the pretended stuff. The old Minister listened attentively to their words in order that he might repeat them to the Emperor; and then the knaves asked for more silk and gold, saying that it was necessary to complete what they had begun. However, they put all that was given them into their knapsacks and continued to work with as much apparent diligence as before at their empty looms.

The Emperor now sent another officer of his court to see how the men were getting on and to ascertain whether the cloth would soon be ready. It was just the same with this gentleman as with the Minister: he surveyed the looms on all sides but could see nothing at all but the empty frames.

"Does not the stuff appear as beautiful to you as it did to my lord the Minister?" asked the impostors of the Emperor's second ambassador, at the same time making the same gestures as before and talking of

---

3. **knaves** (nāvz): sly, dishonest people.

Words to Know and Use | **diligence** (dil′ ə jəns) *n.* constant effort

4. LITERARY CONCEPT: Motivation
Ask students why the Emperor sends the Minister to the weavers instead of going himself. (*Possible responses: The Emperor is worried that he might not be able to see the clothes; he has more confidence in his Minister than he has in himself.*)

5. LITERARY CONCEPT: Character
Ask the students what the Minister's reaction to the "cloth" suggests about him. (*Possible responses: He lacks self-confidence; he is dishonest; he is more interested in keeping his job than in finding out the truth.*)

6. LITERARY CONCEPT: Motivation
Ask students why the weavers name the different colors and describe the patterns for the Minister. (*Possible responses: They know he can't really see any cloth, and they are prompting him so that he will be able to describe the cloth to the Emperor; they are trying to make their trick more convincing.*)

Guided Reading for Less-Proficient Students

Continued from page 648

E. What happens when a child points out that the Emperor has no clothes on? (*The crowd recognizes that the child is right; the Emperor and his followers continue to maintain appearances.*) Summarizing

7. ACTIVE READING: Evaluate
Invite a volunteer to explain how, in one way at least, the cloth actually does reveal who is simple-minded and unfit for office. *(Possible response: By believing the rogues' silly story and by being too cowardly to admit they can't see the fabric, the Minister and the messenger show that they are foolish, dishonest, and unfit for responsible office.)*

8. VOCABULARY: Synonyms
Point out that the author uses synonyms—*knaves, rogues,* and *impostors*—to describe the two dishonest men. Explain that impostors are people who deceive by pretending to be something they are not. Have students supply some other synonyms for these words. *(Possible responses: fakes, phonies, crooks, con men, swindlers, cheats)* ★

THE SERMON (detail)   1566   Pieter Bruegel the Elder   National Gallery of Art, Budapest, Hungary.

the design and colors which were not there.

"I certainly am not stupid!" thought the messenger. "It must be that I am not fit for my good, profitable office! That is very odd; however, no one shall know anything about it." And accordingly he praised the stuff he could not see and declared that he was delighted with both colors and patterns. "Indeed, please Your Imperial Majesty," said he to his sovereign when he returned, "the cloth which the weavers are preparing is extraordinarily magnificent."

The whole city was talking of the splendid cloth which the Emperor had ordered to be woven at his own expense.

And now the Emperor himself wished to see the costly manufacture while it was still on the loom. Accompanied by a select number of officers of the court, among whom were the two honest men who had already admired the cloth, he went to the crafty impostors, who, as soon as they were aware of the Emperor's approach, went on working more diligently than ever, although they still did not pass a single thread through the looms.

"Is not the work absolutely magnificent?" said the two officers of the crown already mentioned. "If Your Majesty will only be pleased to look at it! What a splendid design! What glorious colors!" and at the same time they pointed to the empty frames, for they imagined that everyone but themselves could see this exquisite piece of workmanship.

"How is this?" said the Emperor to himself. "I can see nothing! This is indeed a terrible affair! Am I a simpleton? Or am I unfit

Words to Know and Use	**sovereign** (sǎv′ rən) *n.* a monarch; royal ruler **exquisite** (eks′ kwi zit) *adj.* beautiful; outstanding

650

to be an emperor? That would be the worst thing that could happen. Oh, the cloth is charming!" said he aloud. "It has my entire approbation."[4] And he smiled most graciously and looked at the empty looms, for on no account would he say that he could not see what two of the officers of his court had praised so much. All his retinue[5] now strained their eyes, hoping to discover something on the looms, but they could see no more than the others; nevertheless they all exclaimed, "Oh! How beautiful!" and advised His Majesty to have some new clothes made from this splendid material for the approaching procession. "Magnificent! Charming! Excellent!" resounded on all sides, and everyone was uncommonly gay. The Emperor shared in the general satisfaction and presented the impostors with the riband[6] of an order of knighthood to be worn in their buttonholes, and the title of "Gentlemen Weavers."

The rogues sat up the whole of the night before the day on which the procession was to take place, and had sixteen lights burning so that everyone might see how anxious they were to finish the Emperor's new suit. They pretended to roll the cloth off the looms, cut the air with their scissors, and sewed with needles without any thread in them. "See!" cried they at last. "The Emperor's new clothes are ready!"

And now the Emperor, with all the grandees of his court, came to the weavers; and the rogues raised their arms as if in the act of holding something up, saying, "Here are Your Majesty's trousers! Here is the scarf! Here is the mantle![7] The whole suit is as light as a cobweb; one might fancy one has nothing at all on when dressed in it; that, however, is the great virtue of this delicate cloth."

"Yes, indeed!" said all the courtiers, although not one of them could see anything of this exquisite manufacture.

"If Your Imperial Majesty will be graciously pleased to take off your clothes, we will fit on the new suit in front of the looking glass."

The Emperor was accordingly undressed, and the rogues pretended to array him in his new suit, the Emperor turning round from side to side before the looking glass.

"How splendid His Majesty looks in his new clothes, and how well they fit!" everyone cried out. "What a design! What colors! These are indeed royal robes!"

"The canopy which is to be borne over Your Majesty in the procession is waiting," announced the Chief Master of the Ceremonies.

"I am quite ready," answered the Emperor. "Do my new clothes fit well?" asked he, turning himself round again before the looking glass in order that he might appear to be examining his handsome suit.

The lords of the bedchamber, who were to carry His Majesty's train, felt about on the ground as if they were lifting up the ends of the mantle, and pretended to be carrying something; for they would by no means betray anything like simplicity or unfitness for their office.

So now the Emperor walked under his

---

4. **approbation** (ap′ rə bā′ shən): official approval.
5. **retinue** (ret′ ′n yo͞o′): a group of attendants or servants.
6. **riband** (rib′ band′): a decorative ribbon.
7. **mantle**: a royal robe.

Multicultural Connections

To explore the role of clothing in different areas of society, ask students these questions:

1. In this story, the emperor set the standard for what was considered fashionable. Who or what sets the fashion standards in your school or community? Is there one standard for everyone, or does each group have its own standard?

2. Do you associate different clothing with different cultures within our society? Do you make assumptions about a person's background based on their clothing?

3. If you were an immigrant to the United States, would you change your style of dress so that you could fit in, or would you wear the styles that you were familiar with? Explain.

high canopy in the midst of the procession, through the streets of his capital; and all the people standing by, and those at the windows, cried out, "Oh, how beautiful are our Emperor's new clothes! What a magnificent train there is to the mantle! And how gracefully the scarf hangs!" In short, no one would allow that he could not see these much-admired clothes, because in doing so, he would have declared himself either a simpleton or unfit for his office. Certainly, none of the Emperor's various suits had ever excited so much admiration as this.

"But the Emperor has nothing at all on!" said a little child. "Listen to the voice of innocence!" exclaimed his father, and what the child had said was whispered from one to another.

"But he has nothing at all on!" at last cried out all the people. The Emperor was <u>vexed</u>, for he knew that the people were right; but he thought, "The procession must go on now!" And the lords of the bedchamber took greater pains than ever to appear holding up a train, although in reality there was no train to hold. ❧

Responding to Reading

1. Jot down your reaction to the ending of this tale.

2. In your opinion, why is a child the one who tells the truth about the Emperor's new clothes?

3. Why do you think the Emperor and his court continue their procession even after the truth is known?

4. Why do you think the rogues are able to carry out their scheme?
   Think about
   • which people they say can see the clothes
   • why they target the Emperor for their scheme
   • how the other members of court react

5. What common human failings does the story portray?

Words to Know and Use	**vexed** (vekst) *adj.* troubled **vex** *v.*

652

The Fatal Flower

LAURENCE YEP

Long ago in a faraway kingdom there was a girl called Gem who hated the way she looked. She was so ashamed that she refused to leave the house. Instead, she would stand in her little courtyard and peek through the gates at the other girls as they passed by in the village lane. "What pretty eyes she has," she would sigh. "Why can't I have eyes like that?" Or she would stare enviously at someone else. "Look at how graceful she is. Why can't I walk like that?"

Her exasperated mother would tell her that she looked fine. "You should go outside. You've got two eyes and a nose and a mouth, all in the right place. Why do you have to complain all the time?"

"Because other girls have their eyes, noses, and mouths arranged much better than me," Gem insisted. "I'm so repulsive that they'll just laugh."

"It's different flowers for different eyes," her mother said. Though her mother coaxed and scolded, Gem remained inside trying to make herself beautiful.

From herbs her family gathered for her, she tried to make all sorts of pills, lotions, and ointments. Some were to make her skin smooth as silk. Others were to make her hair shiny and full. Whichever one she tried, she was always disappointed; and the smells from all her brews almost drove her family from the house. Eyes watering from the smoke and holding his nose against the stench, her father found her by the stove getting ready to throw out her latest failure. "I can't stand it anymore. They say there's a wise woman who has the power to change things. Maybe she can make you into what you want to be. Follow the river to the hill."

By now, Gem was desperate enough to try anything. The next morning before sunrise, she sneaked out with a piece of cloth wrapped around her head as a veil.

Keeping to the high riverbank, she followed the wide, muddy river until she reached the hill. The wise woman's hut sat upon the top, surrounded by terraced fields where herbs grew in neat, well-tended rows. Harvested herbs and flowers sat drying on the hut's roof or were hanging inside from the ceiling, so the hill smelled like a dusty garden of flowers.

Outside the little hut was a woman with black skin. She was winnowing rice—separating the harvested grains from the chaff and bits of straw. She would lay out handfuls of the harvest on a big, flat, round

| Words to Know and Use | **repulsive** (ri pul' siv) *adj.* offensive; disgusting |
| | **stench** (stench) *n.* a strong, foul smell |

653

TEXT ANNOTATIONS

1. LITERARY CONCEPT: Setting
Ask students why they think this type of setting—"long ago in a faraway kingdom"—is a common one in folk tales. (Possible responses: An unspecific setting suggests that the story could happen anywhere; a remote setting makes magic people and events plausible.)

2. LITERARY CONCEPT: Figurative Language
Call on a volunteer to explain this expression. (Possible responses: Different things appeal to different people; beauty is in the eye of the beholder.) ★

3. LITERARY SIDELIGHT
Point out that a common character in folklore is the wise old man or woman with magic powers. Invite students to name such characters that they have encountered in other tales. (Possible responses: Merlin, Cinderella's fairy godmother, Toby in "The People Could Fly")

Guided Reading for Less-Proficient Students

These questions can help guide students through the reading. Ask each question at the point of the selection where the capital letter and arrow appear in the margin. In addition, you may wish to use appropriate Active Reading annotations.

A. Why doesn't Gem ever leave her house? (She is ashamed of how she looks.) Recalling

B. Why does Gem visit the wise woman? (She hopes the woman will make her beautiful.) Recalling

C. What must Gem do to get her wish? (She must find a special flower in the mountains.) Recalling

D. What warning does the wise woman give? (that beauty doesn't always bring happiness) Recalling

Continued on page 654

4. ACTIVE READING: Evaluate
Ask students what they think of Gem's attitude toward herself, especially in the light of what her mother has already said about her looks. *(Any response is valid.)*

5. LITERARY CONCEPT: Figurative Language
Ask students what the wise woman seems to be saying to Gem with her comments about the rice and the chaff. *(Possible responses: Gem is foolish to think so much about becoming pretty, since prettiness is useless; things should be valued for what they are, not what they look like.)* ★

6. LITERARY CONCEPT: Folklore
Explain that in folklore it is common for a main character to set out on a quest—a journey to find something rare or accomplish an important task. Ask volunteers to describe the quests of other heroes in folklore. *(Possible responses: King Arthur's knights' quest for the Holy Grail; Odin's quest for the water of knowledge; Psyche's quest to find Eros)*

7. LITERARY CONCEPT: Figurative Language
Have a volunteer identify the metaphor used to describe the river. *("a cold, steely blue ribbon")* ★

Art Note

In China, fan painting has been a highly regarded art. This work shows the delicate, fluid style of Chen Shu (1660–1736). Called *Mallows, Asters, Beetle and Butterfly*, the fan was painted by Chen in her seventy-sixth year. Note how she energized the work with the lively butterfly. Note also the delicate strokes she used in the painting. *What kind of person do you think would have used this fan?*

---

tray woven from bamboo and toss the contents into the air. The grain, still in its brown hulls, would rattle down, while the breeze would blow the chaff and straw away.

Kneeling before the wise woman, Gem bowed. "I look like a monster, but I hear you have the power to change me into someone beautiful."

B ▶
4

The wise woman calmly poured the winnowed rice into a basket. "First, let's see what I have to work with."

"You've been warned." Trembling, Gem unwrapped her veil. "Just look at me. I'm too gruesome to live."

The wise woman put another handful of harvested grain upon the tray. With a powerful jerk of her arms, she tossed it up into the air. Once again, the brown rice pattered down upon the tray like hard drops of rain. "Rice is ugly, but it fills the belly." Then she nodded to the chaff and bits of straw that shone like flakes of gold as they whirled

around in the breeze. "While that fluff is pretty but useless."

5

Gem touched her forehead against the dirt, pleading with the wise woman to help her. With a sigh, the wise woman put her tray down and patted Gem on the shoulder. "Deep in the mountains there once lived a king and his daughter. The king was also a powerful wizard, and his daughter was almost as magical. When she died, she changed into a creeper with thin vines from which grow tiny yellow flowers like five-pointed stars. If your heart is set upon becoming beautiful, you must bring me a flower from that vine, and I will grant your wish."

6
◀ C

So Gem traveled beside the river until it had narrowed into a cold, steely blue ribbon and the land had slanted upward into steeper and steeper hills. Though she looked everywhere, she saw nothing. Just as she was about to turn back in discouragement, she heard a voice. "Why are you wearing that veil?"

7

She looked all around, but she saw no one.

"Are you

MALLOWS, ASTERS, BEETLE AND BUTTERFLY
1735 Chen Shu Chengxun tang collection, Hong Kong.

654   UNIT SIX   THEMES IN WORLD FOLKLORE

Guided Reading for Less-Proficient Students

Continued from page 653

E. What happens when Gem uses the magic potion? *(Gem becomes beautiful.)* Recalling

F. Why do the king's men want the heart of a beautiful girl? *(Doctors say that soup made from the heart will cure the king's fever.)* Summarizing

G. How does the beautiful Gem manage to escape the king's men? *(The wise woman changes her appearance back to what it was originally.)* Recalling

H. How does Gem feel about her looks at the end of the story? *(that they're good enough)* Inferring deaf?" the voice repeated from overhead.

Leaning her head back, she saw a little woman perched on the branch of a tree. She wore an embroidered blouse and skirt, and Gem could see a pair of bird's claws peeking out from the dress as the strange little woman clung to a tree branch.

The little woman leaned her head to one side like a bird and studied Gem. "What's wrong?"

"Everything," the girl said, and explained her quest. "Do you know where the flowers grow?"

The little woman folded her arms smugly. "I certainly do."

Gem clung to the trunk of the tree. "Oh, please tell me."

The little woman leaned down and felt the veil. "First, you must bring me a piece of cloth as long as the river."

Gem thought long and hard while the bird-woman watched expectantly. Finally, Gem broke off a straight twig from a nearby branch. With a sharp rock, she made an elaborate show of marking the stick into ten equal units. Then she presented her homemade ruler to the bird-woman. "First, you must tell me the exact length of the river."

The bird-woman waved the ruler in annoyance. "I can't measure the whole river."

"Then I can't make a cloth as long as it. But," Gem said, and unwound her veil, "until you can measure the river, why don't you keep this as a sample gift?"

The bird-woman took the cloth, drawing it back and forth in her hands as she stared at Gem. "If I were a human, I'd be more ashamed of my fat, sloppy feet than my face."

Gem glanced at the woman's great, ugly claws but said only, "Where are the flowers?"

The bird-woman wrapped the cloth around her shoulders. "I'll show you." Leaping lightly to the ground, she began to hop along like a bird. Gem followed her among the trees until they came to a shadowy place where red pine trees grew in a circle. Though the scent of the pine was thick, Gem could smell another sweet fragrance that she could not name.

And in the center of the clearing was a tree about Gem's height around which grew a tangle of slender vines without any roots. Tiny yellow flowers rose from the tips of the vines like constellations of stars.

Excited, Gem was going to pluck handfuls of the flower, but the bird-woman stopped her. "If I can have only a sample cloth, you can take only a sample flower."

Gem tried to hide her disappointment, because the flowers were so small. "Well," she sighed, "one flower will have to do." Carefully, she selected the largest of the flowers. Tucking it away safely in a sleeve, Gem reached the wise woman late in the afternoon.

"Now, please keep your promise," Gem said triumphantly.

The wise woman took the tiny stalk between her fingers. "Remember. Beauty does not always bring happiness. Do you still wish it?"

"With all my heart."

"To my mind, a girl who is clever enough to find the flower does not need to be beautiful too." The wise woman shrugged. "But so be it. Fetch me some water from the well."

8. ACTIVE READING: Review
Ask students what character traits Gem has revealed in dealing with the bird-woman. If necessary, help students by reading the following example of a think-aloud, or model one of your own.

Think-Aloud Script Gem needs the flower, but there's no way she can get a piece of cloth as long as a river. She's smart—she outwits the bird-woman by making a ruler and asking the length of the river. Fortunately, the bird-woman doesn't get angry about it. Gem is polite and gives the bird-woman the veil as a sort of consolation prize. When the woman insults humans' "fat, sloppy feet," Gem doesn't retaliate by insulting the woman's claws. Gem is careful and avoids an argument. She may not be beautiful, but she certainly is smart!

9. LITERARY CONCEPT: Theme
Ask students to evaluate this statement of the main message of the story—"beauty does not always bring happiness." Invite students to comment on whether physical beauty actually brings unhappiness sometimes. (Any response is valid.)

TWO BEAUTIFUL LADIES: LADY WITH FAN (detail) 1863 Ju Qing
Art Gallery, Institute of Chinese Studies, The Chinese University of Hong Kong.

Gem found a bucket and brought the water as the wise woman had asked. In the meantime, the wise woman had started a fire beneath a small stove. At the wise woman's directions, the eager girl filled a pot with water and placed it upon the top of the stove.

Then, murmuring a spell, the wise woman began to twirl the flower between her palms, faster and faster, harder and harder, until she squeezed the juice from the flower. Instantly, the hut was filled with a sweet scent that overpowered all the other fragrances. When she had wrung out the last drop, she threw the flower itself into the hole beneath the stove where the fire burned. The crushed flower disappeared in a flash of light.

Under the wise woman's watchful eye, Gem kept feeding the fire until the whole pot had almost boiled away. Carefully pouring the remaining contents into a small jar, the wise woman handed it to Gem.

"Wash your face with the first drop," the wise woman instructed. "Rub any warts and moles with the second. Swallow the third."

As the sun set, Gem skipped home clutching the jar to her chest. People turned to stare at the stranger, because no one but her own family had ever seen her. Soon, Gem said to herself, they will all be wishing they could be me.

She burst into her home, holding the jar triumphantly in the air. "I found the wise woman," she told her astounded family.

With elaborate caution, Gem poured the first drop onto her palm and washed her cheeks. Though it was only a drop, the fluid kept spreading magically until her whole face felt cool and tingly.

The second drop she massaged onto any bumps on her face, and wherever she touched, the spot burned with a pleasant warmth.

Then, raising the jar and closing her eyes, she drank the third drop. "Ai yah. Ai yah," she murmured.

"Are you feeling sick?" her mother asked anxiously.

"No." Gem hugged herself. "At least I don't think so." She gave a shiver. "But I feel as though there's lightning bouncing around inside. And each bit of lightning is tiny as an ant and they're all racing around under my skin. What kind of evil trick has the wise woman played on me?"

Terrified, Gem put her hands to her face and began to cry.

"Quick," her worried mother said. "We'll go to a doctor." The mother grabbed her wrists and tried to pull Gem toward the door.

As her mother tugged at her, Gem was forced to lower her hands. When the mother saw her daughter, she stopped in midstep.

"How terrible is it?" Gem asked. When her mother could only gape, Gem turned to her father. "Am I even more hideous?" When he only stared too, she begged her brothers to tell her, but they were as stunned as their parents.

Desperately Gem flung some water into a bowl and stared down, waiting for the water to calm down enough so she could see her reflection. She blinked when she saw the beautiful stranger gazing up at her. The stranger's face had eyebrows like the leaf of the willow, eyes like kernels of apricots, a mouth like a cherry, a face shaped like a melon seed.

As the sun set, Gem skipped home clutching the jar to her chest.

Cautiously, hardly daring to believe, she raised a hand to touch her face. Upon the surface of the water, the lovely stranger also raised a delicate hand.

"It worked," she said. "It worked!"

Word of her beauty quickly spread through the countryside, for there was no one as lovely as she.

About that time, though, the king of the land fell sick with a terrible fever that burned through his body like flames through

10

11

12

◄ E

10. ACTIVE READING: Question
Why haven't these villagers—Gem's neighbors—ever seen her before? *(Possible responses: Gem has always refused to go outside, thinking herself too ugly; Gem has been wearing a cloth as a veil.)*

11. LITERARY CONCEPT: Suspense
Ask students how this paragraph builds suspense. *(Possible responses: We don't know whether the spell has made Gem ugly or beautiful; her family's speechlessness keeps us from finding out what has happened.)*

12. LITERARY CONCEPT: Figurative Language
Ask students to list the similes the author uses to describe Gem. *(eyebrows like willow leaves, eyes like apricot kernels, mouth like a cherry, face shaped like a melon seed)* Make sure students understand that these images are meant to connote great beauty.

For Alternative Learning Styles
Students may wish to draw the transformed Gem. Have them consider what the similes are saying about the shapes and colors of her features. ★

an old log. Hurriedly his doctors examined him and, after a lengthy <u>consultation</u> among themselves, went to his heir, the prince. "Everyone has the elements of yin and yang.[1] His Highness burns because he has too much fiery yang and must be cooled with yin. Because his illness is so severe, it must be quickly countered with a powerful dose."

"What are you waiting for?" the prince demanded. "Do it!"

13 The doctors bowed deeply, and their chief hardly dared to look up at the angry prince. "We regret to inform you that yin is most concentrated in the heart of a beautiful girl. We must cut it out."

The prince paled. "Is there no other way?"

The chief doctor apologized and said, "It would take too long to gather it from other sources. He must have a broth made from such a heart as soon as possible, or His Highness will surely die."

The prince took a breath and then nodded. "So be it." That very night he sent men racing from the palace across the kingdom to fetch back the most beautiful girls.

In her village, Gem woke to the frightened cries and the wailing. Her sleepy father staggered into the lane to find out what was happening. Hastily he scurried back, wide-eyed with the news. "Everyone **14** with a pretty daughter is telling the king's men to come here for you. They want to **F ▶** cut out your heart."

"Quickly. Go hide in the hills," her mother ordered her daughter. "We'll put up a fuss and distract them for as long as we can."

Gem slid out of the courtyard gate and darted away from the lights by the village gates. Moving a cart against the village walls, she managed to climb to the top of a wall. To her dismay, she saw men with torches ringing the village.

She dropped back down within the village and tried to hide, but the other villagers, fearing for the lives of their own daughters, pointed at Gem and called to the king's men. Not knowing where else to go, she stumbled into the temple of the goddess of mercy. As she heard the mob coming toward her, she collapsed in despair.

The next instant there was a flash of light, and the wise woman was standing there with her arms folded in front of her. With a cry, Gem crawled on her hands and knees toward the wise woman. "Save me. This cursed beauty will be my death."

The wise woman looked down at her sternly. "Make up your mind. Are you too **15** beautiful or too ugly to live?"

However, as the terrified girl begged for help, the wise woman's expression softened. From her sleeve, she produced another small jar. "I thought you might be needing this, so I saved the last three drops. Use them as before."

Shaking with fright, Gem took the jar from the wise woman, who disappeared just

---

1. **yin and yang:** in Chinese philosophy, the two primary forces in the universe. The first is passive and negative; the second, active and positive.

Words to Know and Use	**consultation** (kän′ səl tā′ shən) *n.* a meeting to discuss or decide something

as quickly as she had come. Hastily Gem rubbed one drop on her face, dotted her face with the second, and swallowed the third.

As the mob burst into the temple, they found Gem cowering upon the floor of the temple. Sure that they had found the most beautiful girl, they yanked her to her feet; but when they saw her, they became angry. "She's just an ordinary girl," their captain said. "They've just been playing a trick on us."

And kicking and slapping the villagers who had led them there, the soldiers left Gem alone in the temple. ◄ G

As it turned out, the king's fever broke that night and he recovered. And when he was well and heard what had almost happened, he dismissed all his old doctors and hired new ones.

As for Gem, she found her looks were adequate for her needs. ❧

16
◄ H

Responding to Reading

1. What feelings did you have about Gem? Jot down your reactions in your journal or notebook.

2. What do you think are Gem's strengths and weaknesses?

3. What does the story reveal about Chinese values?

   Think about
   • why it is dangerous to stand apart from the crowd
   • the advice given to Gem by her mother and the wise woman

4. If you could become more handsome or more beautiful, as Gem did, would you? Explain your feelings.

16. LITERARY CONCEPT: Folklore
Explain that changes in shape or form constitute a common theme in folklore. Point out that the change is often a punishment, as with Echo and Narcissus. Ask students how Gem's transformation is different from theirs. (Possible responses: Hers was the granting of a wish, not a punishment; she got to change back when her new form began to cause her trouble.)

Responding to Reading

1. Any response is valid.

2. **Possible responses:** Strengths: determination, intelligence; weaknesses: obsession with her looks, self-pity, stubbornness

3. **Possible responses:** that the Chinese find peace in being ordinary, that they see dissatisfaction with one's lot in life as a source of danger and unhappiness, that they feel people should not stand out from the crowd

4. Any response is valid.

ENCOURAGING INDEPENDENT READING

Anpao: An American Indian Odyssey, novel based on Blackfoot and Cherokee oral tales, by Jamake Highwater

The Superlative Horse, ancient Chinese story retold by Jean Merrill

When Shlemiel Went to Warsaw and Other Stories, Yiddish folk tales retold by Isaac Bashevis Singer

Comprehension Check

1. What is Echo's punishment? (She can say nothing except the last few words she has heard.)

2. What is Narcissus' punishment? (He falls in love with his own reflection, which will never love him back.)

3. Why does everyone pretend to see the Emperor's new clothes? (No one wants to be judged a simpleton or an incompetent.)

4. Who finally tells the truth about the Emperor's clothes? (a young child)

5. What does Gem want to change? (her looks)

6. What does the wise woman make for Gem? (a magic potion that makes her beautiful)

7. Why is Gem in danger when she's beautiful? (The king's men want her heart for medicine.)

8. How does Gem avoid this danger? (The wise woman restores Gem's former appearance.)

Student Response

Responding to Reading

1. Possible response: Beauty seems a dangerous thing in both cultures: Gem is threatened simply for being beautiful, perhaps because standing out by virtue of one's beauty was not desirable to the Chinese, and Narcissus' cruelty and his ultimate fate suggest that beauty can go to a person's head and make him or her behave badly. Beauty seems to have been valued more highly by the Greeks.

2. Possible responses: "The Emperor's New Clothes," since the Emperor neglects his duties and he and his courtiers are dishonest and gullible; "The Fatal Flower," since the king's doctors would kill an innocent girl just to cure a fever and since the prince sends soldiers to terrorize the people

3. Possible responses: Narcissus might want a lighted mirror in which to admire himself; the Emperor would probably be tempted by the latest high-fashion clothing; Gem would probably want personal-care items—skin creams, shampoos, makeup.

Literary Concept: Literary Folk Tale

Children would enjoy the silliness of the Emperor and his courtiers, the rogues' pretending to make the clothes, the embarrassment of the Emperor when people realize he has no clothes on, and the child's role as the truthteller.

Writing Options

The Writing Options are designed to meet varied student interests and abilities. Have each student choose one writing activity to complete.

Journal Update Ask students to write topics for modern tales about vain people.

Vocabulary Practice

Answers to Exercise
King Elmer was a most **repulsive sovereign**. He was a selfish **rogue** with an **excessively** bad **stench**. He became so **vexed** with his **exquisite** wife, who worked with **diligence** in a **consultation** with his enemies, that he threw her out of his **realm**.

Responding to Reading

Comparing the Selections

1. On the basis of what you learned from these tales, how are the Greek and Chinese attitudes towards beauty alike and different?

2. In your opinion, which selection is more critical of those in power, "The Emperor's New Clothes" or "The Fatal Flower"?

Broader Connections

3. What modern products do you think would tempt Narcissus, the Emperor, and Gem?

Literary Concept: Literary Folk Tale

Although Hans Christian Andersen relied on the folklore of Denmark for many of his tales, he also invented new stories and gave new twists to old ones. His works are called **literary folk tales** because they have their origin in writing, not oral retellings. Andersen's stories were written for children. What do you think children would like about this story?

Writing Options

1. In a **letter** from Gem to the organizers of a beauty pageant, express her thoughts about the pageant's effects on contestants.

2. Choose a well-known person for the Narcissus "I Love Myself" Prize. Write a **testimonial** explaining that person's qualifications.

Vocabulary Practice

Exercise Recopy the paragraph below, replacing each boldfaced word with a word from the list.

King Elmer was a most **offensive ruler**. He was a selfish **crook** with an **overly** bad **odor**. He became so **annoyed** with his **beautiful** wife, who worked with **persistence** in a **meeting** with his enemies, that he threw her out of his **kingdom**.

Words to Know and Use
consultation
diligence
excessively
exquisite
realm
repulsive
rogue
sovereign
stench
vexed

The Spelling Connection

Spelling Pattern: Adding Suffixes If the final syllable of a base word ending in a consonant is not accented, you usually do *not* double the final consonant before adding a suffix.

Example: label labeled labeling

Words with Suffixes from the Selections

accustom	accustomed	water	watering
remember	remembered	travel	traveled
chatter	chattered	murmur	murmuring

Other Words with Suffixes

custom	customer	credit	credited
profit	profitable	focus	focused

Exercise Answer with spelling words.

1. If a lemonade stand makes money, it is ___.
2. An honest salesperson doesn't try to cheat his ___.
3. If you are used to something, you're ___ to it.
4. Money added to your bank account is ___ to you.
5. Instead of a sprinkler, use the ___ can.

*O*ptions for Learning (Multimodal/Cross-Curricular Activities)

1 • **Rogue's Business** Imagine that the two rogues in "The Emperor's New Clothes" set up shop in your town. Work in a small group to devise products they might sell, and create a brochure about the products.

2 • **The Selling of Beauty** Create a television ad in which either Gem or Narcissus endorses a beauty product, such as "Gem Lotion." Act out your ad in class.

*H*ans Christian Andersen   1805–1875

At the age of fourteen, Hans Christian Andersen, the son of a poor washerwoman and a shoemaker, went to Copenhagen, the capital of Denmark, hoping to win fame in the theater. He failed as an actor, a dancer, and a singer before he finally found patrons who arranged for his education.

Later, he turned to writing. In 1835 he published a cheap booklet called *Tales Told for Children.* His tales became immensely popular, gaining him fame across Europe. Andersen went on to write 168 tales, including "The Princess and the Pea," and "The Ugly Duckling."

Interestingly, Andersen never thought highly of his tales, perhaps because he always hoped his success would come in the theater. Also, he had no particular liking for children.

*L*aurence Yep   1948–

Yep published his first short story as a college freshman. When only twenty-five, he published his first book. Two years later he wrote his second book, *Dragonwings,* which won ten awards, including a Newbery Medal Honor Award. He has written over seventeen books and two plays, many of them reflecting his Chinese heritage.

His books, such as *Child of the Owl*

and *Sea Glass,* often focus on characters caught between two cultures. Yep says that his books are popular among teenagers because "I'm always pursuing the theme of being an outsider—an alien—and many teenagers feel they're aliens."

Yep has also taught at various schools, including the University of California at Berkeley, where he was a writer in residence.

■ *A biography of Moira Kerr can be found on page 631.*

Cross-Curricular Projects

Science/Math Have interested students research the ideal conditions for hearing an echo, and ask them to use the speed of sound waves to calculate how long it takes to hear an echo in various settings.

Health Gem visits a wise old woman who gathers and dries herbs for use as medicines. Have students research Chinese herbal medicine with an eye to finding out why practitioners of this ancient art are still popular today.

Social Studies Ask volunteers to find out about the role of women in ancient China. Ask them to discover how and why that role has changed in modern China.

Objectives

- To write in the narrative, descriptive, informative, literary, or persuasive mode
- To use appropriate strategies for writing in a chosen format
- To draft, revise, edit, and share a piece of writing of one's choice

Teaching Strategies

DISCUSSING THE ASSIGNMENT

Since students have their choice of assignments and formats, you might suggest that they consider the following when deciding which to do: the kind of assignment they enjoyed most; the one they found most difficult, with an eye toward improving their skill; or the assignment that intrigues them most.

Remind students to make their own PASSkeys and keep them handy as they write. Use these strategies to offer help and encouragement on each of the assignments that follow.

A. Narrative Writing

Prewrite and Explore Suggest to students that this assignment is an excellent opportunity to write a humorous piece. Suggest that they brainstorm to create a supernatural being with a problem—one that can only be solved by the creation of their chosen appliance. Students might even enjoy giving the appliance a personality.

Draft and Discover One narrative strategy is to have students' stories begin in the present with the main characters reflecting on the "good old days." Their reflections serve as a flashback that tells how the appliance was created.

Revise Your Writing If students use dialogue in their myths, remind them that it should reflect their characters' personalities.

WRITER'S CHOICE

As you discovered in this unit, the forms of folklore are many and varied. In this workshop your writing opportunities are varied as well. You can pick a format of your choice—one that you've enjoyed before. You can make your own PASSkey and create your own steps. So go ahead! Choose the assignment you like best, loosen up your writing arm, and let your imagination fly.

A. Narrative Writing: Where Did It Come From?

It's hard to imagine, but long ago when the world was young, there were no VCR's, microwave ovens, soft drink machines, or even blow dryers. How did these miraculous devices originate? Which gods or goddesses, heroes or heroines, might have been responsible? Write a myth that explains the "origin" of a modern technological device.

> **NEED MORE HELP?**
> A **myth** is a story—a narrative. For more about writing a narrative, see the Writer's Workshop on pages 174–178.

Prewrite and Explore You might start by listing six to eight technological devices you use or see others use daily. Then you can choose a device and brainstorm, perhaps with friends, about its "mythical" origin. Feel free to make up new gods and heroes, giving them appropriate names, duties, and supernatural powers.

> **NEED MORE HELP?**
> For more about cause and effect, see the Reader's Workshop on page 182.

Draft and Discover You can write your myth in chronological order. As you write, think about causes and effects. For example, the device you've chosen is an effect, and the actions of your characters are its causes. Make the effects of actions clear.

Revise Your Writing Use the checklist on page 177 to revise your work. Ask a classmate to help.

B. Descriptive/Informative Writing: As Great-Grandma Used to Say . . .

Every family has its own stories and sayings, just as every culture has its own folklore. Some stories feature things that family members have done or seen. Other favorites may spring from a family's ethnic heritage. Write about the place that stories and sayings have in your family. Describe the people who recite them and the ways that other family members respond.

ADDITIONAL RESOURCES

Unit Six Resource Book
Writer's Workshop Worksheets, p. 41
Writer's Workshop: Peer and Self-Evaluation, p. 42
Assessment Guidelines, p. 43

Technology and Enrichment
 Writer's Databank Software: Files 7–10, Techniques for Elaboration
Elaboration, Revision, and Proofreading Transparencies
Fine Art Transparency Pack

Links to
Writer's Craft

For more about specific modes of writing, see *The Writer's Craft,* Grade 7, "Observation and Description," (pages 48–61), "Narrative and Literary Writing," (pages 70–85), "Informative Writing: Explaining How," (pages 94–107), "Informative Writing: Explaining What," (pages 116–129), or "Persuasion," (pages 138–151).

Prewrite and Explore Try jotting notes about who tells your family's folklore and when, where, why, and how it's told. Then you can rough out one or two general statements about the importance of this folklore to your family.

Draft and Discover You might open with a description of a family storyteller in action. Then, in two or three paragraphs, you can explain your ideas about the role of folklore in your family. Include examples and anecdotes, and don't forget to state your own feelings.

Revise Your Writing Use the checklists for descriptive writing, page 112, and informative writing, page 573, as revision guides.

◀ **NEED HELP?**
....
For more about descriptive writing, see the Writer's Workshop on pages 109–113. For more about informative writing, see the Writer's Workshop on pages 569–573.

C. Writing About Literature: Watch That Trickster!

Talk about sly! You have to get up pretty early in the morning to outwit tricksters like Lazy Peter, Anansi the spider, and Anansi's friend Turtle. Find and read more trickster tales from several cultures. Then write a paper comparing and contrasting two of the tricksters.

Prewrite and Explore You might make a chart to help you explore the two tricksters' likenesses and differences. Chart areas like looks, personality, and powers. As you fill in the spaces with the tricksters' traits, include supporting details from the tales.

◀ **NEED HELP?**
....
For more on writing about literature, see the Writer's Workshop on pages 457–461.

Draft and Discover One approach is to describe the first trickster in a paragraph, covering each area in your chart. In the next paragraph, describe the second trickster, covering the same areas and noting the tricksters' likenesses and differences. Another approach is to use one paragraph for likenesses and differences in both tricksters' looks, a second for likenesses and differences in their personalities, and so on. Include transitions such as on the other hand, like, unlike, in the same way, and in contrast.

Revise Your Writing Look at the checklist on page 461. Then, with a friend, create a checklist for a comparison-and-contrast paper.

D. Narrative Writing: Lights, Camera, Action!

What if the tales from this unit were made into modern movies? Can you picture Phaëthon in his father's chariot, pulling up for a drive-through burger and fries? Update a tale from this unit by rewriting it as a movie script. Give your script a modern setting, and feel free to add modern twists.

B. Descriptive/Informative Writing

Prewrite and Explore If students claim they don't have any stories and sayings in their families but would like to try this project, tell them to invent something! You might suggest students read a few of James Thurber's sketches about his strange family or review "Aunt Millicent."

Draft and Discover If students invent a family member, suggest that they organize the body of their work into three paragraphs. That way they can explain how "Uncle George" affects three different family members—each in a different way.

Students who write about real family storytellers might want to capture a saying or story on tape and play it back as they draft.

Revise Your Writing Suggest that students describe their family storyteller by using a photograph of the person as a guide. As they revise, have them begin with the speaker's most noticeable characteristic—a calm, level gaze, for example—and continue from there.

C. Writing About Literature

Prewrite and Explore Remind students that the tricksters they compare and contrast don't have to be from the same tale. In addition to charts, remind students that they can use Venn diagrams or even double word webs to note their character's traits. Point out that students might also compare and contrast the tricksters' methods of operation, choice of victims, and usual outcomes.

Draft and Discover Remind students that organization is key to writing effective comparison and contrast papers. Encourage students to use one of the approaches discussed in the text and to end their papers with a two- or three-sentence summary.

Revise Your Writing You may want students who choose this option to meet in small groups to revise together. A helpful guide might be the comparison/contrast worksheet (p. 10) in the Thinking Skills Transparency Pack.

Multicultural Connections

Trickster Tales Since students have read about Anansi the spider and Lazy Peter, have them find and retell a trickster tale from another country.

Students may work in pairs or individually to tell their tales. Encourage them to use visual and auditory aids such as large pictures drawn on cardboard or oak tag and homemade sound effects to accompany the retelling. Here is a partial list of tricksters from which students might choose:

1. Anansi stories from Ghana

2. other African tales featuring the tortoise, the hare, and the monkey

3. Native American trickster tales featuring the raven and the coyote

4. Aesop's fables featuring the crow and the fox

D. Narrative Writing

Prewrite and Explore Suggest that students choose a selection that is full of conflict, as that is what makes great drama. Students might make storyboards, which are like comic strips, except that each panel shows a scene from the drama. Under each panel students write brief notes to explain what's happening in each one.

Draft and Discover A good strategy for writing a script is to have students imagine their favorite actor or actress as the main character. That way, they can write dialogue the way the star would say it and compose stage directions with specific people in mind.

Revise Your Writing Encourage students to pay special attention to the dialogue as they revise. Remind them that whatever their actors say, their dialogue must reflect the personality of the character who speaks.

E. Informative Writing

Prewrite and Explore Once students have chosen selections, formed theories, and researched material, have them make graphic organizers. Here is a model for a cause-and-effect format:

Draft and Discover Suggest that students describe their effects with powerful images (Prometheus on the cliff; Phaëthon losing control of the fiery chariot). If they describe a cause-and-effect chain, be sure they explain how each effect becomes a new cause.

Revise Your Writing Have students revise for clarity to be sure causes are believable and effects logical for the cultures from which their tales come. Remind students that their bibliographies should be in standard format.

· · · · · · · · · **NEED HELP?**
For more about writing a script, see the Writer's Workshop on pages 237–241.

Prewrite and Explore Choose a tale to dramatize, and list its main events. Each main event can become a scene in your script. You can use scene charts to plan details about each scene's modern setting, characters, and action. Consider working in a small group.

Draft and Discover Follow standard drama format, beginning with a cast of characters. Then, scene by scene, write dialogue and stage directions.

Revise Your Writing Have friends "walk through" your script, reading it aloud. Make needed changes so that the tale will work as drama.

E. Informative Writing: What Caused That Tale?

Although legends, myths, and folk tales are entertaining, they also pass along history and cultural values. Choose a tale from this unit, and do some detective work. First, speculate about the reasons that might have caused the people to tell that tale. Then research the culture from which the tale comes in order to support your theory. Finally, in a cause-and-effect essay, explain why and how the tale probably originated.

Prewrite and Explore Which story's origins and purpose can you form a theory to explain? For example, do you have a good idea of why "The People Could Fly" was told? Choose a tale and write a statement that expresses why you think it was told. Then head for the library to track down information about the culture that told it. Look for facts or statistics that support your theory—or change your theory to fit the facts you find. Take notes, including bibliography notes.

· · · · · · · · · **NEED HELP?**
For more about writing an informative report, see the Writer's Workshop on pages 339–343.

Draft and Discover You are explaining the cause of an effect—the tale you chose. State your main idea clearly at the beginning. Then support your theory with several reasons, using facts and details from your notecards. Conclude with a powerful restatement of your main idea. Add a list of your sources.

Revise Your Writing Use the checklist on page 342. Ask a friend to read your draft and respond to it.

F. Persuasive Writing: Get Out the Vote!

In this unit, you've met characters with great personal strengths as well as those with supernatural powers. Choose one whose strengths or powers would be useful in modern politics. Then write a campaign pamphlet urging people to elect your character president.

Multicultural Connections

Sun gods The myth of the sun god Apollo and Phaëthon, Apollo's son, originated so the early Greeks could explain the sun's path across the sky. Share with students that many countries besides Greece had myths about the sun. Have students work in small groups to research the following:

1. the Japanese sun god, who was the ancestor of all the emperors

2. the Inca god, whose image was also a calendar

3. the bonfire sun of the early Australian aborigines

4. the ancient Egyptian sun god, Ra, who used the sun as a ship

Prewrite and Explore You might create a chart with spaces to list the strengths and powers of several "candidates." Choose the one best suited to the job, and try a focused freewriting about why he or she would be a good president. Then sketch a layout for your pamphlet, including both verbal and visual elements.

Draft and Discover Draft the text of your pamphlet, using ideas and words from your freewriting. Introduce your candidate at the beginning. Use logic to explain his or her strong points, and choose words that have connotations that will help persuade readers.

Revise Your Writing Check the text of your pamphlet for errors in reasoning, and write a call to action for the conclusion. Then add illustrations and other visual elements to create a finished product.

◀ **NEED HELP?**

For more about persuasive writing, see the Writer's Workshops on pages 388–392 and 512–516.

G. Narrative Writing: Fix-It Time

"The People Could Fly" uses fantasy to deal with a real problem. The fantasy may not offer a practical solution—but it makes the problem clear and unforgettable. Think of a current problem that you care about, and come up with a fantasy solution. Then write the story of what happens once your solution is used.

Prewrite and Explore Freewrite to focus your observations of a problem that you care about. Next, brainstorm for fantasy solutions. Then close your eyes for a moment. Form detailed mental pictures of what might happen if your fantasy solution came true.

Draft and Discover As you write the tale of what happens when your solution is used, keep your imagination humming. Reach for descriptive, sensory details to bring your mental pictures to life. Be sure you clearly show the problem as well as the solution.

Revise Your Writing Find a "grabber" action scene to open your story. Be sure you show readers why the problem concerns you. See if you can add transitions to make the order of events clearer to your readers. Then create a satisfying conclusion.

◀ **NEED HELP?**

For more on writing about problems and solutions, see the Writer's Workshop on pages 339–343.

Final Revision

No matter which assignment you chose, be sure to give your draft another look. Before you proofread for errors in grammar, spelling, punctuation, and capitalization, look for ways you can add life to your writing. Try varying sentence beginnings, as shown in the box at the top of the next page.

WRITER'S WORKSHOP   665

F. Persuasive Writing

Prewrite and Explore Here's another opportunity for students to write humor. You may want to suggest that they choose highly improbable characters for their political jobs, such as Phaëthon for Commissioner of Traffic Safety. Charts can list advantages such as "friends in high places" and "experience working under stress."

Draft and Discover As students draft, remind them to present their supporting reasons in separate paragraphs and to keep their strongest reason until last.

Revise Your Writing Remind students that their last few sentences should be a call to action.

G. Narrative Writing

Prewrite and Explore Share with students that this assignment is a chance to express wishes too far-fetched to ever come true—but here they can! Have students list the problems that they care about the most, and choose the one they'd feel most virtuous about fixing.

Draft and Discover Suggest that students think of the paper as a story, with strong characters and setting and with a monumental conflict that's about to be resolved. Have students begin writing in the middle, in the scene where the biggest changes occur.

Revise Your Writing Students might revise by creating two different tones—the first, a sorrowful one; the second, when the fantasy takes over, a warm, light, joyful one. Have students use thesauruses to develop and maintain these tones throughout the respective sections.

REVISION TIPS

■ Remind students to describe characters and situations in precise language, using comparisons, figurative language, and sensory details.

- Have students revise their dialogue so characters show, not tell, what's going on.

- Have them proofread to remove every grammatical, typographical, and mechanical error they can find.

Use the following sentences as oral practice to help students vary sentence beginnings. (Possible revisions are given.)

1. Phaëthon should be our next Traffic Commissioner. He has experience. *(For Traffic Commissioner, it's got to be Phaëthon. Surely he's the most experienced candidate of all!)*

2. Uncle George is certainly a character, a man with stories no one else's uncle ever thought of. *(Without exception, Uncle George is the oddest man we know. His stories are all original.)*

Publish and Present

You might want to have a display of students' papers to showcase the last (and best) work of the school year. Use the largest space you have in the classroom, such as a chalkboard that stretches the length of a side wall. Masks and other regalia can be set up on a long table underneath the papers. Encourage students to photograph the display and place the photo as a memento in their journals or learning logs.

Reflect on Your Writing

You might want to have students answer these questions instead of or in addition to those in the text:

1. Did I achieve the purpose I set for myself?

2. In what way is this paper the best work I've done this year?

Closure

Now that students have written their last assignment in seventh grade, suggest that they keep their writing skills sharp by making entries in their journals at least once a week during vacation.

NEED MORE HELP?
See the Language Workshop on pages 668–670.

THE EDITOR'S EYE: VARYING SENTENCE BEGINNINGS

Your writing can sound immature when all your sentences start with their subjects. Instead, try starting some sentences with an adverb or a prepositional phrase.

Problem	*Coyote* is the loner among all the animals. *He* often disagrees with the others. *No one* can predict what he'll do.
Improved	*Among all the animals,* Coyote is the loner. *Often* he disagrees with the others. No one can predict what he'll do.

Publish and Present

Here are some suggestions for sharing your work with others.

Face Value   Make a mask that represents a central character in your writing. Decorate it with colors, designs, and objects related to the character. Read your work and display the mask to classmates.

Variety Show   With others who have done the same assignment, create a group presentation. Read your writings for class members and play appropriate background music during your presentation.

Reflect on Your Writing

FOR YOUR PORTFOLIO ▶

Write brief answers to the following questions. Attach them to your paper when you put it in your portfolio.

1. How did you decide which assignment you would complete?
2. How did your writing process for this paper differ from the processes you followed in previous Writer's Workshops?

Assessment Guidelines

These guidelines may help you assess student writing:

Content
- Assignment follows prompts and guidelines, yet still offers creative ideas.
- Narratives use such elements as character, setting, and plot and contain specific details.
- Expository and persuasive papers follow the conventions of the genre.

Style
- Sentences are varied, and paragraphing is appropriate.
- Tone and point of view have been consistently maintained throughout the assignment.

Usage and Mechanics
- Standard English is used throughout.
- Errors in spelling, capitalization, and punctuation are avoided.

See *Unit Six Resource Book*, page 43.

WORKSHOP

SELF-ASSESSMENT

Portfolio Review

Guided Assignment   Write a one-page essay in which you explain your achievements this year as a writer.

Prewrite and Explore   Read through your Portfolio, taking notes. Choose the writings you feel best about, and pinpoint what you like about your work. Decide which aspects of your writing were weakest at the beginning of the year. Where do you see improvement now? Then list two or three aspects of your writing that you'd like to strengthen. Consider your level of comfort with each part of the writing process (prewriting, drafting, revising, proofreading, and publishing).

Draft and Discover   Using your notes and lists, draft your essay. You might begin either with your strengths or with areas you'd like to improve. Use examples from your own work to explain your points.

Revise Your Writing   Find the organization that's emerging in your draft, and work to make it clear. Keep reshaping your paragraphs and sentences until they say exactly what you think and feel, and they're easy for readers to follow. Then add an introduction that will catch readers' attention and a conclusion that will give readers a sense of completion. Design a checklist that a friend can use to offer helpful responses and a checklist that you can use on your own.

Proofread   Find and correct any errors in grammar, spelling, and mechanics. A friend might help. Then make a clean copy of your essay.

Publish and Present   Share your essay with a small group of classmates. As a group, discuss what you enjoy most—and least—about writing.

Objectives

■ To review the writing assignments completed during the past year

■ To analyze and evaluate one's writing, identifying weaknesses, strengths, and improvements

■ To draft, revise, and edit an assessment of one's writing in the form of an essay

Teaching Strategies

Have students read the directions for the portfolio review. Ask volunteers to explain with which aspects of their writing they feel most and least satisfied. Have the class discuss why it is useful to review their progress as writers and to identify strengths and weaknesses.

Prewrite and Explore Have students make graphic organizers to summarize the points they want to make in their writing. Example:

Strengths	Weaknesses	Improvements

Draft and Discover Suggest that students begin with a sentence that gives their overall reactions to the year's writing. Then, in separate paragraphs, have them write main idea sentences from their graphic organizers and support them with details from individual assignments.

Revise Your Writing Have students shape their first sentences into introductions and write conclusions that summarize or otherwise complete the assessment.

Proofread Suggest that students proofread for correct punctuation with transitions.

Publish and Present Have students place their essays at the front of their portfolios, followed by the year's work in the order in which it was produced.

Closure

Point out that students should be happy with whatever they've learned and be confident that they'll continue to improve in the future.

Objectives

■ To understand that varying sentences adds interest to writing

■ To develop and use strategies for varying sentences

Teaching Strategies

Explain to students that they'll do a "boredom test" on some of their past assignments. Have them skim a few papers and note the following points: Are their sentences mostly in subject-verb-object order? Are many the same length? Do many—even the ones with wonderful imagery and precise language—have the same rhythm? Tell students that if so, they flunk the boredom test! Now they'll try to remedy the situation.

Have the class scan the workshop, noting its three subheads. Work with students through the first subsection, encouraging them to give examples from their past work and challenging them to apply the strategies. If you think students will be embarrassed, do it yourself first, using some of the work you've written in the past.

Then point out the following problems students might encounter.

■ Remind them that not all words ending in -ly are adverbs; *lovely* and *friendly*, for example, are adjectives. Have them perform the adverb test on all -ly words: if the word answers the question *how, when, where,* or *to what extent,* it is an adverb.

■ To keep students from making modifying errors with participial phrases, give them this rule: Place the subject and the participial phrase that modifies it right next to each other.

SENTENCE VARIETY

Have you ever read a story by a third grader? The plot may be wild, but the sentences are usually tame: short, simple, subject-verb-object. Even a hair-raising story gets dull when it's told in a monotonous way. Mature writers learn to vary their sentence lengths and structures—and so can you.

Varying Sentence Beginnings

You can add variety by changing the beginnings of some of your sentences.

1. Begin with an **appositive,** a phrase that identifies the subject.

The young fellow, Kelfala, was a clown.
His friends, Shortie Bumpie and Longie Tallie, followed Kelfala.

2. Begin with a **prepositional phrase.** Prepositions, words such as *with, over, on, in,* and *at,* show relationships in space or time.

With Wambuna, Kelfala had no success.
Even *after failure,* he wouldn't give up.

3. Begin with an **adverb** or adverb phrase. Adverbs modify verbs and may end in -ly.

Finally he asked two friends for help.
A week later, his chance came.

4. Begin with a **participial phrase.** A participle is an adjective formed by adding -ing to a verb.

Carrying a mysterious packet, Kelfala set out.
Trailing Wambuna silently, he followed her to a stream.

5. Begin with a **quote.**

"Wait a minute, Kelfala," one of his friends said.
"The trick was mine, see?" and with that, Kelfala hopped.

668   UNIT SIX   THEMES IN WORLD FOLKLORE

ADDITIONAL RESOURCES
Unit Six Resource Book
Language Workshop Practice, p. 47

Links to
Writer's Craft

For more about sentence variety, see *The Writer's Craft,* Grade 7, "Sentence Composing," pages 46–47.

Changing the inner structures of some of your sentences is another way to avoid monotony.

1. Put the object or complement first.

> *This* the young men admired about Wambuna.
> *Her head* she carried erect.

2. Combine sentence ideas by using words like *when, if, while, because,* or *although.*

> *When she laughed,* she showed ivory-white teeth.
> Kelfala loved her *because she was clever and beautiful.*

Varying Sentence Length

When you have too many short sentences in a row, you can join some of them, changing the rhythm of your writing.

1. Join simple sentences with a comma and a conjunction.

> Kelfala's trick worked. He didn't marry Wambuna.
> Kelfala's trick worked, *but* he didn't marry Wambuna.

2. Create compound subjects, verbs, or objects.

> Wambuna smiled. The young men smiled too. Then they laughed.
> Wambuna and the young men smiled and laughed.

3. Insert a phrase from one sentence into another sentence.

> Wambuna sauntered off. She was heading toward her garden.
> Wambuna sauntered off toward her garden.

◀ **NEED MORE HELP?** ·········
See the Language
Workshop on pages
462–464.

Exercise 1   Concept Check   Revise each of the following sentences five times. Add a different kind of beginning each time. Use details from "Where the Girl Saved Her Brother."

1. The Cheyenne girl rescued her brother.
2. Her people have never forgotten her bravery.

LANGUAGE WORKSHOP   669

Work through the last two subsections with students as you did with the one on the previous page.

Remind students that when they vary sentences by using compound elements, they set off items in a series with commas. If only two compound elements are used, students should join them with *and, but,* or *or.*

Write these sentences on the board for practice in sentence variety.

1. Prometheus brought fire to the human race. He was punished for his kindness.

2. He stole the fire from the gods. He offered it to the people.

3. The people thanked him many times over.

4. Zeus was not happy with Prometheus. He lashed Prometheus to a rock. He ordered two vultures to eat his liver. He made him suffer for many years.

5. Eventually another hero saved Prometheus. That hero was named Heracles.

Answers to Exercise 1
Possible responses are given.

1. a. On the plains of Montana the Cheyenne girl rescued her brother.
b. Counting coup, the Cheyenne girl rescued her brother.
c. "Ai-y-eee!" cried the Cheyenne girl as she rescued her brother.
d. The Cheyenne girl screamed a war cry, rode into the midst of the enemy, and rescued her brother.
e. When the Cheyenne girl saw that her brother was outnumbered, she rode to his aid and rescued him.

2. a. Wisely, her people have never forgotten her bravery.
b. Her bravery they never forgot.
c. After that daring rescue, her people never forgot her bravery.
d. "You honor your tribe, Buffalo Calf Road Woman," said the people, and they never forgot her bravery.
e. Buffalo Calf Road Woman, a Cheyenne girl, showed bravery that her people never forgot.

Grammar Games: Sentence Variety

Divide students into groups of about five. Have each group assign one person as its recorder. Tell the first person in each group to think of a very simple sentence, which the recorder writes. Then have each team member add to the sentence a phrase, such as an appositive or a prepositional phrase. The recorder writes each new sentence as it is spoken. At the end of the four additions, the group may revise the sentence until satisfied with the result. Ask the recorder of each team to read the first and final sentence to the class, showing how the group has improved the sentence.

Answers to Exercise 2

(Answers will vary. A possible revision is given.)

Once there lived an ordinary-looking girl named Gem who considered herself ugly and refused to leave her house. "Please make me beautiful," she begged a wise woman of her town. Feeling sorry for Gem, the woman told her how to find a magic flower that would make her beautiful. Traveling for many days, Gem finally found the flower in a distant forest. Sure enough, it made Gem beautiful.

However, to Gem's surprise, beauty became a curse when soldiers almost killed her. Rushing back to the wise woman, Gem begged to be plain again. Her wish was granted, and her life was saved.

In this interesting story, Gem learned a lesson about a complicated kind of vanity. Conceited in reverse and greedy for beauty, Gem had desired much more than she ever needed.

Answers to Exercise 3

Check students' chosen sentences and their rewrites. Their final comments should indicate that the sentences they wrote are static, monotonous, and boring. The sentences they copied from the tale, however, are varied and interesting.

Answers to Exercise 4

Check students' assignments; note whether they followed directions.

Closure

Assure students that practice in varying sentences is valuable, since, like embossed stationery, sentence variety gives their writing a professional touch. Suggest that students list in their journals the strategies they've just learned, and encourage them to use appropriate strategies as they write letters or notes during the summer.

Vary sentence beginnings, sentence structures, and sentence lengths.

The girl called Gem looked fine. She thought she looked ugly. She would not leave the house. She talked to a wise woman. She learned of a magic flower. It could make her beautiful. She found the flower. It grew in a distant forest. She became beautiful. Beauty was a curse for her. That was a surprise. Soldiers almost killed her. She wanted to be plain again. The wise woman helped her. Gem learned a lesson. The story is interesting. It shows a complicated kind of vanity. Gem was conceited in reverse. She was also greedy. She was greedy for beauty. She wanted more than she needed.

Exercise 3   Looking at Style   Look at Leo Tolstoy's "The Old Grandfather and His Little Grandson," on page 615. Then follow the directions.

1. From the story, copy an example of each sentence variety technique listed below.

   a. a short, simple sentence followed by a long, intricate sentence

   b. two sentence ideas combined by using *when*

   c. a sentence that begins with an adverb phrase, followed by two sentences that begin with their subjects

2. Rewrite the story so that each sentence starts with its subject. How is the effect different from the effect of the original?

Exercise 4   Revising Your Writing   Reread the paper you wrote for the Writer's Workshop on pages 662–666. Revise it by adding variety to your sentence beginnings, sentence structures, and sentence lengths.

Additional Practice

Join these sentences to change their rhythm.

1. This zoo is one of the most advanced in the nation. Its habitats are authentic.
2. Kevin is one of the zookeepers. He tells wonderful elephant jokes.
3. Monkeys chattered in the trees. The tigers paid no attention to them.
4. The lions prowled over their habitat. The cheetahs explored. The panthers slept.
5. Many people were there. It was a beautiful day. They were visiting the zoo.
6. Little children were being dragged along by their parents. Some cried. Some laughed. Parents looked tired.
7. It's fun to watch people at a zoo. Many mimic the animals.
8. Sunday at the zoo is usually busy. This Sunday was no exception.

VOCABULARY
WORKSHOP

GREEK ROOTS

The ancient Greeks passed on not only their myths but some of their language as well. Many of our English words are based on Greek **roots,** or combining forms.

A root may appear at the beginning, in the middle, or at the end of a word. A prefix or suffix may be added to it. For example, the suffix *-ic* is used to form adjectives. The Greek root *phobia* (fear), with this suffix added, gives us the word *phobic,* "fearful." Roots are sometimes joined with other roots. *Graph* (writing) plus *logy* (study of) gives us *graphology,* "the study of handwriting." Study the Greek roots below. They can help you figure out the meanings of many words.

phobia—fear	psycho—mind	graph—writing
genes—origin	hydro—water	patri—father
stere—strong	techni—skilled	anthropo—human
phon—sound	pyro—fire	philo—to love
arch—first	zoo—animal	logi, logy—reason, study of
soph—wisdom	typos, typi—type, example	
biblio—book		

Exercise   The following words are made from the Greek roots above. By thinking like a detective, you can guess their meanings. First, copy the word on your paper and draw lines between the parts to separate the roots. Next, write the roots' meanings. Then write your guess of each word's meaning. Check your guesses in a dictionary.

Example: zoo/phobia   animal + fear = fear of animals

1. hydroplane	**6.** logical	**11.** photograph	**16.** technology
2. psychology	**7.** philanthropy	**12.** bibliography	**17.** pyrogenic
3. stereophonic	**8.** philosophy	**13.** bibliophile	**18.** genealogy
4. archetype	**9.** zoology	**14.** pyrotechnics	**19.** patriarch
5. archeology	**10.** stereotype	**15.** anthropology	**20.** phonograph

ADDITIONAL RESOURCES
Unit Six Resource Book
Vocabulary Workshop Practice, p. 48

Objective

■ To learn to decode words with Greek roots

Teaching Strategies

Have students read the introductory paragraph on page 671 and study the roots in the box. Ask them to tell any English words they know that contain these roots.

Answers to Exercise
(Shortened answers are given.)

1. a plane that can take off and land in water

2. the study of the mind

3. relating to the splitting of solid sound into dimensional parts

4. the first of a kind

5. the study of the first examples

6. relating to reason

7. the practice of doing good for humanity

8. the love or study of wisdom

9. the study of animals

10. a strong or fixed type of something

11. writing with light

12. a list of books (from which information is taken for writing)

13. someone who loves books

14. fire skills; the manufacture and use of fireworks

15. the study of humans

16. a body of advanced knowledge

17. something which brings forth fire, such as a volcano

18. the study of (a person's) origins; family history

19. the founding father of a family

20. sound writing; an instrument that records sound

Additional Practice

Have students "decode" these phobias.

1. acrophobia *(fear of high places)*
2. agoraphobia *(fear of public places)*
3. ailurophobia *(fear of cats)*
4. arachnophobia *(fear of spiders)*
5. xenophobia *(fear of people of foreign origin)*
6. gynophobia *(fear of women)*
7. herpetophobia *(fear of snakes)*
8. numerophobia *(fear of numbers)*

672

Handbook Contents

READER'S HANDBOOK

GLOSSARY

The **glossary** is an alphabetical listing of words from the selections, with meanings. The glossary gives the following information:

1. The entry word broken into syllables.

2. The pronunciation of each word. The **respelling** is shown in parentheses. The Pronunciation Key below shows the symbols for the sounds of letters and key words that contain those sounds.

A **primary accent** ' is placed after the syllable that is stressed the most when the word is spoken. A **secondary accent** ' is placed after a syllable that has a lighter stress.

3. The part of speech of the word. These abbreviations are used:

n. noun　　*v.* verb　　*adj.* adjective
adv. adverb　　*prep.* preposition

4. The meaning of the word. The definitions listed in the glossary apply to selected ways a word is used in these selections.

5. Related forms. Words with suffixes such as *-ing, -ed, -ness,* and *-ly* are often listed under the base word.

1. entry word ········
2. respelling ····
def er en tial (def' ər en' shəl)
3. part of speech ······ *adj.* showing courteous regard ······ 4. meaning
or respect

Pronunciation Key

Symbol	Key Words	Symbol	Key Words	Symbol	Key Words	Symbol	Key Words
a	at, gas	o͞o	tool, crew	ə ⎰ a	in ago	ch	chin
ā	ape, day	o͝o	look, pull	e	in agent	sh	she
ä	car, lot	yo͞o	use, cute, few	i	in insanity	th	thin
e	elf, ten	yo͝o	cure	o	in comply	th	then
ē	even, me	oi	oil, coin	⎱ u	in focus	zh	leisure
i	is, hit	ou	out, sour			ŋ	ring
ī	bite, fire	u	up, cut			'	able (ā' b'l)
ō	own, go	ᵤr	fur, bird				
ô	law, horn	er	perhaps, murder				

Foreign Symbols

Symbol	Key Words	Symbol	Key Words
a	salle	n	mon
ë	coer	ô	abuelos
ö	feu	r	gringos
ü	rue		

From *Webster's New World Dictionary, Third Edition,* Copyright © 1988 by Simon & Schuster Inc.

674　　READER'S HANDBOOK

A

a bode (ə bōd′) *n.* a home

a bra sion (ə brā′ zhən) *n.* a scrape on the skin

a brupt ly (ə brupt′ lē) *adv.* suddenly

ac com mo da tion (ə käm′ ə dā′ shən) *n.* a room and food in hotels, ships, trains, etc.

ack nowl edge (ak näl′ ij) *v.* to recognize the status or rights of

ac qui si tion (ak′ wə zish′ ən) *n.* the act of getting something

ad ap ta tion (ad′ əp tā′ shən) *n.* a thing changed to suit new conditions

ad here (ad hir′) *v.* to be loyal

al ien ate (āl′ yən āt′) *v.* to cause someone to become unfriendly

al lot (ə lät′) *v.* to give out as a share or portion

a lum nus (ə lum′ nəs) *n.* a graduate of a particular school; *plural*—**alumni** (ə lum′ nī′)

a mi a bly (ā′ mē ə blē) *adv.* agreeably; pleasantly

an guished (aŋ′ gwisht) *adj.* filled with pain, mental or physical; extremely upset **anguish** *v.*

an tag o nism (an tag′ ə niz′ əm) *n.* hostility; unfriendliness

ap pal ling (ə pôl′ iŋ) *adj.* horrifying; dreadful **appall** *v.*

ap ti tude (ap′ tə tood′) *n.* a natural ability

ar chive (är′ kīv) *n.* a storehouse for records of the past

a ris to crat ic (ə ris′ tə krat′ ik) *n.* wealthy, privileged people

ar tic u late (är tik′ yoo lit) *adj.* able to express oneself clearly in words

as cer tain (as′ ər tān) *v.* to find out

au di tion (ô dish′ ən) *n.* a test of skill or ability, usually of a musician or actor; a tryout

B

base less (bās′ lis) *adj.* having no foundation in fact

beck on (bek′ 'n) *v.* to summon or call someone, usually by a gesture or nod

be mused (bē myoozd′) *adj.* confused; bewildered **bemuse** *v.*

ben e fac tor (ben′ ə fak′ tər) *n.* a person who provides money or help

binge (binj) *n.* a period of uncontrolled eating or drinking

bleak (blēk) *adj.* harsh and dreary

brash ness (brash′ nəs) *n.* recklessness; foolish daring

brood ing (brood′ iŋ) *adj.* full of worry; troubled **brood** *v.*

C

cap size (kap′ sīz′) *v.* to be overturned or upset

caul dron (kôl′ drən) *n.* a large kettle

cha os (kā′ äs′) *n.* a state of disorder and confusion

cher ish (cher′ ish) *v.* to hold dear; treasure

cla mor (klam′ ər) *n.* a loud noise; uproar

com bat ant (kəm bat′ 'nt) *n.* fighter

com mun ing (kə myoon′ iŋ) *adj.* talking together privately **commune** *v.*

com pas sion ate (kəm pash′ ən it) *adj.* showing concern or sympathy

com pe tence (käm′ pə təns) *n.* a state of being capable

com pet i tive (kəm pet′ ə tiv) *adj.* relating to rivalry among businesses, groups, or individuals

con cus sion (kən kush′ ən) *n.* a strong shaking

con fines (kän′ fīns′) *n.* limits; boundaries

con found (kən found′) *v.* to bewilder; confuse

con sen sus (kən sen′ səs) *n.* an opinion shared by most; general agreement

con sul ta tion (kän′ səl tā′ shən) *n.* a meeting to discuss or decide something

con sump tion (kən sump′ shən) *n.* the act of eating or drinking

con temp tu ous (kən temp′ choo əs) *adj.* lacking respect; scornful

con tort ed (kən tôrt′ əd) *adj.* twisted or pulled out of shape **contort** *v.*

con vic tion (kən vik′ shən) *n.* a strong belief

cow er (kou′ ər) *v.* crouch or shrink down in fear

cringe (krinj) *v.* to shrink back from something unpleasant

croon (kroon) *v.* to sing softly

cryp tic (krip′ tik) *adj.* puzzling; mysterious

cu bi cle (kyoo′ bi kəl) *n.* a small compartment used for work or sleep

cull (kul) *v.* to remove from a group something or someone that is not as good as the rest

cul ti vat ed (kul′ tə vāt′ id) *adj.* planted or prepared for planting as opposed to wild, **cultivate** *v.*

cyn i cal (sin′ i kəl) *adj.* mistrustful of others′ sincerity

D

de fi ant (dē fī′ ənt) *adj.* refusing to obey or act in a way acceptable to others

de i ty (dē′ ə tē) *n.* a god; a divine being

de lib er ate (di lib′ ər āt′) *v.* to carefully consider

de mol ish (di mäl′ ish) *v.* to wreck; destroy

der i va tion (der′ ə vā′ shən) *n.* origin; source

de scend ant (dē sen′ dənt) *n.* an immediate or remote offspring of a person

des o la tion (des′ ə lā′ shən) *n.* feeling of loneliness and misery

des per ate ly (des′ pər it lē) *adv.* acting in a manner that shows extreme need or hopelessness

de ten tion (di ten′ shən) *n.* punishment of being held against one′s will, as in having to stay after school

dex ter ous ly (deks′ tər əs lē) *adv.* skillfully

dil i gence (dil′ ə jəns) *n.* constant effort

din gy (din′ jē) *adj.* somewhat dark and unclean; shabby

dis a bled (dis ā′ bəld) *n.* people with an illness or physical handicap that limits their activities

dis creet ly (di skrēt′ lē) *adv.* in a polite way; tactfully

dis si pate (dis′ ə pāt′) *v.* to gradually disappear

dis suade (di swād′) *v.* to persuade not to do something

dis tinc tive (di stiŋk′ tiv) *adj.* different from others; characteristic

di vert (də vʉrt′) *v.* to shift; to turn aside

di vulge (də vulj′) *v.* to reveal

drawl (drôl) *v.* to speak in a slow manner, stretching the vowel sounds

du bi ous ly (dōō′ bē əs lē) *adv.* in a doubtful way; skeptically

E

e lec tive (ē lek′ tiv) *n.* a school subject or course chosen by the student rather than assigned

e lite (ā lēt′) *n.* a group regarded as the best

e lo quence (el′ ə kwəns) *n.* forceful, convincing speech

e lude (ē lōōd′) *v.* to avoid or get away from by being sly or quick

em u late (em′ yōō lāt′) *v.* to imitate or copy

en dow (en dou′) *v.* to provide with a quality or a talent

en dure (en door′) *v.* to withstand; put up with; tolerate

en grossed (en grōst′) *adj.* completely occupied; absorbed **engross** *v.*

en ter pris ing (ent′ ər prī′ ziŋ) *adj.* adventurous; energetic

es sence (es′ əns) *n.* the basic nature of a thing

et i quette (et′ i kit) *n.* the proper way to behave toward others; good manners

e va sion (ē vā′ zhən) *n.* the act of avoiding or escaping from

e vic ted (ē vikt′ ′d) *adj.* to be forced to move from a rented house or apartment **evict** *v.*

ex as per a tion (eg zas′ pər ā′ shən) *n.* annoyance; irritation

ex ces sive ly (ek ses′ iv lē) *adv.* overly; too much

ex ot ic (eg zät′ ik) *adj.* strange; unusual

ex pe di en cy (ek spē′ dē ən sē) *n.* suitability for the purpose at hand

ex pire (ek spīr′) *v.* to die

ex plic it (eks plis′ it) *adj.* plain; straightforward

ex qui site (eks′ kwi zit) *adj.* beautiful; outstanding

F

fa tigue (fə tēg′) *n.* extreme weariness or exhaustion

feign (fān) *v.* to pretend

fe roc i ty (fə räs′ ə tē) *n.* extreme fierceness; savagery

fe ver ish ly (fē′ vər ish lē) *adv.* in a highly emotional or nervous way

flip pant (flip′ ənt) *adj.* lacking in seriousness; silly and disrespectful

flour ish (flʉr′ ish) *v.* to thrive; grow vigorously

flus tered (flus′ tərd) *adj.* nervous or confused **fluster** *v.*

676   Reader's Handbook

G

gen ial ly (jēn′ yəl lē) *adv.* in a friendly way

girth (gᵤrth) *n.* the distance around something

glim mer (glim′ ər) *v.* to give off a flickering dim light

glow er (glou′ ər) *v.* to stare in an angry way; scowl

grope (grōp) *v.* to touch or feel about in search of something

gruff (gruf) *adj.* rough and husky

gul li ble (gul′ ə bəl) *adj.* easily fooled or tricked

H

har ried (har′ ēd) *adj.* worried; distressed **harry** *v.*

heft (heft) *v.* to lift something to see how heavy it is

hi er ar chy (hī′ ər är′ kē) *n.* a group of people organized according to rank or authority

hoax (hōks) *n.* a trick or deception

hov er (huv′ ər) *v.* to fly or flutter over a place as if suspended

hu mil i ty (hyōō mil′ ə tē) *n.* lack of pride

I

i di o syn cra sy (id′ ē ō′ siŋ′ krə sē) *n.* a personal way of acting; odd mannerism

im mense (im mens′) *adj.* very large; enormous

im mense ly (im mens′ lē) *adv.* very much; enormously

im merse (im mᵤrs′) *v.* to involve oneself completely

im paled (im pāld′) *adj.* pierced through **impale** *v.*

im per a tive (im per′ ə tiv) *adj.* absolutely necessary

im promp tu (im prämp′ tōō′) *adj.* without preparation; on the spur of the moment

in ad e quate (in ad′ i kwət) *adj.* not enough

in com pre hen si ble (in′ käm′ prē hen′ sə bəl) *adj.* not capable of being understood

in con sol a ble (in′ kən sōl′ ə bəl) *adj.* brokenhearted; not able to be comforted

in cred u lous (in krej′ ōō ləs) *adj.* unable or unwilling to believe something

in crim i nate (in krim′ i nāt′) *v.* to cause someone to appear guilty

in def i nite ly (in def′ ə nit lē) *adv.* for an unlimited length of time

in dif fer ence (in dif′ ər əns) *n.* a lack of interest or concern

in dig nant (in dig′ nənt) *adj.* angry because of an action that seems wrong

in ev i ta ble (in ev′ i tə bəl) *adj.* sure to happen; unavoidable

in scrip tion (in skrip′ shən) *n.* a brief message permanently marked or engraved on a surface

in sin u a tion (in sin′ yōō ā′ shən) *n.* a suggestion or hint intended to insult

in so lent (in′ sə lənt) *adj.* boldly showing no respect

in tense (in tens′) *adj.* firm; very serious

in ter ven ing (in′ tər ven′ iŋ) *adj.* coming between **intervene** *v.*

in trep id (in trep′ id) *adj.* very brave

in tri cate (in′ tri kit) *adj.* elaborately detailed

in val id (in′ və lid) *n.* a sickly or disabled person

i rate (ī rāt′) *adj.* angry

J

jeer ing (jir′ iŋ) *adj.* mocking; rude, taunting **jeer** *v.*

L

le git i mate (lə jit′ ə mət) *adj.* normal; according to the rules

lib er a tion (lib′ ər ā′ shən) *n.* the state of freedom reached after a struggle

lin ger (liŋ′ gər) *v.* to continue to stay; delay leaving

loath some (lōth′ səm) *adj.* deserving of hate; disgusting

M

ma lig nant (mə lig′ nənt) *adj.* wishing or causing evil; very harmful

mil i tant (mil′ i tənt) *n.* a person fighting for a cause

mim i cry (mim′ ik rē) *n.* an act of imitation

min i mize (min′ ə mīz′) *v.* to reduce to the smallest possible amount

mor bid ly (môr′ bid lē) *adv.* in a gloomy, depressed way

mo rose (mə rōs′) *adj.* in low spirits; gloomy

N

niche (nich) *n.* the place a person occupies in society

nov el ty (näv′ əl tē) *n.* something new, original, or unusual

O

ob scured (əb skyoord′) *adj.* hidden from view **obscure** *v.*

ob sessed (əb sest′) *adj.* greatly preoccupied with something **obsess** *v.*

oc cult (ə kult′) *adj.* supernatural

o men (ō′ mən) *n.* an event or sign believed to point toward a future happening

om in ous ly (äm′ ə nəs lē) *adv.* in a threatening or evil way

op ti mis tic (äp′ tə mis′ tik) *adj.* hopeful about the future; confident

P

pains tak ing (pānz′ tāk′ iŋ) *adj.* very careful

pal lid (pal′ id) *adj.* pale; lacking normal color

pas sive (pas′ iv) *adj.* inactive, but receiving action; lacking in energy or willpower

pend ing (pen′ diŋ) *prep.* while waiting for; until

per pet u al (pər pech′ oo əl) *adj.* endless; lasting forever

per sist ent (pər sist′ ənt) *adj.* refusing to stop; continuing stubbornly

pig men ta tion (pig mən tā′ shən) *n.* a skin color

pil fer ing (pil′ fər iŋ) *n.* stealing **pilfer** *v.*

plac id (plas′ id) *adj.* calm; at peace

pon der (pän′ dər) *v.* to think deeply; carefully consider

pre cept (prē′ sept′) *n.* a rule of conduct

pred e ces sor (pred′ ə ses′ ər) *n.* a person who comes before

pre lim i nary (prē lim′ ə ner′ ē) *n.* a match or competition before the main contest; *plural* **preliminaries**

pre oc cu pa tion (prē äk′ yoo pā′ shən) *n.* a state of being wrapped up or engrossed in something

pri or i ty (prī ôr′ ə tē) *n.* something that must receive attention first

prod i gy (präd′ ə jē) *adj.* of a child with extraordinary talent or genius

pro lif ic (prō lif′ ik) *adj.* producing many children

prom in ent (präm′ ə nənt) *adj.* well-known; widely recognized

proph e cy (präf′ ə sē) *n.* a prediction; foretelling of future events

Q

quiv er (kwiv′ ər) *v.* to tremble or shake

R

ra tion al ize (rash′ ən əl īz′) *v.* to explain or make excuses for

rav age (rav′ ij) *v.* to violently attack, causing severe damage

realm (relm) *n.* a kingdom

re coil (ri koil′) *v.* to draw back from something distasteful or painful

ref uge (ref′ yooj) *n.* a safe place

re ha bil i ta tion (rē′ hə bil′ ə tā′ shən) *n.* the restoring of a person's ability to lead a useful life

re lin quish (ri liŋ′ kwish) *v.* to give up

rel ish (rel′ ish) *v.* to enjoy

re luc tant ly (ri luk′ tənt lē) *adv.* unwillingly

re plen ished (ri plen′ ishd) *adj.* added to; resupplied **replenish** *v.*

re pris al (ri prī′ zəl) *n.* an injury done in response to an injury received; retaliation

re pul sive (ri pul′ siv) *adj.* offensive; disgusting

re sil ient (ri zil′ yənt) *adj.* flexible and springy

re tal i ate (ri tal′ ē āt′) *v.* to get revenge; get even

rev er ie (rev′ ər ē) *n.* a daydream

re vive (ri vīv′) *v.* to regain consciousness; wake up

rogue (rōg) *n.* a rascal

rote (rōt) *n.* memorization without understanding

S

sanc tion (saŋk′ shən) *v.* to give approval for

sanc tu ar y (saŋk′ choo er′ ē) *n.* shelter; protection

sa vor (sā′ vər) *v.* to take great pleasure in

scheme (skēm) *v.* to plot or plan in a secretive way

scowl (skoul) *v.* to look angry by drawing the eyebrows together and frowning

sear (sir) *v.* to burn the surface; scorch

sem i nar y (sem' ə ner' ē) *n.* a school where people are trained to become ministers, priests, or rabbis

se nile (sē' nīl') *adj.* showing the mental confusion sometimes found in old people

shrewd ly (shro͞od' lē) *adv.* wisely; in a clever way

slack en (slak' ən) *v.* to lessen; let up

sloth (slōth) *n.* laziness

slug gish (slug' ish) *adj.* moving at a slow pace

sneer ing (snir' iŋ) *adj.* having a mocking smile **sneer** *v.*

snip ing (snīp' iŋ) *n.* attacking someone in a sly or deceitful way **snipe** *v.*

sol ace (säl' is) *n.* comfort

sor cer y (sôr' sər ē) *n.* magic

sov er eign (säv' rən) *n.* a monarch; royal ruler

spec u lat ing (spek' yo͞o lāt' iŋ) *adj.* thinking about different possibilities; guessing what might happen **speculate** *v.*

spell bound (spel' bound') *adj.* as if in a trance; fascinated

spend thrift (spend' thrift') *n.* a person who wastes money

squan der (skwän' dər) *v.* to spend carelessly

stark (stärk) *adv.* entirely; completely

stench (stench) *n.* a strong, foul smell

strick en (strik' ən) *adj.* suddenly affected by pain; wounded

stri dent (strīd' 'nt) *adj.* having a harsh sound

stu pen dous (sto͞o pen' dəs) *adj.* huge; tremendous

sub con scious ly (sub kän' shəs lē) *adv.* without being fully aware

suit or (so͞ot' ər) *n.* a man seeking a woman's love

sul len (sul' ən) *adj.* gloomy; acting moody

su per flu ous (sə pʉr' flo͞o əs) *adj.* unnecessary; not important

surge (sʉrj) *v.* to suddenly push forward in a violent way

sur plus (sʉr' plus') *adj.* extra

sus te nance (sus' tə nəns) *n.* nourishment; assistance

swarth y (swôrth' ē) *adj.* having darkish skin

T

tac tic (tak' tik) *n.* a method used to accomplish something; a strategy

taunt (tônt) *v.* to make fun of; jeer

te di ous (tē' dē əs) *adj.* boring; dull

trans fixed (trans fikst') *adj.* unable to move because of awe or fear **transfix** *v.*

trans for ma tion (trans' fər mā' shən) *n.* a change

trib ute (trib' yo͞ot) *n.* an action or gift that honors a deserving individual

tu mul tu ous ly (to͞o mul' cho͞o əs lē) *adv.* in a wild and disorderly way

ty rant (tī' rənt) *n.* a ruler with unlimited power

U

ul ti mate (ul' tə mit) *adj.* final; most important

un nerve (un nʉrv') *v.* to take away courage; to make nervous

un seem ly (un sēm' lē) *adj.* not decent or proper

up hol ster y (up hōl' stər ē) *n.* the soft fabric covering furniture

V

van quish (vaŋ' kwish) *v.* to conquer, defeat

ven om (ven' əm) *n.* bitterness; hatred

ve ran da (və ran' də) *n.* a long open porch, usually with a roof

vexed (vekst) *adj.* troubled **vex** *v.*

vil est (vīl' ist) *adj.* most horrible or unpleasant

W

wield ing (wēld' iŋ) *adj.* handling and using **wield** *v.*

wil y (wīl' ē) *adj.* crafty; sly

wretch ed (rech' 'd) *adj.* deserving contempt; inferior

Z

zeal (zēl) *n.* enthusiasm; eagerness

LITERARY AND READING TERMS

Act   An act is a major section of a play. Each act may be further divided into smaller sections called **scenes.** *The Monsters Are Due on Maple Street* has two acts.
   See *Drama* and *Scene.*

Alliteration   Alliteration is the repetition of consonant sounds at the beginnings of words. Writers use alliteration to emphasize certain words and to give their writing a musical quality. Note the repetition of the c̲ sound in this line from "The Highwayman":

"Over the c̲obbles he c̲lattered and c̲lashed"

Allusion   An allusion is a reference to a famous person, place, event, or other work of literature. In "Aunt Millicent," Grandma makes an allusion to the story "Rikki-tikki-tavi."

Analysis   Analysis is the process of breaking something down into its elements and examining each one. When you analyze a literary work, you examine its various parts in order to understand the work as a whole.

Author's Purpose   An author's purpose may be to entertain, to explain or inform, to express an opinion, or to persuade readers to do or believe something. The author may combine two or three purposes, but one is usually most important.

Autobiography   An autobiography is a form of nonfiction in which one person tells the story of his or her life. *Nadja on My Way* is an example of autobiography.
   See *Nonfiction.*

Biography   A biography is the story of a person's life written by another person. The subjects of biographies are often famous people, as in Jacobs's "Eleanor Roosevelt."
   See *Nonfiction.*

Cast of Characters   In a drama, the cast of characters is given at the beginning of the script. It is a list of all the characters in the play, usually in order of appearance.
   See *Drama.*

Cause and Effect   Events are often related by cause and effect. This relationship occurs when one event brings about a second event. The first event in time is the cause; the second event is the effect. This statement from "The Noble Experiment" shows a cause and effect: "He pointed out that I couldn't play for a few days anyhow because of my bum arm."

Character   A character is a person, an animal, or an imaginary creature that takes part in the action of a literary work. Generally, a work focuses on one or more **main characters.** Less important characters are called **minor characters.**

Characterization   Characterization refers to the techniques a writer uses to create and develop a character. There are four basic methods of developing a character: 1) a physical description of the character; 2) the character's thoughts, speech, or actions; 3) the thoughts, speech, and actions of other characters; 4) direct comments on a character's nature.

Chronological Order   Chronological order refers to the order in which events happen in time. The biography "Eleanor Roosevelt" follows chronological order, beginning with Eleanor's birth and ending with her death.

Climax   The climax, or turning point, is the high point of interest in the plot of a story or play. At the climax, the conflict is resolved and the outcome of the plot becomes clear. The climax of "The Smallest Dragonboy," for example, occurs when Keevan Impresses the dragon at the hatching.
   See *Plot.*

Comparison   The process of identifying similarities is called comparison. In "All Summer in a Day," the writer compares Margot to "an old photograph dusted from an album, whitened away." Both Margot and the photograph are pale and fragile.

Conflict   Conflict is a struggle between two opposing forces. In an **external conflict,** such as the battle between Rikki and the cobras in "Rikki-tikki-tavi," a character struggles against some outside person or force. **Internal conflict** occurs when the struggle is within a character. Martin in "The Medicine Bag" experiences internal conflict when caught between feelings of shame and pride toward his grandfather.
    See *Plot.*

Connecting   The process of relating the content of a literary work to the reader's own knowledge or experience is called connecting. For example, in *Nadja on My Way* when the author describes her feelings before competing, the reader may remember similar feelings in his or her own experience.

Connotation   Connotation refers to the suggestions and associations that go along with a given word, stretching well beyond its dictionary meaning. For example, the word *mother* is defined as "a female parent," but the word suggests images of love, warmth, and security.

Context Clues   Context clues are the words or phrases before or after an unfamiliar word that help explain its meaning. Context clues may define the word, give a synonym for it, give an example of its meaning, provide comparisons or contrasts, or enable readers to infer the meaning.

Contrast   The pointing out of differences between two or more things is called contrast. In "Last Cover" the narrator contrasts himself with his brother Colin:

I was following in my father's footsteps, true to form, but Colin threatened to break the family tradition.

Denotation   Denotation is the dictionary definition of a word.
    See *Connotation.*

Description   Description is a picture, in words, of a scene, a character, or an object. A description might appeal to the reader's senses or provide detailed information about characters or events.

Dialect   Dialect is a form of language as it is spoken in a certain place or among a certain group of people. A dialect has its own pronunciations, spellings, and expressions. Mrs. Pratchett in *Boy* speaks the dialect of the British working class: "Let's 'ave a look at some of them titchy ones."

Dialogue   A conversation between two or more characters is called dialogue. In most literary forms, dialogue is set off by quotation marks. In plays, however, dialogue simply follows the name of the character who is speaking and does not require quotation marks.

Drama   A drama, or play, is a form of literature meant to be performed by actors before an audience. In drama, the story is told through the dialogue and the actions of the characters.
    See *Act, Cast of Characters, Dialogue, Scene,* and *Stage Directions.*

Drawing Conclusions   Combining several pieces of information to make a decision is called drawing a conclusion. Conclusions can be drawn from a combination of stated facts and inferences the reader makes.
    See *Inference.*

Essay   A short nonfiction work that deals with one subject is called an essay. Some essays emphasize personal feelings, such as "Homeless." Others focus more on the presentation of information, as in "America the Not-so-Beautiful."

See *Nonfiction*.

Evaluating   Evaluating is the process of judging the worth of something or someone. A work of literature or its elements may be evaluated by standards such as entertainment, believability, originality, or emotional power.

Exaggeration   The extreme overstating of an idea is called exaggeration. In *Driving Miss Daisy*, Florine exaggerates, "I told you a million times."

Exposition   Exposition is the beginning of a plot in a story or play. It introduces main characters, describes the setting, and often establishes the conflict. For example, the opening paragraphs of "Old Sly Eye" provide the exposition for the story.

External Conflict   See *Conflict*.

Fable   A fable is a brief story that teaches a lesson about human nature. Many fables feature animals that act and speak like humans. Fables often end with a stated moral that summarizes the lesson. "The Wolf in Sheep's Clothing" is an example of a fable.

See *Moral*.

Fact and Opinion   A fact is a statement that can be proved, such as "April has thirty days." In contrast, an opinion is a statement that cannot be proved, such as "April is the nicest month of the year." Opinions usually reflect personal beliefs and are often debatable.

Fantasy   A fantasy is a type of fiction that takes place in an unreal, invented world, such as Pern in "The Smallest Dragonboy." Fantasies often involve magic or characters with extraordinary powers.

Fiction   Fiction is prose writing that tells an imaginary story. The term usually refers to novels and short stories. Writers of fiction may invent the entire work, or they may loosely base their story on real people or events.

See *Character, Conflict, Plot, Setting, Theme*.

Figurative Language   Figurative language goes beyond dictionary meanings of words to create fresh and original descriptions. In a figurative expression, the words are not literally true, and one thing may be described in terms of another. For example, the speaker in "For My Father" says of her father that "the desert had dried his soul." The three most common forms of figurative expressions are the simile, the metaphor, and personification.

See *Metaphor, Simile,* and *Personification*.

Flashback   In a literary work a flashback is a scene that interrupts the present action to describe an event that took place at an earlier time. For example, a flashback in "Last Cover" explains how Colin found Bandit.

Foil   A character who provides a striking contrast to a main character is called a foil. A foil helps make the personal qualities of the main character more obvious. For example, in "The Revolt of the Evil Fairies," Rat Joiner is a foil to the narrator.

Folk Tale   A folk tale is a simple story that has been handed down by word of mouth from one generation to another. The characters in folk tales may be animals, humans, or superhumans. Folk tales usually occur in the distant past and may involve supernatural events. "The Force of Luck" is a folk tale.

Folklore   The traditions, customs, and stories that are passed along by word of mouth within a culture are known as its folklore. Folklore includes various forms of literature, such as legends, folk tales, myths, and fables.

Foreshadowing   Foreshadowing refers to a writer's use of hints that suggest events that will occur later in a story. For example, in "Old

Sly Eye" the father warns Alben, "I wouldn't want to come home and find Old Sly Eye had done to us what he's done to others." His comments foreshadow the confrontation between Alben and the panther.

Form Form is a term that describes a literary work's structure or organization. In poetry, form describes the physical arrangement of words and lines on a page. Some poems follow a very predictable pattern with the same number of syllables in each line and the same number of lines in each stanza. Other poems, like E. E. Cummings's "old age sticks," have an irregular form.

Free Verse Poetry with no regular patterns of rhyme, rhythm, or line length is called free verse. Poets use free verse to capture the sounds and rhythms of ordinary language. "I'll Walk the Tightrope" is written in free verse.
See *Poetry.*

Generalization A generalization is a broad statement made about an entire group, such as "Novels take longer to read than short stories." Not all generalizations are true. Some are too broad or not backed up by evidence, like the statement "All seventh graders are tall."

Genre The term used to identify the major categories of literature is called genre. There are four main literary genres: fiction, nonfiction, poetry, and drama.

Hero A hero is a character whose actions win great admiration, often for his or her courage or nobility. A hero can be a real person, such as Jackie Robinson or Eleanor Roosevelt, or a fictional creation, such as Keevan in "The Smallest Dragonboy."

Imagery Words and phrases that appeal to the reader's senses are known as imagery. Writers use details to help the reader imagine how things look, feel, smell, sound, and taste.

Note the imagery in these lines from "Looking North to Taos."

> I saw the pueblo beneath the blue
> mountain, the older
> buildings crumbling,
> melting into mud.

Inference An inference is a logical guess or conclusion based on evidence. Based on details in selections and their own experience, readers can figure out more than the words say. For example, in "The Emperor's New Clothes" the Emperor is described as "so excessively fond of new clothes that he spent all his money in dress. He did not trouble himself in the least about his soldiers." From these details and their own knowledge, readers could infer that the Emperor is vain and concerned only about himself.

Internal Conflict See *Conflict.*

Irony Irony is a contrast between what is expected and what actually exists or happens. For example, most readers of "A Man Who Had No Eyes" believe that the successful and prosperous Mr. Parsons is sighted, only to discover at the end that he is blind.

Jargon A specialized vocabulary used by those in a certain profession is called jargon.

Legend A legend is a story handed down from the past about a specific person, usually someone of heroic accomplishments. Legends usually have some basis in historical fact. "Where the Girl Saved Her Brother" is an example of a legend.

Main Idea The main idea is the central point that a writer is making. Usually, the term is used in discussions of nonfiction. The main idea may refer to the central message of the entire work or simply the topic sentence of a paragraph.

Metaphor A comparison of two unlike things that have something in common is called a metaphor. A metaphor does not use direct words of comparison such as *like* and *as*. The following metaphor from "All Summer in a Day" describes Margot: "If she spoke at all, her voice would be a ghost."

See *Figurative Language*.

Minor Character See *Character*.

Mood The mood, or atmosphere, is the feeling created in the reader by a literary work. In "All Summer in a Day," Ray Bradbury creates a mood of tension and anticipation. Writers use many techniques to establish the mood, such as word choice, dialogue, description, and plot events.

Moral A moral is the lesson taught by a story. Morals are often stated directly in fables.

See *Fable*.

Motivation A motivation is a reason that explains why a character acts, feels, or thinks a certain way. Gem in "The Fatal Flower" is motivated by her desire for beauty.

Myth A myth is a traditional story, usually of unknown authorship, that tells about the actions of gods or heroes or explains how something came to be. Myths may explain such things as human nature, the origin of the world, mysteries of nature, or social customs. Most myths were once believed to be true and were tied to a particular society's religious beliefs. "Phaëthon" is an example of a myth.

Narrative Any writing that tells a story is called a narrative. The events in a narrative may be real or imagined. Narratives dealing with real events include biographies and autobiographies. Fictional narratives include myths, short stories, novels, and narrative poems.

Narrative Poetry Poetry that tells a story is called narrative poetry. Like any story, narrative poetry has characters, setting, and plot. Narrative poems also have elements of poetry, such as rhyme, rhythm, imagery, and figurative language. "The Highwayman" is an example of narrative poetry.

Narrator The narrator is the teller of a story.

See *Point of View*.

Nonfiction Writing that tells about real people, places, and events is called nonfiction. Types of nonfiction include biographies, autobiographies, articles, and essays.

Novel A novel is a work of fiction which is longer and more complex than a short story. The setting, plot, and characters of a novel are developed in detail.

Onomatopoeia Onomatopoeia is the use of words that by their sound suggest their meaning. *Whirr, buzz, pop,* and *sizzle* are examples of onomatopoeia. In "The Highwayman" the words *tlot-tlot* imitate the sound of horse hooves hitting the road.

Personification The giving of human qualities to an animal, object, or idea is called personification. In "Anansi and His Visitor, Turtle," for example, the spider and turtle converse as if they were human.

Persuasion Persuasion is a type of writing that is meant to sway the reader's feelings, beliefs, or actions. Persuasion normally is used to appeal to both the mind and emotions of the reader.

Play See *Drama*.

Plot Plot is the sequence of related events that make up a story; it is the action, or what happens in the story. Most plots follow a regular pattern. The **exposition** introduces the characters and the conflict they face. Complications set in as the characters try to resolve the conflict. Eventually, the plot reaches a **climax,** the highest point of interest or suspense. The final stage is the **resolution,** in which loose ends are tied up and the story is brought to a close.

Poetry   Poetry is a type of literature that expresses ideas and feelings in compact, imaginative, and musical language. Poets combine words in patterns to touch the reader's senses, emotions, and mind. Normally, poems are written in lines, which are often grouped in stanzas. Many poems contain a regular rhythm and some use rhyme.

See *Alliteration, Figurative Language, Form, Free Verse, Imagery, Narrative Poetry, Rhyme, Rhythm,* and *Stanza.*

Point of View   The perspective from which a story is told is called its point of view. The most common points of view are first person, third-person omniscient, and third-person limited.

In the **first-person** point of view, the narrator is one of the characters in the story and uses first-person pronouns such as *I, me,* and *we.* The reader sees the events of the story and other characters only through the eyes of the narrator. "Lose Now, Pay Later" uses first-person point of view.

In the **third-person** point of view, the narrator is not in the story and relates the story using third-person pronouns such as *he, she,* or *it.* In the **third-person omniscient,** or all-knowing, point of view, the narrator knows everything about the characters and can see into their minds. "The Emperor's New Clothes," which brings us into the minds of the Emperor and his advisors, is an example of omniscient narration.

In the **third-person limited** point of view, the narrator brings us into the mind of only one character. "The Smallest Dragonboy," which limits its focus to Keevan's thoughts and actions, is an example of this type of narration.

Predicting   Using what you know to guess what will happen in the future is called predicting. Good readers gather information as they read and combine that information with prior knowledge to predict the events in a story.

Problem Solving   The process of identifying a problem and considering possible solutions is known as problem solving. First, the problem is defined. Second, the causes of the problem are identified. Third, a list of possible solutions is made and possible outcomes of each of the solutions are considered. Finally, a solution is chosen and applied.

Prose   Prose is the ordinary form of spoken and written language, that is, language that does not possess the regular rhythmic pattern of poetry.

Questioning   The process of raising questions while reading is called questioning. Good readers ask themselves questions in an effort to understand characters and events. They look for the answers as they continue to read.

Repetition   Repetition is the repeated use of any element of language—a sound, a word, a phrase, a line, or a grammatical structure. Writers use repetition to stress important ideas and to create memorable sound effects, as in these lines from "The Charge of the Light Brigade."

Theirs not to make reply,
Theirs not to reason why,
Theirs but to do and die;

Resolution   See *Plot.*

Reviewing   The process of pausing while reading to recall previous events and check understanding is called reviewing. Readers stop to reflect on what they know, to make some inferences about what is happening, and to better understand what they are reading.

Rhyme   Rhyme is the repetition of identical or similar sounds. Two words rhyme when their accented syllables and all the sounds following these syllables sound the same. *Dog* and *log* are rhymes, as are *letter* and *better.*

The most common form of rhyme is **end rhyme,** where the rhyme occurs at the end of the lines of poetry. **Internal rhyme** takes place when rhymes occur within lines. Note both the internal and end rhymes found in these lines from "Wishes."

I want to <u>sail</u> on a swallow's <u>tail</u> and
peep through the sky's blue <u>glass</u>.
I want to <u>see</u> if the dreams in <u>me</u> shall
perish or come to <u>pass</u>.
See *Poetry*.

Rhythm   The pattern of stressed and unstressed syllables in poetry is called rhythm. When the stressed syllables—the syllables that are emphasized—are arranged in a consistent pattern, the poem has a regular beat. Note the rhythm in these lines from "If I Can Stop One Heart from Breaking." The stressed syllables are marked by ∕; the unstressed ones by ⌣.

⌣ ∕ ⌣　∕　⌣　∕　⌣　∕　⌣
If I can stop one Heart from breaking

⌣　∕　⌣　∕　⌣　∕
I shall not live in vain
See *Poetry*.

Satire   Satire is a literary technique that makes fun of foolish behaviors or ideas. A satire usually offers a humorous criticism of something that needs to be changed for the good of society. For example, "Upon the Waters" makes fun of the bureaucracy of the welfare system.

Scanning   In reading, scanning is the process of searching for a particular fact or piece of information. When you scan, your eyes sweep across a page, looking for key words that may lead you to the information you want.

Scene   A scene is a unit of action in a play that takes place in one setting at one time. For example, in *Driving Miss Daisy* one scene takes place in Daisy's kitchen; the next occurs at Boolie's workplace. Each scene of the play presents an episode in the plot.

Science Fiction   Science fiction is fiction based on real or imagined scientific developments. These stories are often set in imaginary places and usually take place in the future. "Lose Now, Pay Later" is science fiction.

Screenplay   A script from which a movie is produced is called a screenplay. Screenplays often have more scenes than stage plays because it is easier to show changes in time or place on film than on a stage. Consequently, screenplays tend to have many stage directions and often include camera instructions. The version of *Driving Miss Daisy* in this book is a screenplay.

Setting   Setting is the time and place of the action of a story, poem, or play. Sometimes the setting is clear and well-defined; at other times, it is left to the reader's imagination. Setting may include geographic location, the historical period (past, present, or future), season, time of day, and customs and manners of the society.
See *Fiction*.

Short Story   A work of fiction that can generally be read in one sitting is called a short story. Short stories usually focus on one or two main characters who face a single problem or conflict.
See *Fiction*.

Simile   A simile is a comparison of two unlike things that have some quality in common. Similes make a direct comparison, using words such as *like, as,* or *resembles*. Note the following simile from *Boy:* "What is left looks rather like a gigantic black pancake."
See *Figurative Language*.

Skimming   Skimming is reading quickly to find the main idea or to get an overview. When you skim, you read only the title, the headings, the words in special type, and the first sentence of each paragraph. You also read charts, graphs, and time lines.

Sound Effects See *Alliteration, Onomatopoeia, Poetry, Repetition, Rhyme,* and *Rhythm.*

Speaker The speaker in a poem is the voice that talks to the reader. The speaker is comparable to a narrator in a work of fiction. In some poems, the speaker expresses the feelings of the poet, as in "There Is No Word for Goodbye." In other poems the speaker and poet are not the same.

Stage Directions Instructions to the actors, director, and stage crew in a play script are called stage directions. These instructions may suggest scenery, lighting, music, sound effects, and how actors should move or speak. In this book, stage directions appear within parentheses in italic type.
   See *Drama.*

Stanza A group of lines in poetry is called a stanza. A stanza is like a paragraph in prose. "The Charge of the Light Brigade," for example, has seven stanzas.
   See *Poetry.*

Stereotype A broad generalization about something or someone that leaves no room for individual differences is called a stereotype. A stereotype is often used to judge people unfairly on the basis of race, ethnic background, or physical appearance.

Style Style is the way in which a piece of literature is written. Style refers to *how* something is said rather than to *what* is said. Many elements contribute to style, including word choice, sentence length, tone, and figurative language. The style of *Boy,* for example, can be described as playful, relying on exaggeration, humor, and colorful words.

Summarizing To summarize means to tell briefly in your own words the main ideas of a piece of writing, omitting unimportant details.

Surprise Ending An unexpected twist in the plot at the end of a story is called a surprise ending. "Hearts and Hands" is an example of a story with a surprise ending.

Suspense The feeling of growing tension and excitement felt by a reader is called suspense. Writers create suspense by raising questions in the readers' minds about what might happen in the plot. For example, a suspenseful moment occurs in "Old Sly Eye" when Alben is trapped in the loft.

Symbol A symbol is a person, a place, an object, or an action that stands for something outside itself. The bald eagle, for example, is a symbol of the United States.
   Literary symbols take on their meaning within the context of the work of literature. In "Dream Deferred," for instance, the "raisin in the sun" might be a symbol of dreams that have been denied, lost, or forgotten.

Teleplay A play written for television is called a teleplay. In a teleplay, the stage directions usually include camera instructions.

Theme A theme is the message about life or human nature communicated by a work of literature. In most cases the reader must infer the theme. One way of figuring out a theme is to apply the lessons learned by the main characters to all people. For example, one theme of "The Christmas Hunt" is that a child's parents sometimes know best.

Tone A writer's attitude toward his or her subject is called tone. A writer's tone may be amused, objective, angry, or any number of other attitudes. The tone of "Formula" might be considered dreamy or escapist.

Visualizing The process of forming a mental picture from a written description is called visualizing. Good readers use details supplied by the writer to picture characters, settings, and events in their mind.

JAMES BERRY

RAY BRADBURY

SANDRA CISNEROS

Sherwood Anderson *(1876–1941)* grew up in Ohio. After serving in the Spanish-American War, he managed a paint factory in Ohio, even though he had very little formal education. One day he pretended to lose his mind and walked out. He then moved to Chicago and began writing. With the help of Carl Sandburg and others, he published his first notable work, *Winesburg, Ohio,* which brought him national recognition.

James Berry *(1924–)* grew up in Jamaica but emigrated to England in 1948. Currently he divides his time between the two countries. A well-known poet and critic, Berry won first prize in the National Poetry Competition of Great Britain in 1981. His collections of poetry include *Chain of Days* and *Fractured Circles.* Of Jamaica, Berry says, "No one has reported our stories, or the way we saw things. It's the function of writers and poets to bring in the left-out side of the human family."

Ray Bradbury *(1920–)* was writing stories by the age of twelve, and in high school he put out his own magazine. Bradbury says about his early writing, "I was in love with everything I did. I did not warm to a subject, I boiled over." Bradbury tries to write one thousand words each day and at least one story a week. Though he writes about future technology and space travel, he has never learned to drive a car and rarely flies in airplanes. His favorite way to get around is by bicycle.

Russell Gordon Carter *(1892–1957)* was a young political writer for Woodrow Wilson's presidential campaign and fought in the First World War before he began to write for *Youth's Companion,* a magazine for adolescents. He quickly became popular for stories based on historical events, such as "Brothers of the Frontiers" and "A Patriot Lad of Old Boston." In his lifetime, he published over fifty books and hundreds of stories.

Sandra Cisneros *(1954–)* grew up with six brothers in a Mexican-American family in Chicago. For her, books were an escape from poverty and loneliness. Today, she mixes the Spanish she heard as a child into poems, short stories, and novels about everyday Hispanic life. *The House on Mango Street,* from which "Bums in the Attic" is taken, won the Before Columbus Book Award. She has won many other honors and grants, including two National Endowment for the Arts fellowships.

*These pages provide author biographies for literature lessons that do not already include this information.

Lucille Clifton *(1936–)* is the great-great-granddaughter of a woman who was brought from West Africa as a slave in 1830. Clifton published her first book in 1969 and has written poetry and prose for children and adults ever since. Her writing focuses on black urban families. She was Poet Laureate of Maryland from 1979 to 1982, and in 1984 she won the Coretta Scott King Award for her children's book *Everett Anderson's Goodbye.*

LUCILLE CLIFTON

Margaret Danner *(1915–1984)* began writing poetry in middle school and won first prize in a poetry competition when she was in the eighth grade. After college she became the first African-American assistant editor at *Poetry,* a magazine that publishes works of many great poets. *Poetry* published some of Danner's poems. She received several awards that allowed her to travel to Africa, and much of her poetry is about that continent.

Julia Fields *(1938–)* grew up in Bessemer, Alabama. Later, she taught high school English in Birmingham and wrote poetry on the side. In 1968, she received a grant from the National Endowment for the Arts and also released her first volume of work, *Poems.* She has since been poet-in-residence at several colleges and universities, helping others to find their own poetic voices and continuing to write and publish her own work.

Robert Frost *(1874–1963)* drew his inspiration from his life in rural New England. His poems reflect the spirit of New England's independence and stubbornness. He claimed that he started out as such a poor student that he didn't read a book until he was fifteen. Yet at the end of his life, he was the only poet ever to have won four Pulitzer Prizes and participate in a presidential inauguration; he recited a poem when John F. Kennedy was sworn in as president. On his eighty-eighth birthday, he received a Congressional Gold Medal and had a mountain in Vermont named after him. "One can never tell how the race will turn out until the end," he said. "I'm a lucky man."

ROBERT FROST

O. Henry *(1862–1910),* whose real name was William Sydney Porter, left school at the age of fifteen and worked as a pharmacist, a ranch hand, a newspaper columnist, a publisher, and a bank teller. He was convicted of embezzling from the bank and spent three years in jail. O. Henry spent the last eight years of his life in New York City, where his career as a writer prospered. He wrote more than 250 short stories and several novels. His stories are famous for their surprise endings, irony, and humor.

O. HENRY

Langston Hughes *(1902–1967)* was at different times a janitor, a teacher, a farmer, a cook, a waiter, a doorman, a sailor, a busboy, and a poet. While a busboy, he left his poems on the table of Vachel Lindsay, a well-known poet. Hughes became famous overnight. He wrote poems, short stories, novels, plays, songs, and a newspaper column. He is best known for his poetry about African Americans; their search for justice and a better life; and their beauty, strength, and heritage. He founded three theaters, taught at several universities, and won many awards for his work.

LANGSTON HUGHES

Ana Maria Iza *(1941–)* was born in Quito, Ecuador, and attended its Universidad Central. However, she so enjoyed the time she spent singing at the music conservatory there that she switched her attention to music. She became a soprano with the choir of the prestigious Ecuadorian Casa de la Cultura. Iza has received several prizes and awards in Ecuadorian poetry competitions, and she published her first volume of poetry, *Pedaza de Nada* (Bits of Nothing), when she was only twenty-eight.

Shirley Jackson *(1919–1965)* was born and raised in California. After attending Syracuse University, she settled in Vermont with her husband. She wrote many humorous stories about her husband and four children, fictionalizing their lives in *Life Among the Savages* and *Raising Demons*. However, she is best known for writing horror stories such as "The Lottery" and the novels *The Haunting of Hill House* and *We Have Always Lived in the Castle*. Many of Jackson's stories have been made into plays, movies, and television dramas.

GEORGIA DOUGLAS JOHNSON

Georgia Douglas Johnson *(1886–1966)* helped pave the way for later African-American poets, including Langston Hughes and Mari Evans. In Washington, D.C., Johnson started a weekly open house for young poets, which Hughes attended. She was active in the pan-Africa movement, worked for women's and minority rights, and served as a commissioner at the U.S. Department of Labor. Johnson was also a playwright, but some producers refused to stage three of her plays about a lynching of a black person by a white mob.

MacKinlay Kantor *(1904–1977)* was encouraged to write by his mother, a newspaper editor. However, it was years before Kantor found a successful market for his work in the "pulps," cheap popular magazines. Often paid only a penny a word, Kantor quickly produced stories with surprise endings and melodramatic climaxes. He also wrote murder mysteries. In 1956, Kantor won the Pulitzer Prize for *Andersonville*, a novel about the conditions in a southern Civil War prison camp. Kantor's last historical novel, *Valley Forge*, was published in 1975 in honor of the nation's bicentennial.

MACKINLAY KANTOR

Edna Mason Kaula *(1906–   )* has lived in Australia, New Zealand, Indonesia, Holland, Central Africa, and the United States. She studied to be an artist in Holland and later added writing to her skills. She has made lengthy visits to many countries in Africa. On some of her visits, she witnessed ceremonies never before seen by a non-African. She has written and illustrated many popular books for adults and children about the places she has been.

Janice Mirikitani says that "For My Father," written to her stepfather, describes the pain of "being an Asian-American in a country that treated you as a foreigner." This pain clearly fueled a desire to help others as well as to express her own feelings. Mirikitani is president of the Glide Foundation in San Francisco, California, which feeds the poor, houses the homeless, and helps victims of drugs, battering, and AIDS. She continues to publish her own work, and her efforts on the behalf of other writers and artists have resulted in many awards. These include California's Woman of the Year and San Francisco's Woman Warrior in Arts and Culture.

JANICE MIRIKITANI

Pat Mora *(1942–   )* is the author of three poetry collections, two of which have received Southwest Book Awards. Much of her writing describes both the visual beauty and cultural diversity of the Southwest, and the harmony that exists in nature and among Mexican and Anglo peoples. Her work has appeared in many textbooks and has been translated into Spanish, Italian, and Bengali. She presently lives in Ohio, continues to write, and gives readings of her poetry, essays, and children's books.

PAT MORA

Alfred Noyes *(1880–1958)* was born and raised in Wolverhampton, England. While still an undergraduate in college, he published his first collection of poems. By 1910 he had written his first biography and eight full books of poetry. Noyes wrote "The Highwayman" in only two days. His readers so loved his ballads and narrative poetry that he soon became the most popular poet in England. Noyes continued writing until 1942, when glaucoma took his eyesight.

Anna Quindlen *(1952–   )* published her first story in *Seventeen* magazine in 1974, the year she graduated from Barnard College. In 1981 she began writing columns for *The New York Times,* which have made her famous. In 1991 she won a Pulitzer Prize for her syndicated weekly column, "Public and Private." Quindlen says that mixing up fact and fiction, being too curious, and asking too many questions are "the kinds of things you are not supposed to do at fifteen, but get you a Pulitzer Prize at thirty-nine."

ANNA QUINDLEN

ANDREW A. ROONEY

JUAN A. A. SEDILLO

LESLIE MARMON SILKO

Andrew A. Rooney *(1919–   ),* born in Albany, New York, won writing prizes and wrote for magazines in high school and college. During World War II he wrote for the military newspaper *Stars and Stripes.* In 1949 Rooney began his career with CBS. When he read "An Essay on War" on television in 1971, not only did the essay win an award, but Rooney began his on-camera career. In 1978 he joined the popular CBS news program *60 Minutes.* He has written ten books, won four Emmy awards, and six Writers Guild Awards.

Juan A. A. Sedillo *(1902–1982)* had a long, distinguished career in law and government. From 1932 to 1936 he served in the New Mexico state senate but then left New Mexico for Europe, where he practiced law. He joined the U.S. Army and fought in World War II, in which he was awarded a Bronze Star and five battle stars. After the war, Sedillo became a chief defense counsel for the German war crimes trials, then chief legal officer for the U.S. military government in Germany. Next he was a judge in the American Zone in Berlin, then a State Department advisor, and finally a staff member with the U.S. diplomatic corps in Morocco. In later life, Sedillo returned to New Mexico to become a judge.

Leslie Marmon Silko *(1948–   )* was born in Albuquerque, New Mexico. Her ancestry is a mixture of Laguna Pueblo Indian, Mexican, and European. She grew up on the Laguna Pueblo Reservation and still lives there. Silko wrote many short stories and poems before her first novel, *Ceremony,* won her fame as a Native American writer in 1977. Silko has received several grants and awards for her writing, including a MacArthur Foundation five-year grant. Silko feels that Native American rituals and traditions are seeds of renewal and identity.

Mary TallMountain *(1918–   )* was three years old when her mother, a member of the Koykon-Athabascan people of Nulato, Alaska, was fatally stricken with tuberculosis. The Nulato village council approved Mary's adoption by a white couple. After her adoptive parents died, TallMountain moved to San Francisco in 1945 where she ran her own business. A bout with illness left her almost penniless, and she nearly became homeless. TallMountain decided to become a voice for the homeless. She moved to one of the poorest parts of the city and wrote about the people there. She still lives in California and writes about her heritage.

Alfred, Lord Tennyson *(1809–1892)* found fame only after much misfortune. He and his family were plagued by poverty, his earliest poetry received terrible reviews, and his best friend, Arthur Hallam, died suddenly. Tennyson became so depressed he did not publish anything for the next nine years. In 1850, Tennyson's luck changed. His poem *In Memoriam,* written in honor of Arthur Hallam, became hugely popular. Queen Victoria so liked his work that she made him Poet Laureate of England and Lord Tennyson.

ALFRED, LORD TENNYSON

Yoshiko Uchida *(1921–1992)* wrote stories on brown wrapping paper when she was ten. When she attended college in Berkeley, California, she found much prejudice against Japanese Americans. During World War II her family was imprisoned along with thousands of other Japanese-American families. Finally, Uchida was allowed to leave to study at Smith College. In 1952 she received a Ford Foundation Fellowship to collect folk tales in Japan. Uchida wrote more than twenty-five books, including *Journey Home, The Best Bad Thing, A Jar of Dreams,* and the award-winning *Journey to Topaz.*

YOSHIKO UCHIDA

WRITER'S
HANDBOOK

THE WRITING PROCESS

Writing is a process—a series of steps taken to create a finished product. The process a writer uses is unique to him or her and may not be the same for every writing experience. You need to develop your own writing process, one that works best for you.

Many writers focus their thinking and writing in stages similar to the ones outlined on these pages and shown in the graphic below. Use these stages as a guide, but feel free to go backward or forward in the procedure and to shorten or even skip some stages if you are comfortable doing so.

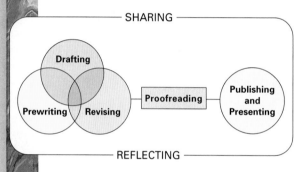

Prewriting and Exploring

Before you write, you think and plan. The following steps might help you get started:

1. Clarify the Assignment

When you are given a writing assignment, make sure you understand what you are being asked to write. To clarify your task, fill out as much of a PASSkey as you can for the assignment by answering the following questions:

P = Purpose
Is the purpose stated in the assignment?
Do I want to express ideas or feelings? to inform? to entertain? to analyze? to persuade?

A = Audience
Who will read my writing?
How much about the subject do my readers know?
How much more do they need to know?
What might they find interesting?
How do I want my audience to respond?

S = Subject
Has a topic been assigned?
What topic do I know about or want to explore?
What topic can I handle well in the length that has been assigned?

S = Structure
Has a structure or form been assigned?
What organization would help me accomplish my purpose?
What should the final product look like?

2. Get Ideas for a Topic

Try some of these different ways of finding topics:

Recalling   Remember events and scenes from your past. Look through family photo albums, scrapbooks, diaries, or your journal to jog your memory. Talk to family members or old friends. Think of the first time you did something.

Brainstorming   With a partner or a small group of classmates, think of and jot down as many ideas as possible. One person's ideas will spur another's. Keep the atmosphere positive and don't stop to evaluate. Ideas should be generated, not judged.

Listing Write a topic or category at the top of a page and list every idea you can think of that relates to it. Go in as many different directions as your imagination will allow.

Freewriting Choose a topic you want to explore and write the first thing that pops into your head. For about three minutes, keep writing everything that comes into your mind. Don't worry about grammar, spelling, or punctuation, and don't stop to read what you've written. After a few minutes, stop writing, read what you wrote, and pick out any ideas that you want to explore further.

Webbing Write a central idea in the middle of your page and circle it. Outside the circle write related ideas. Circle each and draw a line connecting it to the central idea. Do the same for each related idea, as in the idea web below.

3. Choose and Limit Your Topic

Choose a topic that excites you—one you know about or would like to learn about. Narrow your topic to a size you can deal with in the length of your paper. For example, "my family" is too broad a topic to cover in a short composition, but a topic like "my brother's funny habits" could be handled easily.

4. Gather Information

Although different kinds of writing require you to gather information in different ways, most writing involves doing some research and/or using your imagination. If you write an informative or persuasive paper, you must do research to get facts and statistics. If you write about your own experience, you will delve into your memory. If you create fiction or drama, you will use your imagination, but you might do research as well. When you write about literature, you study the literary work itself. For whatever type of writing you do, make notes on a piece of paper, index cards, or a computer screen to record your thoughts .

5. Organize Your Ideas

After you have all the information and ideas you need, organize your notes into the order in which you wish to present your ideas. You can organize by outlining, numbering, using graphic devices, arranging index cards, or moving sections of notes around on a computer screen.

Draft and Discover

When you draft, you begin to put your ideas on paper, following any notes, graphics, or outlines you have made. Drafting is a time to let ideas flow without concern for spelling and punctuation. Errors can be corrected later.

Revise Your Writing

When you revise, you judge the strengths and weaknesses of your paper. You can do this by yourself or with a peer reader. Try to improve what you said and how you said it.

Look for ways you can improve your writing by asking yourself questions about the content. The revision questions on the next page will help you get started.

Revision Questions

- Are the ideas clear and focused on the topic?

- Is the purpose of the writing clear?

- Do any parts need more details?

- Do the ideas flow in a logical order?

- Is the tone consistently the way I want it?

- Will this produce the response I want from the audience?

- Can I add a more exciting beginning?

- Does the piece end in a satisfying way?

When you are satisfied with the content of your writing, check for mistakes in grammar, usage, capitalization, punctuation, and spelling. Use proofreading symbols to mark these errors. Then make a clean, corrected copy of your paper.

Proofreading Symbols

Symbol	Meaning	Example
∧	insert	leson
≡	capitalize	douglass
/	lowercase	History
∼	transpose	veiw
ℓ	take out	lots of
¶	paragraph	¶ The
⊙	add a period	slavery⊙
∧	add a comma	Finally∧

Publish and Present

You communicate with others by sharing your writing. Here are a few possible ways to do this.

- Read your writing aloud to classmates.

- Trade papers with a classmate so that you can read each other's work.

- Publish everyone's work in your own magazine.

- Submit your writing to a school newspaper.

- Tape-record a reading of your work.

- Videotape classmates acting out your writing.

Reflect on Your Writing

After you have completed your writing, think about it and the process you went through to complete it. What have you discovered about your own writing process? Should you change your method the next time around? By learning from what you do each time, you will constantly improve your personal writing process.

TIPS FOR BETTER PARAGRAPHS

Paragraphs are the building blocks of writing. Whether a paragraph stands by itself or is part of a longer composition, such as an essay or a story, it needs to be solidly constructed.

The following information will help you understand paragraphs and give you tips for constructing better paragraphs.

What Is a Paragraph?

A **paragraph** is a group of related sentences that work together to develop a main idea or accomplish a single purpose. Each paragraph that follows has a single main idea or purpose. In the model below, the first sentence states the main idea.

> Away from Allenswood, Eleanor's old uncertainty about her looks came back again. She saw herself as too tall, too thin, too plain. She worried about her buckteeth, which she had thought made her look horselike. The old teasing began again, especially on the part of Uncle Ted's daughter, "Princess" Alice Roosevelt, who seemed to take pleasure in making Eleanor feel uncomfortable.
>
> William J. Jacobs, "Eleanor Roosevelt"

In the next model paragraph, no one sentence states the main idea. Instead, all the sentences work together for a single purpose—to describe Rikki-tikki-tavi, a mongoose.

> He was a mongoose, rather like a little cat in his fur and his tail, but quite like a weasel in his head and his habits. His eyes and the end of his restless nose were pink. He could scratch himself anywhere he pleased with any leg, front or back, that he chose to use. He could fluff up his tail till it looked like a bottle brush, and his war cry as he scuttled through the long grass was *Rikk-tikk-tikki-tikki-tchk!*
>
> Rudyard Kipling, "Rikki-tikki-tavi"

Unity and Coherence

Well-written paragraphs, such as the previous models, reflect two characteristics: unity and coherence. A paragraph has **unity** when all the sentences tell about one main idea or serve a single purpose. In the example below, one of the sentences strays from the topic. Can you tell which one?

> I never saw my sister in better form. Sarah hit every note in the songs, and her acting was superb. The woman sitting next to me in the audience cried when Sarah gave her farewell speech. I noticed other people in the audience with tears in their eyes. Sometimes boys get embarrassed when they cry, but I don't know why they should. The audience belonged to Sarah that night.

The sentence that begins "Sometimes boys get embarrassed" has nothing to do with the description of Sarah's performance. The sentence breaks the unity of the paragraph. It strays from the point and may confuse readers.

A paragraph has **coherence** when the sentences flow smoothly and logically from beginning to end. In a well-written paragraph, the relationship between the sentences is clear to the reader. Compare the following two paragraphs. Which has more coherence?

> Theaters in ancient Athens were built outside, nestled in the hills. A circular stone floor, called the orchestra, served as the performing stage. The stone seats were set into the hillside. There stood a large building called a skene. This was just a building that the actors used for costume changes. It served as a scenic background for the action of a play. Everything was done on a grand scale to entertain the thousands of people in the audience.

> Theaters in ancient Athens were built outside, nestled in the hills. *At the bottom* of the hills, a circular stone pit, called the orchestra, served as the performing stage. Stone seats, *rising above* the orchestra, were

set into the hillside. *Behind* the orchestra, there stood a large building called a skene. *Originally,* this was just a building that the actors used for costume changes. *Later,* it served as a scenic background for the action of a play. Everything was done on a grand scale to entertain the thousands of people in the audience.

The second paragraph in the pair is more coherent because it makes use of **transitions,** the words in italic type. Transitions are the connecting words that let readers know how the details in a paragraph are related.

Some common transitions show relationships of time and space. Others point out comparison and contrast and other logical relationships.

When you revise your paragraphs, check to make sure that your sentences are clearly connected to one another. When necessary, add transition words to help make the relationships clearer.

The chart below lists words and phrases commonly used as transitions.

Transition Words and Phrases

Time Order	before	after	next
	then	meanwhile	yesterday
	during	first	second
Spatial Order	above	below	behind
	around	to the left	on top of
	inside	outside	in front of
Order of Importance	first	most important	strongest
	second	less important	most significant
	third	least important	weakest
Comparison	as	than	like
	similarly	in the same way	by comparison
	neither/nor	either/ or	also
Contrast	yet	but	however
	unlike	instead	in contrast
	nevertheless	on the contrary	on the other hand
Cause and Effect	because	therefore	for this reason
	if/then	thus	so
	as a result	since	due to

---

698   WRITER'S HANDBOOK

Making Your Main Idea Clear

There are two ways of getting across the main idea of your paragraph. One way is to come right out and state your main idea in a **topic sentence.** A topic sentence identifies your topic and tells what you want to say about it. Often, writing that explains or persuades makes use of topic sentences.

The topic sentence may be the first sentence of the paragraph, as in the example below.

> Whenever the white man treats an Indian as they treat each other, then we shall have no more wars. We shall all be alike—brothers of one father and mother, with one sky above us and one country around us and one government for all. Then the Great Spirit Chief who rules above will smile upon this land and send rain to wash out the bloody spots made by brothers' hands from the face of the earth. For this time the Indian race are waiting and praying. I hope that no more groans of wounded men and women will ever go to the ear of the Great Spirit Chief above, and that all people may be one people.
>
> Chief Joseph, "Chief Joseph Speaks"

A topic sentence may appear elsewhere in a paragraph. Sometimes, the second sentence in a paragraph serves as the topic sentence. At other times, it may be the last sentence of the paragraph.

A good topic sentence does more than state the main idea of a paragraph. It also catches readers' interest and makes them want to read on. Compare the following topic sentences.

> I am going to explain the second reason why our class should "adopt" a family for the holidays.

> Besides helping the "adopted family," our holiday basket project will build class spirit.

The second sentence is more interesting and more specific than the first. It tells readers what the paragraph will be about and makes them curious to find out more. Use the checklist below to improve your own topic sentences.

Topic Sentence Checklist

1. Does the sentence tell what the paragraph is about?

2. Is the main idea stated clearly?

3. Is the sentence interesting enough to catch the reader's attention?

4. Is the main idea narrow enough to be developed in one paragraph?

5. Does the sentence cover all the related ideas in the paragraph?

Another way of getting across main ideas is to use an **implied main idea.** Unlike a topic sentence, an implied main idea is not stated directly but is communicated by all the paragraph's sentences working together.

Narrative and descriptive writing often make use of implied main ideas. In the following model, all the sentences work together to describe the lonely appearance of Margot, the main character in the story.

> Margot stood alone. She was a very frail girl who looked as if she had been lost in the rain for years, and the rain had washed out the blue from her eyes and the red from her mouth and the yellow from her hair. She was an old photograph dusted from an album, whitened away, and if she spoke at all her voice would be a ghost. Now she stood, separate, staring at the rain and the loud, wet world beyond the huge glass.
>
> Ray Bradbury, "All Summer in a Day"

Elaboration

A well-constructed paragraph needs details that support its main idea or help to accomplish its purpose. The chart below lists some common types of **elaboration,** or ways of adding supporting details, that you might use to develop your paragraphs.

A well-developed paragraph feels complete. It doesn't leave out important information or state ideas without explaining them. Do you think the following paragraph is well developed?

> You probably don't care much about fruit flies. However, plenty of scientists do. Thousands of experiments have been conducted with fruit flies. They are a valuable source of scientific knowledge.

This paragraph leaves too many questions unanswered. Why do scientists conduct experiments with fruit flies? What have scientists learned from them? Now read another version of the paragraph, one with more elaboration.

> You probably don't care much about fruit flies. However, plenty of scientists do. Fruit flies are a perfect subject for genetics, the branch of biology that deals with heredity. A fruit fly only lives about two weeks. In the course of a year, twenty-seven generations of fruit flies are born and die. Their short life cycle gives scientists a unique opportunity to study how and why traits are passed on to other generations. As a result, fruit flies have contributed more to the study of genetics than any other animal.

When you revise your paragraphs, look for places where you need more information or details.

Types of Elaboration

Type	Definition	Example
Facts/Statistics	Statements that can be proved	The capital of Cameroon is Yaoundé.
Sensory Details	Words that appeal to the five senses	The canary with the silky orange feathers sang loudly in a staccato rhythm.
Reasons	Logical statements to support an idea	Rita deserved to win. She offered the best plan for improving the school. She also worked very hard and listened to everyone's ideas.
Examples	Specific cases or instances that illustrate a main idea	Picking wildflowers and littering are two ways that people ruin national parks.
Quotations	Someone's exact words	"Women who smoke face a greater risk of cancer," said Dr. Peavy.

Paragraphing

When you begin drafting, you often do not know how many paragraphs you will write or what the main idea of each paragraph will be. The following guidelines will help you organize your ideas into effective paragraphs.

Guidelines for Paragraphing

As you draft:

- **Look for related details.**
  Group them together as a paragraph.

- **Look for changes in main ideas.**
  Start a new paragraph with each new idea.

- **Recognize changes in setting or speaker.**
  Whenever the setting or speaker changes, begin a new paragraph.

As you revise:

- **Look for overloaded or overly long paragraphs.**
  Break these down into smaller paragraphs, each focusing on one main idea.

- **Look for strings of short paragraphs.**
  These paragraphs may need to be grouped together or need further elaboration.

- **Make sure each paragraph has a main idea or clear purpose.**
  If you can't tell what the main idea is, how will your reader be able to?

- **Watch out for paragraphs that overlap one another.**
  If two paragraphs cover the same topic, revise one or both of them.

RESEARCH AND REPORT WRITING

This section gives you a brief overview of the steps involved in writing research papers and reports. For further help in this area, consult the Writer's Workshop on Informative Writing on page 569.

Finding a Topic

These tips on finding an idea can make writing easier:

1. Choose a topic that truly interests you. That way you won't get bored and your work will be easier to finish.

2. Check the library. See whether there are enough books and articles available for you to adequately research your subject.

3. Limit your topic. Many topic ideas start out too big. A topic like diabetes may be too large because there is simply too much to say. Choose a smaller topic, such as juvenile diabetes, the causes and treatment of diabetes, or the discovery and history of diabetes. A smaller topic makes a report more manageable.

4. Jot down major points you think you might cover in your report. You may need to look through books to get some general ideas for what you might write about. These general ideas will help you focus your research.

Using the Library

After choosing and focusing your topic, begin your search for information. Like most researchers, you will probably begin with the resources in the library. However, research can also include interviews, TV programs, and many other nonprint sources.

The Card Catalog The card catalog lists all the materials in the library and tells you where to find them. There are three cards for every book: a **title card,** an **author card,** and a **subject card.** Begin by looking up your subject, but don't panic if you can't find what you want right away. You may need to look under a different heading.

Computerized Catalogs Most public libraries now have computerized catalogs. Instructions for using them are usually posted next to the terminals. Generally, you type in your subject; the title of the book; or the last name, then first name, of the author.

Call Numbers Most libraries arrange nonfiction books according to the Dewey Decimal System. The Dewey Decimal System assigns every book a number in one of ten categories. This **call number** is usually printed on the spine of the book. The books are then arranged on the library shelves in numerical order. When you use a card catalog or computer, you are given the call numbers to help you locate the book. Find the area of the library containing those numbers, and search for your book.

Reference Section

The reference section of your library contains all kinds of books that provide facts and statistics, including the different types of materials mentioned below. Ask the librarian for help if you have trouble finding any source.

Readers' Guide to Periodical Literature This journal lists, by subject, articles in current magazines and newspapers. Find the most current *Readers' Guide* and look up the subject of your report. After you find an article that looks promising, write the name and date of the magazine and the page number. Then go to the magazine area and ask the librarian for the issue of the magazine you need. For more information about using the *Readers' Guide,* see page 390.

General Encyclopedias Encyclopedias are often a good place to start your research, since they give a general overview of a subject.

Beware of depending on them, however. If you use only an encyclopedia entry, you haven't done any serious research. You need to find more current and detailed information by using other sources as well.

Specialized Dictionaries and Encyclopedias These books focus on a particular area of knowledge. You can find dictionaries for ballet, biographies, and slang, for example, and encyclopedias on science, sports, and so on.

Almanacs and Yearbooks Since these books are published yearly, they have up-to-date facts and statistics. Check the table of contents and the index of the most current almanac to find your subject.

Atlases These books of maps also contain information on other geographical topics, such as population, temperature, and weather.

Parts of a Book

With the help of a card catalog or computer, you will find many nonfiction books on your topic. By scanning the parts of a book, you can decide immediately whether the book will be useful to you or not.

Title Page This gives the full title of a book, the place of publication, and the names of authors, editors, and publishers.

Copyright Page This page has the publication date, so you can decide how current the information in the book is. A 1972 book on Russia, for instance, will not discuss the breakup of the Soviet Union.

Foreword, Preface, or Introduction These pages contain important background information, such as the author's purpose for writing or the method used to collect the information.

Table of Contents This is a summary of the contents of the book, arranged in order of appearance. These pages are especially important because they may quickly show you whether the book discusses your topic and whether the coverage is detailed enough for your purposes.

Text This is the body of the book. A quick look can help you decide whether the book is too simple or too technical for your needs.

Glossary This is a dictionary at the back of the book that defines technical terms used in the text.

Index Found at the back of the book, this is an alphabetical list of the subjects in the book, together with the page numbers where they can be found. Check the index to see how many pages are devoted to your topic.

Taking Notes

When you find facts and details you can use, take notes. Using index cards can make note-taking easy for you.

Begin by recording important information about each source you use on a **source card** or **bibliography card.** Include the author or editor, last name first; the title of the book or name of the article (for magazines and encyclopedias); the city and publisher; the year (or date for a magazine) of publication; and the library call number (for nonfiction books). You will use the information on these cards later, when you compile your **bibliography** or list of **works cited.** Notice the example below.

Source Card

```
                                    362.196462
                                         D.

Dolger, Henry, M.D., and Bernard Seeman.
    How to Live with Diabetes. New York:
    Norton, 1977.
```

Then use one note card for each fact or idea you might want to include in your report. On the first line, write the title of the source. On the second line, write the page numbers. Then write the fact. You will use these cards to organize your outline and write your paper. To see how note cards look, see the example below.

Note Card

How to Live with Diabetes	**Title**
36–37	**Pages**
	Information
In juvenile diabetes, the pancreas does not produce enough insulin. Without insulin injections, patients can die.	

When to Take a Note   As you read, keep your topic in mind. When you find information that will help you get your ideas across, stop and take a note. Look for the following:

- details about the main ideas you plan to cover in your paper
- important dates and facts
- important people
- interesting events or examples
- conflicting opinions
- special terms or jargon

Summarizing and Quoting   Whenever you can, summarize information in your own words. If you want to include someone else's idea, be sure you say whose idea it is. You might choose to quote someone's exact words because they are clever, famous, or memorable. If so, copy them word for word, and mark the beginning and end with quotation marks.

Remember that **plagiarism** is the use of someone else's words or ideas without giving that person credit. Plagiarism is against the law. Always give credit to your sources.

If your teacher requires you to credit sources within your report, put the source in parentheses at the end of the passage that contains someone else's words or ideas. Use these guidelines:

Crediting Sources Within Your Paper

- **Work by one author**   At the end of your sentence, put the author's last name and the page number in parentheses.
(Pray 234)

- **Work by more than one author**   Put all the last names and the page number in parentheses.
(Dolger and Seeman 32)

- **Works with no author**   Put the title or a shortened version of the title and the page number in parentheses.
("Diabetes" 12)

- **Nonprint works**   Put the name of the person interviewed, the television program, or other nonprint work in parentheses.
(Curtis)

Outlining

An outline helps you organize your main points and supporting details in logical order. Begin by reviewing your note cards. Group the cards into separate piles, putting together those that are about similar ideas. Then review the groups, thinking about what they have in common. Your groups can help you organize your outline into headings and subheadings.

In a topic outline, use phrases, not complete sentences, in a form similar to that shown on the next page.

Outline

Title ──────────→ Kinds of Diabetes
Roman numeral ──────→ I. Type One: Juvenile diabetes
Capital letter ──────→ A. Lack of insulin
Arabic numeral ──────→ 1. Hormone produced by pancreas
Capitalize each line ────→ 2. Enables body to store and use sugar
                                      and starch
                            B. Symptoms
Indent each subdivision ──→ 1. Severe thirst
                               2. Weight loss
                               3. Sugar accumulates in blood
Lowercase letter ──────→ a. Not converted to energy in body
                                  b. Excreted as waste in urine
                            II. Type Two: Adult diabetes

Guidelines for Listing Works Cited

On a separate sheet of paper at the end of your report, you must list the sources you used while writing. This list is sometimes called a **bibliography.** You can compile the information from your source cards. List sources in alphabetical order by the name of the author. The guidelines and examples below show the correct format and punctuation for several different kinds of sources. Remember to underline any information that appears in italics.

Books   Author or editor, last name first; book title; city and publisher; year of publication

Covelli, Pat. *Borrowing Time: Growing Up with Juvenile Diabetes.* New York: Crowell, 1977.

Dolger, Henry, M.D., and Bernard Seeman. *How to Live with Diabetes.* New York: Norton, 1977.

Magazine articles   Author, if one is named; article title; name and date of magazine; page numbers

"Diabetes to Go." *Prevention* Apr. 1992: 12–13.

Encyclopedia articles   Author, if listed; title of the entry; encyclopedia name; year of publication

Roth, Jesse. "Diabetes." *The World Book Encyclopedia.* 1988 ed.

Interviews   Name of person interviewed; type of interview (personal or telephone); date

Curtis, Frank. Personal interview. Sept. 25, 1992.

Television programs   Name of program; narrator or other person providing information; name of series; network; local station; date

"A Desert Blooming." Writ. Marshall Riggan. *Living Wild.* PBS. WTTW, Chicago. 29 Apr. 1984.

Recordings   Artist; title of work; title of recording; type of recording; manufacturer; catalog number; year

U2. "MLK." *The Unforgettable Fire.* Audiocassette. RCA, 90231-4, 1984.

WRITING LETTERS

Business Letters

A business letter is written for a specific purpose—for example, requesting information or ordering a product. It requires a formal writing style and a specific format. Business letters have six parts: the **heading,** the **inside address,** the **salutation,** the **body,** the **closing,** and the **signature.** These six parts can be arranged in either **block form** or **modified block form.**

Block Form and Modified Block Form

For any business letter, use plain white 8 1/2" X 11" paper, whether you type the letter or write it by hand. In **block form** all parts begin at the left margin. Use this form only when you type a letter. In **modified block form** the heading, the closing, and the signature are aligned near the right margin, and the other parts are at the left margin. With this form new paragraphs may be indented.

BLOCK FORM

```
37254 Breezeway Terrace
Spokane, Washington 77777      Heading
October 8, 19—


United States Forest Service
Gifford Pinchot National Forest
P.O. Box 8944                  Inside
Vancouver, Washington 98668    Address

Dear Sir or Madam:            Salutation

                              Body
During my vacation I spoke with
Ms. Julie Pizarro, a ranger stationed
in the Gifford Pinchot National
Forest. I told her that I was
interested in a career in the Forest
Service in your area. She suggested
that I write to you for information.

Please send me any material you have
that describes the qualifications I
would need to join the Forest Service.
Thank you for your time and attention.

Yours truly,                  Closing
Maya Garber
Maya Garber                   Signature
```

MODIFIED BLOCK FORM

```
                    451 Pine Street
Heading             Ames, Iowa 55555
                    June 6, 19—

Credit Manager
Threads Express, Inc.
P.O. Box 14367               Inside Address
Ithaca, New York 11111

Dear Sir or Madam:            Salutation

                              Body
  I shop regularly at one of your
stores, and I saw a report on our
local television news about your new
credit line for young people.

  Please send me an application form
for your special "Kid's Charge" card.
I understand that my parents must
cosign the application. Thank you for
your prompt response.

Closing             Sincerely,

Signature           Mark O'Neill
                    Mark O'Neill
```

Heading The heading of a letter tells where and when you are writing. It gives your street address on the first line; your city, state, and ZIP code on the second line; and the month, day, and year on the third line. The heading should be placed about an inch below the top of the page.

Inside Address The inside address tells to whom the letter is being sent. Place the inside address at the left margin at least four lines below the heading. On the first line you should place the name of the receiver (if you know the person's name). If there is room, place the person's title on the same line, separated from the name by a comma. Otherwise, place the title on the next line. If you do not know the name of the person who will receive the letter, use the person's title or the name of the department. On the following lines, place the name and address of the organization or company, including the city, state, and ZIP code.

Salutation The salutation of a business letter is the way you greet the person to whom you are writing. The salutation should be positioned two lines below the inside address. Begin with the word *Dear,* follow it by the name of the person, and end with a colon. Use only the person's last name, preceded by a title such as *Mr., Mrs., Ms., Dr.,* or *Professor.* If you do not know the person's name, use a general salutation such as *Ladies and Gentlemen.* Another alternative is to write to a department or to a position within a company. The following forms are acceptable:

Dear Mr. Allen: Dear Sir or Madam:
Dear Ms. Kreutzer: Dear Customer
Dear Mrs. Jackson: Service Department:
                       Dear Editor:

Body The body, the main part of the letter in which you write your message, begins two spaces below the salutation. The body may contain a single paragraph or several paragraphs. Leave a space between each paragraph.

Closing The closing is placed two lines below the body, in line with the heading. Closings commonly used for business letters include *Sincerely, Sincerely yours,* and *Very truly yours.* Note that only the first word is capitalized and that the closing ends with a comma.

Signature Type or print your name four spaces below the closing, and sign your name in the space between.

Friendly Letters

A friendly letter has all the parts of a business letter except the inside address. Notice that a friendly letter is not formal in tone; its salutation might read *Hey Susie!* or *Howdy, John,* while its closing might read *Your pal* or *Missing you.* Notice that the salutation is followed by a comma instead of the colon that is used in a business letter. Indent each paragraph, and write clearly so that your reader can follow what you are saying.

Heading	813 King Drive, #2 Dallas, Texas 33333 March 12, 19—

Dear José,   **Salutation**
                              Body
I am very sorry I can't accept your invitation to visit you at your summer place in Michigan. I have already signed up to go to scuba-diving camp during that week in June! Maybe you could go to the camp with me, and we could go to Michigan from there. Could you ask your parents? Hurry and write me back to tell me what they say.

Closing   Take it easy,
Signature   Stan

LANGUAGE HANDBOOK

WORD ORIGINS

The words *grammar* and *glamour* are related. Back in the Middle Ages, when few people could read and write, learning was often associated with magic. A *glamorous* person was one who possessed the secrets of magic because he or she knew *grammar*—the art of reading and writing.

USING THE LANGUAGE HANDBOOK

Think of this handbook as your owner's manual for the English language. The handbook gives you basic information about how our language works. It explains the most common terms for describing the parts and functions of the language. It also helps you to avoid common errors so that you can improve your writing and speaking.

SECTION 1: PARTS OF SPEECH PREVIEW

All words in our language are classified into eight different groups called the *parts of speech*.

Each part of speech plays a different role in a sentence. Before you learn what each role is, learn to recognize what part of speech a word is. The examples below show how one part of speech differs from another.

Noun   A noun is a word that names a person, a place, a thing, or an idea.

> Examples: student   Cleveland   soccer   cooperation
> The *students* went to *Cleveland* to play a *game* of *soccer.*

Pronoun   A pronoun is a word used in place of a noun or another pronoun.

> Examples: he   it   ourselves   everybody   whom   that   I
> The coach made sure *everybody* was on the bus before *he* got on.

Verb   A verb is a word that expresses an action or a state of being. The forms of verbs usually change to show the time of the action.

> Examples: borrow   snicker   invent   do   is   look
> When Jeff *lost* Jim's shinguards, Jim *was* angry.

Adjective   An adjective is a word that modifies, or defines by describing, a noun or a pronoun. It tells *which one, how many, what kind,* or *how much.* Often, it comes before the noun it modifies.

> Examples: silly   monstrous   purple   strong   shiny   few
> Bill used *two elastic* bandages to wrap his *sore* shin.

ADDITIONAL RESOURCES
Technology and Enrichment
Grammar & Usage Copy Masters
  Exercises, pp. 1–7
  Tests, pp. 101–104

Adverb   An adverb is a word that modifies, or defines by describing, a verb, an adjective, or another adverb. It tells *where, when, how,* or *to what extent.*

> Examples: never   quite   frequently   soon   happily   here
> *Often* the losing team *valiantly* tries to make a comeback.

Preposition   A preposition is a word that shows how the noun or pronoun that follows it is related to some other word in the sentence. Many prepositions show direction, position, or relation in time.

> Examples: at   during   between   from   after   of   to
> The ball rolled *toward* the goal *in* the last minute *of* the game.

Conjunction   A conjunction is a word that connects words or groups of words.

> Examples: and   or   but   yet   because   although
> Both Marius *and* I tried to prevent the goal, *but* we were too slow.

Interjection   An interjection is a word or group of words that shows strong or sudden emotion. An interjection can stand by itself.

> Examples: gee   oh   oops   look out   wow
> *Oh!* The loss was so disappointing!

Parts of Speech at a Glance

Every word in a sentence is a particular part of speech. Notice the following illustration.

You will be learning more about each of the parts of speech in later sections of this handbook. For now, see how many you can recognize in the following exercises.

Exercise 1

1. verb, adjective
2. adverb, noun
3. verb, adjective
4. adverb, conjunction
5. preposition, pronoun
6. interjection, adjective
7. adverb, noun
8. noun, verb
9. pronoun, adverb
10. adjective, conjunction

Exercise 2

1. noun
2. conjunction
3. adverb
4. adjective
5. preposition
6. adjective
7. pronoun
8. preposition

LITERARY MODEL
from "Lose Now, Pay Later" by Carol Farley

Exercise 1   Concept Check

Identifying Parts of Speech   Write the part of speech of each italicized word.

1. The Underground Railroad *was* not a *real* railroad; it had no trains, no engines, and no steel tracks.
2. It was a network of escape routes used by slaves trying *courageously* to reach freedom in the free states and in *Canada.*
3. The people who *helped* the *runaway* slaves were called conductors.
4. The conductors *secretly* led the slaves from one stopping place, *or* station, to another along the route.
5. Benjamin Baker was a Quaker *from* New York *who* acted as a conductor.
6. *Oh!* He risked everything—his money, his freedom, and his life—to help *complete* strangers make their way to freedom.
7. A former slave, Harriet Tubman, *rightly* gained fame for her *work* as a conductor on the Underground Railroad.
8. Because of her *success* in leading slaves to the "Promised Land" of freedom, she *became* known as the "Moses" of her people.
9. *Nobody* knows how many slaves used the Underground Railroad *then.*
10. A *low* estimate is forty thousand people, *and* a high estimate is one hundred thousand.

Exercise 2   Application in Literature

Parts of Speech   Write the part of speech of each italicized word.

(1) Swoodies aren't cold like ice cream or warm like cooked *pudding,* (2) *but* they're a blending of both in temperature and texture.   (3) The flavor melts *instantly,* and your whole mouth and brain are flooded with tastes and impressions.   (4) Like that *first* swoodie I tried, coconut-almond-marshmallow; (5) suddenly, as my mouth separated the individual tastes, my brain burst into memories associated *with* each flavor.   (6) I felt as if I were lying on a *warm* beach, all covered with coconut suntan oil (7)—then I heard myself giggling and singing as a group of *us* roasted marshmallows around a campfire (8)—then I relived the long-ago moments of biting *into* the special Christmas cookies my grandmother made with almonds when I was little.

(9) *"Wow!"* Trinja looked at me, and I see that she had just experienced the same kind of reactions.   (10) We scarfed up the rest of that *swoodie* in just a few more bites, and we moved on to another flavor.

Exercise 3   Drafting Skill

Adding Words   On your paper, write words to complete the following paragraphs. Choose the most exciting words you can think of, but be sure to use the parts of speech indicated on the blanks.

When Mika heard the soldiers' (1) __(noun)__, she felt (2) __(adjective)__ at first. But (3) __(adverb)__ her courage (4) __(verb)__. She grasped her (5) __(noun)__ firmly and hid (6) __(preposition)__ the kitchen cupboard. Suddenly, the shouting stopped, (7) __(conjunction)__ the voices seemed farther away.

(8) " __(interjection)__ !" she thought. "Now (9) __(pronoun)__ can (10) __(verb)__ !"

9. interjection
10. noun

Exercise 3
Answers will vary. Sample answers are provided.

1. shouts
2. frightened
3. then
4. returned
5. kitten
6. inside
7. and
8. Wow!
9. I
10. escape

SECTION 2: UNDERSTANDING SENTENCES

A *sentence* is a group of words that expresses a complete thought. A sentence must have a *subject* and *predicate*.

Subjects and Predicates

The **subject** tells whom or what a sentence is about, and the **predicate** tells what the subject does or is. The complete subject and the complete predicate together contain all the words in the sentence.

Complete Subject	Complete Predicate
Gloria Cooper	edited a book.
The book	listed funny mistakes from headlines.
The mistakes	had appeared in newspapers around the country.

Simple Subjects and Verbs

In every sentence there are a few words that are more important than the rest. These key words are the simple subject and the simple predicate, or verb. The **simple subject** is the key word in the complete subject. The **simple predicate,** or **verb,** is the key word in the complete predicate. Consider this sentence:

A dark mysterious *shadow*   suddenly *appeared* in the doorway.

Shadow is the key word in the complete subject. It names the thing that appeared. The simple subject is a noun or pronoun, not a modifier. *Appeared* is the key word in the complete predicate; it tells what the shadow did. *Appeared* is the verb.

Subjects and Verbs at a Glance

The **complete subject** includes all the words that identify the person, place, thing, or idea the sentence is about.	The **complete predicate** includes all the words that tell or ask something about the subject.

Bright yellow **daffodils** **cheer** the patients in the ward.

The **simple subject** tells whom or what the sentence is about. It may be one or several words, but it does not include modifiers.	The **simple predicate,** or **verb,** tells what the subject does or is. It may be one word or several, but it does not include modifiers.

ADDITIONAL RESOURCES
Technology and Enrichment
Grammar & Usage Copy Masters
    Exercises, pp. 8–18
    Tests, pp. 105–110
 Grammar Test Generator

Exercise 1 Concept Check

Subjects and Predicates Copy the sentences below. Draw a line to separate the complete subject from the complete predicate. Circle the simple subject, and draw two lines under the verb.

1. Apollo drove an incredible chariot.
2. The magnificent chariot sparkled in the sunlight.
3. Phaëthon begged for his own ride.
4. His father feared the outcome.
5. The new driver felt confident at first.
6. He grabbed the reins.
7. The mighty horses snorted fire.
8. The inexperienced Phaëthon suddenly zoomed through the sky.
9. The foolish boy fell out of the chariot.
10. The story ended in tragedy.

Finding the Verb

A verb can express an action, state that something exists, or link the subject to another word that describes the subject.

To understand a sentence, you must find the verb. Here are some guidelines that tell you what verbs do.

An **action verb** says what the subject of the sentence does. The action may or may not be something you can see.

> Armand *jumped* six feet.
> Robin *said* no.
> Jill *loves* classical music.

A **linking verb** links the subject of the sentence with a word in the predicate that renames or modifies the subject. It does not refer to an action.

> A pizza *is* a cheese pie. (links *pizza* with *pie*)
> The pizza *is* huge. (links *pizza* with *huge*)

The most common linking verbs are *am, are, were, being, is, was, be,* and *been*. Other familiar linking verbs include *look, appear, seem, become, remain, feel, sound, taste, grow,* and *smell*. Many linking verbs can also be used as action verbs.

> That face *looked* mean. (linking verb)
> Those eyes *looked* right through me. (action verb)

Exercise 1

1. (Apollo) / <u>drove</u> an incredible chariot.
2. The magnificent (chariot) / <u>sparkled</u> in the sunlight.
3. (Phaëthon) / <u>begged</u> for his own ride.
4. His (father) / <u>feared</u> the outcome.
5. The new (driver) / <u>felt</u> confident at first.
6. (He) / <u>grabbed</u> the reins.
7. The mighty (horses) / <u>snorted</u> fire.
8. The inexperienced (Phaëthon) / suddenly <u>zoomed</u> through the sky.
9. The foolish (boy) / <u>fell</u> out of the chariot.
10. The (story) / <u>ended</u> in tragedy.

A **helping verb** helps the main verb express meaning. Some forms of verbs such as *is, has,* and *do* can be used to help other verbs. When they are used in this way, they are called **helping verbs.** The verb they help is called the **main verb.** Together, the helping verb and the main verb make up a **verb phrase.**

I *do love* pizza.   *Have* you *seen* Marie?

Helping Verbs and Main Verbs at a Glance

The parts of a verb phrase often appear next to one another. However, sometimes the parts of the verb phrase are separated by words that are not part of the verb phrase.

> **QUICK TIP**   To find the verb of a sentence, use these methods:
>
> 1. Look for a word that tells the main action, expresses a state of being, or links the subject with a description.
> 2. Look for helping verbs. Examples are *is, am, are, was, were, be, been, have, has, had, do, does, did, shall, will, should, would,* and *could.*
> 3. Look for all the verbs that make up the verb phrase.

Exercise 2   Concept Check

Identifying Verbs   Write the verb or verb phrase in each of the following sentences. Tell whether the verb or verb phrase shows action or is a linking verb. Be sure to include any helping verbs.

1. In March of 1987, a tugboat from New York became famous.
2. It was towing a barge of garbage.

3. A barge is a large flat-bottomed boat.

4. It can hold a great deal of cargo.

5. This barge carried 3,186 tons of New York's garbage.

6. According to the original plan, North Carolina would buy the rotten garbage for its methane gas.

7. However, officials in North Carolina changed their minds.

8. They would no longer accept New York's garbage.

9. The smelly barge traveled to different places for two months.

10. Finally it returned, still full, to New York City.

Compound Sentence Parts

A *compound subject* or a *compound verb* has two or more parts.

This sentence has a compound subject:

> *Clams* and *shrimp* are shellfish.

This sentence has a compound verb:

> The sailboat *pitches* and *rolls* in the bay.

QUICK TIP   You can make your writing more concise and less repetitive and choppy by using compound subjects and verbs, as follows:

Choppy	The bridge heaved. The bridge swayed.
Improved	The bridge heaved and swayed.

Exercise 3   Concept Check

Compound Subjects and Verbs   Write the compound subject or compound verb in each of the following sentences. Tell whether it is a compound subject or a compound verb.

1. Eng and Chang were the original Siamese twins.

2. The twins were joined at birth and were never separated.

3. They looked alike but had different personalities.

4. The connective ligament between their chests stretched and grew with them.

5. Tragically, their father and five of their brothers and sisters died of the deadly disease cholera.

3. is; linking

4. can hold; action

5. carried; action

6. would buy; action

7. changed; action

8. would accept; action

9. traveled; action

10. returned; action

Exercise 3

1. Eng, Chang; compound subject

2. were joined, were separated; compound verb

3. looked, had; compound verb

4. stretched, grew; compound verb

5. father, five; compound subject

Exercise 4

Answers may vary. Sample answers are provided.

1. Robert Hunter discovered the twins in Siam and made them famous.

2. The twins could run, dive, and swim.

3. Hunter managed the twins and exhibited them in the United States.

4. Audiences and doctors were fascinated by the twins.

5. The twins performed tricks and answered questions for the audience.

6. Their American shows and European exhibitions were sold out.

7. They were unhappy with their new manager, fired him, and became their own managers.

8. Later, Chang and Eng became successful farmers.

9. Both men fell in love with sisters and married them.

10. The Siamese twins and their twenty-one children achieved a fairly normal life.

Exercise 4   Revision Skill

Combining Sentences   Combine the sentences in each item into a single sentence with either a compound subject or compound verb. You may add, change, or delete words as necessary.

Example   The twins had to find work. Their mother had to find work too.

Answer   The twins and their mother had to find work.

1. Robert Hunter discovered the twins in Siam. He made them famous.

2. The twins could run. The twins could dive. They could swim.

3. Hunter managed the twins. Hunter exhibited them in the United States.

4. Audiences were fascinated by the twins. Doctors were also fascinated by them.

5. The twins performed tricks for the audience. They answered questions for the audience.

6. Their American shows were sold out. Their European exhibitions were sold out.

7. They were unhappy with their new manager. They fired him. They became their own managers.

8. Later, Chang became a successful farmer. Eng also became a successful farmer.

9. Both men fell in love with sisters. They married the sisters.

10. The Siamese twins achieved a fairly normal life. Their twenty-one children had a normal life too.

Kinds of Sentences

One way to make your writing and speech interesting is to use different kinds of sentences. You can use all of these four types of sentences.

A *declarative sentence* makes a statement.

> The book *Stolen Continents* tells about the European invasion of the Americas.

An *interrogative sentence* asks a question.

> How many people lived in America before the Europeans came?

An *imperative sentence* makes a request or commands someone to do something.

> Tell me what happened to all those people.

An *exclamatory sentence* expresses strong feeling.

> Oh, how terribly the people suffered!

An **end mark** is the punctuation at the end of a sentence. The end mark you use depends on what kind of sentence you write. Use a period (.) after a declarative sentence, a question mark (?) after an interrogative sentence, a period (.) after an imperative sentence, and an exclamation point (!) after an exclamatory sentence.

Exercise 5   Concept Check

Kinds of Sentences   On your paper, write *Declarative, Interrogative, Imperative,* or *Exclamatory* to show what kind each sentence is. Then write the correct punctuation mark.

1. Washington, D.C., is a very exciting city to visit
2. Can you imagine the sense of history a visit will give you
3. Oh, what a weird feeling you get at Ford's Theatre, where Lincoln was shot
4. Did you know you can watch money being printed in Washington
5. Be sure to see the Federal Bureau of Investigation
6. What an impressive sight the Washington Monument is
7. The Vietnam Veterans Memorial is the most-visited monument
8. The wall evokes more emotion than other monuments do
9. What would you say if you met a politician in the Capitol
10. When you visit Washington, just dress casually

Exercise 6   Revision Skill

Revising Sentences   Rewrite each sentence from Exercise 5 as a different kind of sentence. Tell what kind of sentence the new sentence is. Add or delete words as necessary.

Sentence Fragments

> **A *sentence fragment* is a group of words that does not express a complete idea.**

A fragment leaves out important information such as the subject or the verb.

Fragment   Colonies on the moon. (There is no verb.)

Sentence   Colonies on the moon are being planned.

Exercise 7

The revisions of fragments may vary. Sample answers are provided.

1. Sentence

2. Sentence

3. Fragment: Mountain lions are also called cougars, panthers, or pumas.

4. Fragment: Unlike lions and tigers, mountain lions cannot roar.

5. Sentence

6. Fragment: Wildlife sanctuaries are important.

7. Sentence

8. Fragment: Mountain lions can kill animals eight times their size.

9. Fragment: Mountain lions fight each other to the death.

10. Sentence

Exercise 8

Revisions of fragments may vary. Sample answers are provided.

(1) There are thirty-seven different species of dolphins. (2) Some are among the most intelligent animals in the world. (3) Dolphins are our friends. (4) Like us, dolphins are mammals, not fish. (5) They seem to develop ties with humans. (6) Conservationists are working to protect the dolphins. (7) The dolphins are being killed by people fishing for tuna. (8) Dolphins get caught in the huge nets and drown. (9) Fishing fleets used to kill 250,000 dolphins every year. (10) New laws have been passed to protect the dolphins.

Fragment	Trapped several miles beneath the earth's surface. (There is no subject.)
Sentence	The miners were trapped several miles beneath the earth's surface.

Exercise 7   Concept Check

Identifying Fragments   Write *Sentence* or *Fragment* on your paper for each of the following. Then change all the fragments to complete sentences.

1. Mountain lions are beautiful wild animals.
2. Most of them live in rugged high country.
3. Also called cougars, panthers, or pumas.
4. Unlike lions and tigers, cannot roar.
5. In some areas, mountain lions are nearly extinct.
6. Wildlife sanctuaries important.
7. Some states do not allow hunters to kill the animals.
8. Can kill animals eight times their size.
9. Fight each other to the death.
10. Mountain lions usually will not attack humans.

Exercise 8   Proofreading Skill

Correcting Fragments   Rewrite the following paragraph and turn any fragments into complete sentences. Add correct punctuation.

(1) There are thirty-seven different species of dolphins (2) Some are among the most intelligent animals in the world (3) Dolphins our friends (4) Like us, mammals, not fish (5) Seem to develop ties with humans (6) Conservationists are working to protect the dolphins (7) Being killed by people fishing for tuna (8) Get caught in the huge nets and drown (9) Fishing fleets used to kill 250,000 dolphins every year (10) New laws have been passed to protect the dolphins

Run-on Sentences

A *run-on sentence* occurs when two or more sentences are written as one.

Sometimes, when people are in a hurry, they incorrectly write two sentences as one. The result is a **run-on sentence.** The end mark may accidentally be left off the end of the first sentence. Sometimes a comma is incorrectly used to separate the sentences. This is known as a **comma splice.**

Run-on	A deer stood by the roadside it was blinded by our headlights.
Corrected	A deer stood by the roadside. It was blinded by our headlights.
Run-on (comma splice)	Maria is from Peru, she speaks fluent Spanish.
Corrected	Maria is from Peru. She speaks fluent Spanish.

To correct a run-on, use one of the methods described below.

Correcting Run-on Sentences

- Add an end mark to the first sentence and begin the second sentence with a capital letter.
- Add a semicolon after the first sentence.
- Add a comma after the first sentence and use a conjunction such as *and, or, nor, for, but, so,* or *yet* to begin the second.

Run-on	Maria is from Peru, she speaks fluent Spanish.
Corrected	Maria is from Peru; she speaks fluent Spanish.
Corrected	Maria is from Peru, and she speaks fluent Spanish.

◀ **PUNCTUATION NOTE**
· · · · · · · · · · · · · ·
When you combine two sentences using a conjunction, always place a comma before the conjunction.

Exercise 9   Concept Check

Run-ons   Decide if each of the following is a correct sentence or a run-on. If it is correct, write *Correct* on your paper. If it is a run-on, rewrite it correctly.

1. I enjoy history; it is my favorite subject.
2. History teaches us about people in the past those ancient guys did some wonderful and terrible things.
3. I'm learning that people really haven't changed that much over the ages.
4. Incan history is fascinating, Incas were amazing people.
5. Have you learned about the Incas let me tell you about them.

Exercise 9
Rewritten sentences may vary. Sample answers are provided.

1. Correct

2. History teaches us about people in the past; those ancient guys did some wonderful and terrible things.

3. Correct

4. Incan history is fascinating. Incas were amazing people.

5. Have you learned about the Incas? Let me tell you about them.

Exercise 10

Answers may vary. Sample answers are provided.

1. The Incas were great architects. They were masterful road builders.

The Incas were great architects, and they were masterful road builders.

2. The main Incan royal road began at Quito. It ended at Cuzco.

The main Incan royal road began at Quito, and it ended at Cuzco.

3. The Incas had impressive roads. They had no horses or vehicles.

The Incas had impressive roads, but they had no horses or vehicles.

4. Atahualpa had golden ornaments in his hair. He wore an emerald necklace.

Atahualpa had golden ornaments in his hair; he wore an emerald necklace.

5. The Incas were brave soldiers. They were destroyed by smallpox and civil war.

The Incas were brave soldiers, but they were destroyed by smallpox and civil war.

Exercise 11

Answers will vary. Sample answers are provided.

(1) The first computers were huge. It took an entire room to hold them. (2) Today they are small; many people have them at home. (3) Home computers are useful and fun. (4) Some people use them for work. Thousands of new businesses are started each year by home computer users. (5) Some people use them to play games. (6) They can be used for shopping, and they can also be used for banking and paying bills. (7) You can even use them to talk to other people all over the country. (8) Computers are especially helpful with school work. They allow you to easily correct typing errors. (9) You can store an entire encyclopedia on compact disc. (10) What other uses are there for a home computer? You can probably name several.

Exercise 10   Revision Skill

Correcting Run-ons   Each sentence below is a run-on. Correct each sentence in two different ways.

Example	Manco Capac was the first Incan emperor, Atahualpa was the last.
Separate	Manco Capac was the first Incan emperor. Atahualpa was the last.
Combined	Manco Capac was the first Incan emperor, and Atahualpa was the last.

1. The Incas were great architects, they were masterful road builders.

2. The main Incan royal road began at Quito it ended at Cuzco.

3. The Incas had impressive roads, they had no horses or vehicles.

4. Atahualpa had golden ornaments in his hair, he wore an emerald necklace.

5. The Incas were brave soldiers they were destroyed by smallpox and civil war.

Exercise 11   Revision Skill

Sentence Review   Rewrite the following paragraph, correcting all sentence fragments and run-ons.

(1) The first computers were huge, took an entire room to hold them. (2) Today they are small many people have them at home. (3) Home computers useful, fun. (4) Some people use them for work, thousands of new businesses are started each year by home computer users. (5) Play games. (6) They can be used for shopping they can also be used for banking and paying bills. (7) Even talk to other people all over the country. (8) Computers are especially helpful with school work, they allow you to easily correct typing errors. (9) Entire encyclopedia on compact disc. (10) What other uses are there for a home computer you can probably name several.

Prepositions show relationships. Conjunctions link words together. Interjections express feelings.

Three Parts of Speech at a Glance

Interjection
Shows emotion

Preposition
Shows relationship between the animals and the couch

Help! The cat **and** the baby alligator are **under** the couch!

Conjunction
Connects *cat* and *baby alligator*

Prepositions and Prepositional Phrases

A *preposition* is a word that shows the relationship of its object to some other word in the sentence.

The word *preposition* can be divided into two parts: *pre,* meaning "before," and *position.* A preposition is a word that is *positioned before* its object to show how that object relates in time or space to some other word in the sentence. The **object of a preposition** is a noun or a pronoun. The examples below are **prepositional phrases:** the preposition plus its object.

> *on* the hook *(on* is a preposition; *hook* is its object)
> *during* the storm *(during* is a preposition; *storm* is its object)

The job of a preposition is to show how its object relates to another word in the sentence, usually a word that comes before the prepositional phrase.

> The coat *on* the hook belongs *to* me. *(Hook* is connected to *coat* by the preposition *on; me* is connected to *belongs* by the preposition *to.)*

◀ **WRITING TIP**
When you write, try beginning some sentences with a prepositional phrase to add an interesting twist.

ADDITIONAL RESOURCES
Technology and Enrichment
Grammar & Usage Copy Masters
 Exercises, pp. 19–24
 Tests, pp. 111–114
 Grammar Test Generator

Exercise 1
1. <u>for</u> her <u>work</u>
   <u>with</u> homeless <u>people</u>

2. <u>in</u> <u>Yugoslavia</u>
   <u>to</u> <u>Calcutta</u>

▶

SHOW WHAT?

Many prepositions show relationships in **space**. (The sign is *above* the door.) Others show relationships in **time**. (We went to the movies *after* dinner.)

Words Often Used as Prepositions

about	below	from	past
above	beneath	in	through
across	beside	inside	to
after	between	into	toward
against	beyond	near	under
along	but (except)	of	underneath
among	by	off	until
around	down	on	up
as	during	out	with
before	except	outside	within
behind	for	over	without

WRITING TIP

Make sure when you write that your prepositional phrases are close to the words they tell about.
Unclear: Ali stared at the huge spider with a terrified look.
Clear: With a terrified look, Ali stared at the huge spider.

QUICK TIP   Remember that a preposition must have an object. In a sentence, if one of the words in the list is used without an object, it is an adverb. Prepositions always have objects; adverbs never do.

Preposition   He fell *down* the steps.
Adverb   He fell *down*.

Exercise 1   Concept Check

Prepositional Phrases   Write the prepositional phrases that appear in the following sentences. Draw one line under each preposition. Draw two lines under its object. There may be more than one phrase in a sentence.

Example   Mother Teresa saved many lives in Calcutta.
Answer   <u>in</u> <u>Calcutta</u>

1. Mother Teresa won the Nobel Peace Prize for her work with homeless people.
2. Born in Yugoslavia, Mother Teresa joined a religious order, which sent her to Calcutta.

722   LANGUAGE HANDBOOK

3. With three million inhabitants, Calcutta has one of the largest populations in the world.

4. Most Calcuttans live below an average American's standard of living.

5. Many poor Calcuttans without homes live from day to day.

6. Through Mother Teresa's efforts, however, schools and hospitals have been established for the needy.

7. She has helped lepers beyond hope and poor people near death.

8. Orphanages and youth centers were created under her supervision.

9. Until her arrival, it seemed that no one cared about these people.

10. Mother Teresa focused international attention on the poor within big cities around the world.

Exercise 2   Drafting Skill

Using Prepositional Phrases   Complete the following story by writing prepositional phrases to fit the blanks.

(1) Last night I dreamed about traveling __?__. (2) My best friend, Kim, went __?__. (3) __?__, Kim and I saw many new things. (4) At first we just strolled __?__, looking __?__. (5) Then we rode a boat __?__. (6) Later we hiked __?__. (7) We enjoyed talking __?__. (8) Kim stayed __?__ the whole time. (9) We went __?__ and did not return __?__. (10) When I woke up, I saw my suitcase __?__.

Conjunctions and Interjections

A *conjunction* is a word that connects words or groups of words.

An *interjection* is a word or short group of words used to express feelings such as anger, fear, joy, or surprise.

Conjunctions can be used to combine sentences or sentence parts.

Two Sentences	Gossip is sometimes fun. Gossip is often hurtful to people.
Combined Sentence	Gossip is sometimes fun, *but* it is often hurtful to people.
Combined Sentence Parts	Gossip can be both fun *and* hurtful at the same time.

Common conjunctions include *and, or, nor, for, but, so,* and *yet.*

IN THE END

Ending sentences with prepositions is a practice that some people just won't put up with. Other people feel that prepositions at the ends of sentences are just fine. Check with your teacher to see what his or her view is.

3. <u>With</u> three million <u>inhabitants</u>
   <u>of</u> the largest <u>populations</u>
   <u>in</u> the <u>world</u>

4. <u>below</u> an average American's
   <u>standard</u>
   <u>of</u> <u>living</u>

5. <u>without</u> <u>homes</u>
   <u>from</u> <u>day</u>
   <u>to</u> <u>day</u>

6. <u>Through</u> Mother Teresa's <u>efforts</u>
   <u>for</u> the <u>needy</u>

7. <u>beyond</u> <u>hope</u>
   <u>near</u> <u>death</u>

8. <u>under</u> her <u>supervision</u>

9. <u>Until</u> her <u>arrival</u>
   <u>about</u> these <u>people</u>

10. <u>on</u> the <u>poor</u>
    <u>within</u> big <u>cities</u>
    <u>around</u> the <u>world</u>

Exercise 2
Answers may vary. Sample answers are provided.

1. to Jamaica
2. with me
3. On our trip
4. near the ocean
   for shells
5. on the water
6. up a mountain
7. with Jamaican children
8. with me
9. on a raft trip
   until Tuesday
10. on the floor

Exercise 3

1. Hey, interjection
2. Yeah, interjection
   or, conjunction
3. but, conjunction
   and, conjunction
4. Wow, interjection
   and, conjunction
5. Gee, interjection
   yet, conjunction

Exercise 4

Answers will vary. Sample answers are provided.

I enjoy mystery stories <u>and</u> stories about ancient cultures <u>of Europe</u>. *(conjunction; prepositional phrase)* One story that combines both <u>of my interests</u> is the story of Atlantis. *(prepositional phrase)* No one knows exactly where Atlantis was, <u>or</u> if it even existed. *(conjunction)* However, this ancient city is mentioned by the ancient Greek philosopher Plato. *(no change)* According to Plato, Atlantis was a powerful, wealthy city <u>with a large population</u>. *(prepositional phrase)* It was on an island in the Mediterranean Sea. *(no change)* Its power did not last <u>for long</u>. *(prepositional phrase)* <u>In his account</u>, Plato says that earthquakes caused Atlantis to disappear into the sea. *(prepositional phrase)* Modern science has confirmed that the ancient island of Thera was destroyed by a volcano. *(no change)* <u>Wow,</u> that must have been some explosion! *(interjection)* Could Thera be Atlantis? *(no change)* No one really knows, <u>but</u> I find the mystery fascinating. *(conjunction)*

An interjection expresses feeling. If an interjection expresses strong emotion, it is punctuated with an exclamation point. An interjection that expresses only mild emotion is punctuated by a comma.

> *Help!* I'm falling! (strong emotion)
>
> *Oh,* I guess I'll live. (mild emotion)

Common interjections include *oh, ah, alas, gee, gosh, oops, well, wow, help, so, whew, hooray, hey,* and *yeah.*

Exercise 3   Concept Check

Conjunctions and Interjections   Write the conjunctions and interjections in the following sentences. Tell whether each is a conjunction or an interjection.

1. Hey, isn't that a scarab beetle charm around your neck?
2. Yeah, such ornaments, made of stone or metal, were popular in ancient Egypt.
3. Egyptians had gold, but they had to import silver and iron.
4. Wow! Did you know that Egyptians pioneered in the fields of mathematics, medicine, astronomy, and architecture?
5. Gee, I never knew how much the Egyptians influenced our culture, yet they lived so long ago.

Exercise 4   Revision Skill

Adding Interest to Your Writing   Rewrite the following paragraph. Make it more lively by adding prepositional phrases, conjunctions, and interjections. Underline each addition you make and, in the margin of your paper, write what part of speech the addition is. You may combine sentences and add words if necessary.

I enjoy mystery stories. I also enjoy stories about ancient cultures. One story that combines both is the story of Atlantis. No one knows exactly where Atlantis was. No one knows if it even existed. However, this ancient city is mentioned by the ancient Greek philosopher Plato. According to Plato, Atlantis was a powerful, wealthy city. It was on an island in the Mediterranean Sea. Its power did not last. Plato says that earthquakes caused Atlantis to disappear into the sea. Modern science has confirmed that the ancient island of Thera was destroyed by a volcano. That must have been some explosion! Could Thera be Atlantis? No one really knows. I find the mystery fascinating.

A *noun* is a word that names a person, a place, a thing, or an idea.

Persons	Eleanor Roosevelt, baby, host, Aladdin, vice-president
Places	Houston, park, arcade, rain forest
Things	concert, skateboard, television, football
Ideas	cooperation, friendship, wonder, honor

QUICK TIP To find out whether a word is a noun, simply see if it makes sense in one of these blanks:

_____ is _____ are

Nouns	*Houston* is	*friends* are
Not Nouns	*to* is	*see* are

Types of Nouns

If a noun names a particular person, place, thing, or idea, it is a *proper noun*.

Michael Jordan	EPCOT Center	Nile
Florida	Felicia	Hinduism

If a noun names a kind of person, place, thing, or idea, it is a *common noun*.

player	auditorium	river
state	woman	religion

A noun made up of more than one word is called a *compound noun*.

You may have noticed that some nouns—like *vice-president, rain forest, football,* and *Michael Jordan*—are made up of more than one word.

spacewalk	great-grandfather	time capsule
basketball	Zuni Pueblo	Lake Ontario

QUICK TIP A compound noun might be spelled as one word, like *spacewalk;* with a hyphen, like *great-grandfather;* or as two words, like *Zuni Pueblo.*

◀ **PLACE NAMES**

Many place names in the Americas come from Native American languages. *Mexico* comes from the name of Mexítli, an Aztec war god. *Missouri* comes from words meaning "people of the big canoes"; *Mississippi,* from words meaning "big river."

USING NOUNS 725

ADDITIONAL RESOURCES
Technology and Enrichment
Grammar & Usage Copy Masters
 Exercises, pp. 25–33
 Tests, pp. 115–118
 Grammar Test Generator

Exercise 1

1. homeroom (compound noun), roll, cards, bulletin, home, parents

2. principal, Mr. Belton (proper noun), loudspeaker (compound noun), students, year, experiences, friendships

3. students, chairs

4. Victor (proper noun), Teresa (proper noun), rows, novel

5. year

Exercise 2

Answers will vary. Sample answers are provided.

1. actor: Richard Gere

2. city: New Orleans

3. planet: Venus

4. nation: Nigeria

5. game: Monopoly

6. singer: Suzanne Vega

7. university: Princeton University

8. car: Buick

9. teacher: Ms. Powell

10. company: IBM

LITERARY MODEL
from "Seventh Grade"
by Gary Soto ▶

Exercise 1   Application in Literature

Types of Nouns   Write the nouns in the following passage. Label the three proper nouns and the two compound nouns.

(1) In homeroom, roll was taken, emergency cards were passed out, and they were given a bulletin to take home to their parents. (2) The principal, Mr. Belton, spoke over the crackling loudspeaker, welcoming the students to a new year, new experiences, and new friendships. (3) The students squirmed in their chairs and ignored him. (4) Victor sat calmly, thinking of Teresa, who sat two rows away, reading a paperback novel. (5) This would be his lucky year.

Exercise 2   Concept Check

Proper Nouns   On your paper write a proper noun that names an example of the person or thing named by each common noun.

Example   mountain   **Answer**   Mount Everest

1. actor	5. game	8. car
2. city	6. singer	9. teacher
3. planet	7. university	10. company
4. nation		

Using Nouns

Nouns are used as *subjects, direct objects, indirect objects, predicate nouns,* and *objects of prepositions*.

Think of the **subject** as naming the actor in a sentence—whom or what the sentence is about. The **direct object** names the thing or person who *receives* the action.

Bill threw the ball.

Bill names the actor, so it is the subject. To determine the direct object, ask yourself *what* he threw. The direct object is *ball*.

An **indirect object** names a person or thing to whom something is done or given.

Bill threw Jack the ball.

You already know what Bill threw (direct object)—the ball. To whom did he throw it? The indirect object is *Jack*. To have an indirect object, a sentence must have a direct object. However, a sentence can have a direct object without an indirect object.

When the noun after the verb refers to the subject, it is called a **predicate noun.**

> Bill is our best pitcher.

Since *pitcher* renames the subject *Bill, pitcher* is a predicate noun. It is a noun in the predicate that names the same person, place, thing, or idea as the subject.

You remember that a preposition takes an object. A noun can function as the **object of a preposition.**

> Bill is the best pitcher on our team.

Team is the object of the preposition *on*.

Uses of Nouns at a Glance

> The **indirect object** tells to whom or for whom something is done or given.

> The **direct object** tells who or what receives the action of the verb.

Mr. Achebe sent **Maud** a **turtle** for her **birthday.**

> The **subject** tells the person, place, thing, or idea that the sentence is about.

> The **object of a preposition** comes after a preposition such as *of, at, on, to,* or *for.*

Maud is the **goalie** on our soccer **team.**

> A **predicate noun** comes after a linking verb such as *is, are,* or *seems.* It renames or describes the subject.

Exercise 3   Concept Check

Uses of Nouns   Decide what job each italicized noun is doing in the sentence. Write *Subject, Direct Object, Indirect Object, Object of a Preposition,* or *Predicate Noun.*

1. For my *birthday,* Dad gave me plane *tickets.*

2. He also gave my *sister tickets.*

3. My *dad* was a *winner* on a television quiz show.

4. Dad won the *prize* in a lucky *spin* of the wheel.

5. I sent *Jane* the good *news.*

Exercise 4   Drafting Skill

Nouns in Sentences   Think of an interesting noun that can be used to complete each sentence. Write the noun on a sheet of paper. Then identify the noun as *Subject, Direct Object, Indirect Object, Object of a Preposition,* or *Predicate Noun.*

> **Example**   _____?_____ is a large city.
>
> **Answer**   San Juan, Subject

1. Puerto Rico is a beautiful _____?_____ .
2. We will stay there for a _____?_____ .
3. I will buy my _____?_____ a gift in Old San Juan.
4. Tourism is an important _____?_____ here.
5. You can reach Puerto Rico by _____?_____ .
6. One afternoon we visited a _____?_____ .
7. The _____?_____ was covered with beautiful white sand.
8. We ate fresh _____?_____ almost every day.
9. The _____?_____ include scuba diving, swimming, and fishing.
10. I sent my _____?_____ a postcard.

Using Plural Forms of Nouns

A noun is *singular* if it names one person, place, thing, or idea. It is *plural* if it names more than one person, place, thing, or idea.

1. To form the plurals of most nouns, add -s.

bicycle	hairstyle	pet	kitchen
bicycles	*hairstyles*	*pets*	*kitchens*

2. When a singular noun ends in *s, sh, ch, x,* or *z,* add -es.

gas	bush	couch	box
gases	*bushes*	*couches*	*boxes*

3. For most singular nouns that end in *o,* add -s. For a few nouns that end in *o* preceded by a consonant, add -es.

stereo	radio	potato	hero
stereos	*radios*	*potatoes*	*heroes*

CONFUSED?

How did we get so many rules? Over time, the English language has borrowed words and rules from many other languages. That's why our spellings and plurals are so mixed up.

4. **If a singular noun ends in *y* with a consonant before it, change the *y* to *i* and add *-es*. If the noun ends in *y* with a vowel before it, add *-s* to form the plural.**

comedy	baby	joy	donkey
comedies	*babies*	*joys*	*donkeys*

5. **For some nouns ending in *f*, add *-s*. For other nouns ending in *f* or *fe*, change the *f* to *v* and add *-es* or *-s*. Since there is no rule, you must memorize such words.**

chief	roof	life	thief
chiefs	*roofs*	*lives*	*thieves*

6. **Some nouns are spelled the same in the singular and in the plural.**

sheep	quail	deer	tuna

◀ **ANIMAL NAMES**

A number of nouns that name animals can be the same in the singular and the plural. Here are just a few:

bass	elk
carp	deer
fish	grouse
moose	pike
quail	salmon
sheep	shrimp
trout	tuna

7. **The plurals of some nouns are formed in ways that are unusual.**

ox	woman	child	mouse
oxen	*women*	*children*	*mice*

8. **For a compound noun written as one word, form the plural by changing the last word in the compound to its plural form.**

grandfather	butterfly	stepchild	snowstorm
grandfathers	*butterflies*	*stepchildren*	*snowstorms*

Exercise 5   Concept Check

Plural Nouns   Write the correct plural form of each noun.

1. country
2. fish
3. studio
4. cave
5. box
6. child
7. belief
8. stitch
9. bridge
10. shelf
11. woman
12. calf
13. hobby
14. shrimp
15. turkey
16. porch
17. building
18. lady
19. fox
20. photo

◀ **HOW DO YOU KNOW?**

Most dictionaries show the plurals of nouns when the plurals are formed in unusual ways. If you are unsure how to spell the plural of a noun, look the noun up in a dictionary.

Exercise 5

1. countries	11. women
2. fish	12. calves
3. studios	13. hobbies
4. caves	14. shrimp
5. boxes	15. turkeys
6. children	16. porches
7. beliefs	17. buildings
8. stitches	18. ladies
9. bridges	19. foxes
10. shelves	20. photos

Exercise 6
1. rodeos
2. families
3. highways
4. deer—no change
5. sandwiches
6. calves
7. heroes
8. feet
9. clowns
10. lives

Exercise 7
1. Steve's
2. twins'
3. mouse's
4. piano's
5. fish's
6. baby's
7. families'
8. box's
9. thieves'
10. horses'
11. children's
12. doctors'
13. sheep's
14. class's
15. men's

Exercise 6   Revision Skill

Plural Nouns   Rewrite the following sentences. Change the italicized singular nouns to their correct plural forms.

1. My parents and I love *rodeo*.
2. Last year two *family* went to a rodeo in Arizona.
3. Luckily, the *highway* between here and there were good.
4. At one stop we had a chance to pet some tame *deer*.
5. We brought along some *sandwich* to eat.
6. Some contestants roped *calf*.
7. My *hero* were the bull riders.
8. People stamped their *foot* and cheered.
9. Of course, everyone loves to see the *clown*.
10. Rodeo clowns often save the *life* of contestants.

Using Possessive Forms of Nouns

A *possessive noun* is one that shows ownership or belonging.

▶ 1. **If a noun is singular, add 's to form the possessive.**

　　a flower's petals　　　　Juanita's luck

2. **If a noun is plural and already ends in *s*, add an apostrophe.**

　　the wolves' territory　　　six years' time

3. **If a noun is plural and does not end in *s*, add 's.**

　　the geese's feathers　　　the deer's tracks

Exercise 7 Concept Check

Possessive Nouns   On a separate piece of paper, write the possessive forms of these nouns.

1. Steve	6. baby	11. children
2. twins	7. families	12. doctors
3. mouse	8. box	13. sheep
4. piano	9. thieves	14. class
5. fish	10. horses	15. men

Exercise 8   Revision Skills

Possessive Nouns   Rewrite the following sentences. Change the italicized nouns to their correct possessive forms.

1. I like Victoria *Chess* illustrations.
2. The *woman* travels took her all over the world.
3. She observed the world with an *artist* eye.
4. Her *pens* points are made of metal.
5. Many *illustrators* backgrounds include art school.
6. You should see *viewers* reactions to her lizard drawings!
7. Her *cats* names are Mrs. Bloom, Zazou, and Pearl.
8. *Pearl* specialty is hunting.
9. According to Chess, *children* laughter inspires her.
10. Two books illustrated by her are on our *library* shelves.

Exercise 9   Revision Skill

Noun Usage Review   Each sentence below has one error in the form of a plural or possessive noun. Find the error and write the word correctly on your paper.

1. The earthes closest neighbor is the moon.
2. Today we know that our planets orbit takes it around the sun.
3. Early people, though, had different believes.
4. Six planets orbits are larger than the earth's orbit.
5. Today, big telescopes can study valley's on the moon.
6. Telescopes show that Marses surface has dark areas, bright areas, and polar caps.
7. Scientists have spotted Mars's giant canal's.
8. During World War II, noise's were interfering with radio communication.
9. At first scientists thought the noises came from other radioes.
10. They thought their enemy's were making the sounds.
11. Imagine those scientists surprise!
12. Studys show that the noises were made by sunspots.
13. They look like dark patches on the sun's surface.
14. A sunspots surface is cooler than the rest of the surface of the sun.
15. Men's and womens's knowledge about the planets grows daily.

Exercise 8
1. Chess's
2. woman's
3. artist's
4. pens'
5. illustrators'
6. viewers'
7. cats'
8. Pearl's
9. children's
10. library's

Exercise 9
1. earth's
2. planet's
3. beliefs
4. planets'
5. valleys
6. Mars's
7. canals
8. noises
9. radios
10. enemies
11. scientists'
12. Studies
13. patches
14. sunspot's
15. women's

Exercise 1

1. you, S
   them, O

2. their, P
   them, O

Note: *themselves* is a reflexive pronoun

3. his, P

4. we, S
   you, O

5. I, S

6. My, P
   I, S

A *pronoun* is a word that is used in place of a noun or another pronoun.

Noun	Take the *clothes* to the shelter for the homeless.
Pronoun	Take *them* to the shelter for the homeless.
Noun	*Belia* is working there today.
Pronoun	*She* is working there today.

Personal Pronouns

A *personal pronoun* refers to a particular person, place, object, or idea.

Like the nouns they replace, pronouns have different jobs in a sentence. Personal pronouns have three forms: **subject, object,** and **possessive.** The form of a personal pronoun depends on its job in a sentence. For example, *I* is used as a subject, *me* as an object, and *my* or *mine* as a possessive.

Forms of Personal Pronouns

	Subject	Object	Possessive
Singular	I	me	my, mine
	you	you	your, yours
	she, he, it	her, him, it	her, hers, his, its
Plural	we	us	our, ours
	you	you	your, yours
	they	them	their, theirs

Exercise 1   Application in Literature

Identifying Pronoun Forms   Write all the personal pronouns in the following passage. Write *S* above the subject pronouns, *O* above the object pronouns, and *P* above the possessive pronouns.

LITERARY MODEL
from "Hearts and Hands" by O. Henry

(1) "Don't you worry about them, miss," said the other man. (2) "All marshals handcuff themselves to their prisoners to keep them from getting away. (3) Mr. Easton knows his business." (4) "Will we see you again soon in Washington?" asked the girl. (5) "Not soon, I think," said Easton. (6) "My butterfly days are over, I fear."

ADDITIONAL RESOURCES
Technology and Enrichment
Grammar & Usage Copy Masters
  Exercises, pp. 34–42
  Tests, pp. 119–122
 Grammar Test Generator

Personal Pronouns at a Glance

She wrote the poem.

> A subject pronoun can be used as the **subject** of a sentence.

The poet was **she.**

> A subject pronoun can be used as a **predicate pronoun** after a linking verb.

We gave **him** the idea.

> An object pronoun can be used as an **indirect object.**

The idea came from **us.**

> An object pronoun can be used as the **object of a preposition.**

My friend welcomed **me.**

> Possessive pronouns are used to show ownership or possession.

> An object pronoun can be used as a **direct object.**

Using the Subject Form

The subject form of a pronoun (*I, you, he, she, it, we,* and *they*) is used as the subject of a sentence or as a predicate pronoun. A **predicate pronoun,** like a predicate noun, is one that follows a linking verb and renames or identifies the subject of a sentence.

Subject	**Predicate Pronoun**
She won first prize.	The winner was *she.*
Tina and *I* were cheerleaders.	The cheerleaders were Tina and *I.*

> **QUICK TIP** A sentence with a predicate pronoun will still make sense if you reverse the order of the subject and pronoun:
> The winner was *she. She* was the winner.

Using the Object Form

The object form of a pronoun (*me, you, him, her, it, us,* and *them*) is needed if the pronoun is used as a direct object, an indirect object, or an object of a preposition.

Direct Object	The coach called *her.*
Indirect Object	The boy gave *her* the money.
Object of Preposition	The cook gave samples to *them.*

Exercise 2

1. I

2. she

3. us

4. we

5. him

6. him

7. him

8. they

9. he

10. I

Exercise 3

1. Mary Godwin was born in London in 1797. *No error*

2. When she was sixteen, the poet Percy Bysshe Shelley fell in love with <u>her.</u>

3. The two of <u>them</u> ran away to Italy and married in 1816.

4. Life was adventurous for the Shelleys, but many did not approve of <u>them</u> and their wild lifestyle.

5. When Percy drowned in 1822, Mary was devastated. *No error*

6. Her husband had left <u>her</u> no money, and she had young children to raise.

7. It was <u>she</u> who wrote *Frankenstein.*

8. However, it did not earn much for <u>her</u> while she was alive.

Exercise 2   Concept Check

Using Subject and Object Pronouns   Write the correct pronoun.

1. (I, Me) was surprised to learn that *Frankenstein* was written in 1816 by Mary Shelley.

2. It was (she, her) who married the famous poet, Percy Bysshe Shelley.

3. She would probably be surprised to learn that her story is still popular with (we, us).

4. However, there is one point that (we, us) often confuse.

5. Most people call the monster "Frankenstein," but in the book no name is given to (he, him).

6. Frankenstein is the name of the mad scientist who created (he, him).

7. In most movies the monster is evil; people are terrified of (he, him).

8. In the novel the monster is kind toward others until (they, them) become hostile toward him.

9. Because of their hostility, (he, him) becomes a true monster.

10. Actually, (I, me) found the story to be sad, not scary.

Exercise 3   Proofreading Skill

Correcting Pronoun Forms   Rewrite the following paragraph, correcting all pronoun errors.

(1) Mary Godwin was born in London in 1797. (2) When she was sixteen, the poet Percy Bysshe Shelley fell in love with she. (3) The two of they ran away to Italy and married in 1816. (4) Life was adventurous for the Shelleys, but many did not approve of they and their wild lifestyle. (5) When Percy drowned in 1822, Mary was devastated. (6) Her husband had left she no money, and she had young children to raise. (7) It was her who wrote *Frankenstein.* (8) However, it did not earn much for she while she was alive.

Using the Possessive Form

Possessive pronouns show ownership or belonging. Unlike possessive nouns (such as *student's*), possessive pronouns do not contain an apostrophe.

Do not confuse possessive pronouns with contractions that sound similar. If the word you are writing takes the place of two words, it is a contraction and needs an apostrophe.

Possessive Pronouns	its	your	their
Contractions	it's (it is)	you're (you are)	they're (they are)

Exercise 4 Revision Skill

Pronouns and Contractions Rewrite each sentence, correcting errors in the use of pronouns and contractions. If a sentence is already correct, write *Correct.*

1. Your always going to get disagreements about which boxing match was the greatest fight of the century.
2. Some people would cast they're vote for the fight between Joe Louis and Max Schmeling in 1938.
3. The fight gained international attention because of it's participants.
4. The Germans, under the rule of Adolf Hitler, felt confident that their boxer, Schmeling, would win.
5. Louis had already lost one match to Schmeling, but Louis's fans never lost they're belief in his ability.
6. Its hard for some people to forget that night in New York City.
7. When Louis entered the ring, one fan yelled, "You're victory will be for the U.S.A., Joe!"
8. Another fan screamed, "It's going to be a sad trip back to Germany for Schmeling!"
9. The announcer predicted, "Your going to remember this great fight!"
10. The crowd voiced it's approval for Louis; in two minutes and four seconds, he knocked out Schmeling.

Pronouns in Compounds

Sometimes two pronouns, or a pronoun and a noun, are joined by *and, or,* or *nor* to form a compound. Don't let a compound confuse you. Remember that the way a pronoun is used always determines its form. A pronoun in a compound subject must be in the subject form. A pronoun in a compound object must be in the object form.

Compound Subject
Toshiro and *I* disagreed about the meaning of the poem.

Compound Predicate Pronoun
The co-captains of the debate team are *she* and *I.*

Compound Direct Object
The school sent *Yolanda* and *me* to the state finals.

Compound Indirect Object
The teacher gave *Raheem* and *me* two tickets.

Compound Object of a Preposition
This is a special evening for *you* and *me.*

Exercise 4
1. You're
2. their
3. its
4. Correct
5. their
6. It's
7. Your
8. Correct
9. You're
10. its

Exercise 5

1. I
2. She
3. we
4. me
5. her
6. he
7. he
8. Correct
9. "her"
10. him

Exercise 5   Revision Skill

Compound Pronouns   Read each sentence. If the italicized pronoun is correct, write *Correct*. If the pronoun is incorrect, rewrite it correctly.

1. Pam, Ravi, and *me* worked together on a paper about Norse myths.
2. *Her* and Ravi suggested that we research Loki, the trickster.
3. The librarian and *us* searched the card catalog until we found information about Loki and other Norse gods.
4. Finding out about Loki's two wives surprised neither Pam nor *I*.
5. The librarian also told Ravi and *she* about the travels of Loki and Thor, the god of thunder.
6. When Thor's hammer was missing, *him* and Loki knew that the giant Thrym had taken it.
7. Two gods planned to recover the hammer; they were Thor and *him*.
8. Pam drew attention to Thor disguising himself as a bride; Ravi and *she* enjoyed that part.
9. Thrym thought that Thor was a goddess; he invited Loki and *"she"* into his home.
10. Thrym was tricked by Thor and *he;* the two gods left with the hammer.

Interrogative Pronouns: Who and Whom

Interrogative pronouns are used to ask a question.

The interrogative pronouns are *who, whom, whose, which,* and *what.* Two of these pronouns, *who* and *whom,* are often confused. *Who* is a subject pronoun. It is used as a subject or as a predicate pronoun.

Subject	*Who* is coming to dinner?
Predicate Pronoun	The captain of the team is *who?*

Whom is an object pronoun. It is used as a direct object, an indirect object, or an object of a preposition.

Direct Object	*Whom* do you admire most?
Indirect Object	She gave *whom* the pen?
Object of a Preposition	To *whom* was the pen given?

QUICK TIP   To tell whether *who* or *whom* should be used, try answering the question with a statement that uses a personal pronoun.

Who is coming to dinner?   *She* is coming to dinner.

Whom do you admire most?   You admire *him* the most.

To whom was the pen given?   The pen was given to *her*.

If your answer contains a subject pronoun, use *who* in your question. If the answer contains an object pronoun, use *whom* in your question.

Exercise 6   Revision Skill

Who and ***Whom***   Write the correct pronouns.

1. In your opinion, (who, whom) is the better journalist, Connie Chung or Diane Sawyer?
2. (Who, Whom) do you prefer as an interviewer?
3. (Who, Whom) was featured on the cover of *Vogue,* which caused a stir among other journalists?
4. (Who, Whom) did Marlon Brando once embarrass during an interview?
5. After Richard Nixon resigned as president, (whom, who) did he allow to interview him?

Pronouns and Their Antecedents

Pronouns usually refer back to a noun or to another pronoun. The noun or pronoun that a pronoun stands for is the pronoun's **antecedent.**

Have you read the story of *Gilgamesh? He* was a king of ancient Sumer. (The antecedent of *He* is *Gilgamesh.*)

The *story* of Gilgamesh has *its* roots in oral literature. (The antecedent of *its* is *story.*)

The antecedent may appear before the pronoun in the same sentence, or it may be in a preceding sentence, as in the first example above.

◄ **WHO CARES ABOUT *WHOM*?** · · · · · · · ·
Many people seldom use *whom* in conversation. They break grammatical rules by saying *"Who* do you like best?" and *"Who* should I call next?" Most experts think that such talk is fine in conversation, but they advise that *whom* should be used in formal writing and speaking.

◄ **PRONOUNS WITHOUT ANTECEDENTS** · · · · · · · ·
Most pronouns need a clear antecedent. However, some do not, as in the following examples:
Who went to the game?
It looks like rain.
What was the question?

Exercise 6
1. who
2. Whom
3. Who (Sawyer)
4. Whom (Chung)
5. whom (Sawyer)

Exercise 7

1. he, Carver

2. His, Carver
   It, research

3. They, products

4. him, Carver

5. It, success

Exercise 7   Concept Check

Pronouns and Their Antecedents   Write the pronouns in the following sentences. Then write the antecedent of each pronoun.

Example   George Washington Carver was born in Missouri; his mother was a slave.

Answer   *his, George Washington Carver*

1. As a boy, Carver was fascinated by plants and rocks; he studied botany in college.
2. His research focused on agriculture. It led to many profitable new crops for farmers in the South.
3. Carver created hundreds of products from peanuts. They included soap, fertilizer, cosmetics, and fabric.
4. Carver joined Tuskegee Institute in Alabama after Booker T. Washington hired him.
5. Carver's success was legendary. It inspired countless people.

Indefinite Pronouns

An *indefinite pronoun* is one that does not refer to a particular person or thing.

The following chart lists singular and plural indefinite pronouns:

Singular Indefinite Pronouns

another	each	everything	nothing
anybody	either	neither	one
anyone	everybody	nobody	somebody
anything	everyone	no one	someone

Plural Indefinite Pronouns

both	few	many	several

An indefinite pronoun must agree in number with its antecedent.

The singular possessive pronouns *his, her,* and *its* are used with singular indefinite pronouns.

Someone lost *her* purse. (The antecedent of the possessive pronoun is *someone,* which is singular. Therefore, the singular form *her* is correct.)

His or her may be used when the person referred to could be either male or female, as in the following example:

> *Someone* must have forgotten *his or her* book.

The plural possessive *their* is used with plural indefinite pronouns.

> *Few* were willing to change *their* plans. (The antecedent of the possessive pronoun is *few. Few* is plural. Therefore, the plural form *their* is correct.)

QUICK TIP   Don't be fooled by words that come between a possessive pronoun and its antecedent.

> *One* of them left *his or her* coat there. (The antecedent of *his or her* is the singular pronoun *one,* not the plural *them.*)

> *Many* in the audience voiced *their* displeasure. (The antecedent of *their* is the plural pronoun *Many,* not the singular noun *audience.*)

Exercise 8   Revision Skill

Agreement with Indefinite Antecedents   Write the correct possessive pronouns.

1. Each of my aunts has extended (her, their) invitation for lodging when we visit Montreal next month.
2. Both will be pleased to open (her, their) homes to us.
3. Either should have a spare room in (her, their) house.
4. Anyone would want to spend (his or her, their) time seeing a Montreal Canadiens hockey game.
5. Many in the crowd at the Forum show (its, their) appreciation by cheering wildly.
6. We may also visit McGill University; somebody there may show us (his or her, their) room.
7. Each of the metro stations has good maps on (its, their) walls.
8. Those men probably work in the Underground City because neither is carrying (his, their) coat.
9. Several stores in Montreal have beautiful exhibits in (its, their) windows.
10. We will meet new people everywhere; perhaps a few will show us (his or her, their) hospitality.

USING PRONOUNS   739

◀ **NONSEXIST LANGUAGE**
In the old days, the masculine pronouns *he, him,* and *his* were used to refer to all people, as in this sentence: *A firefighter needs to take good care of his equipment.* Nowadays, masculine pronouns are often replaced with phrases such as *he or she* and *his or her,* as in this sentence: *A firefighter needs to take good care of his or her equipment.*

Exercise 8
1. her
2. their
3. her
4. his or her
5. their
6. his or her
7. its
8. his
9. their
10. their

Exercise 9

1. Each of us must choose <u>his or her</u> topic by Wednesday.

2. This book was written by Isaac Asimov; <u>it's</u> a good one.

3. Ms. Washington suggested it to Kai, Jenny, and <u>me</u>.

4. At the library, Kai and <u>I</u> learned about Asimov's work as a scientist, teacher, and writer.

5. Correct

6. Both must have studied <u>their</u> books constantly.

7. "<u>Whom</u> did he write for?" I asked the librarian.

8. The librarian said, "<u>You're</u> going to be surprised at how many books he has written."

9. If I had to choose my favorite writer, I would have a hard time deciding between <u>him</u> and Anne McCaffrey.

10. The author of this book about comets was <u>he</u>.

11. His wife and <u>he</u> wrote a number of books together.

12. Many children's books were written by <u>her</u> and him.

13. Correct

14. <u>Its</u> title is *Nightfall*.

15. <u>Their</u> work is still in print, along with dozens of other Asimov books.

Exercise 9　Revision Skill

Pronoun Usage　Most of the following sentences contain an error in the use of a pronoun or a contraction, or in pronoun agreement. Rewrite the sentences that need correction. If a sentence has no error, write *Correct*.

1. Each of us must choose their topic by Wednesday.

2. This book was written by Isaac Asimov; its a good one.

3. Ms. Washington suggested it to Kai, Jenny, and I.

4. At the library, Kai and me learned about Asimov's work as a scientist, teacher, and writer.

5. When he was three, his family moved to the United States; at seven, he taught his sister to read.

6. Both must have studied his or her books constantly.

7. "Who did he write for?" I asked the librarian.

8. The librarian said, "Your going to be surprised at how many books he has written."

9. If I had to choose my favorite writer, I would have a hard time deciding between he and Anne McCaffrey.

10. The author of this book about comets was him.

11. His wife and him wrote a number of books together.

12. Many children's books were written by she and him.

13. He and Robert Silverberg also wrote a book together.

14. It's title is *Nightfall*.

15. They're work is still in print, along with dozens of other Asimov books.

Exercise 1
1. lived, A
2. worked, A
3. built, A
4. was, L
5. is, L
6. invented, A

SECTION 6: USING VERBS

A *verb* expresses action or a state of being.

> The new model airplane *flew* beautifully.
> These paintings *are* strange.
> I *was* in class.

Action verbs are verbs that tell what a subject does.

> Sabrina *stamped* her foot.   Everyone *laughed*.

A *linking verb* connects the subject of the sentence to a word that renames or describes the subject.

> Jane *is* brilliant.   The water *felt* cold.
> Bill *was* the writer.   The Robs *became* parents.

All the forms of the verb *be* are linking verbs. These include *am, is, are, was, were, be, been,* and *being.* Other common linking verbs are *appear, become, feel, grow, look, seem, smell, sound,* and *taste.*

QUICK TIP Some words can be either action verbs or linking verbs. To see whether a verb is a linking verb, try replacing it with a form of *be.* If the sentence still makes sense, the verb is a linking verb. If it does not, then the verb is an action verb.

> The trumpet player *sounded* terrible. *(The trumpet player is terrible* makes sense, so *sounded* is a linking verb here. *Terrible* modifies *trumpet player.)*

> The fire chief *sounded* the siren. *(The fire chief is the siren* does not make sense. *Sounded* is an action verb here.)

Exercise 1   Concept Check

Types of Verbs   Write the verbs in the following sentences. After each verb, write *A* for action or *L* for linking.

1. Antoine-Joseph Sax lived in Brussels, Belgium.
2. He worked with his father, a maker of instruments.
3. His father built wind and brass instruments, as well as pianos, harps, and guitars.
4. Antoine-Joseph Sax was a talented inventor.
5. One of his best-known inventions is the saxophone.
6. Sax invented several other instruments as well.

ADDITIONAL RESOURCES
Technology and Enrichment
Grammar & Usage Copy Masters
   Exercises, pp. 43–58
   Tests, pp. 123–126

 Grammar Test Generator

7. heard, A

8. performed, A

9. became, L

10. play, A

7. The general public first heard the saxophone in 1844.

8. Sax performed a musical selection by the composer Berlioz.

9. Sax never became rich during his lifetime.

10. Today, however, many people play the saxophone.

Verb Phrases

A *verb phrase* consists of a main verb and one or more helping verbs.

Often the **main verb** of a sentence appears with one or more **helping verbs.** A main verb with one or more helping verbs is called a **verb phrase.** Notice the helping verbs in italics below.

will ride   *could be* growing   *had been* looking

The following chart names the most common helping verbs.

Helping Verbs	
Forms of *be*	am, is, are, was, were, be, been, being
Forms of *do*	do, does, did
Forms of *have*	have, has, had
Other Verbs	can will shall may must could would should might

Verbs at a Glance

An **action verb** tells what action the subject is doing.

Dani **climbed** to the tree's top. She **grabbed** its highest branch.

A **linking verb** connects a subject (*Clay*) to a word in the predicate (*hoarse*).

Clay **has sounded** hoarse since his performance.

Helping Verb   Main Verb

Exercise 2 Concept Check

Types of Verbs   Write the complete verb in each sentence. Underline the helping verb once and the main verb twice. Then write *A* if the verb shows action and *L* if the verb links the subject to a word in the predicate.

1. For hundreds of years, Shanghai has been a major seaport.
2. On a map of China, you can see the city's key position on the East China Sea.
3. Shanghai must be one of the busiest places in the world!
4. The Communist government of mainland China has ruled Shanghai since 1949.
5. Shanghai has continued its trade with the non-Communist world.

Exercise 3 Drafting Skill

Helping Verbs   Add a helping verb to complete the meaning of each sentence.

1. Next week my sister ___?___ return from Shanghai.
2. She ___?___ written me about the city several times.
3. "You ___?___ see the Temple of the Jade Buddha," she wrote.
4. "That temple ___?___ be the most wonderful place in the city."
5. I ___?___ like to see the jade statue inside that temple.

The Tenses of Verbs

Every verb has several different forms that are used to refer to different times. These forms are called the *tenses* of the verb.

Tenses of Verbs

Present	Shows an action that happens now or that happens regularly or constantly
	Now: Lisa *walks* the dog. Regularly: He *sets* the alarm every night. Constantly: Marie *lives* in Paris.
Past	Shows an action that was completed in the past
	Roberto *changed* the tire.
Future	Shows an action that will happen in the future
	Lorena *will call* me tomorrow.

Exercise 2
1. has been, L
2. can see, A
3. must be, L
4. has ruled, A
5. has continued, A

Exercise 3
Answers will vary. Sample answers are provided.
1. will
2. has
3. should
4. must
5. would

Exercise 4

1. have heard, present perfect

2. calls, present

3. ruled, past

4. had made, past perfect

5. will learn, future

Exercise 5

1. has broken

2. had refused

3. ordered

4. shoots

5. will escape

6. will read

7. viewed

8. have related

9. believed

10. have enjoyed

TENSE CHANGES

There are three ways to change the tense of a verb: (1) change the ending—*walk, walked;* (2) change the spelling—*see, saw, seen;* (3) change the helping verb—*will play, has played.*

Present Perfect	Shows an action that was completed at an indefinite time in the past or that began in the past and continues into the present
	We *have ridden* these horses all summer.
Past Perfect	Shows a past action that came before another past action
	Lee *had bought* his gifts before he left.

Exercise 4   Concept Check

Identifying Tenses   Identify the verb and its tense in each sentence.

1. Yes, I have heard of William Tell.
2. My Swiss cousin calls him a national hero.
3. Gessler, a cruel man, ruled Switzerland.
4. He had made life miserable for his subjects.
5. Now you will learn about heroic William Tell.

Exercise 5   Drafting Skill

Using Tenses   Complete the following sentences with the verb forms given in parentheses. Write the complete sentences.

1. A man said, "This man (present perfect of *break)* a law!"
2. William Tell (past perfect of *refuse)* to kneel before Gessler's hat.
3. Gessler (past of *order)* him to prove his skill with a crossbow.
4. In this picture, Tell (present of *shoot)* an apple off his son's head.
5. In the next chapter he (future of *escape)* from Gessler's soldiers.
6. Tomorrow we (future of *read)* about other legendary heroes.
7. Yesterday I (past of *view)* a great film about Robin Hood.
8. For years, people (present perfect of *relate)* stories about King Arthur.
9. When I was younger, I (past of *believe)* most of the stories.
10. Recently I really (present perfect of *enjoy)* stories about knights.

Principal Parts of Verbs

Every verb has four *principal parts.* The principal parts of verbs are the *present,* the *present participle,* the *past,* and the *past participle.*

744   LANGUAGE HANDBOOK

The principal parts of verbs are used to make the verb tenses. Most verbs are regular, like those in the chart below. **Regular verbs** add *-ed* or *-d* to the present form to show the past tense. The past form never uses a helping verb. The past participle is the same as the past form, but it always uses a helping verb.

Regular Verbs

Present	Present Participle	Past	Past Participle
walk	(is) walking	walked	(have) walked
clap	(is) clapping	clapped	(have) clapped
wait	(is) waiting	waited	(have) waited

Verbs that do not form the past tense by adding *-ed* or *-d* are **irregular verbs.** In some cases the past and the past participle are the same, but in many cases they are not. Learn as many of the irregular forms as you can from the chart below.

REMEMBER!
The past form **never** uses a helping verb. The past participle **always** uses a helping verb.

Irregular Verbs

Present	Past	Past Participle	Present	Past	Past Participle
begin	began	(have) begun	ride	rode	(have) ridden
break	broke	(have) broken	ring	rang	(have) rung
bring	brought	(have) brought	rise	rose	(have) risen
choose	chose	(have) chosen	run	ran	(have) run
come	came	(have) come	say	said	(have) said
do	did	(have) done	see	saw	(have) seen
drink	drank	(have) drunk	sing	sang	(have) sung
eat	ate	(have) eaten	speak	spoke	(have) spoken
fall	fell	(have) fallen	steal	stole	(have) stolen
freeze	froze	(have) frozen	swim	swam	(have) swum
give	gave	(have) given	take	took	(have) taken
go	went	(have) gone	teach	taught	(have) taught
grow	grew	(have) grown	throw	threw	(have) thrown
have	had	(have) had	wear	wore	(have) worn
know	knew	(have) known	write	wrote	(have) written

Exercise 6

1. rode
2. sang
3. swam
4. begun
5. known
6. grew
7. rang
8. chosen
9. gave
10. went
11. frozen
12. broken
13. did
14. rose
15. written

Exercise 6   Concept Check

Irregular Verbs   Write the correct verb form.

1. Last week my father and I (ride, rode) up to Vermont.
2. On the way we played games and (sung, sang) songs.
3. On our first night in Vermont, we stayed in a motel and (swam, swum) in the pool.
4. The next morning we got back on the road, and by 9 A.M. we had (begun, began) to see signs for Jericho.
5. I have long (knew, known) about Jericho because of "Snowflake" Bentley.
6. Wilson Bentley (grew, grown) up in Jericho, Vermont.
7. When the school bell (rang, rung), Bentley ignored it.
8. His mother, a teacher, had (chose, chosen) to teach him at home.
9. When he was young, his parents (gave, given) him a microscope.
10. During snowstorms, Bentley (went, gone) outside with a camera.
11. He took pictures of snowflakes that had (froze, frozen) on a black tray.
12. If the snowflake had (broke, broken), he didn't photograph it.
13. Bentley (did, done) other artistic work as well.
14. Some days he (rose, risen) early to study dew or frost on windows.
15. He has (wrote, written) a book that has hundreds of his pictures.

Confusing Verb Pairs

The following verb pairs are sometimes confused.

Let means "to permit or allow." *Leave* means "to cause or allow to remain."

> *Let* me help you.
> *Leave* those books with me.

Lie means "to rest in a flat position." *Lie* never has a direct object. *Lay* means "to place." It almost always takes a direct object.

> Mom will *lie* down on the hammock this afternoon.
> *Lay* those packages on the table.

Sit means "to occupy a seat." *Sit* never has a direct object. *Set* means "to place." *Set* almost always has a direct object.

> Please *sit* down.
> Please *set* the groceries on the counter over there.

Rise means "to go upward." It never has a direct object. Raise means "to lift" or "to make something go up." It usually has a direct object.

We shall *rise* tomorrow morning at ten o'clock.
The mechanic *raised* the hood of the car.

	Present	Past	Past Participle
Let and *Leave*	let	let	(have) let
	leave	left	(have) left
Lie and *Lay*	lie	lay	(have) lain
	lay	laid	(have) laid
Sit and *Set*	sit	sat	(have) sat
	set	set	(have) set
Rise and *Raise*	rise	rose	(have) risen
	raise	raised	(have) raised

MORE CONFUSION
. . . .
Two other verbs that are sometimes confused are *learn* and *teach. Learn* means "to gain knowledge or skill." *Teach* means "to help someone learn."
Today we *learned* to yodel.
Ms. Montalva *taught* us how to yodel.

Exercise 7   Concept Check

Confusing Verbs   Write the correct verb form.

1. Even in these polluted times, many fascinating creatures (lie, lay) at the bottoms of tide pools.

2. (Leave, Let) me tell you about a few of them.

3. (Sitting, Setting) beneath rocks or clumps of seaweed, small crabs hide from sea gulls and other predators.

4. The globe-shaped sea urchins are covered with spines that cause predators to (let, leave) them alone.

5. (Lie, Lay) an urchin on your hand and watch it cling to your palm.

6. If you (sit, set) a crab down on the sand, it scuttles off in a peculiar sideways motion.

7. Other creatures such as starfish and sand dollars are (lying, laying) in tide pools.

8. When the tide (rises, raises), sea water floods into the tide pools, bringing food to the inhabitants.

9. The tiny barnacles open their hard shells and (rise, raise) their legs to move particles of food toward their mouths.

10. Tide pools are fragile ecosystems, so feel free to look at the creatures in them, but then (let, leave) them alone.

Exercise 7
1. lie
2. Let
3. Sitting
4. leave
5. Lay
6. set
7. lying
8. rises
9. raise
10. leave

Exercise 8

1. has written
2. has given
3. Let
4. sits
5. went
6. had chosen
7. had taken
8. raise
9. grew
10. gave

Exercise 9

(1) The great white shark was <u>lying</u> on the sandy bottom, ready to <u>rise</u> to attack any unsuspecting prey. (2) Allan, a scuba diver who <u>wore</u> a tank and flippers, <u>swam</u> closer and closer to the shark. (3) He had just <u>begun</u> his dive when he suddenly <u>saw</u> the shark. (4) Allan <u>knew</u> that great whites are called "man-eaters" because they attack more people than any other shark. (5) Allan slowly began to back away. <u>Correct</u> (6) Whenever possible, he never <u>broke</u> his rule, "<u>Let</u> sleeping sharks <u>lie</u>."

Exercise 8   Proofreading Skill

Verb Review   Each of the following sentences contains one error in verb usage. Write the correct verb.

1. Angela Bates has wrote an excellent article in *National Parks* magazine about Nicodemus, Kansas.
2. In her article she has gave a brief history of the town.
3. Leave me tell you what her article says.
4. The small town of Nicodemus, Kansas, sets on Highway 24.
5. After the Civil War, many former slaves go to that town.
6. They had chose new lives on the Kansas frontier.
7. They had took the name Nicodemus from an African prince, the first slave in the United States to buy his freedom.
8. These former slaves believed that they could rise crops in Kansas.
9. The African-American pioneers faced many hardships, but the town growed nonetheless.
10. In 1973 the U.S. government gived Nicodemus the status of National Historic Landmark.

Exercise 9   Revision Skill

Verb Usage Review   Rewrite the following paragraph, correcting any errors in verb usage.

(1) The great white shark was laying on the sandy bottom, ready to raise to attack any unsuspecting prey. (2) Allan, a scuba diver who weared a tank and flippers, swimmed closer and closer to the shark. (3) He had just began his dive when he suddenly seen the shark. (4) Allan knowed that great whites are called "man-eaters" because they attack more people than any other shark. (5) Allan slowly began to back away. (6) Whenever possible, he never breaked his rule, "Leave sleeping sharks lay."

Understanding Adjectives

An *adjective* is a word that modifies a noun or a pronoun.

golden apples	*furry* critters	*silly* conversation
unbelievable story	*perfect* alibi	*old* clothes

Articles

The most widely used of all adjectives are the words *a, an,* and *the.* These adjectives are called **articles.** *The* is the **definite article** because it points to specific persons, places, things, or groups.

the Buddhist temple	*the* open window	*the* Laplanders

A and *an* are **indefinite articles** because they do not refer to specific items. Use *a* before a consonant sound. Use *an* before a vowel sound.

a tangerine	*an* honor	*an* orange

Common and Proper Adjectives

Proper *adjectives* are adjectives that are formed from proper nouns.

A **proper noun,** you may recall, is a word that names a particular person, place, thing, or idea. Here are some examples of proper nouns and adjectives:

Proper Noun	Proper Adjective	Example
Russia	Russian	Russian dance
England	English	English tea
Texas	Texas	Texas chili
Sunday	Sunday	Sunday brunch

Notice that some proper nouns change their form when they become adjectives. For example, *Asia* becomes *Asian.* However, some proper nouns and adjectives, like *Texas,* have the same form.

All other adjectives, except articles, are called **common adjectives.** Examples of common adjectives include *blue, clear, extraordinary, final, fluffy, lovable, quiet, round, salty,* and *weird.*

PRONOUNS AS ADJECTIVES

The demonstrative pronouns *this, these, that,* and *those* can act as adjectives and modify nouns: *this* plant or *those* islands. Some possessive pronouns can also act as adjectives: *my* family or *their* car.

ADDITIONAL RESOURCES
Technology and Enrichment
Grammar & Usage Copy Masters
Exercises, pp. 59–68
Tests, pp. 127–130

 Grammar Test Generator

Exercise 1

1. One, C
   fine, C
   Mexican, P

2. strange, C

3. solid, C
   enormous, C
   hot, C

4. next, C

5. dramatic, C
   small, C
   western, C

6. Paricutín, P
   several, C
   unusual, C
   past, C
   few, C

7. American, P

8. Oregon, P
   tremendous, C

9. violent, C

10. Gray, C
    nearby, C

Exercise 1   Concept Check

Identifying Adjectives   Write the adjectives in the following sentences on your paper. Then label each one *P* for proper adjective or *C* for common adjective. Ignore the articles.

Example   Volcanoes are spectacular and dangerous.

Answer   spectacular, C   dangerous, C

1. One fine day in February of 1943, a Mexican farmer went out to plow his fields.
2. As he worked, he heard a strange sound coming from the ground.
3. The solid ground burst open, and an enormous mound of hot ash appeared.
4. By the next morning, a volcano stood where the farmer's field had been.
5. This dramatic eruption occurred in Paricutín, a small town in western Mexico.
6. The Paricutín volcano is one of several unusual eruptions that have happened in the past few decades.
7. For example, an American volcano made headlines in May of 1980.
8. Mount St. Helens, in the state of Washington near the Oregon border, caused tremendous damage when it erupted.
9. The violent blast laid waste to hundreds of miles of land.
10. Gray clouds rose from the site and blocked out the sun in Washington and in nearby states.

Predicate Adjectives

REMINDER

Linking verbs include forms of the verb *to be* (*is, am, are, was, were, be, been,* and *being*) and verbs like *become, feel, grow, look, seem, smell,* and *taste.*

▶ **When an adjective is separated from the noun or pronoun it modifies by a linking verb, it is a *predicate adjective*.**

Exercise 2   Concept Check

Predicate Adjectives   Write each sentence on your paper. Circle the linking verb. Underline the subject once. Then underline the predicate adjective or adjectives twice.

1. Central Italy is beautiful throughout the year.
2. Of all the cities in central Italy, Rome is the most famous.
3. In the late afternoon, the shadows around the ancient monuments grow long.
4. At that time of day, Rome looks even more splendid than usual.
5. Visitors become thoughtful and dream about Rome's past.
6. Visitors to Rome's underground catacombs are sometimes frightened.
7. This network of underground passages, built by early Christians, is dark and eerie.
8. Because tombs for the dead were cut into the walls, the walls are full of skeletons.
9. These burial places were sacred.
10. When the Romans persecuted the Christians, these tombs became useful for holding secret meetings.

Understanding Adverbs

An *adverb* modifies a verb, an adjective, or another adverb.

Modifying Verbs	works *slowly*	runs *there*
Modifying Adjectives	*very* little	*extremely* hot
Modifying Adverbs	*so* clearly	*too* easily

Adverbs tell *how, where, when,* or *to what extent* about the words they modify. As you can see from the following examples, adverbs can make writing more specific and more interesting.

How	grew *rapidly*	calls *loudly*	jumps *high*
Where	came *here*	went *back*	ran *out*
When	called *yesterday*	stop *now*	*never* ask
To What Extent	*almost* ready	*quite* often	*too* slow

Many adverbs are formed by adding *-ly* to an adjective.

    crisp + *-ly* = crisply   neat + *-ly* = neatly

Commonly used adverbs that do *not* end in *-ly* are listed in the chart on the next page.

Exercise 2

1. Central <u>Italy</u> (is) <u>beautiful</u> throughout the year.

2. Of all the cities in central Italy, <u>Rome</u> (is) the most <u>famous</u>.

3. In the late afternoon, the <u>shadows</u> around the ancient monuments (grow) <u>long</u>.

4. At that time of day, <u>Rome</u> (looks) even more <u>splendid</u> than usual.

5. <u>Visitors</u> (become) <u>thoughtful</u> and dream about Rome's past.

6. <u>Visitors</u> to Rome's underground catacombs (are) sometimes <u>frightened</u>.

7. This <u>network</u> of underground passages, built by early Christians, (is) <u>dark</u> and <u>eerie</u>.

8. Because tombs for the dead were cut into the walls, the <u>walls</u> (are) <u>full</u> of skeletons.

9. These burial <u>places</u> (were) <u>sacred</u>.

10. When the Romans persecuted the Christians, these <u>tombs</u> (became) <u>useful</u> for holding secret meetings.

Questionable
Adverbs

Some adverbs are used to ask questions. These adverbs are known as **interrogatives.**
How does a plane fly? *When* is the first day of spring? *Where* do meteorites come from? *Why* do stars twinkle?

Commonly Used Adverbs

afterward	hard	never	so	very
almost	here	next	soon	well
already	how	not	still	when
also	instead	now	straight	where
back	late	often	then	why
even	long	quick	there	yes
far	low	rather	today	yesterday
fast	more	seldom	tomorrow	yet
forth	near	slow	too	

Exercise 3   Concept Check

Finding Adjectives and Adverbs   Make two columns on your paper. In one column write all the adjectives (except articles) you find in the following paragraph. Write all the adverbs in the second column.

(1) The phoenix is a famous bird in Greek mythology.
(2) Supposedly, only one of these amazing golden creatures actually existed at any one time. (3) It lived for exactly five hundred years.
(4) Then, the old phoenix would burn itself to death. (5) Amazingly, a new phoenix would immediately rise from the warm ashes.
(6) Because the bird continually re-created itself, it is now used as a powerful symbol of rebirth, determination, and survival.

Adjective or Adverb?

Sometimes people confuse adverbs and adjectives. Remember that an adjective modifies a noun or a pronoun. An adverb modifies a verb, an adjective, or another adverb.

Adjective   These are *good hockey* skates. (*good* and *hockey* modify the noun *skates*.)

Adverb   Pedro skates *well*. (*well* modifies the verb *skates*)

An adjective, not an adverb, is used after a linking verb such as *is, am, was, were, be, looks, feels, grows, sounds, smells, tastes, becomes*, or *seems*. The linking verb connects the adjective to a noun or pronoun that it modifies.

Adjective after a linking verb   That song sounds *beautiful*.
Adverb modifying an action verb   Marika sings *beautifully*.

Do not use an adverb after a linking verb.

Incorrect	She sounds *angrily*.
Correct	She sounds *angry*.

Incorrect	The food here tastes *badly*.
Correct	The food here tastes *bad*.

Do not use an adjective to modify a verb, an adjective, or another adverb.

Incorrect	John writes *careless*.
Correct	John writes *carelessly*.

Incorrect	Many TV programs are *real* boring.
Correct	Many TV programs are *really* boring.

Exercise 4   Concept Check

Choosing the Correct Modifier   Write the modifier that is correct.

1. Vice-President Al Gore has studied the environment for a (real, really) long time.
2. He believes that solving environmental problems is (terrible, terribly) important to our future.
3. In his book *Earth in the Balance*, Mr. Gore writes (forceful, forcefully) about these issues.
4. Dumping toxic wastes into the air and water is (bad, badly) policy for the future.
5. Mr. Gore sounds (angry, angrily) when he speaks about those who have broken laws meant to protect our resources.

Exercise 5   Proofreading Skill

Using Modifiers Correctly   Decide whether the italicized modifiers in the following paragraph are used correctly. If the modifier is correct, write *Correct* on your paper. If the modifier needs to be changed, write the correct form on your paper.

(1) Some people think that it's *extreme* late to start to clean up our nation's waterways. (2) Our rivers, streams, and lakes once smelled and tasted *sweet*. (3) Now, the water in many of our major waterways tastes *badly*. (4) It also smells *real* funny. (5) We *sure* can do something about this situation! (6) We can move *quick* to ban the dumping of wastes into the water.

Exercise 4
1. really
2. terribly
3. forcefully
4. bad
5. angry

Exercise 5
1. extremely
2. Correct
3. bad
4. really
5. surely
6. quickly

Exercise 6

Answers may vary. Sample answers are provided.

1. Some people might think that there were hardly any black soldiers who fought in the Civil War.

2. This could not be further from the truth.

3. In fact, there were scarcely any eligible African-American men who stayed out of the war.

4. These men felt that there wasn't anything else they could do but fight against the system that had enslaved them.

5. They did not want to let anyone else do their fighting.

6. Many had come from the South and didn't ever want to return.

7. However, rather than say to themselves, "We're never going back there," they willingly put on their uniforms.

8. They never had any second thoughts about fighting for freedom.

9. One can think of nothing more noble than a willingness to risk death or a return to slavery in order to free others.

10. We will never forget their bravery.

Avoiding Double Negatives

Do not use two negative words together in the same sentence.

Some of the most commonly used adverbs are the negative words *no, not, none, nothing,* and *never.* Other negatives include the adverbs *hardly* and *scarcely* and contractions that contain *n't,* the shortened form of *not: can't, don't, doesn't, won't, wouldn't, isn't,* and *aren't.* If two of these words are used in a sentence when only one is needed, the result is a **double negative.**

Double Negative	I *don't* have *nothing* to lose.
Correct	I don't have anything to lose.
Correct	I have nothing to lose.
Double Negative	You *can't* have *none* of that food.
Correct	You can't have any of that food.
Correct	You can have none of that food.
Double Negative	Those boys *won't never* come back.
Correct	Those boys won't ever come back.
Correct	Those boys will never come back.

Exercise 6   Proofreading Skill

Correcting Double Negatives   Rewrite the following sentences, correcting all double negatives.

1. Some people might think that there weren't hardly any black soldiers who fought in the Civil War.

2. This could not be no further from the truth.

3. In fact, there weren't scarcely any eligible African-American men who stayed out of the war.

4. These men felt that there wasn't nothing else they could do but fight against the system that had enslaved them.

5. They did not want to let no one else do their fighting.

6. Many had come from the South and didn't never want to return.

7. However, rather than say to themselves, "We're not never going back there," they willingly put on their uniforms.

8. They never had no second thoughts about fighting for freedom.

9. One can't think of nothing more noble than a willingness to risk death or a return to slavery in order to free others.

10. We won't never forget their bravery.

Adjectives and Adverbs in Comparisons

**When you use a modifier to compare one thing with another, use the *comparative form.*

When you use a modifier to compare one thing with more than one other thing, use the *superlative form.*

Modifier	That math test was hard.
Comparative Form	That math test was harder than the science test.
Superlative Form	That math test was the hardest test I ever took.

Short modifiers such as the adjective *thin* and the adverb *soon* change their forms by adding *-er* for the comparative and *-est* for the superlative. Notice in the examples below that words ending in *n* and *y* may undergo slight spelling changes when *-er* or *-est* is added.

Modifier	Comparative Form	Superlative Form
thin	thinner	thinnest
soon	sooner	soonest
happy	happier	happiest
slow	slower	slowest

Longer modifiers such as the adjective *wonderful* and the adverb *cautiously* add the word *more* to make the comparative, and they add *most* to make the superlative.

Modifier	Comparative Form	Superlative Form
wonderful	more wonderful	most wonderful
cautiously	more cautiously	most cautiously
important	more important	most important
practical	more practical	most practical

Never use *more* and the *-er* ending together, or *most* and the *-est* ending together.

Incorrect	more prettier	most beautifullest
Correct	prettier	most beautiful

Exercise 7

1. saddest

2. shyest

3. more frequently

4. most thrilling

5. more exciting

6. greater

7. more cruelly

8. more glorious

9. saddest

10. more courageously

Exercise 7   Revision Skill

Comparison of Modifiers   Find the errors in adjective and adverb forms in the following sentences. Write the correct forms on your paper.

1. Of all the stories that I have read, "All Summer in a Day" is probably the sadder.

2. In this story the main character, Margot, is the most shyest child in the class.

3. The story takes place on Venus, where it rains more frequentlier than it does on Earth.

4. In the story, a group of children have gathered on the most thrillingest day of their life.

5. This day is most exciting than any other day because the sun will come out for an hour.

6. No child in the class has greatest expectations than Margot because she alone remembers how the sun looks and feels.

7. Margot's envious classmates behave most cruelly than anyone could imagine: they lock Margot in a closet.

8. Then they run outside where the sun feels gloriouser than anything else they could dream of.

9. Suddenly, the sadder sound they ever heard begins: it is the dripping of the rain.

10. The student who acts most courageously than the rest of the class will open the closet door.

Unusual Form Changes

Some modifiers change their forms completely and use different words for the comparative and superlative.

Modifier	Comparative Form	Superlative Form
good	better	best
bad	worse	worst
badly	worse	worst
well	better	best
much	more	most
little	less	least

Exercise 8 Concept Check

Unusual Forms   Find the errors in modifier forms in the following sentences. Write the modifiers correctly.

1. The United States has the bestest basketball players on earth.
2. That U.S. basketball players are more better than their competitors was proved in the 1992 Olympics.
3. The U.S. Olympic team was so better that people called them "the Dream Team."
4. Even the less skilled player on the U.S. team was still very talented.
5. It might seem useless to challenge a team of the world's very better players.
6. What could be worst than to play against a team of such greats as Michael Jordan, Larry Bird, and Magic Johnson?
7. However, other teams actually played their better game against the Americans.
8. No matter how badlier they played, other teams still enjoyed being on the same court with "the Dream Team."
9. The actual game was least important to them than the joy of playing against the best.
10. The more difficult problem they had was getting autographs from the U.S. players!

Using Demonstrative Adjectives

A **demonstrative pronoun,** such as *this, that, these,* or *those,* points out a specific person or thing. When such a word is used as a modifier, it becomes a **demonstrative adjective.**

This and *that* modify singular nouns. *These* and *those* modify plural nouns.

this book	*these* books
that brick	*those* bricks

Kind and *sort* are singular. They are used with the demonstrative adjectives *this* and *that. Kinds* and *sorts* are plural and are used with the demonstrative adjectives *these* and *those.*

this kind	*these* kinds	*that* sort	*those* sorts

Never use *here* or *there* with demonstrative adjectives.

Incorrect	*This here* water is salty.
Correct	*This* water is salty.

Exercise 9
Answers may vary slightly.

(1) This invention of mine is bound to catch on. (2) After all, we need this sort of thing. (3) With my invention that pen you are now using will not be needed. (4) This kind of writing tool will be outdated. (5) Here's how this invention works. (6) To use the invention, you first put on these headphones. (7) Then you concentrate on those ideas you want to write about. (8) Magically, those ideas appear on paper. (9) Of course, this idea of mine is just a fantasy right now. (10) However, these kinds of wild ideas have come true in the past. Who knows what the future might bring!

Exercise 10
Answers may vary slightly.

1. Benjamin Franklin was <u>an</u> eminent American statesman, scientist, and inventor.

2. <u>These</u> are just a few of his inventions: the lightning rod, bifocals, and the Franklin stove.

3. As a boy, he dreamed of going to sea, but his father said it wouldn't get him <u>anywhere.</u>

4. At age twelve, he became <u>an</u> apprentice printer, but he wanted to do <u>more important</u> work.

5. When he was seventeen, he thought he could do no <u>worse</u> on his own.

6. When he arrived in Philadelphia, he was <u>terribly</u> poor.

7. He began publishing a newspaper and *Poor Richard's Almanack,* one of the <u>most popular</u> books ever printed.

8. The success of <u>that book</u> helped him become famous.

9. Most of us remember Franklin for the kite experiment, which was perhaps his <u>most dangerous</u> scientific investigation.

10. He seemed to be <u>happiest</u> when he was busy.

11. He was known to be <u>an</u> honest man.

12. One of his <u>proudest</u> achievements was signing both the Declaration of Independence and the U.S. Constitution.

13. Franklin thought mail was delivered <u>more slowly</u> than it should have been; he became the country's first postmaster general.

14. Franklin was a <u>really</u> extraordinary person.

15. We <u>can</u> never have enough of this kind of ingenuity in the world.

Exercise 9   Revision Skill

Demonstrative Adjectives   Rewrite the following paragraph, correcting the errors that you find.

(1) This here invention of mine is bound to catch on. (2) After all, we need these sort of thing. (3) With my invention those pen you are now using will not be needed. (4) These kind of writing tool will be outdated. (5) Here's how this here invention works. (6) To use the invention, you first put on these here headphones. (7) Then you concentrate on those there ideas you want to write about. (8) Magically, that ideas appear on paper. (9) Of course, this here idea of mine is just a fantasy right now. (10) However, these kind of wild ideas have come true in the past. Who knows what the future might bring!

Exercise 10   Revision Skill

Modifier Review   All of the following sentences contain errors in the use of modifiers. Rewrite the sentences correctly.

1. Benjamin Franklin was a eminent America statesman, scientist, and inventor.
2. These here are just a few of his inventions: the lightning rod, bifocals, and the Franklin stove.
3. As a boy, he dreamed of going to sea, but his father said it wouldn't get him nowhere.
4. At age twelve, he became a apprentice printer, but he wanted to do importanter work.
5. When he was seventeen, he thought he could do no worst on his own.
6. When he arrived in Philadelphia, he was terrible poor.
7. He began publishing a newspaper and *Poor Richard's Almanack,* one of the much popular books ever printed.
8. The success of that there book helped him become famous.
9. Most of us remember Franklin for the kite experiment, which was perhaps his dangerousest scientific investigation.
10. He seemed to be most happyest when he was busy.
11. He was known to be a honest man.
12. One of his most proud achievements was signing both the Declaration of Independence and the U.S. Constitution.
13. Franklin thought mail was delivered more slower than it should have been; he became the country's first postmaster general.
14. Franklin was a real extraordinary person.
15. We can't never have enough of this kind of ingenuity in the world.

SECTION 8: SUBJECT—VERB AGREEMENT

Singular and Plural

**A noun that names one person, place, thing, or idea is *singular*.
A noun that names more than one is *plural*.**

Singular	Plural
spaceship	spaceships
country	countries
notebook	notebooks

Verbs also have singular and plural forms.

Singular	Plural
I dream	we dream
you dream	you dream
he, she, or it dreams	they dream

Some verbs have special singular or plural forms, as shown in the following chart.

	Be	Have	Do
Singular Forms	is, am, was	has, had	does, did
Plural Forms	are, were	have, had	do, did

Exercise 1 Concept Check

Identifying Singular and Plural Words   Tell whether the italicized word in each sentence is singular or plural.

1. I have seen *bats* flying around at night above the trees in my yard.
2. Bats are nocturnal animals—that is, they *come* out only at night.
3. *Do* you know that a single bat can eat its weight in insects?
4. One bat *eats* about twenty thousand bugs in a week.
5. I read once that bats *are* the only mammals capable of true flight.
6. Bats *migrate* to warmer climates in the winter.
7. The largest bat in the world actually *has* a six-foot wingspan.
8. Bats are not really blind; that *is* a myth.
9. They *depend* on their hearing more than on their sight, however.
10. *People* think bats are nasty, but most are actually quite harmless.

◀ **AN ODD COUPLE**

The pronouns *I* and *you* are a bit strange. *I* always refers to one person. *You* can refer to one person or to more than one person. Even when they refer to only one person, both pronouns are used with plural verbs (except in the expressions *I am* and *I was*):

I *do* I *have*
you *do* you *have*

ADDITIONAL RESOURCES
Technology and Enrichment
Grammar & Usage Copy Masters
Exercises, pp. 69–74
Tests, pp. 131–134
 Grammar Test Generator

Exercise 1
1. plural
2. plural
3. plural
4. singular
5. plural
6. plural
7. singular
8. singular
9. plural
10. plural

Exercise 2

1. are

2. were

3. are

4. haven't

5. were

Agreement of Subject and Verb

A verb must agree with its subject.

In a sentence the verb must agree with its subject. If the subject is singular, the verb must be singular. If the subject is plural, the verb must be plural.

A <u>scrapbook</u> <u>is</u> a place for storing memories. (The subject, *scrapbook,* is singular. Therefore, a singular verb, *is,* is used.)

<u>Journals</u> <u>are</u> good places to record your ideas. (The subject, *journals,* is plural. Therefore, a plural verb, *are,* is used.)

My <u>journal</u>, my <u>scrapbook</u>, and my <u>sketchbook</u> <u>are</u> very important to me. (The subject—*journal, scrapbook, and sketchbook*—is plural. Therefore, a plural verb, *are,* is used.)

QUICK TIP   Sometimes a prepositional phrase appears between a subject and its verb. Remember, however, that a verb never agrees with a word that appears in a prepositional phrase.

<u>One</u> (of the explorers) <u>claims</u> to have seen a sea serpent. (The verb *claims* agrees with *one,* the subject of the sentence. It does not agree with *explorers,* which is part of a prepositional phrase.)

<u>Some</u> parts (of the space shuttle) <u>were</u> faulty, and they are what caused the explosion. (The verb *were* does not agree with *space shuttle,* which appears in a prepositional phrase. Instead, it agrees with its real subject, *parts.*)

Exercise 2   Drafting Skill

Making Subjects and Verbs Agree   Write the correct verbs.

1. The pictures on my wall (is, are) of Parguera, a fishing village on Puerto Rico, an island in the West Indies.
2. My parents (was, were) born in San Juan, the capital of Puerto Rico.
3. The people of this island (is, are) known for the beautiful baskets, pottery, and straw rugs that they make.
4. The United States and Puerto Rico (hasn't, haven't) always been friendly.
5. Puerto Ricans (was, were) having problems cooperating with the United States until Luis Muñoz Marín became friendly with people in Franklin D. Roosevelt's administration.

6. The U.S. Congress and Harry Truman (is, are) credited with allowing Puerto Rico to become a commonwealth of the United States in 1952.

7. Now Puerto Rico (is, are) a place that attracts tourists from all over the world.

8. Many people in Puerto Rico (works, work) in the clothing industry.

9. One of the island's most beautiful places (is, are) El Yunque, a mountain covered by a rain forest.

10. My family and I (is, are) going to Puerto Rico in June.

Agreement with Compound Subjects

A subject made up of two or more parts is known as a *compound subject*.

A compound subject with parts joined by the conjunction *and* is plural and always takes a plural verb.

Flutes and drums are the most common instruments around the globe.

If the parts of a compound subject are joined by *or* or *nor*, the verb agrees with the part that is closest to the verb.

An afghan or some other handmade item makes a nice gift. (The singular verb *makes* agrees with the nearer noun, *item*.)

Neither the earth nor the other planets have existed forever. (The plural verb *have existed* agrees with the nearer noun, *planets*.)

Neither the other planets nor the earth has existed forever. (The singular verb *has existed* agrees with the nearer noun, *earth*.)

Exercise 3   Drafting Skill

Choosing the Correct Verb   Write the correct verb.

1. The other students in my geography class and I (has, have) learned that the Amazon alone carries one-fifth of the world's river water.

2. Neither the Nile River nor the Mississippi River (has, have) as much water as the Amazon.

3. The Amazon and the Nile (is, are) the two longest rivers in the world.

4. When my father visited the Amazon years ago, either a large excursion boat or small guide boats (was, were) available to take people down the river.

5. A large Amazonian crocodile or flesh-eating Amazonian piranhas (is, are) frightening to come across in the wild.

6. are
7. is
8. work
9. is
10. are

Exercise 3
1. have
2. has
3. are
4. were
5. are

Exercise 4

(1) The ancient Greeks and Romans <u>were</u> very inventive people. (2) One of their myths and legends <u>concerns</u> a strange people who live in a faraway land. (3) In the story neither men nor any boy <u>is</u> ever allowed to live in that distant country. (4) All of the inhabitants <u>are</u> women. (5) These women and their daughters <u>are</u> known as Amazons. (6) Each of the Amazons <u>is</u> allowed to interact with societies that contain men. (7) Often everybody hunts together. (No error) (8) However, none of the males can stay in the land of the Amazons. (No error) (9) Many myths and stories about the Amazons <u>have</u> been told over the centuries. (10) Some historians and other scholars <u>believe</u> that the explorer Francisco de Orellana named South America's largest river the Amazon because of fierce women whom he met there.

Agreement with Indefinite Pronouns

Singular indefinite pronouns are used with singular verbs.

Plural indefinite pronouns are used with plural verbs.

Some indefinite pronouns are plural in some sentences and singular in others.

Indefinite Pronouns

Singular			Plural
another	either	nobody	both
anybody	everybody	no one	few
anyone	everyone	one	many
anything	everything	somebody	several
each	neither	someone	

Singular   *Each* of these tornadoes *has caused* terrible destruction.

Plural   *Both* of these tornadoes *have caused* terrible destruction.

These indefinite pronouns are plural in some sentences and singular in others: *all, any, most, none,* and *some.*

Singular   Is *any* of the pie left on the plate?

Plural   Are *any* of the cookies left in the bag?

Exercise 4   Proofreading Skill

Agreement with Compound Subjects and Indefinite Pronouns

Rewrite the following paragraph, correcting any agreement errors.

(1) The ancient Greeks and Romans was very inventive people. (2) One of their myths and legends concern a strange people who live in a faraway land. (3) In the story neither men nor any boy are ever allowed to live in that distant country. (4) All of the inhabitants is women. (5) These women and their daughters is known as Amazons. (6) Each of the Amazons are allowed to interact with societies that contain men. (7) Often everybody hunts together. (8) However, none of the males can stay in the land of the Amazons. (9) Many myths and stories about the Amazons has been told over the centuries. (10) Some historians and other scholars believes that the explorer Francisco de Orellana named South America's largest river the Amazon because of fierce women whom he met there.

Agreement in Inverted Sentences

In most sentences the subject comes before the verb. However, sometimes the subject and the verb are switched around, or **inverted.**

Regular Order   The jumbo jet taxied onto the runway.
                        (The subject, *jet,* comes before the verb, *taxied.*)

Inverted Order   Onto the runway taxied the jumbo jet.
                        (The subject, *jet,* comes after the verb, *taxied.*)

Subjects and verbs are often inverted in questions.

> Are bats really mammals? (The subject is *bats.* The verb is *are.*)

> Is the moray eel or the crown-of-thorns starfish dangerous? (The compound subject is *the moray eel or the crown-of-thorns starfish.* The verb is *is.*)

The words *there, where,* and *here* often begin sentences. Their job is to get the sentence moving. When *there, where,* or *here* begins a sentence, look for the subject later in the sentence.

> There is the entrance to the space museum. (The subject is *entrance.* The verb is *is.*)

> Where do fish go in the winter? *(Fish* is the subject of the verb *do go.*)

A verb must always agree with its subject, even if the subject and the verb are inverted.

Incorrect   On the wall hangs photos of Mr. Guzman when he was a little boy in Puerto Rico.

Correct   On the wall hang photos of Mr. Guzman when he was a little boy in Puerto Rico.

Incorrect   Here is the tickets you ordered.
Correct   Here are the tickets you ordered.

Exercise 5   Proofreading Skill

Agreement in Inverted Sentences   Rewrite the following paragraph, correcting agreement errors.

> (1) Where does the oceans come from? (2) Scientists has thought about this question for many years. (3) There are now a good theory to explain the origin of oceans. (4) According to modern geologists, the early earth was a ball of rock. (5) All over

Exercise 5

(1) Where <u>do</u> the oceans come from? (2) Scientists <u>have</u> thought about this question for many years. (3) There <u>is</u> now a good theory to explain the origin of oceans. (4) According to modern geologists, the early earth was a ball of rock. (No error)

(5) All over the surface of the earth <u>were</u> hundreds of thousands of volcanoes that were constantly erupting. (6) Continually hitting the earth <u>were</u> hundreds of thousands of meteorites. (7) So where <u>do</u> the oceans come in? (8) Quite simply, thrown into the sky by these mighty blasts <u>was</u> a lot of water vapor. (9) This vapor cooled and turned into droplets of liquid water. (No error) (10) In the skies all over the earth <u>were</u> enormous clouds made up of these tiny droplets. (11) Eventually, there <u>were</u> tremendous rainstorms, all over the earth. (12) These rains became the oceans of today. (No error)

Exercise 6

1. have

2. are

3. are

4. have

5. are

6. is

7. converts

8. are

9. go

10. arrives

11. is

12. does

13. are

14. is

15. have

the surface of the earth was hundreds of thousands of volcanoes that were constantly erupting. (6) Continually hitting the earth was hundreds of thousands of meteorites. (7) So where does the oceans come in? (8) Quite simply, thrown into the sky by these mighty blasts were a lot of water vapor. (9) This vapor cooled and turned into droplets of liquid water. (10) In the skies all over the earth was enormous clouds made up of these tiny droplets. (11) Eventually, there was tremendous rainstorms, all over the earth. (12) These rains became the oceans of today.

Exercise 6   Drafting Skill

Review of Subject-Verb Agreement   Write the correct verb.

1. Televisions, radios, and motion pictures (has, have) brought about great changes in the past century.

2. A typhoon in Guam or hungry people in Somalia (is, are) brought directly into our homes over the airwaves.

3. Now new inventions and new discoveries (is, are) promising to bring about even greater changes.

4. Neither television nor motion pictures (has, have) the far-reaching potential of personal computers.

5. Letters and numbers (is, are) stored by computers in a special format that is known as "digital."

6. The music on compact discs (is, are) also in digital form.

7. A digital machine like a computer or a compact disc player (converts, convert) information into 1s and 0s.

8. These 1s and 0s (is, are) easily sent between machines over telephone wires.

9. Today, along telephone wires (goes, go) digital signals carrying all kinds of information.

10. In a flash (arrives, arrive) information sent from across the city or across the world.

11. There (is, are) a strong possibility that in the future all movies, telephone calls, news, photographs, money transactions, and orders for goods and services will travel between homes and businesses over telephone lines.

12. Where (does, do) the digital revolution seem to be taking us?

13. Thinkers in many different fields (is, are) considering this question.

14. Here (is, are) one widely accepted answer.

15. Computers and telephone networks (has, have) the potential of bringing all people of the world closer together.

Proper Nouns and Proper Adjectives

Capitalize proper nouns and proper adjectives.

A **common noun** is the name of a whole class of persons, places, things, or ideas. A **proper noun** is the name of a particular person, place, thing, or idea. A **proper adjective** is an adjective made from a proper noun. Proper nouns and proper adjectives are capitalized, but common nouns and common adjectives are not.

Common Noun	hero	continent
Proper Noun	**H**ercules	**A**frica
Common Adjective	heroic	continental
Proper Adjective	**H**erculean	**A**frican

Names and Titles of People

Capitalize the names of persons and initials that stand for names.

Lucille **C**lifton   **T**oni **C**ade **B**ambara   **R**obert **D**. **B**allard

Capitalize titles and abbreviations for titles that appear before people's names. Capitalize abbreviations such as *Jr.* that appear after a name.

Rev. Martin Luther King, **J**r.   **M**s. Rylant   **D**r. Asimov

Capitalize such words as *mother, father, aunt,* and *uncle* when these words are used as names or when they come just before a name.

Hey, **A**unt Flores, look at the swans!
Here are the car keys, **D**ad.
This painting was done by **U**ncle Tiu.

Do not capitalize words that name family members if these words are preceded by a possessive, such as *your* or *my,* or by an article such as *a* or *the.*

My **a**unt loves swans.   His **u**ncle did that painting.

ADDITIONAL RESOURCES
Technology and Enrichment
Grammar & Usage Copy Masters
   Exercises, pp. 75–83
   Tests, pp. 135–138
 Grammar Test Generator

Exercise 1

1. I enjoy listening to Uncle Amit tell about his childhood in Bombay, India.

2. I love hearing the stories from those sacred Hindu books: the Vedas, the Ramayana, and the Mahabharata.

3. In Hinduism, my uncle's religion, the supreme being is Brahma.

4. My uncle suggested that I read a book by Dr. Mary S. Mistri and Ms. Emily Grant about the Hindu religion.

5. According to Dr. Mistri and Ms. Grant, Brahma has three different forms.

6. At times, Brahma appears as Brahama, the creator; the other two forms are Vishnu, the preserver, and Shiva, the destroyer.

7. Many people in Asia practice the Hindu faith.

8. Perhaps the most famous Hindu of our century was Mohandas K. Gandhi.

The Pronoun I

Capitalize the pronoun _I_.

I read some poems by Derek Walcott.

Religions, Sacred Beings, and Sacred Writings

Capitalize words that name religions, sacred beings, or religious scriptures. Also capitalize adjectives formed from these names.

Allah	Jehovah	the Torah	the Bible
Brahma	Isis	the Virgin Mary	the Vedas
Christian	Islam	Islamic	Confucian

Races, Ethnic Groups, Languages, and Nationalities

Capitalize the names of races, ethnic groups, languages, and nationalities. Also capitalize adjectives formed from such names.

Hispanics	Kenyan coffee	French food	Italian
African American	Swahili	Oriental art	Sioux

Exercise 1   Concept Check

Using Capital Letters   Write the following sentences using correct capitalization.

1. i enjoy listening to uncle amit tell about his childhood in bombay, india.

2. i love hearing the stories from those sacred hindu books: the vedas, the ramayana, and the mahabharata.

3. In hinduism, my uncle's religion, the supreme being is brahma.

4. My uncle suggested that i read a book by dr. mary s. mistri and ms. emily grant about the hindu religion.

5. According to dr. mistri and ms. grant, brahma has three different forms.

6. At times, brahma appears as brahama, the creator; the other two forms are vishnu, the preserver, and shiva, the destroyer.

7. Many people in asia practice the hindu faith.

8. Perhaps the most famous hindu of our century was mohandas k. gandhi.

9. dr. gandhi used the principle of nonviolent action to force the british to give up control of india.

10. In the united states, gandhi's principle of nonviolent action was practiced by rev. martin luther king, jr.

Geographical Names

Capitalize each important word in a geographical name. Do not capitalize prepositions, such as *in* or *of,* or the articles *a, an,* or *the.*

Bodies of Water	the **P**acific **O**cean, the **P**o **R**iver, **G**ulf of **M**exico
Continents	**A**ntarctica, **E**urope, **S**outh **A**merica
Land Forms	**M**ississippi **D**elta, **C**ape **A**nn, the **G**obi **D**esert, **M**ount **C**armel, **C**hallenger **D**eep
Objects in the Universe	**J**upiter, **V**enus, **M**ilky **W**ay
Political Units	**L**atvia, the **E**uropean **E**conomic **C**ommunity, **T**exas, **M**onroe **C**ounty, the **C**herokee **N**ation
Public Areas	**M**uir **W**oods, **B**oston **C**ommon, **Y**ellowstone **N**ational **P**ark
Roads, Highways	**R**oute 66, **S**kyline **D**rive, **P**ennsylvania **A**venue
World Regions	the **F**ar **E**ast, the **S**outhern **H**emisphere, the **B**alkans, **M**icronesia

Directions and Sections

Capitalize names of sections of the United States or the world. Also capitalize any adjectives that come from those names.

The **N**orth had many more factories than the **S**outh.
The **W**estern nations agreed to offer aid by way of **W**est **A**frica.

Do not capitalize nouns or adjectives that merely indicate compass directions or locations.

Walk three blocks **n**orth to the Korean Meeting House.

9. Dr. Gandhi used the principle of nonviolent action to force the British to give up control of India.

10. In the United States, Gandhi's principle of nonviolent action was practiced by Rev. Martin Luther King, Jr.

Organizations, Institutions, Buildings, and Structures

Capitalize all important words in the names of organizations, institutions, buildings, and structures.

Organizations and Institutions	the Libertarian Party, the United Negro College Fund, Oxfam America, Bolivar High School
Buildings	Grand Central Station, the Taj Mahal, the Monadnock Building, the Forbidden Palace
Structures	the Holland Tunnel, the Vietnam Veterans Memorial, Hoover Dam, the Great Wall of China

Events, Documents, and Periods of Time

Capitalize all important words in the names of historical events, documents, and periods of time.

Events	King Philip's War, the 1992 Winter Olympics, Macy's Thanksgiving Day Parade, the California Gold Rush
Documents	the Emancipation Proclamation, the Magna Carta, the Declaration of Independence, the Treaty of Versailles
Periods of Time	the Heroic Age, the Enlightenment, the Mesozoic Era, the Great Depression, the Middle Ages

Months, Days, and Holidays

Capitalize the names of months, days, and holidays, but not the names of seasons.

October	Thursday	Yom Kippur	winter

Time Abbreviations

Capitalize the abbreviations *B.C., A.D., A.M.,* and *P.M.*

Please be at the bus by 7:30 **A.M.**
The first makeup was worn about 4000 **B.C.**
Pompeii was buried by lava in **A.D.** 79.

Exercise 2 Concept Check

Using Capital Letters Write the words and abbreviations in the following sentences that should be capitalized. Begin them with a capital letter.

1. mom and dad were busy preparing for our new year's eve party, so I went for a bike ride down moonwalk avenue.

2. it was almost 3004 a.d., and we had just bought another house in the northern hemisphere of saturn.

3. Only two years ago last spring, we were citizens of Earth, living in new york city near the chrysler building.

4. we were planning to move to a cottage by the gulf of mexico.

5. One morning, however, we read that the interspace treaty had been signed by president shirley pankhurst and by members of congress.

6. "This will allow human beings to live on other friendly planets by labor day," dad said.

7. We had to travel to the capitol in washington, d.c., and apply for space housing.

8. the day before we left, i took pictures of the empire state building and the duck pond in central park.

9. My brother and I now attend saturn high school monday through friday, from eight a.m. to two p.m.

10. I still look through my high-powered telescope at Earth in order to keep an eye on north america.

Sentences and Poetry

Capitalize the first word of every sentence.

Roberto peeled peanuts delicately.

Capitalize the first word of every line of poetry.

And of course there must be something wrong
In wanting to silence any song.

Quotations

Capitalize the first word of a direct quotation.

Borey said, "**A**ll roads, howsoe'er they diverge, lead to Rome."

◀ EXCEPTION
. . . .
Sometimes, especially in modern poetry such as "in the inner city" (page 33) and "For My Father," (page 90) a poet chooses not to capitalize the first word of every line.

Exercise 2

1. Mom and Dad were busy preparing for our New Year's Eve party, so I went for a bike ride down Moonwalk Avenue.

2. It was almost 3004 A.D., and we had just bought another house in the Northern Hemisphere of Saturn.

3. Only two years ago last spring, we were citizens of Earth, living in New York City near the Chrysler Building.

4. We were planning to move to a cottage by the Gulf of Mexico.

5. One morning, however, we read that the Interspace Treaty had been signed by President Shirley Pankhurst and by members of Congress.

6. "This will allow human beings to live on other friendly planets by Labor Day," Dad said.

7. We had to travel to the Capitol in Washington, D.C., and apply for space housing.

8. The day before we left, I took pictures of the Empire State Building and the duck pond in Central Park.

9. My brother and I now attend Saturn High School Monday through Friday, from eight A.M. to two P.M.

10. I still look through my high-powered telescope at Earth in order to keep an eye on North America.

When a quotation is interrupted, it is called a **divided quotation.** Do not capitalize the second part unless it starts a new sentence.

> "Close your booklet," said Mr. Suarez, "and go to lunch."
> "Remind me tomorrow," Sarah said. "**I** have to go now."

Parts of a Letter

In the greeting of a letter, capitalize all important words.

> **D**ear **D**r. **S**imington: **D**ear **S**ir or **M**adam:

In the closing of a letter, capitalize only the first word.

> **Y**ours truly,   **S**incerely yours,

Outlines and Titles

Capitalize the first word of each item in an outline and the letters that introduce major subsections.

> I. **C**ars
>   **A. S**edans
>   1. **C**onvertibles
>   2. **H**ardtops
>   **B. S**ports cars

Capitalize the first word, the last word, and all other important words in titles.

Book	*Boy: Tales of Childhood*
Newspaper	*The Los Angeles Times*
Play	*The Monsters Are Due on Maple Street*
Television Series	*Murder, She Wrote*
Short Story	"Hearts and Hands"
Song	"Simple Gifts"
Work of Art	*Twittering Machine*

The word *the* at the beginning of a title and the word *magazine* are capitalized only when they are part of the formal name.

> *The Boston Globe*   *The New York Times Magazine*
> *Time magazine*

Exercise 3   Concept Check

Using Capital Letters   Copy the following letter, correcting each error in capitalization.

---

521 jefferson ave.
evanston, illinois 60202
may 10, 19—

dear ms. eliot,

I'm sorry that I've missed so many school days because of the flu. I will soon finish reading the novel julie of the wolves. By the end of the week, I also hope to complete my paper on the story "all summer in a day."

Here is the beginning of an outline for my essay on orchestras:

    I. instruments
      A. woodwinds
        1. flutes
        2. clarinets

Finally, I have chosen the poem I want to read at the memorial day parade: robert frost's "mending wall." I especially love the line at the end that says, "good fences make good neighbors."

I hope to be back to school soon.

        yours truly,

        marlena lopez

Exercise 4   Proofreading Skill

Using Capital Letters   Write the following sentences with correct capitalization.

1. i have been reading a wonderful book by diane ackerman.
2. the book is called *the moon by whale light.*
3. it was recommended to me by dad. My mom also loved it.
4. did you know that ms. ackerman writes for *the new yorker*?
5. that's a well-known magazine published in new york city.

Exercise 3

521 Jefferson Ave.
Evanston, Illinois 60202
May 10, 19—

Dear Ms. Eliot,

I'm sorry that I've missed so many school days because of the flu. I will soon finish reading the novel *Julie of the Wolves.* By the end of the week, I also hope to complete my paper on the story "All Summer in a Day."

Here is the beginning of an outline for my essay on orchestras:

    I. Instruments
      A. Woodwinds
        1. Flutes
        2. Clarinets

Finally, I have chosen the poem I want to read at the Memorial Day parade: Robert Frost's "Mending Wall." I especially love the line at the end that says, "Good fences make good neighbors."

I hope to be back to school soon.

        Yours truly,

        Marlena Lopez

Exercise 4

1. I have been reading a wonderful book by Diane Ackerman.
2. The book is called *The Moon by Whale Light.*
3. It was recommended to me by Dad. My mom also loved it.
4. Did you know that Ms. Ackerman writes for *The New Yorker*?
5. That's a well-known magazine published in New York City.

6. Her book tells about her travels to Patagonia, a region of Argentina, in the Southern Hemisphere, where she studied whales.

7. The whales come down the Atlantic coast to the very tip of the South American continent.

8. Ms. Ackerman gives a lively account of the time she swam with a mother whale named Fang.

9. She also tells about observing whales from a boat called *Morning Watch* and from a plane called *Love Juicy.*

10. In her opinion, no answer has been found to the question, What do whales do with the largest brains on earth?

11. The author even showed her sense of humor: one day she went to a Halloween party dressed as a thunderstorm.

12. I made an outline of the animals she discussed in her book:

    I. Bats

    II. Crocodilians

    III. Whales

    IV. Penguins

13. Her book inspired me to write a poem.

Bats are not like rats.
They're more like me.
They fill the night
With mystery.

14. She discusses the differences between the constellations in the Southern Hemisphere and those that appear in the north.

15. I recommended this book and another book by Ackerman, *A Natural History of the Senses,* to Emily, my sister.

6. Her book tells about her travels to patagonia, a region of argentina, in the southern hemisphere, where she studied whales.

7. the whales come down the atlantic coast to the very tip of the south american continent.

8. ms. ackerman gives a lively account of the time she swam with a mother whale named fang.

9. she also tells about observing whales from a boat called *morning watch* and from a plane called *love juicy.*

10. in her opinion, no answer has been found to the question, what do whales do with the largest brains on earth?

11. the author even showed her sense of humor: one day she went to a halloween party dressed as a thunderstorm.

12. I made an outline of the animals she discussed in her book:

    I. bats
    II. crocodilians
    III. whales
    IV. penguins

13. her book inspired me to write a poem.
bats are not like rats.
they're more like me.
they fill the night
with mystery.

14. She discusses the differences between the constellations in the southern hemisphere and those that appear in the north.

15. i recommended this book and another book by ackerman, *a natural history of the senses,* to emily, my sister.

SECTION 10: PUNCTUATION

Imagine trying to get around a large department store without any signs to guide you. Now imagine trying to read a story that contains no punctuation marks. Punctuation marks, like signs, help people to avoid becoming confused.

End Marks

The punctuation marks that show where a sentence ends are called end marks. The three **end marks** are the period, the question mark, and the exclamation point.

The Period

A period is used in each of the following ways:

- at the end of a **declarative** sentence
- at the end of most **imperative** sentences
- after an **indirect question**
- after an **abbreviation** or an **initial**
- after a **number** or **letter** used to label a part of an outline or an item in a list

A **declarative sentence** is one that makes a statement.

> Custer graduated last in his class at West Point.

An **imperative sentence** is one that gives a command or makes a request.

> Please be careful with that Ming Dynasty vase.

An **indirect question** tells that someone has asked a question but does not contain the exact words of the question.

> Yolanda asked whether the violin or the clarinet was harder to learn how to play.

An **abbreviation** is a shortened version of a word.

Mon. (Monday)   Sr. (Sister)
Gov. (Governor)   U.S. (United States)
Co. (Company)   A.D. (*anno Domini*)

◀ **STOP!**
In British English, a period is referred to as a full stop.

◀ **DON'T OVERDO IT!**
If an abbreviation comes at the end of a sentence that ends with a period, use one period, not two.
Incorrect Malcolm was born at 3:30 P.M..
Correct Malcolm was born at 3:30 P.M.

PUNCTUATION   773

ADDITIONAL RESOURCES
Technology and Enrichment
Grammar & Usage Copy Masters
Exercises, pp. 84–100
Tests, pp. 139–142
 Grammar Test Generator

1. The Presidio in San Francisco, Calif., will soon be a national park.

2. Special Features

   1. Hundreds of buildings

   2. Airfield and parade ground

   3. National cemetery

   3. I. Physical Features

      A. Size

         1. Bigger than Central Park in N.Y.

         2. Total size 1,487 acres

4. U.S. Representative Phillip Burton helped save the Presidio.

5. Show me where Crissy Field is.

6. The U.S. Army took over the Presidio in 1846.

7. I asked if the Presidio had been damaged by the earthquake that hit at 5:13 A.M. on Apr. 18, 1906.

8. I've seen the parks in New Orleans, La., and in Lowell, Mass.

9. On Sept. 5, Ms. West and I visited the area around 6:30 P.M.

10. I wonder if the Dept. of Defense still owns the Presidio.

SHORTEST NAMES OF ALL

Some people have names that consist of single letters. One-letter names are not written with periods because they are not initials. Examples include Malcolm X and U Thant, a Burmese secretary-general of the United Nations.

▶ An **initial** is the first letter of a name, used by itself.

　　Robert D. Ballard　　Juan A. A. Sedillo　　E. E. Cummings

In an **outline** or **list,** periods are used to mark divisions or items.

I. Poetry	Ingredients
A. Epic poetry	1. 1/2 pound cooked wild rice
B. Lyric poetry	2. 1/2 pound roasted chestnuts
C. Dramatic poetry	3. 1/4 pound dried mixed fruit

Exercise 1　Concept Check

Using Periods Correctly　Copy the following items, adding periods where needed.

1. The Presidio in San Francisco, Calif, will soon be a national park

2. Special Features

   1 Hundreds of buildings

   2 Airfield and parade ground

   3 National cemetery

3. I Physical Features

   A Size

      1 Bigger than Central Park in N Y

      2 Total size 1,487 acres

4. U S representative Phillip Burton helped save the Presidio

5. Show me where Crissy Field is

6. The U S Army took over the Presidio in 1846

7. I asked if the Presidio had been damaged by the earthquake that hit at 5:13 A M on Apr 18, 1906

8. I've seen the parks in New Orleans, La, and in Lowell, Mass

9. On Sept 5, Ms West and I visited the area around 6:30 P M

10. I wonder if the Dept of Defense still owns the Presidio

The Question Mark and the Exclamation Point

Use a question mark at the end of an interrogative sentence.

An **interrogative sentence** asks a question.

　　Didn't Geronimo write an autobiography**?**
　　Wasn't Crazy Horse a great hero**?**

Remember that a period is used at the end of an indirect question.

> We asked whether Geronimo wrote an autobiography.

Use an exclamation point at the end of an exclamatory sentence.

An **exclamatory sentence** expresses strong feelings.

> Your performance was excellent!   These socks are filthy!

Use an exclamation point at the end of an imperative sentence that expresses excitement. Other imperative sentences should be followed by a period.

> Watch out!   Call the dentist and change your appointment.

Use an exclamation point at the end of a strong interjection.

> Hooray!   Good grief!

Exercise 2   Concept Check

Using Question Marks and Exclamation Points   Copy the following sentences and add the proper end marks.

1. What beautiful pictures those are in your living room
2. Where did you find such unusual works
3. Raoul wondered if the pictures were Japanese woodblock prints
4. Look at these antique portraits by the artist Sharaku
5. Wow Were these women also drawn by the same artist
6. I wondered if you liked the scenes that Hiroshige drew
7. I heard that Van Gogh was a fan of Hiroshige's work
8. When were the first color woodblock prints made
9. Didn't an artist named Harunobu create those first prints
10. We should ask the librarian for a book on Japanese prints

Commas in Compound Sentences and in Series

Use a comma before the conjunction that joins the parts of a compound sentence.

A **compound sentence** contains independent sentences joined with a conjunction such as *and, or, nor, for, but, so,* or *yet.*

> A well-known cowboy film star died in the fire in the Coconut Grove nightclub, **and** over four hundred others died too.

1. What beautiful pictures those are in your living room!

2. Where did you find such unusual works?

3. Raoul wondered if the pictures were Japanese woodblock prints.

4. Look at these antique portraits by the artist Sharaku.

5. Wow! Were these women also drawn by the same artist?

6. I wondered if you liked the scenes that Hiroshige drew.

7. I heard that Van Gogh was a fan of Hiroshige's work.

8. When were the first color woodblock prints made?

9. Didn't an artist named Harunobu create those first prints?

10. We should ask the librarian for a book on Japanese prints.

Exercise 3

(1) Water can be a solid, a liquid, or a gas. (2) Solid water is known as ice, and gaseous water is known as water vapor. (3) Tanya, Pablo, and I did a simple, interesting experiment. (4) Our water-pressure experiment required water, a can, and a nail. (5) Tanya found a hammer and punched holes in the can. (No error) (6) One hole was near the top, one was near the middle, and one was near the bottom. (7) Pablo found thick black tape and covered the holes. (No error) (8) Then Tanya filled the can with water. (No error) (9) I removed the tape, and water spurted from all three holes. (10) The water pressure near the bottom was the greatest, so water from the lowest hole squirted the farthest.

Use commas to separate items in a series.

A **series** contains three or more items. The commas should appear after each item in the series except the last.

> Common birds of the Atlantic seacoast include the cormorant, the sanderling, and the herring gull.

> The pilot put on his helmet, climbed into the cockpit, and waved goodbye to the crowd.

> Marissa held Scruffy, Walter brushed the dog with soapy water, and I rinsed him with the hose.

Use commas between two or more adjectives of equal rank that modify the same noun.

> It was a dark, dreary night.

To decide whether adjectives are of equal rank, try placing the word *and* between them. If *and* sounds natural and if you can reverse the order of the adjectives without changing the meaning, then a comma is needed.

Exercise 3   Proofreading Skill

Commas in Compound Sentences and Items in Series   Rewrite the following paragraph, adding commas where needed.

(1) Water can be a solid a liquid or a gas. (2) Solid water is known as ice and gaseous water is known as water vapor. (3) Tanya, Pablo and I did a simple interesting experiment. (4) Our water-pressure experiment required water a can and a nail. (5) Tanya found a hammer and punched holes in the can. (6) One hole was near the top one was near the middle and one was near the bottom. (7) Pablo found thick black tape and covered the holes. (8) Then Tanya filled the can with water. (9) I removed the tape and water spurted from all three holes. (10) The water pressure near the bottom was the greatest so water from the lowest hole squirted the farthest.

Commas with Introductory Elements

Use a comma to separate an introductory word or phrase from the rest of a sentence.

So, is the hive full of honey yet?
Tumbling out of bed, the toddler bumped his head.
Due to heavy snow, there were many accidents on Route 22.

Commas with Interrupters

Use a comma before and after a word or group of words that interrupts a sentence.

This is, by the way, why we call crazy people lunatics.
In ancient days, if you can believe it, people thought that craziness had a lunar, or moon-related, cause.

Use a comma to set off nouns used in direct address.

A **noun of direct address** is the name of the person you are speaking to.

Well, Thor, what's the news from Asgard?

Use a comma after most appositives.

An **appositive** is a word or group of words that renames or identifies the person or thing referred to before it.

Mount Ararat, a mountain mentioned in the Bible, is in Turkey.

Exercise 4 Concept Check

Using Commas Correctly   Copy the following sentences, adding commas where needed.

1. Apollo the son of Zeus was the god of light.
2. Yes he rode across the sky each day from east to west.
3. At night I believe he took a boat back to the east.
4. Just today Melvin I heard the story of Clytie a wood nymph.
5. Well she was really in love with Apollo.
6. He however paid her no attention.
7. All day long she would sit and watch Apollo the sun god.
8. As his chariot moved across the sky she followed with her eyes.
9. Clytie just pined away Pat and was turned into a heliotrope.
10. That flower by the way always keeps turned toward the sun.

◀ SPEAKING OF
PHRASES . . . .
A comma usually isn't needed after a single introductory prepositional phrase: *In the garage* I saw a 1932 Ford.
A comma *is* needed after two or more introductory prepositional phrases: *In the garage at the end of our street,* I saw a 1932 Ford.

Exercise 4

1. Apollo, the son of Zeus, was the god of light.

2. Yes, he rode across the sky each day from east to west.

3. At night, I believe, he took a boat back to the east.

4. Just today, Melvin, I heard the story of Clytie, a wood nymph.

5. Well, she was really in love with Apollo.

6. He, however, paid her no attention.

7. All day long she would sit and watch Apollo, the sun god.

8. As his chariot moved across the sky, she followed with her eyes.

9. Clytie just pined away, Pat, and was turned into a heliotrope.

10. That flower, by the way, always keeps turned toward the sun.

Commas in Quotations

Use a comma to set off a direct quotation from the rest of a sentence.

A **direct quotation** is one that gives the exact words of a speaker. An explanatory phrase, such as *he said,* may come before the quotation, after it, or in the middle of it. If the explanatory phrase comes first, put the comma right after it.

> John said, "We must unite."

If the phrase comes last, put the comma inside the quotation marks that end the quotation.

> "We must unite," John said.

If the explanatory words come in the middle of the quotation, use commas both before (inside the quotation marks) and after the explanatory words.

> "We must unite," John said, "or we will be defeated."

Do not use a comma to set off an indirect quotation. An **indirect quotation** is one that does not give the speaker's exact words but restates them in different words.

> Ulysses S. Grant said that persons of African descent would make excellent soldiers.

Commas in Dates, Addresses, and Letters

Use commas to separate the parts of dates and addresses.

In writing dates, use a comma between the day of the month and the year. If no day of the month is given, it is not necessary to use a comma between the month and the year.

> On May 20, 1992, Chris won the championship.
> The concert was on Friday, June 2, 1993.
> The celebration took place in November 1993.

In writing addresses, use a comma after the name of the street and after the name of the city. Do not use a comma before the ZIP code. Study the following examples:

> Her address is 735 Halsted Street, Chicago, Illinois 60604.
> She lived in Cairo, Egypt, after leaving Tulsa, Oklahoma.
> We arrived at 525 East Fiftieth Street, New York City.

Use a comma after the salutation of a friendly letter. Use a comma after the closing of a friendly or a business letter.

Dear Jackie,   Sincerely yours,   Your pal,

Exercise 5   Concept Check

Correct Comma Usage   Copy the following sentences, adding commas where needed.

1. "You know" said Jade "I'd like to travel a lot."
2. In July 1990 she made this announcement.
3. Last week she returned from a week in Tangier Morocco.
4. She said "Many places there are named for Ibn Batuta."
5. On June 13 1325 Ibn Batuta left Morocco on his first journey.
6. Before he was through his travels had taken him 75,000 miles!
7. He traveled as far as Quanzhou China I think.
8. "For twenty-nine years he traveled through the known world" said Jade.
9. After returning Ibn Batuta dictated his life story.
10. A library in Paris France has his manuscript.

Exercise 6   Proofreading Skill

Checking for Comma Errors   Write the following paragraph, correcting all errors in comma usage.

(1) Yes our summer's trip will certainly be a welcome treat. (2) This year, my family will visit Spain, Algeria and Morocco. (3) We will not be sightseeing however. (4) My mother a history teacher wants to do some research. (5) Much of it centers on Casablanca Morocco. (6) I asked her why she wanted to go there. (7) She said that Casablanca is very historic, and she told me why. (8) In November 1943, an important meeting took place there. (9) President Franklin D. Roosevelt met there I believe with Winston Churchill. (10) The meeting took place I have read, during World War II.

Exercise 7   Revision Skill

Using Commas and End Marks   Copy the following sentences, adding end marks and commas as needed.

1. Emile said "Stop I want to take a picture"
2. I asked if he had ever seen an iceberg before

Exercise 5

1. "You know," said Jade, "I'd like to travel a lot."

2. In July 1990 she made this announcement. (No error)

3. Last week she returned from a week in Tangier, Morocco.

4. She said, "Many places there are named for Ibn Batuta."

5. On June 13, 1325, Ibn Batuta left Morocco on his first journey.

6. Before he was through, his travels had taken him 75,000 miles!

7. He traveled as far as Quanzhou, China, I think.

8. "For twenty-nine years he traveled through the known world," said Jade.

9. After returning, Ibn Batuta dictated his life story.

10. A library in Paris, France, has his manuscript.

Exercise 6

(1) Yes, our summer's trip will certainly be a welcome treat. (2) This year, my family will visit Spain, Algeria, and Morocco. (3) We will not be sightseeing, however. (4) My mother, a history teacher, wants to do some research. (5) Much of it centers on Casablanca, Morocco. (6) I asked her why she wanted to go there. (No error) (7) She said that Casablanca is very historic, and she told me why. (No error) (8) In November 1943 an important meeting took place there. (9) President Franklin D. Roosevelt met there, I believe, with Winston Churchill. (10) The meeting took place, I have read, during World War II.

Exercise 7

Answers may vary. Sample answers are provided.

1. Emile said, "Stop! I want to take a picture."

2. I asked if he had ever seen an iceberg before.

3. He hadn't, and he wanted a picture of one.

4. Icebergs can be dangerous, you know.

5. On April 14, 1912, a terrible accident happened.

6. Didn't the *Titanic,* the world's biggest passenger ship, hit an iceberg and sink?

7. While photographing, Emile asked, "How are icebergs formed?"

8. Many icebergs are near the North Pole, Greenland, and Antarctica.

9. What a lot of icebergs Cape Farewell, Greenland, has!

10. "Well, it's not surprising," said Mr. Wong, our science teacher.

11. "The icebergs, Emile, break off of the Greenland icecap," he said.

12. Every spring, thousands of new icebergs form, and some of them are huge!

13. Emile asked how big an iceberg could get.

14. "A really big one," said Mr. Wong, "might be a mile long!"

15. Wow! I'd like to see an iceberg that size.

3. He hadn't and he wanted a picture of one

4. Icebergs can be dangerous, you know

5. On April 14 1912, a terrible accident happened

6. Didn't the *Titanic* the world's biggest passenger ship hit an iceberg and sink

7. While photographing Emile asked, "How are icebergs formed"

8. Many icebergs are near the North Pole Greenland and Antarctica

9. What a lot of icebergs Cape Farewell, Greenland has

10. "Well it's not surprising," said Mr. Wong our science teacher

11. "The icebergs Emile break off of the Greenland icecap" he said

12. Every spring, thousands of new icebergs form and some of them are huge

13. Emile asked how big an iceberg could get

14. "A really big one" said Mr. Wong "might be a mile long"

15. Wow I'd like to see an iceberg that size

The Semicolon

Use a semicolon (;) to join the parts of a compound sentence if no conjunction is used.

> We looked outside the tent; it was still raining.

Use a semicolon to separate items in a series if the items contain commas.

> The expedition's leaders were from Beijing, China; from Katmandu, Nepal; and from London, England.

The Colon

Use a colon (:) to introduce a list of items.

A sentence containing a word or phrase such as *these, the following,* or *here* is often followed by a colon. The colon only follows a complete sentence; it never comes directly after a verb.

| **Incorrect** | The winning dogs are: Rover, Fido, and Rex. |
| **Correct** | These are the winning dogs: Rover, Fido, and Rex. |

Use a colon between hours and minutes when given as numbers.

> 12:00 A.M.   4:46 P.M.

Exercise 8 Concept Check

Using Semicolons and Colons Read each sentence. If no additional punctuation is needed, write *Correct.* If the sentence needs a semicolon or a colon, write the sentence correctly.

1. Annie hurried to the museum she, Takao, and I were meeting there at 300.
2. There were the following three exhibits one of photography, one of Chinese art, and one of paintings by the artist Velázquez.
3. "Velázquez" was only part of his name; his full name was Diego Rodríguez de Silva y Velázquez.
4. He was connected to the court in the following way he was the king's painter, and he and his family lived at court.
5. Look at the people in this painting the artist, the princess, and the courtiers.
6. The museum stays open late on Thursdays it doesn't close until 900 P.M.
7. I had a chance to see my favorite picture it's called *The Infanta Margarita.*
8. Velázquez painted it early in his career; it was his first portrait of the Spanish royal princess.
9. This may not be his best-known work *Las Meninas,* or *The Maids of Honor,* is probably more famous.
10. Tonight at 800 there is a television show about Velázquez.

The Hyphen

Use a hyphen (-) to show a word break at the end of a line. Be sure to break words between syllables.

> Writing a report can be an excellent coopera-
> tive learning project.

Use a hyphen between the words that make up a compound modifier used before a noun.

> Paolo wrote a sixteen-line poem.
> I have a king-size headache.

Use hyphens in compound nouns.

> editor-in-chief   stick-in-the-mud
> great-grandchild   ex-president

◀ REMINDER
· · · · · · · · · · · · ·
If you're not sure how to break a word between syllables, look up the word in a dictionary.

Exercise 9

1. blue-eyed

2. great-grandfather

3. high-pitched

4. ultra-sonic (word break at end of line)

5. two-thirds

6. king-size

7. vi-brate (word break at end of line)

8. twenty-six

9. vice-president

10. four-fifths

Use hyphens in compound numbers from twenty-one to ninety-nine.

seventy-six trombones   ninety-nine bottles

Use a hyphen in a fraction.

one-half   six-tenths   two-thirds

Exercise 9   Concept Check

Using Hyphens   Write the words that need hyphens in the following sentences, adding the hyphens that are needed.

1. My blue eyed cat cannot hear sounds.
2. My great grandfather wears a hearing aid.
3. Dogs can hear high pitched sounds that we don't hear.
4. Sounds too high for humans to hear are called ultra sonic sounds.
5. About two thirds of the students know that vibrations cause sound.
6. Listen to this king size rubber band vibrate when I pluck it.
7. When sound waves hit our eardrums, our eardrums begin to vi brate.
8. I tried an experiment with the twenty six students in my class.
9. The vice president of the class held up her wristwatch.
10. Everyone saw it, but only four fifths of the students in the room could hear it.

The Apostrophe

Use an apostrophe (') to make the possessive form of a noun.

Make the possessive of a singular noun by adding an apostrophe and *s* even if the noun already ends in *s*.

the boss**'s**   my friend**'s**   a chimpanzee**'s**

Make the possessive of a plural noun that ends in *s* by adding just an apostrophe.

the countries' borders   the boys' locker room

Make the possessive of a plural noun that does not end in *s* by adding an apostrophe and *s*.

the oxen**'s** salt lick   the children**'s** toys

Use an apostrophe to show that one or more letters have been left out of a contraction.

> don't (do not)   wouldn't (would not)   could've (could have)

Use an apostrophe and _s_ to show the plurals of a letter or a word referred to as a word.

> There are six _and_**'s** in that sentence!
> How many _i_**'s** are there in the word _Mississippi?_

Exercise 10   Concept Check

Using Apostrophes   Write the words and letters that need apostrophes in the following sentences. Add the needed apostrophes.

1. My brother and I both attend my fathers high school.
2. Kondo is trying out for the mens soccer team.
3. He said, "Its a popular sport."
4. His grades are all As and Bs.
5. Our parents wont let him play if his grades fall.
6. Our parents trophies show that they were both competitive swimmers.
7. Some students interests are limited to one area.
8. My brothers and sisters arent like that.
9. There are no _cant_s in their vocabularies.
10. My youngest sisters interests include track and computers.

Exercise 11   Proofreading Skill

Using Punctuation Correctly   Write correctly any sentences that need additional punctuation in the following paragraph. If a sentence needs no additional punctuation, write _Correct._

(1) At the age of twenty five, Jim Thorpe was called "the finest all-around athlete in the world." (2) He excelled in a number of sports football, track, and baseball. (3) The boys early education was rugged. (4) His school day began at 545 A.M. and ended at 900 P.M. (5) His first school taught Thorpe more than academic subjects it also taught him sports. (6) The boy would watch the players at practice. (7) Later, he tried to imitate the players moves. (8) Thorpe's reputation as a good player grew. (9) Then the following series of problems struck his father was injured in an accident; the boy left school; Jims mother and brother died. (10) Shortly thereafter, Jim returned to school. (11) This time, he went to Pennsylvania's Carlisle Indian School. (12) This school had a first rate football coach named Glenn S. "Pop" Warner.

Exercise 12

1. The Grimm <u>brothers'</u> stories are full of numbers.

2. "I <u>didn't</u> notice that," said Fatima.

3. Listen to these <u>titles:</u> "The Six Swans," "The Twelve Brothers," and "The Wolf and the Seven Goats."

4. Those fairy <u>tales'</u> titles are amazing.

5. They are some of the <u>best-known</u> fairy tales in the world.

6. I like "The Frog <u>Prince";</u> that's the story where a princess kisses a frog.

7. A frog finds the toy she <u>lost;</u> she kisses him, and he turns into a prince.

8. My father and mother collect old <u>children's</u> books.

9. My <u>parents'</u> collection includes several books of fairy tales from around the world.

10. Mother said, "These books aren't just for kids; even <u>middle-aged</u> people enjoy them."

Exercise 12   Revision Skill

Using Semicolons, Colons, Hyphens, and Apostrophes   Write the following sentences, adding any needed punctuation.

1. The Grimm brothers stories are full of numbers.
2. "I didnt notice that," said Fatima.
3. Listen to these titles "The Six Swans," "The Twelve Brothers," and "The Wolf and the Seven Goats."
4. Those fairy tales titles are amazing.
5. They are some of the best known fairy tales in the world.
6. I like "The Frog Prince" that's the story where a princess kisses a frog.
7. A frog finds the toy she lost she kisses him, and he turns into a prince.
8. My father and mother collect old childrens books.
9. My parents collection includes several books of fairy tales from around the world.
10. Mother said, "These books aren't just for kids; even middle aged people enjoy them."

Quotation Marks

Use quotation marks (" ") at the beginning and the end of a direct quotation.

> The kids in the haunted house yelled, **"**Let us out of here!**"**

▶ Capitalize the first word of a quotation. Separate the quotation from the rest of the sentence with one or more commas. A comma or period before a quotation comes before the quotation marks. A comma or period after a quotation goes inside the quotation marks.

> Mr. Sandoz said, **"**Now you're on your own,**"** just as we got to the mouth of the cave.
> **"**Help!**"** said Timothy. **"**I can't see anything in here.**"**

A question mark or exclamation point goes inside the quotation marks if it is part of the quotation; it goes outside the quotation marks if it is not part of the quotation.

> Ms. Lee asked, **"**How many planets are there in the solar system**?"**
> Did Ms. Lee say, **"**There are nine known planets**"?**

Use quotation marks around both parts of a divided quotation.

Do not capitalize the first letter of the first word of the second part of a divided quotation unless it begins a new sentence.

> "Listen!" said Mr. Sandoz. "You can hear the bats down there."
> "Can you imagine," said Mr. Sandoz, "how many of them there must be?"

When punctuating dialogue, begin a new paragraph to indicate a new speaker.

> "Hello, class," said Ms. Lee. "You'll probably want to know something about me. Any questions?"
> "Yes," said Sue Washington. "What did you do before you were a teacher?"
> "I spent thirty years as a professional astronomer."

Exercise 13   Concept Check

Using Quotation Marks and Other Punctuation   Write the following sentences, adding quotation marks and other punctuation as needed.

1. What an exciting photograph exclaimed Carlos
2. This picture he said shows the eruption of a volcano
3. Did Carlos say This picture shows the eruption of a volcano
4. Our science teacher said The center of the earth is extremely hot
5. How hot is it asked Coretta
6. Mr. Red Deer said It can reach 13,000 degrees Fahrenheit
7. Is the hot melted rock called magma I asked
8. Yes said Mr. Red Deer The magma bursts through the earth's crust
9. What did Mr. Red Deer say asked Coretta, about a ring of fire
10. The Ring of Fire said Carlos, is an area with many active volcanoes

Exercise 14   Revision Skill

Punctuating Dialogue   Rewrite the following passage using correct paragraphing and punctuation.

> Oh, nuts I spilled liquid soap all over my blouse said Barbara. Sue replied Im sure you can wash it out Yes complained Barbara but then my blouse will be wet for the rest of the day I think Id better go home and start this week over If this is only Monday, what will Friday be like

Exercise 13

1. "What an exciting photograph!" exclaimed Carlos.

2. "This picture," he said, "shows the eruption of a volcano."

3. Did Carlos say, "This picture shows the eruption of a volcano"?

4. Our science teacher said, "The center of the earth is extremely hot."

5. "How hot is it?" asked Coretta.

6. Mr. Red Deer said, "It can reach 13,000 degrees Fahrenheit."

7. "Is the hot melted rock called magma?" I asked.

8. "Yes," said Mr. Red Deer. "The magma bursts through the earth's crust."

9. "What did Mr. Red Deer say," asked Coretta, "about a ring of fire?"

10. "The Ring of Fire," said Carlos, "is an area with many active volcanoes."

Exercise 14

Punctuation may vary slightly.

"Oh, nuts! I spilled liquid soap all over my blouse," said Barbara.

Sue replied, "I'm sure you can wash it out."

"Yes," complained Barbara, "but then my blouse will be wet for the rest of the day. I think I'd better go home and start this week over. If this is only Monday, what will Friday be like?"

IN PRINT

Titles and names that are underlined in writing appear in italics in print.

Punctuating Titles

Use quotation marks to set off the titles of short stories, poems, essays, magazine articles, chapters, television episodes, reports, and songs.

Short Story	"Charles," by Shirley Jackson
Poem	"A Dream Deferred," by Langston Hughes
Essay	"Homeless," by Anna Quindlen
Song	"Ave Maria," by Franz Schubert
Television Episode	"The Trouble with Tribbles"

▶ **Underline the titles of books, newspapers, magazines, movies, television series, plays, works of art, and long musical compositions.**

Book	Kipling's <u>Jungle Book</u>
Newspaper	<u>The Boston Globe</u>
Movie	<u>Malcolm X</u>
Television Series	<u>Star Trek</u>
Long Musical Composition	Puccini's <u>La Bohème</u>

Underline the names of planes, trains, and ships.

the <u>Titanic</u>   <u>Air Force One</u>

Exercise 15   Concept Check

Punctuating Titles   Write the titles given in the following sentences. Underline them or use quotation marks as needed.

1. I just finished reading a book called Trains.
2. I need it for my report, which is titled Art and the Train.
3. I've always wanted to ride on a train like the Orient Express.
4. I know there's a book called Murder on the Orient Express by Agatha Christie.
5. There are lots of songs about trains, including City of New Orleans.
6. Didn't Emily Dickinson write a poem called The Railway Train?
7. I read an article about train whistles in an old issue of Cricket magazine.
8. The article was called The Language of Train Whistles.
9. I know that Key, Lock, and Lantern is a periodical about trains.
10. In your bibliography did you include Toby's story Lost in Grand Central Station?

Exercise 16   Proofreading Skill

Using Quotation Marks and Punctuating Titles   Write the following passage, correcting any errors in punctuation or paragraphing that you find.

(1) Omar and I just finished writing a report called Early Trains. (2) We included drawings, maps, and early railroad songs, such as I've Been Working on the Railroad. (3) Was I surprised when I read, "Early trains were rather slow!" (4) In 1829 the fastest train in the world was the Rocket. (5) "I think" said Omar "that its top speed was thirty-five miles an hour." (6) I said, "Is that what we wrote in our report?" (7) My teacher said that "he liked our approach." (8) "This report shows a lot of work, he said. (9) "I want to put it in the library. (10) I'll put it next to that book called "Railroads."

Exercise 17   Revision Skill

Using Punctuation Marks Correctly   Write the following sentences, correcting any errors in punctuation.

1. On May 27 1907 Rachel Carson was born in Springdale Pennsylvania
2. Juanita said, Wasnt she an environmentalist
3. What a difference she made in this world exclaimed Walt
4. She did part time work for the Bureau of Fisheries and she later got a full time job.
5. Was Under the Sea Wind her first book
6. I asked if Ms Carsons next book was successful
7. Thats the book that was published on July 2 1951
8. The book The Sea Around Us was a huge success it stayed on the best-seller list for eighty six weeks.
9. Carson had several concerns the sea its life forms and the use of pesticides
10. Pesticides were used frequently and Carson wondered if they were safe
11. She worked with several experts, including Dr Wilhelm C Huepner of the National Cancer Institute.
12. Some critics made fun of Carsons warnings an article in Time magazine called her book "unfair"
13. Over a two year period however the U S government stopped using the most dangerous pesticide.
14. She wrote an article called Teach Your Child to Wonder but I havent read it.
15. Rachel Carson was extraordinary she was a good writer and a gifted scientist.

14. She wrote an article called "Teach Your Child to Wonder," but I haven't read it.

15. Rachel Carson was extraordinary; she was a good writer and a gifted scientist.

Punctuation and paragraphing may vary slightly.

(1) Omar and I just finished writing a report called "Early Trains." (2) We included drawings, maps, and early railroad songs, such as "I've Been Working on the Railroad." (3) Was I surprised when I read, "Early trains were rather slow"!

(4) In 1829 the fastest train in the world was the Rocket. (5) "I think," said Omar, "that its top speed was thirty-five miles an hour."

(6) I said, "Is that what we wrote in our report?"

(7) My teacher said that he liked our approach. (8) "This report shows a lot of work," he said. (9) "I want to put it in the library. (10) I'll put it next to that book called Railroads."

Exercise 17

1. On May 27, 1907, Rachel Carson was born in Springdale, Pennsylvania.

2. Juanita said, "Wasn't she an environmentalist?"

3. "What a difference she made in this world!" exclaimed Walt.

4. She did part-time work for the Bureau of Fisheries, and she later got a full-time job.

5. Was Under the Sea Wind her first book?

6. I asked if Ms. Carson's next book was successful.

7. That's the book that was published on July 2, 1951.

8. The book The Sea Around Us was a huge success; it stayed on the best-seller list for eighty-six weeks.

9. Carson had several concerns: the sea, its life forms, and the use of pesticides.

10. Pesticides were used frequently, and Carson wondered if they were safe.

11. She worked with several experts, including Dr. Wilhelm C. Huepner of the National Cancer Institute.

12. Some critics made fun of Carson's warnings; an article in Time magazine called her book "unfair."

13. Over a two-year period, however, the U.S. government stopped using the most dangerous pesticide.

Index of Fine Art

Index of Skills

Literary Terms

Action, 239, 240, 420
Acts, 155, 680
Alliteration, 680
Allusion, 476, 680
American slave tales, 618
  dialect in, 618
Author's purpose, 44, 85, 106, 680
Autobiography, 42, 43, 55, 152, 222, 680
  diaries, 42
  journal, 42
  memoirs, 42
Ballad, 235
Biographer, 42
Biography, 42, 43, 283, 680
Briticisms, 222, 236
Camera directions, 155, 157, 489
Cast of characters, 155, 680
Character development, 398, 680
Characterization, 23, 41, 140, 680
Characters, 15 , 75, 155 , 237, 239, 509, 680
  dynamic, 398, 405
  main, 15, 296, 353, 454, 458, 680
  minor, 15, 336, 405, 680
  static, 398, 405
Classic stories, 336
Climax, 15, 156, 189, 190, 454, 680, 684
Complications, 15, 23, 684
Conflict, 15, 34, 156, 189, 238, 296, 681
  external, 189, 283, 385, 681
  internal, 189, 283, 313, 566, 681
  introduced in exposition, 566
Connotation, 465, 515, 665, 681
Denotation, 465, 681
Description, 385, 546, 681
Dialect, 26, 222, 420, 681
  in American slave tale, 618
Dialogue, 155, 156, 171, 173, 175, 179, 238, 240,
    313, 643, 681
Diaries, 42
Drama, 155, 237, 681

action in, 239, 240, 420
acts, 155, 680
camera directions in, 155, 157, 489
cast of characters, 155
characters in, 237, 239, 509
climax in, 156, 454
conflict in, 156, 238
dialect in, 420
dialogue in, 155, 156, 171, 238, 240
elements of, 155–56
exposition in, 509
lighting in, 155, 157
plot in, 509
props, 155, 157, 240
reading, strategies for, 156
resolution, 156
scenery, 155
scenes, 155–56, 239, 420
script, 155–56, 420
setting in, 157, 171, 237, 239, 240, 509
sound, 155
sound effects, 157
stage directions, 155, 156, 157, 172, 173, 238,
    240, 420, 489, 511, 687
teleplay, 157, 172, 687
Dynamic characters, 398, 405
End rhyme, 685–86
Essay, 42, 47, 681–82
  formal, 42
  informal, 42, 47
  persuasive, 235, 376
Exaggeration, 208, 376, 682
Exposition, 15, 509, 566, 682, 684
External conflict, 189, 283, 385, 681
Fables, 584, 585, 682
  moral in, 585
  themes in, 607, 616
Fact, 682
Fantasy, 251, 665, 682
Fiction, 682
  characterization in, 23, 41, 140, 680
  characters in, 15, 75, 155, 237, 239, 680

Reading and Critical Thinking Skills

*G*rammar, Usage, and Mechanics

*W*riting Skills, Modes, and Formats

Salutation, in letters, 706–707

Self-assessment, 62, 113, 178, 241, 290, 343, 346, 392, 461, 516, 573, 666, 667 , 696

Sensory details, 109, 111, 112, 266, 269, 665, 700

Signal words, 174, 177
  see also Transitions

Signature, in letters, 706–707

Statistics
  used in elaboration, 700
  in persuasive writing, 388, 390, 391

Supporting details, 459, 664

Supporting an opinion, 111, 391, 455, 514

Thesis statement, 460

Topic sentence, 699

Transitions, 289, 342, 570, 572, 663, 665, 698
  see also Signal words

Unity, in writing, 697

Word choice, 344, 391, 513, 515

Words often confused, 344–46

Writing about literature, 366, 457–61, 512–16, 663
  analyzing character, 83, 457–61, 510
  analyzing a poem, 89
  analyzing theme, 272
  character sketch, 556
  comparing and contrasting characters, 190, 209, 477, 532, 567, 592, 630
  comparing and contrasting selections, 386
  personal response, 34, 106, 171, 218, 234, 265, 269, 272, 365, 385, 405, 454, 476, 488, 509, 531, 537, 547, 566, 592, 611, 629, 639, 652
  responding to characters, 23, 24, 55, 140, 152, 172, 208, 209, 283, 313, 317, 336, 419, 556, 604, 621, 635, 642, 647, 659
  responding to speaker, 320, 371, 535

Writing letters
  business letters, 706–707
  friendly letters, 707

Writing process, 694–701
  coherence in, 697–98
  conclusions, 342, 458, 460, 570, 665, 667
  details, 61, 62, 111
  elaboration in, 699–700
  implied main idea in, 699
  introductions, 61, 112, 289, 341, 569, 665, 667
  main idea in, 697, 699–700, 701
  organization, 59, 60, 61, 106, 111, 177, 286, 289, 391

paragraphs in, 697–701
  topic sentence in, 699
  transitions, 289, 342, 570, 572, 663, 665, 698
  unity in, 697
  writing with computers, 61, 112, 177, 240, 290, 341, 515, 572, 574
    see also Drafting; Prewriting; Proofreading; Publishing and presenting; Revising; Self-assessment

*V*ocabulary Skills

Analogies, 303, 477

Antonyms, 56, 76, 386, 510, 547

Briticisms, 222, 236

Connotation, 465, 515, 665, 681
  negative, 465
  neutral, 465
  positive, 465

Context clues, 24, 107, 117, 141, 190, 235, 314, 406, 465, 522, 567, 605, 643, 681
  antonyms, 56, 76, 386, 510, 547
  definition and restatement, 117, 681
  example, 117, 681
  inference, 35, 117, 284, 337, 366, 681
  synonyms, 76, 153, 172, 266, 386, 510, 532, 556, 630, 660, 681

Denotation, 209, 465, 681

Dialect, 26, 234, 420, 618, 681

Dictionaries, 131
  specialized, 703

Glossary, 703

Homonyms, 343, 344

Jargon, 93, 683

Loaded language, 520

Persuasion, language of, 347

Prefixes, 671

Restatement clues. *See* Context clues

Roots, Greek, 671

Specialized vocabulary. *See* Jargon

Suffixes, 671

Synonyms, 76, 153, 172, 266, 386, 510, 532, 556, 630, 660, 681

There, They're, and *Their,* 343

*R*esearch and Study Skills

Speaking, Listening, and Viewing

Index of Titles and Authors

Page numbers that appear in italics refer to biographical information.

Acknowledgments

(continued from page iv)

Estate of Margaret Danner: "I'll Walk the Tightrope" by Margaret Danner. Reprinted by permission of Naomi Washington for the Estate of Margaret Danner.

Dell Books, a division of Bantam Doubleday Dell Publishing Group, Inc.: "Lose Now, Pay Later" by Carol Farley; copyright © 1991 by Carol Farley, from *2041: Twelve Short Stories About the Future* by Jane Yolen, Editor. Used by permission of Dell Books, a division of Bantam Doubleday Dell Publishing Group, Inc.

Mari Evans: "The Rebel," from *I Am a Black Woman* by Mari Evans, published by William Morrow & Co., 1970. By permission of the author.

Farrar, Straus & Giroux, Inc., and Murray Pollinger, Literary Agent: "The Bicycle and the Sweetshop," "The Great Mouse Plot," and "Mr. Coombes," from *Boy* by Roald Dahl; copyright © 1984 by Roald Dahl. English editions published by Jonathan Cape Limited and Penguin Books Ltd. "Charles," from *The Lottery and Other Stories* by Shirley Jackson; copyright 1948, 1949 by Shirley Jackson, renewal copyright © 1976, 1977 by Laurence Hyman, Barry Hyman, Mrs. Sarah Webster, and Mrs. Joanne Schnurer. Reprinted by permission of Farrar, Straus & Giroux, Inc.

Julia Fields: "Aardvark" by Julia Fields, from *Nine Black Poets*. By permission of the author.

Harcourt Brace Jovanovich, Inc.: "Seventh Grade," from *Baseball in April and Other Stories* by Gary Soto; copyright © 1990 by Gary Soto. "Without Commercials," from *Horses Make a Landscape Look More Beautiful* by Alice Walker; copyright © 1984 by Alice Walker. Reprinted by permission of Harcourt Brace Jovanovich, Inc. "What Do We Do with a Variation," from *When I Dance* by James Berry; copyright © 1991, 1988 by James Berry. Reprinted by permission of Harcourt Brace Jovanovich, Inc., and June Hall Literary Agency Ltd., a division of Peters, Fraser & Dunlop Ltd.

HarperCollins Publishers: "The Fatal Flower," from *Tongues of Jade* by Laurence Yep; text copyright © 1991 by Laurence Yep. Chapter ll from *The Endless Steppe* by Esther Hautzig; copyright © 1968 by Esther Hautzig. Reprinted by permission of HarperCollins Publishers.

Lawrence Hill Books: "Last Cover," from *The Best Nature Stories of Paul Annixter* by Paul Annixter; copyright © 1974 Jane and Paul Annixter. By permission of the publisher, Lawrence Hill Books (Brooklyn, New York).

Henry Holt and Company, Inc.: "A Minor Bird," from *The Poetry of Robert Frost* by Robert Frost, edited by Edward Connery Lathem; copyright 1928, © 1969 by Holt, Rinehart and Winston, copyright © 1956 by Robert Frost. "Upon the Waters" (pp. 187–197), from *Rites of Passage* by Joanne Greenberg; copyright © 1966, 1967, 1968, 1969, 1970, 1971, 1972 by Joanne Greenberg. Reprinted by permission of Henry Holt and Company, Inc.

Houghton Mifflin Company: "Aunt Millicent" by Mary Steele, from *Dream Time,* edited by Gascoigne, Goodman, and Tyrrell; copyright © 1989 by Mary Steele. Reprinted by permission of Houghton Mifflin Co. All rights reserved.

Interlink Publishing Group, Inc.: "A Blind Man Catches a Bird," from *Children of Wax: African Folk Tales* by Alexander McCall Smith; copyright © 1990 Alexander McCall Smith.

Estate of MacKinlay Kantor: "A Man Who Had No Eyes" by MacKinlay Kantor. By permission of Tim Kantor and Layne Shroder, children of deceased author.

Virginia Kidd, Literary Agent for Anne McCaffrey: "The Smallest Dragonboy" by Anne McCaffrey; copyright © 1973 by Anne McCaffrey, first appeared in *Science Fiction Tales*. Reprinted by permission of the author and the author's agent, Virginia Kidd.

Little, Brown and Company: "How Odin Lost His Eye," from *Adventures with the Giants* by Catharine F. Sellew; copyright 1950 by Catharine F. Sellew, copyright © renewed 1978 by Catharine F. Sellew. *The Arrow and the Lamp: The Story of Psyche* retold by Margaret Hodges; text copyright © 1989 by Margaret Hodges. By permission of Little, Brown and Company.

Liveright Publishing Corporation: "old age sticks," from *Complete Poems, 1913-1962* by E. E. Cummings; copyright © 1923, 1925, 1931, 1935, 1938, 1939, 1940, 1944, 1945, 1946, 1947, 1948, 1949, 1950, 1951, 1952, 1953, 1954, 1955, 1956, 1957, 1958, 1959, 1960, 1961, 1962 by the Trustees for the E. E. Cummings Trust, copyright © 1961, 1963, 1968 by Marion Morehouse Cummings.

Macmillan Publishing Company: Excerpts from "Eleanor Roosevelt," from *Great Lives: Human Rights* by William Jay Jacobs; copyright © 1990 William Jay Jacobs. Reprinted with the permission of Charles Scribner's Sons, an imprint of Macmillan Publishing Company.

Janice Mirikitani: "For My Father," from *Awake in the River; Poetry and Prose* by Janice Mirikitani, Isthmus Press, 1978, San Francisco, CA. By permission of the author.

Museum of New Mexico Press: "The Force of Luck," from *Cuentos: Tales from the Hispanic Southwest* by José Griego y Maestas and Rudolfo Anaya; copyright © 1980. Reprinted with permission of the Museum of New Mexico Press.

Hugh Noyes for Literary Estate of Alfred Noyes: "The Highwayman" by Alfred Noyes. Permission of Hugh Noyes, for Trustees of Alfred Noyes Literary Estate.

Harold Ober Associates, Inc.: "Stolen Day" by Sherwood Anderson; copyright © 1941by United Newspapers Magazine Corp., copyright renewed © 1968 by Eleanor Copenhaver Anderson. Reprinted by permission of Harold Ober Associates, Inc.

Penguin Books Canada Limited: Excerpts from *Little by Little* by Jean Little; copyright © 1987 Jean Little. Reprinted by permission of Penguin Books Canada Limited.

The Putnam Publishing Group: "Kelfala's Secret Something" by Adjai Robinson, from *Three African Tales;* copyright © 1979 by Adjai Robinson. Reprinted by permission of The Putnam Publishing Group. "Anansi and His Visitor, Turtle," from *African Village Folk Tales* by Edna Mason Kaula; copyright © 1968 by Edna Mason Kaula. Reprinted by permission of Philomel Books.

Random House, Inc.: "Where the Girl Saved Her Brother" told by Strange Owl, from *The Sound of Flutes and Other Indian Legends,* edited by Richard Erdoes; copyright © 1976 by Richard Erdoes. Reprinted by permission of Pantheon Books, a division of Random House, Inc. "Dream Deferred," from *The Panther and the Lash* by Langston Hughes; copyright © 1951 by Langston Hughes. "Homeless," from *Living Out Loud* by Anna Quindlen; copyright © 1987 by Anna Quindlen. "America the Not-so-Beautiful," from *Not That You Asked* by Andrew A. Rooney; copyright © 1989 by Essay Productions. Excerpts from *The Autobiography of Malcolm X* by Malcolm X with Alex Haley; copyright © 1964 by Alex Haley and Malcolm X. Copyright © 1965 by Alex Haley and Betty Shabazz. Reprinted by permission of Random House, Inc. "The People Could Fly," from *The People Could Fly: American Black Folktales,* told by Virginia Hamilton; text copyright © 1985 by Virginia Hamilton. Reprinted by permission of Alfred A. Knopf, Inc. Excerpts from *Nadja on My Way* by Nadja Salerno-Sonnenberg; copyright © 1989 by Nadja Salerno-Sonnenberg. Reprinted by permission of Crown Publishers, Inc.

Marian Reiner, Literary Agent: "The Women's 400 Meters," from *The Sidewalk Racer and Other Poems of Sports and Motion* by Lillian Morrison; copyright © 1965, 1967, 1968, 1977 by Lillian Morrison. Reprinted by permission of Marian Reiner for the author.

Scholastic, Inc.: "Prometheus," from *Heroes, Gods and Monsters of the Greek Myths* retold by Bernard Evslin; copyright © 1966 by Scholastic, Inc. Chapters 2 and 3 from *Exploring the Titanic* by Robert D. Ballard; copyright © 1991 by The Madison Press Ltd. Reprinted by permission of Scholastic, Inc.

The Rod Serling Trust: *The Monsters Are Due on Maple Street* by Rod Serling; copyright © 1960 Rod Serling; © 1988 Carolyn Serling, Jodi Serling, and Anne Serling. Reprinted by permission of the Rod Serling Trust. All rights reserved.

Virginia Driving Hawk Sneve: "The Medicine Bag" by Virginia Driving Hawk Sneve, first printed in *Boys' Life,* March 1975. Reprinted by permission of the author.

Mary TallMountain: "There Is No Word for Goodbye" by Mary TallMountain, from *The Blue Cloud Quarterly.* Reprinted by permission of the author.

Twentieth Century Fox Film Corp.: "Funny Boy" by Allan Burns, from the series entitled *Room 222;* copyright © 1969 Twentieth Century Fox Film Corporation. All rights reserved.

Estate of Yoshiko Uchida: "Oh Broom, Get to Work" by Yoshiko Uchida; copyright © 1977. Reprinted by permission of the Estate of Yoshiko Uchida.

Franklin Watts, Inc.: "A Crush," from *A Couple of Kooks and Other Stories About Love* by Cynthia Rylant; copyright © 1990 by Cynthia Rylant. Reprinted with permission of Orchard Books, New York.

Western Publishing Company, Inc.: "Old Sly Eye" by Russell Gordon Carter, from *Story Parade;* copyright © 1945 Story Parade, renewed in 1973. Used by permission of Western Publishing Company, Inc.

Wylie, Aitken & Stone: "The Time We Climbed Snake Mountain" by Leslie Marmon Silko; copyright © 1972 by Leslie Marmon Silko. By permission of Sarah Chalfant, Literary Agent of Wylie, Aitken & Stone for the author.

The Zanuck Company and Scholastic, Inc.: Adaptation of *Driving Miss Daisy* by Alfred Uhry, from *Literary Cavalcade Magazine,* January 1990. By permission of The Zanuck Company and Scholastic, Inc.

The authors and editors have made every effort to trace the ownership of all copyrighted selections found in this book and to make full acknowledgment for their use.

Illustrations

Illustrations by Rich Lo: 475, 611, 610. Illustrations by Jerry Nelson: 15, 42, 84, 155, 584.   Maps by Robert Voigts: 17, 192, 222, 377, 538, 587, 593, 597, 608, 610, 612, 615, 619, 622, 625, 633, 636, 640, 646, 648, 653.

Author Photographs

AP/Wide World Photos: Alfred Uhry 456, MacKinlay Kantor 690 bottom, Andrew A. Rooney, 692 top.   © Archive Photos: Rod Serling 173.   Arte Publico Press: Judith Ortiz Cofer 548, Pat Mora 691 top.   Avon Books: Carol Farley 77.   © Sophie Baker: Roald Dahl 236.   The Chicago Defender: Alfred Duckett 154.   Cox Studios: Virginia Hamilton 631 middle.   Culver

Pictures: Rudyard Kipling 338, Hans Christian Andersen 661 top, Alfred Lord Tennyson 693 top. Richard Erdoes: Rachel Strange Owl 644 middle.   Bernard Evslin: 644 top.   © June Finfer, Filmedia Ltd.: Yoshiko Uchida 693 bottom.   Historical Pictures/Stock Montage: Emily Dickinson 372 top, Leo Tolstoy 617 bottom, Aesop 617 top, O. Henry, 689 bottom.   By permission of the Houghton Library, Harvard University: e.e. cummings 221 bottom. © 1987 Elizabeth Gilliland: Lillian Morrison 321 top.   The Granger Collection, New York: Malcolm X 478, Langston Hughes 690 top.   Rubén Guzmán: Sandra Cisneros 688 bottom.   Virginia Kidd, literary agent: Anne McCaffrey 267.   Photo by Jay Kay Klein: Ray Bradbury 688 middle.   © 1991 George T. Kruse: Janice Mirikitani 691 top.   Photo by Michael LeRoy: Allan Burns 511. © Lee Marmon: Leslie Marmon Silko 692 bottom.   Photo by Jim Marshall: Alice Walker 483. Photo by Margaret Miller: Cynthia Rylant 407.   Courtesy, Moorland-Spingarn Research Center, Howard University, Washington, D.C.: Georgia Douglas Johnson 690 bottom. Collection of the National Palace Museum, Taipei, Taiwan, Republic of China: Po Chü-i 372 bottom.   National Portrait Gallery, Smithsonian Institution, Washington, D.C./Art Resource, New York: Robert Frost 689 middle.   Photo by Barbara Nitke: Robert Ballard 108.   Courtesy, *The New York Times:* Anna Quindlen 691 bottom.   NYT Pictures: Frank Horne 321 bottom. Photo by Christian Steiner: Nadja Salerno-Sonnenberg 315.   Schomburg Center for Research in Black Culture, The New York Public Library, Astor, Lenox and Tilden Foundations: Toni Cade Bambara 36, Ted Poston 191.   Photo by Bob Tradelius: Joanne Greenberg 142.   Photo by Ian West: Mary Steele 210.   Photo by K. Yep: Laurence Yep 661, bottom.

Miscellaneous Art Credits

viii STOP LIGHT 1986 © C. J. Yao. Courtesy, Styria Studio, New York.   x DAKOTA PIPE CLAN MAGIC Oscar Howe Courtesy, Mr. and Mrs. Peter A. Hassrick.   xii THE STARRY NIGHT 1889 Vincent van Gogh Oil on canvas, 29 x 36 1/4 inches (73.4 x 92.1 cm). Collection, The Museum of Modern Art, New York. Acquired through the Lillie P. Bliss Bequest. Photograph © 1992 The Museum of Modern Art, New York.   xiv THE BOATING PARTY 1893-94 Mary Cassatt National Gallery of Art, Washington, D.C. Chester Dale Collection.   xvi YO Y MI FUTURO (I and my future) 1951 Jesús Guerrero Galván Collection, Pascual Gutiérrez Roldán.   xviii THREE FOLK MUSICIANS 1967 Romare Bearden Courtesy, the estate of Romare Bearden and ACA Galleries, New York.   3 The Hermitage, St. Petersburg, Russia.   4 top EXOTIC LANDSCAPE 1910 Henri Rousseau (1844-1910) Oil on canvas 45 3/4 x 64 inches Norton Simon Foundation, Pasadena, California; bottom Small beaded pouch, about 1915. Photo 1989 Benson L. Lanford and Robert W. Gilmore.   5 top © 1988 from *Exploring the Titanic* by Robert D. Ballard. A Scholastic/Madison Press Book, bottom LE PETIT DEJEUNER 1986 Jennifer Hornyak Courtesy, Gallery Claude Lafitte, Montreal, Canada.   14 Mural in Philadelphia (detail) 1992 Meg Fish. Courtesy of the artist.   17 © 1991 H. Richard Johnson/FPG.   26 PAINTED BRONZE 1960 © Jasper Johns/VAGA, New York Courtesy, Leo Castelli Gallery, New York.   37 Underwood Photo Archives.   38 The Bettmann Archive.   44 AP/Wide World Photos.   48 © 1991 Michael Simpson/FPG.   67 Illustration by Lynn Rowe Reed.   68 © Barry Seidman/The Stock Market. 78 © 1987 Tom Bean/The Stock Market.   86 The Hermitage, St. Petersburg, Russia.   90 Courtesy, California Historical Society.   91 H. Armstrong Roberts.   93, 94, 96-97, 100, 103 © 1988 From *Exploring the Titanic* by Robert D. Ballard. A Scholastic/Madison Press Book.   95 Joseph Carvalho collection.   99 Courtesy, 7C's Press/Titanic Historical Society, Inc., Old Orchard, Mass.   118 *Monkey Island* by Paula Fox. Copyright © 1991 by Paula Fox. Jacket painting copyright © 1991 by Rene Ade. Reproduced with permission of the publisher, Orchard Books, New York.   119 From *The Witch of Blackbird Pond* by Elizabeth George Speare. Copyright © 1958 by Elizabeth George Speare. Reprinted by permission of Houghton Mifflin Company. All rights reserved.   119 *Against the Storm* by Gaye Hicyilmaz. Copyright © 1992 by Little, Brown and Company, Inc. Used by permission.   122 UPI/Bettmann.   123 From *The World*

Book Encyclopedia © 1992 World Book, Inc. By permission of the publisher. 131 D. Lada/H. Armstrong Roberts. 143 Courtesy AU Sports Memorabilia. 147 inset UPI/Bettmann. 157 Culver Pictures. 183 SHIFTING EMBRACE (detail) 1990 Philemona Williamson Collection of Mr. and Mrs. Clarence Otis, photo by Manu Sassoonian, Courtesy, June Kelly Gallery, New York. 184 © James van der Zee Institute. 211 © John Running. 217 UPI/ Bettmann. 229 THE APPRENTICE 1981 Terry Mimnaugh bronze, edition of 15 from a series "What Little Boys Are Made Of." 246 From *Roll of Thunder, Hear My Cry* by Mildred D. Taylor, jacket illustration by Jerry Pinkney. Copyright © 1976 by the Dial press. Used by permission of Dial Books for Young Readers, a division of Penguin Books USA Inc. 247 *Maniac Magee* by Jerry Spinelli. Copyright © 1990 by Little, Brown and Company, Inc. Used by permission. 247 From *Brother Eagle, Sister Sky* by Susan Jeffers. Copyright © 1991 by Susan Jeffers. Used by permission of Dial Books for Young Readers, a division of Penguin Books USA, Inc. 250 RECLINING WOMAN (detail) Will Barnet © 1992 Will Barnet/VAGA, New York. 251 From *The Dragonlover's Guide to Pern* by Jody Lynn Nye with Anne McCaffrey, illustrations by Todd Cameron Hamilton. Copyright © 1989 by Bill Fawcett and Associates. Reprinted by permission of Ballantine Books, a division of Random House, Inc. 268 Illustration by Judy Pedersen. 273 Franklin Roosevelt Library. 295 LORD OF THE RIMROCK (detail) Leon Parson Print from National Wildlife Galleries, Fort Myers Florida. 296 The Bettmann Archive. 304 H. Abernathy/H. Armstrong Roberts. 316 © 1990 David Madison/Duomo. 322 © Norman Myers/Bruce Coleman Inc. 348 *The Hobbit* by J.R.R. Tolkien. © 1938. Reprinted with permission of Houghton Mifflin Company. All rights reserved. 349 Jacket illustration by Eric Velasquez from *The Gift of the Girl Who Couldn't Hear* by Susan Shreve. Text copyright © 1991 by Susan Shreve. Illustration copyright © by Eric Velasquez. By permission of Tambourine Books, a division of William Morrow & Company, Inc. 349 *Anpao* by Jamake Highwater. Cover reprinted by permission of HarperCollins Publishers. 352 Photo copy by Peter Schaff. 353 © Joe McDonald/Animals, Animals. 368 H. Armstrong Roberts. 373 © David Woodfall/TSW. 375 © Matt Lambert/TSW. 397 Illustration by Patty Dryden. 398 © Greenlar/The Image Works. 400, 401 Illustrations © 1992 by Norman Green. 408 Original illustration by Charles Mikolaycak for *The Highwayman.* Courtesy of the Kerlan Collection at the University of Minnesota. Used with permission of the illustrator and Lathrop, Lee and Shepard Publishers. 415 D. Degnan/H. Armstrong Roberts. 420 © Stephen Ellison/Shooting Star. 424, 451 © Shooting Star. 431 Globe Photos © Rangefinders. 437, 440 Photofest. 466 *The Flawed Glass* by Ian Strachan. Copyright © 1990 by Little, Brown Inc. Used by permission. 467 Reprinted with permission of Bradbury Press, an Affiliate of Macmillan, Inc., from *One-Eyed Cat* by Paula Fox. Jacket Illustration by Neil Waldman. Copyright © 1984 Bradbury Press. 467 Jacket illustration by Susan Bonners from *The Clay Marble* by Mingfong Ho. Jacket illustration copyright © 1991 by Susan Bonners. Reprinted by permission of Farrar, Straus & Giroux, Inc. 470 THE LIBRARIES ARE APPRECIATED (detail) 1943 Jacob Lawrence Philadelphia Museum of Art, Louis A. Stern Collection. 471 UPI/Bettmann. 479 Bill Bachman/Leo de Wys. 484 © Steve Leonard/TSW. 521, 522 © Brian Milne/Animals, Animals. 534 © Michael Dich/Animals, Animals. 549 The Bancroft Library, University of California, Berkeley. 557 AP/Wide World Photos. 578 Reprinted with the permission of Macmillan Publishing Company from *The House of Dies Drear* by Virginia Hamilton. Illustrated by Eros Keith. Copyright © 1968 Macmillan Publishing Company. 579 *The Adventures of Tom Sawyer* by Mark Twain. By permission of Tom Doherty Associates/Tor Books. 579 *Risk n' Roses* by Jan Slepian. © 1977 Reprinted with permission of Philomel Books, a division of Putnam. 582, 586 © Michael Holford. 582, 607 The Granger Collection, New York. 583, 618 A DRAWING BASED ON A SPIRITUAL 1958 Charles White Courtesy, Heritage Gallery, Los Angeles. 583, 632 Arapaho spear. Oklahoma Museum of Natural History, University of Oklahoma, Norman. 583, 615, 645 © Carmine Fantasia. 595 International Procession, from Girard Foundation Collection in the Museum of International Folk Art, a unit of The Museum of New Mexico, Santa Fe. Photograph by Michel Monteaux.

Skills Trace Charts

The charts that follow show the scope of skills presented in McDougal Littell's *Literature and Language* series.

LITERARY TERMS AND TECHNIQUES	GRADE 6	GRADE 7	GRADE 8
Act	188, 623	155, 680	208, 738
Alliteration	623	680	97, 738
Allusion		476, 680	144, 738
Antagonist			249, 738, 743
Author's Purpose	55, 90, 145, 340	44, 85, 106, 680	40, 440, 593, 738
Autobiography	48, 49, 50, 393, 623	42, 43, 55, 152, 222, 680	40, 41, 47, 53, 56, 60, 738, 742
Ballad		235	669
Biography	48, 49, 145, 245, 623	42, 43, 283, 680	40, 41, 163, 186, 296, 738, 742
Briticisms		222, 236	
Camera Directions		155, 157, 489	
Cast of Characters	188, 206, 623	155, 680	207, 738
Characterization	45, 180, 292, 473, 624	23, 41, 140, 680	37, 53, 167, 582, 738
Characters	15, 45, 48, 73, 82, 91, 96, 97, 138, 167, 188, 189, 206, 208, 245, 292, 473, 486, 623, 625, 627	15, 23, 41, 75, 140, 155–56, 176, 237–41, 296, 336, 353, 405, 454, 457–61, 680	25, 31, 37, 53, 87, 168, 200, 207, 208, 298, 420, 582, 720, 721, 722, 738, 745
dynamic/static		398, 405	103, 738
main/minor	15, 45, 73, 208, 627	15, 296, 336, 353, 405, 454, 458, 566, 680	15, 16, 249, 738, 740, 745
Chronological Order	395, 624	43, 106, 680	56, 66, 167, 229, 739
Climax/Turning Point	15, 188, 624, 628	15, 156, 189, 238, 296, 681	15, 168, 200, 224, 739, 743
Colloquialism			724, 726-28
Complications	15	15, 684	15, 743
Concrete Poetry	230, 233, 400, 624, 626		
Conflict	15, 26, 123, 189, 204, 208, 357, 473, 604, 624	15, 34, 156, 189, 238, 283, 296, 313, 385, 566, 681	15, 25, 113, 154, 166, 168, 200, 443, 451, 720, 739
Connotation		465, 515, 665, 681	38, 692
Denotation		209, 465, 681	
Description/Details	68, 210, 245, 624	385, 546, 681	457, 741
Dialect	29, 452, 618, 624	26, 222, 420, 618, 681	146, 739
Dialogue	91, 188, 208, 210, 248, 486, 625	155, 156, 171, 173, 175, 179, 238, 240, 313, 643, 681	31, 167, 207, 208, 318, 726, 739, 741
Diaries	48	42	40, 539, 739
Drama	156, 188-89, 190, 206, 239, 240, 248, 249, 254, 420, 486, 487, 520, 522, 625, 628	55, 156, 157, 171, 172, 173, 237, 238, 239, 240, 420, 489, 509, 511, 680, 681, 687	207-208, 224, 226, 342, 360, 403, 494, 569, 580, 721, 738, 739, 744
End Rhyme	629	685-86	89, 91, 97, 456, 744
Essay	48, 56, 103-107, 131, 205	42, 47, 235, 376, 681-82	40, 296, 378, 739, 742
Exposition (in plot)	15	15, 509, 566, 682, 684	15, 740, 743
Fable	539, 580, 588, 625	584, 585, 607, 616, 682	649, 685-86, 708-10, 740, 742
Fantasy	91	251, 665, 682	241, 249
Fiction	15, 16, 26, 45, 48, 72, 82, 91, 97, 123, 138, 167, 180, 188, 189, 208, 245, 272, 294, 473, 486, 604, 623, 624, 625	6, 15, 16, 23, 34, 41, 75, 83, 123, 140, 155, 156, 171, 175, 177, 184, 189, 190, 192, 237, 238, 239, 240, 296, 336, 405, 454, 479, 488, 531, 566, 616, 680, 681, 682, 684-85, 687	15-17, 28, 32, 80, 103, 129, 138, 146, 189, 241, 267, 321, 386, 399, 433, 443, 467, 582, 606, 740
Figurative Language	625	92, 268, 682	738, 740, 742
Figures of Speech *see* Hyperbole, Metaphor, Personification, Simile			

LITERARY TERMS AND TECHNIQUES	GRADE 6	GRADE 7	GRADE 8
Poetry	33, 81, 91, 98, 132, 144, 164, 183, 230, 233, 244, 356, 359, 400, 401, 417, 440, 448, 455, 624, 626, 628	84, 85, 86, 89, 217, 220, 268, 269, 270, 272, 316, 371, 408, 414, 419, 460, 464, 476, 479, 482, 535, 683, 684, 685, 686, 687	45, 76, 89-91, 99, 112, 153, 162, 202, 248, 251, 317, 337, 377, 453, 475, 592, 596, 743
Point of View	72, 83, 88, 103, 628	83, 190, 216, 405, 685	169, 451, 593, 617, 631, 743
Pourquoi Tales			692
Props	188, 522	155, 157, 240	207, 342
Protagonist			249, 738, 743
Puns	91		
Radio play	190, 628		226, 744
Repetition	89, 96, 97, 138, 361, 629	419, 685	89, 91, 744
in poetry		84, 86, 419	
Resolution	15, 625	15, 156, 685	15, 200, 224, 443, 451, 723, 743
Rhyme	89, 96, 97, 138, 629	84, 220, 371, 408, 414, 685-86	89, 91, 97, 453, 456, 738, 743, 744
Rhythm	89, 96, 97, 138, 629	84, 86, 89, 220, 371, 408, 414, 460, 464, 686	89, 91, 340, 738, 741–44
in poetry		84, 86, 89	
Sarcasm		208	741
Satire		140, 686	
Scenery	188	155	207, 744
Scenes	188, 623, 629	155-56, 239, 420, 680, 686	208, 569, 722, 738, 744
Screenplay		420, 686	
Script	188	155, 420	207, 580, 721
Sensory Details	310, 441, 629	109, 111, 112, 266, 269, 272	47, 89, 206, 741
Setting	15, 29, 34, 45, 48, 96, 97, 126, 132, 138, 180, 188, 209, 418, 630	15, 34, 75, 123, 155, 157, 171, 184, 192, 237, 239, 240, 336, 337, 509, 566, 616, 686	15, 91, 154, 166, 168, 200, 207, 208, 226, 742, 743, 744, 745
Simile	149, 151, 451, 625, 630	85, 130, 272, 686	90, 102, 206, 257, 740, 744
Sound/Sound Devices *see* Alliteration; Onomatopoeia; Rhyme; Rhythm			
Speaker	186, 448, 451, 630	316, 535, 687	453, 745
Stage Directions and Staging	188, 189, 190, 206, 248, 254, 260	155, 156, 157, 172, 173, 238, 240, 420, 489, 511, 687	207, 360, 403, 745
Stanzas	183, 186, 233, 630	84, 479, 482, 687	89, 251, 255, 745
Stereotypes		484, 488, 687	28, 31, 379, 396, 745
Style	214, 326	283, 313, 464, 519, 687	453, 722, 745
Surprise Ending		41, 687	396, 456, 657, 745
Suspense	204, 473, 631	265, 687	31, 167, 335, 742, 745
Symbol	400, 447, 631	630, 643, 687	476, 745
Tall Tale			649, 650, 669
Teleplay		155-56, 157, 172, 687	
Theme	82, 90, 101, 146, 204, 272, 536, 574, 604, 631	16, 85, 171, 270, 320, 479, 482, 584–85, 604, 607, 616, 687	16, 90, 422, 476, 598, 649, 680, 691, 705, 738, 745
Tone	277, 456	313, 482, 687	724, 745
Turning Point *see* Climax			
Word Choice/Diction	98, 359	85, 313, 344, 391, 482, 513, 515	57, 59, 90, 116, 118, 123, 169, 206, 228, 230, 299, 360, 362, 426, 457, 575, 598, 600, 679

READING AND CRITICAL THINKING SKILLS	GRADE 6	GRADE 7	GRADE 8
Skimming and Scanning	16, 34, 57, 208, 254, 326, 423, 531, 630	16, 83, 107, 208, 239, 267, 287, 294, 337, 346, 385, 389, 390, 459, 512, 533, 571, 686	16, 90, 298, 361, 635, 641, 722, 728, 744, 745
Stereotypes		484, 687	28, 31, 379, 396, 745
Summarizing	34, 47, 82, 531, 587, 608, 631	284, 396, 459, 483, 606, 687, 704	249, 299, 304, 634, 745, 760
Supporting Details	26, 34, 45, 46, 204, 262, 268, 302, 340, 361, 404, 418, 449, 473, 520, 554, 587, 601, 608	23, 55, 75, 83, 106, 130, 140, 171, 189, 192, 208, 216, 220, 269, 272, 283, 320, 336, 365, 371, 415, 445, 454, 537, 570, 577, 624	31, 46, 58, 78, 117–18, 169, 255, 257, 396, 481–82, 636–37, 720, 745
Synthesizing	90	130, 322, 366, 371	6, 16, 37, 41, 53, 78, 90, 113, 154, 186, 200, 203, 385, 476, 538, 556
Visualizing	16, 90, 98, 102, 400, 631	16, 85, 90, 176, 316, 377, 514, 537, 665, 687	6, 16, 25, 27, 31, 80, 88, 89, 90, 113, 136, 258, 454, 465, 600, 696, 745

WRITING SKILLS, MODES, AND FORMATS	GRADE 6	GRADE 7	GRADE 8
The Writing Process			
Prewriting	59–60, 104–105, 149–50, 208–209, 276–77, 321, 378, 423, 477–78, 524–25, 606, 607, 608, 609, 611, 636	59–60, 110, 111, 175–76, 239, 287, 288, 340–41, 388–91, 458–59, 512–14, 570–71, 663, 694–95	58, 117, 168, 229, 298, 361, 425, 481, 573, 574, 635–36, 720, 721, 722, 723, 725, 752–53, 758
Drafting	61, 106, 150–51, 209, 278, 321, 379, 478–79, 526, 606, 607, 608, 609, 611, 637	60–61, 111–12, 176–77, 240, 289, 341, 460, 514–15, 572–73, 662, 663, 664, 665, 667, 694, 695	59, 118, 169, 230, 298–99, 362, 482, 575, 636–37, 720, 721, 722, 723, 753
Revising and Editing (proofreading)	61, 65, 106, 110, 151, 155, 213–14, 278, 282, 322, 326, 379, 383, 424, 428, 479, 483, 526, 530, 606, 607, 608, 609, 611, 614, 637–38	61, 62, 112, 113, 177, 178, 180–81, 240–41. 244, 289, 290, 291, 293, 342, 346, 392, 395, 460–61, 515–16, 518, 519, 572–76, 662, 663, 664, 665–66, 667, 669–70, 694, 695–96	59, 60, 63, 118–19, 122, 169, 170, 173, 230, 231, 234, 299, 300, 303, 362, 363, 366, 426, 427, 430, 482, 483, 486, 575, 576, 579, 637, 638, 640, 720, 721, 722, 723, 725, 727–28, 753, 755, 767–68, 772, 773–74, 778, 781, 788, 791, 793, 794, 795, 797, 801, 802, 810, 811, 815–16, 819, 823, 825
Publishing and Presenting	62, 107, 152, 211, 279, 323, 380, 425, 480, 527, 610, 611, 638	62, 113, 178, 241, 290, 343, 392, 461, 516, 573, 666, 667, 694, 696	60, 119, 170, 231, 300, 363, 427, 483, 576, 638, 724, 725, 753
Reflecting	62, 107, 152, 211, 279, 323, 380, 425, 480, 527, 610, 636, 638	62, 113, 178, 241, 290, 343, 392, 461, 516, 573, 666, 694, 696	60, 119, 170, 231, 363, 427, 483, 576, 638, 724
Audience	58, 103, 148, 207, 275, 319, 323, 340, 376, 421, 476, 523, 607, 623	58, 109, 174, 237, 286, 339, 388, 391, 512, 515, 569	56, 115, 166, 227, 295, 298, 359–63, 423, 479, 572, 633, 729, 752
Conclusions	276, 422, 424, 477, 526	342, 458, 460, 570, 665, 667	57, 230, 297, 424, 426, 480, 573, 634, 637
Introductions	275, 376, 422, 424, 476	61, 112, 289, 341, 569, 665, 667	230, 299, 426, 482, 572, 633, 637, 638
Journal Writing	45, 46, 50, 56, 68, 72, 73, 85, 91, 117, 123, 131, 132, 145, 165, 180, 190, 204, 221, 231, 234, 292, 311, 359	17, 48, 68, 78, 90, 192, 211, 251, 273, 313, 353, 368, 377, 415, 471, 479, 534, 538, 549, 557, 607, 618	56, 66, 78, 80, 88, 91, 97, 99, 100, 113, 144, 155, 163, 186, 189, 203, 209, 224, 258, 267, 293, 321, 337, 342, 386, 399, 457, 467, 494, 539, 569, 582, 596, 601, 650, 671, 707
Organization	58, 61, 106, 149–50, 210, 230, 272, 277, 278, 305, 324, 359, 379, 395, 424, 526, 606, 625, 637	59, 60, 61, 106, 111, 177, 286, 289, 391, 571–72, 662, 663, 664, 665, 667, 695, 701, 704–705	59, 117, 118, 167, 168, 229, 235, 251, 298, 358, 361, 423, 426, 482, 573, 574, 575, 635, 636, 723, 752, 753, 760–61
Outlining	526, 646–47	571–72, 695, 704–705	235, 358, 636, 723, 760–61
Paragraphing	59, 384, 639–43	60, 391, 663, 697–701	59, 230, 575, 754–57

	GRADE 6	GRADE 7	GRADE 8
Elements of Writing Style			
Peer Review/Editing	61, 106, 151, 210, 278, 322, 379, 425, 479, 526	61, 112, 177, 178, 241, 289, 291, 342, 392, 461, 515, 518, 572–73, 575, 667, 694	59, 60, 117, 118–19, 169, 230–31, 298, 299, 362, 426–27, 482, 575, 637, 638, 721, 722, 723, 725, 752
Portfolios	62, 107, 152, 211, 279, 323, 380, 425, 480, 611	62, 113, 178, 241, 290, 293, 343, 346, 392, 461, 516, 573, 666, 667, 696	60, 119, 170, 300, 363, 576, 638, 724, 725
Purpose	148, 207, 275, 319, 376, 421, 423, 476, 523	58, 109, 174, 237, 286, 339, 388, 391, 512, 515, 569	56, 115, 166, 227, 296, 359, 423, 479, 572, 633, 752
Sentence Combining	610, 612–14	460, 462–64	300, 301–302
Sensory Details	310, 441, 611, 629	109, 111, 112, 266, 269, 665, 700	47, 58, 117–18, 169, 481–82, 636–37, 720
Sentence Variety	613, 656	459, 664	300, 301–302
Thesis Statement		289, 342, 570, 572, 663, 665, 698	425
Transitions	156, 320, 322, 323, 324–26, 422, 424, 479, 607, 640	289, 342, 570, 572, 663, 665, 698	228, 230, 573, 575, 755
Word Choice	98, 359	85, 313, 344, 391, 482, 513, 515	57, 59, 116, 118, 119, 123, 169, 228, 230, 299, 360, 362, 426, 457, 466, 575
Writing with Computers	62, 106, 151, 211, 279, 322, 378, 424, 479, 525	61, 112, 177, 240, 290, 341, 515, 572, 574	119, 169, 230, 299, 363, 426, 481, 575, 635
Writing Modes	(Numbers listed represent the types of activities presented)		
Expressive and Personal Writing	17, 27, 34, 36, 46, 56, 58–62, 72, 88, 101, 103–107, 124, 146, 154, 166, 181, 186, 233, 303, 316, 341, 363, 400, 405, 419, 448, 456, 560, 623	17, 24, 25, 35, 36, 48, 58–62, 92, 107, 130, 141, 174, 190, 209, 216, 220, 266, 272, 284, 314, 320, 366, 368, 371, 376, 406, 435, 471, 477, 479, 534, 537, 538, 547, 549, 557, 567, 586, 605, 618, 667	56–60, 66, 78, 80, 88, 91, 97, 99, 100, 113, 144, 155, 163, 186, 189, 203, 209, 224, 258, 267, 293, 321, 337, 342, 386, 399, 457, 467, 494, 539, 582, 596, 601, 650, 671, 692, 707, 722–23
Observation and Description	98, 101, 102, 124, 138, 148–52, 230, 233, 419, 474, 606–607	26, 41, 47, 76, 89, 109–113, 266, 269, 284, 414, 416, 662–63, 699	115–19, 187, 457, 466, 478, 707, 720, 756
Narrative and Imaginative Writing	27, 28, 34, 35, 36, 46, 56, 72, 83, 88, 96, 101, 124, 125, 131, 146, 166, 181, 183, 186, 205, 207–11, 212–14, 246, 273, 292, 303, 310, 317, 341, 358, 363, 374, 394, 419, 441, 451, 456, 520, 549, 560, 578, 588, 604, 606, 609, 627	24, 35, 41, 83, 92, 107, 141, 153, 154, 172, 174–78, 190, 191, 209, 210, 216, 220, 235, 237–41, 266, 267, 284, 286–90, 303, 314, 320, 337, 339–43, 366, 376, 386, 406, 414, 455, 478, 482, 488, 510, 514, 532, 547, 556, 567, 605, 630, 643, 660, 662, 663–64, 665–66, 699	26, 31, 46, 78, 79, 88, 97, 98, 102, 113, 136, 145, 154, 164, 166–70, 187, 201, 206, 209, 225, 226, 241, 250, 257, 266, 294, 319, 336, 337, 340, 357, 379, 385, 397, 403, 421, 422, 441, 452, 453, 466, 477, 570, 594, 600, 605, 617, 631, 680, 681, 682, 692, 705, 718, 720
Informative (Expository) Writing: Analysis	146, 166, 246, 275–79, 292, 317, 319, 341, 523–27, 604, 607	35, 37, 44, 90, 131, 143, 182, 184, 217, 265, 296, 341, 353, 414, 457–61	38, 135, 164, 201, 227–31, 296–300, 441, 477
Informative (Expository) Writing: Classification	34, 35, 47, 55, 57, 59, 68, 84, 96, 104–105, 132, 167, 209, 221, 246, 277, 279, 475, 486, 525, 540, 590, 664	25, 68, 111, 123, 154, 211, 236, 239, 268, 272, 273, 287, 304, 315, 322, 336, 373, 389, 408, 456, 483, 484, 522, 534, 548, 577, 645, 663, 664, 667, 695	17, 28, 42, 47, 55, 103, 117, 138, 226, 229, 241, 251, 258, 267, 306, 342, 358, 373, 380, 398, 399, 422, 425, 433, 442, 481, 493, 574, 582, 596, 632, 635, 650, 682, 707, 720, 723, 725, 752
Persuasive Writing	36, 48, 146, 147, 229, 341, 358, 374, 376–80, 400, 419, 421–25, 447, 608, 628	47, 235, 339–43, 366, 376, 388–91, 455, 477, 482, 512–16, 664–65	26, 114, 266, 340, 359–63, 367, 379, 385, 397, 423–27, 441, 452, 456, 570, 632, 721–22
Writing about Literature	26, 45, 55, 56, 82, 146, 151, 186, 229, 273, 302, 310, 357, 374, 394, 404, 441, 451, 474, 479–80, 521, 549, 559, 560, 578, 588, 604, 606–610	23, 24, 34, 55, 83, 89, 106, 140, 152, 171, 172, 190, 208, 209, 218, 234, 265, 269, 272, 283, 313, 317, 320, 336, 365, 366, 371, 385, 386, 405, 419, 454, 457–61, 476, 477, 488, 509, 510, 512–16, 531, 532, 535, 537, 547, 556, 566, 567, 592, 604, 611, 621, 629, 630, 635, 639, 642, 647, 652, 659, 663	26, 77, 80, 87, 97, 100, 113, 144, 154, 163, 164, 176, 187, 201, 203, 224, 249, 294, 295, 338, 378, 385, 422, 454, 476, 479–83, 539, 569, 572–76, 593, 594, 598, 600, 630, 632, 657, 673, 696, 705, 714, 722

WRITING SKILLS, MODES, AND FORMATS	GRADE 6	GRADE 7	GRADE 8
Writing Formats and Structures			
Advertisement	36, 147, 229, 317, 447	77, 92, 107, 386, 483, 532, 661	26, 114, 164, 359–63, 441, 721
Anecdote	88, 316, 623	141	424–25
Article	83, 166, 205, 275–79, 419, 604	89, 209, 286–90, 532, 630	54, 97, 113, 136, 225, 250, 357, 441, 617
Autobiographical Incident/ Personal Narrative	58–62, 88, 456	35, 56, 58–62, 174–78, 366, 406, 616	31, 56–60, 201, 379, 385, 397, 421, 441, 452, 456, 682, 722–23
Biography/ Biographical Sketch	148–52		478
Brochure/Handbook	27, 36, 147, 317, 376–80, 474–475, 521	266, 386–87, 567	79, 164
Cause–Effect	35, 181	61, 182, 184, 664	250, 294, 456, 570
Character Sketch	124, 166, 229, 323, 363	153, 209, 266, 556	115–19, 187, 225, 477, 594
Column	138, 233	24, 284, 510	46, 102, 225
Comparison/Contrast	27, 56, 124, 138, 151, 181, 190, 205, 292, 303, 310, 325, 374, 378, 394, 441, 474, 478–79, 532, 567	35, 112, 153, 190, 209, 211, 314, 386, 419, 477, 532, 567	26, 201, 266
Definition	292, 475	153, 267	466
Description	83, 148–52, 292, 363, 404	41, 109–13, 284	115–19, 136, 145, 154, 187, 294, 319, 336, 452, 466, 720
Dialogue	35, 131, 146, 181, 212–14, 273, 358, 374, 404, 451, 456, 549	41, 56, 154, 190, 266, 284, 488, 567, 643	31, 136, 154, 164, 397, 466, 572–76, 594, 600, 617, 692, 718
Diary/Journal/Log Entry	27, 35, 46, 56, 83, 205, 303	24, 56, 83, 406	26, 46, 78, 88, 255, 294, 319, 357, 452, 570, 631
Drama	56, 125, 206, 317, 521	24, 56, 154, 172, 191, 210, 237–41, 266, 337, 455, 511	359–63, 398, 422, 571, 721
Editorial	374, 419	47, 339–43	423–27
Epilogue/Sequel	39, 273, 394, 441	24, 414, 488, 510, 567, 630	145, 250, 379, 680, 692, 718
Essay	48, 56, 101, 103–07, 131, 146, 205, 292, 305, 317	47, 92, 141, 235, 314, 366, 371, 482, 605, 630	54, 88, 187, 201, 319, 421, 452, 570, 631
Evaluation	34, 46, 101, 124, 186, 229, 374, 441, 474, 521	92, 109–13, 376, 390, 455, 512–16	296–300, 385, 397, 479–83, 705, 722
Explanation	56, 83, 101, 103–07, 146–47, 166, 181, 275–79, 310, 317, 523–27, 607	76, 83, 286–90, 366, 376, 569–73	38, 164, 201, 227–31, 296–300, 397, 421, 477, 631, 633–38, 692, 723
Folklore	181, 549, 560, 588, 606	616, 631, 643, 662–64	669, 681, 705, 720–23
Greeting Card	46		27
Interview	88, 146, 181, 183, 419, 609	25, 142, 236, 285, 315	257, 595
Last Will and Testament	273		38, 225
Letter	27, 58–62, 72, 88, 186, 205, 246, 341, 404, 421–25, 441, 521, 578, 607	35, 92, 141, 209, 216, 220, 314, 376, 455, 510, 532, 605, 660, 706–07	26, 38, 46, 78, 88, 187, 201, 226, 294, 379, 385, 397, 403, 421, 456, 477
Literary Analysis	131, 146, 186, 441, 457–61, 476–80, 608	35, 272, 457–61, 510	154, 224, 479–83, 572–76, 593, 705, 722
Memo/Notes	124, 166, 273, 310, 400	24, 76, 92, 107, 235, 266, 455, 547	340, 570, 631, 718
Memoir	58–62, 88	35, 56, 141, 175–178, 366, 406, 477	31, 56–60, 201, 385, 397, 421, 441, 452, 456, 682, 722–23
Monologue	166, 358		31, 257, 336, 441, 452, 477, 600, 605
Opinion	35, 46, 56, 101, 103–07, 124, 186, 205, 358, 400, 419, 521, 608	92, 109–13, 130, 190, 216, 376, 390, 455, 512–16, 547	97, 296–300, 385, 397, 479–83, 605, 705, 722
Parable	394		570
Poem	72, 101, 124, 166, 233, 303, 341, 363, 400, 405, 419, 448, 560	130, 220, 235, 272, 320, 371, 419, 477, 537	98, 102, 206, 337, 453, 594, 680
Predictions	27, 83, 353, 441	56, 130, 172, 190	209, 241

WRITING SKILLS, MODES, AND FORMATS	GRADE 6	GRADE 7	GRADE 8
Writing Formats and Structures			
Problem–Solution	35, 143, 292, 296, 341, 376–80, 419	339–43, 376	359–63
Proposal/Plan	146, 358, 447	76	
Report	102, 147, 522–27, 561, 607	25, 89, 141, 190, 337, 547, 569–73, 702–05	54, 88, 98, 136, 165, 250, 294–300, 320, 466, 571, 594, 633–38, 723
Review	441, 476–80, 521	109–13, 512–16	397, 479–83, 705, 722
Rewriting (Rewrite)	27, 83, 96, 273, 419, 578	190, 210, 303, 510	145, 226, 295, 422, 617, 680–81, 705
Scene *see* Drama			
Song Lyrics	36, 138, 456	25, 153, 337, 567	136, 669, 680
Speech	166, 181, 303, 319–323, 358, 400	36, 191, 386, 388–91, 406, 477, 488	55, 164, 187, 357, 385, 680
Story	46, 207–11, 419, 609	130, 235, 406, 665	38, 54, 166–70, 319, 336, 617
Summary	28, 146, 246, 447, 474, 608	172, 284, 337, 366, 414, 510, 514, 556, 605	299, 421, 482, 760

GRAMMAR, USAGE, AND MECHANICS	GRADE 6	GRADE 7	GRADE 8
Parts of Speech			
Parts of Speech	618, 650–52, 662, 664	708–11	762–64
Understanding Sentences			
Subjects	107–110, 153–55, 281–82, 653–54, 656, 667–68, 673–74, 700–701	63–64, 241–43, 462–63, 712–13, 715–16, 726–28, 733–36, 759–64	232–33, 302, 427–30, 765–71, 775–79
Predicates	653–54, 667	291, 712–13	232–33, 765, 790–91
Objects	107–110, 667–68, 675	63–65, 462–63, 727–28, 733–36	770–71, 775–79
Complete Sentences	152–55, 653–61	290–93, 460, 462–64, 717–18	232–33, 765–66, 768
Compound Sentences	380, 610, 612–14, 713–14, 718	460, 462–64, 775–76, 780–81, 786–87	300–303, 815–16, 821–21, 827
Compound Sentence Parts	656–57, 664–65	715–16, 776	815–16, 827
Fragments	152–55, 210, 658–59	290–93, 717–18	232–33, 765–66, 768
Run–on Sentences	153–55, 659–61	290–93, 298, 718–20	231–34, 766–68
Prepositions, Conjunctions, and Interjections			
Prepositions	281, 651, 662–64	668, 709–711, 721–23	763, 770, 799–800, 802
Conjunctions	380–81, 610, 612–13, 651, 664–65, 713–14	460, 462–63, 709–711, 719, 721, 723–24	302, 763, 815, 820, 827
Interjections	651, 664–65	709–711, 721, 723–24, 775, 786–87	763, 814, 827
Nouns			
Classes of Nouns	663, 666–67	725–26	769–70
Plurals	62–65, 280, 669–71	242, 728–30, 759–61	771–72, 774, 798–800, 822–23, 827
Possessives	62–65, 671–72, 720–21	63, 730–31, 782–84, 786–87	773–74, 822–23, 827

LANGUAGE AND VOCABULARY SKILLS	GRADE 6	GRADE 7	GRADE 8
Analogies	303, 358	303, 477	174, 319, 540, 618
Antonyms	27, 46, 111, 181, 229, 273, 310, 474, 578, 604	56, 76, 386, 510, 547	54, 88, 129, 187, 201, 225, 294, 379, 421, 441, 540-41, 570-71, 618, 631, 705
Briticisms		222, 236	
Colloquialisms			724, 726-28
Connotation/Denotation		209, 465, 515, 665, 681	38, 692
Context Clues	35, 37, 46, 56, 83, 124, 146, 156, 158, 166, 181, 205, 246, 273, 303, 317, 341, 343, 374, 419, 521, 549, 588, 624	24, 35, 56, 76, 107, 117, 141, 153, 172, 190, 235, 266, 284, 315, 337, 366, 386, 406, 465, 510, 522, 532, 547, 556, 567, 605, 630, 643, 660, 681	26, 38, 64, 78, 129, 145, 164, 187, 201, 319, 396, 433, 540, 594, 619, 669, 680, 692, 718, 739
Dialect	29, 452, 624	26, 222, 420, 618, 681	146, 739, 771–72
Dictionaries	84, 618, 645, 666, 670	131, 703, 729, 781	729, 759, 769, 772
Formal and Informal English	154	737	63, 232, 723–24, 726–28, 765, 776
Glossary	618, 645	674, 703	732, 759
Homonyms		343, 344–46	669
Idioms			729, 741
Jargon/Specialized Vocabulary	47, 97, 190, 278, 475	93, 683	
Loaded Language		465, 520	431
Persuasion, Language of		347	360, 367, 671
Prefixes	429	671	606
Roots, Greek		671	
Spelling Tips	63, 64, 108, 429, 481, 688	63, 114	485, 577, 769
Standard and Nonstandard English			724, 726-28, 796
Suffixes	429	671	606
Synonyms	27, 46, 111, 181, 229, 273, 310, 521, 560, 578, 604	76, 153, 172, 266, 386, 510, 532, 556, 630, 660, 681	54, 88, 129, 187, 201, 225, 294, 379, 421, 441, 540-41, 570-71, 618, 631, 705
Thesaurus	111, 689		169
Word Origins	28, 615, 672	173, 709–09, 725, 728	320, 769

RESEARCH AND STUDY SKILLS	GRADE 6	GRADE 7	GRADE 8
Almanacs	645	703	759
Atlases	607, 645	703	759
Author Cards, (in card catalog)	644	702	758
Bibliographies	525, 645-46	390, 572, 664, 703-705	634–35, 637, 759-60
Books (parts of)	645	703	759
Call Numbers	644	702	759
Card Catalogs	644	702	635, 758
Computerized Catalog Systems	644	702	635, 758
Dewey Decimal System	644	571, 702	758
Dictionaries	84	131, 703, 729, 781	729, 759, 769, 772
Encyclopedias	606, 644-46	337, 570, 702-703, 705	635, 723, 758-59
Glossary	618, 645	674, 703	732, 759
Index (using an)	645	703	759

RESEARCH AND STUDY SKILLS

	GRADE 6	GRADE 7	GRADE 8
Note-Taking	525, 644-46	288, 390, 571, 664, 703-704	635–36, 759–60
Outlining	646-47	571-72, 704-705	636. 760–61
Periodicals	607, 646	42, 108, 390, 750	635
Plagiarism	525	572, 704	636, 760
Readers' Guide to Periodical Literature	420, 525, 644	36, 390, 571, 702	635, 758
Reading Rates			90, 641, 744
Research Activities	36, 57, 84, 125, 139, 147, 247, 274, 318, 342, 375, 420, 522, 561	25, 36, 57, 77, 89, 108, 154, 173, 191, 211, 236, 285, 338, 367, 372, 387, 407, 456, 478, 483, 511, 532, 533, 547, 567, 569-73, 644, 664	27, 39, 55, 79, 88, 98, 114, 165, 188, 226, 295, 320, 341, 358, 398, 442, 478, 571, 595, 632-38, 670, 693, 706, 719, 722
SQ3R			306, 745
Summarizing	47, 607, 646	284, 315, 337, 396, 459, 483, 606, 687, 704	299, 760
Works Cited, *see* Bibliography			

SPEAKING, LISTENING, AND VIEWING SKILLS

	GRADE 6	GRADE 7	GRADE 8
Dramatic Reading	28, 36, 47, 66, 125, 138, 166, 189, 206, 215, 233, 247, 304, 318, 322, 327, 364, 375, 475, 480, 579, 589, 605	25, 57, 77, 142, 153, 154, 173, 210, 221, 241, 245, 285, 338, 456, 511, 617, 631, 661, 664, 666	39, 98, 137, 188, 226, 295, 358, 362, 363, 398, 422, 478, 571, 580, 595, 632, 706, 719
Interviewing	84, 318, 342	25, 142, 236, 285, 315, 548, 568	27, 79, 226, 398, 478, 595, 632
Listening	47, 66, 154, 216, 327	142, 314, 315, 396, 518, 696	27, 39, 358, 422
Oral Reports	36, 37, 47, 57, 84, 125, 139, 147, 206, 247, 274, 304, 318, 342, 405, 420, 442, 522, 561	17, 25, 38, 44, 57, 77, 108, 142, 154, 173, 210, 236, 303, 315, 367, 387, 407, 478, 483, 511, 548, 568, 606, 644	27, 79, 98, 114, 165, 188, 320, 358, 398, 443, 478, 595, 670, 693, 719
Public Speaking	36, 37, 47, 57, 84, 125, 139, 147, 206, 247, 274, 285, 304, 318, 322, 327, 342, 405, 420, 442, 522, 561	17, 25, 36, 38, 44, 57, 77, 108, 142, 154, 173, 181, 191, 210, 236, 285, 303, 315, 367, 387, 407, 478, 483, 511, 516, 533, 548, 568, 606, 644	27, 79, 98, 114, 165, 188, 226, 231, 235, 320, 358, 398, 443, 478, 595, 670, 693, 719
Videotape	28, 323	108, 173, 338, 407, 483, 511, 696	226, 363
Working in Groups	36, 37, 46, 47, 50, 66, 97, 107, 126, 139, 152, 187, 189, 206, 211, 214, 230, 248, 279, 311, 323, 342, 375, 384, 405, 562, 606	56, 86, 93, 140, 142, 157, 180, 191, 192, 217, 222, 265, 273, 315, 316, 322, 367, 407, 478, 548, 568, 586, 643, 661, 663–664, 669	39, 53, 98, 119, 137, 168, 295, 298, 304, 358, 398, 404, 422, 426-27, 440, 443, 451, 478, 493, 576, 601, 721